ST/ESA/SER.A/234

Department of Economic and Social Affairs
Population Division

WORLD FERTILITY REPORT: 2003

United Nations
New York

The Department of Economic and Social Affairs of the United Nations Secretariat is a vital interface between global policies in the economic, social and environmental spheres and national action. The Department works in three main interlinked areas: (i) it compiles, generates and analyses a wide range of economic, social and environmental data and information on which States Members of the United Nations draw to review common problems and take stock of policy options; (ii) it facilitates the negotiations of Member States in many intergovernmental bodies on joint courses of action to address ongoing or emerging global challenges; and (iii) it advises interested Governments on the ways and means of translating policy frameworks developed in United Nations conferences and summits into programmes at the country level and, through technical assistance, helps build national capacities.

NOTE

The designations employed in this report and the material presented in it do not imply the expression of any opinion whatsoever on the part of the Secretariat of the United Nations concerning the legal status of any country, territory, city or area or of its authorities, or concerning the delimitation of its frontiers of boundaries.

The designations "more developed", "less developed" and "least developed" for countries, areas or regions are intended for statistical convenience and do not necessarily express a judgement about the stage reached by a particular country or area in the development process.

The term "country" as used in the text of this report also refers, as appropriate, to territories or areas.

This publication has been issued without formal editing.

ST/ESA/SER.A/234

United Nations publication
Sales No.
ISBN

PREFACE

The Population Division of the Department of Economic and Social Affairs of the United Nations Secretariat is responsible for providing the international community with up-to-date and scientifically objective information on population and development. According to its mandate, the Population Division provides guidance to the United Nations General Assembly, Economic and Social Council and the Commission on Population and Development on population and development issues and undertakes regular studies on population levels and trends, population estimates and projections, population policies and population and development interrelationships.

In particular, the Population Division is concerned with the following substantive areas: the study of patterns of fertility, mortality, international and internal migration, including their levels, trends and differentials as well as their causes and consequences; the analysis of age and parity patterns of fertility, and its proximate determinants, such as, marriage and contraceptive use; estimates and projections of population size, distribution, and age and sex structure; the documentation and analysis of population policies at the national and international levels; and the study of the relationship between socio-economic development and population change.

The work of the Population Division is published in a variety of formats, including electronically, to meet the needs of diverse audiences. These publications and materials are used by Governments, national and international organizations, research institutions and individuals engaged in social and economic planning, research and training, and by the general public.

This report is the first of its kind to be issued on topics related to reproductive behaviour. It presents information on fertility, marriage, contraceptive use and national policies with respect to childbearing for 192 countries of the world. The data are compiled from civil registration, population censuses and nationally representative sample surveys and, in the case of national policies, Government's responses to United Nations inquiries and other sources.

For each country, available data on 24 indicators are presented for two dates. Time series of age-specific fertility rates and total fertility rates from different sources are presented for each country in graphic form. The observed series of total fertility rates are supplemented on the graphs with estimates from *World Population Prospects: the 2002 Revision*. In addition to this report, the United Nations Population Division has issued a wall chart, *World Fertility Patterns 2004*, which provides selected information from this report for all countries.

The Population Division gratefully acknowledges the assistance and cooperation of the Statistics Division of the Department of Economic and Social Affairs of the United Nations Secretariat, the Council of Europe and the Demographic and Health Surveys in providing a large part of the data used in this report.

This report as well as other population information may be accessed on the World Wide Web site of the Population Division at www.unpopulation.org. For further information concerning this publication, please contact the office of Mr. Joseph Chamie, Director, Population Division, Department of Economic and Social Affairs, United Nations, New York, NY 10017, USA; telephone number (212) 963-3179; fax number (212) 963-2147.

CONTENTS

I. COUNTRY PROFILES

II. Selected indicators

III. Definitions and sources

TABLES

The tables presented in this report make use of the following symbols:

Two dots (..) indicate that data are not available or are not separately reported.

An em dash (—) indicates that the amount is nil or negligible.

A hyphen (-) indicates that the item is not applicable.

A minus sign (-) before a figure indicates a decrease.

A full stop (.) is used to indicate decimals.

Use of a hyphen (-) between years, for example, 1995-2000, signifies the full period involved, from 1 July of the first year to 1 July of the second year.

Numbers and percentages in tables do not necessarily add to totals because of rounding.

Countries and areas are grouped geographically into six major areas: Africa; Asia; Europe; Latin America and the Caribbean; Northern America; and Oceania. Africa and Asia are further divided into Eastern Asia, South-eastern Asia, South Central Asia, Sub-Saharan Africa and Northern Africa/Western Asia (considered here as a single region). In addition, for statistical convenience, the regions are classified as belonging to either of two categories: more developed or less developed. The less developed regions include all the regions of Africa, Asia (excluding Japan), and Latin America and the Caribbean, as well as Melanesia, Micronesia and Polynesia. The more developed regions comprise Australia/New Zealand, Europe, Northern America and Japan.

The following abbreviations have been used:

AHS	Arab-Gulf Family and Child Health Survey
HIV/AIDS	Human Immunodeficiency Virus/Acquired Immunodeficiency Syndrome
CPS	Contraceptive Prevalence Survey
DHS	Demographic and Health Survey
EUROSTAT	Statistical Office of the European Communities
FFS	Fertility and Family Survey
FHS	Family Health Survey
KAP	Survey of Knowledge, Attitudes and Practices
MCH	Maternal and Child Health Survey
MICS	Multiple Indicator Cluster Survey (UNICEF)
RHS	Reproductive Health Survey
UNPD	United Nations Population Division
USSR	Union of Soviet Socialist Republics
WFS	World Fertility Survey

INTRODUCTION

The twentieth century ushered in significant global demographic transformations. A central component of these changes has been the sharp decline in levels of fertility in almost all countries and regions of the world. Over the past 40 years, for example, the average number of children per couple has fallen by half, i.e., from five to nearly two and a half children. In addition, the number of countries with fertility rates below the replacement level of 2.1 children per couple has increased from 5 to 60 countries.

Fundamental to these changes in childbearing are shifts in marriage patterns and increases in the use of contraception. While marriage or some form of consensual union continues to be nearly universal, both men and women are marrying much later compared to 30 years ago. In addition, increasing numbers of married couples are experiencing divorce and separation.

Contraceptive use has increased substantially in most countries both among young and older couples. The use of contraception by couples who have reached their desired family size is having a considerable impact on fertility surpassing the effect of changes in marriage patterns. In addition, Governments' policies and programmes on fertility levels and contraceptive use have played a major role in altering childbearing behaviour and reducing overall fertility.

In an attempt to document these critical changes, this volume presents data on fertility, marriage patterns, contraceptive use and national policies with respect to childbearing for 192 countries of the world. In addition to the often used summary indicators of fertility (total fertility rate), marriage (age at marriage) and contraceptive use (prevalence of any method), other indicators have been included that increase the understanding of changes in reproductive and marriage behaviour that have taken place since 1970, that is, over the course of a generation.

A summary of the major findings is presented in the section following this introduction. After the summary, in Part I, individual country profiles using available data on 24 indicators are presented for two dates, around 1970 and around 1990. The data are compiled from a variety of sources, including civil registration, population censuses and nationally representative sample surveys and, in the case of national policies, Government's responses to United Nations Population Inquiries. The basic criterion for inclusion of data is their validity. No attempt was made to adjust the data for coverage, undercount or other non-sampling errors. In Part II data on 13 selected indicators are presented for all countries. In addition, three tables compare the total fertility rates presented in this report to estimates published in the United Nations 2002 Revision of *World Population Prospects*. Finally, the definitions and the sources of data utilized in this report are provided in Part III.

تقرير الخصوبة العالمي لعام 2003
موجز تنفيذي

تقرير الخصوبة العالمي لعام 2003، الذي أعدته شعبة السكان التابعة لإدارة الشؤون الاقتصادية والاجتماعية بالأمانة العامة للأمم المتحدة، يعرض مجموعة من التقديرات والمؤشرات الرئيسية للخصوبة والزواج واستعمال وسائل منع الحمل في 192 بلدا، مشيرا في معظمه إلى فترتي السبعينات والتسعينات، ولكنه عند الضرورة يغطي فترات أسبق من ذلك أو فترات أحدث من ذلك عند الإمكان. ومجموعة البيانات المعروضة في التقرير تتيح تقييم التغيرات غير المسبوقة التي حدثت في مجالات الزواج واستعمال وسائل منع الحمل والخصوبة منذ فترة السبعينات. وعلى وجه التحديد، يوثق التقرير النتائج الرئيسية التالية:

1 - **حدث في جميع أنحاء العالم تحول رئيسي في توقيت الزواج إلى مراحل عمرية أكبر** - ارتفعت القيمة الوسيطة لمتوسط سن الأعزب عند الزواج على مستوى العالم من 25.4 إلى 27.2 سنة للرجل ومن 21.5 إلى 23.2 سنة للمرأة. وفي حالة البلدان المتقدمة النمو، كانت الزيادة مدهشة بقدر أكبر، إذ ارتفع الوسيط من 25.2 إلى 28.8 سنة للرجل ومن 22.0 إلى 26.1 سنة للمرأة.

2 - **أصبح الرجال والنساء يمضون فترات أطول من حياتهم في حالة عزوبة** - انخفضت النسبة المئوية الوسيطة للأشخاص الذين سبق لهم الزواج من الفئة العمرية 25-29 من 85 في المائة في السبعينات إلى 76 في المائة في التسعينات في حالة المرأة، ومن 68 في المائة إلى 56 في المائة في حالة الرجل. وهنا أيضا كانت الانخفاضات في النسبة المئوية لمن سبق لهم الزواج من الفئة العمرية 25-29 أكثر ضخامة في حالة البلدان المتقدمة النمو، حيث انخفضت القيم الوسيطة من 85 في المائة إلى 62 في المائة للرجال ومن 74 في المائة إلى 43 في المائة للنساء.

3 - **تأخر الزواج لدى البالغين صغار السن لم يُحدث بعد انخفاضات ملحوظة في النسبة المئوية للأشخاص الذين تزوجوا مرة واحدة على الأقل خلال عمرهم** - لا يزال انتشار الزواج أو غيره من أشكال الاقتران الرضائي يكاد يكون عاما. ففي السبعينات، بلغت نسبة من تزوجوا

مرة واحدة على الأقل من جميع الرجال والنساء من الفئة العمرية 45-49 سنة 89 في المائة أو أكثر في ثلاثة من كل أربعة بلدان، وبحلول التسعينات، كانت هذه النسبة لا تزال قريبة من 89 في المائة.

4 - زادت معدلات الطلاق في معظم البلدان المتوافر عنها بيانات

- في البلدان المتقدمة النمو، ارتفع المعدل الوسيط للطلاق من 13 طلاقا لكل 100 من الرجال والنساء في السبعينات إلى 24 طلاقا لكل 100 من الرجال و 27 طلاقا لكل 100 من النساء في التسعينات. وفي البلدان النامية، ارتفع المعدل الوسيط للطلاق من 7 طلاقات إلى 12 طلاقا لكل 100 من الرجال ومن 5 طلاقات إلى 15 طلاقا لكل 100 من النساء. أي أن الأمر لم يقتصر على نزوع الناس إلى التأخر في الزواج، بل أخذ يزداد أيضا عدم استقرار الرباطات الزواجية. ومن الواضح أن كلا هذين الاتجاهين له آثار كبيرة على السلوك الإنجابي.

5 - حدثت زيادة هائلة في استعمال وسائل تنظيم الأسرة - فيما بين السبعينات والتسعينات، زاد استعمال وسائل منع الحمل بين النساء المتزوجات أو المقترنات حاليا في تسعة من كل عشرة من البلدان المتوافر عنها بيانات. وزاد المستوى الوسيط لاستعمال وسائل منع الحمل على مستوى العالم من 38 في المائة من النساء المتزوجات أو المقترنات حاليا في السبعينات إلى 52 في المائة في التسعينات. وفي حالة البلدان النامية، ارتفع المعدل الوسيط لانتشار وسائل منع الحمل من 27 في المائة إلى 40 في المائة فيما بين هاتين الفترتين. وبحلول التسعينات، بلغ معدل انتشار وسائل منع الحمل في نسبة الربع من جميع البلدان النامية 62 في المائة أو أكثر.

6 - زاد عموما استعمال الطرق الحديثة لمنع الحمل في البلدان النامية - ارتفع المعدل الوسيط لاستعمال الطرق الحديثة لمنع الحمل في البلدان النامية من 18 إلى 30 في المائة بين فترتي السبعينات والتسعينات. بيد أن استعمال الطرق الحديثة لمنع الحمل لا يزال نادرا في نسبة تبلغ الربع من جميع البلدان النامية، حيث لا تزال مستويات الاستعمال أقل من 12 في المائة.

7 - فيما بين عامي 1970 و 2000، حدث لسكان العالم انخفاض ضخم وغير مسبوق في معدلات الخصوبة، يعزى معظمه إلى انخفاض الخصوبة الذي شهدته البلدان النامية (الشكل الأول) - هبط متوسط مستويات الخصوبة في العالم النامي من أكثر من 5.9 أطفال لكل امرأة في السبعينات إلى حوالي 3.9 أطفال لكل امرأة في التسعينات. وكان المعدل الوسيط لانخفاض الخصوبة في البلدان النامية بين فترتي السبعينات والتسعينات في حدود 1.8 طفل لكل امرأة، ويبدو أن نسبة تبلغ الربع من جميع البلدان النامية حققت انخفاضات بلغت 2.6 طفل أو أكثر للمرأة الواحدة.

8 - بينما كانت الخصوبة مرتفعة بصورة متسقة في البلدان النامية في السبعينات، أصبحت مستويات الخصوبة متباينة حاليا على نطاق واسع فيما بين البلدان النامية - فمعدل الخصوبة لا يزال يجاوز 5 أطفال للمرأة الواحدة في عدد من أقل البلدان نموا، ولكنه وصل إلى ما دون مستويات الإحلال في حوالي 20 من البلدان النامية.

9 - انخفضت عموما منذ السبعينات مستويات الخصوبة في البلدان المتقدمة النمو، التي شهد العديد منها "طفرة إنجابية" خلال فترتي الخمسينات والستينات - بلغ الانخفاض الوسيط في الخصوبة الكلية للبلدان المتقدمة النمو 0.8 طفل للمرأة الواحدة بين السبعينات والتسعينات. وبحلول أواخر التسعينات، لم يتجاوز عدد البلدان المتقدمة النمو التي أفادت بأن الخصوبة الكلية لديها بلغت 2 طفل أو أكثر للمرأة الواحدة أربعة بلدان، هي ألبانيا وأيسلندا ونيوزيلندا والولايات المتحدة الأمريكية. وعلاوة على ذلك، كان مستوى الخصوبة في 14 من البلدان المتقدمة النمو أدنى من 1.3 طفل للمرأة الواحدة، وهو مستوى للخصوبة غير مسبوق في الانخفاض في التاريخ المسجل للكتل السكانية الكبيرة.

10 - تتباين مستويات عدم الإنسال تباينا كبيرا فيما بين المناطق الرئيسية - في التسعينات نزعت نسب النساء اللائي لم ينجبن من الفئة العمرية 45-49 سنة إلى الارتفاع في البلدان المتقدمة النمو وبلدان منطقة البحر الكاريبي. ففي أربعة من كل خمسة من البلدان المتقدمة النمو المتوافر عنها بيانات، بلغت نسبة اللائي لم ينجبن من النساء من الفئة العمرية 45-49

سنة 7 في المائة على الأقل، وفي تسعة من البلدان النامية، تجاوزت نسبة اللائي لم ينجبن 10 في المائة. وكانت مستويات عدم الإنسال منخفضة نسبيا في التسعينات في أفريقيا وآسيا ومعتدلة في أمريكا اللاتينية. وفيما بين السبعينات والتسعينات، هبطت مستويات عدم الإنسال في أفريقيا، حيث تناقصت حالات العقم الناتج عن الأمراض المنقولة عن طريق الاتصال الجنسي خلال السبعينات والثمانينات.

11 - **كانت التحولات السلوكية الكبرى المتصلة بأشكال الاقتران، والزواج، واستعمال وسائل منع الحمل، هي التي مهدت السبيل أمام حدوث التغيرات البالغة التي طرأت على مستويات الخصوبة منذ السبعينات** ـ أدت السياسات الحكومية المتعلقة بإتاحة وسائل منع الحمل دورا مهما في تعديل السلوك الإنجابي. ففي عام 1976، أفاد 52 في المائة من جميع الحكومات أنه لا توجد لديها أي مبادرات لتعديل مستويات الخصوبة، ولكن هذه النسبة انخفضت بحلول عام 2001 إلى 32 في المائة (الشكل 2). وظل الدعم الحكومي لتنظيم الأسرة يزداد ازديادا مطردا منذ السبعينات. وبحلول عام 2001، كانت نسبة قدرها 92 في المائة من جميع الحكومات تدعم برامج تنظيم الأسرة وتوزيع وسائل منع الحمل إما بصورة مباشرة (75 في المائة)، عن طريق مرافق حكومية، أو بصورة غير مباشرة (17 في المائة)، عن طريق دعم أنشطة المنظمات غير الحكومية، مثل رابطات تنظيم الأسرة.

وقد اختيرت البيانات المتعلقة بالخصوبة والزواج واستعمال وسائل منع الحمل والسياسات المتصلة بالإنجاب المعروضة في هذا التقرير بحيث تعكس التحولات الكبرى التي حدثت في السلوك الإنجابي والزواجي منذ السبعينات، أي على مدى جيل بأكمله. وأدرجت في ذلك مؤشرات تعكس التغيرات التي حدثت حسب فئات المواليد فضلا عن مؤشرات أخرى تبين الاتجاهات الحاصلة من منظور الفترات المختلفة. وقد استمدت البيانات من مصادر متنوعة، منها السجلات المدنية والتعدادات السكانية والدراسات الاستقصائية ذات التمثيل الوطني. ولم يجر تعديل البيانات المعروضة لأغراض تصويب أخطاء التغطية أو نقص الحصر أو غير ذلك من أخطاء أخذ العينات. ومن ثم فإن قيم بعض المؤشرات، وبخاصة المؤشرات المتصلة بالبلدان النامية ذات البيانات الناقصة، قد لا تكون متفقة مع القيم

التي نشرتها شعبة السكان في **التوقعات السكانية العالمية: تنقيح عام 2002**، نظرا إلى أن هذه القيم الأخيرة قد عُدلت حسب الاقتضاء. وتُعرض في التقرير لكل بلد من البلدان قيم 43 مؤشرا لكل تاريخ بعينه، حيثما كانت البيانات متوافرة.

وترد أدناه مناقشة أكثر تفصيلا لنتائج هذا التقرير. ووحدة التحليل المتخذة لأغراض مناقشة هذه النتائج هي البلد، وموضع التركيز الرئيسي هو تغيرات توزيع البلدان حسب مختلف المؤشرات.

لا يزال انتشار الزواج أو غيره من أشكال الاقتران الرضائي يكاد يكون عاما. ففي السبعينات، بلغت نسبة من تزوجوا مرة واحدة على الأقل من جميع الرجال وجميع النساء من الفئة العمرية 45-49 سنة 89 في المائة على الأقل في ثلاثة من كل أربعة بلدان، وبحلول التسعينات، كانت هذه النسبة لا تزال قريبة من 89 في المائة. وعلاوة على ذلك، بلغت نسبة الرجال من الفئة العمرية 45-49 سنة الذين سبق لهم الزواج أو الاقتران في نسبة تبلغ الربع من جميع البلدان المتوافر عنها البيانات ذات الصلة 97 في المائة أو أكثر في السبعينات و 98 في المائة أو أكثر في التسعينات. وبالمثل، بلغت نسبة النساء من الفئة العمرية 45-49 سنة اللائي سبق لهن الزواج أو الاقتران في نسبة الربع من جميع البلدان 98 في المائة على الأقل.

وفي السبعينات، بلغ معدل انتشار الزواج أعلى قيمة له في بلدان آسيا ولا يزال مرتفعا حاليا، وإن كانت هناك بعض حالات حدثت فيها انخفاضات ملموسة في نسب من سبق لهم الزواج، لا سيما في حالة الرجال في اليابان وحالة النساء في سنغافورة أو في الأراضي الفلسطينية المحتلة وإسرائيل وبروني دار السلام وماليزيا وميانمار. وتتسم بلدان أفريقيا هي الأخرى عموما بارتفاع معدل الزواج أو الاقتران الرضائي، حيث أفادت ثلاثة أرباعها أنه بحلول التسعينات بلغت نسبة من سبق لهم الزواج أو الاقتران من الفئة العمرية 45-49 سنة 96 في المائة على الأقل في حالة الرجال و 98 في المائة على الأقل في حالة النساء. وفي الواقع أن عددا من البلدان في أفريقيا يبدو أنه شهد حدوث زيادة ملموسة في نسب من سبق لهم الزواج من

الفئة العمرية 45-49 سنة، خصوصا في حالة الرجال. ومن أمثلة هذه البلدان أوغندا وبنن وبوركينا فاسو وجمهورية أفريقيا الوسطى والكاميرون. وعلى النقيض من ذلك، سجلت انخفاضات هامة في نسب من سبق لهم الزواج من النساء والرجال من الفئة العمرية 45-49 سنة في بوتسوانا وجنوب أفريقيا وريونيون.

والزواج أو الاقتران الرضائي أقل انتشارا إلى حد ما في بلدان أمريكا اللاتينية وبخاصة في منطقة البحر الكاريبي بالمقارنة بالمناطق الأخرى في العالم النامي. فبحلول التسعينات لم تتجاوز نسبة من سبق لهم الزواج أو الاقتران من الفئة العمرية 45-49 سنة في نصف بلدان منطقة البحر الكاريبي 72 في المائة من الرجال و 70 في المائة من النساء. وعلاوة على ذلك، سُجل حدوث انخفاضات كبيرة فيما بين السبعينات والتسعينات في نسب من سبق لهم الزواج في بربادوس وجامايكا وجزر الأنتيل الهولندية وسانت لوسيا. وفي بقية بلدان أمريكا اللاتينية، غلب على نسب من سبق لهم الزواج من الفئة العمرية 45-49 سنة أن تكون أعلى من ذلك، ولكن بحلول التسعينات، وُجد أن ما لا يقل عن 10 في المائة من الرجال و 9 في المائة من النساء من الفئة العمرية 45-49 سنة في نصف بلدان المنطقة لم يسبق لهم الزواج أو الاقتران. وهذه الأرقام تمثل تغيرا عما كان في السبعينات، حيث غلب أن تكون نسب من لم يسبق لهم الزواج أعلى من ذلك. وفيما بين السبعينات والتسعينات، شهد ما لا يقل عن نصف البلدان في أمريكا اللاتينية زيادات ملموسة في نسب الرجال والنساء من الفئة العمرية 45-49 سنة الذين سبق لهم الزواج أو الاقتران. بيد أن الاقتران الرضائي شائع في أمريكا اللاتينية ومنطقة البحر الكاريبي، ويجب توخي الحذر لدى تفسير البيانات المتعلقة بنسب من سبق لهم الزواج حيث أن الاتجاهات المرصودة قد تكون ناجمة جزئيا عن حدوث تحسن مع الزمن في الإبلاغ بحالات الاقتران الرضائي وليس عن تغير فعلي في معدل انتشار الزواج.

وفي أوروبا وأمريكا الشمالية واستراليا/نيوزيلندا، لا يزال معدل انتشار الزواج أو الاقتران الرضائي مرتفعا، حيث تتجاوز نسب من سبق لهم الزواج أو الاقتران من الفئة العمرية 45-49 سنة 86 في المائة من الرجال و 89 في المائة من النساء في ثلاثة من كل أربعة بلدان في تلك المناطق. بيد أنه فيما بين السبعينات والثمانينات، شهد ما لا يقل عن ثلاثة

أرباع البلدان المعنية انخفاضا في نسب من سبق لهم الزواج من الرجال، وكانت الانخفاضات ملحوظة بأكبر درجة في بلدان الشمال الأوروبي وفي لاتفيا وأيسلندا وهولندا والولايات المتحدة. وكانت الانخفاضات في نسب النساء اللائي سبق لهن الزواج أقل شيوعا، ولكنها كانت كبيرة في عدد من البلدان، وخصوصا في أيسلندا والدانمرك والسويد.

وتتيح البيانات المتوافرة إجراء مقارنة لنسب الرجال والنساء الذين تزوجوا أو اقترنوا بحلول الفترة العمرية 25-29 سنة في السبعينات والتسعينات. وتبين هذه المقارنة حدوث تحول رئيسي على مستوى العالم في توقيت الزواج: فقد انخفضت النسبة الوسيطة للنساء اللائي سبق لهن الزواج من الفئة العمرية 25-29 سنة من 85 في المائة إلى 76 في المائة، وانخفضت النسبة المناظرة للرجال من الفئة العمرية 25-29 سنة من 68 في المائة إلى 56 في المائة. وعلاوة على ذلك، حدث في ثلاثة أرباع جميع البلدان المتوافر عنها البيانات المطلوبة انخفاض في نسب من سبق لهم الزواج بحلول الفترة العمرية 25-29 سنة. وهذه الانخفاضات ملحوظة بأكبر درجة في بلدان أوروبا وأمريكا الشمالية واستراليا/نيوزيلندا حيث يعمد الشباب بصورة متزايدة إلى تأخير السن الذي يقترنون عنده، ولكن هناك اتجاهات مماثلة يمكن ملاحظتها في جميع المناطق الأخرى. وهذه التغيرات تنذر بحدوث انخفاض شامل وعام في معدل انتشار الزواج والاقتران الرضائي في المستقبل وسط الفئة العمرية 45-49 سنة.

وتتضح هذه التغيرات أيضا في الارتفاع المستمر في السن عند الزواج. فمتوسط سن الأعزب عند الزواج، الذي هو مؤشر لمتوسط طول فترة العزوبة، ازداد من فترة السبعينات إلى فترة التسعينات في ثلاثة أرباع جميع البلدان المتوافر عنها بيانات. وعلى مستوى العالم، زادت القيمة الوسيطة لمتوسط سن الأعزب عند الزواج من 25.4 إلى 27.2 سنة في حالة الرجال ومن 21.5 إلى 23.2 سنة في حالة النساء. وسُجلت زيادات كبيرة بشكل خاص في متوسط سن الأعزب عند الزواج في فئة البلدان المتقدمة النمو، حيث زاد هذا المتوسط بأكثر من أربع سنوات في استراليا وأيرلندا وأيسلندا وإيطاليا وبلجيكا والدانمرك والسويد وسويسرا وفرنسا وفنلندا وكندا والمملكة المتحدة والنرويج وهنغاريا وهولندا والولايات المتحدة. أما في البلدان النامية، فقد نزعت الزيادات في متوسط سن الأعزب

عند الزواج إلى أن تكون أقل من ذلك مقدارا، خصوصا في حالة الرجال. بيد أنه سجلت زيادات بمقدار 3 سنوات أو أكثر في قلة من البلدان في جميع المناطق، منها تونس والجزائر والجماهيرية العربية الليبية والسودان وقطر والكويت وماليزيا والمغرب وملديف في آسيا وشمال أفريقيا؛ وفي جزر الأنتيل الهولندية وجزر البهاما وجزر فرجن التابعة للولايات المتحدة وسانت لوسيا وغواديلوب وغيانا وغيانا الفرنسية ومارتينيك في أمريكا اللاتينية ومنطقة البحر الكاريبي. وكما ذُكر سابقا، فإن بعض هذه الزيادات في أمريكا اللاتينية ومنطقة البحر الكاريبي قد تكون ناتجة عن تغيرات في مدى الإبلاغ بحالات الاقتران الرضائي.

وازدادت معدلات الطلاق في معظم البلدان المتوافر عنها بيانات. فقد ارتفع المعدل الوسيط للطلاق في البلدان المتقدمة النمو من 13 طلاقا لكل 100 من الرجال والنساء في السبعينات إلى 24 طلاقا لكل 100 من الرجال و 27 طلاقا لكل 100 من النساء في التسعينات. وفي مجموعة البلدان النامية المتوافر عنها بيانات، زاد المعدل الوسيط للطلاق من 7 إلى 12 طلاقا لكل 100 من الرجال ومن 5 إلى 15 طلاقا لكل 100 من النساء. وفي ثلاثة أرباع جميع البلدان، المتقدمة النمو والنامية، المتوافر عنها بيانات لفترة السبعينات وإلى فترة التسعينات، زادت معدلات الطلاق، وفي نصف هذه البلدان، كانت الزيادات في حدود ما يتراوح من 6 إلى 7 لكل 000 1. أي أن الأمر لم يقتصر على نزوع الناس إلى الزواج في سن متأخر نسبيا، بل أخذ يزداد أيضا عدم استقرار الرباطات الزواجية. ومن الواضح أن كلا هذين الاتجاهين له آثار كبيرة على السلوك الإنجابي.

فيما بين السبعينات والتسعينات، ازداد استعمال وسائل منع الحمل بين النساء المتزوجات أو المقترنات حاليا في 90 في المائة من جميع البلدان المتوافر عنها بيانات لهاتين الفترتين. وزاد المعدل الوسيط لاستعمال وسائل منع الحمل على مستوى العالم من 38 في المائة من النساء المتزوجات أو المقترنات حاليا إلى 52 في المائة. بيد أن هذه الأرقام العالمية تحجب الفروق الهامة القائمة بين البلدان المتقدمة النمو والبلدان النامية.

ففي البلدان المتقدمة النمو، كان استعمال وسائل منع الحمل مرتفعا بالفعل في السبعينات، حيث كان ما لا يقل عن نصف جميع النساء المتزوجات أو المقترنات حاليا في البلدان المتقدمة النمو يستعملن وسائل منع الحمل. بل إنه في ثلاثة أرباع جميع البلدان المتقدمة النمو، كان ما لا يقل عن ثلثي جميع النساء المتزوجات أو المقترنات حاليا يستعملن وسائل منع الحمل في السبعينات. وبحلول التسعينات، ازداد معدل استعمال وسائل منع الحمل في 14 من البلدان المتقدمة النمو البالغ عددها 44 بلدا، ولكنه انخفض في ستة منها. وكثيرا ما كانت الانخفاضات التي سجلت في معدل استعمال وسائل منع الحمل ناتجة عن التناقص في استعمال الطرق التقليدية لمنع الحمل وتزايد الاعتماد على الطرق الحديثة. بيد أن بعض هذه الفروق قد لا تكون حقيقية، لكونها ناتجة عن تغييرات في إجراءات جمع البيانات لا عن تغيرات فعلية في السلوك. وعلى الرغم من ذلك، فإن البيانات تدل على أن البلدان المتقدمة النمو ككل شهدت زيادة ملحوظة في استعمال الطرق الحديثة لمنع الحمل، حيث ارتفع المعدل الوسيط لهذا الاستعمال من 54 إلى 61 في المائة من النساء المتزوجات أو المقترنات حاليا. وعلى الصعيد القطري، سجلت جميع البلدان المتوافر عنها بيانات لفترتي السبعينات والتسعينات حدوث زيادة في معدل انتشار الطرق الحديثة، إلا في النمسا، حيث انخفض هذا المعدل بحوالي 10 نقاط مئوية. وفي حالة النمسا، يمكن أن يكون هذا التغير ناتجا في جزء منه عن استعمال إجراءات مختلفة في جمع البيانات.

وفي البلدان النامية، كان معدل انتشار منع الحمل في السبعينات أقل بقدر ملحوظ مما أصبح عليه في التسعينات. ففي البلدان النامية المتوافر عنها معلومات، ارتفع المعدل الوسيط لانتشار منع الحمل من 27 في المائة إلى 40 في المائة فيما بين هاتين الفترتين. وبحلول التسعينات، بلغ معدل انتشار منع الحمل في نسبة الربع من جميع البلدان النامية 62 في المائة أو أكثر. بيد أنه في ربع آخر من جميع البلدان النامية، ظل معدل انتشار منع الحمل أدنى من 24 في المائة من جميع النساء المتزوجات أو المقترنات حاليا. بل وكانت معدلات استعمال الطرق الحديثة أدنى من ذلك. وعلى الرغم من أن المعدل الوسيط لاستعمال الطرق الحديثة لمنع الحمل في البلدان النامية ارتفع من 18 إلى 30 في المائة فيما بين السبعينات والتسعينات، لا يزال استعمال الطرق الحديثة نادرا في كثير من البلدان النامية، حيث تقل معدلات انتشار

هذه الطرق في ربع هذه البلدان عن 12 في المائة. وتشمل هذه الفئة الأخيرة أفغانستان واليمن في آسيا و 25 بلدا في أفريقيا.

وبحلول التسعينات، بلغ معدل انتشار الطرق الحديثة لمنع الحمل مستويات مرتفعة في عدد من البلدان النامية. ففي تونس وجنوب أفريقيا والجزائر وريونيون وزمبابوي ومصر، كان أكثر من نصف جميع النساء المتزوجات أو المقترنات حاليا يستعملن الطرق الحديثة لمنع الحمل بحلول التسعينات. وفي آسيا، تحققت معدلات مماثلة أو تفوق ذلك في إسرائيل وإندونيسيا وأوزبكستان وتايلند وتركمانستان وجمهورية إيران الإسلامية وجمهورية كوريا وجمهورية كوريا الشعبية الديمقراطية وسنغافورة والصين والفلبين وفييت نام وكازاخستان ومنطقة هونغ كونغ الصينية الإدارية الخاصة ومنغوليا. وفي أمريكا اللاتينية ومنطقة البحر الكاريبي، فاقت معدلات استعمال الطرق الحديثة لمنع الحمل 50 في المائة في أكثر من نصف جميع البلدان المتوافر عنها بيانات. ومعظم هذه البلدان سجل زيادات باهرة في استعمال الطرق الحديثة لمنع الحمل فيما بين السبعينات والتسعينات. وعلى مدى تلك الفترة، شهد ما لا يقل عن النصف من جميع البلدان النامية المتوافر عنها بيانات ارتفاعا في معدل استعمال الطرق الحديثة لمنع الحمل بمقدار 20 نقطة مئوية أو أكثر.

وموجز القول في هذا الصدد هو أنه قد قُطعت أشواط كبيرة في تلبية الطلب على الطرق الحديثة لمنع الحمل في البلدان النامية، ولكن لا تزال معدلات استعمال الطرق الحديثة لمنع الحمل منخفضة في كثير من بلدان أفريقيا وفي بعض بلدان آسيا وأمريكا اللاتينية ومنطقة البحر الكاريبي. وكالمتوقع، فإن معدلات استعمال الطرق الحديثة لمنع الحمل يغلب أن تكون منخفضة في حالة أقل البلدان نموا وغيرها من البلدان المنخفضة الدخل عنها في حالة البلدان المتوسطة الدخل.

انخفضت الخصوبة فيما بين السبعينات والتسعينات انخفاضا ملحوظا على مستوى العالم. فقد هبط المعدل الوسيط للخصوبة الكلية لجميع البلدان المتوافر عنها بيانات من 5.4 أطفال إلى 2.9 طفل لكل امرأة على مدى الفترة المذكورة. ومعظم هذا الانخفاض ناتج عن تناقص الخصوبة في

البلدان النامية، التي تغير فيها المعدل الوسيط للخصوبة الكلية من 5.9 أطفال إلى 3.9 أطفال لكل امرأة فيما بين السبعينات والتسعينات. وشهدت البلدان المتقدمة النمو أيضا انخفاضات ملموسة في الخصوبة، وإن كانت أصغر نسبيا، حيث هبط المعدل الوسيط للخصوبة الكلية من 2.3 إلى 1.4 طفل لكل امرأة على مدى تلك الفترة ذاتها.

وفيما عدا جمهورية الكونغو الديمقراطية وغينيا وغينيا الفرنسية ومالي، يبدو أن سائر البلدان النامية المتوافر عنها بيانات لفترتي السبعينات والتسعينات شهدت حدوث انخفاضات في مستويات الخصوبة، وإن كان يحتمل أن تكون تقديرات التغير مشوبة بالتحيز من جراء تفاوت أخطاء الإبلاغ في البيانات الأساسية. وعلى الرغم من ذلك، فإن البيانات المعروضة في هذا التقرير تعطي صورة عامة تؤكدها تقييمات أخرى لاتجاهات الخصوبة. وكان الانخفاض الوسيط في الخصوبة في البلدان النامية فيما بين السبعينات والتسعينات في حدود 1.8 طفل لكل امرأة، ويبدو أن نسبة الربع من جميع البلدان النامية حققت انخفاضات بلغت 25.6 طفل أو أكثر لكل امرأة. والصين هي إحدى البلدان في هذه الفئة، حيث خفضت خصوبتها بحوالي 4 أطفال لكل امرأة منذ عام 1970. ومن البلدان الأخرى التي أفيد بأنها حققت انخفاضات كبيرة في الخصوبة تركيا وتايلند وتونس والجزائر وجمهورية إيران الإسلامية والمكسيك. وعلى النقيض من ذلك، انخفضت الخصوبة ببطء (بأقل من طفل واحد منذ عام 1970) أو لم تنخفض إطلاقا في 21 بلدا ناميا، منها 13 بلدا في أفريقيا جنوب الصحراء الكبرى.

وفيما يتعلق بالبلدان المتقدمة النمو، كانت انخفاضات الخصوبة هي القاعدة، وإن كانت صغيرة المقدار ولكن ليست بالهينة بالنظر إلى انخفاض مستويات الخصوبة الكلية الذي أصبحت تتسم به معظم هذه البلدان بالفعل بحلول السبعينات. وبلغ الانخفاض الوسيط في الخصوبة الكلية للبلدان المتقدمة النمو 0.8 طفل لكل امرأة، وبحلول التسعينات لم يتجاوز عدد البلدان المتقدمة النمو التي أبلغت بمعدل كلي للخصوبة قدره 2 طفل أو أكثر لكل امرأة أربعة بلدان، هي ألبانيا وأيسلندا ونيوزيلندا والولايات المتحدة الأمريكية. أما في السبعينات، فقد كانت مستويات الخصوبة 2 طفل على الأقل لكل امرأة في 36 من البلدان المتقدمة النمو.

وباعتبـار أن مسـتوى الخصـوبة البـالغ 2.1 طفـل لكـل امـرأة يمثل المسـتوى الـذي يكفـل تمـام الإحـلال السكاني عنـدما يكون معـدل الوفيـات منخفضـا، كانت مستويات الخصوبة في 12 من البلدان المتقدمة النمو دون مستوى الإحـلال في السبعينات بينمـا لم تبلغ الخصوبة هذا المستوى مـن الانخفاض إلا في بلد واحد فقط من البلدان النامية. وبحلول التسعينات، زاد عدد البلدان المتقدمة النمو التي يقل مسـتوى خصوبتها عن مستوى الإحلال إلى 41 بلدا، وبلغ هذا العدد في حالة البلدان النامية 19 بلدا. وفي 14 من البلدان المتقدمـة النمـو، كـان معدل الخصوبة الكلية أقل مـن 1.3 طفل لكـل امـرأة، وهو مستوى لـم يسبق لـه مثيل في التـاريخ المسجل للكتل السكانية الكبيرة.

وترافقت مـع الانخفاض العـالمي في الخصـوبة تحـولات كبيـرة في توقيت الإنجاب. ففي نسبة النصف من جميع البلدان النامية، انخفض متوسط السن الـذي يبـدأ عنـده إنجـاب المرأة للأطفال، مـع تنـاقص معدلات الخصوبة لدى النساء الأكبر سنا. وفي البلدان المتقدمة النمو، نزع الاتجاه الرئيسي إلى ارتفـاع متوسط سـن الإنجاب نتيجـة لإرجـاء المرأة لبدء الإنجاب. وتفيد البيانات المتعلقة بمتوسط السن عند ولادة الطفل الأول بـأن هذا المتوسط آخذ في الارتفاع عموما في كل من البلدان المتقدمة النمو والبلدان النامية. وكانت الزيادات في متوسط سن الأمهات عند إنجـاب الطفل الأول أكثر وضوحا في حالة البلدان المتقدمة النمو، حيث زاد متوسط هذا السن في ثلاثة أرباع هذه البلدان بما لا يقل عن 1.7 سنة فيما بين السبعينات والتسعينات. وفي البلدان النامية، كانت هذه الزيادات أقل مقدارا، حيث بلغت 0.5 سنة على الأقل في ثلاثة أربـاع جميـع البلدان النامية المتوافر عنهـا بيانـات لهاتين الفتـرتين. ويتضح من ذلك أنه لا تزال توجد فروق هامـة في توقيت المولود الأول بين البلدان المتقدمة النمو والبلدان النامية. وفي التسعينات، بلغت القيمة الوسيطة لمتوسط السن عند ولادة الطفل الأول 26.4 سنة في البلدان المتقدمـة النمـو و 22.1 سنة فقط في البلدان النامية.

وحدثت أيضـا تغيرات مهمـة فيمـا يتعلق بمستوى عدم الإنسال بـين النسـاء مـن الفئـة العمريـة 45-49 سـنة. وعلـى الـرغم مـن قلـة عـدد البلدان المتوافر عنها بيانات قابلة للمقارنة لفترتي السبعينات والتسعينات، فإن الأدلـة المتاحة تبين حدوث انخفاض مهم في عدم الإنسال في أفريقيا، حيث كانت

الأمراض المنقولة عن طريق الاتصال الجنسي سببا مهما من أسباب العقم في الخمسينات والستينات. وفي أمريكا اللاتينية أيضا، هبطت عموما مستويات عدم الإنسال. وفي المناطق الرئيسية الأخرى حدثت زيادات وانخفاضات في مستويات عدم الإنسال، ولكن في حين أن مستويات عدم الإنسال في التسعينات كانت منخفضة إلى حد ما في أفريقيا وآسيا (حيث لم تتجاوز إطلاقا 9 في المائة وكانت في معظم البلدان أقل من 5 أو 7 في المائة، على التوالي)، فإنها كانت مرتفعة في منطقة البحر الكاريبي والبلدان المتقدمة النمو. ففي ثلاثة من كل أربعة من البلدان المتقدمة النمو في التسعينات، كان 7 في المائة على الأقل من النساء من الفئة العمرية 45-49 سنة غير منجبات، وفي ثلاثة أرباع بلدان منطقة البحر الكاريبي المتوافر عنها بيانات بشأن هذا الموضوع، كانت نسبة النساء غير المنجبات من الفئة العمرية 45-49 سنة 8 في المائة على الأقل. وسُجلت مستويات عدم الإنسال المرتفعة بصفة خاصة (أعلى من 10 في المائة) في استونيا وأوروغواي والبرتغال وجزر الأنتيل الهولندية وجمهورية مولدوفا ورومانيا وسويسرا وفرنسا وفنلندا وكندا ولكسمبرغ.

حدثت تغيرات كبرى في الآراء التي تعتنقها الحكومات والإجراءات التي تتخذها فيما يتعلق بمستويات الخصوبة واتجاهاتها. ففي عام 1976، أفاد 52 في المائة من جميع الحكومات بأنه لا توجد لديها أي مبادرات لتعديل مستويات الخصوبة، ولكن هذه النسبة انخفضت بحلول عام 2001 إلى 32 في المائة (انظر الشكل الثاني). وأخذ الدعم الحكومي لتنظيم الأسرة يزداد ازديادا مطردا منذ السبعينات. وبحلول عام 2001، أصبح 92 في المائة من جميع الحكومات يدعم برامج تنظيم الأسرة وتوزيع وسائل منع الحمل إما بصورة مباشرة (75 في المائة) عن طريق مرافق حكومية، أو بصورة غير مباشرة (17 في المائة) عن طريق دعم أنشطة المنظمات غير الحكومية، مثل رابطات تنظيم الأسرة.

وتغيرت تغيرا ملموسا أيضا آراء الحكومات بشأن مدى مناسبة مستويات الخصوبة. ففي حين أنه في عام 1976، كانت نسبة الحكومات التي تريد خفض الخصوبة 27 في المائة من جميع الحكومات، فإن هذه النسبة ارتفعت بحلول عام 2001 إلى 45 في المائة. وفي حالة البلدان

النامية، كانت النسبة التي تريد خفض الخصوبة أعلى من ذلك في عام 2001، إذ بلغت 58 في المائة. وكانت هناك زيادة أيضا في نسبة الحكومات التي تريد رفع مستوى الخصوبة: من 9 في المائة في عام 1976 إلى 13 في المائة في عام 2001. ونتيجة لذلك، انخفض الوزن النسبي للحكومات التي تريد الإبقاء على مستويات الخصوبة الراهنة من 13 في المائة إلى 10 في المائة. وهذا يعني أنه يوجد حاليا عدد أكبر من الحكومات يريد تغيير مستويات خصوبة سكانه ويوجد لديه استعداد لتصميم مبادرات مناسبة لتحقيق هذه الأهداف.

الشكل الأول

توزيع 160 بلدا حسب مستوى الخصوبة الكلية حوالي عامي 1970 و 2000

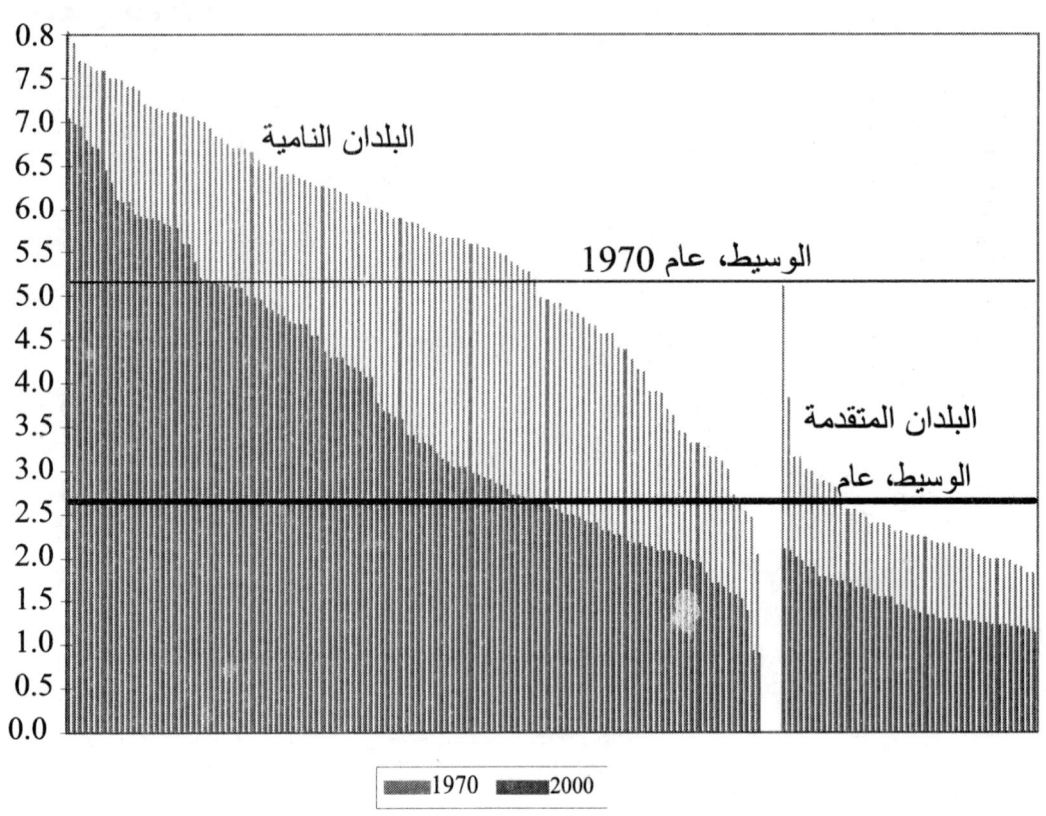

البلدان النامية

الوسيط، عام 1970

البلدان المتقدمة

الوسيط، عام

1970 ∎∎∎ 2000 ∎∎∎

الشكل الثاني - سياسات الحكومات بشأن مستوى الخصوبة: 1976 و 2001

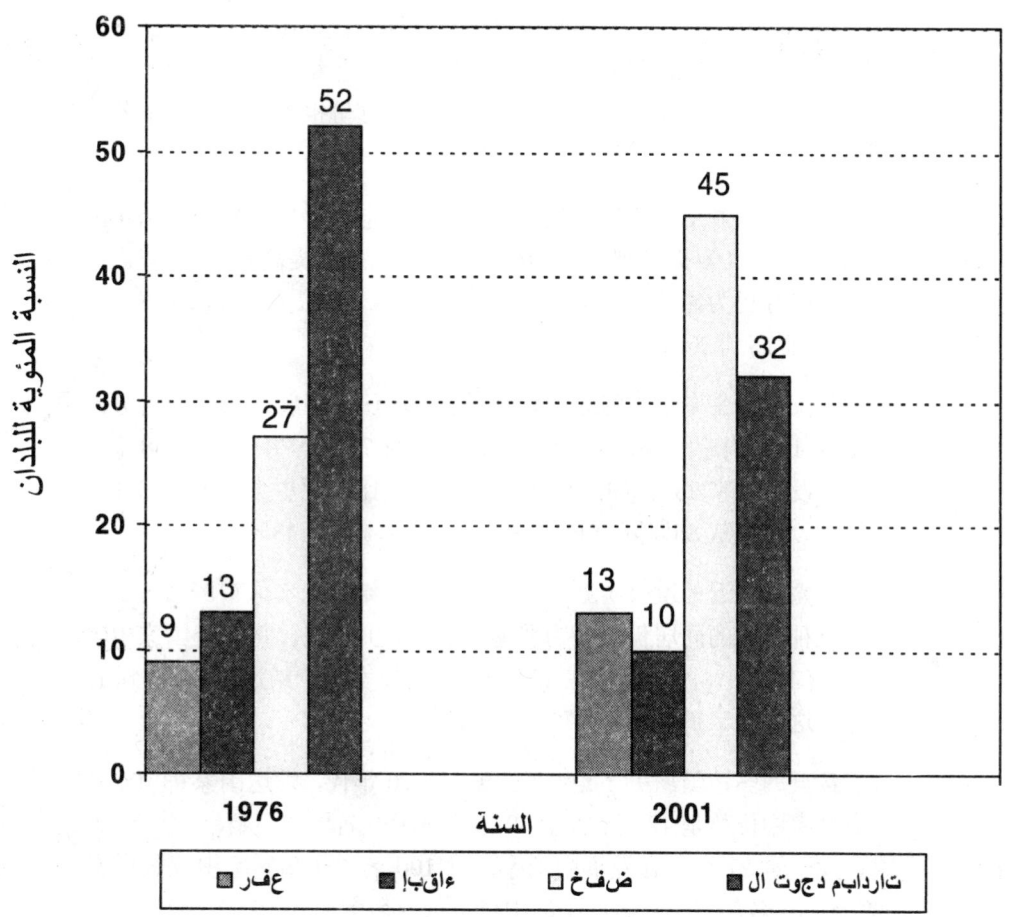

2003 年世界生育率报告

提要

《2003 年世界生育率报告》由联合国秘书处经济及社会事务部人口司编制，汇编了 192 个国家的生育率、结婚率和使用避孕药具的重要估计数和指标，大多指的是 1970 年代和 1990 年代，必要时也涵盖更早期阶段，在可能的情况下则包括更近时期。有了这一组数据就可以对 1970 年代以来在结婚率、避孕药具的使用和生育率方面发生的空前变化进行评估。特别是，这份报告记载了以下各项重大统计结果：

1. 全世界的婚龄发生了向后推迟的重大变化。全世界男子平均初婚年龄中位数值从 25.4 岁提高到 27.2 岁，妇女从 21.5 岁提高到 23.2 岁。发达国家的增幅更为显著，男子的中位数值从 25.2 岁提高到 28.8 岁，女子从 22 岁提高到 26.1 岁。

2. 无论男女，一生中单身的时间都更长。25 至 29 岁曾婚妇女的百分比中位数从 1970 年代的 85％降至 1990 年代的 76％，男子则从 68％降至 56％。发达国家 25 至 29 岁曾婚人口的百分比降幅更大，曾婚妇女的百分比中位数值从 85％降至 62％，男子从 74％降至 43％。

3. 青年人婚龄推迟并没有明显缩小一生中至少结婚一次人口的百分比。婚姻或某种形式的同居仍然极为普遍。在 1970 年代，每四个国家中，就有三个国家 89％以上年龄在 45 至 49 岁的男女至少结过一次婚，到 1990 年代，这一数字仍然接近 89％。

4. 在有数据的多数国家中，离婚率上升。1970 年代，发达国家每 100 名男女离婚率中位数是 13 名，到 1990 年代每 100 名男子离婚率中位数是 24 名，女子是 27 名。在发展中国家，每 100 名男子离婚率中位数从 7 名增加到 12 名，每 100 名女子的中位数从 5 名增加到 15 名。这就是说，不仅出现了晚婚的趋势，婚姻的不稳定性也在日趋上升。这两种趋势显然对生殖行为产生重大影响。

5. 采取计划生育的人数显著增加。在 1970 年代至 1990 年代期间，在可提供资料的国家中，每十个中有九个国家使用避孕药具的已婚或同居妇女的人数有所增加。从 1970 年代至 1990 年代，世界范围使用避孕药具的已婚或同居妇女的中位数从 38％上升到 52％。发展中国家在这段期间的中位数值从 27％上升到 40％。到 1990 年代，在所有发展中国家中，四分之一国家的避孕率已上升到 62％或更高。

6. 发展中国家使用现代避孕方法的人数普遍增加。发展中国家使用现代避孕方法的中位数从 1970 年代的 18％上升到 1990 年代的 30％。但是，在所有发展中国家中，有四分之一国家仍然很少使用现代避孕方法，使用率仍然低于12%。

7. 在 1970 至 2000 年期间，主要由于发展中国家生育率下降，世界人口的生育水平空前大幅下降（图一）。发展中世界的平均生育水平从 1970 年代的每名妇女逾 5.9 名子女减少到 1990 年代的每名妇女约 3.9 名子女。在 1970 年代至 1990 年代期间，发展中国家生育率下降的中位数大约是每名妇女减少 1.8 名子女，有四分之一的发展中国家是每名妇女减少 2.6 名子女，或减少得更多。

8. 在 1970 年代，发展中国家的生育率普遍很高，如今发展中国家的生育水平则差异很大。因此，在一些最不发达国家，生育率仍保持在每名妇女有五名以上子女，但是在大约 20 个发展中国家，则低于更替水平。

9. 发达国家的生育水平自 1970 年代以来普遍下降，其中很多国家在 1950 年代和 1960 年代期间经历了婴儿高潮期。在 1970 年代至 1990 年代期间，发达国家总生育率下降的中位数是每名妇女 0.8 名子女。到 1990 年代后期，只有四个发达国家——阿尔巴尼亚、冰岛、新西兰和美利坚合众国——报告的总生育率是每名妇女两名子女或更多。此外，在 14 个发达国家中，每名妇女的生育率低于 1.3 名子女，在有记载的历史中，这种大规模人口的低生育率水平是前所未有的。

10. 在主要地区之间，无子女人口差别很大。在 1990 年代，发达国家和加勒比国家年龄在 45 至 49 岁之间的无子女妇女的比例一般都较高。在有数据的每五个发达国家中，有四个国家至少有 7% 年龄在 45 至 49 岁之间的妇女是无子女的。有九个发达国家无子女人数的比率超过了 10%。在 1990 年代，非洲和亚洲无子女人口相对较少，拉丁美洲情况属于一般。由于从 1970 年代到 1980 年代非洲性传播疾病造成的不育症减少，在 1970 年代至 1990 年代期间无子女人数也在减少。

11. 同居关系、婚姻和避孕药具使用方面的重大行为转变，使 1970 年代以来生育水平发生巨大变化。政府关于获取避孕药具的政策在转变生殖行为方面发挥重大作用。在 1976 年，有 52% 的国家政府报告说他们没有制定改变生育水平的措施，但是到 2001 年，这一百分比下降到 32%（图 2）。自 1970 年代以来，支持计划生育的政府稳步增加。到 2001 年，有 92% 的国家政府支持计划生育方案，或通过政府设施直接分发避孕药具（75%），或通过支持计划生育协会等非政府组织的活动，间接提供避孕药具（17%）。

本报告选载的生育率、结婚率、避孕药具的使用和生育政策数据，是为了反映 1970 年代以来，也就是在经历了一代人之后，在生殖和婚姻行为方面发生的重大转变。其中列入了按同期出生群分列反映变化的指标和从年代角度出发显示趋势的其他指标。数据的来源很多，包括公民登记、人口普查和有代表性的国内调查。提出的数据没有进行过覆盖面、少计或其他非抽样误差的调整。因此，某些指标值，特别是与没有完整数据的发展中国家有关的指标值可能与人口司在《世界人口前景：2002 年订正本》中公布的数据不符，因为后者已视必要进行过调整。对于可提供数据的每一个国家，都列入了每一个年代的 43 个指标的值。

下文更详细地讨论本报告的主要统计结果。在讨论结果时，分析单位是国家，主要重点是各个指标显示的国家分布情况的变化。

结婚率

婚姻或某种形式的同居仍然极为普遍。1970 年代，在每四个国家中，就有三个国家的 89％45 至 49 岁的男女至少结过一次婚，到 1990 年代，这一数字仍然接近 89％。此外，1970 年代，在有相关数字的所有国家中，四分之一国家的 45 至 49 岁曾婚或曾同居的男子比例为 97％，或更高，在 1990 年代为 98％，或更高。同样，在所有国家中，四分之一的国家至少有 98％45 至 49 岁的妇女曾婚或曾同居。

在 1970 年代，亚洲国家的结婚率最高，现在仍然很高，当然某些国家，特别是日本的男子，新加坡的妇女或在文莱达鲁萨兰国、以色列、马来西亚、缅甸和被占领的巴勒斯坦领土，曾婚人数比例急剧下降。非洲国家的结婚或同居率也很高，其中四分之三的国家报告说，到 1990 年代，至少 96％45 至 49 岁的男子和至少 98％同一年龄组的妇女曾婚或曾同居。事实上，非洲一些国家 45 至 49 岁曾婚人数特别是男子的比例有显著增加。其中的例子有贝宁、布基纳法索，喀麦隆、中非共和国和乌干达。相反，在博茨瓦纳、留尼汪岛和南非，45 至 49 岁曾婚男女的比率显著下降。

与发展中世界其他地区相比，拉丁美洲国家，特别是加勒比区域结婚或同居率不是很高。到 1990 年代，在半数加勒比国家，45 至 49 岁曾婚或曾同居的男子比率最多是 72％，妇女最多是 70％。此外，在 1970 年代至 1990 年代期间，巴巴多斯、牙买加、荷属安的列斯群岛和圣卢西亚曾婚人数比率大幅下降。在拉丁美洲其他国家，45 至 49 岁曾婚人数比率高一些，但是到 1990 年代，在该区域半数国家中，至少有 10％45 至 49 岁的男子和 9％45 岁至 49 岁的妇女从未结过婚，或从未同过居。这些数字代表了从 1970 年代开始发生的变化，1970 年代从未结婚的人数比例往往较高。在 1970 年代至 1990 年代期间，在至少半数的拉丁美洲国家中，45 至 49 岁曾婚或曾同居的男女比例显著增加。但是在拉丁美洲和加勒比，同居现象很普遍，必须审慎地解读曾婚人口比例数据，因为数据反映的趋势部分可能是有关同居的报告方式逐步有所改进所致，而不是结婚率发生了实际变化。

在欧洲、北美和澳大利亚/新西兰，结婚或同居比例仍然很高，在这些区域的每四个国家中，就有三个国家86％以上45至49岁的男子和89％以上45至49岁的妇女曾婚或曾同居。但是，在1970年代至1990年代期间，其中至少四分之三的国家曾婚男子人数比例下降，下降比例最大的是北欧国家以及拉脱维亚、冰岛、荷兰和美国。但是在一些国家，特别是丹麦、冰岛和瑞典，曾婚妇女人数比例下降不是一个普遍现象，不过仍然很显著。

通过现有数据，可以对1970年代和1990年代25至29岁结婚或同居的男女人口比例进行一个比较。这一比较显示，全世界的婚龄发生重大变化：25至29岁曾婚妇女的中位数比例从85％减少到76％，男子从68％减少到56％。此外，在提供所需数据的所有国家中，四分之三的国家显示25至29岁曾婚人口比例下降。欧洲和北美各国以及澳大利亚/新西兰下降的比例最大，这些国家年轻人的婚龄不断推迟，但是所有其他区域也出现明显的相同趋势。这些变化可能预示，今后45至49岁人口的结婚率或同居率将普遍全面下降。

这也反映在婚龄不断提高。因此，在1970年代至1990年期间，在有数据的所有国家中，有四分之三国家的平均初婚年龄（衡量单身生活平均年数的一个指标）提高。在世界范围，男子平均初婚年龄的中位数值从25.4岁提高到27.2岁，妇女从21.5岁提高到23.2岁。发达国家的平均初婚年龄的增幅特别大，下列国家的平均初婚年龄都提高4岁以上：澳大利亚、比利时、加拿大、丹麦、法国、芬兰、匈牙利、冰岛、爱尔兰、意大利、荷兰、挪威、瑞典、瑞士、联合王国和美国。发展中国家特别是男子的平均初婚年龄增幅较小。不过，各个区域都有一些国家平均初婚年龄提高了3岁以上，其中包括亚洲和北非的阿尔及利亚、阿拉伯利比亚民众国、科威特、马尔代夫、马来西亚、摩洛哥、卡塔尔、苏丹和突尼斯以及拉丁美洲和加勒比的巴哈马、瓜德罗普岛、法属圭亚那、圭亚那、马提尼克岛、荷属安的列斯群岛、圣卢西亚和美属维尔京群岛。如上所述，拉丁美洲和加勒比一些国家平均初婚年龄提高是因为改变了有关同居的报告方式。

多数有数据的国家离婚率上升。在发达国家，离婚率中位数从1970年代每100名男女13人离婚增加到1990年代每100名男子24人离婚，每100名妇女27人离婚。在有数据的的发展中国家中，离婚率中位数从每100名男子7人离婚增加到12人离婚，每100名妇女5人离婚增加到15人离婚。在可提供1970年代至1990年代数据的所有国家，不论是发达国家还是发展中国家，有四分之三离婚率上升，其中一半国家上升到每100人有6至7人离婚。这就是说，不仅出现了晚婚的趋势，婚姻的不稳定性也在持续上升。这两种趋势显然都对生殖行为产生重大影响。

避孕药具的使用

在1970年代至1990年代期间，在可提供这两个年代资料的90％的国家中，使用避孕药具的已婚或同居妇女人数上升。世界范围使用避孕药具的已婚或同居妇女的中位数水平从 38% 上升到 52%。但是这些全球数字显示了发达国家与发展中国家之间的重大差别。

发达国家避孕药具的使用率在 1970 年代就很高，当时发达国家至少有一半已婚或同居妇女使用避孕药具。事实上 1970 年代，在四分之三发达国家的已婚或同居妇女中，至少有三分之二的妇女使用避孕药具。到 1990 年代，在 44 个发达国家中，有 14 个国家避孕药具的使用率上升，但是有 6 个国家使用率下降。所记载的避孕药具使用率下降往往是因为使用传统避孕方法的人数减少，依赖现代方法的人数增加。但是其中一些差异可能是一种假象，是数据收集程序的变化造成的，而不是实际的行为变化。但是数据表明，发达国家作为一个整体，使用现代避孕方法人数显著增加，已婚或同居妇女使用这类方法的中位数水平从 54% 上升到 61%。在国家一级，所有可提供 1970 年代和 1990 年代数据的国家使用现代方法的普及率都在上升，奥地利是一个例外，该国的普及率减少了近十个百分点。对于奥地利来说，这一变化可能部分是因为使用不同的数据收集程序造成的。

在发展中国家，1970 年代避孕普及率比 1990 年代要低得多。在有资料的发展中国家，这两个年代之间避孕普及率中位数水平从 27% 上升到 40%。到 1990 年代，有四分之一发展中国家的避孕普及率达到 62% 或更高。但是在另外四分之一发展中国家所有已婚或同居妇女中，避孕普及率仍低于 24%。使用现代方法的人数则更少。尽管从 1970 年代至 1990 年代发展中国家使用现代避孕方法的中位数水平从 18% 上升到 30%，但是在很多发展中国家，很少有人使用现代方法，其中四分之一国家的普及率低于 12%。后者包括亚洲的阿富汗和也门以及非洲的 25 个国家。

到 1990 年代，一些发展中国家使用现代避孕方法的普及率已经很高。因此，在阿尔及利亚、埃及、留尼汪、南非、突尼斯和津巴布韦，到 1990 年代，已有半数以上已婚或同居妇女使用现代避孕方法。下列国家达到同样或更高水平：在亚洲有中国、朝鲜民主主义人民共和国、中国香港特别行政区、印度尼西亚、伊朗伊斯兰共和国、以色列、哈萨克斯坦、蒙古、大韩民国、菲律宾、新加坡、泰国、土库曼斯坦、乌兹别克斯坦和越南。在拉丁美洲和加勒比可提供数据的半数国家，使用现代避孕方法比率超过 50%。其中多数国家在 1970 年代至 1990 年代期间使用现代避孕方法的人数显著增加。在这段时期内，如所预料，在所有可提供数据的发展中国家中，其中至少一半国家使用现代避孕方法的比例上升了 20 个百分点或更高。

总之，发展中国家在满足现代避孕方法需求方面已取得重大进展，但是很多非洲国家以及亚洲、拉丁美洲和加勒比一些国家使用现代避孕方法的比例仍然较低。最不发达国家和其他低收入国家使用现代避孕方法的人数更有可能少于中等收入国家。

生育率

在 1970 年代至 1990 年代期间，世界范围的生育率明显下降。在此期间，可提供数据的所有国家的总生育率中位数从每名妇女 5.4 名子女减少到每名妇女 2.9 名子女，多数是由于发展中国家生育率下降造成的。这些国家总生育率中位数从 1970 年代每名妇女 5.9 名子女减少到 1990 年代每名妇女 3.9 名子女。发达国家的生育率尽管下降的幅度小一些，也很显著。发达国家在同一时期的总生育率中位数从每名妇女 2.3 名子女减少到每名妇女 1.4 名子女。

除刚果民主共和国、法属圭亚那、圭亚那和马里之外，所有可提供 1970 年代和 1990 年代数据的其他发展中国家的生育率都在下降，但由于基本数据方面的不同报告方法的误差，可能在估计变化时产生偏差。不过，本报告提出的数据反映了整体情况，这可从有关生育率趋势的其他评估中得到印证。在 1970 年代至 1990 年代期间，发展中国家生育率下降的中位数大约是每名妇女减少 1.8 名子女，有四分之一的发展中国家是每名妇女减少 2.6 名子女，或减少得更多。中国便属于这一组国家，自 1970 年以来，每名妇女减少生育 4 名子女。报告生育率大幅下降的其他国家包括阿尔及利亚、伊朗伊斯兰共和国、墨西哥、泰国、突尼斯和土耳其。但是有 21 个发展中国家的生育率减速缓慢（自 1970 年以来还不到 1 名子女）或根本没有下降，其中有 13 个国家是在撒哈拉以南非洲。

发达国家生育率下降已成为规律，降幅虽小，却不容小视，因为自 1970 年代以来其中多数国家的总生育率水平已经较低。发达国家总生育率下降的中位数是每名妇女 0.8 名子女。到 1990 年代，只有四个发达国家——阿尔巴尼亚、冰岛、新西兰和美利坚合众国——报告的总生育率是每名妇女两名子女，或更多。在 1970 年代，有 36 个发达国家的生育率是每名妇女至少两名子女。

如果将每名妇女 2.1 名子女作为在死亡率低的情况下确保人口更替的生育水平，在 1970 年代，有 12 个发达国家的生育水平低于更替水平，而只有一个发展中国家有同样低的生育水平。到 1990 年代，生育率低于更替水平的发达国家数目增加到 41 个，发展中国家则是 19 个。有 14 个发达国家的总生育率是每名妇女少于 1.3 名子女，这在有记载的历史中，这种大规模人口的低生育水平是前所未有的。

在世界范围生育率下降的同时，育龄时机也发生重大变化。在半数发展中国家，由于年纪较长妇女的生育率下降，妇女生育的平均年龄降低。在发达国家，生育的平均年龄提高已成为主要趋势，这是因为妇女推迟开始生育的时机。无论是发达国家还是发展中国家的数据都表明，生育头胎子女的平均年龄普遍提高。发达国家母亲生育头胎子女的平均年龄提高得较多，在 1970 年代至 1990 年代期间，其中四分之三国家生育头胎子女的平均年龄至少提高 1.7 岁。发展中国家则不太显著，在可提供这两个年代数据的四分之三的发展中国家，生育头胎子女的平均年龄至少提高了 0.5 岁。因此，发达国家和发展中国家在生育头胎子女的时机方面仍然存在重大差距。在 1990 年期间，发达国家生育头胎子女的平均年龄中位数值是 26.4 岁，发展中国家只是 22.1 岁。

45 至 49 岁之间无子女妇女的人数也发生重大变化。尽管 1970 年代和 1990 年代提供可比数据的国家很少，但仍然有证据表明：非洲无子女人人数大幅减少，该区域性传播疾病是 1950 年代和 1960 年代造成不育症的一个重要原因。拉丁美洲无子女人数也普遍减少。其他主要地区的无子女人数有增也有减。在 1990 年代，非洲和亚洲国家无子女人数比较少（从未超过 9%，多数国家仍然分别低于 5% 或 7%），但是加勒比和发达国家无子女人数比例较高。1990 年代，在每四个发达国家中，其中三个国家至少有 7%45 至 49 岁的妇女是无子女的，在有这方面数据的四分之三的加勒比国家，至少有 8%45 至 49 岁的妇女是无子女的。下列国家无子女人数比例特别高（超过 10%）：加拿大、爱沙尼亚、芬兰、法国、卢森堡、荷属安的列斯群岛、葡萄牙、摩尔多瓦共和国、罗马尼亚、瑞士和乌拉圭。

人口政策

各国政府对于生育水平和趋势的看法和行动发生了重大变化。在 1976 年，有 52% 的国家政府报告说它们没有采取措施改变生育水平，但是到 2001 年，这一百分比降至 32%（见图二）。从 1970 年代以来，支持计划生育的政府稳步增加。到 2001 年，有 92% 的国家政府支持计划生育方案，或通过政府设施直接分发避孕药具（75%），或通过支持计划生育协会等非政府组织的活动，间接提供避孕药具（17%）。

各国政府对于适当的生育水平的看法也发生重大变化。在 1976 年，有 27% 的国家政府希望降低生育率，到 2001 年，希望降低生育率的政府为 45%。在发展中国家，2001 年希望降低生育率的政府的百分比更高，达 58%。希望提高生育率的政府的百分比也在提高，从 1976 年的 9% 提高到 13%。因此，希望维持现有生育水平的政府的比重从 13% 降至 10%。这就是说，如今有更多国家政府希望改变本国人口的生育水平，并打算制定适当措施实现这些目标。

2003 年世界生育率报告

图一. 1970 年和 2000 年 16 个国家的总和生育率水平分布情况

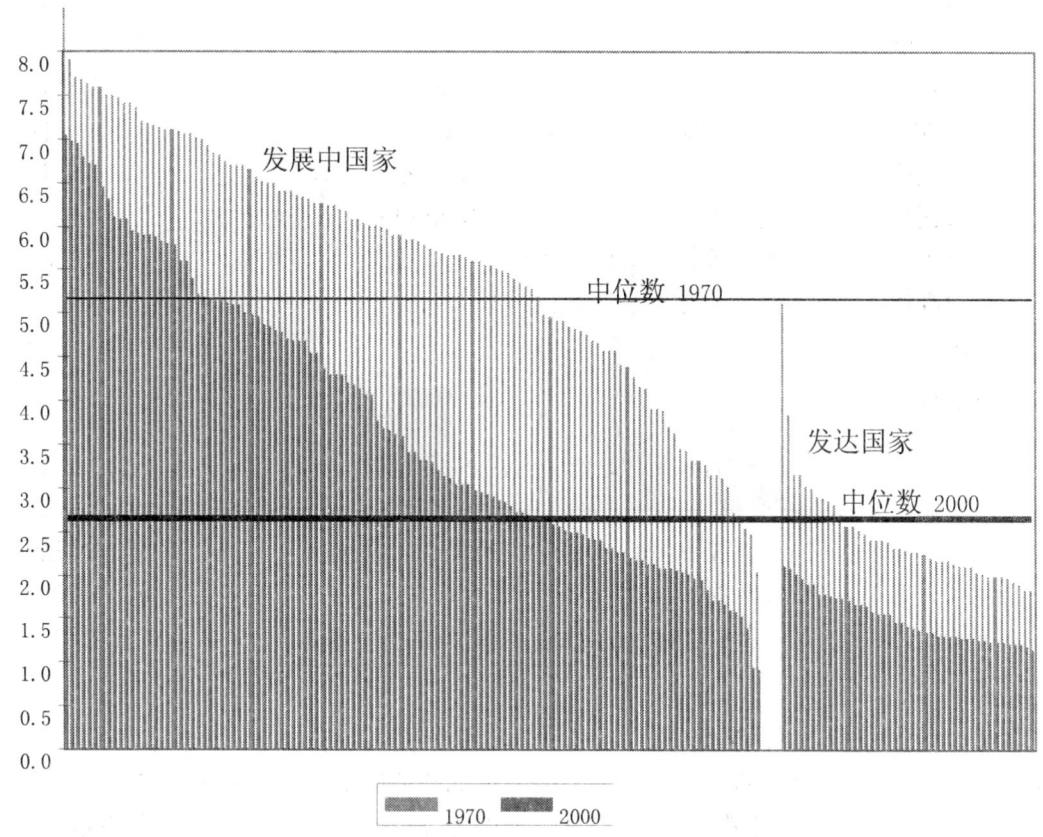

图二. 政府对生育水平采取的政策：1976 年和 2001 年

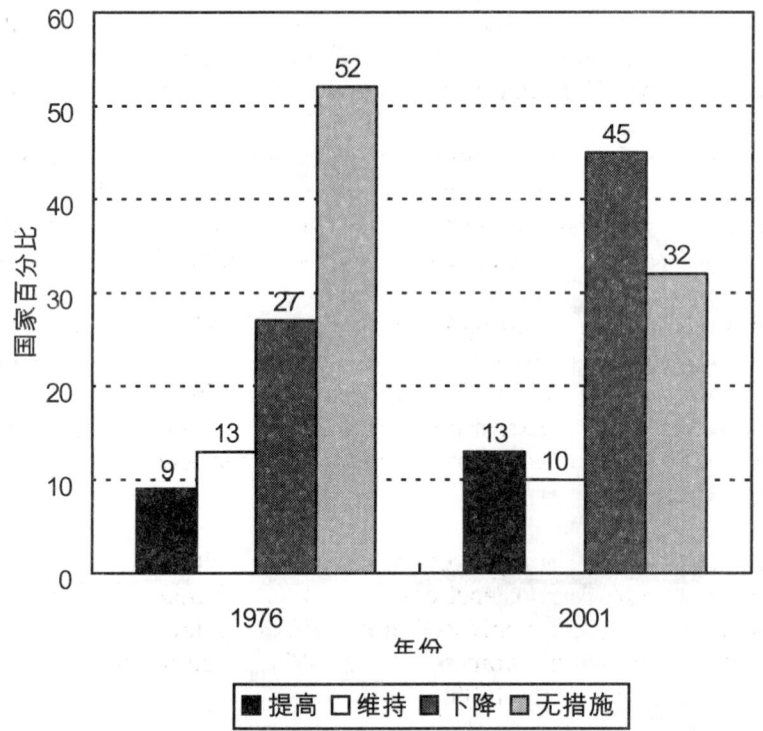

EXECUTIVE SUMMARY

The *World Fertility Report 2003*, prepared by the Population Division of the Department of Economic and Social Affairs of the United Nations Secretariat, presents a compilation of key estimates and indicators of fertility, nuptiality and contraceptive use for 192 countries, referring mostly to the 1970s and to the 1990s but covering earlier when necessary or more recent periods when possible. The set of data presented permit an assessment of the unprecedented changes in nuptiality, contraceptive use and fertility that have occurred since the 1970s. In particular, the report documents the following key findings:

1.	**A major worldwide shift in the timing of marriage to older ages has occurred**. The median value of the singulate mean age at marriage for the world rose from 25.4 to 27.2 years among men and from 21.5 to 23.2 years among women. For developed countries, the increase has been even more striking, with the median rising from 25.2 to 28.8 years for men and 22.0 to 26.1 for women.

2.	**Both men and women are spending longer periods of their life being single**. The median of the percentage ever-married among persons aged 25-29 declined from 85 per cent in the 1970s to 76 per cent in the 1990s for women, and from 68 per cent to 56 per cent for men. Again, the reductions in the percentage of ever-married persons aged 25-29 are more substantial for developed countries, whose median values declined from 85 per cent to 62 per cent among women and from 74 per cent to 43 per cent among men.

3.	**Delayed marriage among young adults has not yet resulted in noticeable reductions in the percentage of persons marrying at least once over their lifetime**. Marriage or some form of consensual union continues to be nearly universal. In the 1970s, in three out of every four countries, 89 per cent or more of all men and all women aged 45-49 had been married at least once and that figure was still close to 89 per cent by the 1990s.

4.	**Divorce rates have increased in most countries with data available**. In developed countries, the median rate of divorce rose from 13 divorces per 100 for men and women in the 1970s to 24 divorces per 100 men and 27 per 100 women in the 1990s. In developing countries, the median rate of divorce increased from 7 to 12 divorces per 100 men and from 5 to 15 divorces per 100 women. That is, not only has there been a tendency for people to marry later, but the instability of marital unions has been rising. Both trends clearly have significant implications for reproductive behaviour.

5.	**A tremendous increase has taken place in the use of family planning**. Between the 1970s and the 1990s, the use of contraception among women currently married or in union increased in nine out of every ten countries with information available. The median level of contraceptive use at the world level increased from 38 per cent of women currently married or in union in the 1970s to 52 per cent in the 1990s. For developing countries, the median prevalence rose from 27 per cent to 40 per cent between those dates. By the 1990s, contraceptive prevalence in a quarter of all developing countries was 62 per cent or higher.

6.	**The use of modern contraceptive methods in developing countries has generally risen**. The median use of modern contraception in developing countries increased from 18 to 30 per cent between the 1970s and the 1990s. However, in a quarter of all developing countries the use of modern contraceptive methods remains rare, with levels of use remaining below 12 per cent.

7.	**Between 1970 and 2000, the world population experienced a major and unprecedented reduction of fertility levels, driven mostly by the decline in fertility in developing countries** (figure I). Average fertility levels in the developing world dropped from over 5.9 children per woman in the 1970s to about 3.9 children per woman in the 1990s. The median fertility reduction in developing countries between the 1970s and the 1990s was of the order of 1.8 children per woman and a quarter of all developing countries appear to have achieved reductions of 2.6 children per woman or more.

8.   **Whereas fertility was uniformly high in developing countries in the 1970s, the fertility levels of developing countries today vary over a wide range**. Thus, fertility remains above 5 children per woman in a number of least developed countries but it has reached below-replacement levels in about 20 developing countries.

9.   **Fertility levels in developed countries, many of which experienced a "baby boom" during the 1950s and 1960s, have generally declined since 1970**. The median reduction in the total fertility of developed countries was 0.8 children per woman between the 1970s and the 1990s. By the late 1990s only four developed countries—Albania, Iceland, New Zealand and the United States of America—reported a total fertility of 2 children per woman or higher. Furthermore, in 14 developed countries, fertility was lower than 1.3 children per woman, an unprecedented low level of fertility in the recorded history of large populations.

10.   **Levels of childlessness vary considerably among major areas**. In the 1990s, the proportions of childless women among those aged 45-49 tended to be high in developed countries and in countries of the Caribbean. At least 7 per cent of women aged 45-49 were childless in four of every five developed countries with data and in nine developed countries the proportion childless surpassed 10 per cent. Levels of childlessness were relatively low in Africa and Asia in the 1990s and moderate in Latin America. Between the 1970s and the 1990s, levels of childlessness declined in Africa, as sterility caused by sexually transmitted diseases decreased during the 1970s and 1980s.

11.   **The profound changes in fertility levels occurring since 1970 have been made possible by major behavioural transformations related to union formation, marriage and the use of contraception**. Government policies on access to contraceptives have played an important role in modifying reproductive behaviour. In 1976, 52 per cent of all Governments reported that they had no intervention to modify fertility levels but by 2001 that percentage had dropped to 32 per cent (figure 2). Government support for family planning has increased steadily since the 1970s. By 2001, 92 per cent of all Governments supported family planning programmes and the distribution of contraceptives either directly (75 per cent), through government facilities, or indirectly (17 per cent), by supporting the activities of non-governmental organizations such as family planning associations.

The data on fertility, nuptiality, contraceptive use and policies relating to childbearing presented in this report were selected to reflect the major transformations of reproductive and nuptiality behaviour that have taken place since 1970, that is, over the course of a generation. Indicators reflecting changes by birth cohort and others indicating trends from a period perspective have been included. Data were derived from a variety of sources, including civil registration, population censuses and nationally representative surveys. The data presented have not been adjusted for coverage, undercount or other non-sampling errors. Thus, the values of certain indicators, particularly those pertaining to developing countries with deficient data, may not match those published by the Population Division in *World Population Prospects: The 2002 Revision*, since the latter have been adjusted as necessary. For each country, the values of 43 indicators are presented for each date, provided data are available.

The key findings of this report are discussed in more detail below. In discussing results, the unit of analysis is the country and the main focus is on changes of the distribution of countries according to the various indicators.

Nuptiality

Marriage or some form of consensual union continues to be nearly universal. In the 1970s, in three out of every four countries, at least 89 per cent of all men and all women aged 45-49 had been married at least once and that figure was still close to 89 per cent by the 1990s. Furthermore, in a quarter of all countries with the relevant data, the proportion of men aged 45-49 ever-married or in union was 97 per cent or higher in the 1970s and 98 per cent or higher in the 1990s. Similarly, in a quarter of all countries, at least 98 per cent of women aged 45-49 had been married or in union.

In the 1970s, the prevalence of marriage was highest in the countries of Asia and it continues to be high, although there have been some instances of significant reductions in the proportions ever marrying, especially among men in Japan and among women in Singapore or in Brunei Darussalam, Israel, Malaysia, Myanmar and the Occupied Palestinian Territory. The countries of Africa are also generally characterized by a high prevalence of marriage or consensual unions, with three-quarters of them reporting that at least 96 per cent of men aged 45-49 and at least 98 per cent of women in the same age group had ever been married or in union by the 1990s. In fact, a number of countries in Africa appear to have experienced significant increases in the proportions ever married by age 45-49, particularly among men. Examples include Benin, Burkina Faso, Cameroon, the Central African Republic and Uganda. In contrast, important reductions in the proportions ever-married among men and women aged 45-49 were recorded in Botswana, Réunion and South Africa.

Marriage or consensual unions are somewhat less prevalent in the countries of Latin America and especially in the Caribbean region compared with other regions of the developing world. By the 1990s in half of the countries of the Caribbean at most 72 per cent of men and 70 per cent of women aged 45-49 had ever been married or in union. Furthermore, significant reductions in the proportions ever married were recorded in Barbados, Jamaica, the Netherlands Antilles and St. Lucia between the 1970s and the 1990s. In the rest of the countries of Latin America, the proportions ever-married among persons aged 45-49 tended to be higher, but by the 1990s in half of the countries of the region at least 10 per cent of men and 9 per cent of women aged 45-49 had never been married or in union. These figures represent a change from the 1970s, when the proportions who never married tended to be higher. Between the 1970s and the 1990s at least half of the countries in Latin America recorded significant increases in the proportions of men and women aged 45-49 who had ever been married or in union. However, in Latin America and the Caribbean consensual unions are common and the data on proportions ever married must be interpreted with caution since the trends observed may be partly due to an improvement in the reporting of consensual unions over time rather than an actual change in the prevalence of marriage.

In Europe, Northern America and Australia/New Zealand, the prevalence of marriage or consensual unions continues to be high, with over 86 per cent of men and over 89 per cent of women aged 45-49 having been married or in union in three out of every four countries in those regions. However, between the 1970s and the 1990s, at least three-quarters of the countries concerned experienced a reduction in the proportions ever married among men, the reductions being most marked in the Nordic countries and in Latvia, Iceland, Netherlands and the United States. Reductions in the proportions ever-married among women were less common but still significant in a number of countries, particularly in Denmark, Iceland and Sweden.

The data available permit a comparison of the proportions of men and women who had married or entered a union by age 25-29 in the 1970s and in the 1990s. This comparison indicates that a major worldwide shift in the timing of marriage has occurred: the median proportion ever-married among women aged 25-29 declined from 85 per cent to 76 per cent, and from 68 per cent to 56 per cent among men aged 25-29. Furthermore, three-quarters of all countries with the required data show a reduction in the proportions ever married by age 25-29. Those reductions are most marked in the countries of Europe, Northern

America and Australia/New Zealand where young people are increasingly postponing the age of entry into unions, but similar trends are noticeable in all other regions. These changes may foreshadow a general overall decline in the prevalence of marriage and consensual unions among persons aged 45-49 in the future.

These changes are also reflected in the continuous rise of the age at marriage. Accordingly, the singulate mean age at marriage (SMAM), an indicator of the mean length of single life, increased from the 1970s to the 1990s in three-quarters of all countries with data available. At the world level, the median value of the SMAM rose from 25.4 to 27.2 years among men and from 21.5 to 23.2 years among women. Particularly large increases in the SMAM were recorded among developed countries, with SMAM rising by more than 4 years in Australia, Belgium, Canada, Denmark, France, Finland, Hungary, Iceland, Ireland, Italy, Netherlands, Norway, Sweden, Switzerland, the United Kingdom and the United States. In developing countries, increases in the SMAM tended to be smaller in magnitude, particularly for men. However, gains of 3 years or more were recorded by a few countries in all regions, including Algeria, the Libyan Arab Jamahiriya, Kuwait, Maldives, Malaysia, Morocco, Qatar, Sudan and Tunisia in Asia and Northern Africa; and the Bahamas, Guadeloupe, French Guiana, Guyana, Martinique, the Netherlands Antilles, St. Lucia and the United States Virgin Islands in Latin America and the Caribbean. As already noted, in Latin America and the Caribbean some of these increases could be the result of changes in the reporting of consensual unions.

Divorce rates increased in most countries with data available. The median rate of divorce in developed countries rose from 13 divorces per 100 for men and women in the 1970s to 24 divorces per 100 men and 27 divorces per 100 women in the 1990s. Among the developing countries with data available, the median rate of divorce increased from 7 to 12 divorces per 100 men and from 5 to 15 divorces per 100 women. In three-quarters of all countries, whether developed or developing, having data for the 1970s and to the 1990s, divorce rates increased and in half of them the increases were of the order of 6 to 7 per 100. That is, not only has there been a tendency for people to marry later, but the instability of marital unions has been rising. Both trends clearly have significant implications for reproductive behaviour.

Contraceptive use

Between the 1970s and the 1990s, the use of contraception among women currently married or in union increased in ninety per cent of all countries with information available for the two dates. The median level of contraceptive use at the world level increased from 38 per cent of women currently married or in union to 52 per cent. However, these global figures mask the important differences between developed and developing countries.

Among developed countries, contraceptive use was already high in the 1970s when at least half of all women who were currently married or in union in developed countries were using contraception. In fact, in three-quarters of all developed countries at least two-thirds of all women currently married or in union were users of contraception in the 1970s. By the 1990s, the level of contraceptive use had increased in at 14 out of 44 developed countries, but it had declined in six of them. The reductions recorded in the level of contraceptive use were often the result of a decline in the use of traditional contraceptive methods and of greater reliance on modern methods. However, some of these differences may be spurious, resulting from changes in data collection procedures rather than from actual changes in behaviour. Nevertheless, the data indicate that developed countries as a whole experienced a marked increase in the use of modern methods of contraception, with the median level of such use rising from 54 to 61 per cent of women currently married or in union. At the country level, all countries with data available for the 1970s and the 1990s recorded an increase in the prevalence of modern methods, except for Austria, where such prevalence dropped by nearly 10 percentage points. In the case of Austria, this change may be partly due to the use of different data collection procedures.

Among developing countries, contraceptive prevalence was markedly lower in the 1970s than in the 1990s. For developing countries with information, the median level of contraceptive prevalence rose from 27 per cent to 40 per cent between those dates. By the 1990s, contraceptive prevalence in a quarter of all developing countries was 62 per cent or higher. However, in another quarter of all developing countries, contraceptive prevalence remained below 24 per cent of all women currently married or in union. Levels of use of modern methods were even lower. Although the median level of use of modern contraceptive methods in developing countries rose from 18 to 30 per cent between the 1970s and the 1990s, use of modern methods remains rare in many developing countries, with a quarter having levels of prevalence below 12 per cent. The latter include Afghanistan and Yemen in Asia and 25 countries in Africa.

By the 1990s, several developing countries had attained high prevalence levels of modern contraceptive methods. Thus, in Algeria, Egypt, Réunion, South Africa, Tunisia and Zimbabwe, over half of all women currently married or in union were using modern methods of contraception by the 1990s. Similar or higher levels had been attained by China, the Democratic People's Republic of Korea, Hong Kong SAR of China, Indonesia, the Islamic Republic of Iran, Israel, Kazakhstan, Mongolia, the Republic of Korea, the Philippines, Singapore, Thailand, Turkmenistan, Uzbekistan and Viet Nam in Asia. In Latin America and the Caribbean, over half of all countries with data available had levels of modern contraceptive use higher than 50 per cent. Most of these countries had recorded impressive increases in the use of modern contraceptive methods between the 1970s and the 1990s. Indeed, over that period, at least half of all developing countries with data had seen their level of use of modern contraceptive methods rise by 20 percentage points or more.

In sum, major strides have been made in satisfying the demand for modern contraceptive methods in developing countries but low levels of modern contraceptive use still persist in many countries of Africa and in some countries of Asia and Latin America and the Caribbean. As would be expected, the least developed countries and other low-income countries are more likely to exhibit low levels of modern contraceptive use than medium-income countries.

Fertility

Between the 1970s and the 1990s, fertility declined markedly at the world level. The median total fertility for all countries with data available dropped from 5.4 to 2.9 children per woman over the period concerned. Most of that reduction was caused by the decline of fertility in developing countries, whose median total fertility changed from 5.9 to 3.9 children per woman between the 1970s and the 1990s. There were also significant, though smaller, reductions in the fertility of developed countries, whose median total fertility declined from 2.3 to 1.4 children per woman over the same period.

Except for the Democratic Republic of Congo, French Guiana, Guinea and Mali, all other developing countries with data available for the 1970s and the 1990s appear to have experienced reductions in fertility levels, though estimates of change may be biased by differential reporting errors in the basic data. Nevertheless, the data presented in this report reveal an overall picture validated by other assessments of fertility trends. The median fertility reduction in developing countries between the 1970s and the 1990s was of the order of 1.8 children per woman and a quarter of all developing countries appear to have achieved reductions of 2.6 children per woman or more. China is one of the countries in this group, having reduced its fertility by about 4 children per woman since 1970. Other countries with large reported reductions of fertility include Algeria, the Islamic Republic of Iran, Mexico, Thailand, Tunisia and Turkey. In contrast, fertility declined slowly (by less than one child since 1970) or not at all in 21 developing countries, 13 of which are in sub-Saharan Africa.

Among developed countries, fertility reductions were the rule, though their magnitude was generally small but significant given the low levels of total fertility that already characterized most of those countries by the 1970s. The median reduction of total fertility among developed countries was of 0.8 children per woman and by the 1990s only four developed countries—Albania, Iceland, New Zealand and the United States of America—reported a total fertility of 2 children per woman or higher. In the 1970s, 36 developed countries had levels of fertility of at least 2 children per woman.

Taking 2.1 children per woman to represent a level of fertility ensuring population replacement when mortality is low, fertility levels in 12 developed countries were below replacement level in the 1970s whereas just one developing country had a similarly low level of fertility. By the 1990s, the number of developed countries with below-replacement fertility had increased to 41 and that of developing countries stood at 19. In 14 developed countries, total fertility was lower than 1.3 children per woman, a level unprecedented for large populations in recorded history.

The worldwide reduction of fertility has been accompanied by major shifts in the timing of childbearing. In half of all developing countries, the mean age at which women have children has decreased as the fertility rates of older women decline. In developed countries, the major tendency has been for the mean age at childbearing to rise as women postpone the beginning of childbearing. Data on the mean age at the birth of the first child indicate that it has generally been rising, both in developed and in developing countries. Increases in the mean age of mothers at the time of the first birth have been more pronounced in developed countries, three-quarters of which have seen their mean age at first birth rise by at least 1.7 years between the 1970s and the 1990s. In developing countries, such increases have been more modest, amounting to at least 0.5 years in three-quarters of all developing countries with data for the two periods. Consequently, important differences in the timing of first births remain between developed and developing countries. In the 1990s, the median value of the mean age at first birth was 26.4 years in developed countries and just 22.1 years in developing countries.

Important changes have also occurred with respect to the level of childlessness among women aged 45-49. Although the countries having comparable data for the 1970s and the 1990s are few, the available evidence suggests that there has been an important reduction of childlessness in Africa, where sexually transmitted diseases were an important cause of sterility in the 1950s and 1960s. In Latin America as well the levels of childlessness have generally dropped. In other major areas there have been both increases and decreases of childlessness but, whereas levels of childlessness in the 1990s are fairly low in Africa and Asia (never surpassing 9 per cent and remaining in most countries below 5 or 7 per cent, respectively), they are high in the Caribbean and in developed countries. Thus, in three out of every four developed countries, at least 7 per cent of women aged 45-49 were childless in the 1990s and in three-quarters of Caribbean countries with data on the subject, the proportion of childless women among those aged 45-49 was at least 8 per cent. Particularly high levels of childlessness (above 10 per cent) were recorded in Canada, Estonia, Finland, France, Luxembourg, the Netherlands Antilles, Portugal, the Republic of Moldova, Romania, Switzerland and Uruguay.

Population policies

Major changes in the views and actions of Governments with regard to fertility levels and trends have taken place. In 1976, 52 per cent of all Governments reported that they had no intervention to modify fertility levels but by 2001 that percentage had dropped to 32 per cent (see figure II). Government support for family planning has increased steadily since the 1970s. By 2001, 92 per cent of all Governments supported family planning programmes and the distribution of contraceptives either directly (75 per cent), through government facilities, or indirectly (17 per cent), by supporting the activities of non-governmental organizations such as family planning associations.

The views of Governments on the adequacy of fertility levels have also changed considerably. Thus, whereas in 1976, 27 per cent of all Governments wanted to lower fertility, by 2001, 45 per cent did.

Among developing countries, the percentage wishing to reduce fertility was even higher in 2001, amounting to 58 per cent. There was also an increase in the percentage of Governments wishing to raise fertility: from 9 per cent in 1976 to 13 per cent in 2001. As a consequence, the relative weight of Governments wishing to maintain current fertility levels declined from 13 per cent to 10 per cent. That is, today more Governments wish to change the fertility levels of their populations and are prepared to devise adequate interventions to achieve such goals.

Figure I. Distribution of 160 countries by total fertility level around 1970 and 2000

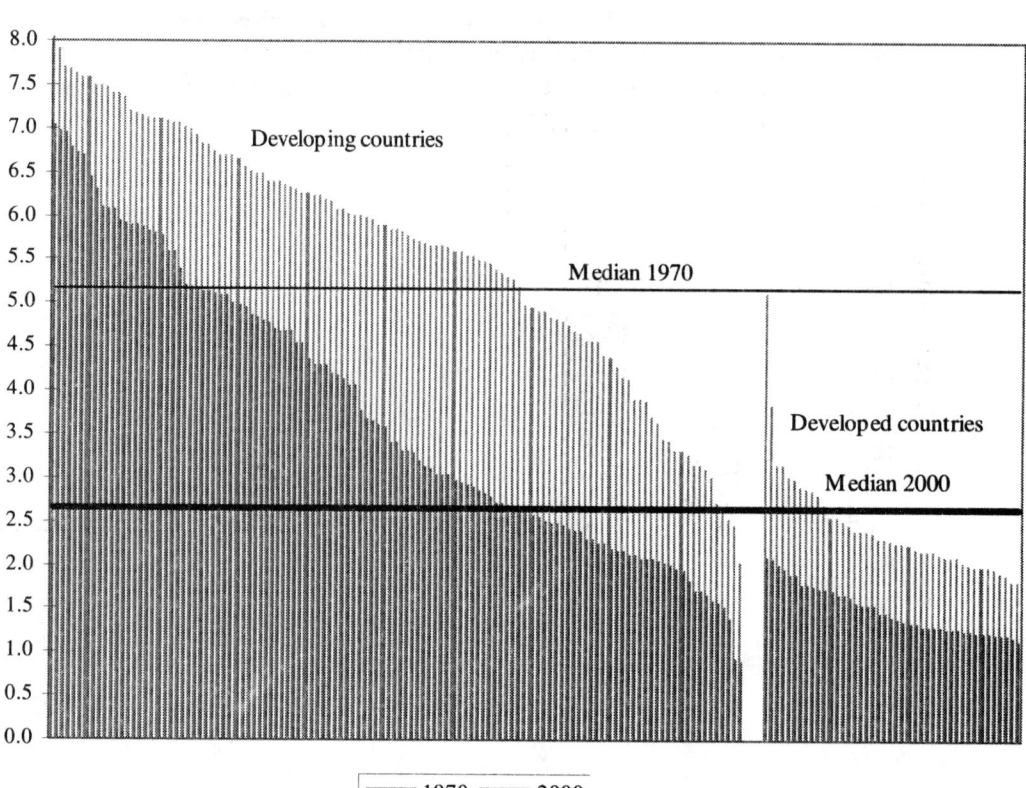

Figure II. Government policies on the level of fertility: 1976 and 2001

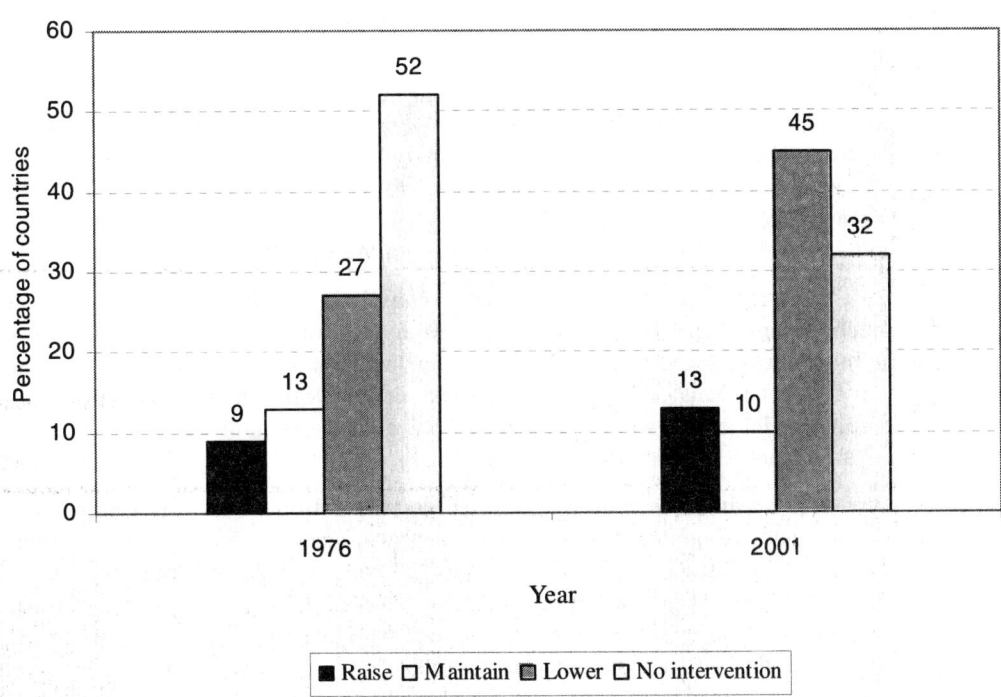

Résumé

Élaboré par la Division de la population du Département des affaires économiques et sociales du Secrétariat de l'Organisation des Nations Unies, le *Rapport mondial sur la fécondité 2003* rassemble des estimations et des indicateurs clefs concernant la fécondité, la nuptialité et l'utilisation des contraceptifs dans 192 pays, essentiellement pour les années 70 et 90 mais aussi pour des périodes plus anciennes quand il y a lieu ou plus récentes dans la mesure du possible. Cet ensemble de données permet d'évaluer les changements sans précédent survenus dans ces trois domaines depuis les années 70. Le Rapport met notamment en lumière les éléments suivants :

1.   **L'élévation de l'âge du mariage constitue un changement radical à l'échelle mondiale**. L'âge moyen des célibataires au moment du mariage dans le monde est passé de 25,4 à 27,2 ans pour les hommes et de 21,5 à 23,2 pour les femmes. Dans les pays développés, cette évolution a été encore plus frappante, les chiffres étant passés de 25,2 à 28,8 ans pour les hommes et de 22 à 26,1 pour les femmes.

2.   **Les hommes comme les femmes restent célibataires plus longtemps**. En moyenne, le pourcentage de non-célibataires âgés de 25 à 29 ans est tombé de 85 % dans les années 70 à 76 % dans les années 90 pour les femmes et de 68 % à 56 % pour les hommes. Là encore, la réduction est plus sensible dans les pays développés, où les chiffres moyens ont chuté de 85 % à 62 % pour les femmes et de 74 % à 43 % pour les hommes.

3.   **Le mariage tardif des jeunes adultes ne s'est pas encore traduit par une réduction sensible de la proportion d'individus mariés au moins une fois dans leur vie**. Le mariage, ou toute autre forme d'union consensuelle, demeure quasiment universel. Dans les années 70, dans trois pays sur quatre, au moins 89 % des hommes et des femmes âgés de 45 à 49 ans avaient été mariés au moins une fois et ce chiffre avoisinait toujours 89 % dans les années 90.

4.   **Le taux de divorce a augmenté dans la plupart des pays pour lesquels on disposait de données**. Dans les pays développés, le taux moyen de divorce est passé de 13 pour 100 hommes et femmes dans les années 70 à 24 pour 100 hommes et 27 pour 100 femmes dans les années 90. Dans les pays en développement, ce taux est passé de 7 à 12 divorces pour 100 hommes et de 5 à 15 pour 100 femmes. Ainsi, non seulement tend-on à se marier plus tard mais les mariages sont plus instables, deux tendances qui ont indiscutablement des répercussions sur le comportement procréateur.

5.   **Le recours à la planification familiale a très fortement augmenté**. Entre les années 70 et les années 90, le recours à la contraception par les femmes mariées ou vivant en couple a augmenté dans neuf pays sur 10 pour lesquels on disposait de données. À l'échelle mondiale, le taux moyen d'utilisation des contraceptifs est passé de 38 % pour les femmes mariées ou vivant en couple dans les années 70 à 52 % dans les années 90. Dans les pays en développement, le taux moyen de prévalence est passé de 27 % à 40 % pour la même période. Dans les années 90, le taux de prévalence contraceptive avait atteint au moins 62 % dans un quart des pays en développement.

6.   **En règle générale, l'utilisation de méthodes contraceptives modernes dans les pays en développement a progressé**. Dans les pays en développement, l'utilisation de moyens contraceptifs modernes est passé, en

moyenne, de 18 % à 30 % entre les années 70 et les années 90. Cependant, dans un quart de ces pays, l'utilisation de méthodes contraceptives modernes demeure rare (moins de 12 %).

7. **De 1970 à 2000, la population mondiale a connu une chute considérable et sans précédent des taux de fécondité, essentiellement en raison de la baisse de la fécondité dans les pays en développement** (figure 1). Les taux moyens de fécondité dans les pays en développement ont chuté de plus de 5,9 enfants par femme dans les années 70 à environ 3,9 enfants par femme dans les années 90. En moyenne, la baisse de la fécondité dans ces pays entre les années 70 et les années 90 était de l'ordre de 1,8 enfant par femme et, dans un quart des pays en développement, il semble que cette baisse ait été d'au moins 2,6 enfants par femme.

8. **Alors que, dans les années 70, le taux de fécondité était uniformément élevé dans les pays en développement, aujourd'hui, il varie considérablement.** En effet, les taux de fécondité sont supérieurs à 5 enfants par femme dans un certain nombre de pays les moins avancés mais ils ont atteint des niveaux inférieurs au taux de renouvellement des générations dans une vingtaine de pays en développement.

9. **En règle générale, les taux de fécondité dans les pays développés, dont beaucoup ont connu une explosion de la natalité dans les années 50 et 60, ont diminué depuis 1970.** La réduction moyenne de la fécondité cumulée dans les pays développés était de 0,8 enfant par femme entre les années 70 et les années 90. À la fin des années 90, seuls quatre pays développés (l'Albanie, les États-Unis, l'Islande et la Nouvelle-Zélande) signalaient des taux de fécondité cumulée d'au moins 2 enfants par femme. En outre, dans 14 pays développés, la fécondité était inférieure à 1,3 enfant par femme, du jamais vu dans l'histoire des populations.

10. **Les taux d'infécondité varient sensiblement d'une grande région à l'autre.** Dans les années 90, la proportion de femmes sans enfant âgées de 45 à 49 ans était généralement élevée dans les pays développés et dans les Caraïbes. Au moins 7 % des femmes âgées de 45 à 49 ans étaient sans enfant dans quatre pays développés sur cinq pour lesquels on disposait de données et cette proportion franchissait la barre des 10 % dans neuf pays développés. Dans les années 90, les taux d'infécondité étaient relativement faibles en Afrique et en Asie, et modérés en Amérique latine. Grâce à la baisse de la stérilité due aux maladies sexuellement transmissibles dans les années 70 et 80, les niveaux d'infécondité ont diminué en Afrique entre les années 70 et les années 90.

11. **Les changements profonds dans les taux de fécondité depuis 1970 sont le fruit d'une modification radicale des comportements liée à la formation des unions, au mariage et au recours à la contraception.** Les politiques gouvernementales concernant l'accès aux contraceptifs ont beaucoup contribué à modifier le comportement procréateur. En 1976, 52 % des gouvernements signalaient qu'ils n'étaient intervenus en rien dans la modification des niveaux de fécondité mais, en 2001, cette proportion n'était plus que de 32 % (figure 2). L'assistance apportée par les gouvernements à la planification familiale progresse régulièrement depuis les années 70. En 2001, 92 % des gouvernements contribuaient à des programmes de planification familiale et à la distribution de contraceptifs, directement (75 %) dans des établissements publics ou indirectement (17 %) en appuyant les activités

d'organisations non gouvernementales telles que les associations de planification familiale.

Les données sur la fécondité, la nuptialité et l'utilisation des contraceptifs ainsi que les politiques relatives à la procréation mentionnées dans le présent rapport ont été choisies afin d'illustrer l'évolution radicale des comportements en matière de procréation et de nuptialité depuis 1970, soit en une génération. Les indicateurs qui reflètent des changements par cohorte de naissances et autres tendances révélatrices pour une période donnée ont été pris en compte. Les données provenaient de sources diverses, notamment des registres de l'état civil, des recensements démographiques et autres enquêtes représentatives sur le plan national. Elles n'ont pas été corrigées pour combler les lacunes, remédier au sous-dénombrement ou rectifier toute erreur autre que d'échantillonnage. Ainsi, les valeurs de certains indicateurs, surtout celles qui concernent les pays en développement pour lesquels les données sont insuffisantes, peuvent ne pas correspondre à celles que publie la Division de la population dans son rapport intitulé *World Population Prospects: The 2002 Revision* puisque ces dernières ont été révisées en conséquence. Pour chaque pays, les valeurs des 43 indicateurs sont présentées pour chaque date dans la mesure où l'on dispose des données.

Les principales conclusions du présent rapport sont examinées de manière plus approfondie ci-après. Le pays est l'unité utilisée lors de l'analyse, qui porte essentiellement sur les changements dans la répartition des pays en fonction des divers indicateurs.

Nuptialité

Le mariage, ou toute autre forme d'union consensuelle, demeure quasiment universel. Dans les années 70, dans trois pays sur quatre, au moins 89 % des hommes et des femmes âgés de 45 à 49 ans avaient été mariés au moins une fois et ce chiffre avoisinait toujours 89 % dans les années 90. En outre, dans un quart des pays disposant de données, la proportion d'hommes non célibataires âgés de 45 à 49 ans était d'au moins 97 % dans les années 70 et d'au moins 98 % dans les années 90. De même, dans un quart des pays, au moins 98 % des femmes âgées de 45 à 49 ans avaient été mariées ou avaient vécu en couple.

Dans les années 70, la prévalence du mariage était la plus élevée dans les pays d'Asie et elle continue d'être importante bien que, dans certains cas, une réduction sensible de la proportion de non-célibataires ait été observée, surtout chez les hommes au Japon et chez les femmes à Brunéi Darussalam, en Israël, en Malaisie, au Myanmar, à Singapour et dans le territoire palestinien occupé. De même, les pays d'Afrique se caractérisent généralement par une prévalence élevée du mariage ou des unions consensuelles et les trois quarts d'entre eux indiquent qu'au moins 96 % des hommes âgés de 45 à 49 ans et au moins 98 % des femmes dans le même groupe d'âge étaient non célibataires dans les années 90. De fait, dans plusieurs pays d'Afrique, notamment au Bénin, au Burkina Faso, au Cameroun, en Ouganda et en République centrafricaine, la proportion de non-célibataires âgés de 45 à 49 ans semble avoir nettement augmenté, en particulier chez les hommes. En revanche, une forte baisse de la proportion de non-célibataires chez les hommes et les femmes âgés de 45 à 49 ans a été enregistrée en Afrique du Sud, au Botswana et à la Réunion.

La prévalence du mariage ou des unions consensuelles est légèrement inférieure dans les pays d'Amérique latine, en particulier dans la région des

Caraïbes, par rapport à d'autres régions du monde en développement. Dans les années 90, la moitié des pays des Caraïbes comptaient au plus 72 % d'hommes et 70 % de femmes non célibataires âgés de 45 à 49 ans. En outre, d'importantes réductions du pourcentage de non-célibataires ont été enregistrées aux Antilles néerlandaises, à la Barbade, à la Jamaïque et à Sainte-Lucie entre les années 70 et les années 90. Dans les autres pays d'Amérique latine, la proportion de non-célibataires âgés de 45 à 49 ans était généralement plus élevée mais dans les années 90, la moitié des pays de la région comptaient au moins 10 % d'hommes et 9 % de femmes non célibataires âgés de 45 à 49 ans. Ces chiffres représentent un changement par rapport aux années 70 où la proportion de non-célibataires tendait à être supérieure. Entre les années 70 et les années 90, au moins la moitié des pays d'Amérique latine ont enregistré de fortes hausses de la proportion d'hommes et de femmes non célibataires âgés de 45 à 49 ans. Cependant, en Amérique latine et dans les Caraïbes, les unions consensuelles sont courantes et les données sur la proportion de non-célibataires doivent être interprétées avec prudence car les tendances observées peuvent être en partie imputables à une amélioration progressive de la pratique en matière de déclaration des unions consensuelles plutôt qu'à une véritable évolution de la prévalence du mariage.

En Amérique du Nord, en Australie, en Europe et en Nouvelle-Zélande, la prévalence du mariage ou des unions consensuelles continue d'être élevée : dans ces régions, trois pays sur quatre comptent plus de 86 % d'hommes et plus de 89 % de femmes non célibataires âgés de 45 à 49 ans. Toutefois, entre les années 70 et les années 90, au moins les trois quarts des pays concernés ont connu une réduction de la proportion d'hommes non célibataires; cette réduction a été la plus marquée dans les pays nordiques et aux États-Unis, en Islande, en Lettonie et aux Pays-Bas. La réduction de la proportion de femmes non célibataires était moins courante bien que sensible dans un certain nombre de pays, notamment au Danemark, en Islande et en Suède.

Les données dont on dispose permettent de comparer le pourcentage d'hommes et de femmes âgés de 25 à 29 ans mariés ou vivant en couple dans les années 70 et dans les années 90. Cette comparaison montre que l'âge du mariage dans le monde entier a radicalement changé : en moyenne, la proportion de non-célibataires chez les femmes âgées de 25 à 29 ans est tombée de 85 % à 76 % et de 68 % à 56 % chez les hommes appartenant au même groupe d'âge. En outre, les trois quarts des pays pour lesquels on disposait de données ont connu une réduction de la proportion de non-célibataires âgés de 25 à 29 ans. Ces réductions sont les plus nettes en Amérique du Nord, en Australie, en Europe et en Nouvelle-Zélande, où les jeunes retardent de plus en plus le moment de l'union, mais la même tendance est visible dans toutes les autres régions. Ces changements peuvent présager un déclin global de la prévalence du mariage et des unions consensuelles chez les individus âgés de 45 à 49 ans.

Cette évolution se manifeste également par l'élévation continuelle de l'âge du mariage. Ainsi, entre les années 70 et les années 90, l'âge moyen des célibataires au moment du mariage, indicateur de la durée moyenne du célibat, a augmenté dans les trois quarts des pays pour lesquels on disposait de données. À l'échelle mondiale, il est passé de 25,4 à 27,2 ans pour les hommes et de 21,5 à 23,2 ans pour les femmes. Une hausse très nette de l'âge moyen des célibataires au moment du mariage a été enregistrée dans les pays développés, où il a augmenté de plus de 4 ans en Australie, en Belgique, au Canada, au Danemark, aux États-Unis, en Finlande, en France, en Hongrie, en

Irlande, en Islande, en Italie, en Norvège, aux Pays-Bas, au Royaume-Uni, en Suède et en Suisse. Dans les pays en développement, cette hausse était généralement moins sensible, en particulier chez les hommes. Dans toutes les régions, quelques pays ont néanmoins enregistré une hausse de 3 ans ou plus : en Asie et en Afrique du Nord, c'est le cas de l'Algérie, de la Jamahiriya arabe libyenne, du Koweït, de la Malaisie, des Maldives, du Maroc, du Qatar, du Soudan et de la Tunisie; en Amérique latine et dans les Caraïbes, on peut citer les Antilles néerlandaises, les Bahamas, la Guadeloupe, le Guyana, la Guyane française, la Martinique, Sainte-Lucie et les îles Vierges américaines. Comme indiqué plus haut, en Amérique latine et dans les Caraïbes, certaines de ces augmentations pourraient être dues à l'évolution de la pratique en matière de déclaration des unions consensuelles.

Le taux de divorce a augmenté dans la plupart des pays pour lesquels on disposait de données. Dans les pays développés, le taux moyen est passé de 13 divorces pour 100 hommes et femmes dans les années 70 à 24 divorces pour 100 hommes et 27 pour 100 femmes dans les années 90. Dans les pays en développement pour lesquels on disposait de données, le taux moyen est passé de 7 à 12 divorces pour 100 hommes et de 5 à 15 pour 100 femmes. Dans les trois quarts des pays développés ou en développement pour lesquels on disposait de données pour les années 70 et 90, le taux de divorce a augmenté et dans la moitié d'entre eux, cette augmentation était de l'ordre de 6 à 7 %. Ainsi, non seulement tend-on à se marier plus tard mais les mariages sont plus instables, deux tendances qui ont indiscutablement des répercussions sur le comportement procréateur.

Utilisation des contraceptifs

Entre les années 70 et les années 90, le recours à la contraception par les femmes mariées ou vivant en couple s'est accru dans 90 % des pays pour lesquels on disposait de données portant sur les deux périodes. À l'échelle mondiale, le niveau moyen d'utilisation des contraceptifs est passé de 38 % à 52 % pour les femmes mariées ou vivant en couple. Cependant, ces chiffres dissimulent des écarts importants entre les pays développés et les pays en développement.

Dans les années 70, le taux d'utilisation des contraceptifs était déjà élevé dans les pays développés, où au moins la moitié des femmes mariées ou vivant en couple avaient recours à la contraception. En effet, dans les trois quarts de ces pays, au moins deux tiers des femmes mariées ou vivant en couple utilisaient des contraceptifs à cette époque. Dans les années 90, le taux d'utilisation avait augmenté dans 14 pays développés sur 44 mais diminué dans six d'entre eux. Les réductions enregistrées étaient souvent le fait d'un déclin de l'utilisation des méthodes contraceptives traditionnelles et d'un recours accru aux méthodes modernes. Cependant, certaines de ces différences peuvent être trompeuses car elles tiennent peut-être au changement des méthodes de collecte des données plus qu'à une véritable évolution des comportements. Cela étant, les données montrent que, dans l'ensemble des pays développés, l'usage des méthodes contraceptives modernes a nettement augmenté, le taux moyen d'utilisation étant passé de 54 % à 61 % des femmes mariées ou vivant en couple. À l'échelle nationale, tous les pays pour lesquels on disposait de données pour les années 70 et 90 ont enregistré une augmentation de la prévalence des méthodes modernes, à l'exception de l'Autriche, où elle a chuté de près de 10 points de pourcentage. Dans ce dernier cas, il se peut que cette évolution soit due en partie à l'emploi de méthodes de collecte de données différentes.

Dans les pays en développement, la prévalence de la contraception était nettement plus faible dans les années 70 que dans les années 90. Dans ceux pour lesquels on disposait de données, le taux moyen de prévalence est passé de 27 % à 40 % d'une période à l'autre. Dans les années 90, la prévalence de la contraception dans un quart des pays en développement était d'au moins 62 %. Cependant, dans un autre quart, elle demeurait inférieure à 24 % des femmes mariées ou vivant en couple. Le taux d'utilisation des méthodes modernes était encore plus faible. Bien que le taux d'utilisation moyen des méthodes contraceptives modernes dans les pays en développement soit passé de 18 % à 30 % entre les années 70 et les années 90, le recours aux méthodes modernes demeure rare dans bon nombre de ces pays, dont un quart (parmi lesquels l'Afghanistan et le Yémen en Asie et 25 pays d'Afrique) a des taux de prévalence inférieurs à 12 %.

Dans les années 90, plusieurs pays en développement avaient atteint des taux élevés de prévalence des méthodes contraceptives modernes. Ainsi, en Afrique du Sud, en Algérie, en Égypte, à la Réunion, en Tunisie et au Zimbabwe, plus de la moitié des femmes mariées ou vivant en couple utilisaient des méthodes contraceptives modernes dans les années 90. Des niveaux semblables ou supérieurs ont été atteints en Asie dans les pays et régions suivants : Chine, RAS de Hong Kong, Indonésie, Iran (République islamique d'), Israël, Kazakhstan, Mongolie, Ouzbékistan, Philippines, République de Corée, République populaire démocratique de Corée, Singapour, Thaïlande, Turkménistan et Viet Nam. Dans plus de la moitié des pays d'Amérique latine et des Caraïbes pour lesquels on disposait de données, les taux d'utilisation des méthodes contraceptives modernes étaient supérieurs à 50 %. La plupart de ces pays avaient connu une hausse spectaculaire des taux d'utilisation des méthodes contraceptives modernes entre les années 70 et les années 90. En effet, au cours de cette période, dans la moitié au moins des pays en développement pour lesquels on disposait de données, le taux d'utilisation des méthodes contraceptives modernes avait augmenté d'au moins 20 points de pourcentage.

En bref, de grands progrès ont été faits pour satisfaire la demande en méthodes contraceptives modernes dans les pays en développement mais de faibles taux d'utilisation de ces méthodes persistent toujours dans de nombreux pays d'Afrique et dans certains pays d'Amérique latine, d'Asie et des Caraïbes. Comme on pourrait s'y attendre, les pays les moins avancés et d'autres pays à faible revenu sont plus susceptibles d'enregistrer de faibles taux d'utilisation des méthodes contraceptives modernes que les pays à revenu intermédiaire.

Fécondité

Des années 70 aux années 90, la fécondité a nettement baissé dans le monde entier. En moyenne, la fécondité cumulée pour tous les pays pour lesquels on disposait de données a chuté de 5,4 à 2,9 enfants par femme pour la période considérée. Cette réduction tient pour une large part au déclin de la fécondité dans les pays en développement, où, en moyenne, la fécondité cumulée est tombée de 5,9 à 3,9 enfants par femme entre les années 70 et les années 90. Bien que dans une moindre mesure, une forte baisse de la fécondité a également été observée dans les pays développés, où le taux moyen de fécondité cumulée a chuté de 2,3 à 1,4 enfant par femme au cours de la même période.

À l'exception de la Guinée, de la Guyane française, du Mali et de la République démocratique du Congo, tous les autres pays en développement pour lesquels on disposait de données pour les années 70 et 90 semblent avoir connu une réduction des taux de fécondité même si les estimations des variations sont parfois faussées en raison des diverses erreurs qui peuvent se glisser lors de la communication des données de base. Cela étant, les données contenues dans le présent rapport font apparaître une situation globale corroborée par d'autres évaluations des tendances de la fécondité. Entre les années 70 et les années 90, la réduction moyenne de la fécondité dans les pays en développement était de l'ordre de 1,8 enfant par femme et, dans un quart de ces pays, le nombre d'enfants par femme semblait avoir baissé d'au moins 2,6. Dans cette catégorie de pays, on compte la Chine, où le taux de fécondité a chuté d'environ 4 enfants par femme depuis 1970. Parmi les autres pays où d'importantes réductions ont été signalées, on peut citer l'Algérie, l'Iran (République islamique d'), le Mexique, la Thaïlande, la Tunisie et la Turquie. En revanche, la fécondité a peu baissé (de moins d'un enfant depuis 1970) ou est restée stable dans 21 pays en développement dont 13 sont des pays de l'Afrique subsaharienne.

Dans les pays développés, la réduction de la fécondité était la norme et, bien que de faible ampleur, elle n'en demeurait pas moins importante vu le faible taux de fécondité cumulée qui caractérisait déjà la plupart de ces pays dans les années 70. La réduction moyenne de la fécondité cumulée dans ces pays était de 0,8 enfant par femme, et dans les années 90, seuls quatre pays développés (l'Albanie, les États-Unis, l'Islande, et la Nouvelle-Zélande) ont fait état de niveaux de fécondité cumulée d'au moins 2 enfants par femme alors que l'on en comptait 36 dans les années 70.

En admettant que 2,1 enfants par femme représente un taux de fécondité permettant d'assurer le renouvellement de la population dans les pays où la mortalité est faible, dans les années 70, les niveaux de fécondité étaient inférieurs au niveau de reproduction dans 12 pays développés contre un seul pays en développement avec un niveau de fécondité aussi bas. Dans les années 90, le taux de fécondité était inférieur au niveau de reproduction dans 41 pays développés et dans 19 pays en développement. Dans 14 pays développés, la fécondité cumulée était inférieure à 1,3 enfant par femme, du jamais vu dans l'histoire des populations.

La réduction de la fécondité à l'échelon mondial s'est accompagnée d'une évolution radicale de l'âge de la procréation. Dans la moitié des pays en développement, l'âge moyen auquel les femmes ont des enfants a baissé tandis que les taux de fécondité diminuent chez les femmes âgées. Dans les pays développés, l'âge moyen de procréation tend, en général, à s'élever car les femmes retardent le début de la procréation. Il ressort des données que l'âge moyen à la première naissance est généralement en hausse dans les pays développés comme dans les pays en développement. L'élévation de l'âge moyen de la mère à la première naissance est plus nette dans les pays développés : entre les années 70 et les années 90, l'âge moyen à la première naissance a augmenté d'au moins 1,7 an dans les trois quarts de ces pays. Dans les pays en développement, ces augmentations ont été plus modestes : dans les trois quarts des pays pour lesquels on disposait de données pour ces deux périodes, l'âge moyen a augmenté de 0,5 an. Des écarts importants demeurent donc entre les pays développés et les pays en développement en ce qui concerne l'âge à la première naissance. Dans les années 90, l'âge moyen à la première naissance était de 26,4 ans dans les pays développés contre 22,1 ans seulement dans les pays en développement.

D'importants changements se sont également produits en ce qui concerne le niveau d'infécondité chez les femmes âgées de 45 à 49 ans. Bien que peu de pays disposent de données comparables pour les années 70 et 90, celles dont on dispose donnent à penser que l'infécondité a fortement diminué en Afrique, où les maladies sexuellement transmissibles étaient une cause importante de stérilité dans les années 50 et 60. De même, en Amérique latine, les taux d'infécondité ont généralement chuté. Dans d'autres grandes régions, on constate à la fois une hausse et une baisse du taux d'infécondité mais, alors que, dans les années 90, ce taux était relativement faible en Afrique et en Asie (ne dépassant jamais 9 % et demeurant inférieur à 5 % et 7 %, respectivement, dans la plupart des pays), il était élevé dans les Caraïbes et dans les pays développés. Ainsi, dans trois pays développés sur quatre, au moins 7 % des femmes âgées de 45 à 49 ans étaient sans enfants dans les années 90 et dans les trois quarts des pays des Caraïbes pour lesquels on disposait de données à ce sujet, cette proportion était d'au moins 8 %. Des taux d'infécondité particulièrement élevés (supérieurs à 10 %) ont été enregistrés dans les Antilles néerlandaises, au Canada, en Estonie, en Finlande, en France, au Luxembourg, au Portugal, en République de Moldova, en Roumanie, en Suisse et en Uruguay.

Politiques démographiques

Les vues et les initiatives des gouvernements en ce qui concerne les taux et les tendances de la fécondité ont considérablement évolué. En 1976, 52 % des gouvernements affirmaient n'avoir rien fait pour modifier les taux de fécondité, mais, en 2001, cette proportion n'était plus que de 32 % (voir figure II). L'assistance apportée par les gouvernements à la planification familiale progresse régulièrement depuis les années 70. En 2001, 92 % des gouvernements contribuaient à des programmes de planification familiale et à la distribution de contraceptifs, directement (75 %) dans des établissements publics ou indirectement (17 %) en appuyant les activités d'organisations non gouvernementales telles que les associations de planification familiale.

Les vues des gouvernements concernant l'adéquation des taux de fécondité ont elles aussi beaucoup évolué. Ainsi, alors qu'en 1976, 27 % d'entre eux souhaitaient réduire la fécondité, en 2001, ils étaient 45 % à le vouloir. Dans les pays en développement, la proportion de ceux qui voulaient réduire la fécondité était encore plus élevée en 2001, atteignant 58 %. De même, la proportion de gouvernements souhaitant accroître la fécondité avait augmenté, passant de 9 % en 1976 à 13 % en 2001. Aussi, le pourcentage de gouvernements souhaitant maintenir les taux actuels de fécondité a-t-il baissé de 13 % à 10 % : aujourd'hui un plus grand nombre de gouvernements veulent changer le taux de fécondité de leur population et sont prêts à mettre sur pied des initiatives leur permettant d'atteindre ces objectifs.

Figure I

**Répartition de 160 pays en fonction du niveau de fécondité cumulée
vers 1970 et 2000**

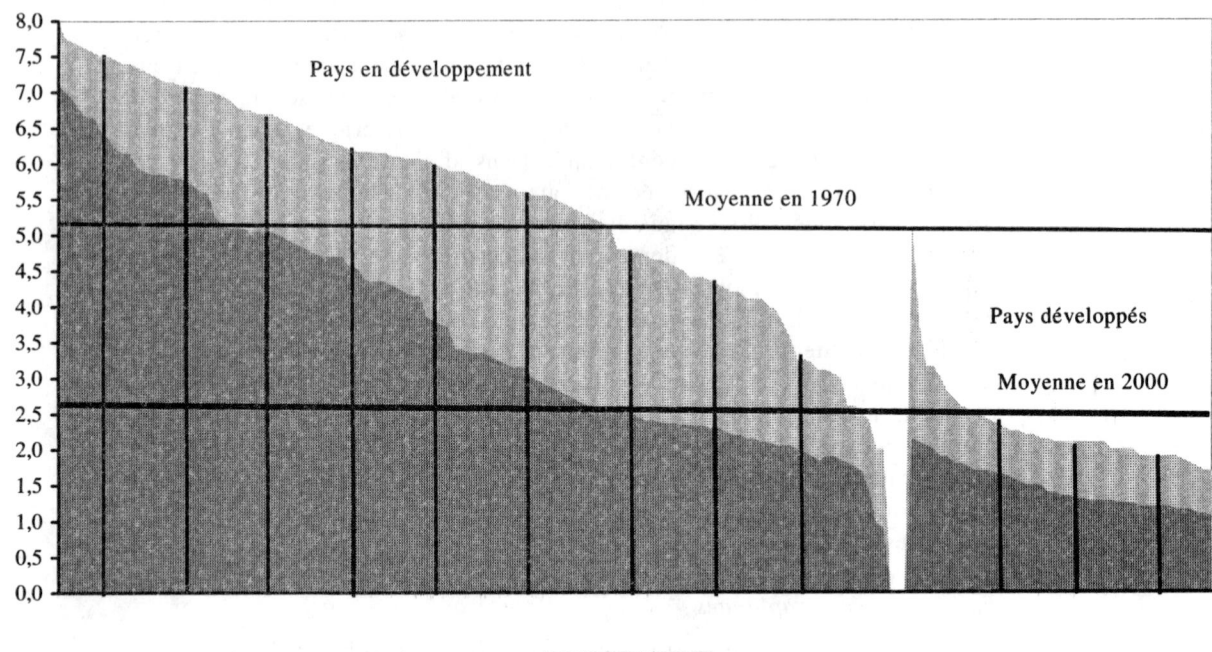

Population Division, DESA, United Nations

Figure II
Politiques gouvernementales concernant le taux de fécondité : 1976 et 2001

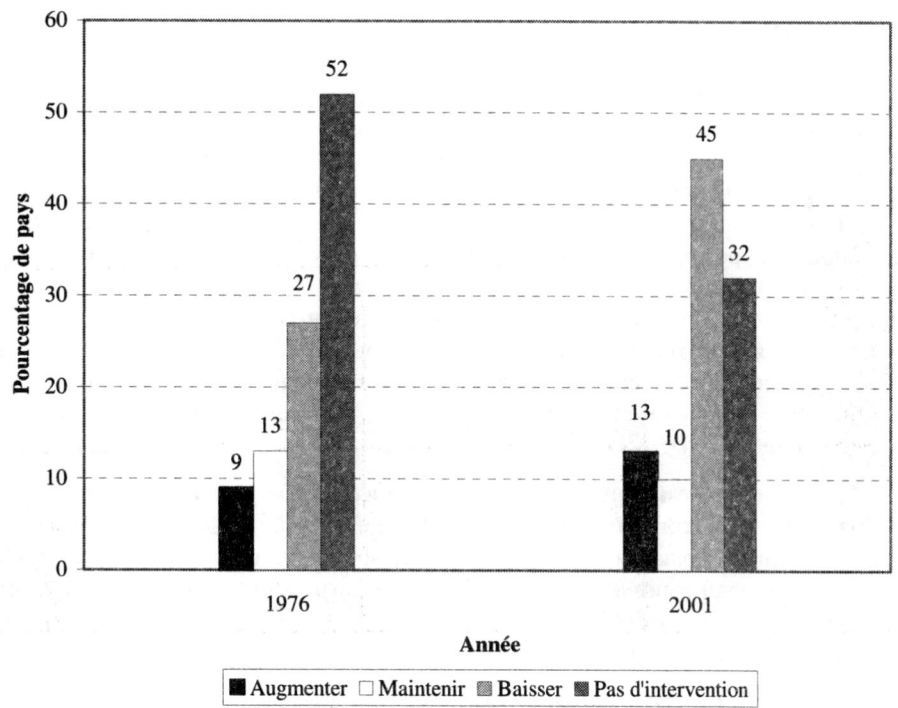

Резюме

Отдел народонаселения Департамента по экономическим и социальным вопросам Секретариата Организации Объединенных Наций подготовил «*Доклад о рождаемости в мире, 2003 год*», в котором представлены основные оценки и показатели, касающиеся рождаемости, брачности и применения противозачаточных средств по 192 странам главным образом за 70-е и 90-е годы, хотя некоторые данные приводятся за более ранние или более поздние периоды. Представленные в докладе данные позволяют дать оценку беспрецедентным по своим масштабам изменениям, которые произошли за период с 70-х годов в области брачности, применения противозачаточных средств и рождаемости. В докладе, в частности, документально подтверждаются следующие основные выводы:

1. **Во всем мире произошло значительное увеличение среднего возраста вступления в брак.** Общемировой медианный возраст вступления в брак вырос с 25,4 до 27,2 года среди мужчин и с 21,5 до 23,2 года среди женщин. В группе развитых стран увеличение медианного возраста было еще более разительным — с 25,2 до 28,8 года среди мужчин и с 22,0 до 26,1 года среди женщин.

2. **Как мужчины, так и женщины проводят более значительную часть своей жизни одинокими.** Медианная доля лиц в возрасте 25–29 лет, когда-либо состоявших в браке, сократилась с 85 процентов в 70-х годах до 76 процентов в 90-х годах среди женщин и с 68 процентов до 56 процентов среди мужчин. Сокращение доли лиц в возрасте 25–29 лет, когда-либо состоявших в браке, также было более существенным в развитых странах, для которых этот медианный показатель сократился с 85 процентов до 62 процентов среди женщин и с 74 процентов до 43 процентов среди мужчин.

3. **Увеличение возраста вступления в первый брак пока не привело к заметному сокращению доли лиц, вступающих в брак по меньшей мере один раз за всю жизнь.** Абсолютное большинство людей вступает в брак или консенсуальный союз. В 70-х годах в трех из каждых четырех стран не менее 89 процентов мужчин и женщин в возрасте 45–49 лет находились в браке по меньшей мере один раз, и этот показатель по-прежнему составлял почти 89 процентов в 90-е годы.

4. **Распространенность разводов увеличилась в большинстве стран, по которым имеются данные.** Медианный суммарный коэффициент разводимости для развитых стран увеличился с 13 разводов на 100 мужчин и женщин в 70-х годах до 24 разводов на 100 мужчин и 27 разводов на 100 женщин в 90-х годах. Медианный суммарный коэффициент разводимости в группе развивающихся стран вырос с 7 до 12 разводов на 100 мужчин и с 5 до 15 разводов на 100 женщин. Это означает, что не только увеличивается возраст вступления в брак, но и снижается стабильность брачных союзов. Обе тенденции имеют, безусловно, серьезные последствия для репродуктивного поведения.

5. **Значительно расширилось применение методов планирования семьи.** В период с 70-х по 90-е годы применение противозачаточных средств замужними женщинами расширилось в девяти из каждых десяти стран, по которым имеется такая информация. Медианная доля замужних женщин, использующих противозачаточные средства, возросла с 38 процентов в 70-х годах до 52 процентов в 90-х годах. Медианный показатель в группе развивающихся стран возрос за этот период с 27 до 40 процентов. К 90-м годам в каждой четвертой развивающейся стране не менее 62 процентов состоящих в браке женщин использовали контрацепцию.

6. **В развивающихся странах в целом расширилось применение современных противозачаточных средств.** В период с 70-х годов по 90-е годы в группе развивающихся странах медианный показатель применения современных противозачаточных средств увеличился с 18 до 30 процентов. Однако в каждой четвертой развивающейся стране менее 12 процентов состоящих в браке женщин используют современные контрацептивы.

7. **В период с 1970 года по 2000 год произошло беспрецедентное сокращение сренемирового уровня рождаемости, обусловленное главным образом снижением рождаемости в развивающихся странах** (диаграмма I). Средний по развивающимся странам уровень рождаемости снизился с более чем 5,9 ребенка на одну женщину в 70-х годах до 3,9 ребенка на одну женщину в 90-х годах, причем в половине стран рождаемость сократилась на 1,8 ребенка на женщину и более, в том числе в каждой четвертой стране – как минимум на 2,6 ребенка на одну женщину.

8. **В то время как в 70-х годах рождаемость в развивающихся странах была повсеместно высока, сегодня она варьирует в широких пределах.** Так, хотя в ряде наименее развитых стран суммарная рождаемость продолжает составлять более 5 детей на одну женщину, она уменьшилась ниже уровня воспроизводства населения в 20 развивающихся странах.

9. **В развитых странах, многие из которых пережили «бэби бум» в 50-е и 60-е годы, рождаемость снизилась после 1970 года.** В половине развитых стран суммарная рождаемость сократилась на 0,8 ребенка на одну женщину и более. К концу 90-х годов рождаемость составляла (или незначительно превышала) 2 ребенка на женщину лишь в четырех развитых странах — в Албании, Исландии, Новой Зеландии и Соединенных Штатах Америки. В то же время в 14 развитых странах суммарная рождаемость была ниже 1,3 ребенка на одну женщину, что представляет собой самый низкий уровень рождаемости за всю документированную историю стран с большим народонаселением.

10. **Уровни бездетности значительно различаются в основных регионах.** В 90-х годах доля бездетных женщин в возрасте 45–49 лет была, как правило, высока в развитых странах и странах Карибского бассейна. В четырех из каждых пяти развитых стран, по которым имеются такие данные, по меньшей мере 7 процентов женщин в возрасте 45–49 лет были бездетными, а в девяти развитых странах доля бездетных женщин превысила 10 процентов. Уровни бездетности относительно низки в Африке и Азии, а в Латинской Америке находятся на среднем уровне. В период с 70-х годов и по 90-е годы показатели бездетности в

Африке сократились, поскольку в 70-е и 80-е годы снизился уровень стерильности, вызванной венерическими заболеваниями.

11. **Глубокие изменения в показателях рождаемости, происшедшие за период с 1970 года, объясняются серьезным изменением отношения к вступлению в брак или консенсуальный союз и к применению контрацепции.** Важную роль в изменении репродуктивного поведения сыграла государственная политика в вопросах, касающихся доступа к противозачаточным средствам. В 1976 году правительства 52 процентов стран сообщили, что они не принимают никаких мер по изменению уровня рождаемости, тогда как к 2001 году доля таких стран снизилась до 32 процентов (диаграмма 2). С 70-х годов правительства все более активно поддерживают практику планирования семьи. К 2001 году правительства 92-х процентов стран поддерживали программы планирования семьи и мероприятия по распределению противозачаточных средств либо напрямую (75 процентов) через государственные учреждения, либо косвенно (17 процентов) путем поддержки деятельности неправительственных организаций, таких, как ассоциации по планированию семьи.

Представленные в докладе данные о рождаемости, брачности, применении противозачаточных средств и политике в отношении деторождения были отобраны таким образом, чтобы продемонстрировать глубокие изменения в области репродуктивного поведения и брачности, которые произошли за период с 1970 года, т.е. на протяжении одного поколения. В доклад включены показатели по реальным и гипотетическим поколениям. Данные собирались из различных источников, включая статистику актов гражданского состояния, переписи населения и общенациональные выборочные обследования. В представленные данные не вносились поправки на неполноту учета, ошибки выборки и другие погрешности. Поэтому некоторые показатели, особенно по развивающимся странам с неполными данными, могут не совпадать с откоректированными показателями, опубликованными Отделом народонаселения в докладе *«Перспективы мирового народонаселения: пересмотренное издание 2002 года.* Для каждой страны представлены имеющиеся данные по 43 показателям и двум периодам.

Основные сделанные в докладе выводы более подробно рассматриваются ниже. При рассмотрении результатов за единицу анализа берется страна и основное внимание уделяется изменениям в распределении стран по значениям различных показателей.

Брачность

Абсолютное большинство людей вступает в брак или консенсуальный союз. В 70-х годах в трех из каждых четырех стран по меньшей мере 89 процентов мужчин и женщин в возрасте 45-49 лет когда-либо состояли в браке. В 90-е годы этот показатель все еще составлял почти 89 процентов. Кроме того, в каждой четвертой стране, по которой имеются данные, доля мужчин в возрасте 45–49 лет, когда-либо состоявших в браке или консенсуальном союзе, составляла 97 процентов или более в 70-х годах и 98 процентов или более в 90-х годах. Точно так же в четверти стран по меньшей мере 98 процентов женщин в возрасте 45–49 лет когда-либо состояли в браке или консенсуальном союзе.

Как в 70-х, так и в 90-х годах брачность была особенно высока в странах Азии, хотя в некоторых случаях и имели место значительные сокращения доли людей, когда-либо состоявших в браке, особенно среди мужчин в Японии и среди женщин в Сингапуре или в Брунее-Даруссаламе, Израиле, Малайзии, Мьянме и на оккупированной палестинской территории. Для стран Африки также в целом характерен высокий показатель брачности — в трех четвертях из них в 90-е годы по меньшей мере 96 процентов мужчин в возрасте 45–49 лет и по меньшей мере 98 процентов женщин той же возрастной группы хотя бы один раз состояли в браке или консенсуальном союзе. В ряде стран Африки произошло существенное увеличение доли лиц, особенно мужчин, когда-либо состоявших в браке к моменту достижения возраста 45–49 лет. В качестве примеров можно привести Бенин, Буркина-Фасо, Камерун, Уганду и Центральноафриканскую Республику. Напротив, в Ботсване, Реюньоне и Южной Африке произошло крупное сокращение доли когда-либо состоявших в браке мужчин и женщин в возрасте 45–49 лет.

Браки или консенсуальные союзы несколько в меньшей степени распространены в странах Латинской Америки, и особенно в Карибском регионе, по сравнению с другими регионами развивающегося мира. К 90-м годам в половине стран Карибского бассейна не более 72 процентов мужчин и 70 процентов женщин в возрасте 45–49 лет когда-либо состояли в браке или союзе. Кроме того, в период с 70-х по 90-е годы было отмечено значительное сокращение доли когда-либо состоявших в браке на Барбадосе, Ямайке, Нидерландских Антильских островах и Сент-Люсии. Хотя в остальных странах Латинской Америки доля когда-либо состоявших в браке лиц в возрасте 45–49 лет, как правило, выше, к 90-м годам в половине стран этого региона по меньшей мере 10 процентов мужчин и 9 процентов женщин в возрасте 45–49 лет никогда не состояли в браке или в союзе. Эти показатели свидетельствуют об изменении ситуации по сравнению с 70-ми годами, когда доля лиц, никогда не состоявших в браке, была, как правило, выше. В период с 70-х по 90-е годы по крайней мере в половине стран Латинской Америки значительно увеличилась доля мужчин и женщин в возрасте 45–49 лет, которые хотя бы один раз состояли в браке или в союзе. Однако в Латинской Америке и Карибском бассейне широко распространены консенсуальные союзы, и к сведениям о доле когда-либо находившихся в браке людей необходимо относиться осторожно, поскольку наблюдаемые тенденции могут отчасти объясняться улучшившимся сбором данных о консенсуальных союзах, а не фактическими изменениями брачности.

В Европе, Северной Америке и Австралии/Новой Зеландии показатель брачности или вступления в консенсуальные союзы остается высоким — более 86 процентов мужчин и более 89 процентов женщин в возрасте 45–49 лет когда-либо состояли в браке или в союзе в 75 процентах стран этих регионов. Однако в период с 70-х по 90-е годы по меньшей мере в 75 процентах соответствующих стран произошло сокращение доли когда-либо состоявших в браке мужчин, причем наиболее заметное сокращение наблюдалось в Скандинавских странах, Латвии, Исландии, Нидерландах и Соединенных Штатах. Доля когда-либо состоявших в браке женщин сократилась меньше, хотя все же существенно в ряде стран, особенно в Дании, Исландии и Швеции.

Имеющиеся данные позволяют сопоставить доли мужчин и женщин в возрасте 25-29 лет, которые когда-либо вступали в брак или в союз, в

70-е и 90-е годы. Это сопоставление свидетельствует о том, что во всем мире значительно изменился возраст вступления в брак: медианная доля когда-либо состоявших в браке женщин в возрасте 25–29 лет сократилась с 85 до 76 процентов, а такая же доля мужчин — с 68 до 56 процентов. В целом, доля людей в возрасте 25-29 лет, когда-либо состоявших в браке, сократилась в 75 процентах всех стран, по которым имеются необходимые данные. Этот показатель сократился больше всего в странах Европы, Северной Америки и Австралии/Новой Зеландии, где все больше молодых людей вступают в союзы в более позднем возрасте, хотя аналогичные тенденции наблюдаются и во всех других регионах. Эти изменения могут привести в будущем к общему снижению показателя брачности и вступления в консенсуальные союзы среди лиц в возрасте 45–49 лет.

Об этих изменениях свидетельствует также постепенное увеличение возраста вступления в брак. Так, расчетный средний возраст вступления в первый брак (СВВБ) — то есть средняя продолжительности жизни до вступления в брак — увеличился за период с 70-х по 90-е годы в 75 процентах всех стран, по которым имеются такие данные. Медианное значение СВВБ по всему миру выросло с 25,4 до 27,2 года среди мужчин и с 21,5 до 23,2 года среди женщин. Особенно сильно СВВБ увеличился в развитых странах — более чем на 4 года в Австралии, Бельгии, Венгрии, Дании, Исландии, Ирландии, Италии, Канаде, Нидерландах, Норвегии, Соединенном Королевстве, Соединенных Штатах, Финляндии, Франции, Швейцарии и Швеции. В развивающихся странах прирост МВВБ был, как правило, меньше, особенно среди мужчин. Однако этот показатель увеличился на 3 года или более в ряде стран каждого региона, включая Алжир, Катар, Кувейт, Ливийскую Арабскую Джамахирию, Малайзию, Мальдивские Острова, Марокко, Судан и Тунис в Азии и Северной Африке; и Багамские острова, Виргинские острова Соединенных Штатов, Гайану, Гваделупу, Мартинику, Нидерландские Антильские острова, Сент-Люсию и Французскую Гвиану в Латинской Америке и Карибском бассейне. Как отмечалось ранее, по отношению к Латинской Америке и Карибскому бассейну увеличение этого показателя в некоторых случаях может быть объяснено изменениями в методах сборе информации о консенсуальных союзах.

Коэффициенты разводимости увеличились в большинстве стран, по которым имеются такие данные. Медианное значение суммарного коэффициента разводимости по развитым странам выросло с 13 разводов на 100 мужчин и женщин в 70-х годах до 24 разводов на 100 мужчин и 27 разводов на 100 женщин в 90-х годах. В развивающихся странах, по которым имеются данные, этот показатель увеличился с 7 до 12 разводов на 100 мужчин и с 5 до 15 разводов на 100 женщин. Показатели разводимости возросли в 75 процентах всех стран, развитых и развивающихся, по которым имеются данные за 70-е и 90-е годы, и в половине из них прирост составил примерно 6–7 разводов на 100 браков. Это означает, что не только увеличился возраст вступления в брак, но и ослабла стабильность брачных союзов. Обе эти тенденции имеют, безусловно, серьезные последствия для репродуктивного поведения.

Применение противозачаточных средств

В период с 70-х по 90-е годы в 90 процентах стран, по которым имеется информация, возросла доля замужних женщин, применяющих противозачаточные средства. Если в 70-е годы в половине стран не более 38 процентов замужних женщин использовали контрацепцию, то в 90-е годы в половине стран таких женщин стало не менее 52 процентов. Однако за этими глобальными показателями скрываются серьезные различия между развитыми и развивающимися странами.

В развитых странах противозачаточные средства уже широко применялись в 70-е годы, когда по меньшей мере половина всех состоявших в браке женщин пользовалась противозачаточными средствами. Более того, в 70-е годы в трех из каждых четырех развитых стран по меньшей мере две трети всех замужних женщин использовали контрацептивы. К 90-м годам масштабы применения противозачаточных средств возросли в 14 из 44 развитых стран и сократились в 6 из них. Сокращение показателей применения противозачаточных средств объяснялось нередко сокращением использования традиционных средств контрацепции. Однако некоторые из этих различий могут быть статистическим артефактом, обусловленным изменениями в процедурах сбора данных, а не фактическими переменами в поведении. В развитых странах в целом заметно расширилось применение современных методов контрацепции — средний показатель их применения женщинами, состоящими в браке или в союзе, вырос с 54 до 61 процента. Применение современных методов расширилось во всех странах, по которым имеются данные за 70-е и 90-е годы. Лишь в Австрии этот показатель снизился почти на 10 процентных пунктов, что частично объяснятся различиями в процедурах сбора данных.

В развивающихся странах в 70-е годы противозачаточные средства использовались много реже, в 70-х годах были гораздо меньше, чем в 90-х годах. В группе развивающихся стран, по которым имеется информация, медианный уровень применения противозачаточных средств вырос в период между этими датами с 27 до 40 процентов. К 90-м годам в каждой четвертой стране не менее 62 процентов замужних женщин применяли противозачаточные средства. Однако в другой четверти всех развивающихся стран противозачаточными средствами пользовалось менее 24 процентов всех женщин, состоявшихся в тот момент в браке или в союзе. Уровни применения современных методов были еще ниже. Хотя медианный уровень применения современных методов контрацепции в развивающихся странах увеличился в период с 70-х по 90-е годы с 18 до 30 процентов, современные методы по-прежнему применяются редко во многих развивающихся странах, причем в каждой четвертой из них этот показатель составляет менее 12 процентов. К числу последних относятся 25 африканцких стран, а также Афганистан и Йемен.

К 90-м годам современные методы контрацепции стали широко применяться в ряде развивающихся стран. Так, в Алжире, Египте, Зимбабве, Реюньоне, Тунисе и Южной Африке современными методами контрацепции пользовалось более половины замужних женщин. Аналогичные или более высокие показатели были достигнуты в ряде азиатских стран-- во Вьетнаме, Гонконге (ОАР Китая), Израиле, Индонезии, Исламской Республике Иран, Казахстане, Китае, Корейской Народно-Демократической Республике, Монголии, Республике Корея, Сингапуре, Таиланде, Туркменистане, Узбекистане и Филиппинах. В более чем половине стран Латинской Америки и Карибского бассейна, по которым имеются данные, показатели применения современных противозачаточных средств составляли более 50 процентов. В большинстве этих развивающихся стран использование современных методов контрацепции резко увеличилось в период с 70-х по 90-е годы. Так, за этот период по меньшей мере в половине всех развивающихся стран, по которым имеются данные, показатель применения современных противозачаточных средств вырос на 20 процентных пунктов или более.

Итак, были достигнуты крупные успехи в удовлетворении спроса на современные противозачаточные средства в развивающихся странах. Вместе с тем современная контрацепция по-прежнему мало используется во многих странах Африки, равно как и в некоторых странах Азии и Латинской Америки и Карибского бассейна. Как и следовало ожидать, низкие уровни применения современных методов контрацепции более характерны для наименее развитых стран и других стран с низким уровнем дохода, чем для стран со средним уровнем дохода.

Рождаемость

В период с 70-х по 90-е годы уровень рождаемости во всем мире значительно снизился. За этот период средний суммарный коэффициент рождаемости по всем странам, по которым имеются данные, сократился с 5,4 до 2,9 ребенка на женщину. Бо́льшая часть этого сокращения вызвана снижением рождаемости в развивающихся странах, где в период с 70-х по 90-е годы медиана суммарной рождаемости уменьшилась с 5,9 до 3,9 ребенка на женщину. Кроме того, существенное, хотя и менее крупное, снижение рождаемости произошло и в развитых странах, где за тот же период медиана суммарной рождаемости сократилась с 2,3 до 1,4 ребенка на женщину.

За исключением Демократической Республики Конго, Французской Гвианы, Гвинеи и Мали, рождаемость снизилась во всех развивающихся странах, по которым имеются данные за 70-е и 90-е годы, хотя ошибки в исходных данных могут искажать оценки масштабов изменений. Тем не менее представленные в докладе данные дают общее представление, подтверждаемое другими оценками тенденций рождаемости. В период с 70-х по 90-е годы суммарная рождаемость в половине развивающихся стран сократилась не менее чем на на 1,8 ребенка на женщину, а в одной четверти развивающихся стран сокращение составило не менее 2,6 ребенка на женщину. Так, в Китае после 1970 года суммарная рождаемость сократилась на 4 ребенка на женщину. Другие страны, в которых произошло значительное снижение рождаемости, включают Алжир, Исламскую Республику Иран, Мексику, Таиланд, Тунис и Турцию. И напротив, уровень рождаемости снизился не намного (менее чем на одного ребенка с 1970 года) или не изменился вообще в 21 развивающейся стране, причем 13 из них — субсахарские африканские страны.

В развитых странах сокращение рождаемости было повсеместным. Величина сокращения была в целом небольшой, но существенной, если учесть, что к 70-м годам уровни рождаемости в большинстве этих стран были уже низки. В группе развитых стран медианное сокращение рождаемсти составило 0,8 ребенка на женщину. В 70-х годах в 36 развитых странах суммарная рождаемость составляла не менее 2 детей на одну женщину. К 90-м годам лишь в четырех развитых странах — Албании, Исландии, Новой Зеландии и Соединенных Штатах Америки — суммарная рождаемость составляла 2 ребенка или более на женщину.

Если 2,1 ребенка на женщину принять в качестве показателя рождаемости, обеспечивающего воспроизводство населения при низком уровне смертности, то в 70-х годах уровни рождаемости в 12 развитых странах были ниже уровней, необходимых для воспроизводства населения, тогда как аналогичный низкий уровень рождаемости наблюдался лишь в одной развивающейся стране. К 90-м годам число развитых стран с уровнем рождаемости ниже уровня воспроизводства увеличилось до 41, а число развивающихся стран — до 19. В 14 развитых странах суммарная рождаемость была ниже 1,3 ребенка на женщину — самый низкий уровень за всю документированную историю стран с большим народонаселением.

Общемировое снижение рождаемости сопровождалось крупными изменениями в возрасте деторождения. В половине всех развивающихся стран сокращение рождаемости в старших детородных возрастах привело к снижению среднего возраста матери. В развитых странах главной тенденцией было увеличение среднего возраста матери вследствие откладывания деторождения. Данные о среднем возрасте женщины при рождении первого ребенка свидетельствуют о том, что этот показатель в целом увеличивается как в развитых, так и в развивающихся странах. Средний возраст женщины при рождении первого ребенка увеличился больше всего в развитых странах — в 75 процентах из них этот показатель увеличился по меньшей мере на 1,7 года в период с 70-х по 90-е годы. Прирост был менее значительным в развивающихся странах и составил 0,5 года и более в 75 процентах стран, по которым имеются данные за оба периода. Поэтому и в 90-е годы сохранялись различия между развитыми и развивающимися странами по среднему возрасту женщин при рождении первого ребенка: медианное значение этого показателя по группе развитых стран составляло 26,4 года против 22,1 года в группе развивающихся стран.

Значительно изменилась доля бездетных женщин в возрасте 45–49 лет. Хотя стран, по которым имеются сопоставимые данные за 70-е и 90-е годы, не так много, имеющаяся информация свидетельствует о том, что доля бездетных женщин существенно сократилась в Африке, где венерические заболевания были серьезной причиной стерильности в 50-е и 60-е годы. В Латинской Америке показатели бездетности также в целом сократились. В других основных регионах наблюдались как увеличения, так и сокращения показателя бездетности. В 90-х годах уровни бездетности были довольно низкими в Африке и Азии, где они не превышали 9 процентов, а в большинстве стран были ниже 5 или 7 процентов, соответственно); в то же время доля бездетных женщин была высока в странах Карибского бассейна и в развитых странах. Так, в 90-е годы в 75 процентах развитых стран по меньшей мере 7 процентов женщин в возрасте 45–49 лет были бездетными, а в 75 процентах стран Карибского бассейна, по которым имеются такие данные, доля бездетных женщин в возрасте 45–49 лет составляла по меньшей мере 8 процентов. Особенно высокие уровни бездетности (более 10 процентов) были зарегистрированы в Канаде, Люксембурге, Нидерландских Антильских островах, Португалии, Республике Молдова, Румынии, Уругвае, Финляндии, Франции, Швейцарии и Эстонии.

Демографическая политика

Произошли существенные изменения во взглядах и действиях правительств в отношении уровней рождаемости и тенденций в этой области. В 1976 году правительства 52 процентов стран сообщили, что они не принимали никаких мер для изменения уровня рождаемости, а к 2001 году доля таких стран сократилась до 32 процентов (см. диаграмму II). С 70-х годов правительства все более активно поддерживают планирование семьи. К 2001 году правительства 92 процентов стран поддерживали программы планирования семьи и мероприятия по распределению противозачаточных средств либо напрямую (75 процентов) — через государственные учреждения — либо косвенно (17 процентов) — путем поддержки деятельности неправительственных организаций, таких, как ассоциации по планированию семьи.

Кроме того, отношение правительств к уровню рождаемости существенно изменилось. Так, в 1976 году правительства 27 процентов стран хотели снизить уровень рождаемости, а к 2001 году к этому стремилось 45 процентов стран. Доля правительств развивающихся стран, желающих снизить уровень рождаемости, еще выше и составляет 58 процентов. Вместе с тем доля правительств, желающих повысить уровень рождаемости, возросла с 9 процентов в 1976 году до 13 процентов в 2001 году. В результате удельный вес правительств, желающих сохранить рождаемость на нынешнем уровне, уменьшилась с 13 процентов до 10 процентов. Иными словам, больше правительств желают сегодня изменить уровень рождаемости своего населения и готовы принять надлежащие меры для достижения таких целей.

Диаграмма I.
**Общие показатели рождаемости 160 стран ориентировочно за 1970 и
2000 годы**

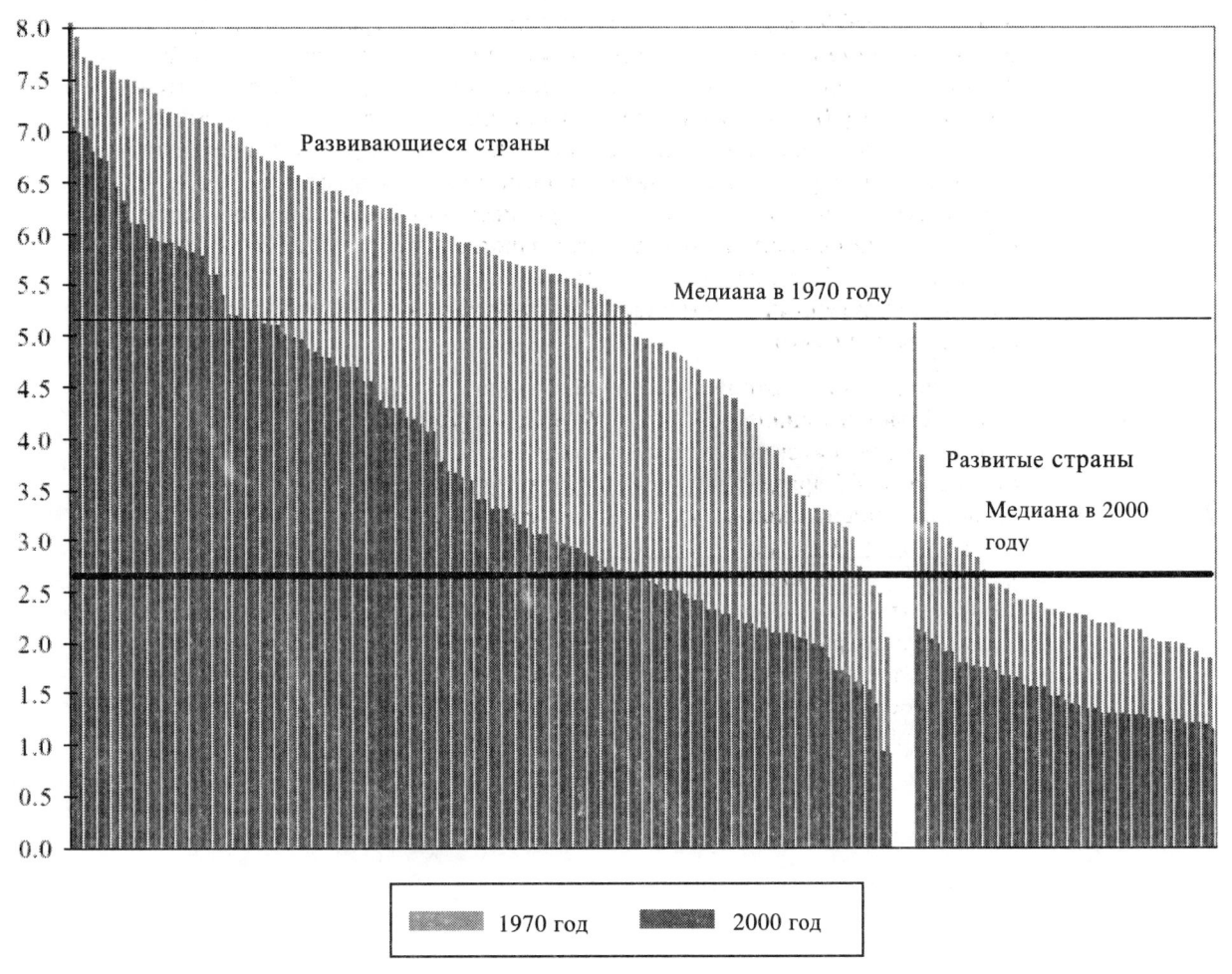

Диаграмма II.
**Государственная политика в отношении рождаемости : 1976 и
2001 годы**

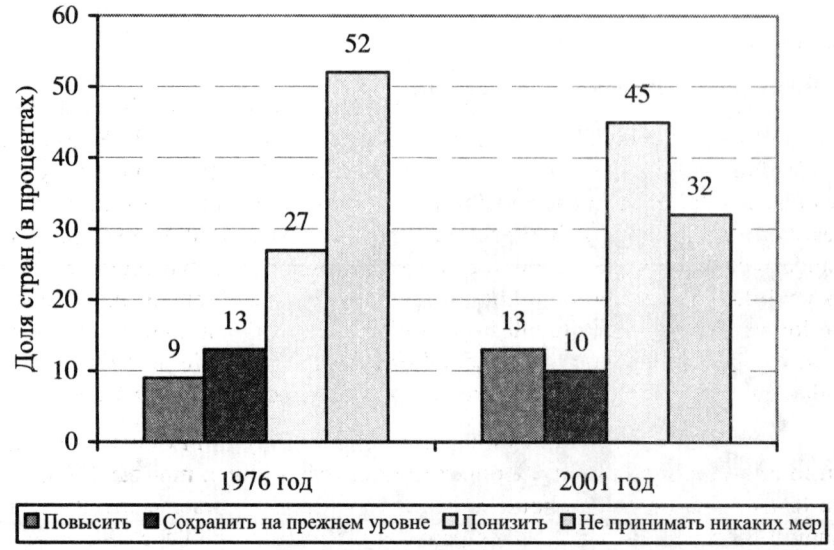

World Fertility Report 2003

Resumen

En el *World Fertility Report 2003*, preparado por la División de Población del Departamento de Asuntos Económicos y Sociales de la Secretaría de las Naciones Unidas, se presenta una recopilación de estimaciones e indicadores básicos de fecundidad, nupcialidad y uso de anticonceptivos para 192 países, con referencia principalmente a los decenios de 1970 y 1990, pero abarcando fechas anteriores, cuando es necesario, o períodos más recientes cuando es posible. El conjunto de datos presentados permite formular una evaluación de los cambios sin precedentes que se han registrado en materia de nupcialidad, uso de anticonceptivos y fecundidad desde el decenio de 1970. En particular, en el informe se documentan las siguientes conclusiones básicas:

1.   **Se ha registrado en todo el mundo un cambio muy importante en la edad en que se contrae matrimonio, que es ahora más tardía.** El valor de la mediana correspondiente a la edad media al contraer matrimonio en el mundo pasó de 25,4 a 27,2 años para los hombres y de 21,5 a 23,2 años para las mujeres. En los países desarrollados, el incremento ha sido aún más notable, ya que la mediana subió de 25,2 a 28,8 años para los hombres y de 22,0 a 26,1 años para las mujeres.

2.   **Tanto los hombres como las mujeres permanecen solteros durante períodos más largos de sus vidas.** La mediana del porcentaje de no solteros entre las personas de 25 a 29 años de edad se redujo del 85% en el decenio de 1970 al 76% en el decenio de 1990 para las mujeres, y del 68% al 56% para los hombres. También en este caso, las reducciones en el porcentaje de las personas algunas vez casadas de 25 a 29 años son más considerables en los países desarrollados, en los que los valores de la mediana descendieron del 85% al 62% entre las mujeres y del 74% al 43% entre los hombres.

3.   **La demora de los adultos jóvenes en contraer matrimonio no se ha traducido aún en reducciones marcadas del porcentaje de personas que contraen matrimonio al menos una vez en sus vidas.** El matrimonio, o alguna forma de unión consensual, sigue siendo casi universal. En el decenio de 1970, en tres de cada cuatro países, el 89% ó más de todos los hombres y todas las mujeres de 45 a 49 años de edad habían estado casados por lo menos una vez y esa cifra continuaba cercana al 89% en el decenio de 1990.

4.   **Las tasas de divorcio han aumentado en la mayoría de los países para los que se dispone de datos.** En los países desarrollados, el valor de la mediana de la tasa de divorcio pasó de 13 divorcios por 100, para hombres y mujeres, en el decenio de 1970 a 24 divorcios por cada 100 hombres y 27 por cada 100 mujeres en el decenio de 1990. En los países en desarrollo, el valor de la mediana de la tasa de divorcio pasó de 7 a 12 divorcios por cada 100 hombres y de 5 a 15 divorcios por cada 100 mujeres. Es decir, que no sólo ha habido una tendencia a casarse más tarde sino que la inestabilidad de las uniones maritales ha ido en aumento. Es evidente que ambas tendencias tienen consecuencias importantes para el comportamiento reproductivo.

5.   **Ha habido un aumento enorme en la utilización de la planificación familiar.** Entre los decenios de 1970 y de 1990, el uso de anticonceptivos entre las mujeres actualmente casadas o en una unión consensual aumentó en 9 de cada 10 países para los que se dispone de información. El valor de la mediana del uso de anticonceptivos en todo el mundo aumentó del 38% de las mujeres actualmente casadas o en una unión consensual en el decenio de 1970 al 52% en el decenio de 1990. En los países en desarrollo, el valor de la mediana del uso de anticonceptivos aumentó del 27% al 40% entre esas fechas. Para el decenio de 1990, la frecuencia del uso de anticonceptivos en una cuarta parte de todos los países en desarrollo era igual o superior al 62%.

6.   **El uso de métodos anticonceptivos modernos en los países en desarrollo ha aumentado en general.** El valor de la mediana del uso de anticonceptivos modernos en países en desarrollo aumentó del 18% al 30% entre el decenio de 1970 y el de 1990. Sin embargo, en una cuarta parte de todos los países en desarrollo el uso de métodos anticonceptivos modernos sigue siendo poco frecuente y se mantiene en un porcentaje inferior al 12%.

7.   **Entre 1970 y 2000, el nivel de fecundidad de la población mundial experimentó una reducción muy importante y sin precedentes, impulsada principalmente por la declinación de la fecundidad en los países en desarrollo** (gráfico I). Los valores medios de la fecundidad en el mundo en desarrollo cayeron, de más de 5,9 hijos por mujer, en el decenio de 1970, a unos 3,9 hijos por mujer en el decenio de 1990. El valor de la mediana de la reducción de la fecundidad en los países en desarrollo entre los decenios de 1970 y 1990 fue de alrededor de 1,8 hijos por mujer, y en una cuarta parte de todos los países en desarrollo se han logrado, al parecer, reducciones iguales o superiores a 2,6 hijos por mujer.

8.   **En tanto que en el decenio de 1970 la fecundidad era uniformemente elevada en los países en desarrollo, los niveles de fecundidad en esos países hoy en día muestran una gran diversidad.** Así, en un cierto número de los países menos adelantados, la fecundidad se mantiene por encima de cinco hijos por mujer, mientras que en unos 20 países en desarrollo está por debajo del crecimiento vegetativo.

9.   **Los niveles de fecundidad en los países desarrollados, en muchos de los cuales se registró un auge de la natalidad en los decenios de 1950 y 1960, han declinado en general desde 1970.** Entre los decenios de 1970 y 1990, el valor de la mediana de la reducción de la fecundidad total en los países en desarrollo fue de 0,8 hijos por mujer. Para fines del decenio de 1990, sólo en cuatro países desarrollados —Albania, Estados Unidos de América, Islandia y Nueva Zelandia— se informaba de una fecundidad total de dos hijos por mujer o superior. Además, en 14 países desarrollados, la fecundidad era inferior a 1,3 hijos por mujer, lo que constituye un nivel de fecundidad muy bajo y sin precedentes en la historia de grandes números de personas.

10.   **Las cifras de personas sin hijos varían considerablemente entre las zonas principales.** En el decenio de 1990, el porcentaje de mujeres de 45 a 49 años de edad sin hijos tendía a ser alto en los países desarrollados y en los países del Caribe. En cuatro de cada cinco países desarrollados para los que se disponía de datos, por lo menos el 7% de las mujeres de 45 a 49 años de edad no tenían hijos, y en nueve países desarrollados el porcentaje de mujeres sin hijos era superior al 10%. Los porcentajes de mujeres sin hijos eran relativamente bajos en África y Asia en el decenio de 1990 y moderados en América Latina. Entre el decenio de 1970 y el de 1990, hubo una disminución del por-

centaje de mujeres sin hijos en África, debido a que la esterilidad causada por las enfermedades de transmisión sexual se redujo en los decenios de 1970 y 1980.

11. **Los profundos cambios de los niveles de fecundidad que se han registrado desde 1970 han sido posibles gracias a transformaciones muy importantes del comportamiento relacionadas con la formación de uniones, el matrimonio y el uso de anticonceptivos.** Las políticas gubernamentales sobre el acceso a los anticonceptivos han desempeñado un importante papel en la modificación del comportamiento reproductivo. En 1976, el 52% de todos los gobiernos informaban que no habían intervenido para modificar los niveles de fecundidad, pero para el año 2001 ese porcentaje se había reducido al 32% (gráfico II). El apoyo gubernamental a la planificación de la familia ha ido aumentando constantemente desde el decenio de 1970. Para el año 2001, el 92% de todos los gobiernos prestaban apoyo a programas de planificación familiar y a la distribución de anticonceptivos, ya sea directamente (75%), mediante servicios gubernamentales, o indirectamente (17%), mediante el apoyo a las actividades de organizaciones no gubernamentales tales como las asociaciones de planificación familiar.

Los datos sobre fecundidad, nupcialidad, uso de anticonceptivos y políticas en materia de procreación que se exponen en el presente informe se seleccionaron de modo que reflejaran las transformaciones más importantes del comportamiento reproductivo y en materia de nupcialidad que han tenido lugar desde 1970, es decir, en el curso de una generación. Se han incluido indicadores que reflejan los cambios por cohorte de nacimientos y otras tendencias indicativas desde la perspectiva de un período. Los datos se obtuvieron de diversas fuentes, incluso el registro civil, los censos de población y encuestas nacionales representativas. Los datos presentados no se han ajustado a fin de tener en cuenta el ámbito de aplicación, la subenumeración y otros errores no provenientes del muestreo. Por eso, los valores de algunos indicadores, en particular los correspondientes a países en desarrollo en que hay deficiencia en los datos, pueden no coincidir con los publicados por la División de Población en *World Population Prospects: The 2002 Revision*, ya que estos últimos se han ajustado según fue necesario. Para cada país se presentan los valores de 43 indicadores para cada fecha, siempre que se disponga de datos.

Las principales conclusiones del presente informe se consideran con más detalle a continuación. Al tratar los resultados, la unidad de análisis es el país y se ha hecho hincapié principalmente en los cambios en la distribución de los países según los distintos indicadores.

Nupcialidad

El matrimonio, o alguna forma de unión consensual, sigue siendo casi universal. En el decenio de 1970, entre tres de cada cuatro países, por lo menos el 89% de todos los hombres y todas las mujeres de 45 a 49 años de edad habían estado casados por los menos una vez, y para el decenio de 1990 esa cifra todavía seguía estando cercana al 89%. Además, en una cuarta parte de todos los países con datos pertinentes, la proporción de hombres de 45 a 49 años de edad alguna vez casados o en una unión consensual era del 97% o más en el decenio de 1970 y del 98% o más en el decenio de 1990. Del mismo modo, en la cuarta parte de todos los países, por lo menos el 98% de las mujeres de 45 a 49 años de edad habían estado casadas o en una unión.

En el decenio de 1970 la prevalencia del matrimonio era máxima en los países de Asia, en los que sigue siendo alta, aunque ha habido algunos casos de reducciones importantes en los porcentajes de las personas algunas vez casadas, especialmente entre los hombres del Japón y las mujeres de Singapur, o en Brunei Darussalam, Israel, Malasia, Myanmar y el Territorio Palestino Ocupado. Los países de África se caracterizan también en general por una elevada prevalencia del matrimonio o de uniones consensuales, y las tres cuartas partes de ellos informan que por lo menos el 96% de los hombres de 45 a 49 años de edad y por lo menos el 98% de las mujeres del mismo grupo de edades han estado casados o en una unión en el decenio de 1990. De hecho, en un cierto número de países de África parecen haberse registrado importantes aumentos de los porcentajes de las personas que a los 45 a 49 años han estado alguna vez casadas, en particular entre los hombres. Entre los ejemplos se encuentran Benin, Burkina Faso, el Camerún, la República Centroafricana y Uganda. Por el contrario, en Botswana, la Reunión y Sudáfrica se registraron reducciones importantes en los porcentajes de personas alguna vez casadas entre los hombres y mujeres de 45 a 49 años de edad.

El matrimonio y las uniones consensuales son algo menos prevalecientes en los países de América Latina, y especialmente en la región del Caribe, en comparación con otras regiones del mundo en desarrollo. Para el decenio de 1990, en la mitad de los países del Caribe a lo sumo el 72% de los hombres y el 70% de las mujeres de 45 a 49 años de edad habían estado alguna vez casados o en una unión. Además, en las Antillas Holandesas, Barbados, Jamaica y Santa Lucía se registraron, entre el decenio de 1970 y el de 1990, reducciones importantes en los porcentajes de las personas algunas vez casadas. En los demás países de América Latina, los porcentajes de personas alguna vez casadas entre las de 45 a 49 años de edad tendían a ser mayores, pero para el decenio de 1990 en la mitad de los países de la región por lo menos el 10% de los hombres y el 9% de las mujeres de 45 a 49 años de edad nunca habían estado casadas o formado parte de una unión consensual. Estas cifras representan un cambio con respecto al decenio de 1970, en que los porcentajes de las personas que nunca estuvieron casadas tendían a ser superiores. Entre el decenio de 1970 y el decenio de 1990, en la mitad, por lo menos, de los países de América Latina se registraron importantes aumentos en los porcentajes de hombres y mujeres de 45 a 49 años de edad que habían estado alguna vez casados o en una unión. Sin embargo, en América Latina y el Caribe las uniones consensuales son comunes y los datos sobre los porcentajes de personas que alguna vez han estado casadas deben interpretarse con cautela ya que las tendencias observadas pueden deberse en parte a que la información sobre las uniones consensuales ha mejorado con el tiempo y no a un cambio real de la prevalencia del matrimonio.

En Europa, América del Norte y Australia/Nueva Zelandia, la prevalencia del matrimonio y las uniones consensuales sigue siendo elevada, ya que más del 86% de los hombres y más del 89% de las mujeres de 45 a 49 años de edad han estado casados o en uniones consensuales en tres de cada cuatro países de esas regiones. Sin embargo, entre el decenio de 1970 y 1990, por lo menos las tres cuartas partes de los países en cuestión experimentaron una reducción en los porcentajes de los hombres alguna vez casados; las reducciones son más notables en los países nórdicos y en Letonia, Islandia, los Países Bajos y los Estados Unidos. Las reducciones en los porcentajes de mujeres alguna vez casadas fueron menos comunes pero sin embargo considerables en un cierto número de países, en particular en Dinamarca, Islandia y Suecia.

Los datos disponibles permiten hacer una comparación de los porcentajes de hombres y mujeres que se habían casado o habían entrado a formar parte de una unión consensual a más tardar a los 25 a 29 años de edad en el decenio de 1970 frente al decenio de 1990. Esa comparación indica que se había registrado en todo el mundo un cambio importante en la edad de contraer matrimonio: el valor de la mediana porcentual de las personas alguna vez casadas disminuyó del 85% al 76% entre las mujeres de 25 a 29 años y del 68% al 56% entre los hombres de 25 a 29 años de edad. Además, en las tres cuartas partes de todos los países para los que se dispone de los datos necesarios se registra una reducción de los porcentajes de personas alguna vez casadas para los 25 a 29 años de edad. Esas reducciones son más acusadas en los países de Europa, América del Norte y Australia/Nueva Zelandia, donde los jóvenes están aplazando en medida cada vez mayor la edad en que entran a formar parte de uniones, pero tendencias similares se observan en todas las demás regiones. Esos cambios pueden anunciar una declinación general de conjunto en el futuro en la prevalencia del matrimonio y las uniones consensuales entre las personas de 45 a 49 años.

Esos cambios se reflejan también en el constante aumento de la edad al casarse. Consiguientemente, la edad media de la población soltera al casarse, que es un indicador de la duración media de la condición de soltero, experimentó un aumento del decenio de 1970 al decenio de 1990 en las tres cuartas partes de todos los países para los que se dispone de datos. A nivel mundial, el valor de la mediana de la edad media de la población soltera al casarse pasó de 25,4 a 27,2 años en los hombres y de 21,5 a 23,2 años en las mujeres. En los países desarrollados se registraron incrementos particularmente considerables de la edad media de la población soltera al casarse: el valor medio creció más de cuatro años en Australia, Bélgica, el Canadá, Dinamarca, los Estados Unidos, Francia, Finlandia, Hungría, Irlanda, Islandia, Italia, los Países Bajos, Noruega, el Reino Unido, Suecia y Suiza. En los países en desarrollo los aumentos de la edad media de la población soltera al casarse tendieron a ser de menor magnitud, sobre todo en el caso de los hombres. Sin embargo, hubo incrementos de tres o más años en unos pocos países de todas las regiones, entre ellos Argelia, la Jamahiriya Árabe Libia, Kuwait, Maldivas, Malasia, Marruecos, Qatar, el Sudán y Túnez, en Asia y África del Norte; y las Antillas Neerlandesas, las Bahamas, Guadalupe, la Guayana Francesa, Guyana, las Islas Vírgenes de los Estados Unidos, Martinica y Santa Lucía en América Latina y el Caribe. Como ya se ha señalado, en América Latina y el Caribe algunos de esos aumentos podrían ser consecuencia de cambios en la manera de suministrar información sobre las uniones consensuales.

Las tasas de divorcio aumentaron en la mayoría de los países para los que se dispone de datos. El valor de la mediana de la tasa de divorcio en los países desarrollados pasó de 13 divorcios por cada 100 hombres y mujeres en el decenio de 1970 a 24 divorcios por cada 100 hombres y 27 divorcios por cada 100 mujeres en el decenio de 1990. Entre los países en desarrollo para los que se dispone de datos, la mediana de la tasa de divorcio aumentó de 7 a 12 divorcios por cada 100 hombres y de 5 a 15 divorcios por cada 100 mujeres. En las tres cuartas partes de todos los países, tanto desarrollados como en desarrollo, para los que se dispone de datos para el decenio de 1970 y el decenio de 1990, las tasas de divorcio aumentaron y en la mitad de ellos los aumentos fueron de alrededor del 6% al 7%. Es decir, que no sólo ha habido una tendencia a que las personas se casen más tarde, sino que la inestabilidad de las uniones maritales también ha ido en aumento. Es evidente que ambas tendencias tienen consecuencias importantes para el comportamiento reproductivo.

Uso de anticonceptivos

Entre el decenio de 1970 y el de 1990, el uso de anticonceptivos entre las mujeres que estaban casadas o formaban parte de una unión en esos períodos aumentó en un 90% en todos los países en que había información disponible para los dos períodos. El valor de la mediana del uso de anticonceptivos a nivel mundial aumentó del 38% de las mujeres que estaban casadas o formaban parte de una unión al 52%. Sin embargo, esas cifras mundiales oscurecen las importantes diferencias entre los países desarrollados y los países en desarrollo.

Entre los países desarrollados, el uso de anticonceptivos ya era elevado en el decenio de 1970, cuando por lo menos la mitad de todas las mujeres de los países desarrollados que estaban casadas o formaban parte de una unión utilizaban anticonceptivos. En realidad, en las tres cuartas partes de todos los países desarrollados, por lo menos los dos tercios de todas las mujeres que estaban casadas o formaban parte de uniones eran usuarias de anticonceptivos para el decenio de 1970. Para el decenio de 1990, el nivel de la utilización de anticonceptivos había aumentado en 14 de 44 países desarrollados, pero en seis de ellos había disminuido. Las reducciones registradas en el uso de anticonceptivos con frecuencia eran el resultado de una reducción en el uso de métodos anticonceptivos tradicionales y de una mayor utilización de métodos modernos. Sin embargo, algunas de esas diferencias pueden ser espurias y deberse a cambios en los procedimientos de recopilación de datos antes que a cambios reales del comportamiento. Sin embargo, los datos indican que en los países desarrollados en su conjunto hubo un pronunciado aumento del uso de métodos anticonceptivos modernos, y el valor de la mediana de ese uso aumentó y pasó del 54% al 61% de las mujeres que estaban casadas o formaban parte de una unión. A nivel de países, en todos los países en que había datos disponibles para los decenios de 1970 y de 1990 se registró un aumento en la prevalencia de los métodos modernos, excepto en Austria, donde esa prevalencia se redujo en casi 10 puntos porcentuales. En el caso de Austria, este cambio puede deberse en parte a la utilización de procedimientos diferentes de recopilación de datos.

Entre los países en desarrollo, la prevalencia de anticonceptivos en el decenio de 1970 fue pronunciadamente inferior a la del decenio de 1990. En los países en desarrollo para los que se disponía de información, el valor de la mediana de la prevalencia de anticonceptivos creció entre esas fechas del 27% al 40%. Para el decenio de 1990, la prevalencia de anticonceptivos en una cuarta parte de todos los países en desarrollo era del 62% o superior. Sin embargo, en otra cuarta parte de todos los países en desarrollo, la prevalencia de anticonceptivos se mantenía por debajo del 24% de todas las mujeres que estaban casadas o formaban parte de una unión consensual. Los índices de utilización de métodos modernos eran aún más bajos. Si bien el valor de la mediana correspondiente a la utilización de métodos anticonceptivos modernos en los países en desarrollo aumentó del 18% al 30% entre el decenio de 1970 y el de 1990, la utilización de métodos modernos sigue siendo poco frecuente en muchos países en desarrollo, y en una cuarta parte de ellos los índices de prevalencia están por debajo del 12%. Entre estos últimos se cuentan el Afganistán y el Yemen en Asia y 25 países de África.

Para el decenio de 1990, varios países en desarrollo habían alcanzado niveles elevados de prevalencia de métodos anticonceptivos modernos. Así, por ejemplo, en Argelia, Egipto, la Reunión, Sudáfrica, Túnez y Zimbabwe, más de la mitad de todas las mujeres que estaban casadas o formaban parte de una unión utilizaban métodos anticonceptivos modernos para el decenio de 1990. Niveles análogos o más altos se habían alcanzado en China, Filipinas, Indonesia, Irán (República Islámica del), Israel, Kazajstán, Mongolia, la Región Administrativa Especial China de Hong Kong, la República de Corea, la República Popular Democrática de Corea, Singapur, Tailandia, Turkmenistán, Uzbekistán y Viet Nam, en Asia. En América Latina y el Caribe, más de la mitad de todos los países para los que se disponía de datos tenían niveles de utilización de anticonceptivos modernos superiores al 50%. En la mayoría de esos países se habían registrado aumentos muy notables en el uso de métodos anticonceptivos modernos entre los decenios de 1970 y 1990. De hecho, en ese período, por lo menos la mitad de todos los países en desarrollo para los que se disponía de datos habían experimentado un aumento de 20 puntos porcentuales o más en el uso de métodos anticonceptivos modernos.

En resumen, se han hecho avances muy importantes en lo que respecta a satisfacer la demanda de métodos anticonceptivos modernos en los países en desarrollo, pero en muchos países de África y en algunos países de Asia y América Latina y el Caribe todavía subsisten niveles bajos de utilización de anticonceptivos modernos. Como cabría esperar, en los países menos adelantados y otros países de bajos ingresos se dan con más frecuencia que en los países de ingresos medianos bajos niveles de uso de anticonceptivos modernos.

Fecundidad

Entre los decenios de 1970 y 1990, la fecundidad disminuyó de manera pronunciada en el plano mundial. El valor de la mediana correspondiente a la fecundidad total de todos los países para los que se disponía de datos descendió de 5,4 a 2,9 hijos por mujer en el período en cuestión. La mayor parte de esa reducción se debió al descenso de la fecundidad en los países en desarrollo, en los que el valor de la mediana de la fecundidad total pasó de 5,9 a 3,9 hijos por mujer entre el decenio de 1970 y el de 1990. Se produjeron también reducciones importantes, aunque más pequeñas, de la fecundidad en los países desarrollados, en los que el valor de la mediana de la fecundidad total descendió de 2,3 a 1,4 hijos por mujer en el mismo período.

Salvo en la Guayana Francesa, Guinea, Malí y la República Democrática del Congo, todos los demás países en desarrollo para los que se disponía de datos para los decenios de 1970 y 1990 parecían haber experimentado reducciones de los niveles de fecundidad, aunque las estimaciones de cambio pueden estar sesgadas por errores diferenciales en el suministro de información sobre los datos básicos. Sin embargo, los datos que se presentan en este informe muestran un panorama de conjunto validado por otras evaluaciones de las tendencias de la fecundidad. El valor de la mediana de la reducción de la fecundidad en los países en desarrollo entre los decenios de 1970 y de 1990 fue de alrededor de 1,8 hijos por mujer, y una cuarta parte de todos los países en desarrollo parecen haber logrado reducciones de 2,6 hijos por mujer o más. China es uno de los países que integran este grupo, ya que su fecundidad se ha reducido en aproximadamente 4 hijos por mujer desde 1970. Otros países que han informado sobre reducciones considerables de la fecundidad incluyen a

Argelia, Irán (República Islámica del), México, Tailandia, Túnez y Turquía. En cambio, la fecundidad disminuyó lentamente (en menos de un hijo desde 1970) o no disminuyó del todo en 21 países en desarrollo, 13 de los cuales se encuentran en el África subsahariana.

Entre los países desarrollados, las reducciones de la fecundidad fueron la norma, si bien su magnitud fue en general escasa pero significativa dados los bajos niveles de fecundidad total que ya habían llegado a caracterizar a la mayoría de esos países en el decenio de 1970. La reducción en el valor de la mediana de la fecundidad total entre los países desarrollados fue de 0,8 hijos por mujer, y para el decenio de 1990 sólo cuatro países desarrollados —Albania, los Estados Unidos de América, Islandia y Nueva Zelandia— informaron que tenían una fecundidad total de 2 o más hijos por mujer. En el decenio de 1970, había 36 países desarrollados en que los niveles de fecundidad eran por lo menos de 2 hijos por mujer.

Si 2,1 hijos por mujer representa un nivel de fecundidad que garantiza el reemplazo de la población cuando la mortalidad es baja, los niveles de fecundidad en 12 países desarrollados estaban por debajo del nivel de reemplazo en el decenio de 1970, y en cambio sólo un país en desarrollo tenía un nivel de fecundidad aproximadamente tan bajo. Para el decenio de 1990, el número de países desarrollados en que la fecundidad estaba por debajo del nivel de reemplazo había aumentado a 41, en tanto que había 19 países en desarrollo en la misma situación. En 14 países desarrollados, la fecundidad total era inferior a 1,3 hijos por mujer, lo que constituye un nivel histórico sin precedentes para poblaciones numerosas.

La reducción de la fecundidad en todo el mundo se ha visto acompañada por cambios muy importantes en la época en que ocurre la procreación. En la mitad de todos los países en desarrollo, la edad media en que las mujeres tienen hijos ha disminuido paralelamente a la reducción de las tasas de fecundidad de las mujeres de más edad. En los países desarrollados, la tendencia principal ha sido que la edad media de procreación ha ido aumentando a medida que las mujeres aplazaban el comienzo de la procreación. Los datos sobre la edad media al nacer el primer hijo indican que en general ha ido en aumento, tanto en los países desarrollados como en los países en desarrollo. El aumento de la edad media de las madres al nacer el primer hijo ha sido más pronunciado en los países desarrollados, en las tres cuartas partes de los cuales la edad media de las madres al ocurrir el primer nacimiento se incrementó en por lo menos 1,7 años entre el decenio de 1970 y el de 1990. En los países en desarrollo, esos incrementos han sido más limitados, y son de por lo menos 0,5 años en las tres cuartas partes de todos los países en desarrollo en los que existen datos correspondientes a los dos períodos. En consecuencia, sigue habiendo importantes diferencias entre los países desarrollados y los países en desarrollo con relación al momento de los primeros nacimientos. En el decenio de 1990, el valor de la mediana de la edad media en el momento del primer nacimiento era de 26,4 años en los países desarrollados y sólo de 22,1 años en los países en desarrollo.

También han ocurrido cambios importantes en lo que respecta al nivel de infecundidad entre las mujeres de 45 a 49 años de edad. Aunque son pocos los países que poseen datos comparables para el decenio de 1970 y el de 1990, los elementos probatorios disponibles sugieren que ha habido una considerable reducción de la infecundidad en África, donde las enfermedades de transmisión sexual fueron una causa importante de esterilidad en los decenios de 1950 y 1960. También en América Latina han descendido en general los niveles de infecundidad. En otras zonas importantes se han registrado tanto aumentos como reducciones en la fecundidad pero, si bien los niveles de infecundidad en el decenio de 1990 son bastante bajos en África y Asia (sin superar nunca el 9% y manteniéndose en la mayoría de los países por debajo del 5% ó 7%, respectivamente), en el Caribe y en los países desarrollados son elevados. Es así que en tres de cada cuatro países desarrollados, por lo menos el 7% de las mujeres de 45 a 49 años no tenían hijos en el decenio de 1990 y en las tres cuartas partes de los países del Caribe en que hay datos sobre la cuestión, el porcentaje de mujeres sin hijos entre las de 45 a 49 años de edad era de por lo menos el 8%. En las Antillas Neerlandesas, el Canadá, Estonia, Finlandia, Francia, Luxemburgo, Portugal, la República de Moldova, Rumania, Suiza y el Uruguay se registraron niveles particularmente elevados de infecundidad (superiores al 10%).

Políticas de población

Ha habido cambios muy importantes en los puntos de vista y en las medidas de los gobiernos respecto de los niveles y tendencias en materia de fecundidad. En 1976 el 52% de todos los gobiernos comunicaban que no habían intervenido en modo alguno para modificar los niveles de fecundidad, pero para el año 2001 ese porcentaje había descendido al 32% (véase el gráfico II). El apoyo gubernamental a la planificación de la familia ha aumentado en forma constante desde el decenio de 1970. Para 2001, el 92% de todos los gobiernos prestaban apoyo a programas de planificación de la familia y de distribución de anticonceptivos, ya sea directamente (75%), por intermedio de servicios gubernamentales, o indirectamente (17%), prestando apoyo a las actividades y organizaciones no gubernamentales tales como las asociaciones de planificación de la familia.

También han variado considerablemente los puntos de vista de los gobiernos sobre si los niveles de fecundidad son o no adecuados. Así, en tanto que en 1976 el 27% de todos los gobiernos deseaban reducir la fecundidad, para el año 2001 el 45% deseaban hacerlo. Entre los países en desarrollo, el porcentaje de los que deseaban reducir la fecundidad era aún mayor en 2001, ya que ascendía al 58%. También había aumentado el porcentaje de los gobiernos que deseaban elevar la fecundidad: del 9% en 1976 había pasado al 13% en 2001. El coeficiente de ponderación relativo de los gobiernos que deseaban mantener los niveles actuales de fecundidad descendió del 13% al 10%. Es decir que, hoy en día hay más gobiernos que desean modificar los niveles de fecundidad de sus poblaciones y están dispuestos a idear tipos de intervención apropiados para el logro de esos objetivos.

Gráfico I

Distribución de 160 países por tasa de fecundidad total, alrededor de los años 1970 y 2000

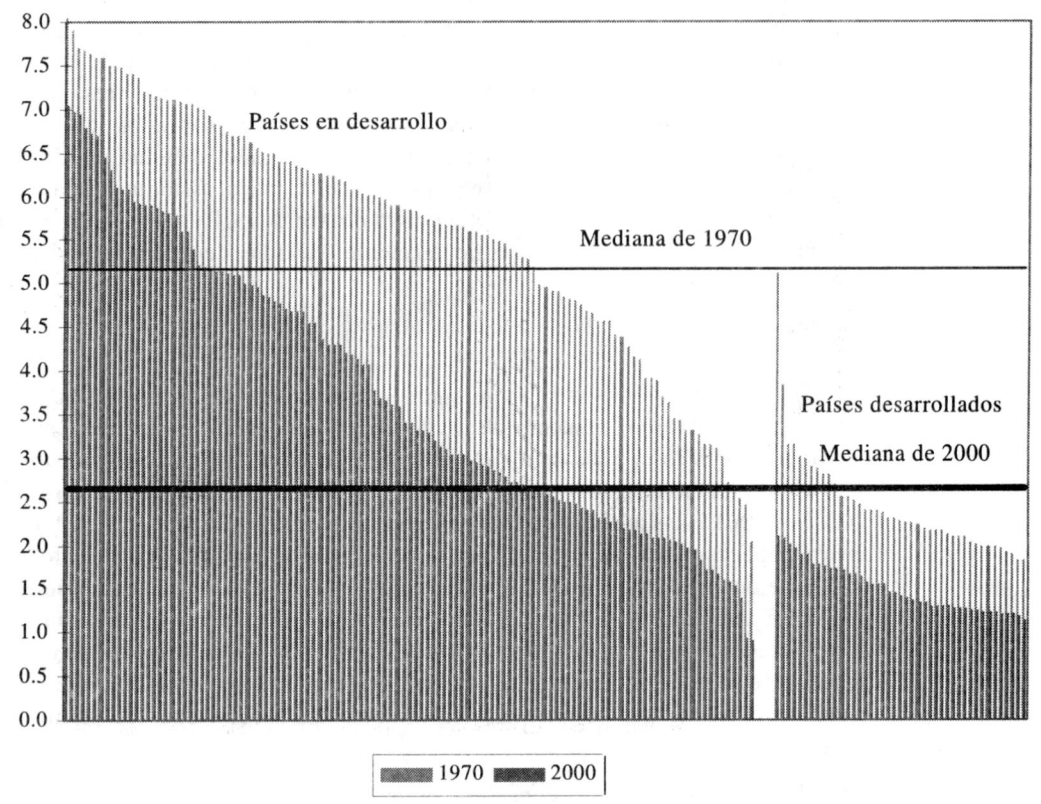

Gráfico II
Políticas gubernamentales sobre la tasa de fecundidad: 1976 y 2001

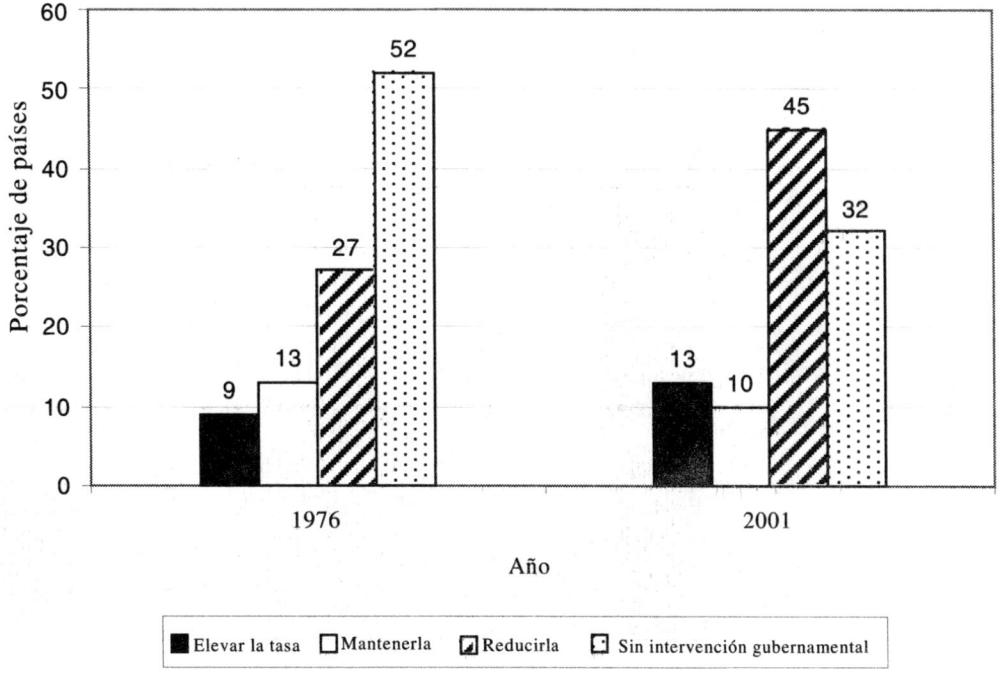

I. COUNTRY PROFILES

Indicator	Period			
	Earlier year		*Later year*	
	Year	*Value*	*Year*	*Value*
Nuptiality				
Annual number of marriages (*thousands*)	..	..	..	..
Annual number of divorces (*thousands*)	..	..	..	..

Indicator	*Year*	*Male*	*Female*	*Year*	*Male*	*Female*
Total first marriage rate (per person)	..	..	..	..	..	..
Total divorce rate (per person)	..	..	..	..	..	..
Mean age at first marriage (years)	..	..	..	..	..	..
SMAM (years)	1979	25.3	17.8	..	..	..
Percentage ever married by age group						
15-19	1979	9.2	53.7	..	..	..
20-24	1979	36.5	90.7	..	..	..
25-29	1979	65.0	97.2	..	..	..
30-34	1979	83.3	98.6	..	..	..
35-39	1979	91.0	99.1	..	..	..
40-44	1979	94.2	99.0	..	..	..
45-49	1979	95.9	99.0	..	..	..

Fertility	*Year*	*Value*	*Year*	*Value*
Annual number of births (*thousands*)	1979	627.6	..	..
Crude birth rate (per 1 000 population)	1979	48.1	..	..
Percentage of extra-marital births among all births	..	..	..	..
Total fertility rate (births per woman)	1973	8.2	..	..
Age-specific fertility rate (per 1 000 women)				
15-19	1973	168	..	..
20-24	1973	359	..	..
25-29	1973	355	..	..
30-34	1973	307	..	..
35-39	1973	235	..	..
40-44	1973	137	..	..
45-49	1973	81	..	..
Mean age at childbearing (years)	1973	30.0	..	..
Mean age at first birth (years)	..	..	..	..
Children ever born per woman				
35-39	..	..	..	..
40-44	..	..	..	..
45-49	..	..	..	..
Percentage of childless women				
35-39	..	..	..	..
40-44	..	..	..	..
45-49	..	..	..	..
Percentage of women with parity three or higher				
35-39	..	..	..	..
40-44	..	..	..	..
45-49	..	..	..	..
Family Planning				
Contraceptive prevalence among women in union				
Percentage using any contraceptive method	1973	1.6	2000	4.8
Percentage using a modern contraceptive method	1973	1.6	2000	3.6
Percentage using condoms	1973	0.0	2000	0.0
Population policies				
Government's view on the level of fertility	1976	Too high	2001	Too high
Government's policy regarding level of fertility	1976	No intervention	2001	No intervention
Government's support for contraceptive methods	1976	Direct support	2001	Direct support

Total fertility rates

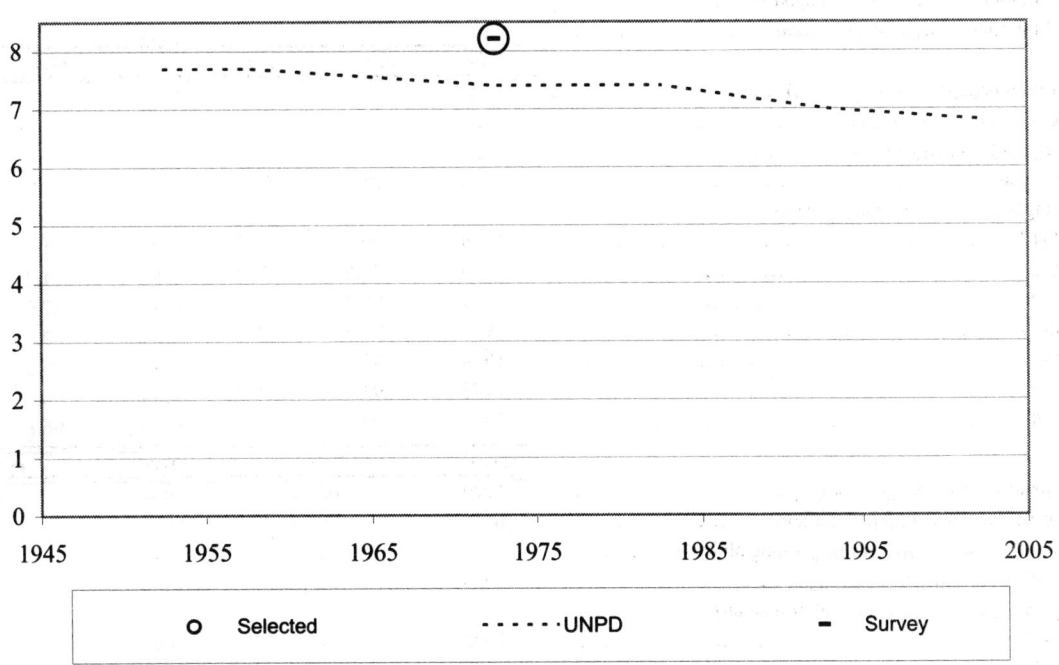

Indicator	Period					
	Earlier year			Later year		
	Year	Value		Year	Value	
Nuptiality						
Annual number of marriages (*thousands*)	1970	14.4		1998	27.9	
Annual number of divorces (*thousands*)	1970	1.6		1991	2.2	
	Year	Male	Female	Year	Male	Female
Total first marriage rate (per person)	1970	..	0.8	1990	..	1.0
Total divorce rate (per person)	..	..	..	..	..	..
Mean age at first marriage (years)	1970	..	21.6	1999	..	23.5
SMAM (years)	..	..	..	1989	27.0	22.9
Percentage ever married by age group						
15-19	..	..	..	1989	1.0	8.3
20-24	..	..	..	1989	11.2	52.2
25-29	..	..	..	1989	57.0	85.9
30-34	..	..	..	1989	87.6	94.0
35-39	..	..	..	1989	95.2	96.8
40-44	..	..	..	1989	96.7	98.2
45-49	..	..	..	1989	96.8	98.6
Fertility	Year	Value		Year	Value	
Annual number of births (*thousands*).............................	1970	69.5		1998	60.1	
Crude birth rate (per 1 000 population)	1970	32.5		1998	15.9	
Percentage of extra-marital births among all births	..	..		..	..	
Total fertility rate (births per woman)	1970	5.1		1999	2.1	
Age-specific fertility rate (per 1 000 women)						
15-19	1970	38		1999	16	
20-24	1970	263		1999	122	
25-29	1970	273		1999	158	
30-34	1970	212		1999	89	
35-39	1970	146		1999	30	
40-44	1970	68		1999	6	
45-49	1970	23		1999	1	
Mean age at childbearing (years)	1970	29.8		1999	29.8	
Mean age at first birth (years)	1967	22.9		1989	24.7	
Children ever born per woman						
35-39	..	..		..	..	
40-44	..	..		..	..	
45-49	..	..		..	..	
Percentage of childless women						
35-39	..	..		..	..	
40-44	..	..		..	..	
45-49	..	..		..	..	
Percentage of women with parity three or higher						
35-39	..	..		..	..	
40-44	..	..		..	..	
45-49	..	..		..	..	
Family Planning						
Contraceptive prevalence among women in union						
Percentage using any contraceptive method	..	..		2000	57.5	
Percentage using a modern contraceptive method	..	..		2000	15.3	
Percentage using condoms	..	..		2000	7.9	
Population policies						
Government's view on the level of fertility	1976	Satisfactory		2001	Satisfactory	
Government's policy regarding level of fertility	1976	Maintain		2001	Maintain	
Government's support for contraceptive methods	1976	Direct support		2001	Direct support	

Total fertility rates

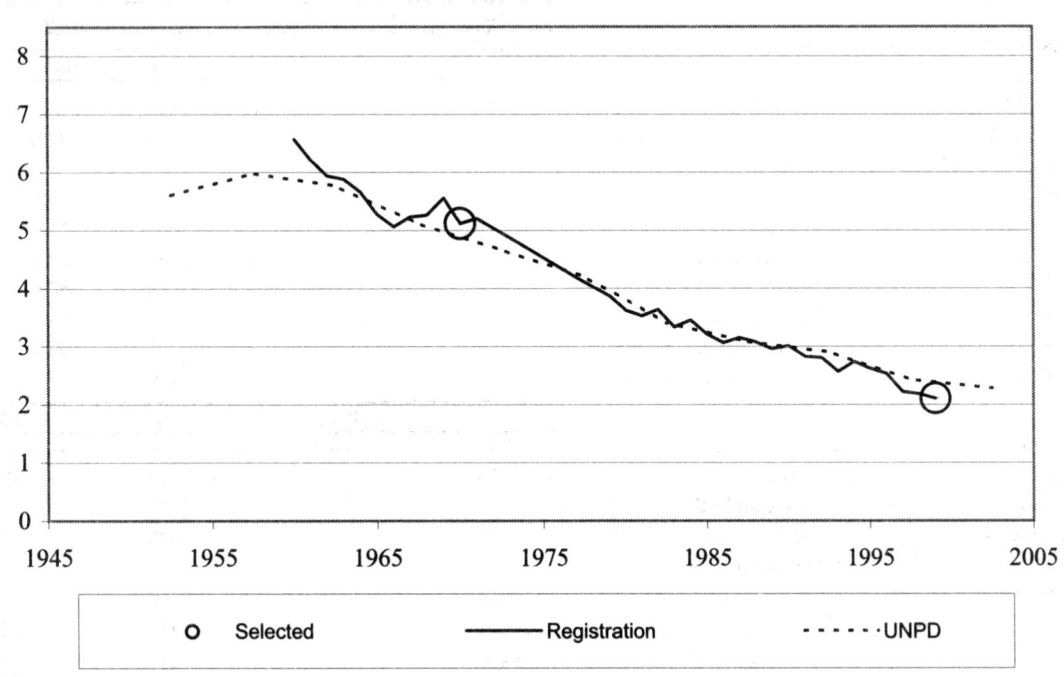

Age-specific fertility rates

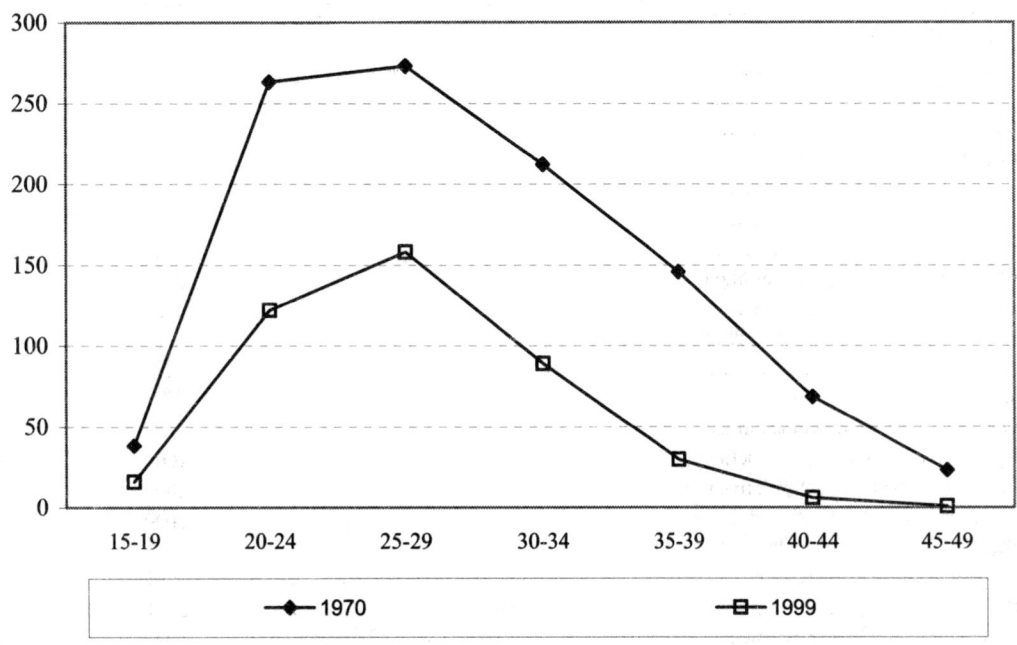

Algeria

Indicator	Period					
	Earlier year			Later year		
	Year	Value		Year	Value	
Nuptiality						
Annual number of marriages (*thousands*)	1985	123.6		2001	194.3	
Annual number of divorces (*thousands*)	..	..		..	..	
	Year	Male	Female	Year	Male	Female
Total first marriage rate (per person)	..	..	..	..	..	..
Total divorce rate (per person)	..	..	..	..	..	..
Mean age at first marriage (years)	..	..	..	..	..	..
SMAM (years)	1977	25.3	21.0	1992	..	25.9
Percentage ever married by age group						
15-19	1977	2.5	23.6	1992	..	3.6
20-24	1977	29.0	69.0	1992	..	29.6
25-29	1977	70.3	89.1	1992	..	65.2
30-34	1977	91.5	96.4	1992	..	86.8
35-39	1977	96.3	98.2	1992	..	93.6
40-44	1977	97.5	98.7	1992	..	96.9
45-49	1977	98.1	99.0	1992	..	98.1
Fertility	Year	Value		Year	Value	
Annual number of births (*thousands*).............................	1970	603.4		2001	618.4	
Crude birth rate (per 1 000 population)	1970	43.9		2001	20.1	
Percentage of extra-marital births among all births	1964	0.3		..	..	
Total fertility rate (births per woman)	1977	7.4		1996	3.1	
Age-specific fertility rate (per 1 000 women)						
15-19	1977	97		1996	19	
20-24	1977	285		1996	109	
25-29	1977	342		1996	150	
30-34	1977	336		1996	154	
35-39	1977	267		1996	125	
40-44	1977	129		1996	58	
45-49	1977	27		1996	13	
Mean age at childbearing (years)	1977	30.5		1996	31.3	
Mean age at first birth (years)[a]	..	..		1992	24.9	
Children ever born per woman						
35-39	..	..		1992	5.4	
40-44	..	..		1992	6.8	
45-49	..	..		1992	7.6	
Percentage of childless women						
35-39	..	..		1992	9.7	
40-44	..	..		1992	6.4	
45-49	..	..		1992	3.9	
Percentage of women with parity three or higher						
35-39	..	..		1992	81.5	
40-44	..	..		1992	87.3	
45-49	..	..		1992	90.2	
Family Planning						
Contraceptive prevalence among women in union						
Percentage using any contraceptive method	..	..		2000	64.0	
Percentage using a modern contraceptive method	..	..		2000	50.1	
Percentage using condoms	..	..		2000	1.5	
Population policies						
Government's view on the level of fertility	1976	Satisfactory		2001	Too high	
Government's policy regarding level of fertility	1976	No intervention		2001	Lower	
Government's support for contraceptive methods	1976	Direct support		2001	Direct support	

[a]Median age at first birth among women aged 25-29 at the date of the survey

Total fertility rates

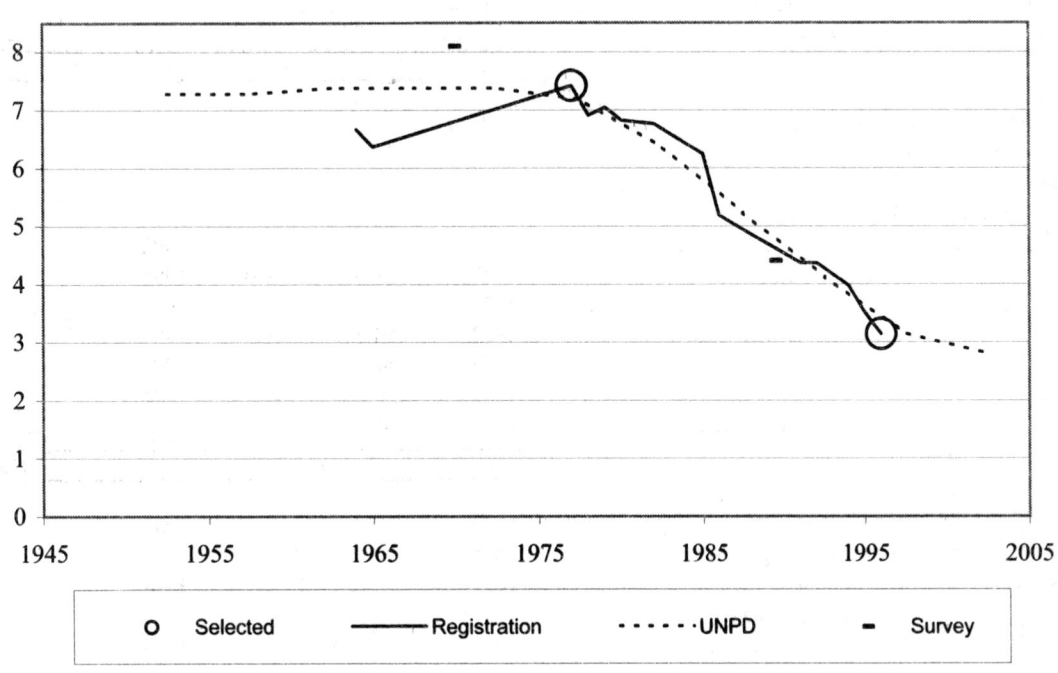

O Selected	—— Registration	· · · · · UNPD	– Survey	

Age-specific fertility rates

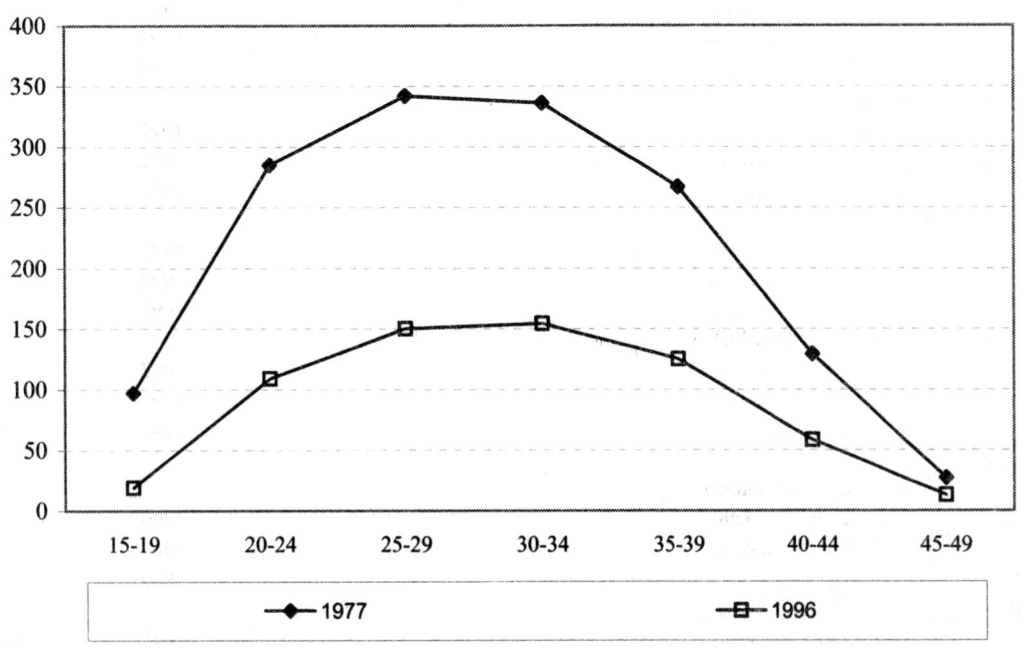

◆ 1977	◻ 1996

Indicator	Period			
	Earlier year		Later year	
	Year	Value	Year	Value
Nuptiality				
Annual number of marriages (*thousands*)	..	..	..	..
Annual number of divorces (*thousands*)	..	..	..	..

	Year	Male	Female	Year	Male	Female
Total first marriage rate (per person)	..	..	..	..	..	..
Total divorce rate (per person)	..	..	..	..	..	..
Mean age at first marriage (years)	..	..	..	..	..	..
SMAM (years)	1970	24.5	19.4	..	..	..
Percentage ever married by age group						
15-19	1970	7.6	35.7	..	..	..
20-24	1970	41.7	82.8	..	..	..
25-29	1970	71.4	88.4	..	..	..
30-34	1970	82.9	91.3	..	..	..
35-39	1970	86.7	90.0	..	..	..
40-44	1970	91.9	95.3	..	..	..
45-49	1970	92.5	95.4	..	..	..

Fertility	Year	Value	Year	Value
Annual number of births (*thousands*)	..	..	..	..
Crude birth rate (per 1 000 population)	..	..	..	..
Percentage of extra-marital births among all births	..	..	..	..
Total fertility rate (births per woman)	..	..	..	..
Age-specific fertility rate (per 1 000 women)				
15-19	..	..	..	..
20-24	..	..	..	..
25-29	..	..	..	..
30-34	..	..	..	..
35-39	..	..	..	..
40-44	..	..	..	..
45-49	..	..	..	..
Mean age at childbearing (years)	..	..	..	..
Mean age at first birth (years)	..	..	..	..
Children ever born per woman				
35-39	..	..	..	..
40-44	..	..	..	..
45-49	..	..	..	..
Percentage of childless women				
35-39	..	..	..	..
40-44	..	..	..	..
45-49	..	..	..	..
Percentage of women with parity three or higher				
35-39	..	..	..	..
40-44	..	..	..	..
45-49	..	..	..	..
Family Planning				
Contraceptive prevalence among women in union				
Percentage using any contraceptive method	..	..	2001	6.2
Percentage using a modern contraceptive method	..	..	2001	4.5
Percentage using condoms	..	..	2001	0.3
Population policies				
Government's view on the level of fertility	..	..	2001	Satisfactory
Government's policy regarding level of fertility	..	..	2001	Maintain
Government's support for contraceptive methods	..	..	2001	Direct support

Total fertility rates

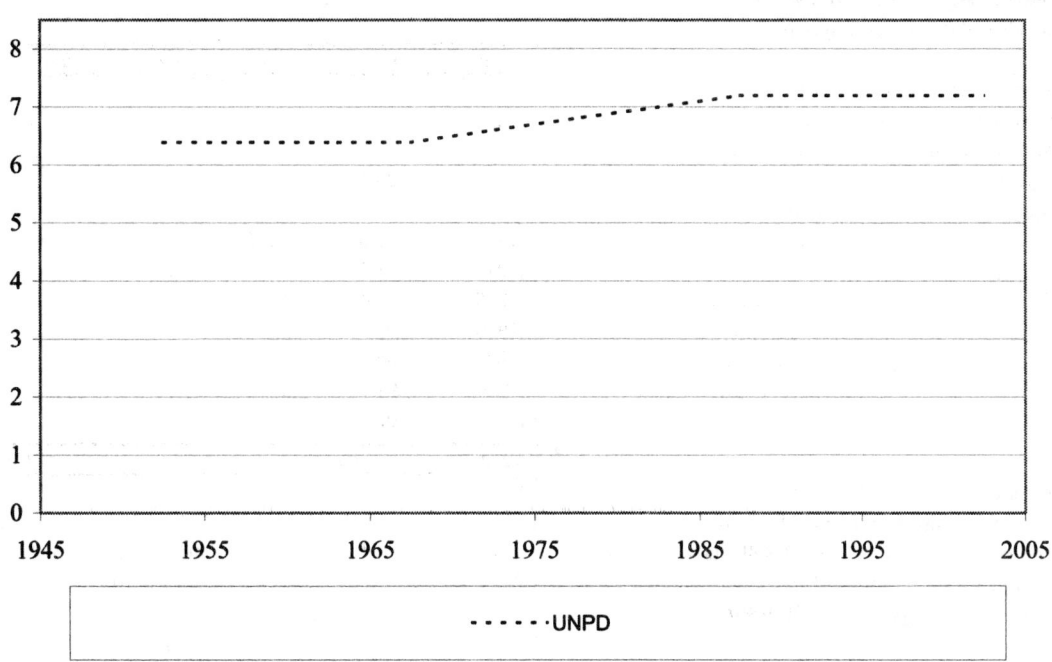

Indicator	Period					
	Earlier year			Later year		
	Year	Value		Year	Value	

Nuptiality

Indicator	Year	Value		Year	Value	
Annual number of marriages (*thousands*)	1970	175.3		2001	130.5	
Annual number of divorces (*thousands*)	..	..		..	..	

Indicator	Year	Male	Female	Year	Male	Female
Total first marriage rate (per person)	..	..	..	..	..	..
Total divorce rate (per person)	..	..	..	..	..	..
Mean age at first marriage (years)	..	..	..	..	..	..
SMAM (years)	1970	26.4	23.1	1991	25.8	23.3
Percentage ever married by age group						
15-19	1970	1.9	10.8	1991	2.7	12.4
20-24	1970	21.2	44.0	1991	25.6	45.2
25-29	1970	57.9	72.6	1991	61.1	73.8
30-34	1970	76.8	83.8	1991	80.4	85.2
35-39	1970	82.9	87.2	1991	87.6	89.5
40-44	1970	85.6	88.4	1991	89.8	90.8
45-49	1970	87.2	89.0	1991	90.6	91.3

Fertility

Indicator	Year	Value	Year	Value
Annual number of births (*thousands*)	1970	544.5	2001	683.5
Crude birth rate (per 1 000 population)	1970	22.7	2001	18.2
Percentage of extra-marital births among all births	..	..	1998	53.0
Total fertility rate (births per woman)	1970	3.2	2000	2.5
Age-specific fertility rate (per 1 000 women)				
15-19	1970	68	2000	66
20-24	1970	163	2000	117
25-29	1970	175	2000	127
30-34	1970	123	2000	106
35-39	1970	71	2000	60
40-44	1970	26	2000	18
45-49	1970	7	2000	2
Mean age at childbearing (years)	1970	28.1	2000	27.9
Mean age at first birth (years)	..	..	1987	23.7
Children ever born per woman				
35-39	1970	2.7	1991	2.7
40-44	1970	2.9	1991	2.8
45-49	1970	2.9	1991	2.8
Percentage of childless women				
35-39	1970	13.8	..	..
40-44	1970	12.8	..	..
45-49	1970	13.8	..	..
Percentage of women with parity three or higher				
35-39	1970	41.1	..	..
40-44	1970	42.8	..	..
45-49	1970	41.7	..	..

Family Planning

Indicator	Year	Value	Year	Value
Contraceptive prevalence among women in union				
Percentage using any contraceptive method	..	..	..	..
Percentage using a modern contraceptive method	..	..	..	..
Percentage using condoms	..	..	..	..

Population policies

Indicator	Year	Value	Year	Value
Government's view on the level of fertility	1976	Too low	2001	Satisfactory
Government's policy regarding level of fertility	1976	Raise	2001	No intervention
Government's support for contraceptive methods	1976	Limits	2001	Indirect support

Total fertility rates

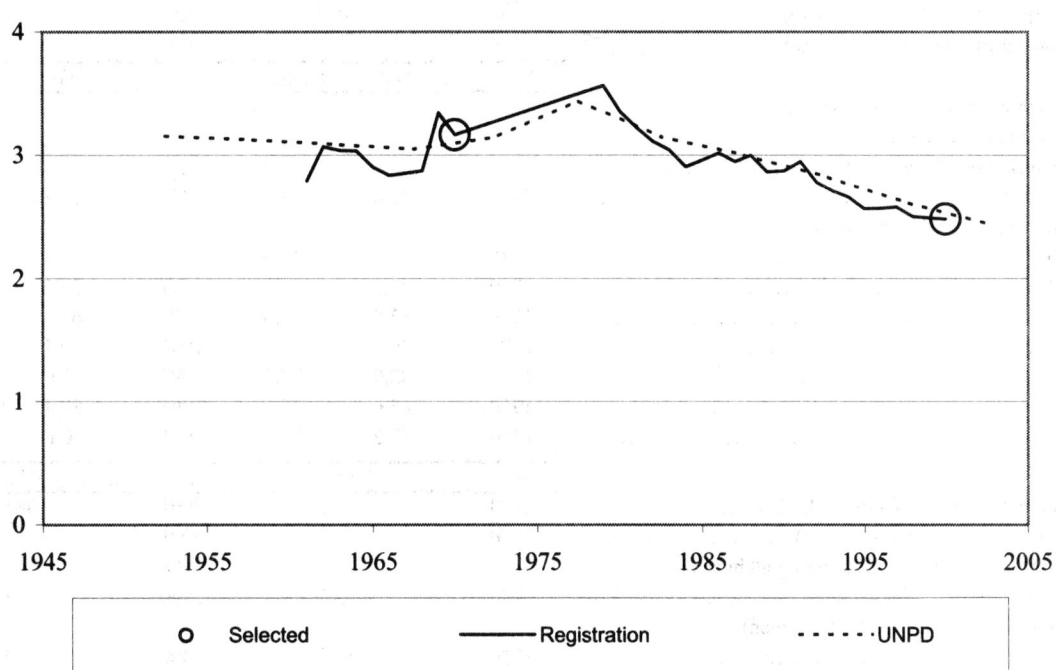

Age-specific fertility rates

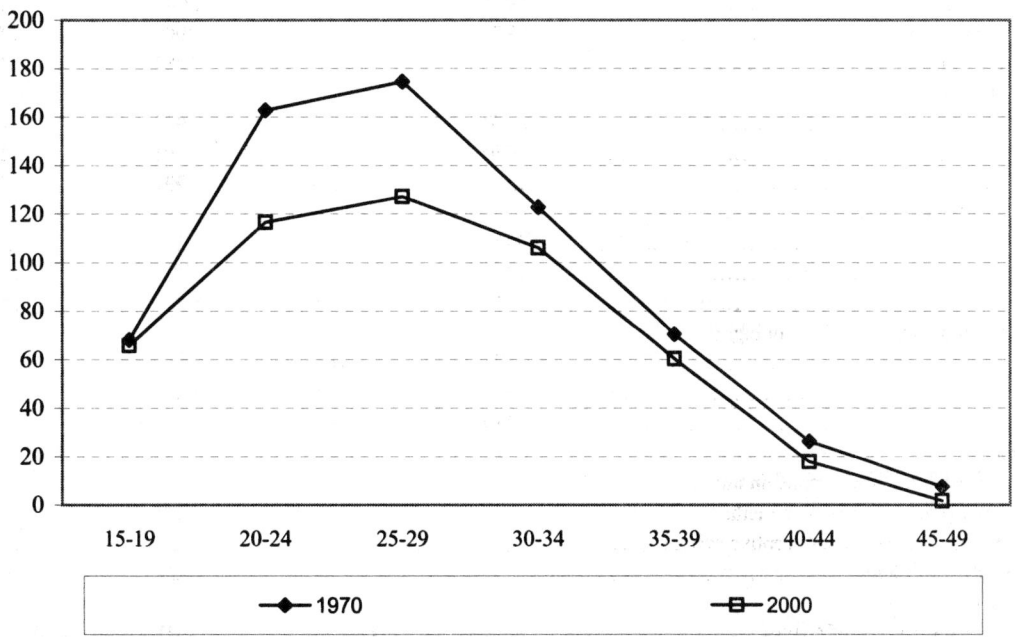

Indicator	Period					
	Earlier year			Later year		
	Year	Value		Year	Value	
Nuptiality						
Annual number of marriages (*thousands*)	1970	18.3		2001	12.3	
Annual number of divorces (*thousands*)	1970	2.4		2001	1.8	
	Year	Male	Female	Year	Male	Female
Total first marriage rate (per person)	1982	1.0	1.0	1997	0.4	0.4
Total divorce rate (per person)	..	..	..	1996	0.1	0.1
Mean age at first marriage (years)	1982	26.0	22.8	1997	27.1	22.9
SMAM (years)	1979	..	..	2000	..	23.0
Percentage ever married by age group						
15-19	1979	..	..	2000	..	8.6
20-24	1979	30.1	57.1	2000	..	52.5
25-29	1979	76.7	82.4	2000	..	86.5
30-34	1979	92.7	91.6	2000	..	94.7
35-39	1979	97.2	95.5	2000	..	94.2
40-44	1979	98.5	96.1	2000	..	93.1
45-49	1979	99.1	96.4	2000	..	94.3
Fertility	Year	Value		Year	Value	
Annual number of births (*thousands*).............................	1970	55.7		2001	32.1	
Crude birth rate (per 1 000 population)	1970	22.1		2001	8.4	
Percentage of extra-marital births among all births	1970	1.7		2001	15.3	
Total fertility rate (births per woman)	1970	3.2		1998	1.9	
Age-specific fertility rate (per 1 000 women)						
15-19	1970	41		1998	57	
20-24	1970	216		1998	169	
25-29	1970	169		1998	97	
30-34	1970	115		1998	39	
35-39	1970	66		1998	15	
40-44	1970	21		1998	2	
45-49	1970	5		1998	0	
Mean age at childbearing (years)	1970	27.8		2001	24.8	
Mean age at first birth (years)	1985	22.5		2000	23.0	
Children ever born per woman						
35-39	..	..		2000	2.5	
40-44	..	..		2000	2.6	
45-49	..	..		2000	2.7	
Percentage of childless women						
35-39	..	..		2000	7.2	
40-44	..	..		2000	8.8	
45-49	..	..		2000	8.9	
Percentage of women with parity three or higher						
35-39	..	..		2000	48.9	
40-44	..	..		2000	53.6	
45-49	..	..		2000	55.3	
Family Planning						
Contraceptive prevalence among women in union						
Percentage using any contraceptive method	..	..		2000	60.5	
Percentage using a modern contraceptive method	..	..		2000	22.3	
Percentage using condoms	..	..		2000	6.9	
Population policies						
Government's view on the level of fertility	1976	--		2001	Too low	
Government's policy regarding level of fertility	1976	--		2001	Raise	
Government's support for contraceptive methods	1976	--		2001	Direct support	

Total fertility rates

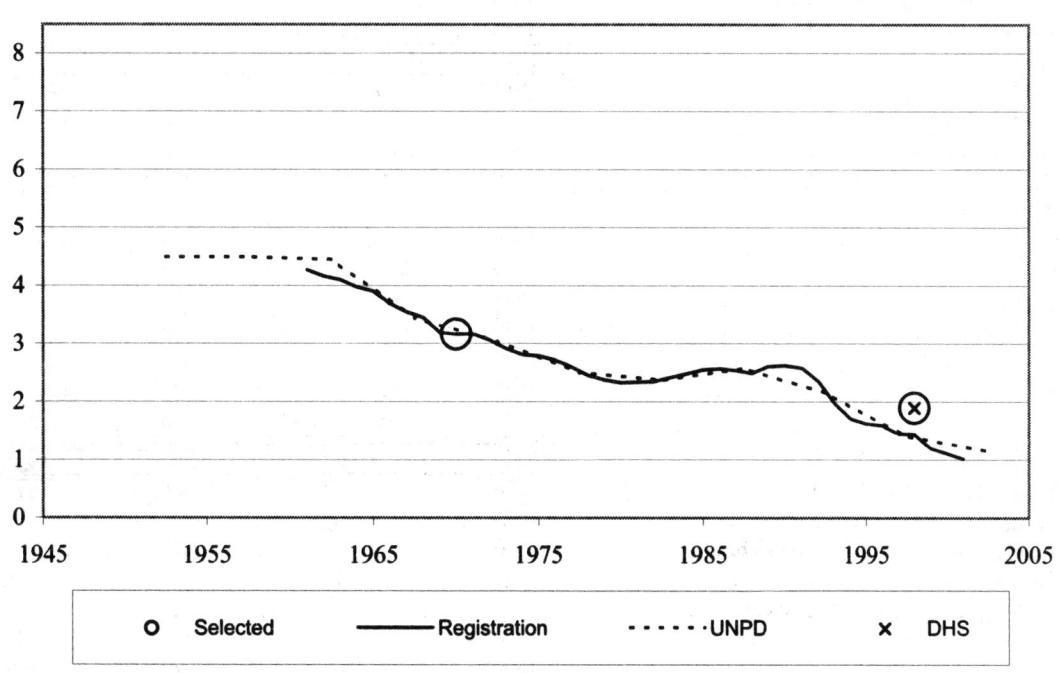

Age-specific fertility rates

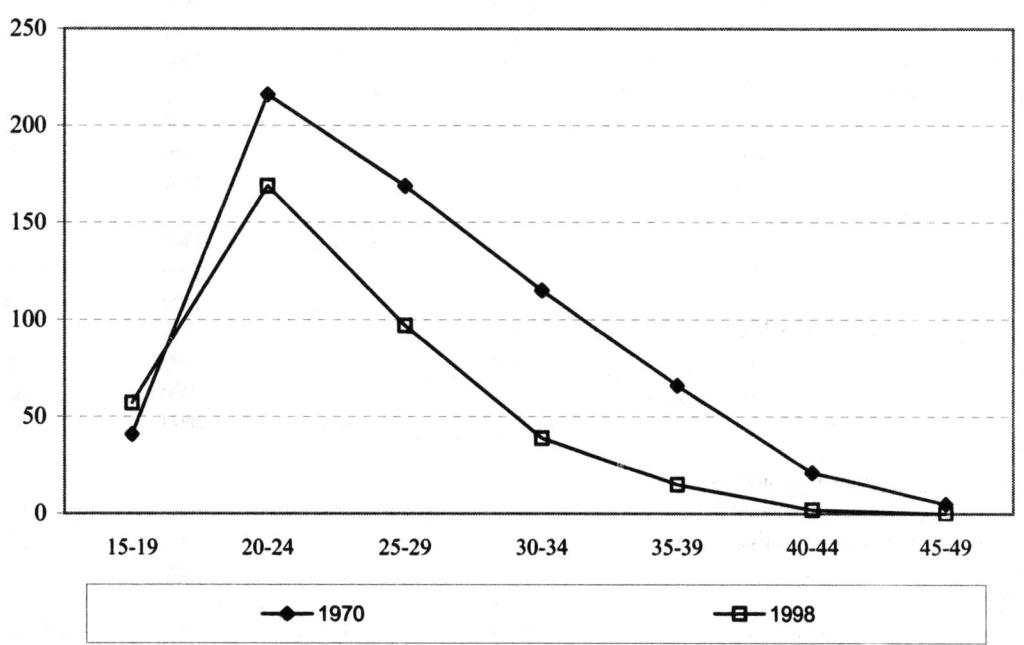

Indicator	Period					
	Earlier year			Later year		
	Year	Value		Year	Value	
Nuptiality						
Annual number of marriages (*thousands*)	1970	116.1		2001	109.1	
Annual number of divorces (*thousands*)	1970	12.2		2000	49.9	
	Year	Male	Female	Year	Male	Female
Total first marriage rate (per person)	1976	0.8	0.8	1996	0.6	0.6
Total divorce rate (per person)	1970	0.1	0.1	1996	0.3	0.3
Mean age at first marriage (years)	1976	25.1	22.5	1996	28.5	26.4
SMAM (years)	1971	24.4	21.5	2000	30.9	28.7
Percentage ever married by age group						
15-19	1971	1.4	8.8	2000	0.1	0.6
20-24	1971	36.1	64.3	2000	5.5	13.0
25-29	1971	74.3	88.4	2000	31.4	47.2
30-34	1971	86.1	93.5	2000	60.3	72.9
35-39	1971	89.1	95.0	2000	75.8	83.8
40-44	1971	90.0	95.2	2000	83.9	89.3
45-49	1971	91.0	95.1	2000	89.1	92.8
Fertility	Year	Value		Year	Value	
Annual number of births (*thousands*)	1970	257.5		2000	249.6	
Crude birth rate (per 1 000 population)	1970	20.6		2000	13.0	
Percentage of extra-marital births among all births	1970	8.3		1996	27.4	
Total fertility rate (births per woman)	1970	2.9		2000	1.7	
Age-specific fertility rate (per 1 000 women)						
15-19	1970	51		2000	17	
20-24	1970	172		2000	56	
25-29	1970	190		2000	107	
30-34	1970	102		2000	110	
35-39	1970	45		2000	49	
40-44	1970	12		2000	9	
45-49	1970	1		2000	0	
Mean age at childbearing (years)	1970	27.1		2000	29.6	
Mean age at first birth (years)	..	..		1996	27.7	
Children ever born per woman						
35-39	1976	2.7		1986	2.2	
40-44	1976	3.0		1986	2.5	
45-49	1976	2.9		1986	2.7	
Percentage of childless women						
35-39	1976	3.8		1986	11.9	
40-44	1976	3.7		1986	9.7	
45-49	1976	4.8		1986	9.0	
Percentage of women with parity three or higher						
35-39	1976	54.2		1986	38.6	
40-44	1976	58.8		1986	46.0	
45-49	1976	56.0		1986	54.5	
Family Planning						
Contraceptive prevalence among women in union						
Percentage using any contraceptive method	..	..		1986	76.1	
Percentage using a modern contraceptive method	..	..		1986	72.2	
Percentage using condoms	..	..		1986	4.4	
Population policies						
Government's view on the level of fertility	1976	Satisfactory		2001	Satisfactory	
Government's policy regarding level of fertility	1976	No intervention		2001	No intervention	
Government's support for contraceptive methods	1976	Indirect support		2001	Indirect support	

Total fertility rates

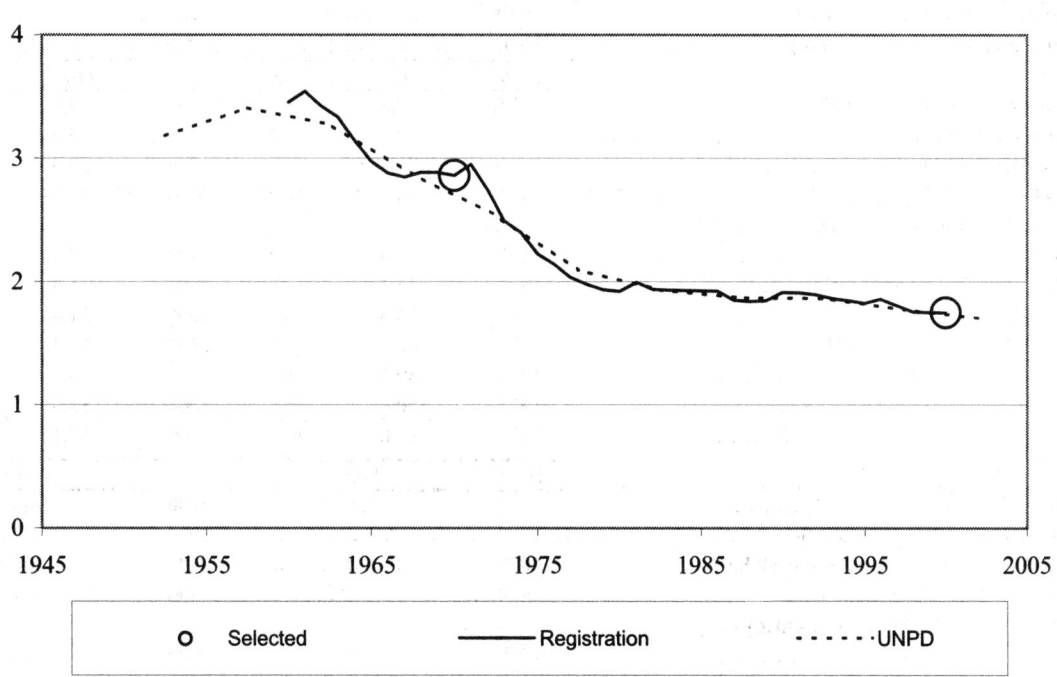

O Selected	—— Registration	· · · · · UNPD	

Age-specific fertility rates

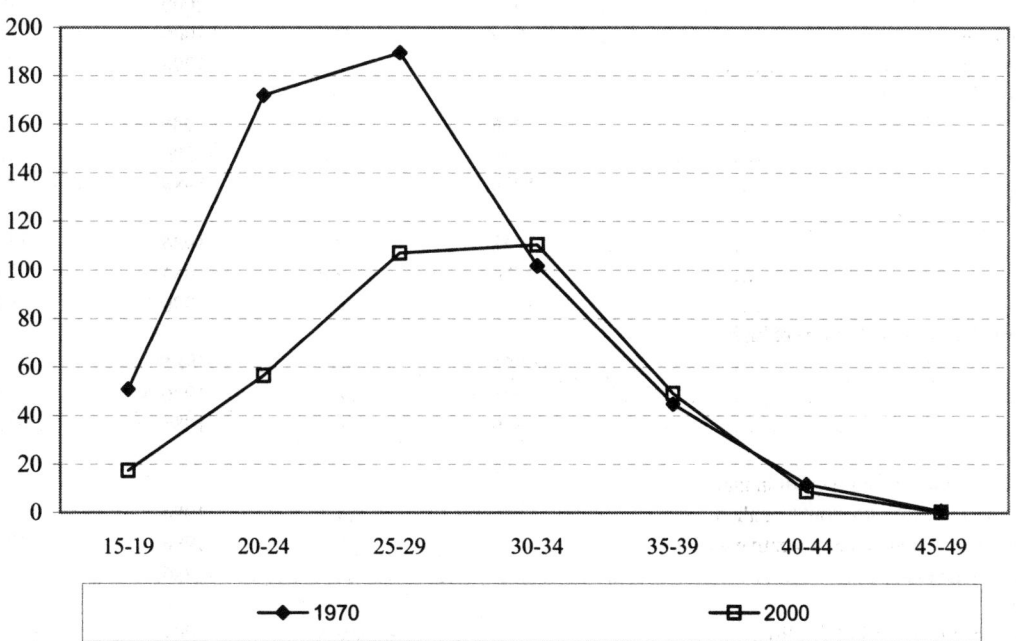

◆ 1970	□ 2000

Austria

Indicator	Year	Value		Year	Value	
		Earlier year			*Later year*	
	Year	*Value*		*Year*	*Value*	
Nuptiality						
Annual number of marriages (*thousands*)	1970	52.8		2001	34.2	
Annual number of divorces (*thousands*)	1970	10.4		2001	20.6	
	Year	*Male*	*Female*	*Year*	*Male*	*Female*
Total first marriage rate (per person)	1975	0.7	0.8	1998	0.5	0.5
Total divorce rate (per person)	1970	0.2	0.2	1997	0.2	0.3
Mean age at first marriage (years)	1975	25.5	22.7	1998	29.2	26.7
SMAM (years)	1971	26.0	21.9	1991	28.9	26.1
Percentage ever married by age group						
15-19	1971	0.6	7.0	1991	0.6	2.7
20-24	1971	25.8	55.0	1991	11.5	25.7
25-29	1971	66.4	81.4	1991	42.8	61.4
30-34	1971	82.3	87.7	1991	69.3	79.9
35-39	1971	88.2	89.4	1991	81.9	87.8
40-44	1971	91.5	89.6	1991	87.7	91.5
45-49	1971	93.0	88.4	1991	90.3	92.4
Fertility	*Year*	*Value*		*Year*	*Value*	
Annual number of births (*thousands*).............................	1970	112.3		2001	75.5	
Crude birth rate (per 1 000 population)	1970	15.0		2001	9.3	
Percentage of extra-marital births among all births	1970	12.8		2001	33.1	
Total fertility rate (births per woman)	1970	2.3		2001	1.3	
Age-specific fertility rate (per 1 000 women)						
15-19	1970	59		2001	14	
20-24	1970	155		2001	61	
25-29	1970	116		2001	91	
30-34	1970	76		2001	66	
35-39	1970	41		2001	25	
40-44	1970	11		2001	5	
45-49	1970	1		2001	0	
Mean age at childbearing (years)	1970	26.7		2001	28.4	
Mean age at first birth (years)	1985	24.3		2001	23.0	
Children ever born per woman						
35-39	1981	2.0		1995-1996	1.7	
40-44	1981	2.2		1995-1996	2.0	
45-49	1981	2.4		1995-1996	2.0	
Percentage of childless women						
35-39	1981	15.4		1995-1996	13.9	
40-44	1981	14.2		1995-1996	7.6	
45-49	1981	15.1		1995-1996	9.0	
Percentage of women with parity three or higher						
35-39	1981	29.2		1995-1996	19.2	
40-44	1981	36.9		1995-1996	27.3	
45-49	1981	39.8		1995-1996	28.4	
Family Planning						
Contraceptive prevalence among women in union						
Percentage using any contraceptive method	1982	71.4		1996	50.8	
Percentage using a modern contraceptive method	1982	56.3		1996	46.8	
Percentage using condoms	1982	4.0		1996	7.2	
Population policies						
Government's view on the level of fertility	1976	Satisfactory		2001	Too low	
Government's policy regarding level of fertility	1976	No intervention		2001	Raise	
Government's support for contraceptive methods	1976	Direct support		2001	Indirect support	

Total fertility rates

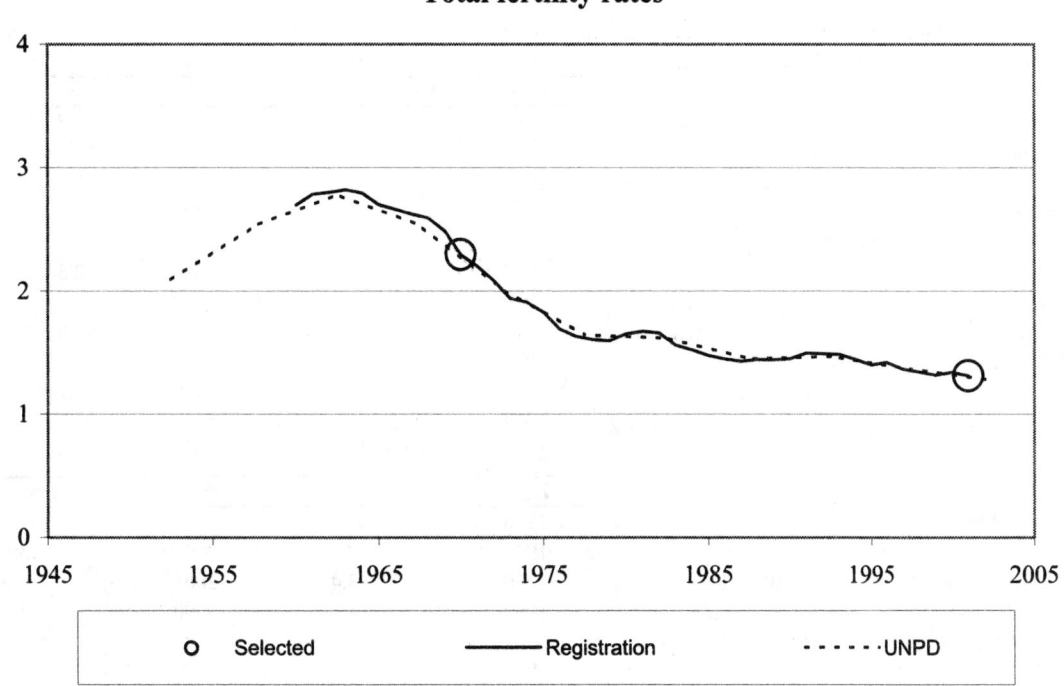

Age-specific fertility rates

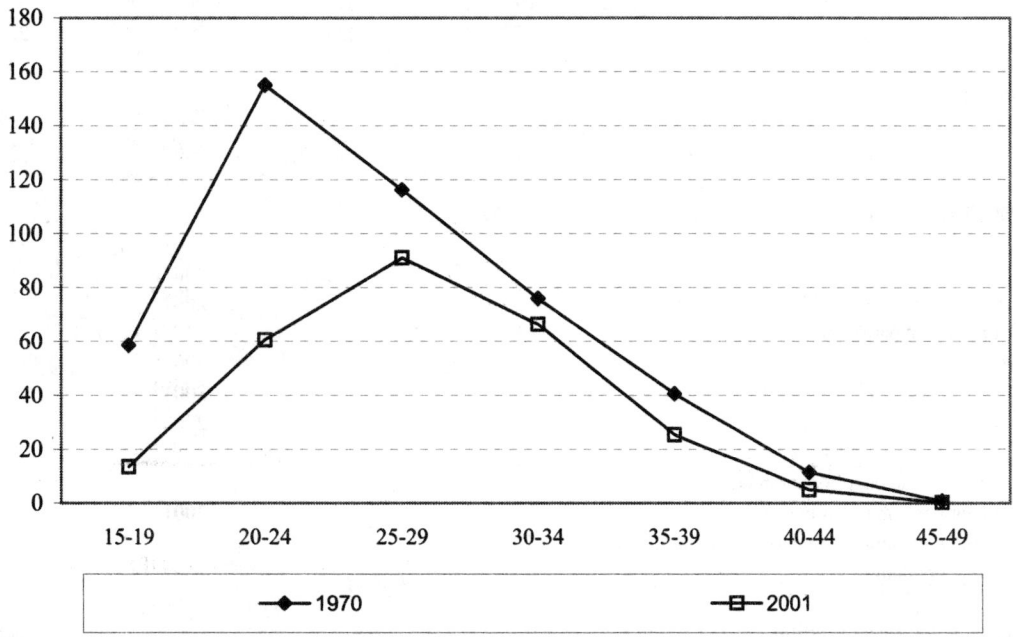

Indicator	Period					
	Earlier year			Later year		
	Year	Value		Year	Value	
Nuptiality						
Annual number of marriages (*thousands*)	1970	35.2		2001	41.9	
Annual number of divorces (*thousands*)	1970	6.8		1997	5.8	
	Year	Male	Female	Year	Male	Female
Total first marriage rate (per person)	1982	1.0	0.9	1998	0.5	0.6
Total divorce rate (per person)	..	..	..	1996	0.1	0.1
Mean age at first marriage (years)	1982	27.0	23.5	1998	27.3	23.3
SMAM (years)	..	..	..	1999	27.0	23.9
Percentage ever married by age group						
15-19	1979	..	..	1999	2.5	12.8
20-24	1979	20.3	48.8	1999	16.8	49.0
25-29	1979	69.5	82.4	1999	57.0	76.1
30-34	1979	90.6	92.8	1999	85.6	86.7
35-39	1979	96.7	96.6	1999	94.7	90.7
40-44	1979	98.2	97.6	1999	97.6	93.9
45-49	1979	98.9	97.9	1999	98.3	96.1
Fertility	Year	Value		Year	Value	
Annual number of births (*thousands*)	1970	151.0		2001	110.4	
Crude birth rate (per 1 000 population)	1970	27.7		2001	13.6	
Percentage of extra-marital births among all births	1970	3.4		2001	6.6	
Total fertility rate (births per woman)	1970	4.6		2000	2.1	
Age-specific fertility rate (per 1 000 women)						
15-19	1970	37		2000	44	
20-24	1970	233		2000	151	
25-29	1970	234		2000	133	
30-34	1970	205		2000	58	
35-39	1970	143		2000	19	
40-44	1970	50		2000	9	
45-49	1970	10		2000	..	
Mean age at childbearing (years)	1970	29.6		2000	26.1	
Mean age at first birth (years)	..	..		2001	24.7	
Children ever born per woman						
35-39	..	..		2001	2.6	
40-44	..	..		2001	3.0	
45-49	..	..		2001	..	
Percentage of childless women						
35-39	..	..		2001	12.4	
40-44	..	..		2001	11.8	
45-49	..	..		2001	..	
Percentage of women with parity three or higher						
35-39	..	..		2001	53.5	
40-44	..	..		2001	63.1	
45-49	..	..		2001	..	
Family Planning						
Contraceptive prevalence among women in union						
Percentage using any contraceptive method	..	..		2001	55.4	
Percentage using a modern contraceptive method	..	..		2001	11.9	
Percentage using condoms	..	..		2001	3.2	
Population policies						
Government's view on the level of fertility	..	--		2001	Satisfactory	
Government's policy regarding level of fertility	..	--		2001	Maintain	
Government's support for contraceptive methods	..	--		2001	Direct support	

Total fertility rates

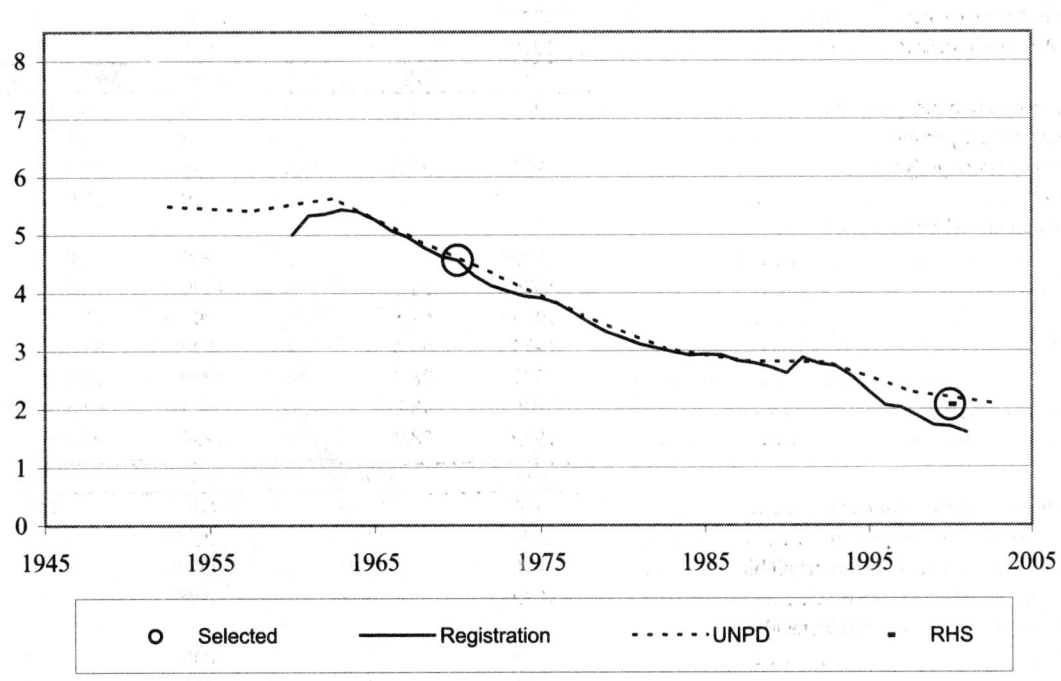

Age-specific fertility rates

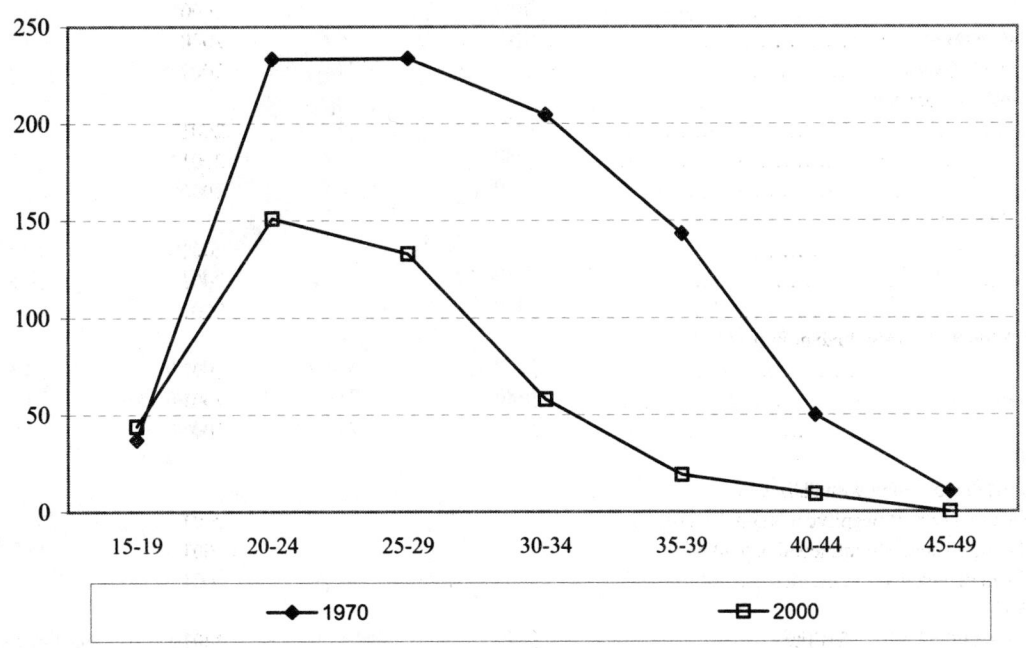

Indicator	Period			
	Earlier year		Later year	
	Year	Value	Year	Value
Nuptiality				
Annual number of marriages (*thousands*)	1970	1.4	1996	2.6
Annual number of divorces (*thousands*)	..	..	..	..

Indicator	Year	Male	Female	Year	Male	Female
Total first marriage rate (per person)	..	..	..	..	..	..
Total divorce rate (per person)	1975	0.1	0.0	1996	0.2	0.2
Mean age at first marriage (years)	..	..	..	..	..	..
SMAM (years)	1970	26.0	22.4	1990	29.1	27.2
Percentage ever married by age group						
15-19	1970	1.3	10.1	1990	0.9	3.7
20-24	1970	27.9	52.0	1990	13.7	25.2
25-29	1970	62.6	74.0	1990	41.5	50.8
30-34	1970	76.6	81.6	1990	63.1	64.5
35-39	1970	81.9	83.5	1990	75.2	72.6
40-44	1970	85.2	83.5	1990	82.0	79.0
45-49	1970	86.9	85.6	1990	85.4	82.8

Indicator	Year	Value	Year	Value
Fertility				
Annual number of births (*thousands*).............................	1970	4.3	1999	6.4
Crude birth rate (per 1 000 population)	1970	25.1	1999	21.4
Percentage of extra-marital births among all births	1970	28.6	1996	56.2
Total fertility rate (births per woman)	1970	3.5	1996	2.3
Age-specific fertility rate (per 1 000 women)				
15-19	1970	77	1996	62
20-24	1970	199	1996	114
25-29	1970	183	1996	115
30-34	1970	112	1996	96
35-39	1970	82	1996	55
40-44	1970	33	1996	13
45-49	1970	4	1996	4
Mean age at childbearing (years)	1970	27.8	1996	27.8
Mean age at first birth (years)	1970	22.8	1996	23.5
Children ever born per woman				
35-39	1980	4.1	1990	3.0
40-44	1980	4.8	1990	3.6
45-49	1980	5.2	1990	4.3
Percentage of childless women				
35-39	1980	9.1	1990	10.9
40-44	1980	9.1	1990	8.3
45-49	1980	8.2	1990	8.2
Percentage of women with parity three or higher				
35-39	1980	67.6	1990	54.6
40-44	1980	73.7	1990	64.1
45-49	1980	73.8	1990	70.2
Family Planning				
Contraceptive prevalence among women in union				
Percentage using any contraceptive method	..	..	1988	61.7
Percentage using a modern contraceptive method	..	..	1988	60.1
Percentage using condoms	..	..	1988	2.3
Population policies				
Government's view on the level of fertility	1976	Satisfactory	2001	Too high
Government's policy regarding level of fertility	1976	No intervention	2001	Lower
Government's support for contraceptive methods	1976	Indirect support	2001	Direct support

Total fertility rates

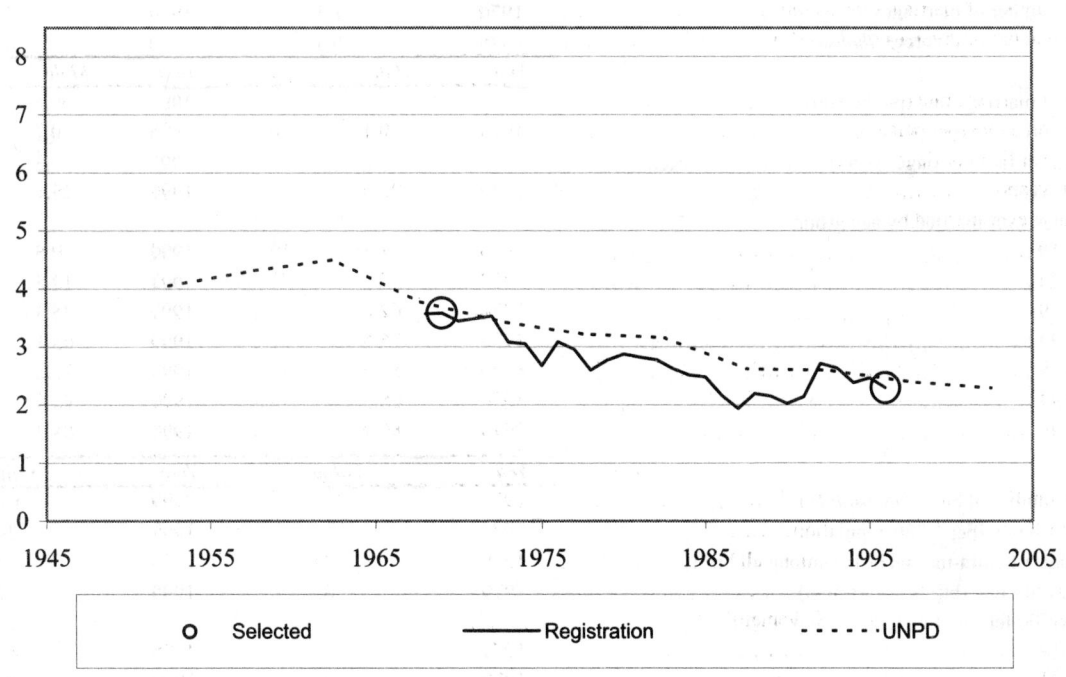

Age-specific fertility rates

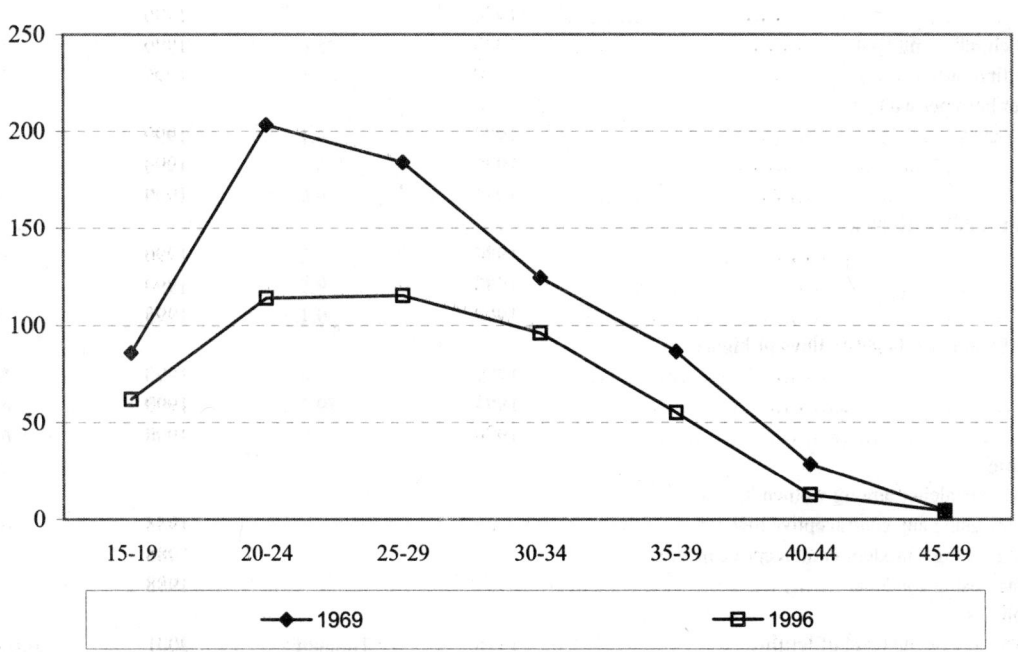

Indicator	Period			
	Earlier year		Later year	
	Year	Value	Year	Value
Nuptiality				
Annual number of marriages (*thousands*)	1976	1.3	2000	4.0
Annual number of divorces (*thousands*)	1976	0.4	2000	0.8

Indicator	Year	Male	Female	Year	Male	Female
Total first marriage rate (per person)	..	..	..	1997	0.5	0.8
Total divorce rate (per person)	1976	0.1	0.2	1995	0.1	0.2
Mean age at first marriage (years)	..	..	..	1997	27.3	24.2
SMAM (years)	..	..	..	1991	28.4	25.6
Percentage ever married by age group						
15-19	..	..	..	1991	0.5	6.7
20-24	..	..	..	1991	12.8	40.9
25-29	..	..	..	1991	45.3	68.8
30-34	..	..	..	1991	73.8	80.9
35-39	..	..	..	1991	88.6	88.3
40-44	..	..	..	1991	92.9	92.3
45-49	..	..	..	1991	93.5	96.2

Indicator	Year	Value	Year	Value
Fertility				
Annual number of births (*thousands*)........................	..	..	2001	13.5
Crude birth rate (per 1 000 population)	..	..	2001	20.6
Percentage of extra-marital births among all births	..	..	..	..
Total fertility rate (births per woman)	1971	6.7	1999	2.8
Age-specific fertility rate (per 1 000 women)				
15-19	1971	288	1999	14
20-24	1971	411	1999	113
25-29	1971	328	1999	157
30-34	1971	188	1999	136
35-39	1971	95	1999	100
40-44	1971	24	1999	40
45-49	1971	6	1999	9
Mean age at childbearing (years)	1971	25.6	1999	30.6
Mean age at first birth (years)	..	..	1997	25.3
Children ever born per woman				
35-39	1971	6.1	1995	4.3
40-44	1971	6.1	1995	5.2
45-49	1971	6.0	1995	6.1
Percentage of childless women				
35-39	1971	8.2	1995	12.3
40-44	1971	9.5	1995	9.6
45-49	1971	9.1	1995	8.9
Percentage of women with parity three or higher				
35-39	1971	81.4	1995	76.9
40-44	1971	79.2	1995	63.1
45-49	1971	79.0	1995	64.3
Family Planning				
Contraceptive prevalence among women in union				
Percentage using any contraceptive method	..	..	1995	61.8
Percentage using a modern contraceptive method	..	..	1995	30.6
Percentage using condoms	..	..	1995	9.6
Population policies				
Government's view on the level of fertility	1976	Too high	2001	Satisfactory
Government's policy regarding level of fertility	1976	No intervention	2001	Lower
Government's support for contraceptive methods	1976	Indirect support	2001	Direct support

Total fertility rates

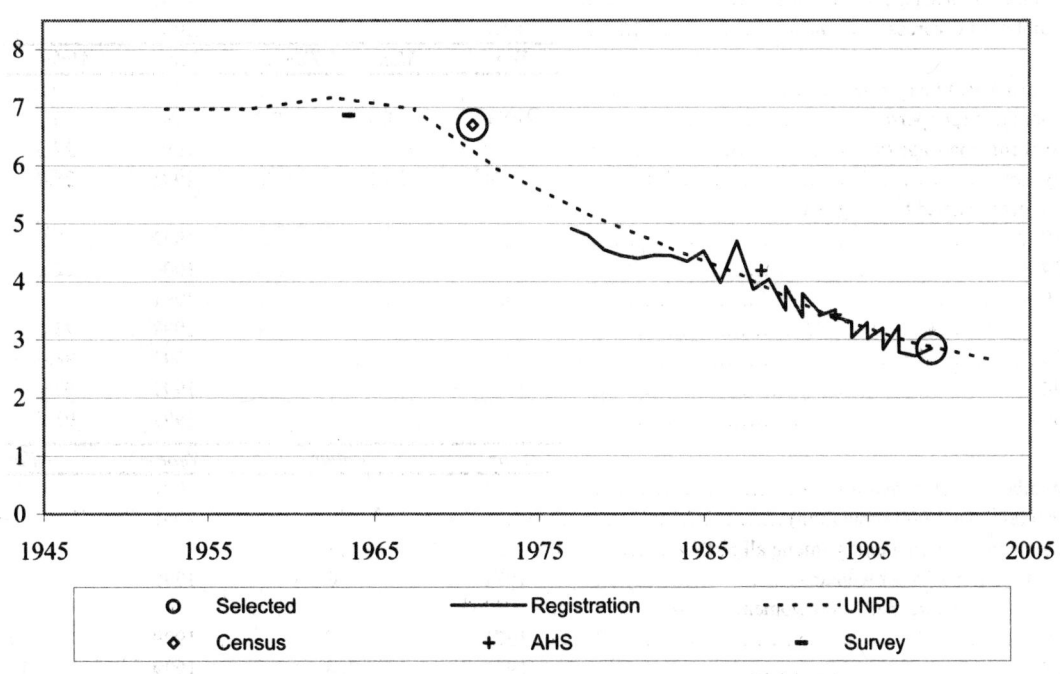

Age-specific fertility rates

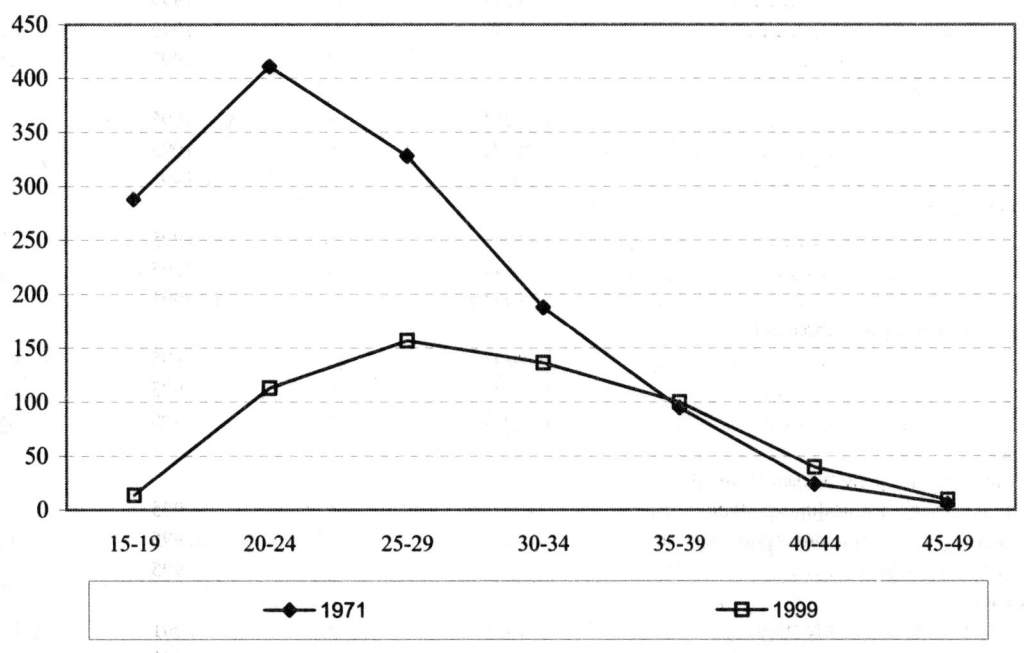

Bangladesh

Indicator	Period			
	Earlier year		Later year	
	Year	Value	Year	Value
Nuptiality				
Annual number of marriages (*thousands*)	1980	805.8	1997	1 181.0
Annual number of divorces (*thousands*)	..	..	..	..

	Year	Male	Female	Year	Male	Female
Total first marriage rate (per person)	..	..	..	..	..	..
Total divorce rate (per person)	..	..	..	..	..	..
Mean age at first marriage (years)	..	..	..	..	..	..
SMAM (years)	1974	24.0	16.4	2000	..	18.7
Percentage ever married by age group						
15-19	1974	7.7	75.5	2000	..	48.1
20-24	1974	39.9	96.8	2000	..	81.5
25-29	1974	77.5	99.1	2000	..	95.8
30-34	1974	94.3	99.4	2000	..	99.9
35-39	1974	97.8	99.6	2000	..	99.8
40-44	1974	98.5	99.5	2000	..	100.0
45-49	1974	98.9	99.7	2000	..	100.0

Fertility	Year	Value	Year	Value
Annual number of births (*thousands*)................................	..	..	..	..
Crude birth rate (per 1 000 population)	..	..	..	..
Percentage of extra-marital births among all births	..	..	..	..
Total fertility rate (births per woman)	1973	6.1	1997	3.4
Age-specific fertility rate (per 1 000 women)				
15-19	1973	219	1997	147
20-24	1973	304	1997	193
25-29	1973	260	1997	163
30-34	1973	214	1997	103
35-39	1973	142	1997	50
40-44	1973	64	1997	20
45-49	1973	12	1997	5
Mean age at childbearing (years)	1973	27.5	1997	26.0
Mean age at first birth (years)[a]	1975-1976	16.5	1999-2000	18.2
Children ever born per woman				
35-39	1975-1976	6.7	1999-2000	4.3
40-44	1975-1976	7.1	1999-2000	5.1
45-49	1975-1976	6.8	1999-2000	6.1
Percentage of childless women				
35-39	1975-1976	1.6	1999-2000	2.5
40-44	1975-1976	2.7	1999-2000	2.2
45-49	1975-1976	2.7	1999-2000	1.7
Percentage of women with parity three or higher				
35-39	1975-1976	93.5	1999-2000	80.1
40-44	1975-1976	91.1	1999-2000	86.2
45-49	1975-1976	89.5	1999-2000	92.4
Family Planning				
Contraceptive prevalence among women in union				
Percentage using any contraceptive method	1975-1976	7.7	1999-2000	53.8
Percentage using a modern contraceptive method	1975-1976	5.0	1999-2000	43.4
Percentage using condoms	1975-1976	0.7	1999-2000	4.3
Population policies				
Government's view on the level of fertility	1976	Too high	2001	Too high
Government's policy regarding level of fertility	1976	Lower	2001	Lower
Government's support for contraceptive methods	1976	Direct support	2001	Direct support

[a]Median age at first birth among women aged 25-29 at the date of the survey for both dates

Total fertility rates

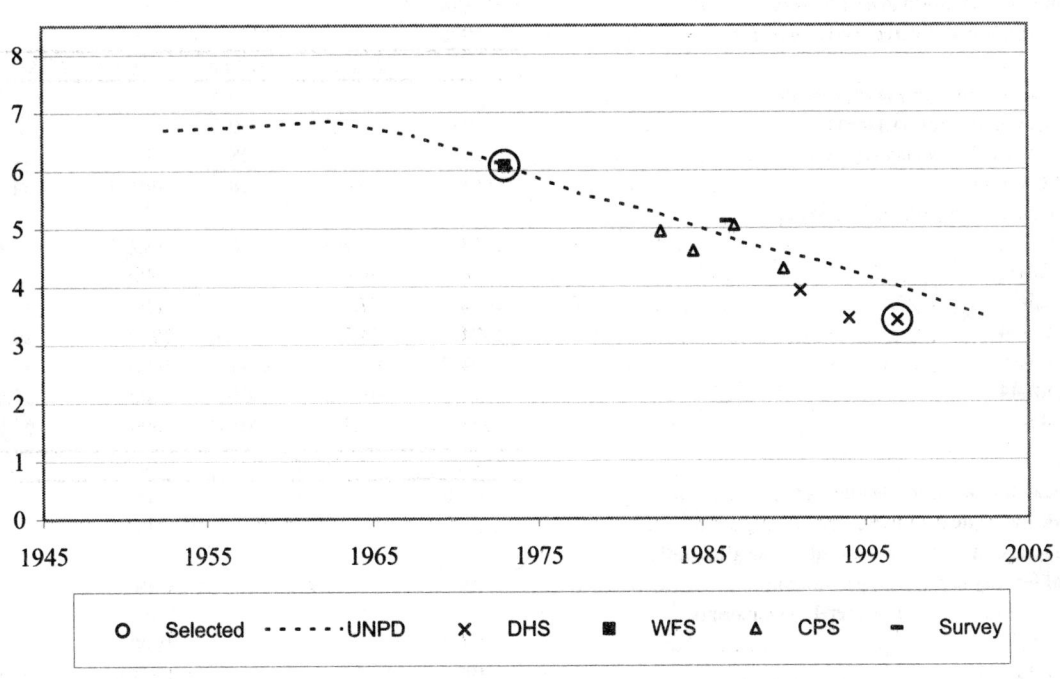

Age-specific fertility rates

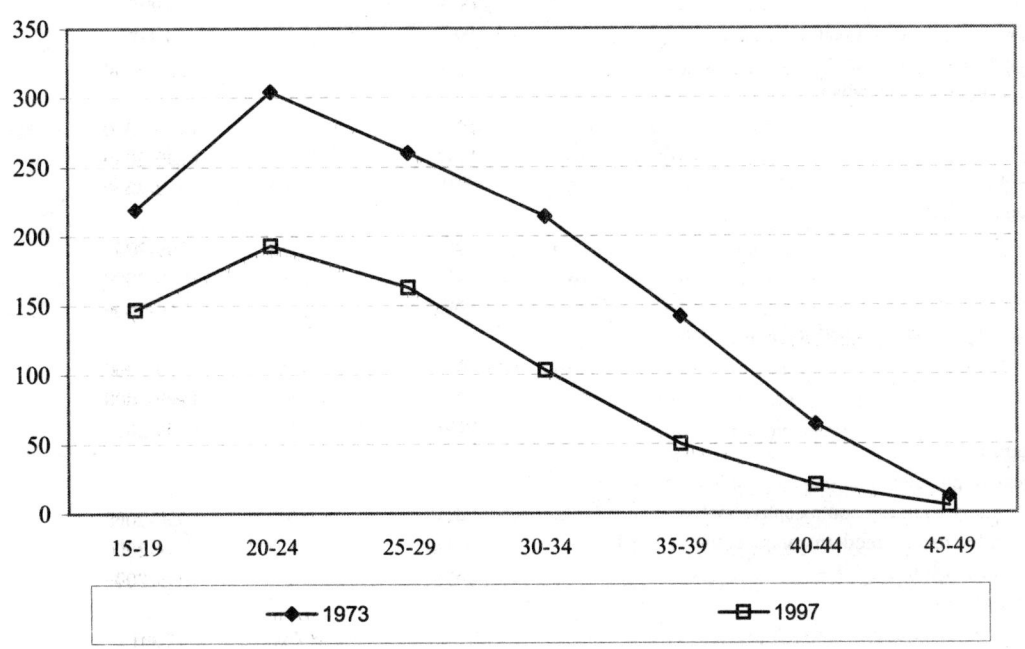

Indicator	Period			
	Earlier year		Later year	
	Year	Value	Year	Value
Nuptiality				
Annual number of marriages (*thousands*)	1970	1.1	1995	3.7
Annual number of divorces (*thousands*)	1970	0.1	1995	0.4

Indicator	Year	Male	Female	Year	Male	Female
Total first marriage rate (per person)	1978	0.4	0.3	1991	0.7	0.7
Total divorce rate (per person)	1970	0.1	0.1	1991	0.2	0.2
Mean age at first marriage (years)	1978	31.7	28.0	1991	32.3	29.9
SMAM (years)	1970	31.7	28.5	1990	34.3	31.8
Percentage ever married by age group						
15-19	1970	0.2	0.9	1990	0.2	0.6
20-24	1970	4.7	12.0	1990	2.3	6.7
25-29	1970	22.7	34.2	1990	12.9	21.4
30-34	1970	43.9	49.1	1990	29.0	35.7
35-39	1970	55.2	55.4	1990	44.0	47.3
40-44	1970	63.2	61.5	1990	55.4	53.3
45-49	1970	68.5	63.6	1990	62.8	59.8

Fertility	Year	Value	Year	Value
Annual number of births (*thousands*).............................	1970	4.9	1996	3.5
Crude birth rate (per 1 000 population)	1970	20.4	1996	13.3
Percentage of extra-marital births among all births	1970	70.9	..	..
Total fertility rate (births per woman)	1970	3.0	1988	1.6
Age-specific fertility rate (per 1 000 women)				
15-19	1970	94	1988	44
20-24	1970	164	1988	87
25-29	1970	156	1988	89
30-34	1970	102	1988	65
35-39	1970	60	1988	28
40-44	1970	25	1988	3
45-49	1970	4	1988	0
Mean age at childbearing (years)	1970	27.2	1988	26.8
Mean age at first birth (years)	..	..	..	..
Children ever born per woman				
35-39	1980	3.3	..	..
40-44	1980	3.9	..	..
45-49	1980	4.3	..	..
Percentage of childless women				
35-39	1980	11.5	..	..
40-44	1980	10.7	..	..
45-49	1980	11.6	..	..
Percentage of women with parity three or higher				
35-39	1980	56.9	..	..
40-44	1980	64.2	..	..
45-49	1980	66.7	..	..
Family Planning				
Contraceptive prevalence among women in union				
Percentage using any contraceptive method	1981	46.5	1988	55.0
Percentage using a modern contraceptive method	1981	44.6	1988	53.2
Percentage using condoms	1981	5.4	1988	7.2
Population policies				
Government's view on the level of fertility	1976	Too high	2001	Satisfactory
Government's policy regarding level of fertility	1976	Lower	2001	No intervention
Government's support for contraceptive methods	1976	Direct support	2001	Direct support

Total fertility rates

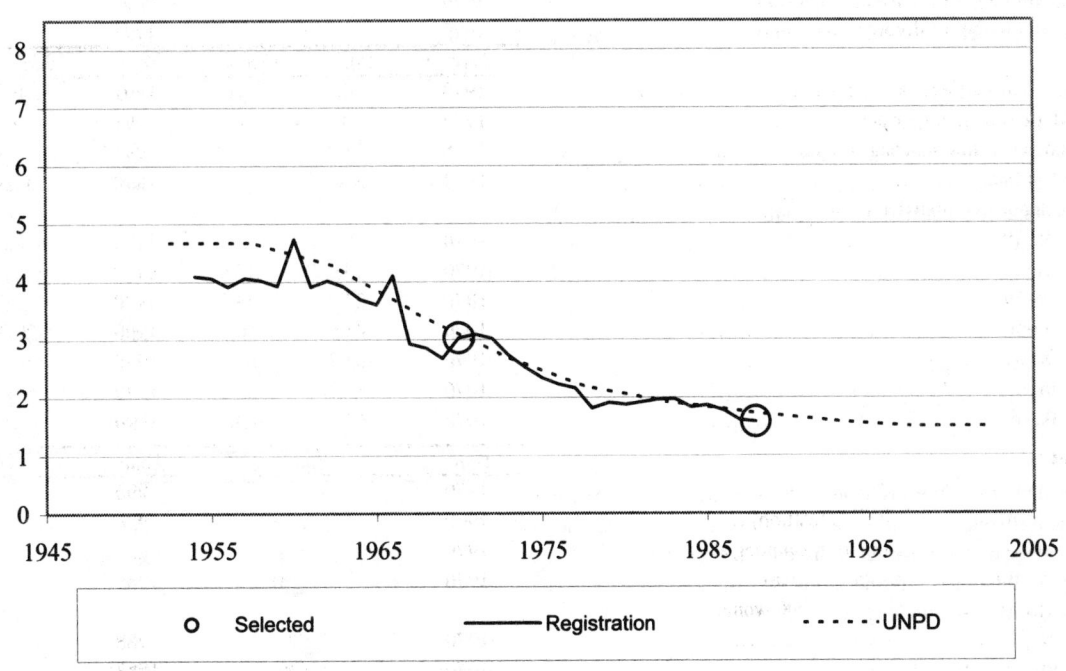

O   Selected   Registration   - - - - - UNPD

Age-specific fertility rates

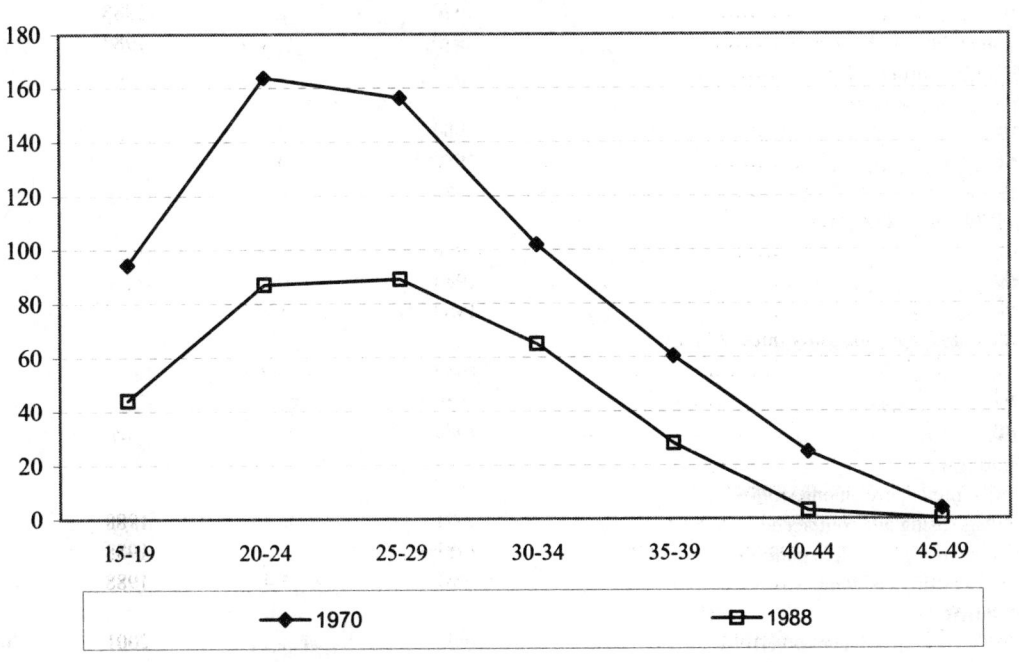

◆ 1970   ▭ 1988

Indicator	Period					
	Earlier year			Later year		
	Year	Value		Year	Value	
Nuptiality						
Annual number of marriages (*thousands*)	1970	83.7		1999	73.0	
Annual number of divorces (*thousands*)	1970	17.1		2000	43.5	
	Year	Male	Female	Year	Male	Female
Total first marriage rate (per person)	1978	1.1	1.0	1998	0.7	0.7
Total divorce rate (per person)	..	..	..	..	..	..
Mean age at first marriage (years)	1978	24.2	22.2	1998	24.6	22.4
SMAM (years)	..	..	..	1999	25.4	22.8
Percentage ever married by age group						
15-19	1979	..	..	1999	1.0	6.3
20-24	1979	36.2	60.3	1999	29.8	54.9
25-29	1979	81.3	87.9	1999	72.3	84.4
30-34	1979	91.7	94.0	1999	87.1	92.5
35-39	1979	95.3	95.8	1999	91.1	95.0
40-44	1979	97.1	95.5	1999	93.1	96.0
45-49	1979	98.3	94.1	1999	94.6	96.3
Fertility	Year	Value		Year	Value	
Annual number of births (*thousands*)	1970	146.7		2001	91.7	
Crude birth rate (per 1 000 population)	1970	16.2		2001	9.2	
Percentage of extra-marital births among all births	1970	7.3		2001	20.5	
Total fertility rate (births per woman)	1970	2.3		2001	1.3	
Age-specific fertility rate (per 1 000 women)						
15-19	1970	20		2001	27	
20-24	1970	162		2001	104	
25-29	1970	135		2001	73	
30-34	1970	87		2001	37	
35-39	1970	43		2001	12	
40-44	1970	12		2001	2	
45-49	1970	1		2001	0	
Mean age at childbearing (years)	1970	27.7		2001	25.8	
Mean age at first birth (years)	..	..		2001	23.4	
Children ever born per woman						
35-39	..	..		1999	1.8	
40-44	..	..		1999	1.9	
45-49	..	..		1999	1.9	
Percentage of childless women						
35-39	..	..		1999	6.8	
40-44	..	..		1999	6.0	
45-49	..	..		1999	6.1	
Percentage of women with parity three or higher						
35-39	..	..		1999	12.3	
40-44	..	..		1999	15.6	
45-49	..	..		1999	17.3	
Family Planning						
Contraceptive prevalence among women in union						
Percentage using any contraceptive method	..	..		1995	50.4	
Percentage using a modern contraceptive method	..	..		1995	42.1	
Percentage using condoms	..	..		1995	4.8	
Population policies						
Government's view on the level of fertility	1976	Satisfactory		2001	Too low	
Government's policy regarding level of fertility	1976	Maintain		2001	Raise	
Government's support for contraceptive methods	1976	Direct support		2001	Direct support	

Total fertility rates

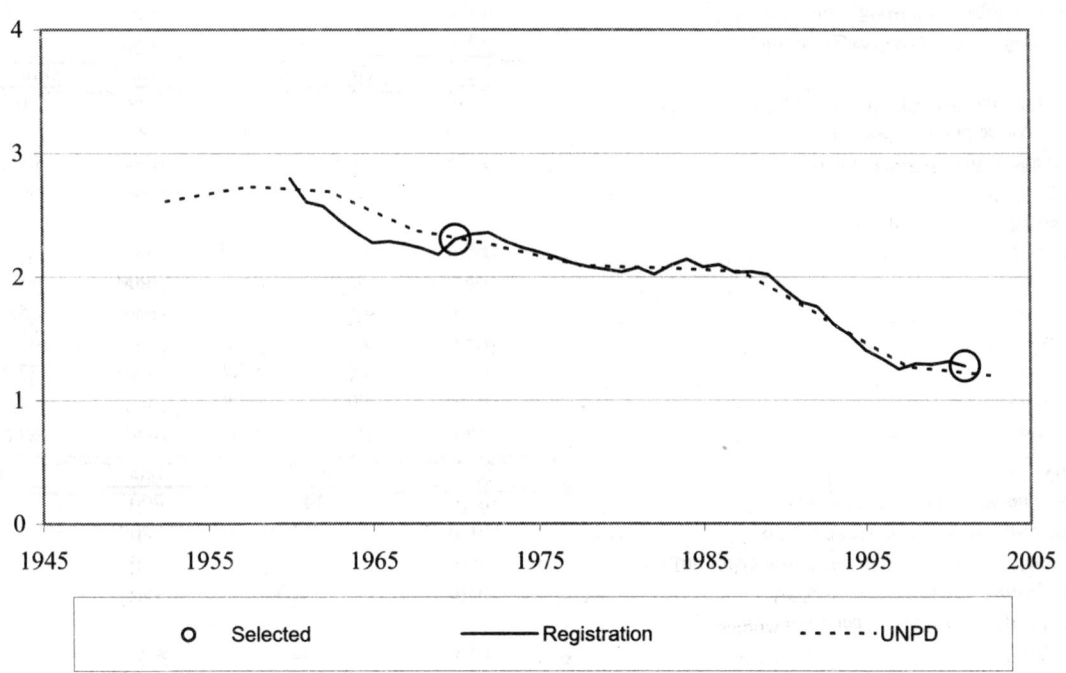

O Selected	—— Registration	· · · · · UNPD

Age-specific fertility rates

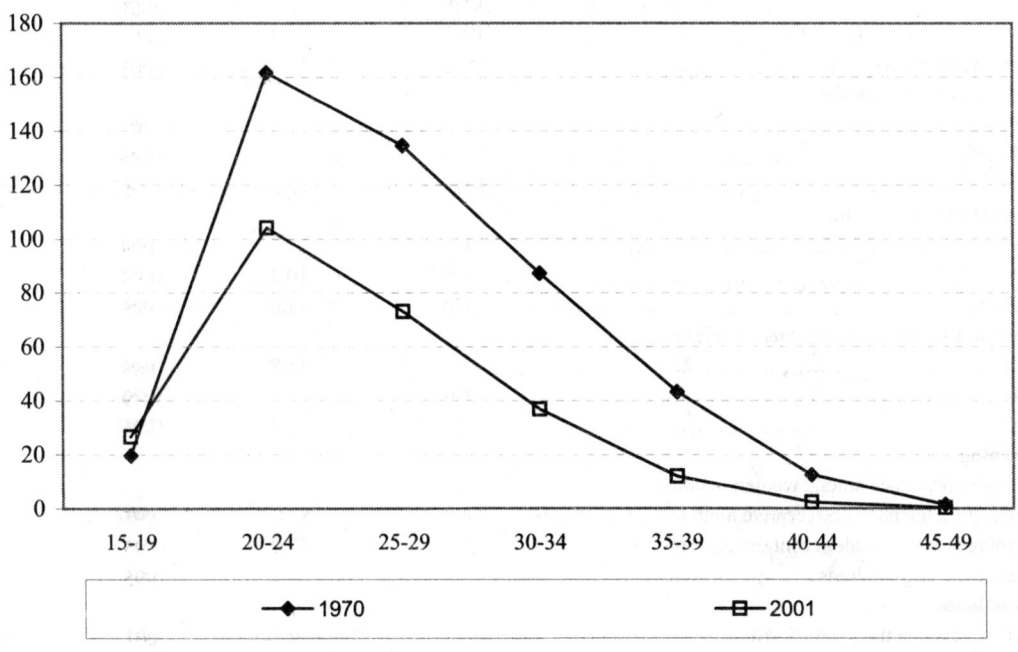

◆ 1970	▫ 2001

Indicator	Period					
	Earlier year			**Later year**		
	Year	Value		Year	Value	
Nuptiality						
Annual number of marriages (*thousands*)	1970	73.2		2001	42.1	
Annual number of divorces (*thousands*)	1970	6.4		2000	27.0	
	Year	Male	Female	Year	Male	Female
Total first marriage rate (per person)	1975	0.9	0.9	1995	0.5	0.6
Total divorce rate (per person)	1970	0.1	0.1	1995	0.4	0.4
Mean age at first marriage (years)	1975	24.2	22.1	1995	27.4	25.3
SMAM (years)	1970	24.2	21.4	2000	30.3	27.9
Percentage ever married by age group						
15-19	1970	1.0	6.9	2000	0.1	1.1
20-24	1970	35.5	59.9	2000	5.7	16.5
25-29	1970	78.0	88.3	2000	35.2	53.7
30-34	1970	87.5	92.7	2000	63.8	76.2
35-39	1970	89.9	93.4	2000	77.2	85.3
40-44	1970	90.7	92.9	2000	84.9	90.3
45-49	1970	91.7	92.3	2000	89.5	93.2
Fertility	Year	Value		Year	Value	
Annual number of births (*thousands*)	1970	142.2		2001	114.0	
Crude birth rate (per 1 000 population)	1970	14.7		2000	11.2	
Percentage of extra-marital births among all births	1970	2.8		1995	17.3	
Total fertility rate (births per woman)	1970	2.3		1995	1.5	
Age-specific fertility rate (per 1 000 women)						
15-19	1970	32		1995	9	
20-24	1970	150		1995	61	
25-29	1970	144		1995	132	
30-34	1970	77		1995	81	
35-39	1970	36		1995	23	
40-44	1970	10		1995	4	
45-49	1970	1		1995	0	
Mean age at childbearing (years)	1970	27.1		1995	28.5	
Mean age at first birth (years)[a]	1970	24.3		1990	26.4	
Children ever born per woman						
35-39	1970	2.2		1992	1.8	
40-44	1970	2.3		1992	..	
45-49	1970	2.2		1992	..	
Percentage of childless women						
35-39	1970	9.1		1992	12.4	
40-44	1970	10.2		1992	..	
45-49	1970	12.0		1992	..	
Percentage of women with parity three or higher						
35-39	1970	35.8		1992	22.6	
40-44	1970	36.3		1992	..	
45-49	1970	33.8		1992	..	
Family Planning						
Contraceptive prevalence among women in union						
Percentage using any contraceptive method	1976	87.0		1992	78.4	
Percentage using a modern contraceptive method	1976	47.0		1992	74.3	
Percentage using condoms	1976	8.0		1992	4.7	
Population policies						
Government's view on the level of fertility	1976	Satisfactory		2001	Satisfactory	
Government's policy regarding level of fertility	1976	No intervention		2001	No intervention	
Government's support for contraceptive methods	1976	Indirect support		2001	Direct support	

[a]Mean age at first birth within current marriage

Total fertility rates

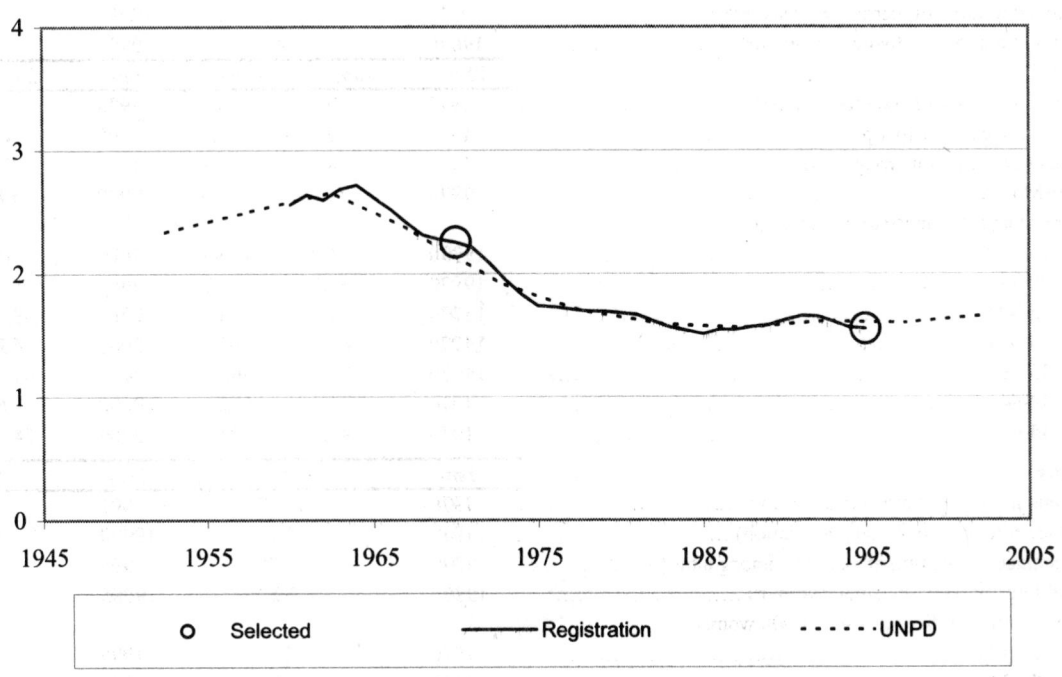

Age-specific fertility rates

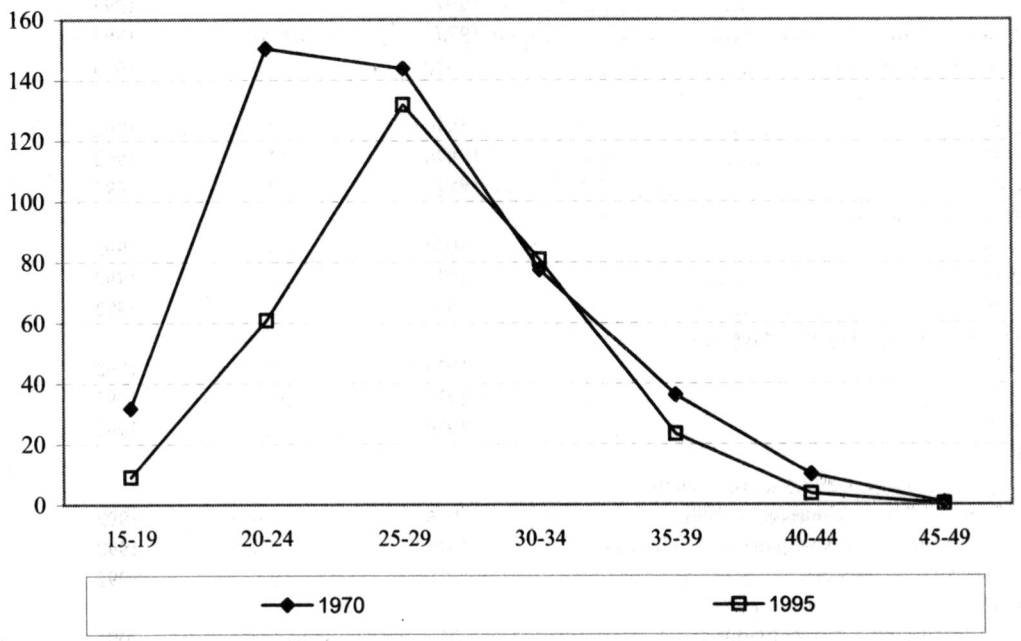

Indicator	Period					
	Earlier year			Later year		
	Year	Value		Year	Value	
Nuptiality						
Annual number of marriages (*thousands*)	1970	0.7		1999	1.5	
Annual number of divorces (*thousands*)	1968	0.0		1998	0.0	
	Year	Male	Female	Year	Male	Female
Total first marriage rate (per person)	..	..	..	1997	0.8	0.8
Total divorce rate (per person)	..	..	..	..	..	..
Mean age at first marriage (years)	..	..	..	..	..	..
SMAM (years)	1970	26.0	22.6	1991	28.4	26.2
Percentage ever married by age group						
15-19	1970	1.8	11.4	1991	1.4	7.9
20-24	1970	24.3	41.1	1991	18.1	30.9
25-29	1970	50.8	59.8	1991	39.8	48.2
30-34	1970	60.1	63.8	1991	53.2	59.5
35-39	1970	63.1	66.6	1991	64.2	67.5
40-44	1970	66.0	67.0	1991	71.6	72.1
45-49	1970	68.7	67.9	1991	74.7	76.0
Fertility	Year	Value		Year	Value	
Annual number of births (*thousands*)	1970	4.5		1999	6.2	
Crude birth rate (per 1 000 population)	1970	37.1		1999	26.5	
Percentage of extra-marital births among all births	1970	43.7		1997	58.1	
Total fertility rate (births per woman)	1970	6.2		1998	3.2	
Age-specific fertility rate (per 1 000 women)						
15-19	1970	142		1998	80	
20-24	1970	309		1998	187	
25-29	1970	302		1998	173	
30-34	1970	239		1998	112	
35-39	1970	173		1998	64	
40-44	1970	75		1998	21	
45-49	1970	9		1998	5	
Mean age at childbearing (years)	1970	28.5		1998	27.3	
Mean age at first birth (years)	..	..		..	..	
Children ever born per woman						
35-39	1980	6.0		1991	5.0	
40-44	1980	6.9		1991	5.7	
45-49	1980	6.9		1991	6.3	
Percentage of childless women						
35-39	1980	5.5		1991	6.1	
40-44	1980	4.4		1991	5.4	
45-49	1980	6.4		1991	6.1	
Percentage of women with parity three or higher						
35-39	1980	83.2		1991	77.9	
40-44	1980	85.9		1991	81.1	
45-49	1980	82.4		1991	85.0	
Family Planning						
Contraceptive prevalence among women in union						
Percentage using any contraceptive method	..	..		1991	46.7	
Percentage using a modern contraceptive method	..	..		1991	41.8	
Percentage using condoms	..	..		1991	1.9	
Population policies						
Government's view on the level of fertility	..	..		2001	Satisfactory	
Government's policy regarding level of fertility	..	..		2001	No intervention	
Government's support for contraceptive methods	..	..		2001	Indirect support	

Total fertility rates

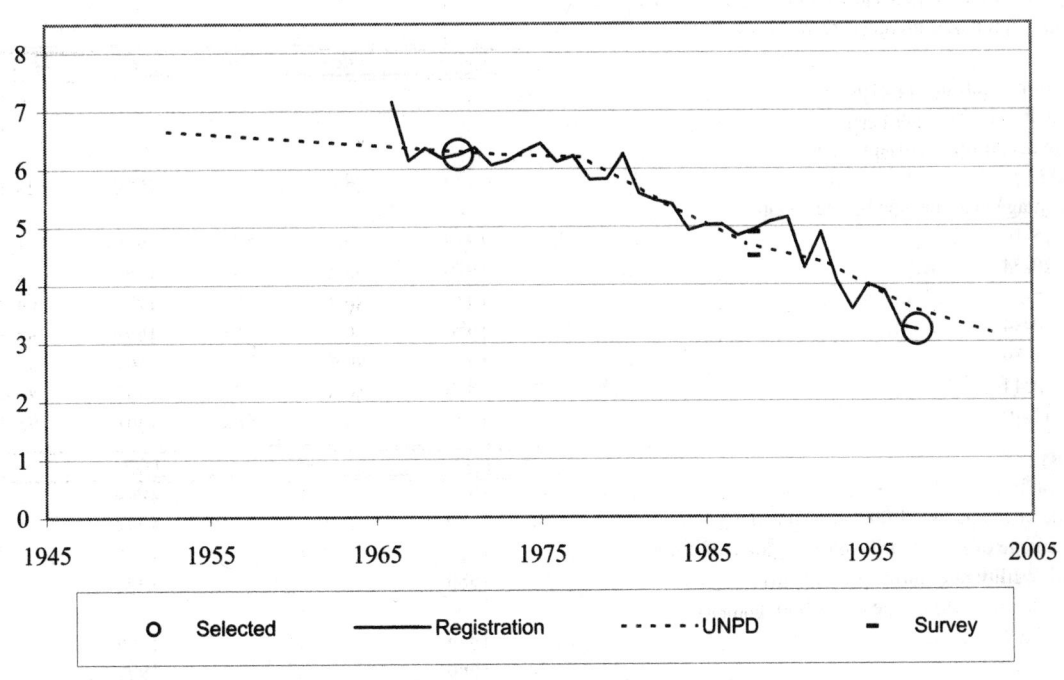

| | O | Selected | —— Registration | · · · · · UNPD | – Survey |

Age-specific fertility rates

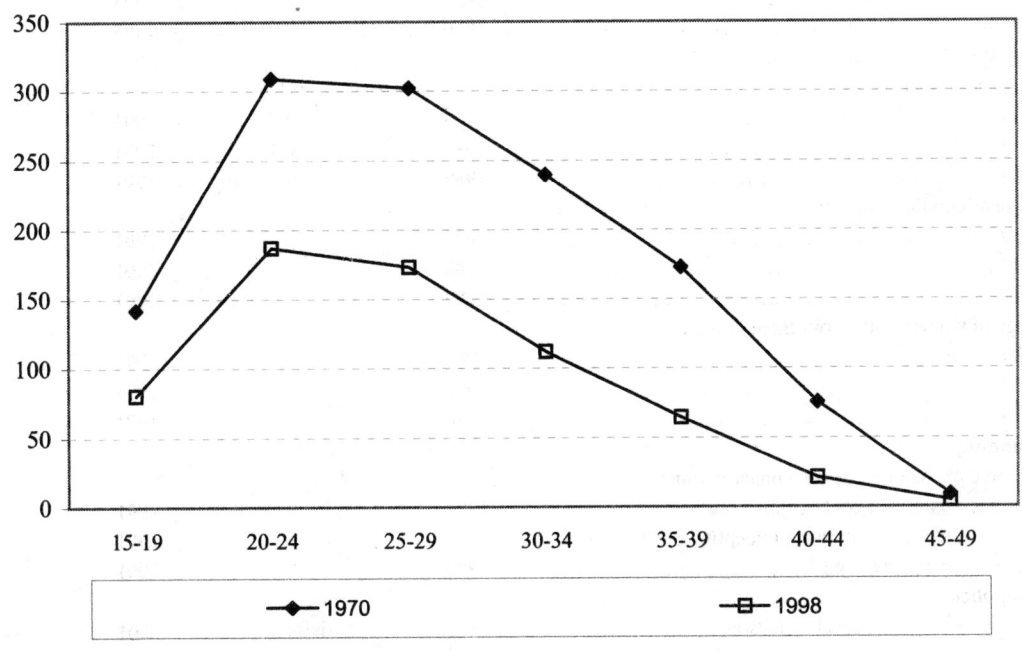

| | ◆ 1970 | ☐ 1998 |

Benin

Indicator	Period					
	Earlier year			**Later year**		
	Year	Value		Year	Value	
Nuptiality						
Annual number of marriages (*thousands*)	..	..		..	..	
Annual number of divorces (*thousands*)	..	..		..	..	
	Year	Male	Female	Year	Male	Female
Total first marriage rate (per person)	..	..	..	..	..	..
Total divorce rate (per person)	..	..	..	..	..	..
Mean age at first marriage (years)	..	..	..	..	..	..
SMAM (years)	1979	24.7	17.7	1996	..	19.9
Percentage ever married by age group						
15-19	1979	5.3	52.2	1996	..	29.1
20-24	1979	33.8	90.1	1996	27.3	79.5
25-29	1979	70.7	97.1	1996	64.9	94.3
30-34	1979	86.3	98.4	1996	89.8	98.4
35-39	1979	90.8	98.6	1996	97.3	99.4
40-44	1979	92.3	98.3	1996	96.8	99.8
45-49	1979	93.5	98.2	1996	98.7	99.7
Fertility	Year	Value		Year	Value	
Annual number of births (*thousands*)	..	..		2001	263.7	
Crude birth rate (per 1 000 population)	..	..		2001	41.1	
Percentage of extra-marital births among all births	..	..		..	..	
Total fertility rate (births per woman)	1980	7.1		1999	5.8	
Age-specific fertility rate (per 1 000 women)						
15-19	1980	151		1999	108	
20-24	1980	314		1999	255	
25-29	1980	329		1999	267	
30-34	1980	278		1999	243	
35-39	1980	193		1999	165	
40-44	1980	99		1999	87	
45-49	1980	51		1999	31	
Mean age at childbearing (years)	1980	29.4		1999	29.6	
Mean age at first birth (years)[a]	..	..		2001	20.2	
Children ever born per woman						
35-39	1982	5.7		2001	5.6	
40-44	1982	6.1		2001	6.4	
45-49	1982	6.3		2001	7.2	
Percentage of childless women						
35-39	1982	..		2001	1.3	
40-44	1982	..		2001	1.0	
45-49	1982	..		2001	2.5	
Percentage of women with parity three or higher						
35-39	1982	..		2001	89.8	
40-44	1982	..		2001	92.3	
45-49	1982	..		2001	91.4	
Family Planning						
Contraceptive prevalence among women in union						
Percentage using any contraceptive method	1982	9.2		2001	18.6	
Percentage using a modern contraceptive method	1982	0.5		2001	7.2	
Percentage using condoms	1982	0.1		2001	1.3	
Population policies						
Government's view on the level of fertility	1976	Satisfactory		2001	Satisfactory	
Government's policy regarding level of fertility	1976	No intervention		2001	No intervention	
Government's support for contraceptive methods	1976	Indirect support		2001	Direct support	

[a]Median age at first birth among women aged 25-29 at the date of the survey

Total fertility rates

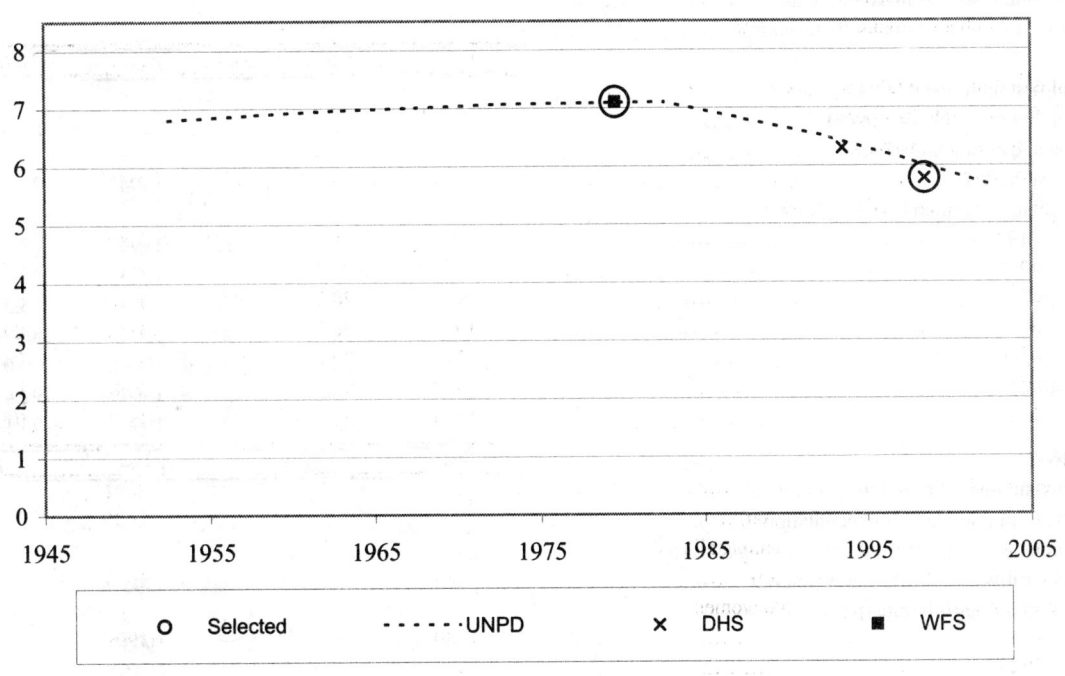

Age-specific fertility rates

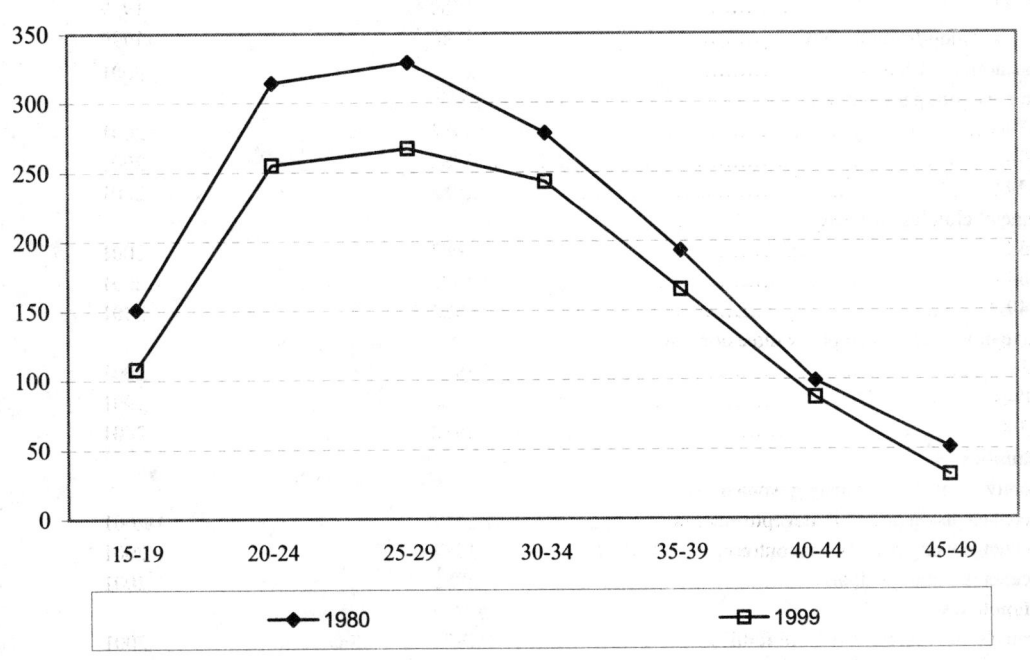

Indicator	Period					
	Earlier year			Later year		
	Year	Value		Year	Value	

Nuptiality

	Year	Value		Year	Value	
Annual number of marriages (*thousands*)	..	..		..	..	
Annual number of divorces (*thousands*)	..	..		..	..	

	Year	Male	Female	Year	Male	Female
Total first marriage rate (per person)	..	..	..	..	..	..
Total divorce rate (per person)	..	..	..	..	..	..
Mean age at first marriage (years)	..	..	..	..	..	..
SMAM (years)	..	..	..	1994	23.8	20.5
Percentage ever married by age group						
15-19	..	..	..	1994	7.9	26.6
20-24	..	..	..	1994	45.5	69.9
25-29	..	..	..	1994	73.2	87.6
30-34	..	..	..	1994	86.9	91.6
35-39	..	..	..	1994	90.0	94.5
40-44	..	..	..	1994	92.4	93.7
45-49	..	..	..	1994	93.1	93.1

Fertility

	Year	Value	Year	Value
Annual number of births (*thousands*)	..	..	..	..
Crude birth rate (per 1 000 population)	..	..	..	..
Percentage of extra-marital births among all births	..	..	..	..
Total fertility rate (births per woman)	..	..	1993	5.6
Age-specific fertility rate (per 1 000 women)				
15-19	..	..	1993	120
20-24	..	..	1993	267
25-29	..	..	1993	242
30-34	..	..	1993	195
35-39	..	..	1993	174
40-44	..	..	1993	95
45-49	..	..	1993	24
Mean age at childbearing (years)	..	..	1993	29.4
Mean age at first birth (years)	..	..	..	..
Children ever born per woman				
35-39	..	..	..	..
40-44	..	..	..	..
45-49	..	..	..	..
Percentage of childless women				
35-39	..	..	..	..
40-44	..	..	..	..
45-49	..	..	..	..
Percentage of women with parity three or higher				
35-39	..	..	..	..
40-44	..	..	..	..
45-49	..	..	..	..

Family Planning

	Year	Value	Year	Value
Contraceptive prevalence among women in union				
Percentage using any contraceptive method	..	..	1994	18.8
Percentage using a modern contraceptive method	..	..	1994	18.8
Percentage using condoms	..	..	1994	0.3

Population policies

	Year	Value	Year	Value
Government's view on the level of fertility	1976	Satisfactory	2001	Too high
Government's policy regarding level of fertility	1976	No intervention	2001	Lower
Government's support for contraceptive methods	1976	Direct support	2001	Direct support

Total fertility rates

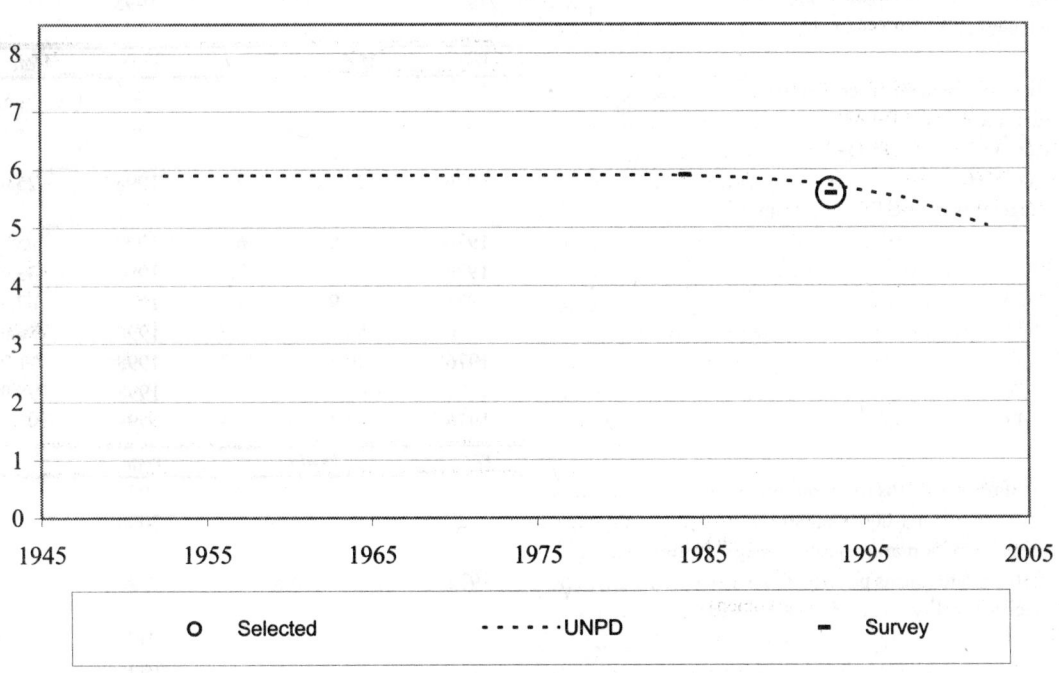

O Selected	····· UNPD	─ Survey

Age-specific fertility rates

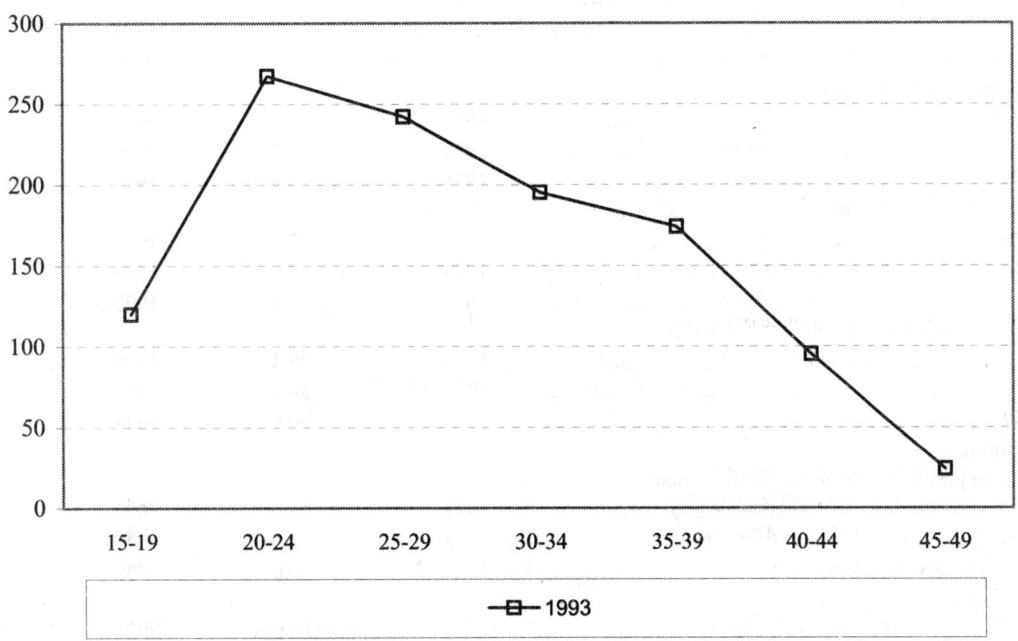

─□─ 1993

Indicator	Period					
	Earlier year			Later year		
	Year	Value		Year	Value	

Nuptiality

Indicator	Year	Value		Year	Value	
Annual number of marriages (*thousands*)	1970	17.8		1995	21.7	
Annual number of divorces (*thousands*)	..	..		..	..	

Indicator	Year	Male	Female	Year	Male	Female
Total first marriage rate (per person)	..	..	..	..	..	..
Total divorce rate (per person)	..	..	..	..	..	..
Mean age at first marriage (years)	..	..	..	..	..	..
SMAM (years)	1976	24.6	22.1	1998	25.4	22.8
Percentage ever married by age group						
15-19	1976	3.9	16.1	1998	5.2	12.2
20-24	1976	39.2	57.0	1998	33.6	53.4
25-29	1976	72.9	79.1	1998	67.5	80.5
30-34	1976	86.5	87.5	1998	86.6	90.7
35-39	1976	90.5	90.3	1998	91.7	94.3
40-44	1976	92.8	92.0	1998	95.9	96.1
45-49	1976	94.2	92.3	1998	97.7	96.3

Fertility

Indicator	Year	Value	Year	Value
Annual number of births (*thousands*).....................	..	..	2000	264.9
Crude birth rate (per 1 000 population)	..	..	2000	31.8
Percentage of extra-marital births among all births	..	..	..	..
Total fertility rate (births per woman)	1974	6.5	1996	4.4
Age-specific fertility rate (per 1 000 women)				
15-19	..	..	1996	88
20-24	..	..	1996	209
25-29	..	..	1996	208
30-34	..	..	1996	171
35-39	..	..	1996	120
40-44	..	..	1996	60
45-49	..	..	1996	18
Mean age at childbearing (years)	..	..	1996	29.1
Mean age at first birth (years)[a]	..	..	1998	21.0
Children ever born per woman				
35-39	1976	5.1	1998	4.2
40-44	1976	5.7	1998	5.0
45-49	1976	5.9	1998	5.1
Percentage of childless women				
35-39	1976	7.9	1998	5.4
40-44	1976	7.0	1998	3.9
45-49	1976	7.0	1998	4.2
Percentage of women with parity three or higher				
35-39	1976	78.4	1998	74.3
40-44	1976	80.8	1998	77.6
45-49	1976	80.9	1998	77.9

Family Planning

Indicator	Year	Value	Year	Value
Contraceptive prevalence among women in union				
Percentage using any contraceptive method	1983	26.0	2000	53.4
Percentage using a modern contraceptive method	1983	12.0	2000	27.3
Percentage using condoms	1983	0.0	2000	3.3

Population policies

Indicator	Year	Value	Year	Value
Government's view on the level of fertility	1976	Satisfactory	2001	Satisfactory
Government's policy regarding level of fertility	1976	No intervention	2001	No intervention
Government's support for contraceptive methods	1976	Direct support	2001	Direct support

[a]Median age at first birth among women aged 25-29 at the date of the survey

Total fertility rates

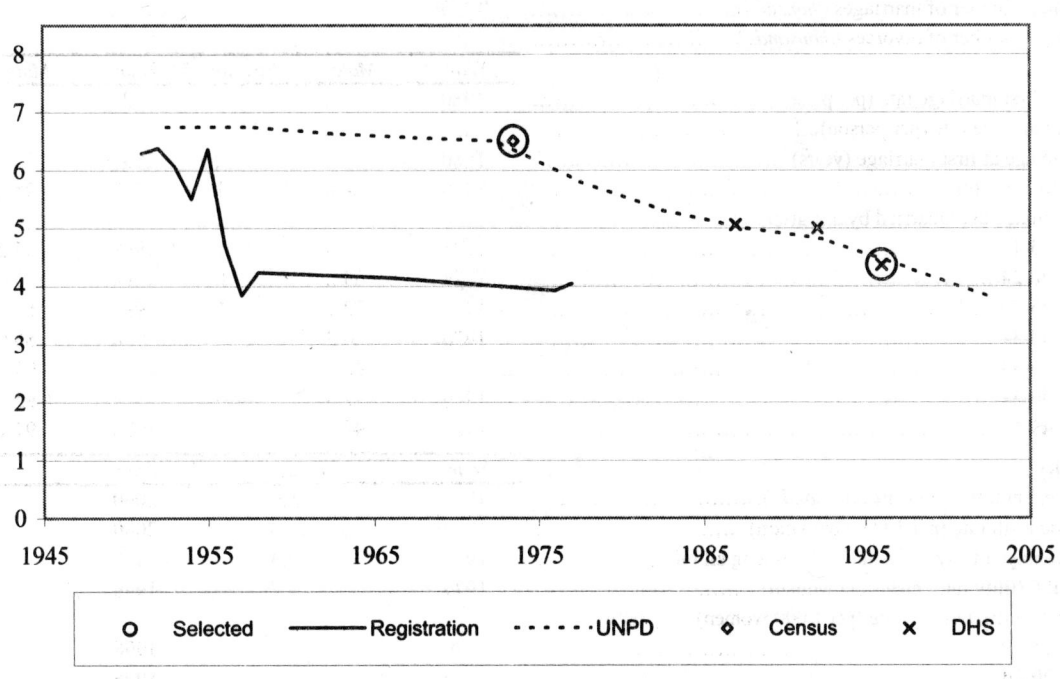

Age-specific fertility rates

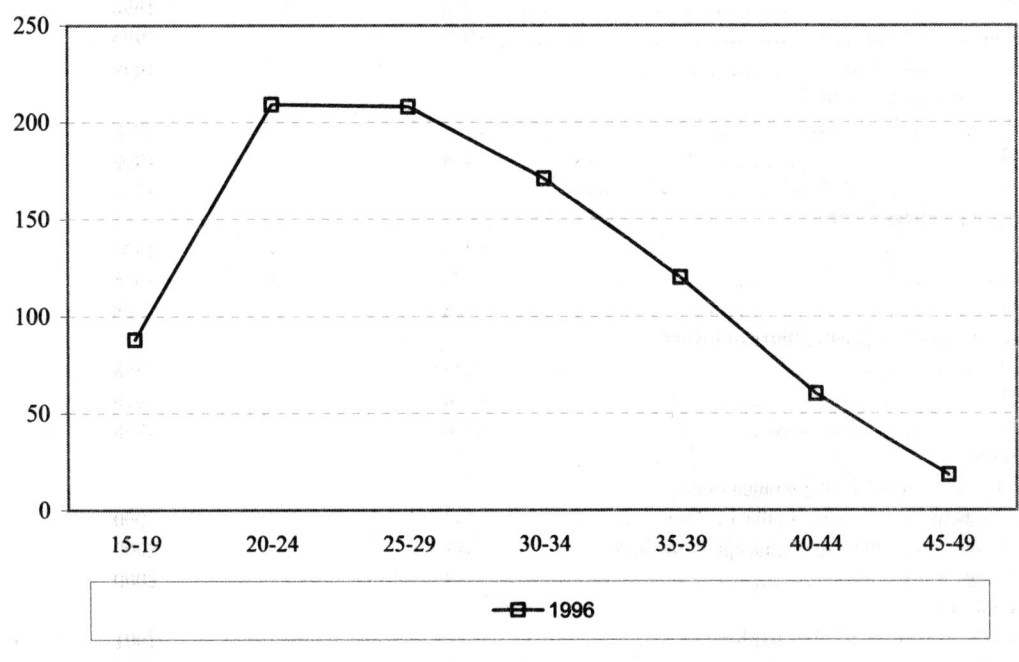

Indicator	Period					
	Earlier year			Later year		
	Year	Value		Year	Value	
Nuptiality						
Annual number of marriages (*thousands*)	..	..		1998	22.4	
Annual number of divorces (*thousands*)	..	..		2000	1.4	
	Year	Male	Female	Year	Male	Female
Total first marriage rate (per person)	1980	..	0.7	1991	0.6	0.7
Total divorce rate (per person)	..	..	..	1991	0.0	0.0
Mean age at first marriage (years)	1980	..	22.0	1991	26.1	22.4
SMAM (years)	..	..	..	..	..	..
Percentage ever married by age group						
15-19	..	..	..	..	..	..
20-24	..	..	..	..	..	..
25-29	..	..	..	..	..	..
30-34	..	..	..	..	..	..
35-39	..	..	..	..	..	..
40-44	..	..	..	..	..	..
45-49	..	..	..	..	..	..
Fertility	Year	Value		Year	Value	
Annual number of births (*thousands*)............................	1970	79.3		2000	39.1	
Crude birth rate (per 1 000 population)	1970	21.4		2000	9.8	
Percentage of extra-marital births among all births	1970	5.3		1990	7.4	
Total fertility rate (births per woman)	1970	2.7		1998	1.6	
Age-specific fertility rate (per 1 000 women)						
15-19	1970	47		1998	26	
20-24	1970	178		1998	113	
25-29	1970	145		1998	91	
30-34	1970	94		1998	51	
35-39	1970	54		1998	24	
40-44	1970	20		1998	6	
45-49	1970	3		1998	1	
Mean age at childbearing (years)	1970	27.5		1998	26.7	
Mean age at first birth (years)	1970	23.0		1990	23.6	
Children ever born per woman						
35-39	..	..		..	..	
40-44	..	..		..	..	
45-49	..	..		..	..	
Percentage of childless women						
35-39	..	..		..	..	
40-44	..	..		..	..	
45-49	..	..		..	..	
Percentage of women with parity three or higher						
35-39	..	..		..	..	
40-44	..	..		..	..	
45-49	..	..		..	..	
Family Planning						
Contraceptive prevalence among women in union						
Percentage using any contraceptive method	..	..		2000	47.5	
Percentage using a modern contraceptive method	..	..		2000	15.7	
Percentage using condoms	..	..		2000	3.1	
Population policies						
Government's view on the level of fertility	..	--		2001	Too low	
Government's policy regarding level of fertility	..	--		2001	No intervention	
Government's support for contraceptive methods	..	--		2001	Indirect support	

Total fertility rates

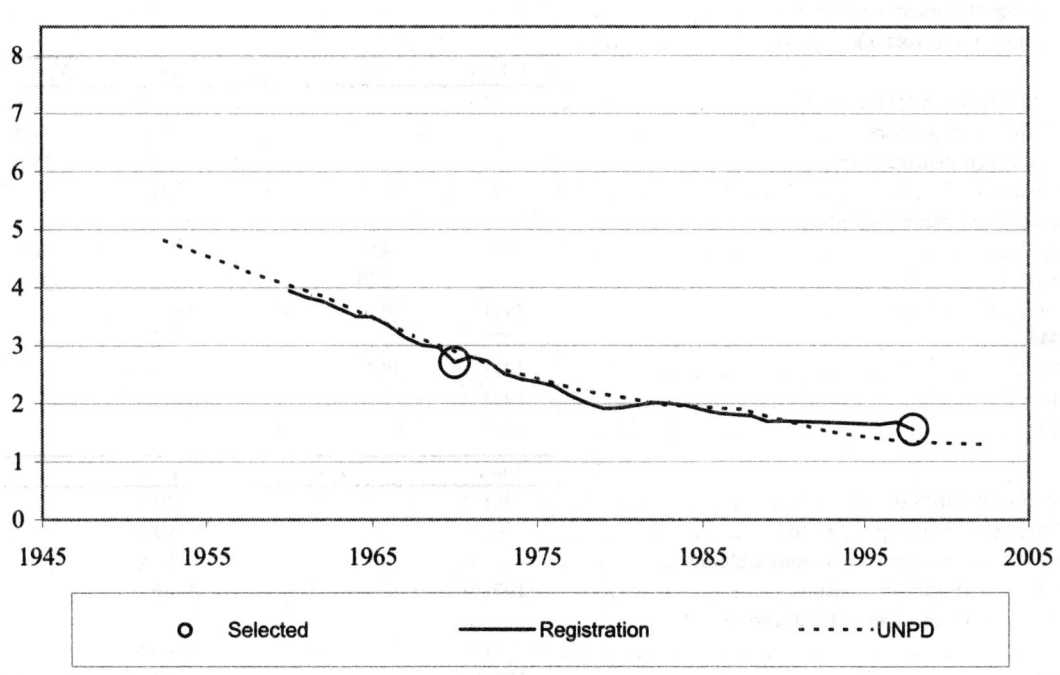

Age-specific fertility rates

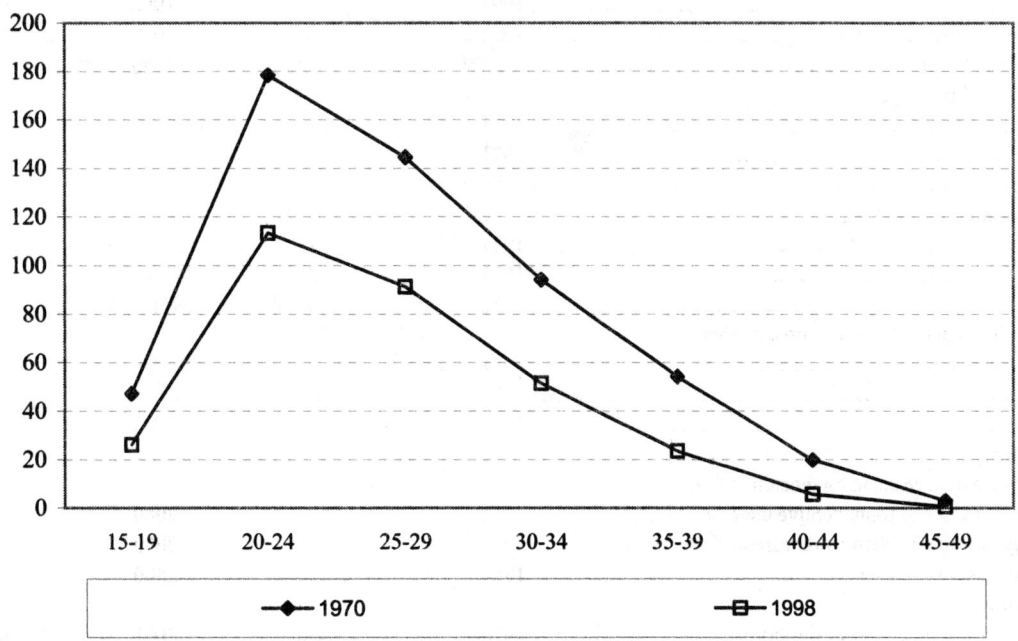

Indicator	Period			
	Earlier year		Later year	
	Year	Value	Year	Value
Nuptiality				
Annual number of marriages (*thousands*)	..	..	1987	1.9
Annual number of divorces (*thousands*)	..	..	..	..

Indicator	Year	Male	Female	Year	Male	Female
Total first marriage rate (per person)	..	..	..	..	..	..
Total divorce rate (per person)	..	..	..	..	..	..
Mean age at first marriage (years)	..	..	..	..	..	..
SMAM (years)	1971	29.5	24.9	1991	30.9	26.9
Percentage ever married by age group						
15-19	1971	4.9	12.7	1991	2.3	5.4
20-24	1971	12.0	43.6	1991	9.0	27.2
25-29	1971	38.2	63.3	1991	29.1	48.0
30-34	1971	63.5	72.8	1991	53.6	61.6
35-39	1971	75.6	79.7	1991	70.8	68.9
40-44	1971	84.0	83.2	1991	80.0	74.7
45-49	1971	87.8	86.5	1991	85.1	77.5

Fertility	Year	Value	Year	Value
Annual number of births (*thousands*)...........................	1981	45.0	2001	53.7
Crude birth rate (per 1 000 population)	1981	48.1	2001	32.0
Percentage of extra-marital births among all births	..	..	..	..
Total fertility rate (births per woman)	1971	6.5	1986	5.0
Age-specific fertility rate (per 1 000 women)				
15-19	1971	96	1986	125
20-24	1971	277	1986	212
25-29	1971	276	1986	202
30-34	1971	243	1986	191
35-39	1971	198	1986	148
40-44	1971	138	1986	83
45-49	1971	71	1986	38
Mean age at childbearing (years)	1971	30.8	1986	29.6
Mean age at first birth (years)	..	..	..	..
Children ever born per woman				
35-39	1971	5.1	1991	4.6
40-44	1971	5.6	1991	5.6
45-49	1971	5.6	1991	6.1
Percentage of childless women				
35-39	1971	6.1	1991	3.9
40-44	1971	6.2	1991	3.9
45-49	1971	6.5	1991	3.9
Percentage of women with parity three or higher				
35-39	1971	80.1	1991	80.5
40-44	1971	80.6	1991	83.9
45-49	1971	77.9	1991	84.3
Family Planning				
Contraceptive prevalence among women in union				
Percentage using any contraceptive method	1984	27.8	2000	40.4
Percentage using a modern contraceptive method	1984	18.6	2000	38.8
Percentage using condoms	1984	1.2	2000	11.2
Population policies				
Government's view on the level of fertility	1976	Too high	2001	Too high
Government's policy regarding level of fertility	1976	Lower	2001	Lower
Government's support for contraceptive methods	1976	Direct support	2001	Direct support

Total fertility rates

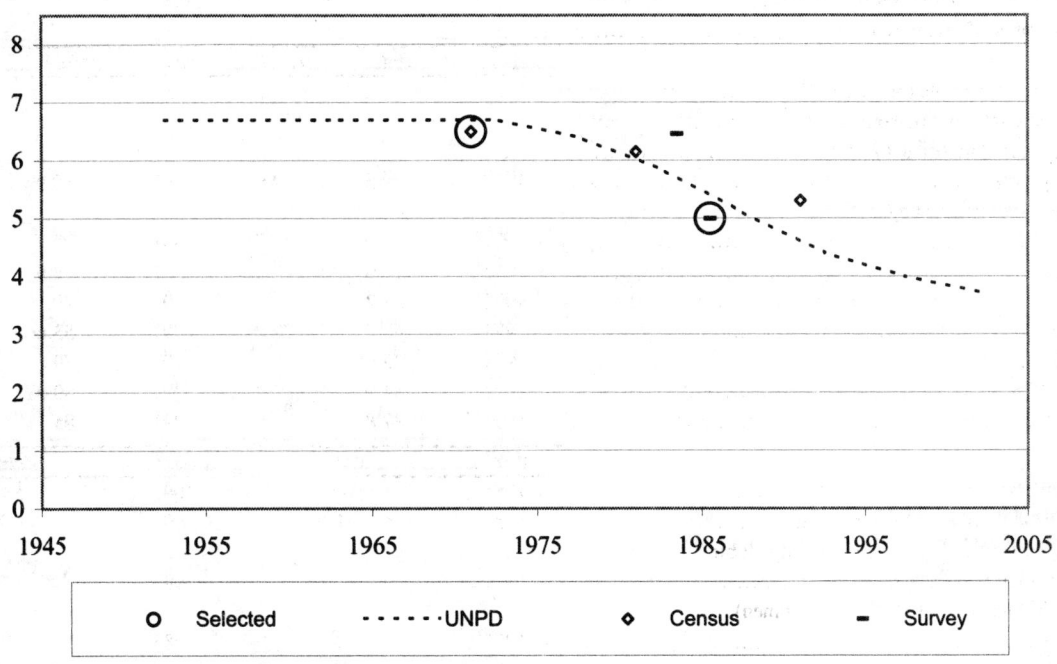

Age-specific fertility rates

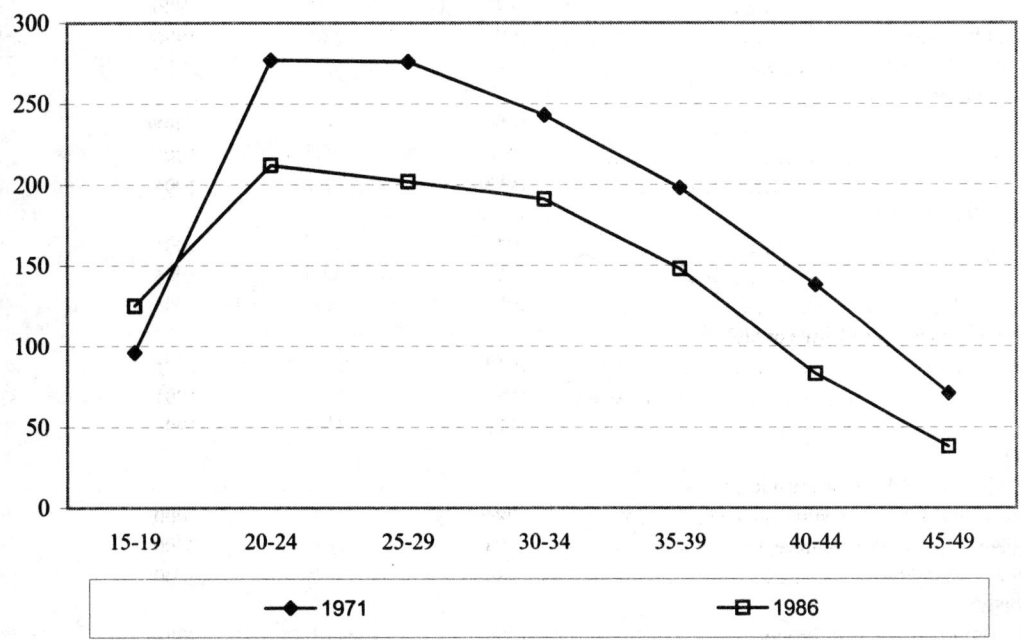

Indicator	Period					
	Earlier year			Later year		
	Year	Value		Year	Value	

Nuptiality

Indicator	Year	Value		Year	Value	
Annual number of marriages (*thousands*)	..	..		..	..	
Annual number of divorces (*thousands*)	..	..		..	..	

	Year	Male	Female	Year	Male	Female
Total first marriage rate (per person)	..	..	..	..	..	..
Total divorce rate (per person)	..	..	..	..	..	..
Mean age at first marriage (years)	1978	28.5	25.6	1995	27.5	24.6
SMAM (years)	1970	26.2	23.0	1996	25.4	23.4
Percentage ever married by age group						
15-19	1970	1.5	12.6	1996	4.3	16.8
20-24	1970	25.0	49.2	1996	29.0	52.6
25-29	1970	62.9	75.2	1996	65.0	78.5
30-34	1970	81.8	85.2	1996	86.3	89.8
35-39	1970	88.4	89.2	1996	92.6	91.8
40-44	1970	91.2	90.3	1996	98.5	93.8
45-49	1970	93.0	91.2	1996	97.0	94.8

Fertility

Indicator	Year	Value		Year	Value	
Annual number of births (*thousands*)	..	..		..	..	
Crude birth rate (per 1 000 population)	..	..		..	..	
Percentage of extra-marital births among all births	..	..		..	..	
Total fertility rate (births per woman)	1980	3.9		1994	2.6	
Age-specific fertility rate (per 1 000 women)						
15-19	1980	58		1994	88	
20-24	1980	182		1994	153	
25-29	1980	204		1994	126	
30-34	1980	160		1994	81	
35-39	1980	109		1994	45	
40-44	1980	52		1994	16	
45-49	1980	13		1994	3	
Mean age at childbearing (years)	1980	29.4		1994	26.5	
Mean age at first birth (years)[a]	..	..		1996	22.1	
Children ever born per woman						
35-39	1970	4.8		1996	3.0	
40-44	1970	5.3		1996	3.5	
45-49	1970	5.5		1996	3.9	
Percentage of childless women						
35-39	1970	13.7		1996	9.8	
40-44	1970	13.4		1996	7.9	
45-49	1970	13.5		1996	8.8	
Percentage of women with parity three or higher						
35-39	1970	68.7		1996	53.8	
40-44	1970	69.7		1996	62.8	
45-49	1970	69.7		1996	67.5	

Family Planning

Indicator	Year	Value	Year	Value
Contraceptive prevalence among women in union				
Percentage using any contraceptive method	..	..	1996	76.7
Percentage using a modern contraceptive method	..	..	1996	70.3
Percentage using condoms	..	..	1996	4.4

Population policies

Indicator	Year	Value	Year	Value
Government's view on the level of fertility	1976	Satisfactory	2001	Satisfactory
Government's policy regarding level of fertility	1976	No intervention	2001	No intervention
Government's support for contraceptive methods	1976	Indirect support	2001	Direct support

[a] Median age at first birth among women aged 25-29 at the date of the survey

Total fertility rates

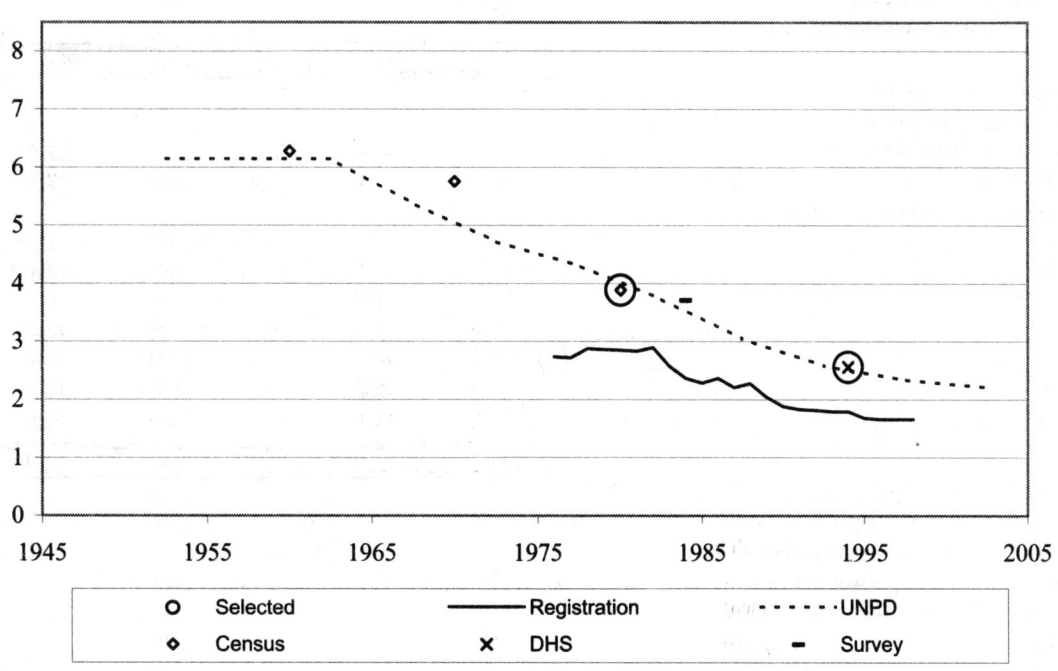

Age-specific fertility rates

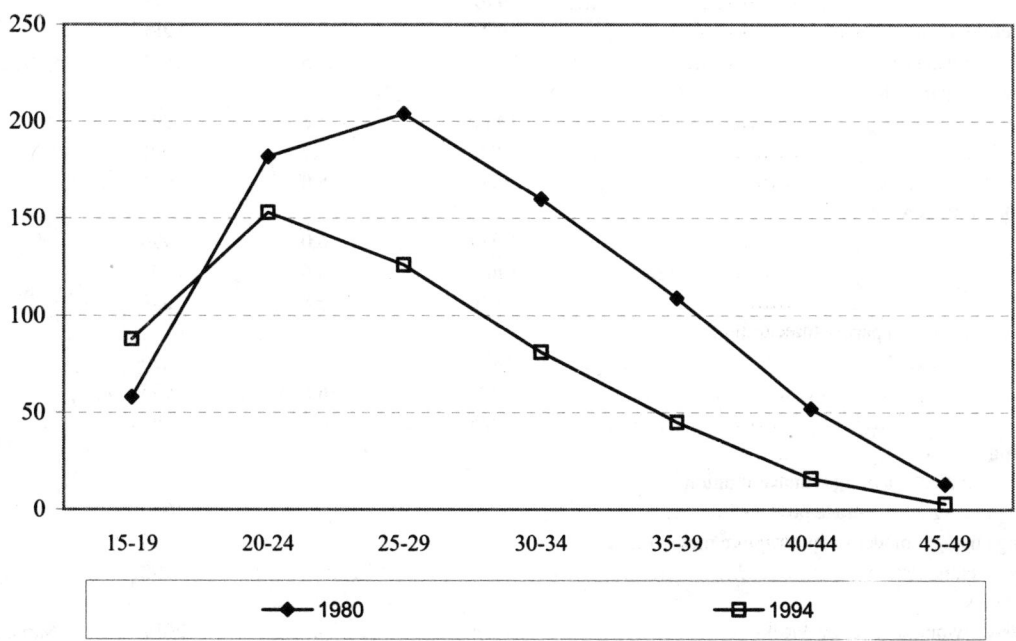

Brunei Darussalam

Indicator	Period					
	Earlier year			Later year		
	Year	Value		Year	Value	
Nuptiality						
Annual number of marriages (*thousands*) ....…..………...	1970	0.6		2000	2.2	
Annual number of divorces (*thousands*) ....………..….	1970	0.1		2001	0.4	
	Year	Male	Female	Year	Male	Female
Total first marriage rate (per person) ....……….....……..	..	..	..	..	..	..
Total divorce rate (per person) ....……..........…….	..	..	..	..	..	..
Mean age at first marriage (years) ....………….......	1977	29.9	23.5	1986	27.1	26.5
SMAM (years) ....…………..........................	1971	26.3	22.4	1991	27.3	25.1
Percentage ever married by age group						
15-19 ....…………………………..............	1971	2.0	14.7	1991	1.2	8.0
20-24 ....…………………………………......	1971	23.5	55.7	1991	18.6	38.2
25-29 ....…………………………………......	1971	61.7	82.4	1991	55.3	67.5
30-34 ....…………………………………......	1971	82.9	90.3	1991	79.8	80.5
35-39 ....…………………………………......	1971	91.0	93.4	1991	90.6	85.4
40-44 ....…………………………………......	1971	92.9	94.7	1991	93.7	88.4
45-49 ....…………………………………......	1971	94.5	95.5	1991	95.2	91.3
Fertility	Year	Value		Year	Value	
Annual number of births (*thousands*)...............…………..	1970	4.8		2000	7.5	
Crude birth rate (per 1 000 population) ....………..	1970	37.0		2000	22.1	
Percentage of extra-marital births among all births ....…	..	..		1982	0.4	
Total fertility rate (births per woman) ....………..	1970	5.8		2000	2.4	
Age-specific fertility rate (per 1 000 women)						
15-19 ....……………………..............	1970	78		2000	31	
20-24 ....……………………..............	1970	323		2000	93	
25-29 ....……………………..............	1970	302		2000	129	
30-34 ....……………………..............	1970	233		2000	113	
35-39 ....……………………..............	1970	153		2000	84	
40-44 ....……………………..............	1970	57		2000	28	
45-49 ....……………………..............	1970	23		2000	2	
Mean age at childbearing (years) ....…………....	1970	28.9		2000	29.8	
Mean age at first birth (years) ....………….......	1978	23.5		1988	24.8	
Children ever born per woman						
35-39 ....……………………..............	1960	4.6		..	..	
40-44 ....……………………..............	1960	4.7		..	..	
45-49 ....……………………..............	1960	5.0		..	..	
Percentage of childless women						
35-39 ....……………………..............	1960	6.0		..	..	
40-44 ....……………………..............	1960	6.6		..	..	
45-49 ....……………………..............	1960	6.8		..	..	
Percentage of women with parity three or higher						
35-39 ....……………………..............	1960	78.1		..	..	
40-44 ....……………………..............	1960	76.8		..	..	
45-49 ....……………………..............	1960	76.1		..	..	
Family Planning						
Contraceptive prevalence among women in union						
Percentage using any contraceptive method ....…	..	..		..	..	
Percentage using a modern contraceptive method	..	..		..	..	
Percentage using condoms ....…………….......	..	..		..	..	
Population policies						
Government's view on the level of fertility ....…….	..	..		2001	Satisfactory	
Government's policy regarding level of fertility ....…	..	..		2001	No intervention	
Government's support for contraceptive methods ....…	..	..		2001	No support	

Total fertility rates

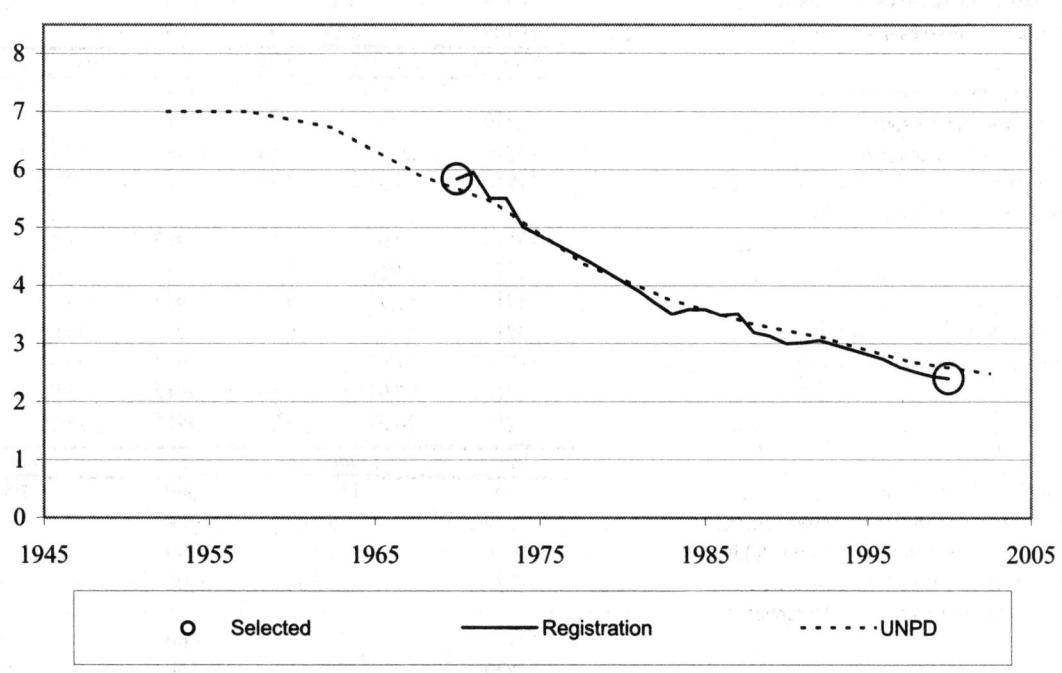

Age-specific fertility rates

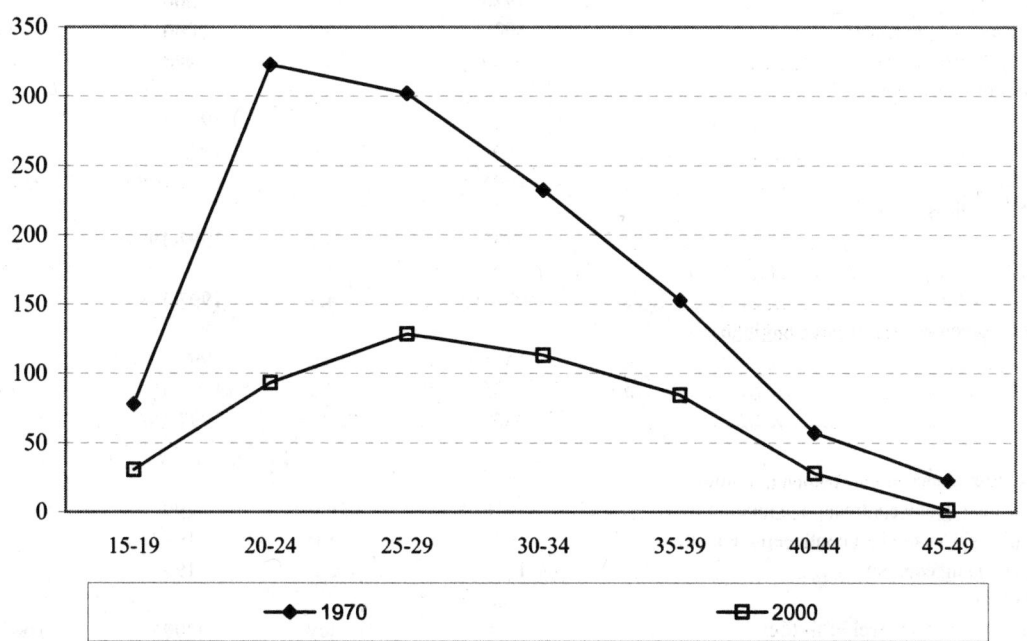

Indicator	Period					
	Earlier year			Later year		
	Year	Value		Year	Value	
Nuptiality						
Annual number of marriages (*thousands*)	1970	73.1		2001	32.0	
Annual number of divorces (*thousands*)	1970	9.9		2001	10.3	
	Year	Male	Female	Year	Male	Female
Total first marriage rate (per person)	1975	0.9	1.0	1997	0.5	0.5
Total divorce rate (per person)	1970	0.3	0.3	1997	0.1	0.2
Mean age at first marriage (years)	1970	..	21.4	1997	26.5	23.1
SMAM (years)	1975	24.5	20.8	1985	24.9	21.1
Percentage ever married by age group						
15-19	1975	4.3	17.8	1985	3.1	16.5
20-24	1975	36.6	72.0	1985	37.0	71.6
25-29	1975	78.1	91.8	1985	75.5	90.6
30-34	1975	91.0	96.1	1985	87.1	95.2
35-39	1975	95.0	97.6	1985	91.5	97.0
40-44	1975	97.1	98.0	1985	94.3	97.7
45-49	1975	97.9	97.8	1985	96.0	98.2
Fertility	Year	Value		Year	Value	
Annual number of births (*thousands*).....................	1970	138.7		2001	68.2	
Crude birth rate (per 1 000 population)	1970	16.3		2001	8.6	
Percentage of extra-marital births among all births	1970	8.5		2001	42.0	
Total fertility rate (births per woman)	1970	2.2		2001	1.2	
Age-specific fertility rate (per 1 000 women)						
15-19	1970	72		2001	45	
20-24	1970	188		2001	87	
25-29	1970	111		2001	72	
30-34	1970	46		2001	33	
35-39	1970	15		2001	10	
40-44	1970	3		2001	2	
45-49	1970	0		2001	0	
Mean age at childbearing (years)	1970	24.7		2001	25.1	
Mean age at first birth (years)	1970	22.1		2001	23.1	
Children ever born per woman						
35-39	1975	2.0		1997-1998	1.6	
40-44	1975	2.0		1997-1998	1.7	
45-49	1975	2.0		1997-1998	..	
Percentage of childless women						
35-39	1975	3.0		1997-1998	8.3	
40-44	1975	3.2		1997-1998	8.2	
45-49	1975	4.3		1997-1998	..	
Percentage of women with parity three or higher						
35-39	1975	16.9		1997-1998	10.2	
40-44	1975	17.2		1997-1998	13.0	
45-49	1975	20.1		1997-1998	..	
Family Planning						
Contraceptive prevalence among women in union						
Percentage using any contraceptive method	1976	76.0		1997	41.5	
Percentage using a modern contraceptive method	1976	8.0		1997	25.4	
Percentage using condoms	1976	2.0		1997	10.7	
Population policies						
Government's view on the level of fertility	1976	Too low		2001	Too low	
Government's policy regarding level of fertility	1976	Raise		2001	Raise	
Government's support for contraceptive methods	1976	Direct support		2001	Indirect support	

Total fertility rates

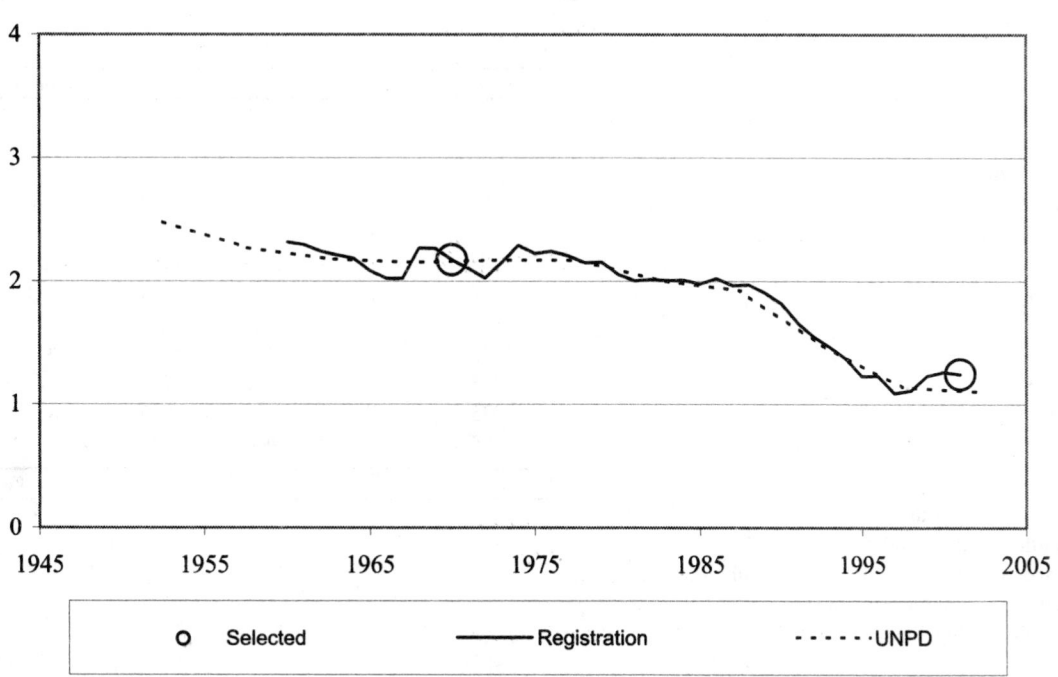

| | Selected | —— Registration | ····· UNPD |

Age-specific fertility rates

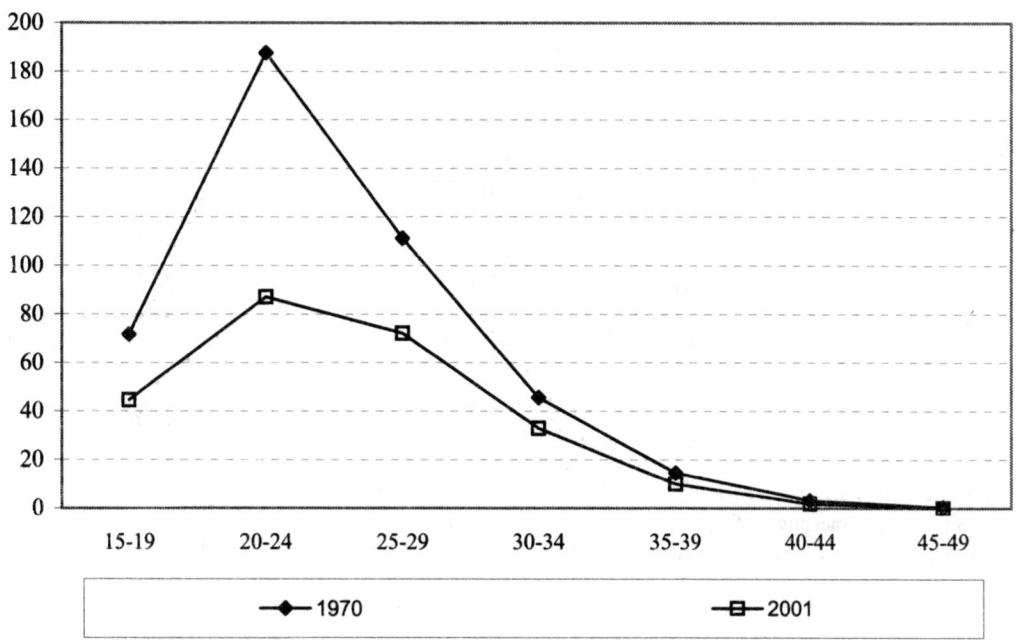

| —◆— 1970 | —☐— 2001 |

Indicator	Period			
	Earlier year		Later year	
	Year	Value	Year	Value
Nuptiality				
Annual number of marriages (*thousands*)	..	..	..	..
Annual number of divorces (*thousands*)	..	..	..	..

	Year	Male	Female	Year	Male	Female
Total first marriage rate (per person)	..	..	..	..	..	..
Total divorce rate (per person)	..	..	..	..	..	..
Mean age at first marriage (years)	..	..	..	..	..	..
SMAM (years)	1975	27.0	17.4	1999	26.4	18.9
Percentage ever married by age group						
15-19	1975	4.0	53.9	1999	1.4	34.8
20-24	1975	25.4	92.6	1999	22.1	90.3
25-29	1975	55.1	96.9	1999	61.0	97.9
30-34	1975	76.3	97.9	1999	89.7	99.4
35-39	1975	86.4	98.1	1999	98.5	99.6
40-44	1975	90.4	97.9	1999	98.7	99.8
45-49	1975	93.3	98.0	1999	99.7	99.8

Fertility	Year	Value	Year	Value
Annual number of births (*thousands*)........................	..	..	..	..
Crude birth rate (per 1 000 population)	..	..	..	..
Percentage of extra-marital births among all births	..	..	..	..
Total fertility rate (births per woman)	1985	7.2	1996	6.8
Age-specific fertility rate (per 1 000 women)				
15-19	1985	152	1996	144
20-24	1985	328	1996	305
25-29	1985	321	1996	293
30-34	1985	279	1996	264
35-39	1985	215	1996	214
40-44	1985	104	1996	112
45-49	1985	38	1996	28
Mean age at childbearing (years)	1986	29.4	1996	29.5
Mean age at first birth (years)[a]	..	..	1999	19.0
Children ever born per woman				
35-39	1985	4.8	1999	6.2
40-44	1985	4.8	1999	7.2
45-49	1985	4.8	1999	7.7
Percentage of childless women				
35-39	1985	4.4	1999	1.6
40-44	1985	5.7	1999	1.2
45-49	1985	6.0	1999	1.1
Percentage of women with parity three or higher				
35-39	1985	86.7	1999	93.7
40-44	1985	85.3	1999	94.3
45-49	1985	85.3	1999	95.8
Family Planning				
Contraceptive prevalence among women in union				
Percentage using any contraceptive method	..	..	1999	11.9
Percentage using a modern contraceptive method	..	..	1999	4.8
Percentage using condoms	..	..	1999	1.2
Population policies				
Government's view on the level of fertility	1976	Satisfactory	2001	Too high
Government's policy regarding level of fertility	1976	No intervention	2001	Lower
Government's support for contraceptive methods	1976	No support	2001	Direct support

[a]Median age at first birth among women aged 25-29 at the date of the survey

Total fertility rates

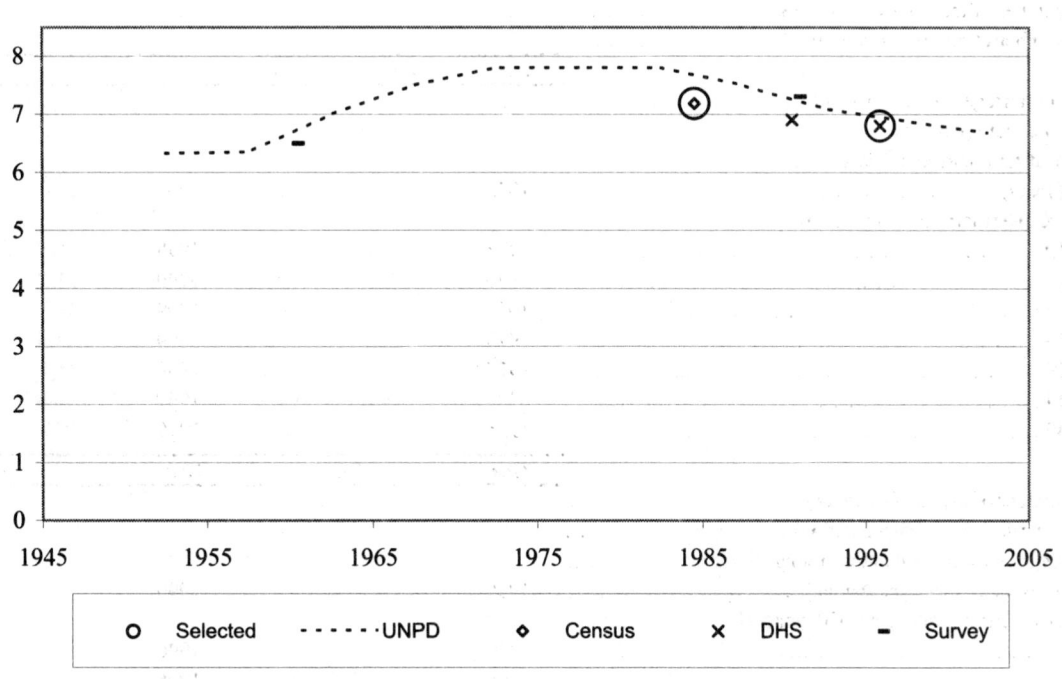

O	Selected	- - - - UNPD	◇ Census	✕ DHS	– Survey

Age-specific fertility rates

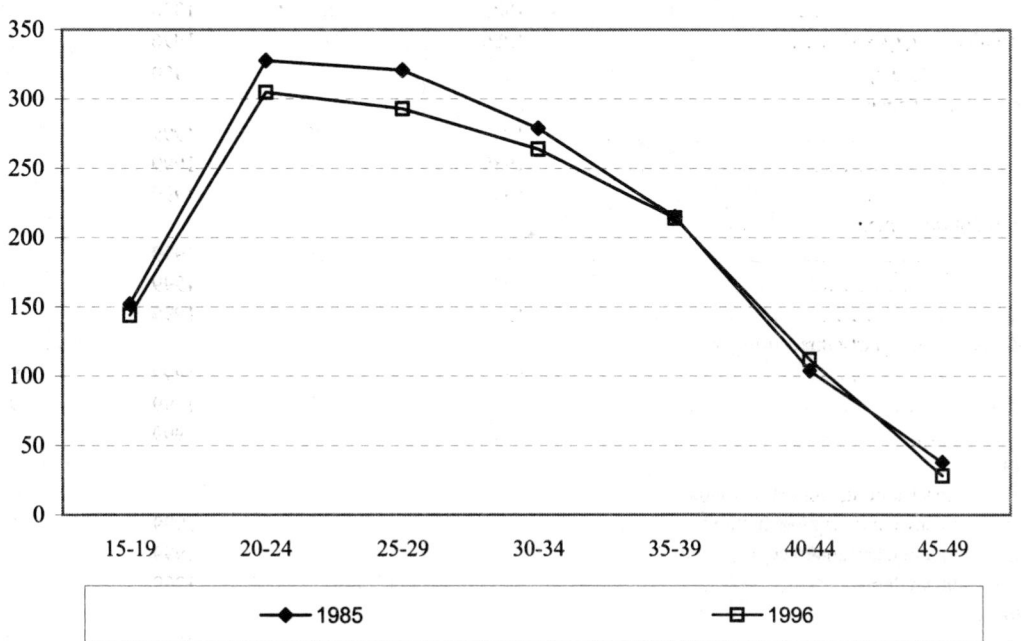

◆ 1985	⊟ 1996

Burundi

Indicator	Period					
	Earlier year			Later year		
	Year	Value		Year	Value	
Nuptiality						
Annual number of marriages (*thousands*)	..	..		..	..	
Annual number of divorces (*thousands*)	..	..		..	..	
	Year	Male	Female	Year	Male	Female
Total first marriage rate (per person)	..	..	..	..	..	..
Total divorce rate (per person)	..	..	..	..	..	..
Mean age at first marriage (years)	..	..	..	..	..	..
SMAM (years)	1971	23.7	21.7	1990	25.7	22.5
Percentage ever married by age group						
15-19	1971	2.9	12.0	1990	0.8	7.0
20-24	1971	45.4	66.2	1990	26.7	60.2
25-29	1971	82.4	92.6	1990	70.5	86.5
30-34	1971	94.7	96.5	1990	89.0	94.4
35-39	1971	98.7	98.3	1990	94.8	96.5
40-44	1971	99.1	98.0	1990	96.6	97.4
45-49	1971	99.4	98.9	1990	97.4	98.0
Fertility	Year	Value		Year	Value	
Annual number of births (*thousands*)	1965	147.9		1998	291.0	
Crude birth rate (per 1 000 population)	1965	46.1		1998	46.2	
Percentage of extra-marital births among all births	..	..		..	..	
Total fertility rate (births per woman)	1980	7.9		1985	7.0	
Age-specific fertility rate (per 1 000 women)						
15-19	1980	93		1985	52	
20-24	1980	282		1985	271	
25-29	1980	336		1985	324	
30-34	1980	328		1985	292	
35-39	1980	261		1985	238	
40-44	1980	200		1985	131	
45-49	1980	82		1985	82	
Mean age at childbearing (years)	1980	31.6		1985	31.5	
Mean age at first birth (years)[a]	..	..		1997	20.9	
Children ever born per woman						
35-39	..	..		1987	5.6	
40-44	..	..		1987	6.6	
45-49	..	..		1987	7.3	
Percentage of childless women						
35-39	..	..		1987	2.8	
40-44	..	..		1987	1.7	
45-49	..	..		1987	2.1	
Percentage of women with parity three or higher						
35-39	..	..		1987	91.4	
40-44	..	..		1987	90.6	
45-49	..	..		1987	93.6	
Family Planning						
Contraceptive prevalence among women in union						
Percentage using any contraceptive method	..	..		2000	15.7	
Percentage using a modern contraceptive method	..	..		2000	10.0	
Percentage using condoms	..	..		2000	0.2	
Population policies						
Government's view on the level of fertility	1976	Satisfactory		2001	Too high	
Government's policy regarding level of fertility	1976	No intervention		2001	Lower	
Government's support for contraceptive methods	1976	No support		2001	Direct support	

[a]Median age at first birth among women aged 25-29 at the date of the survey

Total fertility rates

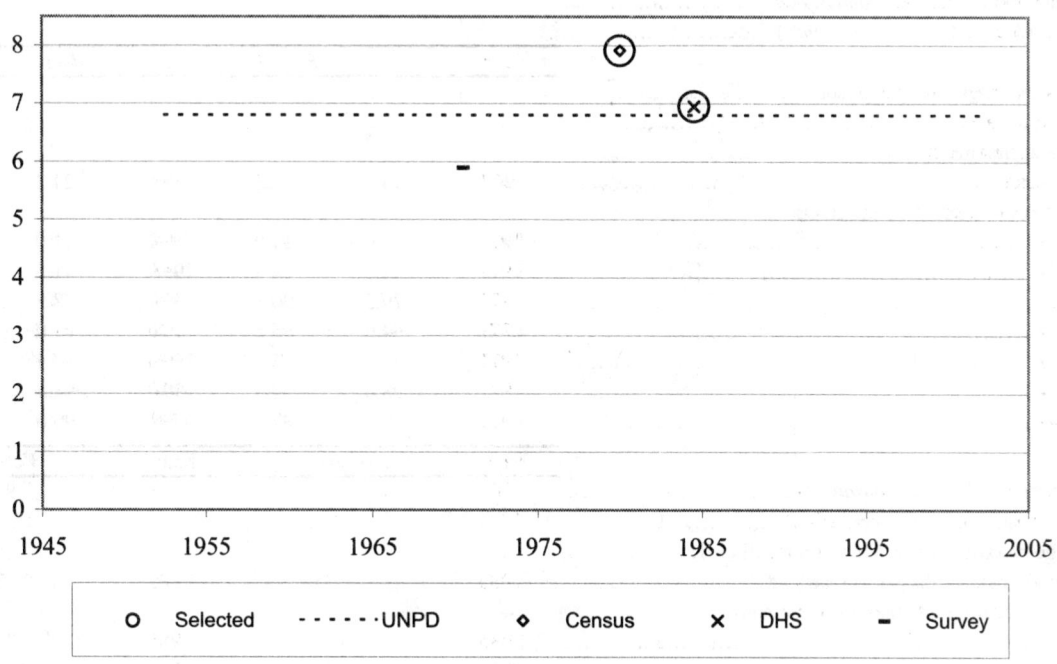

Age-specific fertility rates

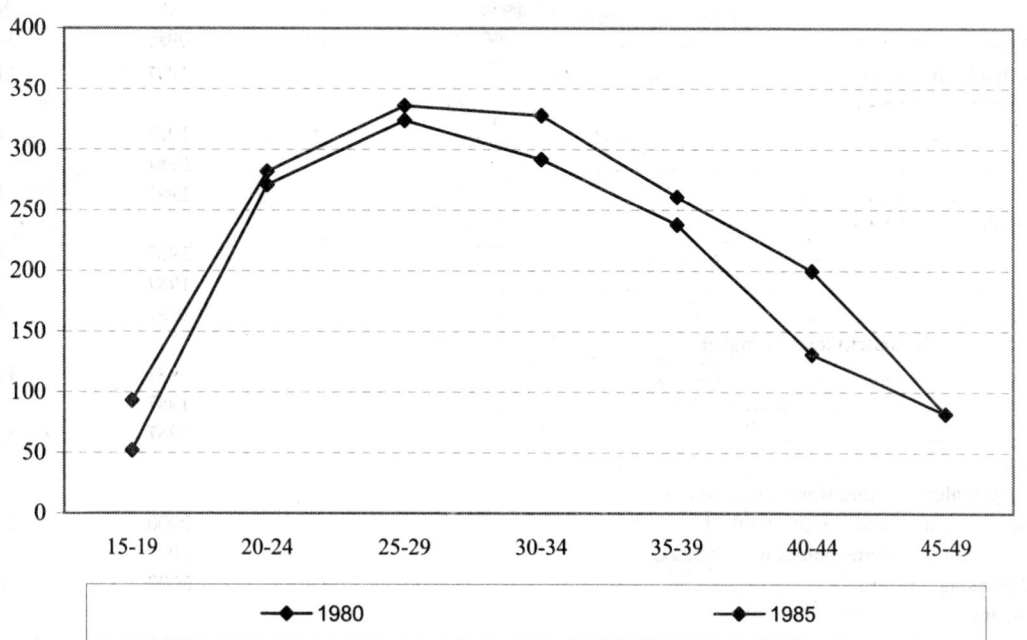

Cambodia

Indicator	Period					
	Earlier year			Later year		
	Year	Value		Year	Value	

Nuptiality

	Year	Value		Year	Value	
Annual number of marriages (*thousands*)	..	..		..	..	
Annual number of divorces (*thousands*)	..	..		..	..	

	Year	Male	Female	Year	Male	Female
Total first marriage rate (per person)	..	..	..	..	..	..
Total divorce rate (per person)	..	..	..	..	..	..
Mean age at first marriage (years)	..	..	..	..	..	..
SMAM (years)	1962	24.4	21.3	1998	24.2	22.5
Percentage ever married by age group						
15-19	1962	2.0	14.9	1998	3.0	12.4
20-24	1962	34.2	68.4	1998	41.5	60.6
25-29	1962	79.5	90.6	1998	78.5	83.2
30-34	1962	94.6	95.8	1998	93.0	90.0
35-39	1962	97.2	97.1	1998	97.4	93.2
40-44	1962	98.0	97.8	1998	98.5	94.6
45-49	1962	98.2	97.9	1998	99.0	95.8

Fertility

	Year	Value	Year	Value
Annual number of births (*thousands*)................................	..	..	..	..
Crude birth rate (per 1 000 population)	..	..	..	..
Percentage of extra-marital births among all births	..	..	..	..
Total fertility rate (births per woman)	1960	7.0	1996	5.2
Age-specific fertility rate (per 1 000 women)				
15-19	1960	102	1996	23
20-24	1960	306	1996	221
25-29	1960	323	1996	246
30-34	1960	295	1996	236
35-39	1960	233	1996	182
40-44	1960	118	1996	103
45-49	1960	25	1996	26
Mean age at childbearing (years)	1960	30.0	1996	31.1
Mean age at first birth (years)[a]	..	..	2000	21.5
Children ever born per woman				
35-39	..	..	2000	4.4
40-44	..	..	2000	5.2
45-49	..	..	2000	5.6
Percentage of childless women				
35-39	..	..	2000	8.1
40-44	..	..	2000	7.6
45-49	..	..	2000	8.2
Percentage of women with parity three or higher				
35-39	..	..	2000	77.7
40-44	..	..	2000	80.5
45-49	..	..	2000	82.5
Family Planning				
Contraceptive prevalence among women in union				
Percentage using any contraceptive method	..	..	2000	23.8
Percentage using a modern contraceptive method	..	..	2000	18.5
Percentage using condoms	..	..	2000	0.9
Population policies				
Government's view on the level of fertility	1976	Too low	2001	Too high
Government's policy regarding level of fertility	1976	Raise	2001	Lower
Government's support for contraceptive methods	1976	Limits	2001	Direct support

[a]Median age at first birth among women aged 25-29 at the date of the survey

Total fertility rates

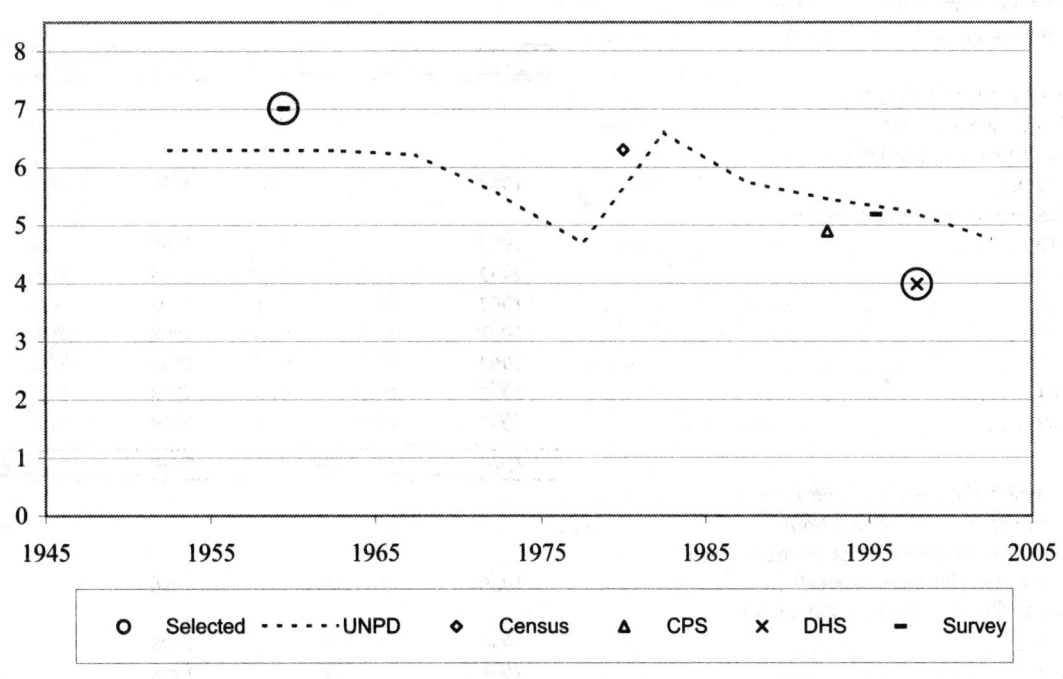

Age-specific fertility rates

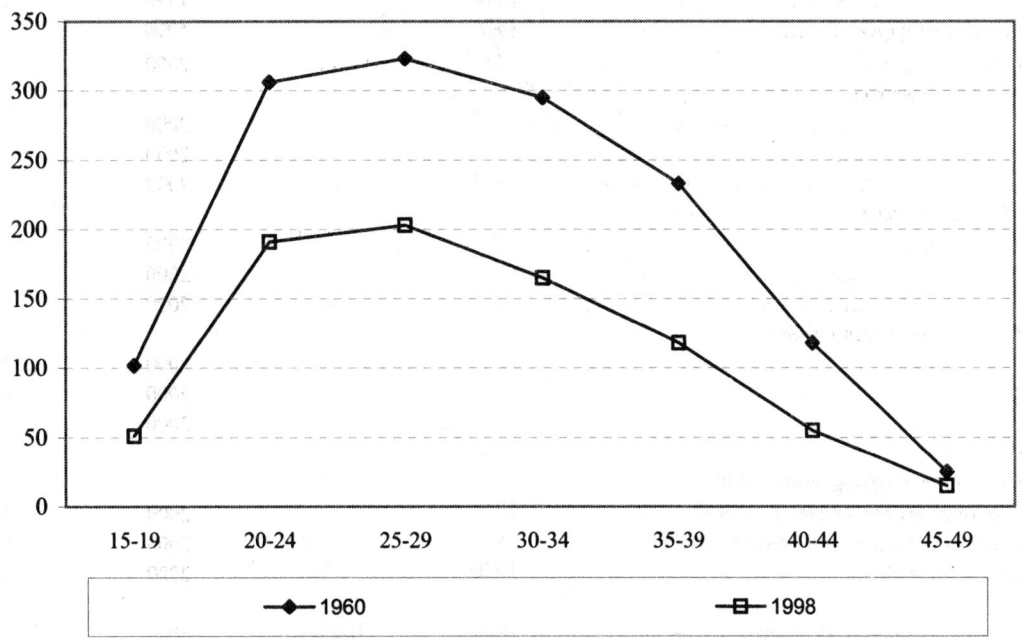

Cameroon

Indicator	Period					
	Earlier year			Later year		
	Year	Value		Year	Value	
Nuptiality						
Annual number of marriages (*thousands*) ....……........……	..	..		..	..	
Annual number of divorces (*thousands*) ....……........…	..	..		..	..	
	Year	Male	Female	Year	Male	Female
Total first marriage rate (per person) ....…................…	..	..	..	..	..	..
Total divorce rate (per person) ....…...……	..	..	..	..	..	..
Mean age at first marriage (years) ....…......	..	..	..	..	..	..
SMAM (years) ....…................................……..	1976	26.4	18.8	1998	26.6	20.2
Percentage ever married by age group						
15-19	1976	2.9	45.6	1998	4.2	35.8
20-24	1976	23.6	80.2	1998	28.0	73.6
25-29	1976	58.2	90.8	1998	58.2	89.1
30-34	1976	77.8	93.9	1998	82.0	94.7
35-39	1976	84.3	94.9	1998	93.7	96.7
40-44	1976	87.4	95.4	1998	96.9	98.9
45-49	1976	89.0	95.7	1998	99.2	98.5
Fertility	Year	Value		Year	Value	
Annual number of births (*thousands*)........................…	..	..		..	..	
Crude birth rate (per 1 000 population) ....…	..	..		..	..	
Percentage of extra-marital births among all births	..	..		..	..	
Total fertility rate (births per woman) ....…	1976	6.4		1996	5.2	
Age-specific fertility rate (per 1 000 women)						
15-19	1976	187		1996	142	
20-24	1976	295		1996	237	
25-29	1976	277		1996	244	
30-34	1976	220		1996	189	
35-39	1976	155		1996	136	
40-44	1976	106		1996	63	
45-49	1976	41		1996	20	
Mean age at childbearing (years) ....…	1976	28.8		1996	28.5	
Mean age at first birth (years)[a]	..	..		1998	20.3	
Children ever born per woman						
35-39	1978	4.9		1998	5.2	
40-44	1978	5.2		1998	6.1	
45-49	1978	5.2		1998	6.4	
Percentage of childless women						
35-39	..	..		1998	5.7	
40-44	..	..		1998	4.4	
45-49	..	..		1998	8.0	
Percentage of women with parity three or higher						
35-39	..	..		1998	80.9	
40-44	..	..		1998	83.6	
45-49	..	..		1998	81.8	
Family Planning						
Contraceptive prevalence among women in union						
Percentage using any contraceptive method	1978	2.4		1998	19.3	
Percentage using a modern contraceptive method	1978	0.6		1998	7.1	
Percentage using condoms ....…...	1978	0.2		1998	2.1	
Population policies						
Government's view on the level of fertility ....…	1976	Too low		2001	Too high	
Government's policy regarding level of fertility ....…	1976	No intervention		2001	Lower	
Government's support for contraceptive methods	1976	Indirect support		2001	Indirect support	

[a]Median age at first birth among women aged 25-29 at the date of the survey

Total fertility rates

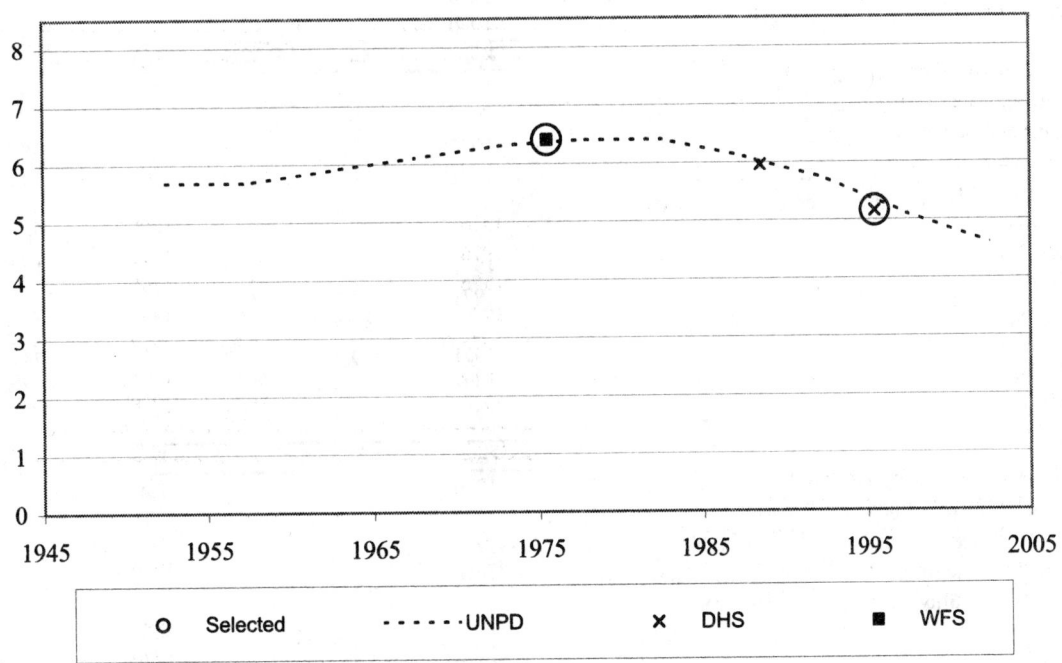

Age-specific fertility rates

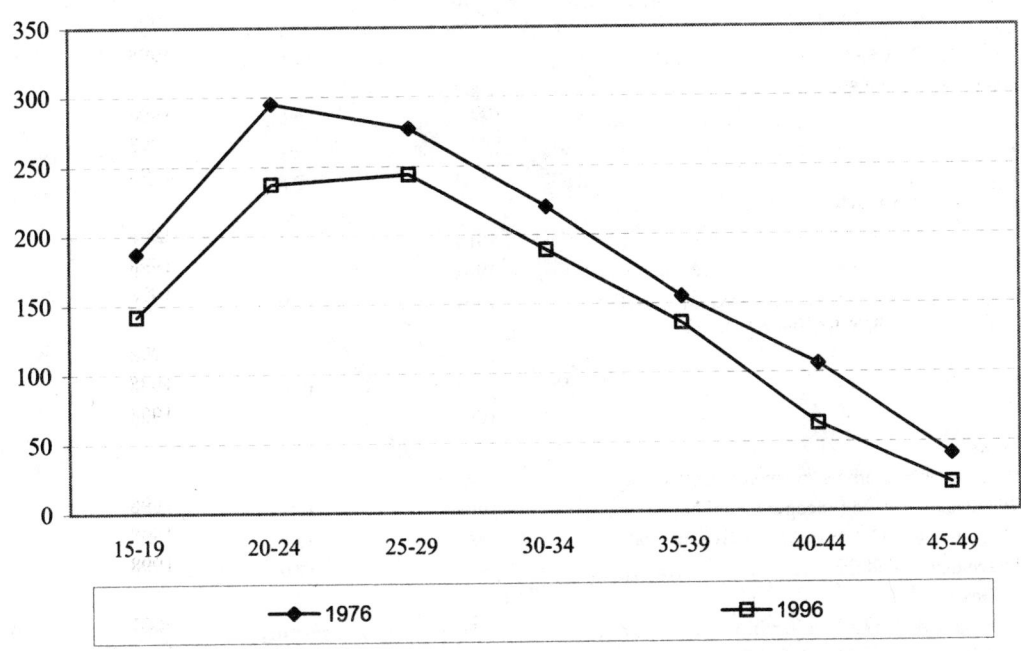

Canada

Indicator	Period					
	Earlier year			**Later year**		
	Year	Value		Year	Value	
Nuptiality						
Annual number of marriages (*thousands*)	1970	188.4		1999	155.7	
Annual number of divorces (*thousands*)	1970	29.2		2000	71.1	
	Year	Male	Female	Year	Male	Female
Total first marriage rate (per person)	1975	0.8	0.8	1997	0.6	0.7
Total divorce rate (per person)	1973	0.2	0.2	1995	0.3	0.3
Mean age at first marriage (years)	1975	25.2	22.8	1997	30.3	28.8
SMAM (years)	1971	24.4	22.0	2002	29.6	26.8
Percentage ever married by age group						
15-19	1971	1.6	7.5	2002	0.8	3.2
20-24	1971	32.4	56.5	2002	14.0	26.7
25-29	1971	74.4	84.6	2002	41.5	57.6
30-34	1971	86.7	90.9	2002	62.3	74.9
35-39	1971	89.7	92.7	2002	74.0	82.6
40-44	1971	90.6	93.1	2002	80.7	86.3
45-49	1971	90.9	93.0	2002	86.1	89.4
Fertility	Year	Value		Year	Value	
Annual number of births (*thousands*)	1970	372.0		2001	328.4	
Crude birth rate (per 1 000 population)	1970	17.5		2001	10.6	
Percentage of extra-marital births among all births	1970	9.6		2000	38.4	
Total fertility rate (births per woman)	1970	2.3		1997	1.6	
Age-specific fertility rate (per 1 000 women)						
15-19	1970	42		1997	20	
20-24	1970	138		1997	64	
25-29	1970	143		1997	104	
30-34	1970	79		1997	84	
35-39	1970	38		1997	33	
40-44	1970	11		1997	5	
45-49	1970	1		1997	0	
Mean age at childbearing (years)	1970	27.1		1997	28.5	
Mean age at first birth (years)	1970	23.7		1997	26.7	
Children ever born per woman						
35-39	1961	2.8		1991	1.8	
40-44	1961	2.9		1991	2.0	
45-49	1961	2.8		1991	2.2	
Percentage of childless women						
35-39	1961	8.3		1991	19.8	
40-44	1961	9.4		1991	15.9	
45-49	1961	11.9		1991	13.7	
Percentage of women with parity three or higher						
35-39	1961	49.7		1991	25.2	
40-44	1961	49.0		1991	29.4	
45-49	1961	44.6		1991	37.8	
Family Planning						
Contraceptive prevalence among women in union						
Percentage using any contraceptive method	1984	73.1		1995	74.7	
Percentage using a modern contraceptive method	1984	69.7		1995	73.3	
Percentage using condoms	1984	7.9		1995	9.4	
Population policies						
Government's view on the level of fertility	1976	Satisfactory		2001	Satisfactory	
Government's policy regarding level of fertility	1976	No intervention		2001	No intervention	
Government's support for contraceptive methods	1976	Direct support		2001	Indirect support	

Total fertility rates

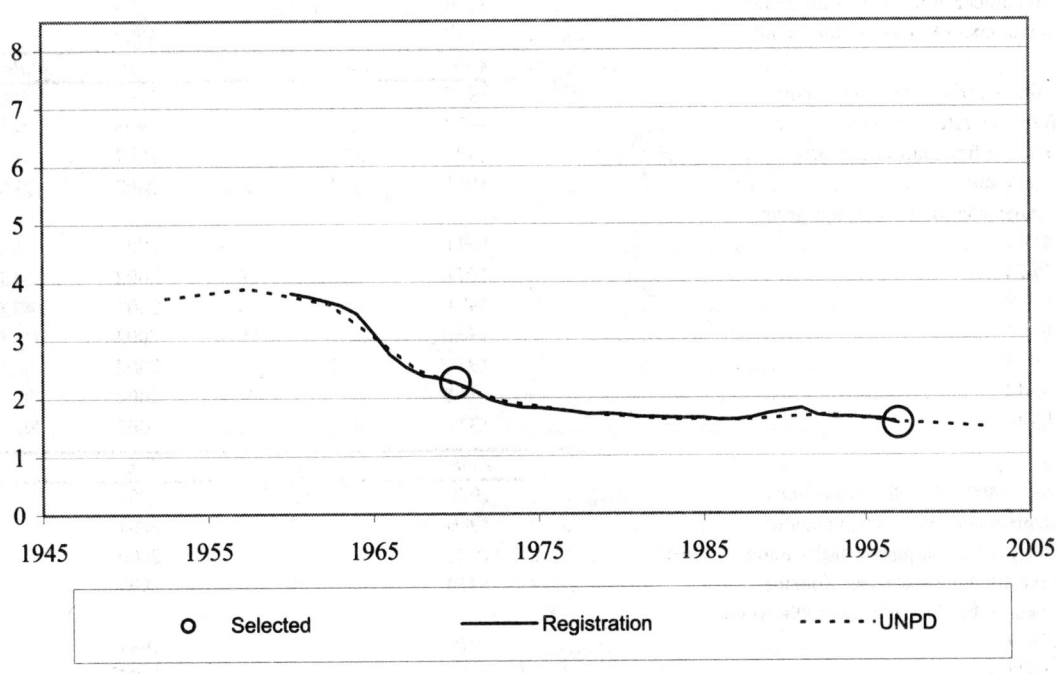

Age-specific fertility rates

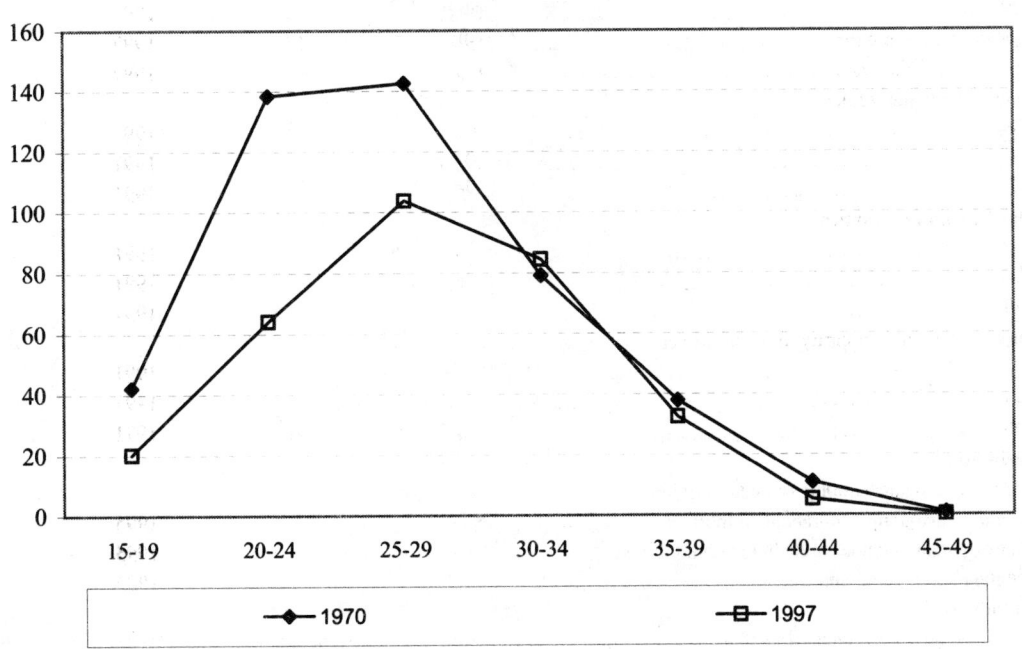

Indicator	Period			
	Earlier year		Later year	
	Year	Value	Year	Value
Nuptiality				
Annual number of marriages (*thousands*)	1970	1.0	1994	1.2
Annual number of divorces (*thousands*)	..	..	..	..

Indicator	Year	Male	Female	Year	Male	Female
Total first marriage rate (per person)	..	..	..	..	..	..
Total divorce rate (per person)	..	..	..	..	..	..
Mean age at first marriage (years)	..	..	..	..	..	..
SMAM (years)	1980	27.3	23.6	1990	28.1	25.7
Percentage ever married by age group						
15-19	1980	0.8	4.6	1990	1.1	6.7
20-24	1980	15.9	31.7	1990	14.7	32.3
25-29	1980	56.4	59.3	1990	47.5	53.4
30-34	1980	75.3	72.5	1990	70.8	65.6
35-39	1980	82.0	79.2	1990	80.7	70.2
40-44	1980	86.3	80.6	1990	81.2	74.6
45-49	1980	88.0	80.0	1990	85.5	77.7

Fertility	Year	Value	Year	Value
Annual number of births (*thousands*)	1970	9.4	1992	9.7
Crude birth rate (per 1 000 population)	1970	34.4	1992	22.2
Percentage of extra-marital births among all births	1970	50.8	..	..
Total fertility rate (births per woman)	1982	5.8	1996	4.2
Age-specific fertility rate (per 1 000 women)				
15-19	1982	77	1996	104
20-24	1982	225	1996	208
25-29	1982	279	1996	188
30-34	1982	261	1996	159
35-39	1982	200	1996	113
40-44	1982	88	1996	61
45-49	1982	23	1996	2
Mean age at childbearing (years)	1979	30.8	1996	28.5
Mean age at first birth (years)	..	..	..	..
Children ever born per woman				
35-39	..	..	..	..
40-44	..	..	..	..
45-49	..	..	..	..
Percentage of childless women				
35-39	..	..	..	..
40-44	..	..	..	..
45-49	..	..	..	..
Percentage of women with parity three or higher				
35-39	..	..	..	..
40-44	..	..	..	..
45-49	..	..	..	..
Family Planning				
Contraceptive prevalence among women in union				
Percentage using any contraceptive method	..	..	1998	52.9
Percentage using a modern contraceptive method	..	..	1998	46.0
Percentage using condoms	..	..	1998	3.0
Population policies				
Government's view on the level of fertility	1976	Satisfactory	2001	Too high
Government's policy regarding level of fertility	1976	No intervention	2001	Lower
Government's support for contraceptive methods	1976	Direct support	2001	Direct support

Total fertility rates

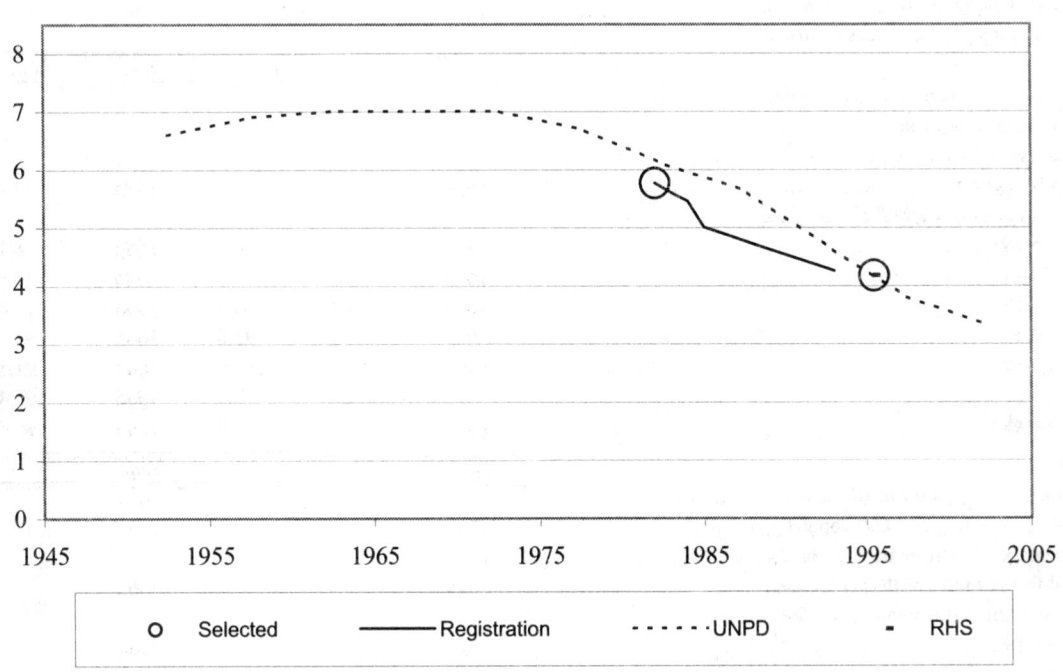

Age-specific fertility rates

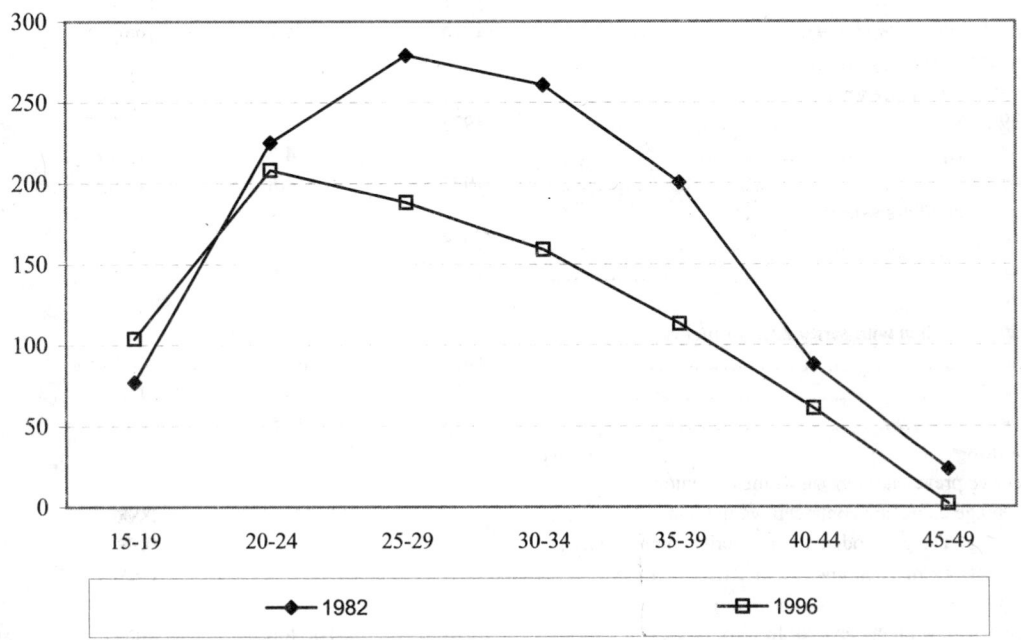

Indicator	Period					
	Earlier year			Later year		
	Year	Value		Year	Value	

Nuptiality

	Year	Value		Year	Value	
Annual number of marriages (*thousands*)	..	..		..	..	
Annual number of divorces (*thousands*)	..	..		..	..	

	Year	Male	Female	Year	Male	Female
Total first marriage rate (per person)	..	..	..	..	..	..
Total divorce rate (per person)	..	..	..	..	..	..
Mean age at first marriage (years)	..	..	..	..	..	..
SMAM (years)	1975	23.3	18.4	1995	24.4	19.7
Percentage ever married by age group						
15-19	1975	13.4	46.8	1995	8.1	42.3
20-24	1975	49.8	81.7	1995	45.6	81.2
25-29	1975	74.5	90.4	1995	76.6	90.8
30-34	1975	84.0	93.6	1995	93.7	94.2
35-39	1975	89.1	94.9	1995	91.3	95.3
40-44	1975	91.9	95.3	1995	95.4	98.3
45-49	1975	92.8	95.0	1995	99.0	98.1

Fertility

	Year	Value	Year	Value
Annual number of births (*thousands*)............................	..	..	..	..
Crude birth rate (per 1 000 population)	..	..	..	..
Percentage of extra-marital births among all births	..	..	..	..
Total fertility rate (births per woman)	1975	5.8	1993	5.2
Age-specific fertility rate (per 1 000 women)				
15-19	1975	172	1993	157
20-24	1975	278	1993	234
25-29	1975	251	1993	232
30-34	1975	209	1993	196
35-39	1975	136	1993	123
40-44	1975	78	1993	61
45-49	1975	45	1993	27
Mean age at childbearing (years)	1975	28.7	1993	28.4
Mean age at first birth (years)[a]	..	..	1994-1995	19.4
Children ever born per woman				
35-39	1975	4.5	1994-1995	4.8
40-44	1975	4.7	1994-1995	5.7
45-49	1975	4.8	1994-1995	5.8
Percentage of childless women				
35-39	1975	15.2	1994-1995	7.5
40-44	1975	17.0	1994-1995	7.9
45-49	1975	17.0	1994-1995	8.4
Percentage of women with parity three or higher				
35-39	1975	64.9	1994-1995	74.8
40-44	1975	63.7	1994-1995	78.7
45-49	1975	63.5	1994-1995	75.9

Family Planning

	Year	Value	Year	Value
Contraceptive prevalence among women in union				
Percentage using any contraceptive method	..	..	2000	27.9
Percentage using a modern contraceptive method	..	..	2000	6.9
Percentage using condoms	..	..	2000	0.9

Population policies

	Year	Value	Year	Value
Government's view on the level of fertility	1976	Too low	2001	Satisfactory
Government's policy regarding level of fertility	1976	No intervention	2001	No intervention
Government's support for contraceptive methods	1976	No support	2001	Indirect support

[a]Median age at first birth among women aged 25-29 at the date of the survey

Total fertility rates

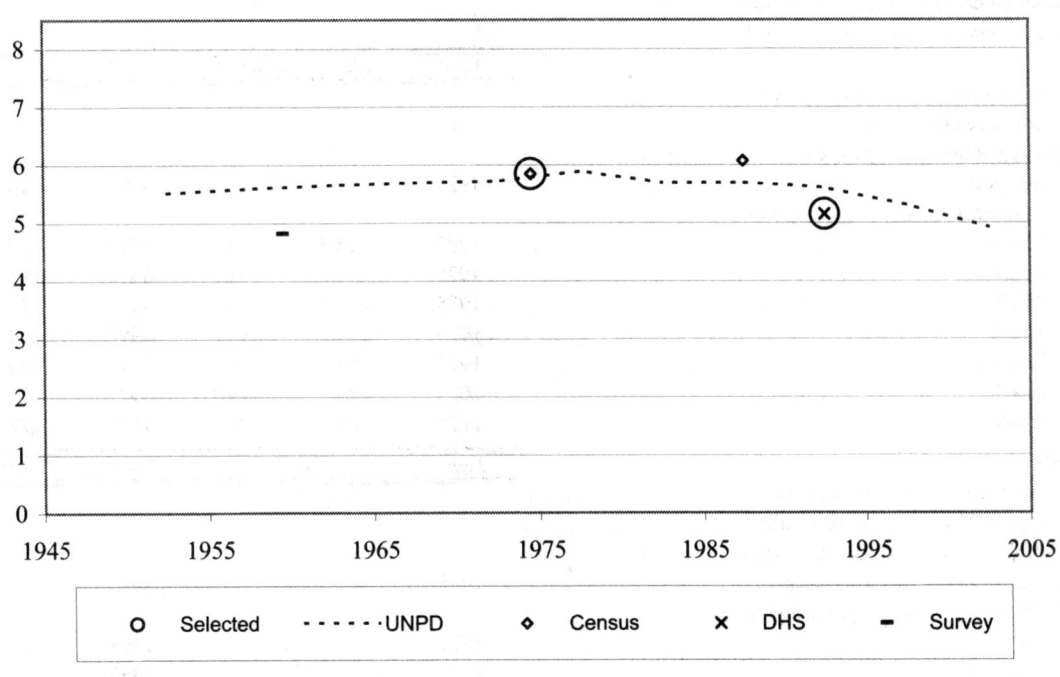

O Selected	······UNPD	◇ Census	✕ DHS	− Survey

Age-specific fertility rates

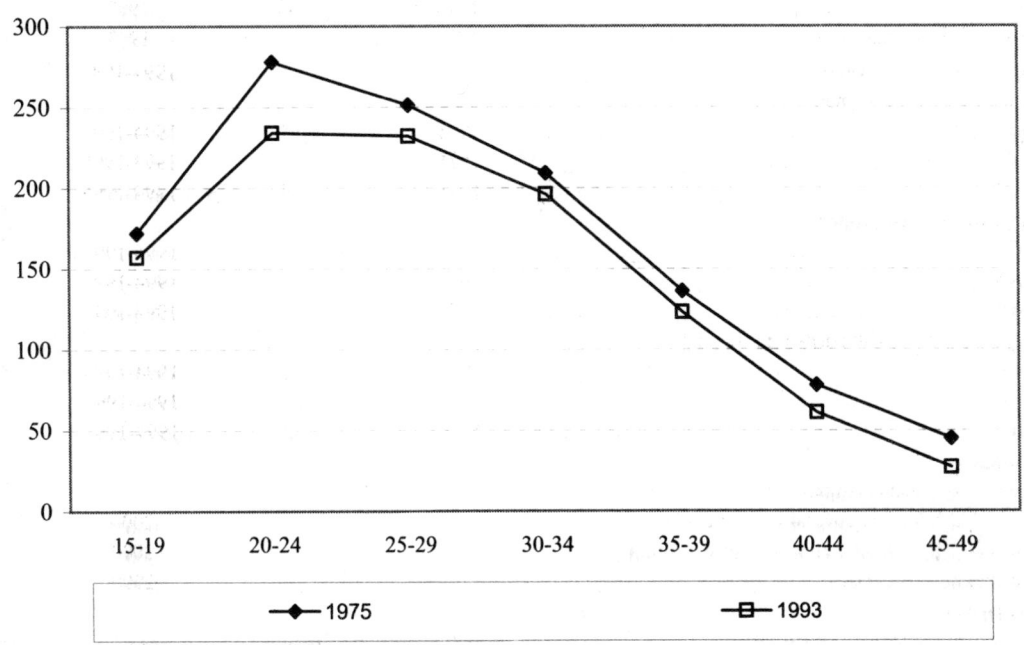

◆ 1975	□ 1993

Chad

Indicator	Period					
	Earlier year			*Later year*		
	Year	*Value*		*Year*	*Value*	
Nuptiality						
Annual number of marriages (*thousands*)	..	..		..	..	
Annual number of divorces (*thousands*)	..	..		..	..	
	Year	*Male*	*Female*	*Year*	*Male*	*Female*
Total first marriage rate (per person)	..	..	..	..	..	..
Total divorce rate (per person)	..	..	..	..	..	..
Mean age at first marriage (years)	..	..	..	..	..	..
SMAM (years)	1964	23.0	16.5	1996	24.1	18.1
Percentage ever married by age group						
15-19	1964	10.1	72.6	1996	5.9	48.6
20-24	1964	53.9	97.6	1996	43.7	92.2
25-29	1964	83.0	99.2	1996	75.2	98.4
30-34	1964	93.3	99.7	1996	95.1	99.6
35-39	1964	96.2	99.7	1996	98.4	99.7
40-44	1964	97.7	99.8	1996	99.3	100.0
45-49	1964	98.2	99.8	1996	100.0	99.9
Fertility	*Year*	*Value*		*Year*	*Value*	
Annual number of births (*thousands*).............................	..	..		..	..	
Crude birth rate (per 1 000 population)	..	..		..	..	
Percentage of extra-marital births among all births	..	..		..	..	
Total fertility rate (births per woman)	..	..		1995	6.6	
Age-specific fertility rate (per 1 000 women)						
15-19	..	..		1995	194	
20-24	..	..		1995	314	
25-29	..	..		1995	313	
30-34	..	..		1995	255	
35-39	..	..		1995	168	
40-44	..	..		1995	68	
45-49	..	..		1995	13	
Mean age at childbearing (years)	..	..		1995	28.0	
Mean age at first birth (years)[a]	..	..		1996-1997	18.2	
Children ever born per woman						
35-39	..	..		1996-1997	6.3	
40-44	..	..		1996-1997	6.7	
45-49	..	..		1996-1997	6.9	
Percentage of childless women						
35-39	..	..		1996-1997	2.7	
40-44	..	..		1996-1997	4.0	
45-49	..	..		1996-1997	4.3	
Percentage of women with parity three or higher						
35-39	..	..		1996-1997	90.8	
40-44	..	..		1996-1997	89.0	
45-49	..	..		1996-1997	88.6	
Family Planning						
Contraceptive prevalence among women in union						
Percentage using any contraceptive method	..	..		2000	7.9	
Percentage using a modern contraceptive method	..	..		2000	2.1	
Percentage using condoms	..	..		2000	0.0	
Population policies						
Government's view on the level of fertility	1976	Satisfactory		2001	Satisfactory	
Government's policy regarding level of fertility	1976	No intervention		2001	No intervention	
Government's support for contraceptive methods	1976	Limits		2001	Indirect support	

[a]Median age at first birth among women aged 25-29 at the date of the survey

Total fertility rates

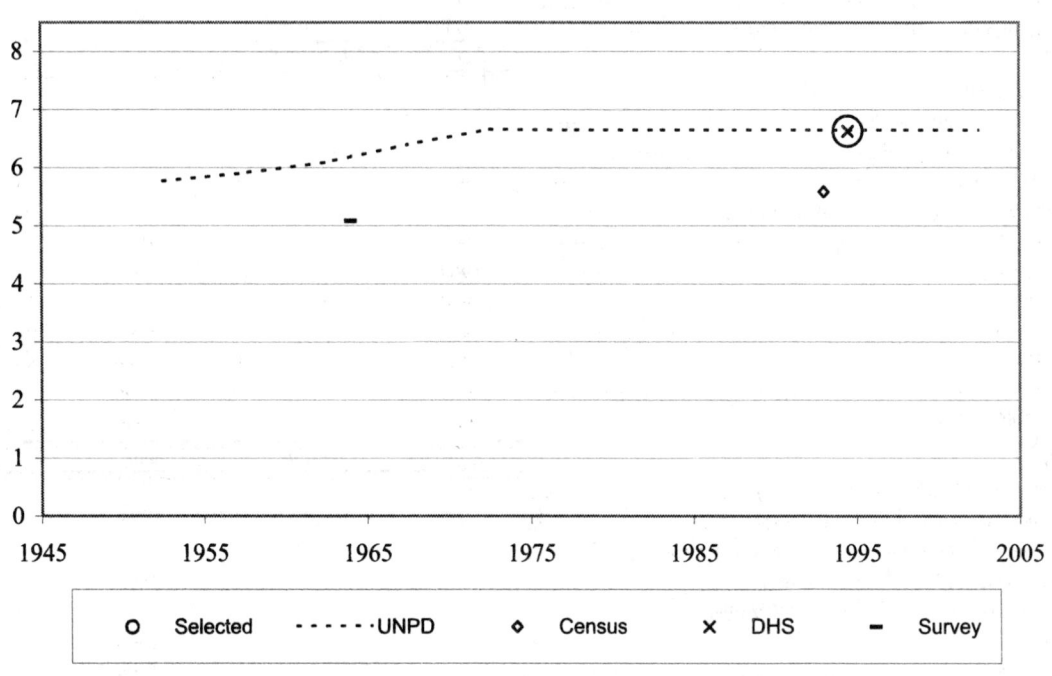

Age-specific fertility rates

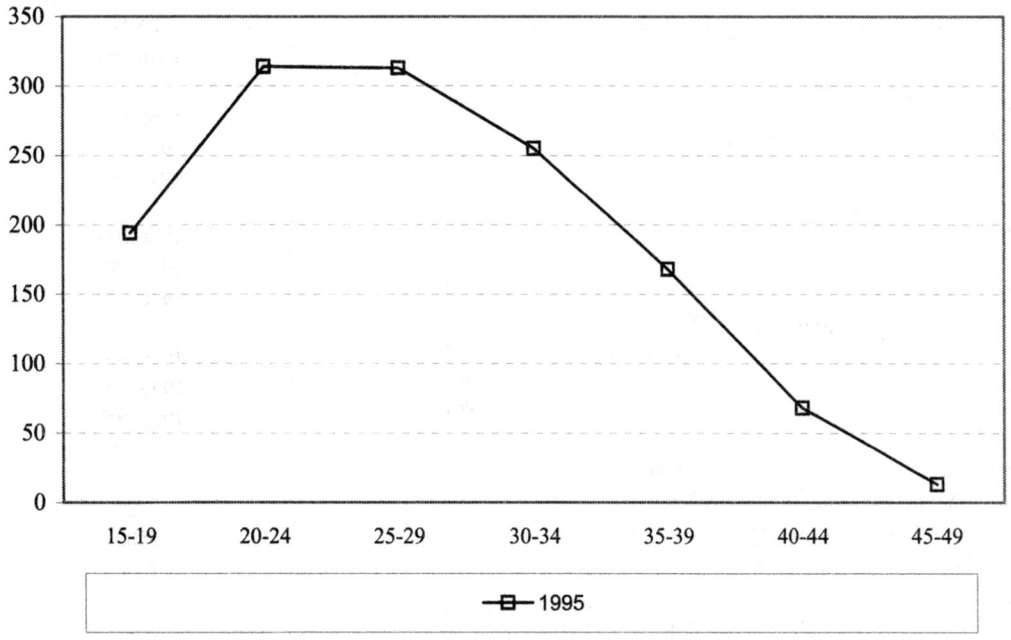

Indicator	Period			
	Earlier year		Later year	
	Year	Value	Year	Value
Nuptiality				
Annual number of marriages (*thousands*)	1970	1.1	1994	0.9
Annual number of divorces (*thousands*)	1971	0.2	1991	0.4

Indicator	Year	Male	Female	Year	Male	Female
Total first marriage rate (per person)	..	..	..	..	..	..
Total divorce rate (per person)	..	..	..	..	..	..
Mean age at first marriage (years)	..	..	..	..	..	..
SMAM (years)	..	..	..	..	..	..
Percentage ever married by age group						
15-19	..	..	..	..	..	..
20-24	..	..	..	..	..	..
25-29	..	..	..	..	..	..
30-34	..	..	..	..	..	..
35-39	..	..	..	..	..	..
40-44	..	..	..	..	..	..
45-49	..	..	..	..	..	..

Fertility	Year	Value	Year	Value
Annual number of births (*thousands*).............................	1970	1.8	1994	1.8
Crude birth rate (per 1 000 population)	1970	14.8	1994	12.8
Percentage of extra-marital births among all births	1964	10.7	1995	27.2
Total fertility rate (births per woman)	..	..	..	..
Age-specific fertility rate (per 1 000 women)				
15-19	..	..	..	..
20-24	..	..	..	..
25-29	..	..	..	..
30-34	..	..	..	..
35-39	..	..	..	..
40-44	..	..	..	..
45-49	..	..	..	..
Mean age at childbearing (years)	..	..	..	..
Mean age at first birth (years)	..	..	..	..
Children ever born per woman				
35-39	1961	1.9	..	..
40-44	1961	1.9	..	..
45-49	1961	2.0	..	..
Percentage of childless women				
35-39	1961	15.7	..	..
40-44	1961	17.8	..	..
45-49	1961	18.1	..	..
Percentage of women with parity three or higher				
35-39	1961	26.5	..	..
40-44	1961	27.1	..	..
45-49	1961	28.9	..	..
Family Planning				
Contraceptive prevalence among women in union				
Percentage using any contraceptive method	..	..	..	..
Percentage using a modern contraceptive method	..	..	..	..
Percentage using condoms	..	..	..	..
Population policies				
Government's view on the level of fertility	..	--	..	--
Government's policy regarding level of fertility	..	--	..	--
Government's support for contraceptive methods	..	--	..	--

Total fertility rates

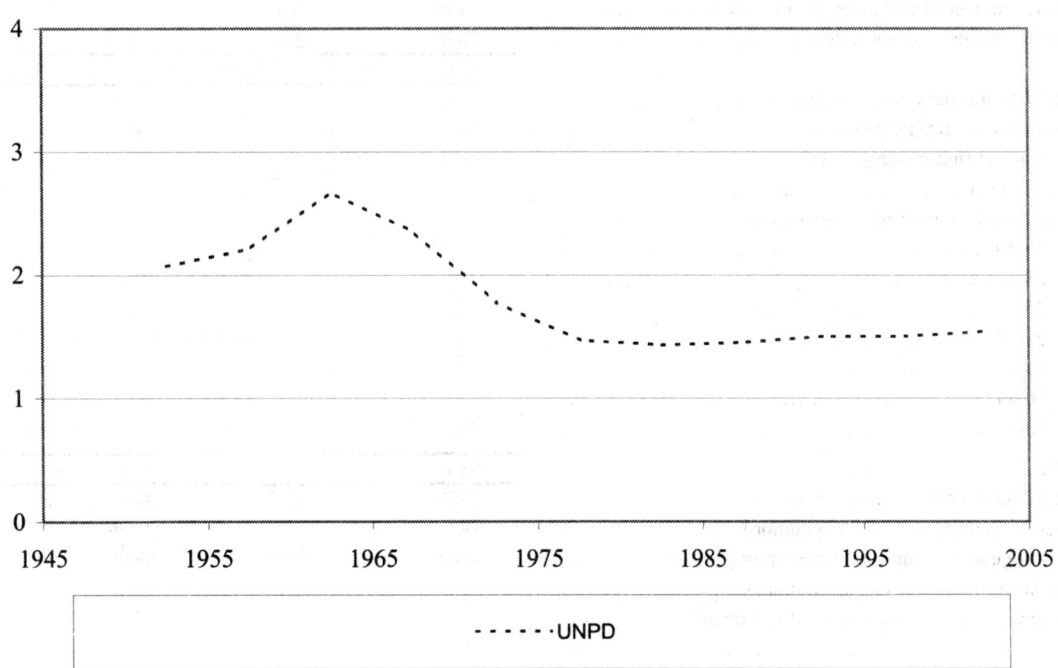

Indicator	Period			
	Earlier year		Later year	
	Year	Value	Year	Value
Nuptiality				
Annual number of marriages (*thousands*)	1970	71.6	1999	69.8
Annual number of divorces (*thousands*)	1977	2.8	1998	6.3

Indicator	Year	Male	Female	Year	Male	Female
Total first marriage rate (per person)	1974	0.9	0.9	1998	0.6	0.6
Total divorce rate (per person)	1984	0.0	0.0	1997	0.0	0.0
Mean age at first marriage (years)	1974	27.1	24.8	1998	27.6	25.5
SMAM (years)	1970	25.7	23.4	1992	25.8	23.4
Percentage ever married by age group						
15-19	1970	1.6	9.2	1992	5.3	11.7
20-24	1970	26.4	43.9	1992	25.4	43.8
25-29	1970	62.6	70.3	1992	59.8	69.8
30-34	1970	80.4	80.2	1992	77.8	79.9
35-39	1970	85.3	85.4	1992	85.4	84.1
40-44	1970	87.9	86.6	1992	88.3	86.1
45-49	1970	89.0	87.0	1992	89.3	86.6

Indicator	Year	Value	Year	Value
Fertility				
Annual number of births (*thousands*).............................	1970	262.0	1999	250.7
Crude birth rate (per 1 000 population)	1970	27.6	1999	16.7
Percentage of extra-marital births among all births	1970	18.8	1998	45.8
Total fertility rate (births per woman)	1970	3.3	1999	2.1
Age-specific fertility rate (per 1 000 women)				
15-19	1970	69	1999	65
20-24	1970	173	1999	100
25-29	1970	168	1999	106
30-34	1970	118	1999	84
35-39	1970	81	1999	49
40-44	1970	40	1999	13
45-49	1970	7	1999	1
Mean age at childbearing (years)	1970	28.4	1999	27.4
Mean age at first birth (years)	1970	24.1	1998	23.4
Children ever born per woman				
35-39	1982	3.1	1992	2.5
40-44	1982	3.8	1992	2.9
45-49	1982	4.3	1992	3.2
Percentage of childless women				
35-39	1982	9.9	1992	8.7
40-44	1982	9.3	1992	7.9
45-49	1982	10.1	1992	8.4
Percentage of women with parity three or higher				
35-39	1982	57.6	1992	..
40-44	1982	65.2	1992	..
45-49	1982	67.4	1992	..
Family Planning				
Contraceptive prevalence among women in union				
Percentage using any contraceptive method	..	..	..	..
Percentage using a modern contraceptive method	..	..	..	..
Percentage using condoms	..	..	..	..
Population policies				
Government's view on the level of fertility	1976	Too high	2001	Satisfactory
Government's policy regarding level of fertility	1976	No intervention	2001	No intervention
Government's support for contraceptive methods	1976	Direct support	2001	Direct support

Total fertility rates

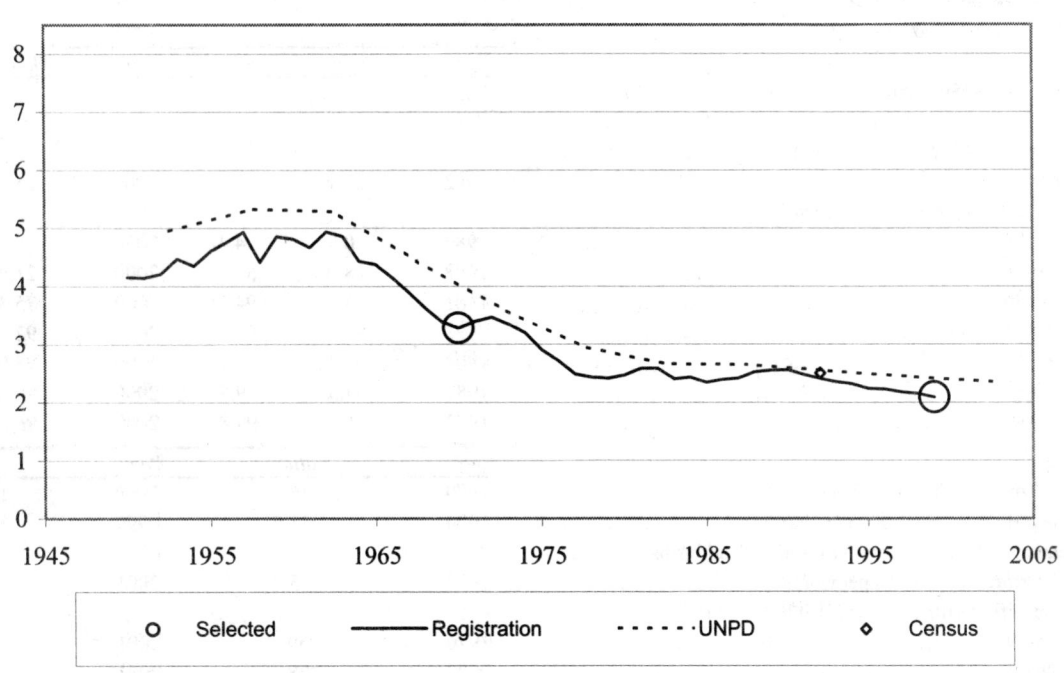

Age-specific fertility rates

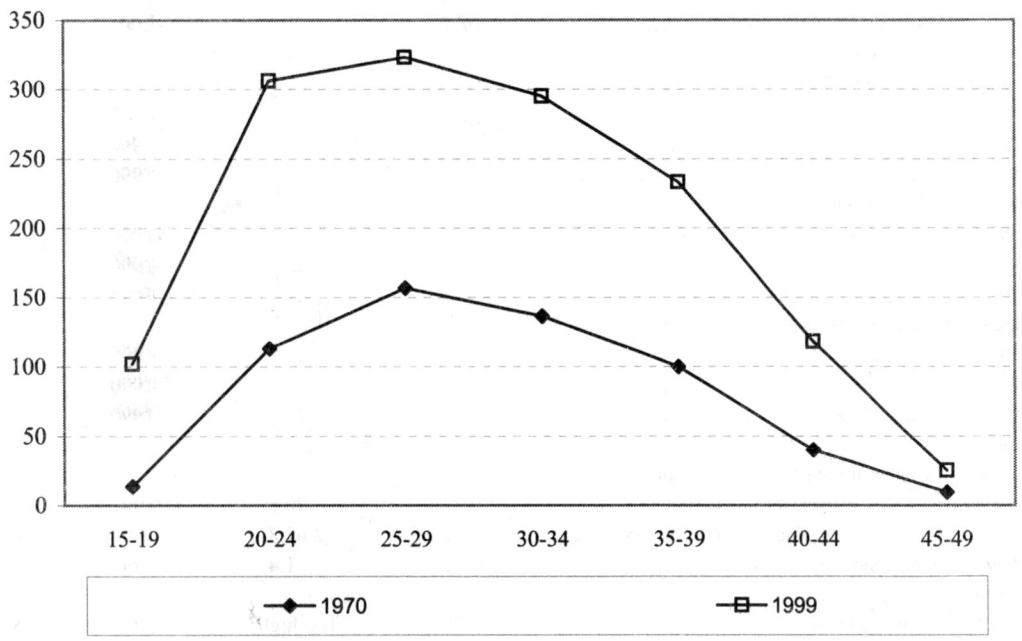

China

Indicator	Period					
	Earlier year			*Later year*		
	Year	Value		Year	Value	
Nuptiality						
Annual number of marriages (*thousands*)	..	..		1998	8 918.0	
Annual number of divorces (*thousands*)	..	..		1998	1 191.0	
	Year	Male	Female	Year	Male	Female
Total first marriage rate (per person)	..	..	..	..	..	..
Total divorce rate (per person)	..	..	..	..	..	..
Mean age at first marriage (years)	..	..	..	..	..	..
SMAM (years)	1982	25.1	22.4	2000	25.1	23.3
Percentage ever married by age group						
15-19	1982	0.9	4.4	2000	0.3	1.2
20-24	1982	28.0	53.5	2000	21.4	42.5
25-29	1982	76.4	94.7	2000	75.3	91.3
30-34	1982	91.2	99.3	2000	92.5	98.7
35-39	1982	93.2	99.7	2000	95.9	99.5
40-44	1982	94.3	99.8	2000	96.2	99.7
45-49	1982	95.6	99.8	2000	96.0	99.8
Fertility	Year	Value		Year	Value	
Annual number of births (*thousands*)	1970	27 360.0		1999	19 090.0	
Crude birth rate (per 1 000 population)	1970	33.0		1999	15.2	
Percentage of extra-marital births among all births	..	..		..	..	
Total fertility rate (births per woman)	1970	5.7		2001	1.4	
Age-specific fertility rate (per 1 000 women)						
15-19	1970	39		2001	3	
20-24	1970	278		2001	108	
25-29	1970	308		2001	115	
30-34	1970	252		2001	40	
35-39	1970	179		2001	9	
40-44	1970	83		2001	2	
45-49	1970	10		2001	1	
Mean age at childbearing (years)	1970	29.9		2001	26.7	
Mean age at first birth (years)	..	..		..	..	
Children ever born per woman						
35-39	..	..		1990	2.5	
40-44	..	..		1990	3.2	
45-49	..	..		1990	4.0	
Percentage of childless women						
35-39	..	..		1990	1.2	
40-44	..	..		1990	1.1	
45-49	..	..		1990	1.2	
Percentage of women with parity three or higher						
35-39	..	..		1990	42.9	
40-44	..	..		1990	68.1	
45-49	..	..		1990	84.0	
Family Planning						
Contraceptive prevalence among women in union						
Percentage using any contraceptive method	1982	70.6		1997	83.8	
Percentage using a modern contraceptive method	1982	67.8		1997	83.3	
Percentage using condoms	1982	1.4		1997	3.4	
Population policies						
Government's view on the level of fertility	1976	Too high		2001	Satisfactory	
Government's policy regarding level of fertility	1976	Lower		2001	Maintain	
Government's support for contraceptive methods	1976	Direct support		2001	Direct support	

Total fertility rates

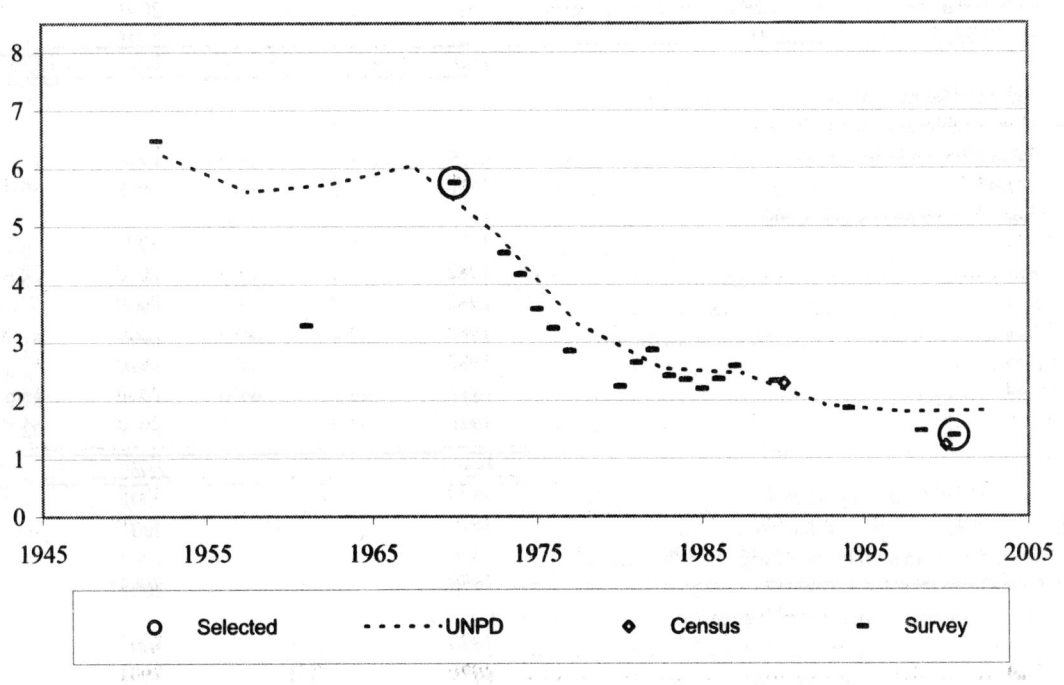

Age-specific fertility rates

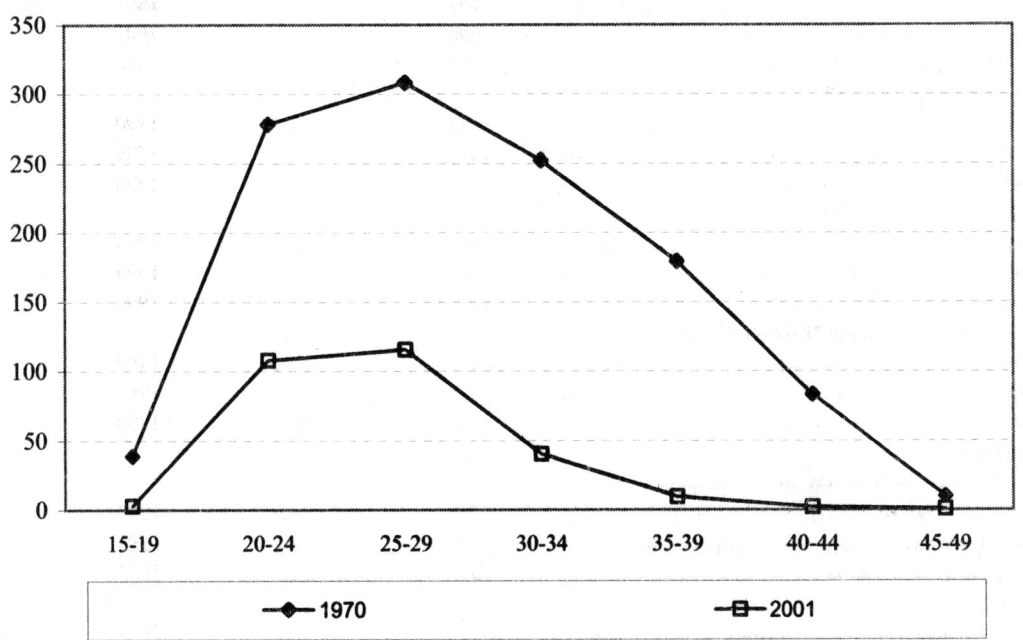

Indicator	Period			
	Earlier year		Later year	
	Year	Value	Year	Value
Nuptiality				
Annual number of marriages (*thousands*)	1970	20.4	2002	32.1
Annual number of divorces (*thousands*)	1984	3.3	2001	13.4

	Year	Male	Female	Year	Male	Female
Total first marriage rate (per person)	1975	0.9	0.8	1998	0.5	0.5
Total divorce rate (per person)	..	..	..	..	..	..
Mean age at first marriage (years)	1975	28.9	24.8	1998	29.7	26.7
SMAM (years)	1971	30.2	23.8	1996	30.7	28.6
Percentage ever married by age group						
15-19	1971	0.5	2.9	1996	0.8	1.7
20-24	1971	7.9	32.4	1996	6.0	14.7
25-29	1971	36.5	79.9	1996	29.1	48.0
30-34	1971	65.5	94.4	1996	61.7	73.5
35-39	1971	80.5	97.0	1996	81.8	85.4
40-44	1971	88.7	97.1	1996	89.9	91.0
45-49	1971	92.8	96.2	1996	92.5	94.1

	Year	Value	Year	Value
Fertility				
Annual number of births (*thousands*)...............................	1970	79.1	2001	48.2
Crude birth rate (per 1 000 population)	1970	20.0	2001	7.2
Percentage of extra-marital births among all births	1970	0.1	1998	5.1
Total fertility rate (births per woman)	1970	3.3	2001	0.9
Age-specific fertility rate (per 1 000 women)				
15-19	1970	18	2001	4
20-24	1970	135	2001	29
25-29	1970	230	2001	58
30-34	1970	159	2001	61
35-39	1970	86	2001	28
40-44	1970	30	2001	5
45-49	1970	5	2001	0
Mean age at childbearing (years)	1970	29.5	2001	30.1
Mean age at first birth (years)	1970	25.2	1998	28.3
Children ever born per woman				
35-39	1971	3.8	..	..
40-44	1971	4.2	..	..
45-49	1971	4.0	..	..
Percentage of childless women				
35-39	1971	3.8	..	..
40-44	1971	3.9	..	..
45-49	1971	5.0	..	..
Percentage of women with parity three or higher				
35-39	1971	72.6	..	..
40-44	1971	73.3	..	..
45-49	1971	67.1	..	..
Family Planning				
Contraceptive prevalence among women in union				
Percentage using any contraceptive method	1972	49.6	1992	86.2
Percentage using a modern contraceptive method	1972	43.3	1992	79.7
Percentage using condoms	1972	3.5	1992	34.5
Population policies				
Government's view on the level of fertility	..	..	..	--
Government's policy regarding level of fertility	..	..	..	--
Government's support for contraceptive methods	..	..	..	--

Total fertility rates

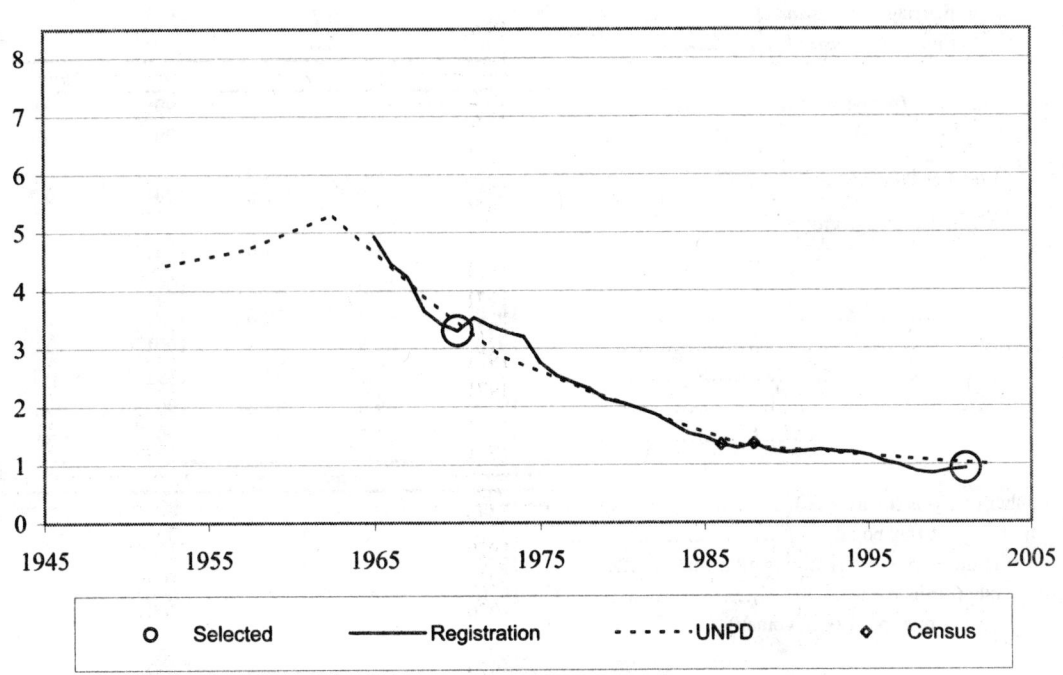

Age-specific fertility rates

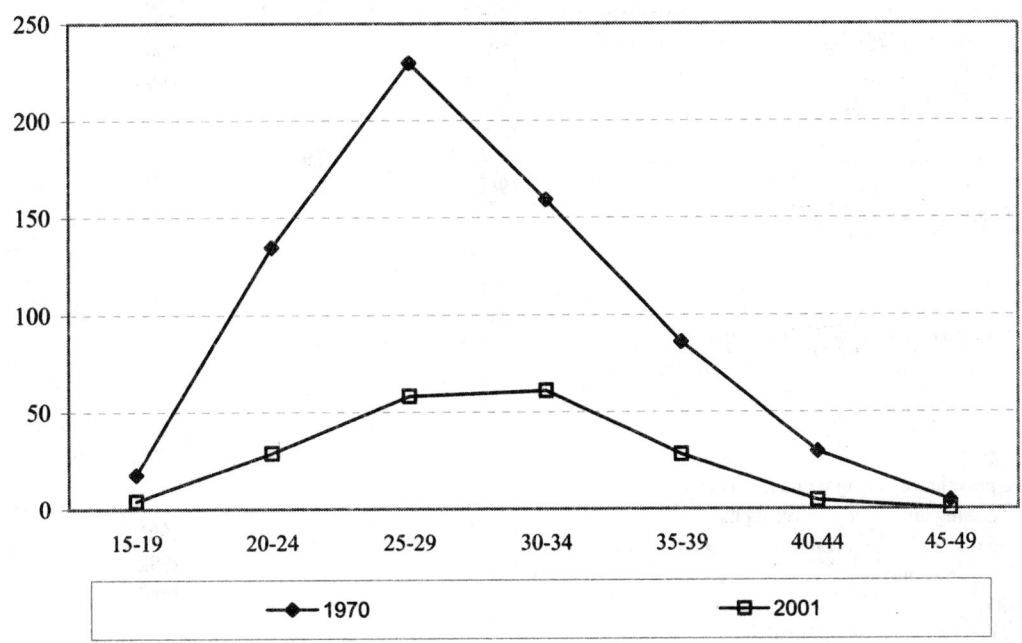

Indicator	Period					
	Earlier year			Later year		
	Year	Value		Year	Value	
Nuptiality						
Annual number of marriages (*thousands*)	1970	0.2		2002	1.2	
Annual number of divorces (*thousands*)	1970	0.0		2001	0.3	
	Year	Male	Female	Year	Male	Female
Total first marriage rate (per person)	..	..	..	1998	0.9	0.7
Total divorce rate (per person)	..	..	..	1997	0.1	0.1
Mean age at first marriage (years)	..	..	..	1998	30.6	27.9
SMAM (years)	1970	29.0	25.6	1991	29.2	27.1
Percentage ever married by age group						
15-19	1970	1.2	2.0	1991	0.8	2.3
20-24	1970	11.5	28.5	1991	9.9	22.3
25-29	1970	42.7	59.6	1991	49.1	67.0
30-34	1970	69.5	88.5	1991	79.0	86.0
35-39	1970	83.3	93.6	1991	90.1	91.4
40-44	1970	89.6	95.2	1991	93.3	93.1
45-49	1970	92.5	95.6	1991	95.0	96.0
Fertility	Year	Value		Year	Value	
Annual number of births (*thousands*)..........................	1970	2.7		2001	3.2	
Crude birth rate (per 1 000 population)	1970	10.9		2001	7.5	
Percentage of extra-marital births among all births	1970	0.7		..	..	
Total fertility rate (births per woman)	1970	2.0		2000	0.9	
Age-specific fertility rate (per 1 000 women)						
15-19	1970	3		2000	5	
20-24	1970	68		2000	26	
25-29	1970	130		2000	64	
30-34	1970	90		2000	56	
35-39	1970	78		2000	26	
40-44	1970	35		2000	5	
45-49	1970	4		2000	0	
Mean age at childbearing (years)	1970	31.1		2000	29.8	
Mean age at first birth (years)	1970	25.0		1998	28.3	
Children ever born per woman						
35-39	1960	3.4		..	..	
40-44	1960	2.9		..	..	
45-49	1960	2.4		..	..	
Percentage of childless women						
35-39	..	..		..	..	
40-44	..	..		..	..	
45-49	..	..		..	..	
Percentage of women with parity three or higher						
35-39	..	..		..	..	
40-44	..	..		..	..	
45-49	..	..		..	..	
Family Planning						
Contraceptive prevalence among women in union						
Percentage using any contraceptive method	..	..		..	..	
Percentage using a modern contraceptive method	..	..		..	..	
Percentage using condoms	..	..		..	..	
Population policies						
Government's view on the level of fertility	..	..		..	--	
Government's policy regarding level of fertility	..	..		..	--	
Government's support for contraceptive methods	..	..		..	--	

Total fertility rates

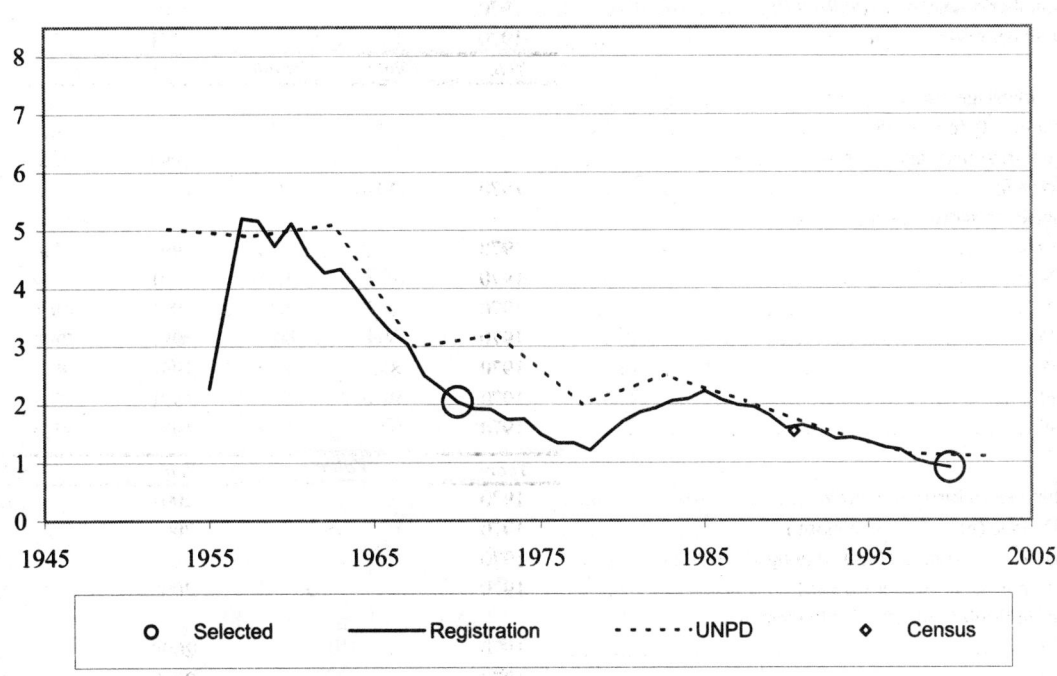

Age-specific fertility rates

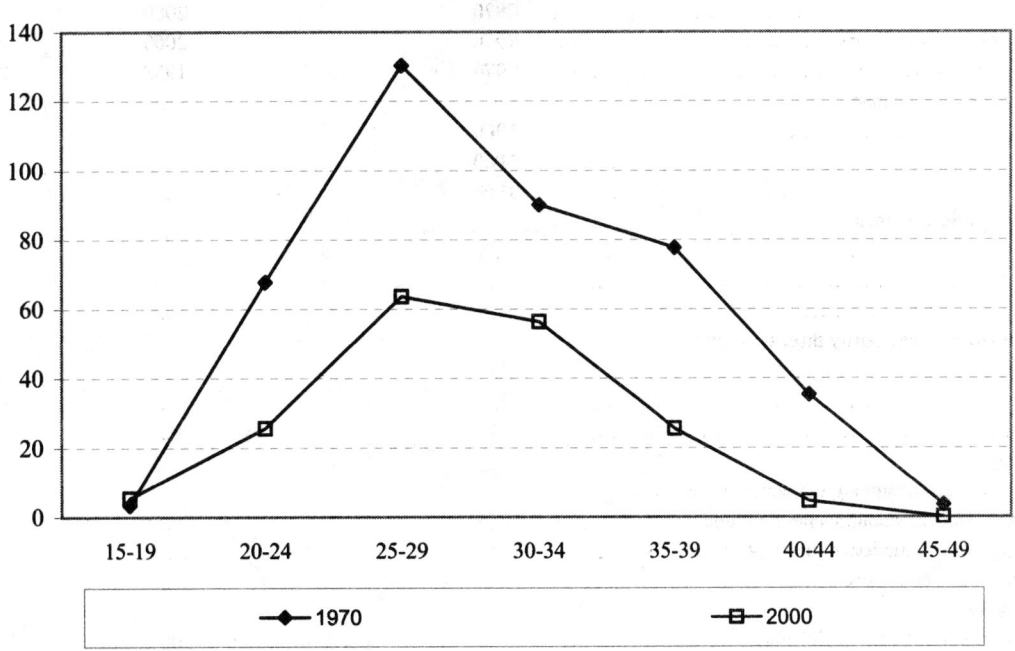

Colombia

Indicator	Period					
	Earlier year			Later year		
	Year	Value		Year	Value	
Nuptiality						
Annual number of marriages (*thousands*)	1970	54.6		1986	70.4	
Annual number of divorces (*thousands*)	..	..		1994	3.7	
	Year	Male	Female	Year	Male	Female
Total first marriage rate (per person)	..	..	..	..	..	..
Total divorce rate (per person)	..	..	..	..	..	..
Mean age at first marriage (years)	..	..	..	..	..	..
SMAM (years)	1973	26.3	22.5	2000	27.0	23.1
Percentage ever married by age group						
15-19	1973	3.0	13.5	2000	3.3	17.6
20-24	1973	24.7	48.8	2000	26.9	50.1
25-29	1973	58.0	70.9	2000	54.0	74.1
30-34	1973	76.4	80.0	2000	75.0	83.7
35-39	1973	82.8	83.2	2000	80.1	90.0
40-44	1973	86.7	84.1	2000	85.2	89.9
45-49	1973	88.0	85.1	2000	89.0	92.4
Fertility	Year	Value		Year	Value	
Annual number of births (*thousands*)	..	..		..	..	
Crude birth rate (per 1 000 population)	..	..		..	..	
Percentage of extra-marital births among all births	..	..		..	..	
Total fertility rate (births per woman)	1974	4.7		1998	2.6	
Age-specific fertility rate (per 1 000 women)						
15-19	1974	101		1998	85	
20-24	1974	230		1998	146	
25-29	1974	221		1998	131	
30-34	1974	172		1998	94	
35-39	1974	130		1998	49	
40-44	1974	62		1998	17	
45-49	1974	23		1998	3	
Mean age at childbearing (years)	1974	29.0		1998	26.9	
Mean age at first birth (years)[a]	1976	21.3		2000	21.8	
Children ever born per woman						
35-39	1973	5.4		2000	2.7	
40-44	1973	6.1		2000	3.2	
45-49	1973	6.4		2000	3.7	
Percentage of childless women						
35-39	1973	9.0		2000	7.9	
40-44	1973	8.6		2000	7.8	
45-49	1973	8.7		2000	8.1	
Percentage of women with parity three or higher						
35-39	1973	..		2000	50.0	
40-44	1973	..		2000	57.6	
45-49	1973	..		2000	66.6	
Family Planning						
Contraceptive prevalence among women in union						
Percentage using any contraceptive method	1976	42.5		2000	76.9	
Percentage using a modern contraceptive method	1976	30.4		2000	64.0	
Percentage using condoms	1976	1.7		2000	6.1	
Population policies						
Government's view on the level of fertility	1976	Too high		2001	Satisfactory	
Government's policy regarding level of fertility	1976	Lower		2001	Lower	
Government's support for contraceptive methods	1976	Direct support		2001	Direct support	

[a]Median age at first birth among women aged 25-29 at the date of the survey for both dates

Total fertility rates

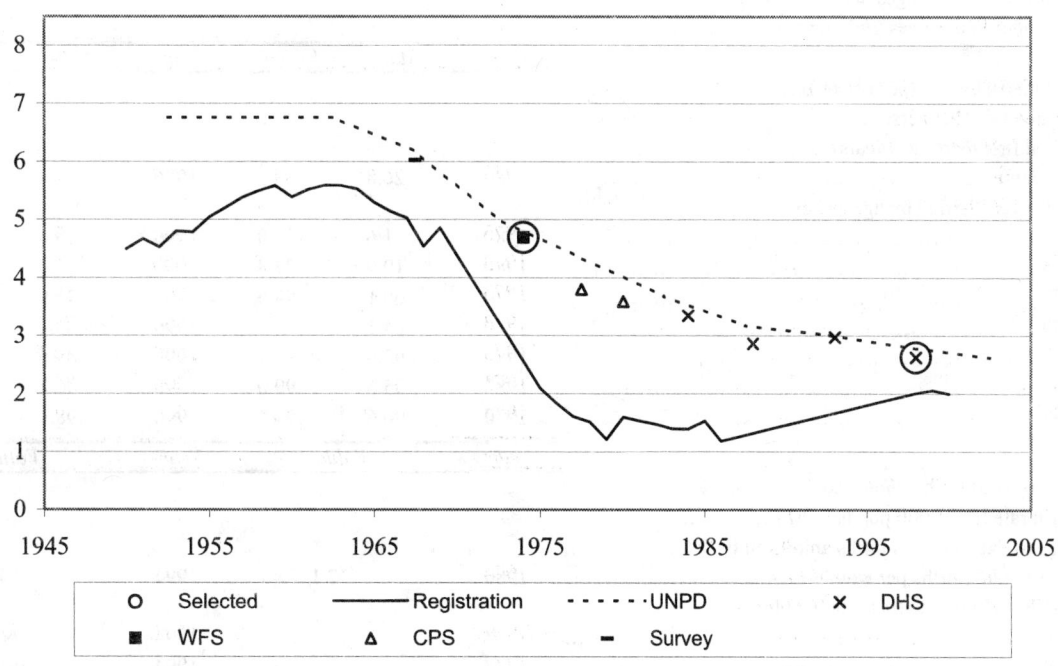

Age-specific fertility rates

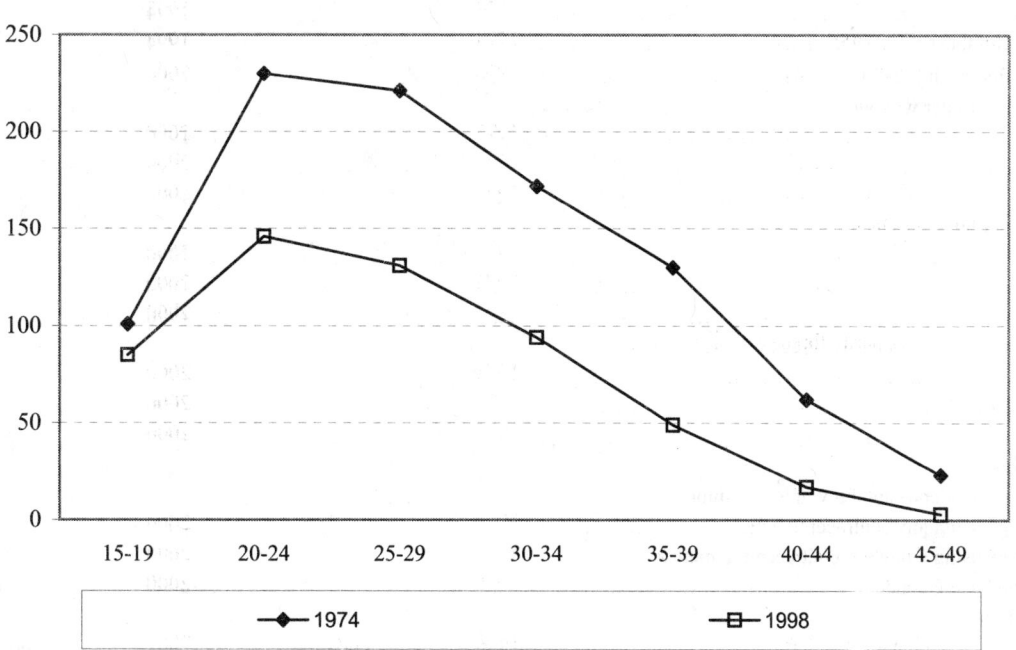

Indicator	Period					
	Earlier year			Later year		
	Year	Value		Year	Value	

Nuptiality

Indicator	Year	Value		Year	Value	
Annual number of marriages (*thousands*)	..	..		..	..	
Annual number of divorces (*thousands*)	..	..		..	..	

Indicator	Year	Male	Female	Year	Male	Female
Total first marriage rate (per person)	..	..	..	..	..	..
Total divorce rate (per person)	..	..	..	..	..	..
Mean age at first marriage (years)	..	..	..	..	..	..
SMAM (years)	1980	26.8	19.8	1996	28.5	23.6
Percentage ever married by age group						
15-19	1980	1.6	31.0	1996	3.1	11.5
20-24	1980	19.9	77.8	1996	15.0	48.4
25-29	1980	60.1	94.5	1996	41.9	76.9
30-34	1980	84.1	98.4	1996	83.1	92.8
35-39	1980	92.0	99.1	1996	88.6	98.6
40-44	1980	95.6	99.0	1996	96.3	99.5
45-49	1980	96.6	99.2	1996	98.1	100.0

Fertility

Indicator	Year	Value	Year	Value
Annual number of births (*thousands*).............................	..	..	..	..
Crude birth rate (per 1 000 population)	..	..	..	..
Percentage of extra-marital births among all births	..	..	..	..
Total fertility rate (births per woman)	1980	7.1	1994	5.1
Age-specific fertility rate (per 1 000 women)				
15-19	..	..	1994	66
20-24	..	..	1994	196
25-29	..	..	1994	237
30-34	..	..	1994	246
35-39	..	..	1994	164
40-44	..	..	1994	78
45-49	..	..	1994	29
Mean age at childbearing (years)	..	..	1994	30.4
Mean age at first birth (years)[a]	..	..	1996	22.4
Children ever born per woman				
35-39	..	..	1996	5.3
40-44	..	..	1996	6.4
45-49	..	..	1996	7.1
Percentage of childless women				
35-39	..	..	1996	5.4
40-44	..	..	1996	4.7
45-49	..	..	1996	2.4
Percentage of women with parity three or higher				
35-39		..	1996	81.3
40-44	..	..	1996	82.6
45-49	..	..	1996	87.6

Family Planning

Indicator	Year	Value	Year	Value
Contraceptive prevalence among women in union				
Percentage using any contraceptive method	..	..	2000	25.7
Percentage using a modern contraceptive method	..	..	2000	19.3
Percentage using condoms	..	..	2000	0.7

Population policies

Indicator	Year	Value	Year	Value
Government's view on the level of fertility	1976	Too high	2001	Too high
Government's policy regarding level of fertility	1976	No intervention	2001	Lower
Government's support for contraceptive methods	1976	No support	2001	Direct support

[a]Median age at first birth among women aged 25-29 at the date of the survey

Total fertility rates

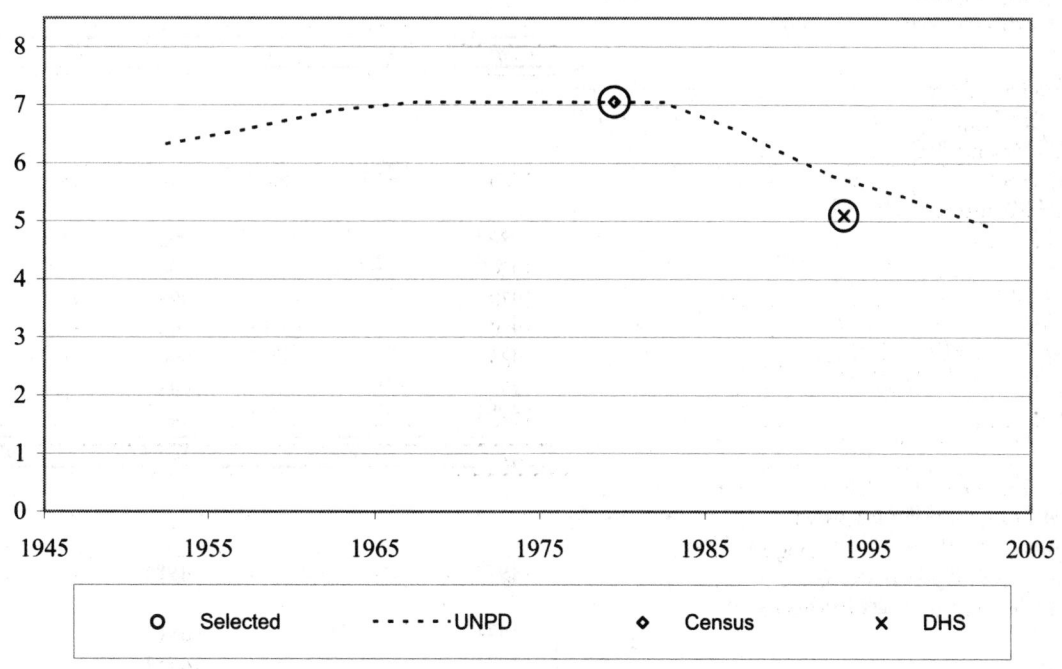

Age-specific fertility rates

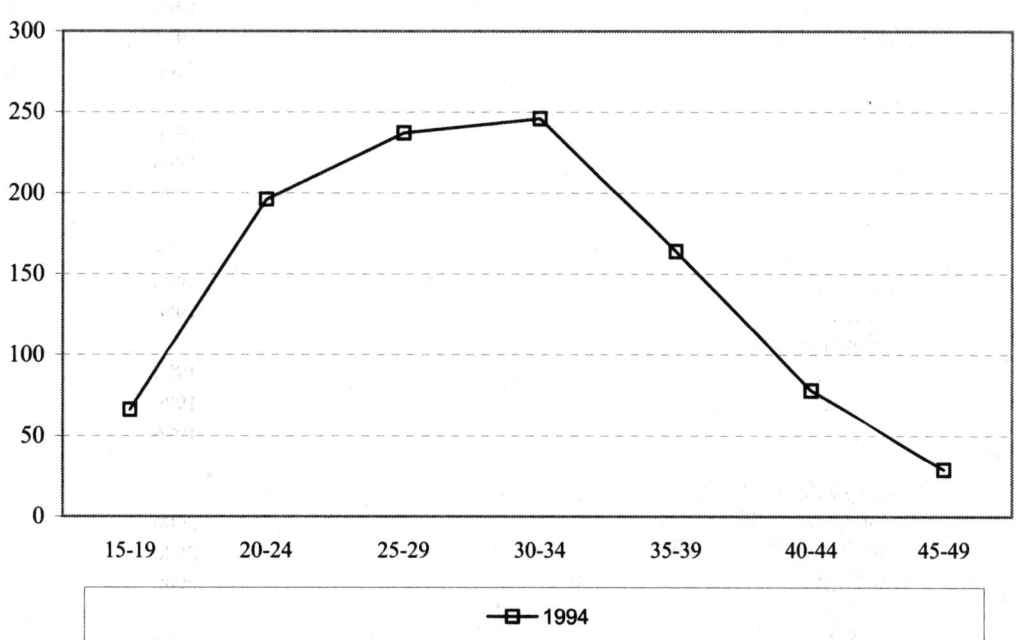

Indicator	Period			
	Earlier year		**Later year**	
	Year	Value	Year	Value
Nuptiality				
Annual number of marriages (*thousands*)	..	..	..	..
Annual number of divorces (*thousands*)	..	..	..	..

	Year	Male	Female	Year	Male	Female
Total first marriage rate (per person)	..	..	..	..	..	..
Total divorce rate (per person)	..	..	..	..	..	..
Mean age at first marriage (years)	..	..	..	..	..	..
SMAM (years)	1984	27.9	22.6	..	..	..
Percentage ever married by age group						
15-19	1984	1.4	18.1	..	..	..
20-24	1984	12.9	53.6	..	..	..
25-29	1984	48.2	76.3	..	..	..
30-34	1984	77.0	86.1	..	..	..
35-39	1984	87.9	90.8	..	..	..
40-44	1984	91.9	92.8	..	..	..
45-49	1984	92.8	93.1	..	..	..

Fertility	Year	Value	Year	Value
Annual number of births (*thousands*)	..	..	..	..
Crude birth rate (per 1 000 population)	..	..	..	..
Percentage of extra-marital births among all births	..	..	..	..
Total fertility rate (births per woman)	1974	7.0	1984	5.9
Age-specific fertility rate (per 1 000 women)				
15-19	1974	156	1984	138
20-24	1974	305	1984	250
25-29	1974	305	1984	267
30-34	1974	255	1984	240
35-39	1974	203	1984	176
40-44	1974	122	1984	89
45-49	1974	52	1984	28
Mean age at childbearing (years)	1974	29.7	1984	29.4
Mean age at first birth (years)	..	..	..	..
Children ever born per woman				
35-39	..	..	..	..
40-44	..	..	..	..
45-49	..	..	..	..
Percentage of childless women				
35-39	..	..	..	..
40-44	..	..	..	..
45-49	..	..	..	..
Percentage of women with parity three or higher				
35-39	..	..	..	..
40-44	..	..	..	..
45-49	..	..	..	..
Family Planning				
Contraceptive prevalence among women in union				
Percentage using any contraceptive method	..	..	..	..
Percentage using a modern contraceptive method	..	..	..	..
Percentage using condoms	..	..	..	..
Population policies				
Government's view on the level of fertility	1976	Satisfactory	2001	Too high
Government's policy regarding level of fertility	1976	No intervention	2001	Lower
Government's support for contraceptive methods	1976	Direct support	2001	Direct support

Total fertility rates

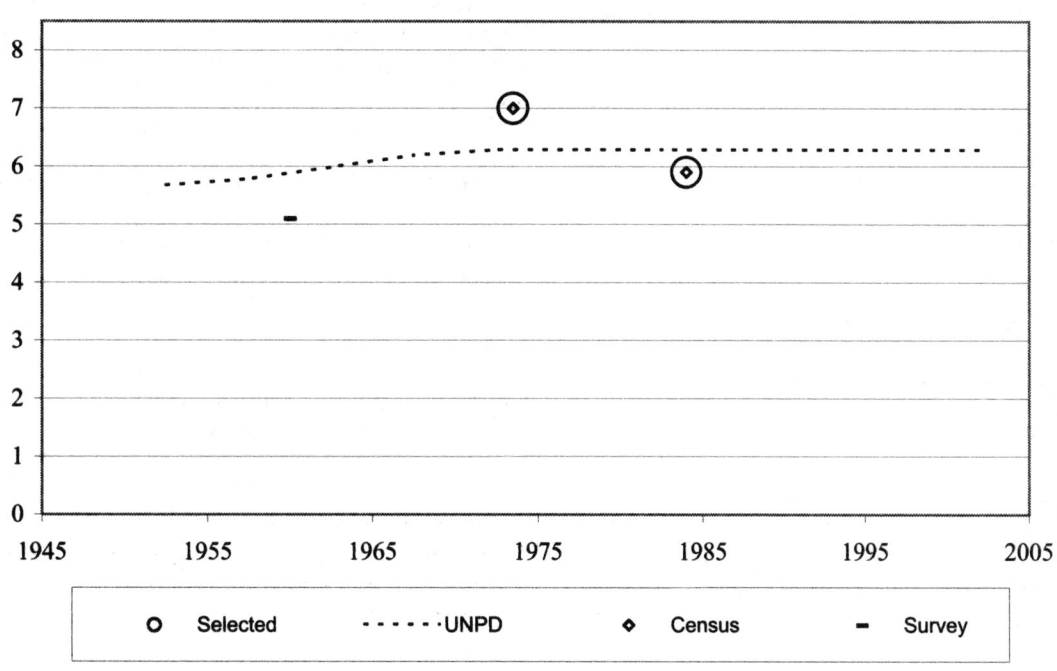

Age-specific fertility rates

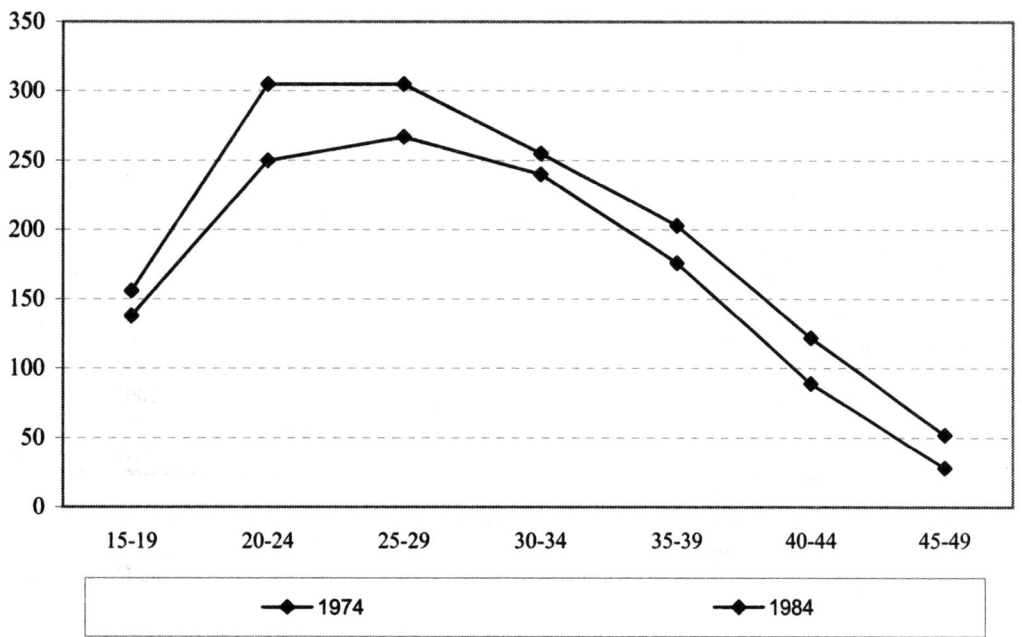

Costa Rica

Indicator	Period					
	Earlier year			Later year		
	Year	Value		Year	Value	
Nuptiality						
Annual number of marriages (*thousands*)	1970	11.0		1997	24.3	
Annual number of divorces (*thousands*)	1970	0.2		1998	7.2	
	Year	Male	Female	Year	Male	Female
Total first marriage rate (per person)	..	..	..	1991	0.5	0.5
Total divorce rate (per person)	1970	0.0	0.0	1981	0.1	0.1
Mean age at first marriage (years)	..	..	..	1991	24.3	27.2
SMAM (years)	1973	25.4	21.7	1986	..	20.9
Percentage ever married by age group						
15-19	1973	1.9	15.1	1986	..	20.0
20-24	1973	29.2	51.3	1986	..	59.0
25-29	1973	65.0	73.5	1986	..	83.0
30-34	1973	80.6	82.3	1986	..	91.0
35-39	1973	85.9	85.2	1986	..	92.0
40-44	1973	88.4	85.8	1986	..	93.0
45-49	1973	89.7	85.4	1986	..	91.0
Fertility	Year	Value		Year	Value	
Annual number of births (*thousands*)............................	1970	57.8		1999	78.5	
Crude birth rate (per 1 000 population)	1970	33.4		1999	21.9	
Percentage of extra-marital births among all births	1970	29.4		1997	48.2	
Total fertility rate (births per woman)	1970	4.9		1999	2.4	
Age-specific fertility rate (per 1 000 women)						
15-19	1970	103		1999	84	
20-24	1970	237		1999	131	
25-29	1970	231		1999	122	
30-34	1970	188		1999	84	
35-39	1970	144		1999	46	
40-44	1970	69		1999	14	
45-49	1970	12		1999	1	
Mean age at childbearing (years)	1970	29.0		1999	26.7	
Mean age at first birth (years)	1973	22.5		1997	22.6	
Children ever born per woman						
35-39	1973	5.5		..	..	
40-44	1973	6.4		..	..	
45-49	1973	6.7		..	..	
Percentage of childless women						
35-39	1973	9.9		..	..	
40-44	1973	9.5		..	..	
45-49	1973	10.7		..	..	
Percentage of women with parity three or higher						
35-39	1973	76.2		..	..	
40-44	1973	78.0		..	..	
45-49	1973	76.9		..	..	
Family Planning						
Contraceptive prevalence among women in union						
Percentage using any contraceptive method	1976	64.4		1993	75.0	
Percentage using a modern contraceptive method	1976	53.5		1993	64.6	
Percentage using condoms	1976	8.8		1993	15.7	
Population policies						
Government's view on the level of fertility	1976	Too high		2001	Satisfactory	
Government's policy regarding level of fertility	1976	No intervention		2001	Lower	
Government's support for contraceptive methods	1976	Direct support		2001	Direct support	

Total fertility rates

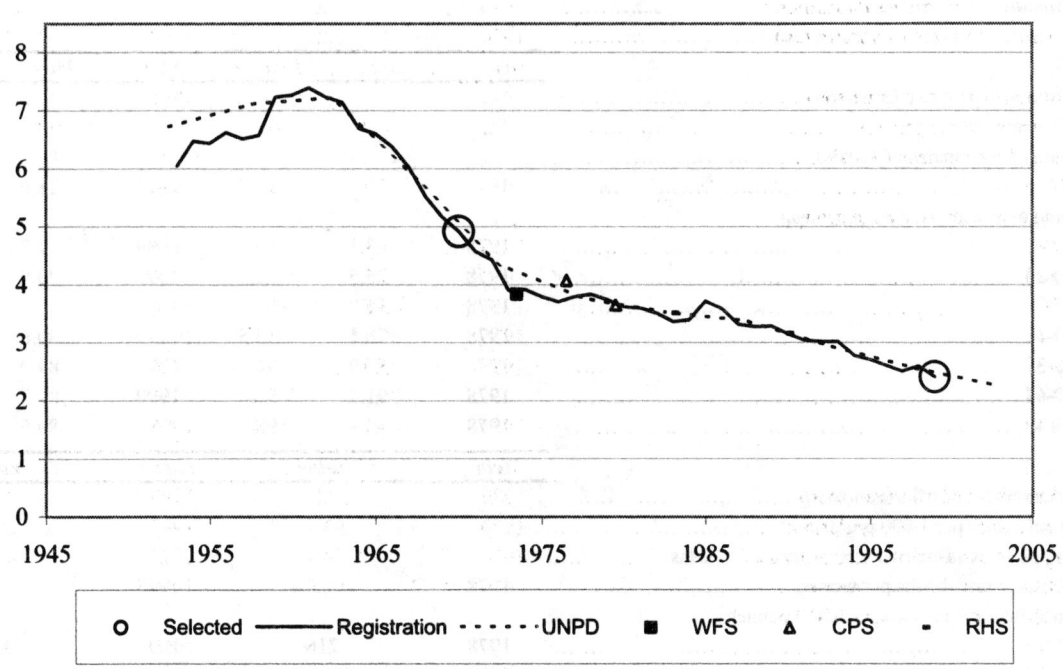

Age-specific fertility rates

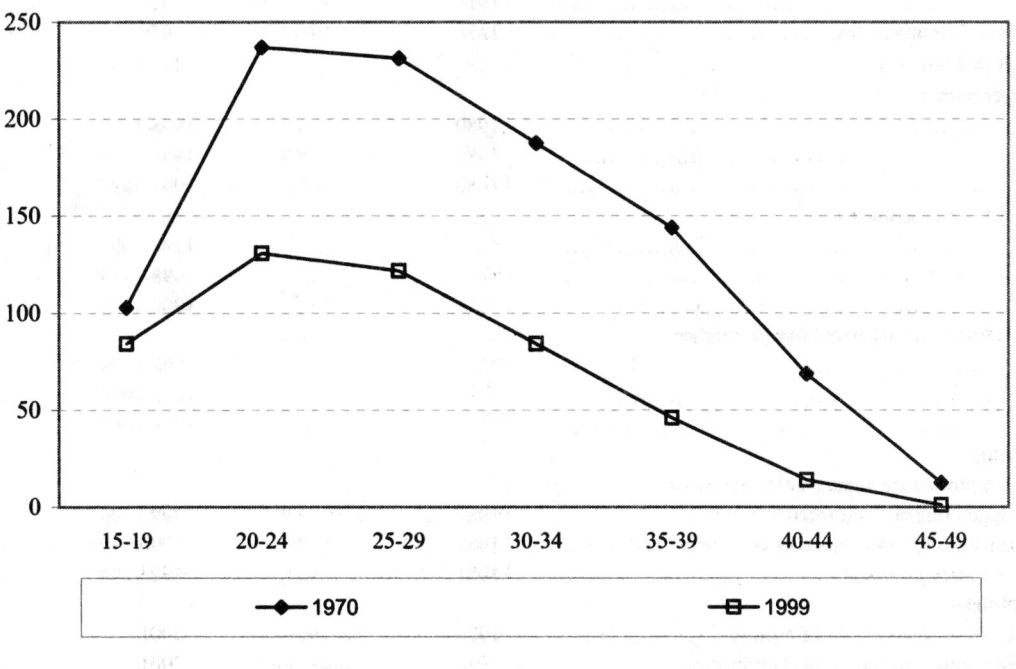

Indicator	Period					
	Earlier year			**Later year**		
	Year	*Value*		*Year*	*Value*	
Nuptiality						
Annual number of marriages (*thousands*)	..	..		..	..	
Annual number of divorces (*thousands*)	..	..		..	..	
	Year	*Male*	*Female*	*Year*	*Male*	*Female*
Total first marriage rate (per person)	..	..	..	..	..	..
Total divorce rate (per person)	..	..	..	..	..	..
Mean age at first marriage (years)	..	..	..	..	..	..
SMAM (years)	1978	27.0	18.7	1999	28.0	22.0
Percentage ever married by age group						
15-19	1978	3.1	53.8	1999	1.7	25.4
20-24	1978	25.5	82.9	1999	20.9	64.2
25-29	1978	55.8	91.8	1999	45.8	82.7
30-34	1978	78.1	95.5	1999	80.6	92.3
35-39	1978	86.9	96.7	1999	89.0	95.1
40-44	1978	91.8	97.6	1999	89.3	98.8
45-49	1978	93.9	98.4	1999	89.5	99.3
Fertility	*Year*	*Value*		*Year*	*Value*	
Annual number of births (*thousands*)	..	..		..	..	
Crude birth rate (per 1 000 population)	..	..		..	..	
Percentage of extra-marital births among all births	..	..		..	..	
Total fertility rate (births per woman)	1978	7.4		1997	5.1	
Age-specific fertility rate (per 1 000 women)						
15-19	1978	216		1997	126	
20-24	1978	313		1997	210	
25-29	1978	300		1997	234	
30-34	1978	248		1997	195	
35-39	1978	203		1997	148	
40-44	1978	132		1997	78	
45-49	1978	60		1997	33	
Mean age at childbearing (years)	1978	29.4		1992	29.4	
Mean age at first birth (years)[a]	..	..		1998-1999	19.5	
Children ever born per woman						
35-39	1980	5.9		1998-1999	5.4	
40-44	1980	6.7		1998-1999	6.3	
45-49	1980	6.9		1998-1999	6.6	
Percentage of childless women						
35-39	..	..		1998-1999	3.1	
40-44	..	..		1998-1999	2.5	
45-49	..	..		1998-1999	2.2	
Percentage of women with parity three or higher						
35-39	..	..		1998-1999	83.4	
40-44	..	..		1998-1999	86.3	
45-49	..	..		1998-1999	86.5	
Family Planning						
Contraceptive prevalence among women in union						
Percentage using any contraceptive method	1981	2.9		1998-1999	15.0	
Percentage using a modern contraceptive method	1981	0.5		1998-1999	7.3	
Percentage using condoms	1981	0.0		1998-1999	1.8	
Population policies						
Government's view on the level of fertility	1976	Satisfactory		2001	Too high	
Government's policy regarding level of fertility	1976	Maintain		2001	Lower	
Government's support for contraceptive methods	1976	No support		2001	Direct support	

[a]Median age at first birth among women aged 25-29 at the date of the survey for both dates

Total fertility rates

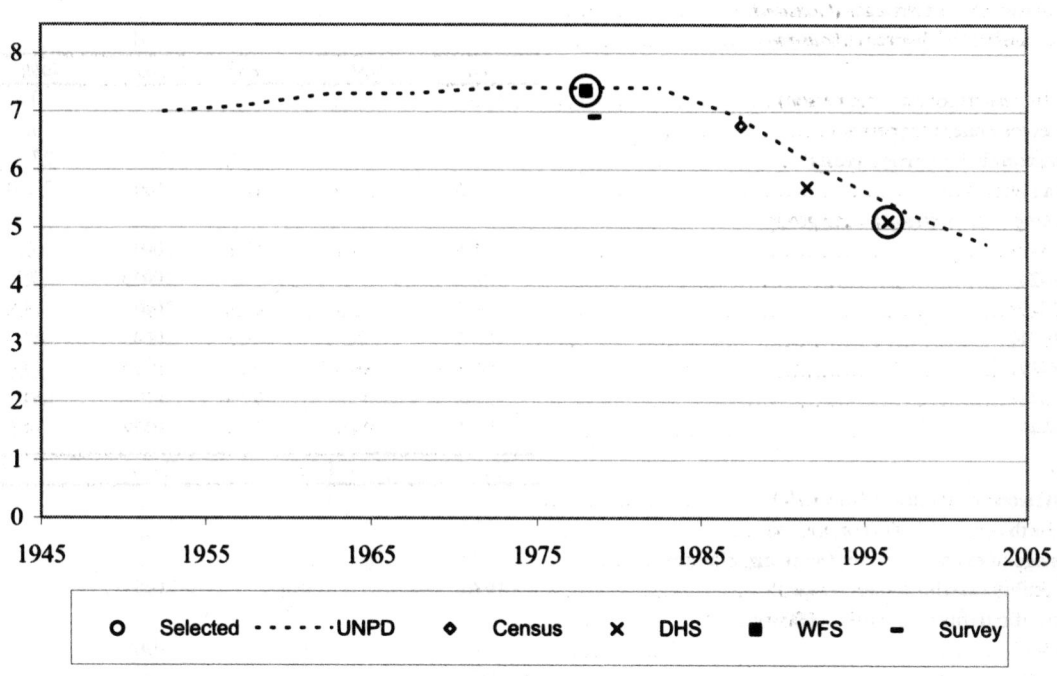

Age-specific fertility rates

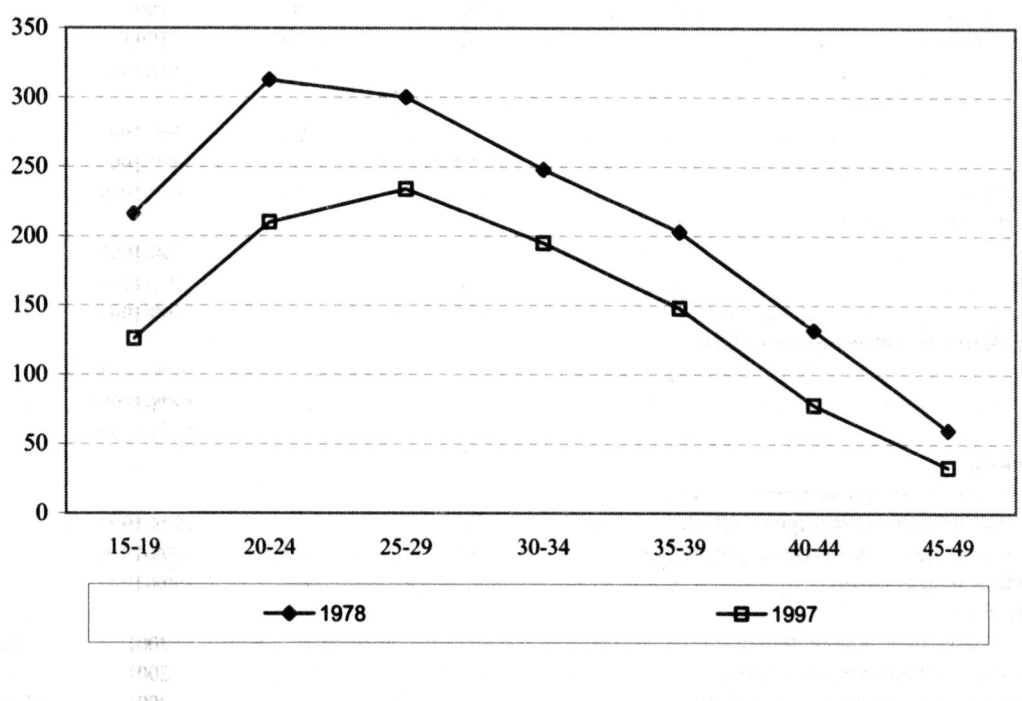

Indicator	Period					
	Earlier year			Later year		
	Year	Value		Year	Value	

Nuptiality

Indicator	Year	Value		Year	Value	
Annual number of marriages (*thousands*)	..	..		2001	22.1	
Annual number of divorces (*thousands*)	..	..		2001	4.7	

Indicator	Year	Male	Female	Year	Male	Female
Total first marriage rate (per person)	1970	..	0.9	1997	0.6	0.7
Total divorce rate (per person)	..	..	..	1997	0.1	0.1
Mean age at first marriage (years)	1970	..	21.4	1997	27.6	24.4
SMAM (years)	..	..	..	2001	29.8	26.2
Percentage ever married by age group						
15-19	..	..	..	2001	0.3	2.4
20-24	..	..	..	2001	7.7	25.8
25-29	..	..	..	2001	38.1	61.5
30-34	..	..	..	2001	66.2	82.2
35-39	..	..	..	2001	77.5	89.5
40-44	..	..	..	2001	83.4	92.2
45-49	..	..	..	2001	87.4	93.5

Fertility	Year	Value	Year	Value
Annual number of births (*thousands*)	1970	61.1	2001	41.0
Crude birth rate (per 1 000 population)	1970	13.8	2001	9.2
Percentage of extra-marital births among all births	1970	5.4	2001	9.4
Total fertility rate (births per woman)	1970	1.8	2001	1.4
Age-specific fertility rate (per 1 000 women)				
15-19	1970	48	2001	15
20-24	1970	136	2001	72
25-29	1970	98	2001	97
30-34	1970	54	2001	62
35-39	1970	23	2001	24
40-44	1970	6	2001	4
45-49	1970	1	2001	0
Mean age at childbearing (years)	1970	26.0	2001	27.9
Mean age at first birth (years)	1970	23.1	2000	25.5
Children ever born per woman				
35-39	..	..	1991	1.9
40-44	..	..	1991	1.9
45-49	..	..	1991	2.0
Percentage of childless women				
35-39	..	..	1991	10.7
40-44	..	..	1991	9.3
45-49	..	..	1991	9.3
Percentage of women with parity three or higher				
35-39	..	..	1991	16.7
40-44	..	..	1991	18.8
45-49	..	..	1991	21.3
Family Planning				
Contraceptive prevalence among women in union				
Percentage using any contraceptive method	..	..	..	..
Percentage using a modern contraceptive method	..	..	..	..
Percentage using condoms	..	..	..	..
Population policies				
Government's view on the level of fertility	..	--	2001	Too low
Government's policy regarding level of fertility	..	--	2001	Raise
Government's support for contraceptive methods	..	--	2001	Direct support

Total fertility rates

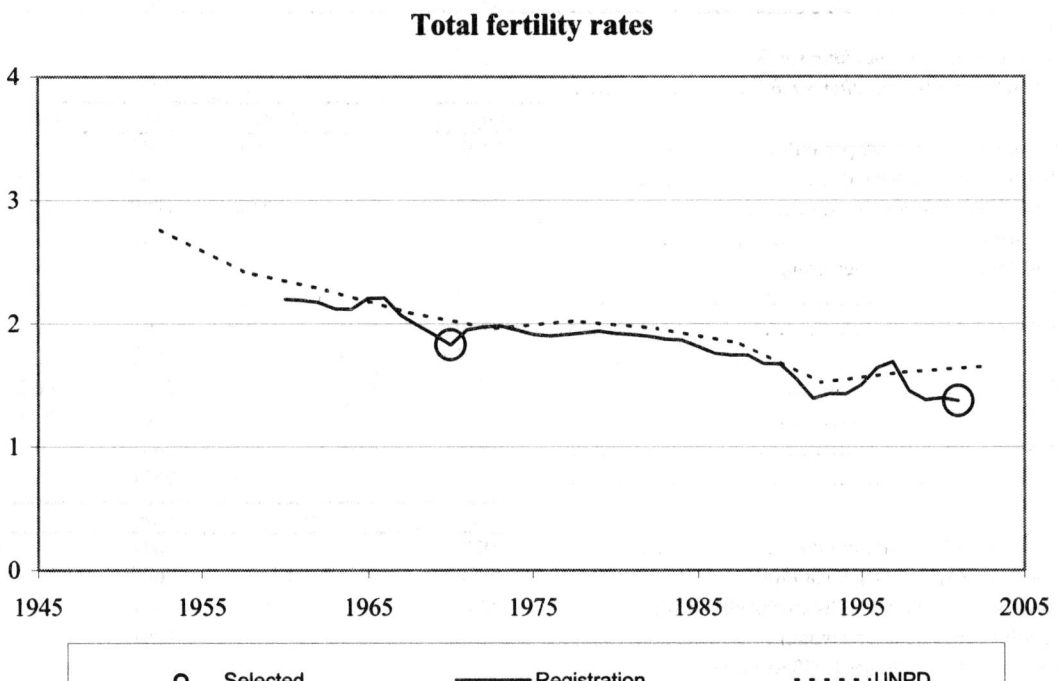

Age-specific fertility rates

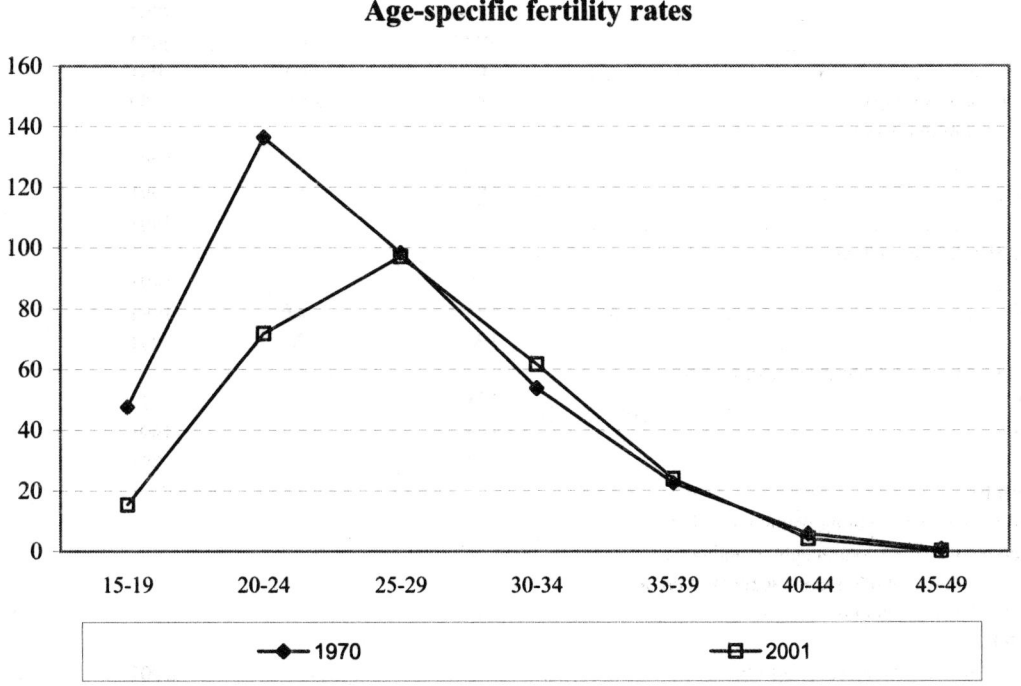

Indicator	Period					
	Earlier year			Later year		
	Year	Value		Year	Value	
Nuptiality						
Annual number of marriages (*thousands*)	1970	115.2		2000	57.0	
Annual number of divorces (*thousands*)	1970	24.8		2000	37.9	
	Year	Male	Female	Year	Male	Female
Total first marriage rate (per person)	1972	1.1	1.1	1996	0.6	0.7
Total divorce rate (per person)	1971	0.4	0.4	1996	0.4	0.4
Mean age at first marriage (years)	1972	28.6	25.8	1996	30.1	27.1
SMAM (years)	1970	23.4	19.5	..	..	..
Percentage ever married by age group						
15-19	1970	4.6	29.6	..	..	..
20-24	1970	37.3	70.4	..	..	..
25-29	1970	71.5	86.0	..	..	..
30-34	1970	82.7	89.9	..	..	..
35-39	1970	85.4	90.7	..	..	..
40-44	1970	85.8	90.5	..	..	..
45-49	1970	85.2	89.9	..	..	..
Fertility	Year	Value		Year	Value	
Annual number of births (*thousands*)..........................	1970	237.0		2000	143.5	
Crude birth rate (per 1 000 population)	1970	27.7		2000	12.8	
Percentage of extra-marital births among all births	..	..		..	..	
Total fertility rate (births per woman)	1970	3.7		2000	1.6	
Age-specific fertility rate (per 1 000 women)						
15-19	1970	128		2000	51	
20-24	1970	227		2000	97	
25-29	1970	164		2000	89	
30-34	1970	116		2000	55	
35-39	1970	73		2000	22	
40-44	1970	26		2000	4	
45-49	1970	4		2000	0	
Mean age at childbearing (years)	1970	26.7		2000	26.1	
Mean age at first birth (years)	1982	21.9		1996	23.1	
Children ever born per woman						
35-39	1981	3.0		..	..	
40-44	1981	3.4		..	..	
45-49	1981	3.7		..	..	
Percentage of childless women						
35-39	1981	7.3		..	..	
40-44	1981	7.6		..	..	
45-49	1981	9.1		..	..	
Percentage of women with parity three or higher						
35-39	1981	51.7		..	..	
40-44	1981	57.9		..	..	
45-49	1981	59.4		..	..	
Family Planning						
Contraceptive prevalence among women in union						
Percentage using any contraceptive method	..	..		..	..	
Percentage using a modern contraceptive method	..	..		2000	72.1	
Percentage using condoms	..	..		2000	5.0	
Population policies						
Government's view on the level of fertility	1976	Satisfactory		2001	Satisfactory	
Government's policy regarding level of fertility	1976	No intervention		2001	No intervention	
Government's support for contraceptive methods	1976	Direct support		2001	Direct support	

Total fertility rates

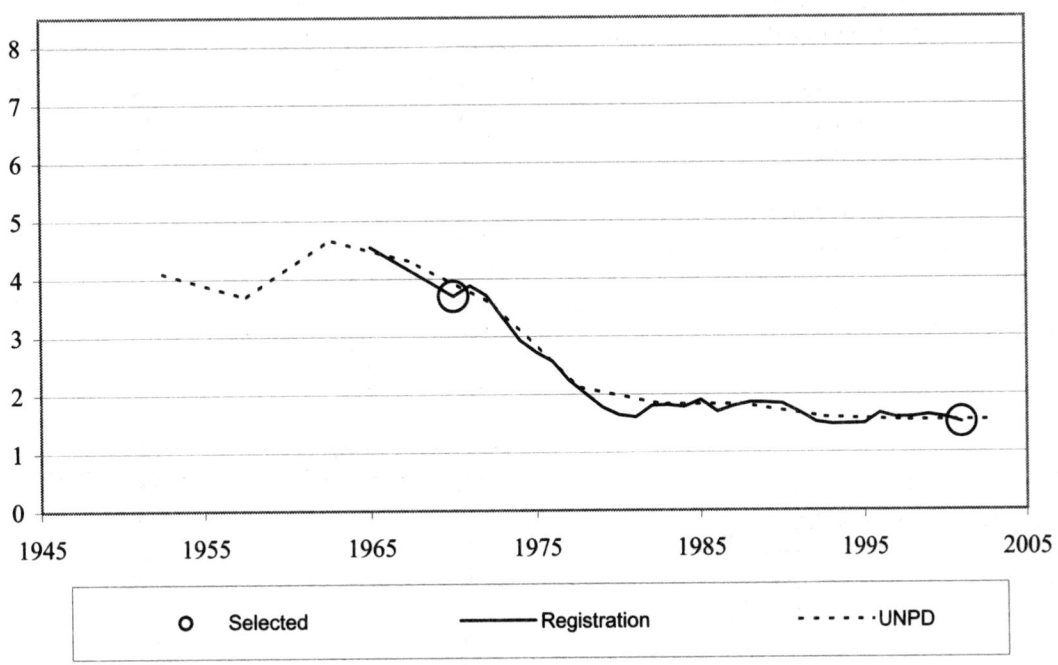

Age-specific fertility rates

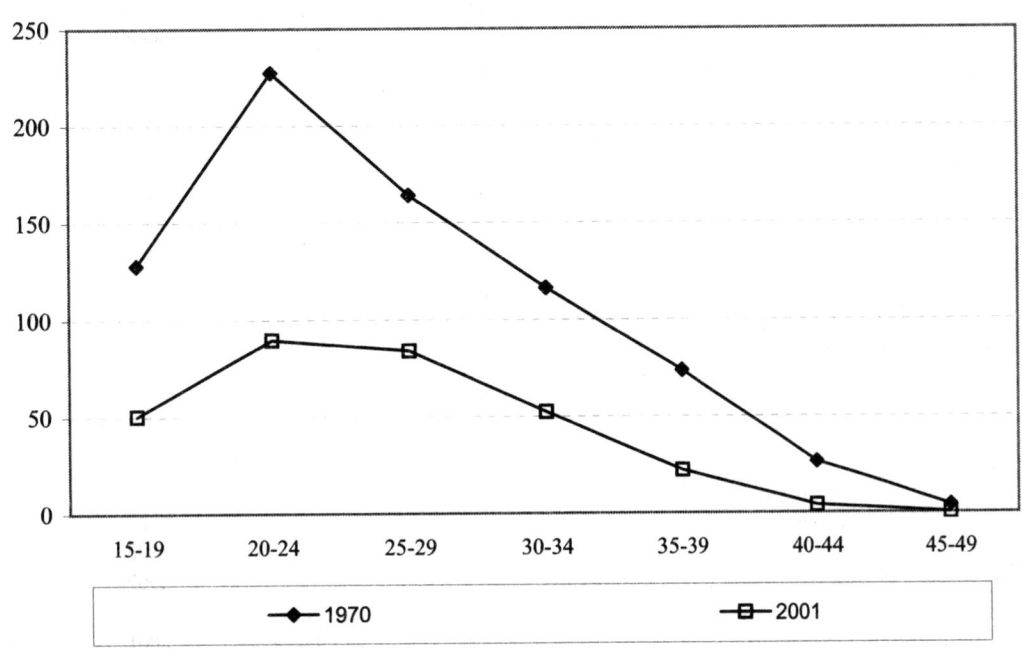

Indicator	Period			
	Earlier year		Later year	
	Year	Value	Year	Value
Nuptiality				
Annual number of marriages (*thousands*)	1970	4.4	2001	10.6
Annual number of divorces (*thousands*)	1970	0.1	2001	1.2

Indicator	Year	Male	Female	Year	Male	Female
Total first marriage rate (per person)	1975	1.2	1.1	1997	1.1	1.1
Total divorce rate (per person)	1980	..	0.0	2000	..	0.2
Mean age at first marriage (years)	1975	26.6	23.8	1997	28.5	26.0
SMAM (years)	1973	25.9	24.2	1992	27.0	23.1
Percentage ever married by age group						
15-19	1973	0.7	3.8	1992	0.6	7.5
20-24	1973	17.6	39.4	1992	18.1	50.8
25-29	1973	65.4	74.5	1992	58.8	81.1
30-34	1973	92.2	90.2	1992	84.3	89.7
35-39	1973	97.0	92.2	1992	93.1	92.1
40-44	1973	97.2	95.4	1992	96.2	93.0
45-49	1973	97.3	95.0	1992	97.2	94.0

Indicator	Year	Value	Year	Value
Fertility				
Annual number of births (*thousands*)	1970	11.8	2000	8.4
Crude birth rate (per 1 000 population)	1970	19.5	2000	11.2
Percentage of extra-marital births among all births	1970	0.2	2000	2.3
Total fertility rate (births per woman)	1970	2.7	2000	1.6
Age-specific fertility rate (per 1 000 women)				
15-19	1970	21	2000	9
20-24	1970	150	2000	70
25-29	1970	181	2000	120
30-34	1970	113	2000	83
35-39	1970	60	2000	30
40-44	1970	19	2000	7
45-49	1970	4	2000	0
Mean age at childbearing (years)	1970	28.6	2000	28.7
Mean age at first birth (years)	1975	24.0	2001	28.6
Children ever born per woman				
35-39	1973	3.1	1992	2.2
40-44	1973	3.6	1992	2.2
45-49	1973	3.7	1992	2.3
Percentage of childless women				
35-39	1973	3.0	1992	3.4
40-44	1973	3.4	1992	3.5
45-49	1973	4.4	1992	4.2
Percentage of women with parity three or higher				
35-39	1973	61.1	1992	38.0
40-44	1973	68.5	1992	39.1
45-49	1973	67.5	1992	42.4
Family Planning				
Contraceptive prevalence among women in union				
Percentage using any contraceptive method	..	..	..	..
Percentage using a modern contraceptive method	..	..	..	..
Percentage using condoms	..	..	..	..
Population policies				
Government's view on the level of fertility	1976	Satisfactory	2001	Too low
Government's policy regarding level of fertility	1976	No intervention	2001	Raise
Government's support for contraceptive methods	1976	No support	2001	Indirect support

Total fertility rates

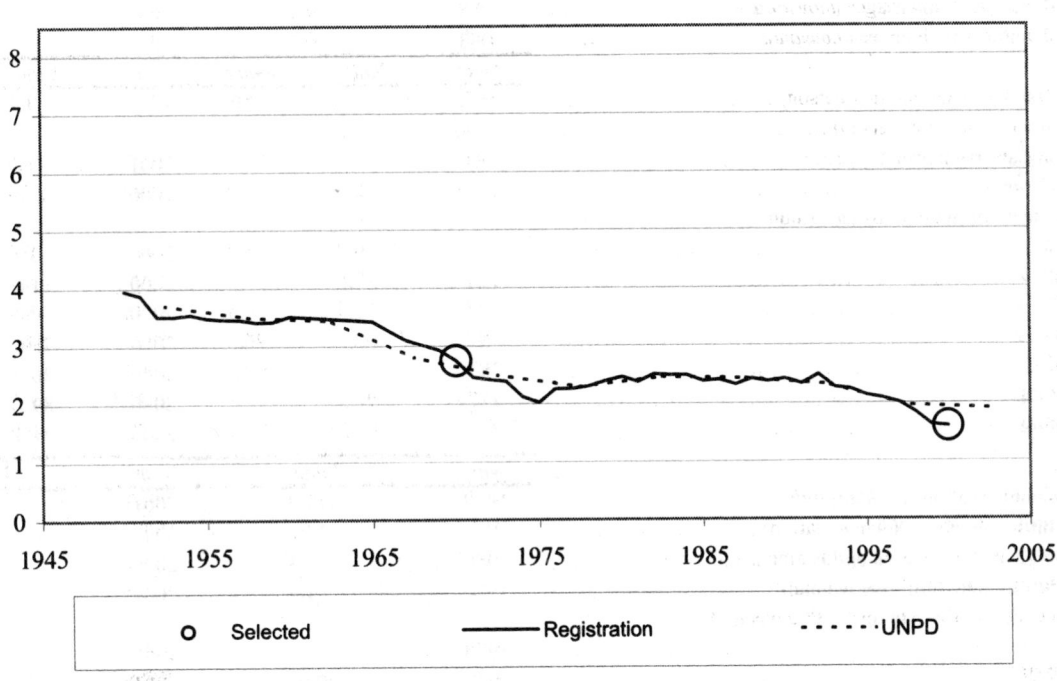

Age-specific fertility rates

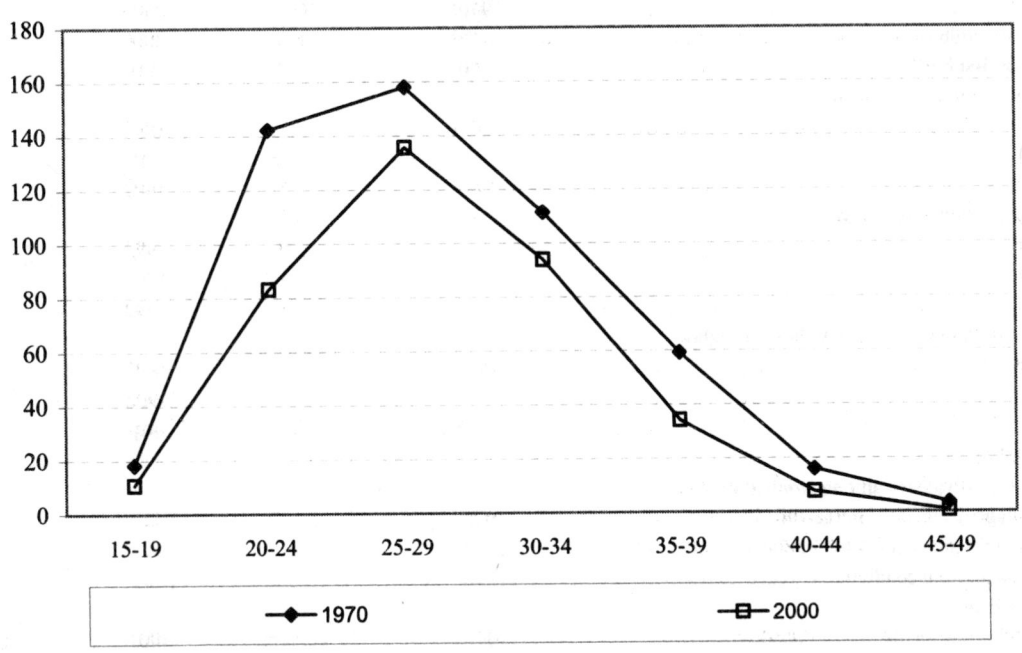

Indicator	Period					
	Earlier year			*Later year*		
	Year	Value		Year	Value	
Nuptiality						
Annual number of marriages (*thousands*)	1985	80.7		2002	52.7	
Annual number of divorces (*thousands*)	1985	30.5		2001	31.6	
	Year	Male	Female	Year	Male	Female
Total first marriage rate (per person)	1970	..	0.9	1997	0.5	0.5
Total divorce rate (per person)	..	..	..	1997	0.4	0.4
Mean age at first marriage (years)	1970	..	21.6	2001	..	24.8
SMAM (years)	..	..	..	2000	28.0	25.3
Percentage ever married by age group						
15-19	..	..	..	2000	0.2	1.2
20-24	..	..	..	2000	11.6	27.2
25-29	..	..	..	2000	50.7	72.4
30-34	..	..	..	2000	78.6	90.3
35-39	..	..	..	2000	86.2	94.3
40-44	..	..	..	2000	89.1	95.8
45-49	..	..	..	2000	91.5	96.5
Fertility	Year	Value		Year	Value	
Annual number of births (*thousands*)	1970	147.9		2001	90.7	
Crude birth rate (per 1 000 population)	1970	15.1		2001	8.8	
Percentage of extra-marital births among all births	1970	5.4		2001	23.5	
Total fertility rate (births per woman)	1970	1.9		2001	1.1	
Age-specific fertility rate (per 1 000 women)						
15-19	1970	48		2001	11	
20-24	1970	173		2001	60	
25-29	1970	102		2001	91	
30-34	1970	41		2001	47	
35-39	1970	13		2001	15	
40-44	1970	3		2001	3	
45-49	1970	0		2001	0	
Mean age at childbearing (years)	1970	25.0		2001	27.5	
Mean age at first birth (years)	1970	22.5		2001	25.3	
Children ever born per woman						
35-39	..	..		1991	2.0	
40-44	..	..		1991	2.0	
45-49	..	..		1991	2.0	
Percentage of childless women						
35-39	..	..		1991	5.8	
40-44	..	..		1991	5.5	
45-49	..	..		1991	6.2	
Percentage of women with parity three or higher						
35-39	..	..		1991	23.0	
40-44	..	..		1991	24.2	
45-49	..	..		1991	23.6	
Family Planning						
Contraceptive prevalence among women in union						
Percentage using any contraceptive method	1970	66.0		1997	72.0	
Percentage using a modern contraceptive method	1970	25.0		1997	62.6	
Percentage using condoms	1970	13.0		1997	12.7	
Population policies						
Government's view on the level of fertility	1976	--		2001	Too low	
Government's policy regarding level of fertility	1976	--		2001	Raise	
Government's support for contraceptive methods	1976	--		2001	Indirect support	

Total fertility rates

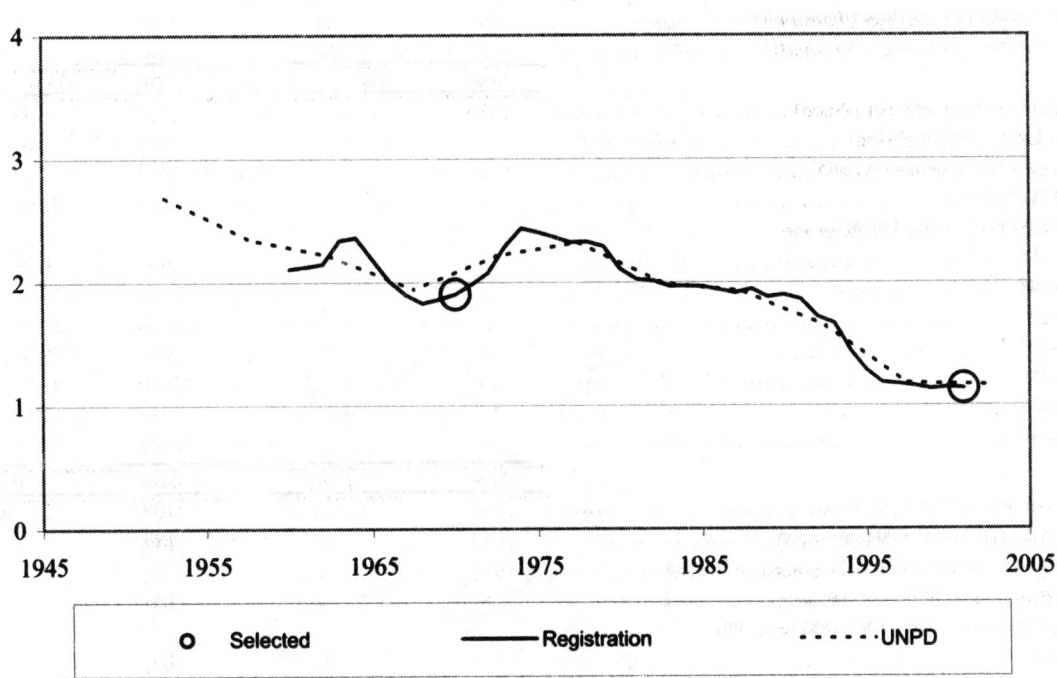

Age-specific fertility rates

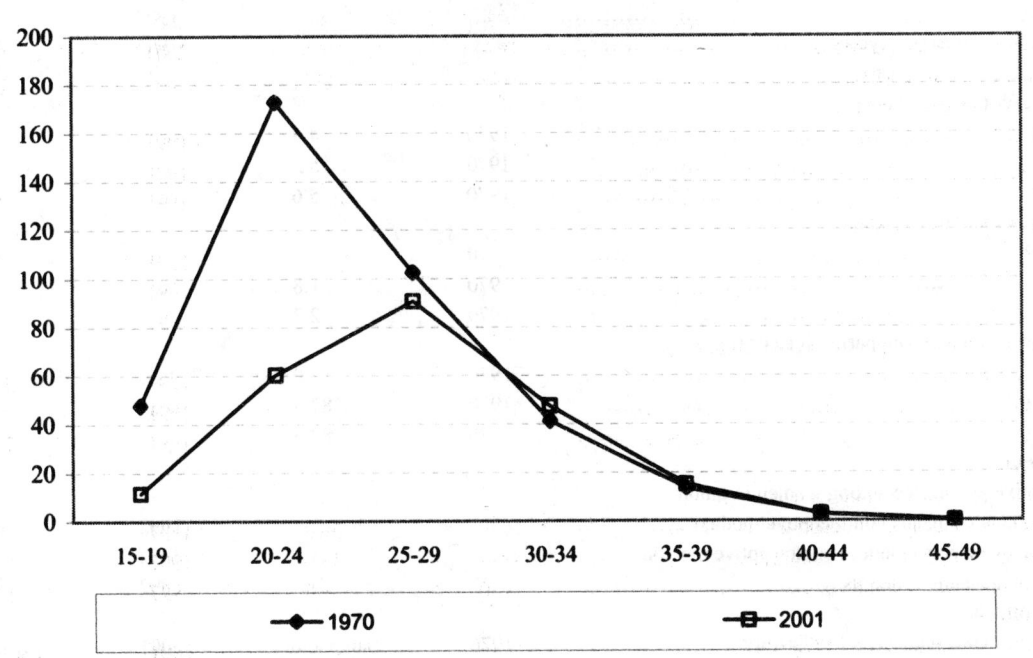

Indicator	Period					
	Earlier year			Later year		
	Year	Value		Year	Value	

Nuptiality

	Year	Value		Year	Value	
Annual number of marriages (*thousands*)	..	..		..	..	
Annual number of divorces (*thousands*)	..	..		..	..	

	Year	Male	Female	Year	Male	Female
Total first marriage rate (per person)	..	..	..	..	..	..
Total divorce rate (per person)	..	..	..	..	..	..
Mean age at first marriage (years)	..	..	..	..	..	..
SMAM (years)	..	..	..	..	..	..
Percentage ever married by age group						
15-19	..	..	..	..	..	..
20-24	..	..	..	..	..	..
25-29	..	..	..	..	..	..
30-34	..	..	..	..	..	..
35-39	..	..	..	..	..	..
40-44	..	..	..	..	..	..
45-49	..	..	..	..	..	..

Fertility

	Year	Value	Year	Value
Annual number of births (*thousands*)	..	..	1993	420.6
Crude birth rate (per 1 000 population)	..	..	1993	19.8
Percentage of extra-marital births among all births	..	..	..	..
Total fertility rate (births per woman)	..	..	1993	2.2
Age-specific fertility rate (per 1 000 women)				
15-19	..	..	1993	0
20-24	..	..	1993	49
25-29	..	..	1993	265
30-34	..	..	1993	101
35-39	..	..	1993	19
40-44	..	..	1993	3
45-49	..	..	1993	1
Mean age at childbearing (years)	..	..	1993	28.7
Mean age at first birth (years)	..	..	..	..
Children ever born per woman				
35-39	1970	4.5	..	..
40-44	1970	5.3	..	..
45-49	1970	5.6	..	..
Percentage of childless women				
35-39	1970	2.3	..	..
40-44	1970	1.8	..	..
45-49	1970	2.2	..	..
Percentage of women with parity three or higher				
35-39	1970	87.0	..	..
40-44	1970	87.8	..	..
45-49	1970	87.6	..	..

Family Planning

	Year	Value	Year	Value
Contraceptive prevalence among women in union				
Percentage using any contraceptive method	..	..	1992	61.8
Percentage using a modern contraceptive method	..	..	1992	53.0
Percentage using condoms	..	..	1992	0.0

Population policies

	Year	Value	Year	Value
Government's view on the level of fertility	1976	Satisfactory	2001	Satisfactory
Government's policy regarding level of fertility	1976	Maintain	2001	Maintain
Government's support for contraceptive methods	1976	Direct support	2001	Direct support

Total fertility rates

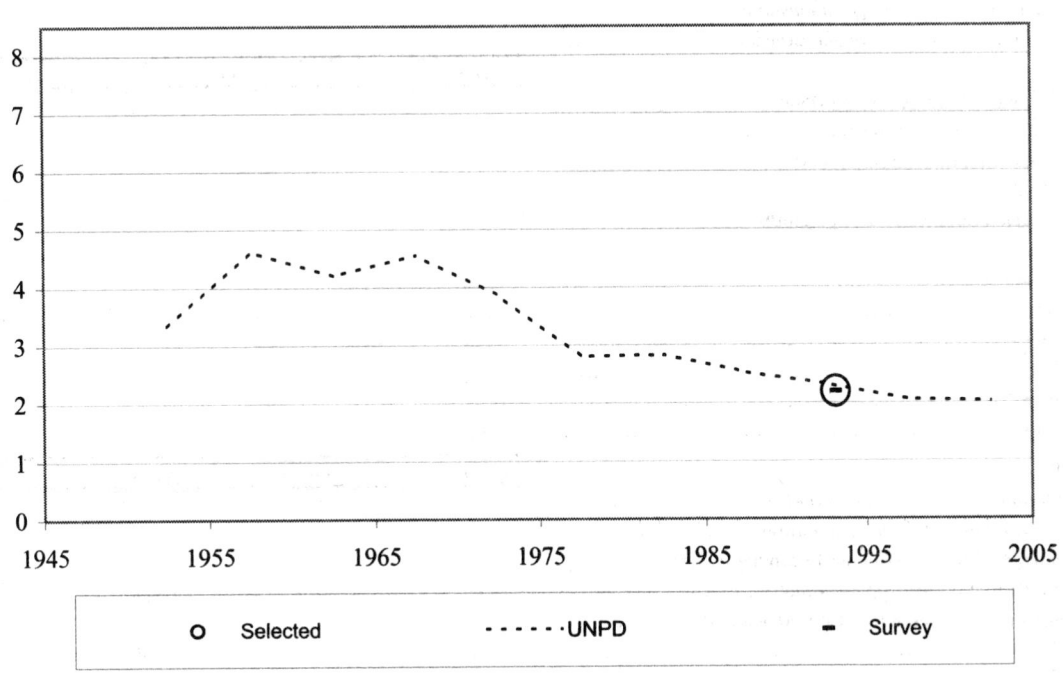

Age-specific fertility rates

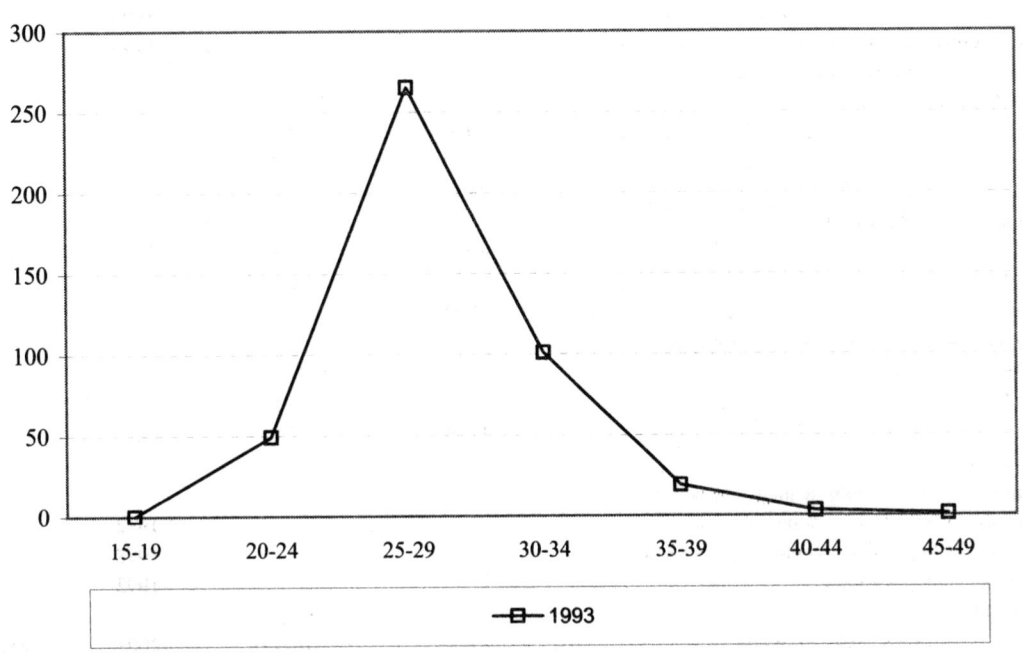

Indicator	Period			
	Earlier year		Later year	
	Year	Value	Year	Value
Nuptiality				
Annual number of marriages (*thousands*)	..	..	..	..
Annual number of divorces (*thousands*)	..	..	..	..

Indicator	Year	Male	Female	Year	Male	Female
Total first marriage rate (per person)	..	..	..	..	..	..
Total divorce rate (per person)	..	..	..	..	..	..
Mean age at first marriage (years)	..	..	..	..	..	..
SMAM (years)	1984	24.9	20.0	..	..	..
Percentage ever married by age group						
15-19	1984	4.7	32.3	..	..	..
20-24	1984	33.9	74.2	..	..	..
25-29	1984	71.1	89.1	..	..	..
30-34	1984	86.6	93.4	..	..	..
35-39	1984	93.0	95.4	..	..	..
40-44	1984	94.7	96.0	..	..	..
45-49	1984	95.4	96.4	..	..	..

Indicator	Year	Value	Year	Value
Fertility				
Annual number of births (*thousands*)...........................	..	..	..	..
Crude birth rate (per 1 000 population)	..	..	..	..
Percentage of extra-marital births among all births	..	..	..	..
Total fertility rate (births per woman)	1971	6.3	1984	6.7
Age-specific fertility rate (per 1 000 women)				
15-19	..	..	..	..
20-24	..	..	..	..
25-29	..	..	..	..
30-34	..	..	..	..
35-39	..	..	..	..
40-44	..	..	..	..
45-49	..	..	..	..
Mean age at childbearing (years)	..	..	..	..
Mean age at first birth (years)	..	..	..	..
Children ever born per woman				
35-39	..	..	..	..
40-44	..	..	..	..
45-49	..	..	..	..
Percentage of childless women				
35-39	..	..	..	..
40-44	..	..	..	..
45-49	..	..	..	..
Percentage of women with parity three or higher				
35-39	..	..	..	..
40-44	..	..	..	..
45-49	..	..	..	..
Family Planning				
Contraceptive prevalence among women in union				
Percentage using any contraceptive method	..	..	2001	31.4
Percentage using a modern contraceptive method	..	..	2001	4.4
Percentage using condoms	..	..	2001	2.3
Population policies				
Government's view on the level of fertility	1976	Satisfactory	2001	Satisfactory
Government's policy regarding level of fertility	1976	No intervention	2001	No intervention
Government's support for contraceptive methods	1976	Direct support	2001	Direct support

Total fertility rates

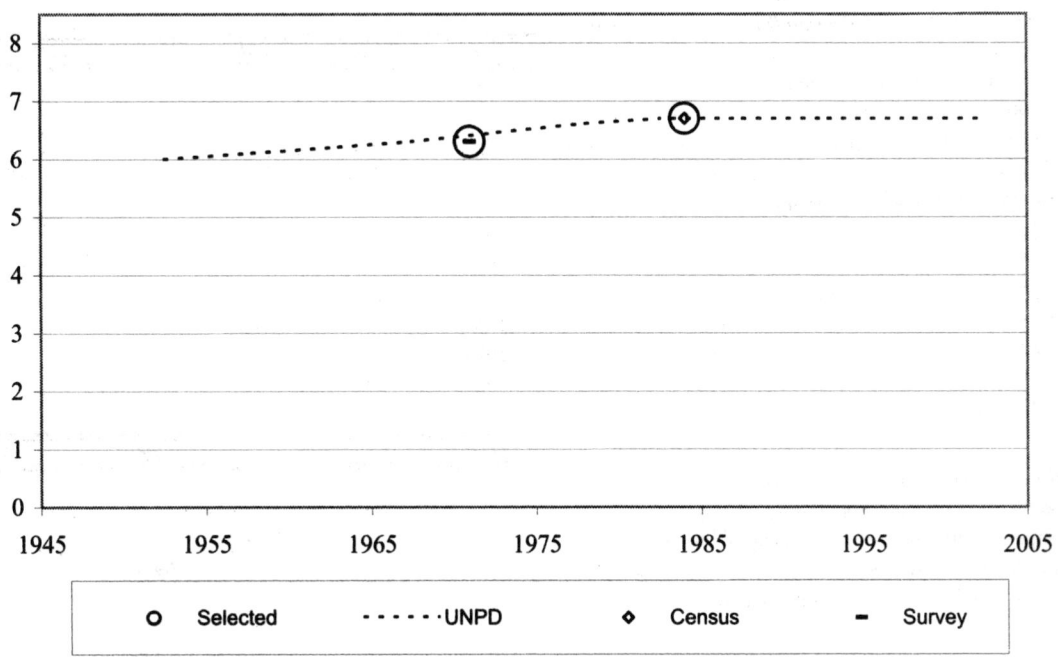

Indicator	Period					
	Earlier year			Later year		
	Year	Value		Year	Value	
Nuptiality						
Annual number of marriages (*thousands*)	..	..		1992	1.3	
Annual number of divorces (*thousands*)	..	..		..	..	
	Year	Male	Female	Year	Male	Female
Total first marriage rate (per person)	..	..	..	..	..	..
Total divorce rate (per person)	..	..	..	..	..	..
Mean age at first marriage (years)	..	..	..	..	..	..
SMAM (years)	..	..	..	..	..	..
Percentage ever married by age group						
15-19	..	..	..	..	..	..
20-24	..	..	..	..	..	..
25-29	..	..	..	..	..	..
30-34	..	..	..	..	..	..
35-39	..	..	..	..	..	..
40-44	..	..	..	..	..	..
45-49	..	..	..	..	..	..
Fertility	Year	Value		Year	Value	
Annual number of births (*thousands*)	..	..		..	..	
Crude birth rate (per 1 000 population)	..	..		..	..	
Percentage of extra-marital births among all births	..	..		..	..	
Total fertility rate (births per woman)	..	..		1993	4.7	
Age-specific fertility rate (per 1 000 women)						
15-19	..	..		1993	49	
20-24	..	..		1993	213	
25-29	..	..		1993	243	
30-34	..	..		1993	212	
35-39	..	..		1993	153	
40-44	..	..		1993	51	
45-49	..	..		1993	16	
Mean age at childbearing (years)	..	..		1993	29.8	
Mean age at first birth (years)	..	..		..	..	
Children ever born per woman						
35-39	..	..		..	..	
40-44	..	..		..	..	
45-49	..	..		..	..	
Percentage of childless women						
35-39	..	..		..	..	
40-44	..	..		..	..	
45-49	..	..		..	..	
Percentage of women with parity three or higher						
35-39	..	..		..	..	
40-44	..	..		..	..	
45-49	..	..		..	..	
Family Planning						
Contraceptive prevalence among women in union						
Percentage using any contraceptive method	..	..		..	..	
Percentage using a modern contraceptive method	..	..		..	..	
Percentage using condoms	..	..		..	..	
Population policies						
Government's view on the level of fertility	..	..		..	..	
Government's policy regarding level of fertility	..	..		..	..	
Government's support for contraceptive methods	..	..		..	..	

Total fertility rates

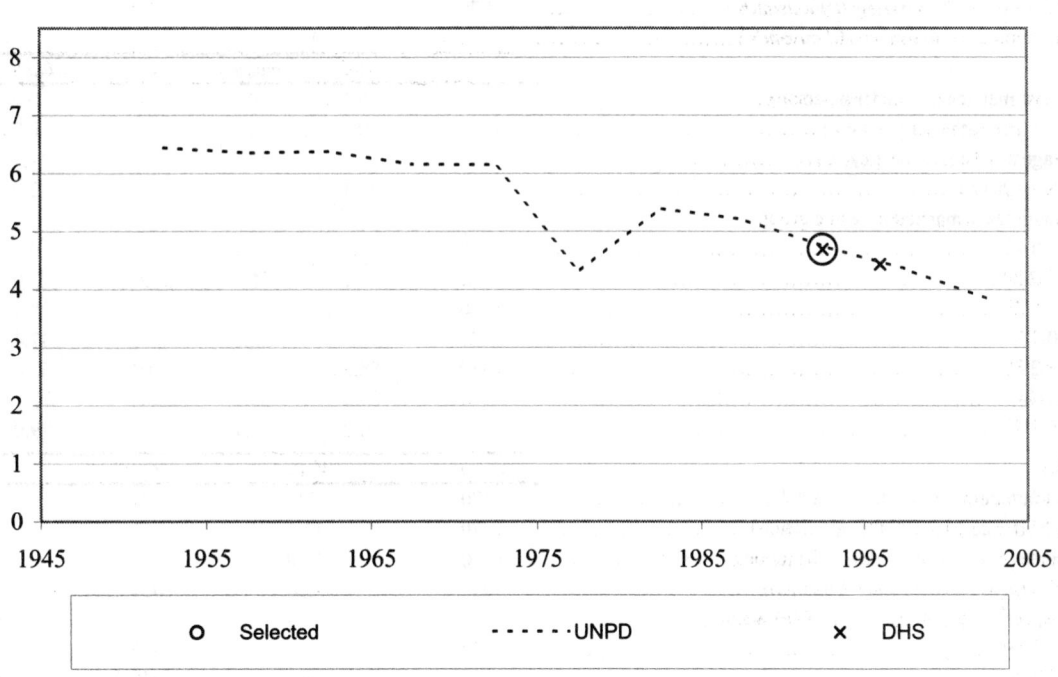

Age-specific fertility rates

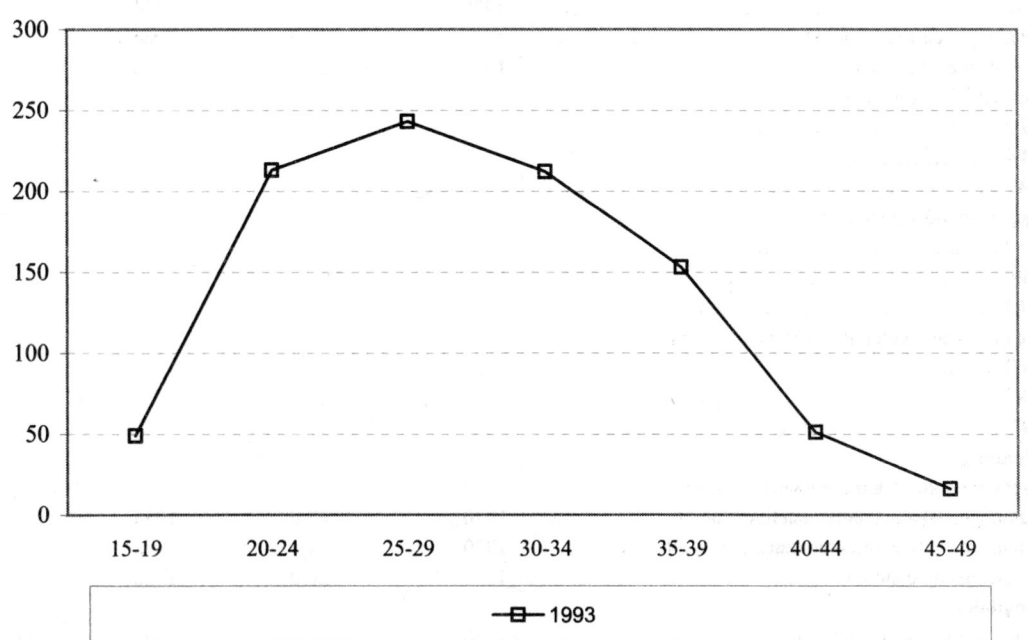

Indicator	Period					
	Earlier year			Later year		
	Year	Value		Year	Value	

Nuptiality

Indicator	Year	Value		Year	Value	
Annual number of marriages (*thousands*)	1970	36.4		2001	36.6	
Annual number of divorces (*thousands*)	1970	9.5		2000	14.4	

Indicator	Year	Male	Female	Year	Male	Female
Total first marriage rate (per person)	1974	0.6	0.7	1997	0.6	0.6
Total divorce rate (per person)	1970	0.5	0.5	1997	0.2	0.3
Mean age at first marriage (years)	1970	..	22.8	1997	31.5	29.3
SMAM (years)	1970	25.1	22.1	2001	32.9	30.7
Percentage ever married by age group						
15-19	1970	0.3	4.1	2001	0.1	0.7
20-24	1970	27.2	55.3	2001	3.6	9.1
25-29	1970	70.8	86.2	2001	18.7	32.6
30-34	1970	85.0	92.6	2001	47.4	61.6
35-39	1970	88.3	93.7	2001	62.8	73.9
40-44	1970	89.4	93.4	2001	72.2	81.1
45-49	1970	90.2	93.1	2001	79.0	86.8

Fertility

Indicator	Year	Value		Year	Value	
Annual number of births (*thousands*)	1970	70.8		2001	65.5	
Crude birth rate (per 1 000 population)	1970	14.4		2001	12.2	
Percentage of extra-marital births among all births	1970	11.0		1997	45.1	
Total fertility rate (births per woman)	1970	2.0		2001	1.7	
Age-specific fertility rate (per 1 000 women)						
15-19	1970	32		2001	8	
20-24	1970	129		2001	51	
25-29	1970	139		2001	126	
30-34	1970	67		2001	115	
35-39	1970	25		2001	43	
40-44	1970	5		2001	7	
45-49	1970	0		2001	0	
Mean age at childbearing (years)	1970	26.8		2001	29.7	
Mean age at first birth (years)	1970	23.8		1995	27.4	
Children ever born per woman						
35-39	..	..		..	..	
40-44	..	..		..	..	
45-49	..	..		..	..	
Percentage of childless women						
35-39	..	..		..	..	
40-44	..	..		..	..	
45-49	..	..		..	..	
Percentage of women with parity three or higher						
35-39	..	..		..	..	
40-44	..	..		..	..	
45-49	..	..		..	..	

Family Planning

Indicator	Year	Value		Year	Value	
Contraceptive prevalence among women in union						
Percentage using any contraceptive method	1970	67.0		1988	78.0	
Percentage using a modern contraceptive method	1970	54.0		1988	72.0	
Percentage using condoms	1970	20.0		1988	22.0	

Population policies

Indicator	Year	Value		Year	Value	
Government's view on the level of fertility	1976	Satisfactory		2001	Satisfactory	
Government's policy regarding level of fertility	1976	No intervention		2001	No intervention	
Government's support for contraceptive methods	1976	Direct support		2001	Indirect support	

Total fertility rates

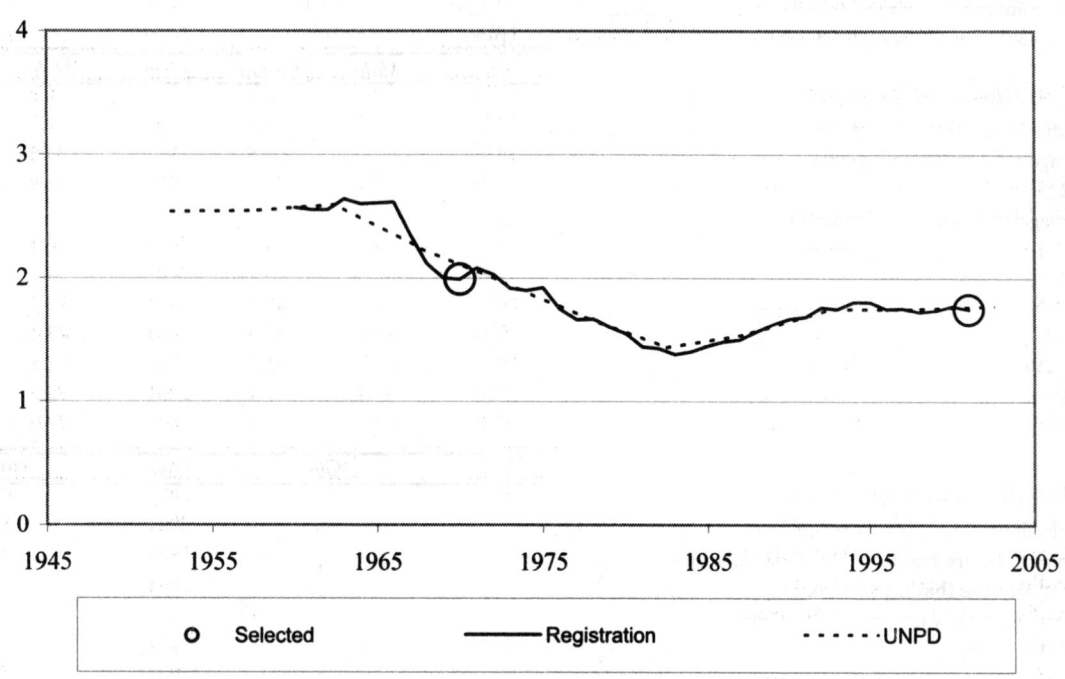

Age-specific fertility rates

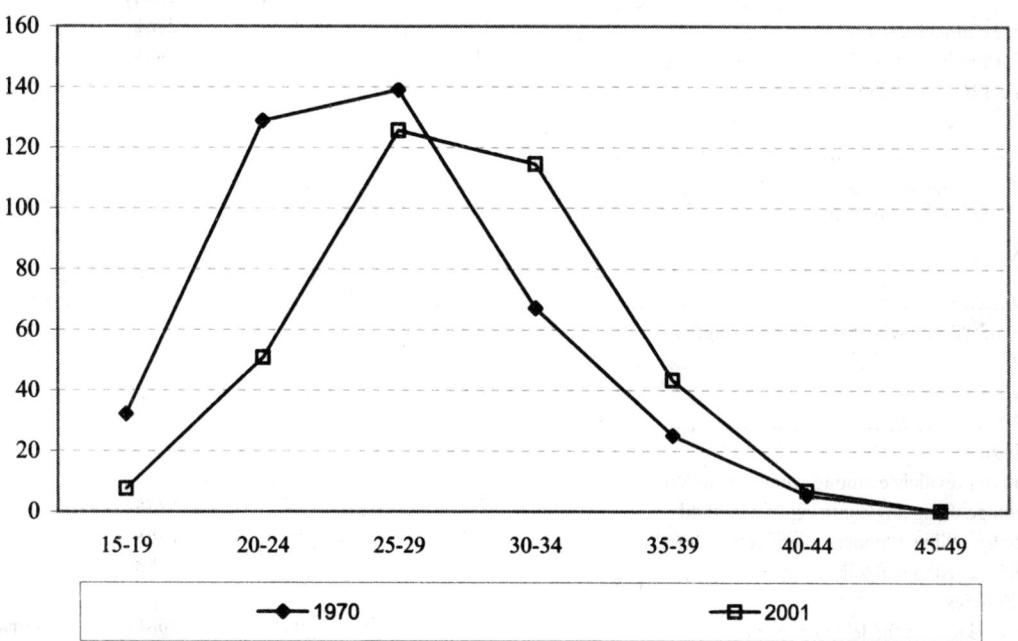

Djibouti

Indicator	Period					
	Earlier year			**Later year**		
	Year	Value		Year	Value	
Nuptiality						
Annual number of marriages (*thousands*)	1962	1.1		..	..	
Annual number of divorces (*thousands*)	1970	0.7		..	..	
	Year	Male	Female	Year	Male	Female
Total first marriage rate (per person)	..	..	..	..	..	..
Total divorce rate (per person)	..	..	..	..	..	..
Mean age at first marriage (years)	..	..	..	..	..	..
SMAM (years)	..	..	..	..	..	..
Percentage ever married by age group						
15-19	..	..	..	..	..	..
20-24	..	..	..	..	..	..
25-29	..	..	..	..	..	..
30-34	..	..	..	..	..	..
35-39	..	..	..	..	..	..
40-44	..	..	..	..	..	..
45-49	..	..	..	..	..	..
Fertility	Year	Value		Year	Value	
Annual number of births (*thousands*)....................	..	..		..	..	
Crude birth rate (per 1 000 population)	..	..		..	..	
Percentage of extra-marital births among all births	..	..		..	..	
Total fertility rate (births per woman)	..	..		1991	6.0	
Age-specific fertility rate (per 1 000 women)						
15-19	..	..		1991	31	
20-24	..	..		1991	155	
25-29	..	..		1991	270	
30-34	..	..		1991	317	
35-39	..	..		1991	257	
40-44	..	..		1991	121	
45-49	..	..		1991	44	
Mean age at childbearing (years)	..	..		1991	32.3	
Mean age at first birth (years)	..	..		..	..	
Children ever born per woman						
35-39	..	..		..	..	
40-44	..	..		..	..	
45-49	..	..		..	..	
Percentage of childless women						
35-39	..	..		..	..	
40-44	..	..		..	..	
45-49	..	..		..	..	
Percentage of women with parity three or higher						
35-39	..	..		..	..	
40-44	..	..		..	..	
45-49	..	..		..	..	
Family Planning						
Contraceptive prevalence among women in union						
Percentage using any contraceptive method	..	..		..	..	
Percentage using a modern contraceptive method	..	..		..	..	
Percentage using condoms	..	..		..	..	
Population policies						
Government's view on the level of fertility	..	..		2001	Too high	
Government's policy regarding level of fertility	..	..		2001	No intervention	
Government's support for contraceptive methods	..	..		2001	Direct support	

Total fertility rates

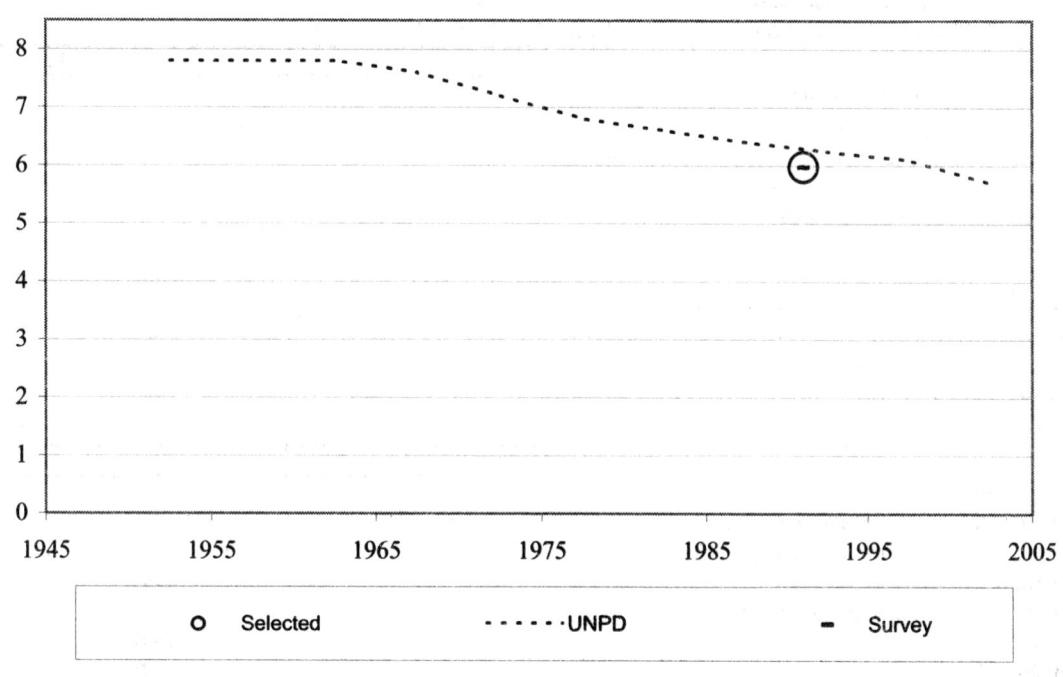

Age-specific fertility rates

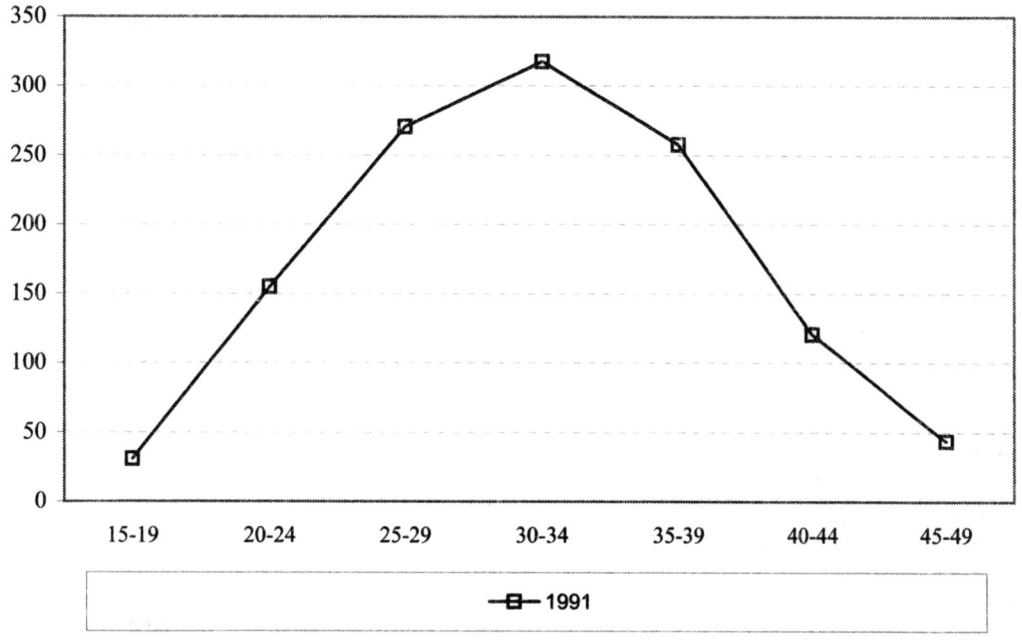

Dominican Republic

Indicator	Period					
	Earlier year			Later year		
	Year	Value		Year	Value	
Nuptiality						
Annual number of marriages (*thousands*)	1970	17.0		1998	28.7	
Annual number of divorces (*thousands*)	1970	3.8		2001	8.4	
	Year	Male	Female	Year	Male	Female
Total first marriage rate (per person)	1984	0.6	0.6	..	..	..
Total divorce rate (per person)	1970	0.0	0.0	1984	0.0	0.1
Mean age at first marriage (years)	1984	32.9	29.8	..	..	..
SMAM (years)	1970	26.1	19.6	1996	25.6	21.3
Percentage ever married by age group						
15-19	1970	6.0	22.4	1996	4.4	28.9
20-24	1970	24.2	60.8	1996	32.3	66.1
25-29	1970	51.3	78.0	1996	70.3	86.1
30-34	1970	65.1	83.1	1996	85.6	94.6
35-39	1970	70.6	84.6	1996	89.6	95.5
40-44	1970	73.8	83.5	1996	96.0	97.3
45-49	1970	76.5	82.7	1996	97.3	98.9
Fertility	Year	Value		Year	Value	
Annual number of births (*thousands*)	1970	163.0		2000	189.3	
Crude birth rate (per 1 000 population)	1970	36.9		2000	22.5	
Percentage of extra-marital births among all births	1970	62.7		..	..	
Total fertility rate (births per woman)	1973	5.7		1999	2.9	
Age-specific fertility rate (per 1 000 women)						
15-19	1973	123		1999	60	
20-24	1973	286		1999	150	
25-29	1973	265		1999	157	
30-34	1973	233		1999	108	
35-39	1973	166		1999	57	
40-44	1973	54		1999	26	
45-49	1973	15		1999	29	
Mean age at childbearing (years)	1973	28.6		1999	28.7	
Mean age at first birth (years)[a]	1975	19.8		1999	21.1	
Children ever born per woman						
35-39	1970	5.6		1999	3.1	
40-44	1970	5.8		1999	3.9	
45-49	1970	6.0		1999	4.2	
Percentage of childless women						
35-39	1970	12.9		1999	7.9	
40-44	1970	15.7		1999	2.5	
45-49	1970	15.1		1999	4.5	
Percentage of women with parity three or higher						
35-39	1970	74.8		1999	67.3	
40-44	1970	71.4		1999	78.7	
45-49	1970	71.8		1999	77.2	
Family Planning						
Contraceptive prevalence among women in union						
Percentage using any contraceptive method	1975	31.7		2000	64.7	
Percentage using a modern contraceptive method	1975	26.0		2000	62.5	
Percentage using condoms	1975	1.5		2000	0.9	
Population policies						
Government's view on the level of fertility	1976	Too high		2001	Too high	
Government's policy regarding level of fertility	1976	Lower		2001	Lower	
Government's support for contraceptive methods	1976	Direct support		2001	Direct support	

[a]Median age at first birth among women aged 25-29 at the date of the survey for both dates

Total fertility rates

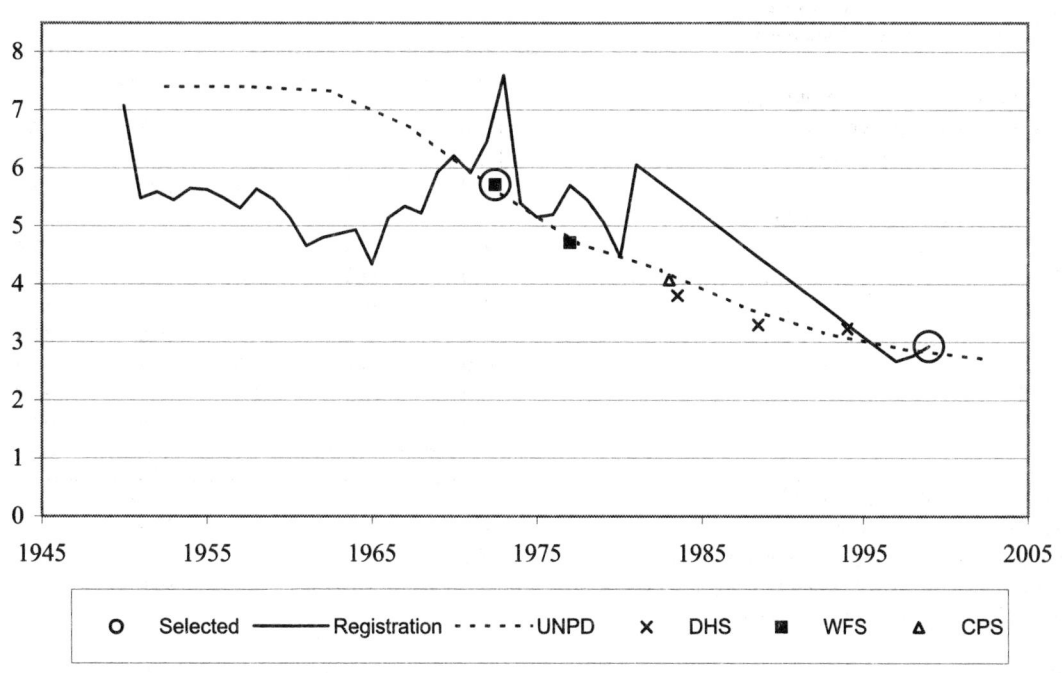

Age-specific fertility rates

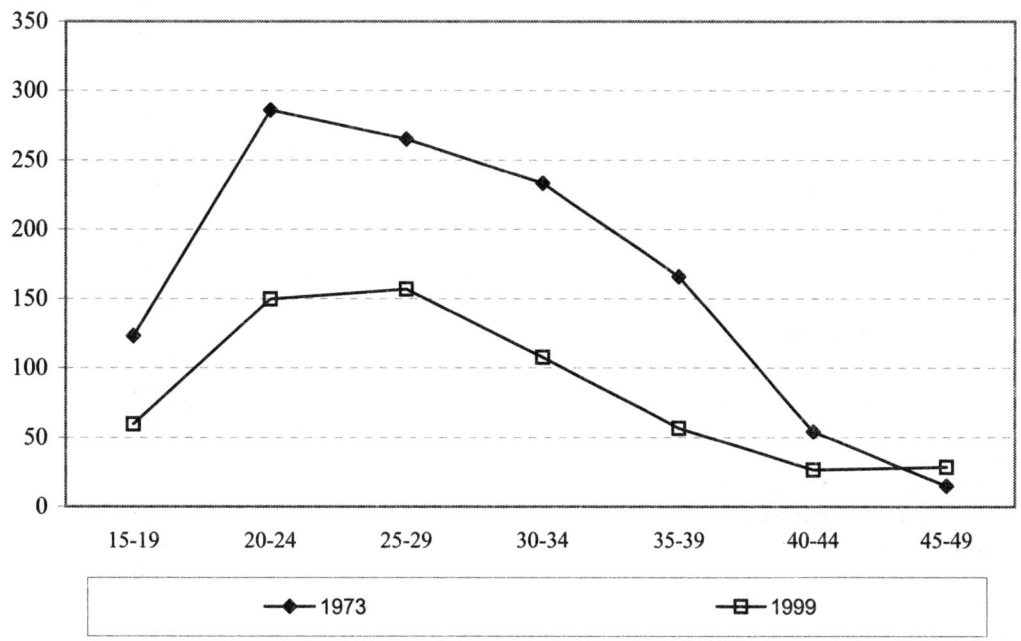

Indicator	Period					
	Earlier year			Later year		
	Year	Value		Year	Value	
Nuptiality						
Annual number of marriages (*thousands*)	..	..		..	..	
Annual number of divorces (*thousands*)	..	..		..	..	
	Year	Male	Female	Year	Male	Female
Total first marriage rate (per person)	..	..	..	1989	0.7	0.7
Total divorce rate (per person)	1970	0.0	0.0	1997	0.1	0.1
Mean age at first marriage (years)	..	..	..	1989	27.2	24.7
SMAM (years)	1974	25.0	21.2	2001	24.6	21.5
Percentage ever married by age group						
15-19	1974	3.9	19.5	2001	7.0	22.0
20-24	1974	34.0	59.3	2001	38.0	57.0
25-29	1974	66.9	78.7	2001	65.6	75.5
30-34	1974	81.9	85.7	2001	79.3	83.6
35-39	1974	86.6	88.0	2001	85.4	86.4
40-44	1974	89.0	88.5	2001	88.1	87.1
45-49	1974	90.1	88.9	2001	89.6	87.9
Fertility	Year	Value		Year	Value	
Annual number of births (*thousands*).............................	1970	230.2		..	..	
Crude birth rate (per 1 000 population)	1970	37.3		..	..	
Percentage of extra-marital births among all births	1966	32.0		..	..	
Total fertility rate (births per woman)	1977	5.3		1997	3.3	
Age-specific fertility rate (per 1 000 women)						
15-19	1977	103		1997	89	
20-24	1977	240		1997	172	
25-29	1977	261		1997	155	
30-34	1977	203		1997	119	
35-39	1977	163		1997	76	
40-44	1977	81		1997	37	
45-49	1977	17		1997	10	
Mean age at childbearing (years)	1977	29.3		1997	28.0	
Mean age at first birth (years)	1970	22.7		1998	23.0	
Children ever born per woman						
35-39	1974	5.6		2001	3.2	
40-44	1974	6.4		2001	3.7	
45-49	1974	6.7		2001	4.2	
Percentage of childless women						
35-39	1974	7.8		2001	9.0	
40-44	1974	7.3		2001	7.8	
45-49	1974	7.5		2001	7.5	
Percentage of women with parity three or higher						
35-39	1974	80.3		2001	58.6	
40-44	1974	82.0		2001	66.8	
45-49	1974	81.8		2001	71.5	
Family Planning						
Contraceptive prevalence among women in union						
Percentage using any contraceptive method	1979	33.6		1999	65.8	
Percentage using a modern contraceptive method	1979	25.7		1999	50.1	
Percentage using condoms	1979	1.0		1999	2.7	
Population policies						
Government's view on the level of fertility	1976	Too high		2001	Too high	
Government's policy regarding level of fertility	1976	No intervention		2001	Lower	
Government's support for contraceptive methods	1976	Direct support		2001	Direct support	

Total fertility rates

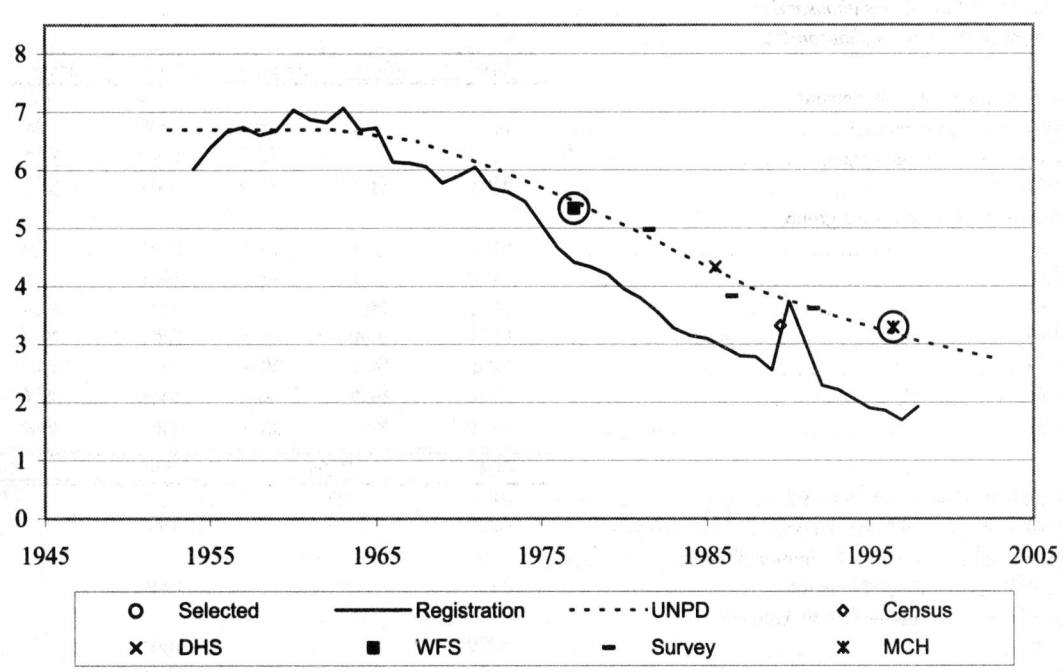

Age-specific fertility rates

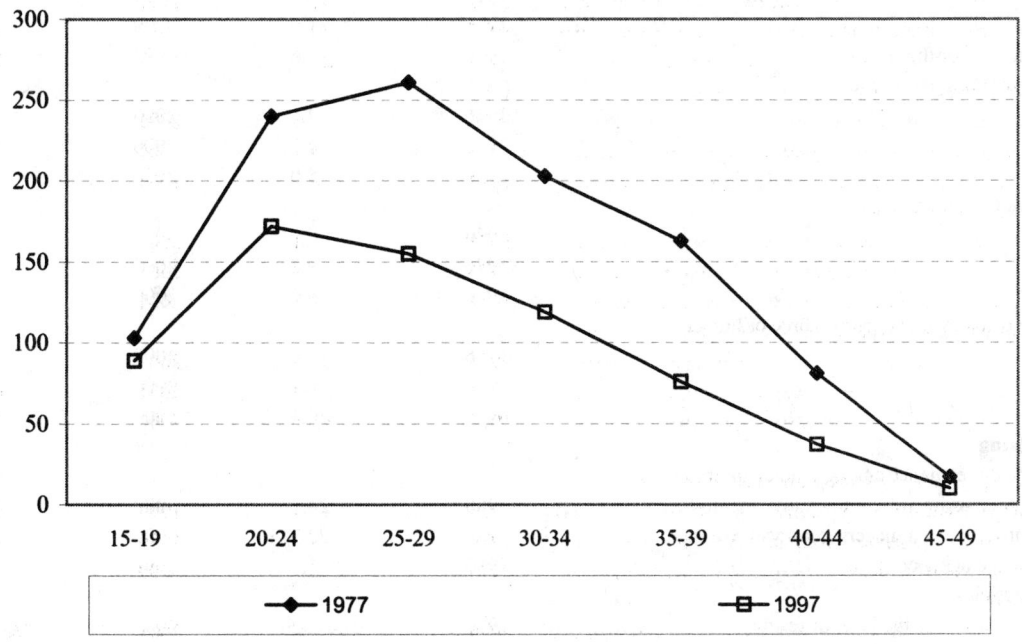

Indicator	Period					
	Earlier year			Later year		
	Year	Value		Year	Value	
Nuptiality						
Annual number of marriages (*thousands*)	..	..		..	..	
Annual number of divorces (*thousands*)	..	..		..	..	
	Year	Male	Female	Year	Male	Female
Total first marriage rate (per person)	..	..	..	..	..	..
Total divorce rate (per person)	1970	0.2	0.2	1996	0.2	0.1
Mean age at first marriage (years)	1973	27.3	21.2	1996	25.7	23.6
SMAM (years)	1976	26.7	21.4	1996	27.9	22.3
Percentage ever married by age group						
15-19	1976	3.8	21.8	1996	2.1	14.5
20-24	1976	19.7	61.1	1996	11.8	56.1
25-29	1976	56.7	86.0	1996	49.2	87.1
30-34	1976	83.0	92.9	1996	82.2	94.9
35-39	1976	92.8	95.3	1996	94.3	97.4
40-44	1976	94.6	95.1	1996	97.6	98.1
45-49	1976	96.2	96.1	1996	98.6	98.6
Fertility	Year	Value		Year	Value	
Annual number of births (*thousands*)	1970	1 161.5		1999	1 693.0	
Crude birth rate (per 1 000 population)	1970	35.1		1999	27.0	
Percentage of extra-marital births among all births	1969	0.0		..	..	
Total fertility rate (births per woman)	1970	5.4		1999	3.6	
Age-specific fertility rate (per 1 000 women)						
15-19	1970	22		1999	19	
20-24	1970	157		1999	193	
25-29	1970	288		1999	226	
30-34	1970	257		1999	163	
35-39	1970	213		1999	88	
40-44	1970	96		1999	26	
45-49	1970	45		1999	7	
Mean age at childbearing (years)	1970	31.9		1999	29.0	
Mean age at first birth (years)	1976	26.6		1995	27.1	
Children ever born per woman						
35-39	1976	4.4		2000	4.2	
40-44	1976	4.7		2000	4.9	
45-49	1976	5.0		2000	5.4	
Percentage of childless women						
35-39	1976	8.4		2000	6.3	
40-44	1976	9.2		2000	5.2	
45-49	1976	9.0		2000	4.8	
Percentage of women with parity three or higher						
35-39	1976	74.8		2000	78.7	
40-44	1976	74.9		2000	83.1	
45-49	1976	76.4		2000	84.4	
Family Planning						
Contraceptive prevalence among women in union						
Percentage using any contraceptive method	1980	24.2		2000	56.1	
Percentage using a modern contraceptive method	1980	22.7		2000	53.9	
Percentage using condoms	1980	1.1		2000	1.0	
Population policies						
Government's view on the level of fertility	1976	Too high		2001	Too high	
Government's policy regarding level of fertility	1976	Lower		2001	Lower	
Government's support for contraceptive methods	1976	Direct support		2001	Direct support	

Total fertility rates

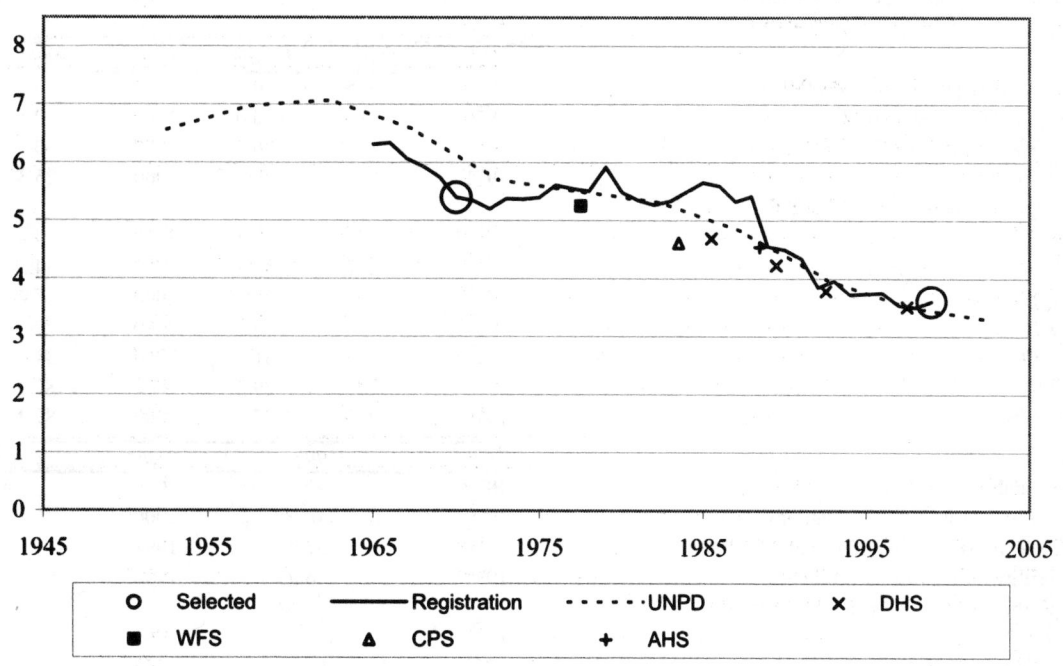

Age-specific fertility rates

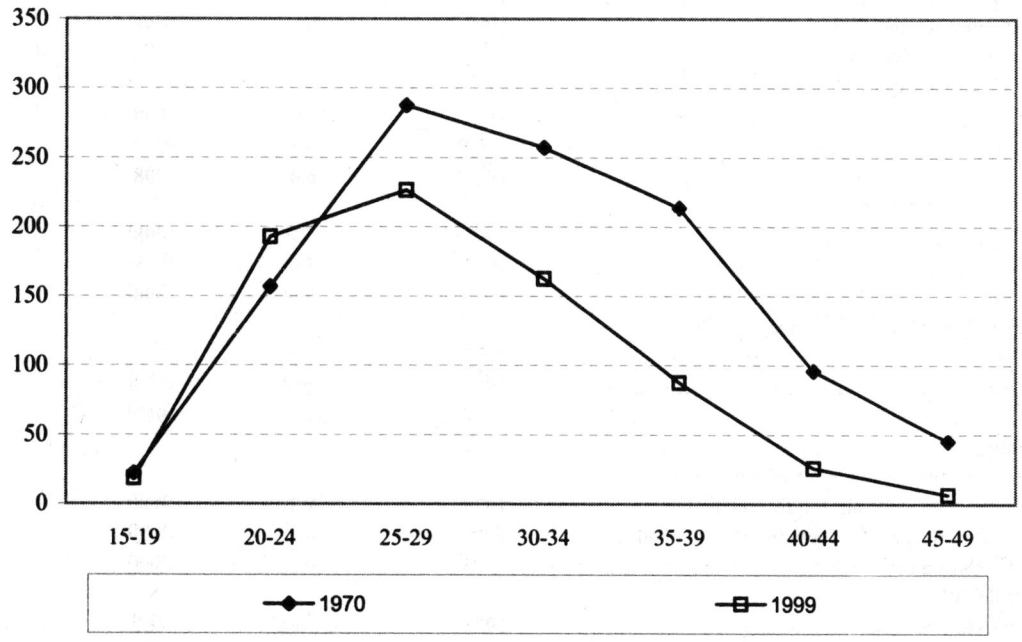

El Salvador

Indicator	Period					
	Earlier year			Later year		
	Year	Value		Year	Value	

Nuptiality

	Year	Value		Year	Value	
Annual number of marriages (*thousands*)	1970	11.8		2000	28.2	
Annual number of divorces (*thousands*)	1970	0.8		2000	3.4	

	Year	Male	Female	Year	Male	Female
Total first marriage rate (per person)	1974	0.5	0.5	1997	0.5	0.4
Total divorce rate (per person)	1970	0.0	0.0	1997	0.1	0.1
Mean age at first marriage (years)	1974	29.6	26.2	1997	30.7	28.3
SMAM (years)	1971	24.7	19.0	2000	25.3	22.3
Percentage ever married by age group						
15-19	1971	3.4	20.4	2000	4.5	15.9
20-24	1971	32.7	56.3	2000	34.5	49.9
25-29	1971	64.2	74.6	2000	63.4	71.9
30-34	1971	77.5	79.9	2000	77.4	81.3
35-39	1971	82.5	81.5	2000	84.9	85.2
40-44	1971	84.4	79.2	2000	87.9	85.9
45-49	1971	85.5	77.7	2000	89.4	86.3

Fertility

	Year	Value	Year	Value
Annual number of births (*thousands*)	1970	141.5	2000	150.2
Crude birth rate (per 1 000 population)	1970	40.0	2000	23.9
Percentage of extra-marital births among all births	1970	67.8	1998	72.8
Total fertility rate (births per woman)	1971	6.0	1996	3.6
Age-specific fertility rate (per 1 000 women)				
15-19	1971	143	1996	116
20-24	1971	291	1996	211
25-29	1971	273	1996	167
30-34	1971	226	1996	118
35-39	1971	181	1996	68
40-44	1971	71	1996	29
45-49	1971	22	1996	8
Mean age at childbearing (years)	1971	28.8	1996	27.0
Mean age at first birth (years)	1971	22.1	1998	23.0
Children ever born per woman				
35-39	1971	5.6	1998	3.7
40-44	1971	6.3	1998	4.2
45-49	1971	6.4	1998	4.9
Percentage of childless women				
35-39	1971	5.4	1998	4.2
40-44	1971	5.9	1998	4.0
45-49	1971	6.0	1998	4.5
Percentage of women with parity three or higher				
35-39	1971	82.2	1998	68.1
40-44	1971	82.9	1998	75.1
45-49	1971	81.2	1998	78.7

Family Planning

	Year	Value	Year	Value
Contraceptive prevalence among women in union				
Percentage using any contraceptive method	1975	19.3	1998	59.7
Percentage using a modern contraceptive method	1975	18.0	1998	54.1
Percentage using condoms	1975	0.5	1998	2.5

Population policies

	Year	Value	Year	Value
Government's view on the level of fertility	1976	Too high	2001	Too high
Government's policy regarding level of fertility	1976	Lower	2001	Lower
Government's support for contraceptive methods	1976	Direct support	2001	Direct support

Total fertility rates

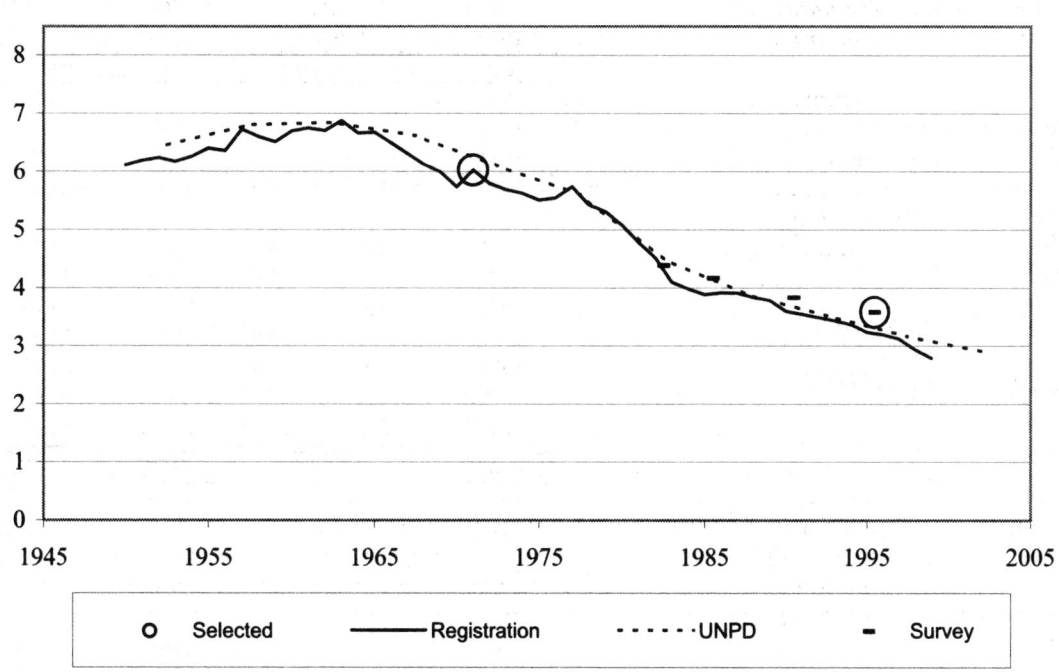

Age-specific fertility rates

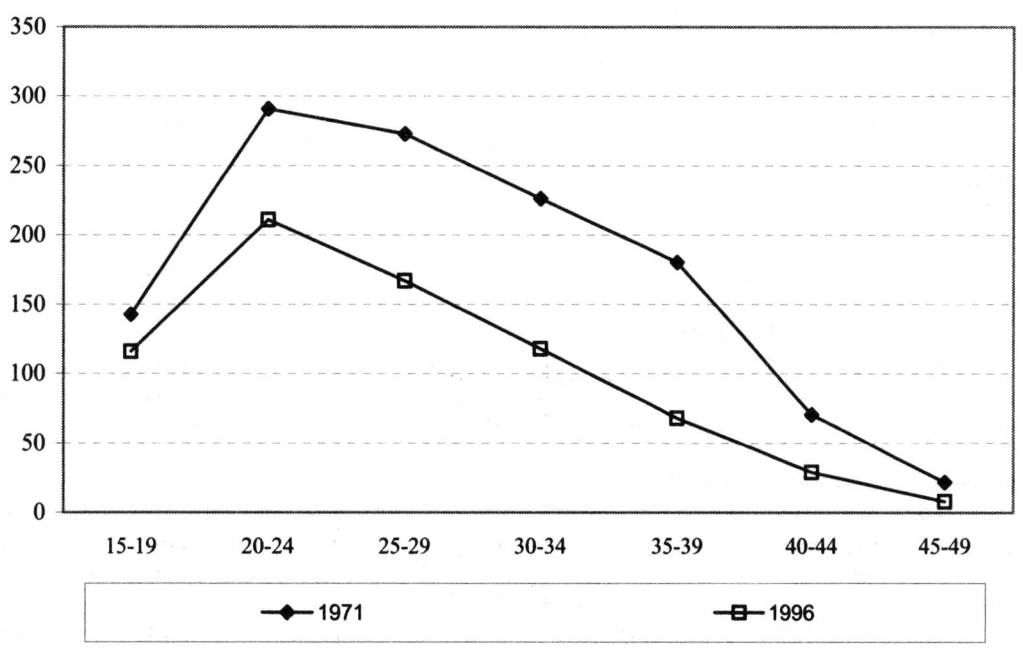

Indicator	Period					
	Earlier year			Later year		
	Year	Value		Year	Value	
Nuptiality						
Annual number of marriages (*thousands*) ....……........	1966	0.2		..	..	
Annual number of divorces (*thousands*)	..	..		..	..	
	Year	Male	Female	Year	Male	Female
Total first marriage rate (per person)	..	..	..	..	..	..
Total divorce rate (per person)	..	..	..	..	..	..
Mean age at first marriage (years)	..	..	..	..	..	..
SMAM (years)	1983	26.9	21.7	..	..	..
Percentage ever married by age group						
15-19	1983	2.1	26.3	..	..	..
20-24	1983	21.8	62.8	..	..	..
25-29	1983	58.3	79.3	..	..	..
30-34	1983	75.9	86.3	..	..	..
35-39	1983	81.6	90.7	..	..	..
40-44	1983	86.5	93.5	..	..	..
45-49	1983	88.6	93.4	..	..	..
Fertility	Year	Value		Year	Value	
Annual number of births (*thousands*).............................	..	..		..	..	
Crude birth rate (per 1 000 population)	..	..		..	..	
Percentage of extra-marital births among all births	..	..		..	..	
Total fertility rate (births per woman)	1983	5.5		..	..	
Age-specific fertility rate (per 1 000 women)						
15-19	..	..		..	..	
20-24	..	..		..	..	
25-29	..	..		..	..	
30-34	..	..		..	..	
35-39	..	..		..	..	
40-44	..	..		..	..	
45-49	..	..		..	..	
Mean age at childbearing (years)	..	..		..	..	
Mean age at first birth (years)	..	..		..	..	
Children ever born per woman						
35-39	..	..		..	..	
40-44	..	..		..	..	
45-49	..	..		..	..	
Percentage of childless women						
35-39	..	..		..	..	
40-44	..	..		..	..	
45-49	..	..		..	..	
Percentage of women with parity three or higher						
35-39	..	..		..	..	
40-44	..	..		..	..	
45-49	..	..		..	..	
Family Planning						
Contraceptive prevalence among women in union						
Percentage using any contraceptive method	..	..		..	..	
Percentage using a modern contraceptive method	..	..		..	..	
Percentage using condoms ....…...	..	..		..	..	
Population policies						
Government's view on the level of fertility	1976	Too low		2001	Satisfactory	
Government's policy regarding level of fertility	1976	No intervention		2001	Maintain	
Government's support for contraceptive methods	1976	No support		2001	No support	

Total fertility rates

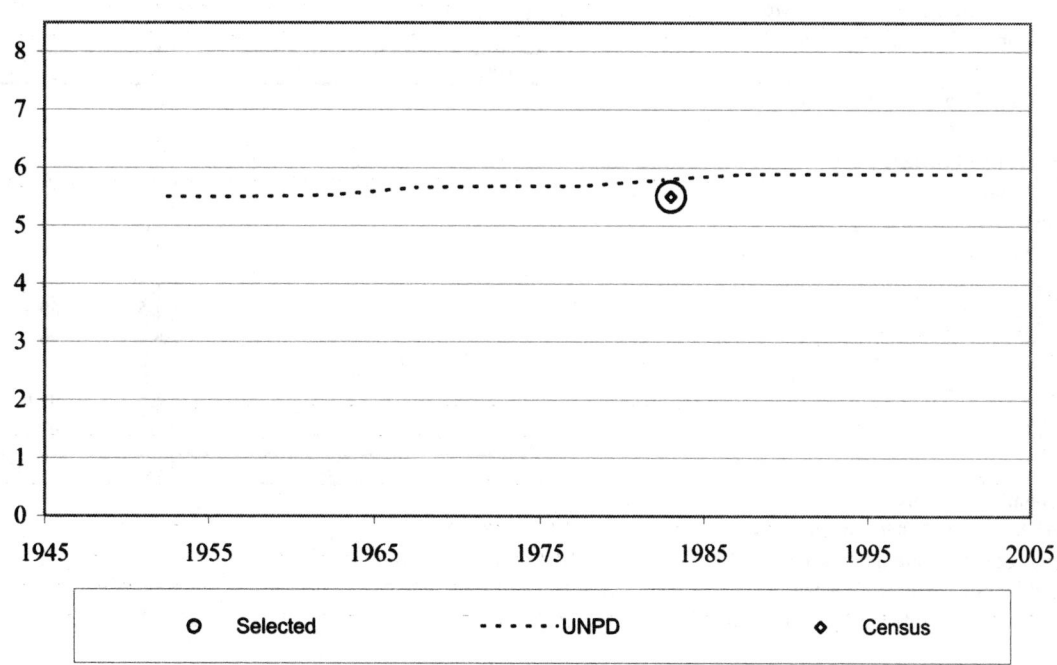

Indicator	Period					
	Earlier year			Later year		
	Year	Value		Year	Value	
Nuptiality						
Annual number of marriages (*thousands*)	..	..		..	..	
Annual number of divorces (*thousands*)	..	..		..	..	
	Year	Male	Female	Year	Male	Female
Total first marriage rate (per person)	..	..	..	..	..	..
Total divorce rate (per person)	..	..	..	..	..	..
Mean age at first marriage (years)	..	..	..	..	..	..
SMAM (years)	..	..	..	1995	25.3	19.6
Percentage ever married by age group						
15-19	..	..	..	1995	1.5	37.7
20-24	..	..	..	1995	31.4	78.1
25-29	..	..	..	1995	69.5	92.1
30-34	..	..	..	1995	90.7	95.7
35-39	..	..	..	1995	98.3	98.2
40-44	..	..	..	1995	95.6	97.3
45-49	..	..	..	1995	99.0	98.1
Fertility	Year	Value		Year	Value	
Annual number of births (*thousands*)............................	..	..		..	..	
Crude birth rate (per 1 000 population)	..	..		..	..	
Percentage of extra-marital births among all births	..	..		..	..	
Total fertility rate (births per woman)	..	..		2000	5.2	
Age-specific fertility rate (per 1 000 women)						
15-19	..	..		2000	85	
20-24	..	..		2000	199	
25-29	..	..		2000	214	
30-34	..	..		2000	213	
35-39	..	..		2000	183	
40-44	..	..		2000	102	
45-49	..	..		2000	51	
Mean age at childbearing (years)	..	..		2000	30.9	
Mean age at first birth (years)[a]	..	..		2002	20.6	
Children ever born per woman						
35-39	..	..		2002	4.7	
40-44	..	..		2002	5.7	
45-49	..	..		2002	6.2	
Percentage of childless women						
35-39	..	..		2002	5.3	
40-44	..	..		2002	3.1	
45-49	..	..		2002	3.4	
Percentage of women with parity three or higher						
35-39	..	..		2002	79.7	
40-44	..	..		2002	84.5	
45-49	..	..		2002	87.4	
Family Planning						
Contraceptive prevalence among women in union						
Percentage using any contraceptive method	..	..		2002	8.0	
Percentage using a modern contraceptive method	..	..		2002	5.1	
Percentage using condoms	..	..		2002	0.6	
Population policies						
Government's view on the level of fertility	..	--		2001	Too high	
Government's policy regarding level of fertility	..	--		2001	Lower	
Government's support for contraceptive methods	..	--		2001	Direct support	

[a]Median age at first birth among women aged 25-29 at the date of the survey

Total fertility rates

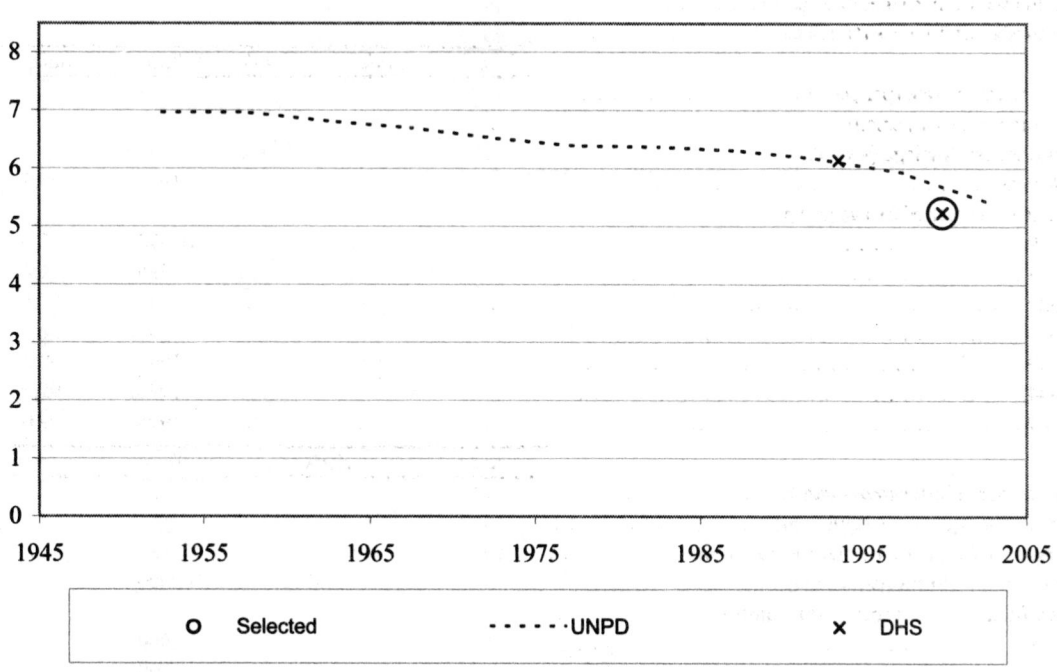

O	Selected	· · · · · ·UNPD		×	DHS

Age-specific fertility rates

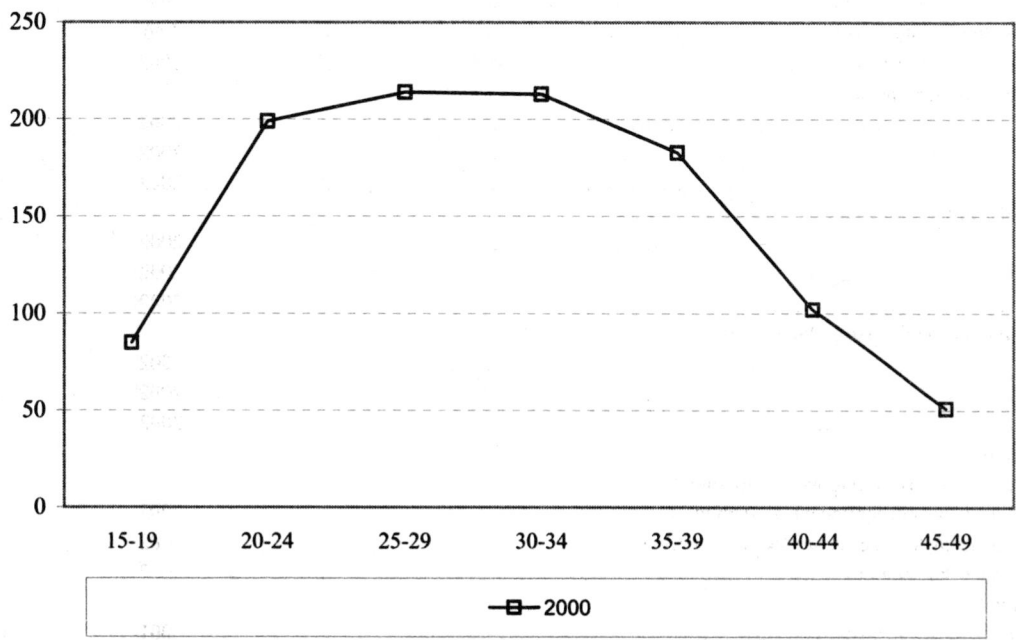

—□— 2000

Indicator	Period					
	Earlier year			Later year		
	Year	Value		Year	Value	

Nuptiality

Indicator	Year	Value		Year	Value	
Annual number of marriages (*thousands*)	1970	12.4		2001	5.6	
Annual number of divorces (*thousands*)	1970	4.4		2001	4.3	

Indicator	Year	Male	Female	Year	Male	Female
Total first marriage rate (per person)	1970	..	1.0	1997	0.3	0.4
Total divorce rate (per person)	..	..	..	1996	0.5	0.5
Mean age at first marriage (years)	1970	..	23.5	1997	26.3	24.1
SMAM (years)	..	..	..	1989	24.5	22.1
Percentage ever married by age group						
15-19	1979	..	..	1989	2.6	9.4
20-24	1979	36.6	59.0	1989	34.8	59.4
25-29	1979	76.3	84.9	1989	75.7	83.7
30-34	1979	86.5	90.5	1989	86.9	89.9
35-39	1979	89.9	92.2	1989	90.1	92.6
40-44	1979	92.3	93.0	1989	91.2	93.3
45-49	1979	93.7	92.4	1989	92.4	93.2

Fertility

Indicator	Year	Value	Year	Value
Annual number of births (*thousands*)	1970	21.6	2001	12.6
Crude birth rate (per 1 000 population)	1970	15.8	2001	9.3
Percentage of extra-marital births among all births	1970	14.1	2001	56.2
Total fertility rate (births per woman)	1970	2.2	2001	1.3
Age-specific fertility rate (per 1 000 women)				
15-19	1970	33	2001	24
20-24	1970	159	2001	81
25-29	1970	131	2001	83
30-34	1970	73	2001	53
35-39	1970	30	2001	22
40-44	1970	7	2001	4
45-49	1970	1	2001	0
Mean age at childbearing (years)	1970	26.7	2001	27.2
Mean age at first birth (years)	1970	24.1	2001	24.2
Children ever born per woman				
35-39	..	..	1994	2.1
40-44	..	..	1994	2.1
45-49	..	..	1994	2.0
Percentage of childless women				
35-39	..	..	1994	7.8
40-44	..	..	1994	6.6
45-49	..	..	1994	10.8
Percentage of women with parity three or higher				
35-39	..	..	1994	32.1
40-44	..	..	1994	25.2
45-49	..	..	1994	27.7

Family Planning

Indicator			Year	Value
Contraceptive prevalence among women in union				
Percentage using any contraceptive method	..	..	1994	70.3
Percentage using a modern contraceptive method	..	..	1994	56.4
Percentage using condoms	..	..	1994	16.1

Population policies

Indicator			Year	Value
Government's view on the level of fertility	..	..	2001	Too low
Government's policy regarding level of fertility	..	..	2001	No intervention
Government's support for contraceptive methods	..	..	2001	Indirect support

Total fertility rates

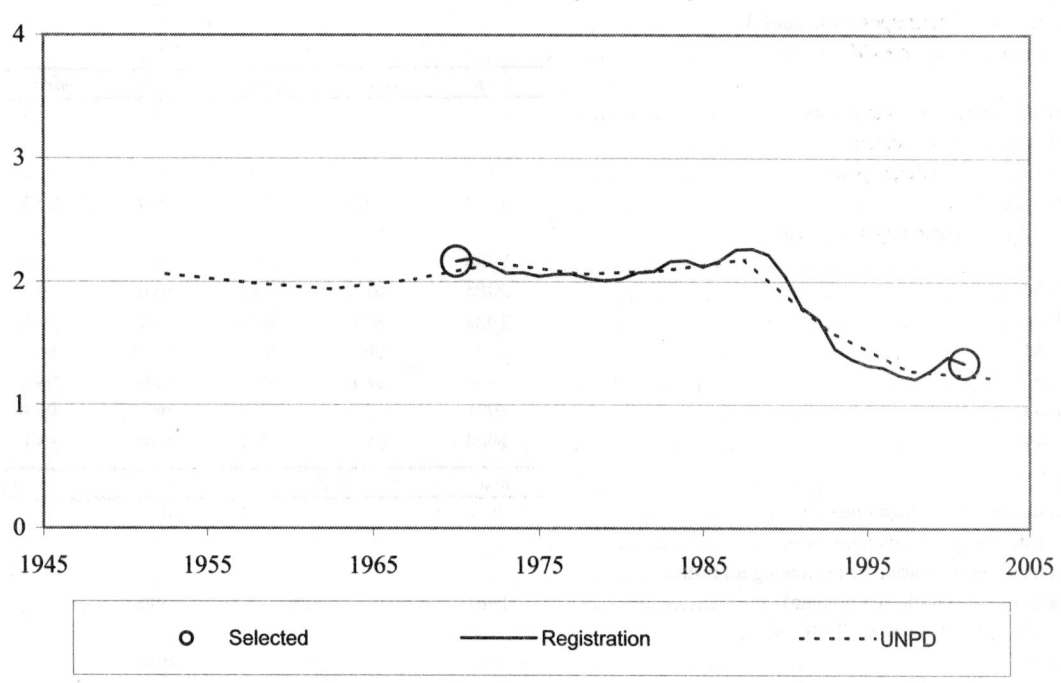

Age-specific fertility rates

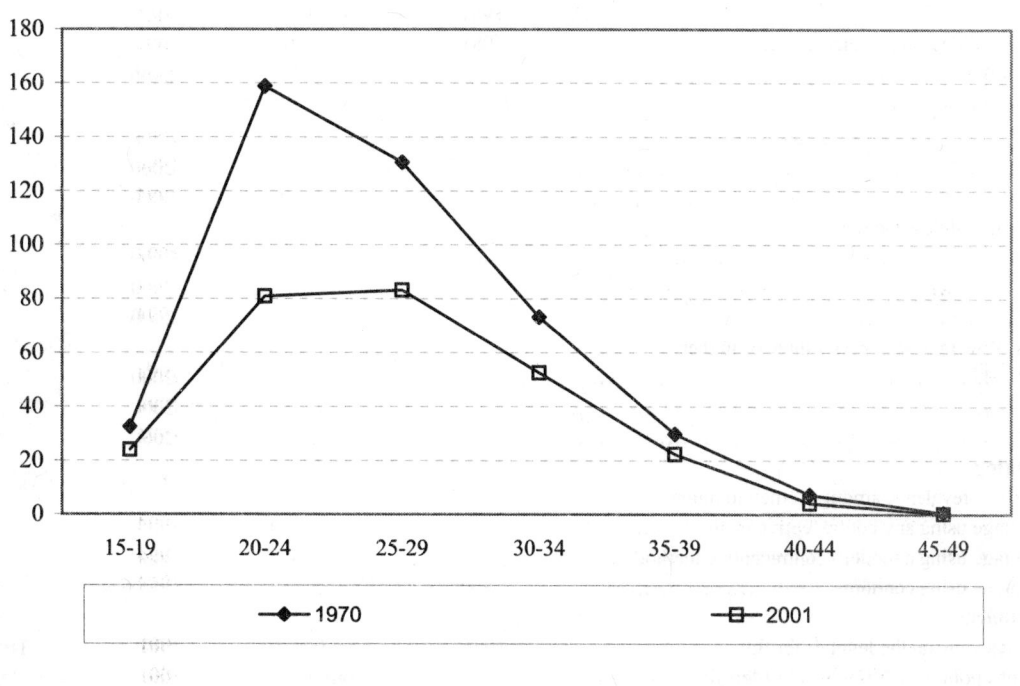

Ethiopia

Indicator	Period					
	Earlier year			Later year		
	Year	Value		Year	Value	

Nuptiality

Indicator	Year	Value		Year	Value	
Annual number of marriages (*thousands*)	..	..		..	..	
Annual number of divorces (*thousands*)	..	..		..	..	

Indicator	Year	Male	Female	Year	Male	Female
Total first marriage rate (per person)	..	..	..	..	..	..
Total divorce rate (per person)	..	..	..	..	..	..
Mean age at first marriage (years)	..	..	..	..	..	..
SMAM (years)	1984	23.3	17.1	2000	25.8	20.5
Percentage ever married by age group						
15-19	1984	6.1	60.9	2000	3.4	30.0
20-24	1984	47.4	94.4	2000	23.7	73.1
25-29	1984	84.6	98.6	2000	70.8	90.4
30-34	1984	96.0	99.0	2000	86.4	97.5
35-39	1984	98.6	99.2	2000	98.4	98.8
40-44	1984	99.1	99.3	2000	99.0	99.6
45-49	1984	99.5	99.2	2000	98.7	99.9

Fertility

Indicator	Year	Value	Year	Value
Annual number of births (*thousands*)	..	..	..	..
Crude birth rate (per 1 000 population)	..	..	..	..
Percentage of extra-marital births among all births	..	..	..	..
Total fertility rate (births per woman)	1981	6.8	1998	5.9
Age-specific fertility rate (per 1 000 women)				
15-19	1981	115	1998	110
20-24	1981	273	1998	244
25-29	1981	299	1998	264
30-34	1981	264	1998	248
35-39	1981	225	1998	183
40-44	1981	125	1998	100
45-49	1981	65	1998	24
Mean age at childbearing (years)	1981	30.6	1998	29.8
Mean age at first birth (years)[a]	..	..	2000	20.1
Children ever born per woman				
35-39	..	..	2000	5.7
40-44	..	..	2000	6.7
45-49	..	..	2000	7.2
Percentage of childless women				
35-39	..	..	2000	3.5
40-44	..	..	2000	1.8
45-49	..	..	2000	2.4
Percentage of women with parity three or higher				
35-39	..	..	2000	87.8
40-44	..	..	2000	91.2
45-49	..	..	2000	91.2

Family Planning

Indicator	Year	Value	Year	Value
Contraceptive prevalence among women in union				
Percentage using any contraceptive method	..	..	2000	8.1
Percentage using a modern contraceptive method	..	..	2000	6.3
Percentage using condoms	..	..	2000	0.3

Population policies

Indicator	Year	Value	Year	Value
Government's view on the level of fertility	1976	Satisfactory	2001	Too high
Government's policy regarding level of fertility	1976	No intervention	2001	Lower
Government's support for contraceptive methods	1976	Indirect support	2001	Direct support

[a]Median age at first birth among women aged 25-29 at the date of the survey

Total fertility rates

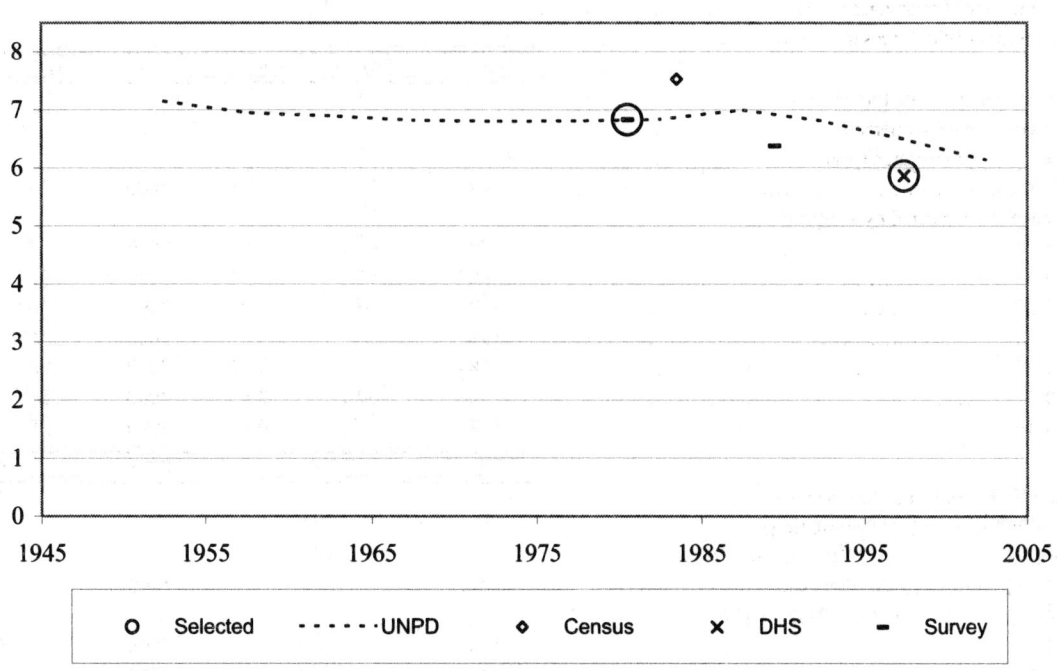

Age-specific fertility rates

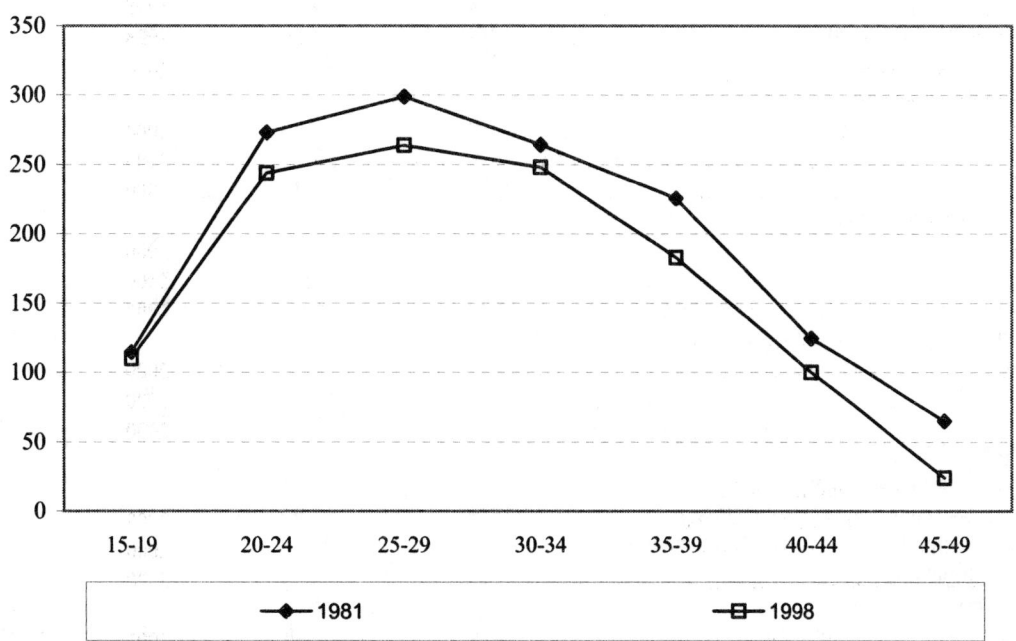

Indicator	Period					
	Earlier year			Later year		
	Year	Value		Year	Value	
Nuptiality						
Annual number of marriages (*thousands*)	1970	4.1		1998	8.1	
Annual number of divorces (*thousands*)	1970	0.3		..	..	
	Year	Male	Female	Year	Male	Female
Total first marriage rate (per person)	1975	1.0	0.9	1987	0.8	0.8
Total divorce rate (per person)	..	..	..	..	..	..
Mean age at first marriage (years)	1975	26.7	23.5	1987	27.1	23.6
SMAM (years)	1976	24.7	21.7	1996	26.1	22.9
Percentage ever married by age group						
15-19	1976	2.7	14.0	1996	1.8	10.3
20-24	1976	35.1	63.4	1996	22.7	54.1
25-29	1976	75.1	86.9	1996	64.8	81.6
30-34	1976	89.9	94.1	1996	85.0	89.5
35-39	1976	94.3	95.8	1996	90.9	92.4
40-44	1976	96.1	96.7	1996	94.0	94.4
45-49	1976	97.0	96.9	1996	94.9	95.4
Fertility	Year	Value		Year	Value	
Annual number of births (*thousands*)	1970	15.5		1999	16.9	
Crude birth rate (per 1 000 population)	1970	29.9		1999	21.0	
Percentage of extra-marital births among all births	1978	17.3		..	..	
Total fertility rate (births per woman)	1972	4.1		1986	3.4	
Age-specific fertility rate (per 1 000 women)						
15-19	1972	58		1986	62	
20-24	1972	248		1986	207	
25-29	1972	215		1986	191	
30-34	1972	162		1986	122	
35-39	1972	90		1986	66	
40-44	1972	43		1986	24	
45-49	1972	10		1986	8	
Mean age at childbearing (years)	1972	28.4		1986	27.7	
Mean age at first birth (years)	1970	23.3		1987	22.3	
Children ever born per woman						
35-39	1966	5.8		1986	3.7	
40-44	1966	6.3		1986	4.3	
45-49	1966	6.4		1986	4.9	
Percentage of childless women						
35-39	1966	6.8		1986	7.3	
40-44	1966	7.6		1986	5.7	
45-49	1966	8.2		1986	5.8	
Percentage of women with parity three or higher						
35-39	1966	80.3		1986	72.5	
40-44	1966	80.1		1986	78.0	
45-49	1966	78.9		1986	80.2	
Family Planning						
Contraceptive prevalence among women in union						
Percentage using any contraceptive method	1974	41.0		..	..	
Percentage using a modern contraceptive method	1974	35.1		..	..	
Percentage using condoms	1974	6.0		..	..	
Population policies						
Government's view on the level of fertility	1976	Too high		2001	Satisfactory	
Government's policy regarding level of fertility	1976	Lower		2001	Lower	
Government's support for contraceptive methods	1976	Direct support		2001	Direct support	

Total fertility rates

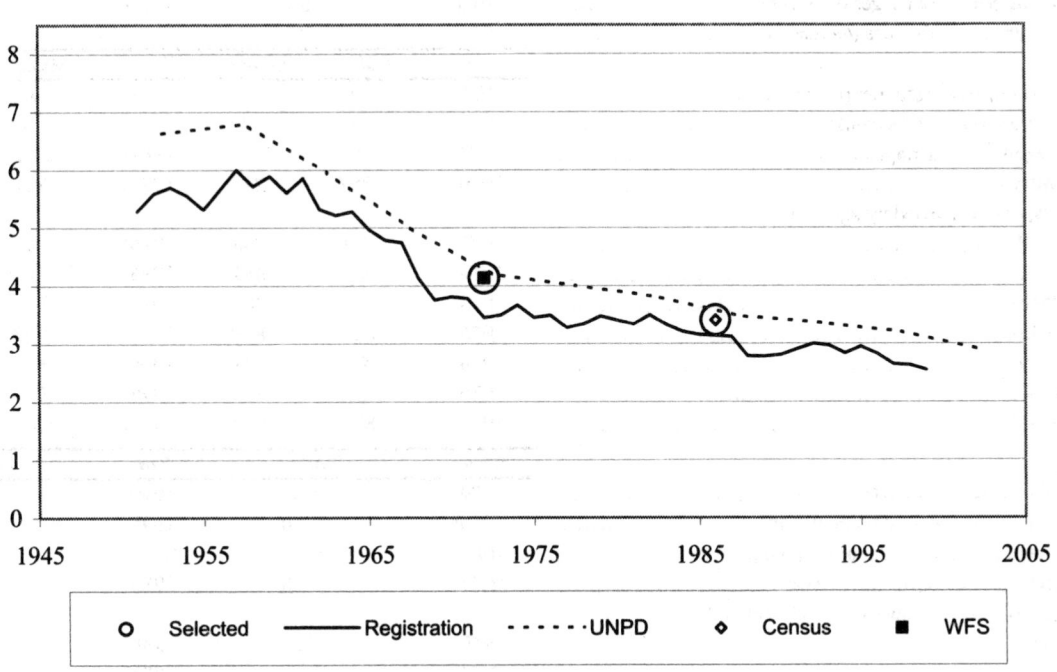

Age-specific fertility rates

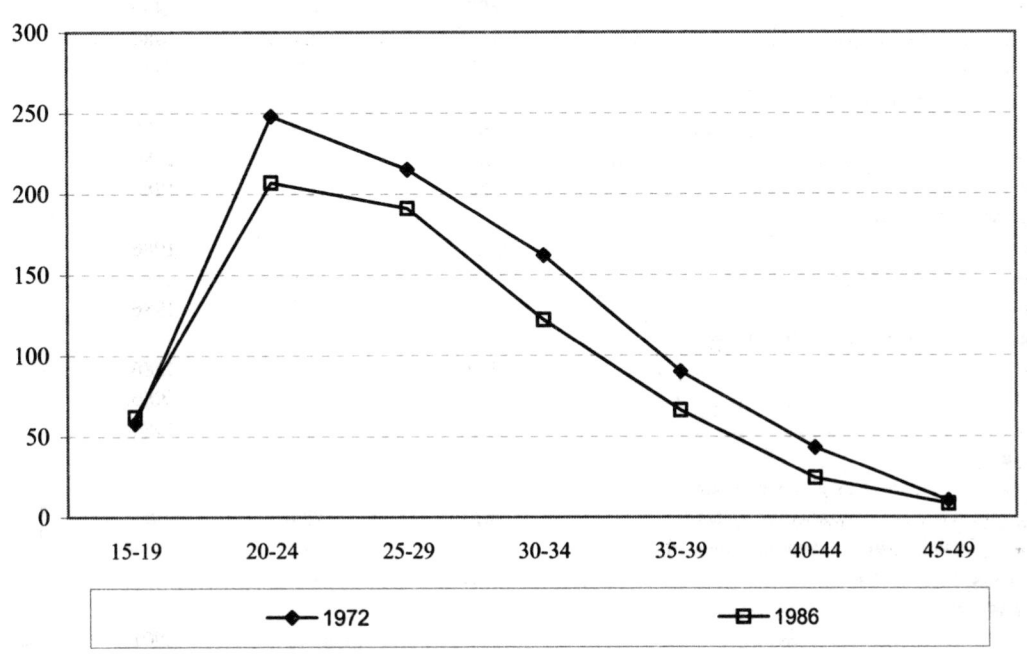

Finland

Indicator	Period					
	Earlier year			Later year		
	Year	Value		Year	Value	
Nuptiality						
Annual number of marriages (*thousands*)	1970	40.7		2001	24.8	
Annual number of divorces (*thousands*)	1970	6.0		2001	13.6	
	Year	Male	Female	Year	Male	Female
Total first marriage rate (per person)	1973	0.7	0.8	1998	0.5	0.6
Total divorce rate (per person)	1970	0.3	0.3	1997	0.3	0.3
Mean age at first marriage (years)	1973	25.5	23.6	1998	29.6	27.6
SMAM (years)	1970	25.6	22.5	2000	32.3	30.2
Percentage ever married by age group						
15-19	1970	1.0	5.4	2000	0.1	0.5
20-24	1970	28.4	48.0	2000	4.7	10.5
25-29	1970	68.3	78.2	2000	24.4	37.8
30-34	1970	80.2	86.1	2000	47.6	60.3
35-39	1970	83.8	88.0	2000	61.9	72.7
40-44	1970	85.2	88.2	2000	71.4	80.4
45-49	1970	87.8	87.9	2000	78.6	85.9
Fertility	Year	Value		Year	Value	
Annual number of births (*thousands*)	1970	64.6		2002	55.5	
Crude birth rate (per 1 000 population)	1970	14.0		2001	10.8	
Percentage of extra-marital births among all births	1970	5.8		2001	39.5	
Total fertility rate (births per woman)	1970	1.8		2001	1.7	
Age-specific fertility rate (per 1 000 women)						
15-19	1970	32		2001	11	
20-24	1970	117		2001	60	
25-29	1970	112		2001	114	
30-34	1970	64		2001	103	
35-39	1970	31		2001	48	
40-44	1970	9		2001	10	
45-49	1970	1		2001	0	
Mean age at childbearing (years)	1970	27.1		2001	29.6	
Mean age at first birth (years)	1970	24.4		2001	27.5	
Children ever born per woman						
35-39	..	..		2000	1.8	
40-44	..	..		2000	1.9	
45-49	..	..		2000	1.9	
Percentage of childless women						
35-39	..	..		2000	21.1	
40-44	..	..		2000	16.8	
45-49	..	..		2000	15.7	
Percentage of women with parity three or higher						
35-39	..	..		2000	26.4	
40-44	..	..		2000	29.4	
45-49	..	..		2000	26.2	
Family Planning						
Contraceptive prevalence among women in union						
Percentage using any contraceptive method	1971	77.0		1989	77.4	
Percentage using a modern contraceptive method	1971	54.0		1989	75.4	
Percentage using condoms	1971	31.0		1989	20.1	
Population policies						
Government's view on the level of fertility	1976	Too low		2001	Satisfactory	
Government's policy regarding level of fertility	1976	Raise		2001	No intervention	
Government's support for contraceptive methods	1976	Direct support		2001	Direct support	

Total fertility rates

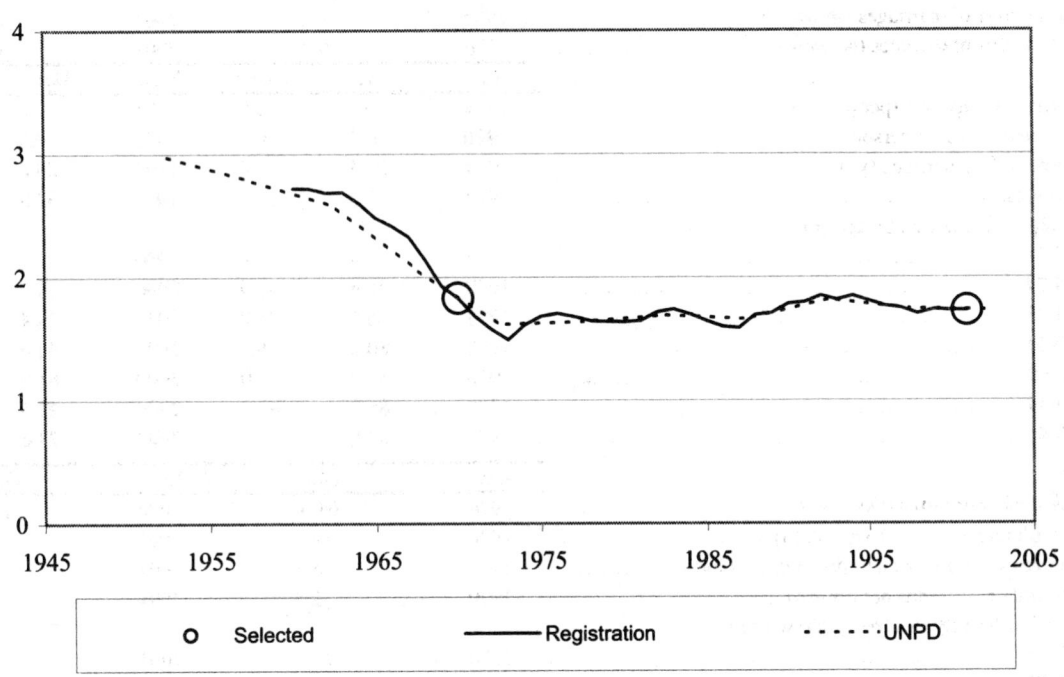

Age-specific fertility rates

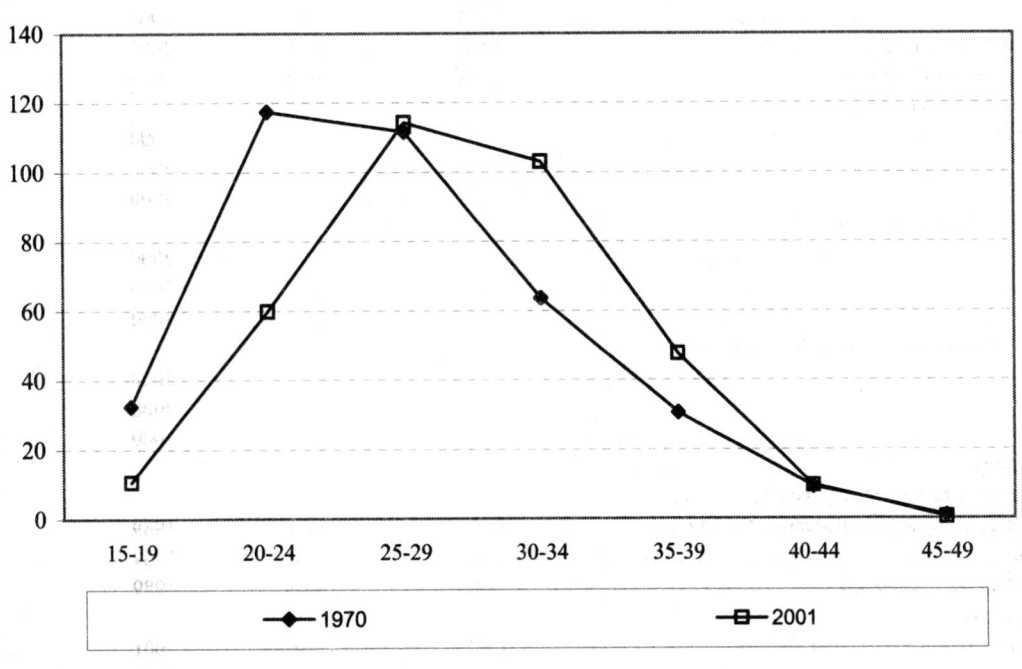

Indicator	Period			
	Earlier year		Later year	
	Year	Value	Year	Value
Nuptiality				
Annual number of marriages (*thousands*)	1970	393.7	2001	304.7
Annual number of divorces (*thousands*)	1970	40.0	1999	116.8

Indicator	Year	Male	Female	Year	Male	Female
Total first marriage rate (per person)	1974	0.8	0.8	1996	0.5	0.5
Total divorce rate (per person)	1970	0.1	0.1	1993	0.2	0.2
Mean age at first marriage (years)	1974	24.8	22.6	1996	29.9	27.9
SMAM (years)	1975	25.3	23.0	2000	32.3	30.2
Percentage ever married by age group						
15-19	1975	0.4	3.5	2000	0.0	0.3
20-24	1975	22.8	45.1	2000	2.7	8.8
25-29	1975	69.2	80.4	2000	24.9	38.8
30-34	1975	84.4	89.5	2000	51.7	62.0
35-39	1975	87.2	92.0	2000	66.5	74.6
40-44	1975	88.0	92.3	2000	77.8	83.6
45-49	1975	88.8	91.8	2000	85.2	88.6

Indicator	Year	Value	Year	Value
Fertility				
Annual number of births (*thousands*)	1970	850.4	2001	774.6
Crude birth rate (per 1 000 population)	1970	16.7	2001	13.1
Percentage of extra-marital births among all births	1970	6.8	2000	42.6
Total fertility rate (births per woman)	1970	2.5	1999	1.8
Age-specific fertility rate (per 1 000 women)				
15-19	1970	37	1999	10
20-24	1970	167	1999	61
25-29	1970	150	1999	133
30-34	1970	88	1999	105
35-39	1970	41	1999	42
40-44	1970	11	1999	8
45-49	1970	1	1999	0
Mean age at childbearing (years)	1970	27.2	1999	29.4
Mean age at first birth (years)[a]	1970	24.4	1999	28.7
Children ever born per woman				
35-39	..	..	1994	2.1
40-44	..	..	1994	2.2
45-49	..	..	1994	2.2
Percentage of childless women				
35-39	..	..	1994	11.3
40-44	..	..	1994	7.7
45-49	..	..	1994	12.0
Percentage of women with parity three or higher				
35-39	..	..	1994	31.9
40-44	..	..	1994	36.7
45-49	..	..	1994	30.2
Family Planning				
Contraceptive prevalence among women in union				
Percentage using any contraceptive method	1972	64.0	1994	74.6
Percentage using a modern contraceptive method	1972	21.0	1994	69.3
Percentage using condoms	1972	8.0	1994	5.0
Population policies				
Government's view on the level of fertility	1976	Too low	2001	Too low
Government's policy regarding level of fertility	1976	Raise	2001	No intervention
Government's support for contraceptive methods	1976	Direct support	2001	Indirect support

[a] Mean age at first birth within current marriage

Total fertility rates

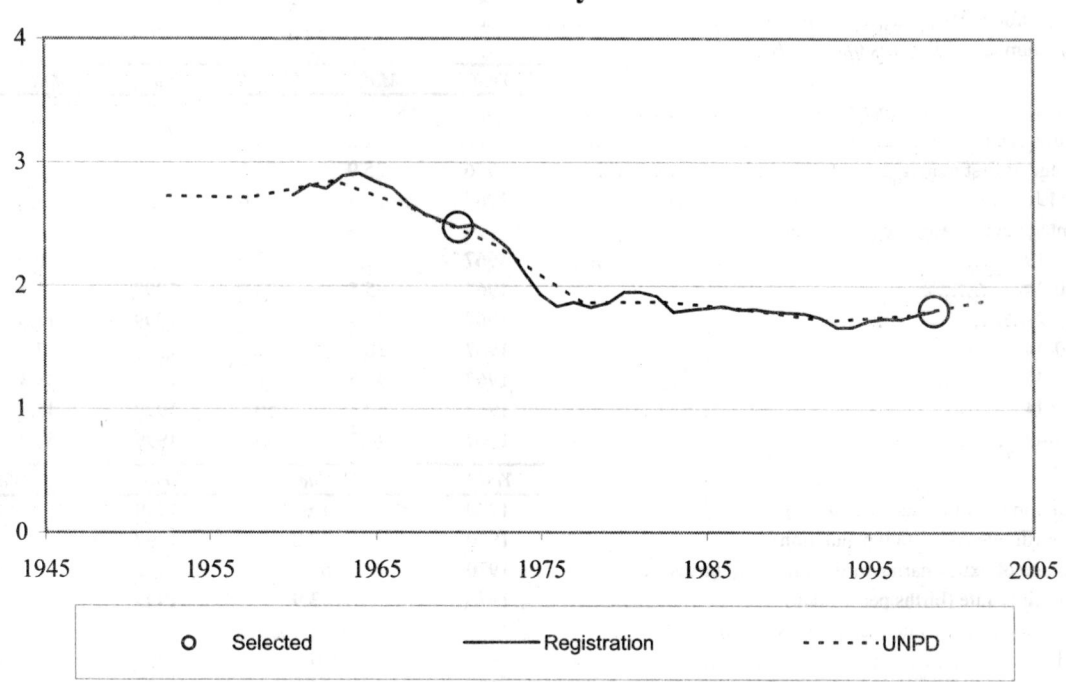

Age-specific fertility rates

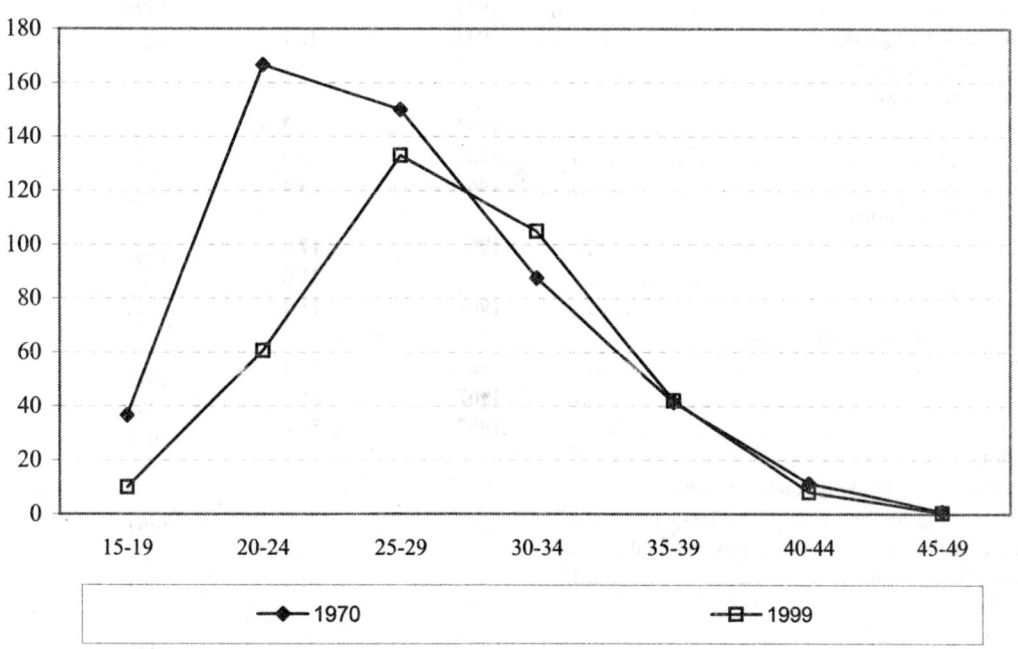

Indicator	Period					
	Earlier year			Later year		
	Year	Value		Year	Value	

Nuptiality

	Year			Year		
Annual number of marriages (*thousands*)	..	..		..	..	
Annual number of divorces (*thousands*)	..	..		..	..	

	Year	Male	Female	Year	Male	Female
Total first marriage rate (per person)	..	..	..	..	..	..
Total divorce rate (per person)	..	..	..	..	..	..
Mean age at first marriage (years)	1976	25.9	22.7	..	..	..
SMAM (years)	1967	28.4	24.4	1999	34.2	31.7
Percentage ever married by age group						
15-19	1967	0.4	3.0	1999	0.0	0.8
20-24	1967	5.5	25.0	1999	1.4	6.5
25-29	1967	26.6	41.4	1999	11.6	21.3
30-34	1967	38.1	47.7	1999	27.5	31.6
35-39	1967	42.5	49.8	1999	38.3	41.2
40-44	1967	50.3	50.3	1999	45.3	45.4
45-49	1967	46.3	53.2	1999	51.9	51.4

Fertility

	Year	Value	Year	Value
Annual number of births (*thousands*).............................	1970	1.6	1999	4.9
Crude birth rate (per 1 000 population)	1970	32.2	1999	31.0
Percentage of extra-marital births among all births	1970	63.1	1986	74.6
Total fertility rate (births per woman)	1973	3.9	1999	4.1
Age-specific fertility rate (per 1 000 women)				
15-19	1973	101	1999	97
20-24	1973	263	1999	178
25-29	1973	177	1999	230
30-34	1973	120	1999	187
35-39	1973	80	1999	105
40-44	1973	34	1999	29
45-49	1973	6	1999	0
Mean age at childbearing (years)	1973	27.1	1999	28.2
Mean age at first birth (years)	1967	24.1	..	..
Children ever born per woman				
35-39	1967	3.7	..	..
40-44	1967	3.7	..	..
45-49	1967	3.4	..	..
Percentage of childless women				
35-39	1967	17.9	..	..
40-44	1967	21.6	..	..
45-49	1967	23.2	..	..
Percentage of women with parity three or higher				
35-39	1967	58.4	..	..
40-44	1967	55.4	..	..
45-49	1967	50.2	..	..

Family Planning

Contraceptive prevalence among women in union				
Percentage using any contraceptive method	..	..	..	..
Percentage using a modern contraceptive method	..	..	..	..
Percentage using condoms	..	..	..	..

Population policies

Government's view on the level of fertility	..	--	..	--
Government's policy regarding level of fertility	..	--	..	--
Government's support for contraceptive methods	..	--	..	--

Total fertility rates

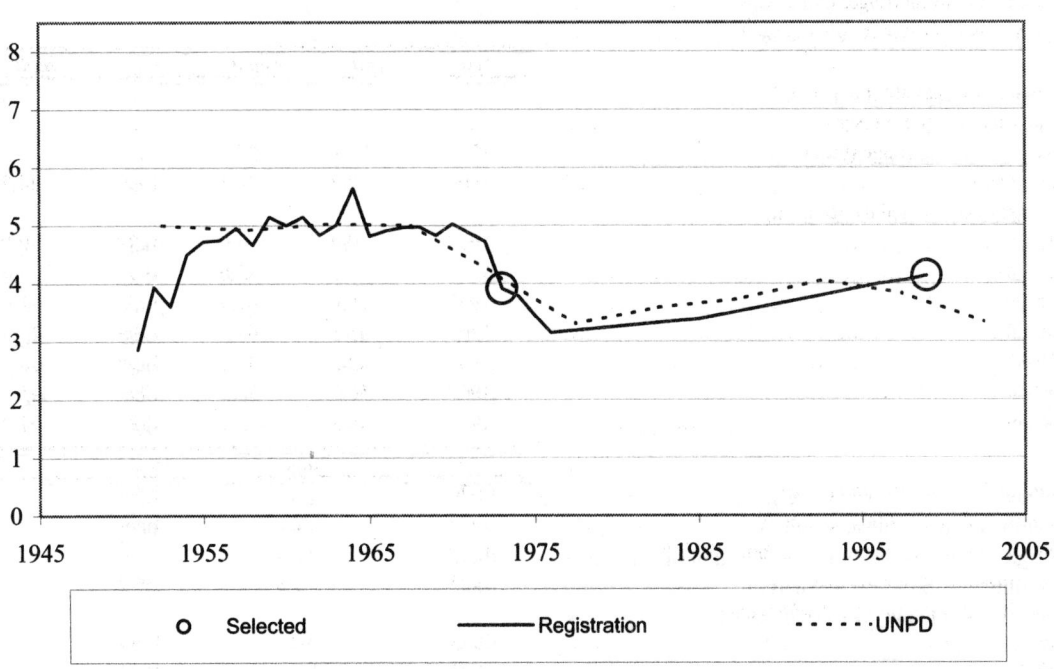

Age-specific fertility rates

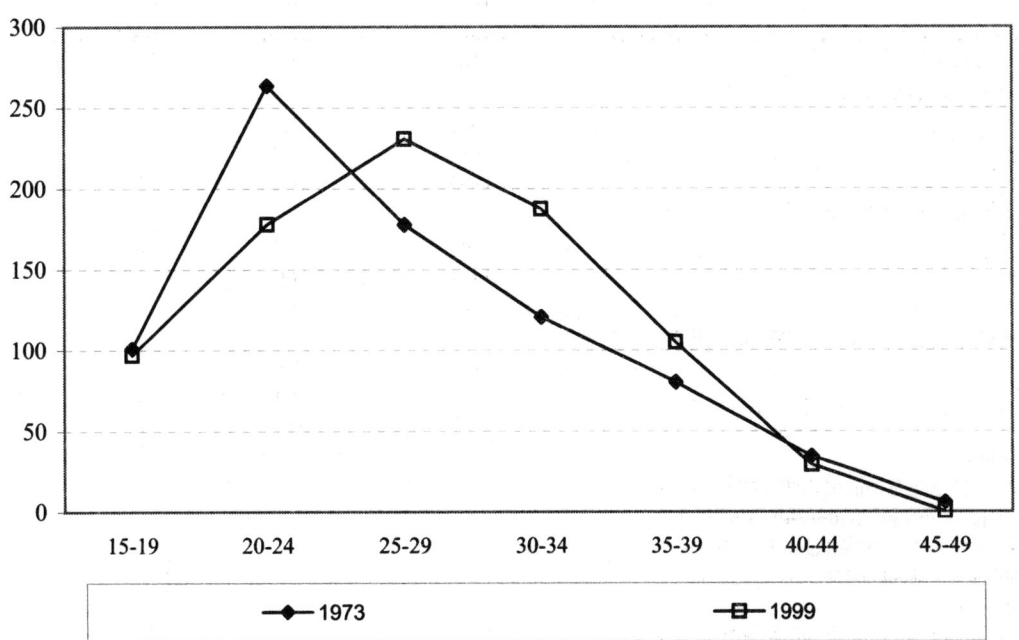

French Polynesia

Indicator	Period					
	Earlier year			Later year		
	Year	Value		Year	Value	
Nuptiality						
Annual number of marriages (*thousands*)	1972	0.9		1993	1.2	
Annual number of divorces (*thousands*)	1969	0.1		..	..	
	Year	Male	Female	Year	Male	Female
Total first marriage rate (per person)	..	..	..	..	..	..
Total divorce rate (per person)	..	..	..	..	..	..
Mean age at first marriage (years)	..	..	..	..	..	..
SMAM (years)	1977	28.5	25.8	1996	32.1	29.9
Percentage ever married by age group						
15-19	1977	1.0	3.7	1996	0.3	1.5
20-24	1977	12.5	28.1	1996	6.8	15.2
25-29	1977	41.8	55.7	1996	23.7	37.1
30-34	1977	60.0	71.1	1996	44.6	55.9
35-39	1977	67.5	75.4	1996	59.3	67.3
40-44	1977	73.4	76.9	1996	69.3	75.2
45-49	1977	76.7	80.4	1996	77.0	81.0
Fertility	Year	Value		Year	Value	
Annual number of births (*thousands*)	1970	4.4		2000	4.9	
Crude birth rate (per 1 000 population)	1970	40.5		2000	21.2	
Percentage of extra-marital births among all births	1968	54.9		..	..	
Total fertility rate (births per woman)	1968	6.7		..	..	
Age-specific fertility rate (per 1 000 women)						
15-19	1968	109		..	..	
20-24	1968	379		..	..	
25-29	1968	353		..	..	
30-34	1968	249		..	..	
35-39	1968	156		..	..	
40-44	1968	79		..	..	
45-49	1968	11		..	..	
Mean age at childbearing (years)	1968	28.4		..	..	
Mean age at first birth (years)	..	..		2000	24.2	
Children ever born per woman						
35-39	..	..		..	..	
40-44	..	..		..	..	
45-49	..	..		..	..	
Percentage of childless women						
35-39	..	..		..	..	
40-44	..	..		..	..	
45-49	..	..		..	..	
Percentage of women with parity three or higher						
35-39	..	..		..	..	
40-44	..	..		..	..	
45-49	..	..		..	..	
Family Planning						
Contraceptive prevalence among women in union						
Percentage using any contraceptive method	..	..		..	..	
Percentage using a modern contraceptive method	..	..		..	..	
Percentage using condoms	..	..		..	..	
Population policies						
Government's view on the level of fertility	..	--		..	--	
Government's policy regarding level of fertility	..	--		..	--	
Government's support for contraceptive methods	..	--		..	--	

Total fertility rates

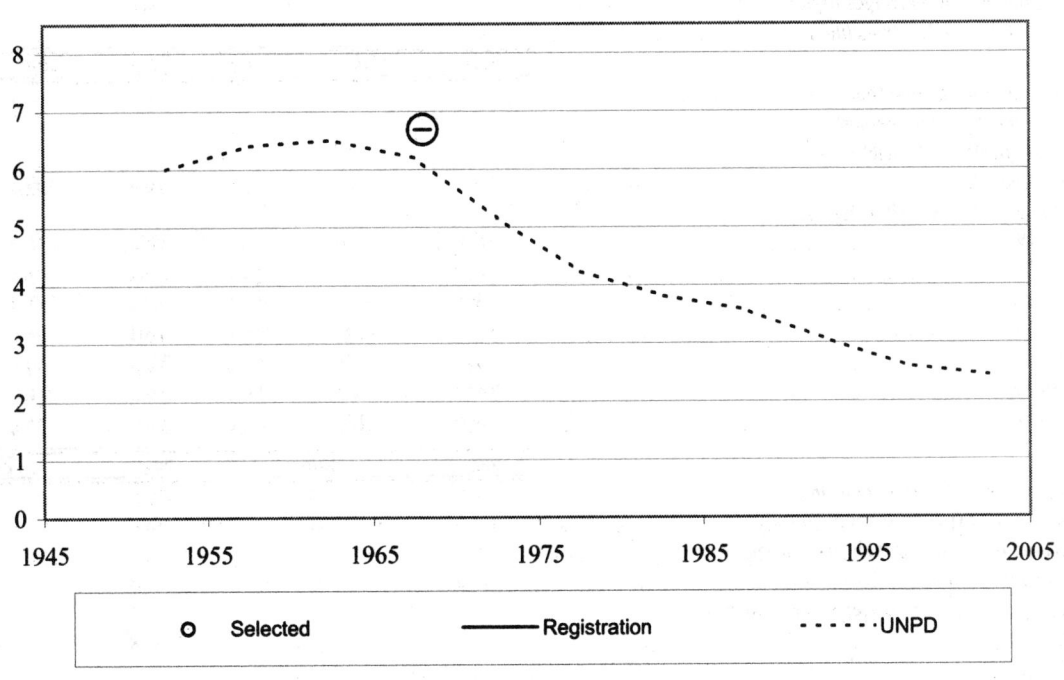

Age-specific fertility rates

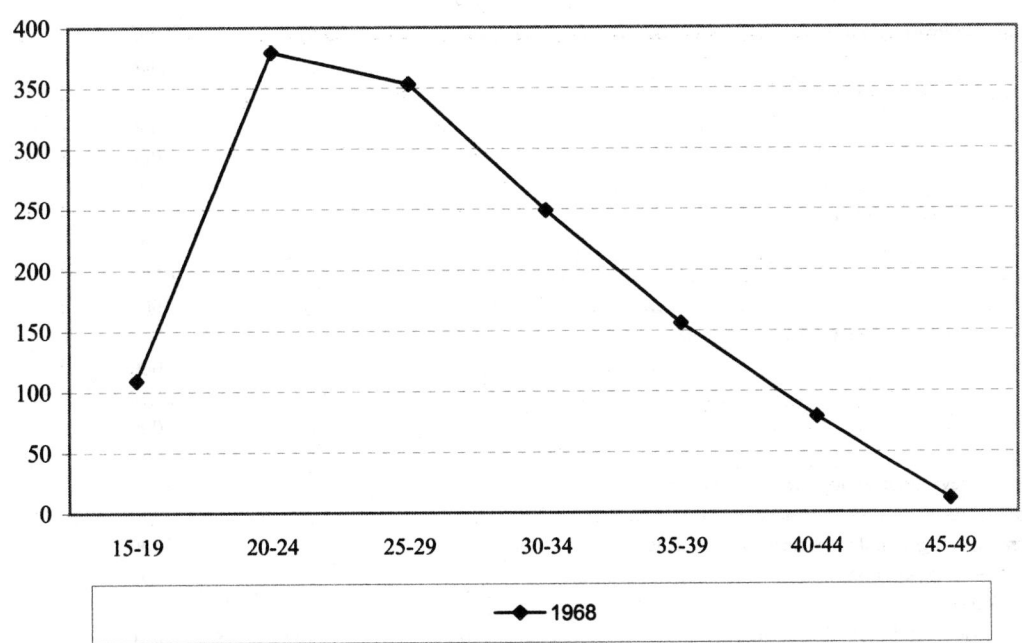

Indicator	Period					
	Earlier year			Later year		
	Year	Value		Year	Value	
Nuptiality						
Annual number of marriages (*thousands*)	..	..		..	..	
Annual number of divorces (*thousands*)	..	..		..	..	
	Year	Male	Female	Year	Male	Female
Total first marriage rate (per person)	..	..	..	..	..	..
Total divorce rate (per person)	..	..	..	..	..	..
Mean age at first marriage (years)	..	..	..	..	..	..
SMAM (years)	1961	25.5	17.7	2001	26.2	22.1
Percentage ever married by age group						
15-19	1961	7.2	62.7	2001	4.0	22.4
20-24	1961	38.6	87.0	2001	29.2	61.3
25-29	1961	65.3	95.1	2001	60.9	82.0
30-34	1961	78.8	96.5	2001	87.1	92.1
35-39	1961	83.0	98.2	2001	92.9	95.9
40-44	1961	89.3	98.4	2001	94.7	96.0
45-49	1961	92.9	98.4	2001	97.5	98.2
Fertility	Year	Value		Year	Value	
Annual number of births (*thousands*)...........................	..	..		..	..	
Crude birth rate (per 1 000 population)	..	..		..	..	
Percentage of extra-marital births among all births	..	..		..	..	
Total fertility rate (births per woman)	..	..		1998	4.3	
Age-specific fertility rate (per 1 000 women)						
15-19	..	..		1998	144	
20-24	..	..		1998	193	
25-29	..	..		1998	178	
30-34	..	..		1998	176	
35-39	..	..		1998	101	
40-44	..	..		1998	48	
45-49	..	..		1998	11	
Mean age at childbearing (years)	..	..		1993	28.0	
Mean age at first birth (years)[a]	..	..		2000	18.7	
Children ever born per woman						
35-39	..	..		2000	4.9	
40-44	..	..		2000	5.9	
45-49	..	..		2000	6.1	
Percentage of childless women						
35-39	..	..		2000	4.5	
40-44	..	..		2000	3.1	
45-49	..	..		2000	7.0	
Percentage of women with parity three or higher						
35-39	..	..		2000	80.7	
40-44	..	..		2000	82.3	
45-49	..	..		2000	81.8	
Family Planning						
Contraceptive prevalence among women in union						
Percentage using any contraceptive method	..	..		2000	32.7	
Percentage using a modern contraceptive method	..	..		2000	11.8	
Percentage using condoms	..	..		2000	5.1	
Population policies						
Government's view on the level of fertility	1976	Too low		2001	Too low	
Government's policy regarding level of fertility	1976	Raise		2001	Raise	
Government's support for contraceptive methods	1976	Limits		2001	No support	

[a]Median age at first birth among women aged 25-29 at the date of the survey

Total fertility rates

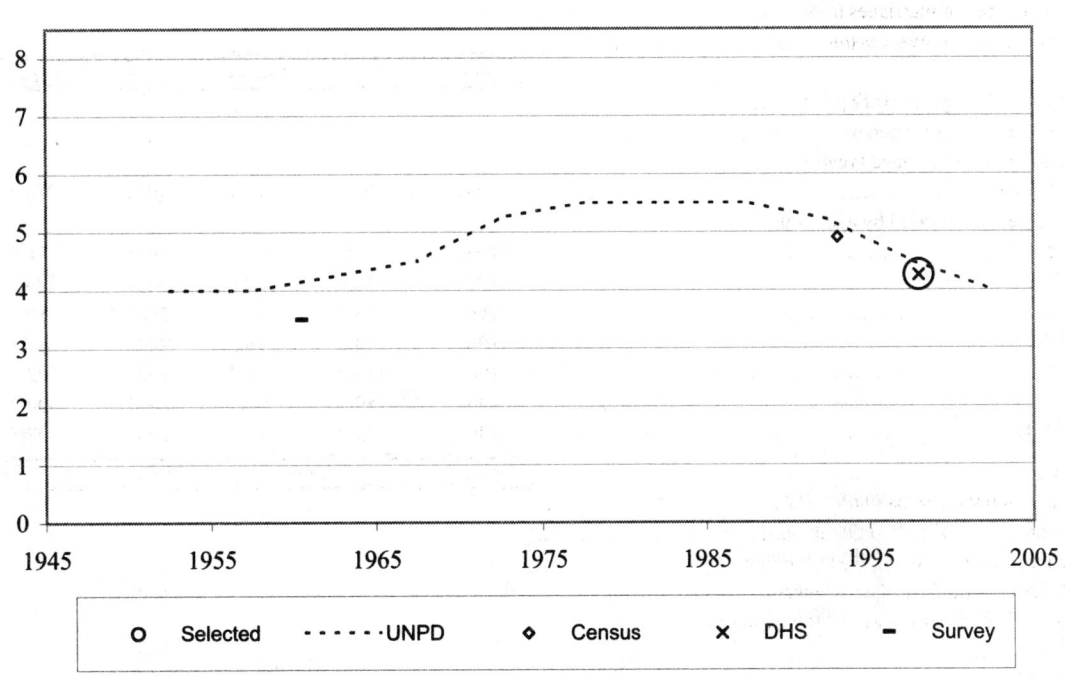

| | Selected | ·····UNPD | Census | DHS | Survey |

Age-specific fertility rates

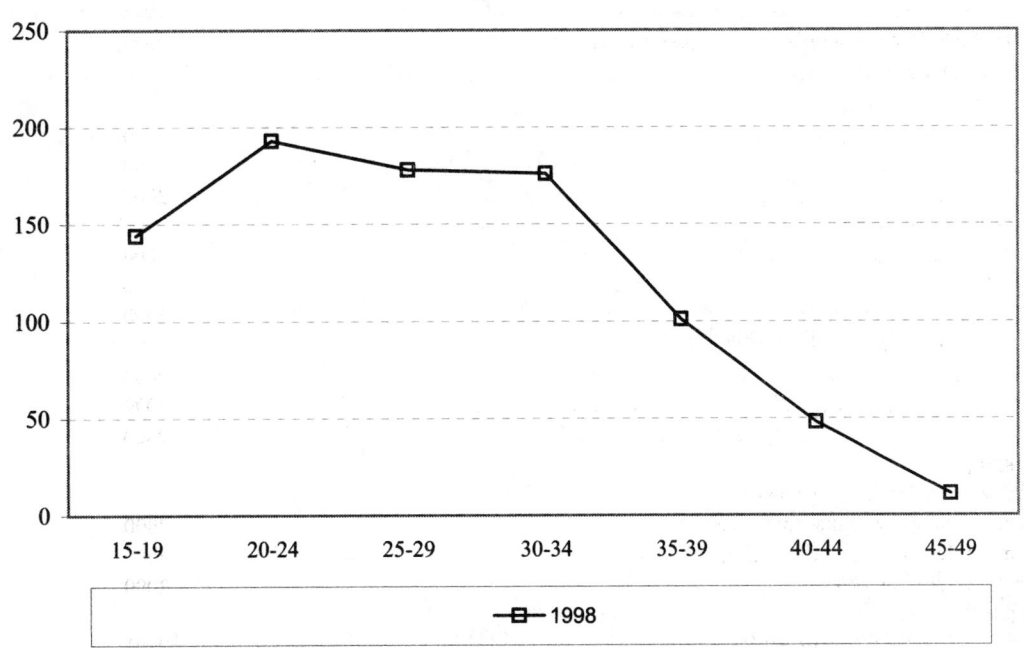

1998

Indicator	Period			
	Earlier year		Later year	
	Year	Value	Year	Value
Nuptiality				
Annual number of marriages (*thousands*)	..	..	..	..
Annual number of divorces (*thousands*)	..	..	..	..

Indicator	Year	Male	Female	Year	Male	Female
Total first marriage rate (per person)	..	..	..	..	..	..
Total divorce rate (per person)	..	..	..	..	..	..
Mean age at first marriage (years)	..	..	..	..	..	..
SMAM (years)	1983	..	..	1993	28.4	19.6
Percentage ever married by age group						
15-19	1983	2.9	55.2	1993	1.7	38.8
20-24	1983	15.9	85.1	1993	12.4	74.8
25-29	1983	47.6	94.9	1993	42.7	90.9
30-34	1983	76.7	97.6	1993	77.1	95.6
35-39	1983	89.3	98.3	1993	88.0	97.3
40-44	1983	[35-44]	[35-44]	1993	93.0	97.7
45-49	1983	95.2	98.7	1993	93.9	97.7

Fertility	Year	Value	Year	Value
Annual number of births (*thousands*)	..	..	..	..
Crude birth rate (per 1 000 population)	..	..	..	..
Percentage of extra-marital births among all births	..	..	..	..
Total fertility rate (births per woman)	1973	6.4	1988	5.9
Age-specific fertility rate (per 1 000 women)				
15-19	1973	200	1988	167
20-24	1973	300	1988	270
25-29	1973	290	1988	238
30-34	1973	210	1988	228
35-39	1973	160	1988	130
40-44	1973	70	1988	78
45-49	1973	40	1988	78
Mean age at childbearing (years)	1973	28.3	1988	29.3
Mean age at first birth (years)	..	..	..	..
Children ever born per woman				
35-39	1973	5.4	..	..
40-44	1973	5.4	..	..
45-49	1973	5.5	..	..
Percentage of childless women				
35-39	1973	7.5	..	..
40-44	1973	9.3	..	..
45-49	1973	7.9	..	..
Percentage of women with parity three or higher				
35-39	1973	78.2	..	..
40-44	1973	75.4	..	..
45-49	1973	76.9	..	..
Family Planning				
Contraceptive prevalence among women in union				
Percentage using any contraceptive method	..	..	2000	9.6
Percentage using a modern contraceptive method	..	..	2000	8.9
Percentage using condoms	..	..	2000	0.1
Population policies				
Government's view on the level of fertility	1976	Satisfactory	2001	Too high
Government's policy regarding level of fertility	1976	No intervention	2001	Lower
Government's support for contraceptive methods	1976	Indirect support	2001	Direct support

Total fertility rates

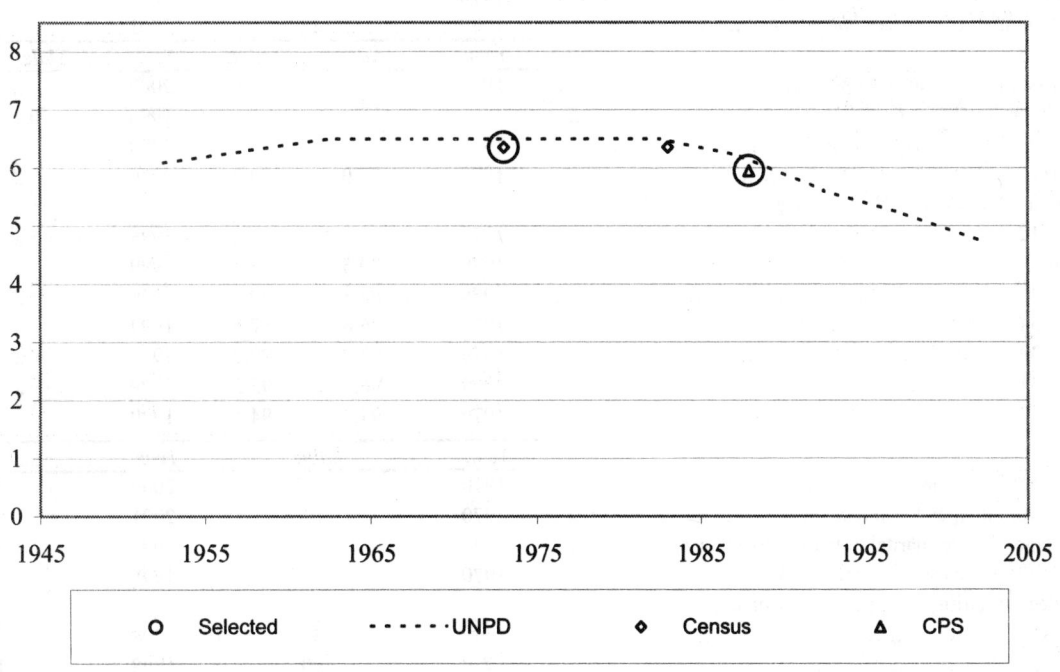

Age-specific fertility rates

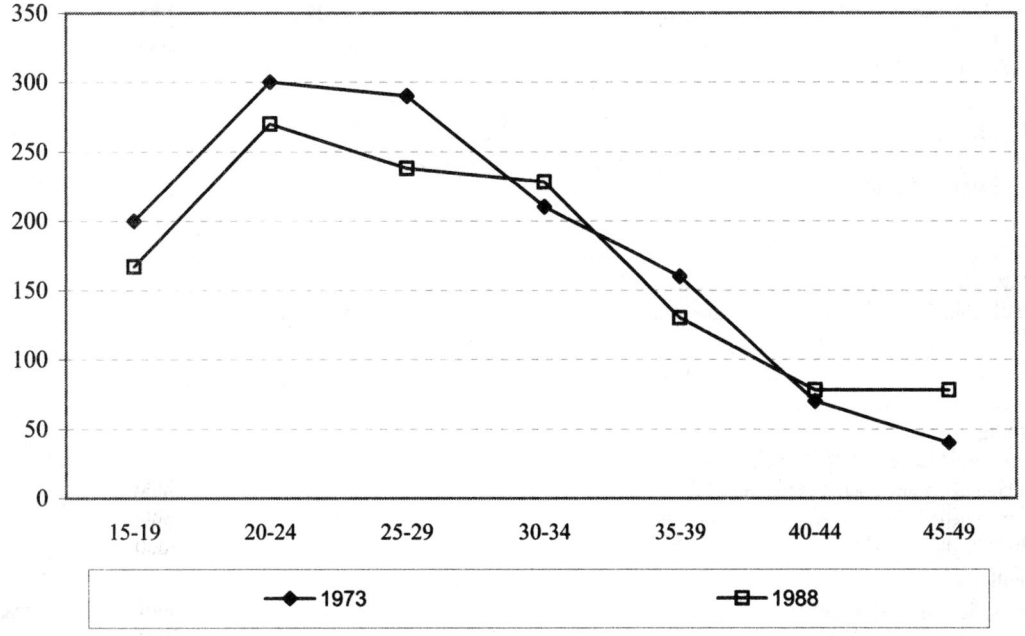

Indicator	Period			
	Earlier year		Later year	
	Year	Value	Year	Value
Nuptiality				
Annual number of marriages (*thousands*)	1970	36.5	2001	13.3
Annual number of divorces (*thousands*)	1970	4.9	2001	2.0

	Year	Male	Female	Year	Male	Female
Total first marriage rate (per person)	1980	..	1.0	2000	..	0.4
Total divorce rate (per person)	..	..	..	1996	0.1	0.1
Mean age at first marriage (years)	1980	..	26.1	2000	..	24.6
SMAM (years)	1979	26.0	23.2	1999	..	24.3
Percentage ever married by age group						
15-19	1979	..	..	1999	..	15.8
20-24	1979	29.5	57.3	1999	..	52.5
25-29	1979	68.3	79.4	1999	..	76.9
30-34	1979	85.6	87.9	1999	..	86.3
35-39	1979	93.2	92.2	1999	..	91.1
40-44	1979	96.3	93.5	1999	..	92.0
45-49	1979	97.9	94.1	1999	..	..

Fertility	Year	Value	Year	Value
Annual number of births (*thousands*)	1970	90.2	2000	40.4
Crude birth rate (per 1 000 population)	1970	19.2	2001	9.3
Percentage of extra-marital births among all births	1975	0.2	2001	44.4
Total fertility rate (births per woman)	1970	2.7	1998	1.7
Age-specific fertility rate (per 1 000 women)				
15-19	1970	36	1998	64
20-24	1970	190	1998	112
25-29	1970	155	1998	92
30-34	1970	94	1998	47
35-39	1970	47	1998	21
40-44	1970	12	1998	7
45-49	1970	2	1998	0
Mean age at childbearing (years)	1970	27.2	2000	25.6
Mean age at first birth (years)	..	..	2000	24.2
Children ever born per woman				
35-39	..	..	..	..
40-44	..	..	..	..
45-49	..	..	..	..
Percentage of childless women				
35-39	..	..	..	..
40-44	..	..	..	..
45-49	..	..	..	..
Percentage of women with parity three or higher				
35-39	..	..	..	..
40-44	..	..	..	..
45-49	..	..	..	..
Family Planning				
Contraceptive prevalence among women in union				
Percentage using any contraceptive method	..	..	2000	40.5
Percentage using a modern contraceptive method	..	..	2000	19.8
Percentage using condoms	..	..	2000	6.3
Population policies				
Government's view on the level of fertility	..	--	2001	Too low
Government's policy regarding level of fertility	..	--	2001	Raise
Government's support for contraceptive methods	..	--	2001	Direct support

Total fertility rates

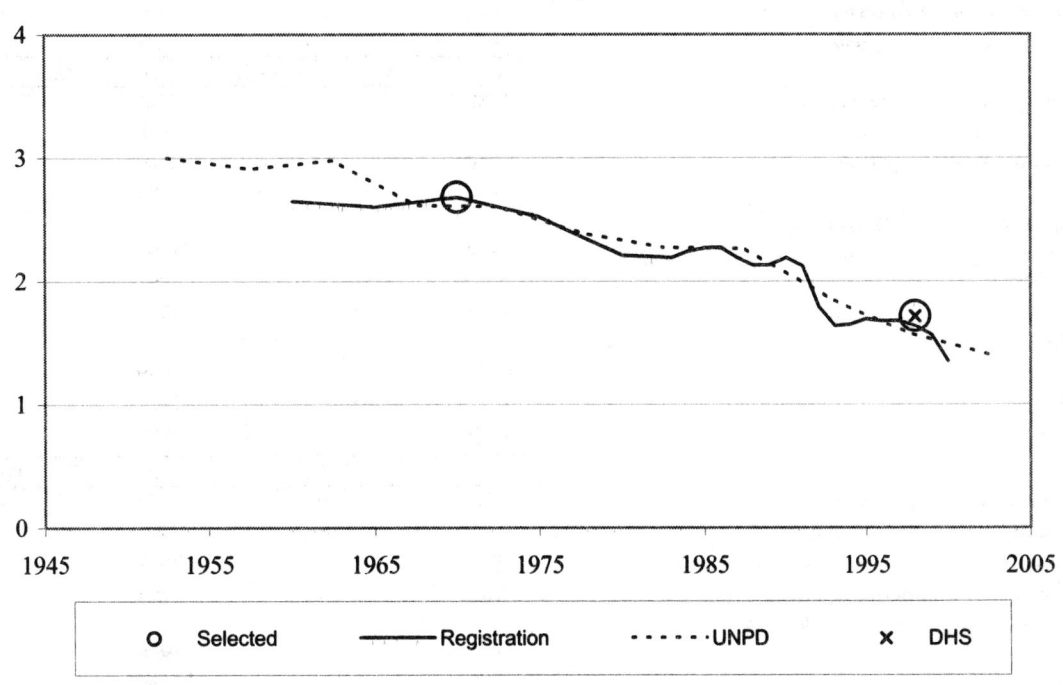

| | O | Selected | —— Registration | · · · · · UNPD | ✕ | DHS |

Age-specific fertility rates

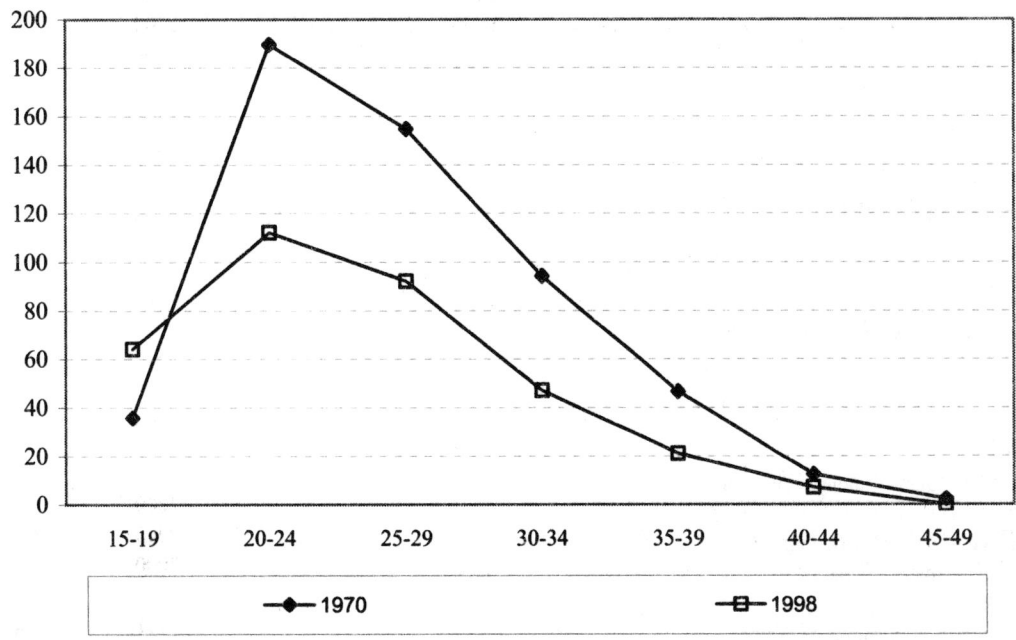

| | ◆ 1970 | □ 1998 |

Indicator	Period					
	Earlier year			Later year		
	Year	Value		Year	Value	
Nuptiality						
Annual number of marriages (*thousands*)	1970	575.2		2001	389.0	
Annual number of divorces (*thousands*)	1970	103.9		2000	194.4	
	Year	Male	Female	Year	Male	Female
Total first marriage rate (per person)	1970	..	1.0	1997	0.5	0.6
Total divorce rate (per person)	..	..	..	1996	0.2	0.3
Mean age at first marriage (years)	1970	..	22.5	1997	29.4	26.8
SMAM (years)	..	..	..	..	..	..
Percentage ever married by age group						
15-19	..	..	..	..	..	..
20-24	..	..	..	..	..	..
25-29	..	..	..	..	..	..
30-34	..	..	..	..	..	..
35-39	..	..	..	..	..	..
40-44	..	..	..	..	..	..
45-49	..	..	..	..	..	..
Fertility	Year	Value		Year	Value	
Annual number of births (*thousands*)	1970	1 047.7		2001	743.5	
Crude birth rate (per 1 000 population)	1970	13.5		2001	8.9	
Percentage of extra-marital births among all births	1970	8.5		2000	23.4	
Total fertility rate (births per woman)	1970	2.0		2000	1.4	
Age-specific fertility rate (per 1 000 women)						
15-19	1970	49		2000	13	
20-24	1970	136		2000	57	
25-29	1970	111		2000	93	
30-34	1970	68		2000	79	
35-39	1970	33		2000	30	
40-44	1970	8		2000	5	
45-49	1970	1		2000	0	
Mean age at childbearing (years)	1970	26.6		2000	28.8	
Mean age at first birth (years)[a]	1970	24.0		2000	28.2	
Children ever born per woman						
35-39	..	..		..	..	
40-44	..	..		..	..	
45-49	..	..		..	..	
Percentage of childless women						
35-39	..	..		..	..	
40-44	..	..		..	..	
45-49	..	..		..	..	
Percentage of women with parity three or higher						
35-39	..	..		..	..	
40-44	..	..		..	..	
45-49	..	..		..	..	
Family Planning						
Contraceptive prevalence among women in union						
Percentage using any contraceptive method	1985	77.9		1992	74.7	
Percentage using a modern contraceptive method	1985	67.6		1992	71.8	
Percentage using condoms	1985	5.7		1992	4.4	
Population policies						
Government's view on the level of fertility	..	--		2001	Too low	
Government's policy regarding level of fertility	..	--		2001	No intervention	
Government's support for contraceptive methods	..	--		2001	No support	

[a]Mean age at first birth within current marriage

Total fertility rates

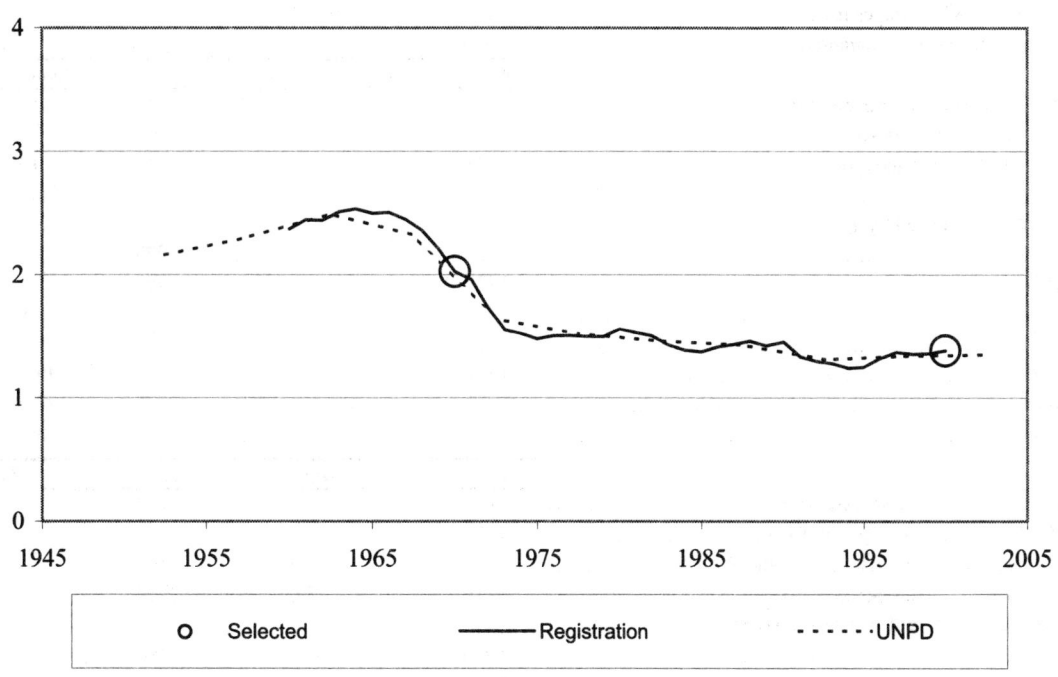

Age-specific fertility rates

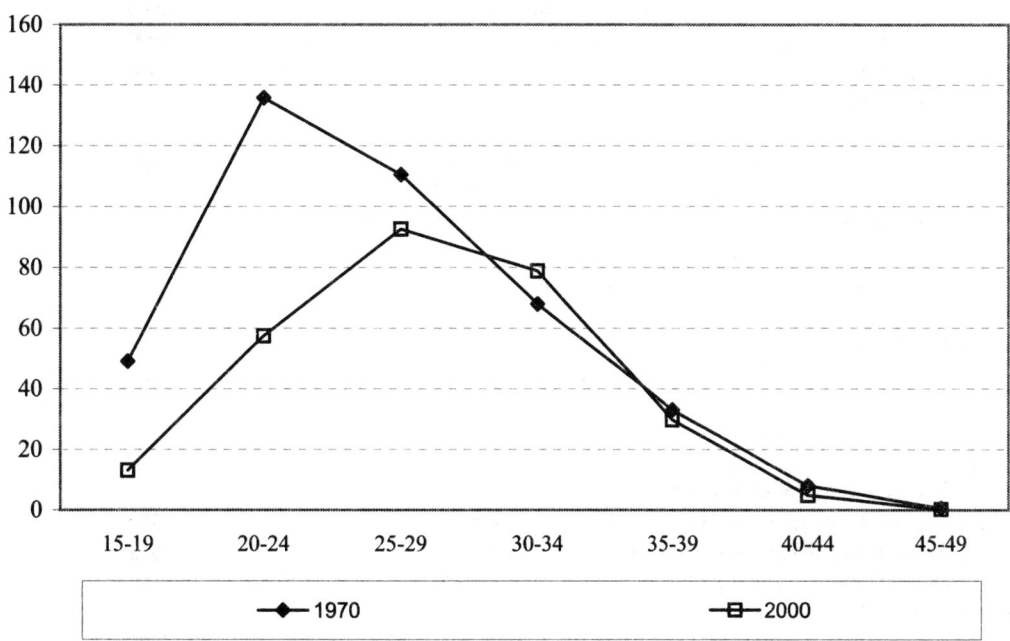

Indicator	Period					
	Earlier year			Later year		
	Year	Value		Year	Value	
Nuptiality						
Annual number of marriages (*thousands*)	..	..		..	..	
Annual number of divorces (*thousands*)	..	..		..	..	
	Year	Male	Female	Year	Male	Female
Total first marriage rate (per person)	..	..	..	..	..	..
Total divorce rate (per person)	..	..	..	..	..	..
Mean age at first marriage (years)	..	..	..	..	..	..
SMAM (years)	1971	..	19.4	1998	26.6	21.2
Percentage ever married by age group						
15-19	1971	..	31.7	1998	3.0	16.4
20-24	1971	..	84.0	1998	25.6	71.0
25-29	1971	..	96.5	1998	58.1	88.8
30-34	1971	..	98.6	1998	85.9	97.7
35-39	1971	..	99.1	1998	96.4	99.1
40-44	1971	..	99.4	1998	97.6	99.8
45-49	1971	..	99.5	1998	98.5	98.6
Fertility	Year	Value		Year	Value	
Annual number of births (*thousands*)...........................	..	..		..	..	
Crude birth rate (per 1 000 population)	..	..		..	..	
Percentage of extra-marital births among all births	..	..		..	..	
Total fertility rate (births per woman)	1968	7.1		1996	4.5	
Age-specific fertility rate (per 1 000 women)						
15-19	1968	132		1996	90	
20-24	1968	257		1996	192	
25-29	1968	266		1996	206	
30-34	1968	242		1996	183	
35-39	1968	169		1996	143	
40-44	1968	135		1996	79	
45-49	1968	50		1996	16	
Mean age at childbearing (years)	1978	30.2		1996	29.7	
Mean age at first birth (years)[a]	..	..		1998	20.9	
Children ever born per woman						
35-39	1979-1980	5.4		1998	4.5	
40-44	1979-1980	6.1		1998	5.4	
45-49	1979-1980	6.7		1998	5.9	
Percentage of childless women						
35-39	..	..		1998	3.2	
40-44	..	..		1998	1.1	
45-49	..	..		1998	2.5	
Percentage of women with parity three or higher						
35-39	..	..		1998	80.5	
40-44	..	..		1998	86.9	
45-49	..	..		1998	90.2	
Family Planning						
Contraceptive prevalence among women in union						
Percentage using any contraceptive method	1979-1980	9.5		1999	22.0	
Percentage using a modern contraceptive method	1979-1980	5.5		1999	13.3	
Percentage using condoms	1979-1980	0.6		1999	2.7	
Population policies						
Government's view on the level of fertility	1976	Too high		2001	Too high	
Government's policy regarding level of fertility	1976	Lower		2001	Lower	
Government's support for contraceptive methods	1976	Direct support		2001	Direct support	

[a]Median age at first birth among women aged 25-29 at the date of the survey

Total fertility rates

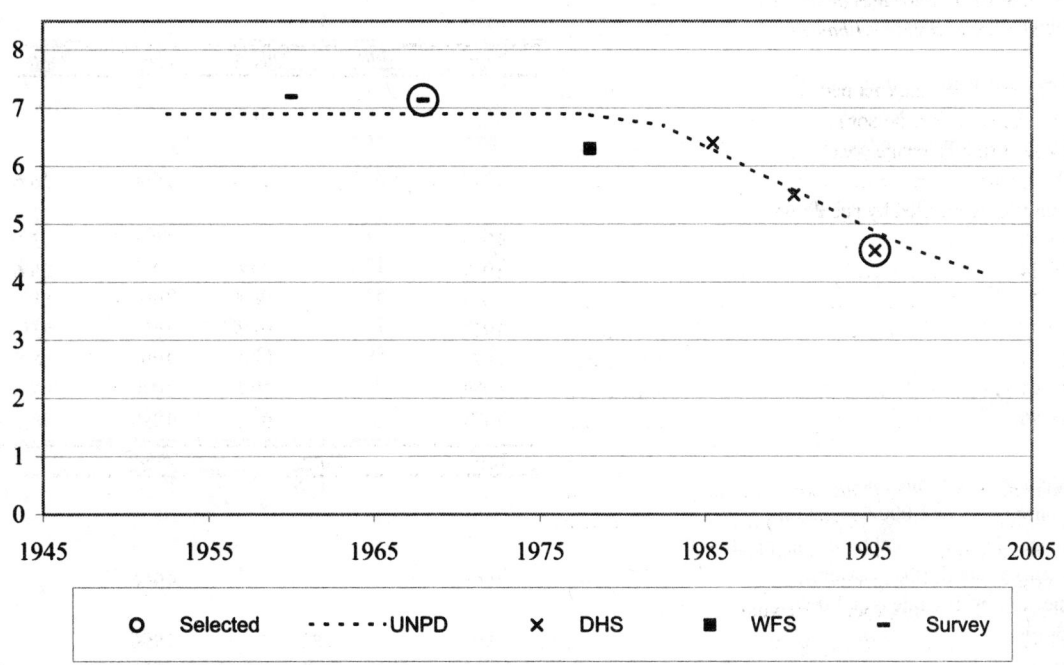

Age-specific fertility rates

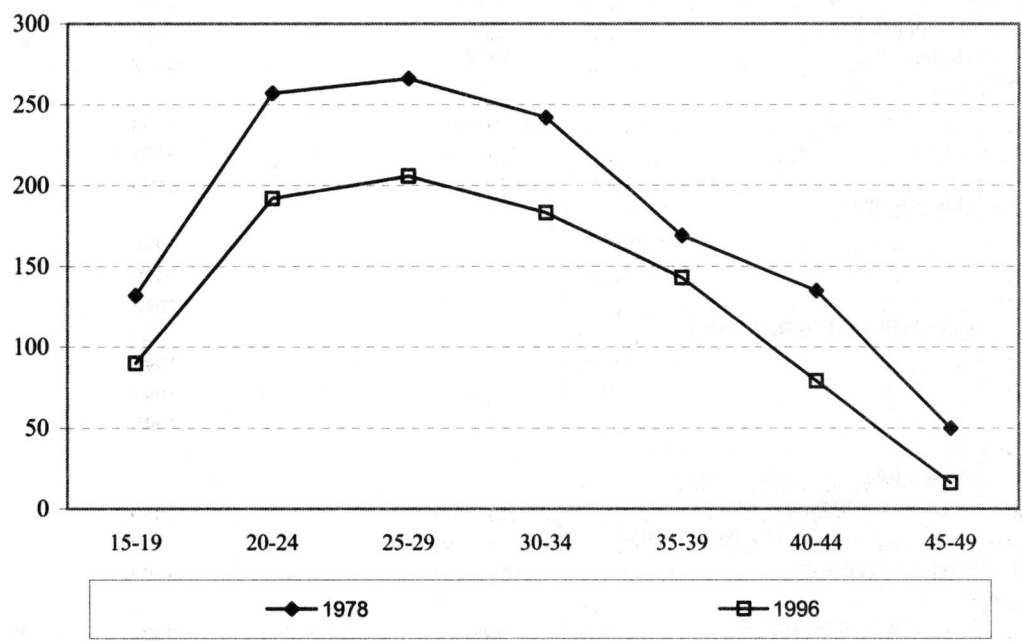

Greece

Indicator	Period					
	Earlier year			Later year		
	Year	Value		Year	Value	
Nuptiality						
Annual number of marriages (*thousands*)	1970	67.4		2001	57.0	
Annual number of divorces (*thousands*)	1970	3.5		2000	11.1	
	Year	Male	Female	Year	Male	Female
Total first marriage rate (per person)	1975	1.2	1.1	1998	0.6	0.6
Total divorce rate (per person)	1970	0.0	0.0	1997	0.1	0.1
Mean age at first marriage (years)	1975	28.7	23.7	1998	30.4	26.6
SMAM (years)	1981	27.6	22.5	1991	29.4	24.5
Percentage ever married by age group						
15-19	1981	1.0	13.8	1991	0.6	5.5
20-24	1981	13.2	52.9	1991	8.4	36.3
25-29	1981	53.9	79.3	1991	39.7	72.5
30-34	1981	79.9	89.0	1991	70.6	87.9
35-39	1981	89.7	92.3	1991	85.8	92.6
40-44	1981	93.3	93.0	1991	91.5	94.1
45-49	1981	94.9	93.7	1991	94.1	94.9
Fertility	Year	Value		Year	Value	
Annual number of births (*thousands*)	1970	144.9		2001	102.3	
Crude birth rate (per 1 000 population)	1970	16.5		2000	9.6	
Percentage of extra-marital births among all births	1970	1.1		1999	3.9	
Total fertility rate (births per woman)	1970	2.4		1999	1.3	
Age-specific fertility rate (per 1 000 women)						
15-19	1970	38		1999	11	
20-24	1970	143		1999	51	
25-29	1970	152		1999	88	
30-34	1970	94		1999	74	
35-39	1970	42		1999	28	
40-44	1970	9		1999	5	
45-49	1970	1		1999	1	
Mean age at childbearing (years)	1970	27.4		1999	28.9	
Mean age at first birth (years)	1970	25.0		1999	27.3	
Children ever born per woman						
35-39	..	..		..	..	
40-44	..	..		..	..	
45-49	..	..		..	..	
Percentage of childless women						
35-39	..	..		..	..	
40-44	..	..		..	..	
45-49	..	..		..	..	
Percentage of women with parity three or higher						
35-39	..	..		..	..	
40-44	..	..		..	..	
45-49	..	..		..	..	
Family Planning						
Contraceptive prevalence among women in union						
Percentage using any contraceptive method	..	..		..	..	
Percentage using a modern contraceptive method	..	..		..	..	
Percentage using condoms	..	..		..	..	
Population policies						
Government's view on the level of fertility	1976	Too low		2001	Too low	
Government's policy regarding level of fertility	1976	Raise		2001	No intervention	
Government's support for contraceptive methods	1976	Limits		2001	No support	

Total fertility rates

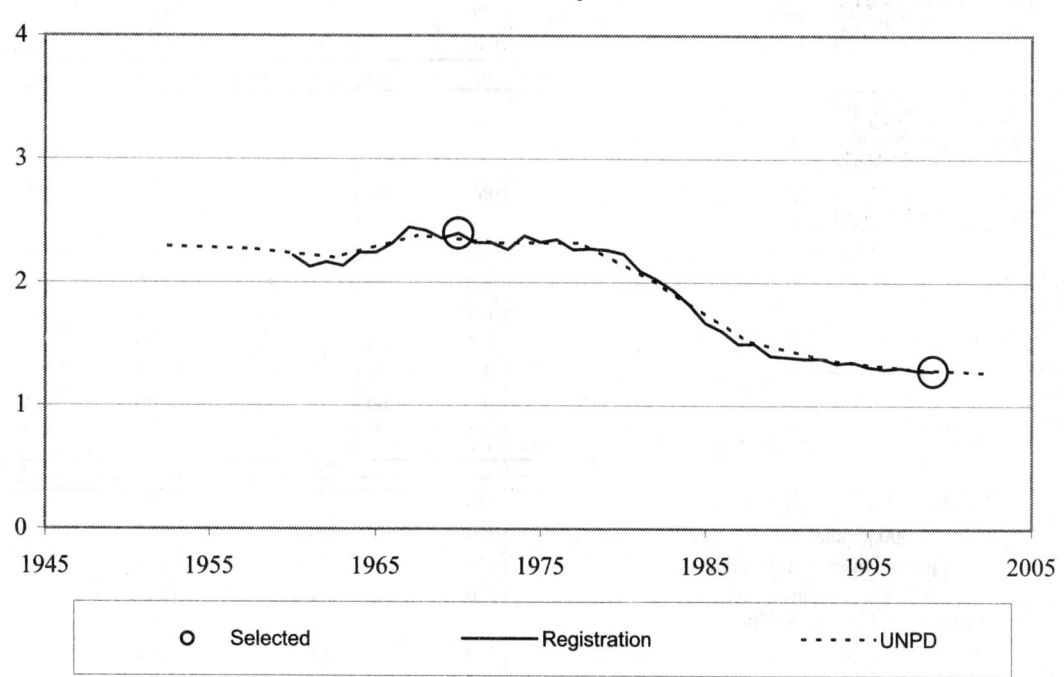

Age-specific fertility rates

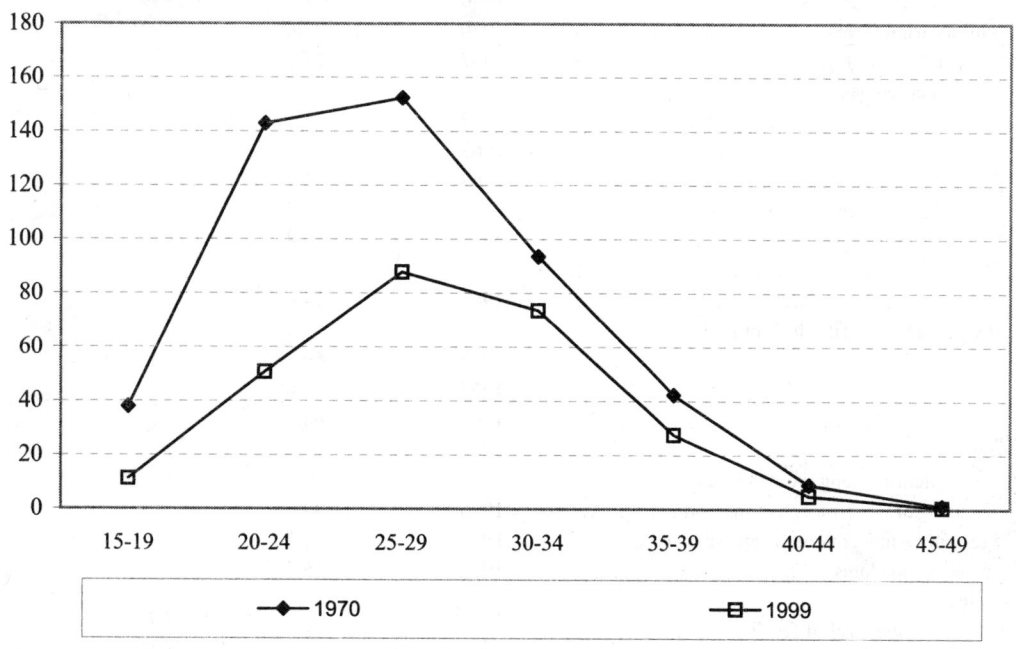

Guadeloupe

Indicator	Period					
	Earlier year			Later year		
	Year	Value		Year	Value	

Nuptiality

Indicator	Year	Value		Year	Value	
Annual number of marriages (*thousands*)	1970	1.9		1992	1.9	
Annual number of divorces (*thousands*)	1970	0.1		1992	0.4	

Indicator	Year	Male	Female	Year	Male	Female
Total first marriage rate (per person)	..	..	..	..	..	..
Total divorce rate (per person)	..	..	..	..	..	..
Mean age at first marriage (years)	..	..	..	..	..	..
SMAM (years)	1967	29.1	25.4	1990	32.3	29.5
Percentage ever married by age group						
15-19	1967	0.2	3.4	1990	0.1	1.1
20-24	1967	6.0	26.5	1990	2.6	11.7
25-29	1967	38.7	50.6	1990	18.3	33.0
30-34	1967	58.1	59.5	1990	41.7	48.4
35-39	1967	64.6	63.3	1990	57.1	58.1
40-44	1967	69.8	66.4	1990	66.7	65.9
45-49	1967	72.8	67.8	1990	72.4	69.8

Fertility

Indicator	Year	Value	Year	Value
Annual number of births (*thousands*)	1970	9.4	1992	7.3
Crude birth rate (per 1 000 population)	1970	29.3	1992	17.9
Percentage of extra-marital births among all births	1970	42.9	1991	61.0
Total fertility rate (births per woman)	1970	4.6	1991	2.2
Age-specific fertility rate (per 1 000 women)				
15-19	1970	65	1991	34
20-24	1970	197	1991	98
25-29	1970	232	1991	136
30-34	1970	209	1991	100
35-39	1970	139	1991	53
40-44	1970	64	1991	14
45-49	1970	9	1991	1
Mean age at childbearing (years)	1970	29.6	1991	28.5
Mean age at first birth (years)	1967	25.1	..	..
Children ever born per woman				
35-39	1967	5.1	..	..
40-44	1967	6.0	..	..
45-49	1967	5.7	..	..
Percentage of childless women				
35-39	1967	10.8	..	..
40-44	1967	12.1	..	..
45-49	1967	14.0	..	..
Percentage of women with parity three or higher				
35-39	1967	69.7	..	..
40-44	1967	69.6	..	..
45-49	1967	64.8	..	..

Family Planning

Indicator	Year	Value	Year	Value
Contraceptive prevalence among women in union				
Percentage using any contraceptive method	1976	43.6	..	..
Percentage using a modern contraceptive method	1976	30.5	..	..
Percentage using condoms	1976	5.7	..	..

Population policies

Indicator	Year	Value	Year	Value
Government's view on the level of fertility	..	--	..	--
Government's policy regarding level of fertility	..	--	..	--
Government's support for contraceptive methods	..	--	..	--

Total fertility rates

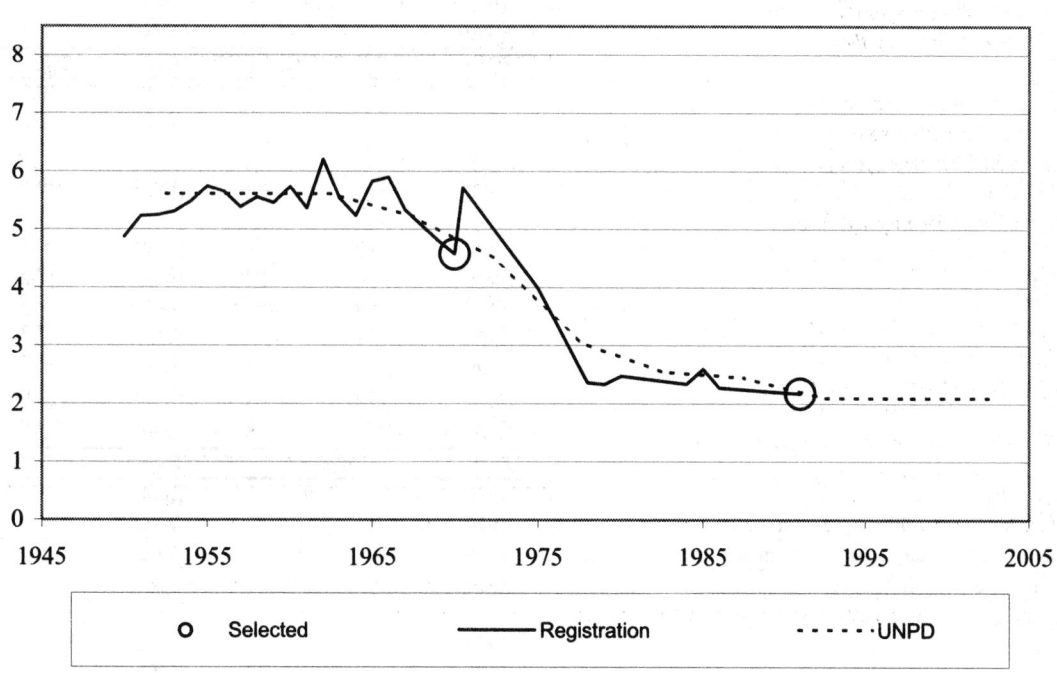

Age-specific fertility rates

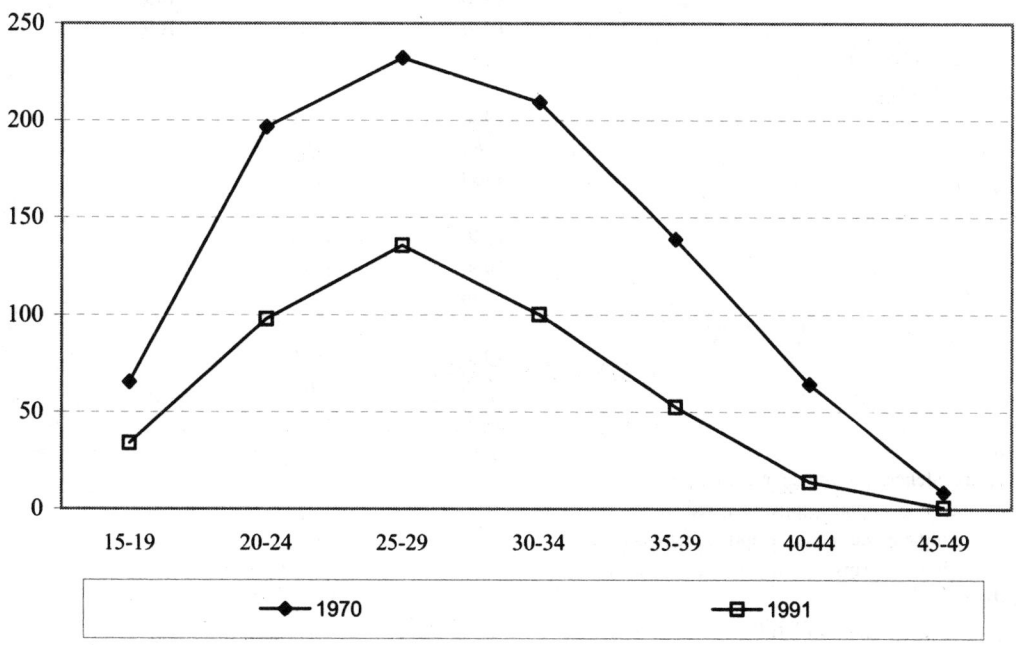

Guam

Indicator	Period					
	Earlier year			Later year		
	Year	Value		Year	Value	
Nuptiality						
Annual number of marriages (*thousands*)	1970	0.9		1999	1.4	
Annual number of divorces (*thousands*)	1970	0.1		1995	0.6	
	Year	Male	Female	Year	Male	Female
Total first marriage rate (per person)	1975	..	..	1992	0.7	0.9
Total divorce rate (per person)	..	..	..	1992	0.6	0.7
Mean age at first marriage (years)	1975	27.1	24.5	1992	27.2	25.2
SMAM (years)	1980	24.5	22.2	1990	26.8	24.4
Percentage ever married by age group						
15-19	1980	3.1	9.9	1990	2.1	5.8
20-24	1980	37.3	59.9	1990	29.3	45.3
25-29	1980	74.6	84.8	1990	58.8	72.3
30-34	1980	88.6	92.2	1990	77.3	84.5
35-39	1980	93.3	93.8	1990	86.2	90.8
40-44	1980	[35-44]	[35-44]	1990	92.0	93.1
45-49	1980	95.1	94.9	1990	94.0	94.8
Fertility	Year	Value		Year	Value	
Annual number of births (*thousands*)	1970	2.9		2000	3.8	
Crude birth rate (per 1 000 population)	1970	33.8		2000	24.5	
Percentage of extra-marital births among all births	1970	9.3		1992	41.3	
Total fertility rate (births per woman)	1970	4.8		1992	3.7	
Age-specific fertility rate (per 1 000 women)						
15-19	1970	96		1992	110	
20-24	1970	280		1992	217	
25-29	1970	267		1992	201	
30-34	1970	161		1992	124	
35-39	1970	103		1992	61	
40-44	1970	41		1992	17	
45-49	1970	3		1992	1	
Mean age at childbearing (years)	1970	27.7		1992	26.6	
Mean age at first birth (years)	..	..		..	..	
Children ever born per woman						
35-39	1960	3.9		..	..	
40-44	1960	4.1		..	..	
45-49	1960	..		..	..	
Percentage of childless women						
35-39	1960	6.9		..	..	
40-44	1960	10.3		..	..	
45-49	1960	..		..	..	
Percentage of women with parity three or higher						
35-39	1960	60.0		..	..	
40-44	1960	56.7		..	..	
45-49	1960	..		..	..	
Family Planning						
Contraceptive prevalence among women in union						
Percentage using any contraceptive method	..	..		..	..	
Percentage using a modern contraceptive method	..	..		..	..	
Percentage using condoms	..	..		..	..	
Population policies						
Government's view on the level of fertility	..	--		..	--	
Government's policy regarding level of fertility	..	--		..	--	
Government's support for contraceptive methods	..	--		..	--	

Total fertility rates

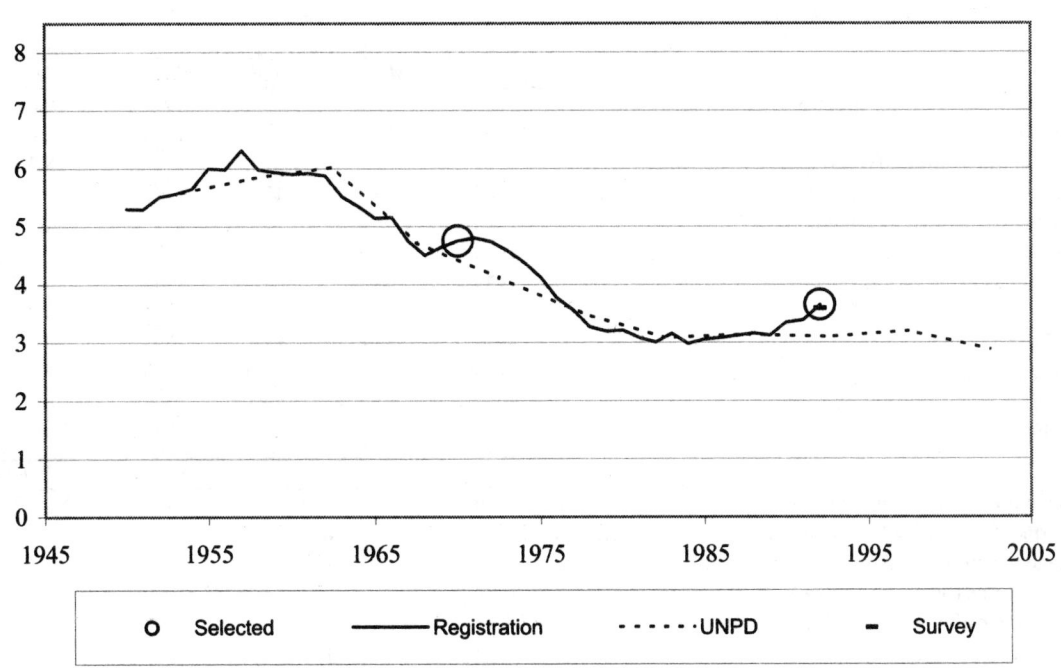

Age-specific fertility rates

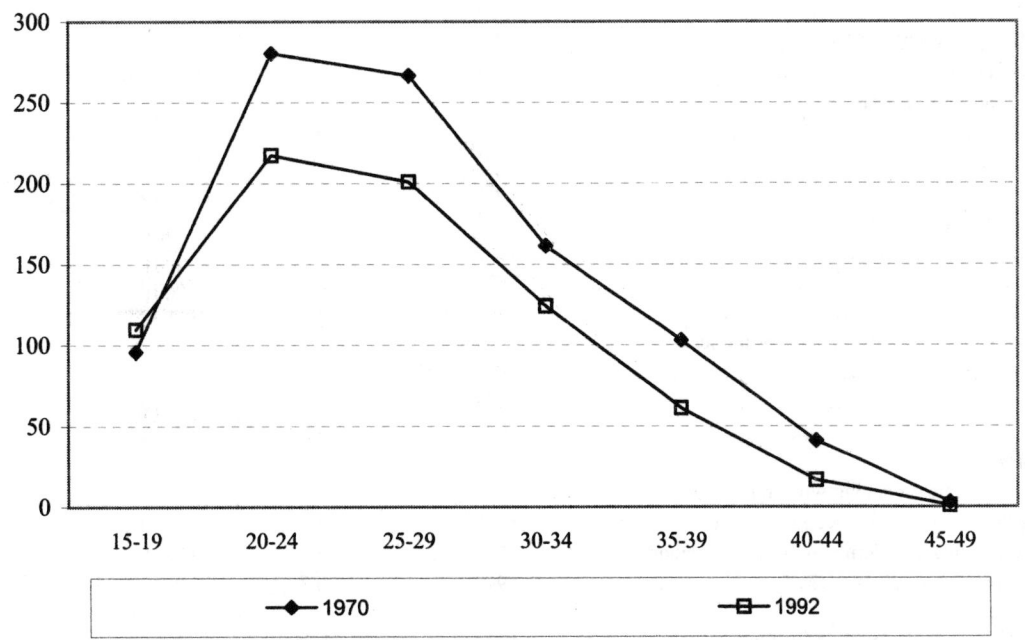

Guatemala

Indicator	Period					
	Earlier year			Later year		
	Year	Value		Year	Value	

Nuptiality

Indicator	Year	Value		Year	Value	
Annual number of marriages (*thousands*)	1970	18.2		1998	53.0	
Annual number of divorces (*thousands*)	1970	0.7		1993	1.5	

Indicator	Year	Male	Female	Year	Male	Female
Total first marriage rate (per person)	..	..	..	1997	0.6	0.6
Total divorce rate (per person)	1965	0.0	0.0	1993	0.0	0.0
Mean age at first marriage (years)	..	..	..	1997	28.3	28.2
SMAM (years)	1973	23.7	19.7	1999	..	20.5
Percentage ever married by age group						
15-19	1973	6.8	28.4	1999	..	26.0
20-24	1973	45.3	67.2	1999	..	69.5
25-29	1973	75.1	82.9	1999	..	89.2
30-34	1973	85.6	88.1	1999	..	92.7
35-39	1973	88.9	89.9	1999	..	96.4
40-44	1973	91.1	89.5	1999	..	94.6
45-49	1973	92.0	89.2	1999	..	95.4

Fertility

Indicator	Year	Value	Year	Value
Annual number of births (*thousands*)	1970	212.2	1999	360.8
Crude birth rate (per 1 000 population)	1970	40.5	1999	32.5
Percentage of extra-marital births among all births	1970	61.9	..	..
Total fertility rate (births per woman)	1972	6.3	1997	5.1
Age-specific fertility rate (per 1 000 women)				
15-19	1972	145	1997	123
20-24	1972	304	1997	277
25-29	1972	285	1997	229
30-34	1972	235	1997	191
35-39	1972	184	1997	136
40-44	1972	80	1997	61
45-49	1972	20	1997	3
Mean age at childbearing (years)	1972	28.8	1997	28.2
Mean age at first birth (years)[a]	1970	22.0	1998-1999	22.7
Children ever born per woman				
35-39	1973	5.6	1998-1999	4.9
40-44	1973	6.2	1998-1999	5.6
45-49	1973	6.5	1998-1999	5.7
Percentage of childless women				
35-39	1973	5.2	1998-1999	4.1
40-44	1973	5.0	1998-1999	5.5
45-49	1973	5.0	1998-1999	3.6
Percentage of women with parity three or higher				
35-39	1973	82.6	1998-1999	78.5
40-44	1973	83.6	1998-1999	82.6
45-49	1973	83.7	1998-1999	87.4

Family Planning

Indicator	Year	Value	Year	Value
Contraceptive prevalence among women in union				
Percentage using any contraceptive method	1978	18.1	1998-1999	38.2
Percentage using a modern contraceptive method	1978	15.2	1998-1999	30.9
Percentage using condoms	1978	0.7	1998-1999	2.3

Population policies

Indicator	Year	Value	Year	Value
Government's view on the level of fertility	1976	Too high	2001	Too high
Government's policy regarding level of fertility	1976	No intervention	2001	Lower
Government's support for contraceptive methods	1976	Direct support	2001	Direct support

[a]Median age at first birth among women aged 25-29 at the date of the survey for both dates

Total fertility rates

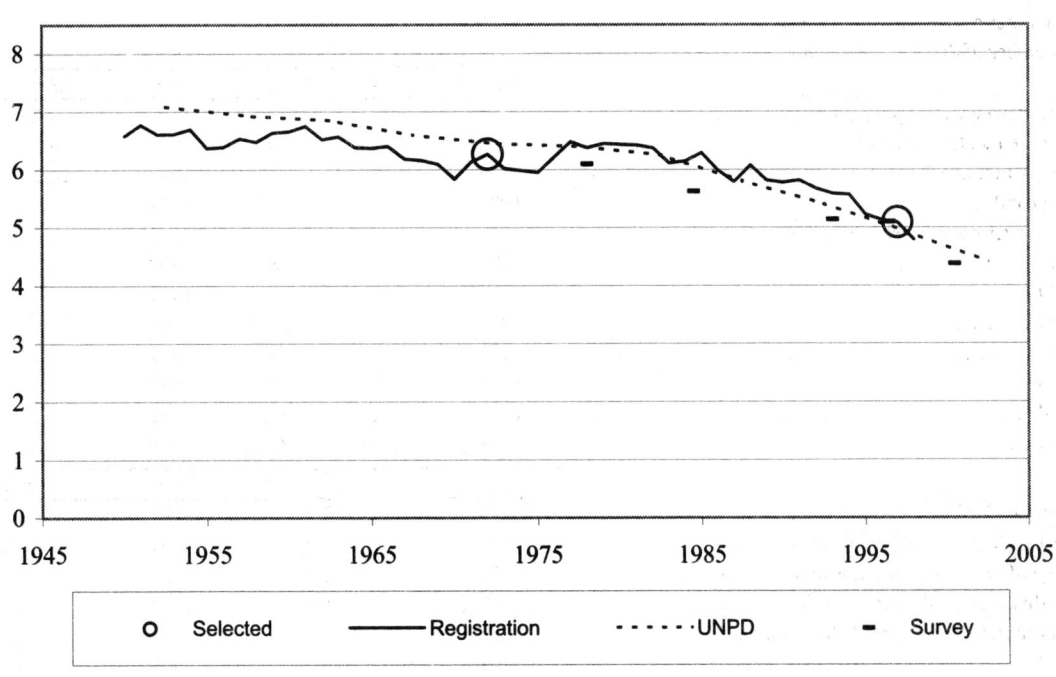

Age-specific fertility rates

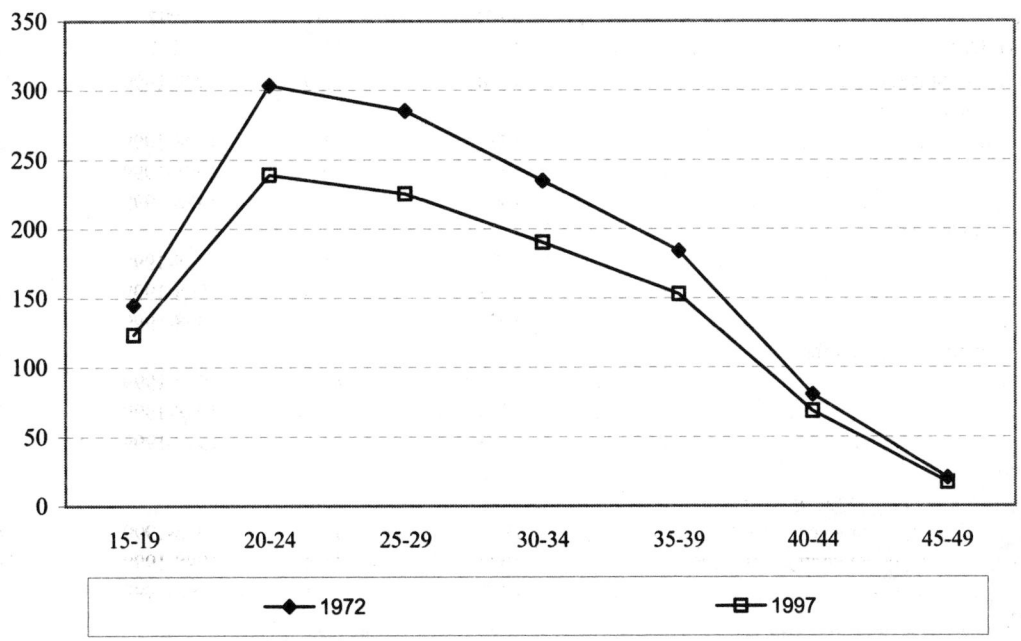

Guinea

Indicator	Period					
	Earlier year			Later year		
	Year	Value		Year	Value	
Nuptiality						
Annual number of marriages (*thousands*) ....…..........	..	..		..	..	
Annual number of divorces (*thousands*) ....…..............	..	..		..	..	
	Year	Male	Female	Year	Male	Female
Total first marriage rate (per person)	..	..	..	..	..	..
Total divorce rate (per person)	..	..	..	..	..	..
Mean age at first marriage (years) ....…...	..	..	..	..	..	..
SMAM (years)	..	..	..	1999	27.7	18.7
Percentage ever married by age group						
15-19	..	..	..	1999	2.4	46.1
20-24	..	..	..	1999	19.7	84.6
25-29	..	..	..	1999	50.2	96.8
30-34	..	..	..	1999	79.7	98.6
35-39	..	..	..	1999	95.2	99.7
40-44	..	..	..	1999	98.0	99.8
45-49	..	..	..	1999	98.9	100.0
Fertility	Year	Value		Year	Value	
Annual number of births (*thousands*)...............................	..	..		..	..	
Crude birth rate (per 1 000 population)	..	..		..	..	
Percentage of extra-marital births among all births	..	..		..	..	
Total fertility rate (births per woman)	1983	5.8		1997	5.8	
Age-specific fertility rate (per 1 000 women)						
15-19	1983	161		1997	172	
20-24	1983	267		1997	249	
25-29	1983	269		1997	253	
30-34	1983	211		1997	231	
35-39	1983	149		1997	151	
40-44	1983	72		1997	75	
45-49	1983	39		1997	37	
Mean age at childbearing (years)	1983	28.8		1997	28.8	
Mean age at first birth (years)[a]	..	..		1999	18.6	
Children ever born per woman						
35-39	..	..		1999	5.5	
40-44	..	..		1999	6.2	
45-49	..	..		1999	6.9	
Percentage of childless women						
35-39	..	..		1999	2.2	
40-44	..	..		1999	2.4	
45-49	..	..		1999	2.1	
Percentage of women with parity three or higher						
35-39	..	..		1999	88.8	
40-44	..	..		1999	90.3	
45-49	..	..		1999	91.6	
Family Planning						
Contraceptive prevalence among women in union						
Percentage using any contraceptive method	..	..		1999	6.2	
Percentage using a modern contraceptive method	..	..		1999	4.2	
Percentage using condoms	..	..		1999	0.6	
Population policies						
Government's view on the level of fertility	1976	Satisfactory		2001	Too high	
Government's policy regarding level of fertility	1976	No intervention		2001	Lower	
Government's support for contraceptive methods	1976	No support		2001	Direct support	

[a]Median age at first birth among women aged 25-29 at the date of the survey

Total fertility rates

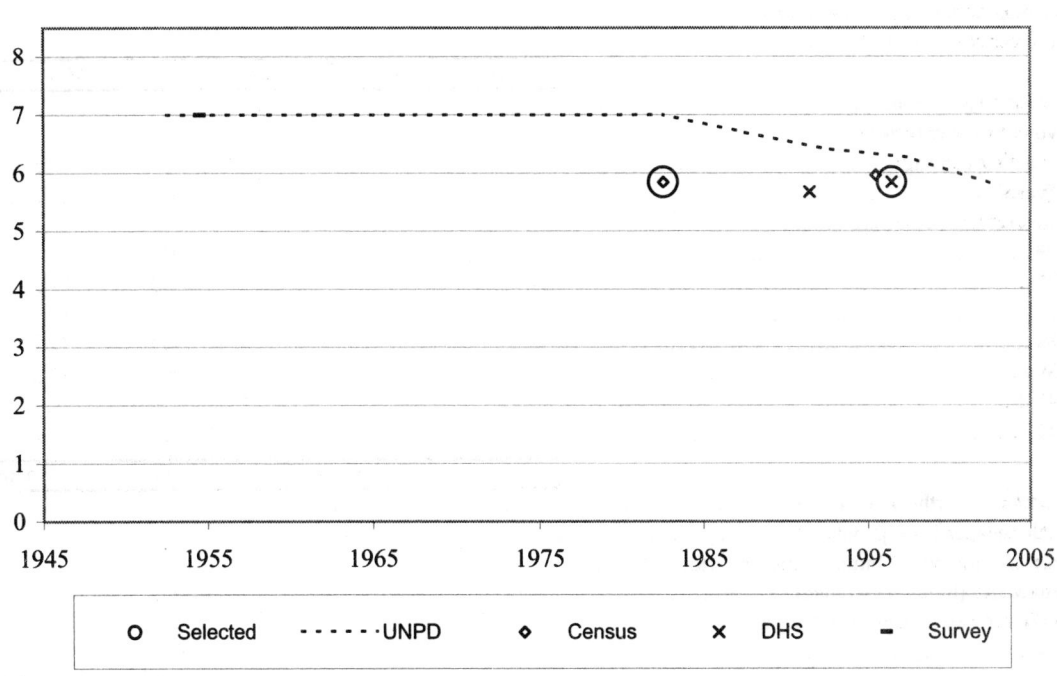

Age-specific fertility rates

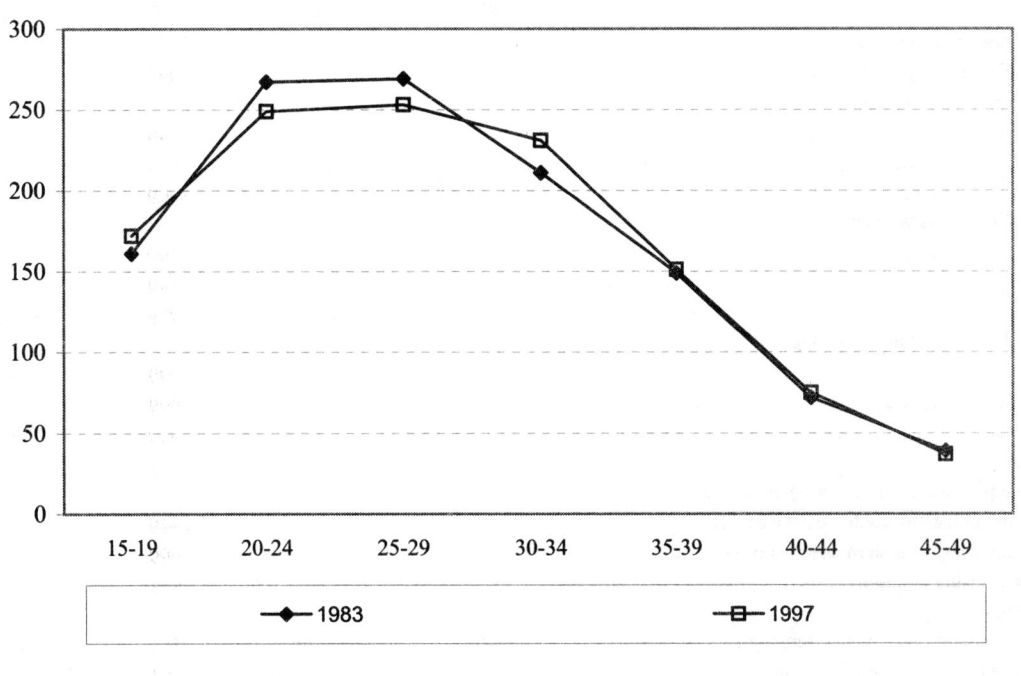

Indicator	Period			
	Earlier year		Later year	
	Year	Value	Year	Value
Nuptiality				
Annual number of marriages (*thousands*)	..	..	..	..
Annual number of divorces (*thousands*)	..	..	..	..

	Year	Male	Female	Year	Male	Female
Total first marriage rate (per person)	..	..	..	..	..	..
Total divorce rate (per person)	..	..	..	..	..	..
Mean age at first marriage (years)	..	..	..	..	..	..
SMAM (years)	..	..	..	..	..	..
Percentage ever married by age group						
15-19	..	..	..	..	..	..
20-24	..	..	..	..	..	..
25-29	..	..	..	..	..	..
30-34	..	..	..	..	..	..
35-39	..	..	..	..	..	..
40-44	..	..	..	..	..	..
45-49	..	..	..	..	..	..

	Year	Value	Year	Value
Fertility				
Annual number of births (*thousands*)	..	..	..	..
Crude birth rate (per 1 000 population)	..	..	..	..
Percentage of extra-marital births among all births	..	..	..	..
Total fertility rate (births per woman)	..	..	..	..
Age-specific fertility rate (per 1 000 women)				
15-19	..	..	..	..
20-24	..	..	..	..
25-29	..	..	..	..
30-34	..	..	..	..
35-39	..	..	..	..
40-44	..	..	..	..
45-49	..	..	..	..
Mean age at childbearing (years)	..	..	..	..
Mean age at first birth (years)	..	..	..	..
Children ever born per woman				
35-39	..	..	..	..
40-44	..	..	..	..
45-49	..	..	..	..
Percentage of childless women				
35-39	..	..	..	..
40-44	..	..	..	..
45-49	..	..	..	..
Percentage of women with parity three or higher				
35-39	..	..	..	..
40-44	..	..	..	..
45-49	..	..	..	..
Family Planning				
Contraceptive prevalence among women in union				
Percentage using any contraceptive method	..	..	2000	7.6
Percentage using a modern contraceptive method	..	..	2000	3.6
Percentage using condoms	..	..	2000	0.1
Population policies				
Government's view on the level of fertility	1976	Satisfactory	2001	Too high
Government's policy regarding level of fertility	1976	No intervention	2001	No intervention
Government's support for contraceptive methods	1976	Indirect support	2001	Direct support

Total fertility rates

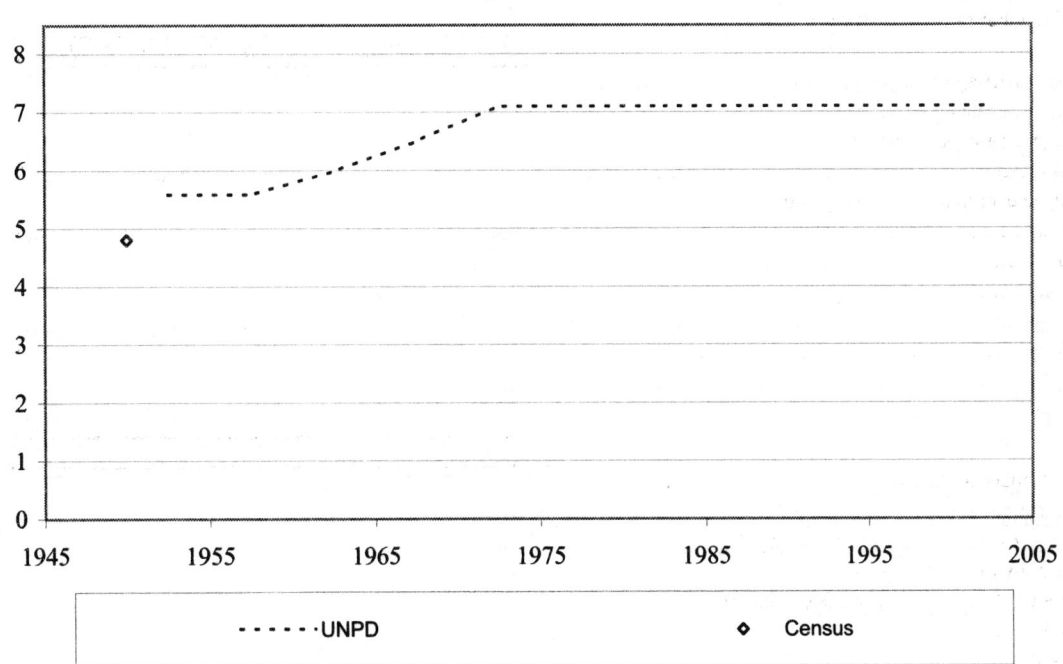

Guyana

Indicator	Period					
	Earlier year			Later year		
	Year	Value		Year	Value	
Nuptiality						
Annual number of marriages (*thousands*)	1968	2.8		..	..	
Annual number of divorces (*thousands*)	1965	0.4		..	..	
	Year	Male	Female	Year	Male	Female
Total first marriage rate (per person)	..	..	..	..	..	..
Total divorce rate (per person)	..	..	..	..	..	..
Mean age at first marriage (years)	..	..	..	..	..	..
SMAM (years)	1970	24.8	21.5	1991	30.1	27.8
Percentage ever married by age group						
15-19	1970	1.6	14.6	1991	0.9	6.9
20-24	1970	28.2	53.3	1991	12.1	26.6
25-29	1970	66.8	75.2	1991	33.9	45.4
30-34	1970	77.0	81.1	1991	54.8	60.8
35-39	1970	81.5	83.4	1991	68.6	70.0
40-44	1970	83.3	83.6	1991	76.4	76.3
45-49	1970	83.4	83.9	1991	80.5	81.7
Fertility	Year	Value		Year	Value	
Annual number of births (*thousands*)	1970	23.7		..	..	
Crude birth rate (per 1 000 population)	1970	33.4		..	..	
Percentage of extra-marital births among all births	1970	37.3		..	..	
Total fertility rate (births per woman)	1973	4.9		..	..	
Age-specific fertility rate (per 1 000 women)						
15-19	1973	114		..	..	
20-24	1973	283		..	..	
25-29	1973	242		..	..	
30-34	1973	184		..	..	
35-39	1973	112		..	..	
40-44	1973	42		..	..	
45-49	1973	6		..	..	
Mean age at childbearing (years)	1973	27.7		..	..	
Mean age at first birth (years)[a]	1977	20.4		..	..	
Children ever born per woman						
35-39	1970	5.9		..	..	
40-44	1970	6.0		..	..	
45-49	1970	5.7		..	..	
Percentage of childless women						
35-39	1970	6.8		..	..	
40-44	1970	8.0		..	..	
45-49	1970	9.8		..	..	
Percentage of women with parity three or higher						
35-39	1970	81.4		..	..	
40-44	1970	79.0		..	..	
45-49	1970	75.8		..	..	
Family Planning						
Contraceptive prevalence among women in union						
Percentage using any contraceptive method	1975	31.4		2000	37.3	
Percentage using a modern contraceptive method	1975	28.3		2000	36.0	
Percentage using condoms	1975	2.9		2000	8.8	
Population policies						
Government's view on the level of fertility	1976	Satisfactory		2001	Satisfactory	
Government's policy regarding level of fertility	1976	No intervention		2001	No intervention	
Government's support for contraceptive methods	1976	No support		2001	Direct support	

[a] Median age at first birth among women aged 25-29 at the date of the survey.

Total fertility rates

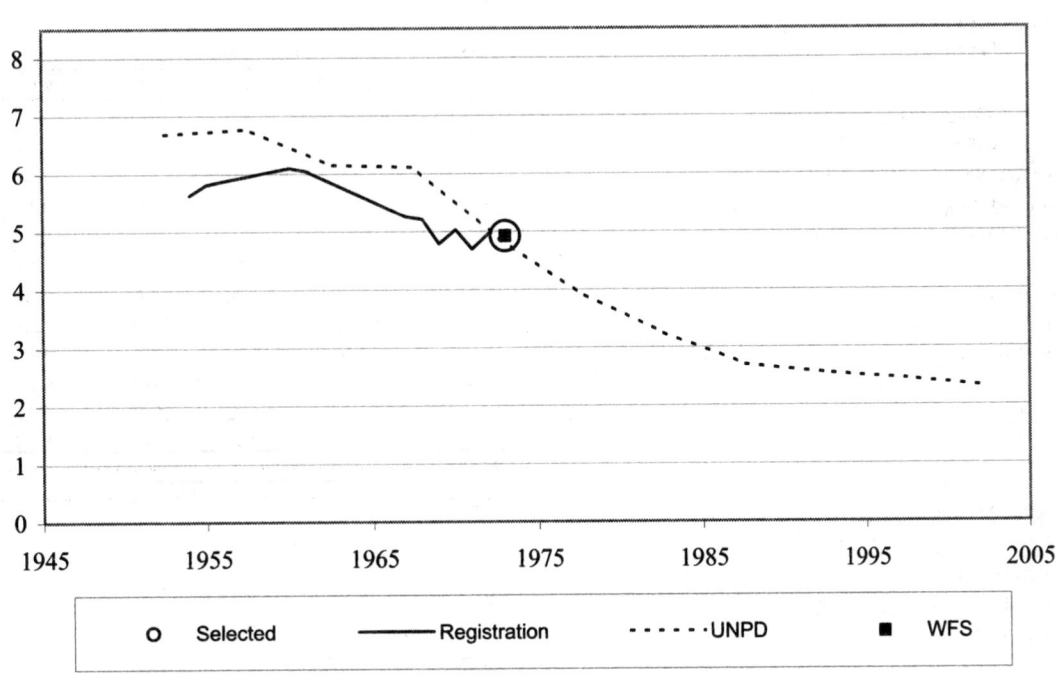

Age-specific fertility rates

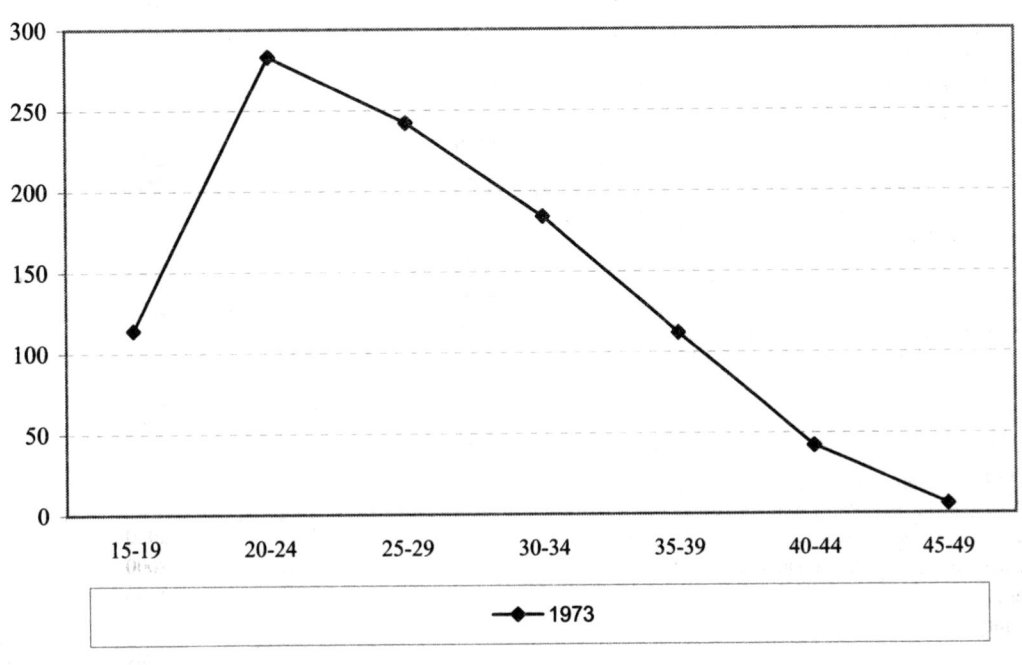

Indicator	Period			
	Earlier year		Later year	
	Year	Value	Year	Value
Nuptiality				
Annual number of marriages (*thousands*)	..	..	..	..
Annual number of divorces (*thousands*)	..	..	..	..

	Year	Male	Female	Year	Male	Female
Total first marriage rate (per person)	..	..	..	..	..	..
Total divorce rate (per person)	..	..	..	..	..	..
Mean age at first marriage (years)	..	..	..	..	..	..
SMAM (years)	1971	28.1	22.4	2000	27.3	22.3
Percentage ever married by age group						
15-19	1971	0.5	5.5	2000	2.6	19.4
20-24	1971	11.5	38.2	2000	29.8	57.3
25-29	1971	44.2	67.2	2000	48.1	79.9
30-34	1971	69.4	78.5	2000	78.0	92.5
35-39	1971	79.9	82.3	2000	93.4	98.5
40-44	1971	84.6	81.7	2000	97.5	97.8
45-49	1971	86.2	80.3	2000	99.4	98.0

	Year	Value	Year	Value
Fertility				
Annual number of births (*thousands*)......................	..	..	..	..
Crude birth rate (per 1 000 population)	..	..	..	..
Percentage of extra-marital births among all births	..	..	..	..
Total fertility rate (births per woman)	1975	5.5	1998	4.7
Age-specific fertility rate (per 1 000 women)				
15-19	1975	57	1998	80
20-24	1975	204	1998	187
25-29	1975	266	1998	204
30-34	1975	226	1998	219
35-39	1975	178	1998	153
40-44	1975	116	1998	75
45-49	1975	54	1998	18
Mean age at childbearing (years)	1975	31.3	1998	30.0
Mean age at first birth (years)[a]	..	..	2000	21.9
Children ever born per woman				
35-39	1977	4.5	2000	4.6
40-44	1977	5.6	2000	5.2
45-49	1977	5.9	2000	5.5
Percentage of childless women				
35-39	..	..	2000	8.9
40-44	..	..	2000	9.9
45-49	..	..	2000	8.8
Percentage of women with parity three or higher				
35-39	..	..	2000	71.8
40-44	..	..	2000	75.6
45-49	..	..	2000	78.8
Family Planning				
Contraceptive prevalence among women in union				
Percentage using any contraceptive method	1977	18.9	2000	27.4
Percentage using a modern contraceptive method	1977	5.4	2000	21.4
Percentage using condoms	1977	1.1	2000	2.2
Population policies				
Government's view on the level of fertility	1976	Too high	2001	Too high
Government's policy regarding level of fertility	1976	Lower	2001	Lower
Government's support for contraceptive methods	1976	Direct support	2001	Direct support

[a]Median age at first birth among women aged 25-29 at the date of the survey

Total fertility rates

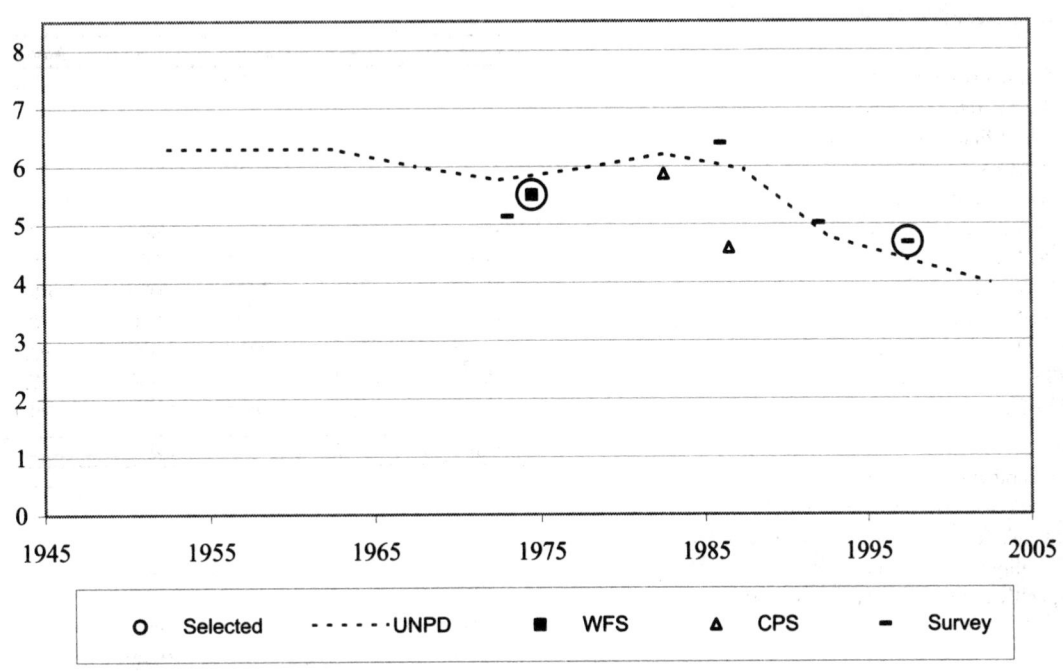

Age-specific fertility rates

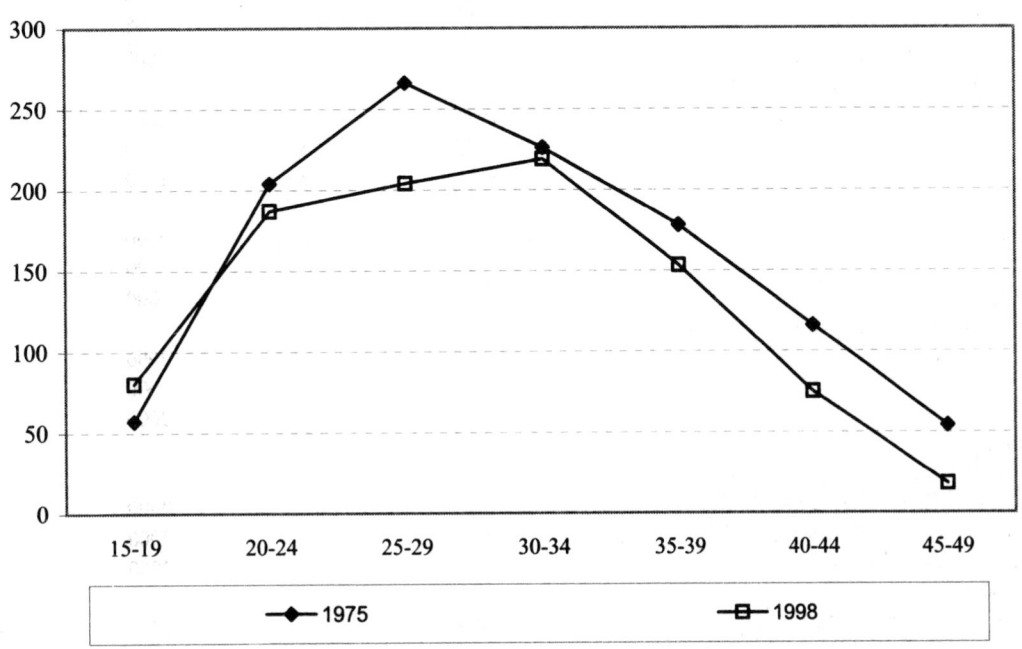

Honduras

Indicator	Period			
	Earlier year		Later year	
	Year	Value	Year	Value
Nuptiality				
Annual number of marriages (*thousands*)	1970	9.7	1987	12.2
Annual number of divorces (*thousands*)	1970	0.5	1987	1.4

Indicator	Year	Male	Female	Year	Male	Female
Total first marriage rate (per person)	..	..	..	..	..	..
Total divorce rate (per person)	..	..	..	..	..	..
Mean age at first marriage (years)	..	..	..	..	..	..
SMAM (years)	1974	24.4	20.0	1996	..	20.4
Percentage ever married by age group						
15-19	1974	4.9	29.2	1996	..	30.5
20-24	1974	41.3	72.0	1996	..	68.3
25-29	1974	73.3	88.5	1996	..	86.8
30-34	1974	86.0	93.3	1996	..	93.7
35-39	1974	90.4	95.0	1996	..	95.6
40-44	1974	92.7	95.0	1996	..	96.4
45-49	1974	93.9	95.1	1996	..	95.6

Fertility	Year	Value	Year	Value
Annual number of births (*thousands*)...................	..	..	..	..
Crude birth rate (per 1 000 population)	..	..	..	..
Percentage of extra-marital births among all births	..	..	..	..
Total fertility rate (births per woman)	1972	7.5	1994	5.0
Age-specific fertility rate (per 1 000 women)				
15-19	1972	171	1994	136
20-24	1972	317	1994	243
25-29	1972	339	1994	210
30-34	1972	307	1994	169
35-39	1972	221	1994	142
40-44	1972	127	1994	78
45-49	1972	18	1994	12
Mean age at childbearing (years)	1972	29.3	1994	28.6
Mean age at first birth (years)	..	..	..	..
Children ever born per woman				
35-39	1974	6.2	..	..
40-44	1974	7.0	..	..
45-49	1974	7.2	..	..
Percentage of childless women				
35-39	1974	5.2	..	..
40-44	1974	5.1	..	..
45-49	1974	5.1	..	..
Percentage of women with parity three or higher				
35-39	1974	85.3	..	..
40-44	1974	86.4	..	..
45-49	1974	86.2	..	..
Family Planning				
Contraceptive prevalence among women in union				
Percentage using any contraceptive method	1981	26.9	2001	61.8
Percentage using a modern contraceptive method	1981	23.5	2001	50.8
Percentage using condoms	1981	0.3	2001	3.2
Population policies				
Government's view on the level of fertility	1976	Too high	2001	Too high
Government's policy regarding level of fertility	1976	Lower	2001	Lower
Government's support for contraceptive methods	1976	Direct support	2001	Direct support

Total fertility rates

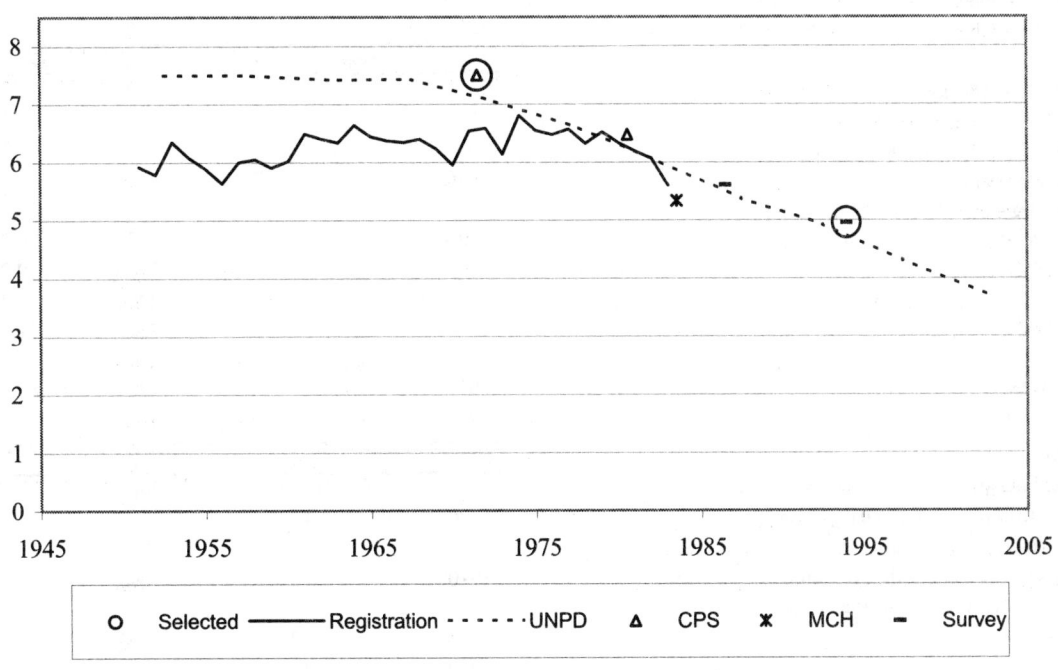

Age-specific fertility rates

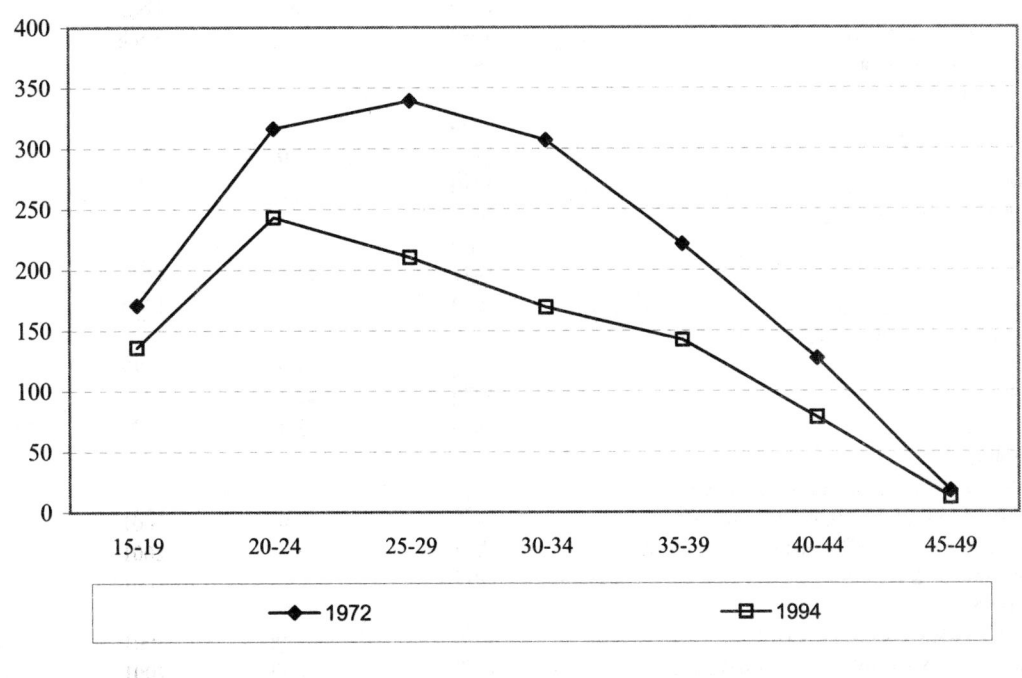

Hungary

Indicator	Period					
	Earlier year			Later year		
	Year	Value		Year	Value	
Nuptiality						
Annual number of marriages (*thousands*)	1970	96.6		2001	43.6	
Annual number of divorces (*thousands*)	1970	22.8		2001	24.4	
	Year	Male	Female	Year	Male	Female
Total first marriage rate (per person)	1975	1.0	1.0	1998	0.5	0.5
Total divorce rate (per person)	1970	0.6	0.6	1997	0.3	0.3
Mean age at first marriage (years)	1975	24.0	21.1	1998	26.7	23.9
SMAM (years)	1970	24.8	20.9	2000	29.1	26.3
Percentage ever married by age group						
15-19	1970	1.4	12.5	2000	0.2	1.9
20-24	1970	32.2	67.7	2000	9.9	24.7
25-29	1970	76.7	89.6	2000	43.2	62.3
30-34	1970	89.2	94.1	2000	71.6	83.5
35-39	1970	93.8	95.4	2000	81.1	91.4
40-44	1970	94.9	94.9	2000	85.7	94.4
45-49	1970	95.7	94.6	2000	89.7	95.3
Fertility	Year	Value		Year	Value	
Annual number of births (*thousands*)	1970	151.8		2002	96.8	
Crude birth rate (per 1 000 population)	1970	14.7		2002	9.8	
Percentage of extra-marital births among all births	1970	5.4		2001	30.3	
Total fertility rate (births per woman)	1970	2.0		2001	1.3	
Age-specific fertility rate (per 1 000 women)						
15-19	1970	53		2001	23	
20-24	1970	159		2001	65	
25-29	1970	109		2001	91	
30-34	1970	51		2001	58	
35-39	1970	19		2001	21	
40-44	1970	4		2001	4	
45-49	1970	0		2001	0	
Mean age at childbearing (years)	1970	25.5		2001	27.6	
Mean age at first birth (years)	1970	22.8		2001	25.3	
Children ever born per woman						
35-39	1970	1.9		1990	1.9	
40-44	1970	2.0		1990	1.9	
45-49	1970	2.1		1990	1.9	
Percentage of childless women						
35-39	1970	10.9		1990	8.9	
40-44	1970	12.8		1990	8.5	
45-49	1970	14.6		1990	8.8	
Percentage of women with parity three or higher						
35-39	1970	23.0		1990	18.2	
40-44	1970	28.0		1990	19.0	
45-49	1970	31.6		1990	18.6	
Family Planning						
Contraceptive prevalence among women in union						
Percentage using any contraceptive method	1974	74.0		1993	77.4	
Percentage using a modern contraceptive method	1974	44.0		1993	68.4	
Percentage using condoms	1974	7.0		1993	7.8	
Population policies						
Government's view on the level of fertility	1976	Satisfactory		2001	Too low	
Government's policy regarding level of fertility	1976	Maintain		2001	Raise	
Government's support for contraceptive methods	1976	Direct support		2001	Direct support	

Total fertility rates

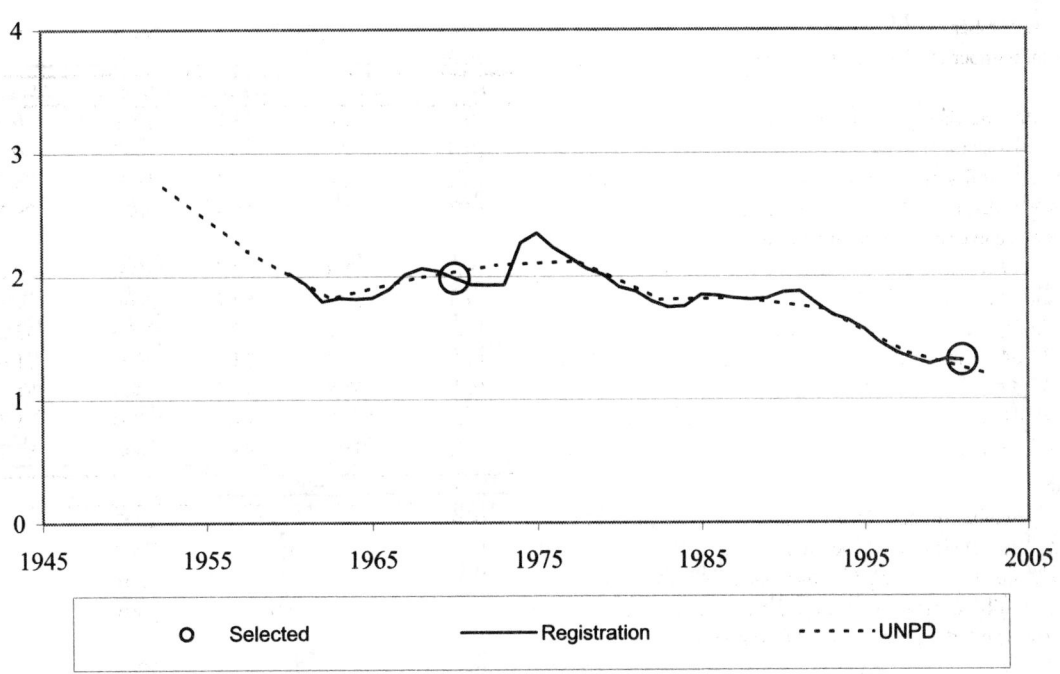

Age-specific fertility rates

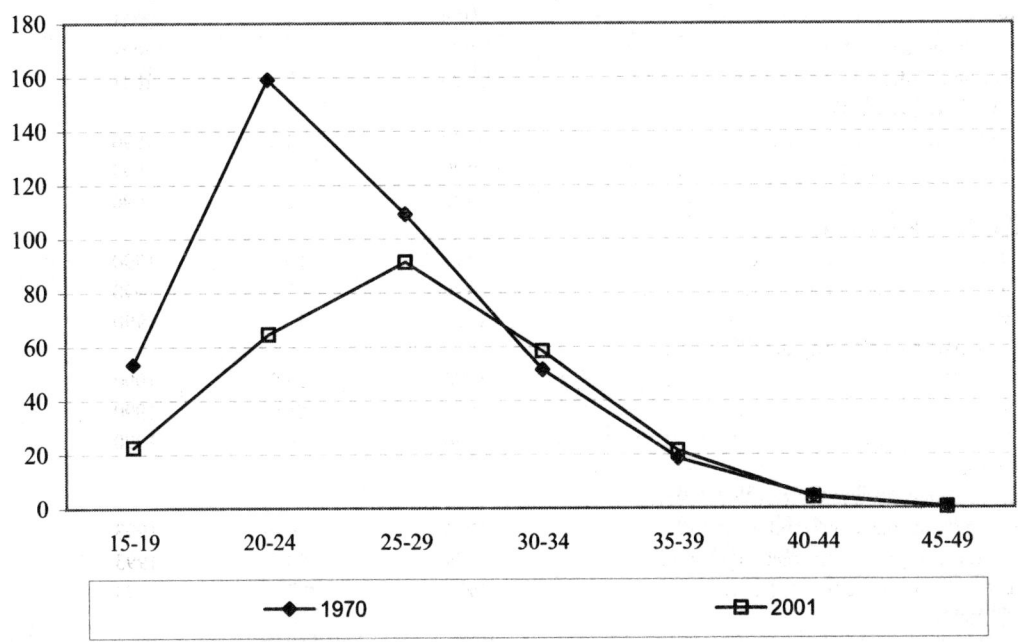

Indicator	Period			
	Earlier year		**Later year**	
	Year	Value	Year	Value
Nuptiality				
Annual number of marriages (*thousands*)	1970	1.6	2000	1.8
Annual number of divorces (*thousands*)	1970	0.2	2001	0.6

Indicator	Year	Male	Female	Year	Male	Female
Total first marriage rate (per person)	1975	0.8	0.8	1997	0.6	0.6
Total divorce rate (per person)	1970	..	0.2	2000	..	0.4
Mean age at first marriage (years)	1975	24.9	23.2	2000	..	29.9
SMAM (years)	1974	24.1	21.9	2000	32.6	30.5
Percentage ever married by age group						
15-19	1974	0.7	3.8	2000	0.4	0.9
20-24	1974	30.2	49.9	2000	4.2	8.2
25-29	1974	69.7	82.9	2000	18.2	27.0
30-34	1974	81.2	90.3	2000	39.2	49.2
35-39	1974	84.4	91.1	2000	54.8	59.9
40-44	1974	85.6	90.7	2000	63.2	67.2
45-49	1974	84.9	89.5	2000	70.0	70.9

Indicator	Year	Value	Year	Value
Fertility				
Annual number of births (*thousands*).............................	1970	4.0	2002	4.0
Crude birth rate (per 1 000 population)	1970	19.7	2002	14.1
Percentage of extra-marital births among all births	1970	29.9	2000	65.2
Total fertility rate (births per woman)	1970	2.8	2000	2.1
Age-specific fertility rate (per 1 000 women)				
15-19	1970	74	2000	22
20-24	1970	166	2000	88
25-29	1970	142	2000	131
30-34	1970	101	2000	112
35-39	1970	57	2000	51
40-44	1970	20	2000	11
45-49	1970	4	2000	1
Mean age at childbearing (years)	1970	27.3	2000	28.9
Mean age at first birth (years)	1970	21.3	2000	25.5
Children ever born per woman				
35-39	..	..	..	..
40-44	..	..	..	..
45-49	..	..	..	..
Percentage of childless women				
35-39	..	..	..	..
40-44	..	..	..	..
45-49	..	..	..	..
Percentage of women with parity three or higher				
35-39	..	..	..	..
40-44	..	..	..	..
45-49	..	..	..	..
Family Planning				
Contraceptive prevalence among women in union				
Percentage using any contraceptive method	..	..	..	..
Percentage using a modern contraceptive method	..	..	..	..
Percentage using condoms	..	..	..	..
Population policies				
Government's view on the level of fertility	1976	Satisfactory	2001	Satisfactory
Government's policy regarding level of fertility	1976	No intervention	2001	Maintain
Government's support for contraceptive methods	1976	Direct support	2001	Direct support

Total fertility rates

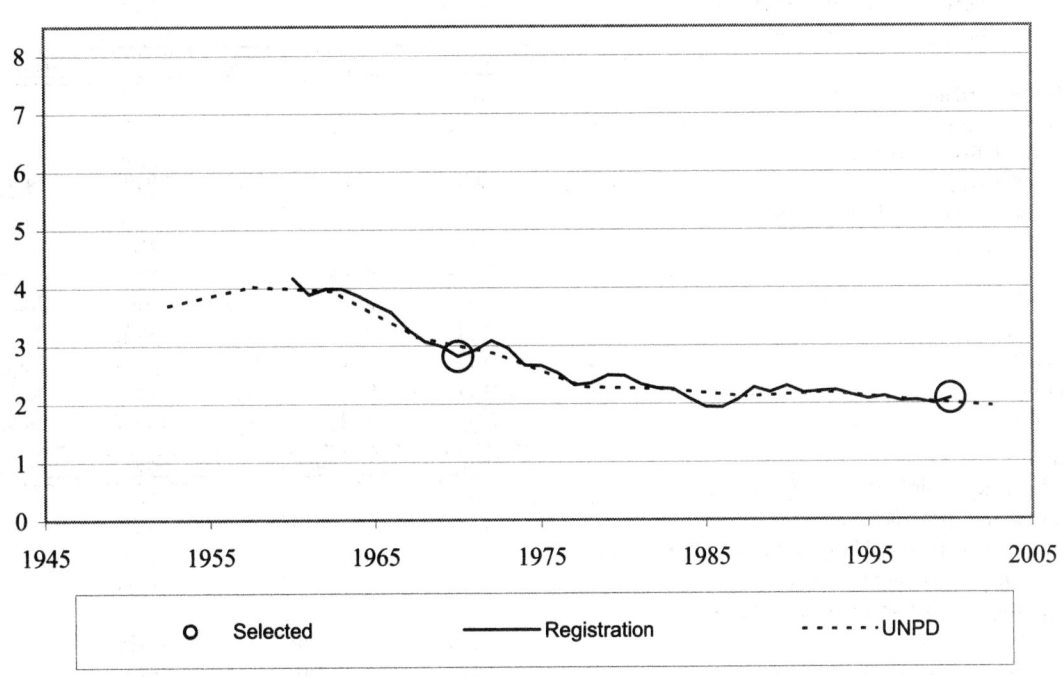

Age-specific fertility rates

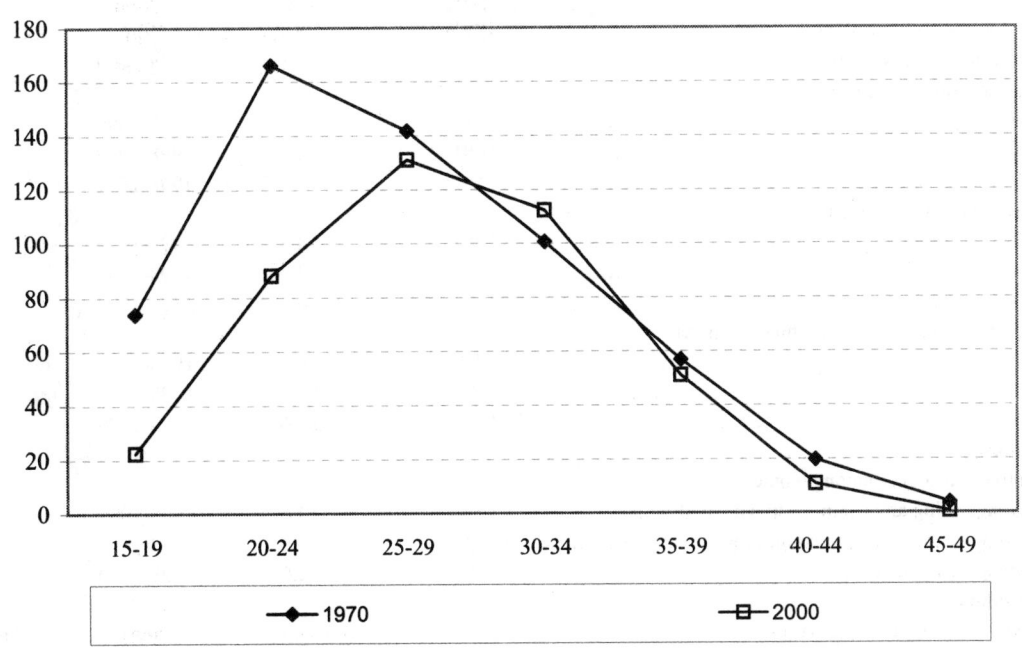

India

Indicator	Period					
	Earlier year			Later year		
	Year	Value		Year	Value	
Nuptiality						
Annual number of marriages (*thousands*)	..	..		..	..	
Annual number of divorces (*thousands*)	..	..		..	..	
	Year	Male	Female	Year	Male	Female
Total first marriage rate (per person)	..	..	..	..	..	..
Total divorce rate (per person)	..	..	..	..	..	..
Mean age at first marriage (years)	..	..	..	..	..	..
SMAM (years)	1971	22.7	17.7	1999	24.9	19.9
Percentage ever married by age group						
15-19	1971	17.7	57.0	1999	4.1	30.0
20-24	1971	49.7	90.9	1999	32.8	78.0
25-29	1971	81.1	98.0	1999	71.5	94.3
30-34	1971	92.7	99.1	1999	91.3	97.9
35-39	1971	96.0	99.5	1999	97.0	98.7
40-44	1971	96.5	99.4	1999	98.2	98.9
45-49	1971	97.1	99.6	1999	98.4	99.2
Fertility	Year	Value		Year	Value	
Annual number of births (*thousands*).........................	..	..		..	..	
Crude birth rate (per 1 000 population)	..	..		..	..	
Percentage of extra-marital births among all births	..	..		..	..	
Total fertility rate (births per woman)	1981	4.9		1997	3.3	
Age-specific fertility rate (per 1 000 women)						
15-19	1981	75		1997	54	
20-24	1981	256		1997	226	
25-29	1981	253		1997	188	
30-34	1981	186		1997	109	
35-39	1981	120		1997	55	
40-44	1981	63		1997	26	
45-49	1981	29		1997	8	
Mean age at childbearing (years)	1981	29.2		1997	27.5	
Mean age at first birth (years)[a]	..	..		1998-1999	19.5	
Children ever born per woman						
35-39	1981	4.3		1998-1999	3.8	
40-44	1981	4.8		1998-1999	4.3	
45-49	1981	5.1		1998-1999	4.6	
Percentage of childless women						
35-39	1981	4.3		1998-1999	4.5	
40-44	1981	4.6		1998-1999	3.8	
45-49	1981	4.5		1998-1999	3.8	
Percentage of women with parity three or higher						
35-39	1981	79.0		1998-1999	73.3	
40-44	1981	80.8		1998-1999	78.4	
45-49	1981	81.6		1998-1999	81.5	
Family Planning						
Contraceptive prevalence among women in union						
Percentage using any contraceptive method	1970	13.6		1998-1999	48.2	
Percentage using a modern contraceptive method	1970	10.0		1998-1999	42.8	
Percentage using condoms	1970	2.6		1998-1999	3.1	
Population policies						
Government's view on the level of fertility	1976	Too high		2001	Too high	
Government's policy regarding level of fertility	1976	Lower		2001	Lower	
Government's support for contraceptive methods	1976	Direct support		2001	Direct support	

[a]Median age at first birth among women aged 25-29 at the date of the survey

Total fertility rates

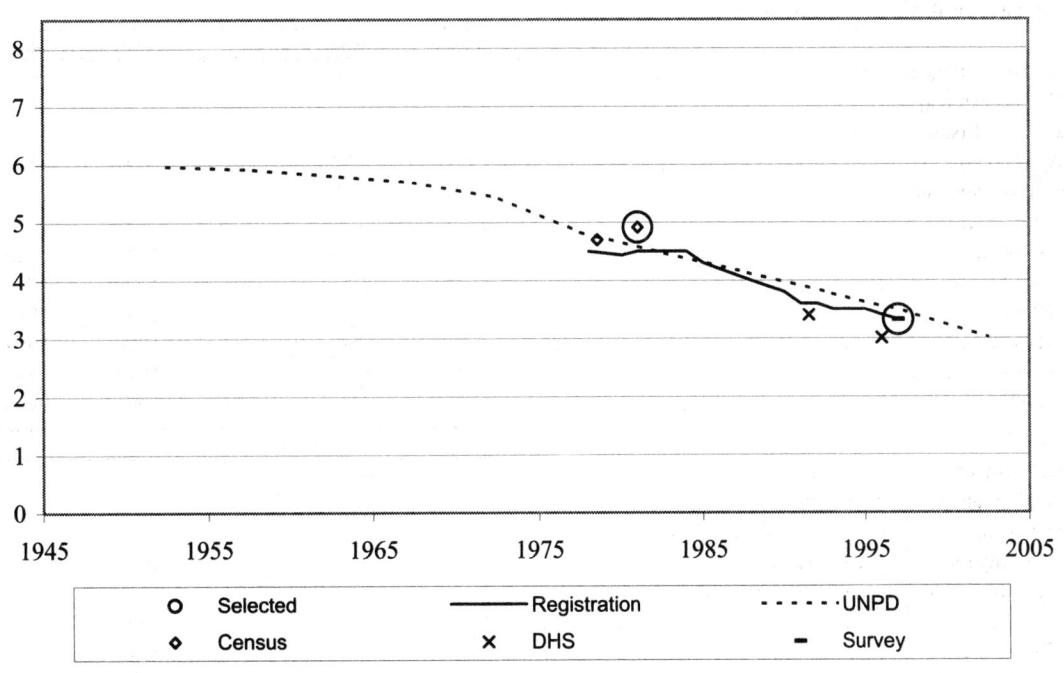

Age-specific fertility rates

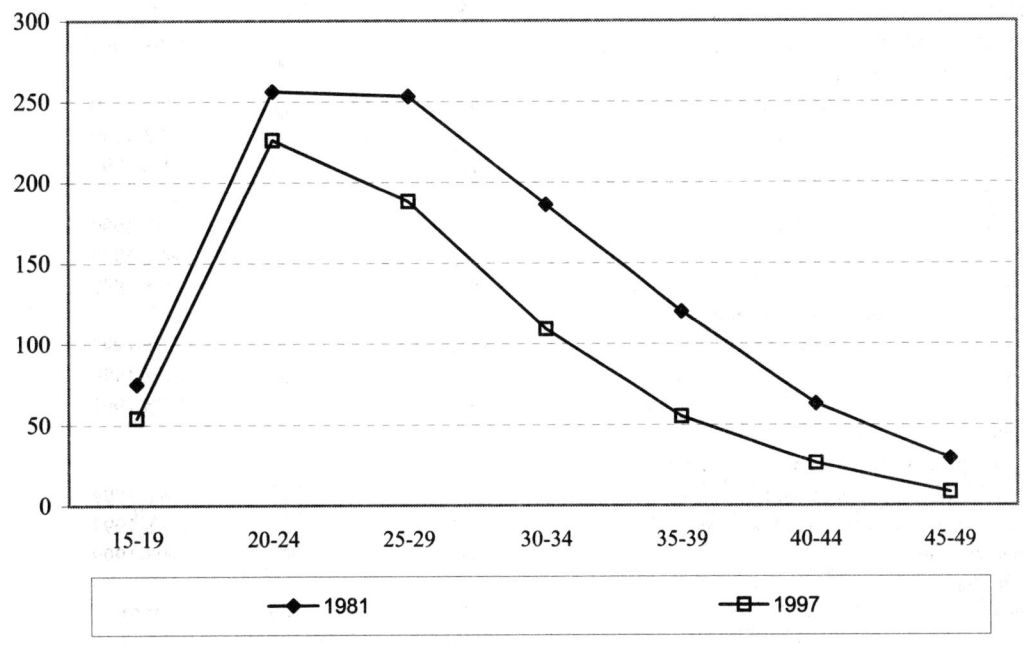

Indicator	Period					
	Earlier year			Later year		
	Year	Value		Year	Value	
Nuptiality						
Annual number of marriages (*thousands*)	1976	935.4		1986	1 249.0	
Annual number of divorces (*thousands*)	1976	106.6		1986	131.9	
	Year	Male	Female	Year	Male	Female
Total first marriage rate (per person)	..	..	..	..	..	..
Total divorce rate (per person)	..	..	..	..	..	..
Mean age at first marriage (years)	..	..	..	..	..	..
SMAM (years)	1971	23.8	19.3	2000	25.9	22.5
Percentage ever married by age group						
15-19	1971	5.1	37.4	2000	3.1	13.3
20-24	1971	41.4	81.5	2000	25.8	56.9
25-29	1971	81.5	95.0	2000	65.6	83.3
30-34	1971	93.9	97.8	2000	88.2	93.1
35-39	1971	97.0	98.6	2000	95.4	96.5
40-44	1971	97.9	98.8	2000	97.8	97.6
45-49	1971	98.2	99.0	2000	98.5	98.0
Fertility	Year	Value		Year	Value	
Annual number of births (*thousands*)	1971	5 317.6		2003	4 851.0	
Crude birth rate (per 1 000 population)	1971	44.7		2003	22.1	
Percentage of extra-marital births among all births	..	..		..	..	
Total fertility rate (births per woman)	1969	5.6		2003	2.6	
Age-specific fertility rate (per 1 000 women)						
15-19	1969	155		2003	51	
20-24	1969	286		2003	131	
25-29	1969	273		2003	143	
30-34	1969	211		2003	99	
35-39	1969	124		2003	66	
40-44	1969	55		2003	19	
45-49	1969	17		2003	4	
Mean age at childbearing (years)	1969	27.9		1996	28.1	
Mean age at first birth (years)[a]	1976	19.4		2003	20.2	
Children ever born per woman						
35-39	1971	5.1		2003	3.0	
40-44	1971	5.2		2003	3.8	
45-49	1971	5.2		2003	4.3	
Percentage of childless women						
35-39	1971	4.8		2003	6.6	
40-44	1971	5.9		2003	5.5	
45-49	1971	6.6		2003	4.9	
Percentage of women with parity three or higher						
35-39	1971	77.8		2003	59.6	
40-44	1971	75.6		2003	71.7	
45-49	1971	73.5		2003	78.6	
Family Planning						
Contraceptive prevalence among women in union						
Percentage using any contraceptive method	1973	8.6		2003	60.3	
Percentage using a modern contraceptive method	1973	7.2		2003	56.7	
Percentage using condoms	1973	0.5		2003	0.9	
Population policies						
Government's view on the level of fertility	1976	Too high		2001	Too high	
Government's policy regarding level of fertility	1976	Lower		2001	Lower	
Government's support for contraceptive methods	1976	Direct support		2001	Direct support	

[a]Median age at first birth among women aged 25-29 at the date of the survey for both dates

Total fertility rates

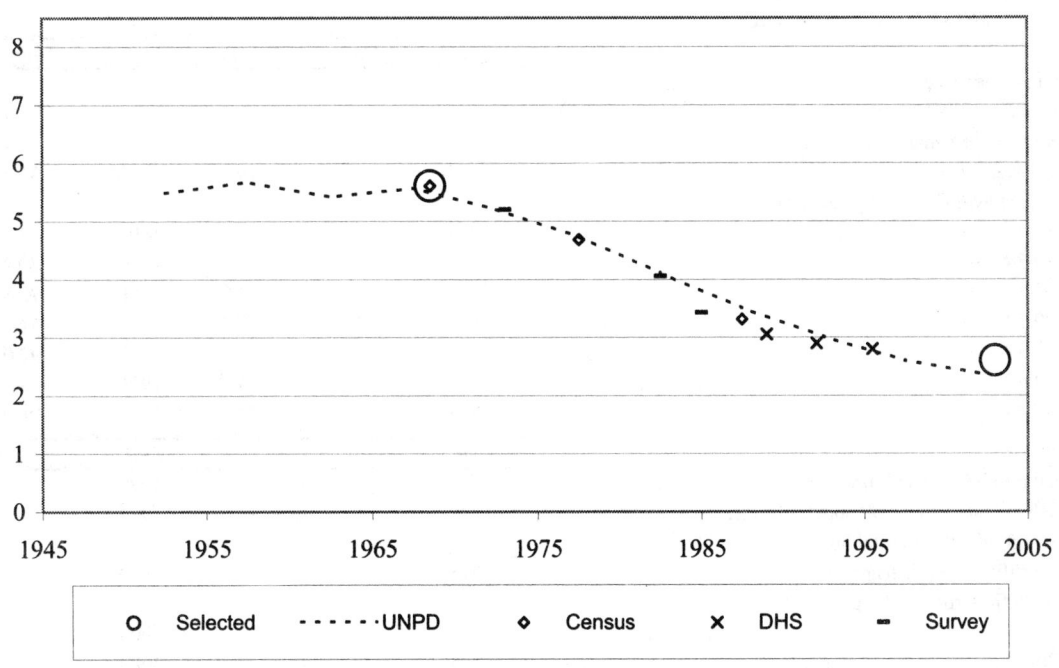

Age-specific fertility rates

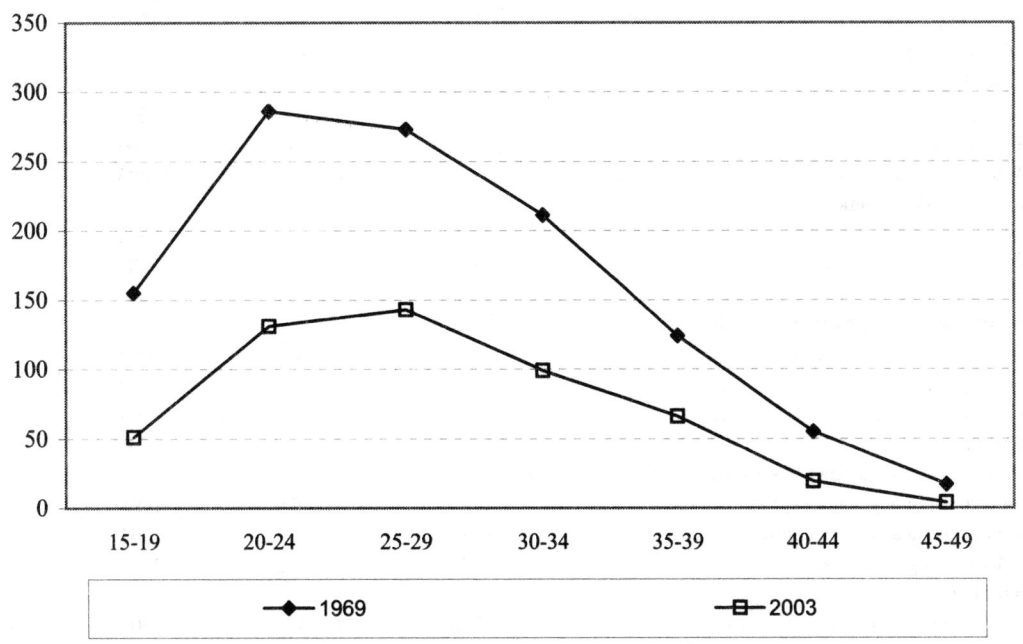

Iran (Islamic Republic of)

Indicator	Period					
	Earlier year			**Later year**		
	Year	Value		Year	Value	
Nuptiality						
Annual number of marriages (*thousands*)	..	..		1986	340.3	
Annual number of divorces (*thousands*)	1970	16.7		1999	51.0	
	Year	Male	Female	Year	Male	Female
Total first marriage rate (per person)	..	..	..	..	..	..
Total divorce rate (per person)	..	..	..	..	..	..
Mean age at first marriage (years)	..	..	..	..	..	..
SMAM (years)	1976	24.2	19.7	1996	25.3	22.1
Percentage ever married by age group						
15-19	1976	6.5	34.3	1996	2.6	17.9
20-24	1976	39.5	78.6	1996	27.4	60.5
25-29	1976	77.6	93.2	1996	72.8	85.2
30-34	1976	92.3	97.3	1996	92.3	93.6
35-39	1976	96.9	98.7	1996	97.0	96.7
40-44	1976	98.2	99.0	1996	98.3	98.1
45-49	1976	98.8	99.2	1996	98.8	98.7
Fertility	Year	Value		Year	Value	
Annual number of births (*thousands*)	1970	1 134.1		1999	1 177.6	
Crude birth rate (per 1 000 population)	1970	39.7		1999	18.8	
Percentage of extra-marital births among all births	..	..		..	..	
Total fertility rate (births per woman)	1975	6.4		2000	2.2	
Age-specific fertility rate (per 1 000 women)						
15-19	1975	174		2000	35	
20-24	1975	278		2000	110	
25-29	1975	263		2000	131	
30-34	1975	230		2000	90	
35-39	1975	177		2000	48	
40-44	1975	124		2000	16	
45-49	1975	36		2000	4	
Mean age at childbearing (years)	1975	29.3		2000	28.3	
Mean age at first birth (years)	..	..		..	..	
Children ever born per woman						
35-39	..	..		1986	5.6	
40-44	..	..		1986	6.4	
45-49	..	..		1986	6.8	
Percentage of childless women						
35-39	..	..		..	..	
40-44	..	..		..	..	
45-49	..	..		..	..	
Percentage of women with parity three or higher						
35-39	..	..		..	..	
40-44	..	..		..	..	
45-49	..	..		..	..	
Family Planning						
Contraceptive prevalence among women in union						
Percentage using any contraceptive method	1977	35.9		1997	72.9	
Percentage using a modern contraceptive method	1977	..		1997	56.0	
Percentage using condoms	1977	3.8		1997	5.4	
Population policies						
Government's view on the level of fertility	1976	Too high		2001	Too high	
Government's policy regarding level of fertility	1976	Lower		2001	Lower	
Government's support for contraceptive methods	1976	Direct support		2001	Direct support	

Total fertility rates

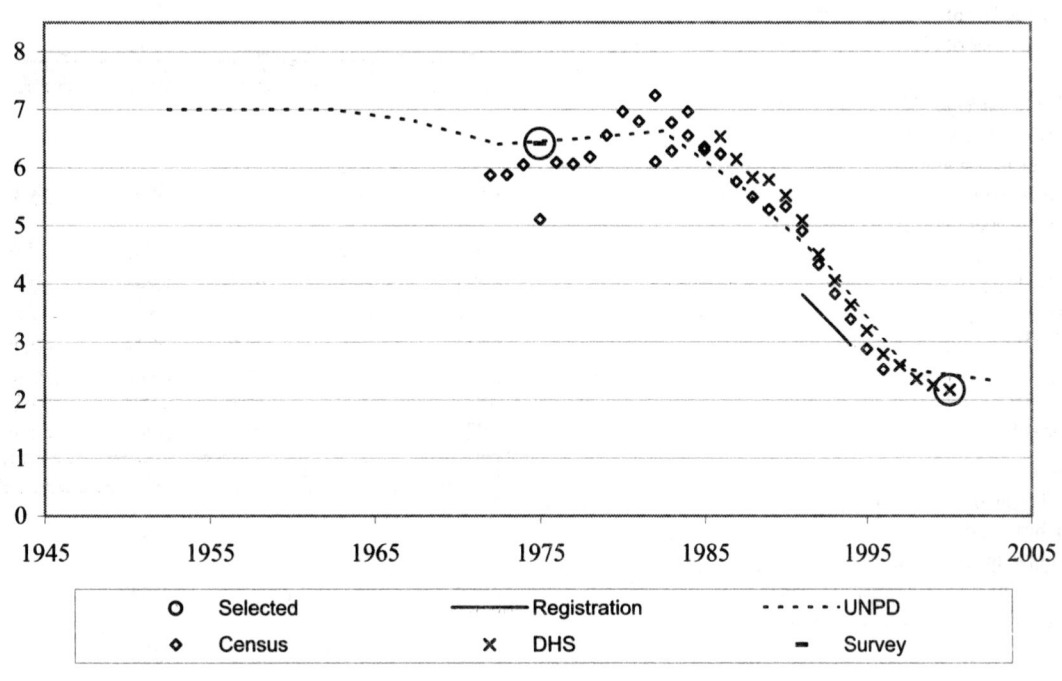

O Selected	—— Registration	····· UNPD
◇ Census	✕ DHS	— Survey

Age-specific fertility rates

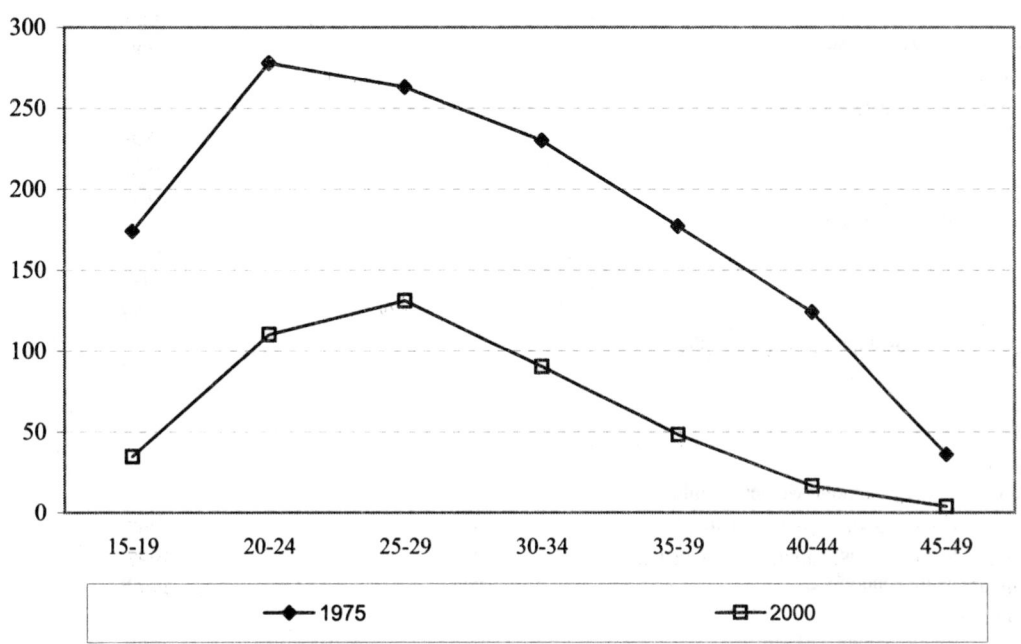

Indicator	Period					
	Earlier year			Later year		
	Year	Value		Year	Value	
Nuptiality						
Annual number of marriages (*thousands*)	1970	38.8		2000	171.1	
Annual number of divorces (*thousands*)	..	..		..	..	
	Year	Male	Female	Year	Male	Female
Total first marriage rate (per person)	..	..	..	..	..	..
Total divorce rate (per person)	..	..	..	..	..	..
Mean age at first marriage (years)	..	..	..	..	..	..
SMAM (years)	1977	25.3	20.8	1987	26.3	22.3
Percentage ever married by age group						
15-19	1977	5.2	32.5	1987	5.8	20.7
20-24	1977	30.1	67.1	1987	27.6	56.5
25-29	1977	68.0	86.1	1987	53.8	80.3
30-34	1977	86.5	92.3	1987	84.4	90.0
35-39	1977	92.6	94.9	1987	93.8	94.6
40-44	1977	93.9	96.3	1987	96.3	95.5
45-49	1977	95.0	96.8	1987	96.9	96.0
Fertility	Year	Value		Year	Value	
Annual number of births (*thousands*).............................	..	..		..	..	
Crude birth rate (per 1 000 population)	..	..		..	..	
Percentage of extra-marital births among all births	..	..		..	..	
Total fertility rate (births per woman)	1974	7.1		1989	5.2	
Age-specific fertility rate (per 1 000 women)						
15-19	..	..		1989	87	
20-24	..	..		1989	211	
25-29	..	..		1989	240	
30-34	..	..		1989	215	
35-39	..	..		1989	173	
40-44	..	..		1989	86	
45-49	..	..		1989	31	
Mean age at childbearing (years)	..	..		1989	30.2	
Mean age at first birth (years)	..	..		..	..	
Children ever born per woman						
35-39	..	..		1987	5.8	
40-44	..	..		1987	6.5	
45-49	..	..		1987	6.7	
Percentage of childless women						
35-39	..	..		1987	5.2	
40-44	..	..		1987	5.4	
45-49	..	..		1987	5.9	
Percentage of women with parity three or higher						
35-39	..	..		1987	81.7	
40-44	..	..		1987	83.8	
45-49	..	..		1987	83.5	
Family Planning						
Contraceptive prevalence among women in union						
Percentage using any contraceptive method	1974	14.5		1989	13.7	
Percentage using a modern contraceptive method	1974	12.9		1989	10.4	
Percentage using condoms	1974	1.4		1989	1.0	
Population policies						
Government's view on the level of fertility	1976	Satisfactory		2001	Satisfactory	
Government's policy regarding level of fertility	1976	Maintain		2001	No intervention	
Government's support for contraceptive methods	1976	Direct support		2001	Direct support	

Total fertility rates

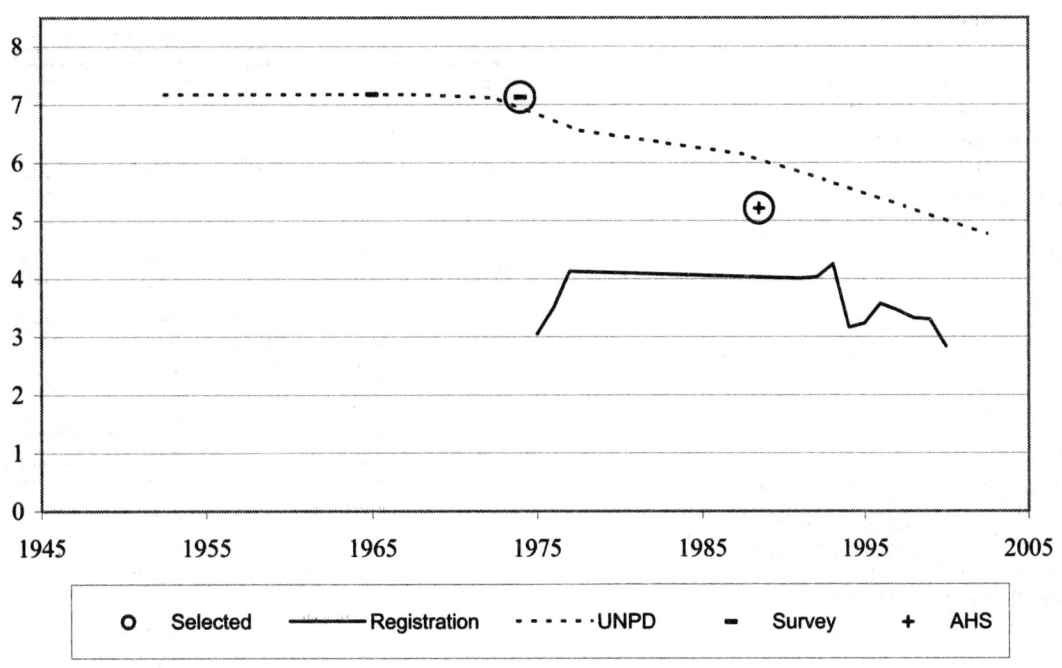

Age-specific fertility rates

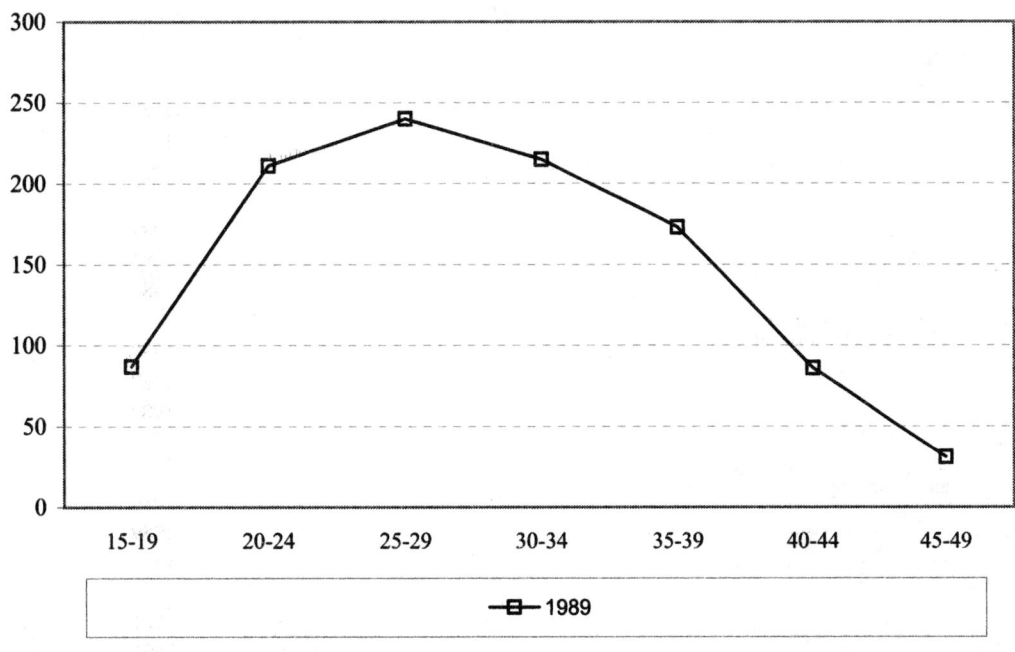

Ireland

Indicator	Period					
	Earlier year			Later year		
	Year	Value		Year	Value	
Nuptiality						
Annual number of marriages (*thousands*)	1970	20.8		2001	19.2	
Annual number of divorces (*thousands*)	..	..		2000	2.6	
	Year	Male	Female	Year	Male	Female
Total first marriage rate (per person)	1974	1.1	1.0	1995	0.6	0.6
Total divorce rate (per person)	..	..	..	..	..	..
Mean age at first marriage (years)	1974	27.2	25.0	1995	29.8	27.9
SMAM (years)	1971	25.8	23.5	2002	32.2	30.9
Percentage ever married by age group						
15-19	1971	0.5	2.1	2002	0.3	0.4
20-24	1971	15.4	31.1	2002	1.1	3.0
25-29	1971	50.8	68.8	2002	13.9	25.0
30-34	1971	67.8	80.6	2002	49.9	61.1
35-39	1971	71.1	82.9	2002	72.9	80.6
40-44	1971	71.0	82.2	2002	82.2	85.9
45-49	1971	71.7	81.8	2002	86.0	89.7
Fertility	Year	Value		Year	Value	
Annual number of births (*thousands*)	1970	64.4		2001	57.9	
Crude birth rate (per 1 000 population)	1970	21.8		2001	15.0	
Percentage of extra-marital births among all births	1970	2.7		2001	31.2	
Total fertility rate (births per woman)	1970	3.9		2001	2.0	
Age-specific fertility rate (per 1 000 women)						
15-19	1970	16		2001	19	
20-24	1970	144		2001	50	
25-29	1970	227		2001	92	
30-34	1970	202		2001	140	
35-39	1970	132		2001	79	
40-44	1970	45		2001	14	
45-49	1970	4		2001	1	
Mean age at childbearing (years)	1970	30.4		2001	30.7	
Mean age at first birth (years)	1975	25.5		2001	28.0	
Children ever born per woman						
35-39	..	..		2002	1.7	
40-44	..	..		2002	2.0	
45-49	..	..		2002	2.0	
Percentage of childless women						
35-39	..	..		2002	13.9	
40-44	..	..		2002	7.6	
45-49	..	..		2002	9.0	
Percentage of women with parity three or higher						
35-39	..	..		2002	19.2	
40-44	..	..		2002	27.3	
45-49	..	..		2002	28.4	
Family Planning						
Contraceptive prevalence among women in union						
Percentage using any contraceptive method	..	..		..	..	
Percentage using a modern contraceptive method	..	..		..	..	
Percentage using condoms	..	..		..	..	
Population policies						
Government's view on the level of fertility	1976	Satisfactory		2001	Satisfactory	
Government's policy regarding level of fertility	1976	Maintain		2001	Maintain	
Government's support for contraceptive methods	1976	No support		2001	Direct support	

Total fertility rates

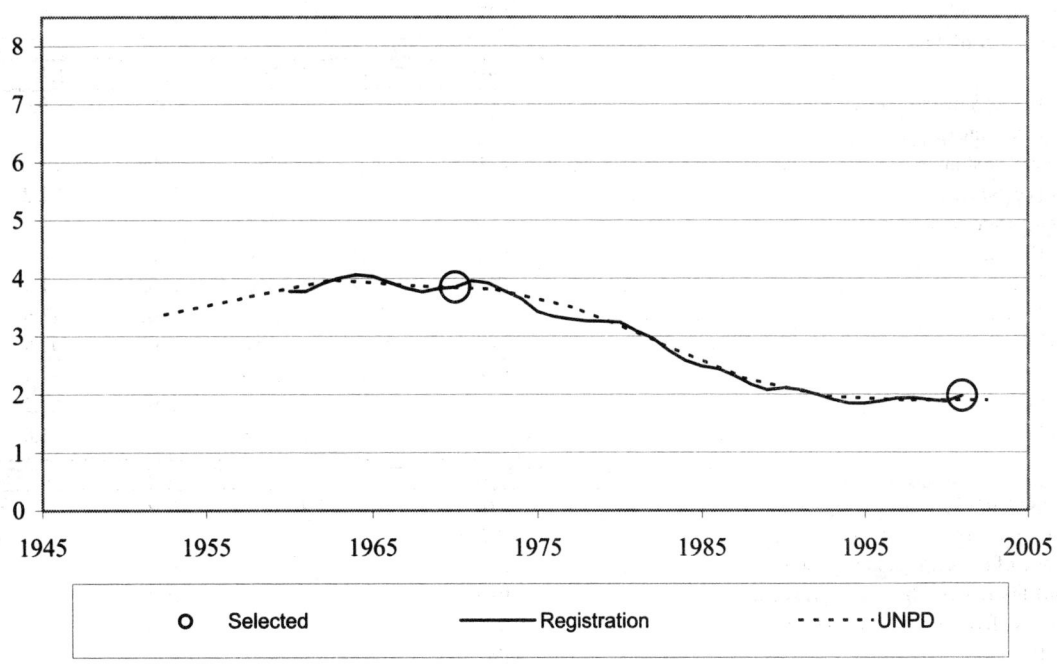

Age-specific fertility rates

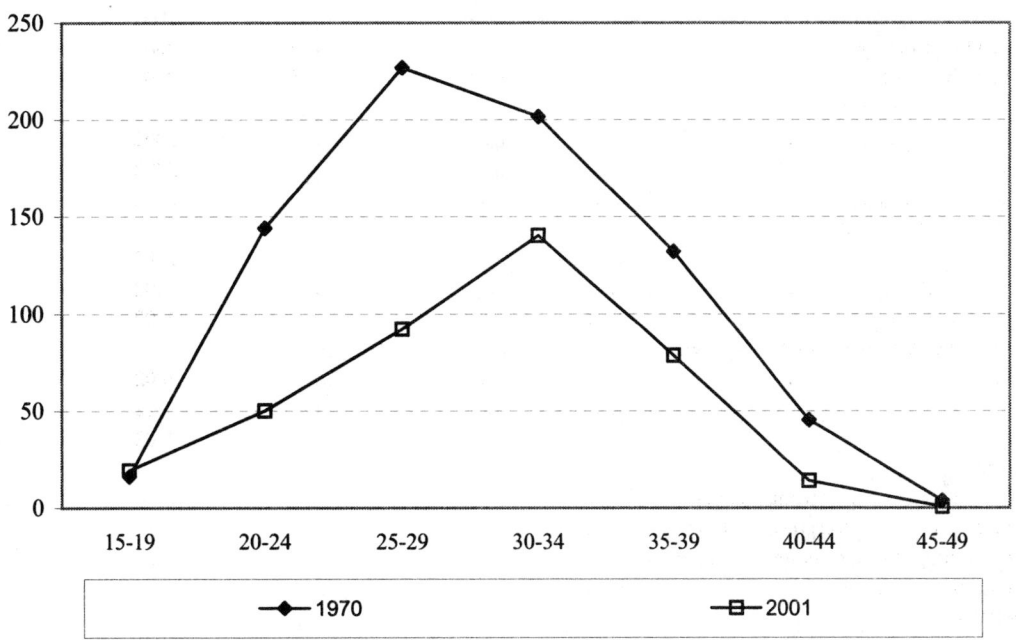

Indicator	Period					
	Earlier year			Later year		
	Year	Value		Year	Value	

Nuptiality

	Year	Value		Year	Value	
Annual number of marriages (*thousands*)	1970	26.6		2001	38.9	
Annual number of divorces (*thousands*)	1970	2.4		2001	11.2	

	Year	Male	Female	Year	Male	Female
Total first marriage rate (per person)	1975	1.0	1.0	1996	0.7	0.7
Total divorce rate (per person)	1971	0.1	0.1	1996	0.1	0.1
Mean age at first marriage (years)	1975	25.5	22.2	1996	27.0	23.9
SMAM (years)	1972	25.4	22.8	1999	27.9	25.0
Percentage ever married by age group						
15-19	1972	1.4	8.7	1999	0.4	4.2
20-24	1972	24.1	54.3	1999	13.3	34.2
25-29	1972	72.4	84.2	1999	50.8	70.2
30-34	1972	90.7	93.3	1999	80.8	86.2
35-39	1972	94.4	96.2	1999	90.0	91.0
40-44	1972	95.3	97.1	1999	93.4	93.2
45-49	1972	96.2	97.7	1999	95.5	94.1

Fertility

	Year	Value		Year	Value	
Annual number of births (*thousands*).............................	1970	80.8		2001	136.6	
Crude birth rate (per 1 000 population)	1970	27.2		2001	21.2	
Percentage of extra-marital births among all births	1970	0.7		1996	3.1	
Total fertility rate (births per woman)	1970	3.9		2000	3.0	
Age-specific fertility rate (per 1 000 women)						
15-19	1970	50		2000	17	
20-24	1970	210		2000	117	
25-29	1970	232		2000	187	
30-34	1970	177		2000	162	
35-39	1970	90		2000	86	
40-44	1970	21		2000	21	
45-49	1970	3		2000	2	
Mean age at childbearing (years)	1970	28.3		2000	29.6	
Mean age at first birth (years)	1970	22.9		1997	21.7	
Children ever born per woman						
35-39	1961	3.3		..	..	
40-44	1961	3.5		..	..	
45-49	1961	3.3		..	..	
Percentage of childless women						
35-39	1961	4.2		..	..	
40-44	1961	6.2		..	..	
45-49	1961	7.1		..	..	
Percentage of women with parity three or higher						
35-39	1961	47.9		..	..	
40-44	1961	49.3		..	..	
45-49	1961	47.2		..	..	

Family Planning

Contraceptive prevalence among women in union						
Percentage using any contraceptive method	..	..		1988	68.0	
Percentage using a modern contraceptive method	..	..		1988	51.9	
Percentage using condoms	..	..		1988	4.0	

Population policies

Government's view on the level of fertility	1976	Too low		2001	Too low	
Government's policy regarding level of fertility	1976	Raise		2001	Raise	
Government's support for contraceptive methods	1976	Direct support		2001	Indirect support	

Total fertility rates

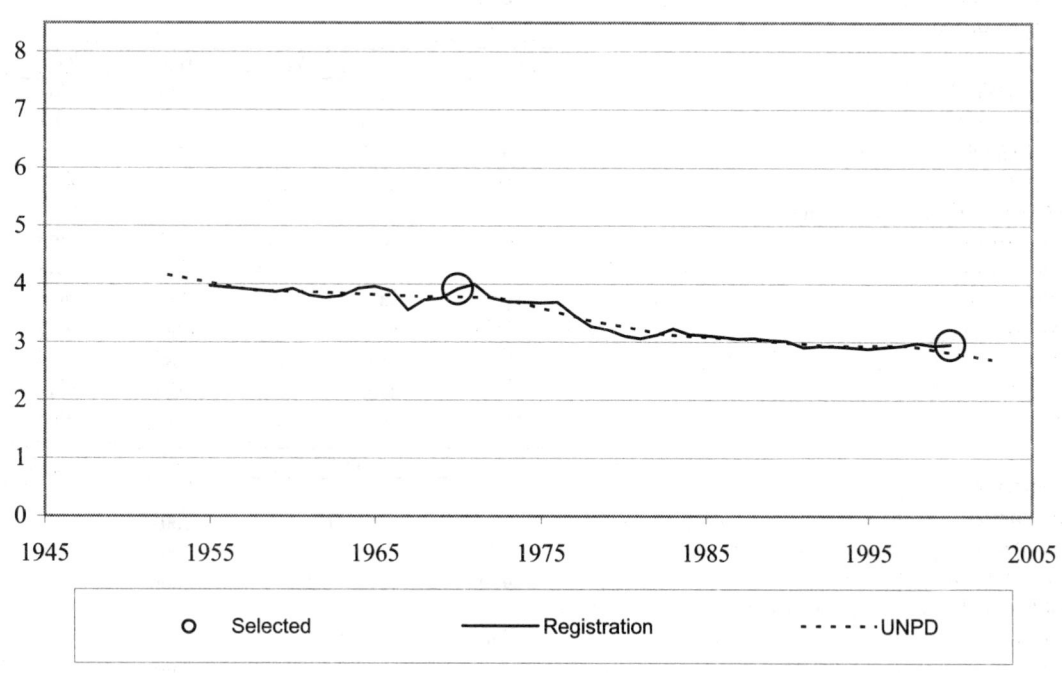

Age-specific fertility rates

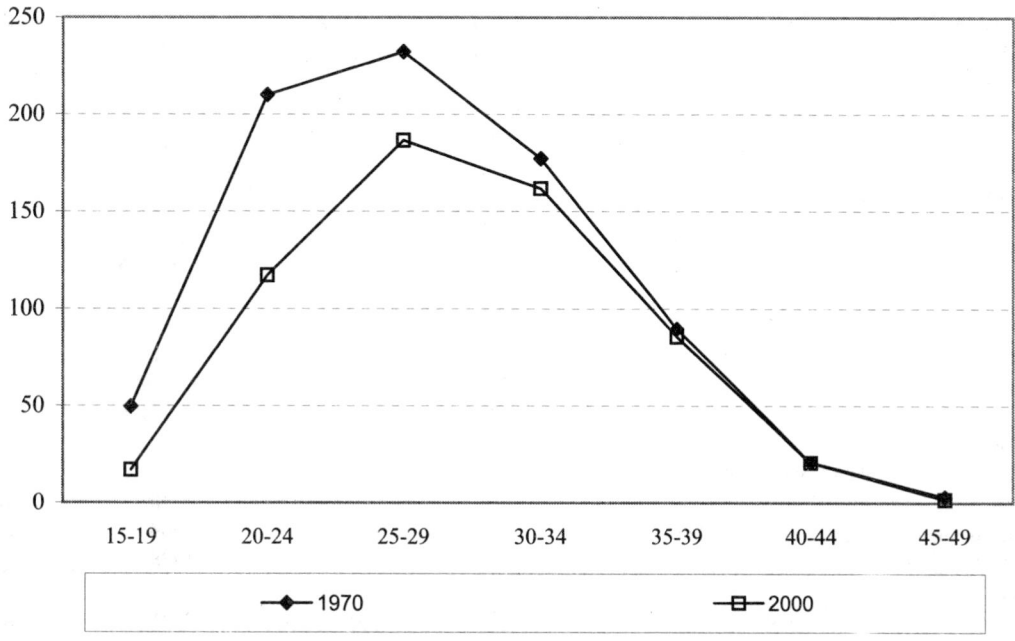

Indicator	Period					
	Earlier year			Later year		
	Year	Value		Year	Value	
Nuptiality						
Annual number of marriages (*thousands*)	1970	395.5		2001	260.9	
Annual number of divorces (*thousands*)	1971	17.1		2000	37.6	
	Year	Male	Female	Year	Male	Female
Total first marriage rate (per person)	1974	1.0	1.0	1996	0.6	0.6
Total divorce rate (per person)	1978	0.0	0.0	1994	0.0	0.0
Mean age at first marriage (years)	1974	27.1	23.8	1996	29.8	26.8
SMAM (years)	1971	27.2	22.6	1999	31.5	28.4
Percentage ever married by age group						
15-19	1971	0.6	6.4	1999	0.1	0.9
20-24	1971	13.4	43.5	1999	3.0	13.3
25-29	1971	54.3	76.8	1999	22.7	45.6
30-34	1971	77.8	85.5	1999	56.6	73.3
35-39	1971	84.9	87.2	1999	76.2	84.5
40-44	1971	87.8	87.0	1999	84.5	89.1
45-49	1971	88.9	86.2	1999	88.7	91.5
Fertility	Year	Value		Year	Value	
Annual number of births (*thousands*)	1970	901.5		2002	537.1	
Crude birth rate (per 1 000 population)	1970	16.7		2002	9.3	
Percentage of extra-marital births among all births	1970	2.2		2000	9.7	
Total fertility rate (births per woman)	1970	2.4		2000	1.2	
Age-specific fertility rate (per 1 000 women)						
15-19	1970	27		2000	7	
20-24	1970	129		2000	33	
25-29	1970	153		2000	76	
30-34	1970	99		2000	84	
35-39	1970	53		2000	40	
40-44	1970	16		2000	8	
45-49	1970	1		2000	0	
Mean age at childbearing (years)	1970	28.3		2000	30.3	
Mean age at first birth (years)	1970	25.0		1995-1996	28.0	
Children ever born per woman						
35-39	..	..		1995-1996	1.6	
40-44	..	..		1995-1996	1.9	
45-49	..	..		1995-1996	2.0	
Percentage of childless women						
35-39	..	..		1995-1996	16.6	
40-44	..	..		1995-1996	10.5	
45-49	..	..		1995-1996	9.2	
Percentage of women with parity three or higher						
35-39	..	..		1995-1996	14.5	
40-44	..	..		1995-1996	22.5	
45-49	..	..		1995-1996	26.1	
Family Planning						
Contraceptive prevalence among women in union						
Percentage using any contraceptive method	1979	78.0		1996	60.2	
Percentage using a modern contraceptive method	1979	32.0		1996	38.9	
Percentage using condoms	1979	13.0		1996	13.7	
Population policies						
Government's view on the level of fertility	1976	Satisfactory		2001	Too low	
Government's policy regarding level of fertility	1976	No intervention		2001	No intervention	
Government's support for contraceptive methods	1976	Indirect support		2001	No support	

Total fertility rates

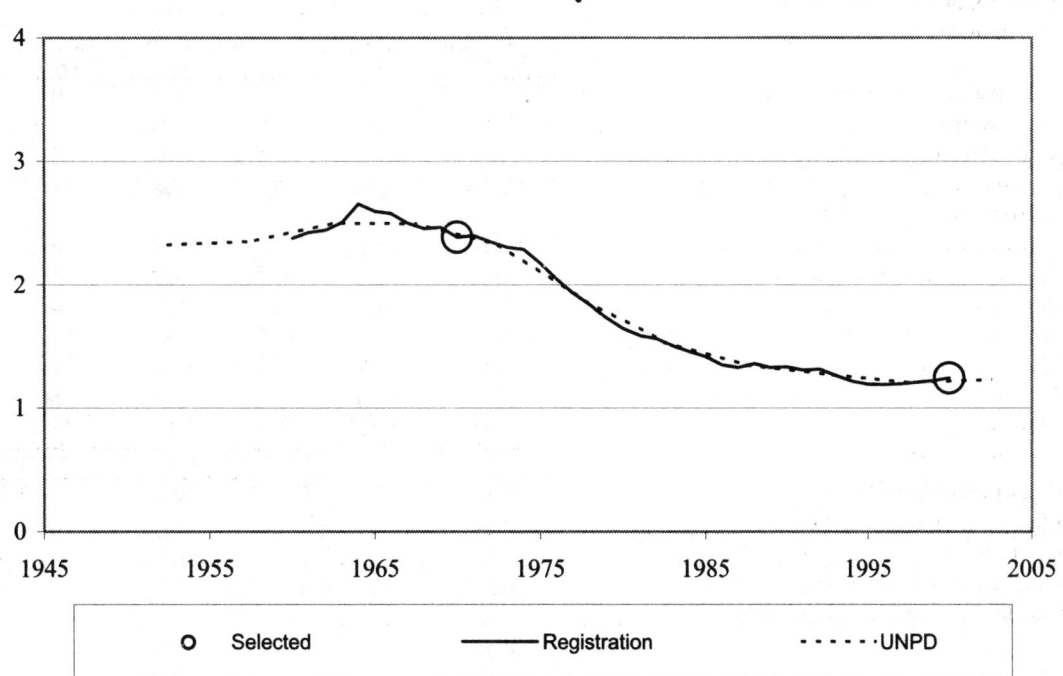

Age-specific fertility rates

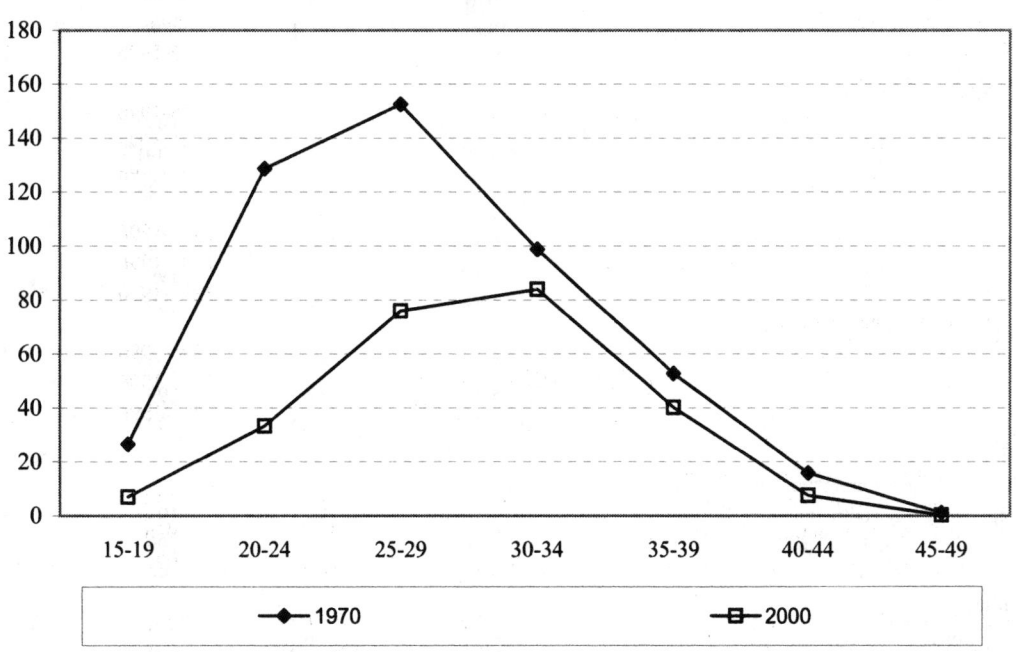

Jamaica

Indicator	Period					
	Earlier year			Later year		
	Year	Value		Year	Value	
Nuptiality						
Annual number of marriages (*thousands*)	1970	8.9		1998	24.1	
Annual number of divorces (*thousands*)	1970	0.6		1999	1.1	
	Year	Male	Female	Year	Male	Female
Total first marriage rate (per person)	..	..	..	..	..	..
Total divorce rate (per person)	1970	0.1	0.1	1995	0.1	0.1
Mean age at first marriage (years)	..	..	..	..	..	..
SMAM (years)	1970	33.0	21.1	1991	34.6	33.2
Percentage ever married by age group						
15-19	1970	0.2	16.5	1991	0.4	0.7
20-24	1970	4.4	51.5	1991	2.2	5.3
25-29	1970	18.3	69.9	1991	10.4	15.8
30-34	1970	33.0	77.5	1991	23.2	28.2
35-39	1970	43.5	80.8	1991	34.7	39.6
40-44	1970	52.4	79.8	1991	44.7	48.8
45-49	1970	59.1	78.9	1991	51.6	54.1
Fertility	Year	Value		Year	Value	
Annual number of births (*thousands*)...........................	1970	64.4		1999	56.9	
Crude birth rate (per 1 000 population)	1970	35.5		1999	22.0	
Percentage of extra-marital births among all births	1964	74.1		1989	86.2	
Total fertility rate (births per woman)	1970	5.5		1996	2.9	
Age-specific fertility rate (per 1 000 women)						
15-19	1970	167		1996	112	
20-24	1970	302		1996	163	
25-29	1970	268		1996	112	
30-34	1970	190		1996	101	
35-39	1970	127		1996	55	
40-44	1970	47		1996	25	
45-49	1970	8		1996	4	
Mean age at childbearing (years)	1970	27.4		1996	26.8	
Mean age at first birth (years)[a]	1975-1976	19.2		..	..	
Children ever born per woman						
35-39	1975-1976	5.1		1991	3.4	
40-44	1975-1976	5.4		1991	4.1	
45-49	1975-1976	5.5		1991	4.6	
Percentage of childless women						
35-39	1975-1976	4.7		1991	8.8	
40-44	1975-1976	6.2		1991	7.3	
45-49	1975-1976	8.2		1991	9.0	
Percentage of women with parity three or higher						
35-39	1975-1976	73.3		1991	60.3	
40-44	1975-1976	73.7		1991	69.2	
45-49	1975-1976	73.9		1991	72.7	
Family Planning						
Contraceptive prevalence among women in union						
Percentage using any contraceptive method	1975-1976	38.3		1997	65.9	
Percentage using a modern contraceptive method	1975-1976	36.2		1997	62.6	
Percentage using condoms	1975-1976	6.6		1997	17.0	
Population policies						
Government's view on the level of fertility	1976	Too high		2001	Too high	
Government's policy regarding level of fertility	1976	Lower		2001	Lower	
Government's support for contraceptive methods	1976	Direct support		2001	Direct support	

[a]Median age at first birth among women aged 25-29 at the date of the survey

Total fertility rates

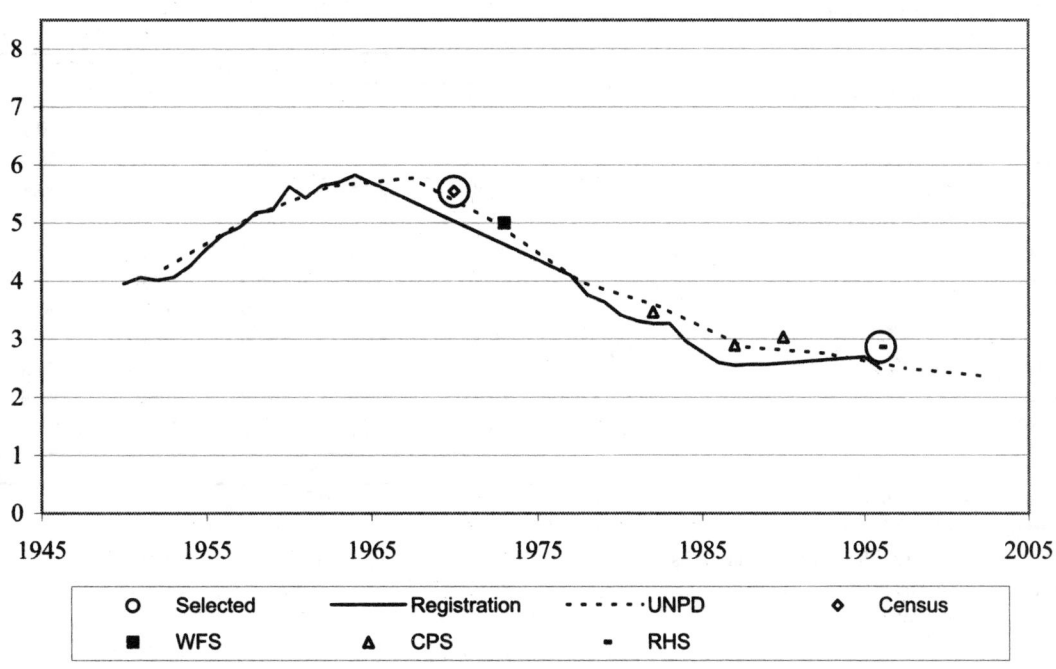

Age-specific fertility rates

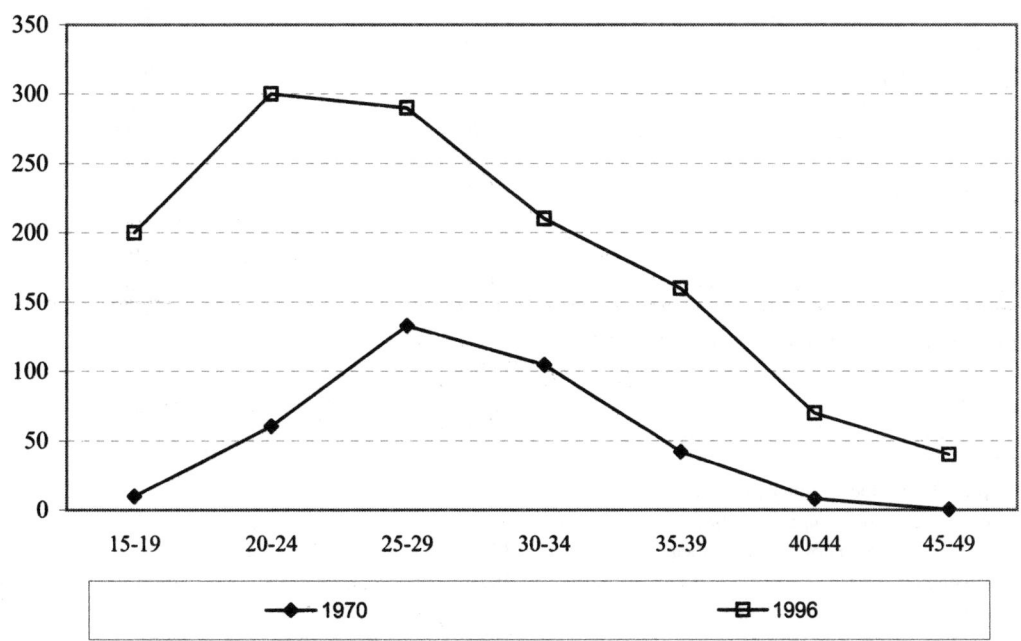

Japan

Indicator	Period					
	Earlier year			Later year		
	Year	Value		Year	Value	

Nuptiality

Indicator	Year	Value		Year	Value	
Annual number of marriages (*thousands*)	1970	1 037.8		2001	800.0	
Annual number of divorces (*thousands*)	1970	97.0		2001	285.9	

Indicator	Year	Male	Female	Year	Male	Female
Total first marriage rate (per person)	1975	0.8	0.8	1998	0.7	0.7
Total divorce rate (per person)	1970	0.1	0.1	1997	0.1	0.2
Mean age at first marriage (years)	1975	27.0	24.5	1998	28.8	26.7
SMAM (years)	1970	27.5	24.7	2000	30.8	28.6
Percentage ever married by age group						
15-19	1970	0.7	2.1	2000	0.5	0.9
20-24	1970	9.9	28.3	2000	7.1	12.1
25-29	1970	53.5	81.9	2000	30.7	46.0
30-34	1970	88.3	92.8	2000	57.1	73.4
35-39	1970	95.3	94.2	2000	74.3	86.2
40-44	1970	97.2	94.7	2000	81.6	91.4
45-49	1970	98.1	96.0	2000	85.4	93.7

Fertility

Indicator	Year	Value		Year	Value	
Annual number of births (*thousands*)	1970	1 955.3		2001	1 170.7	
Crude birth rate (per 1 000 population)	1970	18.9		2001	9.2	
Percentage of extra-marital births among all births	1970	0.9		1998	1.4	
Total fertility rate (births per woman)	1970	2.1		2000	1.3	
Age-specific fertility rate (per 1 000 women)						
15-19	1970	5		2000	5	
20-24	1970	97		2000	39	
25-29	1970	209		2000	98	
30-34	1970	86		2000	91	
35-39	1970	20		2000	31	
40-44	1970	3		2000	4	
45-49	1970	0		2000	0	
Mean age at childbearing (years)	1970	27.8		2000	29.7	
Mean age at first birth (years)	1970	25.9		1998	27.9	
Children ever born per woman						
35-39	1970	2.0		..	..	
40-44	1970	2.3		..	..	
45-49	1970	2.7		..	..	
Percentage of childless women						
35-39	1970	5.9		..	..	
40-44	1970	6.8		..	..	
45-49	1970	7.4		..	..	
Percentage of women with parity three or higher						
35-39	1970	28.8		..	..	
40-44	1970	40.7		..	..	
45-49	1970	53.6		..	..	

Family Planning

Indicator	Year	Value		Year	Value	
Contraceptive prevalence among women in union						
Percentage using any contraceptive method	1971	52.6		2000	55.9	
Percentage using a modern contraceptive method	1971	49.0		2000	..	
Percentage using condoms	1971	38.9		2000	42.1	

Population policies

Indicator	Year	Value		Year	Value	
Government's view on the level of fertility	1976	Satisfactory		2001	Too low	
Government's policy regarding level of fertility	1976	No intervention		2001	No intervention	
Government's support for contraceptive methods	1976	Direct support		2001	Indirect support	

Total fertility rates

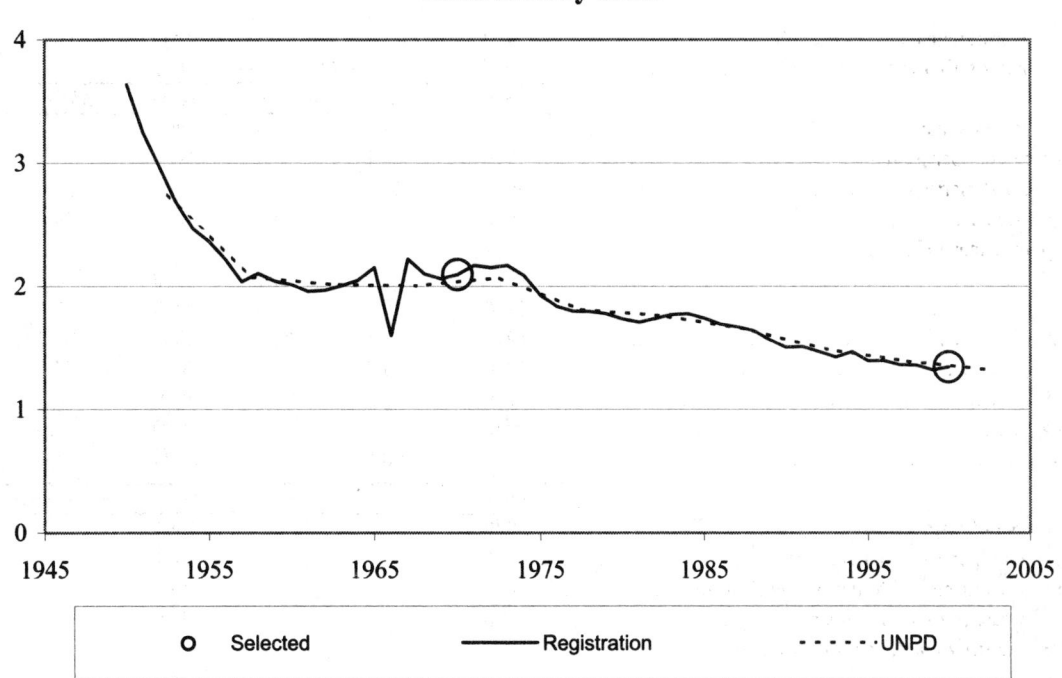

Age-specific fertility rates

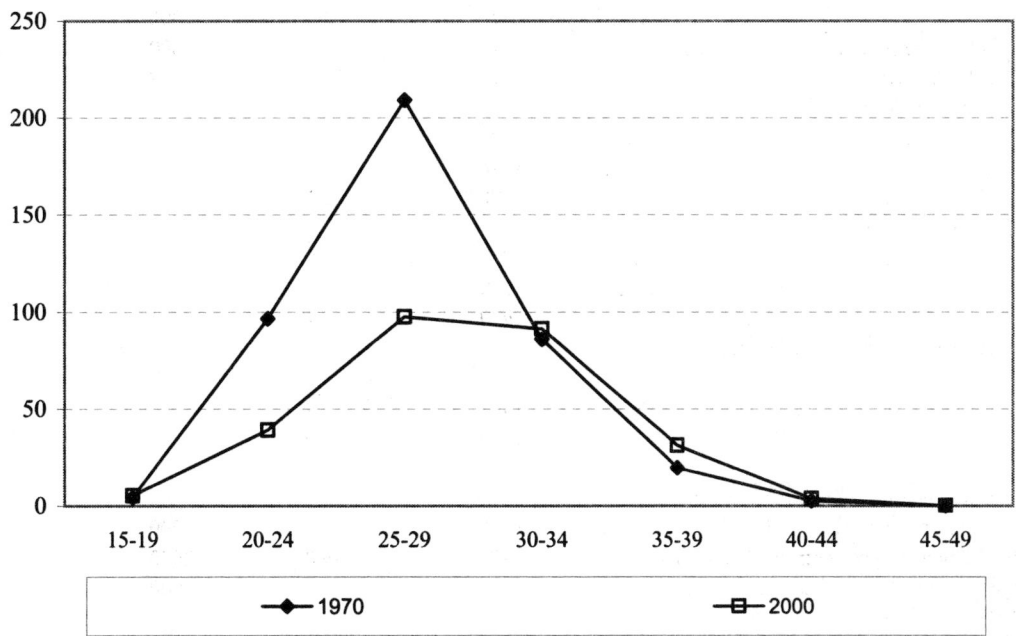

Jordan

Indicator	Period			
	Earlier year		Later year	
	Year	Value	Year	Value
Nuptiality				
Annual number of marriages (*thousands*)	1970	11.7	1998	39.4
Annual number of divorces (*thousands*)	1970	1.5	2000	6.3

Indicator	Year	Male	Female	Year	Male	Female
Total first marriage rate (per person)	1975	1.1	0.8	1997	0.7	0.8
Total divorce rate (per person)	1970	0.1	0.1	1997	0.2	0.2
Mean age at first marriage (years)	1975	26.2	20.7	1997	27.8	23.0
SMAM (years)	1979	25.9	21.5	1994	27.0	24.0
Percentage ever married by age group						
15-19	1979	1.4	20.5	1994	1.5	8.2
20-24	1979	25.7	64.4	1994	16.2	38.8
25-29	1979	66.0	86.7	1994	57.6	66.2
30-34	1979	89.3	93.7	1994	86.2	80.7
35-39	1979	96.2	96.2	1994	95.4	89.8
40-44	1979	97.8	97.4	1994	97.6	94.3
45-49	1979	98.4	97.6	1994	98.4	96.1

Indicator	Year	Value	Year	Value
Fertility				
Annual number of births (*thousands*)	1970	76.8	2000	126.0
Crude birth rate (per 1 000 population)	1970	33.4	2000	25.0
Percentage of extra-marital births among all births	..	..	..	..
Total fertility rate (births per woman)	1974	7.6	2001	3.7
Age-specific fertility rate (per 1 000 women)				
15-19	1974	124	2001	28
20-24	1974	343	2001	150
25-29	1974	365	2001	202
30-34	1974	332	2001	184
35-39	1974	240	2001	122
40-44	1974	103	2001	43
45-49	1974	19	2001	5
Mean age at childbearing (years)	1974	29.5	2001	30.0
Mean age at first birth (years)[a]	1976	19.8	1997	24.7
Children ever born per woman				
35-39	1976	7.1	1997	5.0
40-44	1976	8.4	1997	6.5
45-49	1976	8.6	1997	7.2
Percentage of childless women				
35-39	1976	2.4	1997	14.6
40-44	1976	2.3	1997	8.6
45-49	1976	2.3	1997	7.1
Percentage of women with parity three or higher				
35-39	1976	90.9	1997	78.1
40-44	1976	90.9	1997	87.5
45-49	1976	93.4	1997	88.1
Family Planning				
Contraceptive prevalence among women in union				
Percentage using any contraceptive method	1972	22.3	2002	55.8
Percentage using a modern contraceptive method	1972	17.6	2002	38.6
Percentage using condoms	1972	1.1	2002	3.4
Population policies				
Government's view on the level of fertility	1976	Too high	2001	Too high
Government's policy regarding level of fertility	1976	No intervention	2001	Lower
Government's support for contraceptive methods	1976	Direct support	2001	Direct support

[a]Median age at first birth among women aged 25-29 at the date of the survey for both dates

Total fertility rates

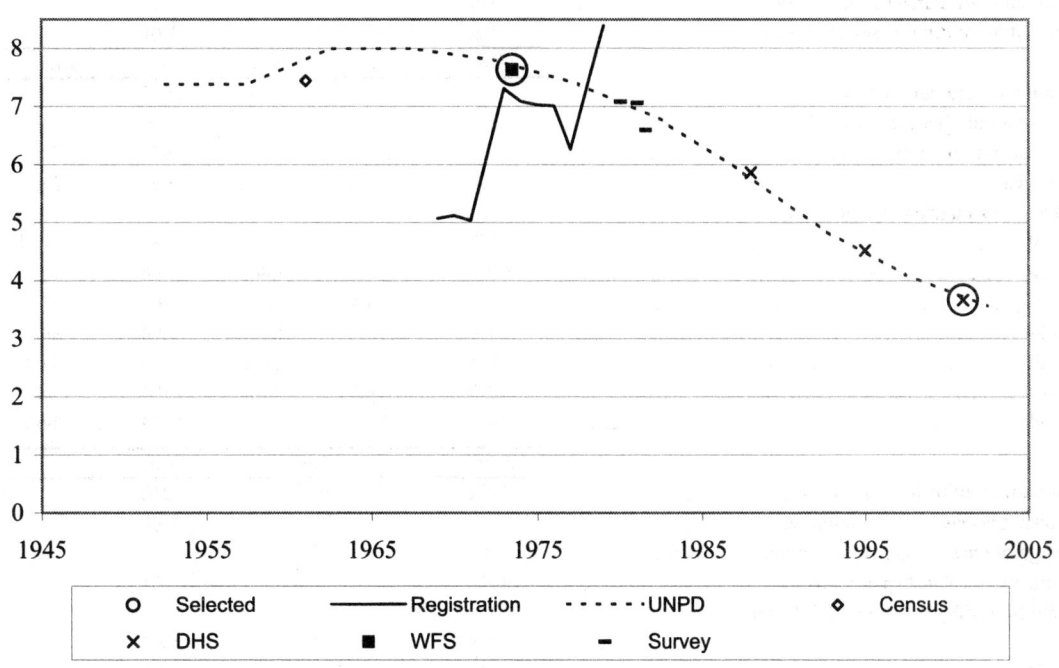

Age-specific fertility rates

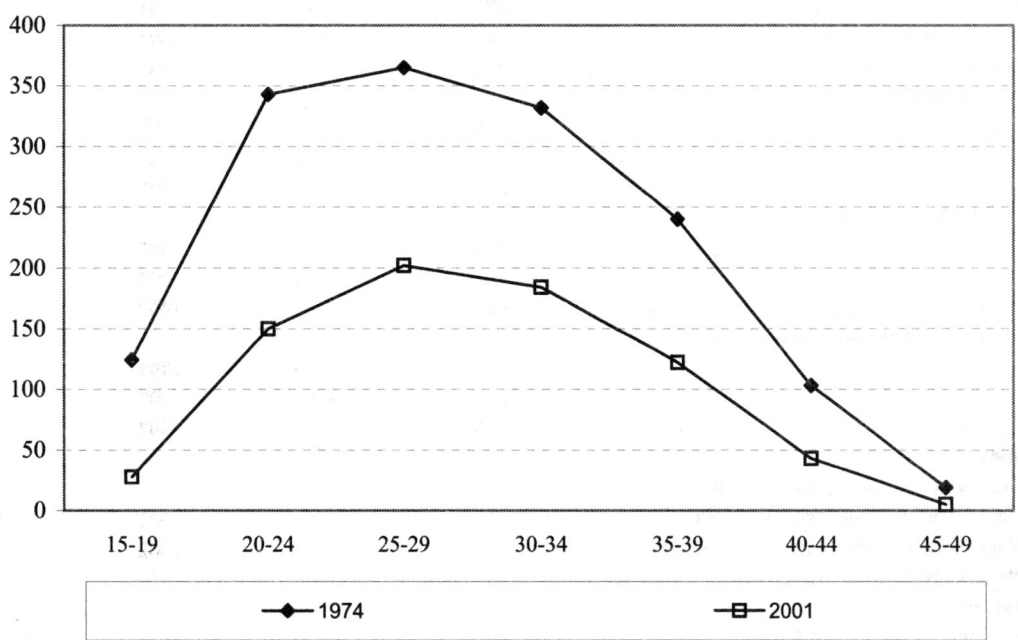

Indicator	Period					
	Earlier year			Later year		
	Year	Value		Year	Value	
Nuptiality						
Annual number of marriages (*thousands*)	1970	124.6		2001	92.9	
Annual number of divorces (*thousands*)	1970	20.9		1999	25.6	
	Year	Male	Female	Year	Male	Female
Total first marriage rate (per person)	..	..	..	1998	0.7	0.7
Total divorce rate (per person)	..	..	..	1997	0.3	0.3
Mean age at first marriage (years)	..	..	..	1998	25.8	23.3
SMAM (years)	..	..	..	1999	26.1	23.4
Percentage ever married by age group						
15-19	1979	..	..	1999	1.4	12.9
20-24	1979	39.6	64.9	1999	25.9	48.2
25-29	1979	84.0	90.1	1999	67.0	73.3
30-34	1979	93.6	95.8	1999	0.0	85.6
35-39	1979	96.7	98.3	1999	91.8	92.3
40-44	1979	98.0	98.6	1999	94.6	95.3
45-49	1979	98.8	98.4	1999	96.1	96.7
Fertility	Year	Value		Year	Value	
Annual number of births (*thousands*).............................	1970	306.7		1999	211.8	
Crude birth rate (per 1 000 population)	1970	23.4		1999	14.2	
Percentage of extra-marital births among all births	1980	10.3		1998	21.8	
Total fertility rate (births per woman)	1970	3.3		1997	2.1	
Age-specific fertility rate (per 1 000 women)						
15-19	1970	30		1997	44	
20-24	1970	192		1997	166	
25-29	1970	178		1997	115	
30-34	1970	135		1997	63	
35-39	1970	83		1997	29	
40-44	1970	34		1997	6	
45-49	1970	9		1997	0	
Mean age at childbearing (years)	1970	28.9		1997	26.1	
Mean age at first birth (years)	..	..		1998	23.5	
Children ever born per woman						
35-39	..	..		1999	2.4	
40-44	..	..		1999	2.7	
45-49	..	..		1999	3.0	
Percentage of childless women						
35-39	..	..		1999	7.7	
40-44	..	..		1999	5.8	
45-49	..	..		1999	5.1	
Percentage of women with parity three or higher						
35-39	..	..		1999	41.2	
40-44	..	..		1999	46.3	
45-49	..	..		1999	47.8	
Family Planning						
Contraceptive prevalence among women in union						
Percentage using any contraceptive method	..	..		1999	66.1	
Percentage using a modern contraceptive method	..	..		1999	52.7	
Percentage using condoms	..	..		1999	4.5	
Population policies						
Government's view on the level of fertility	..	--		2001	Too low	
Government's policy regarding level of fertility	..	--		2001	Raise	
Government's support for contraceptive methods	..	--		2001	Indirect support	

Total fertility rates

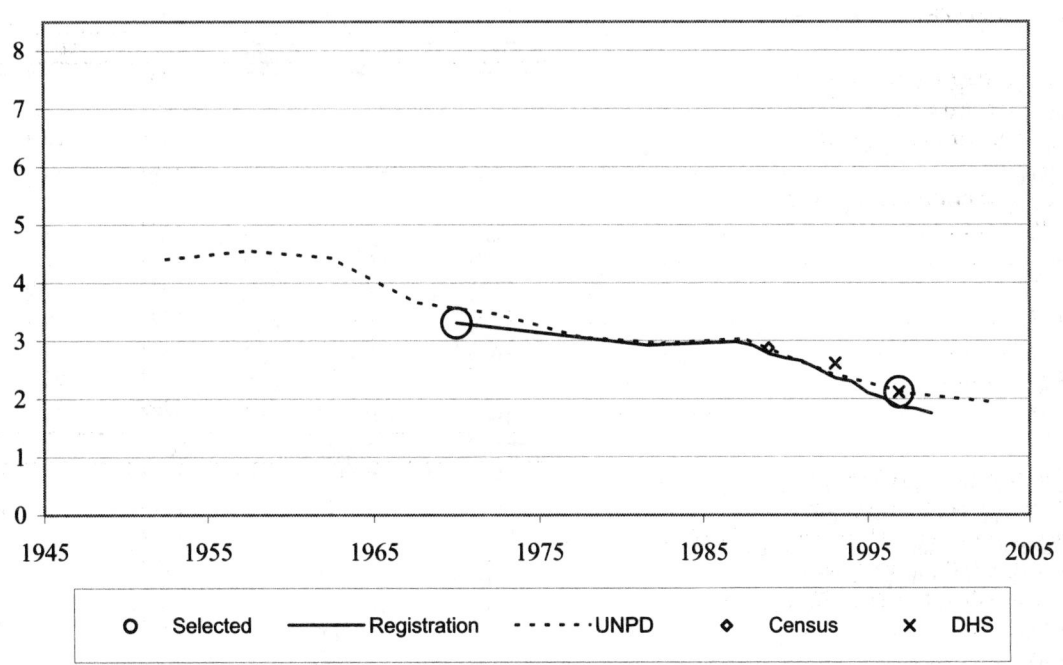

Age-specific fertility rates

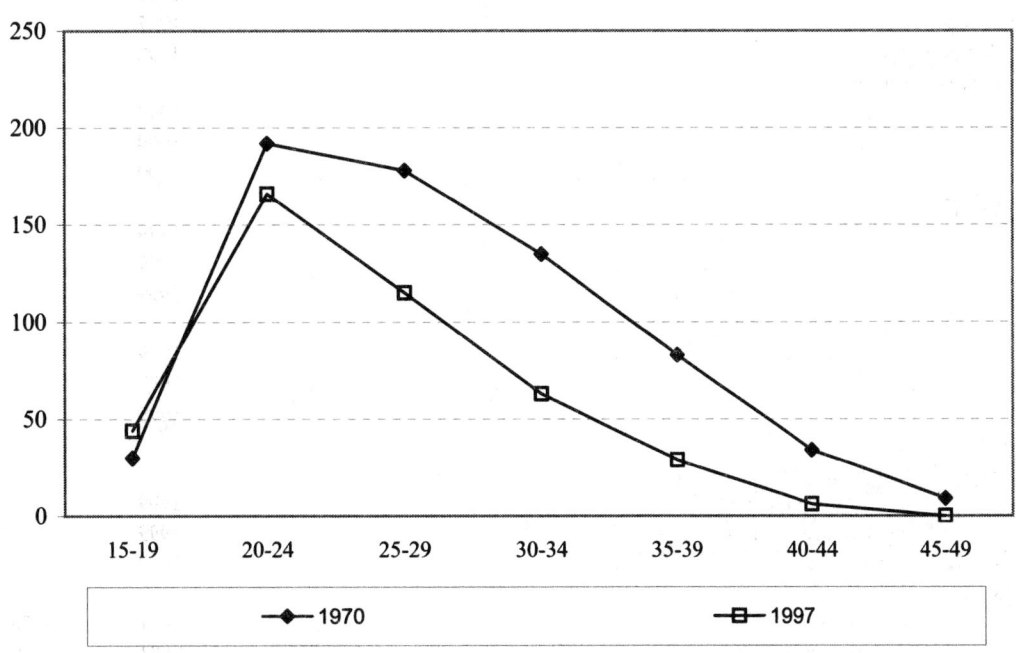

Kenya

Indicator	Period					
	Earlier year			Later year		
	Year	Value		Year	Value	

Nuptiality

	Year	Value		Year	Value	
Annual number of marriages (*thousands*)	..	..		..	..	
Annual number of divorces (*thousands*)	..	..		..	..	

	Year	Male	Female	Year	Male	Female
Total first marriage rate (per person)	..	..	..	..	..	..
Total divorce rate (per person)	..	..	..	..	..	..
Mean age at first marriage (years)	..	..	..	..	..	..
SMAM (years)	1969	25.3	19.2	1998	26.3	21.7
Percentage ever married by age group						
15-19	1969	3.7	35.9	1998	0.7	16.7
20-24	1969	27.5	81.4	1998	22.6	65.1
25-29	1969	67.6	93.5	1998	64.9	87.3
30-34	1969	86.4	96.2	1998	90.6	93.9
35-39	1969	90.9	96.7	1998	96.6	97.2
40-44	1969	93.3	97.2	1998	96.3	97.2
45-49	1969	[40-49]	[40-49]	1998	98.8	98.3

Fertility

	Year	Value		Year	Value	
Annual number of births (*thousands*)	..	..		..	..	
Crude birth rate (per 1 000 population)	..	..		..	..	
Percentage of extra-marital births among all births	..	..		..	..	
Total fertility rate (births per woman)	1969	7.6		1996	4.7	
Age-specific fertility rate (per 1 000 women)						
15-19	1969	132		1996	111	
20-24	1969	331		1996	246	
25-29	1969	337		1996	222	
30-34	1969	294		1996	185	
35-39	1969	223		1996	107	
40-44	1969	135		1996	54	
45-49	1969	68		1996	16	
Mean age at childbearing (years)	1969	30.2		1996	28.3	
Mean age at first birth (years)[a]	..	..		1998	19.6	
Children ever born per woman						
35-39	1969	6.2		1998	5.3	
40-44	1969	6.7		1998	6.4	
45-49	1969	7.0		1998	6.9	
Percentage of childless women						
35-39	1969	4.1		1998	2.4	
40-44	1969	3.9		1998	1.7	
45-49	1969	4.2		1998	2.6	
Percentage of women with parity three or higher						
35-39	1969	87.0		1998	87.7	
40-44	1969	87.0		1998	92.7	
45-49	1969	87.1		1998	91.1	

Family Planning

Contraceptive prevalence among women in union						
Percentage using any contraceptive method	1978	6.7		1998	39.0	
Percentage using a modern contraceptive method	1978	4.2		1998	31.5	
Percentage using condoms	1978	0.1		1998	1.3	

Population policies

Government's view on the level of fertility	1976	Too high		2001	Too high	
Government's policy regarding level of fertility	1976	Lower		2001	Lower	
Government's support for contraceptive methods	1976	Direct support		2001	Direct support	

[a]Median age at first birth among women aged 25-29 at the date of the survey

Total fertility rates

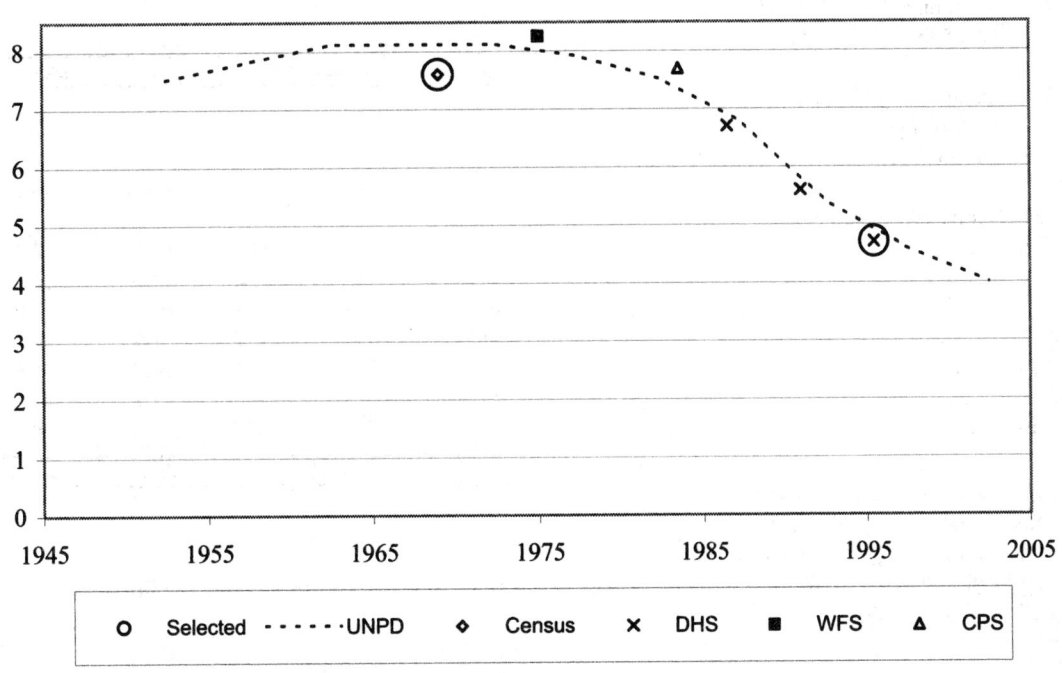

Age-specific fertility rates

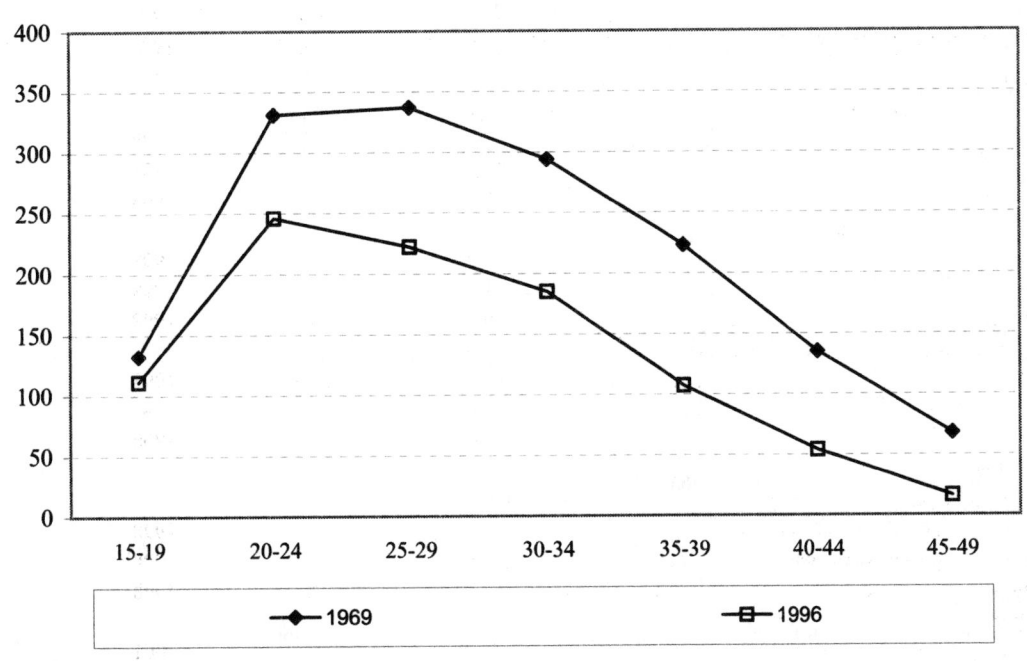

Kuwait

Indicator	Period					
	Earlier year			Later year		
	Year	Value		Year	Value	
Nuptiality						
Annual number of marriages (*thousands*)	1970	2.9		2000	10.8	
Annual number of divorces (*thousands*)	1970	1.1		2000	3.6	
	Year	Male	Female	Year	Male	Female
Total first marriage rate (per person)	..	..	..	1989	..	0.5
Total divorce rate (per person)	1970	0.1	0.2	1992	0.1	0.2
Mean age at first marriage (years)	..	..	..	1989	..	22.2
SMAM (years)	1970	26.5	19.6	1996	27.5	25.2
Percentage ever married by age group						
15-19	1970	3.3	37.7	1996	0.1	5.4
20-24	1970	25.1	79.0	1996	16.6	42.0
25-29	1970	58.2	90.9	1996	57.1	71.9
30-34	1970	83.2	95.1	1996	79.1	83.2
35-39	1970	91.3	96.7	1996	93.6	88.7
40-44	1970	94.8	96.5	1996	96.3	92.8
45-49	1970	96.0	96.8	1996	98.0	94.9
Fertility	Year	Value		Year	Value	
Annual number of births (*thousands*)............................	1970	33.8		2002	43.5	
Crude birth rate (per 1 000 population)	1970	45.3		2002	17.8	
Percentage of extra-marital births among all births	..	..		..	..	
Total fertility rate (births per woman)	1970	6.7		1994	4.3	
Age-specific fertility rate (per 1 000 women)						
15-19	1970	130		1994	30	
20-24	1970	315		1994	183	
25-29	1970	339		1994	237	
30-34	1970	276		1994	201	
35-39	1970	208		1994	141	
40-44	1970	57		1994	61	
45-49	1970	15		1994	16	
Mean age at childbearing (years)	1970	28.8		1994	30.3	
Mean age at first birth (years)	1970	22.4		1986	24.1	
Children ever born per woman						
35-39	1975	5.2		..	..	
40-44	1975	5.7		..	..	
45-49	1975	5.8		..	..	
Percentage of childless women						
35-39	1975	4.9		..	..	
40-44	1975	4.9		..	..	
45-49	1975	5.6		..	..	
Percentage of women with parity three or higher						
35-39	1975	79.7		..	..	
40-44	1975	80.3		..	..	
45-49	1975	79.6		..	..	
Family Planning						
Contraceptive prevalence among women in union						
Percentage using any contraceptive method	..	..		1996	50.2	
Percentage using a modern contraceptive method	..	..		1996	40.9	
Percentage using condoms	..	..		1996	2.9	
Population policies						
Government's view on the level of fertility	1976	Satisfactory		2001	Satisfactory	
Government's policy regarding level of fertility	1976	Maintain		2001	No intervention	
Government's support for contraceptive methods	1976	No support		2001	Indirect support	

Total fertility rates

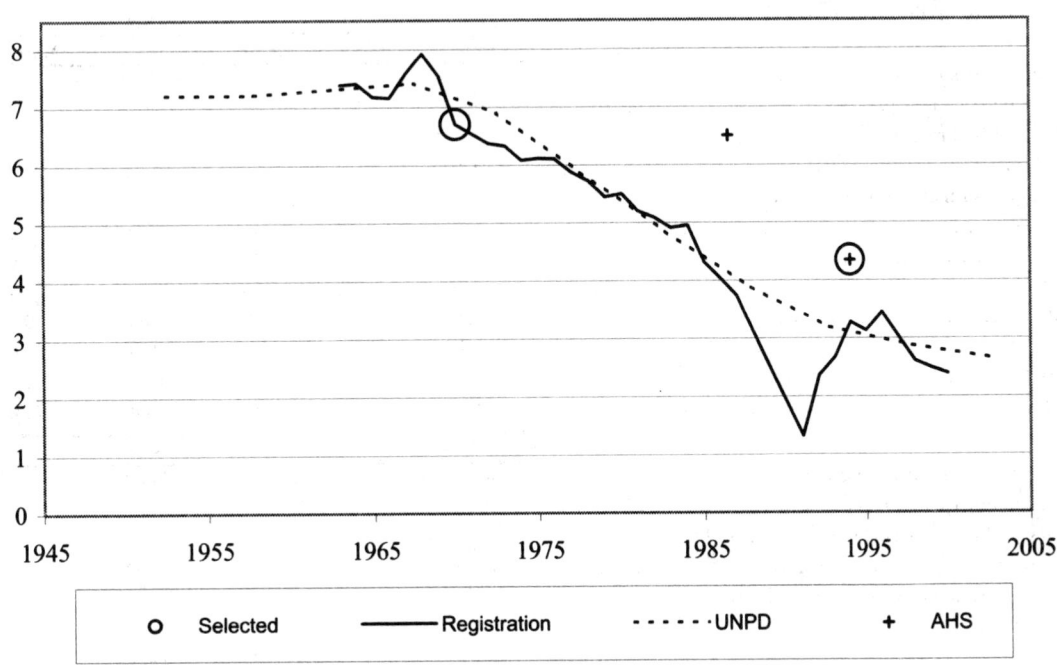

Age-specific fertility rates

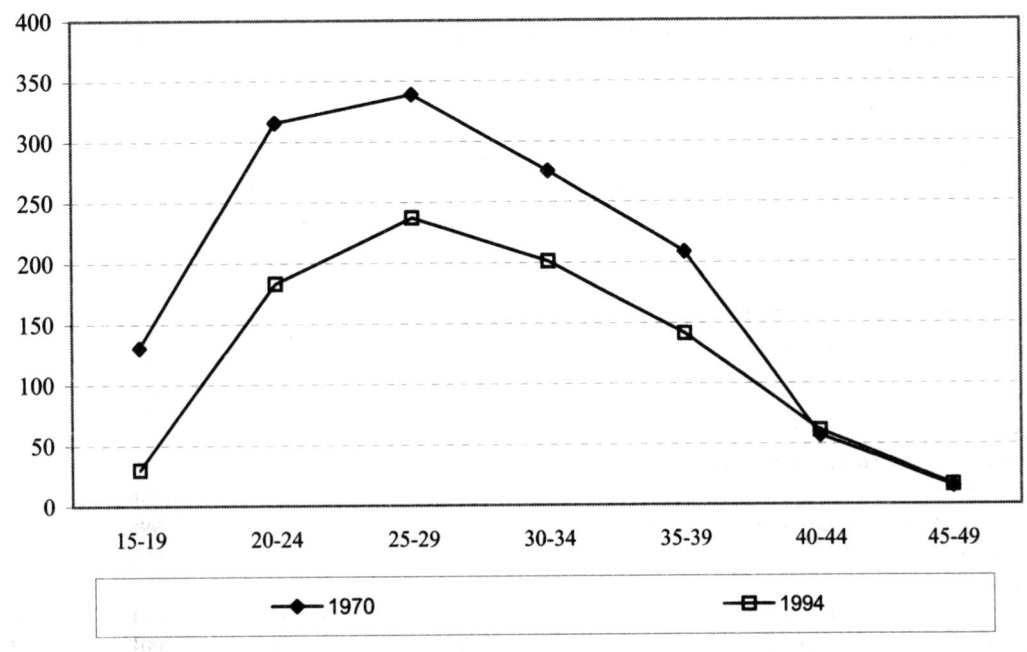

Indicator	Period					
	Earlier year			Later year		
	Year	Value		Year	Value	
Nuptiality						
Annual number of marriages (*thousands*)	1970	27.2		2001	27.5	
Annual number of divorces (*thousands*)	1970	3.6		2001	5.9	
	Year	Male	Female	Year	Male	Female
Total first marriage rate (per person)	1982	1.0	1.0	1998	0.6	0.6
Total divorce rate (per person)	..	..	..	1996	0.2	0.2
Mean age at first marriage (years)	1982	25.1	22.5	1998	25.9	22.8
SMAM (years)	..	..	..	1999	25.0	21.9
Percentage ever married by age group						
15-19	1979	..	..	1999	1.2	11.5
20-24	1979	41.5	70.9	1999	28.4	65.9
25-29	1979	88.0	93.1	1999	76.7	88.4
30-34	1979	95.6	97.2	1999	93.2	94.8
35-39	1979	98.0	98.8	1999	96.5	96.6
40-44	1979	98.6	99.1	1999	97.7	97.5
45-49	1979	99.3	99.1	1999	98.1	98.0
Fertility	Year	Value		Year	Value	
Annual number of births (*thousands*)	1970	90.4		2001	98.1	
Crude birth rate (per 1 000 population)	1970	30.5		2001	19.8	
Percentage of extra-marital births among all births	1980	11.0		1998	27.4	
Total fertility rate (births per woman)	1970	4.9		2000	2.4	
Age-specific fertility rate (per 1 000 women)						
15-19	1970	41		2000	35	
20-24	1970	261		2000	165	
25-29	1970	225		2000	135	
30-34	1970	199		2000	88	
35-39	1970	155		2000	46	
40-44	1970	70		2000	14	
45-49	1970	20		2000	3	
Mean age at childbearing (years)	1970	29.8		2000	27.5	
Mean age at first birth (years)	..	..		1998	23.3	
Children ever born per woman						
35-39	..	..		1997	3.7	
40-44	..	..		1997	4.3	
45-49	..	..		1997	4.9	
Percentage of childless women						
35-39	..	..		1997	3.1	
40-44	..	..		1997	3.1	
45-49	..	..		1997	2.7	
Percentage of women with parity three or higher						
35-39	..	..		1997	74.1	
40-44	..	..		1997	73.8	
45-49	..	..		1997	77.3	
Family Planning						
Contraceptive prevalence among women in union						
Percentage using any contraceptive method	..	..		1997	59.5	
Percentage using a modern contraceptive method	..	..		1997	48.9	
Percentage using condoms	..	..		1997	5.7	
Population policies						
Government's view on the level of fertility	..	--		2001	Satisfactory	
Government's policy regarding level of fertility	..	--		2001	No intervention	
Government's support for contraceptive methods	..	--		2001	Direct support	

Total fertility rates

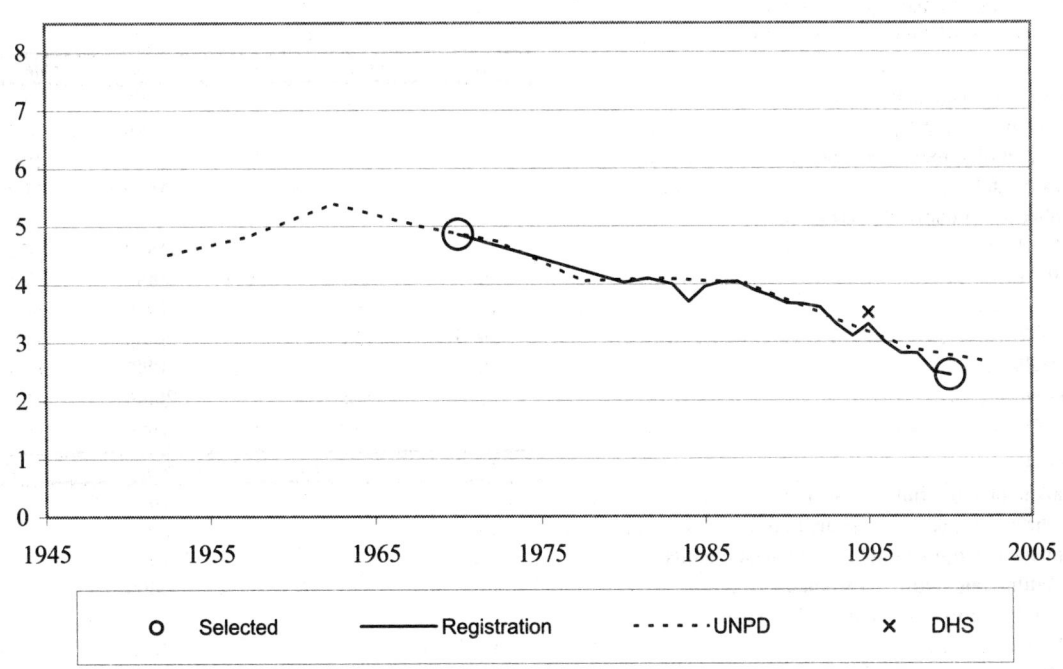

Age-specific fertility rates

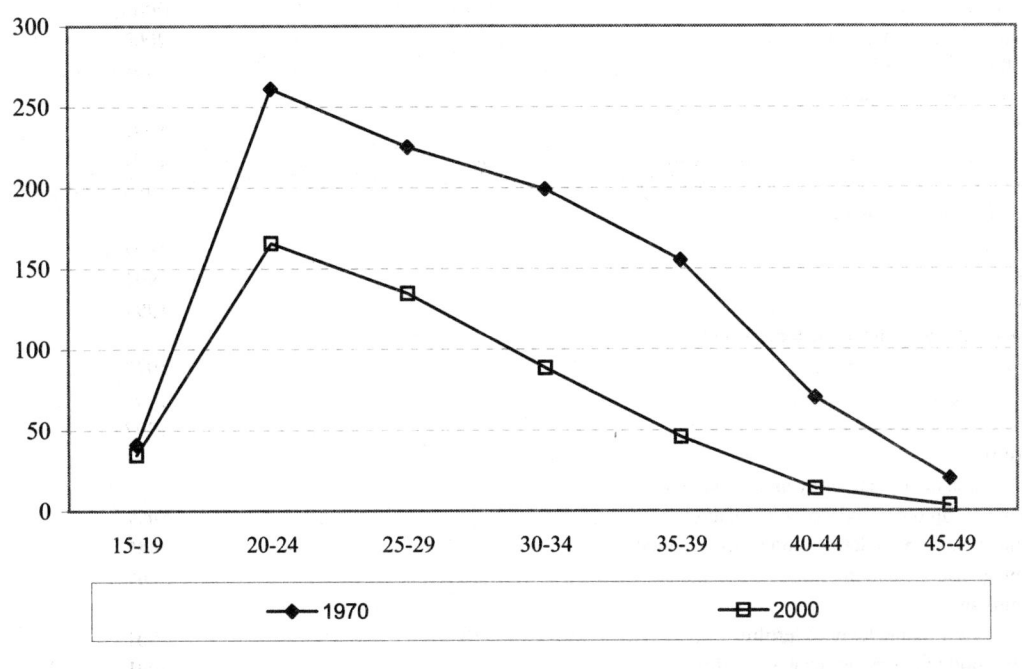

Indicator	Period					
	Earlier year			Later year		
	Year	Value		Year	Value	

Nuptiality

Indicator	Year	Value		Year	Value	
Annual number of marriages (*thousands*)	..	..		..	..	
Annual number of divorces (*thousands*)	..	..		..	..	

Indicator	Year	Male	Female	Year	Male	Female
Total first marriage rate (per person)	..	..	..	..	..	..
Total divorce rate (per person)	..	..	..	..	..	..
Mean age at first marriage (years)	..	..	..	..	..	..
SMAM (years)	..	..	..	2000	..	20.8
Percentage ever married by age group						
15-19	..	..	..	2000	..	26.8
20-24	..	..	..	2000	..	73.0
25-29	..	..	..	2000	..	90.8
30-34	..	..	..	2000	..	95.4
35-39	..	..	..	2000	..	96.6
40-44	..	..	..	2000	..	97.6
45-49	..	..	..	2000	..	98.2

Fertility

Indicator	Year	Value	Year	Value
Annual number of births (*thousands*)	..	..	..	..
Crude birth rate (per 1 000 population)	..	..	..	..
Percentage of extra-marital births among all births	..	..	..	..
Total fertility rate (births per woman)	..	..	1997	4.9
Age-specific fertility rate (per 1 000 women)				
15-19	..	..	1997	102
20-24	..	..	1997	228
25-29	..	..	1997	224
30-34	..	..	1997	172
35-39	..	..	1997	127
40-44	..	..	1997	70
45-49	..	..	1997	53
Mean age at childbearing (years)	..	..	1997	29.6
Mean age at first birth (years)	..	..	..	..
Children ever born per woman				
35-39	..	..	..	..
40-44	..	..	..	..
45-49	..	..	..	..
Percentage of childless women				
35-39	..	..	..	..
40-44	..	..	..	..
45-49	..	..	..	..
Percentage of women with parity three or higher				
35-39	..	..	..	..
40-44	..	..	..	..
45-49	..	..	..	..

Family Planning

Indicator	Year	Value	Year	Value
Contraceptive prevalence among women in union				
Percentage using any contraceptive method	..	..	2000	32.2
Percentage using a modern contraceptive method	..	..	2000	28.9
Percentage using condoms	..	..	2000	0.5

Population policies

Indicator	Year	Value	Year	Value
Government's view on the level of fertility	1976	..	2001	Too high
Government's policy regarding level of fertility	1976	..	2001	Lower
Government's support for contraceptive methods	1976	..	2001	No support

Total fertility rates

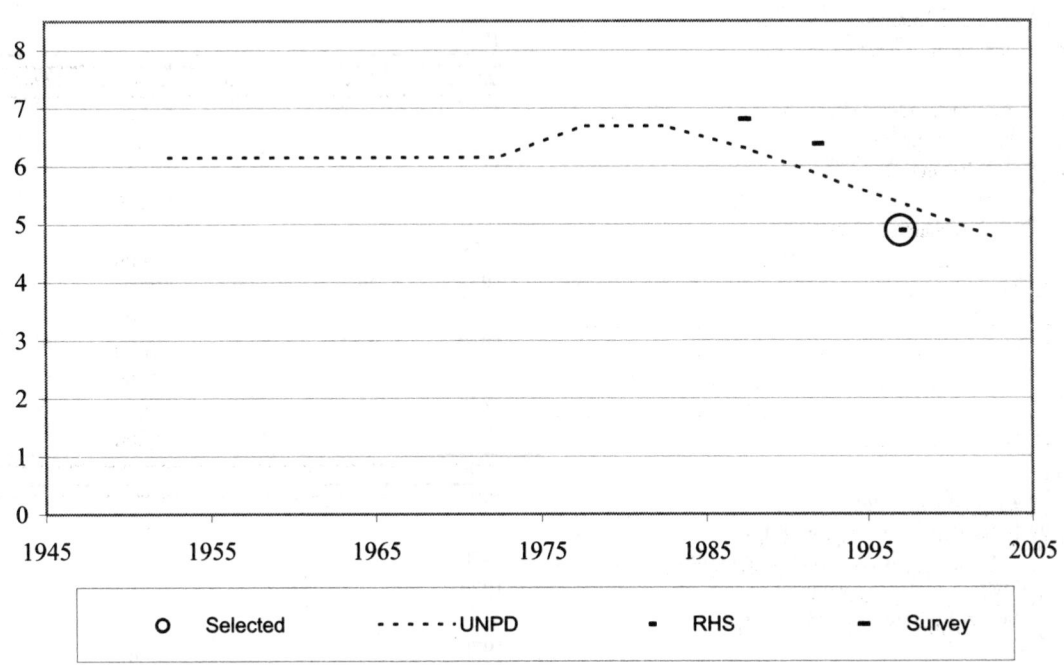

Age-specific fertility rates

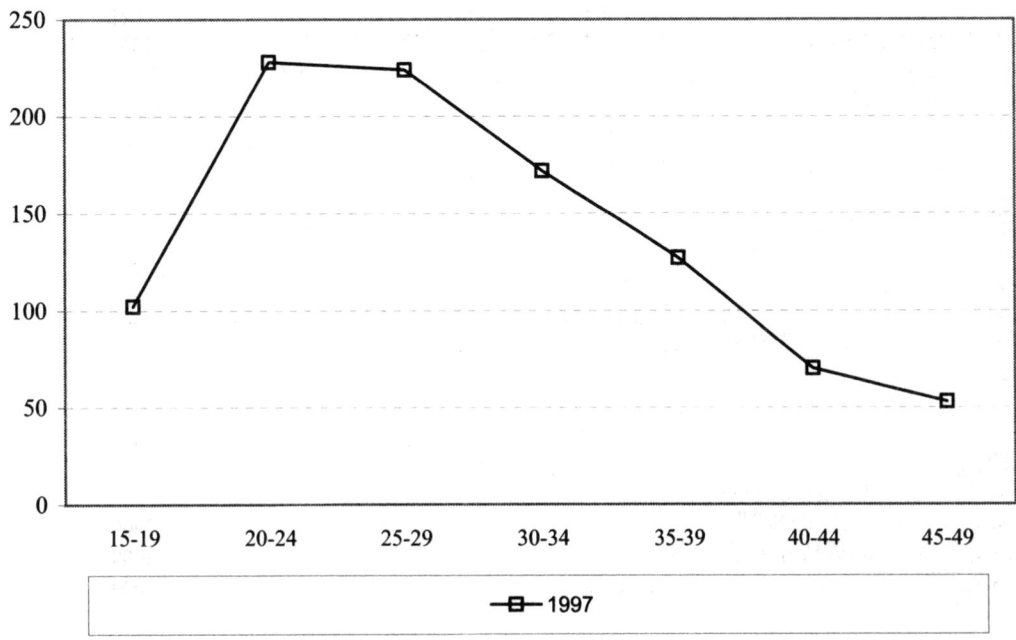

Indicator	Period					
	Earlier year			Later year		
	Year	Value		Year	Value	
Nuptiality						
Annual number of marriages (*thousands*)	1970	24.0		2002	9.7	
Annual number of divorces (*thousands*)	1970	10.9		2001	5.7	
	Year	Male	Female	Year	Male	Female
Total first marriage rate (per person)	1975	..	1.0	1998	0.4	0.4
Total divorce rate (per person)	..	..	..	1997	0.3	0.3
Mean age at first marriage (years)	1975	..	23.3	1998	25.9	23.9
SMAM (years)	..	..	..	2002	29.0	26.9
Percentage ever married by age group						
15-19	1979	..	..	2002	0.3	1.3
20-24	1979	36.7	57.8	2002	10.3	20.6
25-29	1979	77.4	85.2	2002	39.9	55.0
30-34	1979	87.5	91.7	2002	68.3	78.0
35-39	1979	90.9	93.8	2002	82.5	86.4
40-44	1979	93.9	94.3	2002	87.7	89.3
45-49	1979	95.4	93.6	2002	89.6	90.6
Fertility	Year	Value		Year	Value	
Annual number of births (*thousands*)	1970	34.3		2002	20.0	
Crude birth rate (per 1 000 population)	1970	14.6		2002	8.6	
Percentage of extra-marital births among all births	1970	11.4		2001	42.1	
Total fertility rate (births per woman)	1970	2.0		2001	1.2	
Age-specific fertility rate (per 1 000 women)						
15-19	1970	28		2001	18	
20-24	1970	147		2001	75	
25-29	1970	119		2001	77	
30-34	1970	70		2001	47	
35-39	1970	32		2001	20	
40-44	1970	8		2001	5	
45-49	1970	1		2001	0	
Mean age at childbearing (years)	1970	27.0		2001	27.4	
Mean age at first birth (years)	1980	22.9		2001	24.6	
Children ever born per woman						
35-39	..	..		1995	1.9	
40-44	..	..		1995	1.8	
45-49	..	..		1995	1.7	
Percentage of childless women						
35-39	..	..		1995	5.3	
40-44	..	..		1995	6.9	
45-49	..	..		1995	8.3	
Percentage of women with parity three or higher						
35-39	..	..		1995	20.3	
40-44	..	..		1995	17.3	
45-49	..	..		1995	15.0	
Family Planning						
Contraceptive prevalence among women in union						
Percentage using any contraceptive method	..	..		1995	48.0	
Percentage using a modern contraceptive method	..	..		1995	39.3	
Percentage using condoms	..	..		1995	9.6	
Population policies						
Government's view on the level of fertility	..	--		2001	Too low	
Government's policy regarding level of fertility	..	--		2001	Raise	
Government's support for contraceptive methods	..	--		2001	Indirect support	

Total fertility rates

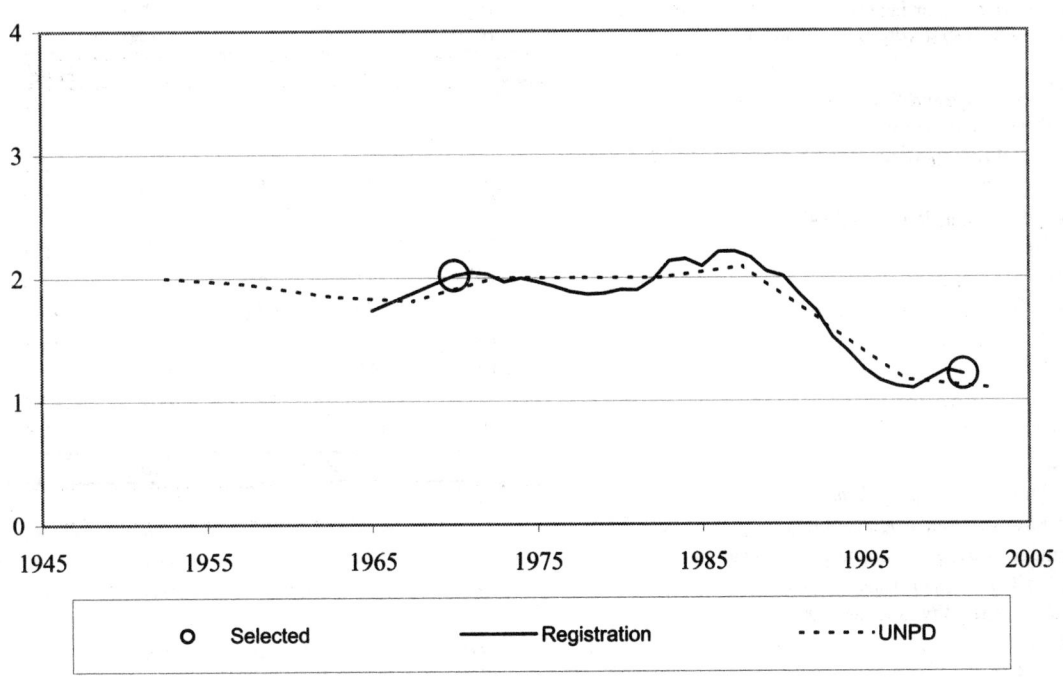

Age-specific fertility rates

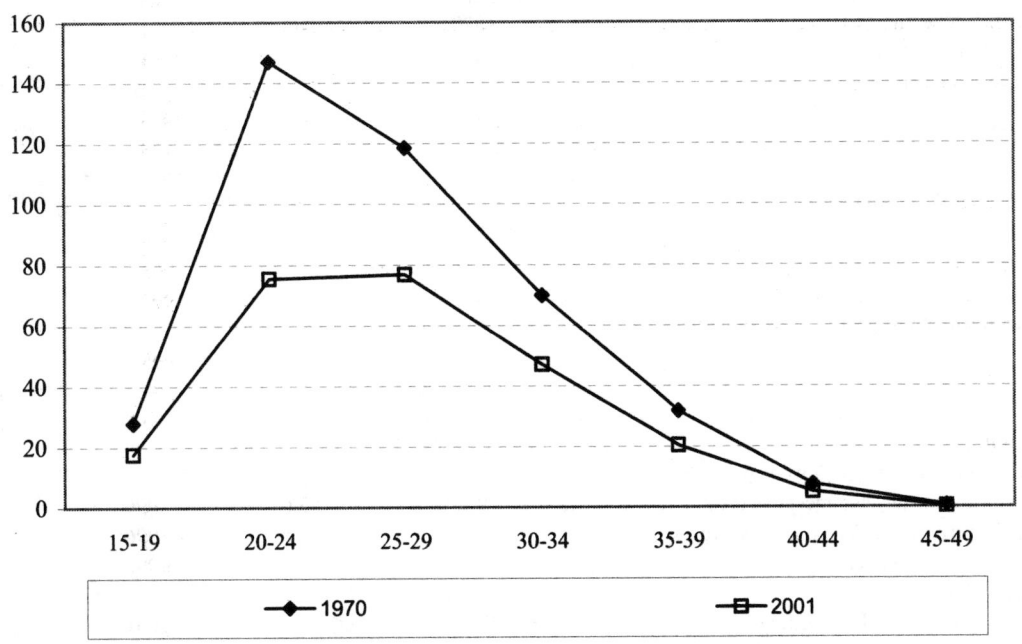

Indicator	Period			
	Earlier year		Later year	
	Year	Value	Year	Value
Nuptiality				
Annual number of marriages (*thousands*)	1970	16.8	2000	32.6
Annual number of divorces (*thousands*)	1970	1.3	2000	4.2

	Year	Male	Female	Year	Male	Female
Total first marriage rate (per person)	..	..	..	..	..	..
Total divorce rate (per person)	..	..	..	..	..	..
Mean age at first marriage (years)	..	..	..	..	..	..
SMAM (years)	1970	28.5	23.2	..	..	..
Percentage ever married by age group						
15-19	1970	1.0	13.2	..	..	..
20-24	1970	11.9	49.1	..	..	..
25-29	1970	45.1	74.9	..	..	..
30-34	1970	74.8	85.8	..	..	..
35-39	1970	85.0	89.9	..	..	..
40-44	1970	91.5	92.4	..	..	..
45-49	1970	94.3	93.1	..	..	..

Fertility	Year	Value	Year	Value
Annual number of births (*thousands*).............................	..	..	..	..
Crude birth rate (per 1 000 population)	..	..	..	..
Percentage of extra-marital births among all births	..	..	..	..
Total fertility rate (births per woman)	1970	4.6	1993	2.5
Age-specific fertility rate (per 1 000 women)				
15-19	1970	40	..	..
20-24	1970	184	..	..
25-29	1970	259	..	..
30-34	1970	214	..	..
35-39	1970	134	..	..
40-44	1970	65	..	..
45-49	1970	18	..	..
Mean age at childbearing (years)	1970	30.2	..	..
Mean age at first birth (years)	..	..	..	..
Children ever born per woman				
35-39	..	..	..	..
40-44	..	..	..	..
45-49	..	..	..	..
Percentage of childless women				
35-39	..	..	..	..
40-44	..	..	..	..
45-49	..	..	..	..
Percentage of women with parity three or higher				
35-39	..	..	..	..
40-44	..	..	..	..
45-49	..	..	..	..
Family Planning				
Contraceptive prevalence among women in union				
Percentage using any contraceptive method	1971	53.0	1996	61.0
Percentage using a modern contraceptive method	1971	23.0	1996	37.0
Percentage using condoms	1971	7.0	1996	..
Population policies				
Government's view on the level of fertility	1976	Satisfactory	2001	Satisfactory
Government's policy regarding level of fertility	1976	No intervention	2001	Lower
Government's support for contraceptive methods	1976	Indirect support	2001	Indirect support

Total fertility rates

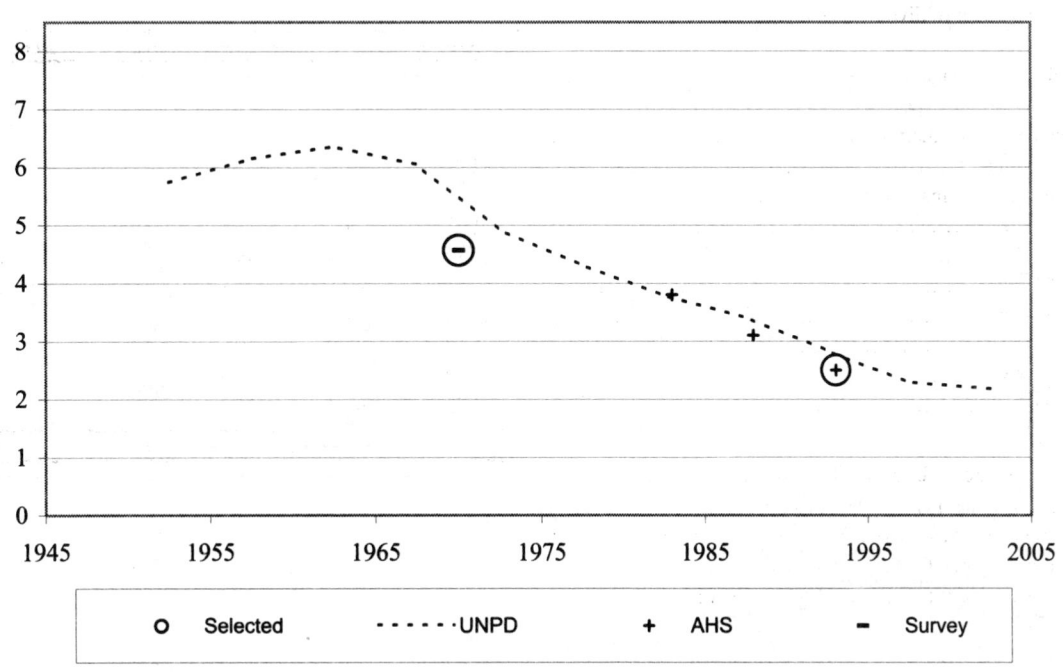

| | O | Selected | ····· UNPD | + AHS | − Survey |

Age-specific fertility rates

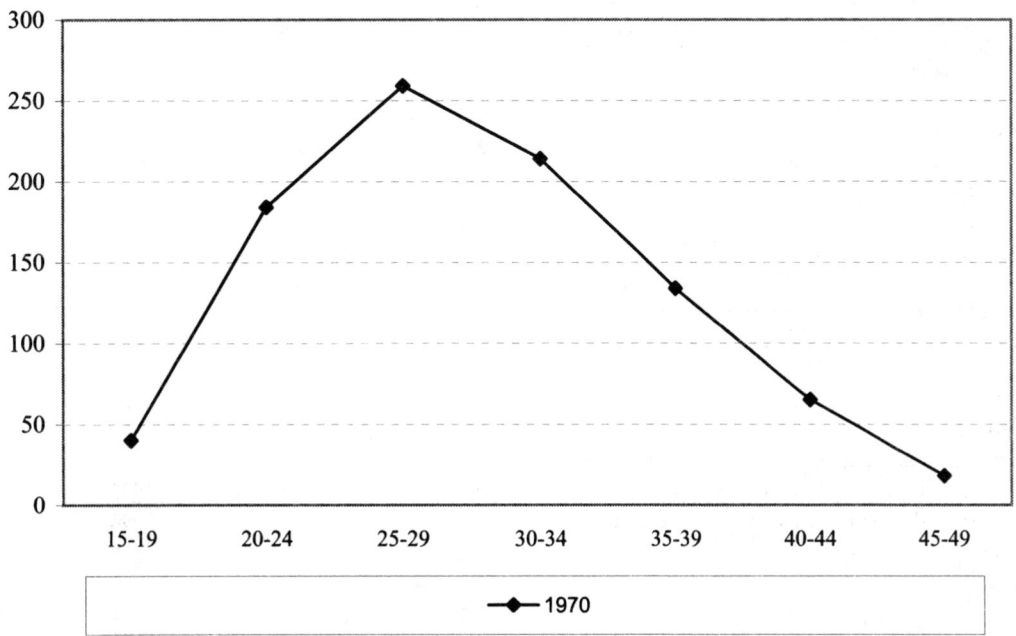

◆ 1970

Indicator	Period					
	Earlier year			Later year		
	Year	Value		Year	Value	

Nuptiality

Indicator	Year	Value		Year	Value	
Annual number of marriages (*thousands*)	..	..		..	..	
Annual number of divorces (*thousands*)	..	..		..	..	

Indicator	Year	Male	Female	Year	Male	Female
Total first marriage rate (per person)	..	..	..	..	..	..
Total divorce rate (per person)	..	..	..	..	..	..
Mean age at first marriage (years)	..	..	..	..	..	..
SMAM (years)	1976	24.8	20.1	1986	25.5	21.3
Percentage ever married by age group						
15-19	1976	3.6	29.4	1986	1.6	18.1
20-24	1976	36.0	79.6	1986	25.9	70.4
25-29	1976	73.4	90.1	1986	70.9	88.2
30-34	1976	88.1	93.3	1986	88.5	92.8
35-39	1976	92.6	94.9	1986	93.6	94.5
40-44	1976	93.8	95.6	1986	95.0	95.5
45-49	1976	95.4	96.5	1986	96.4	96.8

Fertility

Indicator	Year	Value	Year	Value
Annual number of births (*thousands*)	1971	34.9	..	..
Crude birth rate (per 1 000 population)	1971	33.3	..	..
Percentage of extra-marital births among all births	..	..	..	..
Total fertility rate (births per woman)	1975	5.8	1991	4.8
Age-specific fertility rate (per 1 000 women)				
15-19	1975	102	1991	54
20-24	1975	268	1991	186
25-29	1975	258	1991	214
30-34	1975	233	1991	212
35-39	1975	173	1991	149
40-44	1975	94	1991	100
45-49	1975	30	1991	38
Mean age at childbearing (years)	1975	29.7	1991	31.0
Mean age at first birth (years)	..	..	..	..
Children ever born per woman				
35-39	1977	4.6	..	..
40-44	1977	5.0	..	..
45-49	1977	5.2	..	..
Percentage of childless women				
35-39	..	..	..	..
40-44	..	..	..	..
45-49	..	..	..	..
Percentage of women with parity three or higher				
35-39	..	..	..	..
40-44	..	..	..	..
45-49	..	..	..	..

Family Planning

Indicator	Year	Value	Year	Value
Contraceptive prevalence among women in union				
Percentage using any contraceptive method	1977	5.3	2000	30.4
Percentage using a modern contraceptive method	1977	2.4	2000	29.5
Percentage using condoms	1977	0.1	2000	1.8

Population policies

Indicator	Year	Value	Year	Value
Government's view on the level of fertility	1976	Too high	2001	Too high
Government's policy regarding level of fertility	1976	Lower	2001	Lower
Government's support for contraceptive methods	1976	Direct support	2001	Direct support

Total fertility rates

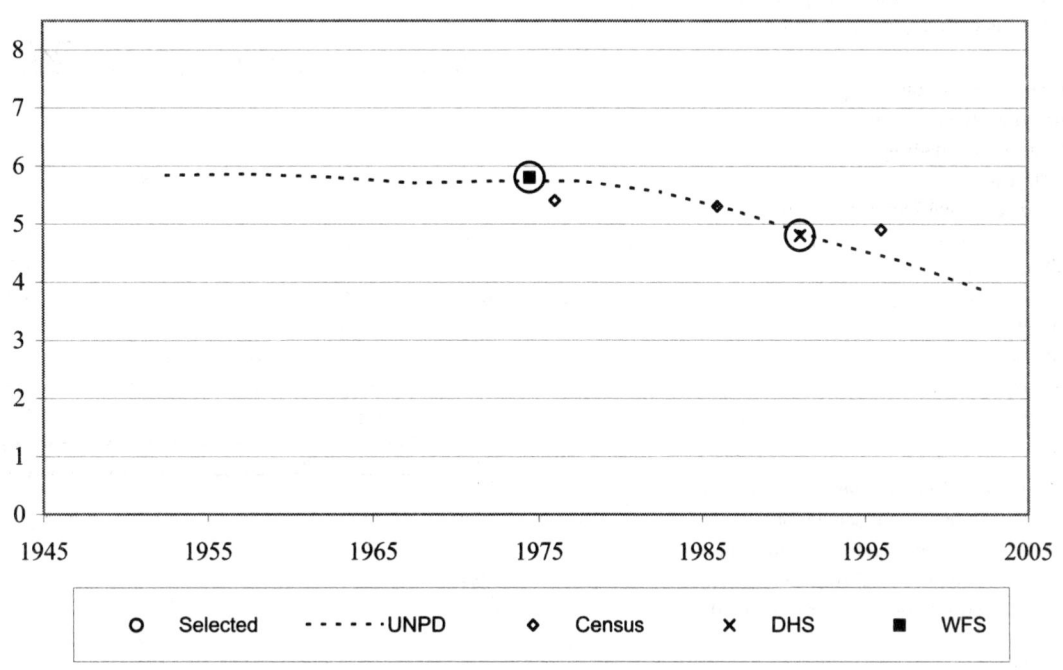

Age-specific fertility rates

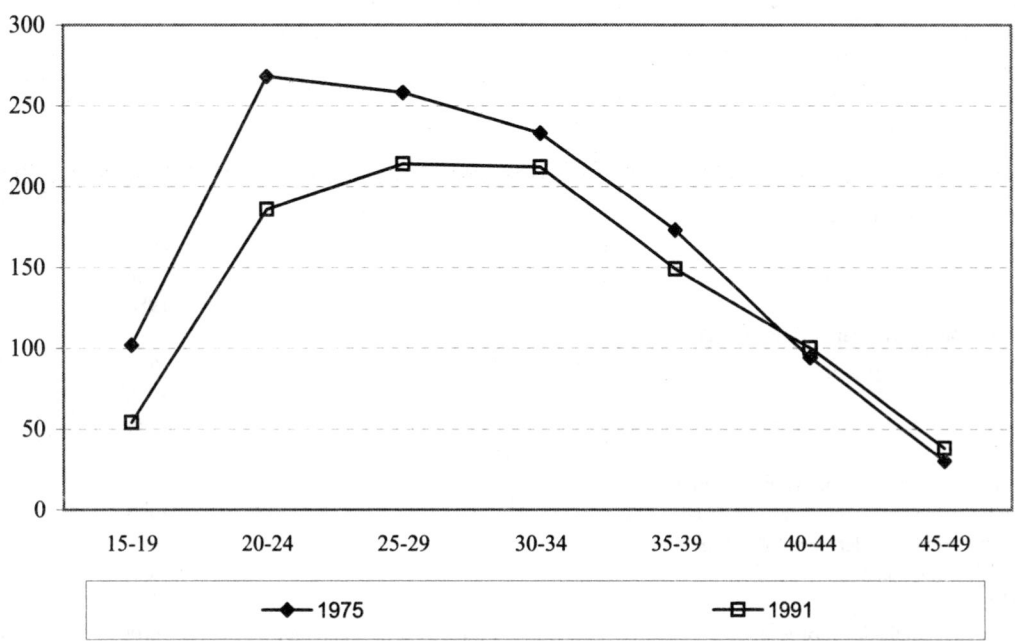

Indicator	Period					
	Earlier year			Later year		
	Year	Value		Year	Value	
Nuptiality						
Annual number of marriages (*thousands*)	..	..		..	..	
Annual number of divorces (*thousands*)	..	..		..	..	
	Year	Male	Female	Year	Male	Female
Total first marriage rate (per person)	..	..	..	..	..	..
Total divorce rate (per person)	..	..	..	..	..	..
Mean age at first marriage (years)	..	..	..	..	..	..
SMAM (years)	1970	26.6	18.7	1986	..	20.2
Percentage ever married by age group						
15-19	1970	2.3	50.5	1986	..	36.0
20-24	1970	25.8	84.5	1986	..	75.3
25-29	1970	60.2	92.8	1986	..	92.1
30-34	1970	79.9	95.2	1986	..	93.8
35-39	1970	87.5	96.6	1986	..	98.8
40-44	1970	91.1	97.2	1986	..	98.3
45-49	1970	93.6	98.3	1986	..	99.5
Fertility	Year	Value		Year	Value	
Annual number of births (*thousands*).............................	..	..		..	..	
Crude birth rate (per 1 000 population)	..	..		..	..	
Percentage of extra-marital births among all births	..	..		..	..	
Total fertility rate (births per woman)	1984	6.6		..	..	
Age-specific fertility rate (per 1 000 women)						
15-19	1984	184		..	..	
20-24	1984	285		..	..	
25-29	1984	272		..	..	
30-34	1984	223		..	..	
35-39	1984	181		..	..	
40-44	1984	114		..	..	
45-49	1984	63		..	..	
Mean age at childbearing (years)	1984	29.5		..	..	
Mean age at first birth (years)[a]	..	..		1986	19.0	
Children ever born per woman						
35-39	..	..		1986	5.3	
40-44	..	..		1986	5.9	
45-49	..	..		1986	6.8	
Percentage of childless women						
35-39	..	..		1986	3.2	
40-44	..	..		1986	3.4	
45-49	..	..		1986	2.6	
Percentage of women with parity three or higher						
35-39	..	..		1986	82.0	
40-44	..	..		1986	80.0	
45-49	..	..		1986	84.6	
Family Planning						
Contraceptive prevalence among women in union						
Percentage using any contraceptive method	..	..		1986	6.4	
Percentage using a modern contraceptive method	..	..		1986	5.5	
Percentage using condoms	..	..		1986	0.0	
Population policies						
Government's view on the level of fertility	1976	Too high		2001	Too high	
Government's policy regarding level of fertility	1976	No intervention		2001	Lower	
Government's support for contraceptive methods	1976	Direct support		2001	Direct support	

[a]Median age at first birth among women aged 25-29 at the date of the survey

Total fertility rates

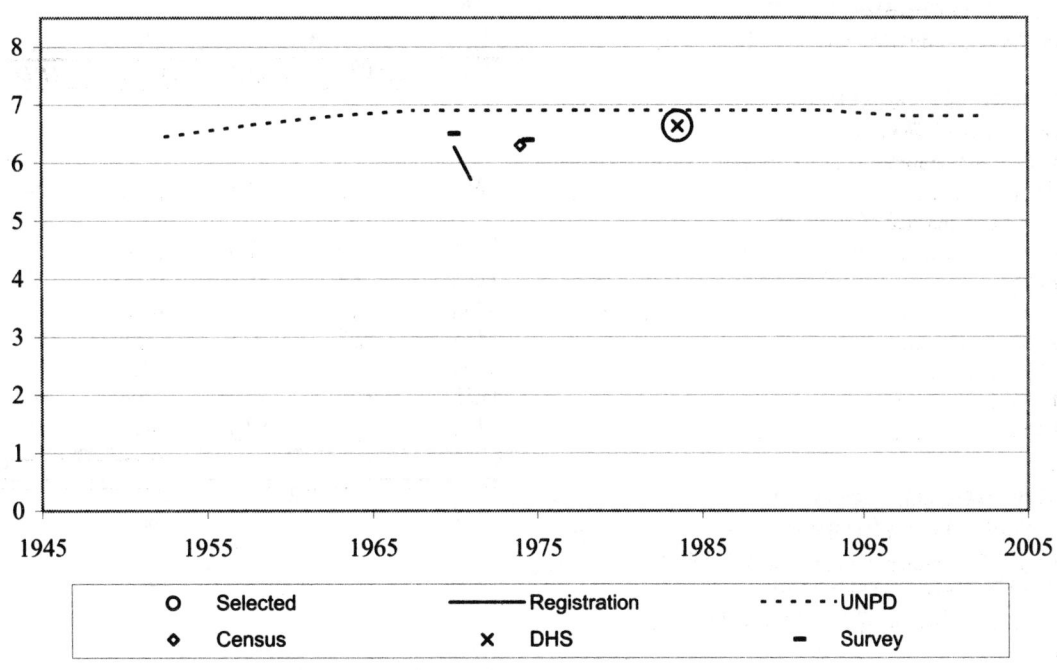

Age-specific fertility rates

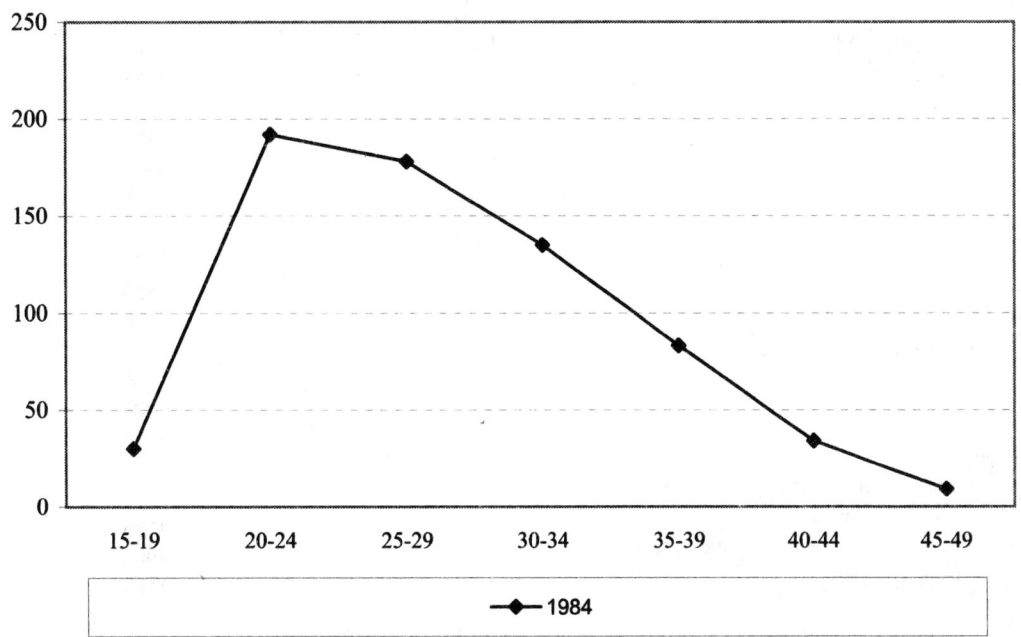

Indicator	Period					
	Earlier year			Later year		
	Year	Value		Year	Value	
Nuptiality						
Annual number of marriages (*thousands*)	1970	14.5		1987	17.9	
Annual number of divorces (*thousands*)	1970	4.0		2000	1.4	
	Year	Male	Female	Year	Male	Female
Total first marriage rate (per person)	..	..	..	..	..	..
Total divorce rate (per person)	..	..	..	..	..	..
Mean age at first marriage (years)	..	..	..	..	..	..
SMAM (years)	1973	24.6	18.7	1995	32.0	29.2
Percentage ever married by age group						
15-19	1973	2.0	39.6	1995	0.1	1.0
20-24	1973	32.3	88.0	1995	1.3	12.2
25-29	1973	78.0	97.4	1995	13.4	41.4
30-34	1973	94.5	98.9	1995	58.0	72.1
35-39	1973	97.5	99.4	1995	89.1	89.5
40-44	1973	98.2	99.4	1995	96.6	96.8
45-49	1973	98.6	99.5	1995	98.5	98.6
Fertility	Year	Value		Year	Value	
Annual number of births (*thousands*)	1970	82.2		2001	99.2	
Crude birth rate (per 1 000 population)	1970	44.3		2001	18.7	
Percentage of extra-marital births among all births	..	..		..	..	
Total fertility rate (births per woman)	1973	6.8		1993	4.1	
Age-specific fertility rate (per 1 000 women)						
15-19	1973	201		1993	7	
20-24	1973	334		1993	74	
25-29	1973	328		1993	181	
30-34	1973	241		1993	229	
35-39	1973	161		1993	193	
40-44	1973	65		1993	109	
45-49	1973	31		1993	24	
Mean age at childbearing (years)	1973	28.0		1993	33.3	
Mean age at first birth (years)	..	..		..	..	
Children ever born per woman						
35-39	1973	7.0		1995	6.1	
40-44	1973	7.5		1995	8.0	
45-49	1973	7.7		1995	9.0	
Percentage of childless women						
35-39	1973	3.3		1995	13.5	
40-44	1973	3.6		1995	5.7	
45-49	1973	3.8		1995	4.3	
Percentage of women with parity three or higher						
35-39	1973	91.3		1995	81.0	
40-44	1973	90.9		1995	91.6	
45-49	1973	90.9		1995	92.2	
Family Planning						
Contraceptive prevalence among women in union						
Percentage using any contraceptive method	..	..		1995	39.7	
Percentage using a modern contraceptive method	..	..		1995	25.6	
Percentage using condoms	..	..		1995	..	
Population policies						
Government's view on the level of fertility	1976	Too low		2001	Satisfactory	
Government's policy regarding level of fertility	1976	Raise		2001	No intervention	
Government's support for contraceptive methods	1976	No support		2001	No support	

Total fertility rates

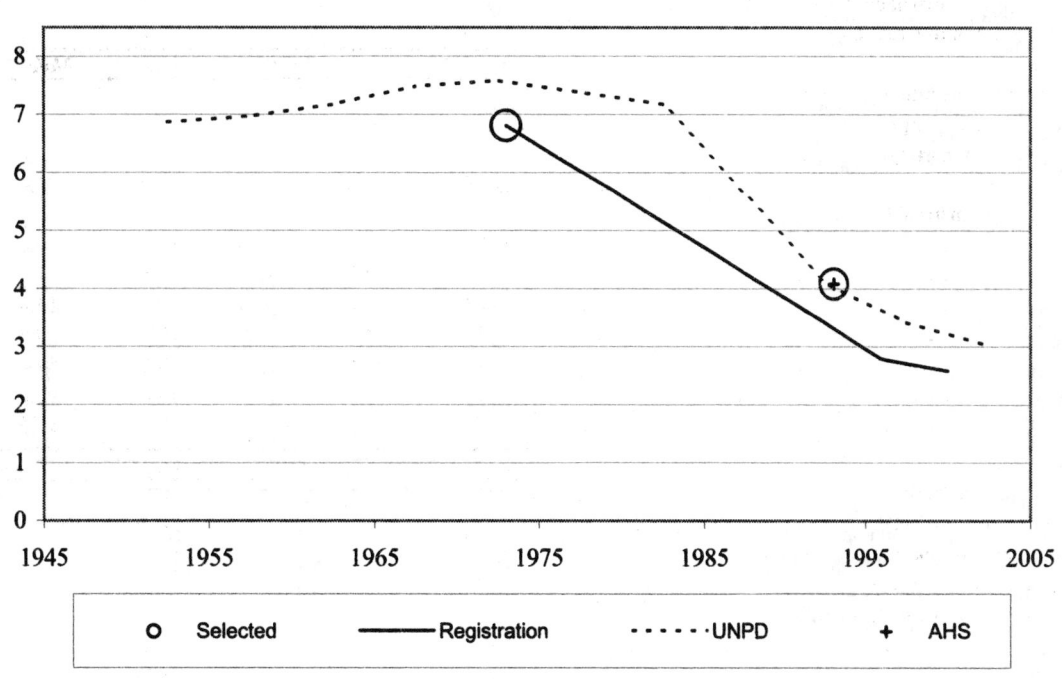

Age-specific fertility rates

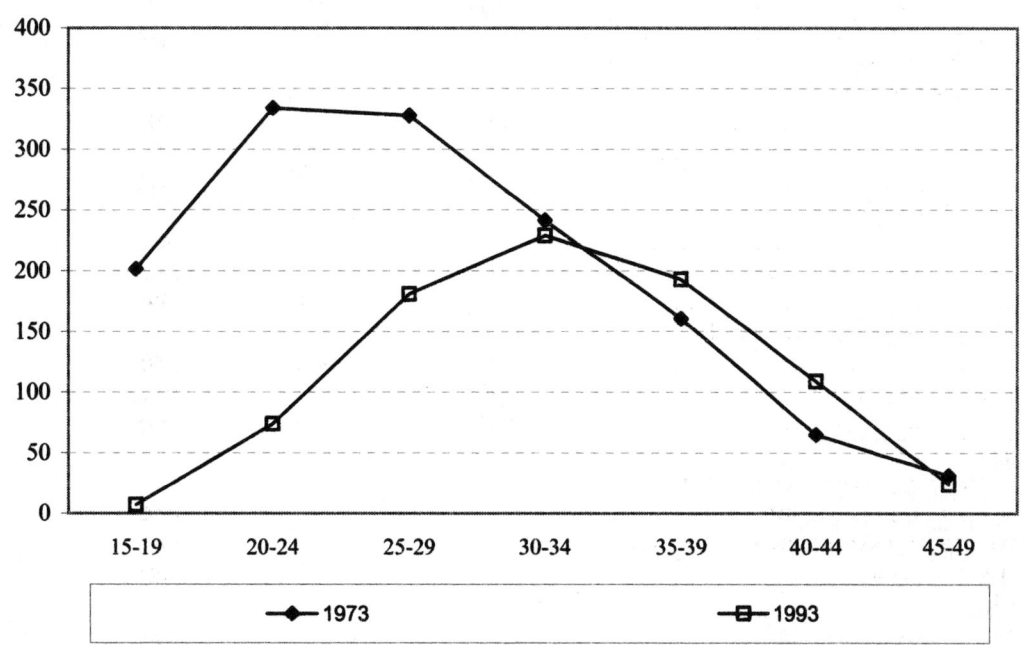

Lithuania

Indicator	Period					
	Earlier year			Later year		
	Year	Value		Year	Value	
Nuptiality						
Annual number of marriages (*thousands*)	1970	29.9		2001	15.8	
Annual number of divorces (*thousands*)	1970	6.9		2001	11.0	
	Year	Male	Female	Year	Male	Female
Total first marriage rate (per person)	1970	..	1.1	1998	0.5	0.6
Total divorce rate (per person)	..	..	..	1997	0.3	0.3
Mean age at first marriage (years)	1970	..	24.0	1998	24.9	22.9
SMAM (years)	..	..	..	2001	26.9	24.8
Percentage ever married by age group						
15-19	1979	..	..	2001	0.5	2.4
20-24	1979	31.7	52.9	2001	17.3	34.9
25-29	1979	76.2	84.8	2001	57.9	73.8
30-34	1979	88.1	91.6	2001	80.5	86.8
35-39	1979	92.1	93.5	2001	88.2	91.0
40-44	1979	94.4	93.5	2001	91.4	92.7
45-49	1979	95.9	92.6	2001	92.2	93.7
Fertility	Year	Value		Year	Value	
Annual number of births (*thousands*)	1970	55.5		2001	31.5	
Crude birth rate (per 1 000 population)	1970	17.7		2001	9.1	
Percentage of extra-marital births among all births	1970	5.1		2001	25.4	
Total fertility rate (births per woman)	1970	2.4		2001	1.3	
Age-specific fertility rate (per 1 000 women)						
15-19	1970	24		2001	22	
20-24	1970	159		2001	86	
25-29	1970	143		2001	83	
30-34	1970	88		2001	45	
35-39	1970	48		2001	19	
40-44	1970	15		2001	4	
45-49	1970	1		2001	0	
Mean age at childbearing (years)	1970	27.8		2001	26.8	
Mean age at first birth (years)	1980	23.8		2001	24.1	
Children ever born per woman						
35-39	..	..		1994-1995	1.8	
40-44	..	..		1994-1995	1.7	
45-49	..	..		1994-1995	1.8	
Percentage of childless women						
35-39	..	..		1994-1995	9.4	
40-44	..	..		1994-1995	12.2	
45-49	..	..		1994-1995	8.9	
Percentage of women with parity three or higher						
35-39	..	..		1994-1995	17.8	
40-44	..	..		1994-1995	16.3	
45-49	..	..		1994-1995	15.4	
Family Planning						
Contraceptive prevalence among women in union						
Percentage using any contraceptive method	..	..		1995	46.6	
Percentage using a modern contraceptive method	..	..		1995	30.5	
Percentage using condoms	..	..		1995	13.1	
Population policies						
Government's view on the level of fertility	..	--		2001	Too low	
Government's policy regarding level of fertility	..	--		2001	Raise	
Government's support for contraceptive methods	..	--		2001	Indirect support	

Total fertility rates

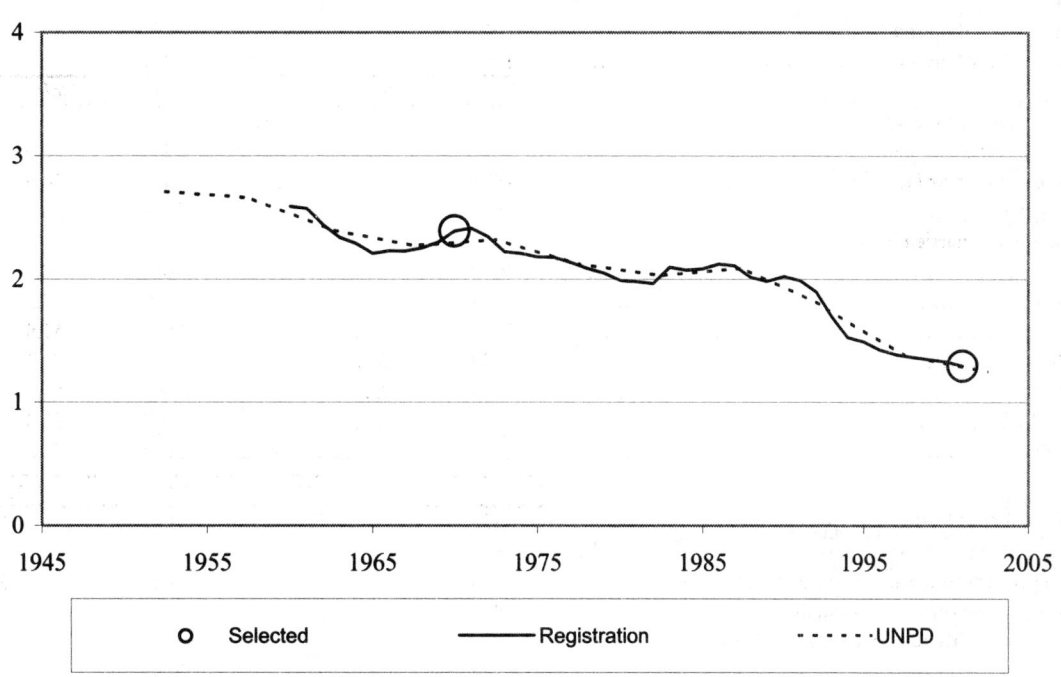

	Selected	Registration	UNPD

Age-specific fertility rates

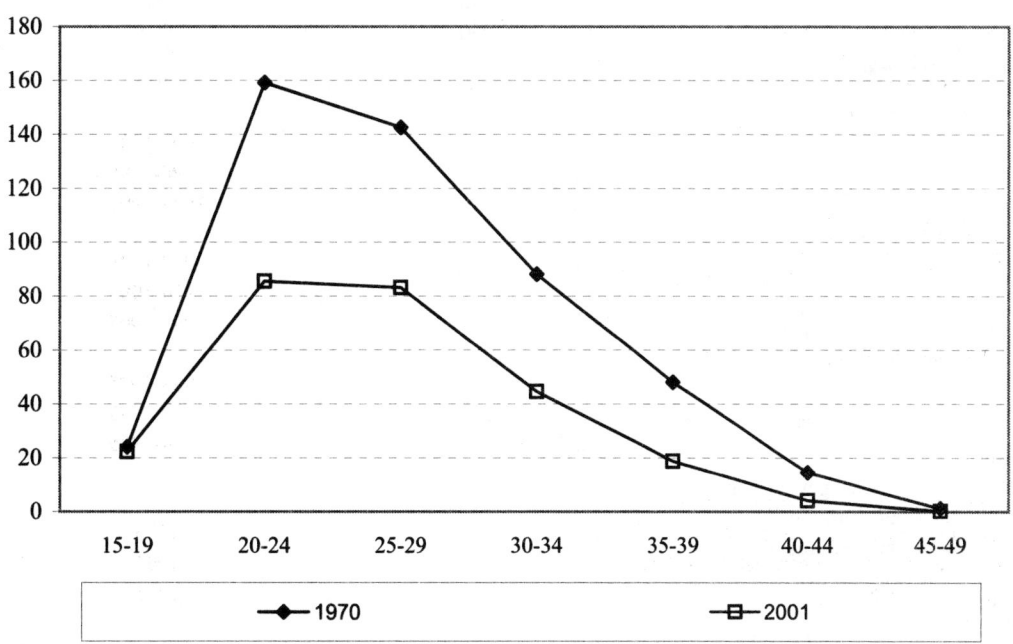

◆ 1970	□ 2001

Luxembourg

Indicator	Period					
	Earlier year			Later year		
	Year	Value		Year	Value	

Nuptiality

	Year	Value		Year	Value	
Annual number of marriages (*thousands*)	1970	2.2		2001	2.0	
Annual number of divorces (*thousands*)	1970	0.2		2001	1.0	

	Year	Male	Female	Year	Male	Female
Total first marriage rate (per person)	1975	0.8	0.8	1996	0.5	0.6
Total divorce rate (per person)	1970	0.1	0.1	1996	0.2	0.2
Mean age at first marriage (years)	1975	24.8	22.2	1996	28.8	26.5
SMAM (years)	1970	25.6	21.4	1991	28.5	26.0
Percentage ever married by age group						
15-19	1970	0.6	6.1	1991	0.4	2.4
20-24	1970	24.0	55.9	1991	10.8	26.2
25-29	1970	67.5	85.4	1991	43.5	62.6
30-34	1970	83.0	91.1	1991	72.0	82.8
35-39	1970	88.3	91.9	1991	84.3	89.3
40-44	1970	90.1	91.4	1991	89.3	92.3
45-49	1970	91.8	89.6	1991	90.9	93.4

Fertility

	Year	Value		Year	Value	
Annual number of births (*thousands*)	1970	4.4		2001	5.5	
Crude birth rate (per 1 000 population)	1970	13.0		2001	12.4	
Percentage of extra-marital births among all births	1970	4.0		1998	17.5	
Total fertility rate (births per woman)	1970	2.0		2001	1.7	
Age-specific fertility rate (per 1 000 women)						
15-19	1970	28		2001	12	
20-24	1970	133		2001	60	
25-29	1970	126		2001	110	
30-34	1970	65		2001	102	
35-39	1970	33		2001	41	
40-44	1970	9		2001	7	
45-49	1970	1		2001	0	
Mean age at childbearing (years)	1970	27.2		2001	29.3	
Mean age at first birth (years)[a]	1970	24.4		2001	28.3	
Children ever born per woman						
35-39	1970	1.9		1991	1.5	
40-44	1970	1.9		1991	1.7	
45-49	1970	1.8		1991	1.8	
Percentage of childless women						
35-39	1970	8.6		1991	22.9	
40-44	1970	9.7		1991	18.8	
45-49	1970	11.8		1991	17.9	
Percentage of women with parity three or higher						
35-39	1970	28.3		1991	17.5	
40-44	1970	28.3		1991	20.6	
45-49	1970	26.5		1991	23.0	

Family Planning

Contraceptive prevalence among women in union						
Percentage using any contraceptive method	..	..		..	..	
Percentage using a modern contraceptive method	..	..		..	..	
Percentage using condoms	..	..		..	..	

Population policies

Government's view on the level of fertility	1976	Too low		2001	Too low	
Government's policy regarding level of fertility	1976	Raise		2001	Raise	
Government's support for contraceptive methods	1976	Indirect support		2001	Indirect support	

[a]Mean age at first birth within current marriage

Total fertility rates

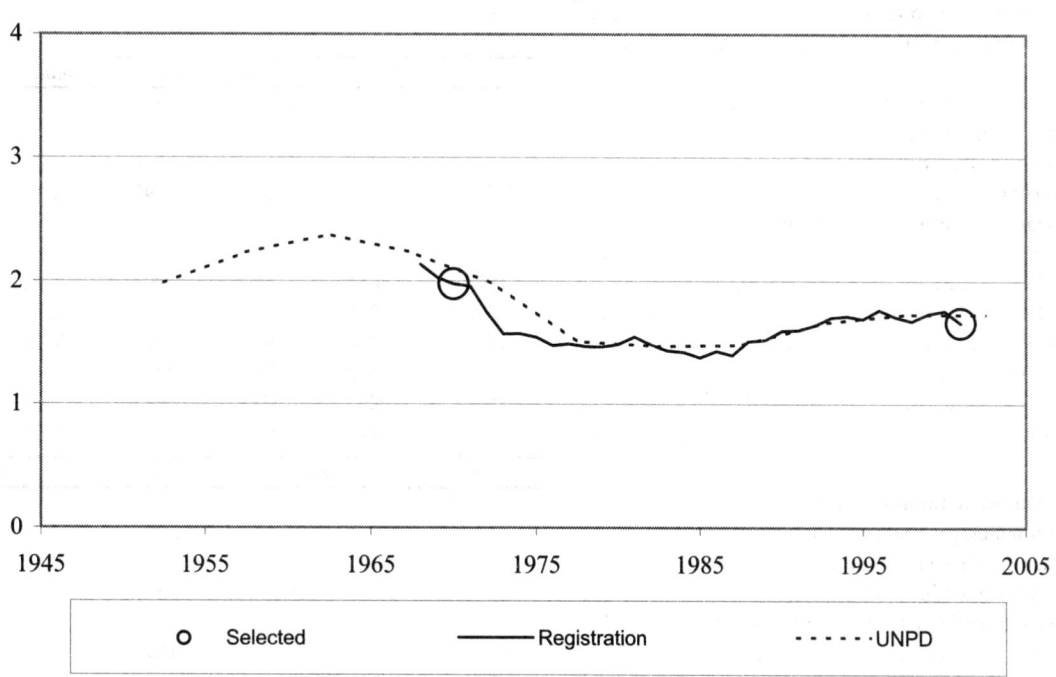

Age-specific fertility rates

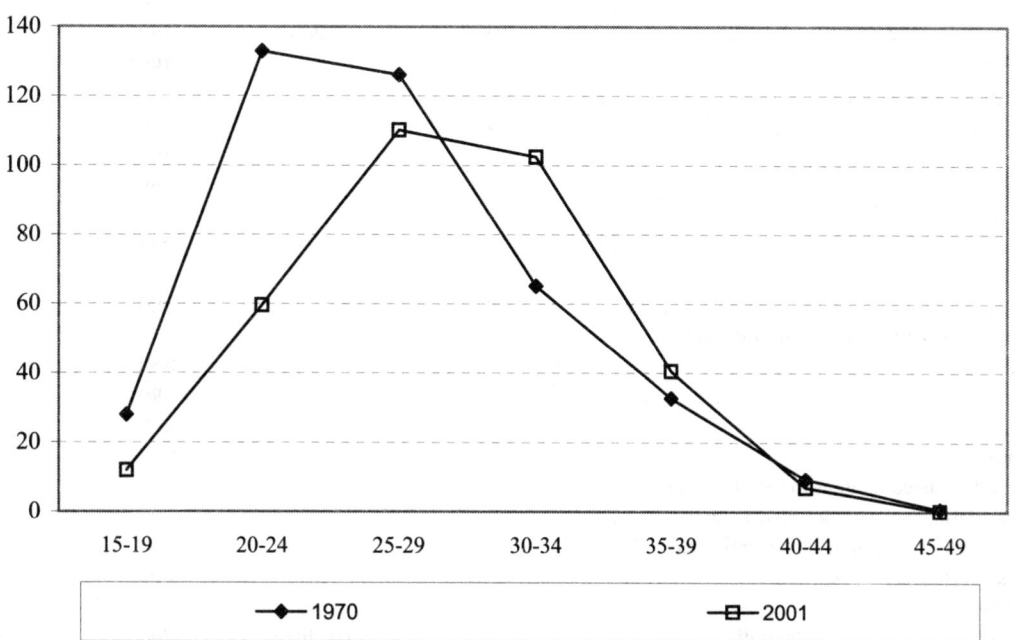

Madagascar

Indicator	Period					
	Earlier year			Later year		
	Year	Value		Year	Value	

Nuptiality

Indicator	Year	Value		Year	Value	
Annual number of marriages (*thousands*)	1970	17.5		..	..	
Annual number of divorces (*thousands*)	..	..		..	..	

Indicator	Year	Male	Female	Year	Male	Female
Total first marriage rate (per person)	..	..	..	..	..	..
Total divorce rate (per person)	..	..	..	..	..	..
Mean age at first marriage (years)	..	..	..	..	..	..
SMAM (years)	1975	23.5	20.3	1997	..	20.6
Percentage ever married by age group						
15-19	1975	9.2	34.4	1997	..	33.7
20-24	1975	47.2	69.3	1997	..	74.3
25-29	1975	79.5	85.9	1997	..	87.6
30-34	1975	91.1	92.3	1997	..	93.9
35-39	1975	94.2	94.4	1997	..	94.4
40-44	1975	95.5	95.1	1997	..	97.6
45-49	1975	96.9	95.7	1997	..	98.7

Fertility

Indicator	Year	Value	Year	Value
Annual number of births (*thousands*)	..	..	1981	403.0
Crude birth rate (per 1 000 population)	..	..	1981	45.0
Percentage of extra-marital births among all births	..	..	..	..
Total fertility rate (births per woman)	1975	6.4	1995	6.1
Age-specific fertility rate (per 1 000 women)				
15-19	1975	132	1995	173
20-24	1975	272	1995	278
25-29	1975	280	1995	264
30-34	1975	232	1995	216
35-39	1975	195	1995	166
40-44	1975	122	1995	93
45-49	1975	45	1995	26
Mean age at childbearing (years)	1975	30.0	1995	28.8
Mean age at first birth (years)[a]	..	..	1997	19.8
Children ever born per woman				
35-39	..	..	1997	5.6
40-44	..	..	1997	6.4
45-49	..	..	1997	7.0
Percentage of childless women				
35-39	..	..	1997	4.5
40-44	..	..	1997	6.0
45-49	..	..	1997	5.4
Percentage of women with parity three or higher				
35-39	..	..	1997	81.4
40-44	..	..	1997	81.5
45-49	..	..	1997	84.3

Family Planning

Indicator	Year	Value	Year	Value
Contraceptive prevalence among women in union				
Percentage using any contraceptive method	..	..	2000	18.8
Percentage using a modern contraceptive method	..	..	2000	11.8
Percentage using condoms	..	..	2000	0.4

Population policies

Indicator	Year	Value	Year	Value
Government's view on the level of fertility	1976	Too high	2001	Too high
Government's policy regarding level of fertility	1976	No intervention	2001	Lower
Government's support for contraceptive methods	1976	Indirect support	2001	Direct support

[a]Median age at first birth among women aged 25-29 at the date of the survey

Total fertility rates

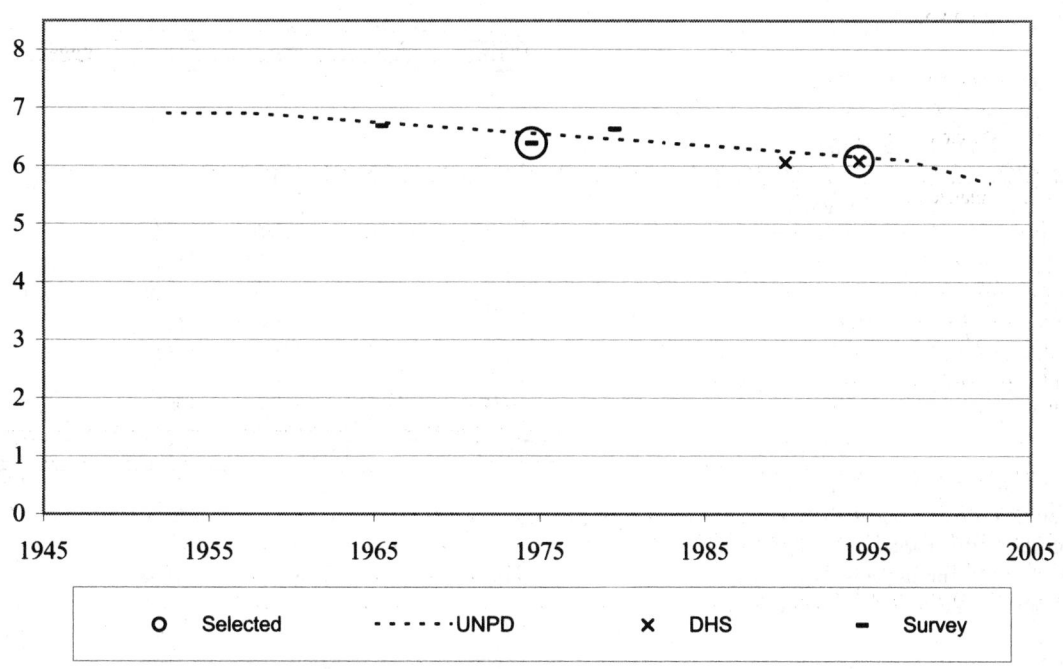

Age-specific fertility rates

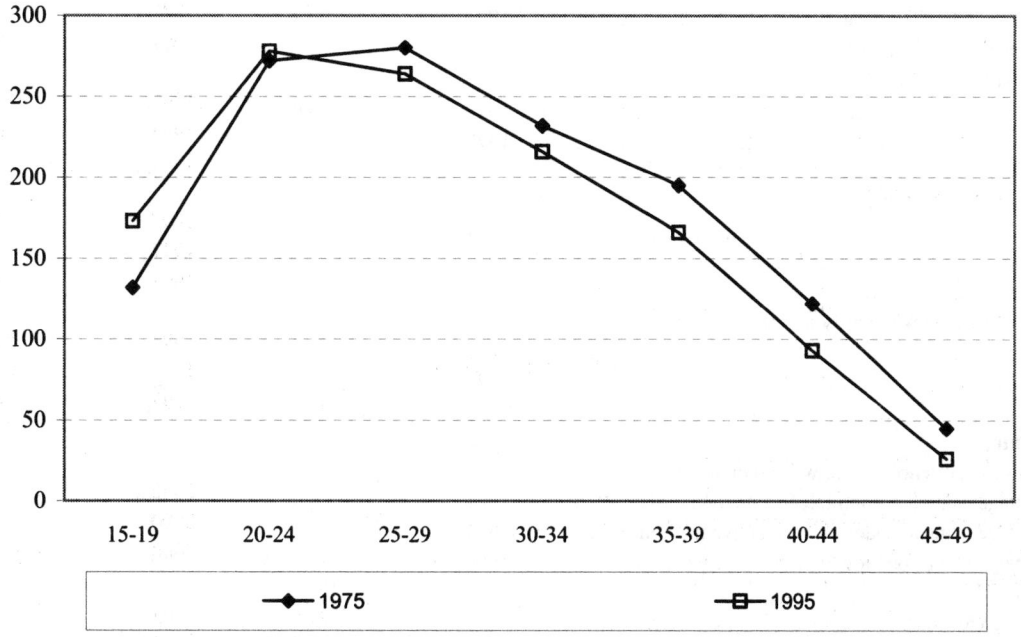

Malawi

Indicator	Earlier year Year	Earlier year Value	Later year Year	Later year Value
Nuptiality				
Annual number of marriages (*thousands*) ....…….........	..	..	..	..
Annual number of divorces (*thousands*) ....……...............	..	..	..	..

Indicator	Year	Male	Female	Year	Male	Female
Total first marriage rate (per person)	..	..	..	..	..	..
Total divorce rate (per person)	..	..	..	..	..	..
Mean age at first marriage (years) ....…	..	..	..	..	..	..
SMAM (years)	1977	22.9	17.8	2000	23.5	18.9
Percentage ever married by age group						
15-19	1977	6.1	51.0	2000	4.0	36.8
20-24	1977	50.7	92.6	2000	41.8	87.7
25-29	1977	86.7	97.8	2000	86.4	98.2
30-34	1977	95.1	98.7	2000	97.0	99.1
35-39	1977	97.1	99.0	2000	98.7	99.7
40-44	1977	97.7	99.0	2000	99.4	99.6
45-49	1977	98.2	99.1	2000	100.0	100.0

Indicator	Year	Value	Year	Value
Fertility				
Annual number of births (*thousands*)..............................	..	..	2001	511.0
Crude birth rate (per 1 000 population)	..	..	2001	45.9
Percentage of extra-marital births among all births	..	..	..	..
Total fertility rate (births per woman)	1977	7.6	1998	6.4
Age-specific fertility rate (per 1 000 women)				
15-19	1977	165	1998	167
20-24	1977	341	1998	307
25-29	1977	334	1998	276
30-34	1977	304	1998	219
35-39	1977	241	1998	169
40-44	1977	119	1998	99
45-49	1977	16	1998	50
Mean age at childbearing (years)	1977	29.3	1998	29.1
Mean age at first birth (years)[a]	..	..	2000	19.2
Children ever born per woman				
35-39	1977	6.0	2000	5.6
40-44	1977	6.7	2000	6.6
45-49	1977	6.9	2000	7.0
Percentage of childless women				
35-39	1977	3.5	2000	2.2
40-44	1977	3.7	2000	1.8
45-49	1977	3.8	2000	2.0
Percentage of women with parity three or higher				
35-39	1977	87.0	2000	87.1
40-44	1977	87.5	2000	91.5
45-49	1977	87.5	2000	90.5
Family Planning				
Contraceptive prevalence among women in union				
Percentage using any contraceptive method	1984	6.9	2000	30.6
Percentage using a modern contraceptive method	1984	1.1	2000	26.1
Percentage using condoms	1984	0.0	2000	1.6
Population policies				
Government's view on the level of fertility	1976	Satisfactory	2001	Too high
Government's policy regarding level of fertility	1976	No intervention	2001	Lower
Government's support for contraceptive methods	1976	Limits	2001	Direct support

[a]Median age at first birth among women aged 25-29 at the date of the survey

Total fertility rates

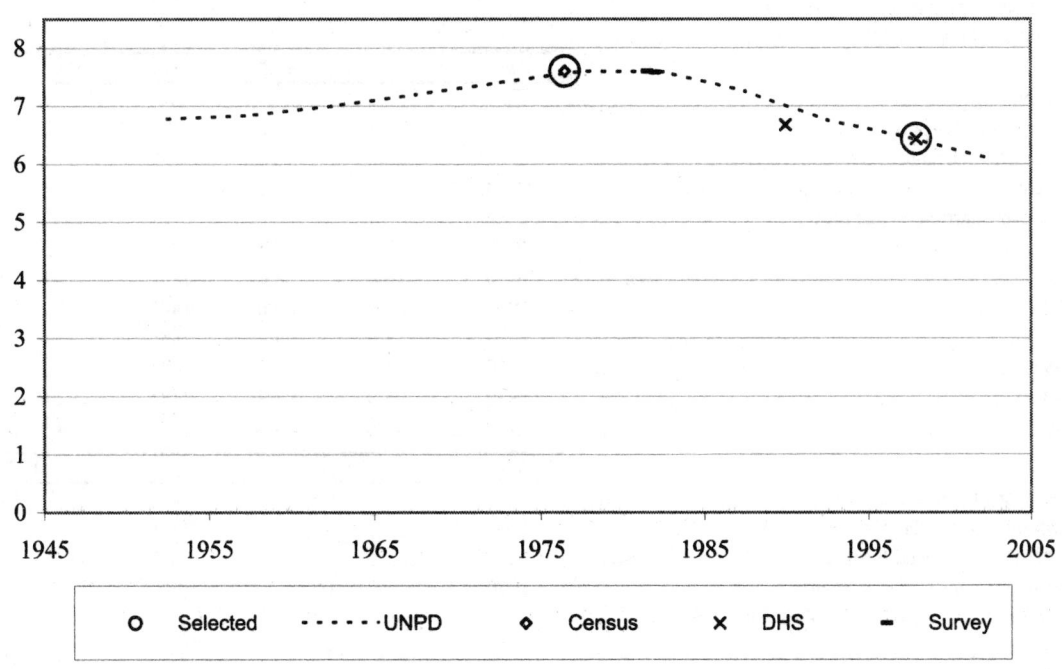

Age-specific fertility rates

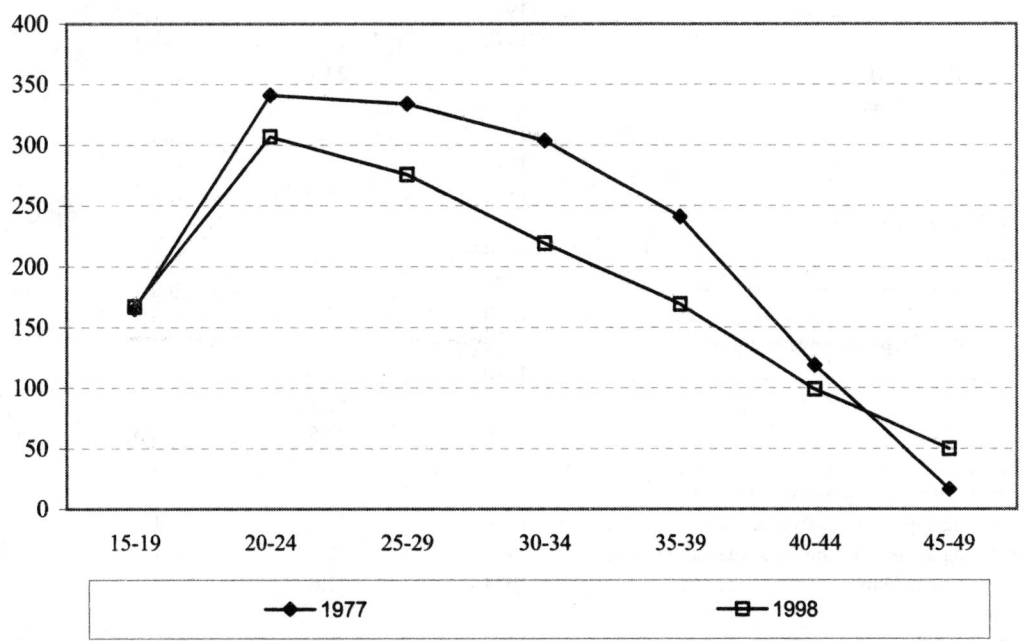

Malaysia

Indicator	Period					
	Earlier year			Later year		
	Year	Value		Year	Value	
Nuptiality						
Annual number of marriages (*thousands*)	..	..		..	..	
Annual number of divorces (*thousands*)	..	..		..	..	
	Year	Male	Female	Year	Male	Female
Total first marriage rate (per person)	..	..	..	..	..	..
Total divorce rate (per person)	..	..	..	..	..	..
Mean age at first marriage (years)	..	..	..	..	..	..
SMAM (years)	1970	25.6	22.1	2000	28.6	25.1
Percentage ever married by age group						
15-19	1970	3.2	17.5	2000	1.1	4.9
20-24	1970	26.6	58.6	2000	11.7	31.5
25-29	1970	68.4	86.6	2000	45.1	70.2
30-34	1970	87.8	94.3	2000	75.3	87.3
35-39	1970	93.6	96.5	2000	87.6	92.2
40-44	1970	95.8	97.8	2000	92.6	93.9
45-49	1970	96.6	98.4	2000	94.9	95.0
Fertility	Year	Value		Year	Value	
Annual number of births (*thousands*).........................	1970	351.5		2000	569.5	
Crude birth rate (per 1 000 population)	1970	32.4		2000	24.5	
Percentage of extra-marital births among all births	..	..		..	..	
Total fertility rate (births per woman)	1970	4.7		1998	3.1	
Age-specific fertility rate (per 1 000 women)						
15-19	1970	54		1998	15	
20-24	1970	233		1998	115	
25-29	1970	236		1998	204	
30-34	1970	216		1998	168	
35-39	1970	126		1998	96	
40-44	1970	54		1998	33	
45-49	1970	15		1998	4	
Mean age at childbearing (years)	1970	29.4		1998	30.1	
Mean age at first birth (years)[a]	1974	22.3		..	..	
Children ever born per woman						
35-39	1970	5.5		..	..	
40-44	1970	5.8		..	..	
45-49	1970	5.6		..	..	
Percentage of childless women						
35-39	1970	2.2		..	..	
40-44	1970	2.7		..	..	
45-49	1970	3.2		..	..	
Percentage of women with parity three or higher						
35-39	1970	82.0		..	..	
40-44	1970	82.1		..	..	
45-49	1970	80.5		..	..	
Family Planning						
Contraceptive prevalence among women in union						
Percentage using any contraceptive method	1974	32.6		1994	54.5	
Percentage using a modern contraceptive method	1974	23.2		1994	29.8	
Percentage using condoms	1974	2.6		1994	5.3	
Population policies						
Government's view on the level of fertility	1976	Too high		2001	Too high	
Government's policy regarding level of fertility	1976	Lower		2001	Lower	
Government's support for contraceptive methods	1976	Direct support		2001	Direct support	

[a]Median age at first birth among women aged 25-29 at the date of the survey

Total fertility rates

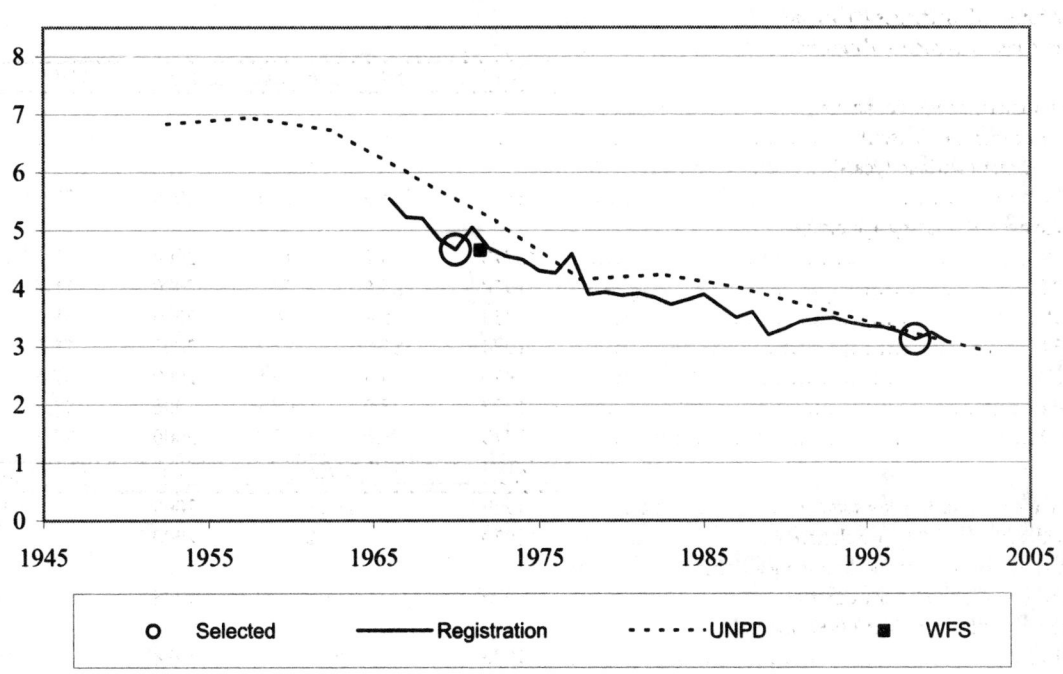

Age-specific fertility rates

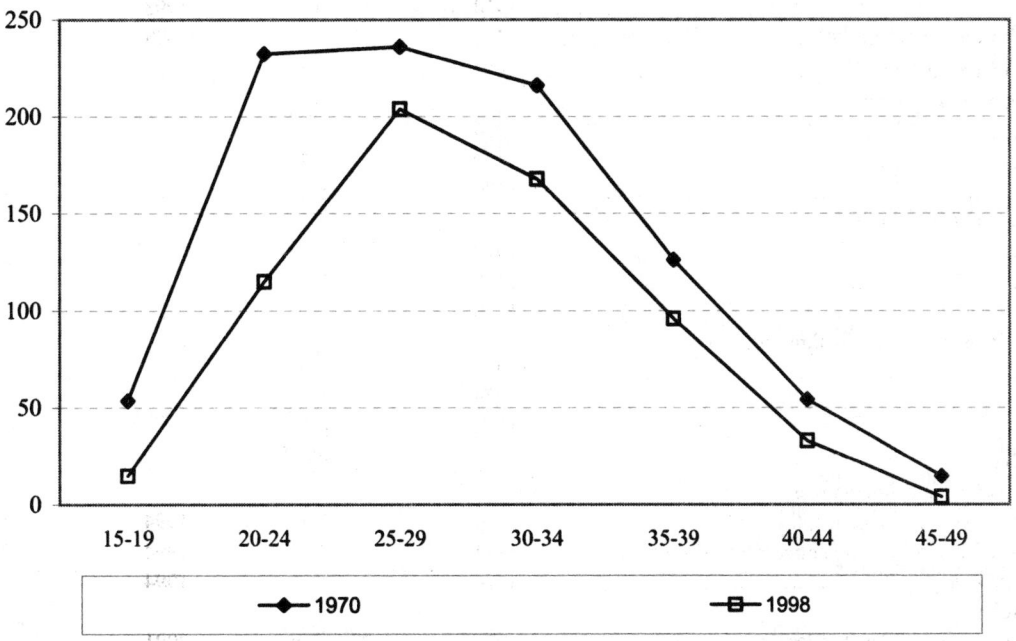

Indicator	Period					
	Earlier year			Later year		
	Year	Value		Year	Value	
Nuptiality						
Annual number of marriages (*thousands*)	1972	4.5		1995	5.0	
Annual number of divorces (*thousands*)	1975	3.6		1995	2.7	
	Year	Male	Female	Year	Male	Female
Total first marriage rate (per person)	..	..	..	..	..	..
Total divorce rate (per person)	..	..	..	..	..	..
Mean age at first marriage (years)	..	..	..	..	..	..
SMAM (years)	1977	22.4	17.5	2000	25.7	21.8
Percentage ever married by age group						
15-19	1977	12.1	56.2	2000	1.3	12.0
20-24	1977	56.9	93.3	2000	25.0	64.1
25-29	1977	84.8	98.6	2000	69.4	91.6
30-34	1977	91.9	99.3	2000	89.6	96.2
35-39	1977	94.9	99.6	2000	95.2	98.4
40-44	1977	95.7	99.3	2000	97.2	98.7
45-49	1977	96.8	99.4	2000	98.3	99.2
Fertility	Year	Value		Year	Value	
Annual number of births (*thousands*)	1974	5.0		1999	5.2	
Crude birth rate (per 1 000 population)	1974	38.9		1999	18.8	
Percentage of extra-marital births among all births	..	..		1996	1.1	
Total fertility rate (births per woman)	..	..		1990	6.4	
Age-specific fertility rate (per 1 000 women)						
15-19	..	..		1990	106	
20-24	..	..		1990	286	
25-29	..	..		1990	303	
30-34	..	..		1990	270	
35-39	..	..		1990	199	
40-44	..	..		1990	96	
45-49	..	..		1990	23	
Mean age at childbearing (years)	..	..		1990	29.6	
Mean age at first birth (years)	..	..		1996	22.1	
Children ever born per woman						
35-39	1977	6.4		2000	5.1	
40-44	1977	6.4		2000	6.3	
45-49	1977	6.3		2000	7.2	
Percentage of childless women						
35-39	1977	4.8		2000	4.7	
40-44	1977	6.1		2000	4.1	
45-49	1977	6.2		2000	3.2	
Percentage of women with parity three or higher						
35-39	1977	87.4		2000	82.5	
40-44	1977	86.1		2000	87.7	
45-49	1977	85.5		2000	90.3	
Family Planning						
Contraceptive prevalence among women in union						
Percentage using any contraceptive method	..	..		..	..	
Percentage using a modern contraceptive method	..	..		..	..	
Percentage using condoms	..	..		..	..	
Population policies						
Government's view on the level of fertility	1976	Satisfactory		2001	Too high	
Government's policy regarding level of fertility	1976	No intervention		2001	Lower	
Government's support for contraceptive methods	1976	No support		2001	Direct support	

Total fertility rates

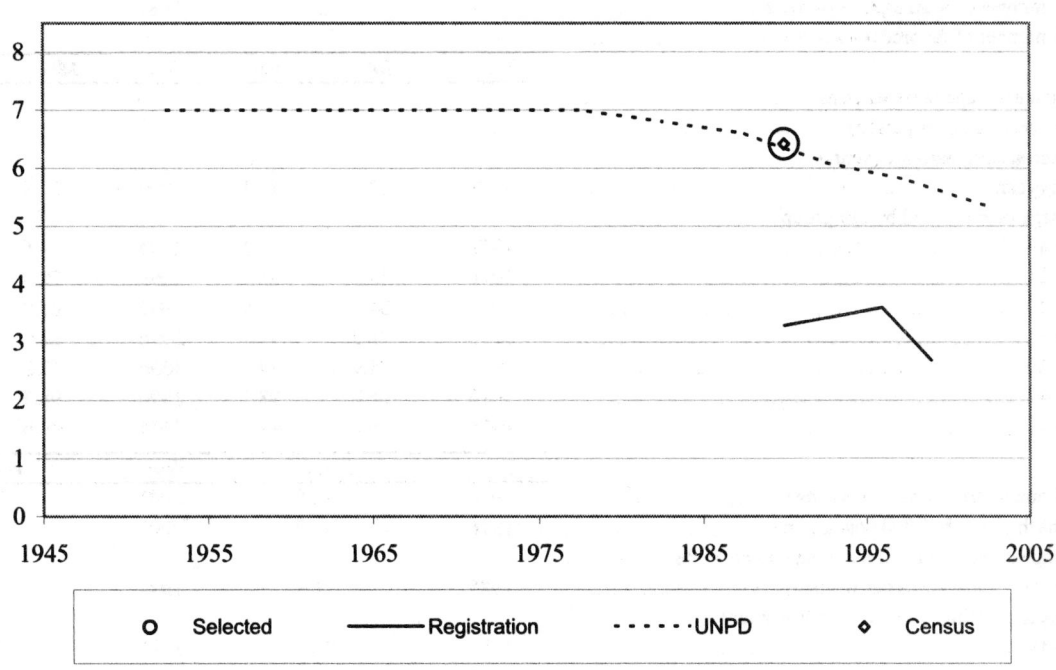

| ○ Selected | —— Registration | · · · · · UNPD | ◇ Census |

Age-specific fertility rates

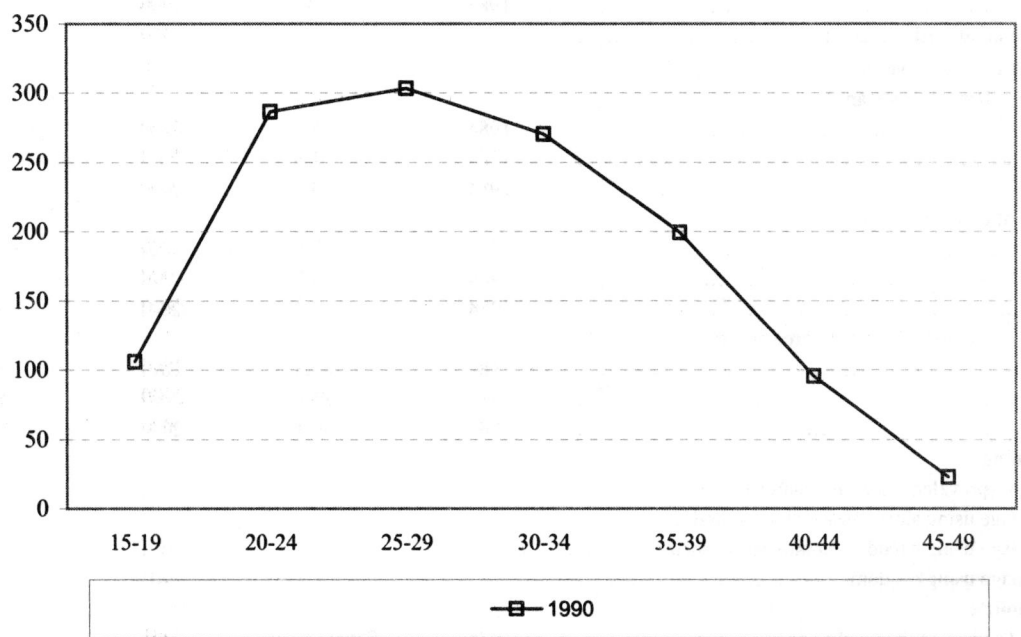

| —□— 1990 |

Indicator	Period					
	Earlier year			Later year		
	Year	Value		Year	Value	
Nuptiality						
Annual number of marriages (*thousands*)	..	..		1987	33.6	
Annual number of divorces (*thousands*)	..	..		..	..	
	Year	Male	Female	Year	Male	Female
Total first marriage rate (per person)	..	..	..	..	..	..
Total divorce rate (per person)	..	..	..	..	..	..
Mean age at first marriage (years)	..	..	..	..	..	..
SMAM (years)	1976	27.6	18.1	1996	25.9	18.4
Percentage ever married by age group						
15-19	1976	1.8	51.1	1996	4.6	49.7
20-24	1976	16.8	88.0	1996	28.9	87.6
25-29	1976	52.4	95.9	1996	67.9	95.8
30-34	1976	80.2	97.5	1996	82.9	98.7
35-39	1976	91.0	98.0	1996	98.3	99.5
40-44	1976	95.0	98.1	1996	98.3	99.9
45-49	1976	96.8	98.3	1996	99.6	99.8
Fertility	Year	Value		Year	Value	
Annual number of births (*thousands*)	1976	272.8		2001	525.7	
Crude birth rate (per 1 000 population)	1976	43.2		2001	50.5	
Percentage of extra-marital births among all births	..	..		..	..	
Total fertility rate (births per woman)	1985	6.9		1994	7.0	
Age-specific fertility rate (per 1 000 women)						
15-19	1985	201		1994	198	
20-24	1985	291		1994	310	
25-29	1985	288		1994	303	
30-34	1985	260		1994	262	
35-39	1985	193		1994	208	
40-44	1985	112		1994	98	
45-49	1985	40		1994	27	
Mean age at childbearing (years)	1985	29.1		1994	28.8	
Mean age at first birth (years)[a]	..	..		2001	18.6	
Children ever born per woman						
35-39	1984	5.5		2001	6.3	
40-44	1984	5.8		2001	7.3	
45-49	1984	5.9		2001	7.9	
Percentage of childless women						
35-39	1984	3.6		2001	3.0	
40-44	1984	3.7		2001	2.6	
45-49	1984	3.7		2001	2.1	
Percentage of women with parity three or higher						
35-39	1984	85.3		2001	89.0	
40-44	1984	85.6		2001	90.6	
45-49	1984	86.1		2001	93.5	
Family Planning						
Contraceptive prevalence among women in union						
Percentage using any contraceptive method	..	..		2001	8.1	
Percentage using a modern contraceptive method	..	..		2001	5.7	
Percentage using condoms	..	..		2001	0.3	
Population policies						
Government's view on the level of fertility	1976	Satisfactory		2001	Too high	
Government's policy regarding level of fertility	1976	No intervention		2001	Lower	
Government's support for contraceptive methods	1976	Direct support		2001	Direct support	

[a]Median age at first birth among women aged 25-29 at the date of the survey

Total fertility rates

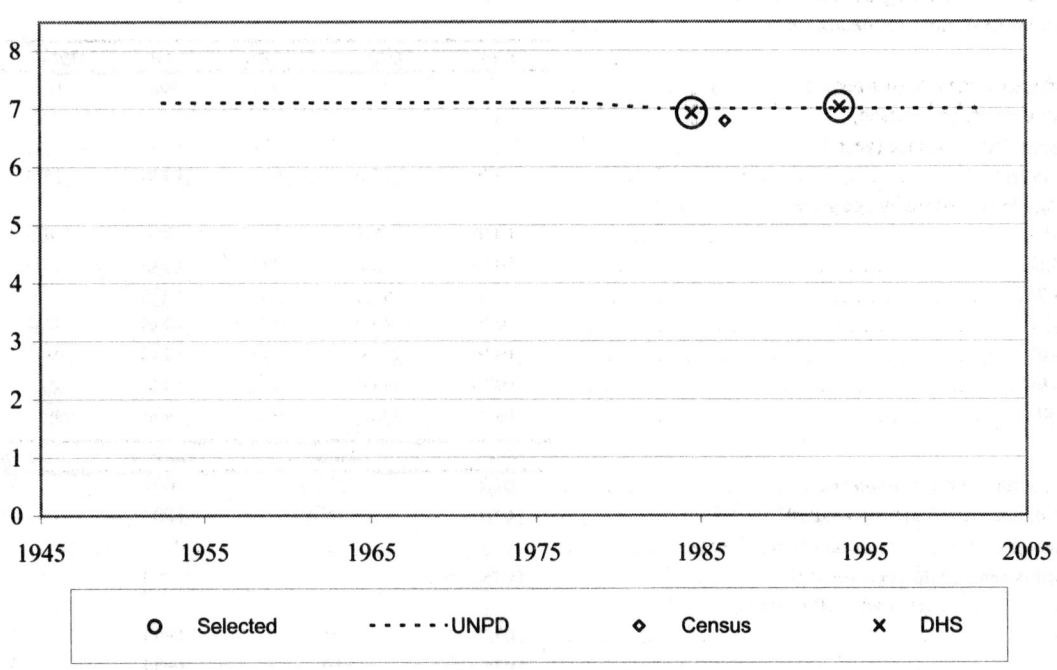

Age-specific fertility rates

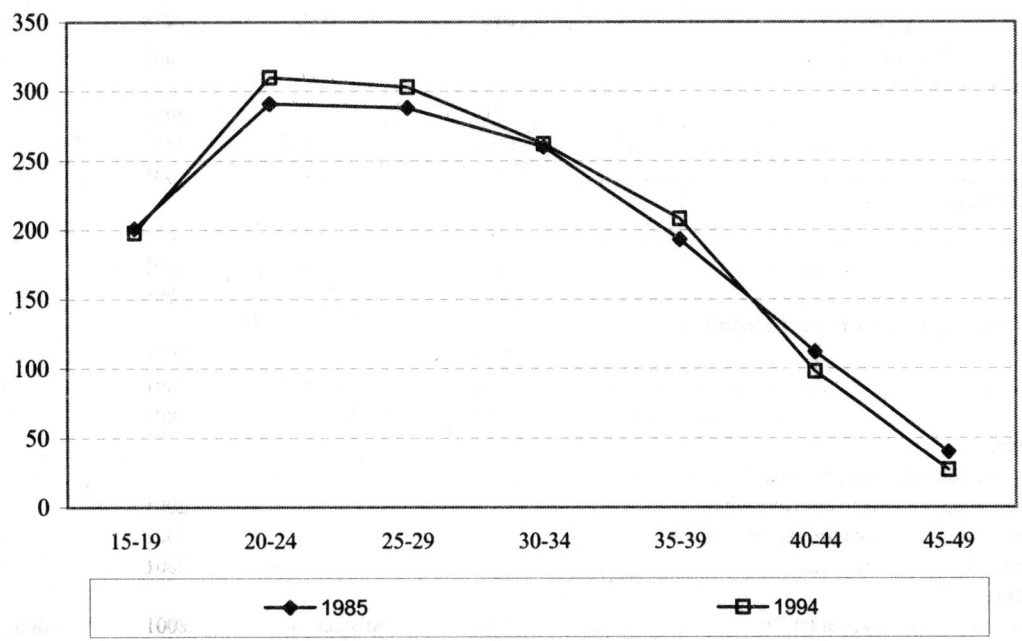

Indicator	Period					
	Earlier year			Later year		
	Year	Value		Year	Value	
Nuptiality						
Annual number of marriages (*thousands*)	1970	2.4		2001	2.2	
Annual number of divorces (*thousands*)	..	..		..	..	
	Year	Male	Female	Year	Male	Female
Total first marriage rate (per person)	1975	1.1	1.0	1998	0.8	0.9
Total divorce rate (per person)	..	..	..	..	..	..
Mean age at first marriage (years)	1975	26.8	24.3	1998	27.3	24.9
SMAM (years)	1967	25.8	24.0	1985	26.2	22.2
Percentage ever married by age group						
15-19	1967	0.3	2.7	1985	0.4	3.0
20-24	1967	15.8	32.8	1985	13.2	33.1
25-29	1967	62.1	66.6	1985	56.2	75.0
30-34	1967	75.2	73.6	1985	81.0	84.9
35-39	1967	80.1	76.0	1985	87.3	84.8
40-44	1967	81.6	77.1	1985	88.6	83.3
45-49	1967	82.4	79.1	1985	88.2	80.7
Fertility	Year	Value		Year	Value	
Annual number of births (*thousands*)	1970	5.3		2001	3.9	
Crude birth rate (per 1 000 population)	1970	17.6		2001	9.8	
Percentage of extra-marital births among all births	1970	1.5		2001	12.9	
Total fertility rate (births per woman)	1975	2.2		2001	1.5	
Age-specific fertility rate (per 1 000 women)						
15-19	1975	17		2001	17	
20-24	1975	119		2001	53	
25-29	1975	150		2001	111	
30-34	1975	91		2001	77	
35-39	1975	42		2001	26	
40-44	1975	14		2001	6	
45-49	1975	0		2001	0	
Mean age at childbearing (years)	1975	28.2		2001	28.6	
Mean age at first birth (years)	..	..		..	..	
Children ever born per woman						
35-39	..	..		..	..	
40-44	..	..		..	..	
45-49	..	..		..	..	
Percentage of childless women						
35-39	..	..		..	..	
40-44	..	..		..	..	
45-49	..	..		..	..	
Percentage of women with parity three or higher						
35-39	..	..		..	..	
40-44	..	..		..	..	
45-49	..	..		..	..	
Family Planning						
Contraceptive prevalence among women in union						
Percentage using any contraceptive method	..	..		..	..	
Percentage using a modern contraceptive method	..	..		..	..	
Percentage using condoms	..	..		..	..	
Population policies						
Government's view on the level of fertility	1976	Satisfactory		2001	Satisfactory	
Government's policy regarding level of fertility	1976	No intervention		2001	No intervention	
Government's support for contraceptive methods	1976	No support		2001	Indirect support	

Total fertility rates

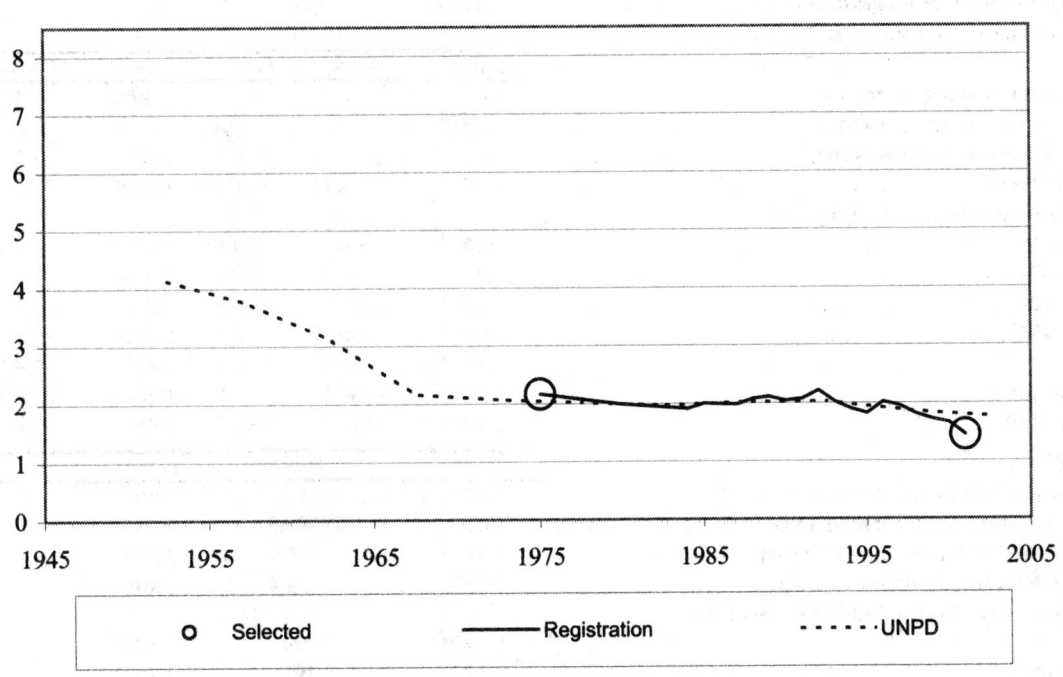

Age-specific fertility rates

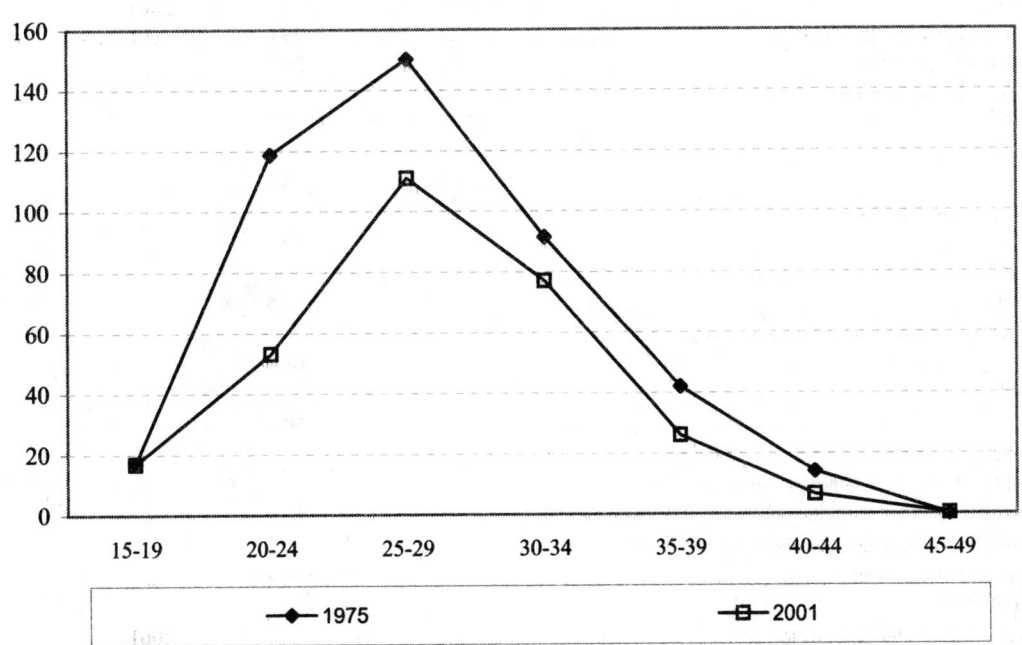

Indicator	Period					
	Earlier year			**Later year**		
	Year	Value		Year	Value	
Nuptiality						
Annual number of marriages (*thousands*)	1970	1.8		1993	1.6	
Annual number of divorces (*thousands*)	1970	0.2		1993	0.3	
	Year	Male	Female	Year	Male	Female
Total first marriage rate (per person)	..	..	..	1992	0.5	0.5
Total divorce rate (per person)	1970	0.1	0.1	..	..	..
Mean age at first marriage (years)	..	..	..	1992	32.9	29.9
SMAM (years)	1967	29.1	26.2	1990	33.0	31.0
Percentage ever married by age group						
15-19	1967	0.2	1.6	1990	0.1	0.5
20-24	1967	5.5	18.8	1990	1.7	6.7
25-29	1967	37.0	44.8	1990	13.4	24.3
30-34	1967	55.4	57.4	1990	36.4	41.9
35-39	1967	64.4	63.9	1990	54.0	54.9
40-44	1967	69.4	65.7	1990	66.5	62.8
45-49	1967	72.6	66.7	1990	70.5	67.2
Fertility	Year	Value		Year	Value	
Annual number of births (*thousands*)........................	1970	9.3		1993	5.9	
Crude birth rate (per 1 000 population)	1970	28.5		1993	15.6	
Percentage of extra-marital births among all births	1970	50.9		1992	65.9	
Total fertility rate (births per woman)	1970	4.4		1992	1.9	
Age-specific fertility rate (per 1 000 women)						
15-19	1970	59		1992	28	
20-24	1970	191		1992	89	
25-29	1970	232		1992	114	
30-34	1970	191		1992	93	
35-39	1970	130		1992	50	
40-44	1970	68		1992	12	
45-49	1970	7		1992	1	
Mean age at childbearing (years)	1970	29.6		1992	28.6	
Mean age at first birth (years)	1967	26.7		..	..	
Children ever born per woman						
35-39	1967	5.3		..	..	
40-44	1967	5.8		..	..	
45-49	1967	5.5		..	..	
Percentage of childless women						
35-39	1967	12.0		..	..	
40-44	1967	14.4		..	..	
45-49	1967	17.6		..	..	
Percentage of women with parity three or higher						
35-39	1967	68.1		..	..	
40-44	1967	67.0		..	..	
45-49	1967	60.4		..	..	
Family Planning						
Contraceptive prevalence among women in union						
Percentage using any contraceptive method	1976	51.3		..	..	
Percentage using a modern contraceptive method	1976	37.9		..	..	
Percentage using condoms	1976	4.6		..	..	
Population policies						
Government's view on the level of fertility	..	--		..	--	
Government's policy regarding level of fertility	..	--		..	--	
Government's support for contraceptive methods	..	--		..	--	

Total fertility rates

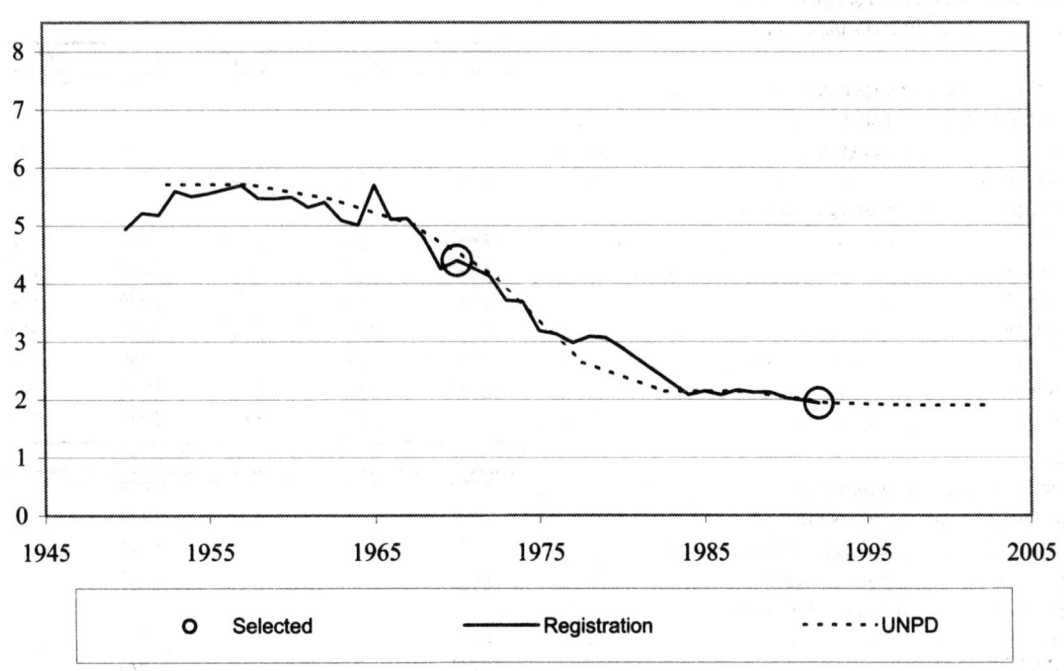

Age-specific fertility rates

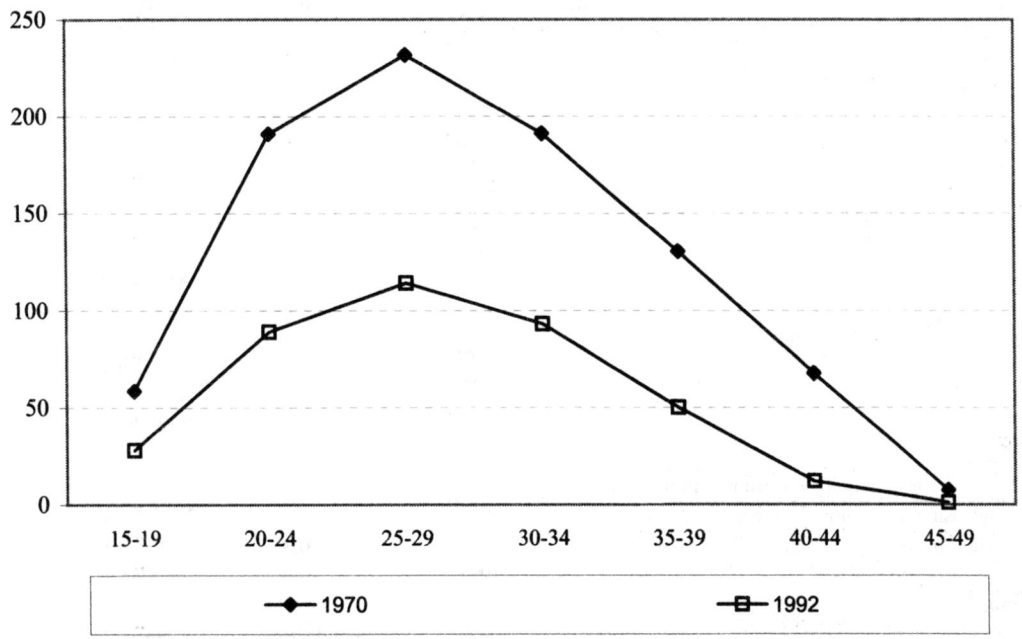

Indicator	Period					
	Earlier year			**Later year**		
	Year	Value		Year	Value	

Nuptiality

Indicator	Year	Value		Year	Value	
Annual number of marriages (*thousands*)	..	..		..	..	
Annual number of divorces (*thousands*)	..	..		..	..	

Indicator	Year	Male	Female	Year	Male	Female
Total first marriage rate (per person)	..	..	..	..	..	..
Total divorce rate (per person)	..	..	..	..	..	..
Mean age at first marriage (years)	..	..	..	..	..	..
SMAM (years)	1977	27.5	19.5	2001	29.5	22.1
Percentage ever married by age group						
15-19	1977	1.8	43.0	2001	0.5	27.8
20-24	1977	19.5	75.6	2001	8.1	60.4
25-29	1977	53.0	90.2	2001	39.7	79.6
30-34	1977	80.5	93.8	2001	75.1	93.3
35-39	1977	90.8	96.2	2001	86.9	96.1
40-44	1977	94.5	96.2	2001	96.0	98.0
45-49	1977	96.2	96.6	2001	99.1	98.0

Fertility

Indicator	Year	Value	Year	Value
Annual number of births (*thousands*)	..	..	..	..
Crude birth rate (per 1 000 population)	..	..	..	..
Percentage of extra-marital births among all births	..	..	..	..
Total fertility rate (births per woman)	1979	6.2	1999	4.7
Age-specific fertility rate (per 1 000 women)				
15-19	1979	155	1999	83
20-24	1979	264	1999	170
25-29	1979	290	1999	215
30-34	1979	242	1999	204
35-39	1979	168	1999	146
40-44	1979	86	1999	85
45-49	1979	44	1999	33
Mean age at childbearing (years)	1979	29.3	1999	30.4
Mean age at first birth (years)[a]	..	..	2000-2001	21.9
Children ever born per woman				
35-39	1981	5.7	2000-2001	5.1
40-44	1981	5.9	2000-2001	5.6
45-49	1981	5.9	2000-2001	6.2
Percentage of childless women				
35-39	..	..	2000-2001	8.3
40-44	..	..	2000-2001	6.9
45-49	..	..	2000-2001	7.0
Percentage of women with parity three or higher				
35-39	..	..	2000-2001	78.6
40-44	..	..	2000-2001	80.2
45-49	..	..	2000-2001	85.2

Family Planning

Indicator	Year	Value	Year	Value
Contraceptive prevalence among women in union				
Percentage using any contraceptive method	1981	0.8	2000-2001	8.0
Percentage using a modern contraceptive method	1981	0.3	2000-2001	5.1
Percentage using condoms	1981	0.0	2000-2001	0.8

Population policies

Indicator	Year	Value	Year	Value
Government's view on the level of fertility	1976	Satisfactory	2001	Satisfactory
Government's policy regarding level of fertility	1976	No intervention	2001	No intervention
Government's support for contraceptive methods	1976	No support	2001	Direct support

[a]Median age at first birth among women aged 25-29 at the date of the survey

Total fertility rates

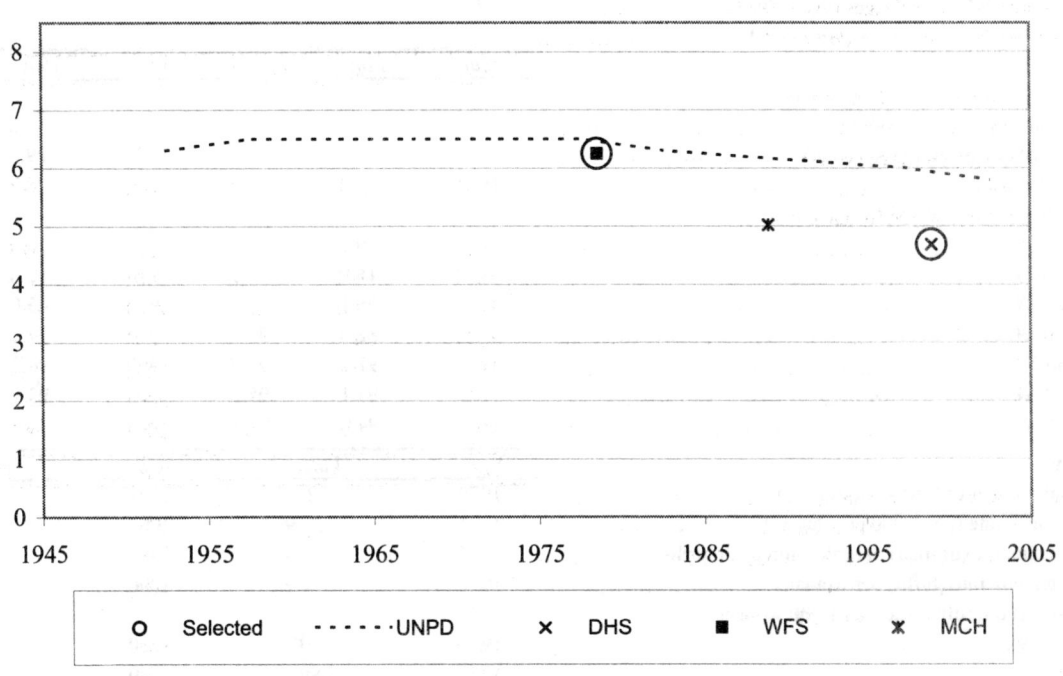

Age-specific fertility rates

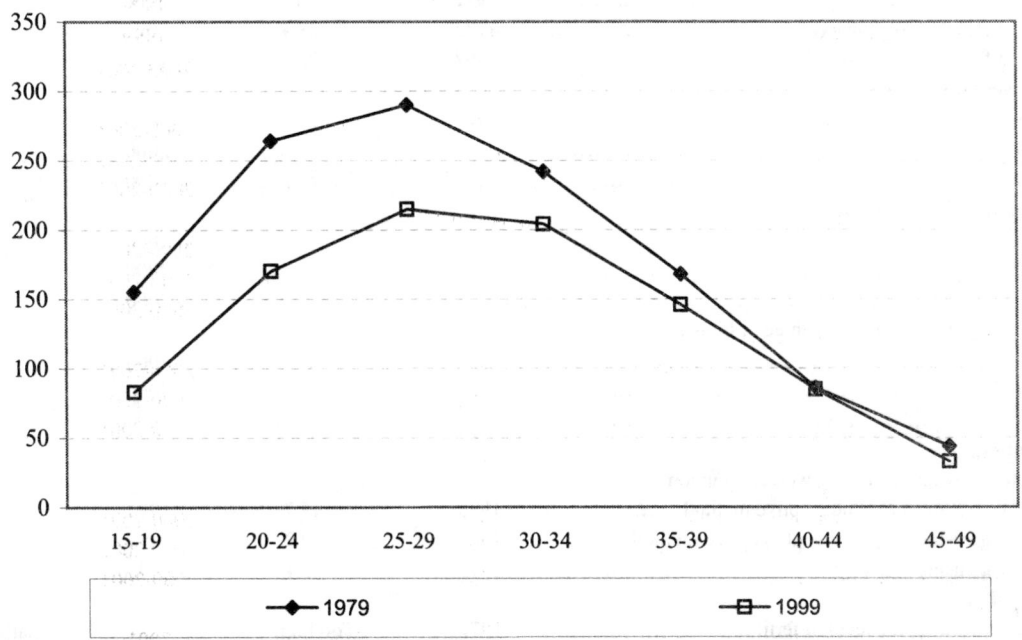

Indicator	Period					
	Earlier year			Later year		
	Year	Value		Year	Value	

Nuptiality

Indicator	Year	Value		Year	Value	
Annual number of marriages (*thousands*)	1970	4.7		2001	10.6	
Annual number of divorces (*thousands*)	..	..		2001	1.5	

	Year	Male	Female	Year	Male	Female
Total first marriage rate (per person)	..	..	..	1997	1.0	1.0
Total divorce rate (per person)	..	..	..	..	..	..
Mean age at first marriage (years)	..	..	..	1997	29.4	25.2
SMAM (years)	1972	27.2	22.5	1990	28.2	23.8
Percentage ever married by age group						
15-19	1972	0.7	13.2	1990	0.6	11.3
20-24	1972	16.0	53.9	1990	12.6	51.3
25-29	1972	56.1	82.7	1990	45.0	76.1
30-34	1972	82.8	92.1	1990	77.1	85.8
35-39	1972	91.2	95.0	1990	90.2	88.8
40-44	1972	93.1	95.6	1990	93.9	91.5
45-49	1972	94.6	96.3	1990	94.7	94.5

Fertility

Indicator	Year	Value	Year	Value
Annual number of births (*thousands*)	1970	22.2	2001	19.7
Crude birth rate (per 1 000 population)	1970	26.9	2001	16.4
Percentage of extra-marital births among all births	1967	0.4	1997	18.2
Total fertility rate (births per woman)	1972	3.4	2000	2.0
Age-specific fertility rate (per 1 000 women)				
15-19	1972	50	2000	39
20-24	1972	189	2000	122
25-29	1972	191	2000	122
30-34	1972	130	2000	77
35-39	1972	88	2000	34
40-44	1972	32	2000	8
45-49	1972	4	2000	1
Mean age at childbearing (years)	1972	28.4	2000	27.2
Mean age at first birth (years)	1967	22.5	1997	24.5
Children ever born per woman				
35-39	..	..	2000	2.3
40-44	..	..	2000	2.6
45-49	..	..	2000	3.0
Percentage of childless women				
35-39	..	..	2000	5.0
40-44	..	..	2000	4.6
45-49	..	..	2000	4.6
Percentage of women with parity three or higher				
35-39	..	..	2000	36.5
40-44	..	..	2000	48.1
45-49	..	..	2000	57.4

Family Planning

Indicator	Year	Value	Year	Value
Contraceptive prevalence among women in union				
Percentage using any contraceptive method	1975	45.7	1991	74.7
Percentage using a modern contraceptive method	1975	29.2	1991	48.9
Percentage using condoms	1975	5.1	1991	13.3

Population policies

Indicator	Year	Value	Year	Value
Government's view on the level of fertility	1976	Too high	2001	Satisfactory
Government's policy regarding level of fertility	1976	Lower	2001	No intervention
Government's support for contraceptive methods	1976	Direct support	2001	Direct support

Total fertility rates

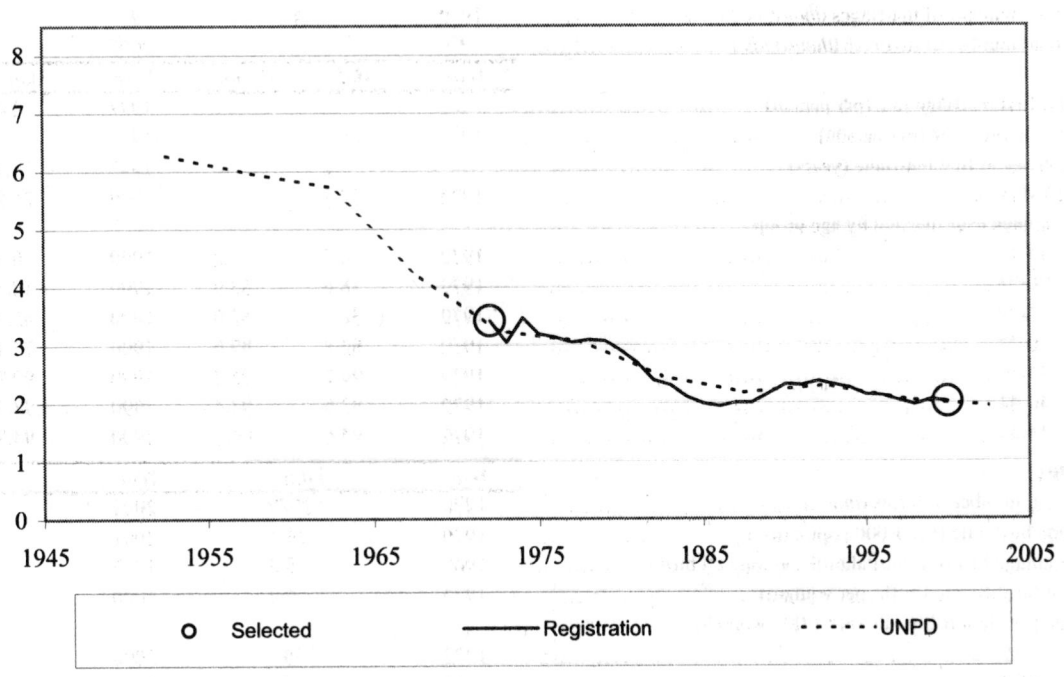

Age-specific fertility rates

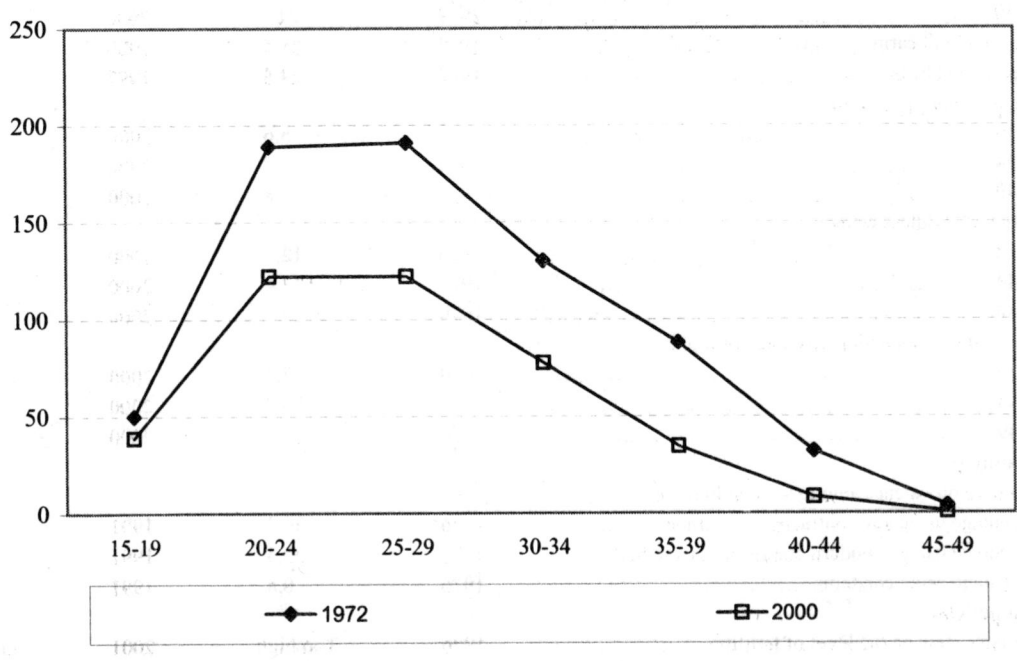

Indicator	Period					
	Earlier year			Later year		
	Year	Value		Year	Value	
Nuptiality						
Annual number of marriages (*thousands*)	1970	356.7		1999	743.9	
Annual number of divorces (*thousands*)	1970	28.8		2000	52.4	
	Year	Male	Female	Year	Male	Female
Total first marriage rate (per person)	..	..	..	1995	0.8	0.7
Total divorce rate (per person)	1976	0.0	0.0	1997	0.1	0.1
Mean age at first marriage (years)	..	..	..	1997	27.3	24.4
SMAM (years)	1970	24.4	21.2	2000	25.0	22.7
Percentage ever married by age group						
15-19	1970	5.2	21.2	2000	5.9	17.1
20-24	1970	38.8	61.5	2000	37.8	52.3
25-29	1970	72.8	82.6	2000	67.9	75.1
30-34	1970	86.2	89.6	2000	83.1	85.6
35-39	1970	90.8	92.2	2000	89.1	89.7
40-44	1970	92.6	92.7	2000	92.2	91.4
45-49	1970	93.6	92.9	2000	93.7	92.2
Fertility	Year	Value		Year	Value	
Annual number of births (*thousands*)	1970	2 132.6		2000	2 798.3	
Crude birth rate (per 1 000 population)	1970	42.1		2000	27.9	
Percentage of extra-marital births among all births	1970	27.3		1993	37.8	
Total fertility rate (births per woman)	1974	6.2		1996	2.7	
Age-specific fertility rate (per 1 000 women)						
15-19	1974	114		1996	75	
20-24	1974	290		1996	146	
25-29	1974	294		1996	144	
30-34	1974	254		1996	102	
35-39	1974	178		1996	56	
40-44	1974	84		1996	19	
45-49	1974	21		1996	3	
Mean age at childbearing (years)	1974	29.2		1996	27.4	
Mean age at first birth (years)	1972	24.4		1995	23.8	
Children ever born per woman						
35-39	1970	5.6		2000	3.2	
40-44	1970	5.9		2000	3.8	
45-49	1970	5.8		2000	4.4	
Percentage of childless women						
35-39	1970	12.3		2000	8.9	
40-44	1970	12.4		2000	7.1	
45-49	1970	12.9		2000	6.6	
Percentage of women with parity three or higher						
35-39	1970	77.2		2000	61.1	
40-44	1970	76.9		2000	68.9	
45-49	1970	75.7		2000	73.7	
Family Planning						
Contraceptive prevalence among women in union						
Percentage using any contraceptive method	1976	30.3		1997	68.4	
Percentage using a modern contraceptive method	1976	23.3		1997	59.5	
Percentage using condoms	1976	0.8		1997	3.7	
Population policies						
Government's view on the level of fertility	1976	Too high		2001	Too high	
Government's policy regarding level of fertility	1976	Lower		2001	Lower	
Government's support for contraceptive methods	1976	Direct support		2001	Direct support	

Total fertility rates

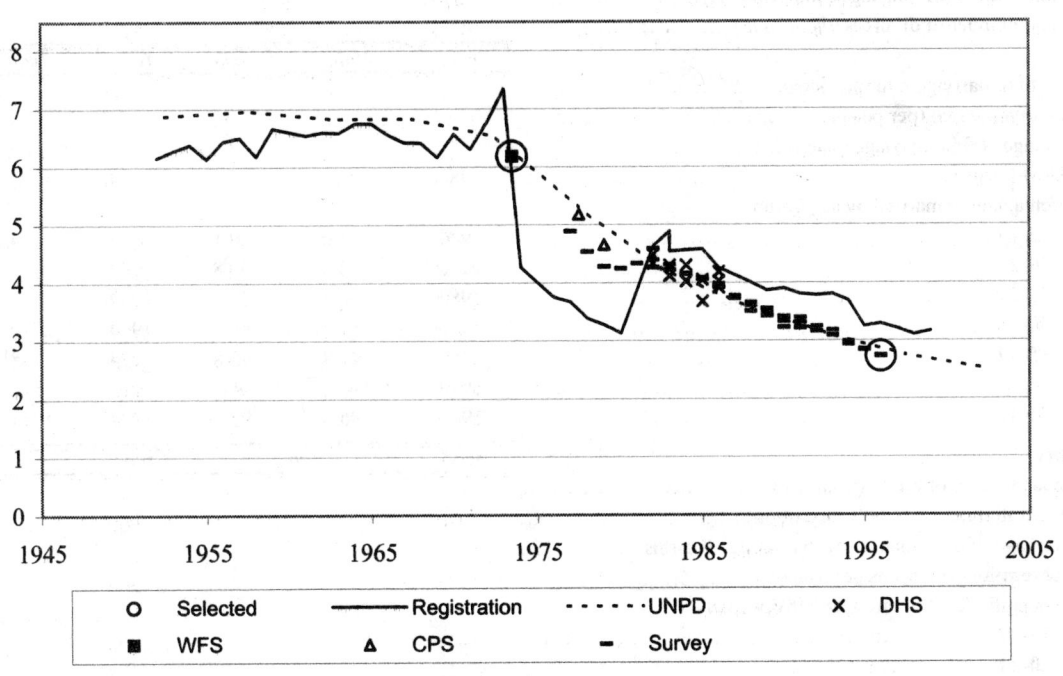

Age-specific fertility rates

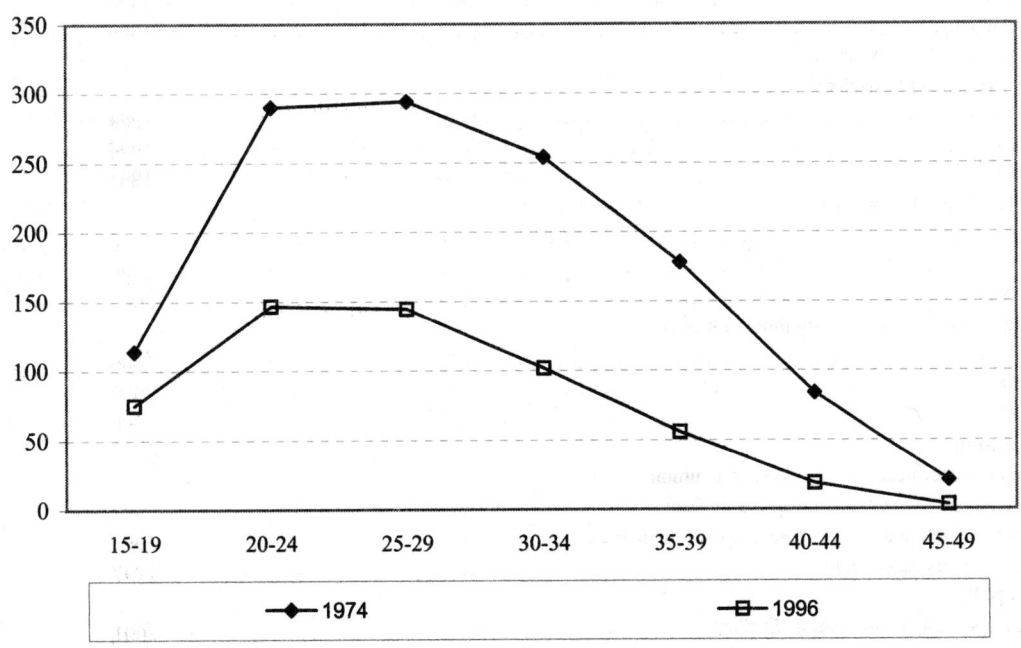

Indicator	Period					
	Earlier year			Later year		
	Year	Value		Year	Value	

Nuptiality

	Year	Value		Year	Value	
Annual number of marriages (*thousands*)	..	..		..	..	
Annual number of divorces (*thousands*)	..	..		..	..	

	Year	Male	Female	Year	Male	Female
Total first marriage rate (per person)	..	..	..	..	..	..
Total divorce rate (per person)	..	..	..	..	..	..
Mean age at first marriage (years)	..	..	..	..	..	..
SMAM (years)	1980	..	..	1994	..	..
Percentage ever married by age group						
15-19	1980	4.6	20.1	1994	4.2	10.2
20-24	1980	32.2	60.8	1994	28.9	43.4
25-29	1980	66.3	81.7	1994	68.7	77.3
30-34	1980	84.2	88.6	1994	[25-34]	[25-34]
35-39	1980	91.9	93.8	1994	88.7	91.5
40-44	1980	[35-44]	[35-44]	1994	[35-44]	[35-44]
45-49	1980	95.6	95.6	1994	94.3	94.5

Fertility

	Year	Value		Year	Value	
Annual number of births (*thousands*)	..	..		..	..	
Crude birth rate (per 1 000 population)	..	..		..	..	
Percentage of extra-marital births among all births	..	..		..	..	
Total fertility rate (births per woman)	..	..		..	..	
Age-specific fertility rate (per 1 000 women)						
15-19	..	..		..	..	
20-24	..	..		..	..	
25-29	..	..		..	..	
30-34	..	..		..	..	
35-39	..	..		..	..	
40-44	..	..		..	..	
45-49	..	..		..	..	
Mean age at childbearing (years)	..	..		..	..	
Mean age at first birth (years)	..	..		..	..	
Children ever born per woman						
35-39	..	..		1994	4.7	
40-44	..	..		1994	5.7	
45-49	..	..		1994	..	
Percentage of childless women						
35-39	..	..		..	..	
40-44	..	..		..	..	
45-49	..	..		..	..	
Percentage of women with parity three or higher						
35-39	..	..		..	..	
40-44	..	..		..	..	
45-49	..	..		..	..	

Family Planning

	Year	Value		Year	Value	
Contraceptive prevalence among women in union						
Percentage using any contraceptive method	..	..		..	..	
Percentage using a modern contraceptive method	..	..		..	..	
Percentage using condoms	..	..		..	..	

Population policies

	Year	Value		Year	Value	
Government's view on the level of fertility	1976	..		2001	Too high	
Government's policy regarding level of fertility	1976	..		2001	Lower	
Government's support for contraceptive methods	1976	..		2001	Direct support	

Total fertility rates

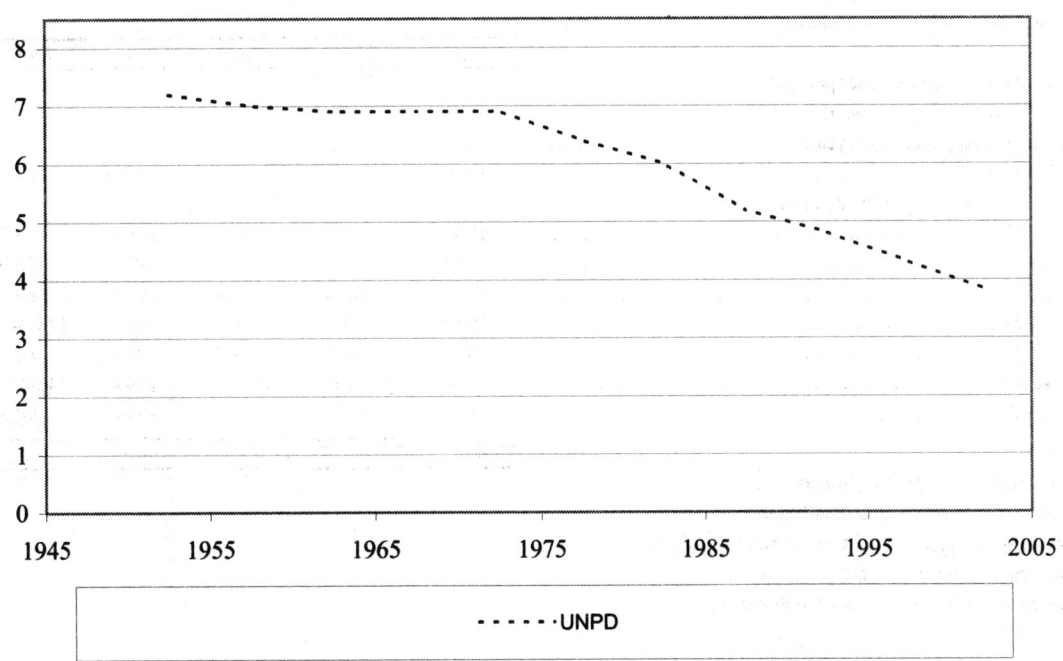

Indicator	Period					
	Earlier year			Later year		
	Year	Value		Year	Value	

Nuptiality

	Year	Value		Year	Value	
Annual number of marriages (*thousands*)	1978	5.2		2001	12.4	
Annual number of divorces (*thousands*)	1978	0.3		2000	0.8	

	Year	Male	Female	Year	Male	Female
Total first marriage rate (per person)	..	..	..	..	..	..
Total divorce rate (per person)	..	..	..	..	..	..
Mean age at first marriage (years)	..	..	..	..	..	..
SMAM (years)	..	..	..	2000	25.7	23.7
Percentage ever married by age group						
15-19	..	..	..	2000	1.3	5.6
20-24	..	..	..	2000	29.3	48.3
25-29	..	..	..	2000	68.8	79.1
30-34	..	..	..	2000	86.6	90.0
35-39	..	..	..	2000	92.8	93.5
40-44	..	..	..	2000	95.8	95.1
45-49	..	..	..	2000	96.6	96.0

Fertility

	Year	Value	Year	Value
Annual number of births (*thousands*)	1965	44.2	2001	49.7
Crude birth rate (per 1 000 population)	1965	40.5	2001	20.3
Percentage of extra-marital births among all births	..	..	1989	19.4
Total fertility rate (births per woman)	1973	7.5	2000	2.3
Age-specific fertility rate (per 1 000 women)				
15-19	1973	83	2000	28
20-24	1973	202	2000	148
25-29	1973	364	2000	136
30-34	1973	368	2000	86
35-39	1973	300	2000	40
40-44	1973	137	2000	14
45-49	1973	44	2000	4
Mean age at childbearing (years)	1973	31.5	2000	27.7
Mean age at first birth (years)	..	..	..	..
Children ever born per woman				
35-39	..	..	..	..
40-44	..	..	..	..
45-49	..	..	..	..
Percentage of childless women				
35-39	..	..	..	..
40-44	..	..	..	..
45-49	..	..	..	..
Percentage of women with parity three or higher				
35-39	..	..	..	..
40-44	..	..	..	..
45-49	..	..	..	..

Family Planning

	Year	Value	Year	Value
Contraceptive prevalence among women in union				
Percentage using any contraceptive method	..	..	2000	67.4
Percentage using a modern contraceptive method	..	..	2000	54.3
Percentage using condoms	..	..	2000	4.3

Population policies

	Year	Value	Year	Value
Government's view on the level of fertility	1976	Satisfactory	2001	Satisfactory
Government's policy regarding level of fertility	1976	Maintain	2001	No intervention
Government's support for contraceptive methods	1976	Direct support	2001	Direct support

Total fertility rates

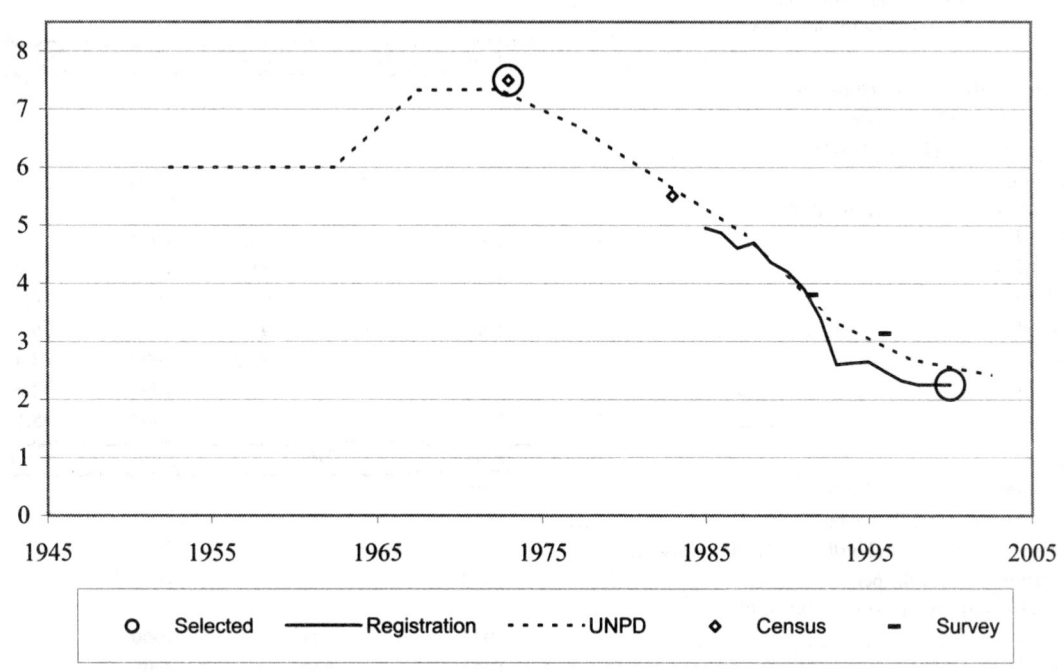

○ Selected	—— Registration	·····UNPD	◇ Census	– Survey

Age-specific fertility rates

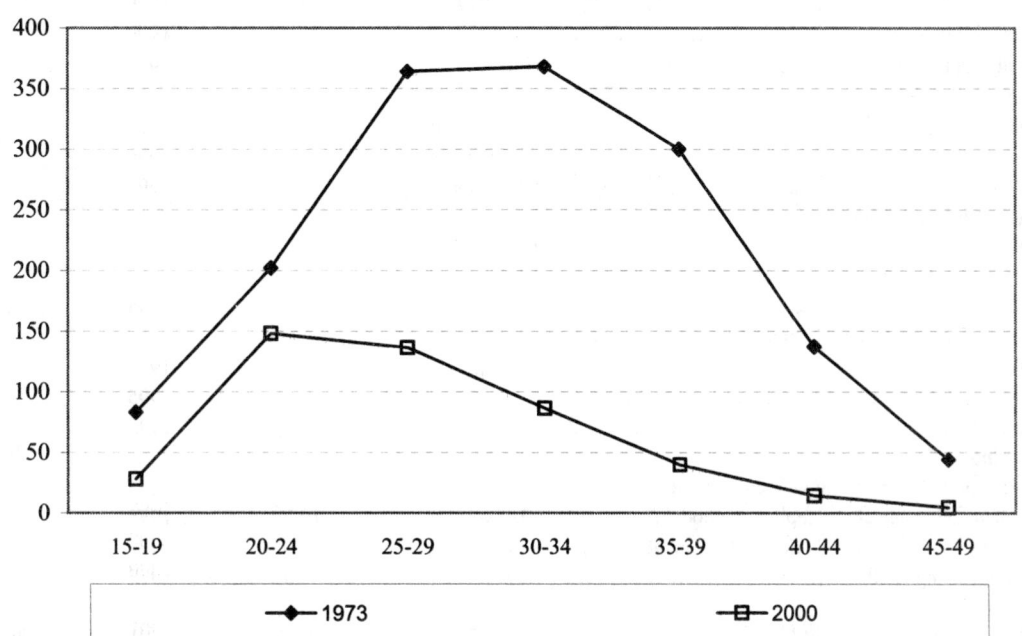

Indicator	Period					
	Earlier year			Later year		
	Year	Value		Year	Value	
Nuptiality						
Annual number of marriages (*thousands*)	..	..		..	..	
Annual number of divorces (*thousands*)	..	..		..	..	
	Year	Male	Female	Year	Male	Female
Total first marriage rate (per person)	..	..	..	..	..	..
Total divorce rate (per person)	..	..	..	..	..	..
Mean age at first marriage (years)	..	..	..	..	..	..
SMAM (years)	1971	25.0	19.1	1994	29.8	25.3
Percentage ever married by age group						
15-19	1971	4.0	33.8	1994	1.1	12.8
20-24	1971	32.1	81.7	1994	11.0	44.1
25-29	1971	72.5	95.0	1994	36.5	64.9
30-34	1971	89.3	97.6	1994	66.7	81.7
35-39	1971	94.6	98.2	1994	85.4	90.8
40-44	1971	96.3	98.2	1994	92.5	95.1
45-49	1971	96.9	97.7	1994	95.1	97.9
Fertility	Year	Value		Year	Value	
Annual number of births (*thousands*)............................	..	..		..	..	
Crude birth rate (per 1 000 population)	..	..		..	..	
Percentage of extra-marital births among all births	..	..		..	..	
Total fertility rate (births per woman)	1977	5.9		1999	3.0	
Age-specific fertility rate (per 1 000 women)						
15-19	1977	93		1999	10	
20-24	1977	265		1999	71	
25-29	1977	296		1999	128	
30-34	1977	222		1999	139	
35-39	1977	178		1999	130	
40-44	1977	98		1999	77	
45-49	1977	29		1999	39	
Mean age at childbearing (years)	1977	29.8		1999	33.3	
Mean age at first birth (years)[a]	..	..		1995	23.3	
Children ever born per woman						
35-39	1979-1980	6.1		1995	3.9	
40-44	1979-1980	7.1		1995	5.5	
45-49	1979-1980	7.1		1995	6.8	
Percentage of childless women						
35-39	..	..		1995	16.9	
40-44	..	..		1995	9.3	
45-49	..	..		1995	3.7	
Percentage of women with parity three or higher						
35-39	..	..		1995	65.6	
40-44	..	..		1995	80.3	
45-49	..	..		1995	85.8	
Family Planning						
Contraceptive prevalence among women in union						
Percentage using any contraceptive method	1979-1980	19.7		1995	50.3	
Percentage using a modern contraceptive method	1979-1980	16.6		1995	42.4	
Percentage using condoms	1979-1980	0.3		1995	1.4	
Population policies						
Government's view on the level of fertility	1976	Too high		2001	Too high	
Government's policy regarding level of fertility	1976	Lower		2001	Lower	
Government's support for contraceptive methods	1976	Direct support		2001	Direct support	

[a]Median age at first birth among women aged 25-29 at the date of the survey

Total fertility rates

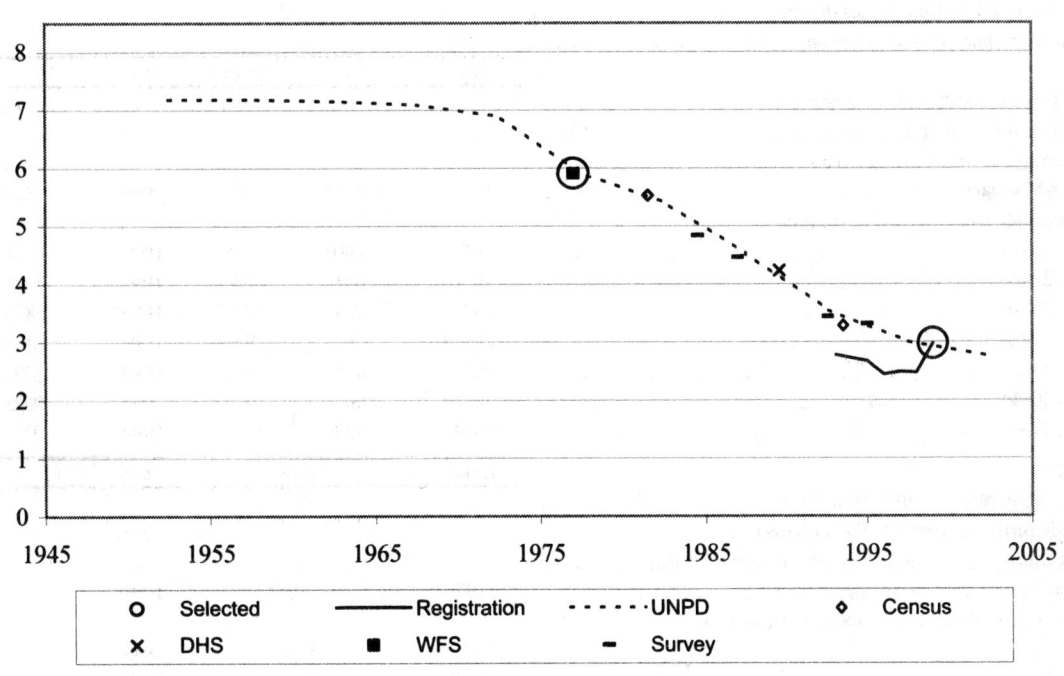

Age-specific fertility rates

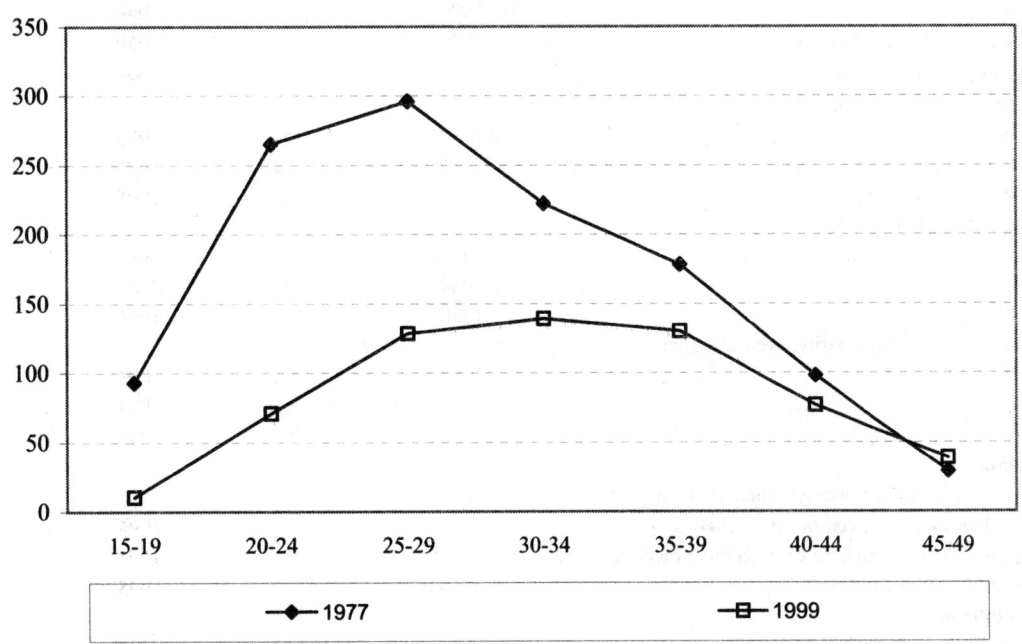

Mozambique

Indicator	Period					
	Earlier year			Later year		
	Year	Value		Year	Value	

Nuptiality

	Year	Value		Year	Value	
Annual number of marriages (*thousands*)	1970	8.2		..	..	
Annual number of divorces (*thousands*)	1970	0.1		..	..	

	Year	Male	Female	Year	Male	Female
Total first marriage rate (per person)	..	..	..	..	..	..
Total divorce rate (per person)	..	..	..	..	..	..
Mean age at first marriage (years)	..	..	..	..	..	..
SMAM (years)	1970	24.7	19.9	1997	22.6	18.0
Percentage ever married by age group						
15-19	1970	4.0	30.8	1997	3.8	47.1
20-24	1970	39.7	78.9	1997	57.6	88.8
25-29	1970	73.2	89.5	1997	87.6	94.1
30-34	1970	86.4	93.4	1997	94.5	97.5
35-39	1970	92.4	94.9	1997	99.2	99.0
40-44	1970	94.5	95.7	1997	100.0	97.4
45-49	1970	95.8	96.0	1997	99.3	97.1

Fertility

	Year	Value	Year	Value
Annual number of births (*thousands*)	..	..	2001	753.3
Crude birth rate (per 1 000 population)	..	..	2001	42.7
Percentage of extra-marital births among all births	..	..	..	..
Total fertility rate (births per woman)	1970	6.7	1995	5.6
Age-specific fertility rate (per 1 000 women)				
15-19	1970	133	1995	173
20-24	1970	294	1995	270
25-29	1970	271	1995	235
30-34	1970	235	1995	198
35-39	1970	196	1995	126
40-44	1970	140	1995	95
45-49	1970	71	1995	25
Mean age at childbearing (years)	1970	30.4	1995	28.5
Mean age at first birth (years)[a]	..	..	1997	18.7
Children ever born per woman				
35-39	1980	5.2	1997	5.0
40-44	1980	5.6	1997	5.7
45-49	1980	5.6	1997	5.9
Percentage of childless women				
35-39	1980	9.3	1997	7.1
40-44	1980	10.8	1997	7.7
45-49	1980	12.3	1997	8.4
Percentage of women with parity three or higher				
35-39	1980	77.2	1997	78.4
40-44	1980	76.7	1997	80.1
45-49	1980	75.1	1997	79.1

Family Planning

	Year	Value	Year	Value
Contraceptive prevalence among women in union				
Percentage using any contraceptive method	..	..	1997	5.6
Percentage using a modern contraceptive method	..	..	1997	5.1
Percentage using condoms	..	..	1997	0.3

Population policies

	Year	Value	Year	Value
Government's view on the level of fertility	1976	Satisfactory	2001	Too high
Government's policy regarding level of fertility	1976	Maintain	2001	Lower
Government's support for contraceptive methods	1976	Direct support	2001	Direct support

[a]Median age at first birth among women aged 25-29 at the date of the survey

Total fertility rates

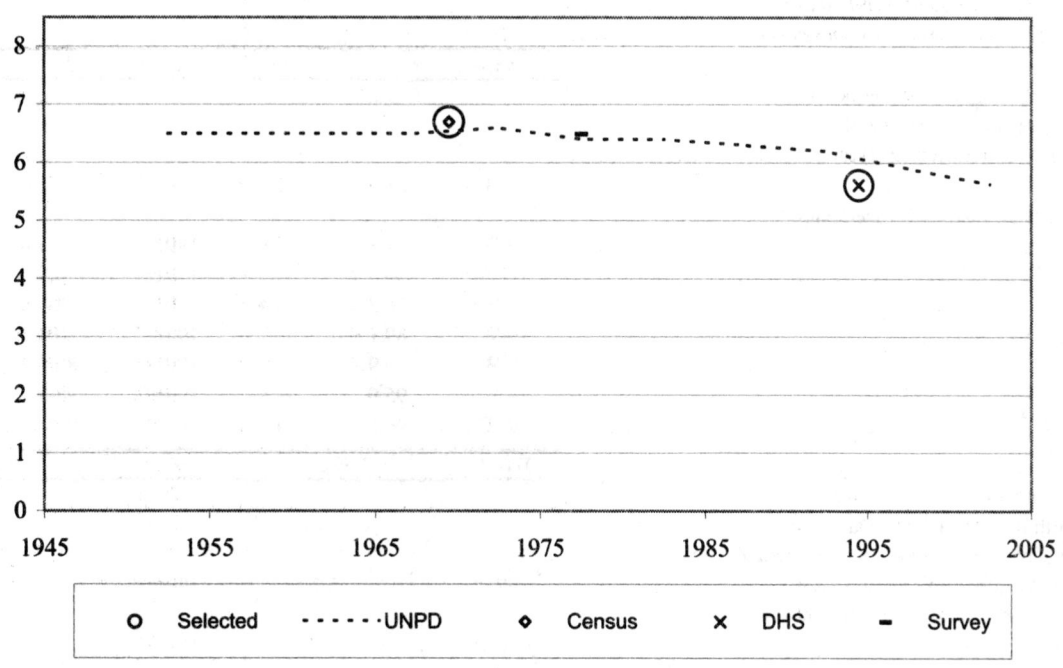

Age-specific fertility rates

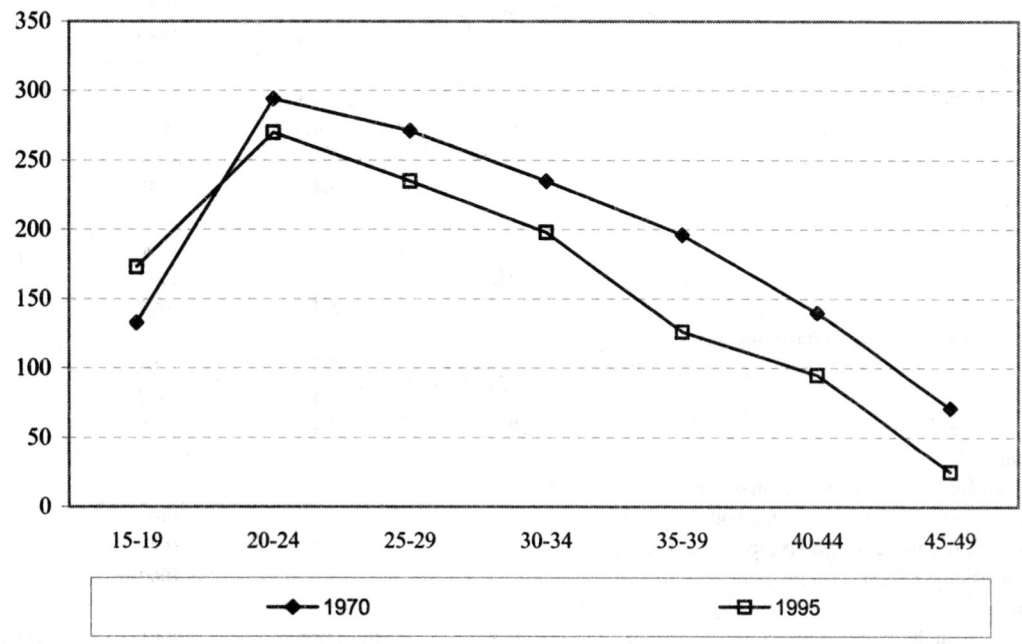

Myanmar

Indicator	Period					
	Earlier year			Later year		
	Year	Value		Year	Value	
Nuptiality						
Annual number of marriages (*thousands*)	..	..		..	..	
Annual number of divorces (*thousands*)	..	..		..	..	
	Year	Male	Female	Year	Male	Female
Total first marriage rate (per person)	..	..	..	..	..	..
Total divorce rate (per person)	..	..	..	..	..	..
Mean age at first marriage (years)	..	..	..	..	..	..
SMAM (years)	1973	23.9	21.3	1991	26.4	24.5
Percentage ever married by age group						
15-19	1973	7.8	22.0	1991	3.3	10.7
20-24	1973	44.8	64.5	1991	30.1	44.0
25-29	1973	76.3	83.4	1991	62.4	67.6
30-34	1973	89.7	90.7	1991	80.4	80.4
35-39	1973	93.9	93.0	1991	88.6	86.2
40-44	1973	95.6	93.8	1991	93.8	89.6
45-49	1973	96.5	94.1	1991	95.7	90.9
Fertility	Year	Value		Year	Value	
Annual number of births (*thousands*).............................	..	..		..	..	
Crude birth rate (per 1 000 population)	..	..		..	..	
Percentage of extra-marital births among all births	..	..		..	..	
Total fertility rate (births per woman)	1973	5.7		1994	2.9	
Age-specific fertility rate (per 1 000 women)						
15-19	..	..		1994	32	
20-24	..	..		1994	121	
25-29	..	..		1994	156	
30-34	..	..		1994	137	
35-39	..	..		1994	93	
40-44	..	..		1994	37	
45-49	..	..		1994	4	
Mean age at childbearing (years)	..	..		1994	29.8	
Mean age at first birth (years)	..	..		..	..	
Children ever born per woman						
35-39	1983	4.4		..	..	
40-44	1983	5.2		..	..	
45-49	1983	5.4		..	..	
Percentage of childless women						
35-39	1983	4.9		..	..	
40-44	1983	4.9		..	..	
45-49	1983	5.4		..	..	
Percentage of women with parity three or higher						
35-39	1983	73.5		..	..	
40-44	1983	77.4		..	..	
45-49	1983	77.4		..	..	
Family Planning						
Contraceptive prevalence among women in union						
Percentage using any contraceptive method	..	..		1997	32.7	
Percentage using a modern contraceptive method	..	..		1997	28.4	
Percentage using condoms	..	..		1997	0.1	
Population policies						
Government's view on the level of fertility	1976	Satisfactory		2001	Satisfactory	
Government's policy regarding level of fertility	1976	No intervention		2001	Maintain	
Government's support for contraceptive methods	1976	No support		2001	Direct support	

Total fertility rates

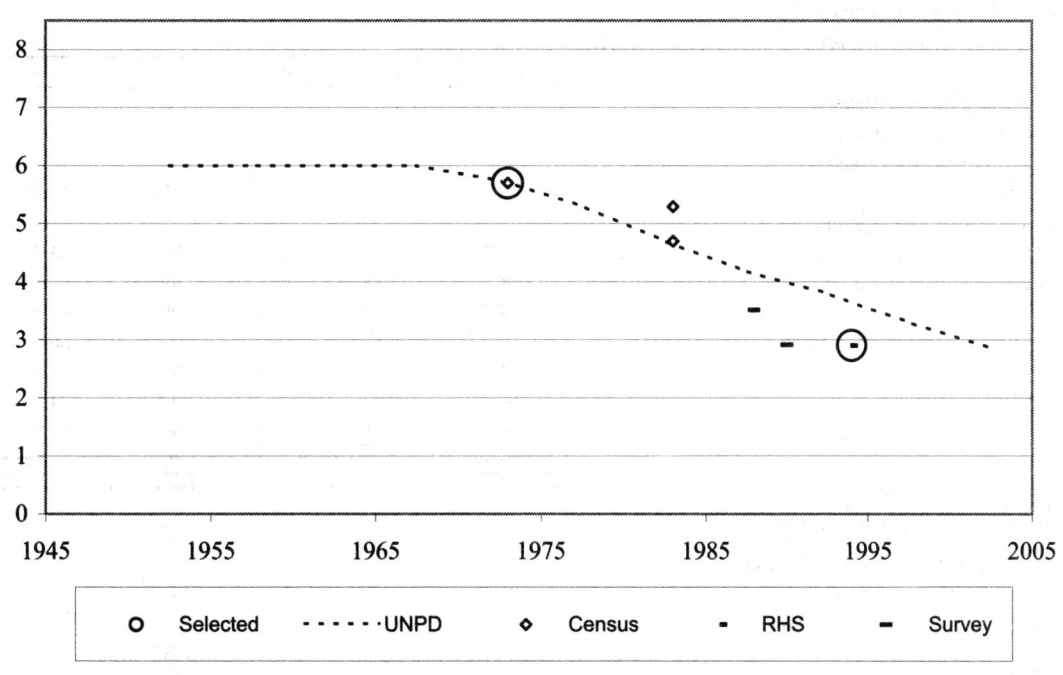

Age-specific fertility rates

Namibia

Indicator	Period					
	Earlier year			Later year		
	Year	Value		Year	Value	

Nuptiality

Annual number of marriages (*thousands*)	..	..		..	..	
Annual number of divorces (*thousands*)	..	..		..	..	

	Year	Male	Female	Year	Male	Female
Total first marriage rate (per person)	..	..	..	..	..	..
Total divorce rate (per person)	..	..	..	..	..	..
Mean age at first marriage (years)	..	..	..	..	..	..
SMAM (years)	1960	27.8	21.8	1992	..	26.4
Percentage ever married by age group						
15-19	1960	0.9	11.2	1992	..	7.7
20-24	1960	15.5	53.5	1992	..	31.0
25-29	1960	42.2	79.6	1992	..	53.0
30-34	1960	69.0	87.5	1992	..	74.2
35-39	1960	81.7	89.5	1992	..	80.8
40-44	1960	85.3	89.9	1992	..	81.1
45-49	1960	86.1	88.6	1992	..	88.1

Fertility

	Year	Value	Year	Value
Annual number of births (*thousands*)	..	..	..	..
Crude birth rate (per 1 000 population)	..	..	..	..
Percentage of extra-marital births among all births	..	..	..	..
Total fertility rate (births per woman)	..	..	1990	5.2
Age-specific fertility rate (per 1 000 women)				
15-19	..	..	1990	101
20-24	..	..	1990	197
25-29	..	..	1990	236
30-34	..	..	1990	197
35-39	..	..	1990	171
40-44	..	..	1990	99
45-49	..	..	1990	38
Mean age at childbearing (years)	..	..	1990	30.3
Mean age at first birth (years)[a]	..	..	1992	21.2
Children ever born per woman				
35-39	..	..	1991	4.6
40-44	..	..	1991	5.6
45-49	..	..	1991	6.1
Percentage of childless women				
35-39	..	..	1991	5.4
40-44	..	..	1991	4.7
45-49	..	..	1991	4.7
Percentage of women with parity three or higher				
35-39	..	..	1991	76.7
40-44	..	..	1991	81.6
45-49	..	..	1991	82.8

Family Planning

Contraceptive prevalence among women in union				
Percentage using any contraceptive method	..	..	1992	28.9
Percentage using a modern contraceptive method	..	..	1992	26.0
Percentage using condoms	..	..	1992	0.3

Population policies

Government's view on the level of fertility	..	--	2001	Too high
Government's policy regarding level of fertility	..	--	2001	Lower
Government's support for contraceptive methods	..	--	2001	Direct support

[a]Median age at first birth among women aged 25-29 at the date of the survey

Total fertility rates

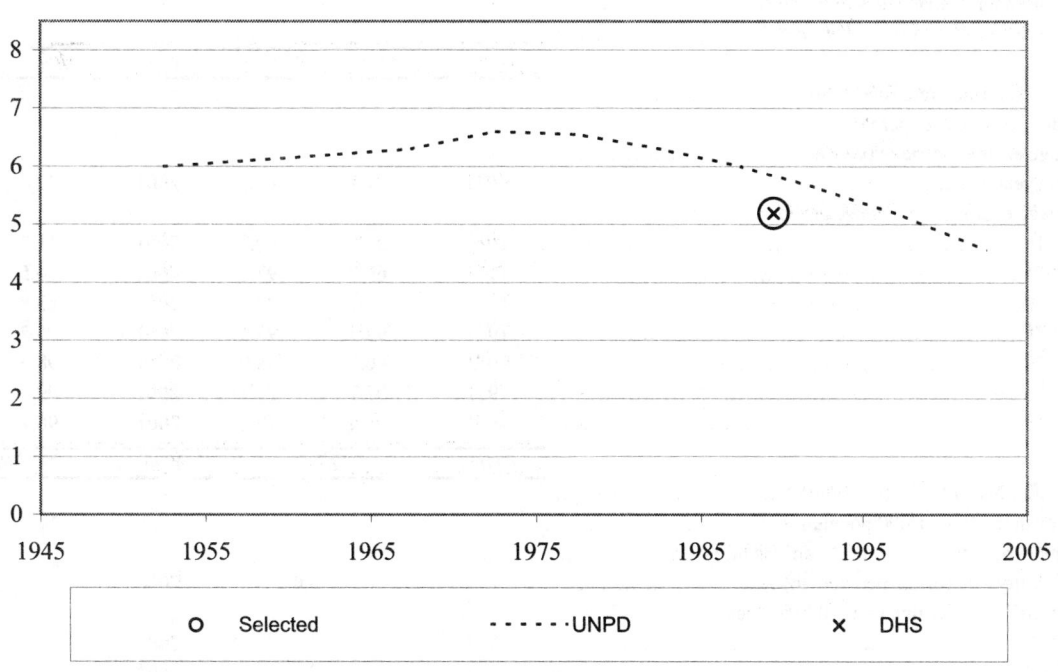

Age-specific fertility rates

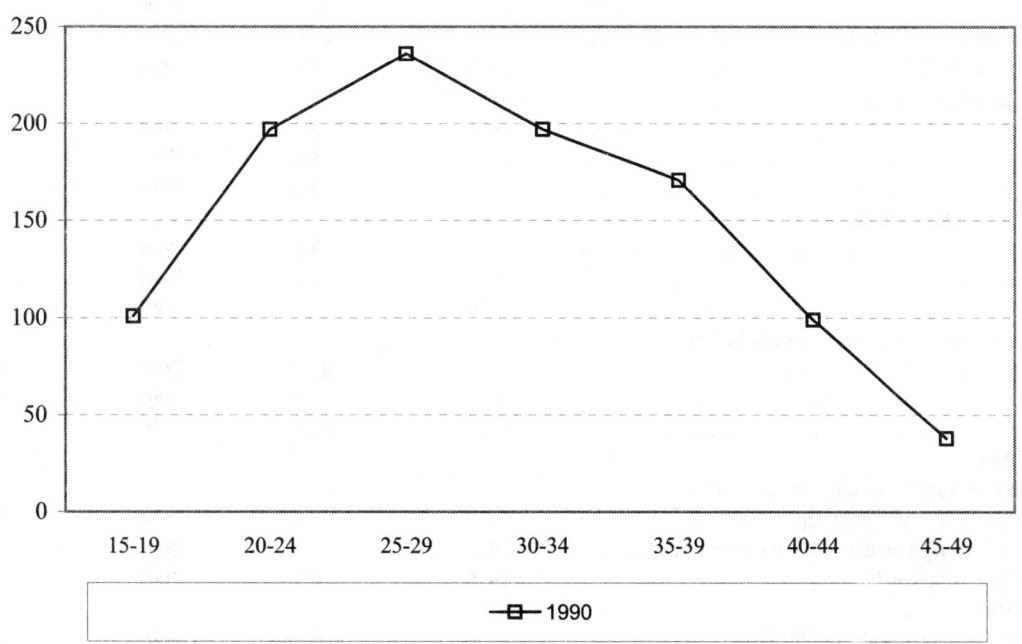

Nepal

Indicator	Period					
	Earlier year			Later year		
	Year	Value		Year	Value	

Nuptiality

Indicator	Year	Value		Year	Value	
Annual number of marriages (*thousands*)	..	..		..	..	
Annual number of divorces (*thousands*)	..	..		..	..	

Indicator	Year	Male	Female	Year	Male	Female
Total first marriage rate (per person)	..	..	..	..	..	..
Total divorce rate (per person)	..	..	..	..	..	..
Mean age at first marriage (years)	..	..	..	..	..	..
SMAM (years)	1971	21.1	17.5	2001	22.6	19.0
Percentage ever married by age group						
15-19	1971	27.0	60.7	2001	11.3	40.3
20-24	1971	66.9	92.1	2001	56.5	82.9
25-29	1971	87.7	97.4	2001	83.8	95.5
30-34	1971	94.3	98.6	2001	95.2	97.5
35-39	1971	96.7	98.9	2001	98.6	98.1
40-44	1971	97.7	99.1	2001	99.1	98.9
45-49	1971	98.4	99.2	2001	98.7	98.6

Fertility

Indicator	Year	Value	Year	Value
Annual number of births (*thousands*).............................	..	..	..	..
Crude birth rate (per 1 000 population)	..	..	..	..
Percentage of extra-marital births among all births	..	..	..	..
Total fertility rate (births per woman)	1974	6.0	2000	4.3
Age-specific fertility rate (per 1 000 women)				
15-19	1974	131	2000	116
20-24	1974	283	2000	260
25-29	1974	287	2000	213
30-34	1974	236	2000	144
35-39	1974	159	2000	84
40-44	1974	79	2000	36
45-49	1974	27	2000	8
Mean age at childbearing (years)	1974	29.0	2000	27.3
Mean age at first birth (years)[a]	1976	19.8	2001	19.7
Children ever born per woman				
35-39	1976	5.1	2001	4.5
40-44	1976	5.5	2001	5.2
45-49	1976	5.8	2001	5.7
Percentage of childless women				
35-39	1976	3.1	2001	4.2
40-44	1976	4.4	2001	2.9
45-49	1976	4.5	2001	3.1
Percentage of women with parity three or higher				
35-39	1976	83.1	2001	86.4
40-44	1976	83.6	2001	88.0
45-49	1976	83.7	2001	89.9

Family Planning

Indicator	Year	Value	Year	Value
Contraceptive prevalence among women in union				
Percentage using any contraceptive method	1976	2.5	2001	39.3
Percentage using a modern contraceptive method	1976	2.5	2001	35.4
Percentage using condoms	1976	0.2	2001	2.9

Population policies

Indicator	Year	Value	Year	Value
Government's view on the level of fertility	1976	Too high	2001	Too high
Government's policy regarding level of fertility	1976	Lower	2001	Lower
Government's support for contraceptive methods	1976	Direct support	2001	Direct support

[a]Median age at first birth among women aged 25-29 at the date of the survey for both dates

Total fertility rates

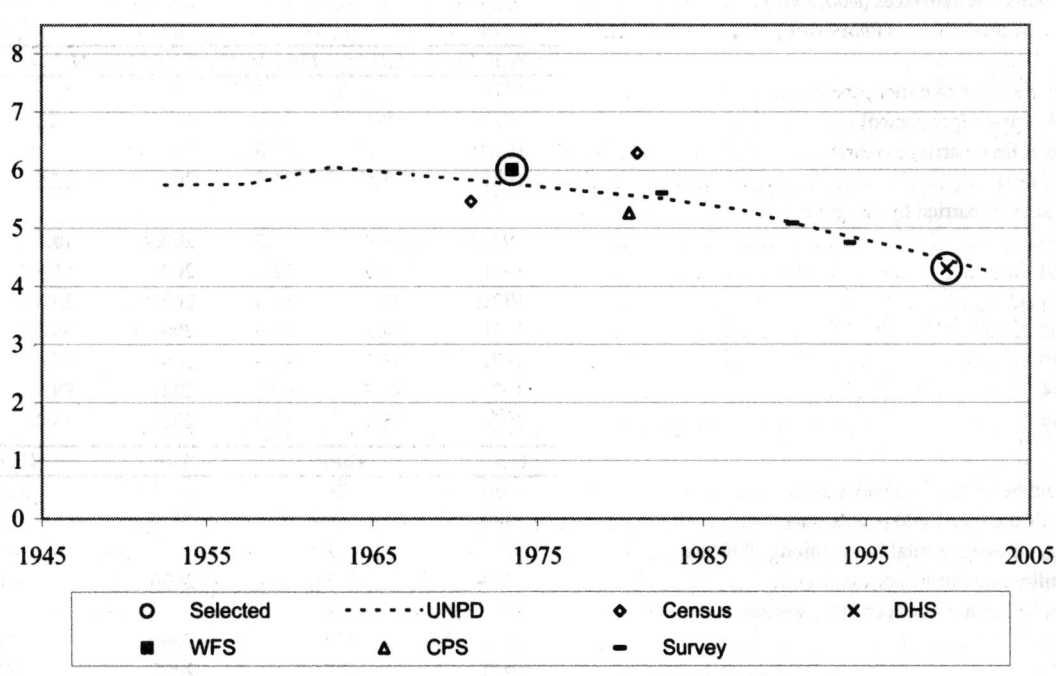

Age-specific fertility rates

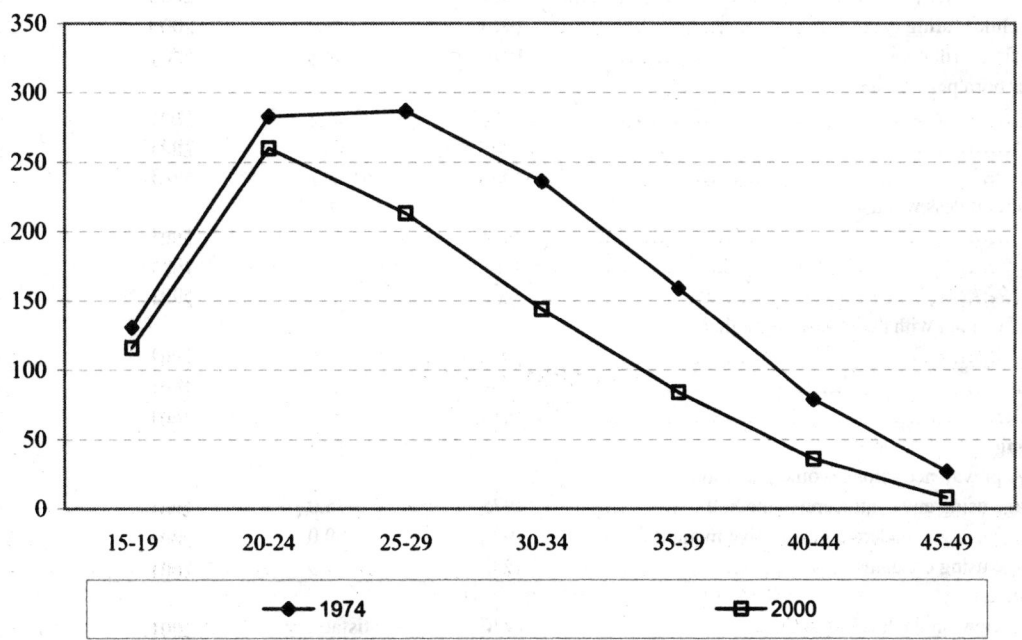

Netherlands

Indicator	Period					
	Earlier year			Later year		
	Year	Value		Year	Value	
Nuptiality						
Annual number of marriages (*thousands*)	1970	123.6		2002	89.3	
Annual number of divorces (*thousands*)	1970	10.3		2001	37.1	
	Year	Male	Female	Year	Male	Female
Total first marriage rate (per person)	1970	..	1.1	1998	0.5	0.6
Total divorce rate (per person)	1970	0.1	0.1	1996	0.2	0.3
Mean age at first marriage (years)	1975	24.7	22.6	1998	30.0	27.6
SMAM (years)	1971	25.1	21.9	2002	32.5	29.9
Percentage ever married by age group						
15-19	1971	0.7	5.2	2002	0.1	0.7
20-24	1971	28.7	54.8	2002	3.4	11.1
25-29	1971	74.4	86.0	2002	20.6	37.6
30-34	1971	86.5	92.0	2002	48.8	64.6
35-39	1971	89.4	92.7	2002	68.8	78.6
40-44	1971	91.4	92.5	2002	78.3	85.1
45-49	1971	93.0	91.9	2002	84.8	89.9
Fertility	Year	Value		Year	Value	
Annual number of births (*thousands*)	1970	238.9		2002	203.1	
Crude birth rate (per 1 000 population)	1970	18.3		2002	12.6	
Percentage of extra-marital births among all births	1970	2.1		2001	27.2	
Total fertility rate (births per woman)	1970	2.6		2001	1.7	
Age-specific fertility rate (per 1 000 women)						
15-19	1970	23		2001	8	
20-24	1970	137		2001	41	
25-29	1970	183		2001	108	
30-34	1970	107		2001	129	
35-39	1970	49		2001	50	
40-44	1970	14		2001	7	
45-49	1970	1		2001	0	
Mean age at childbearing (years)	1970	28.2		2001	30.3	
Mean age at first birth (years)	1970	24.8		2001	28.6	
Children ever born per woman						
35-39	..	..		1993	1.8	
40-44	..	..		1993	..	
45-49	..	..		1993	..	
Percentage of childless women						
35-39	..	..		1993	17.0	
40-44	..	..		1993	..	
45-49	..	..		1993	..	
Percentage of women with parity three or higher						
35-39	..	..		1993	24.0	
40-44	..	..		1993	..	
45-49	..	..		1993	..	
Family Planning						
Contraceptive prevalence among women in union						
Percentage using any contraceptive method	1975	75.0		1993	78.5	
Percentage using a modern contraceptive method	1975	69.0		1993	75.6	
Percentage using condoms	1975	10.0		1993	7.7	
Population policies						
Government's view on the level of fertility	1976	Satisfactory		2001	Satisfactory	
Government's policy regarding level of fertility	1976	No intervention		2001	No intervention	
Government's support for contraceptive methods	1976	Indirect support		2001	Indirect support	

Total fertility rates

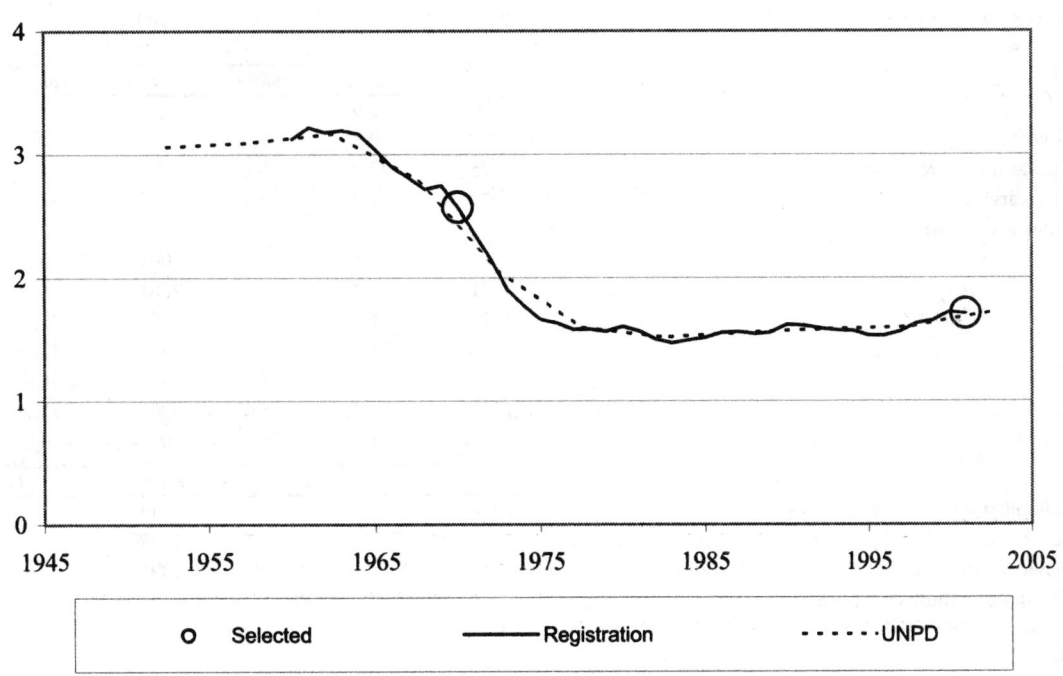

Age-specific fertility rates

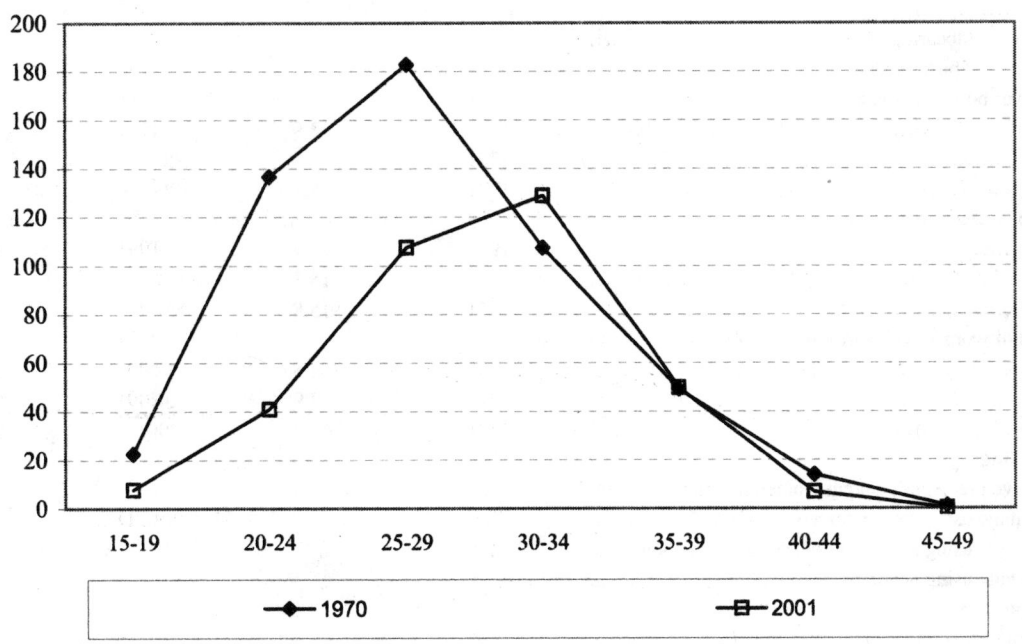

Netherlands Antilles

Indicator	Period					
	Earlier year			Later year		
	Year	Value		Year	Value	
Nuptiality						
Annual number of marriages (*thousands*)	1970	1.4		1999	1.0	
Annual number of divorces (*thousands*)	1974	0.4		1999	0.5	
	Year	Male	Female	Year	Male	Female
Total first marriage rate (per person)	1975	0.9	0.9	..	..	..
Total divorce rate (per person)	1970	0.3	0.3	..	..	..
Mean age at first marriage (years)	1975	27.9	26.4	..	..	..
SMAM (years)	1971	27.3	24.9	2001	32.6	30.2
Percentage ever married by age group						
15-19	1971	0.5	3.5	2001	0.2	0.8
20-24	1971	14.4	28.8	2001	4.6	12.3
25-29	1971	51.6	57.5	2001	21.7	32.8
30-34	1971	72.1	70.9	2001	42.8	46.3
35-39	1971	79.7	75.0	2001	54.6	53.7
40-44	1971	83.0	76.8	2001	62.7	59.0
45-49	1971	84.0	78.9	2001	70.8	66.4
Fertility	Year	Value		Year	Value	
Annual number of births (*thousands*)	1970	4.7		1999	2.8	
Crude birth rate (per 1 000 population)	1970	29.9		1999	13.7	
Percentage of extra-marital births among all births	1970	30.8		1991	54.7	
Total fertility rate (births per woman)	..	..		..	..	
Age-specific fertility rate (per 1 000 women)						
15-19	..	..		..	..	
20-24	..	..		..	..	
25-29	..	..		..	..	
30-34	..	..		..	..	
35-39	..	..		..	..	
40-44	..	..		..	..	
45-49	..	..		..	..	
Mean age at childbearing (years)	..	..		..	..	
Mean age at first birth (years)	..	..		..	..	
Children ever born per woman						
35-39	1971	3.9		2001	2.0	
40-44	1971	4.7		2001	2.2	
45-49	1971	5.1		2001	2.3	
Percentage of childless women						
35-39	1971	15.7		2001	18.0	
40-44	1971	15.3		2001	15.7	
45-49	1971	15.8		2001	15.1	
Percentage of women with parity three or higher						
35-39	1971	62.8		2001	29.4	
40-44	1971	67.9		2001	35.3	
45-49	1971	68.5		2001	38.5	
Family Planning						
Contraceptive prevalence among women in union						
Percentage using any contraceptive method	..	..		..	..	
Percentage using a modern contraceptive method	..	..		..	..	
Percentage using condoms	..	..		..	..	
Population policies						
Government's view on the level of fertility	..	--		..	--	
Government's policy regarding level of fertility	..	--		..	--	
Government's support for contraceptive methods	..	--		..	--	

Total fertility rates

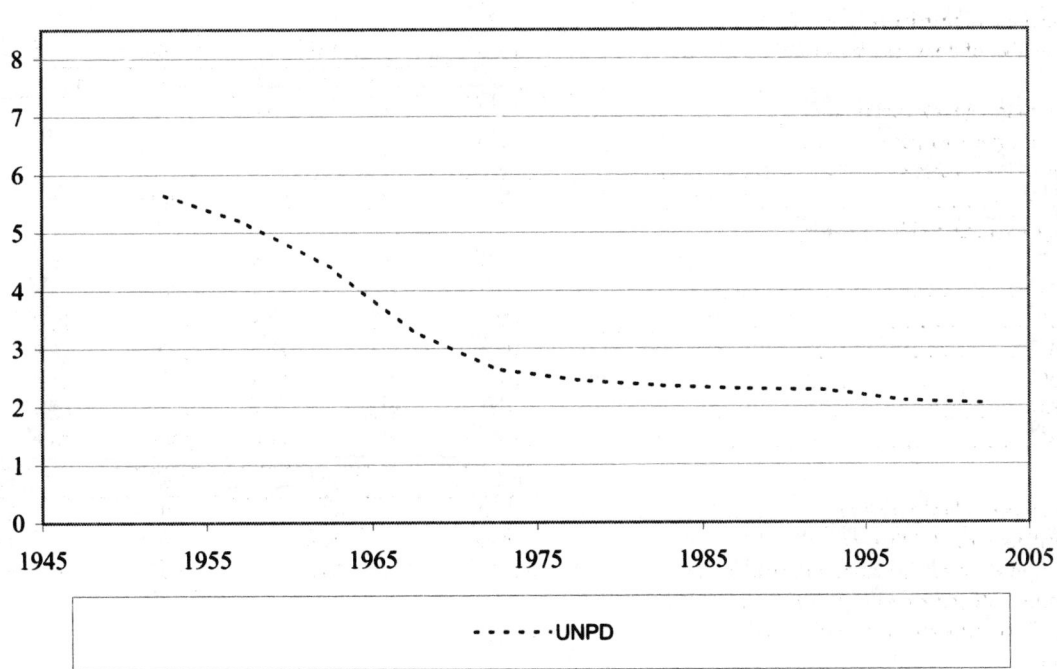

Indicator	Period					
	Earlier year			Later year		
	Year	Value		Year	Value	
Nuptiality						
Annual number of marriages (*thousands*)	1970	1.0		1999	0.9	
Annual number of divorces (*thousands*)	1970	0.1		1999	0.2	
	Year	Male	Female	Year	Male	Female
Total first marriage rate (per person)	1976	0.6	0.6	..	..	..
Total divorce rate (per person)	1976	0.1	0.1	1993	0.1	0.2
Mean age at first marriage (years)	1976	26.2	22.8	..	..	..
SMAM (years)	1969	25.4	21.6	1996	32.5	30.4
Percentage ever married by age group						
15-19	1969	6.2	18.5	1996	0.1	1.2
20-24	1969	21.1	59.1	1996	4.1	13.1
25-29	1969	59.5	78.4	1996	21.6	35.7
30-34	1969	74.4	85.3	1996	42.7	53.7
35-39	1969	79.7	87.9	1996	58.3	65.9
40-44	1969	82.8	87.9	1996	66.9	74.9
45-49	1969	84.1	89.1	1996	75.2	81.1
Fertility	Year	Value		Year	Value	
Annual number of births (*thousands*)...............................	1970	3.9		1999	4.3	
Crude birth rate (per 1 000 population)	1970	35.0		1999	20.8	
Percentage of extra-marital births among all births	1982	45.8		1994	62.5	
Total fertility rate (births per woman)	1970	5.3		1999	2.5	
Age-specific fertility rate (per 1 000 women)						
15-19	1970	127		1999	14	
20-24	1970	311		1999	113	
25-29	1970	243		1999	156	
30-34	1970	180		1999	127	
35-39	1970	126		1999	70	
40-44	1970	62		1999	22	
45-49	1970	8		1999	1	
Mean age at childbearing (years)	1970	27.9		1999	29.5	
Mean age at first birth (years)	1976	23.6		..	..	
Children ever born per woman						
35-39	..	..		..	..	
40-44	..	..		..	..	
45-49	..	..		..	..	
Percentage of childless women						
35-39	..	..		..	..	
40-44	..	..		..	..	
45-49	..	..		..	..	
Percentage of women with parity three or higher						
35-39	..	..		..	..	
40-44	..	..		..	..	
45-49	..	..		..	..	
Family Planning						
Contraceptive prevalence among women in union						
Percentage using any contraceptive method	..	..		..	..	
Percentage using a modern contraceptive method	..	..		..	..	
Percentage using condoms	..	..		..	..	
Population policies						
Government's view on the level of fertility	1976	--		2001	--	
Government's policy regarding level of fertility	1976	--		2001	--	
Government's support for contraceptive methods	1976	--		2001	--	

Total fertility rates

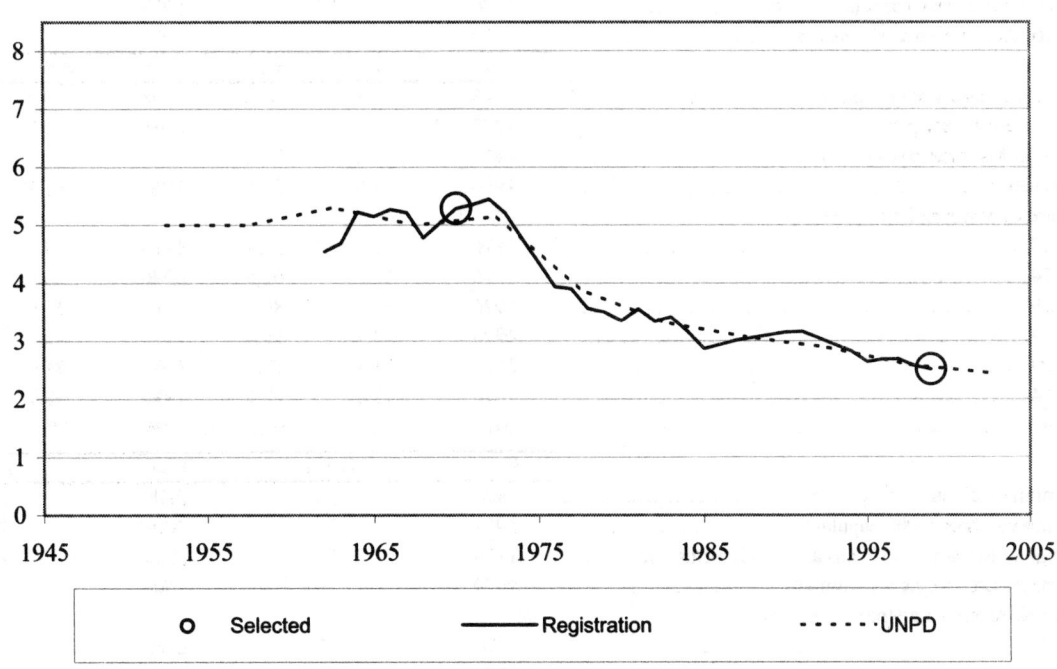

Age-specific fertility rates

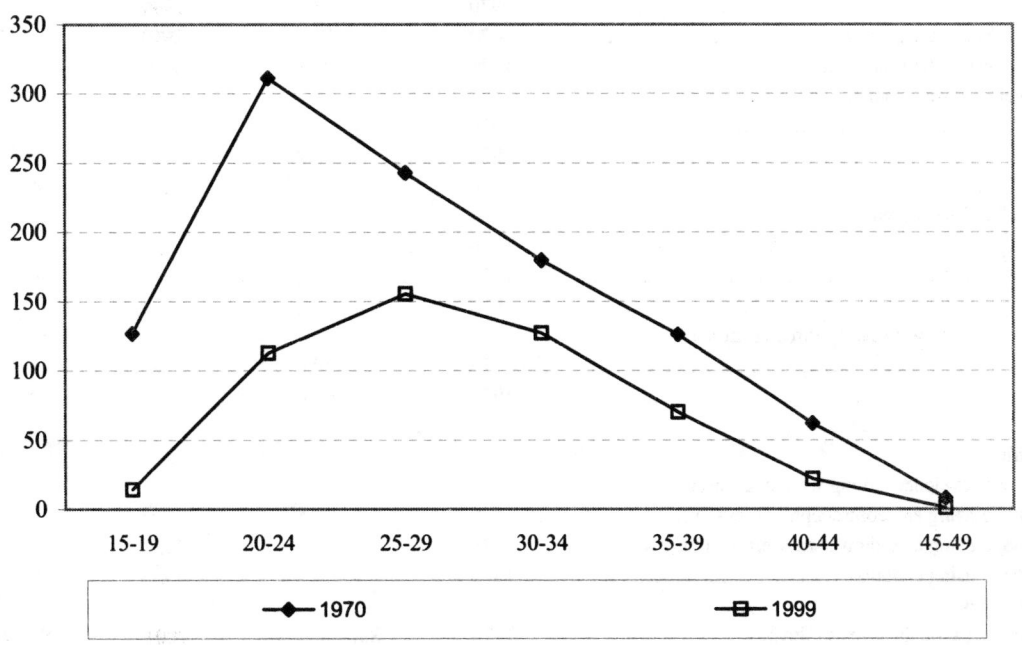

Indicator	Period			
	Earlier year		Later year	
	Year	Value	Year	Value
Nuptiality				
Annual number of marriages (*thousands*)	1970	26.0	1999	21.1
Annual number of divorces (*thousands*)	1970	3.1	1999	9.9

	Year	Male	Female	Year	Male	Female
Total first marriage rate (per person)	1975	0.8	0.8	1998	0.5	0.5
Total divorce rate (per person)	1970	0.1	0.1	1997	0.3	0.3
Mean age at first marriage (years)	1975	25.0	22.4	1998	29.2	27.1
SMAM (years)	1976	24.0	21.5	1996	27.2	25.4
Percentage ever married by age group						
15-19	1976	2.0	10.3	1996	3.0	6.9
20-24	1976	36.3	62.5	1996	23.9	36.7
25-29	1976	76.9	88.2	1996	55.1	67.5
30-34	1976	88.9	93.8	1996	75.7	82.4
35-39	1976	91.8	95.3	1996	85.6	89.2
40-44	1976	92.4	95.6	1996	90.7	93.3
45-49	1976	92.1	95.3	1996	93.3	95.3

	Year	Value	Year	Value
Fertility				
Annual number of births (*thousands*)................................	1970	62.2	2000	56.6
Crude birth rate (per 1 000 population)	1970	22.1	2000	14.8
Percentage of extra-marital births among all births	1970	13.3	1998	42.5
Total fertility rate (births per woman)	1970	3.1	2000	2.0
Age-specific fertility rate (per 1 000 women)				
15-19	1970	62	2000	29
20-24	1970	209	2000	78
25-29	1970	200	2000	116
30-34	1970	100	2000	116
35-39	1970	45	2000	53
40-44	1970	12	2000	10
45-49	1970	1	2000	0
Mean age at childbearing (years)	1970	26.7	2000	29.0
Mean age at first birth (years)	1970	24.0	1998	29.6
Children ever born per woman				
35-39	1976	2.9	..	..
40-44	1976	3.2	..	..
45-49	1976	3.2	..	..
Percentage of childless women				
35-39	1976	5.2	..	..
40-44	1976	5.2	..	..
45-49	1976	6.2	..	..
Percentage of women with parity three or higher				
35-39	1976	59.0	..	..
40-44	1976	63.6	..	..
45-49	1976	61.4	..	..
Family Planning				
Contraceptive prevalence among women in union				
Percentage using any contraceptive method	1976	69.5	1995	74.9
Percentage using a modern contraceptive method	1976	61.5	1995	72.0
Percentage using condoms	1976	8.0	1995	12.4
Population policies				
Government's view on the level of fertility	1976	Satisfactory	2001	Satisfactory
Government's policy regarding level of fertility	1976	No intervention	2001	No intervention
Government's support for contraceptive methods	1976	Direct support	2001	Indirect support

Total fertility rates

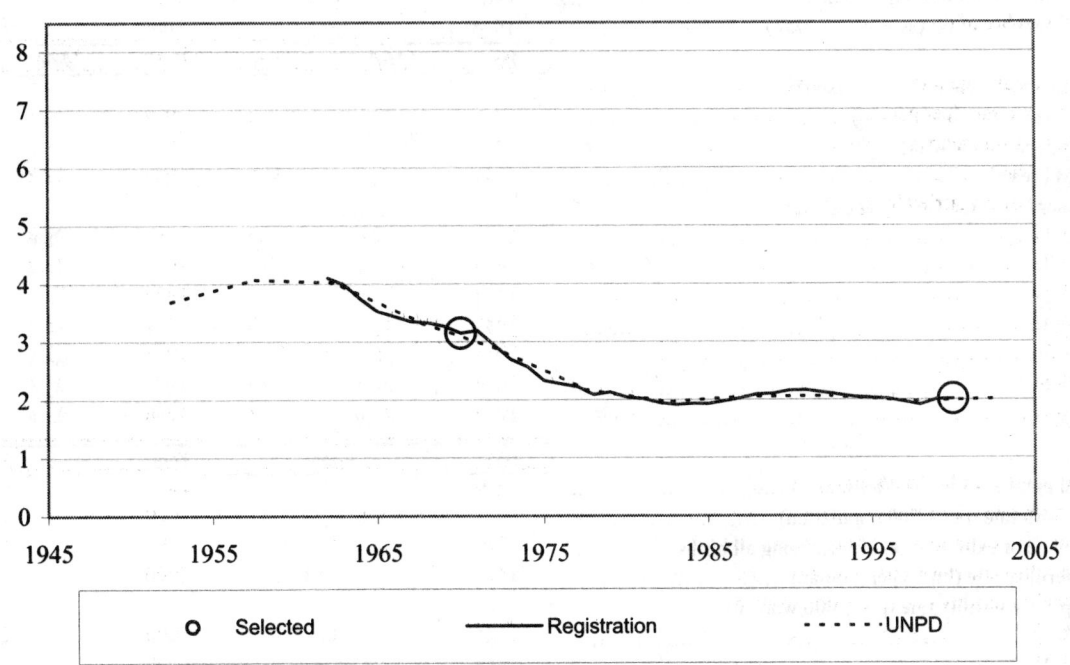

Age-specific fertility rates

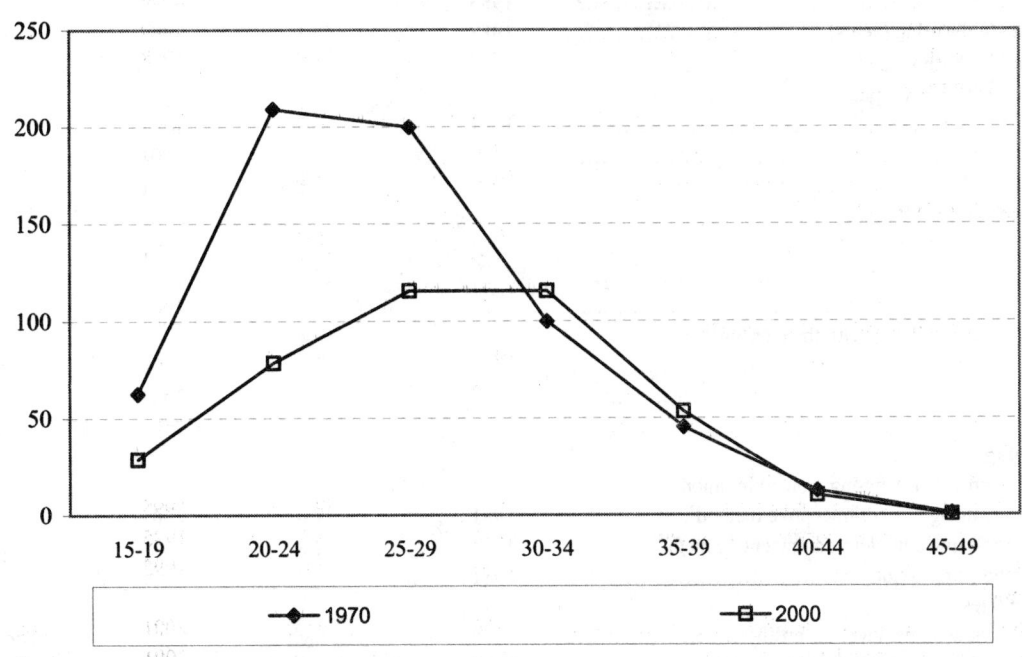

Nicaragua

Indicator	Period					
	Earlier year			Later year		
	Year	Value		Year	Value	
Nuptiality						
Annual number of marriages (*thousands*)	1969	7.4		1999	28.0	
Annual number of divorces (*thousands*)	1975	0.7		1990	0.9	
	Year	Male	Female	Year	Male	Female
Total first marriage rate (per person)	..	..	..	..	..	..
Total divorce rate (per person)	..	..	..	..	..	..
Mean age at first marriage (years)	..	..	..	..	..	..
SMAM (years)	1971	24.7	20.2	1998	24.3	20.6
Percentage ever married by age group						
15-19	1971	4.0	22.1	1998	8.6	31.9
20-24	1971	36.1	62.0	1998	46.4	69.0
25-29	1971	68.2	80.8	1998	74.2	85.9
30-34	1971	81.1	86.2	1998	84.2	93.7
35-39	1971	86.1	88.0	1998	88.3	96.8
40-44	1971	88.4	87.3	1998	92.6	96.0
45-49	1971	89.9	87.3	1998	94.8	97.9
Fertility	Year	Value		Year	Value	
Annual number of births (*thousands*)	..	..		..	..	
Crude birth rate (per 1 000 population)	..	..		..	..	
Percentage of extra-marital births among all births	..	..		..	..	
Total fertility rate (births per woman)	1983	5.8		1999	3.3	
Age-specific fertility rate (per 1 000 women)						
15-19	1983	182		1999	119	
20-24	1983	275		1999	182	
25-29	1983	264		1999	149	
30-34	1983	208		1999	114	
35-39	1983	150		1999	67	
40-44	1983	62		1999	10	
45-49	1983	17		1999	0	
Mean age at childbearing (years)	1983	27.1		1999	26.4	
Mean age at first birth (years)[a]	..	..		1997-1998	19.8	
Children ever born per woman						
35-39	1971	6.2		2001	4.3	
40-44	1971	6.7		2001	5.1	
45-49	1971	6.8		2001	5.7	
Percentage of childless women						
35-39	..	..		2001	4.1	
40-44	..	..		2001	2.8	
45-49	..	..		2001	4.0	
Percentage of women with parity three or higher						
35-39	..	..		2001	73.0	
40-44	..	..		2001	79.8	
45-49	..	..		2001	84.6	
Family Planning						
Contraceptive prevalence among women in union						
Percentage using any contraceptive method	1981	27.0		2001	68.6	
Percentage using a modern contraceptive method	1981	22.8		2001	66.1	
Percentage using condoms	1981	0.8		2001	3.3	
Population policies						
Government's view on the level of fertility	1976	Too high		2001	Too high	
Government's policy regarding level of fertility	1976	No intervention		2001	Lower	
Government's support for contraceptive methods	1976	Direct support		2001	Direct support	

[a]Median age at first birth among women aged 25-29 at the date of the survey

Total fertility rates

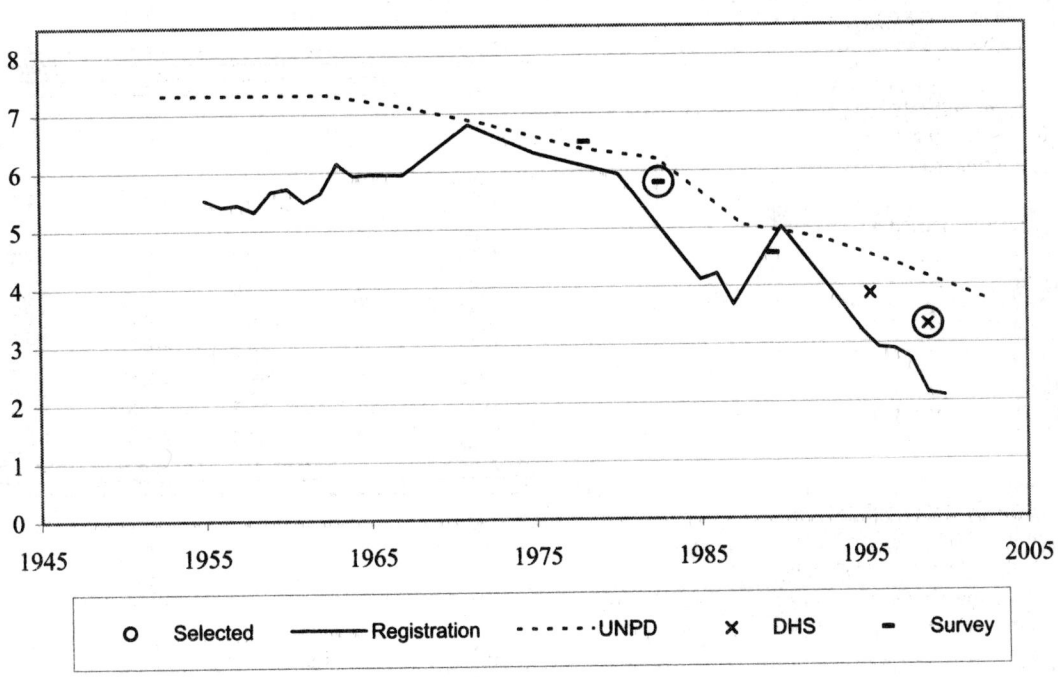

Age-specific fertility rates

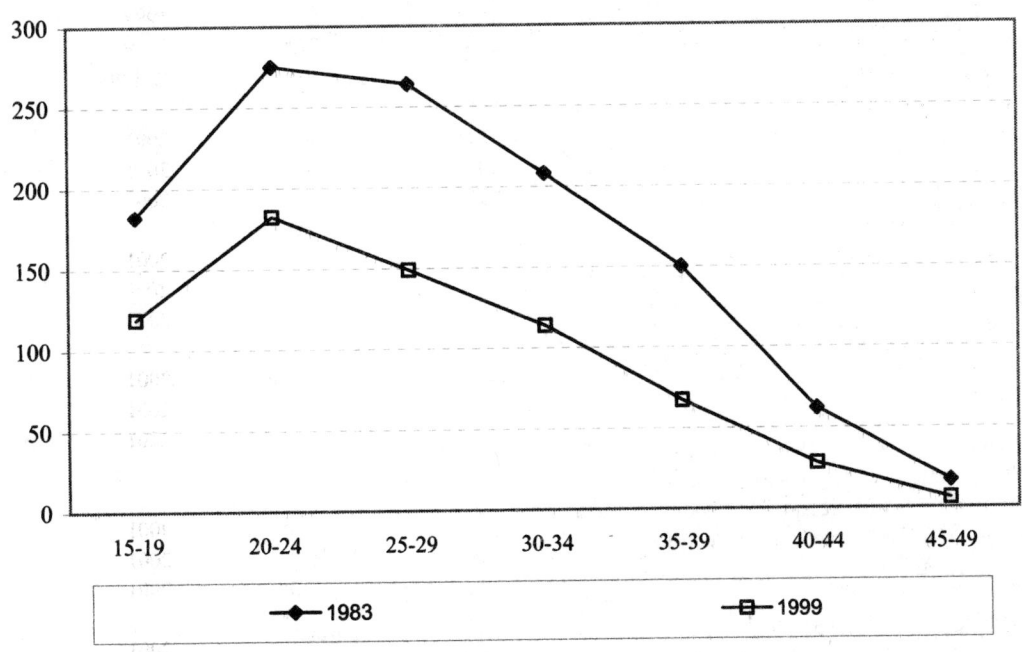

Indicator	Period					
	Earlier year			Later year		
	Year	Value		Year	Value	
Nuptiality						
Annual number of marriages (*thousands*)	..	..		..	..	
Annual number of divorces (*thousands*)	..	..		..	..	
	Year	Male	Female	Year	Male	Female
Total first marriage rate (per person)	..	..	..	..	..	..
Total divorce rate (per person)	..	..	..	..	..	..
Mean age at first marriage (years)	..	..	..	..	..	..
SMAM (years)	1959	21.6	15.8	1998	23.9	17.6
Percentage ever married by age group						
15-19	1959	12.8	86.3	1998	4.2	61.9
20-24	1959	67.5	98.7	1998	41.8	88.9
25-29	1959	90.8	99.5	1998	83.6	97.4
30-34	1959	97.4	99.8	1998	93.8	99.0
35-39	1959	98.8	100.0	1998	98.4	100.0
40-44	1959	99.5	99.8	1998	99.4	99.7
45-49	1959	99.2	99.9	1998	99.6	99.8
Fertility	Year	Value		Year	Value	
Annual number of births (*thousands*).........................	..	..		..	..	
Crude birth rate (per 1 000 population)	..	..		..	..	
Percentage of extra-marital births among all births	..	..		..	..	
Total fertility rate (births per woman)	..	..		1997	7.5	
Age-specific fertility rate (per 1 000 women)						
15-19	..	..		1997	216	
20-24	..	..		1997	322	
25-29	..	..		1997	319	
30-34	..	..		1997	293	
35-39	..	..		1997	206	
40-44	..	..		1997	96	
45-49	..	..		1997	42	
Mean age at childbearing (years)	..	..		1997	28.9	
Mean age at first birth (years)[a]	..	..		2001	19.6	
Children ever born per woman						
35-39	..	..		1998	6.9	
40-44	..	..		1998	7.4	
45-49	..	..		1998	7.6	
Percentage of childless women						
35-39	..	..		1998	1.6	
40-44	..	..		1998	2.9	
45-49	..	..		1998	5.6	
Percentage of women with parity three or higher						
35-39	..	..		1998	93.1	
40-44	..	..		1998	93.1	
45-49	..	..		1998	87.7	
Family Planning						
Contraceptive prevalence among women in union						
Percentage using any contraceptive method	..	..		2000	14.0	
Percentage using a modern contraceptive method	..	..		2000	4.3	
Percentage using condoms	..	..		2000	0.0	
Population policies						
Government's view on the level of fertility	1976	Satisfactory		2001	Too high	
Government's policy regarding level of fertility	1976	No intervention		2001	Lower	
Government's support for contraceptive methods	1976	No support		2001	Direct support	

[a]Median age at first birth among women aged 25-29 at the date of the survey

Total fertility rates

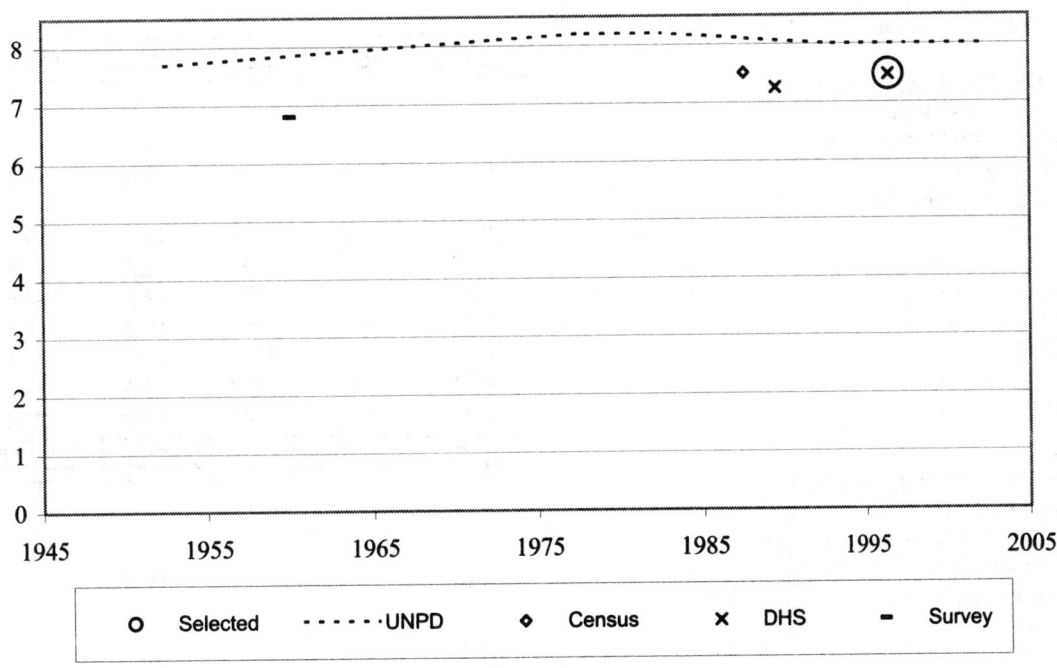

Age-specific fertility rates

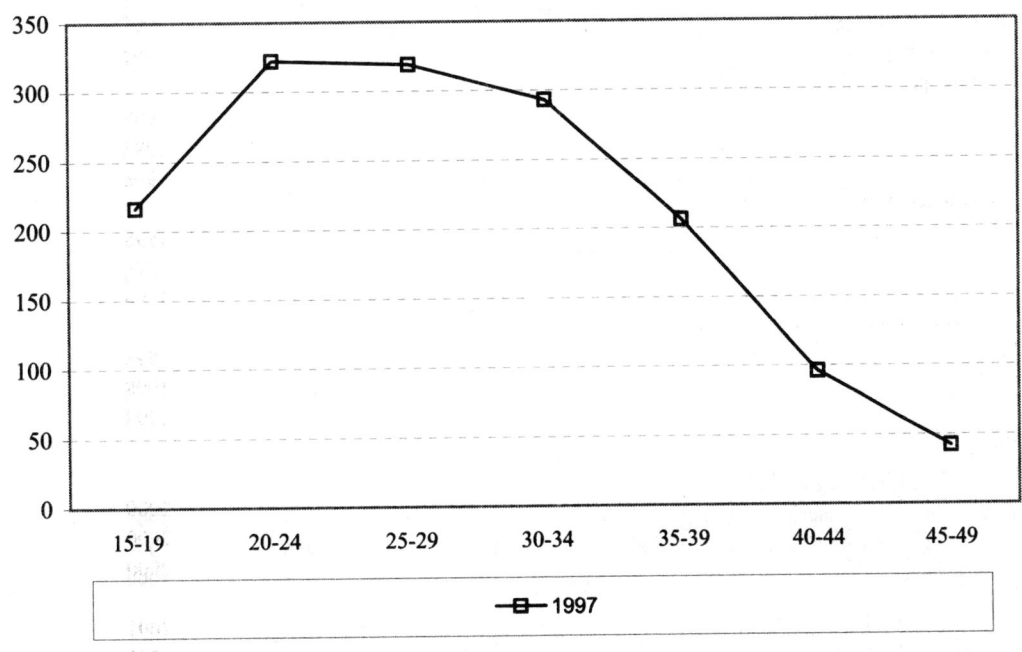

Nigeria

Indicator	Period					
	Earlier year			Later year		
	Year	Value		Year	Value	
Nuptiality						
Annual number of marriages (*thousands*)	..	..		..	..	
Annual number of divorces (*thousands*)	..	..		..	..	
	Year	Male	Female	Year	Male	Female
Total first marriage rate (per person)	..	..	..	..	..	..
Total divorce rate (per person)	..	..	..	..	..	..
Mean age at first marriage (years)	..	..	..	..	..	..
SMAM (years)	..	..	..	1999	27.2	21.4
Percentage ever married by age group						
15-19	..	..	..	1999	3.0	27.5
20-24	..	..	..	1999	17.2	63.5
25-29	..	..	..	1999	58.0	87.0
30-34	..	..	..	1999	84.8	94.9
35-39	..	..	..	1999	94.8	98.1
40-44	..	..	..	1999	97.4	98.7
45-49	..	..	..	1999	100.0	98.9
Fertility	Year	Value		Year	Value	
Annual number of births (*thousands*)	..	..		..	..	
Crude birth rate (per 1 000 population)	..	..		..	..	
Percentage of extra-marital births among all births	..	..		..	..	
Total fertility rate (births per woman)	1980	6.3		1997	5.1	
Age-specific fertility rate (per 1 000 women)						
15-19	1980	173		1997	111	
20-24	1980	284		1997	220	
25-29	1980	274		1997	239	
30-34	1980	231		1997	226	
35-39	1980	147		1997	138	
40-44	1980	100		1997	71	
45-49	1980	60		1997	24	
Mean age at childbearing (years)	1980	29.2		1997	29.3	
Mean age at first birth (years)[a]	..	..		1999	20.4	
Children ever born per woman						
35-39	..	..		1999	5.2	
40-44	..	..		1999	6.0	
45-49	..	..		1999	6.3	
Percentage of childless women						
35-39	..	..		1999	3.5	
40-44	..	..		1999	4.2	
45-49	..	..		1999	3.0	
Percentage of women with parity three or higher						
35-39	..	..		1999	85.6	
40-44	..	..		1999	89.5	
45-49	..	..		1999	88.6	
Family Planning						
Contraceptive prevalence among women in union						
Percentage using any contraceptive method	1982	4.8		1999	15.3	
Percentage using a modern contraceptive method	1982	0.6		1999	8.6	
Percentage using condoms	1982	0.0		1999	1.2	
Population policies						
Government's view on the level of fertility	1976	Satisfactory		2001	Too high	
Government's policy regarding level of fertility	1976	No intervention		2001	Lower	
Government's support for contraceptive methods	1976	Direct support		2001	Direct support	

[a]Median age at first birth among women aged 25-29 at the date of the survey

Total fertility rates

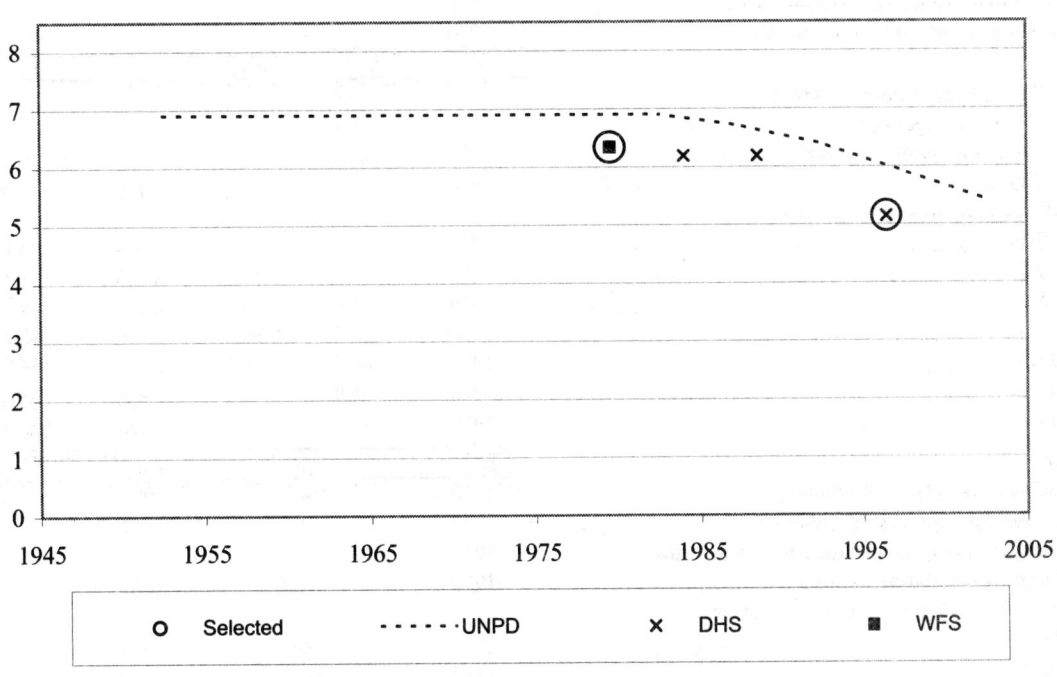

Age-specific fertility rates

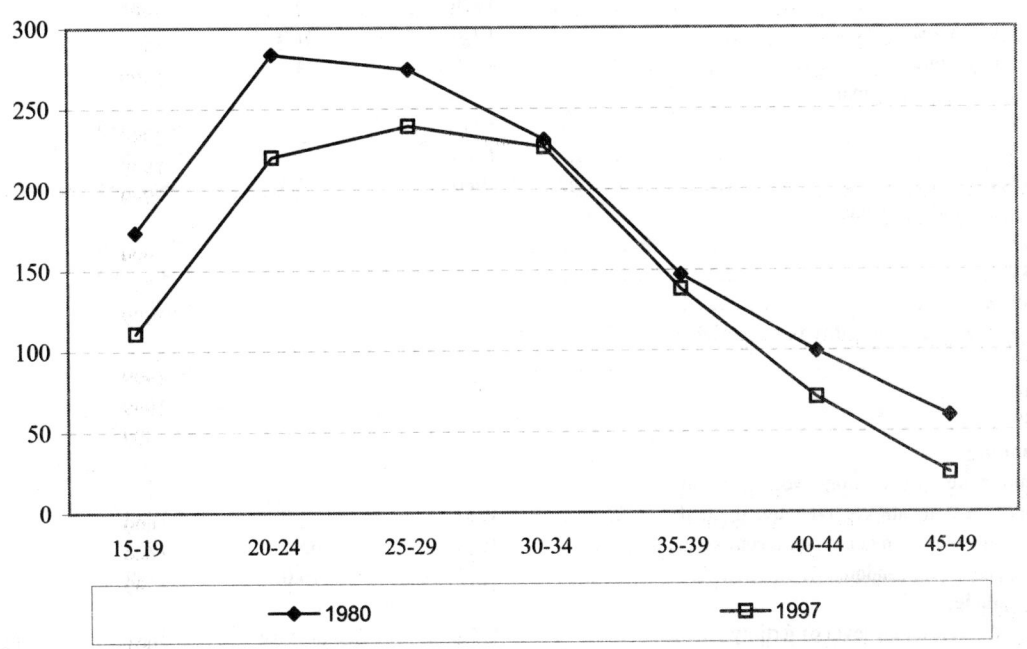

Indicator	Period					
	Earlier year			Later year		
	Year	Value		Year	Value	
Nuptiality						
Annual number of marriages (*thousands*)	1970	29.4		2001	23.0	
Annual number of divorces (*thousands*)	1970	3.4		2001	10.3	
	Year	Male	Female	Year	Male	Female
Total first marriage rate (per person)	1975	0.8	0.8	1998	0.5	0.5
Total divorce rate (per person)	1970	0.1	0.1	1997	0.2	0.3
Mean age at first marriage (years)	1975	25.5	22.9	1998	30.7	28.3
SMAM (years)	1970	24.9	21.9	2002	33.7	31.4
Percentage ever married by age group						
15-19	1970	0.6	4.9	2002	0.1	0.5
20-24	1970	26.9	52.4	2002	3.3	8.7
25-29	1970	68.4	84.0	2002	18.1	31.5
30-34	1970	83.3	92.1	2002	41.9	56.7
35-39	1970	86.4	93.5	2002	59.7	71.2
40-44	1970	86.9	93.1	2002	72.6	81.5
45-49	1970	87.2	91.7	2002	81.8	88.7
Fertility	Year	Value		Year	Value	
Annual number of births (*thousands*)	1970	64.6		2002	55.4	
Crude birth rate (per 1 000 population)	1970	16.6		2002	12.3	
Percentage of extra-marital births among all births	1970	6.9		2001	49.7	
Total fertility rate (births per woman)	1970	2.5		2001	1.8	
Age-specific fertility rate (per 1 000 women)						
15-19	1970	46		2001	11	
20-24	1970	166		2001	62	
25-29	1970	149		2001	123	
30-34	1970	88		2001	108	
35-39	1970	41		2001	45	
40-44	1970	11		2001	7	
45-49	1970	1		2001	0	
Mean age at childbearing (years)	1970	27.0		2001	29.4	
Mean age at first birth (years)	1970	24.0		2001	27.0	
Children ever born per woman						
35-39	1960	2.2		1988-1989	1.8	
40-44	1960	2.4		1988-1989	2.1	
45-49	1960	2.3		1988-1989	2.2	
Percentage of childless women						
35-39	..	..		1988-1989	15.8	
40-44	..	..		1988-1989	9.4	
45-49	..	..		1988-1989	6.6	
Percentage of women with parity three or higher						
35-39	..	..		1988-1989	21.2	
40-44	..	..		1988-1989	28.8	
45-49	..	..		1988-1989	35.8	
Family Planning						
Contraceptive prevalence among women in union						
Percentage using any contraceptive method	1977	71.0		1989	73.8	
Percentage using a modern contraceptive method	1977	65.0		1989	69.2	
Percentage using condoms	1977	16.0		1989	12.5	
Population policies						
Government's view on the level of fertility	1976	Satisfactory		2001	Satisfactory	
Government's policy regarding level of fertility	1976	No intervention		2001	No intervention	
Government's support for contraceptive methods	1976	Direct support		2001	Direct support	

Total fertility rates

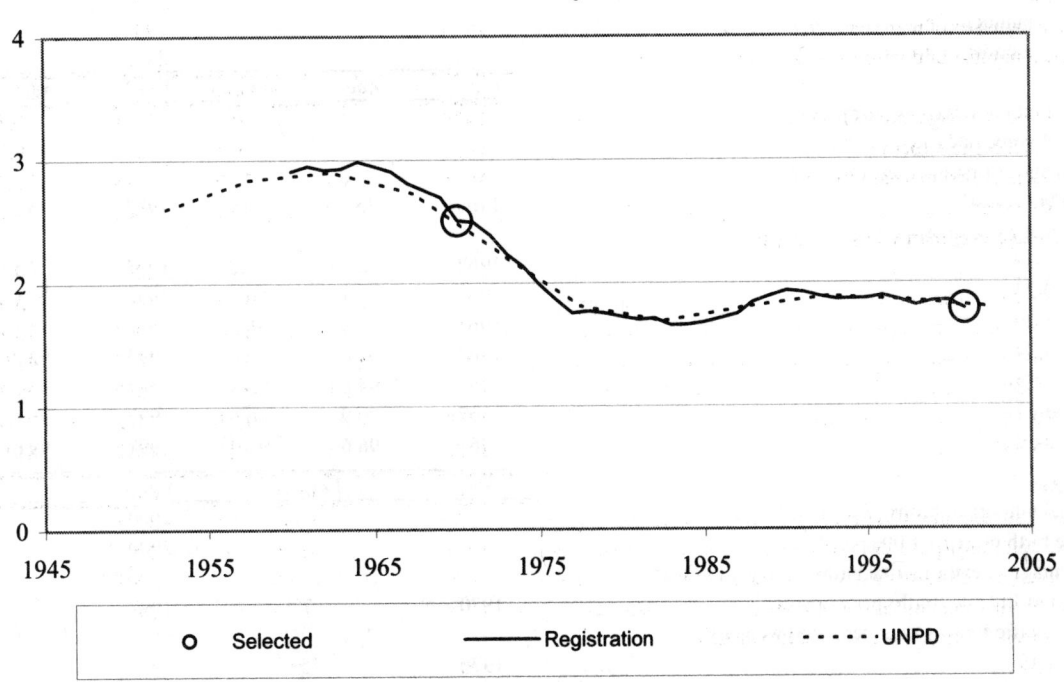

Age-specific fertility rates

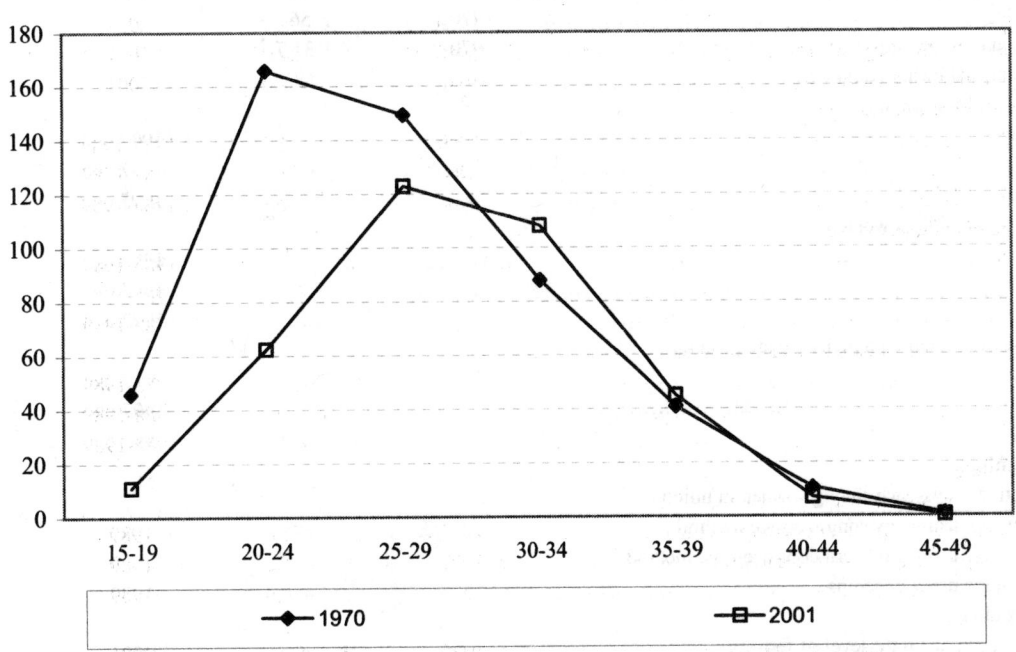

Indicator	Period					
	Earlier year			Later year		
	Year	Value		Year	Value	

Nuptiality

	Year	Value		Year	Value	
Annual number of marriages (*thousands*)	..	..		2000	23.9	
Annual number of divorces (*thousands*)	..	..		2000	3.5	

	Year	Male	Female	Year	Male	Female
Total first marriage rate (per person)	..	..	..	..	..	..
Total divorce rate (per person)	..	..	..	..	..	..
Mean age at first marriage (years)	..	..	..	..	..	..
SMAM (years)	1967	25.2	21.9	1997	25.3	21.7
Percentage ever married by age group						
15-19	1967	2.3	17.2	1997	2.1	24.2
20-24	1967	29.1	60.7	1997	27.9	64.0
25-29	1967	69.9	86.2	1997	71.1	80.1
30-34	1967	91.0	92.0	1997	92.2	83.4
35-39	1967	94.8	95.4	1997	97.6	88.1
40-44	1967	96.9	96.6	1997	98.4	91.2
45-49	1967	96.6	97.0	1997	99.0	92.4

Fertility

	Year	Value		Year	Value	
Annual number of births (*thousands*)	..	..		2000	96.9	
Crude birth rate (per 1 000 population)	..	..		2000	30.8	
Percentage of extra-marital births among all births	..	..		..	..	
Total fertility rate (births per woman)	1970	7.5		1997	6.1	
Age-specific fertility rate (per 1 000 women)						
15-19	1970	55		..	..	
20-24	1970	242		..	..	
25-29	1970	340		..	..	
30-34	1970	343		..	..	
35-39	1970	330		..	..	
40-44	1970	129		..	..	
45-49	1970	56		..	..	
Mean age at childbearing (years)	1970	31.7		..	..	
Mean age at first birth (years)	..	..		..	..	
Children ever born per woman						
35-39	..	..		1997	6.3	
40-44	..	..		1997	7.4	
45-49	..	..		1997	7.5	
Percentage of childless women						
35-39	..	..		1997	4.7	
40-44	..	..		1997	4.6	
45-49	..	..		1997	5.2	
Percentage of women with parity three or higher						
35-39	..	..		1997	89.1	
40-44	..	..		1997	90.2	
45-49	..	..		1997	89.6	

Family Planning

Contraceptive prevalence among women in union						
Percentage using any contraceptive method	..	..		..	..	
Percentage using a modern contraceptive method	..	..		..	..	
Percentage using condoms	..	..		..	..	

Population policies

Government's view on the level of fertility	..	--		2001	--	
Government's policy regarding level of fertility	..	--		2001	--	
Government's support for contraceptive methods	..	--		2001	--	

Total fertility rates

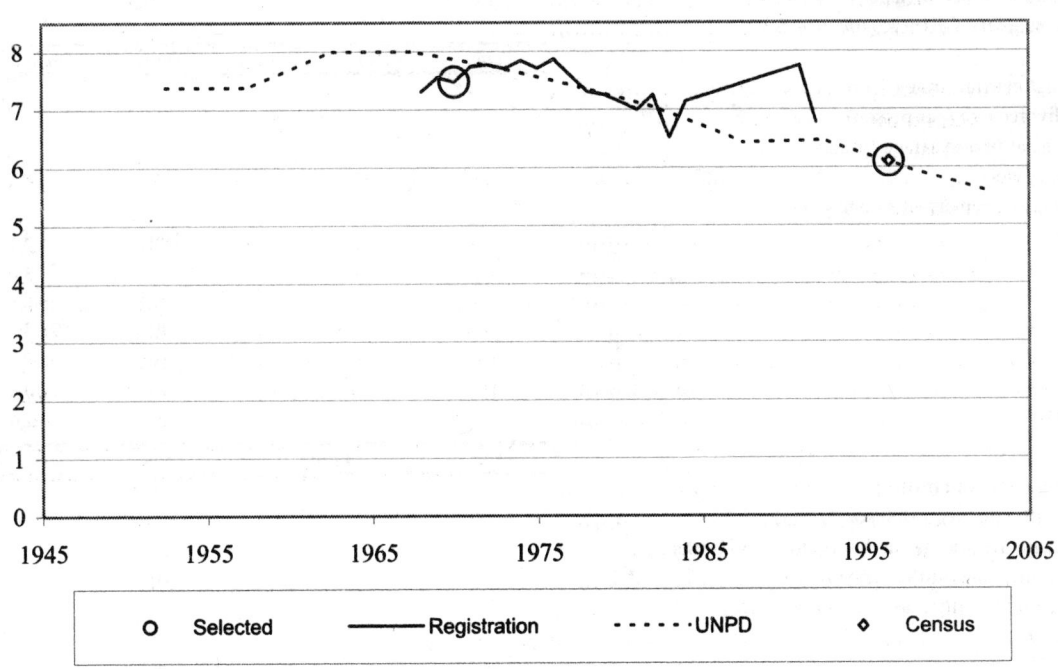

Age-specific fertility rates

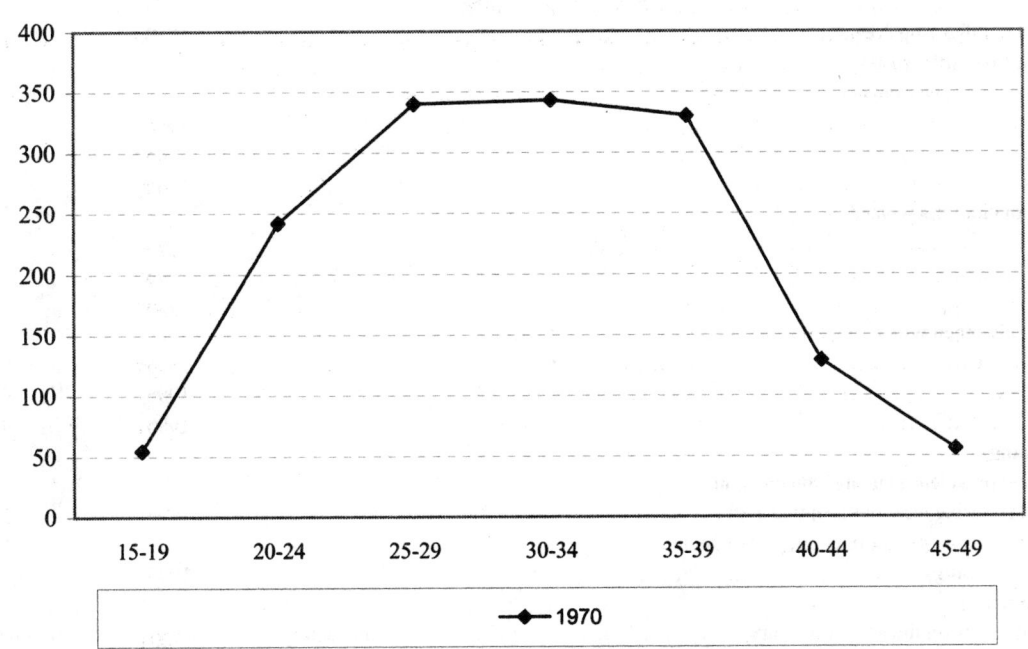

Oman

Indicator	Period			
	Earlier year		Later year	
	Year	Value	Year	Value
Nuptiality				
Annual number of marriages (*thousands*)	..	..	..	..
Annual number of divorces (*thousands*)	..	..	..	..

Indicator	Year	Male	Female	Year	Male	Female
Total first marriage rate (per person)	..	..	..	..	..	..
Total divorce rate (per person)	..	..	..	..	..	..
Mean age at first marriage (years)	..	..	..	..	..	..
SMAM (years)	..	..	..	1995	25.9	21.7
Percentage ever married by age group						
15-19	..	..	..	1995	1.3	15.5
20-24	..	..	..	1995	22.4	61.3
25-29	..	..	..	1995	69.2	90.3
30-34	..	..	..	1995	91.3	97.5
35-39	..	..	..	1995	95.0	99.3
40-44	..	..	..	1995	97.7	99.2
45-49	..	..	..	1995	98.2	99.5

Indicator	Year	Value	Year	Value
Fertility				
Annual number of births (*thousands*)	..	..	..	..
Crude birth rate (per 1 000 population)	..	..	..	..
Percentage of extra-marital births among all births	..	..	..	..
Total fertility rate (births per woman)	..	..	1993	7.4
Age-specific fertility rate (per 1 000 women)				
15-19	..	..	1993	100
20-24	..	..	1993	293
25-29	..	..	1993	340
30-34	..	..	1993	315
35-39	..	..	1993	231
40-44	..	..	1993	120
45-49	..	..	1993	79
Mean age at childbearing (years)	..	..	1993	30.7
Mean age at first birth (years)	..	..	..	..
Children ever born per woman				
35-39	..	..	1995	7.9
40-44	..	..	1995	8.6
45-49	..	..	1995	8.6
Percentage of childless women				
35-39	..	..	1995	3.8
40-44	..	..	1995	2.3
45-49	..	..	1995	2.1
Percentage of women with parity three or higher				
35-39	..	..	1995	93.6
40-44	..	..	1995	93.3
45-49	..	..	1995	93.4
Family Planning				
Contraceptive prevalence among women in union				
Percentage using any contraceptive method	..	..	1995	23.7
Percentage using a modern contraceptive method	..	..	1995	18.2
Percentage using condoms	..	..	1995	1.5
Population policies				
Government's view on the level of fertility	1976	Satisfactory	2001	Too high
Government's policy regarding level of fertility	1976	Maintain	2001	Lower
Government's support for contraceptive methods	1976	No support	2001	No support

Total fertility rates

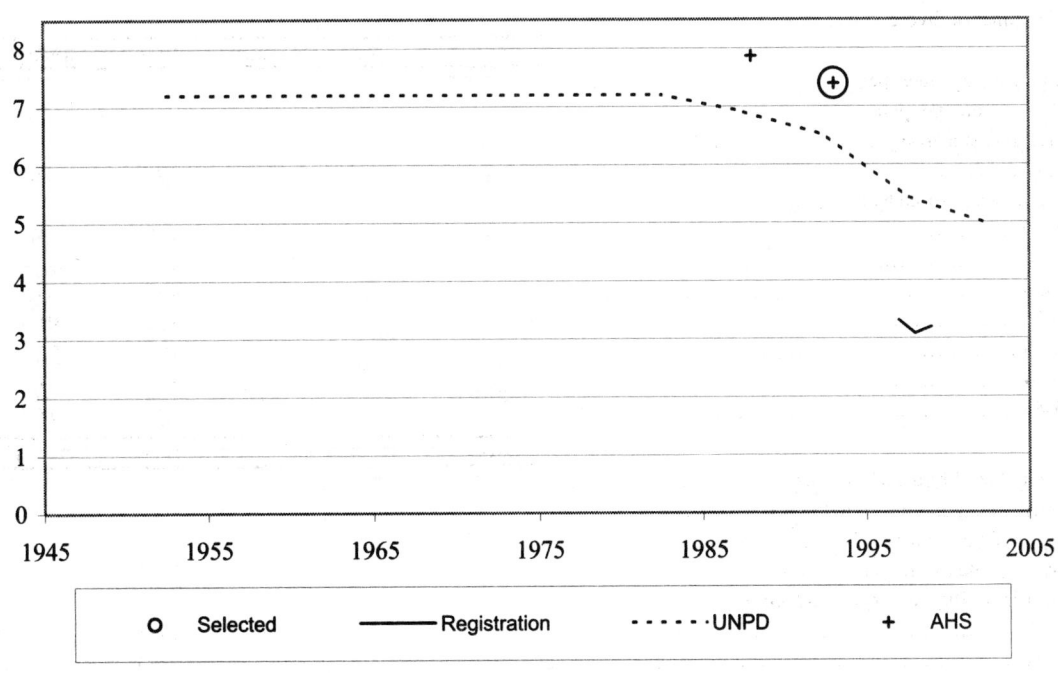

Age-specific fertility rates

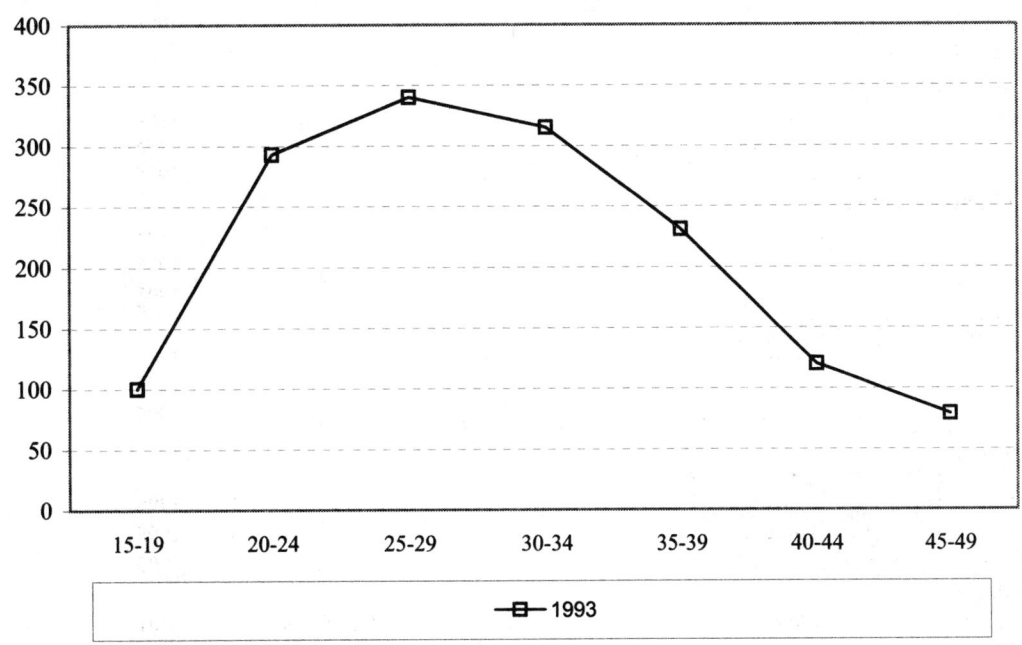

Indicator	Period					
	Earlier year			Later year		
	Year	Value		Year	Value	
Nuptiality						
Annual number of marriages (*thousands*)	..	..		..	..	
Annual number of divorces (*thousands*)	..	..		..	..	
	Year	Male	Female	Year	Male	Female
Total first marriage rate (per person)	..	..	..	..	..	..
Total divorce rate (per person)	..	..	..	..	..	..
Mean age at first marriage (years)	..	..	..	..	..	..
SMAM (years)	1972	25.7	19.7	1998	25.8	21.3
Percentage ever married by age group						
15-19	1972	7.4	34.4	1998	6.1	20.6
20-24	1972	32.2	78.7	1998	30.0	61.4
25-29	1972	63.9	92.8	1998	62.9	93.9
30-34	1972	82.6	96.4	1998	83.9	92.8
35-39	1972	90.8	97.9	1998	91.9	95.6
40-44	1972	93.6	98.1	1998	94.6	96.3
45-49	1972	95.7	98.5	1998	96.2	97.5
Fertility	Year	Value		Year	Value	
Annual number of births (*thousands*)...............................	..	..		..	..	
Crude birth rate (per 1 000 population)	..	..		..	..	
Percentage of extra-marital births among all births	..	..		..	..	
Total fertility rate (births per woman)	1970	6.0		1999	4.8	
Age-specific fertility rate (per 1 000 women)						
15-19	1970	58		1999	65	
20-24	1970	223		1999	211	
25-29	1970	261		1999	258	
30-34	1970	252		1999	206	
35-39	1970	200		1999	128	
40-44	1970	124		1999	61	
45-49	1970	85		1999	26	
Mean age at childbearing (years)	1970	31.8		1999	29.6	
Mean age at first birth (years)[a]	1975	19.9		1990-1991	22.0	
Children ever born per woman						
35-39	1974-1975	5.9		1990-1991	5.5	
40-44	1974-1975	6.9		1990-1991	6.3	
45-49	1974-1975	6.8		1990-1991	6.4	
Percentage of childless women						
35-39	1974-1975	4.4		1990-1991	5.4	
40-44	1974-1975	4.2		1990-1991	5.5	
45-49	1974-1975	2.9		1990-1991	5.5	
Percentage of women with parity three or higher						
35-39	1974-1975	84.9		1990-1991	86.9	
40-44	1974-1975	89.4		1990-1991	90.0	
45-49	1974-1975	88.5		1990-1991	88.4	
Family Planning						
Contraceptive prevalence among women in union						
Percentage using any contraceptive method	1974-1975	5.2		2001	27.6	
Percentage using a modern contraceptive method	1974-1975	3.8		2001	20.2	
Percentage using condoms	1974-1975	1.0		2001	5.5	
Population policies						
Government's view on the level of fertility	1976	Too high		2001	Too high	
Government's policy regarding level of fertility	1976	Lower		2001	Lower	
Government's support for contraceptive methods	1976	Direct support		2001	Direct support	

[a]Median age at first birth among women aged 25-29 at the date of the survey for both dates

Total fertility rates

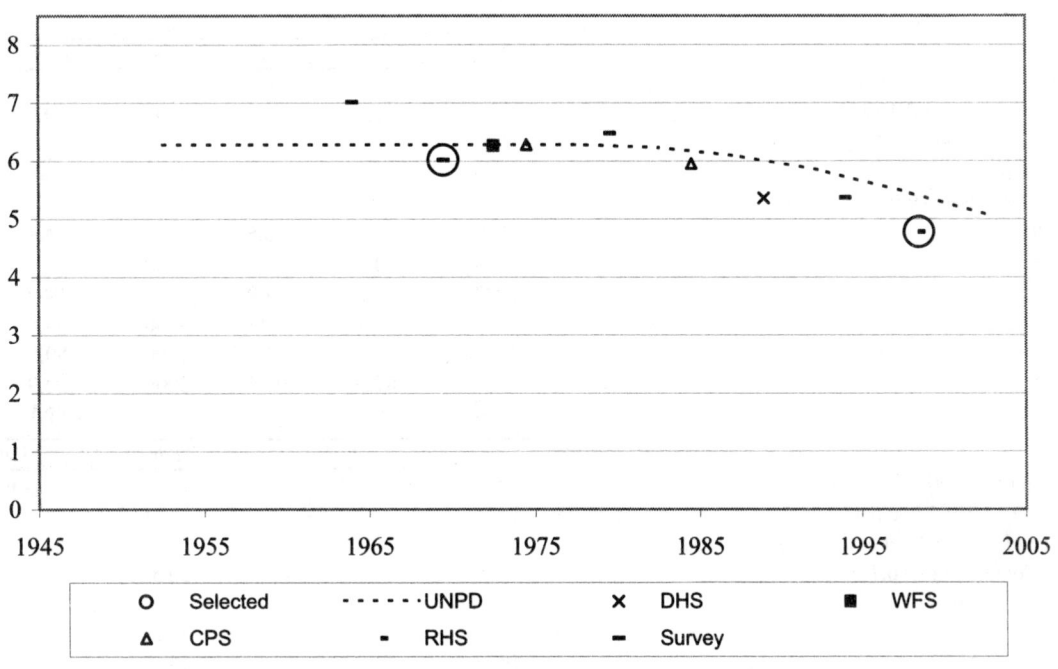

O	Selected	· · · · · UNPD	× DHS	■ WFS
△	CPS	- RHS	- Survey	

Age-specific fertility rates

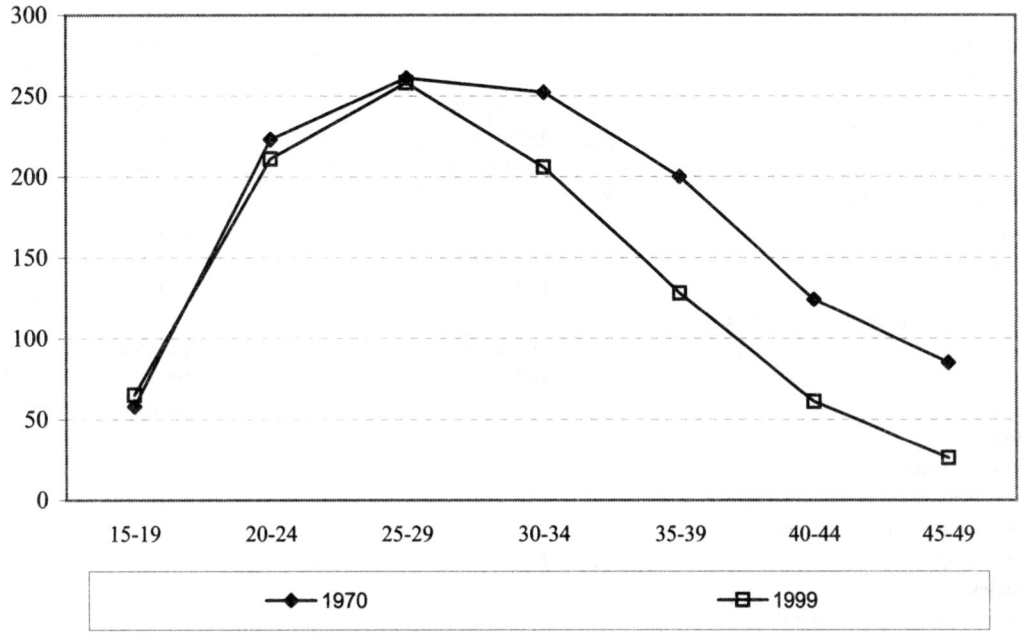

Panama

Indicator	Period					
	Earlier year			Later year		
	Year	Value		Year	Value	
Nuptiality						
Annual number of marriages (*thousands*)	1970	7.3		1999	10.4	
Annual number of divorces (*thousands*)	1970	0.6		2000	2.2	
	Year	Male	Female	Year	Male	Female
Total first marriage rate (per person)	1975	0.4	0.3	..	..	..
Total divorce rate (per person)	1970	0.1	0.1	1997	0.0	0.0
Mean age at first marriage (years)	1975	27.8	24.6	..	..	..
SMAM (years)	1970	24.8	20.4	2000	25.8	21.9
Percentage ever married by age group						
15-19	1970	5.5	26.6	2000	4.8	22.0
20-24	1970	34.2	66.5	2000	32.9	57.6
25-29	1970	65.6	84.9	2000	59.5	75.9
30-34	1970	79.8	91.2	2000	73.8	85.0
35-39	1970	85.0	93.2	2000	80.5	88.7
40-44	1970	87.5	93.4	2000	84.9	90.6
45-49	1970	88.0	93.1	2000	87.1	91.0
Fertility	Year	Value		Year	Value	
Annual number of births (*thousands*)............................	1970	53.3		2000	64.8	
Crude birth rate (per 1 000 population)	1970	35.4		2000	22.7	
Percentage of extra-marital births among all births	1970	70.9		1997	79.9	
Total fertility rate (births per woman)	1970	5.0		2000	2.7	
Age-specific fertility rate (per 1 000 women)						
15-19	1970	134		2000	96	
20-24	1970	280		2000	149	
25-29	1970	246		2000	128	
30-34	1970	174		2000	95	
35-39	1970	115		2000	51	
40-44	1970	40		2000	14	
45-49	1970	8		2000	2	
Mean age at childbearing (years)	1970	27.5		2000	26.6	
Mean age at first birth (years)	1970	21.7		1997	22.3	
Children ever born per woman						
35-39	1975-1976	4.9		1990	3.6	
40-44	1975-1976	5.6		1990	4.2	
45-49	1975-1976	5.8		1990	4.8	
Percentage of childless women						
35-39	1975-1976	1.5		1990	6.3	
40-44	1975-1976	2.5		1990	5.4	
45-49	1975-1976	4.1		1990	5.2	
Percentage of women with parity three or higher						
35-39	1975-1976	70.8		1990	64.4	
40-44	1975-1976	81.1		1990	71.4	
45-49	1975-1976	81.5		1990	76.3	
Family Planning						
Contraceptive prevalence among women in union						
Percentage using any contraceptive method	1975-1976	54.1		..	..	
Percentage using a modern contraceptive method	1975-1976	46.2		..	..	
Percentage using condoms	1975-1976	1.2		..	..	
Population policies						
Government's view on the level of fertility	1976	Too high		2001	Satisfactory	
Government's policy regarding level of fertility	1976	No intervention		2001	Maintain	
Government's support for contraceptive methods	1976	Direct support		2001	Direct support	

Total fertility rates

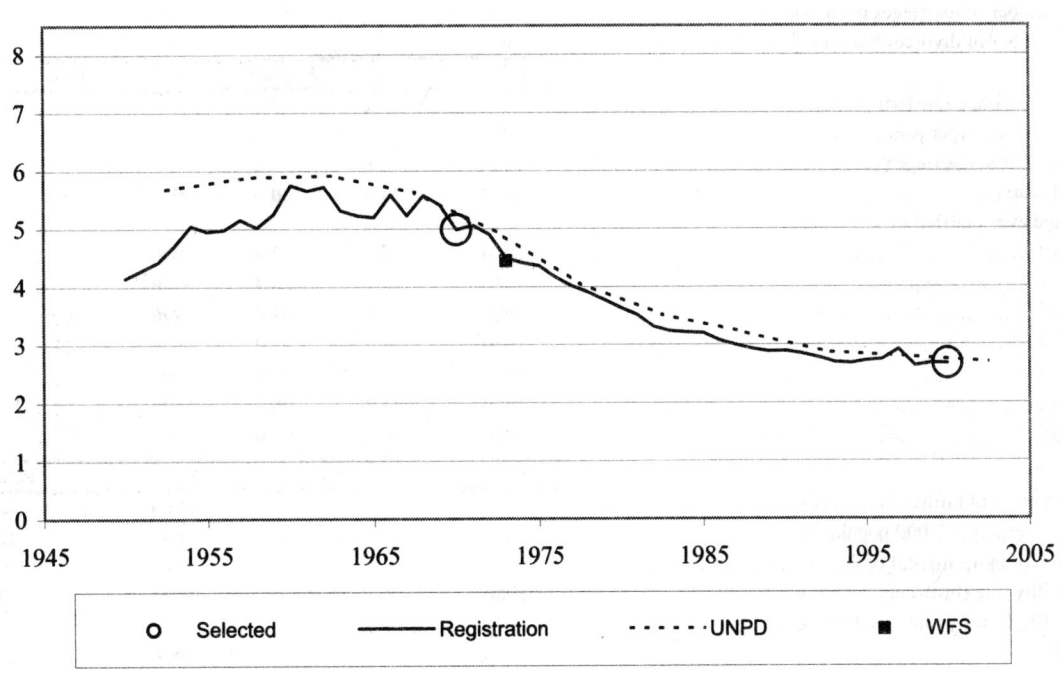

Age-specific fertility rates

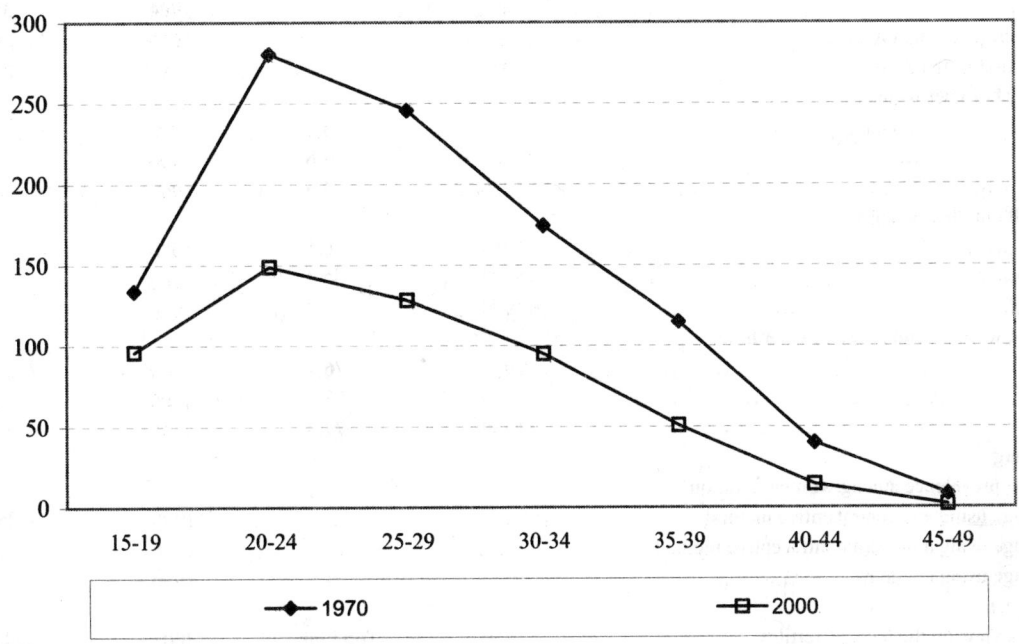

Indicator	Period			
	Earlier year		Later year	
	Year	Value	Year	Value
Nuptiality				
Annual number of marriages (*thousands*)	..	..	..	..
Annual number of divorces (*thousands*)	..	..	..	..

	Year	Male	Female	Year	Male	Female
Total first marriage rate (per person)	..	..	..	..	..	..
Total divorce rate (per person)	..	..	..	..	..	..
Mean age at first marriage (years)	..	..	..	..	..	..
SMAM (years)	1980	24.9	20.6	1996	..	20.8
Percentage ever married by age group						
15-19	1980	4.2	17.6	1996	..	20.8
20-24	1980	36.1	73.4	1996	..	75.1
25-29	1980	70.4	93.4	1996	..	92.8
30-34	1980	86.5	97.0	1996	..	96.6
35-39	1980	91.5	98.0	1996	..	99.0
40-44	1980	93.9	98.1	1996	..	98.7
45-49	1980	94.8	98.6	1996	..	99.8

Fertility	Year	Value	Year	Value
Annual number of births (*thousands*)........................	..	..	1987	122.2
Crude birth rate (per 1 000 population)	..	..	1987	31.9
Percentage of extra-marital births among all births	..	..	..	..
Total fertility rate (births per woman)	1980	6.0	1994	4.8
Age-specific fertility rate (per 1 000 women)				
15-19	..	..	1994	77
20-24	..	..	1994	229
25-29	..	..	1994	234
30-34	..	..	1994	189
35-39	..	..	1994	122
40-44	..	..	1994	82
45-49	..	..	1994	35
Mean age at childbearing (years)	..	..	1994	29.8
Mean age at first birth (years)	..	..	..	..
Children ever born per woman				
35-39	1980	4.3	..	..
40-44	1980	4.6	..	..
45-49	1980	4.6	..	..
Percentage of childless women				
35-39	1980	6.5	..	..
40-44	1980	6.2	..	..
45-49	1980	6.8	..	..
Percentage of women with parity three or higher				
35-39	1980	76.1	..	..
40-44	1980	77.7	..	..
45-49	1980	77.4	..	..
Family Planning				
Contraceptive prevalence among women in union				
Percentage using any contraceptive method	..	..	1996	25.9
Percentage using a modern contraceptive method	..	..	1996	19.6
Percentage using condoms	..	..	1996	0.5
Population policies				
Government's view on the level of fertility	1976	Too high	2001	Too high
Government's policy regarding level of fertility	1976	Lower	2001	Lower
Government's support for contraceptive methods	1976	Direct support	2001	Direct support

Total fertility rates

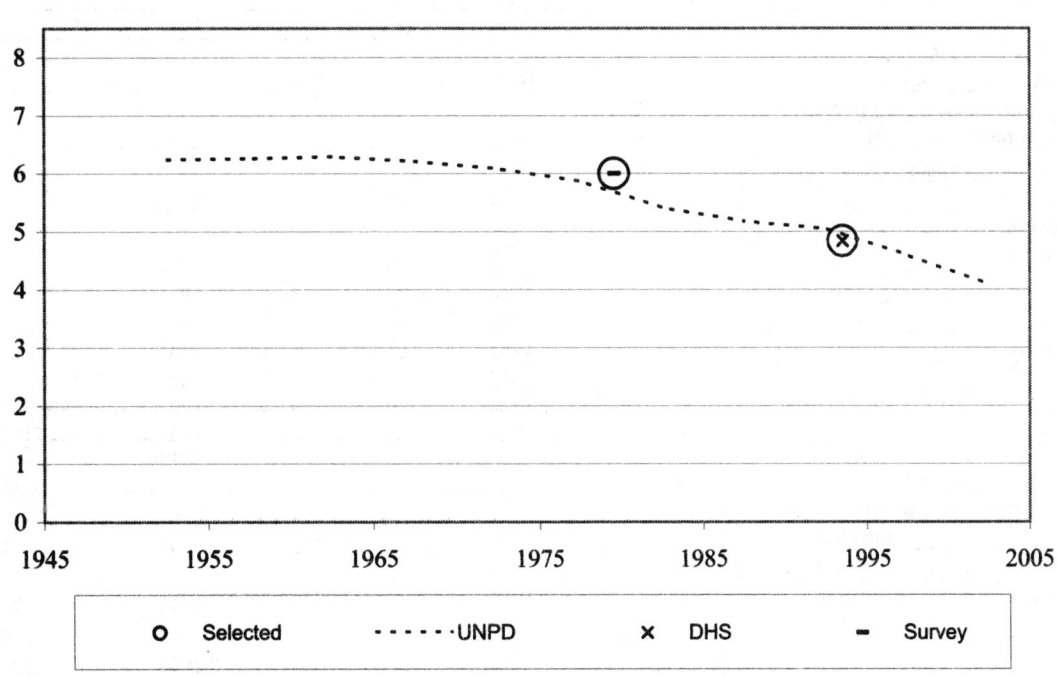

Age-specific fertility rates

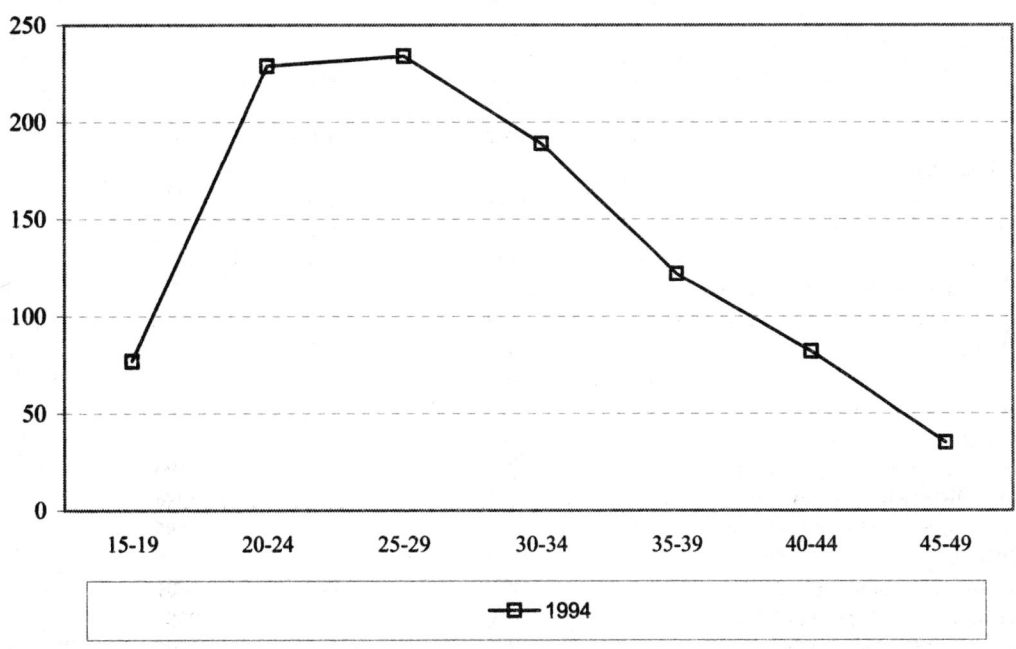

Paraguay

Indicator	Period					
	Earlier year			Later year		
	Year	Value		Year	Value	
Nuptiality						
Annual number of marriages (*thousands*)	..	..		..	..	
Annual number of divorces (*thousands*)	..	..		..	..	
	Year	Male	Female	Year	Male	Female
Total first marriage rate (per person)	..	..	..	..	..	..
Total divorce rate (per person)	..	..	..	..	..	..
Mean age at first marriage (years)	..	..	..	..	..	..
SMAM (years)	1972	26.5	21.7	1992	25.8	21.5
Percentage ever married by age group						
15-19	1972	0.8	11.7	1992	2.1	16.6
20-24	1972	20.3	45.1	1992	27.4	53.5
25-29	1972	57.2	68.8	1992	61.5	74.4
30-34	1972	77.6	78.9	1992	79.4	82.9
35-39	1972	84.6	81.4	1992	86.3	85.7
40-44	1972	87.8	81.3	1992	89.0	85.8
45-49	1972	88.7	80.1	1992	90.1	85.5
Fertility	Year	Value		Year	Value	
Annual number of births (*thousands*).............................	1970	88.0		..	..	
Crude birth rate (per 1 000 population)	1970	37.4		..	..	
Percentage of extra-marital births among all births	1970	42.6		..	..	
Total fertility rate (births per woman)	1977	5.0		1997	4.3	
Age-specific fertility rate (per 1 000 women)						
15-19	1977	86		1997	87	
20-24	1977	221		1997	216	
25-29	1977	239		1997	214	
30-34	1977	207		1997	167	
35-39	1977	150		1997	132	
40-44	1977	74		1997	37	
45-49	1977	16		1997	15	
Mean age at childbearing (years)	1977	29.5		1997	28.7	
Mean age at first birth (years)[a]	..	..		1990	21.6	
Children ever born per woman						
35-39	1979	4.6		1992	4.3	
40-44	1979	5.8		1992	4.9	
45-49	1979	6.3		1992	5.4	
Percentage of childless women						
35-39	..	..		1992	7.6	
40-44	..	..		1992	6.8	
45-49	..	..		1992	6.5	
Percentage of women with parity three or higher						
35-39	..	..		1992	68.9	
40-44	..	..		1992	72.4	
45-49	..	..		1992	74.4	
Family Planning						
Contraceptive prevalence among women in union						
Percentage using any contraceptive method	1977	28.6		1998	57.4	
Percentage using a modern contraceptive method	1977	23.3		1998	47.7	
Percentage using condoms	1977	2.6		1998	7.3	
Population policies						
Government's view on the level of fertility	1976	Satisfactory		2001	Too high	
Government's policy regarding level of fertility	1976	No intervention		2001	No intervention	
Government's support for contraceptive methods	1976	Direct support		2001	Direct support	

[a]Median age at first birth among women aged 25-29 at the date of the survey

Total fertility rates

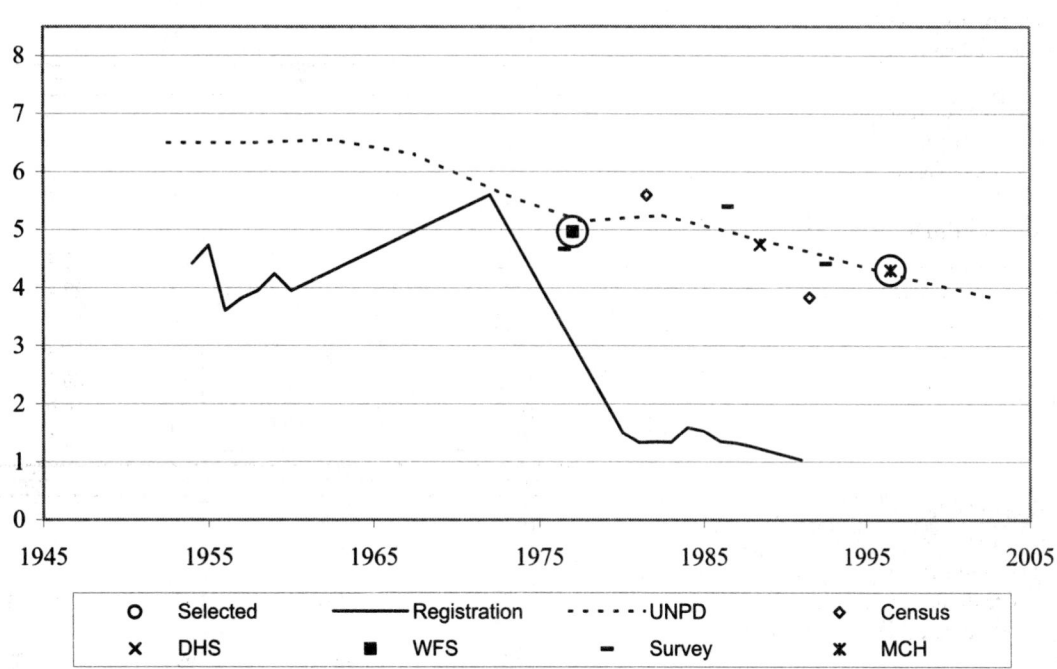

Age-specific fertility rates

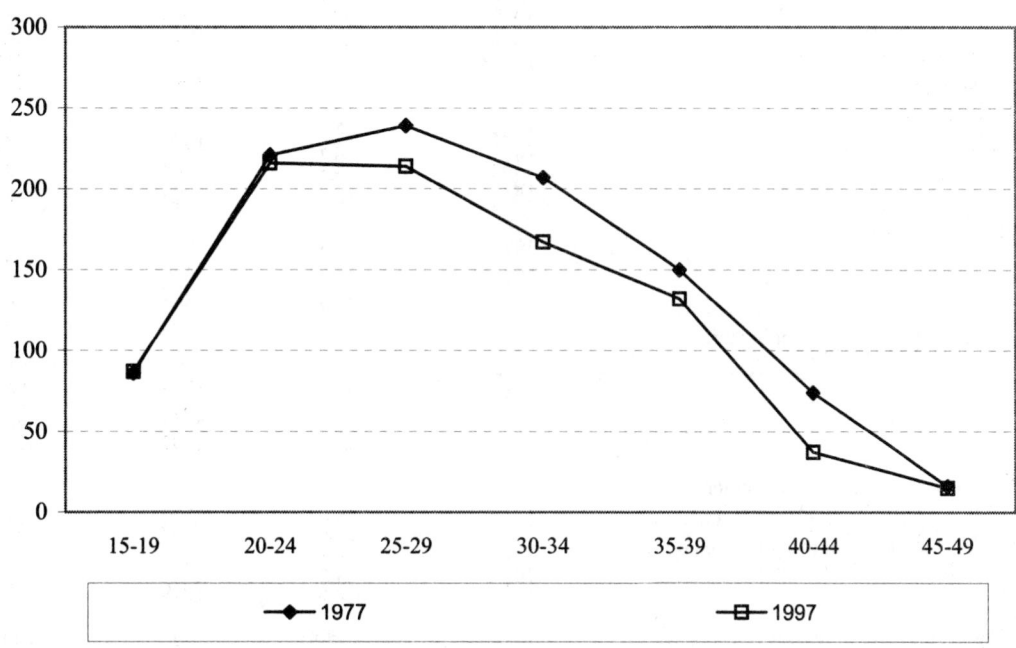

Peru

Indicator	Period					
	Earlier year			Later year		
	Year	Value		Year	Value	
Nuptiality						
Annual number of marriages (*thousands*)	1970	50.8		1998	60.7	
Annual number of divorces (*thousands*)	1968	1.9		1998	2.1	
	Year	Male	Female	Year	Male	Female
Total first marriage rate (per person)	..	..	..	..	..	..
Total divorce rate (per person)	..	..	..	..	..	..
Mean age at first marriage (years)	..	..	..	..	..	..
SMAM (years)	1972	25.2	21.8	1996	26.5	23.1
Percentage ever married by age group						
15-19	1972	5.5	17.0	1996	2.7	12.5
20-24	1972	31.1	55.5	1996	31.4	52.3
25-29	1972	65.3	77.7	1996	60.6	77.1
30-34	1972	82.2	86.0	1996	81.9	89.3
35-39	1972	88.0	88.9	1996	89.0	92.5
40-44	1972	90.3	89.4	1996	94.6	94.7
45-49	1972	91.5	89.8	1996	98.7	95.7
Fertility	Year	Value		Year	Value	
Annual number of births (*thousands*)................................	1970	559.6		2000	607.8	
Crude birth rate (per 1 000 population)	1970	41.8		2000	23.7	
Percentage of extra-marital births among all births	1972	41.3		..	..	
Total fertility rate (births per woman)	1975	5.5		1998	3.0	
Age-specific fertility rate (per 1 000 women)						
15-19	1975	86		1998	70	
20-24	1975	232		1998	148	
25-29	1975	266		1998	143	
30-34	1975	237		1998	122	
35-39	1975	169		1998	83	
40-44	1975	91		1998	34	
45-49	1975	28		1998	7	
Mean age at childbearing (years)	1975	30.0		1998	28.6	
Mean age at first birth (years)[a]	1977/78	23.0		2000	22.2	
Children ever born per woman						
35-39	1972	5.6		2000	3.5	
40-44	1972	6.3		2000	4.2	
45-49	1972	6.6		2000	4.7	
Percentage of childless women						
35-39	1972	6.8		2000	7.7	
40-44	1972	6.9		2000	6.3	
45-49	1972	7.4		2000	6.3	
Percentage of women with parity three or higher						
35-39	1972	82.1		2000	61.8	
40-44	1972	82.9		2000	70.7	
45-49	1972	82.9		2000	74.7	
Family Planning						
Contraceptive prevalence among women in union						
Percentage using any contraceptive method	1970	26.0		2000	68.9	
Percentage using a modern contraceptive method	1970	10.0		2000	50.4	
Percentage using condoms	1970	3.0		2000	5.6	
Population policies						
Government's view on the level of fertility	1976	Satisfactory		2001	Too high	
Government's policy regarding level of fertility	1976	No intervention		2001	Lower	
Government's support for contraceptive methods	1976	Direct support		2001	Direct support	

[a]Median age at first birth among women aged 25-29 at the date of the survey for both dates

Total fertility rates

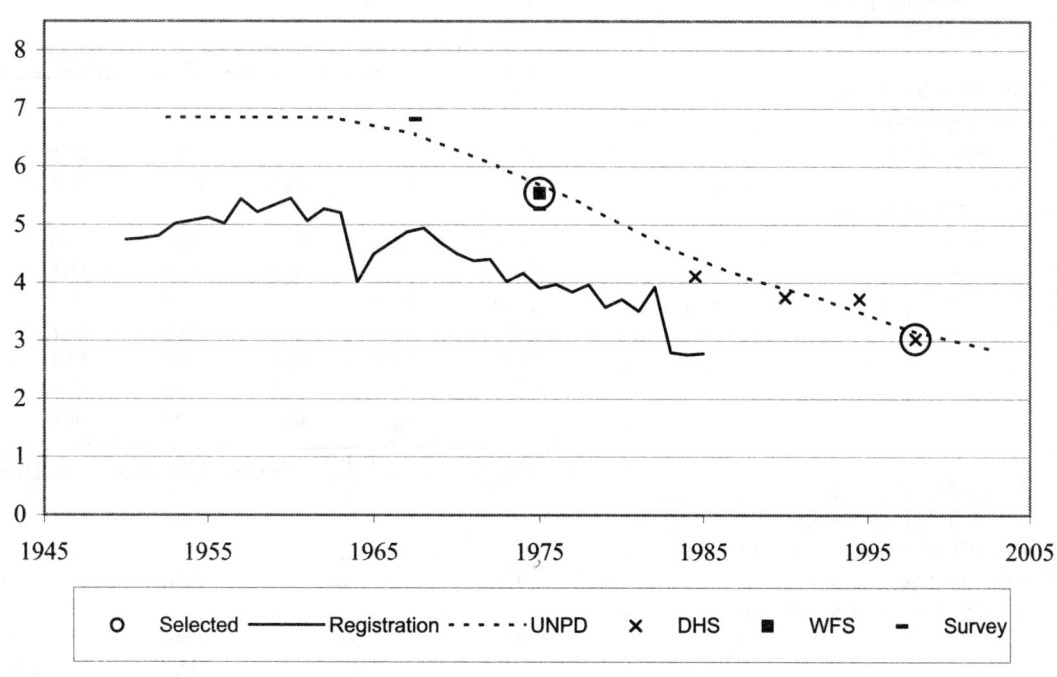

Age-specific fertility rates

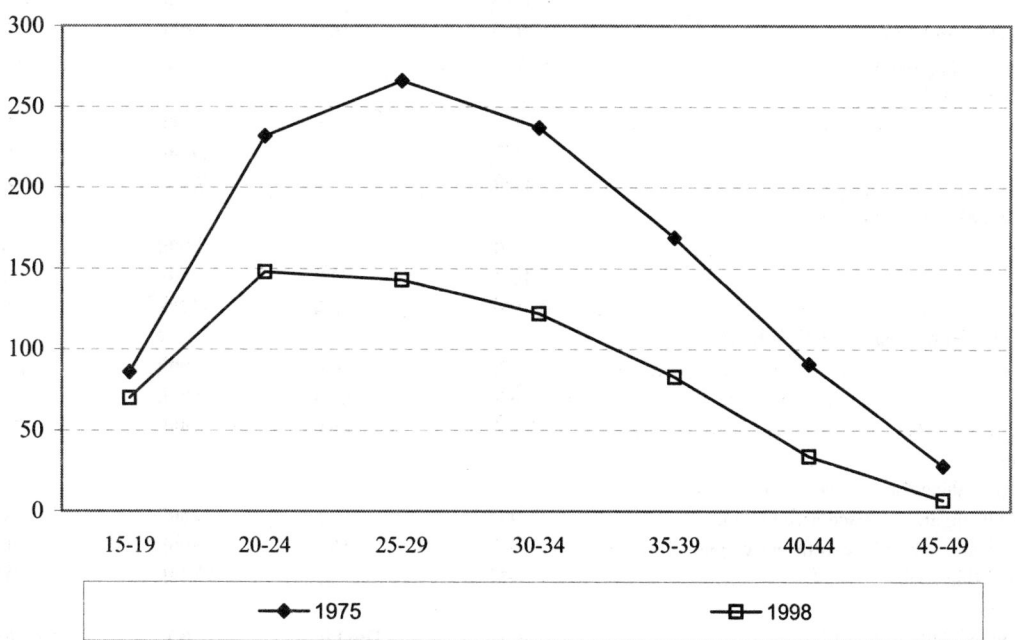

Indicator	Period					
	Earlier year			Later year		
	Year	Value		Year	Value	
Nuptiality						
Annual number of marriages (*thousands*) ....….............	..	..		..	..	
Annual number of divorces (*thousands*)	..	..		..	..	
	Year	Male	Female	Year	Male	Female
Total first marriage rate (per person)	..	..	..	..	..	..
Total divorce rate (per person)	..	..	..	..	..	..
Mean age at first marriage (years)	1974	26.3	23.8	1986	27.0	24.6
SMAM (years)	1970	25.4	22.8	1995	26.6	24.1
Percentage ever married by age group						
15-19	1970	2.5	10.9	1995	3.3	9.6
20-24	1970	30.8	49.8	1995	25.4	42.3
25-29	1970	69.9	78.5	1995	59.9	71.8
30-34	1970	86.9	88.4	1995	80.6	85.7
35-39	1970	92.9	92.0	1995	89.8	91.3
40-44	1970	95.2	92.7	1995	93.6	93.2
45-49	1970	96.3	93.3	1995	95.0	93.8
Fertility	Year	Value		Year	Value	
Annual number of births (*thousands*).............................	..	..		..	..	
Crude birth rate (per 1 000 population)	..	..		..	..	
Percentage of extra-marital births among all births	..	..		..	..	
Total fertility rate (births per woman)	1971	6.0		1996	3.8	
Age-specific fertility rate (per 1 000 women)						
15-19	1971	56		1996	50	
20-24	1971	228		1996	177	
25-29	1971	302		1996	210	
30-34	1971	268		1996	161	
35-39	1971	212		1996	106	
40-44	1971	100		1996	43	
45-49	1971	28		1996	8	
Mean age at childbearing (years)	1971	30.7		1996	29.2	
Mean age at first birth (years)[a]	1978	23.3		1998	23.9	
Children ever born per woman						
35-39	1978	5.2		1998	3.8	
40-44	1978	6.4		1998	4.2	
45-49	1978	6.6		1998	4.7	
Percentage of childless women						
35-39	1978	2.2		1998	9.4	
40-44	1978	2.2		1998	9.7	
45-49	1978	2.4		1998	8.7	
Percentage of women with parity three or higher						
35-39	1978	80.0		1998	67.9	
40-44	1978	85.4		1998	72.8	
45-49	1978	85.0		1998	74.9	
Family Planning						
Contraceptive prevalence among women in union						
Percentage using any contraceptive method	1973	17.6		1998	46.5	
Percentage using a modern contraceptive method	1973	10.8		1998	28.2	
Percentage using condoms	1973	0.8		1998	1.6	
Population policies						
Government's view on the level of fertility	1976	Too high		2001	Too high	
Government's policy regarding level of fertility	1976	Lower		2001	Lower	
Government's support for contraceptive methods	1976	Direct support		2001	Direct support	

[a]Median age at first birth among women aged 25-29 at the date of the survey for both dates

Total fertility rates

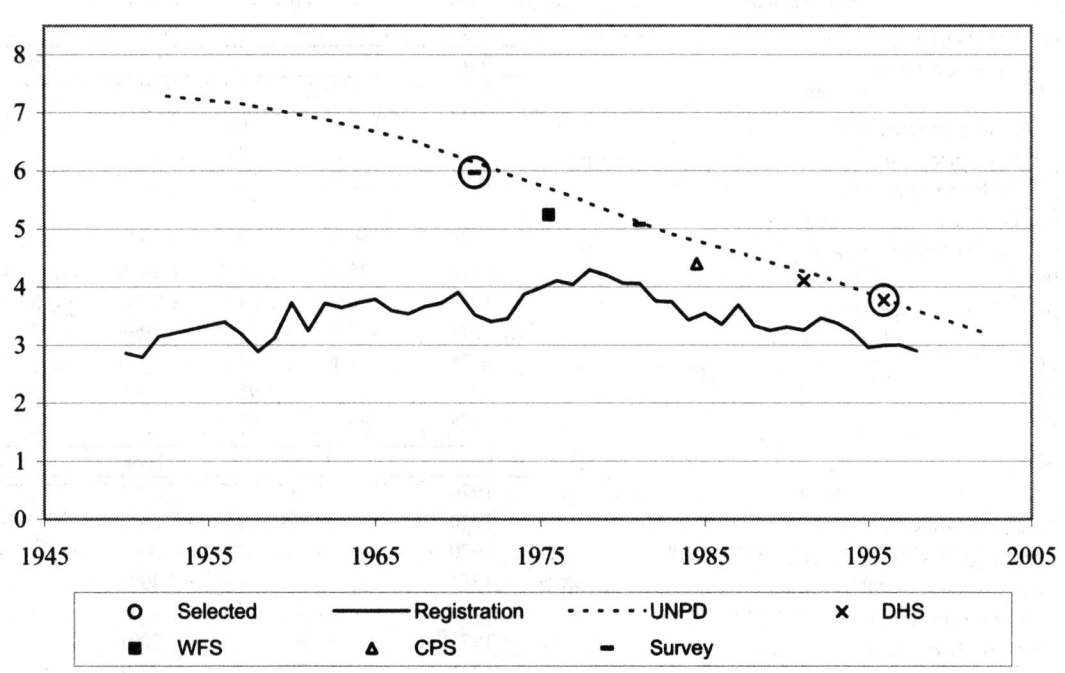

Age-specific fertility rates

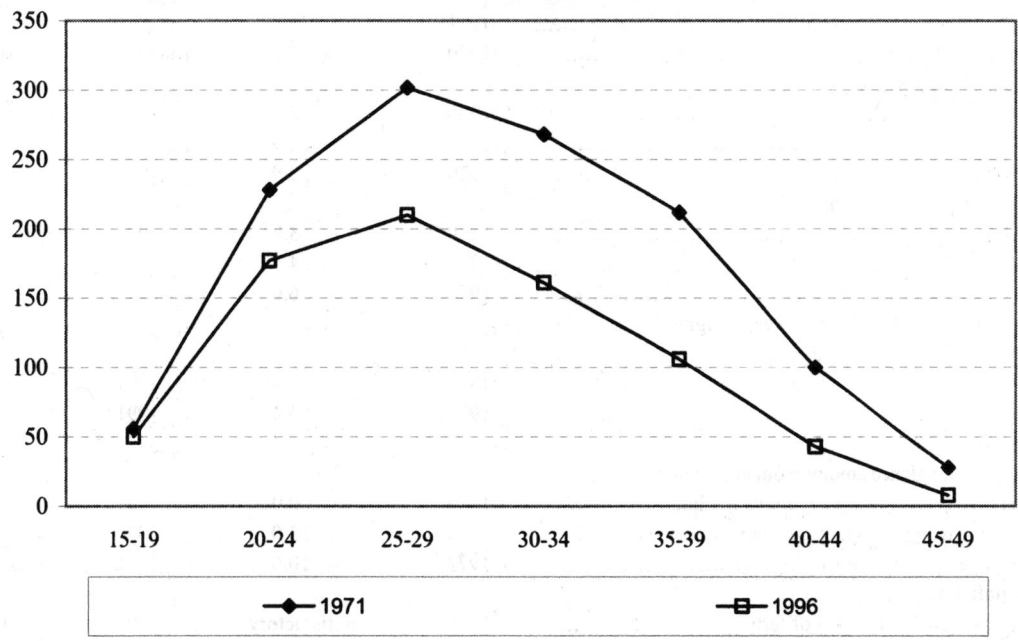

Indicator	Period					
	Earlier year			**Later year**		
	Year	Value		Year	Value	
Nuptiality						
Annual number of marriages (*thousands*)	1970	280.3		2001	195.1	
Annual number of divorces (*thousands*)	1970	34.6		2001	45.3	
	Year	Male	Female	Year	Male	Female
Total first marriage rate (per person)	1975	0.9	0.9	1997	0.6	0.6
Total divorce rate (per person)	1970	0.1	0.1	1997	0.1	0.1
Mean age at first marriage (years)	1970	..	22.8	2001	..	24.1
SMAM (years)	1978	25.7	22.5	1999	28.0	25.2
Percentage ever married by age group						
15-19	1978	0.6	4.9	1999	0.3	1.8
20-24	1978	25.2	53.0	1999	14.4	31.4
25-29	1978	72.9	84.9	1999	54.9	70.3
30-34	1978	87.7	91.4	1999	75.3	85.6
35-39	1978	91.1	94.2	1999	81.1	90.7
40-44	1978	93.2	95.1	1999	86.1	93.1
45-49	1978	95.1	94.7	1999	89.9	93.9
Fertility	Year	Value		Year	Value	
Annual number of births (*thousands*)	1970	546.0		2001	368.2	
Crude birth rate (per 1 000 population)	1970	16.8		2001	9.5	
Percentage of extra-marital births among all births	1970	5.0		2001	13.1	
Total fertility rate (births per woman)	1971	2.3		2001	1.3	
Age-specific fertility rate (per 1 000 women)						
15-19	1971	30		2001	16	
20-24	1971	171		2001	74	
25-29	1971	129		2001	89	
30-34	1971	72		2001	52	
35-39	1971	36		2001	21	
40-44	1971	11		2001	5	
45-49	1971	1		2001	0	
Mean age at childbearing (years)	1971	26.9		2001	27.6	
Mean age at first birth (years)	1970	22.8		2001	24.8	
Children ever born per woman						
35-39	1970	2.6		1991	2.1	
40-44	1970	2.9		1991	2.2	
45-49	1970	2.9		1991	2.3	
Percentage of childless women						
35-39	1970	3.8		1991	9.5	
40-44	1970	4.5		1991	6.1	
45-49	1970	6.0		1991	7.2	
Percentage of women with parity three or higher						
35-39	1970	44.6		1991	26.6	
40-44	1970	52.9		1991	33.1	
45-49	1970	54.4		1991	35.3	
Family Planning						
Contraceptive prevalence among women in union						
Percentage using any contraceptive method	1972	60.0		1991	49.4	
Percentage using a modern contraceptive method	1972	13.0		1991	19.0	
Percentage using condoms	1972	10.0		1991	9.1	
Population policies						
Government's view on the level of fertility	1976	Satisfactory		2001	Too low	
Government's policy regarding level of fertility	1976	Maintain		2001	Raise	
Government's support for contraceptive methods	1976	Direct support		2001	Direct support	

Total fertility rates

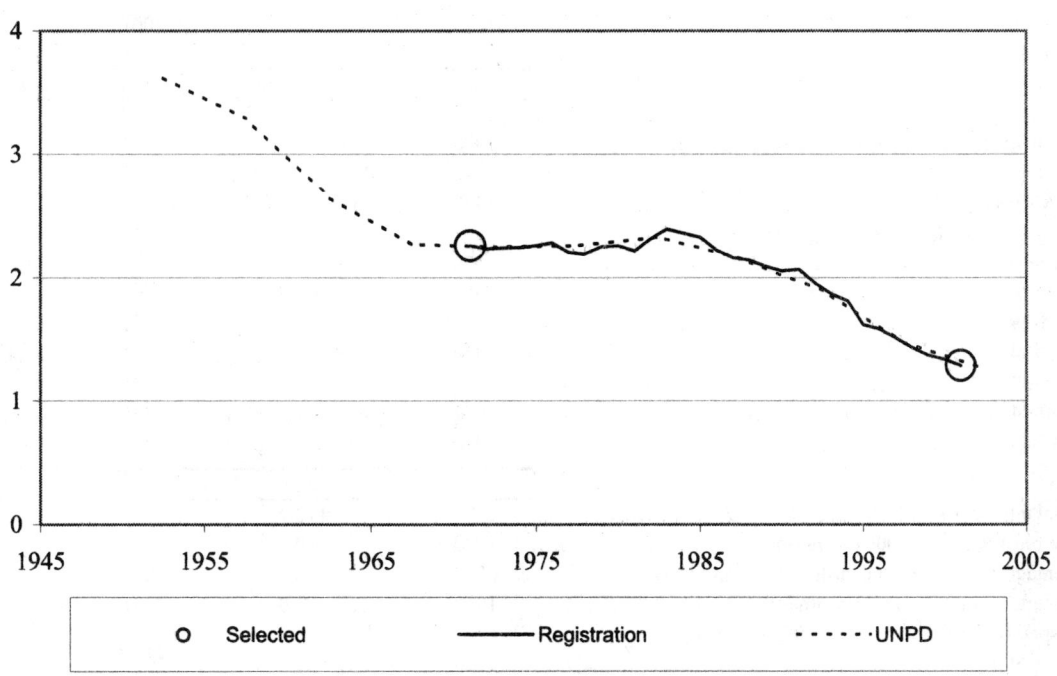

O Selected	—— Registration	·····UNPD

Age-specific fertility rates

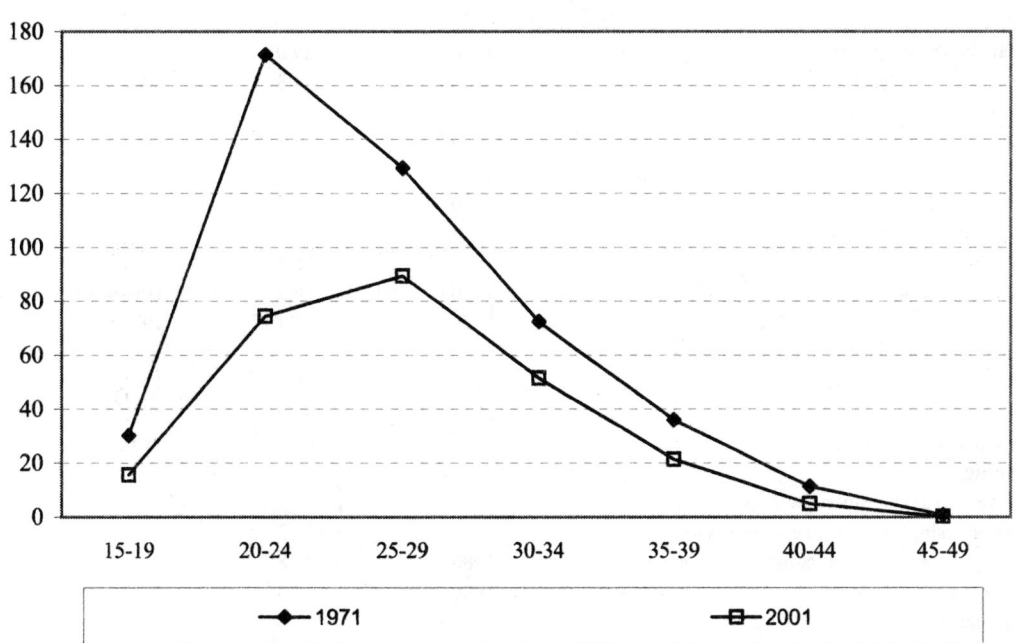

◆ 1971	□ 2001

Indicator	Period					
	Earlier year			Later year		
	Year	Value		Year	Value	
Nuptiality						
Annual number of marriages (*thousands*)	1970	81.5		2001	58.4	
Annual number of divorces (*thousands*)	1970	0.5		2001	18.9	
	Year	Male	Female	Year	Male	Female
Total first marriage rate (per person)	1978	1.0	1.0	1997	0.7	0.8
Total divorce rate (per person)	1970	0.0	0.0	1997	0.2	0.2
Mean age at first marriage (years)	1976	25.5	23.3	1997	27.1	25.0
SMAM (years)	1970	25.6	23.2	1991	26.7	23.9
Percentage ever married by age group						
15-19	1970	1.3	5.3	1991	1.2	5.7
20-24	1970	19.4	39.3	1991	18.9	38.6
25-29	1970	69.2	75.0	1991	60.1	74.8
30-34	1970	86.9	85.0	1991	83.4	88.3
35-39	1970	89.6	87.5	1991	91.3	92.1
40-44	1970	90.6	87.4	1991	94.3	92.9
45-49	1970	91.8	87.5	1991	95.4	93.1
Fertility	Year	Value		Year	Value	
Annual number of births (*thousands*).............................	1970	172.9		2001	112.8	
Crude birth rate (per 1 000 population)	1970	19.1		2001	10.9	
Percentage of extra-marital births among all births	1970	6.9		2001	23.8	
Total fertility rate (births per woman)	1970	3.0		2001	1.5	
Age-specific fertility rate (per 1 000 women)						
15-19	1970	31		2001	20	
20-24	1970	154		2001	55	
25-29	1970	177		2001	92	
30-34	1970	124		2001	83	
35-39	1970	80		2001	35	
40-44	1970	33		2001	6	
45-49	1970	3		2001	0	
Mean age at childbearing (years)	1970	29.0		2001	28.8	
Mean age at first birth (years)	1970	24.8		2001	26.7	
Children ever born per woman						
35-39	1970	2.5		1991	1.9	
40-44	1970	2.8		1991	2.1	
45-49	1970	2.9		1991	2.3	
Percentage of childless women						
35-39	1970	15.6		1991	10.6	
40-44	1970	16.2		1991	10.0	
45-49	1970	17.4		1991	10.8	
Percentage of women with parity three or higher						
35-39	1970	38.2		1991	22.0	
40-44	1970	41.6		1991	26.9	
45-49	1970	43.2		1991	32.8	
Family Planning						
Contraceptive prevalence among women in union						
Percentage using any contraceptive method	1980	66.3		..	..	
Percentage using a modern contraceptive method	1980	32.8		..	..	
Percentage using condoms	1980	5.6		..	..	
Population policies						
Government's view on the level of fertility	1976	Satisfactory		2001	Too low	
Government's policy regarding level of fertility	1976	No intervention		2001	No intervention	
Government's support for contraceptive methods	1976	Direct support		2001	Direct support	

Total fertility rates

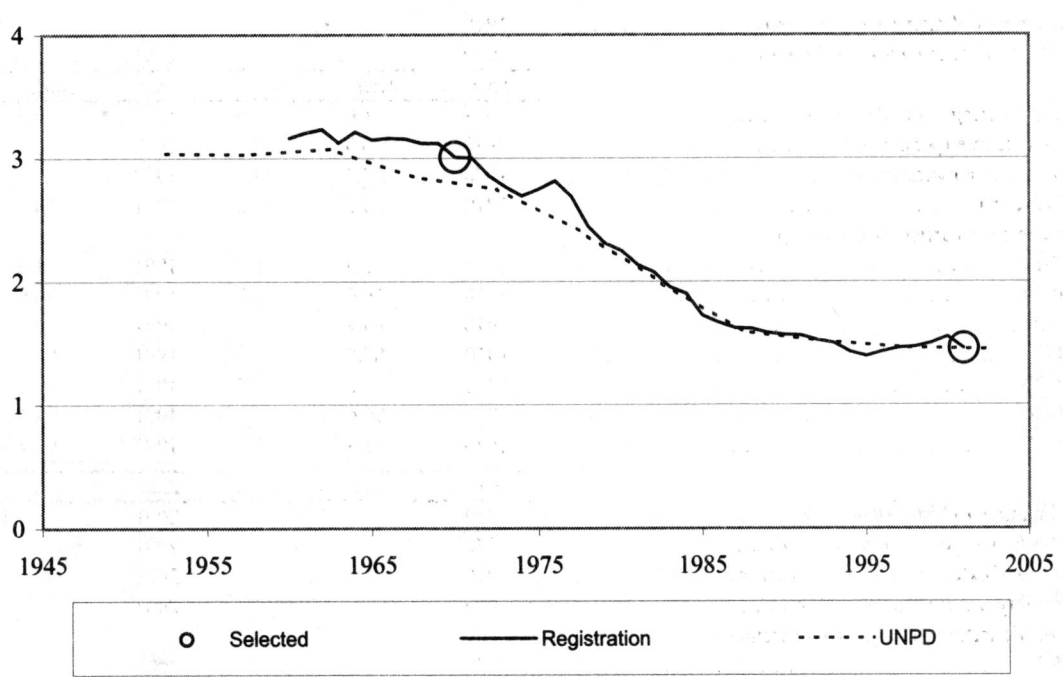

O Selected	—— Registration	· · · · · UNPD

Age-specific fertility rates

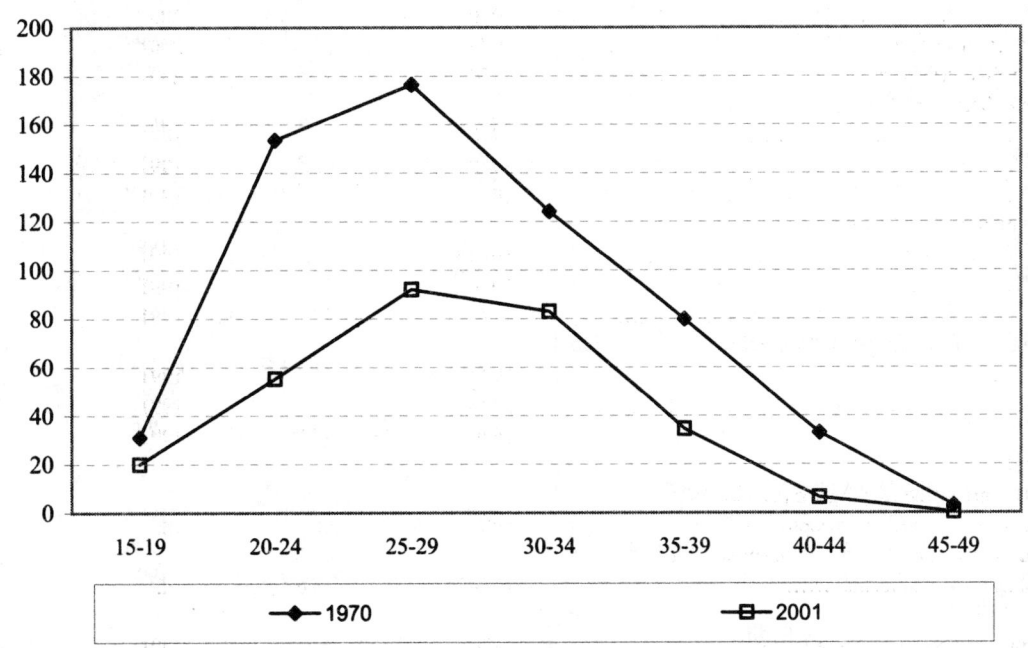

—◆— 1970	—☐— 2001

Indicator	Period					
	Earlier year			Later year		
	Year	Value		Year	Value	
Nuptiality						
Annual number of marriages (*thousands*)	1970	29.7		2001	28.6	
Annual number of divorces (*thousands*)	1970	9.7		2001	13.9	
	Year	Male	Female	Year	Male	Female
Total first marriage rate (per person)	1975	1.0	0.8	1998	0.5	0.5
Total divorce rate (per person)	..	..	..	..	..	..
Mean age at first marriage (years)	1975	25.2	23.3	1998	25.8	23.7
SMAM (years)	1970	24.0	22.1	1996	..	22.6
Percentage ever married by age group						
15-19	1970	4.6	15.6	1996	..	19.5
20-24	1970	38.1	54.7	1996	..	55.0
25-29	1970	73.4	81.3	1996	..	83.9
30-34	1970	85.3	89.8	1996	..	89.5
35-39	1970	88.3	92.3	1996	..	92.4
40-44	1970	89.9	92.8	1996	..	94.4
45-49	1970	90.3	93.5	1996	..	96.9
Fertility	Year	Value		Year	Value	
Annual number of births (*thousands*)...............................	1970	67.4		2001	56.0	
Crude birth rate (per 1 000 population)	1970	24.8		2001	14.6	
Percentage of extra-marital births among all births	1970	19.2		1998	47.0	
Total fertility rate (births per woman)	1970	3.2		2000	2.0	
Age-specific fertility rate (per 1 000 women)						
15-19	1970	73		2000	74	
20-24	1970	194		2000	128	
25-29	1970	182		2000	110	
30-34	1970	103		2000	65	
35-39	1970	56		2000	27	
40-44	1970	21		2000	6	
45-49	1970	3		2000	0	
Mean age at childbearing (years)	1970	27.1		2000	25.8	
Mean age at first birth (years)	1972	22.7		1998	23.3	
Children ever born per woman						
35-39	1970	3.7		1990	2.4	
40-44	1970	3.9		1990	2.7	
45-49	1970	4.3		1990	3.1	
Percentage of childless women						
35-39	1970	4.3		1990	12.6	
40-44	1970	5.4		1990	10.9	
45-49	1970	6.4		1990	9.7	
Percentage of women with parity three or higher						
35-39	1970	60.4		1990	47.5	
40-44	1970	60.7		1990	54.2	
45-49	1970	62.0		1990	59.3	
Family Planning						
Contraceptive prevalence among women in union						
Percentage using any contraceptive method	1974	61.1		1996	77.7	
Percentage using a modern contraceptive method	1974	55.0		1996	67.6	
Percentage using condoms	1974	2.9		1996	6.4	
Population policies						
Government's view on the level of fertility	..	..		..	..	
Government's policy regarding level of fertility	..	..		..	..	
Government's support for contraceptive methods	..	..		..	Direct support	

Total fertility rates

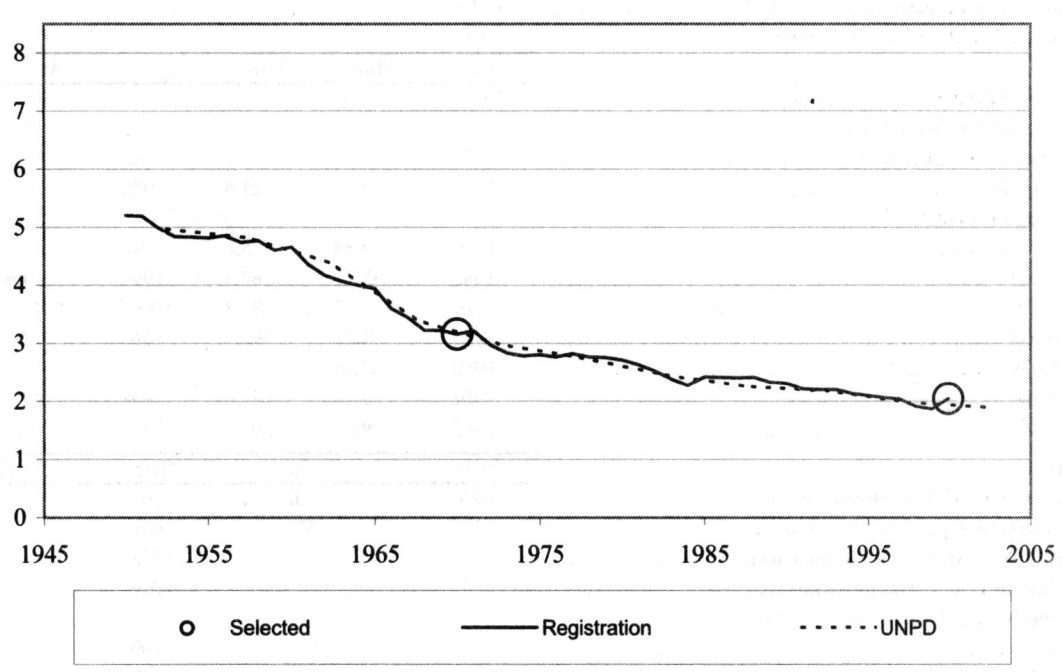

Age-specific fertility rates

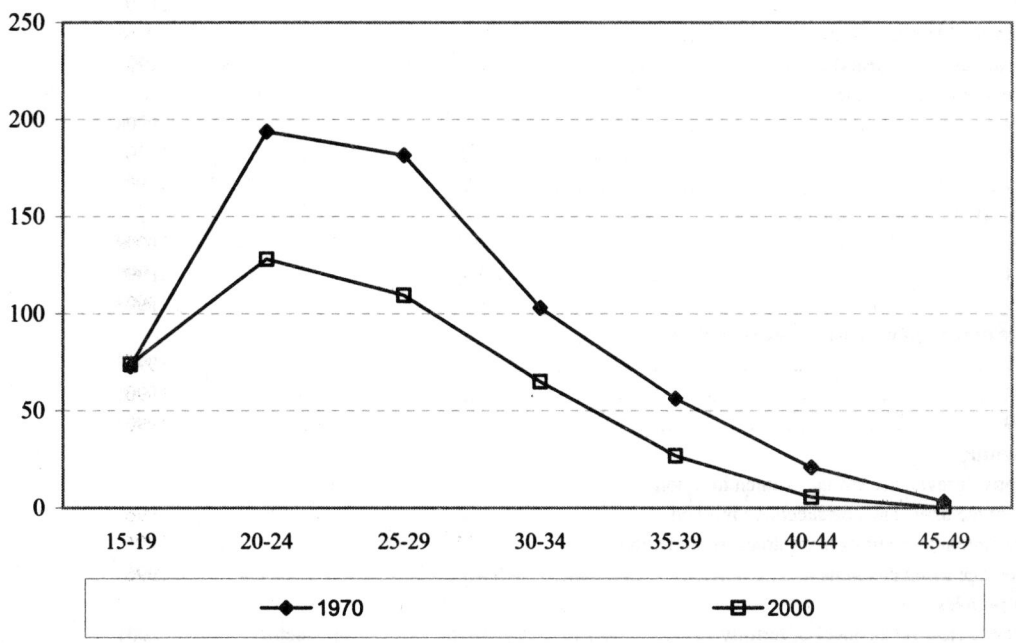

Indicator	Period					
	Earlier year			Later year		
	Year	Value		Year	Value	
Nuptiality						
Annual number of marriages (*thousands*)	..	..		..	..	
Annual number of divorces (*thousands*)	1977	0.3		1990	0.4	
	Year	Male	Female	Year	Male	Female
Total first marriage rate (per person)	..	..	..	..	..	..
Total divorce rate (per person)	..	..	..	1993	0.1	0.2
Mean age at first marriage (years)	..	..	..	..	..	..
SMAM (years)	1982	25.2	21.4	1998	28.7	26.3
Percentage ever married by age group						
15-19	1982	2.8	15.8	1998	0.2	4.2
20-24	1982	27.1	64.3	1998	9.6	32.2
25-29	1982	61.7	91.3	1998	45.1	66.8
30-34	1982	86.9	95.4	1998	77.5	80.2
35-39	1982	94.0	95.9	1998	91.0	89.3
40-44	1982	97.6	97.0	1998	95.5	93.3
45-49	1982	99.0	98.1	1998	97.8	97.0
Fertility	Year	Value		Year	Value	
Annual number of births (*thousands*)...............................	1970	3.6		1999	10.8	
Crude birth rate (per 1 000 population)	1970	32.5		1999	19.0	
Percentage of extra-marital births among all births	..	..		..	..	
Total fertility rate (births per woman)	..	..		1996	4.1	
Age-specific fertility rate (per 1 000 women)						
15-19	..	..		1996	28	
20-24	..	..		1996	154	
25-29	..	..		1996	221	
30-34	..	..		1996	208	
35-39	..	..		1996	136	
40-44	..	..		1996	48	
45-49	..	..		1996	17	
Mean age at childbearing (years)	..	..		1996	30.5	
Mean age at first birth (years)	..	..		1997	24.9	
Children ever born per woman						
35-39	..	..		1998	4.6	
40-44	..	..		1998	5.6	
45-49	..	..		1998	6.6	
Percentage of childless women						
35-39	..	..		1998	14.7	
40-44	..	..		1998	11.6	
45-49	..	..		1998	6.2	
Percentage of women with parity three or higher						
35-39	..	..		1998	76.6	
40-44	..	..		1998	82.0	
45-49	..	..		1998	88.0	
Family Planning						
Contraceptive prevalence among women in union						
Percentage using any contraceptive method	..	..		1998	43.2	
Percentage using a modern contraceptive method	..	..		1998	32.3	
Percentage using condoms	..	..		1998	2.9	
Population policies						
Government's view on the level of fertility	1976	Satisfactory		2001	Satisfactory	
Government's policy regarding level of fertility	1976	Maintain		2001	Maintain	
Government's support for contraceptive methods	1976	No support		2001	Direct support	

Total fertility rates

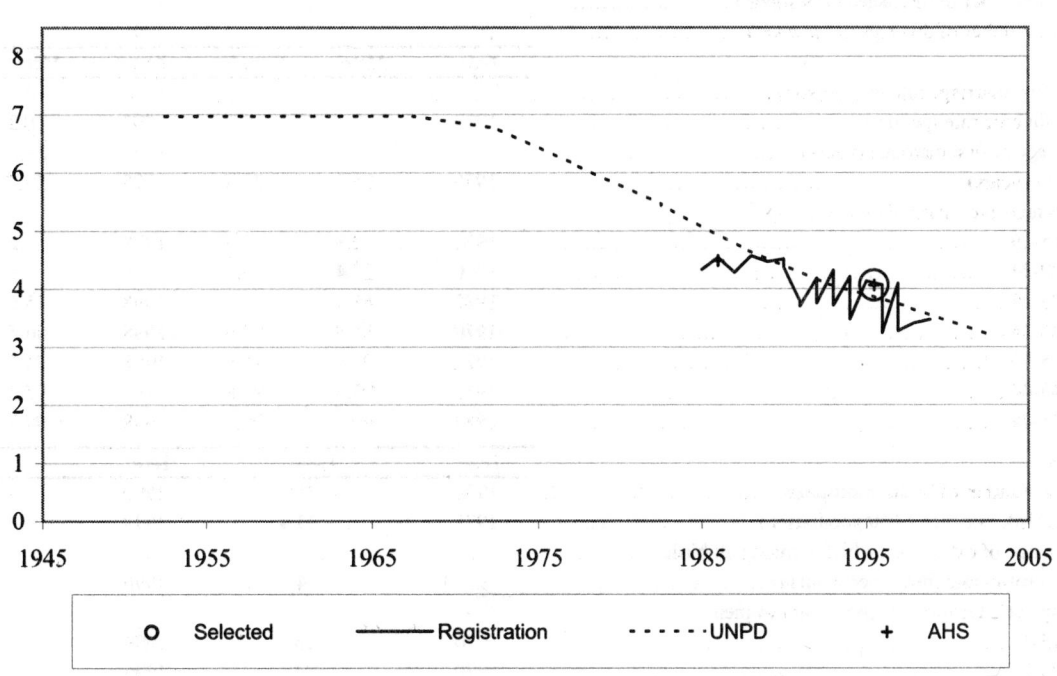

Age-specific fertility rates

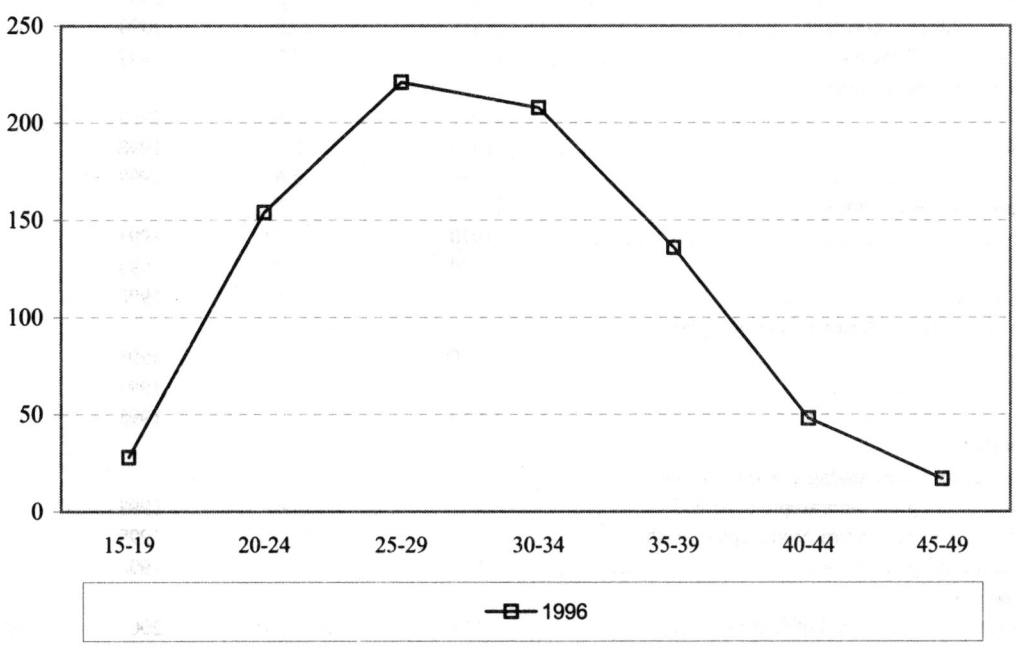

Republic of Korea

Indicator	Period					
	Earlier year			Later year		
	Year	Value		Year	Value	

Nuptiality

Indicator	Year	Value		Year	Value	
Annual number of marriages (*thousands*)	..	..		2001	320.1	
Annual number of divorces (*thousands*)	..	..		2001	135.0	

Indicator	Year	Male	Female	Year	Male	Female
Total first marriage rate (per person)	..	..	..	1998	0.6	0.7
Total divorce rate (per person)	1979	0.1	0.1	1997	0.2	0.2
Mean age at first marriage (years)	..	..	..	1998	29.0	26.2
SMAM (years)	1970	27.2	23.3	1995	29.3	26.1
Percentage ever married by age group						
15-19	1970	0.3	2.9	1995	0.2	0.8
20-24	1970	7.4	42.8	1995	3.7	16.7
25-29	1970	56.6	90.3	1995	35.6	70.4
30-34	1970	93.6	98.6	1995	80.5	93.3
35-39	1970	98.8	99.6	1995	93.4	96.7
40-44	1970	99.6	99.8	1995	97.3	98.1
45-49	1970	99.8	99.9	1995	98.7	99.0

Fertility

Indicator	Year	Value	Year	Value
Annual number of births (*thousands*)	1975	825.8	2001	557.2
Crude birth rate (per 1 000 population)	1975	23.4	2001	11.8
Percentage of extra-marital births among all births	..	..	..	..
Total fertility rate (births per woman)	1970	4.3	2000	1.5
Age-specific fertility rate (per 1 000 women)				
15-19	1970	13	2000	3
20-24	1970	174	2000	40
25-29	1970	298	2000	156
30-34	1970	207	2000	89
35-39	1970	111	2000	18
40-44	1970	43	2000	3
45-49	1970	8	2000	0
Mean age at childbearing (years)	1970	29.8	2000	28.9
Mean age at first birth (years)	1978	25.2	1998	27.1
Children ever born per woman				
35-39	1970	4.5	1990	2.3
40-44	1970	5.3	1990	2.8
45-49	1970	5.6	1990	3.4
Percentage of childless women				
35-39	1970	1.9	1990	2.1
40-44	1970	1.7	1990	1.5
45-49	1970	2.1	1990	1.3
Percentage of women with parity three or higher				
35-39	1970	87.0	1990	35.8
40-44	1970	87.7	1990	58.1
45-49	1970	87.6	1990	75.7

Family Planning

Indicator	Year	Value	Year	Value
Contraceptive prevalence among women in union				
Percentage using any contraceptive method	1971	24.6	1997	80.5
Percentage using a modern contraceptive method	1971	20.3	1997	66.9
Percentage using condoms	1971	3.2	1997	15.1

Population policies

Indicator	Year	Value	Year	Value
Government's view on the level of fertility	1976	Too high	2001	Satisfactory
Government's policy regarding level of fertility	1976	Lower	2001	No intervention
Government's support for contraceptive methods	1976	Direct support	2001	Direct support

Total fertility rates

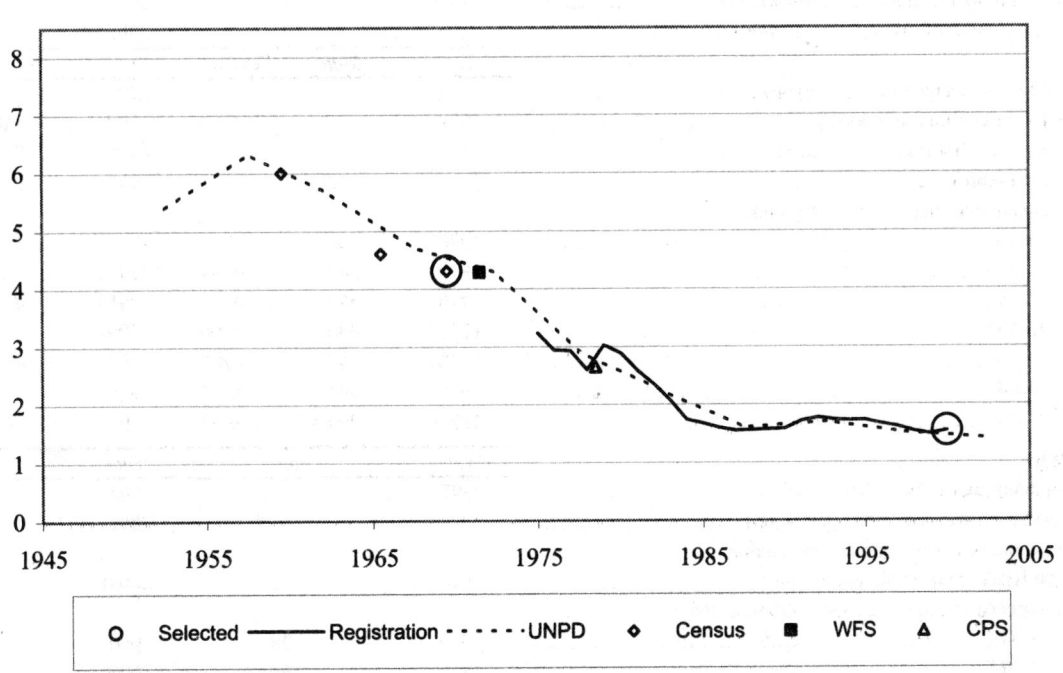

Age-specific fertility rates

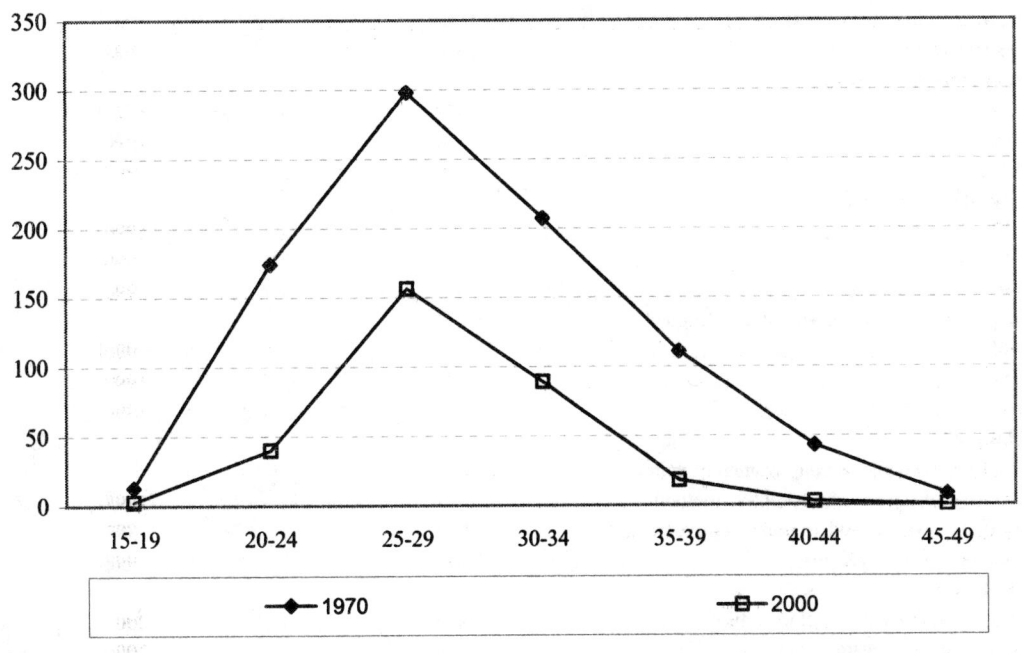

Indicator	Period					
	Earlier year			Later year		
	Year	Value		Year	Value	

Nuptiality

Indicator	Year	Value		Year	Value	
Annual number of marriages (*thousands*)	1970	33.7		2001	21.1	
Annual number of divorces (*thousands*)	1970	7.5		2001	10.8	

Indicator	Year	Male	Female	Year	Male	Female
Total first marriage rate (per person)	1980	..	1.1	1998	0.6	0.6
Total divorce rate (per person)	..	..	..	1991	0.4	0.4
Mean age at first marriage (years)	1980	..	25.6	2001	..	21.9
SMAM (years)	..	..	..	1989	23.8	21.1
Percentage ever married by age group						
15-19	1979	..	..	1989	1.7	11.6
20-24	1979	42.1	66.9	1989	41.4	72.2
25-29	1979	88.6	89.7	1989	85.7	91.2
30-34	1979	96.3	94.0	1989	94.9	95.1
35-39	1979	98.3	95.3	1989	97.4	96.1
40-44	1979	99.0	95.8	1989	98.3	96.4
45-49	1979	99.3	95.9	1989	98.8	96.7

Fertility

Indicator	Year	Value	Year	Value
Annual number of births (*thousands*)	1970	69.8	2001	36.4
Crude birth rate (per 1 000 population)	1970	19.4	2001	10.0
Percentage of extra-marital births among all births	1980	7.4	1998	17.5
Total fertility rate (births per woman)	1969	2.6	2001	1.3
Age-specific fertility rate (per 1 000 women)				
15-19	1969	28	2001	35
20-24	1969	164	2001	98
25-29	1969	135	2001	67
30-34	1969	100	2001	36
35-39	1969	62	2001	12
40-44	1969	21	2001	3
45-49	1969	3	2001	0
Mean age at childbearing (years)	1969	28.2	2001	25.6
Mean age at first birth (years)	..	..	2001	22.8
Children ever born per woman				
35-39	..	..	1989	2.2
40-44	..	..	1989	2.2
45-49	..	..	1989	2.4
Percentage of childless women				
35-39	..	..	1989	8.4
40-44	..	..	1989	9.2
45-49	..	..	1989	10.5
Percentage of women with parity three or higher				
35-39	..	..	1989	31.8
40-44	..	..	1989	31.9
45-49	..	..	1989	37.2

Family Planning

Indicator	Year	Value	Year	Value
Contraceptive prevalence among women in union				
Percentage using any contraceptive method	..	..	2000	62.4
Percentage using a modern contraceptive method	..	..	2000	42.8
Percentage using condoms	..	..	2000	3.5

Population policies

Indicator	Year	Value	Year	Value
Government's view on the level of fertility	1976	--	2001	Satisfactory
Government's policy regarding level of fertility	1976	--	2001	No intervention
Government's support for contraceptive methods	1976	--	2001	Direct support

Total fertility rates

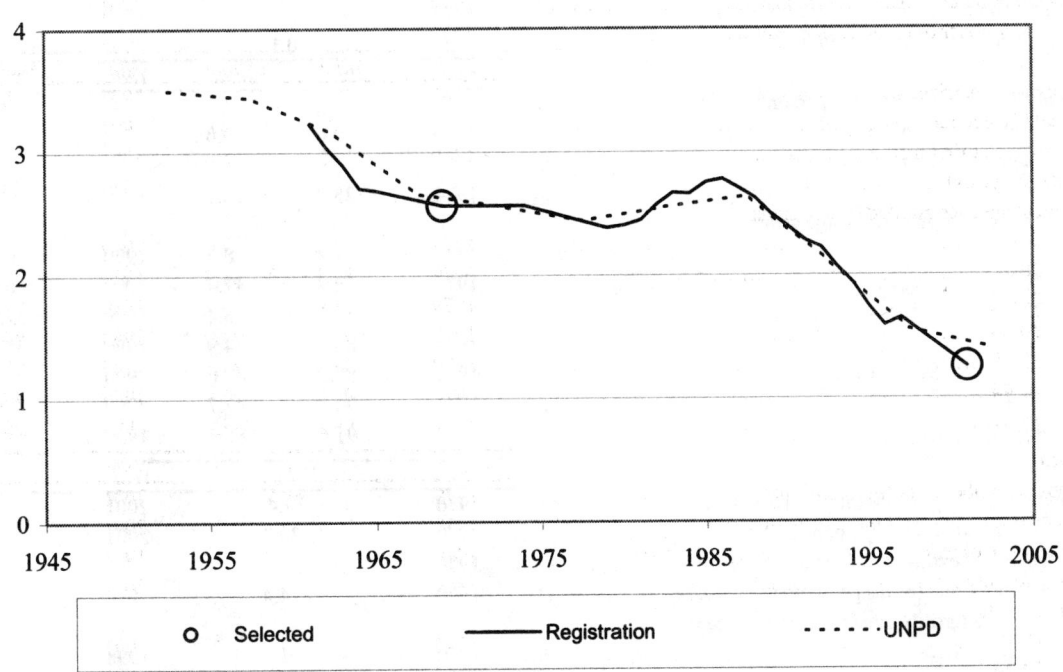

Age-specific fertility rates

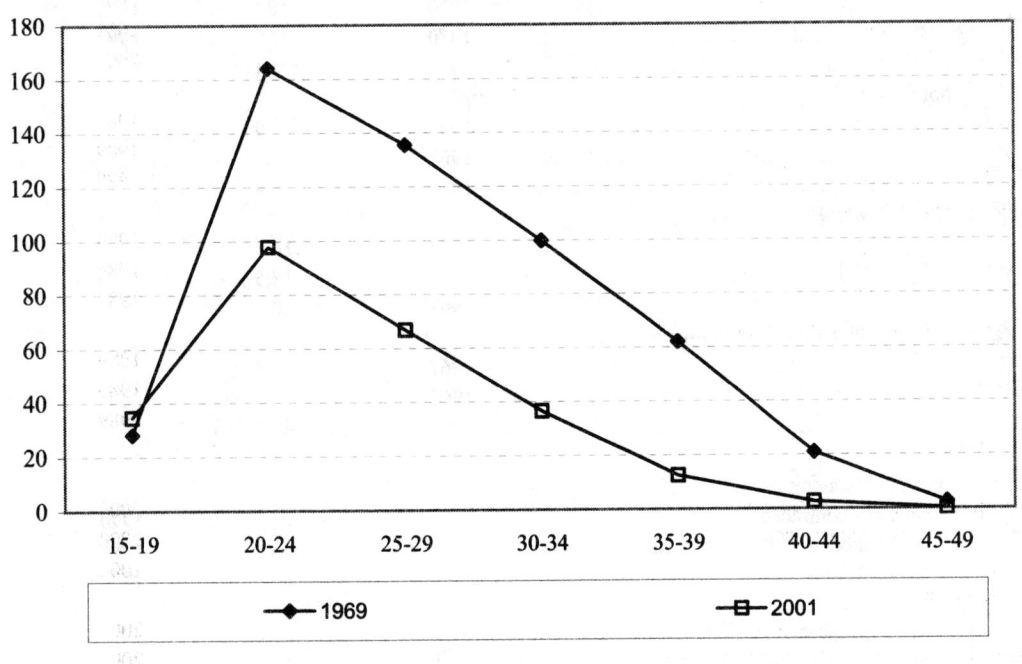

Indicator	Period					
	Earlier year			Later year		
	Year	Value		Year	Value	

Nuptiality

	Year	Value		Year	Value	
Annual number of marriages (*thousands*)	1970	3.0		1999	3.4	
Annual number of divorces (*thousands*)	1970	0.1		2000	0.9	

	Year	Male	Female	Year	Male	Female
Total first marriage rate (per person)	..	..	..	..	..	..
Total divorce rate (per person)	1970	0.0	0.0	..	..	..
Mean age at first marriage (years)	..	..	..	..	..	..
SMAM (years)	1974	25.2	22.5	1990	30.3	28.2
Percentage ever married by age group						
15-19	1974	1.2	8.6	1990	0.1	2.1
20-24	1974	27.4	47.4	1990	6.9	19.4
25-29	1974	72.5	76.4	1990	32.8	44.7
30-34	1974	83.6	84.9	1990	56.6	63.3
35-39	1974	88.3	87.0	1990	71.5	74.5
40-44	1974	90.2	87.7	1990	78.8	80.8
45-49	1974	91.6	87.6	1990	82.1	84.1

Fertility

	Year	Value	Year	Value
Annual number of births (*thousands*)...........................	1970	13.4	2001	14.5
Crude birth rate (per 1 000 population)	1970	30.2	2001	19.8
Percentage of extra-marital births among all births	1970	24.0	1986	49.0
Total fertility rate (births per woman)	1970	4.4	1998	2.3
Age-specific fertility rate (per 1 000 women)				
15-19	1970	62	1998	36
20-24	1970	239	1998	108
25-29	1970	217	1998	131
30-34	1970	171	1998	101
35-39	1970	125	1998	58
40-44	1970	59	1998	19
45-49	1970	8	1998	1
Mean age at childbearing (years)	1970	29.0	1998	28.6
Mean age at first birth (years)	1970	24.1	..	..
Children ever born per woman				
35-39	1967	4.9	..	..
40-44	1967	5.4	..	..
45-49	1967	5.4	..	..
Percentage of childless women				
35-39	1967	16.8	..	..
40-44	1967	18.5	..	..
45-49	1967	20.6	..	..
Percentage of women with parity three or higher				
35-39	1967	69.8	..	..
40-44	1967	70.2	..	..
45-49	1967	67.7	..	..

Family Planning

	Year	Value	Year	Value
Contraceptive prevalence among women in union				
Percentage using any contraceptive method	..	..	1990	66.6
Percentage using a modern contraceptive method	..	..	1990	61.7
Percentage using condoms	..	..	1990	2.7

Population policies

	Year	Value	Year	Value
Government's view on the level of fertility	..	..	..	..
Government's policy regarding level of fertility	..	..	..	..
Government's support for contraceptive methods	..	..	..	..

Total fertility rates

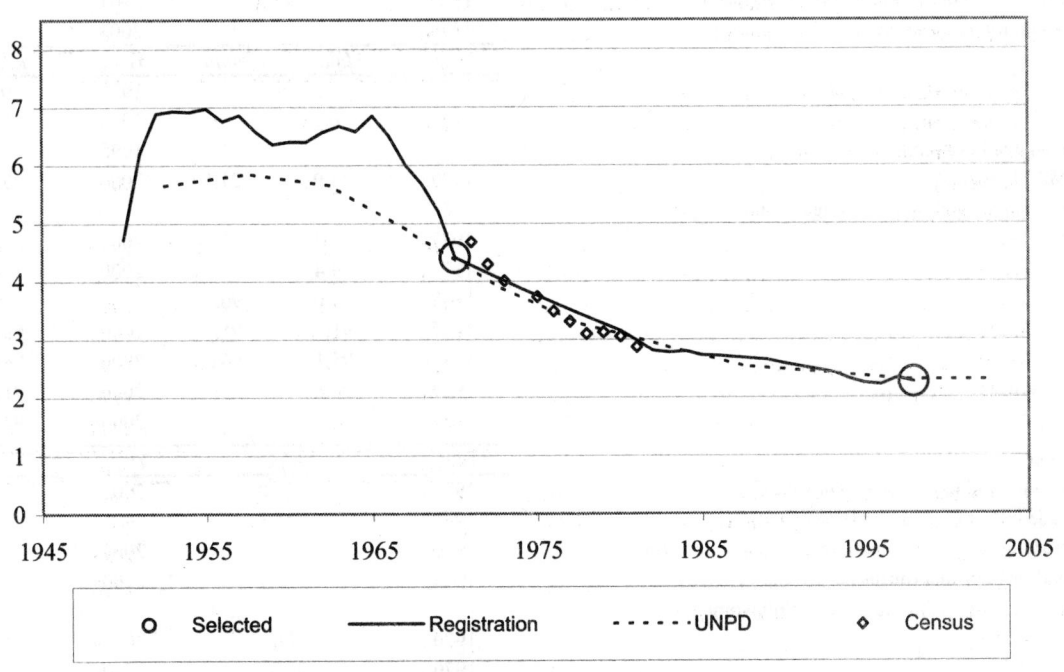

Age-specific fertility rates

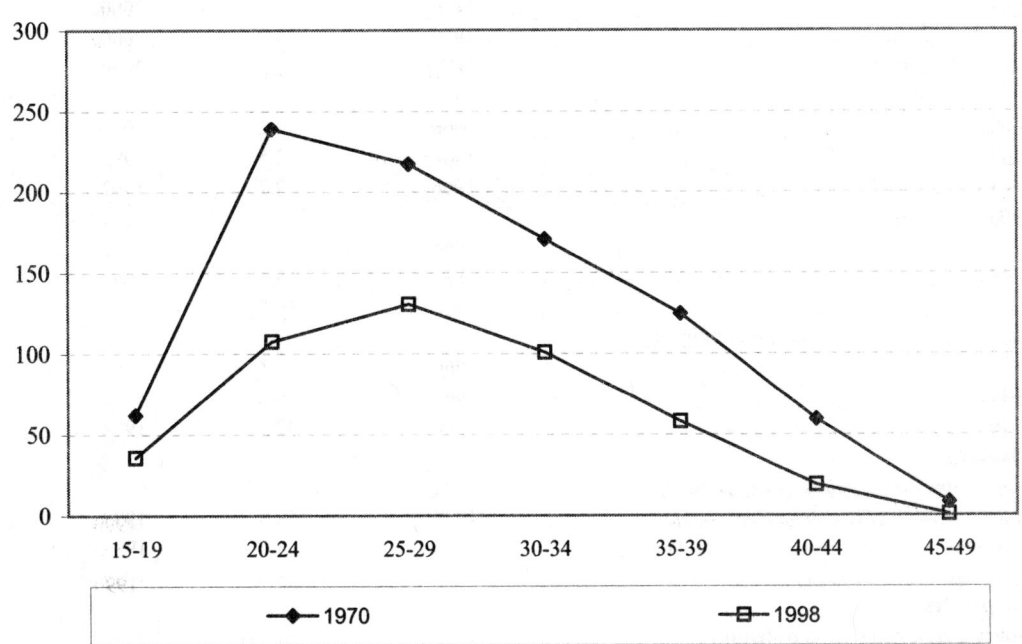

Romania

Indicator	Period					
	Earlier year			Later year		
	Year	Value		Year	Value	

Nuptiality

Indicator	Year	Value		Year	Value	
Annual number of marriages (*thousands*)	1970	145.5		2001	129.9	
Annual number of divorces (*thousands*)	1970	7.9		2001	31.1	

Indicator	Year	Male	Female	Year	Male	Female
Total first marriage rate (per person)	1970	..	0.8	1998	0.7	0.7
Total divorce rate (per person)	1970	0.1	0.1	1997	0.2	0.2
Mean age at first marriage (years)	1970	..	21.9	1998	26.5	23.1
SMAM (years)	1977	24.9	21.1	2000	27.4	24.1
Percentage ever married by age group						
15-19	1977	2.7	15.9	2000	0.2	5.6
20-24	1977	29.4	66.4	2000	13.2	40.8
25-29	1977	77.0	90.1	2000	58.9	78.6
30-34	1977	91.3	95.3	2000	82.4	90.0
35-39	1977	95.1	96.5	2000	88.4	94.3
40-44	1977	96.8	96.8	2000	91.3	95.9
45-49	1977	97.5	96.5	2000	93.8	96.5

Fertility

Indicator	Year	Value	Year	Value
Annual number of births (*thousands*)	1970	427.0	2001	220.4
Crude birth rate (per 1 000 population)	1970	21.1	2001	9.8
Percentage of extra-marital births among all births	1970	3.5	2001	26.7
Total fertility rate (births per woman)	1970	2.9	2000	1.3
Age-specific fertility rate (per 1 000 women)				
15-19	1970	66	2000	39
20-24	1970	202	2000	90
25-29	1970	151	2000	78
30-34	1970	96	2000	37
35-39	1970	48	2000	14
40-44	1970	13	2000	3
45-49	1970	2	2000	0
Mean age at childbearing (years)	1970	26.7	2000	25.7
Mean age at first birth (years)	1970	22.6	2000	23.6
Children ever born per woman				
35-39	1966	2.2	1992	2.1
40-44	1966	2.5	1992	2.3
45-49	1966	2.7	1992	2.3
Percentage of childless women				
35-39	1966	14.8	1992	10.6
40-44	1966	15.6	1992	9.7
45-49	1966	16.5	1992	10.6
Percentage of women with parity three or higher				
35-39	1966	32.3	1992	29.2
40-44	1966	38.8	1992	33.5
45-49	1966	42.9	1992	36.3

Family Planning

Indicator	Year	Value	Year	Value
Contraceptive prevalence among women in union				
Percentage using any contraceptive method	1978	58.0	1999	63.8
Percentage using a modern contraceptive method	1978	5.0	1999	29.5
Percentage using condoms	1978	3.0	1999	8.5

Population policies

Indicator	Year	Value	Year	Value
Government's view on the level of fertility	1976	Satisfactory	2001	Too low
Government's policy regarding level of fertility	1976	Maintain	2001	Raise
Government's support for contraceptive methods	1976	Direct support	2001	Direct support

Total fertility rates

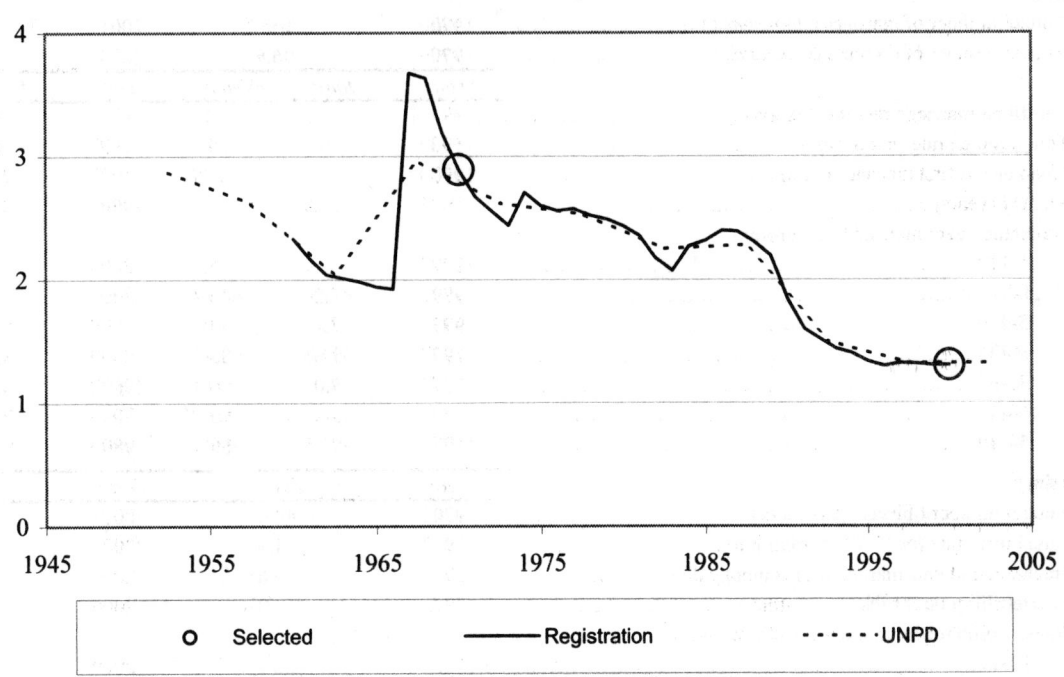

Age-specific fertility rates

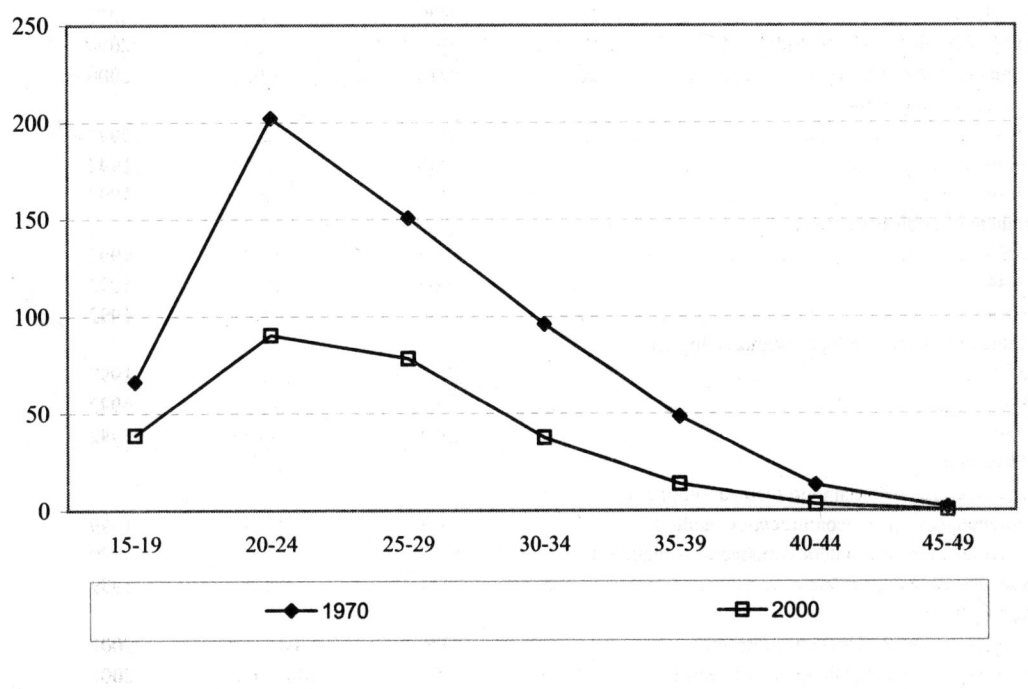

Indicator	Period					
	Earlier year			Later year		
	Year	Value		Year	Value	
Nuptiality						
Annual number of marriages (*thousands*)	1970	1 319.2		2001	1 001.6	
Annual number of divorces (*thousands*)	1970	396.6		2000	627.7	
	Year	Male	Female	Year	Male	Female
Total first marriage rate (per person)	1970	..	1.1	1995	0.7	0.8
Total divorce rate (per person)	1970	..	0.3	1995	0.5	0.6
Mean age at first marriage (years)	1970	..	23.2	1995	24.3	22.0
SMAM (years)	..	..	..	1989	24.4	21.8
Percentage ever married by age group						
15-19	1979	..	..	1989	2.5	10.9
20-24	1979	41.2	64.1	1989	40.0	66.3
25-29	1979	82.1	88.0	1989	79.1	87.9
30-34	1979	91.6	93.4	1989	89.5	93.0
35-39	1979	95.0	96.1	1989	93.2	94.7
40-44	1979	96.8	96.6	1989	95.2	95.5
45-49	1979	98.1	96.0	1989	96.3	96.5
Fertility	Year	Value		Year	Value	
Annual number of births (*thousands*)............................	1970	1 903.7		2001	1 311.6	
Crude birth rate (per 1 000 population)	1970	14.6		2001	9.1	
Percentage of extra-marital births among all births	1970	10.6		2001	28.8	
Total fertility rate (births per woman)	1978	2.0		2001	1.3	
Age-specific fertility rate (per 1 000 women)						
15-19	1970	30		2001	28	
20-24	1970	152		2001	95	
25-29	1970	108		2001	72	
30-34	1970	68		2001	39	
35-39	1970	33		2001	13	
40-44	1970	9		2001	2	
45-49	1970	1		2001	0	
Mean age at childbearing (years)	1970	26.9		2001	25.9	
Mean age at first birth (years)	1979	23.0		1998	23.1	
Children ever born per woman						
35-39	..	..		1994	1.8	
40-44	..	..		1994	1.9	
45-49	..	..		1994	1.8	
Percentage of childless women						
35-39	..	..		1994	7.5	
40-44	..	..		1994	7.0	
45-49	..	..		1994	7.7	
Percentage of women with parity three or higher						
35-39	..	..		1994	17.4	
40-44	..	..		1994	17.4	
45-49	..	..		1994	15.3	
Family Planning						
Contraceptive prevalence among women in union						
Percentage using any contraceptive method	..	..		..	..	
Percentage using a modern contraceptive method	..	..		..	..	
Percentage using condoms	..	..		..	..	
Population policies						
Government's view on the level of fertility	..	--		2001	Too low	
Government's policy regarding level of fertility	..	--		2001	Raise	
Government's support for contraceptive methods	..	--		2001	Direct support	

Total fertility rates

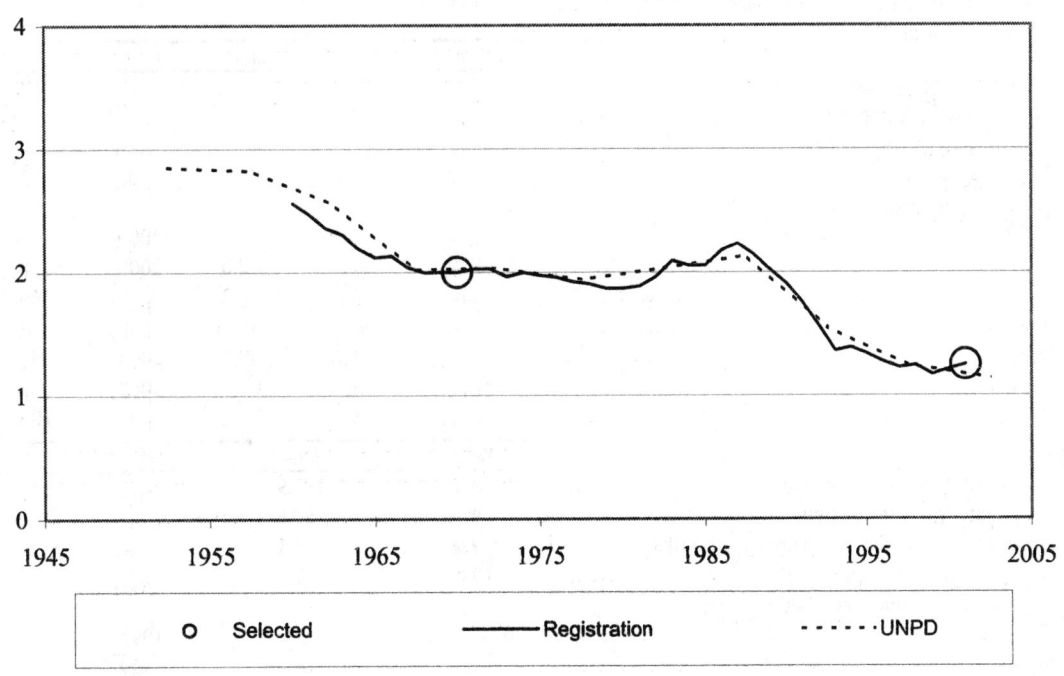

Age-specific fertility rates

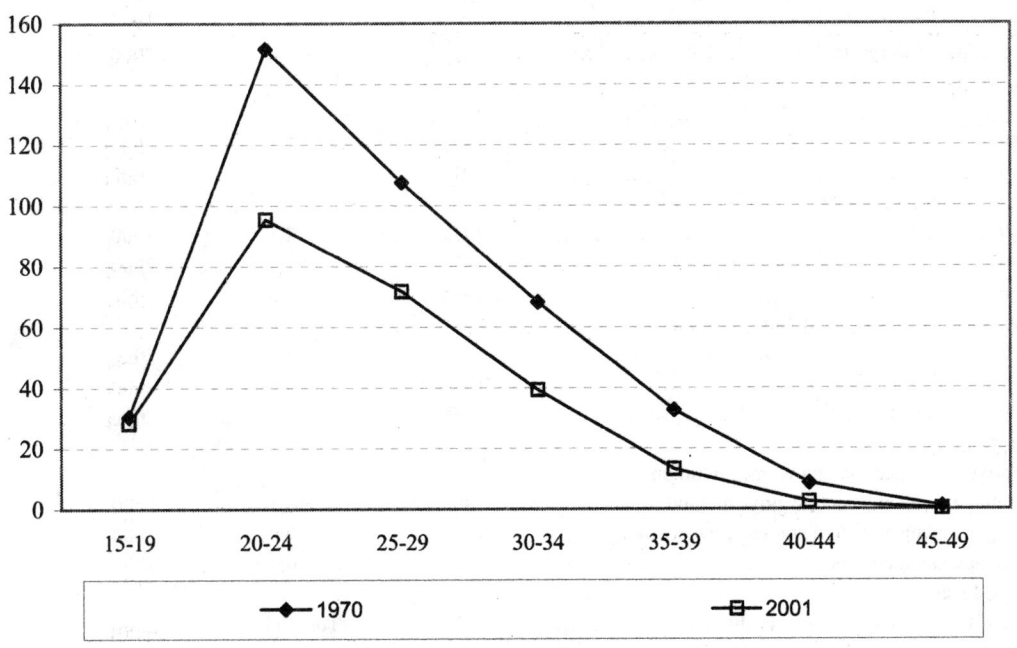

Indicator	Period			
	Earlier year		Later year	
	Year	Value	Year	Value
Nuptiality				
Annual number of marriages (*thousands*)	1970	6.0	..	..
Annual number of divorces (*thousands*)	..	..	..	..

Indicator	Year	Male	Female	Year	Male	Female
Total first marriage rate (per person)	..	..	..	..	..	..
Total divorce rate (per person)	..	..	..	..	..	..
Mean age at first marriage (years)	..	..	..	..	..	..
SMAM (years)	1970	22.6	20.1	2000	25.7	22.7
Percentage ever married by age group						
15-19	1970	3.3	17.6	2000	1.5	7.2
20-24	1970	54.5	82.0	2000	28.7	58.5
25-29	1970	90.0	98.2	2000	66.7	86.7
30-34	1970	97.3	99.6	2000	91.1	95.2
35-39	1970	98.8	99.9	2000	97.2	97.8
40-44	1970	99.5	99.9	2000	96.6	98.1
45-49	1970	99.2	99.9	2000	100.0	98.9

Indicator	Year	Value	Year	Value
Fertility				
Annual number of births (*thousands*)...............................	1970	187.9	..	..
Crude birth rate (per 1 000 population)	1970	50.9	..	..
Percentage of extra-marital births among all births	1978	5.1	..	..
Total fertility rate (births per woman)	1970	7.7	1999	5.9
Age-specific fertility rate (per 1 000 women)				
15-19	..	..	1999	55
20-24	..	..	1999	245
25-29	..	..	1999	278
30-34	..	..	1999	256
35-39	..	..	1999	192
40-44	..	..	1999	122
45-49	..	..	1999	38
Mean age at childbearing (years)	..	..	1999	30.9
Mean age at first birth (years)[a]	..	..	2000	22.0
Children ever born per woman				
35-39	1978	6.2	2000	5.3
40-44	1978	7.1	2000	6.4
45-49	1978	7.3	2000	7.4
Percentage of childless women				
35-39	1978	2.1	2000	2.4
40-44	1978	1.8	2000	1.3
45-49	1978	2.0	2000	1.5
Percentage of women with parity three or higher				
35-39	1978	93.1	2000	90.1
40-44	1978	94.5	2000	91.6
45-49	1978	94.2	2000	96.1
Family Planning				
Contraceptive prevalence among women in union				
Percentage using any contraceptive method	1983	10.1	2000	13.2
Percentage using a modern contraceptive method	1983	0.8	2000	4.3
Percentage using condoms	1983	0.0	2000	0.4
Population policies				
Government's view on the level of fertility	1976	Too high	2001	Too high
Government's policy regarding level of fertility	1976	No intervention	2001	Lower
Government's support for contraceptive methods	1976	No support	2001	Direct support

[a]Median age at first birth among women aged 25-29 at the date of the survey

Total fertility rates

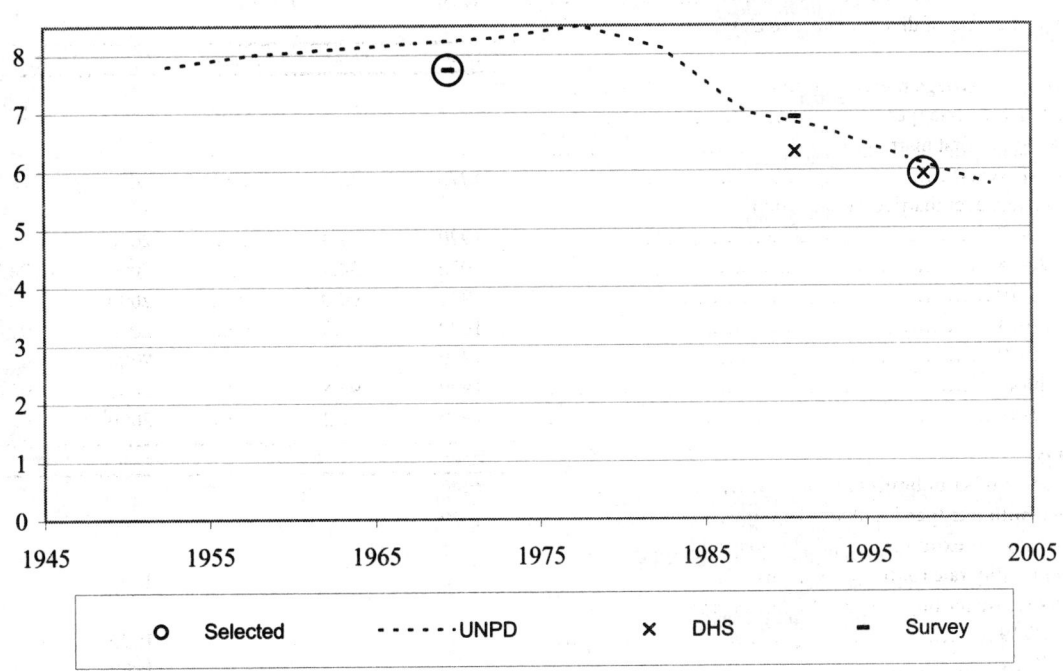

Age-specific fertility rates

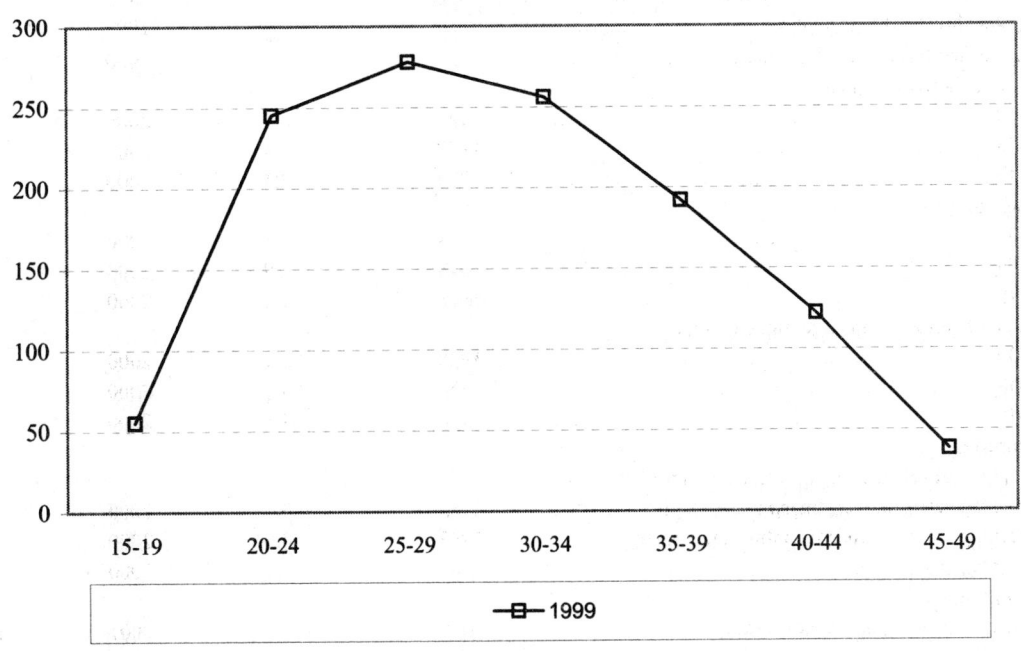

Indicator	Period					
	Earlier year			**Later year**		
	Year	Value		Year	Value	
Nuptiality						
Annual number of marriages (*thousands*)	1970	0.3		2002	0.6	
Annual number of divorces (*thousands*)	1977	0.0		2002	0.1	
	Year	Male	Female	Year	Male	Female
Total first marriage rate (per person)	..	..	..	1998	0.4	0.4
Total divorce rate (per person)	..	..	..	..	..	..
Mean age at first marriage (years)	..	..	..	1998	34.1	31.7
SMAM (years)	1970	32.0	28.7	1991	35.1	33.7
Percentage ever married by age group						
15-19	1970	0.2	1.2	1991	0.5	0.7
20-24	1970	5.0	12.8	1991	2.0	4.8
25-29	1970	23.2	33.9	1991	10.2	15.9
30-34	1970	42.7	49.0	1991	24.4	29.8
35-39	1970	57.1	58.1	1991	39.2	42.6
40-44	1970	66.1	65.7	1991	54.7	51.6
45-49	1970	70.7	67.9	1991	59.7	58.8
Fertility	Year	Value		Year	Value	
Annual number of births (*thousands*).............................	1970	4.0		2002	2.9	
Crude birth rate (per 1 000 population)	1970	39.0		2002	19.4	
Percentage of extra-marital births among all births	1971	72.2		1998	85.8	
Total fertility rate (births per woman)	1975	5.5		2000	2.0	
Age-specific fertility rate (per 1 000 women)						
15-19	1975	162		2000	57	
20-24	1975	275		2000	100	
25-29	1975	271		2000	94	
30-34	1975	195		2000	86	
35-39	1975	128		2000	50	
40-44	1975	59		2000	18	
45-49	1975	9		2000	1	
Mean age at childbearing (years)	1975	27.8		2000	27.9	
Mean age at first birth (years)	1960	20.5		1998	23.1	
Children ever born per woman						
35-39	1980	5.1		1992	3.3	
40-44	1980	5.8		1992	3.9	
45-49	1980	6.2		1992	4.3	
Percentage of childless women						
35-39	1980	7.5		1992	10.8	
40-44	1980	8.3		1992	10.7	
45-49	1980	9.9		1992	9.9	
Percentage of women with parity three or higher						
35-39	1980	75.9		1992	61.8	
40-44	1980	77.0		1992	68.3	
45-49	1980	76.7		1992	73.6	
Family Planning						
Contraceptive prevalence among women in union						
Percentage using any contraceptive method	1981	42.7		1988	47.3	
Percentage using a modern contraceptive method	1981	40.2		1988	46.1	
Percentage using condoms	1981	3.9		1988	5.8	
Population policies						
Government's view on the level of fertility	1976	..		2001	..	
Government's policy regarding level of fertility	1976	..		2001	..	
Government's support for contraceptive methods	1976	..		2001	..	

Total fertility rates

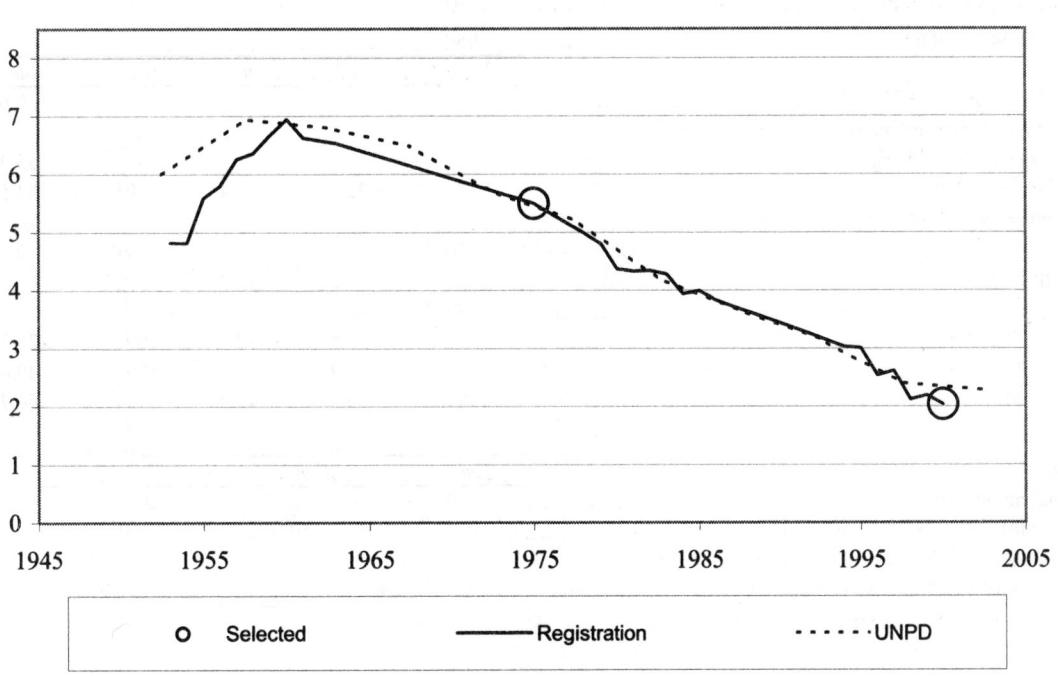

Age-specific fertility rates

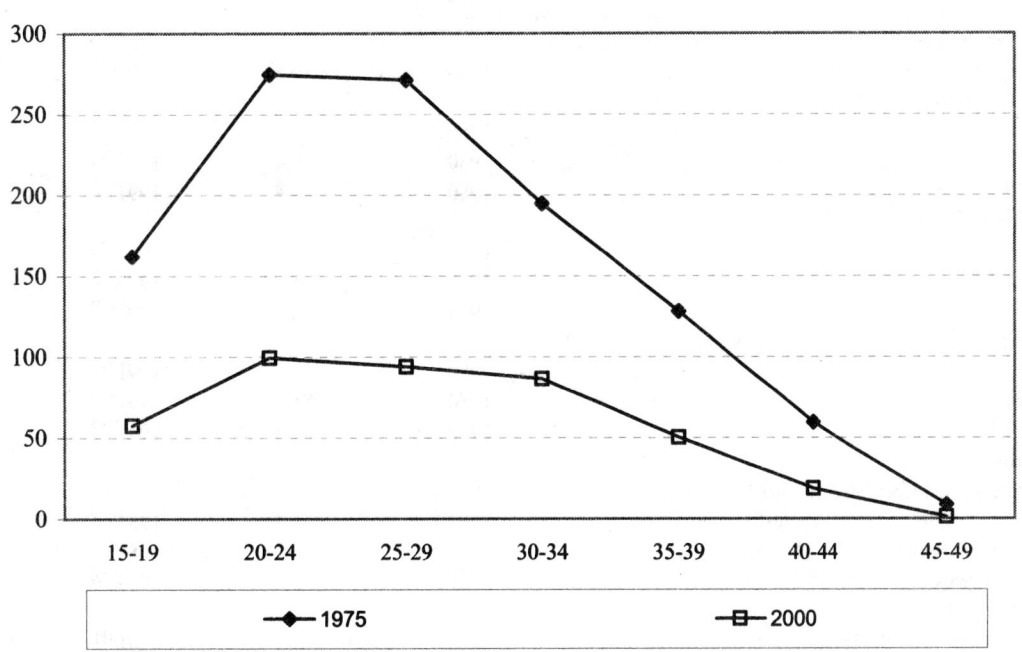

Indicator	Period					
	Earlier year			Later year		
	Year	Value		Year	Value	
Nuptiality						
Annual number of marriages (*thousands*)	1970	0.4		2000	0.7	
Annual number of divorces (*thousands*)	1980	0.0		..	..	
	Year	Male	Female	Year	Male	Female
Total first marriage rate (per person)	..	..	..	1998	0.6	0.6
Total divorce rate (per person)	..	..	..	..	..	..
Mean age at first marriage (years)	..	..	..	1998	35.9	32.5
SMAM (years)	1970	32.8	28.4	1991	34.5	30.9
Percentage ever married by age group						
15-19	1970	0.1	2.3	1991	0.0	0.8
20-24	1970	4.5	14.4	1991	1.8	7.6
25-29	1970	20.7	27.6	1991	10.3	21.8
30-34	1970	36.5	37.5	1991	25.7	34.5
35-39	1970	41.4	44.7	1991	40.0	48.1
40-44	1970	49.3	47.3	1991	54.7	54.2
45-49	1970	57.2	49.4	1991	60.7	58.3
Fertility	Year	Value		Year	Value	
Annual number of births (*thousands*)..........................	1970	3.3		2000	2.2	
Crude birth rate (per 1 000 population)	1970	40.0		2001	18.0	
Percentage of extra-marital births among all births	..	..		..	..	
Total fertility rate (births per woman)	..	..		..	..	
Age-specific fertility rate (per 1 000 women)						
15-19	..	..		..	..	
20-24	..	..		..	..	
25-29	..	..		..	..	
30-34	..	..		..	..	
35-39	..	..		..	..	
40-44	..	..		..	..	
45-49	..	..		..	..	
Mean age at childbearing (years)	..	..		..	..	
Mean age at first birth (years)	1960	19.8		1997	22.1	
Children ever born per woman						
35-39	1980	5.4		1991	3.6	
40-44	1980	6.4		1991	4.3	
45-49	1980	6.4		1991	4.9	
Percentage of childless women						
35-39	1980	5.8		1991	8.6	
40-44	1980	5.8		1991	6.4	
45-49	1980	6.9		1991	7.7	
Percentage of women with parity three or higher						
35-39	1980	80.6		1991	67.2	
40-44	1980	84.6		1991	75.1	
45-49	1980	81.5		1991	78.7	
Family Planning						
Contraceptive prevalence among women in union						
Percentage using any contraceptive method	1981	41.5		1988	58.3	
Percentage using a modern contraceptive method	1981	39.5		1988	54.6	
Percentage using condoms	1981	8.3		1988	7.4	
Population policies						
Government's view on the level of fertility	1976	..		2001	Too high	
Government's policy regarding level of fertility	1976	..		2001	Lower	
Government's support for contraceptive methods	1976	..		2001	Direct support	

Saint Vincent and the Grenadines

Total fertility rates

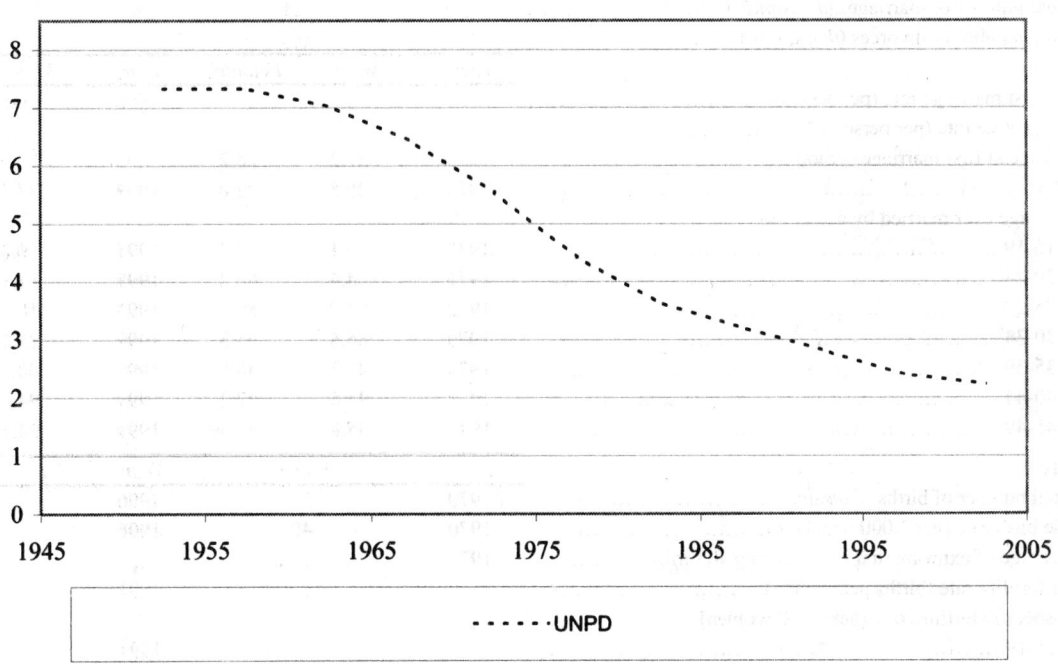

Indicator	Period					
	Earlier year			Later year		
	Year	Value		Year	Value	

Nuptiality

Indicator	Year	Value		Year	Value	
Annual number of marriages (*thousands*)	..	..		..	..	
Annual number of divorces (*thousands*)	..	..		..	..	

Indicator	Year	Male	Female	Year	Male	Female
Total first marriage rate (per person)	..	..	..	..	..	..
Total divorce rate (per person)	..	..	..	..	..	..
Mean age at first marriage (years)	1978	31.2	28.2	..	..	..
SMAM (years)	1971	26.3	22.0	1999	27.4	23.9
Percentage ever married by age group						
15-19	1971	1.4	10.3	1999	1.1	8.3
20-24	1971	25.4	62.2	1999	19.1	50.8
25-29	1971	63.7	89.1	1999	52.7	77.4
30-34	1971	85.4	95.3	1999	74.3	87.4
35-39	1971	90.7	96.1	1999	87.7	91.5
40-44	1971	94.6	97.2	1999	94.6	93.9
45-49	1971	95.8	97.3	1999	94.4	96.6

Fertility

Indicator	Year	Value	Year	Value
Annual number of births (*thousands*)	1970	5.7	1996	5.0
Crude birth rate (per 1 000 population)	1970	40.1	1996	29.7
Percentage of extra-marital births among all births	1975	59.0	..	..
Total fertility rate (births per woman)	..	..	1991	4.9
Age-specific fertility rate (per 1 000 women)				
15-19	..	..	1991	26
20-24	..	..	1991	165
25-29	..	..	1991	251
30-34	..	..	1991	221
35-39	..	..	1991	182
40-44	..	..	1991	103
45-49	..	..	1991	39
Mean age at childbearing (years)	..	..	1991	31.7
Mean age at first birth (years)	1976	27.8	..	..
Children ever born per woman				
35-39	1971	6.2	..	..
40-44	1971	6.7	..	..
45-49	1971	6.8	..	..
Percentage of childless women				
35-39	1971	6.8	..	..
40-44	1971	6.2	..	..
45-49	1971	7.1	..	..
Percentage of women with parity three or higher				
35-39	1971	84.2	..	..
40-44	1971	84.9	..	..
45-49	1971	83.2	..	..

Family Planning

Indicator	Year	Value	Year	Value
Contraceptive prevalence among women in union				
Percentage using any contraceptive method	..	..	..	..
Percentage using a modern contraceptive method	..	..	..	..
Percentage using condoms	..	..	..	..

Population policies

Indicator	Year	Value	Year	Value
Government's view on the level of fertility	..	..	2001	Too high
Government's policy regarding level of fertility	..	..	2001	Lower
Government's support for contraceptive methods	..	..	2001	No support

Total fertility rates

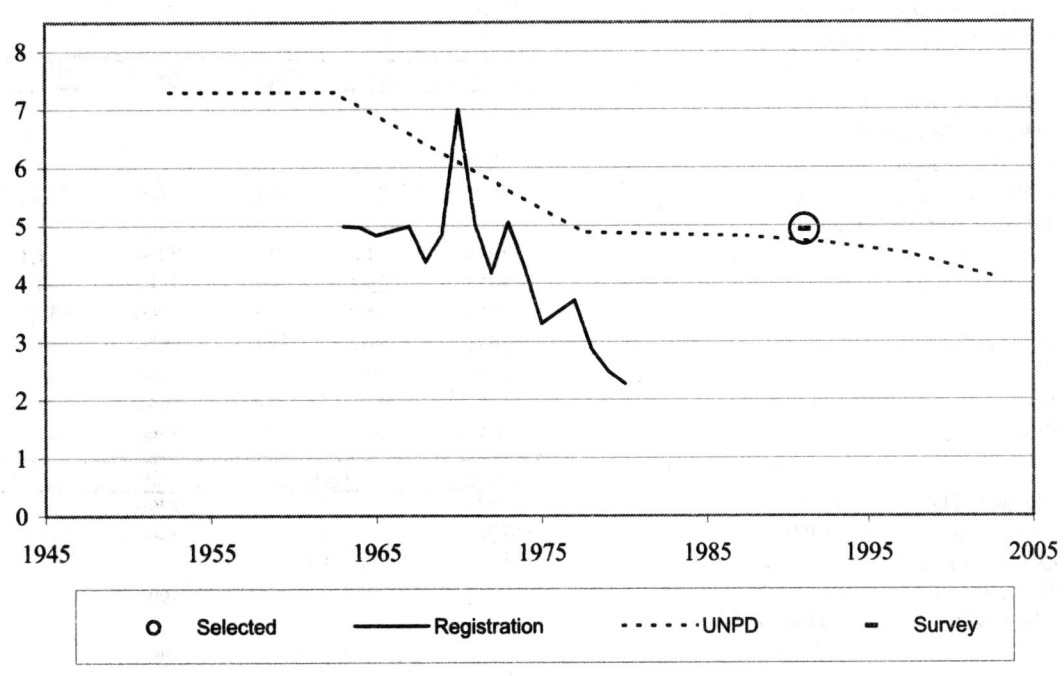

Age-specific fertility rates

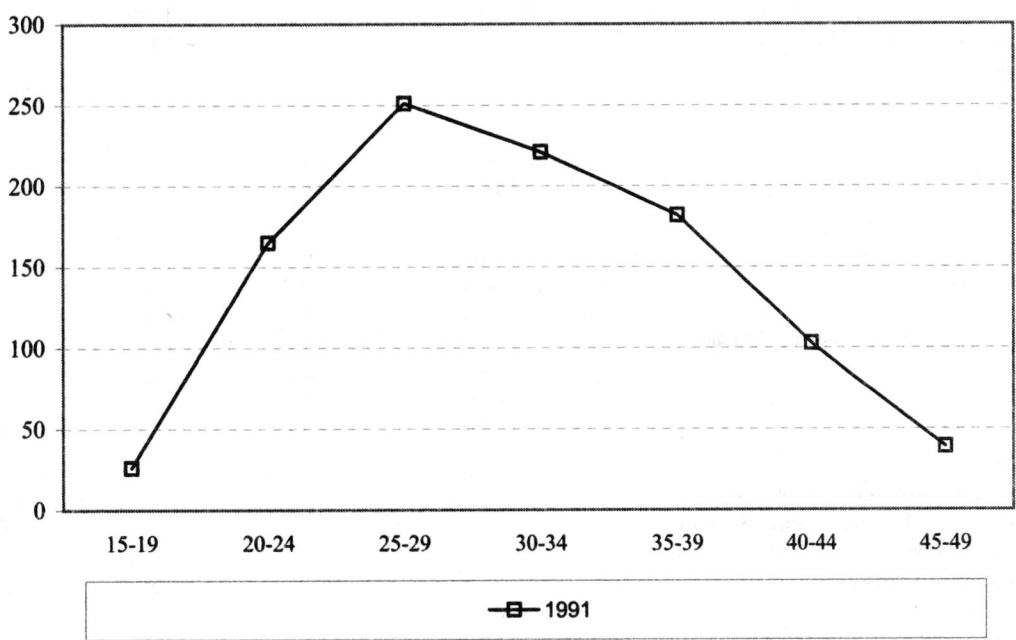

Indicator	Period					
	Earlier year			Later year		
	Year	Value		Year	Value	
Nuptiality						
Annual number of marriages (*thousands*)	1970	0.1		1988	0.0	
Annual number of divorces (*thousands*)	..	..		..	..	
	Year	Male	Female	Year	Male	Female
Total first marriage rate (per person)	..	..	..	..	..	..
Total divorce rate (per person)	..	..	..	..	..	..
Mean age at first marriage (years)	..	..	..	..	..	..
SMAM (years)	1981	21.6	15.6	1991	23.1	17.8
Percentage ever married by age group						
15-19	1981	2.6	24.4	1991	1.9	19.9
20-24	1981	32.9	57.2	1991	28.0	61.7
25-29	1981	65.6	70.6	1991	63.2	74.8
30-34	1981	73.8	73.5	1991	77.6	78.5
35-39	1981	73.1	74.8	1991	81.7	78.4
40-44	1981	70.9	73.4	1991	81.4	78.8
45-49	1981	70.4	69.2	1991	77.4	75.4
Fertility	Year	Value		Year	Value	
Annual number of births (*thousands*)	1970	3.3		1993	5.3	
Crude birth rate (per 1 000 population)	1970	44.5		1993	43.0	
Percentage of extra-marital births among all births	1970	84.7		..	..	
Total fertility rate (births per woman)	..	..		..	..	
Age-specific fertility rate (per 1 000 women)						
15-19	..	..		..	..	
20-24	..	..		..	..	
25-29	..	..		..	..	
30-34	..	..		..	..	
35-39	..	..		..	..	
40-44	..	..		..	..	
45-49	..	..		..	..	
Mean age at childbearing (years)	..	..		..	..	
Mean age at first birth (years)	..	..		..	..	
Children ever born per woman						
35-39	1980	5.7		1991	5.3	
40-44	1980	5.9		1991	5.9	
45-49	1980	5.8		1991	6.2	
Percentage of childless women						
35-39	1980	5.7		1991	2.9	
40-44	1980	6.5		1991	3.3	
45-49	1980	7.8		1991	3.5	
Percentage of women with parity three or higher						
35-39	1980	85.2		1991	83.2	
40-44	1980	84.1		1991	83.2	
45-49	1980	82.5		1991	82.7	
Family Planning						
Contraceptive prevalence among women in union						
Percentage using any contraceptive method	..	..		2000	29.3	
Percentage using a modern contraceptive method	..	..		2000	27.4	
Percentage using condoms	..	..		2000	0.1	
Population policies						
Government's view on the level of fertility	1976	Satisfactory		2001	Too high	
Government's policy regarding level of fertility	1976	No intervention		2001	No intervention	
Government's support for contraceptive methods	1976	No support		2001	Indirect support	

Total fertility rates

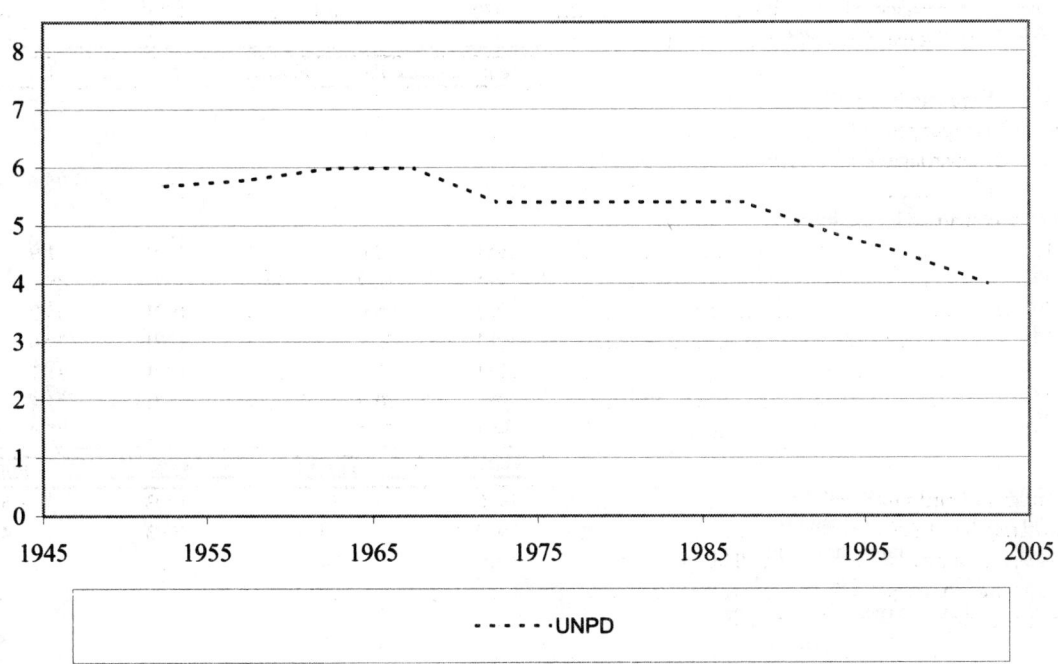

Saudi Arabia

Indicator	Period					
Nuptiality	Year	Value		Year	Value	
Annual number of marriages (*thousands*)	..	..		2000	79.6	
Annual number of divorces (*thousands*)	..	..		2000	18.6	
	Year	Male	Female	Year	Male	Female
Total first marriage rate (per person)	..	..	..	..	..	..
Total divorce rate (per person)	..	..	..	..	..	..
Mean age at first marriage (years)	..	..	..	..	..	..
SMAM (years)	..	..	..	1987	25.6	21.7
Percentage ever married by age group						
15-19	..	..	..	1987	1.0	16.1
20-24	..	..	..	1987	24.0	61.1
25-29	..	..	..	1987	71.0	87.5
30-34	..	..	..	1987	92.6	89.9
35-39	..	..	..	1987	96.6	95.3
40-44	..	..	..	1987	97.6	97.0
45-49	..	..	..	1987	98.6	98.1
Fertility	Year	Value		Year	Value	
Annual number of births (*thousands*)	..	..		2000	624.3	
Crude birth rate (per 1 000 population)	..	..		2000	29.9	
Percentage of extra-marital births among all births	..	..		..	..	
Total fertility rate (births per woman)	..	..		1994	6.1	
Age-specific fertility rate (per 1 000 women)						
15-19	..	..		1994	61	
20-24	..	..		1994	224	
25-29	..	..		1994	287	
30-34	..	..		1994	264	
35-39	..	..		1994	195	
40-44	..	..		1994	119	
45-49	..	..		1994	70	
Mean age at childbearing (years)	..	..		1994	31.4	
Mean age at first birth (years)	..	..		..	..	
Children ever born per woman						
35-39	..	..		1996	6.8	
40-44	..	..		1996	7.7	
45-49	..	..		1996	8.2	
Percentage of childless women						
35-39	..	..		1996	4.4	
40-44	..	..		1996	3.3	
45-49	..	..		1996	3.2	
Percentage of women with parity three or higher						
35-39	..	..		1996	90.8	
40-44	..	..		1996	92.3	
45-49	..	..		1996	92.2	
Family Planning						
Contraceptive prevalence among women in union						
Percentage using any contraceptive method	..	..		1996	31.8	
Percentage using a modern contraceptive method	..	..		1996	28.5	
Percentage using condoms	..	..		1996	0.9	
Population policies						
Government's view on the level of fertility	1976	Satisfactory		2001	Satisfactory	
Government's policy regarding level of fertility	1976	Maintain		2001	Raise	
Government's support for contraceptive methods	1976	Limits		2001	Direct support	

Total fertility rates

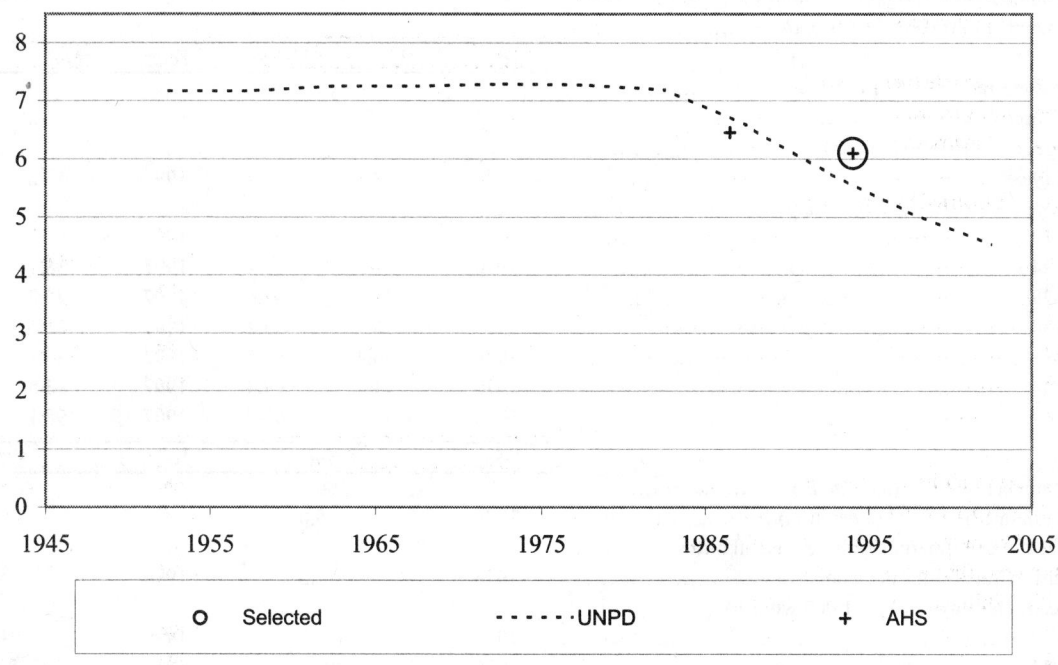

Age-specific fertility rates

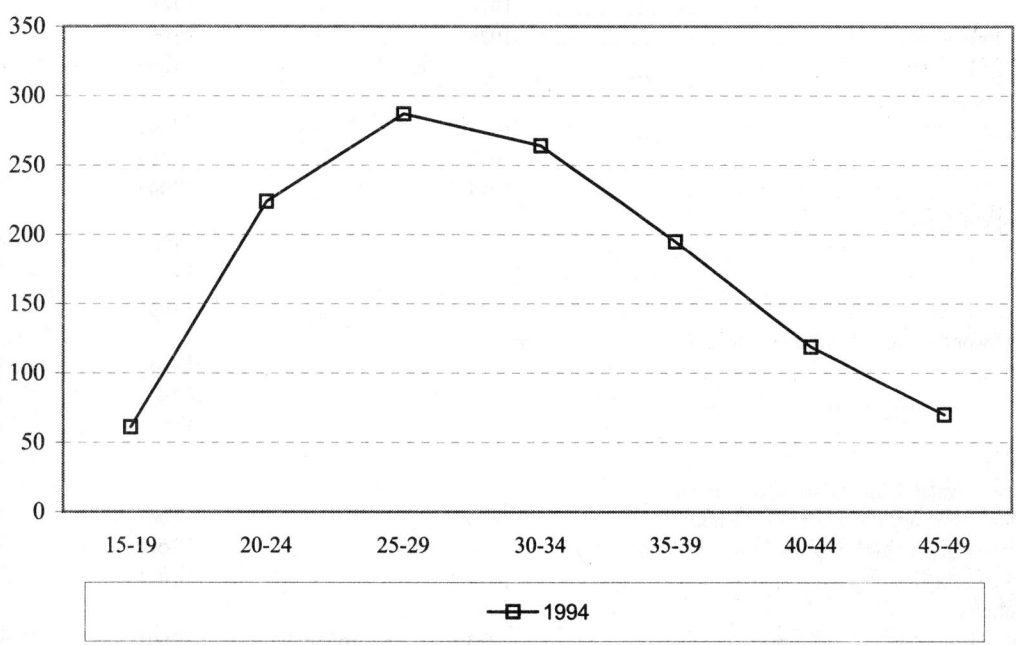

Indicator	Period					
	Earlier year			Later year		
	Year	Value		Year	Value	
Nuptiality						
Annual number of marriages (*thousands*)	..	..		..	..	
Annual number of divorces (*thousands*)	..	..		..	..	
	Year	Male	Female	Year	Male	Female
Total first marriage rate (per person)	..	..	..	..	..	..
Total divorce rate (per person)	..	..	..	..	..	..
Mean age at first marriage (years)	..	..	..	..	..	..
SMAM (years)	1970	28.8	18.7	1997	..	21.5
Percentage ever married by age group						
15-19	1970	0.8	43.3	1997	..	29.0
20-24	1970	9.7	85.4	1997	8.1	62.8
25-29	1970	43.8	97.6	1997	36.2	83.6
30-34	1970	76.7	99.2	1997	62.6	95.3
35-39	1970	90.4	99.5	1997	84.8	98.5
40-44	1970	94.4	99.4	1997	95.8	99.6
45-49	1970	96.7	99.7	1997	98.1	99.9
Fertility	Year	Value		Year	Value	
Annual number of births (*thousands*).............................	1970	200.4		..	..	
Crude birth rate (per 1 000 population)	1970	45.6		..	..	
Percentage of extra-marital births among all births	..	..		..	..	
Total fertility rate (births per woman)	1976	7.2		1996	5.8	
Age-specific fertility rate (per 1 000 women)						
15-19	1976	188		1996	104	
20-24	1976	304		1996	225	
25-29	1976	331		1996	247	
30-34	1976	270		1996	246	
35-39	1976	197		1996	191	
40-44	1976	106		1996	108	
45-49	1976	36		1996	42	
Mean age at childbearing (years)	1976	29.1		1996	30.5	
Mean age at first birth (years)[a]	..	..		1997	20.4	
Children ever born per woman						
35-39	1978	5.9		1997	5.8	
40-44	1978	6.8		1997	6.7	
45-49	1978	7.2		1997	7.6	
Percentage of childless women						
35-39	..	..		1997	2.9	
40-44	..	..		1997	2.4	
45-49	..	..		1997	1.7	
Percentage of women with parity three or higher						
35-39	..	..		1997	86.1	
40-44	..	..		1997	90.1	
45-49	..	..		1997	92.0	
Family Planning						
Contraceptive prevalence among women in union						
Percentage using any contraceptive method	1978	3.8		1997	12.9	
Percentage using a modern contraceptive method	1978	0.6		1997	8.1	
Percentage using condoms	1978	0.3		1997	0.6	
Population policies						
Government's view on the level of fertility	1976	Too high		2001	Too high	
Government's policy regarding level of fertility	1976	No intervention		2001	Lower	
Government's support for contraceptive methods	1976	No support		2001	Direct support	

[a]Median age at first birth among women aged 25-29 at the date of the survey

Total fertility rates

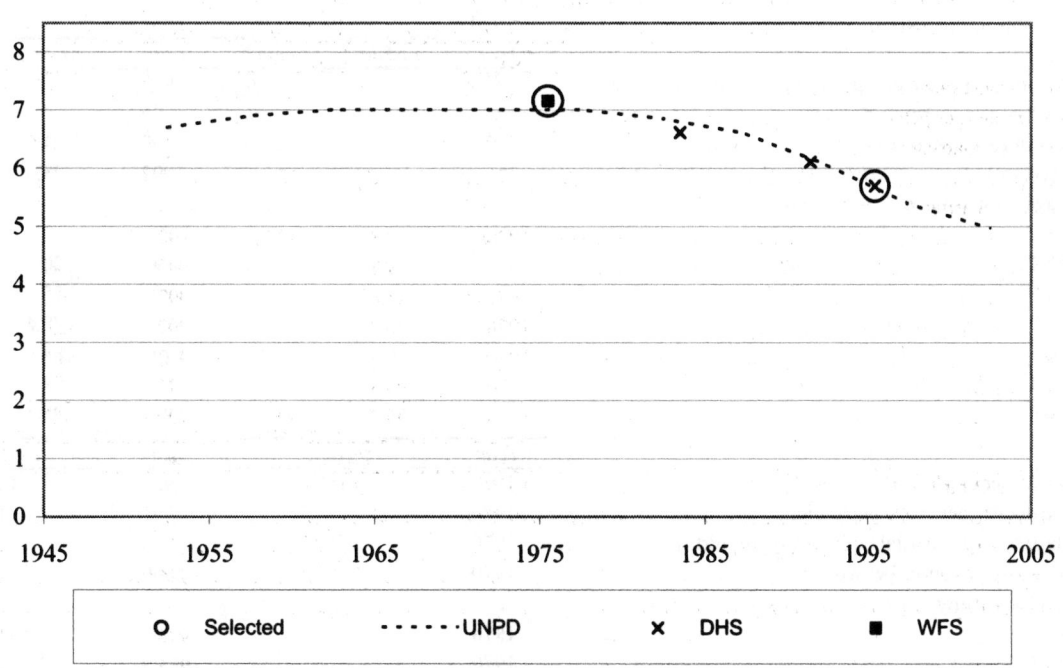

Age-specific fertility rates

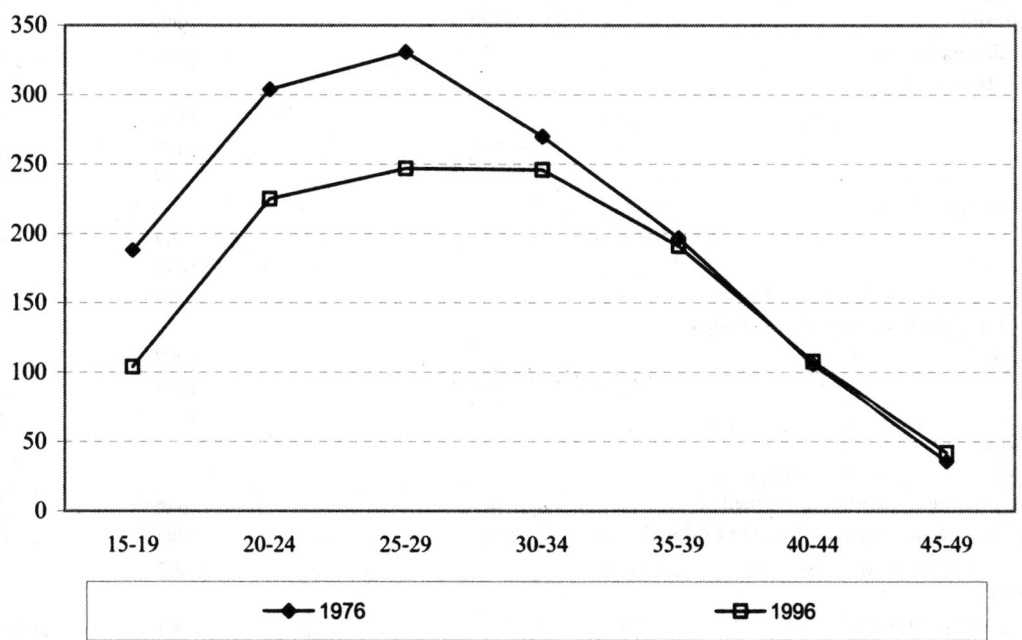

Indicator	Period					
	Earlier year			Later year		
	Year	Value		Year	Value	

Nuptiality

	Year	Value		Year	Value	
Annual number of marriages (*thousands*)	1970	82.1		1999	53.0	
Annual number of divorces (*thousands*)	1970	9.7		2001	8.5	

	Year	Male	Female	Year	Male	Female
Total first marriage rate (per person)	1970	..	0.9	1997	0.6	0.6
Total divorce rate (per person)	..	..	..	1995	0.1	0.1
Mean age at first marriage (years)	1970	..	22.0	1997	27.7	24.2
SMAM (years)	..	..	..	1991	27.4	23.1
Percentage ever married by age group						
15-19	..	..	..	1991	1.9	11.3
20-24	..	..	..	1991	20.5	50.8
25-29	..	..	..	1991	55.2	78.8
30-34	..	..	..	1991	78.4	90.6
35-39	..	..	..	1991	88.6	94.0
40-44	..	..	..	1991	93.4	95.4
45-49	..	..	..	1991	95.5	96.1

Fertility

	Year	Value		Year	Value	
Annual number of births (*thousands*)	1970	157.6		2001	131.4	
Crude birth rate (per 1 000 population)	1970	17.7		2001	12.3	
Percentage of extra-marital births among all births	1970	11.7		2000	20.4	
Total fertility rate (births per woman)	1970	2.3		2000	1.7	
Age-specific fertility rate (per 1 000 women)						
15-19	1970	62		2000	25	
20-24	1970	166		2000	105	
25-29	1970	123		2000	109	
30-34	1970	67		2000	62	
35-39	1970	30		2000	25	
40-44	1970	9		2000	5	
45-49	1970	2		2000	0	
Mean age at childbearing (years)	1970	26.1		2000	27.1	
Mean age at first birth (years)	1970	22.7		2000	25.0	
Children ever born per woman						
35-39	..	..		..	..	
40-44	..	..		..	..	
45-49	..	..		..	..	
Percentage of childless women						
35-39	..	..		..	..	
40-44	..	..		..	..	
45-49	..	..		..	..	
Percentage of women with parity three or higher						
35-39	..	..		..	..	
40-44	..	..		..	..	
45-49	..	..		..	..	

Family Planning

	Year	Value		Year	Value	
Contraceptive prevalence among women in union						
Percentage using any contraceptive method	..	..		2000	58.3	
Percentage using a modern contraceptive method	..	..		2000	32.8	
Percentage using condoms	..	..		2000	17.0	

Population policies

	Year	Value		Year	Value	
Government's view on the level of fertility	..	--		2001	Satisfactory	
Government's policy regarding level of fertility	..	--		2001	Maintain	
Government's support for contraceptive methods	..	--		2001	Direct support	

Total fertility rates

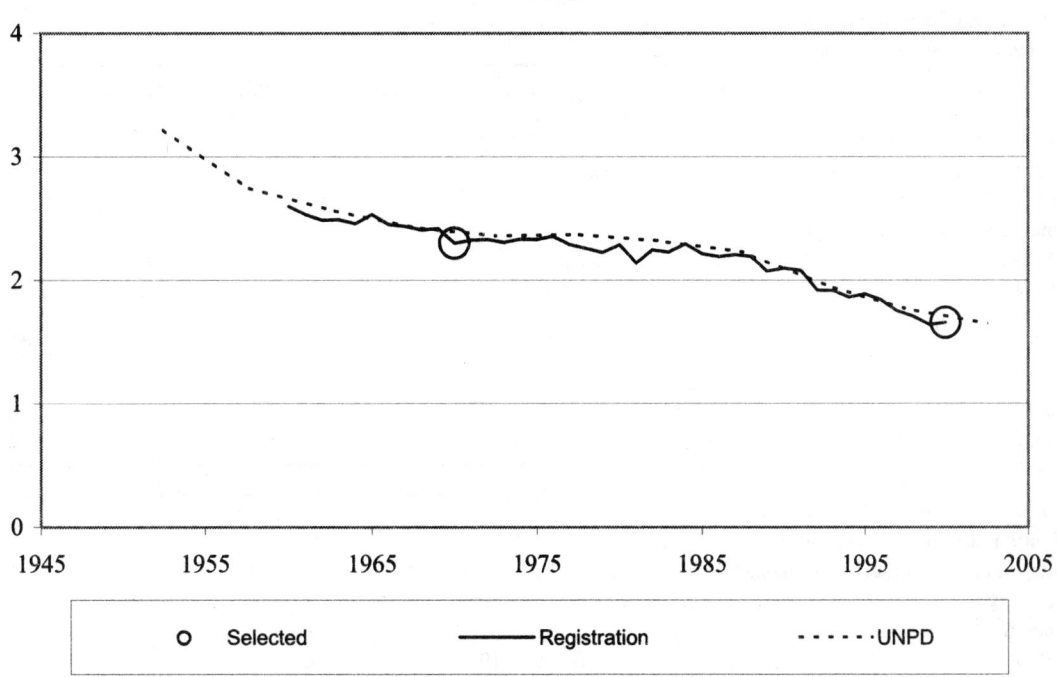

Age-specific fertility rates

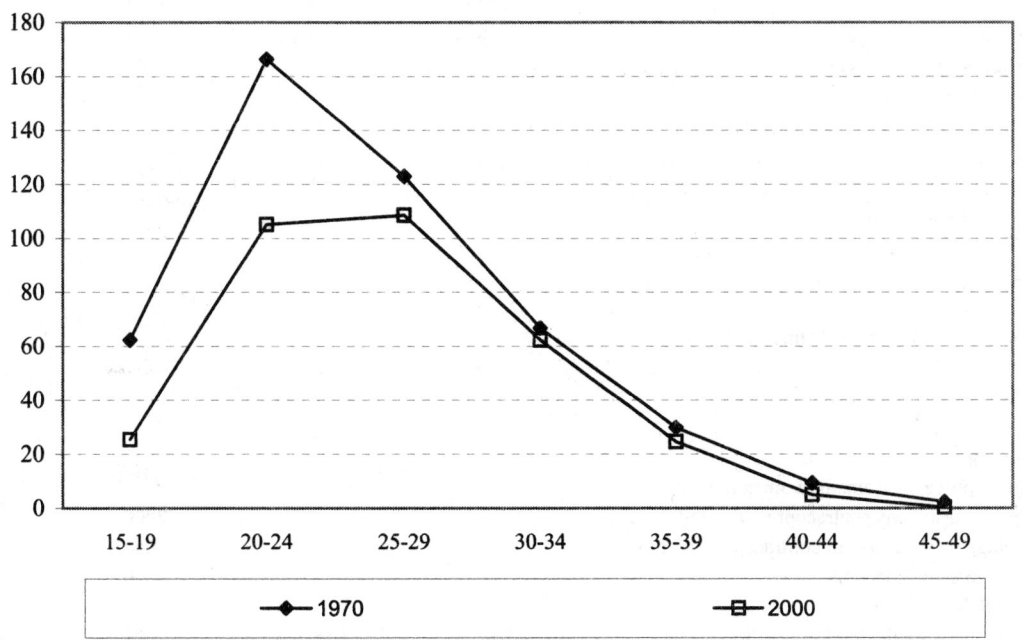

Sierra Leone

Indicator	Period			
	Earlier year		Later year	
	Year	Value	Year	Value
Nuptiality				
Annual number of marriages (*thousands*)	..	..	..	..
Annual number of divorces (*thousands*)	..	..	..	..

	Year	Male	Female	Year	Male	Female
Total first marriage rate (per person)	..	..	..	..	..	..
Total divorce rate (per person)	..	..	..	..	..	..
Mean age at first marriage (years)	..	..	..	..	..	..
SMAM (years)	..	..	..	1992	27.6	19.8
Percentage ever married by age group						
15-19	..	..	..	1992	6.0	47.4
20-24	..	..	..	1992	20.3	73.1
25-29	..	..	..	1992	50.9	88.7
30-34	..	..	..	1992	77.3	92.9
35-39	..	..	..	1992	89.1	97.2
40-44	..	..	..	1992	94.3	96.7
45-49	..	..	..	1992	97.0	98.3

Fertility	Year	Value	Year	Value
Annual number of births (*thousands*)	..	..	..	..
Crude birth rate (per 1 000 population)	..	..	..	..
Percentage of extra-marital births among all births	..	..	..	..
Total fertility rate (births per woman)	1973	6.5	1985	6.3
Age-specific fertility rate (per 1 000 women)				
15-19	1973	212	1985	202
20-24	1973	296	1985	283
25-29	1973	280	1985	271
30-34	1973	210	1985	214
35-39	1973	169	1985	163
40-44	1973	81	1985	80
45-49	1973	54	1985	47
Mean age at childbearing (years)	1973	28.6	1985	28.6
Mean age at first birth (years)	..	..	..	..
Children ever born per woman				
35-39	..	..	..	..
40-44	..	..	..	..
45-49	..	..	..	..
Percentage of childless women				
35-39	..	..	..	..
40-44	..	..	..	..
45-49	..	..	..	..
Percentage of women with parity three or higher				
35-39	..	..	..	..
40-44	..	..	..	..
45-49	..	..	..	..
Family Planning				
Contraceptive prevalence among women in union				
Percentage using any contraceptive method	..	..	2000	4.3
Percentage using a modern contraceptive method	..	..	2000	3.9
Percentage using condoms	..	..	2000	0.1
Population policies				
Government's view on the level of fertility	1976	Too high	2001	Too high
Government's policy regarding level of fertility	1976	No intervention	2001	Lower
Government's support for contraceptive methods	1976	Direct support	2001	Direct support

Total fertility rates

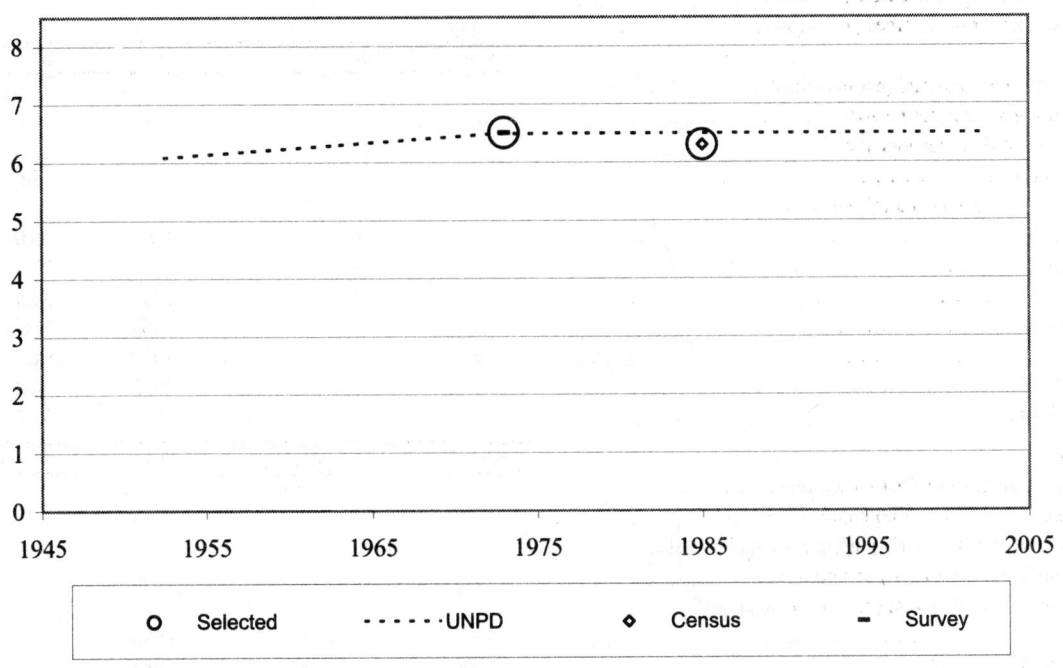

O Selected	····· UNPD	◇ Census	— Survey

Age-specific fertility rates

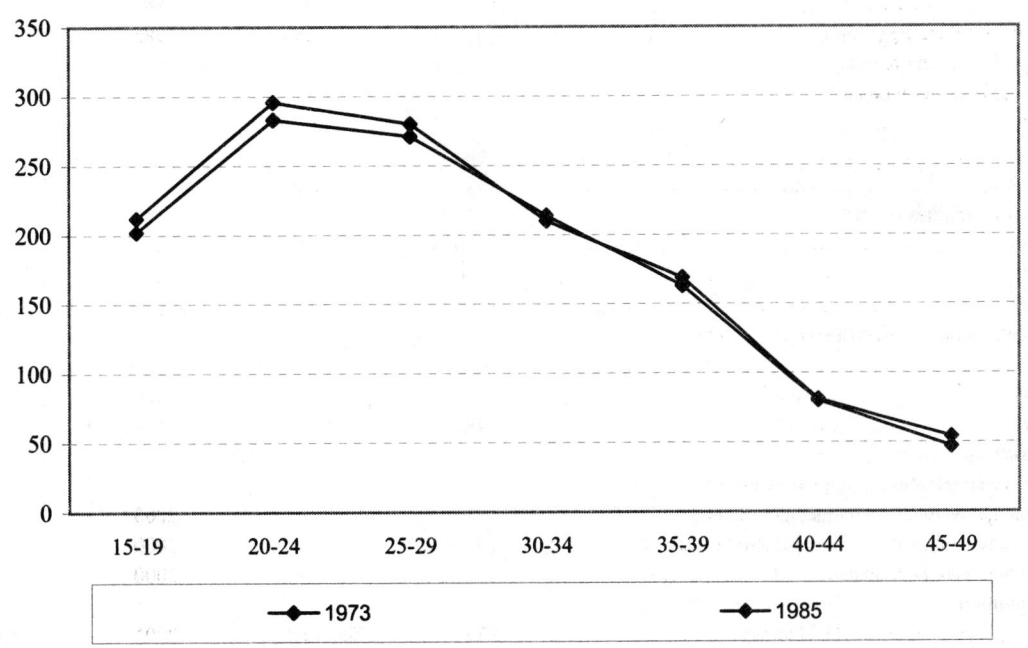

◆ 1973	◆ 1985

Indicator	Period			
	Earlier year		**Later year**	
	Year	Value	Year	Value
Nuptiality				
Annual number of marriages (*thousands*)	1970	15.3	2001	23.8
Annual number of divorces (*thousands*)	1979	1.5	2002	5.5

Indicator	Year	Male	Female	Year	Male	Female
Total first marriage rate (per person)	1976	0.9	0.9	1998	0.8	0.8
Total divorce rate (per person)	1980	0.1	0.1	1997	0.1	0.2
Mean age at first marriage (years)	1976	28.1	24.6	1998	29.0	26.0
SMAM (years)	1970	27.8	24.2	2001	30.0	26.5
Percentage ever married by age group						
15-19	1970	0.5	4.8	2001	0.1	1.0
20-24	1970	11.5	35.4	2001	4.8	16.2
25-29	1970	52.0	77.4	2001	35.8	59.8
30-34	1970	78.5	90.4	2001	69.3	80.5
35-39	1970	89.2	94.9	2001	80.3	84.9
40-44	1970	92.8	96.7	2001	85.2	86.4
45-49	1970	94.1	96.9	2001	89.5	87.5

Fertility	Year	Value	Year	Value
Annual number of births (*thousands*).............................	1970	45.9	2002	40.9
Crude birth rate (per 1 000 population)	1970	22.1	2002	9.8
Percentage of extra-marital births among all births	..	..	..	..
Total fertility rate (births per woman)	1970	3.1	2000	1.7
Age-specific fertility rate (per 1 000 women)				
15-19	1970	26	2000	9
20-24	1970	140	2000	43
25-29	1970	210	2000	113
30-34	1970	139	2000	114
35-39	1970	75	2000	45
40-44	1970	27	2000	8
45-49	1970	5	2000	0
Mean age at childbearing (years)	1970	29.1	2000	30.0
Mean age at first birth (years)	1970	25.0	1998	28.1
Children ever born per woman				
35-39	1980	2.9	1990	1.9
40-44	1980	3.7	1990	2.2
45-49	1980	4.7	1990	2.9
Percentage of childless women				
35-39	1980	2.9	1990	5.4
40-44	1980	2.6	1990	4.0
45-49	1980	2.3	1990	2.7
Percentage of women with parity three or higher				
35-39	1980	56.9	1990	29.5
40-44	1980	68.6	1990	40.5
45-49	1980	77.6	1990	59.3
Family Planning				
Contraceptive prevalence among women in union				
Percentage using any contraceptive method	1973	60.1	1997	62.0
Percentage using a modern contraceptive method	1973	52.8	1997	53.0
Percentage using condoms	1973	17.0	1997	22.0
Population policies				
Government's view on the level of fertility	1976	Satisfactory	2001	Too low
Government's policy regarding level of fertility	1976	No intervention	2001	Raise
Government's support for contraceptive methods	1976	Direct support	2001	No support

Total fertility rates

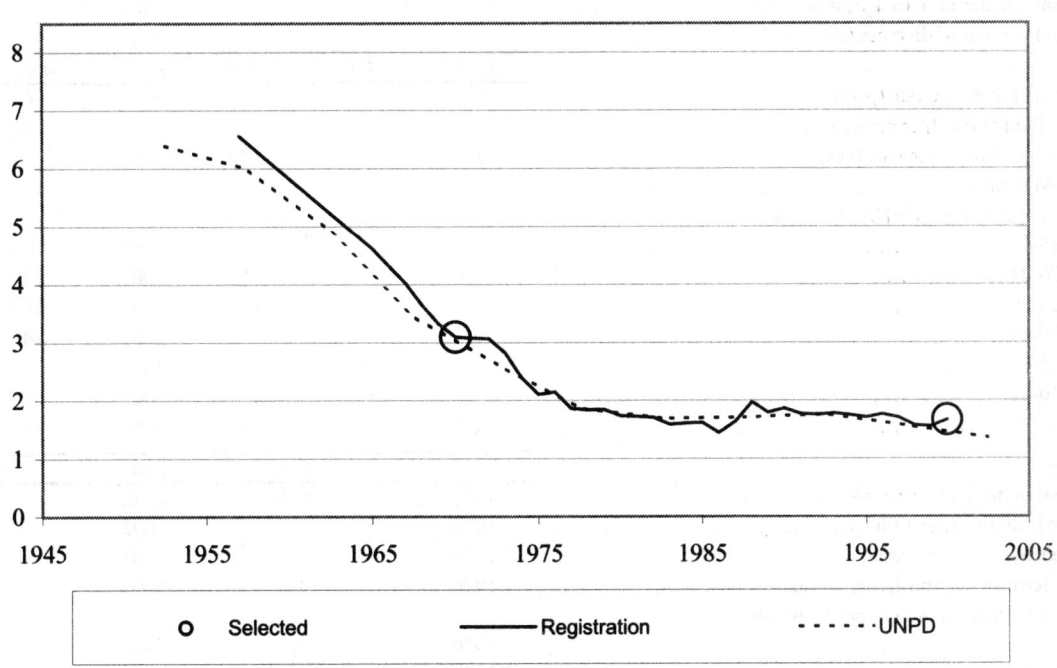

Age-specific fertility rates

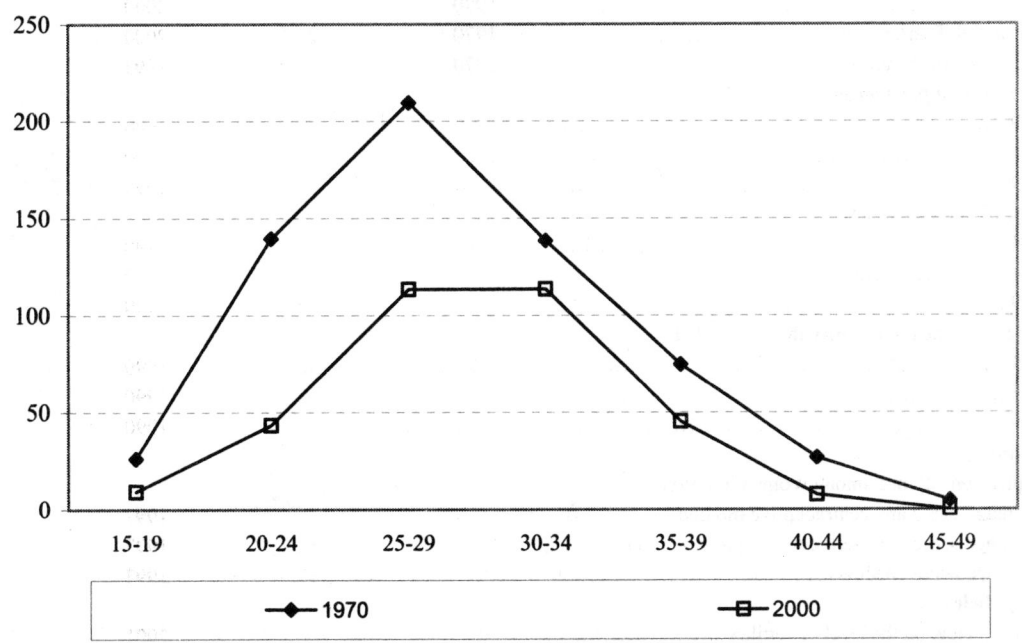

Slovakia

Indicator	Period					
	Earlier year			**Later year**		
	Year	Value		Year	Value	
Nuptiality						
Annual number of marriages (*thousands*)	..	..		2002	25.1	
Annual number of divorces (*thousands*)	1988	8.3		2001	9.8	
	Year	Male	Female	Year	Male	Female
Total first marriage rate (per person)	1970	..	0.9	2001	..	0.5
Total divorce rate (per person)	..	..	..	1995	0.5	0.6
Mean age at first marriage (years)	1970	..	22.0	2001	..	24.2
SMAM (years)	..	..	..	2001	28.3	25.4
Percentage ever married by age group						
15-19	..	..	..	2001	0.4	1.8
20-24	..	..	..	2001	12.0	28.3
25-29	..	..	..	2001	49.0	68.2
30-34	..	..	..	2001	74.2	85.6
35-39	..	..	..	2001	82.7	90.5
40-44	..	..	..	2001	86.7	92.3
45-49	..	..	..	2001	89.9	92.8
Fertility	Year	Value		Year	Value	
Annual number of births (*thousands*)	1970	80.7		2002	50.8	
Crude birth rate (per 1 000 population)	1970	17.7		2002	9.4	
Percentage of extra-marital births among all births	1970	6.2		2001	19.8	
Total fertility rate (births per woman)	1970	2.4		2001	1.2	
Age-specific fertility rate (per 1 000 women)						
15-19	1970	40		2001	21	
20-24	1970	195		2001	73	
25-29	1970	137		2001	84	
30-34	1970	70		2001	43	
35-39	1970	30		2001	15	
40-44	1970	8		2001	3	
45-49	1970	1		2001	0	
Mean age at childbearing (years)	1970	26.3		2001	26.8	
Mean age at first birth (years)	1970	22.6		2001	24.3	
Children ever born per woman						
35-39	..	..		..	..	
40-44	..	..		..	..	
45-49	..	..		..	..	
Percentage of childless women						
35-39	..	..		..	..	
40-44	..	..		..	..	
45-49	..	..		..	..	
Percentage of women with parity three or higher						
35-39	..	..		..	..	
40-44	..	..		..	..	
45-49	..	..		..	..	
Family Planning						
Contraceptive prevalence among women in union						
Percentage using any contraceptive method	..	..		1991	74.0	
Percentage using a modern contraceptive method	..	..		1991	41.0	
Percentage using condoms	..	..		1991	21.0	
Population policies						
Government's view on the level of fertility	..	--		2001	Too low	
Government's policy regarding level of fertility	..	--		2001	Raise	
Government's support for contraceptive methods	..	--		2001	Direct support	

Total fertility rates

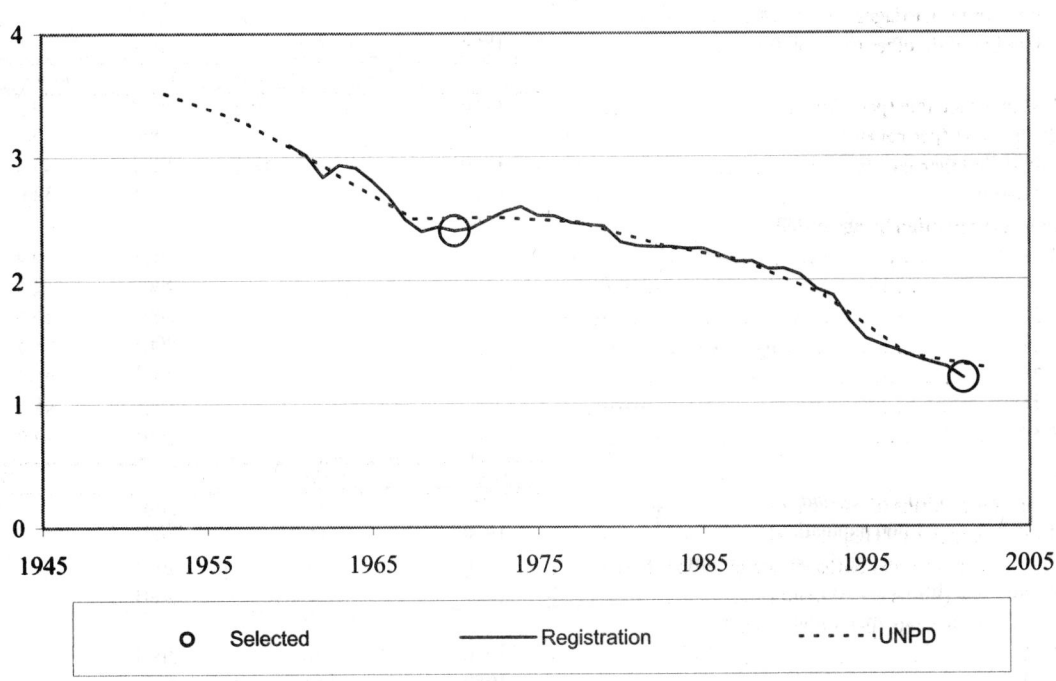

| Selected ○ | Registration —— | UNPD ·····　|

Age-specific fertility rates

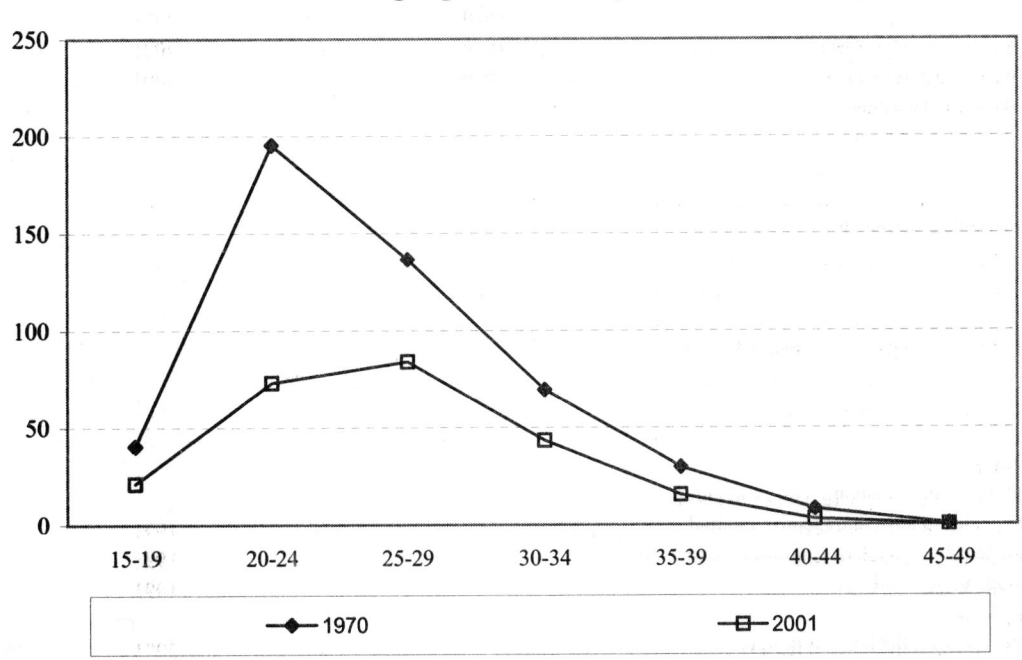

| ◆ 1970 | □ 2001 |

Slovenia

Indicator	Period					
	Earlier year			Later year		
	Year	Value		Year	Value	
Nuptiality						
Annual number of marriages (*thousands*)	1970	14.3		2001	6.9	
Annual number of divorces (*thousands*)	1970	1.9		2001	2.3	
	Year	Male	Female	Year	Male	Female
Total first marriage rate (per person)	1970	..	1.0	1998	0.4	0.5
Total divorce rate (per person)	..	..	..	1996	0.1	0.1
Mean age at first marriage (years)	1970	..	23.1	1998	28.8	26.0
SMAM (years)	..	..	..	2001	32.0	29.8
Percentage ever married by age group						
15-19	..	..	..	2001	0.0	0.3
20-24	..	..	..	2001	2.2	8.3
25-29	..	..	..	2001	20.0	38.7
30-34	..	..	..	2001	48.1	65.6
35-39	..	..	..	2001	65.2	76.9
40-44	..	..	..	2001	71.8	79.5
45-49	..	..	..	2001	74.7	85.6
Fertility	Year	Value		Year	Value	
Annual number of births (*thousands*)..............................	1970	27.4		2001	17.5	
Crude birth rate (per 1 000 population)	1970	15.9		2001	8.8	
Percentage of extra-marital births among all births	1970	8.5		2001	39.4	
Total fertility rate (births per woman)	1970	2.1		2001	1.2	
Age-specific fertility rate (per 1 000 women)						
15-19	1970	42		2001	6	
20-24	1970	152		2001	51	
25-29	1970	114		2001	98	
30-34	1970	70		2001	63	
35-39	1970	34		2001	20	
40-44	1970	10		2001	3	
45-49	1970	1		2001	0	
Mean age at childbearing (years)	1970	26.7		2001	28.5	
Mean age at first birth (years)	1970	23.7		2001	26.7	
Children ever born per woman						
35-39	..	..		1994-1995	1.7	
40-44	..	..		1994-1995	2.0	
45-49	..	..		1994-1995	2.0	
Percentage of childless women						
35-39	..	..		1994-1995	6.9	
40-44	..	..		1994-1995	3.5	
45-49	..	..		1994-1995	2.6	
Percentage of women with parity three or higher						
35-39	..	..		1994-1995	10.5	
40-44	..	..		1994-1995	19.5	
45-49	..	..		1994-1995	19.4	
Family Planning						
Contraceptive prevalence among women in union						
Percentage using any contraceptive method	..	..		1994	73.8	
Percentage using a modern contraceptive method	..	..		1994	59.1	
Percentage using condoms	..	..		1994	7.6	
Population policies						
Government's view on the level of fertility	..	--		2001	Satisfactory	
Government's policy regarding level of fertility	..	--		2001	Raise	
Government's support for contraceptive methods	..	--		2001	Direct support	

Total fertility rates

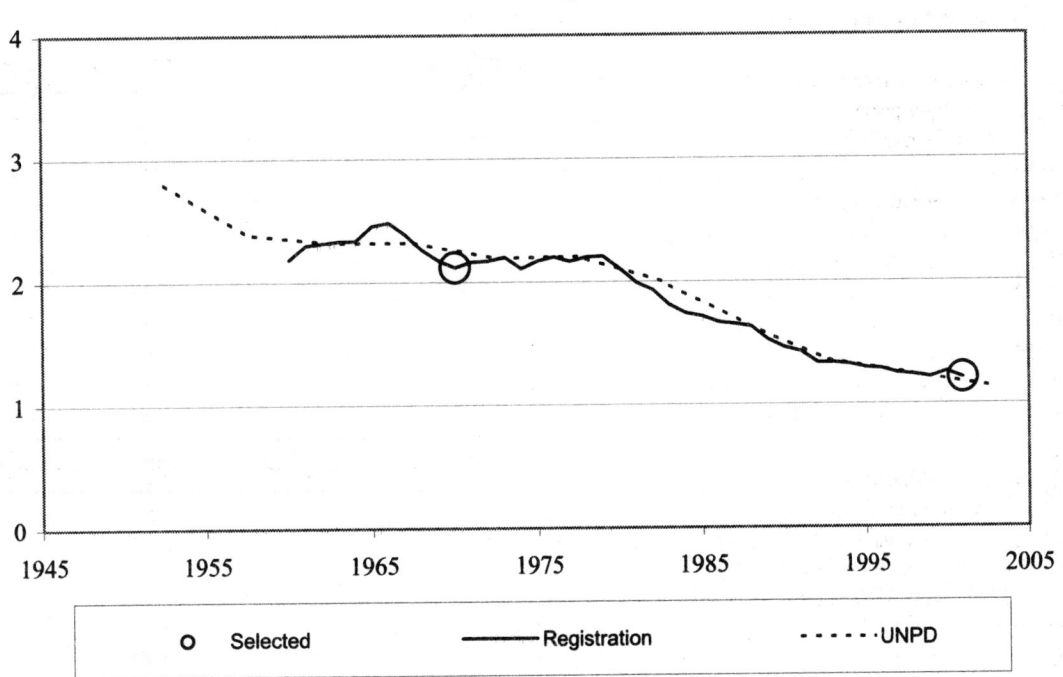

Age-specific fertility rates

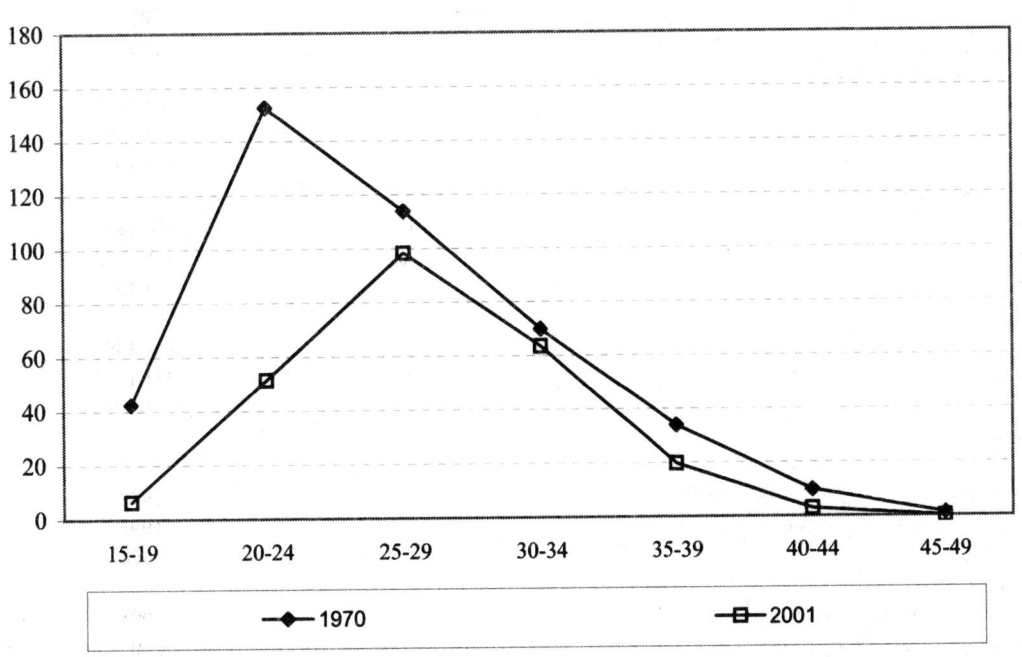

Indicator	Period			
	Earlier year		Later year	
	Year	Value	Year	Value
Nuptiality				
Annual number of marriages (*thousands*)	..	..	..	..
Annual number of divorces (*thousands*)	..	..	..	..

Indicator	Year	Male	Female	Year	Male	Female
Total first marriage rate (per person)	..	..	..	..	..	..
Total divorce rate (per person)	..	..	..	..	..	..
Mean age at first marriage (years)	..	..	..	..	..	..
SMAM (years)	1970	27.4	22.3	..	..	..
Percentage ever married by age group						
15-19	1970	2.1	15.6	..	..	..
20-24	1970	20.8	58.7	..	..	..
25-29	1970	54.6	82.1	..	..	..
30-34	1970	77.0	90.2	..	..	..
35-39	1970	85.3	93.4	..	..	..
40-44	1970	89.6	95.0	..	..	..
45-49	1970	92.4	95.9	..	..	..

Fertility	Year	Value	Year	Value
Annual number of births (*thousands*)	..	..	..	..
Crude birth rate (per 1 000 population)	..	..	..	..
Percentage of extra-marital births among all births	..	..	..	..
Total fertility rate (births per woman)	1973	7.4	1985	6.1
Age-specific fertility rate (per 1 000 women)				
15-19	1973	146	1985	101
20-24	1973	296	1985	280
25-29	1973	328	1985	295
30-34	1973	305	1985	252
35-39	1973	225	1985	177
40-44	1973	141	1985	84
45-49	1973	42	1985	25
Mean age at childbearing (years)	1973	30.1	1985	29.5
Mean age at first birth (years)	..	..	..	..
Children ever born per woman				
35-39	1970	5.0	..	..
40-44	1970	5.7	..	..
45-49	1970	5.9	..	..
Percentage of childless women				
35-39	1970	10.4	..	..
40-44	1970	10.5	..	..
45-49	1970	10.4	..	..
Percentage of women with parity three or higher				
35-39	1970	77.6	..	..
40-44	1970	79.4	..	..
45-49	1970	79.1	..	..
Family Planning				
Contraceptive prevalence among women in union				
Percentage using any contraceptive method	..	..	..	..
Percentage using a modern contraceptive method	..	..	..	..
Percentage using condoms	..	..	..	..
Population policies				
Government's view on the level of fertility	..	..	2001	Too high
Government's policy regarding level of fertility	..	..	2001	Lower
Government's support for contraceptive methods	..	..	2001	Indirect support

Total fertility rates

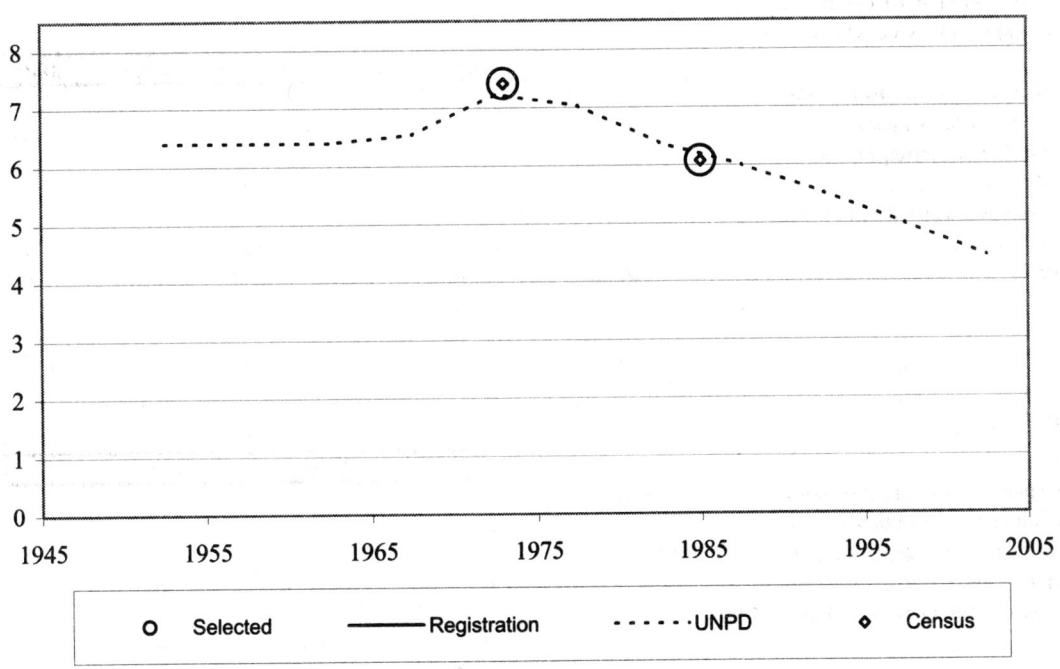

Age-specific fertility rates

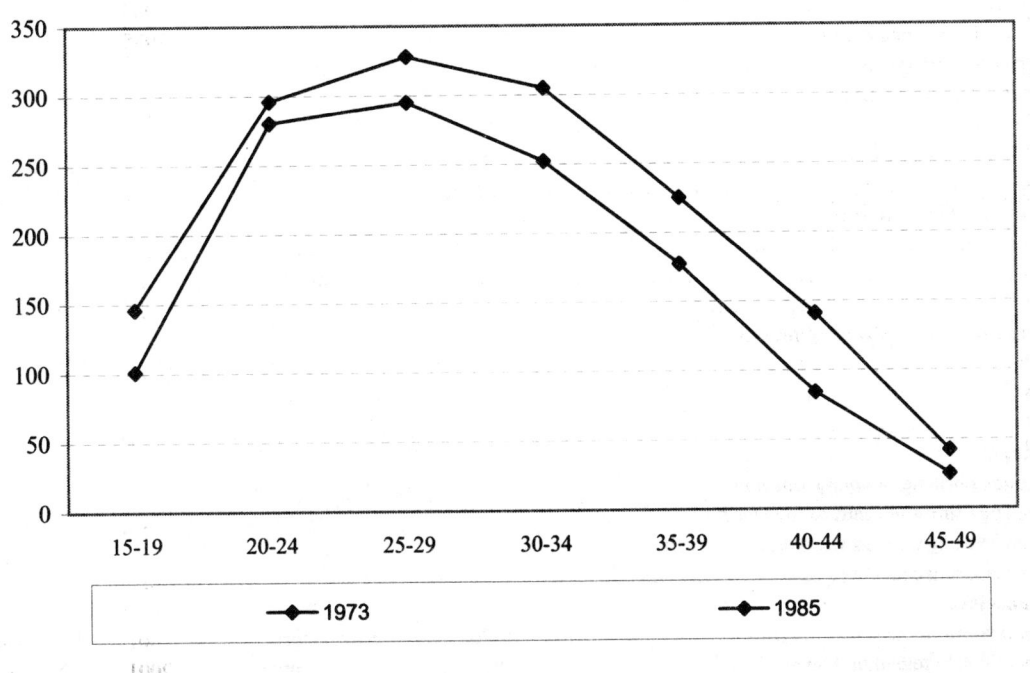

Indicator	Period			
	Earlier year		*Later year*	
	Year	*Value*	*Year*	*Value*
Nuptiality				
Annual number of marriages (*thousands*)	..	..	..	..
Annual number of divorces (*thousands*)	..	..	..	..

Indicator	*Year*	*Male*	*Female*	*Year*	*Male*	*Female*
Total first marriage rate (per person)	..	..	..	..	..	..
Total divorce rate (per person)	..	..	..	..	..	..
Mean age at first marriage (years)	..	..	..	..	..	..
SMAM (years)	..	..	..	..	..	..
Percentage ever married by age group						
15-19	..	..	..	..	..	..
20-24	..	..	..	..	..	..
25-29	..	..	..	..	..	..
30-34	..	..	..	..	..	..
35-39	..	..	..	..	..	..
40-44	..	..	..	..	..	..
45-49	..	..	..	..	..	..

Fertility	*Year*	*Value*	*Year*	*Value*
Annual number of births (*thousands*)...........................	..	..	..	..
Crude birth rate (per 1 000 population)	..	..	..	..
Percentage of extra-marital births among all births	..	..	..	..
Total fertility rate (births per woman)	1975	7.1	..	..
Age-specific fertility rate (per 1 000 women)				
15-19	..	..	..	..
20-24	..	..	..	..
25-29	..	..	..	..
30-34	..	..	..	..
35-39	..	..	..	..
40-44	..	..	..	..
45-49	..	..	..	..
Mean age at childbearing (years)	..	..	..	..
Mean age at first birth (years)	..	..	..	..
Children ever born per woman				
35-39	..	..	..	..
40-44	..	..	..	..
45-49	..	..	..	..
Percentage of childless women				
35-39	..	..	..	..
40-44	..	..	..	..
45-49	..	..	..	..
Percentage of women with parity three or higher				
35-39	..	..	..	..
40-44	..	..	..	..
45-49	..	..	..	..
Family Planning				
Contraceptive prevalence among women in union				
Percentage using any contraceptive method	..	..	..	..
Percentage using a modern contraceptive method	..	..	..	..
Percentage using condoms	..	..	..	..
Population policies				
Government's view on the level of fertility	1976	Satisfactory	2001	Satisfactory
Government's policy regarding level of fertility	1976	No intervention	2001	No intervention
Government's support for contraceptive methods	1976	No support	2001	Direct support

Total fertility rates

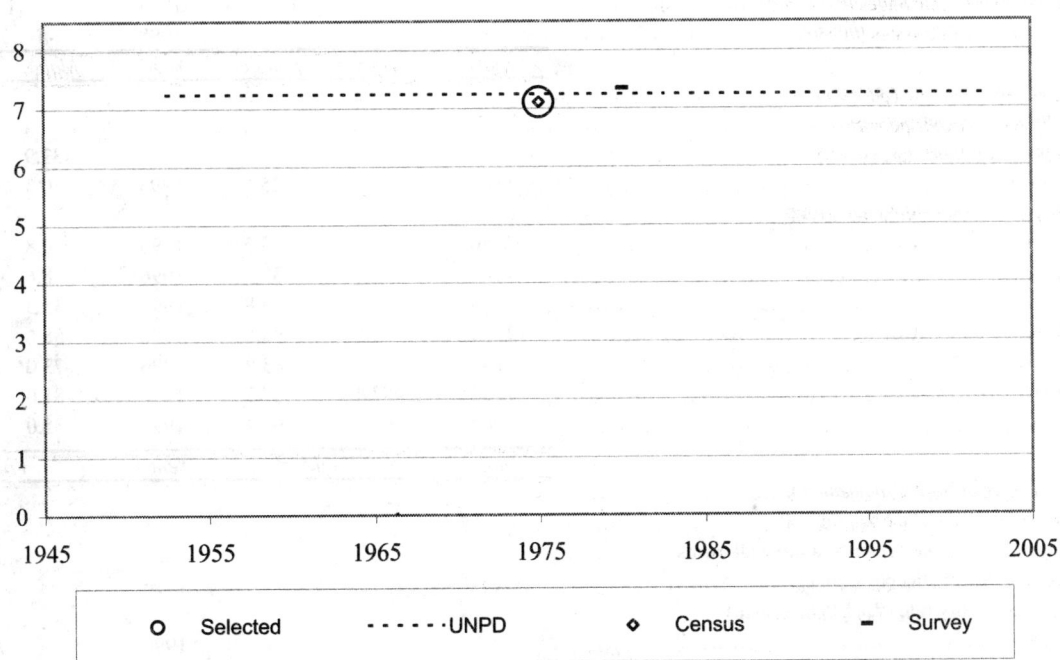

Indicator	Period					
	Earlier year			Later year		
	Year	Value		Year	Value	
Nuptiality						
Annual number of marriages (*thousands*)	..	..		1998	146.7	
Annual number of divorces (*thousands*)	..	..		1998	35.8	
	Year	Male	Female	Year	Male	Female
Total first marriage rate (per person)	..	..	..	..	..	..
Total divorce rate (per person)	..	..	..	..	..	..
Mean age at first marriage (years)	..	..	..	1995	32.9	30.1
SMAM (years)	1980	27.8	25.7	1996	30.3	27.9
Percentage ever married by age group						
15-19	1980	0.9	5.6	1996	0.8	3.4
20-24	1980	17.1	35.8	1996	8.6	22.3
25-29	1980	51.6	62.8	1996	33.3	47.5
30-34	1980	73.5	76.6	1996	58.6	64.1
35-39	1980	82.9	83.9	1996	73.0	73.1
40-44	1980	87.4	87.7	1996	81.0	78.9
45-49	1980	90.1	90.4	1996	85.0	82.8
Fertility	Year	Value		Year	Value	
Annual number of births (*thousands*)............................	..	..		..	..	
Crude birth rate (per 1 000 population)	..	..		..	..	
Percentage of extra-marital births among all births	..	..		..	..	
Total fertility rate (births per woman)	..	..		1996	2.9	
Age-specific fertility rate (per 1 000 women)						
15-19	..	..		1996	78	
20-24	..	..		1996	136	
25-29	..	..		1996	138	
30-34	..	..		1996	108	
35-39	..	..		1996	72	
40-44	..	..		1996	30	
45-49	..	..		1996	10	
Mean age at childbearing (years)	..	..		1996	28.3	
Mean age at first birth (years)[a]	..	..		1998	20.9	
Children ever born per woman						
35-39	..	..		1998	3.2	
40-44	..	..		1998	3.5	
45-49	..	..		1998	4.0	
Percentage of childless women						
35-39	..	..		1998	4.9	
40-44	..	..		1998	4.7	
45-49	..	..		1998	5.2	
Percentage of women with parity three or higher						
35-39	..	..		1998	60.8	
40-44	..	..		1998	64.5	
45-49	..	..		1998	70.2	
Family Planning						
Contraceptive prevalence among women in union						
Percentage using any contraceptive method	1976	37.0		1998	56.3	
Percentage using a modern contraceptive method	1976	35.0		1998	55.1	
Percentage using condoms	1976	2.0		1998	1.7	
Population policies						
Government's view on the level of fertility	1976	Too high		2001	Too high	
Government's policy regarding level of fertility	1976	Lower		2001	Lower	
Government's support for contraceptive methods	1976	Direct support		2001	Direct support	

[a]Median age at first birth among women aged 25-29 at the date of the survey

Total fertility rates

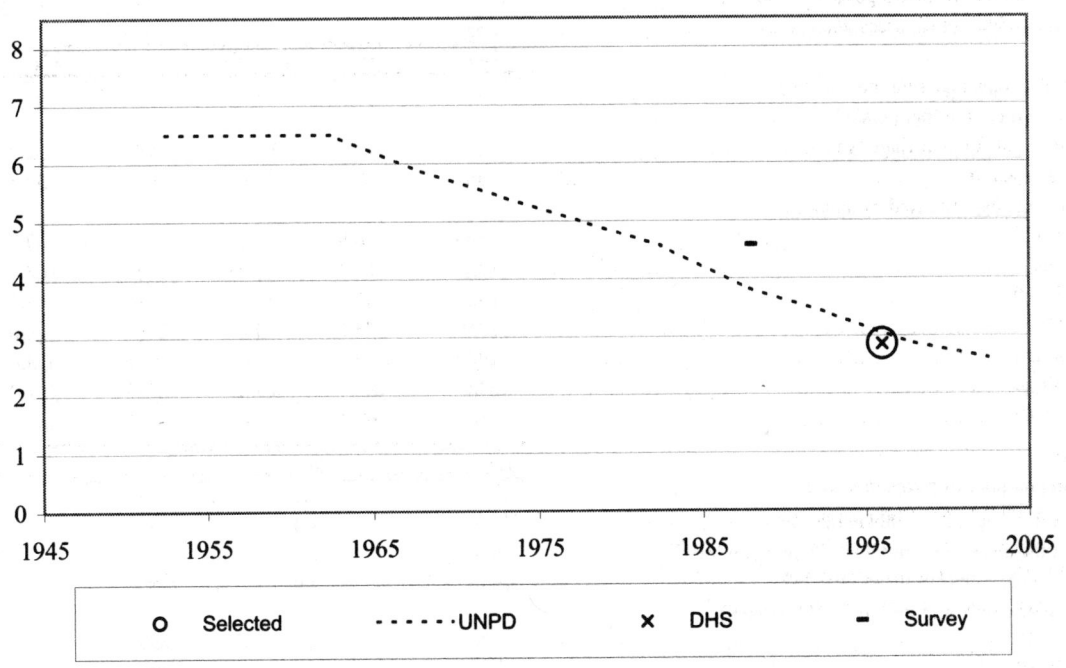

Age-specific fertility rates

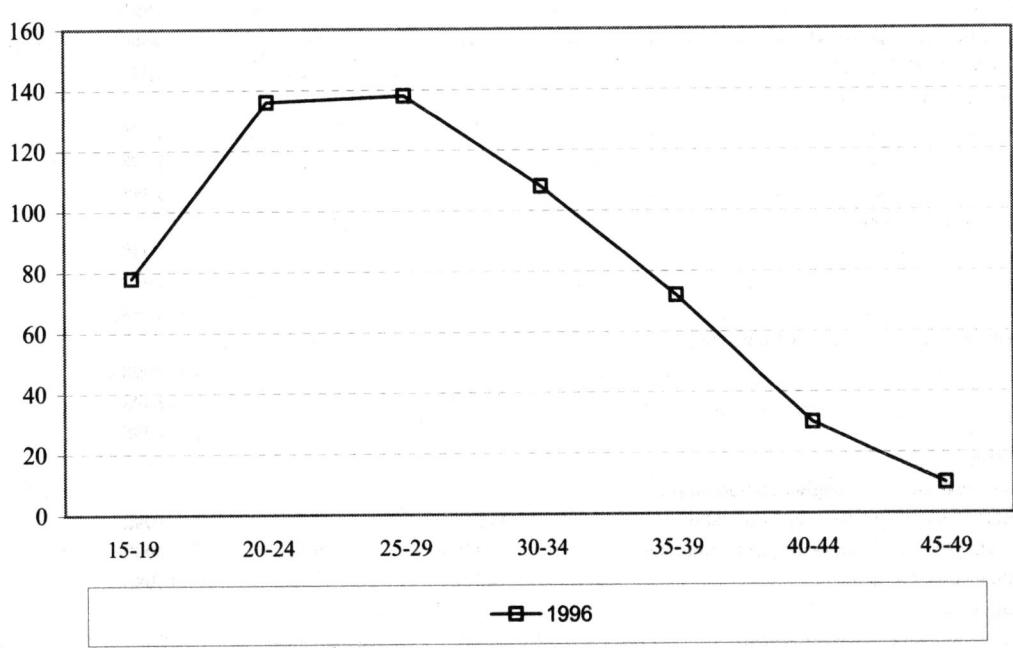

Indicator	Period					
	Earlier year			*Later year*		
	Year	*Value*		*Year*	*Value*	
Nuptiality						
Annual number of marriages (*thousands*)	1970	247.5		1999	206.0	
Annual number of divorces (*thousands*)	1982	21.5		2000	39.0	
	Year	*Male*	*Female*	*Year*	*Male*	*Female*
Total first marriage rate (per person)	1974	1.0	1.0	1997	0.6	0.6
Total divorce rate (per person)	..	..	..	..	..	..
Mean age at first marriage (years)	1974	26.8	24.1	1997	29.4	27.4
SMAM (years)	1970	27.5	23.7	1991	28.4	26.0
Percentage ever married by age group						
15-19	1970	0.6	3.1	1991	0.7	2.4
20-24	1970	9.5	31.7	1991	9.1	22.4
25-29	1970	54.0	73.3	1991	42.4	61.3
30-34	1970	80.9	86.3	1991	74.4	82.8
35-39	1970	86.7	88.4	1991	84.9	88.8
40-44	1970	89.3	88.0	1991	88.4	90.9
45-49	1970	91.2	87.9	1991	90.1	91.8
Fertility	*Year*	*Value*		*Year*	*Value*	
Annual number of births (*thousands*)...............................	1970	656.1		2001	407.1	
Crude birth rate (per 1 000 population)	1970	19.4		2001	10.0	
Percentage of extra-marital births among all births	1970	1.4		2000	17.7	
Total fertility rate (births per woman)	1970	2.9		2000	1.2	
Age-specific fertility rate (per 1 000 women)						
15-19	1970	14		2000	9	
20-24	1970	123		2000	26	
25-29	1970	199		2000	67	
30-34	1970	133		2000	95	
35-39	1970	77		2000	43	
40-44	1970	27		2000	7	
45-49	1970	3		2000	0	
Mean age at childbearing (years)	1970	29.5		2000	30.7	
Mean age at first birth (years)	1975	25.3		2000	29.1	
Children ever born per woman						
35-39	..	..		1994-1995	1.9	
40-44	..	..		1994-1995	2.1	
45-49	..	..		1994-1995	2.5	
Percentage of childless women						
35-39	..	..		1994-1995	9.2	
40-44	..	..		1994-1995	10.5	
45-49	..	..		1994-1995	7.0	
Percentage of women with parity three or higher						
35-39	..	..		1994-1995	21.5	
40-44	..	..		1994-1995	28.3	
45-49	..	..		1994-1995	44.2	
Family Planning						
Contraceptive prevalence among women in union						
Percentage using any contraceptive method	1977	51.0		1995	80.9	
Percentage using a modern contraceptive method	1977	20.0		1995	67.4	
Percentage using condoms	1977	5.0		1995	24.3	
Population policies						
Government's view on the level of fertility	1976	Satisfactory		2001	Too low	
Government's policy regarding level of fertility	1976	No intervention		2001	No intervention	
Government's support for contraceptive methods	1976	Limits		2001	Direct support	

Total fertility rates

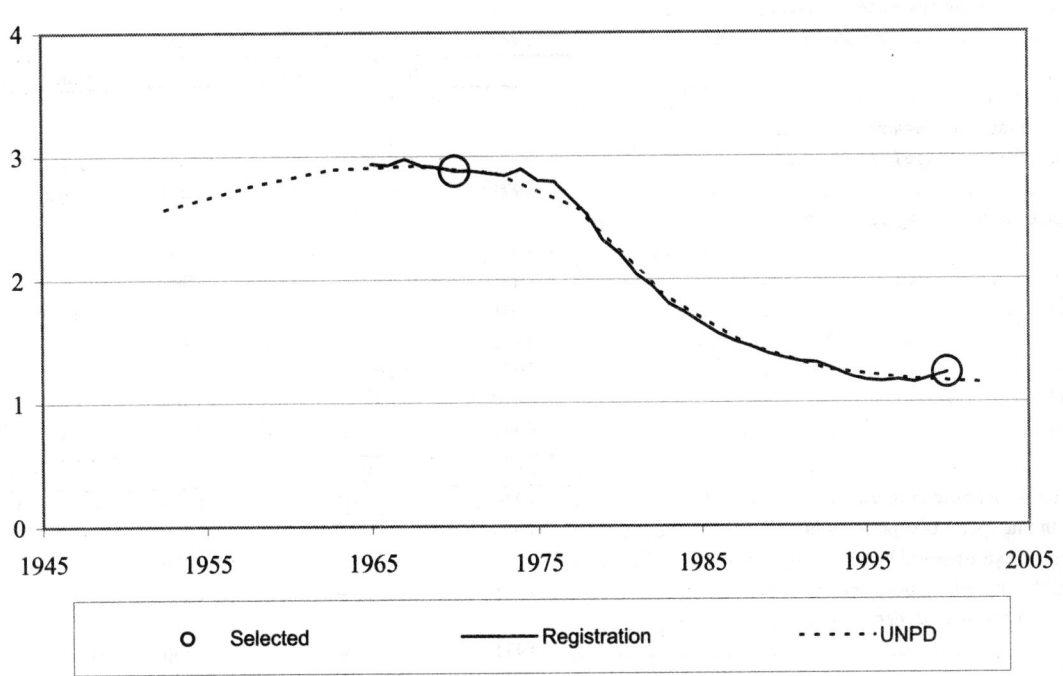

Age-specific fertility rates

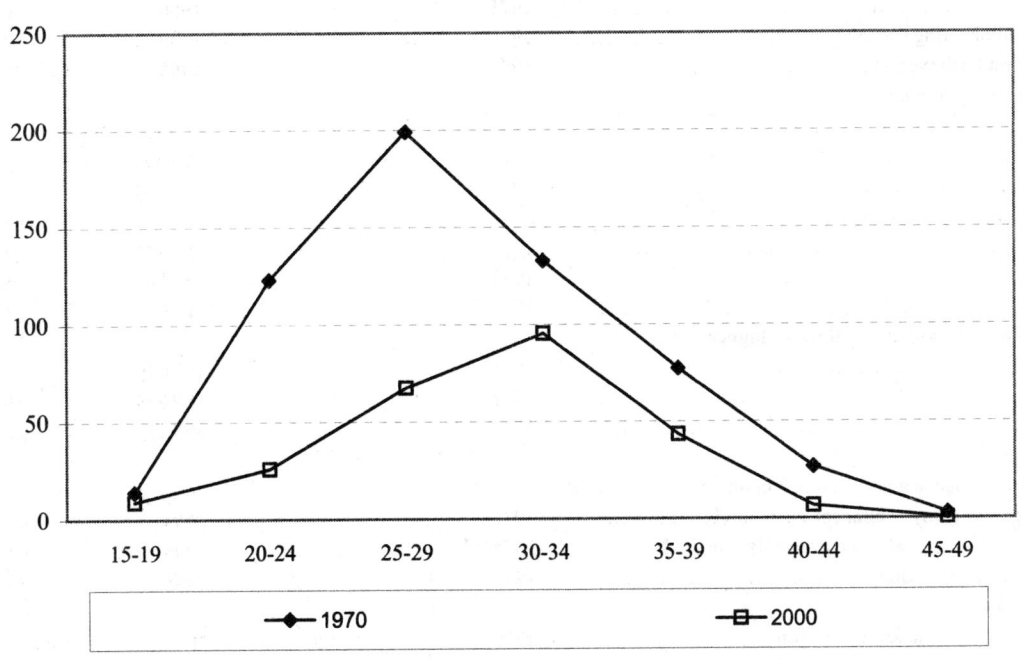

Indicator	Period			
	Earlier year		Later year	
	Year	Value	Year	Value
Nuptiality				
Annual number of marriages (*thousands*)	..	..	..	..
Annual number of divorces (*thousands*)	1972	1.9	1988	2.7

	Year	Male	Female	Year	Male	Female
Total first marriage rate (per person)	..	..	..	..	..	..
Total divorce rate (per person)	..	..	..	..	..	..
Mean age at first marriage (years)	..	..	..	..	..	..
SMAM (years)	1971	28.1	23.5	1993	..	25.3
Percentage ever married by age group						
15-19	1971	0.6	10.6	1993	..	7.1
20-24	1971	13.4	46.8	1993	..	38.8
25-29	1971	46.8	75.4	1993	..	66.3
30-34	1971	74.4	89.1	1993	..	82.3
35-39	1971	86.6	94.2	1993	..	88.9
40-44	1971	90.8	95.3	1993	..	90.8
45-49	1971	92.0	95.9	1993	..	94.8

Fertility	Year	Value	Year	Value
Annual number of births (*thousands*)	1970	367.9	1999	329.1
Crude birth rate (per 1 000 population)	1970	29.4	1999	17.3
Percentage of extra-marital births among all births	..	..	1996	1.4
Total fertility rate (births per woman)	1971	4.2	1996	2.3
Age-specific fertility rate (per 1 000 women)				
15-19	1971	40	1996	29
20-24	1971	184	1996	89
25-29	1971	232	1996	129
30-34	1971	199	1996	111
35-39	1971	131	1996	82
40-44	1971	40	1996	20
45-49	1971	6	1996	2
Mean age at childbearing (years)	1971	29.5	1996	29.6
Mean age at first birth (years)	1981	25.2	1995	26.2
Children ever born per woman				
35-39	1971	4.7	1993	2.6
40-44	1971	5.5	1993	3.0
45-49	1971	5.5	1993	3.8
Percentage of childless women				
35-39	1971	6.3	1993	15.4
40-44	1971	4.0	1993	13.2
45-49	1971	2.7	1993	7.9
Percentage of women with parity three or higher				
35-39	1971	74.2	1993	52.3
40-44	1971	79.0	1993	61.5
45-49	1971	81.4	1993	70.4
Family Planning				
Contraceptive prevalence among women in union				
Percentage using any contraceptive method	1975	43.4	1993	66.1
Percentage using a modern contraceptive method	1975	19.9	1993	43.6
Percentage using condoms	1975	2.3	1993	3.3
Population policies				
Government's view on the level of fertility	1976	Too high	2001	Satisfactory
Government's policy regarding level of fertility	1976	Lower	2001	Lower
Government's support for contraceptive methods	1976	Direct support	2001	Direct support

Total fertility rates

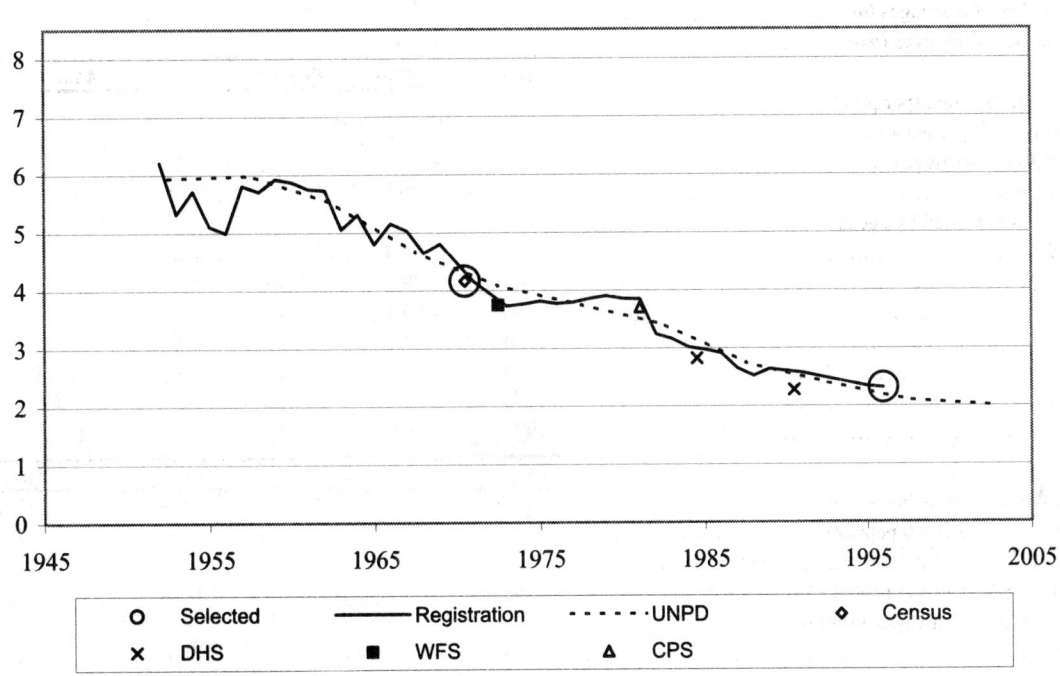

Age-specific fertility rates

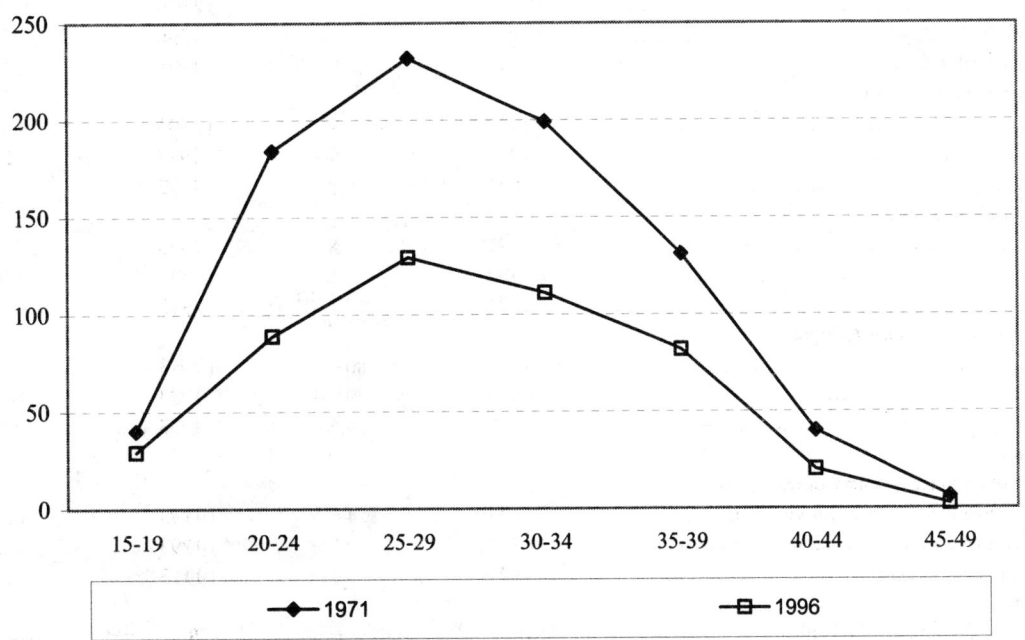

Indicator	Period					
	Earlier year			**Later year**		
	Year	Value		Year	Value	
Nuptiality						
Annual number of marriages (*thousands*)	..	..		..	..	
Annual number of divorces (*thousands*)	..	..		..	..	
	Year	Male	Female	Year	Male	Female
Total first marriage rate (per person)	..	..	..	..	..	..
Total divorce rate (per person)	..	..	..	..	..	..
Mean age at first marriage (years)	..	..	..	..	..	..
SMAM (years)	1973	25.8	18.7	1993	29.1	22.7
Percentage ever married by age group						
15-19	1973	4.4	43.1	1993	1.8	20.6
20-24	1973	29.2	85.0	1993	14.1	55.4
25-29	1973	65.1	95.4	1993	43.2	80.3
30-34	1973	85.0	97.3	1993	67.8	89.7
35-39	1973	92.4	98.2	1993	86.5	96.0
40-44	1973	95.4	98.2	1993	94.0	97.7
45-49	1973	96.5	98.3	1993	96.2	98.4
Fertility	Year	Value		Year	Value	
Annual number of births (*thousands*).........................	..	..		..	..	
Crude birth rate (per 1 000 population)	..	..		..	..	
Percentage of extra-marital births among all births	..	..		..	..	
Total fertility rate (births per woman)	1973	7.1		1992	4.6	
Age-specific fertility rate (per 1 000 women)						
15-19	1973	142		1992	51	
20-24	1973	337		1992	169	
25-29	1973	355		1992	214	
30-34	1973	277		1992	212	
35-39	1973	195		1992	161	
40-44	1973	72		1992	66	
45-49	1973	36		1992	37	
Mean age at childbearing (years)	1973	28.9		1992	30.8	
Mean age at first birth (years)[a]	..	..		1990	22.8	
Children ever born per woman						
35-39	1978-1979	5.8		1990	6.0	
40-44	1978-1979	5.9		1990	7.0	
45-49	1978-1979	6.2		1990	7.5	
Percentage of childless women						
35-39	1978-1979	5.8		1990	8.0	
40-44	1978-1979	7.5		1990	7.0	
45-49	1978-1979	7.1		1990	4.4	
Percentage of women with parity three or higher						
35-39	1978-1979	80.5		1990	84.9	
40-44	1978-1979	79.9		1990	87.1	
45-49	1978-1979	79.5		1990	90.7	
Family Planning						
Contraceptive prevalence among women in union						
Percentage using any contraceptive method	1978-1979	4.6		1993	8.3	
Percentage using a modern contraceptive method	1978-1979	3.7		1993	6.9	
Percentage using condoms	1978-1979	0.1		1993	0.0	
Population policies						
Government's view on the level of fertility	1976	Satisfactory		2001	Too high	
Government's policy regarding level of fertility	1976	No intervention		2001	Lower	
Government's support for contraceptive methods	1976	Direct support		2001	Direct support	

[a]Median age at first birth among women aged 25-29 at the date of the survey

Total fertility rates

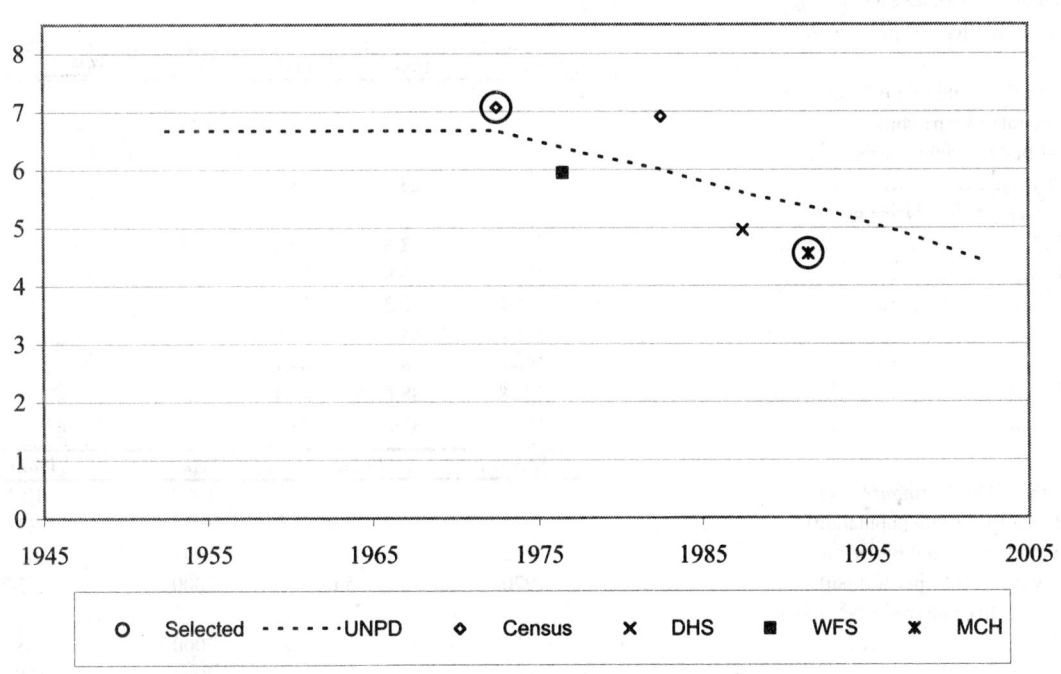

Age-specific fertility rates

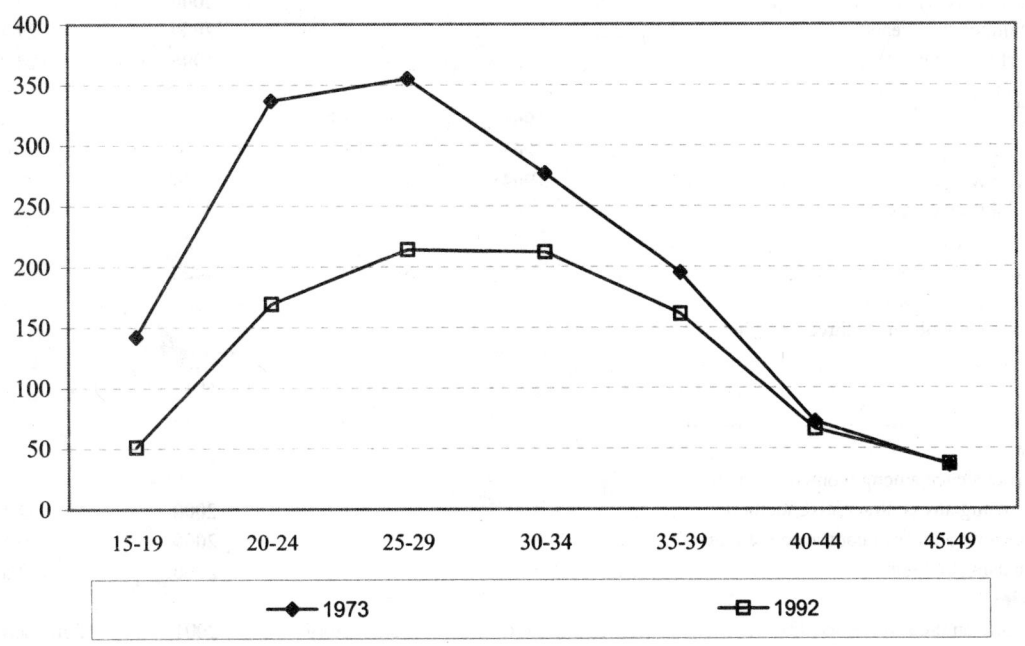

Suriname

Indicator	Period					
	Earlier year			Later year		
	Year	Value		Year	Value	
Nuptiality						
Annual number of marriages (*thousands*)	..	..		..	..	
Annual number of divorces (*thousands*)	..	..		..	..	
	Year	Male	Female	Year	Male	Female
Total first marriage rate (per person)	..	..	..	..	..	..
Total divorce rate (per person)	..	..	..	1991	0.4	0.4
Mean age at first marriage (years)	..	..	..	..	..	..
SMAM (years)	1964	23.6	18.6	..	..	..
Percentage ever married by age group						
15-19	1964	2.8	19.8	..	..	..
20-24	1964	35.9	61.3	..	..	..
25-29	1964	72.3	79.3	..	..	..
30-34	1964	84.0	83.9	..	..	..
35-39	1964	88.8	84.1	..	..	..
40-44	1964	88.6	83.4	..	..	..
45-49	1964	87.2	78.8	..	..	..
Fertility	Year	Value		Year	Value	
Annual number of births (*thousands*)	1972	12.6		1999	10.1	
Crude birth rate (per 1 000 population)	1972	32.9		1999	23.6	
Percentage of extra-marital births among all births	1962	34.1		1997	66.2	
Total fertility rate (births per woman)	1970	5.6		2000	2.7	
Age-specific fertility rate (per 1 000 women)						
15-19	..	..		2000	68	
20-24	..	..		2000	150	
25-29	..	..		2000	148	
30-34	..	..		2000	104	
35-39	..	..		2000	56	
40-44	..	..		2000	16	
45-49	..	..		2000	2	
Mean age at childbearing (years)	..	..		2000	27.4	
Mean age at first birth (years)	..	..		1995	24.2	
Children ever born per woman						
35-39	1964	4.9		..	..	
40-44	1964	5.1		..	..	
45-49	1964	5.0		..	..	
Percentage of childless women						
35-39	..	..		..	..	
40-44	..	..		..	..	
45-49	..	..		..	..	
Percentage of women with parity three or higher						
35-39	..	..		..	..	
40-44	..	..		..	..	
45-49	..	..		..	..	
Family Planning						
Contraceptive prevalence among women in union						
Percentage using any contraceptive method	..	..		2000	42.1	
Percentage using a modern contraceptive method	..	..		2000	40.6	
Percentage using condoms	..	..		2000	2.5	
Population policies						
Government's view on the level of fertility	1976	Satisfactory		2001	Satisfactory	
Government's policy regarding level of fertility	1976	No intervention		2001	No intervention	
Government's support for contraceptive methods	1976	No support		2001	Direct support	

Total fertility rates

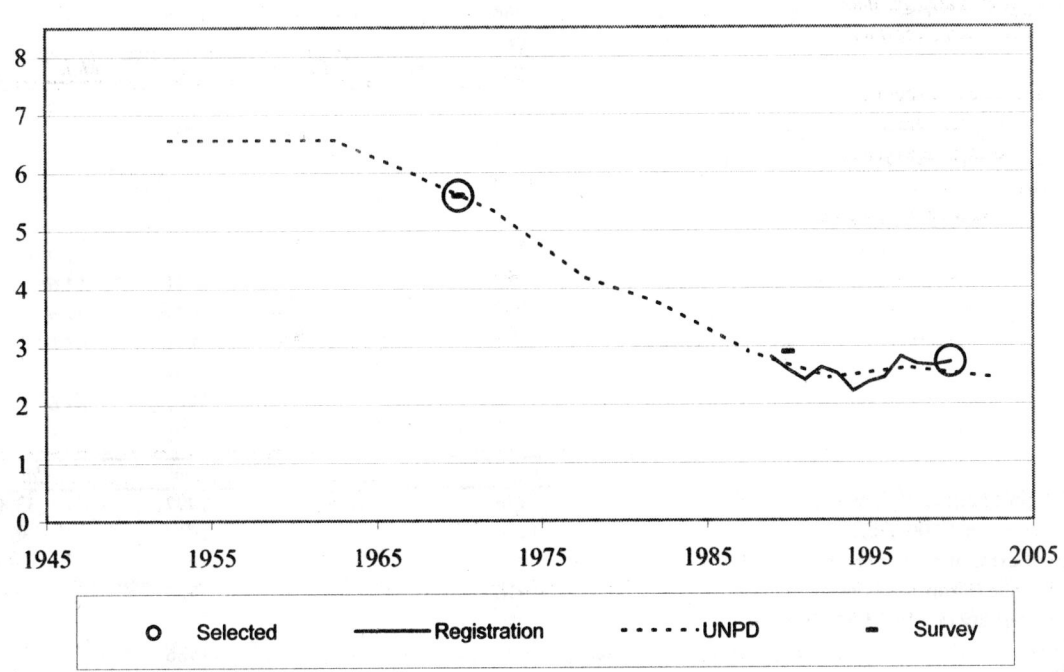

Selected ○   Registration ——   UNPD ·····   Survey –

Age-specific fertility rates

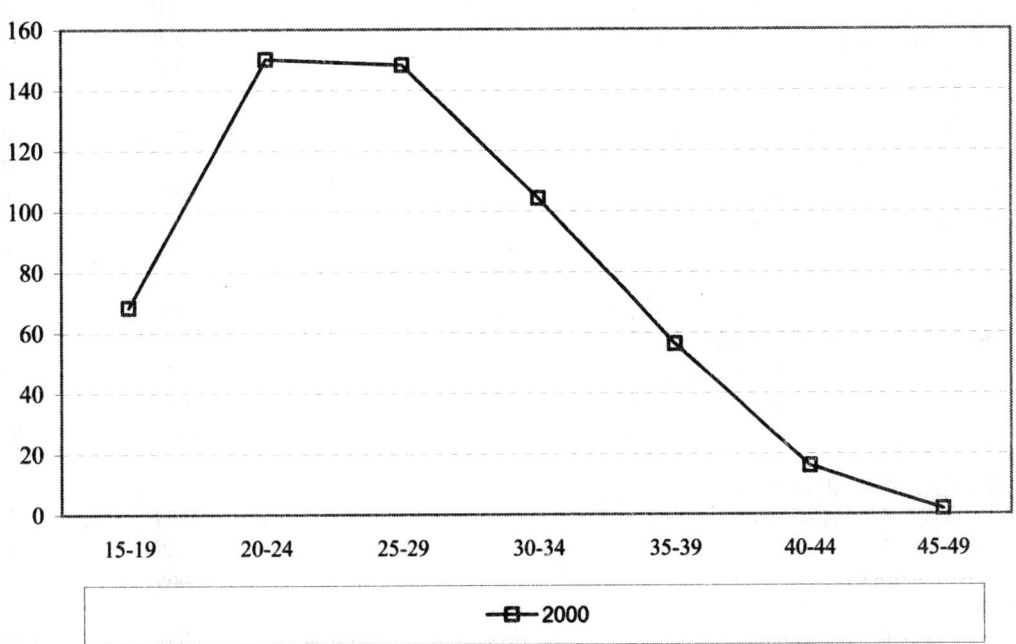

—□— 2000

Swaziland

Indicator	Period					
	Earlier year			**Later year**		
	Year	Value		Year	Value	
Nuptiality						
Annual number of marriages (*thousands*)	1964	0.4		1989	3.1	
Annual number of divorces (*thousands*)	1964	0.0		..	..	
	Year	Male	Female	Year	Male	Female
Total first marriage rate (per person)	..	..	..	..	..	..
Total divorce rate (per person)	..	..	..	..	..	..
Mean age at first marriage (years)	..	..	..	..	..	..
SMAM (years)	..	..	..	1991	29.3	26.0
Percentage ever married by age group						
15-19	..	..	..	1991	1.0	9.1
20-24	..	..	..	1991	14.6	39.7
25-29	..	..	..	1991	41.5	59.9
30-34	..	..	..	1991	65.6	74.7
35-39	..	..	..	1991	80.2	81.8
40-44	..	..	..	1991	84.6	84.7
45-49	..	..	..	1991	90.3	91.0
Fertility	Year	Value		Year	Value	
Annual number of births (*thousands*)	1976	20.5		1997	33.8	
Crude birth rate (per 1 000 population)	1976	41.5		1997	36.4	
Percentage of extra-marital births among all births	..	..		..	..	
Total fertility rate (births per woman)	1976	6.8		1986	5.0	
Age-specific fertility rate (per 1 000 women)						
15-19	..	..		1986	54	
20-24	..	..		1986	205	
25-29	..	..		1986	221	
30-34	..	..		1986	210	
35-39	..	..		1986	175	
40-44	..	..		1986	88	
45-49	..	..		1986	45	
Mean age at childbearing (years)	..	..		1986	31.0	
Mean age at first birth (years)	..	..		..	..	
Children ever born per woman						
35-39	..	..		1997	4.7	
40-44	..	..		1997	5.5	
45-49	..	..		1997	6.0	
Percentage of childless women						
35-39	..	..		1997	6.4	
40-44	..	..		1997	5.7	
45-49	..	..		1997	4.9	
Percentage of women with parity three or higher						
35-39	..	..		1997	75.6	
40-44	..	..		1997	79.3	
45-49	..	..		1997	82.3	
Family Planning						
Contraceptive prevalence among women in union						
Percentage using any contraceptive method	..	..		2000	27.7	
Percentage using a modern contraceptive method	..	..		2000	26.0	
Percentage using condoms	..	..		2000	1.8	
Population policies						
Government's view on the level of fertility	1976	Too high		2001	Too high	
Government's policy regarding level of fertility	1976	Lower		2001	Lower	
Government's support for contraceptive methods	1976	Direct support		2001	Direct support	

Total fertility rates

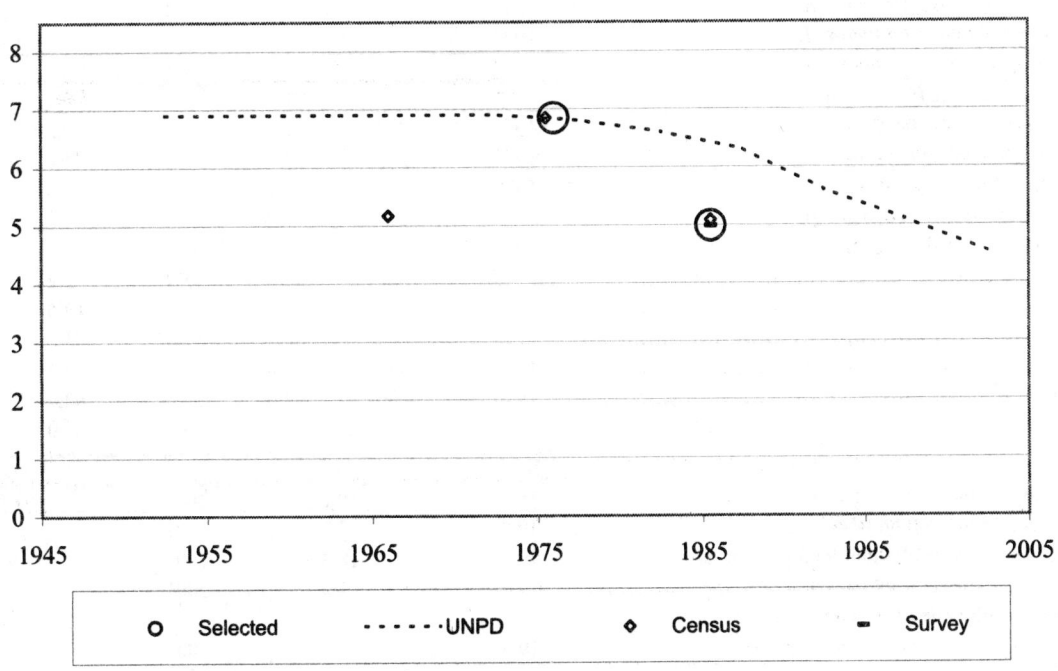

Age-specific fertility rates

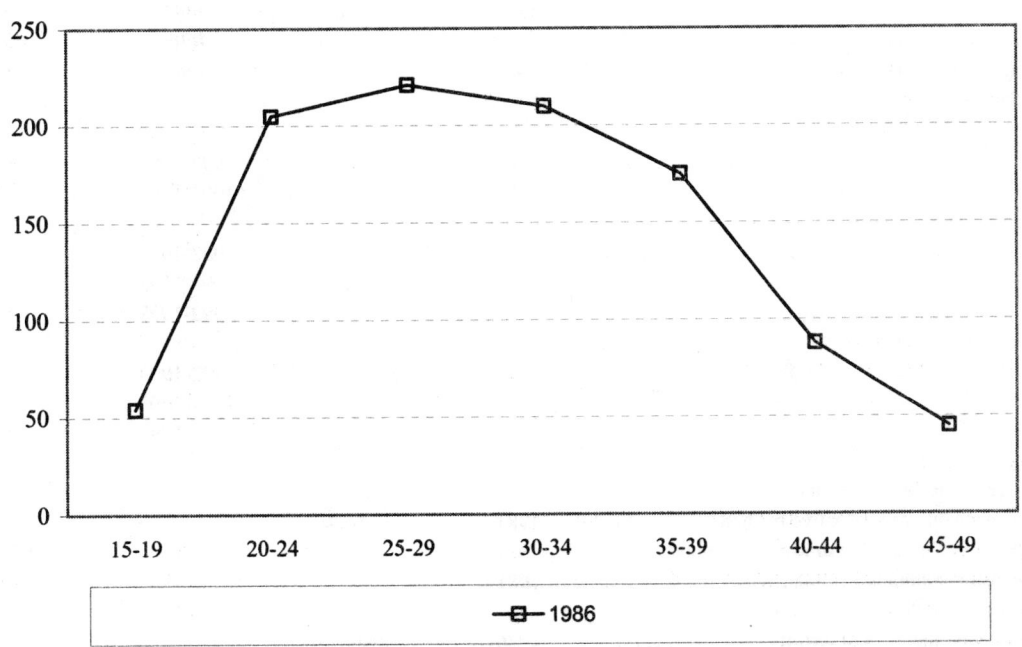

Indicator	Period					
	Earlier year			Later year		
	Year	Value		Year	Value	
Nuptiality						
Annual number of marriages (*thousands*)	1970	43.3		2001	35.8	
Annual number of divorces (*thousands*)	1970	12.9		2001	21.0	
	Year	Male	Female	Year	Male	Female
Total first marriage rate (per person)	1975	0.6	0.6	1997	0.4	0.4
Total divorce rate (per person)	1970	0.2	0.2	1996	0.3	0.3
Mean age at first marriage (years)	1975	27.3	24.9	1997	31.6	29.1
SMAM (years)	1970	26.2	23.7	2001	34.5	32.3
Percentage ever married by age group						
15-19	1970	0.2	2.3	2001	0.1	0.4
20-24	1970	16.9	40.0	2001	2.2	6.7
25-29	1970	59.2	77.0	2001	12.5	23.6
30-34	1970	79.3	88.5	2001	33.8	47.7
35-39	1970	84.5	91.7	2001	50.4	61.4
40-44	1970	85.6	92.4	2001	62.0	71.9
45-49	1970	86.1	92.2	2001	71.0	79.3
Fertility	Year	Value		Year	Value	
Annual number of births (*thousands*)	1970	110.2		2001	91.5	
Crude birth rate (per 1 000 population)	1970	13.7		2001	10.3	
Percentage of extra-marital births among all births	1970	18.4		2001	55.5	
Total fertility rate (births per woman)	1970	1.9		2001	1.6	
Age-specific fertility rate (per 1 000 women)						
15-19	1970	33		2001	7	
20-24	1970	119		2001	47	
25-29	1970	128		2001	104	
30-34	1970	69		2001	103	
35-39	1970	28		2001	44	
40-44	1970	6		2001	8	
45-49	1970	0		2001	0	
Mean age at childbearing (years)	1970	27.0		2001	30.0	
Mean age at first birth (years)	1970	25.9		2001	28.2	
Children ever born per woman						
35-39	..	..		1992-1993	2.0	
40-44	..	..		1992-1993	2.0	
45-49	..	..		1992-1993	..	
Percentage of childless women						
35-39	..	..		1992-1993	11.5	
40-44	..	..		1992-1993	11.5	
45-49	..	..		1992-1993	..	
Percentage of women with parity three or higher						
35-39	..	..		1992-1993	32.4	
40-44	..	..		1992-1993	29.6	
45-49	..	..		1992-1993	..	
Family Planning						
Contraceptive prevalence among women in union						
Percentage using any contraceptive method	1981	78.0		..	..	
Percentage using a modern contraceptive method	1981	72.0		..	..	
Percentage using condoms	1981	..		..	..	
Population policies						
Government's view on the level of fertility	1976	Satisfactory		2001	Satisfactory	
Government's policy regarding level of fertility	1976	No intervention		2001	No intervention	
Government's support for contraceptive methods	1976	Direct support		2001	No support	

Total fertility rates

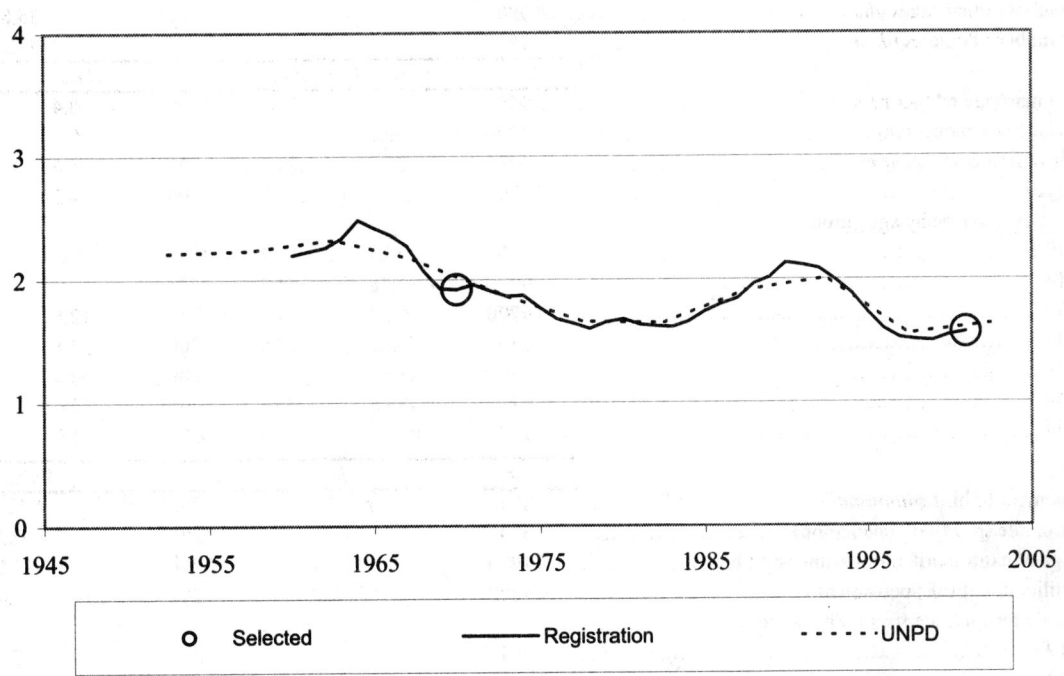

Age-specific fertility rates

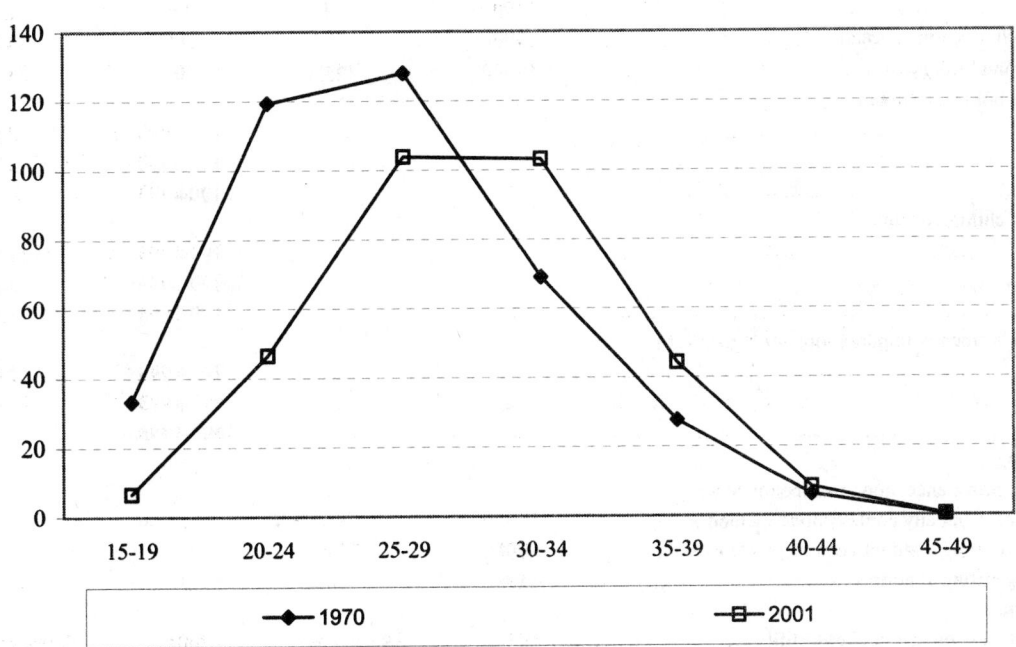

Indicator	Period			
	Earlier year		Later year	
	Year	Value	Year	Value
Nuptiality				
Annual number of marriages (*thousands*)	1970	46.7	2001	36.0
Annual number of divorces (*thousands*)	1970	6.4	2001	15.8

Indicator	Year	Male	Female	Year	Male	Female
Total first marriage rate (per person)	1975	0.6	0.6	1996	0.6	0.7
Total divorce rate (per person)	1970	0.1	0.1	1996	0.2	0.3
Mean age at first marriage (years)	1975	26.7	24.4	1996	29.7	27.3
SMAM (years)	1970	26.0	22.6	2001	31.6	29.1
Percentage ever married by age group						
15-19	1970	0.3	3.7	2001	0.1	0.7
20-24	1970	18.8	45.2	2001	5.1	12.7
25-29	1970	62.9	78.1	2001	24.1	39.9
30-34	1970	82.9	87.0	2001	52.8	67.0
35-39	1970	88.2	88.7	2001	72.6	80.3
40-44	1970	89.8	88.6	2001	82.1	85.9
45-49	1970	90.3	87.8	2001	86.7	88.8

Indicator	Year	Value	Year	Value
Fertility				
Annual number of births (*thousands*)..............................	1970	99.2	2002	72.0
Crude birth rate (per 1 000 population)	1970	16.1	2002	10.0
Percentage of extra-marital births among all births	1970	3.8	2001	11.4
Total fertility rate (births per woman)	1970	2.1	2001	1.4
Age-specific fertility rate (per 1 000 women)				
15-19	1970	22	2001	6
20-24	1970	125	2001	43
25-29	1970	140	2001	93
30-34	1970	84	2001	95
35-39	1970	38	2001	39
40-44	1970	10	2001	6
45-49	1970	1	2001	0
Mean age at childbearing (years)	1970	27.8	2001	30.0
Mean age at first birth (years)[a]	1970	25.3	2001	28.8
Children ever born per woman				
35-39	..	..	1994-1995	1.7
40-44	..	..	1994-1995	1.7
45-49	..	..	1994-1995	1.8
Percentage of childless women				
35-39	..	..	1994-1995	22.5
40-44	..	..	1994-1995	20.4
45-49	..	..	1994-1995	15.6
Percentage of women with parity three or higher				
35-39	..	..	1994-1995	22.5
40-44	..	..	1994-1995	21.9
45-49	..	..	1994-1995	21.9
Family Planning				
Contraceptive prevalence among women in union				
Percentage using any contraceptive method	1980	71.2	1994-1995	82.0
Percentage using a modern contraceptive method	1980	64.9	1994-1995	77.5
Percentage using condoms	1980	8.4	1994-1995	14.2
Population policies				
Government's view on the level of fertility	1976	Satisfactory	2001	Too low
Government's policy regarding level of fertility	1976	No intervention	2001	No intervention
Government's support for contraceptive methods	1976	Indirect support	2001	Direct support

[a]Mean age at first birth within current marriage

Total fertility rates

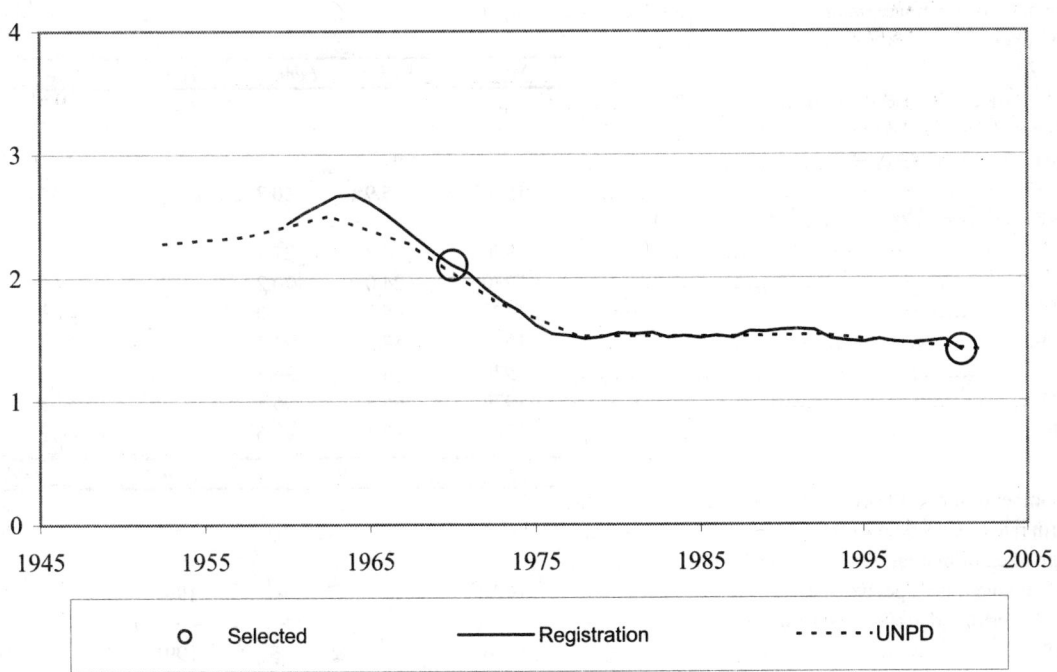

Age-specific fertility rates

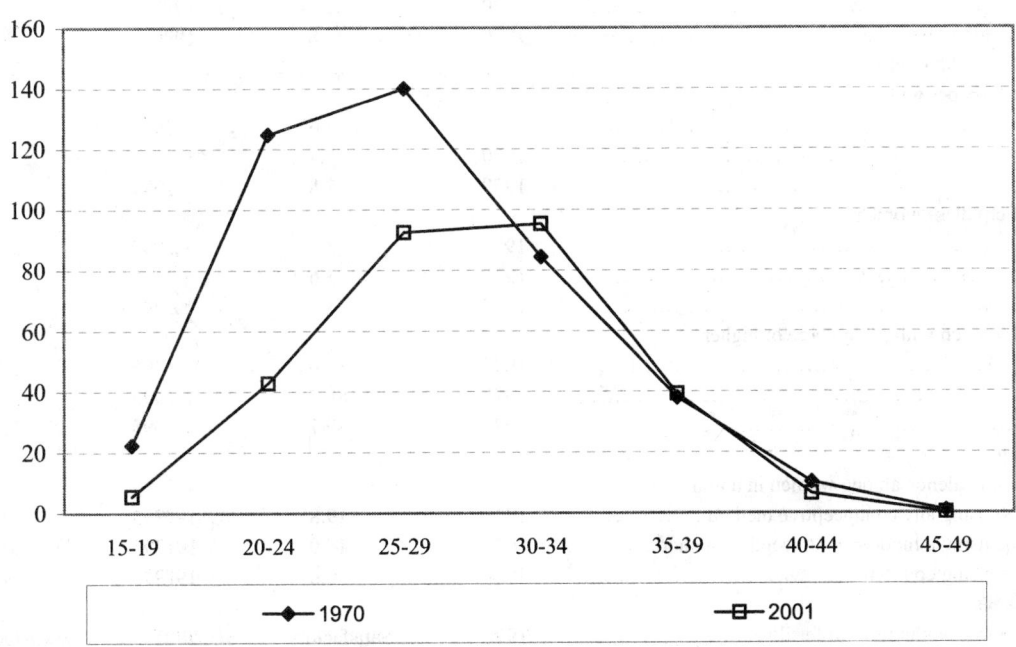

Indicator	Period					
	Earlier year			Later year		
	Year	Value		Year	Value	

Nuptiality

	Year	Value		Year	Value	
Annual number of marriages (*thousands*)	..	..		..	..	
Annual number of divorces (*thousands*)	..	..		..	..	

	Year	Male	Female	Year	Male	Female
Total first marriage rate (per person)	..	..	..	..	..	..
Total divorce rate (per person)	..	..	..	..	..	..
Mean age at first marriage (years)	..	..	..	..	..	..
SMAM (years)	1970	25.9	20.7	..	..	..
Percentage ever married by age group						
15-19	1970	4.2	27.7	..	..	..
20-24	1970	24.0	70.2	..	..	..
25-29	1970	65.3	89.0	..	..	..
30-34	1970	87.5	94.3	..	..	..
35-39	1970	94.1	96.3	..	..	..
40-44	1970	96.3	96.8	..	..	..
45-49	1970	97.3	97.6	..	..	..

Fertility

	Year	Value	Year	Value
Annual number of births (*thousands*).............................	..	..	..	..
Crude birth rate (per 1 000 population)	..	..	..	..
Percentage of extra-marital births among all births	..	..	..	..
Total fertility rate (births per woman)	1970	7.7	1991	4.7
Age-specific fertility rate (per 1 000 women)				
15-19	1970	83	1991	71
20-24	1970	357	1991	184
25-29	1970	389	1991	229
30-34	1970	335	1991	202
35-39	1970	236	1991	155
40-44	1970	123	1991	81
45-49	1970	12	1991	17
Mean age at childbearing (years)	1970	29.8	1991	30.1
Mean age at first birth (years)	..	..	..	..
Children ever born per woman				
35-39	1970	6.6	..	..
40-44	1970	7.4	..	..
45-49	1970	7.8	..	..
Percentage of childless women				
35-39	1970	3.3	..	..
40-44	1970	3.6	..	..
45-49	1970	3.6	..	..
Percentage of women with parity three or higher				
35-39	1970	88.0	..	..
40-44	1970	88.7	..	..
45-49	1970	89.7	..	..

Family Planning

Contraceptive prevalence among women in union				
Percentage using any contraceptive method	1978	19.8	1993	36.1
Percentage using a modern contraceptive method	1978	15.0	1993	28.3
Percentage using condoms	1978	0.6	1993	0.3

Population policies

Government's view on the level of fertility	1976	Satisfactory	2001	Satisfactory
Government's policy regarding level of fertility	1976	No intervention	2001	No intervention
Government's support for contraceptive methods	1976	Direct support	2001	Direct support

Total fertility rates

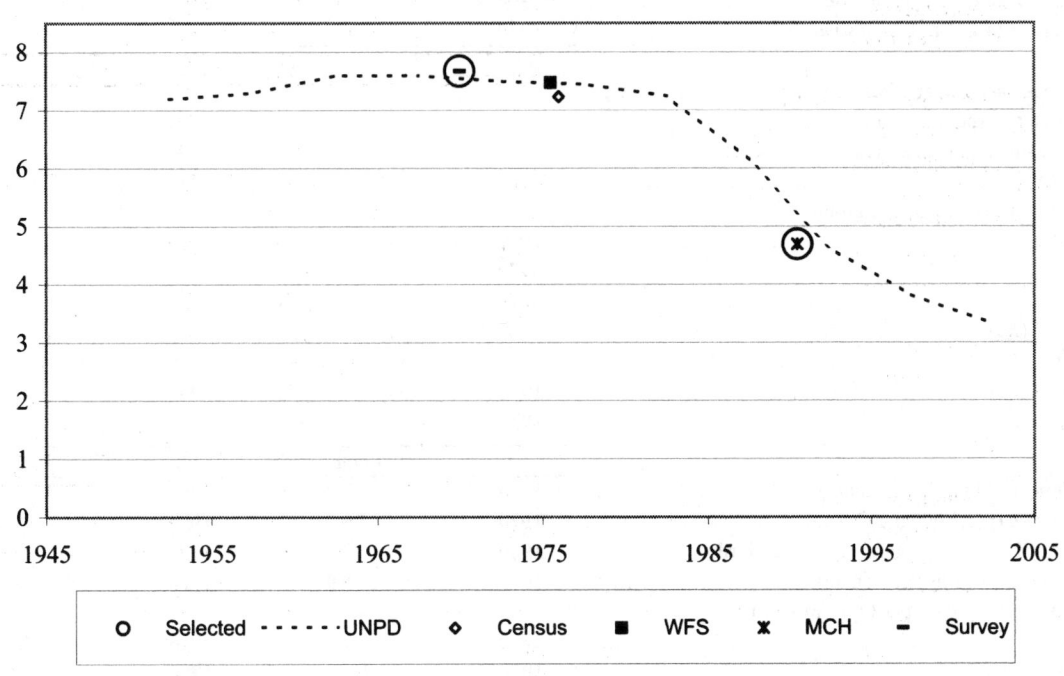

Age-specific fertility rates

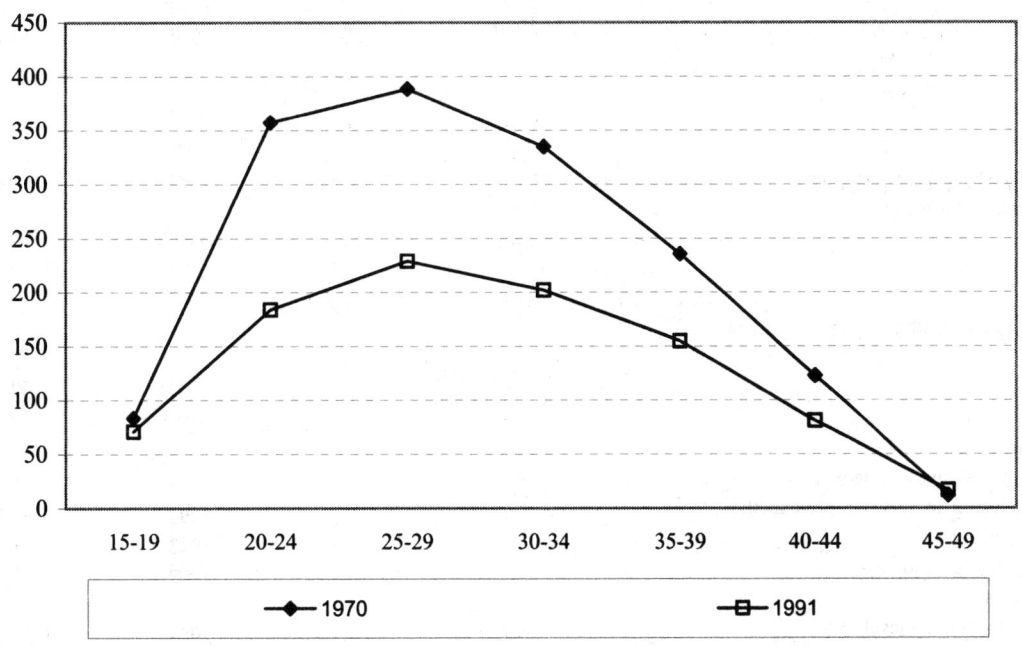

Indicator	Period					
	Earlier year			Later year		
	Year	Value		Year	Value	

Nuptiality

Indicator	Year	Value		Year	Value	
Annual number of marriages (*thousands*)	1970	27.0		1994	38.8	
Annual number of divorces (*thousands*)	1970	3.2		1994	4.4	

Indicator	Year	Male	Female	Year	Male	Female
Total first marriage rate (per person)	..	..	..	1994	0.7	0.7
Total divorce rate (per person)	..	..	..	1994	0.1	0.1
Mean age at first marriage (years)	..	..	..	1994	23.8	20.9
SMAM (years)	..	..	..	1989	23.4	21.2
Percentage ever married by age group						
15-19	1979	..	..	1989	1.3	11.6
20-24	1979	45.0	79.6	1989	44.1	76.9
25-29	1979	90.9	95.6	1989	91.7	94.0
30-34	1979	97.3	98.1	1989	97.5	97.5
35-39	1979	98.5	99.0	1989	98.3	98.3
40-44	1979	99.0	99.2	1989	98.9	98.7
45-49	1979	99.4	99.3	1989	99.0	98.9

Fertility

Indicator	Year	Value	Year	Value
Annual number of births (*thousands*)	1970	102.2	1994	162.2
Crude birth rate (per 1 000 population)	1970	34.8	1994	28.2
Percentage of extra-marital births among all births	1980	7.3	1994	9.3
Total fertility rate (births per woman)	1970	5.9	1993	4.2
Age-specific fertility rate (per 1 000 women)				
15-19	1970	40	1993	54
20-24	1970	261	1993	272
25-29	1970	268	1993	225
30-34	1970	251	1993	160
35-39	1970	216	1993	94
40-44	1970	109	1993	36
45-49	1970	36	1993	7
Mean age at childbearing (years)	1980	30.9	1993	28.1
Mean age at first birth (years)	..	..	..	..
Children ever born per woman				
35-39	..	..	1989	5.0
40-44	..	..	1989	5.6
45-49	..	..	1989	6.0
Percentage of childless women				
35-39	..	..	1989	4.3
40-44	..	..	1989	4.1
45-49	..	..	1989	4.3
Percentage of women with parity three or higher				
35-39	..	..	1989	72.6
40-44	..	..	1989	71.3
45-49	..	..	1989	72.0

Family Planning

Indicator	Year	Value	Year	Value
Contraceptive prevalence among women in union				
Percentage using any contraceptive method	..	..	2000	33.9
Percentage using a modern contraceptive method	..	..	2000	27.3
Percentage using condoms	..	..	2000	0.4

Population policies

Indicator	Year	Value	Year	Value
Government's view on the level of fertility	..	--	2001	Too high
Government's policy regarding level of fertility	..	--	2001	No intervention
Government's support for contraceptive methods	..	--	2001	Direct support

Total fertility rates

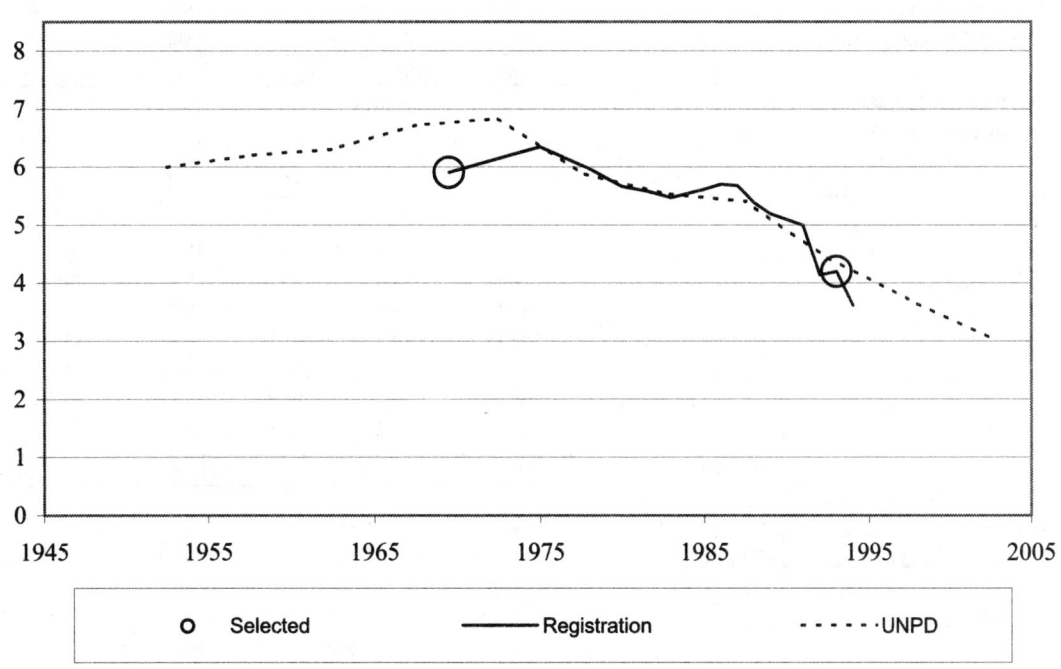

Age-specific fertility rates

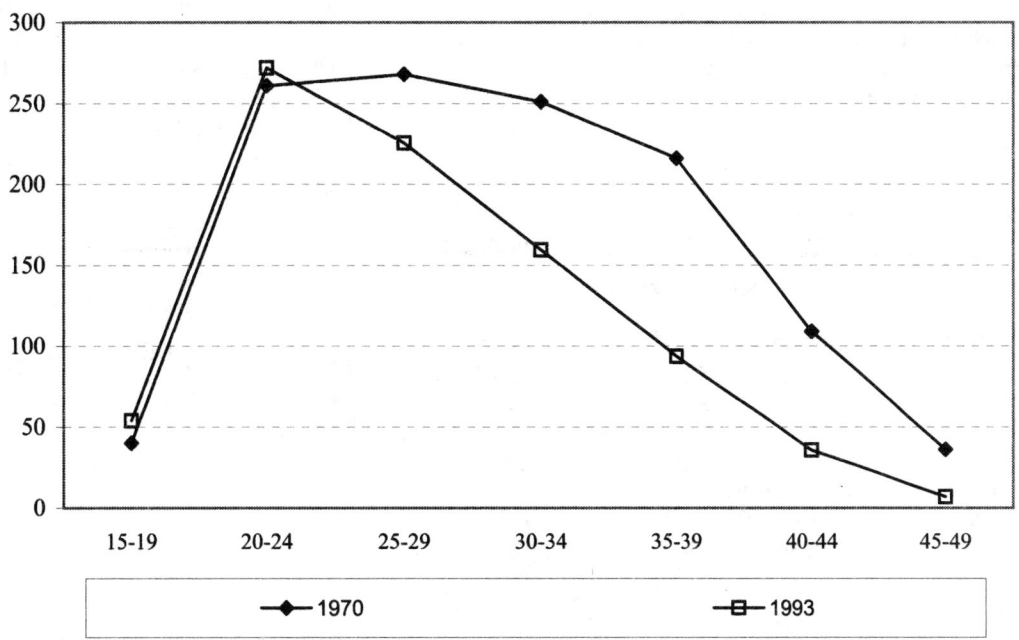

Thailand

Indicator	Period			
	Earlier year		Later year	
	Year	Value	Year	Value
Nuptiality				
Annual number of marriages (*thousands*)	1970	149.0	1995	470.8
Annual number of divorces (*thousands*)	1965	5.1	1995	53.6

Indicator	Year	Male	Female	Year	Male	Female
Total first marriage rate (per person)	..	..	..	..	..	..
Total divorce rate (per person)	..	..	..	..	..	..
Mean age at first marriage (years)	..	..	..	..	..	..
SMAM (years)	1970	24.7	22.0	1990	26.0	23.5
Percentage ever married by age group						
15-19	1970	3.7	18.9	1990	4.0	14.7
20-24	1970	34.9	62.0	1990	29.6	51.6
25-29	1970	75.1	84.4	1990	64.6	74.5
30-34	1970	89.4	91.9	1990	83.5	85.8
35-39	1970	94.2	94.7	1990	91.6	90.4
40-44	1970	96.2	96.1	1990	95.3	92.9
45-49	1970	96.8	97.0	1990	96.8	94.8

Fertility	Year	Value	Year	Value
Annual number of births (*thousands*)	..	..	..	..
Crude birth rate (per 1 000 population)	..	..	..	..
Percentage of extra-marital births among all births	1970	6.2	2001	10.4
Total fertility rate (births per woman)	1967	6.2	1995	2.0
Age-specific fertility rate (per 1 000 women)				
15-19	1967	89	1995	70
20-24	1967	267	1995	119
25-29	1967	299	1995	108
30-34	1967	260	1995	66
35-39	1967	206	1995	26
40-44	1967	100	1995	6
45-49	1967	19	1995	0
Mean age at childbearing (years)	1967	29.9	1995	26.0
Mean age at first birth (years)	1970	23.0	2001	24.3
Children ever born per woman				
35-39	1970	5.3	2000	2.0
40-44	1970	6.1	2000	2.2
45-49	1970	6.4	2000	2.5
Percentage of childless women				
35-39	1970	1.3	2000	7.6
40-44	1970	1.4	2000	6.9
45-49	1970	1.6	2000	6.7
Percentage of women with parity three or higher				
35-39	1970	81.9	2000	25.1
40-44	1970	84.4	2000	35.2
45-49	1970	84.1	2000	45.3
Family Planning				
Contraceptive prevalence among women in union				
Percentage using any contraceptive method	1970	14.4	1997	72.2
Percentage using a modern contraceptive method	1970	13.5	1997	69.8
Percentage using condoms	1970	0.1	1997	1.8
Population policies				
Government's view on the level of fertility	1976	Too high	2001	Satisfactory
Government's policy regarding level of fertility	1976	Lower	2001	Maintain
Government's support for contraceptive methods	1976	Direct support	2001	Direct support

Total fertility rates

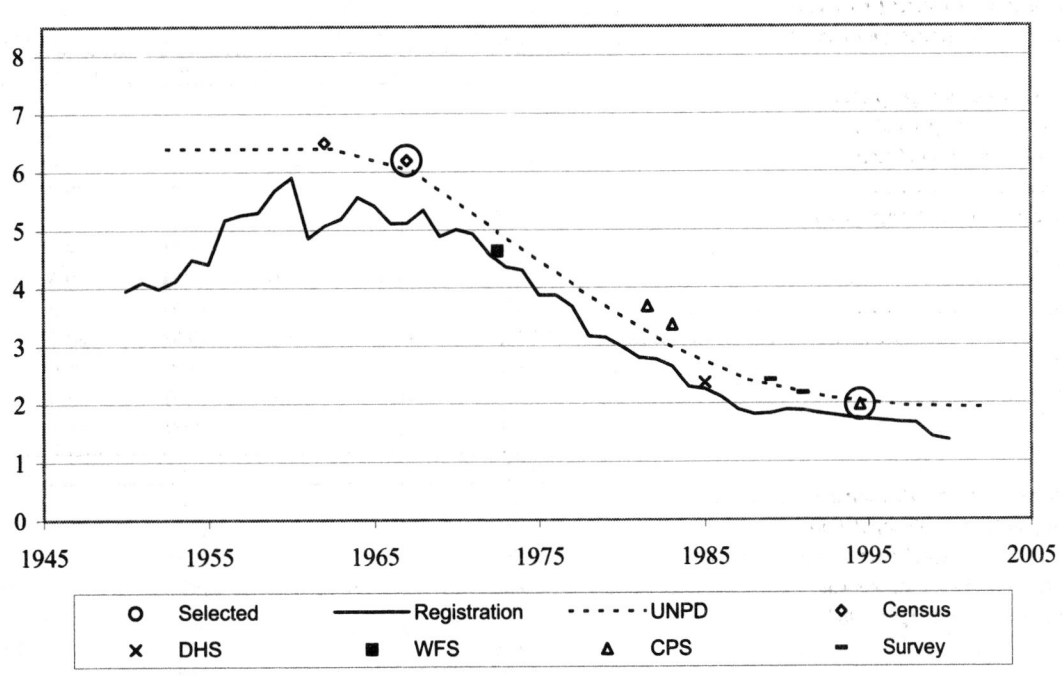

Age-specific fertility rates

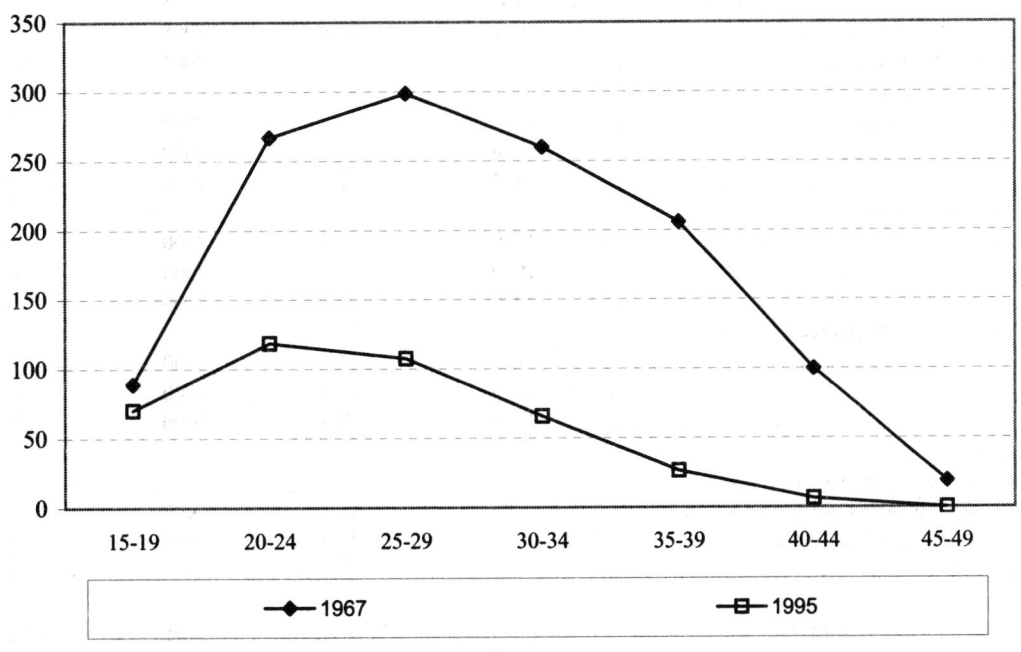

Indicator	Period					
	Earlier year			Later year		
	Year	Value		Year	Value	

Nuptiality

Indicator	Year	Value		Year	Value	
Annual number of marriages (*thousands*)	..	..		2001	13.3	
Annual number of divorces (*thousands*)	..	..		2001	1.4	

Indicator	Year	Male	Female	Year	Male	Female
Total first marriage rate (per person)	1970	..	0.9	1997	0.8	0.8
Total divorce rate (per person)	..	..	..	1997	0.1	0.1
Mean age at first marriage (years)	1970	..	22.1	1997	26.2	23.1
SMAM (years)	..	..	..	1994	26.7	22.9
Percentage ever married by age group						
15-19	..	..	..	1994	1.5	9.1
20-24	..	..	..	1994	21.7	51.3
25-29	..	..	..	1994	62.0	84.5
30-34	..	..	..	1994	83.6	93.9
35-39	..	..	..	1994	92.2	96.0
40-44	..	..	..	1994	95.9	96.6
45-49	..	..	..	1994	97.4	97.2

Fertility

Indicator	Year	Value	Year	Value
Annual number of births (*thousands*)	1970	37.9	2001	27.0
Crude birth rate (per 1 000 population)	1970	23.2	2001	13.3
Percentage of extra-marital births among all births	..	..	..	..
Total fertility rate (births per woman)	1970	3.0	2000	1.9
Age-specific fertility rate (per 1 000 women)				
15-19	1970	43	2000	32
20-24	1970	198	2000	128
25-29	1970	185	2000	133
30-34	1970	103	2000	62
35-39	1970	49	2000	19
40-44	1970	16	2000	3
45-49	1970	3	2000	0
Mean age at childbearing (years)	1970	27.3	2000	26.4
Mean age at first birth (years)[a]	1975	22.1	1987	23.0
Children ever born per woman				
35-39	1970	5.3	2000	2.0
40-44	1970	6.1	2000	2.2
45-49	1970	6.4	2000	2.5
Percentage of childless women				
35-39	1970	1.3	2000	7.6
40-44	1970	1.4	2000	6.9
45-49	1970	1.6	2000	6.7
Percentage of women with parity three or higher				
35-39	1970	81.9	2000	25.1
40-44	1970	84.4	2000	35.2
45-49	1970	84.1	2000	45.3

Family Planning

Indicator	Year	Value	Year	Value
Contraceptive prevalence among women in union				
Percentage using any contraceptive method	..	..	..	..
Percentage using a modern contraceptive method	..	..	..	..
Percentage using condoms	..	..	..	..

Population policies

Indicator	Year	Value	Year	Value
Government's view on the level of fertility	..	--	2001	Too high
Government's policy regarding level of fertility	..	--	2001	Lower
Government's support for contraceptive methods	..	--	2001	Direct support

[a]Median age at first birth among women aged 25-29 at the date of the survey for both dates

Total fertility rates

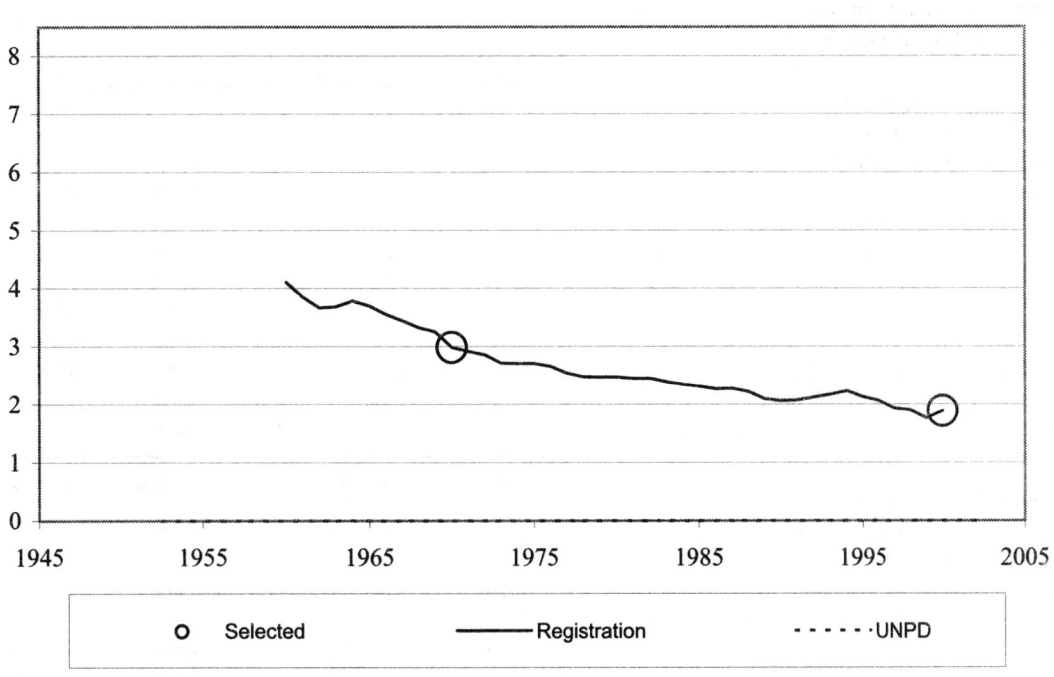

Age-specific fertility rates

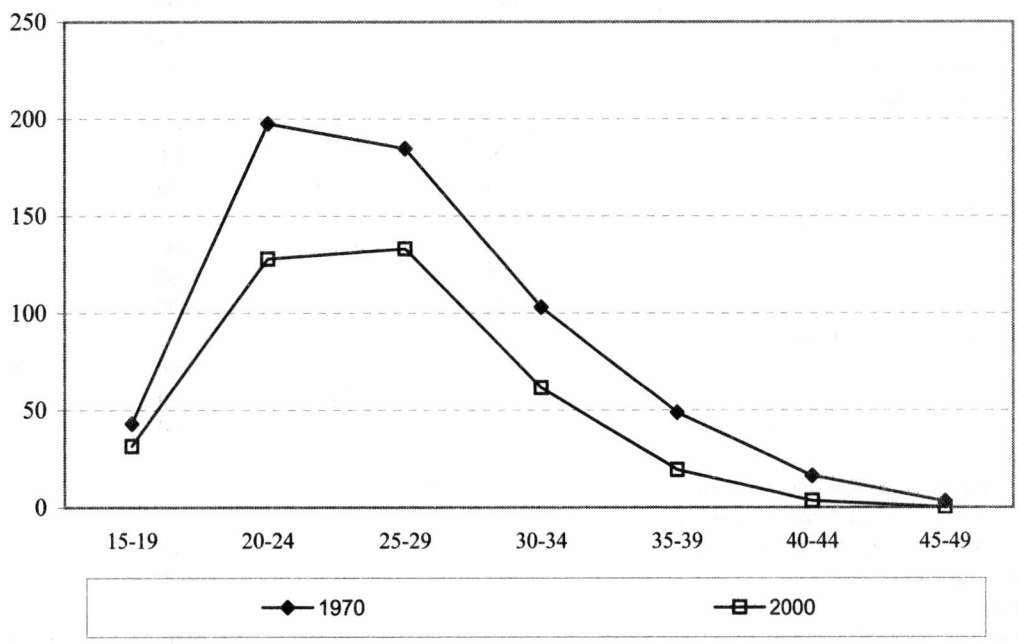

Indicator	Period					
	Earlier year			Later year		
	Year	Value		Year	Value	

Nuptiality

Indicator	Year	Value		Year	Value	
Annual number of marriages (*thousands*)	..	..		..	..	
Annual number of divorces (*thousands*)	..	..		..	..	

Indicator	Year	Male	Female	Year	Male	Female
Total first marriage rate (per person)	..	..	..	..	..	..
Total divorce rate (per person)	..	..	..	..	..	..
Mean age at first marriage (years)	..	..	..	..	..	..
SMAM (years)	1970	26.0	..	1998	27.0	21.3
Percentage ever married by age group						
15-19	1970	2.3	68.6	1998	2.4	19.9
20-24	1970	25.8	[15-24]	1998	18.3	63.4
25-29	1970	64.8	96.9	1998	60.1	92.3
30-34	1970	85.1	98.0	1998	83.9	97.6
35-39	1970	91.6	98.3	1998	94.5	98.9
40-44	1970	93.5	98.2	1998	98.2	99.5
45-49	1970	95.4	98.0	1998	98.9	99.7

Fertility

Indicator	Year	Value	Year	Value
Annual number of births (*thousands*)	1961	84.1	..	..
Crude birth rate (per 1 000 population)	1961	54.7	..	..
Percentage of extra-marital births among all births	..	..	..	..
Total fertility rate (births per woman)	1970	6.6	1996	5.4
Age-specific fertility rate (per 1 000 women)				
15-19	1970	122	1996	89
20-24	1970	292	1996	224
25-29	1970	288	1996	251
30-34	1970	245	1996	214
35-39	1970	194	1996	172
40-44	1970	117	1996	93
45-49	1970	71	1996	37
Mean age at childbearing (years)	1970	30.3	1996	30.2
Mean age at first birth (years)[a]	..	..	1998	18.9
Children ever born per woman				
35-39	..	..	1998	5.1
40-44	..	..	1998	6.1
45-49	..	..	1998	6.7
Percentage of childless women				
35-39	..	..	1998	2.7
40-44	..	..	1998	1.6
45-49	..	..	1998	2.1
Percentage of women with parity three or higher				
35-39	..	..	1998	84.2
40-44	..	..	1998	91.3
45-49	..	..	1998	92.7

Family Planning

Indicator	Year	Value	Year	Value
Contraceptive prevalence among women in union				
Percentage using any contraceptive method	..	..	2000	25.7
Percentage using a modern contraceptive method	..	..	2000	9.3
Percentage using condoms	..	..	2000	1.6

Population policies

Indicator	Year	Value	Year	Value
Government's view on the level of fertility	1976	Satisfactory	2001	Satisfactory
Government's policy regarding level of fertility	1976	No intervention	2001	Maintain
Government's support for contraceptive methods	1976	Indirect support	2001	Direct support

[a]Median age at first birth among women aged 25-29 at the date of the survey

Total fertility rates

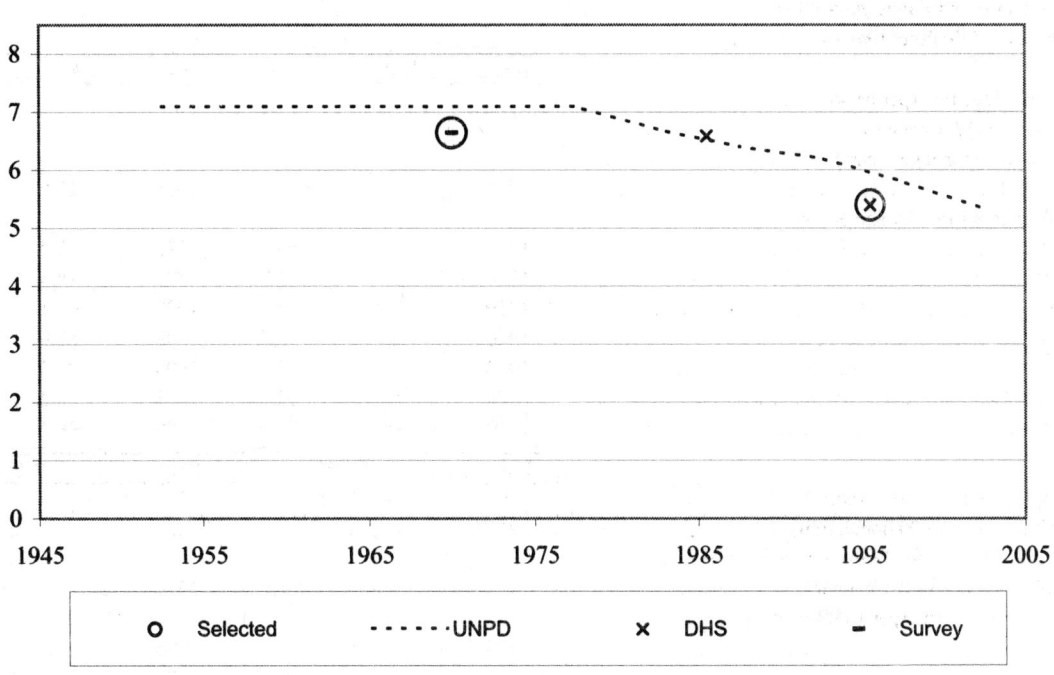

Age-specific fertility rates

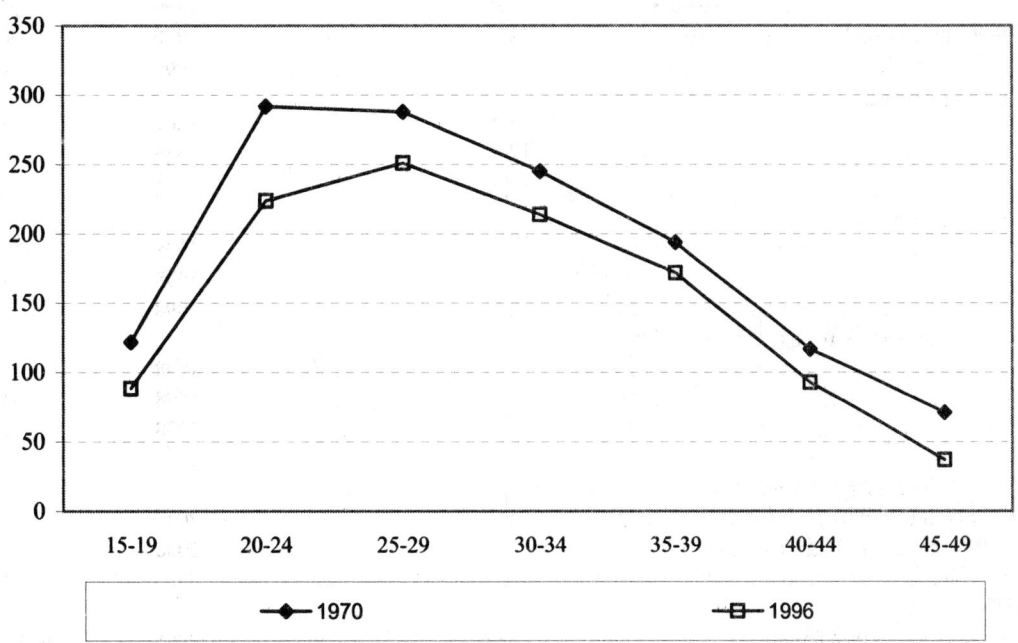

Indicator	Period					
	Earlier year			**Later year**		
	Year	Value		Year	Value	
Nuptiality						
Annual number of marriages (*thousands*)	..	..		2000	0.7	
Annual number of divorces (*thousands*)	..	..		2000	0.1	
	Year	Male	Female	Year	Male	Female
Total first marriage rate (per person)	..	..	..	..	..	..
Total divorce rate (per person)	..	..	..	..	..	..
Mean age at first marriage (years)	..	..	..	..	..	..
SMAM (years)	1976	27.1	24.3	1996	28.0	25.5
Percentage ever married by age group						
15-19	1976	1.2	4.9	1996	1.7	5.0
20-24	1976	18.6	41.0	1996	17.7	33.4
25-29	1976	54.7	73.7	1996	52.4	66.8
30-34	1976	80.5	86.3	1996	73.1	79.8
35-39	1976	89.1	92.1	1996	83.0	87.3
40-44	1976	91.1	93.0	1996	89.8	90.7
45-49	1976	93.4	93.6	1996	92.5	92.9
Fertility	Year	Value		Year	Value	
Annual number of births (*thousands*)	..	..		2000	2.5	
Crude birth rate (per 1 000 population)	..	..		2000	24.6	
Percentage of extra-marital births among all births	..	..		..	..	
Total fertility rate (births per woman)	..	..		..	..	
Age-specific fertility rate (per 1 000 women)						
15-19	..	..		..	..	
20-24	..	..		..	..	
25-29	..	..		..	..	
30-34	..	..		..	..	
35-39	..	..		..	..	
40-44	..	..		..	..	
45-49	..	..		..	..	
Mean age at childbearing (years)	..	..		..	..	
Mean age at first birth (years)	..	..		..	..	
Children ever born per woman						
35-39	1966	5.3		1996	4.1	
40-44	1966	6.5		1996	4.9	
45-49	1966	6.7		1996	..	
Percentage of childless women						
35-39	1966	11.5		1996	14.2	
40-44	1966	9.5		1996	9.8	
45-49	1966	10.2		1996	..	
Percentage of women with parity three or higher						
35-39	1966	76.0		1996	71.2	
40-44	1966	79.2		1996	78.6	
45-49	1966	78.2		1996	..	
Family Planning						
Contraceptive prevalence among women in union						
Percentage using any contraceptive method	..	..		..	..	
Percentage using a modern contraceptive method	..	..		..	..	
Percentage using condoms	..	..		..	..	
Population policies						
Government's view on the level of fertility	1976	Too high		2001	Satisfactory	
Government's policy regarding level of fertility	1976	Lower		2001	Maintain	
Government's support for contraceptive methods	1976	Direct support		2001	Direct support	

Total fertility rates

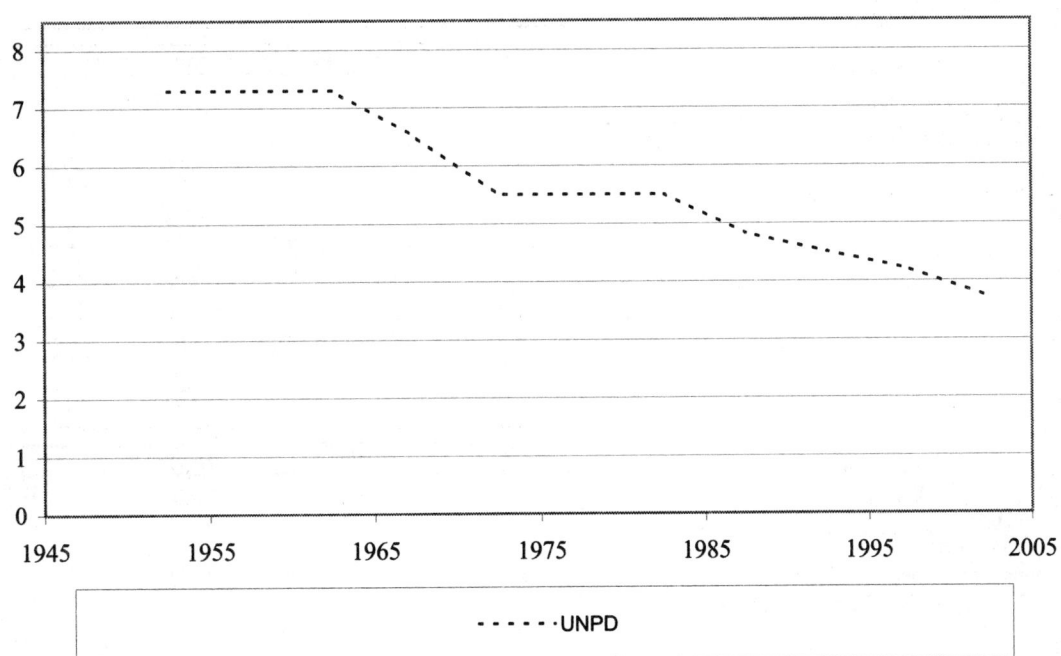

Indicator	Period			
	Earlier year		Later year	
	Year	Value	Year	Value
Nuptiality				
Annual number of marriages (*thousands*)	1970	6.4	1997	7.4
Annual number of divorces (*thousands*)	1970	0.4	1997	1.3

Indicator	Year	Male	Female	Year	Male	Female
Total first marriage rate (per person)	1985	0.7	0.7	1997	0.6	0.6
Total divorce rate (per person)	1972	0.0	0.0	1995	0.1	0.1
Mean age at first marriage (years)	1985	28.9	25.9	..	..	..
SMAM (years)	1970	27.4	24.0	1990	29.8	26.8
Percentage ever married by age group						
15-19	1970	0.7	6.8	1990	1.2	9.0
20-24	1970	15.1	36.1	1990	10.6	27.5
25-29	1970	47.8	62.2	1990	34.8	49.6
30-34	1970	65.3	72.4	1990	55.1	63.1
35-39	1970	73.4	76.6	1990	67.2	70.2
40-44	1970	75.8	78.0	1990	74.3	74.9
45-49	1970	78.0	79.6	1990	78.8	79.3

Fertility	Year	Value	Year	Value
Annual number of births (*thousands*).............................	1970	25.1	1997	18.5
Crude birth rate (per 1 000 population)	1970	25.8	1997	14.5
Percentage of extra-marital births among all births	1970	41.5	..	..
Total fertility rate (births per woman)	1971	3.6	1997	1.7
Age-specific fertility rate (per 1 000 women)				
15-19	1971	85	1997	43
20-24	1971	199	1997	97
25-29	1971	194	1997	88
30-34	1971	131	1997	70
35-39	1971	83	1997	35
40-44	1971	28	1997	9
45-49	1971	4	1997	1
Mean age at childbearing (years)	1971	27.7	1997	27.3
Mean age at first birth (years)	1970	22.2	1997	23.8
Children ever born per woman				
35-39	1977	4.3	1990	3.0
40-44	1977	5.2	1990	3.5
45-49	1977	5.8	1990	4.1
Percentage of childless women				
35-39	..	..	1990	11.7
40-44	..	..	1990	9.5
45-49	..	..	1990	8.3
Percentage of women with parity three or higher				
35-39	..	..	1990	55.2
40-44	..	..	1990	63.5
45-49	..	..	1990	70.3
Family Planning				
Contraceptive prevalence among women in union				
Percentage using any contraceptive method	1971	43.6	2000	38.2
Percentage using a modern contraceptive method	1971	6.5	2000	33.2
Percentage using condoms	1971	9.8	2000	11.7
Population policies				
Government's view on the level of fertility	1976	Too high	2001	Too high
Government's policy regarding level of fertility	1976	Lower	2001	Lower
Government's support for contraceptive methods	1976	Direct support	2001	Direct support

Total fertility rates

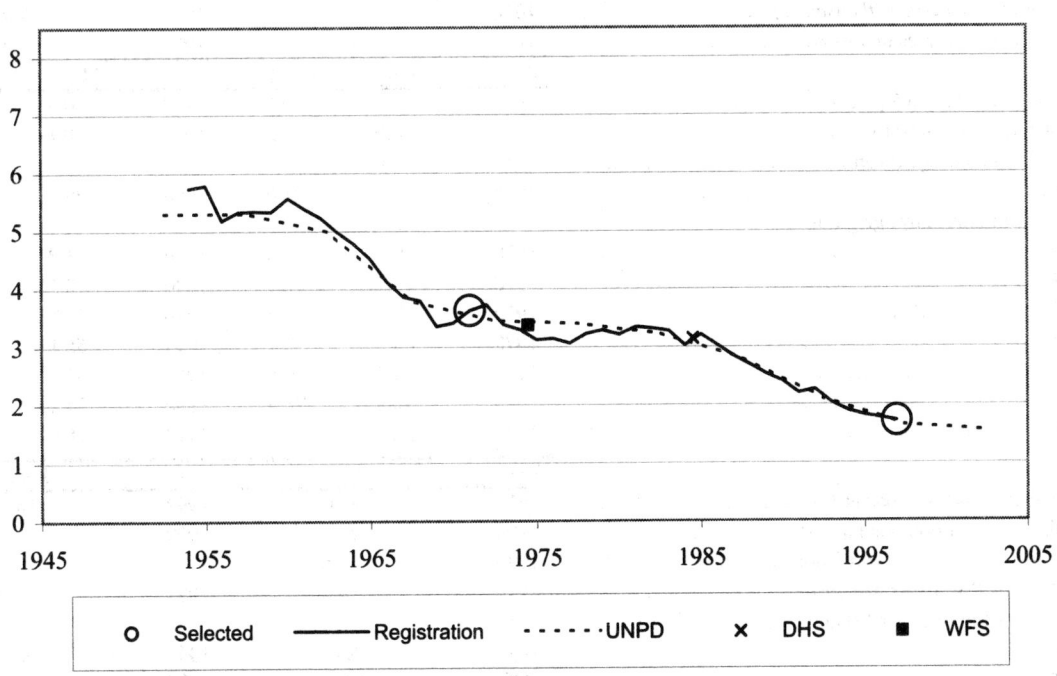

Age-specific fertility rates

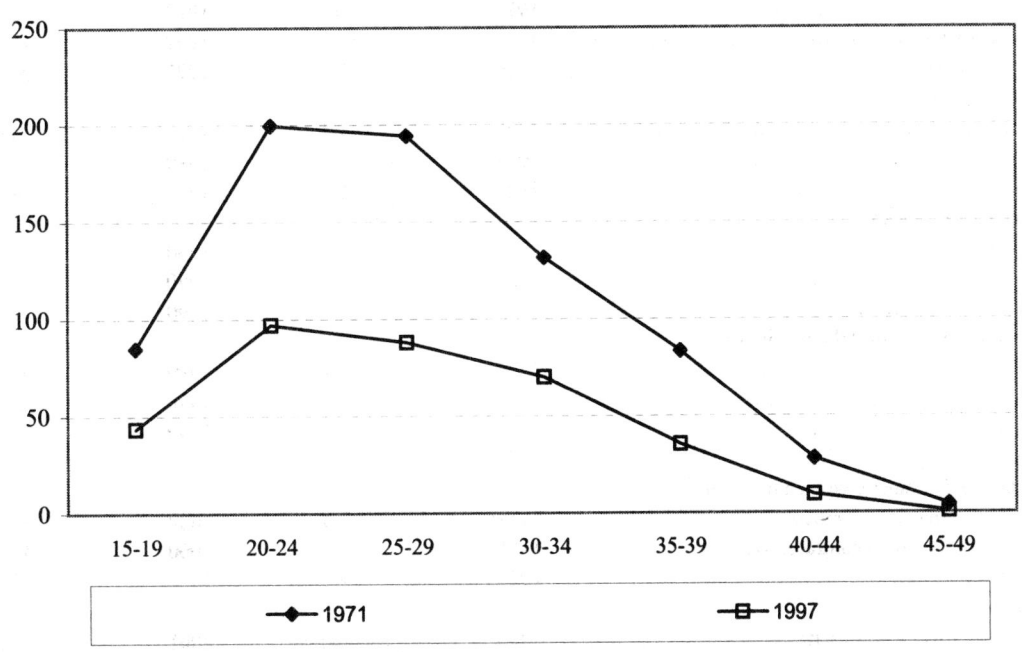

Indicator	Period					
	Earlier year			Later year		
	Year	Value		Year	Value	
Nuptiality						
Annual number of marriages (*thousands*)	1970	34.4		1990	55.6	
Annual number of divorces (*thousands*)	1970	4.3		1993	7.9	
	Year	Male	Female	Year	Male	Female
Total first marriage rate (per person)	..	..	..	1997	0.7	0.7
Total divorce rate (per person)	1971	0.2	0.1	..	..	..
Mean age at first marriage (years)	..	..	..	1997	30.9	26.1
SMAM (years)	1975	27.1	22.6	1994	30.3	26.6
Percentage ever married by age group						
15-19	1975	0.0	10.5	1994	0.0	3.0
20-24	1975	13.7	54.5	1994	3.7	27.7
25-29	1975	57.3	85.5	1994	29.0	62.3
30-34	1975	86.0	95.2	1994	68.8	81.9
35-39	1975	93.6	97.6	1994	90.5	91.1
40-44	1975	96.2	98.4	1994	95.2	95.3
45-49	1975	97.0	98.5	1994	97.0	97.7
Fertility	Year	Value		Year	Value	
Annual number of births (*thousands*)............................	1970	186.4		1999	160.2	
Crude birth rate (per 1 000 population)	1970	36.4		1999	16.9	
Percentage of extra-marital births among all births	1970	0.4		..	..	
Total fertility rate (births per woman)	1970	6.1		1999	2.1	
Age-specific fertility rate (per 1 000 women)						
15-19	1970	46		1999	8	
20-24	1970	254		1999	67	
25-29	1970	302		1999	123	
30-34	1970	273		1999	121	
35-39	1970	206		1999	73	
40-44	1970	96		1999	23	
45-49	1970	40		1999	3	
Mean age at childbearing (years)	1970	30.7		1999	30.7	
Mean age at first birth (years)	1970	23.7		1997	26.9	
Children ever born per woman						
35-39	1978	5.7		..	..	
40-44	1978	6.3		..	..	
45-49	1978	6.5		..	..	
Percentage of childless women						
35-39	1978	3.4		..	..	
40-44	1978	2.9		..	..	
45-49	1978	..		..	..	
Percentage of women with parity three or higher						
35-39	1978	84.1		..	..	
40-44	1978	88.2		..	..	
45-49	1978	..		..	..	
Family Planning						
Contraceptive prevalence among women in union						
Percentage using any contraceptive method	1978	31.4		1994	60.0	
Percentage using a modern contraceptive method	1978	25.1		1994	51.0	
Percentage using condoms	1978	1.3		1994	1.6	
Population policies						
Government's view on the level of fertility	1976	Too high		2001	Too high	
Government's policy regarding level of fertility	1976	Lower		2001	Lower	
Government's support for contraceptive methods	1976	Direct support		2001	Direct support	

Total fertility rates

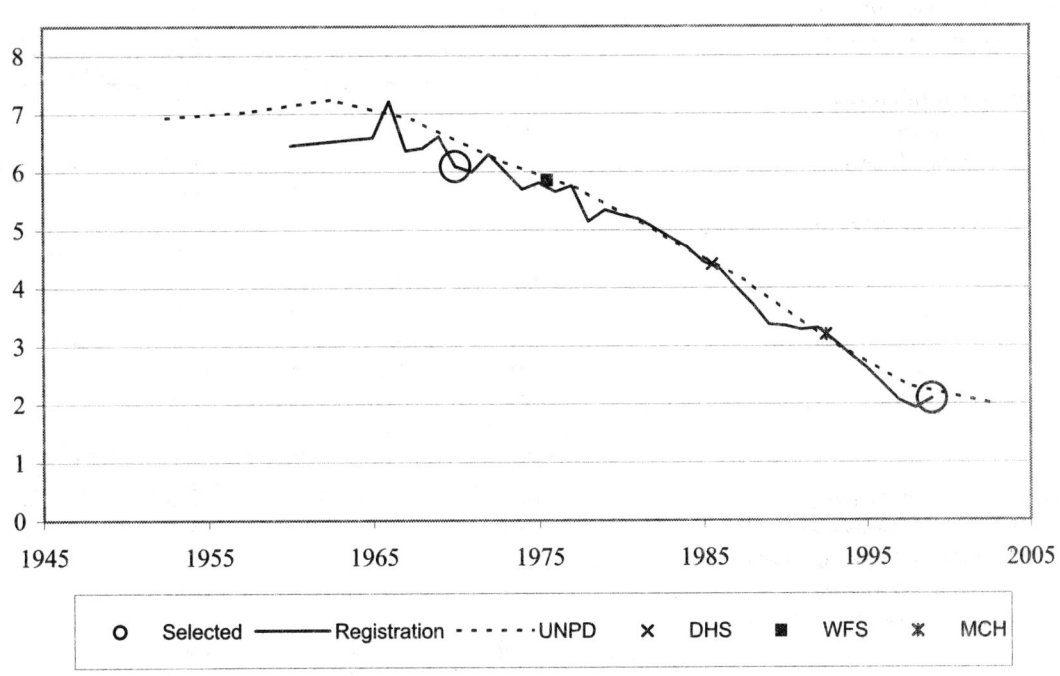

Age-specific fertility rates

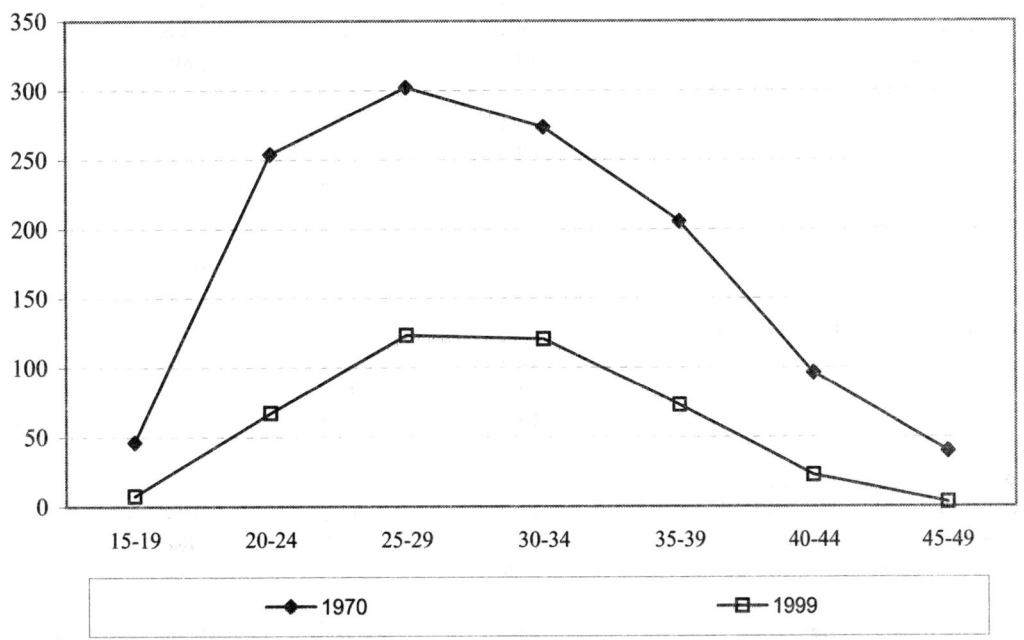

Indicator	Period					
	Earlier year			**Later year**		
	Year	Value		Year	Value	
Nuptiality						
Annual number of marriages (*thousands*)	1980	366.4		1999	475.6	
Annual number of divorces (*thousands*)	1970	9.6		2000	34.9	
	Year	Male	Female	Year	Male	Female
Total first marriage rate (per person)	..	..	..	1999	..	0.8
Total divorce rate (per person)	1970	0.0	0.0	1996	0.1	0.1
Mean age at first marriage (years)	1970	..	19.9	1999	..	22.3
SMAM (years)	1975	23.7	20.1	1998	..	22.0
Percentage ever married by age group						
15-19	1975	9.3	22.0	1998	..	15.5
20-24	1975	40.6	74.2	1998	..	60.7
25-29	1975	78.4	91.1	1998	..	87.1
30-34	1975	89.7	93.9	1998	..	93.5
35-39	1975	95.0	96.9	1998	..	97.6
40-44	1975	95.6	95.9	1998	..	98.2
45-49	1975	97.0	97.1	1998	..	98.3
Fertility	Year	Value		Year	Value	
Annual number of births (*thousands*)........................	1970	1 383.7		2002	1 482.0	
Crude birth rate (per 1 000 population)	1970	39.2		2002	21.1	
Percentage of extra-marital births among all births	1975	3.8		1990	4.5	
Total fertility rate (births per woman)	1970	5.7		2000	2.5	
Age-specific fertility rate (per 1 000 women)						
15-19	1970	89		2000	56	
20-24	1970	293		2000	165	
25-29	1970	283		2000	145	
30-34	1970	222		2000	82	
35-39	1970	157		2000	36	
40-44	1970	62		2000	12	
45-49	1970	31		2000	1	
Mean age at childbearing (years)	1970	29.1		2000	26.6	
Mean age at first birth (years)	1970	20.1		1985	21.7	
Children ever born per woman						
35-39	1970	4.8		1998	3.3	
40-44	1970	5.2		1998	4.0	
45-49	1970	5.1		1998	4.5	
Percentage of childless women						
35-39	1970	5.0		1998	6.0	
40-44	1970	5.4		1998	3.8	
45-49	1970	6.0		1998	3.7	
Percentage of women with parity three or higher						
35-39	1970	80.6		1998	57.1	
40-44	1970	80.6		1998	68.3	
45-49	1970	78.6		1998	76.1	
Family Planning						
Contraceptive prevalence among women in union						
Percentage using any contraceptive method	1978	38.0		1998	63.9	
Percentage using a modern contraceptive method	1978	13.5		1998	37.7	
Percentage using condoms	1978	3.1		1998	8.2	
Population policies						
Government's view on the level of fertility	1976	Too high		2001	Too high	
Government's policy regarding level of fertility	1976	Lower		2001	Lower	
Government's support for contraceptive methods	1976	Direct support		2001	No support	

Total fertility rates

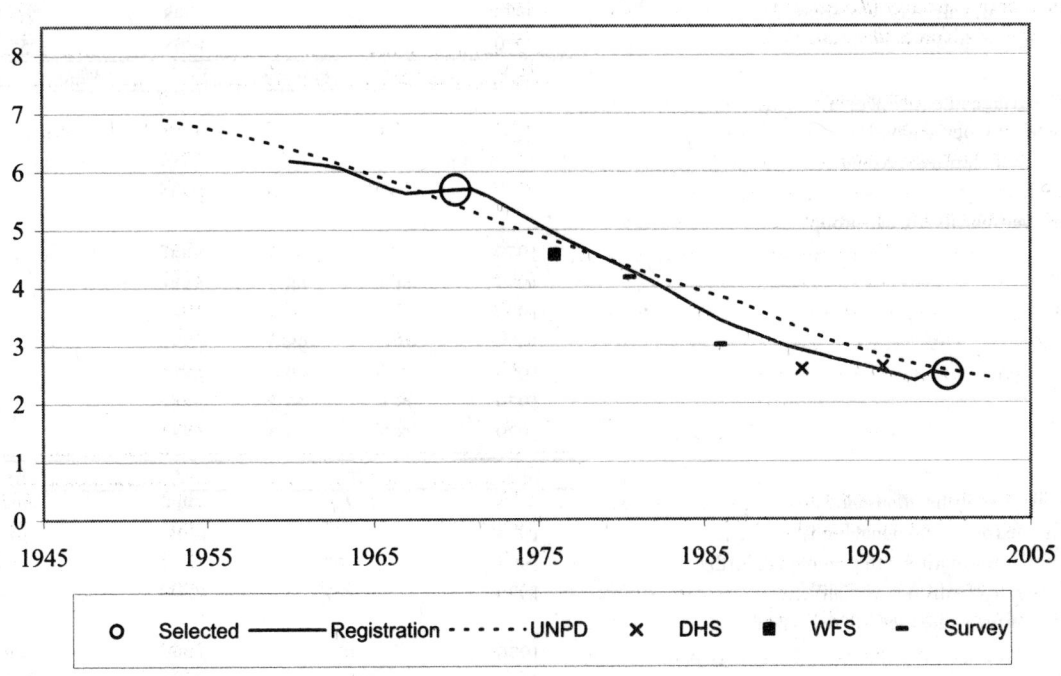

Age-specific fertility rates

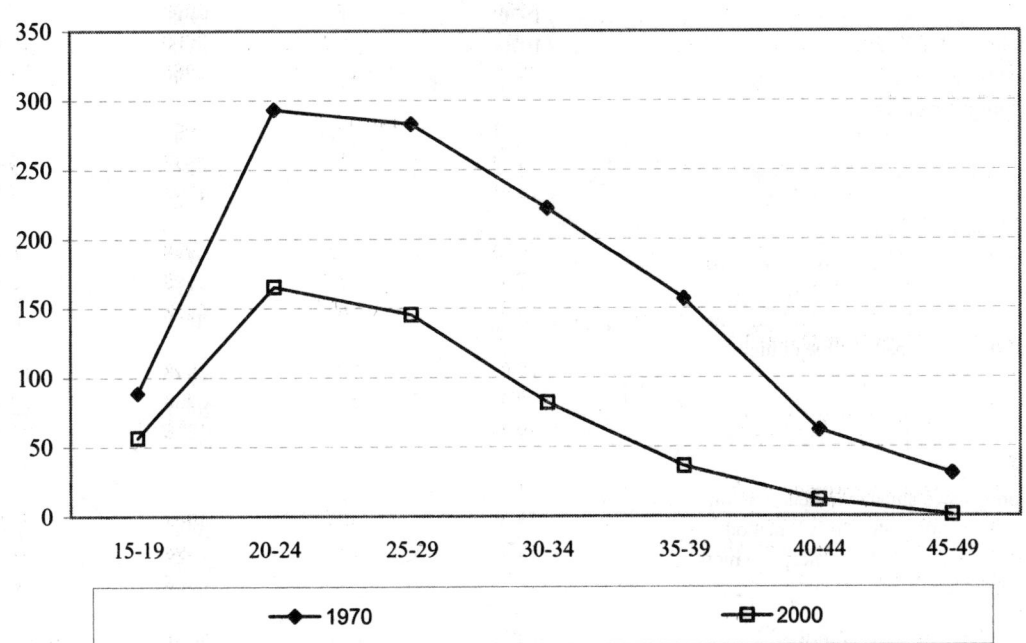

Indicator	Period					
	Earlier year			Later year		
	Year	Value		Year	Value	

Nuptiality

	Year	Value		Year	Value	
Annual number of marriages (*thousands*)	1970	18.8		1998	26.4	
Annual number of divorces (*thousands*)	1970	2.6		1998	5.3	

	Year	Male	Female	Year	Male	Female
Total first marriage rate (per person)	..	..	..	..	..	..
Total divorce rate (per person)	..	..	..	..	..	..
Mean age at first marriage (years)	..	..	..	..	..	..
SMAM (years)	..	..	..	2000	..	23.4
Percentage ever married by age group						
15-19	1979	..	..	2000	..	5.9
20-24	1979	44.5	68.3	2000	..	47.3
25-29	1979	88.5	94.5	2000	..	84.8
30-34	1979	95.7	98.0	2000	..	95.8
35-39	1979	97.3	99.0	2000	..	97.5
40-44	1979	98.1	99.2	2000	..	99.2
45-49	1979	98.7	99.2	2000	..	99.5

Fertility

	Year	Value	Year	Value
Annual number of births (*thousands*).............................	1970	77.1	1998	98.5
Crude birth rate (per 1 000 population)	1970	35.2	1998	20.3
Percentage of extra-marital births among all births	1980	2.9	..	..
Total fertility rate (births per woman)	1970	5.7	1998	3.0
Age-specific fertility rate (per 1 000 women)				
15-19	1970	32	1998	29
20-24	1970	271	1998	192
25-29	1970	276	1998	204
30-34	1970	251	1998	113
35-39	1970	213	1998	50
40-44	1970	62	1998	12
45-49	1970	31	1998	1
Mean age at childbearing (years)	1970	30.4	1998	27.5
Mean age at first birth (years)[a]	..	..	2000	23.3
Children ever born per woman				
35-39	..	..	2000	3.6
40-44	..	..	2000	4.7
45-49	..	..	2000	5.1
Percentage of childless women				
35-39	..	..	2000	5.1
40-44	..	..	2000	2.6
45-49	..	..	2000	1.4
Percentage of women with parity three or higher				
35-39	..	..	2000	75.3
40-44	..	..	2000	84.5
45-49	..	..	2000	83.1

Family Planning

Contraceptive prevalence among women in union				
Percentage using any contraceptive method	..	..	2000	61.8
Percentage using a modern contraceptive method	..	..	2000	53.1
Percentage using condoms	..	..	2000	2.0

Population policies

Government's view on the level of fertility	..	--	2001	Satisfactory
Government's policy regarding level of fertility	..	--	2001	No intervention
Government's support for contraceptive methods	..	--	2001	Direct support

[a]Median age at first birth among women aged 25-29 at the date of the survey

Total fertility rates

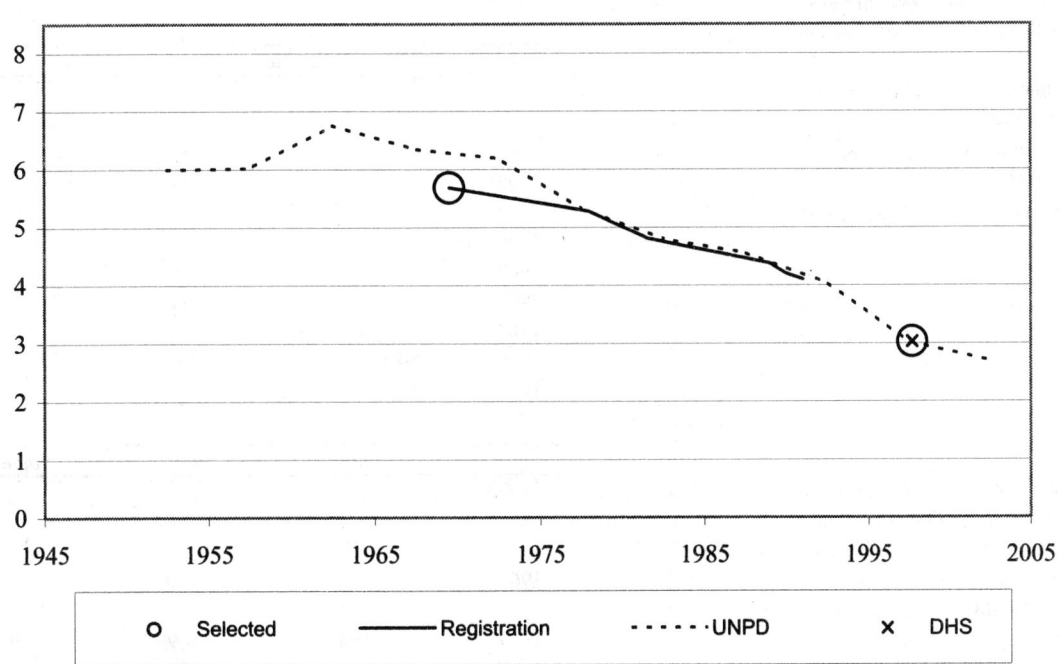

Age-specific fertility rates

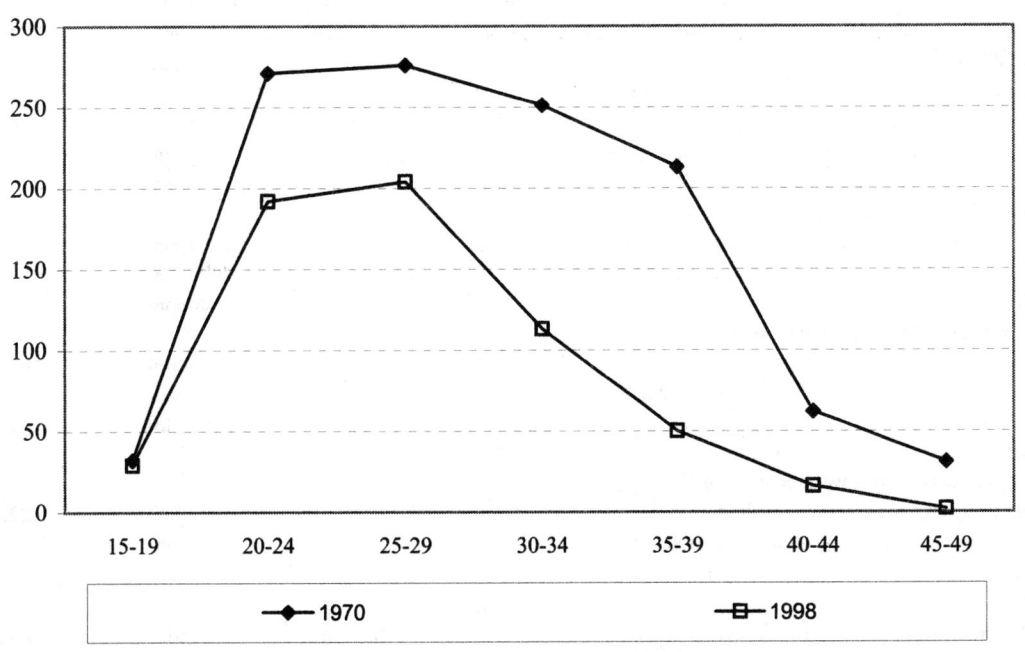

Indicator	Period					
	Earlier year			Later year		
	Year	Value		Year	Value	

Nuptiality

Indicator	Year	Value		Year	Value	
Annual number of marriages (*thousands*)	..	..		..	..	
Annual number of divorces (*thousands*)	..	..		..	..	

Indicator	Year	Male	Female	Year	Male	Female
Total first marriage rate (per person)	..	..	..	..	..	..
Total divorce rate (per person)	..	..	..	..	..	..
Mean age at first marriage (years)	..	..	..	..	..	..
SMAM (years)	1969	23.9	17.7	2001	23.5	19.6
Percentage ever married by age group						
15-19	1969	7.3	49.7	2001	6.5	32.3
20-24	1969	42.6	86.8	2001	45.3	84.7
25-29	1969	69.3	93.2	2001	83.3	93.8
30-34	1969	79.6	94.3	2001	95.4	97.4
35-39	1969	84.1	94.7	2001	95.5	97.8
40-44	1969	85.7	94.0	2001	96.1	99.4
45-49	1969	87.9	94.2	2001	96.5	99.5

Fertility

Indicator	Year	Value	Year	Value
Annual number of births (*thousands*)	..	..	..	..
Crude birth rate (per 1 000 population)	..	..	..	..
Percentage of extra-marital births among all births	..	..	..	..
Total fertility rate (births per woman)	1969	7.1	1999	7.0
Age-specific fertility rate (per 1 000 women)				
15-19	1969	198	1999	190
20-24	1969	341	1999	334
25-29	1969	322	1999	299
30-34	1969	253	1999	261
35-39	1969	189	1999	187
40-44	1969	87	1999	84
45-49	1969	35	1999	39
Mean age at childbearing (years)	1969	28.5	1999	28.7
Mean age at first birth (years)[a]	..	..	2000-2001	18.9
Children ever born per woman				
35-39	..	..	2000-2001	6.1
40-44	..	..	2000-2001	6.9
45-49	..	..	2000-2001	7.4
Percentage of childless women				
35-39	..	..	2000-2001	3.6
40-44	..	..	2000-2001	4.7
45-49	..	..	2000-2001	3.7
Percentage of women with parity three or higher				
35-39	..	..	2000-2001	86.4
40-44	..	..	2000-2001	86.5
45-49	..	..	2000-2001	91.2

Family Planning

Indicator	Year	Value	Year	Value
Contraceptive prevalence among women in union				
Percentage using any contraceptive method	..	..	2000-2001	22.8
Percentage using a modern contraceptive method	..	..	2000-2001	18.2
Percentage using condoms	..	..	2000-2001	1.9

Population policies

Indicator	Year	Value	Year	Value
Government's view on the level of fertility	1976	Too high	2001	Too high
Government's policy regarding level of fertility	1976	Lower	2001	Lower
Government's support for contraceptive methods	1976	Direct support	2001	Direct support

[a]Median age at first birth among women aged 25-29 at the date of the survey

Total fertility rates

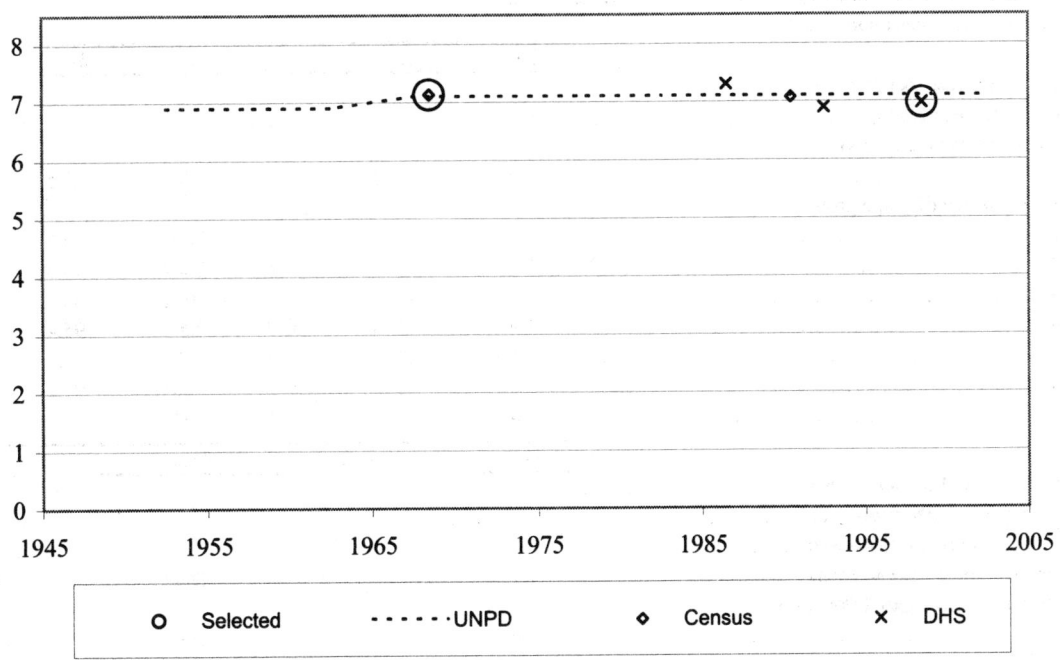

Age-specific fertility rates

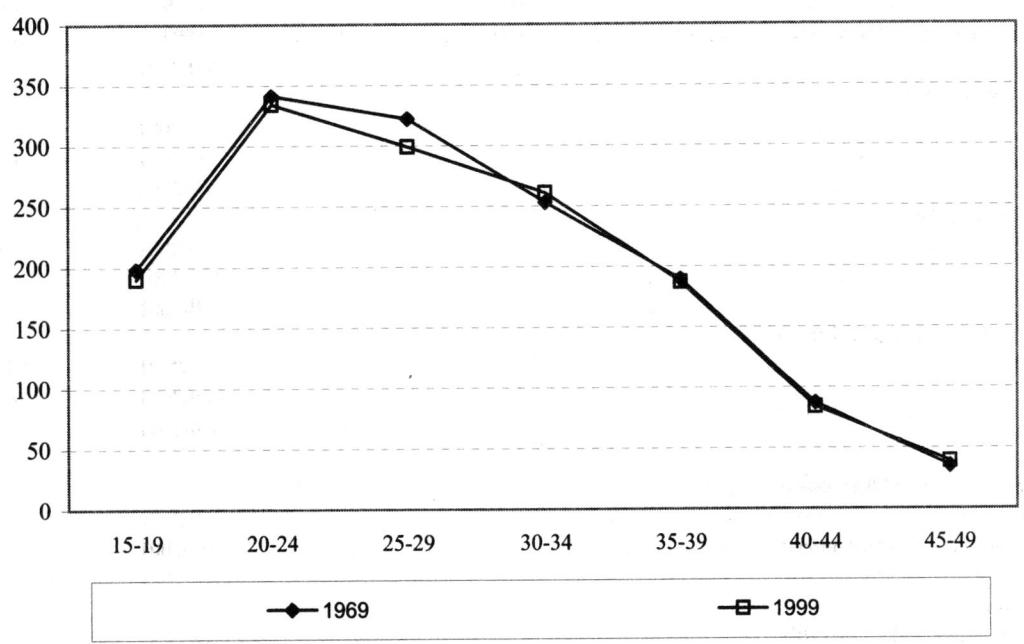

Indicator	Period					
	Earlier year			Later year		
	Year	Value		Year	Value	

Nuptiality

Indicator	Year	Value		Year	Value	
Annual number of marriages (*thousands*)	1970	465.8		2002	317.2	
Annual number of divorces (*thousands*)	1970	135.4		2002	183.5	

Indicator	Year	Male	Female	Year	Male	Female
Total first marriage rate (per person)	1976	0.9	0.9	1998	0.6	0.6
Total divorce rate (per person)	1981	0.5	0.4	1995	0.5	0.5
Mean age at first marriage (years)	1976	24.1	21.8	1998	24.5	21.7
SMAM (years)	1979	24.1	21.4	1999	..	21.7
Percentage ever married by age group						
15-19	1979	..	..	1999	..	10.0
20-24	1979	41.4	67.4	1999	..	64.1
25-29	1979	84.3	90.1	1999	..	92.4
30-34	1979	93.4	94.7	1999	..	97.0
35-39	1979	96.3	96.2	1999	..	97.5
40-44	1979	97.6	95.9	1999	..	98.1
45-49	1979	98.6	94.8	1999	..	..

Fertility

Indicator	Year	Value		Year	Value	
Annual number of births (*thousands*)	1970	719.2		2002	390.7	
Crude birth rate (per 1 000 population)	1970	15.3		2002	8.0	
Percentage of extra-marital births among all births	1970	9.2		2001	18.0	
Total fertility rate (births per woman)	1970	2.1		1998	1.2	
Age-specific fertility rate (per 1 000 women)						
15-19	1970	35		1998	41	
20-24	1970	165		1998	101	
25-29	1970	113		1998	58	
30-34	1970	68		1998	26	
35-39	1970	31		1998	9	
40-44	1970	7		1998	2	
45-49	1970	1		1998	0	
Mean age at childbearing (years)	1970	26.5		1998	24.7	
Mean age at first birth (years)	..	..		..	..	
Children ever born per woman						
35-39	..	..		1989	1.8	
40-44	..	..		1989	1.9	
45-49	..	..		1989	1.9	
Percentage of childless women						
35-39	..	..		1989	7.4	
40-44	..	..		1989	7.2	
45-49	..	..		1989	7.8	
Percentage of women with parity three or higher						
35-39	..	..		1989	16.3	
40-44	..	..		1989	17.9	
45-49	..	..		1989	20.4	

Family Planning

Indicator	Year	Value		Year	Value	
Contraceptive prevalence among women in union						
Percentage using any contraceptive method	..	..		1999	67.5	
Percentage using a modern contraceptive method	..	..		1999	37.6	
Percentage using condoms	..	..		1999	13.5	

Population policies

Indicator	Year	Value		Year	Value	
Government's view on the level of fertility	1976	Satisfactory		2001	Too low	
Government's policy regarding level of fertility	1976	Maintain		2001	Raise	
Government's support for contraceptive methods	1976	Direct support		2001	No support	

Total fertility rates

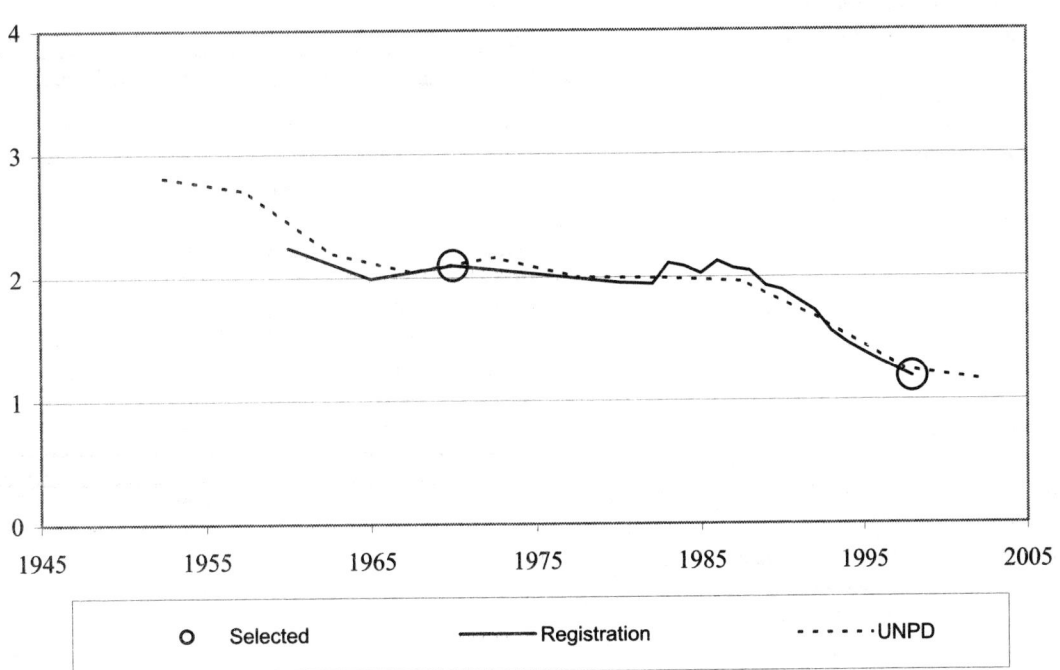

O Selected	—— Registration	····· UNPD

Age-specific fertility rates

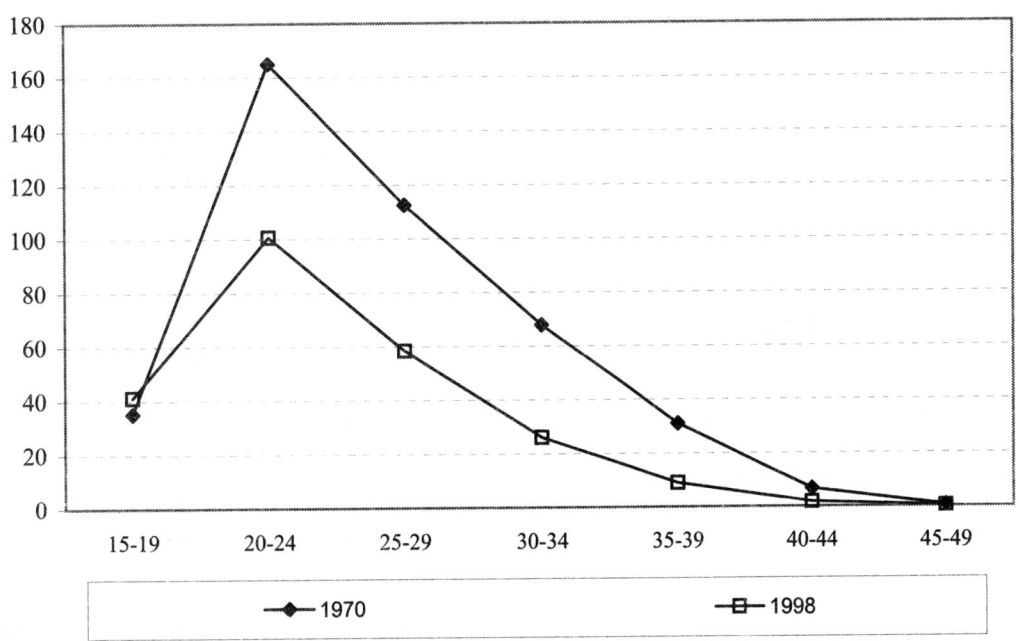

◆ 1970	□ 1998

United Arab Emirates

Indicator	Period					
	Earlier year			Later year		
	Year	Value		Year	Value	
Nuptiality						
Annual number of marriages (*thousands*)	..	..		..	..	
Annual number of divorces (*thousands*)	..	..		..	..	
	Year	Male	Female	Year	Male	Female
Total first marriage rate (per person)	..	..	..	..	..	..
Total divorce rate (per person)	..	..	..	..	..	..
Mean age at first marriage (years)	..	..	..	..	..	..
SMAM (years)	1975	25.9	18.0	1987	25.6	23.1
Percentage ever married by age group						
15-19	1975	8.5	56.5	1987	2.5	18.5
20-24	1975	30.6	87.8	1987	26.6	52.2
25-29	1975	58.0	94.6	1987	68.2	74.5
30-34	1975	82.3	97.4	1987	88.8	90.1
35-39	1975	91.5	98.4	1987	96.7	96.0
40-44	1975	94.8	98.4	1987	97.0	97.7
45-49	1975	95.9	98.6	1987	98.3	98.5
Fertility	Year	Value		Year	Value	
Annual number of births (*thousands*).............................	..	..		1996	47.1	
Crude birth rate (per 1 000 population)	..	..		1996	19.3	
Percentage of extra-marital births among all births	..	..		..	..	
Total fertility rate (births per woman)	..	..		1993	5.0	
Age-specific fertility rate (per 1 000 women)						
15-19	..	..		1993	44	
20-24	..	..		1993	188	
25-29	..	..		1993	257	
30-34	..	..		1993	222	
35-39	..	..		1993	164	
40-44	..	..		1993	92	
45-49	..	..		1993	41	
Mean age at childbearing (years)	..	..		1993	31.0	
Mean age at first birth (years)	..	..		..	..	
Children ever born per woman						
35-39	1975	4.7		1995	6.6	
40-44	1975	4.6		1995	7.6	
45-49	1975	4.6		1995	7.9	
Percentage of childless women						
35-39	1975	5.7		1995	5.3	
40-44	1975	7.8		1995	2.8	
45-49	1975	7.1		1995	3.0	
Percentage of women with parity three or higher						
35-39	1975	73.8		1995	92.3	
40-44	1975	71.0		1995	91.7	
45-49	1975	70.2		1995	92.0	
Family Planning						
Contraceptive prevalence among women in union						
Percentage using any contraceptive method	..	..		1995	27.5	
Percentage using a modern contraceptive method	..	..		1995	23.6	
Percentage using condoms	..	..		1995	2.0	
Population policies						
Government's view on the level of fertility	1976	Satisfactory		2001	Too low	
Government's policy regarding level of fertility	1976	Maintain		2001	Raise	
Government's support for contraceptive methods	1976	No support		2001	Direct support	

Total fertility rates

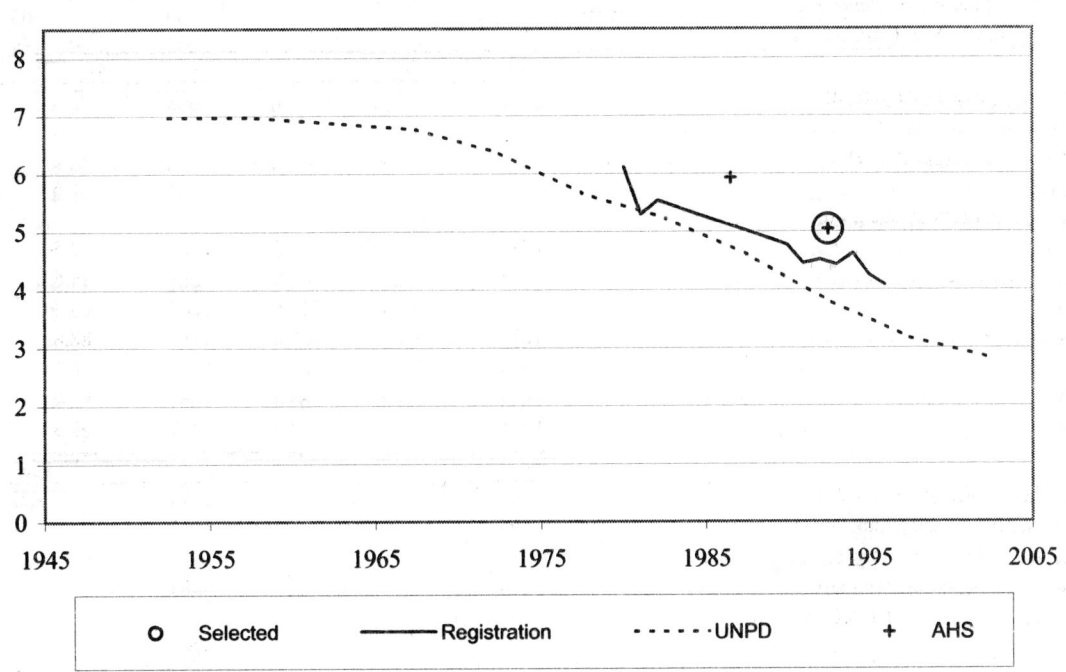

O Selected	—— Registration	- - - - UNPD	+ AHS

Age-specific fertility rates

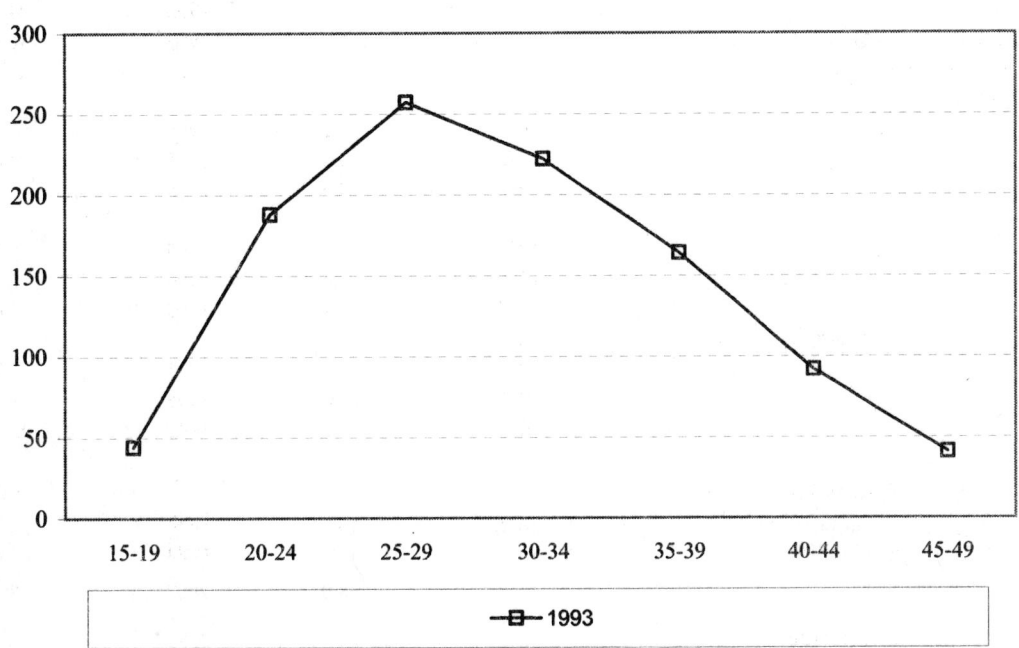

—☐— 1993

Indicator	Period					
	Earlier year			Later year		
	Year	Value		Year	Value	
Nuptiality						
Annual number of marriages (*thousands*)	1970	470.9		2000	305.9	
Annual number of divorces (*thousands*)	1970	62.3		2000	154.3	
	Year	Male	Female	Year	Male	Female
Total first marriage rate (per person)	1970	..	1.0	1996	0.5	0.5
Total divorce rate (per person)	..	..	..	1996	0.3	0.3
Mean age at first marriage (years)	1970	..	22.4	1996	28.8	26.6
SMAM (years)	1971	24.2	21.3	1991	28.4	26.4
Percentage ever married by age group						
15-19	1971	2.0	8.6	1991	0.5	1.7
20-24	1971	36.6	59.7	1991	11.9	24.6
25-29	1971	74.1	86.1	1991	46.3	61.6
30-34	1971	85.7	92.2	1991	72.2	81.8
35-39	1971	88.5	92.8	1991	83.4	89.8
40-44	1971	89.3	92.3	1991	88.5	93.6
45-49	1971	89.6	91.7	1991	90.8	94.8
Fertility	Year	Value		Year	Value	
Annual number of births (*thousands*)	1970	903.9		2001	669.2	
Crude birth rate (per 1 000 population)	1970	16.2		2001	11.2	
Percentage of extra-marital births among all births	1970	8.0		2001	40.1	
Total fertility rate (births per woman)	1972	2.2		2000	1.6	
Age-specific fertility rate (per 1 000 women)						
15-19	1972	48		2000	29	
20-24	1972	141		2000	69	
25-29	1972	143		2000	95	
30-34	1972	71		2000	88	
35-39	1972	30		2000	40	
40-44	1972	8		2000	8	
45-49	1972	0		2000	0	
Mean age at childbearing (years)	1972	26.6		2000	28.5	
Mean age at first birth (years)[a]	..	..		2000	29.1	
Children ever born per woman						
35-39	..	..		..	..	
40-44	..	..		..	..	
45-49	..	..		..	..	
Percentage of childless women						
35-39	..	..		..	..	
40-44	..	..		..	..	
45-49	..	..		..	..	
Percentage of women with parity three or higher						
35-39	..	..		..	..	
40-44	..	..		..	..	
45-49	..	..		..	..	
Family Planning						
Contraceptive prevalence among women in union						
Percentage using any contraceptive method	1970	75.0		2002	84.0	
Percentage using a modern contraceptive method	1970	59.0		2002	81.0	
Percentage using condoms	1970	28.0		2002	18.0	
Population policies						
Government's view on the level of fertility	1976	Satisfactory		2001	Satisfactory	
Government's policy regarding level of fertility	1976	No intervention		2001	No intervention	
Government's support for contraceptive methods	1976	Direct support		2001	Direct support	

[a]Median age at first birth within current marriage

Total fertility rates

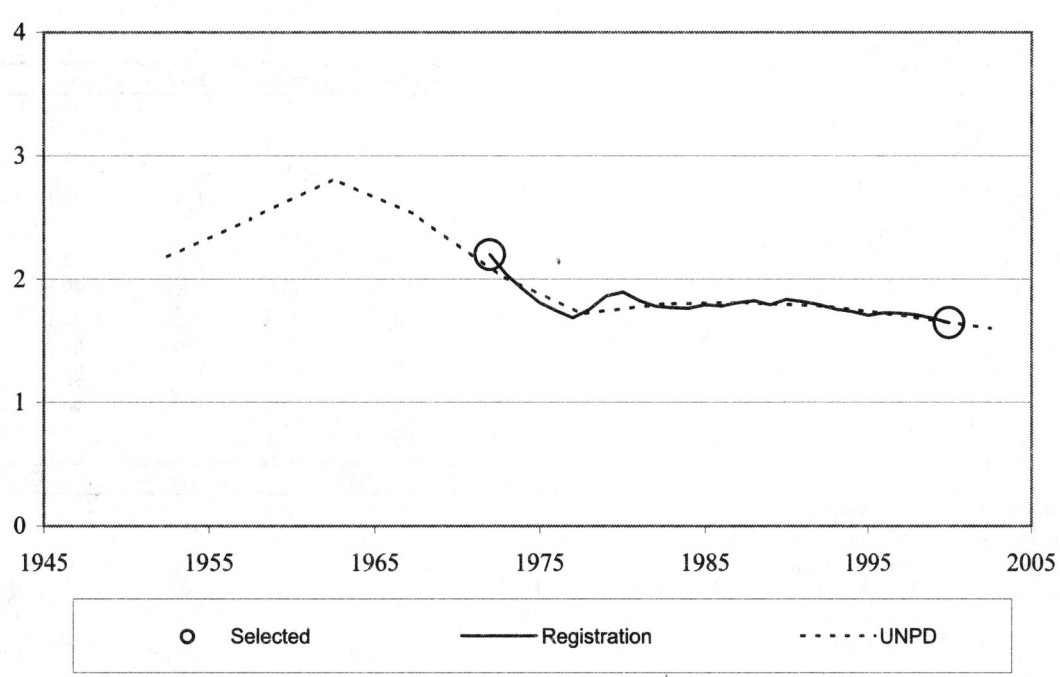

Age-specific fertility rates

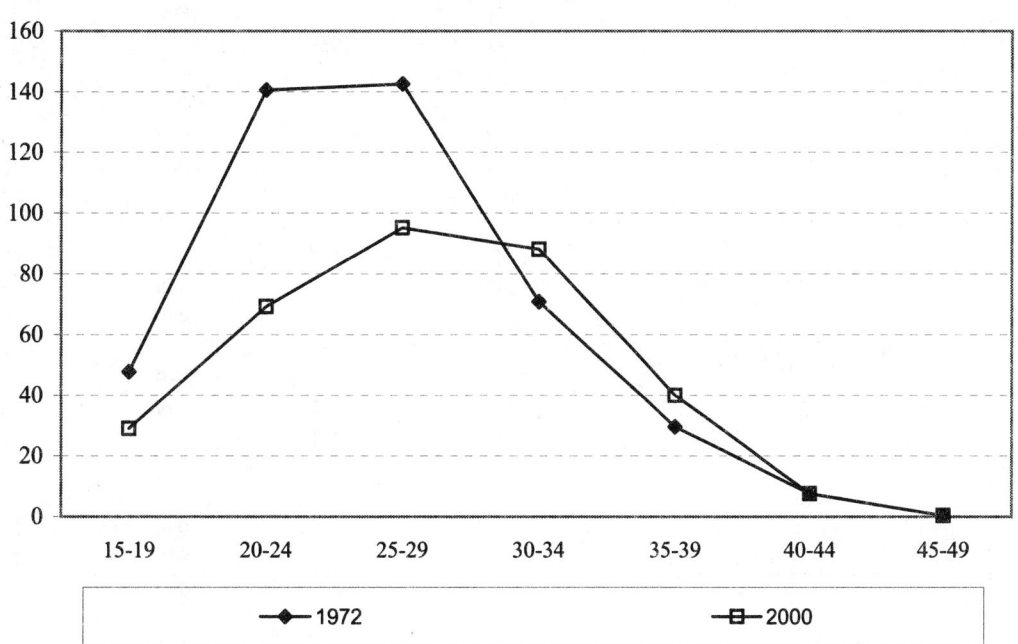

United Republic of Tanzania

Indicator	Period					
	Earlier year			Later year		
	Year	Value		Year	Value	
Nuptiality						
Annual number of marriages (*thousands*)	..	..		..	..	
Annual number of divorces (*thousands*)	..	..		..	..	
	Year	Male	Female	Year	Male	Female
Total first marriage rate (per person)	..	..	..	..	..	..
Total divorce rate (per person)	..	..	..	..	..	..
Mean age at first marriage (years)	..	..	..	..	..	..
SMAM (years)	1978	24.9	19.1	1996	25.1	20.5
Percentage ever married by age group						
15-19	1978	3.5	37.6	1996	2.9	25.3
20-24	1978	34.6	83.9	1996	29.2	75.5
25-29	1978	71.4	94.6	1996	73.1	92.6
30-34	1978	88.2	97.1	1996	93.9	95.5
35-39	1978	92.5	98.1	1996	96.5	98.3
40-44	1978	94.9	98.4	1996	98.3	98.6
45-49	1978	95.6	98.6	1996	97.1	99.3
Fertility	Year	Value		Year	Value	
Annual number of births (*thousands*)................................	..	..		..	..	
Crude birth rate (per 1 000 population)	..	..		..	..	
Percentage of extra-marital births among all births	..	..		..	..	
Total fertility rate (births per woman)	1971	7.1		1998	5.6	
Age-specific fertility rate (per 1 000 women)						
15-19	1971	152		1998	137	
20-24	1971	336		1998	271	
25-29	1971	325		1998	233	
30-34	1971	263		1998	210	
35-39	1971	200		1998	148	
40-44	1971	102		1998	89	
45-49	1971	43		1998	32	
Mean age at childbearing (years)	1971	29.3		1998	29.1	
Mean age at first birth (years)[a]	..	..		1999	19.5	
Children ever born per woman						
35-39	1967	4.8		1999	5.0	
40-44	1967	5.0		1999	6.4	
45-49	1967	5.2		1999	7.0	
Percentage of childless women						
35-39	1967	10.7		1999	3.3	
40-44	1967	11.8		1999	1.9	
45-49	1967	11.3		1999	0.6	
Percentage of women with parity three or higher						
35-39	1967	72.3		1999	81.7	
40-44	1967	71.7		1999	88.5	
45-49	1967	71.8		1999	91.0	
Family Planning						
Contraceptive prevalence among women in union						
Percentage using any contraceptive method	..	..		1999	25.4	
Percentage using a modern contraceptive method	..	..		1999	16.9	
Percentage using condoms	..	..		1999	2.7	
Population policies						
Government's view on the level of fertility	1976	Satisfactory		2001	Too high	
Government's policy regarding level of fertility	1976	No intervention		2001	Lower	
Government's support for contraceptive methods	1976	Direct support		2001	Direct support	

[a]Median age at first birth among women aged 25-29 at the date of the survey

Total fertility rates

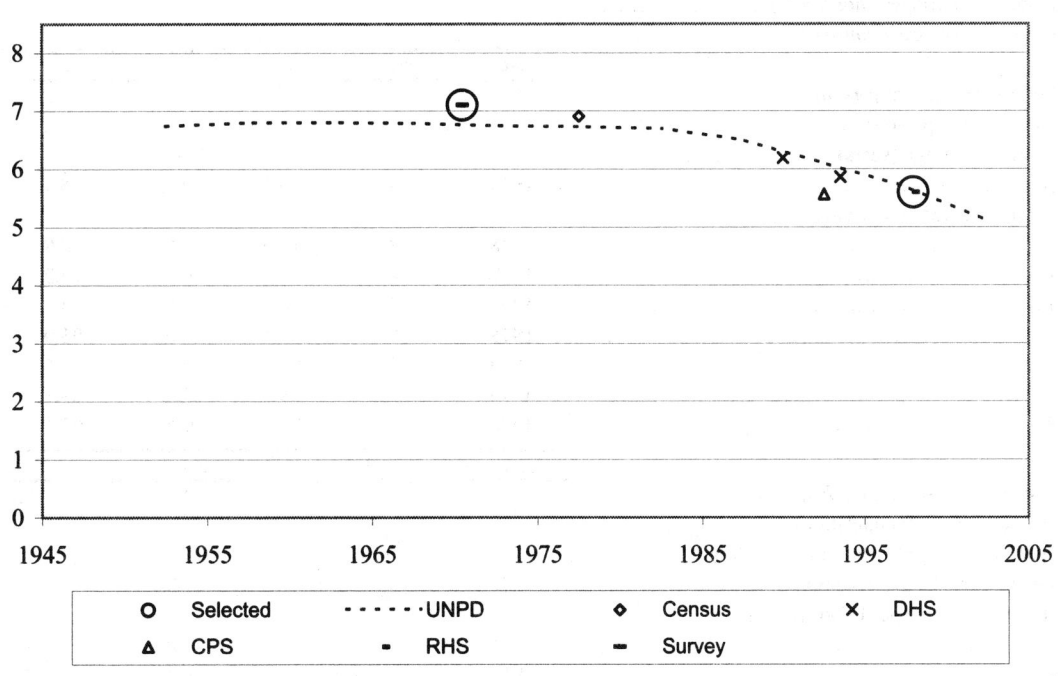

Age-specific fertility rates

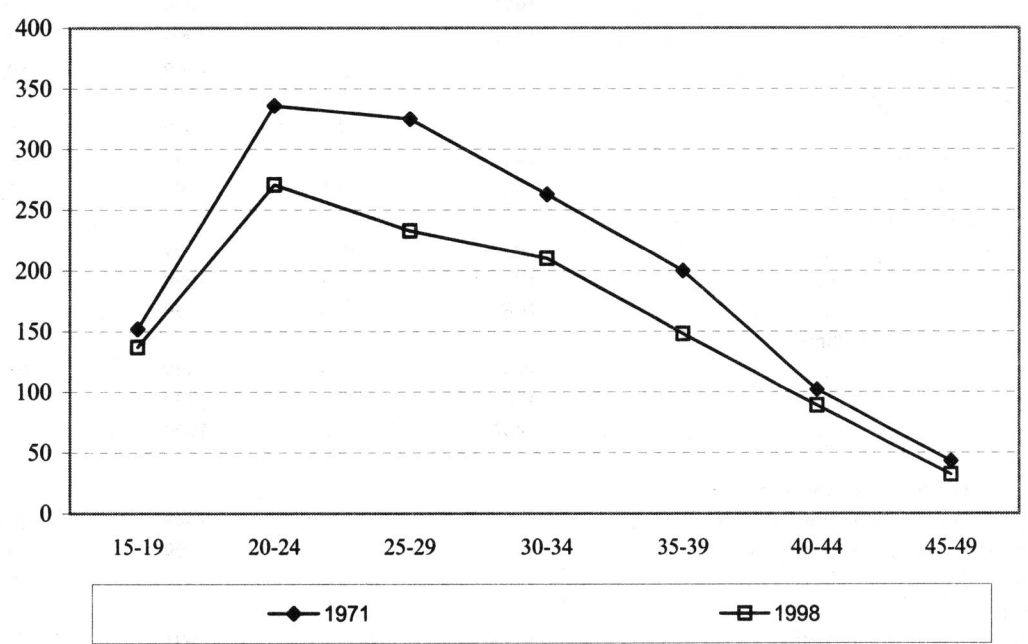

United States of America

Indicator	Period					
	Earlier year			Later year		
	Year	Value		Year	Value	
Nuptiality						
Annual number of marriages (*thousands*)	1970	2 158.8		1998	2 244.0	
Annual number of divorces (*thousands*)	1970	708.0		1998	1 135.0	
	Year	Male	Female	Year	Male	Female
Total first marriage rate (per person)	1975	0.6	0.6	1990	0.6	0.6
Total divorce rate (per person)	1970	0.2	0.2	1990	0.2	0.2
Mean age at first marriage (years)	1975	24.4	22.1	1990	26.5	24.5
SMAM (years)	1970	23.5	21.5	2000	28.6	26.3
Percentage ever married by age group						
15-19	1970	4.1	11.9	2000	1.5	4.1
20-24	1970	44.5	63.7	2000	16.3	27.2
25-29	1970	80.4	87.8	2000	48.3	61.1
30-34	1970	89.3	92.6	2000	69.9	78.1
35-39	1970	91.8	94.1	2000	79.7	85.7
40-44	1970	92.5	94.6	2000	84.3	88.2
45-49	1970	93.4	94.7	2000	88.0	90.0
Fertility	Year	Value		Year	Value	
Annual number of births (*thousands*)	1970	3 731.4		2001	4 025.9	
Crude birth rate (per 1 000 population)	1970	18.2		2001	14.1	
Percentage of extra-marital births among all births	1970	10.7		1999	33.0	
Total fertility rate (births per woman)	1970	2.5		2000	2.1	
Age-specific fertility rate (per 1 000 women)						
15-19	1970	68		2000	49	
20-24	1970	168		2000	112	
25-29	1970	145		2000	121	
30-34	1970	73		2000	94	
35-39	1970	32		2000	40	
40-44	1970	8		2000	8	
45-49	1970	1		2000	0	
Mean age at childbearing (years)	1970	26.1		2000	27.4	
Mean age at first birth (years)	1969	22.5		1998	25.0	
Children ever born per woman						
35-39	1980	2.4		2000	1.8	
40-44	1980	2.9		2000	1.9	
45-49	1980	3.1		2000	..	
Percentage of childless women						
35-39	1980	13.3		2000	20.1	
40-44	1980	10.8		2000	19.0	
45-49	1980	10.9		2000	..	
Percentage of women with parity three or higher						
35-39	1980	43.2		2000	27.8	
40-44	1980	55.4		2000	29.6	
45-49	1980	58.0		2000	..	
Family Planning						
Contraceptive prevalence among women in union						
Percentage using any contraceptive method	1973	69.6		1995	76.4	
Percentage using a modern contraceptive method	1973	63.5		1995	70.5	
Percentage using condoms	1973	9.4		1995	13.3	
Population policies						
Government's view on the level of fertility	1976	Satisfactory		2001	Satisfactory	
Government's policy regarding level of fertility	1976	No intervention		2001	No intervention	
Government's support for contraceptive methods	1976	Direct support		2001	Direct support	

Total fertility rates

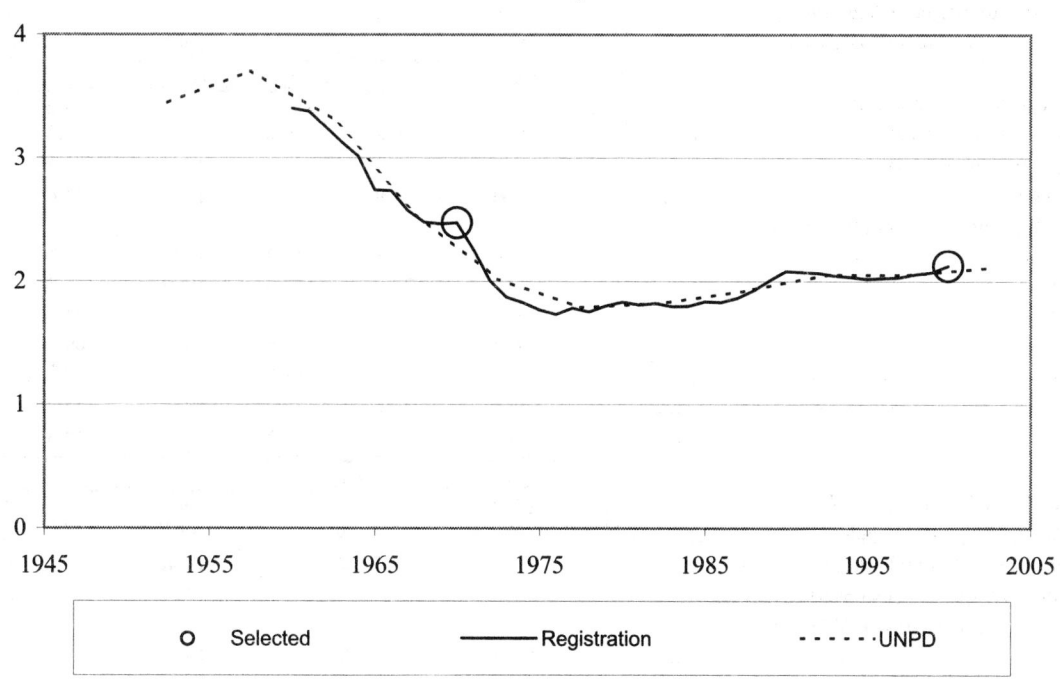

O Selected	—— Registration	- - - - UNPD	

Age-specific fertility rates

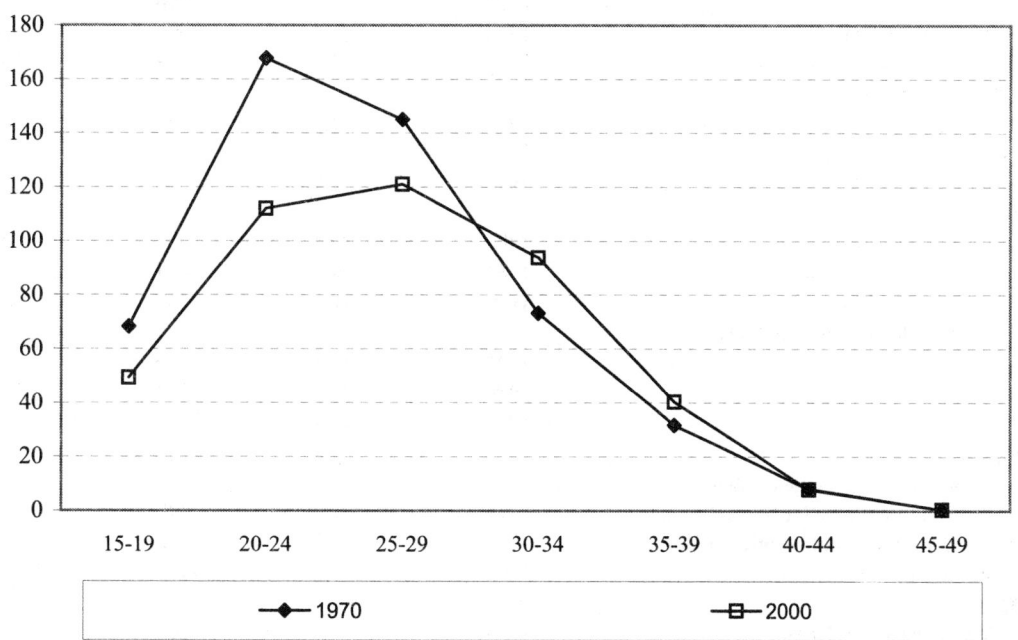

◆ 1970	—□— 2000

Indicator	Period					
	Earlier year			Later year		
	Year	Value		Year	Value	
Nuptiality						
Annual number of marriages (*thousands*)	1970	1.2		1993	3.6	
Annual number of divorces (*thousands*)	1970	0.3		1993	0.5	
	Year	Male	Female	Year	Male	Female
Total first marriage rate (per person)	..	..	..	..	..	..
Total divorce rate (per person)	1972	0.4	0.4	1993	0.6	0.5
Mean age at first marriage (years)	..	..	..	1993	32.2	30.3
SMAM (years)	1960	24.9	20.8	1995	31.6	29.9
Percentage ever married by age group						
15-19	1960	2.8	16.3	1995	4.0	3.2
20-24	1960	33.5	57.9	1995	5.5	15.5
25-29	1960	58.5	75.3	1995	31.5	41.4
30-34	1960	75.8	78.5	1995	49.5	58.0
35-39	1960	82.5	82.2	1995	67.0	73.7
40-44	1960	83.8	85.0	1995	78.7	77.3
45-49	1960	84.0	82.6	1995	85.4	88.5
Fertility	Year	Value		Year	Value	
Annual number of births (*thousands*)	1970	2.9		1993	2.5	
Crude birth rate (per 1 000 population)	1970	38.9		1993	24.4	
Percentage of extra-marital births among all births	1970	44.8		1990	63.4	
Total fertility rate (births per woman)	1970	5.3		1990	3.0	
Age-specific fertility rate (per 1 000 women)						
15-19	1970	230		1990	78	
20-24	1970	288		1990	183	
25-29	1970	250		1990	177	
30-34	1970	161		1990	115	
35-39	1970	96		1990	44	
40-44	1970	31		1990	11	
45-49	1970	4		1990	1	
Mean age at childbearing (years)	1970	26.2		1990	26.7	
Mean age at first birth (years)	..	..		..	..	
Children ever born per woman						
35-39	1970	3.0		..	..	
40-44	1970	2.9		..	..	
45-49	1970	2.7		..	..	
Percentage of childless women						
35-39	1970	6.9		..	..	
40-44	1970	8.2		..	..	
45-49	1970	10.1		..	..	
Percentage of women with parity three or higher						
35-39	1970	56.4		..	..	
40-44	1970	53.0		..	..	
45-49	1970	46.8		..	..	
Family Planning						
Contraceptive prevalence among women in union						
Percentage using any contraceptive method	..	..		..	..	
Percentage using a modern contraceptive method	..	..		..	..	
Percentage using condoms	..	..		..	..	
Population policies						
Government's view on the level of fertility	..	--		2001	..	
Government's policy regarding level of fertility	..	--		2001	..	
Government's support for contraceptive methods	..	--		2001	..	

Total fertility rates

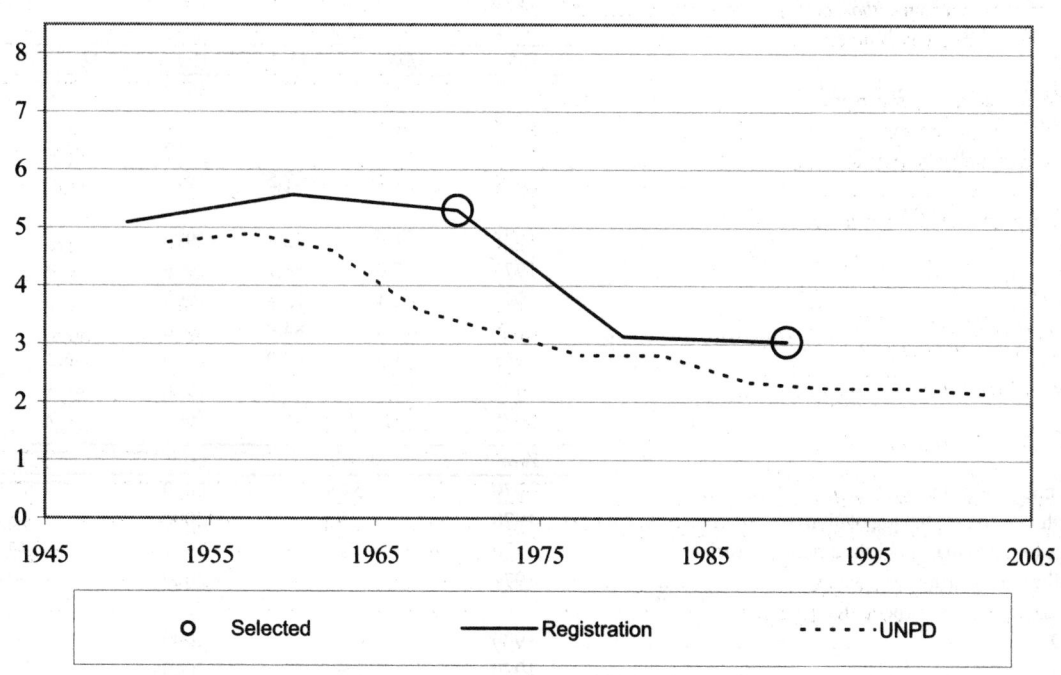

Age-specific fertility rates

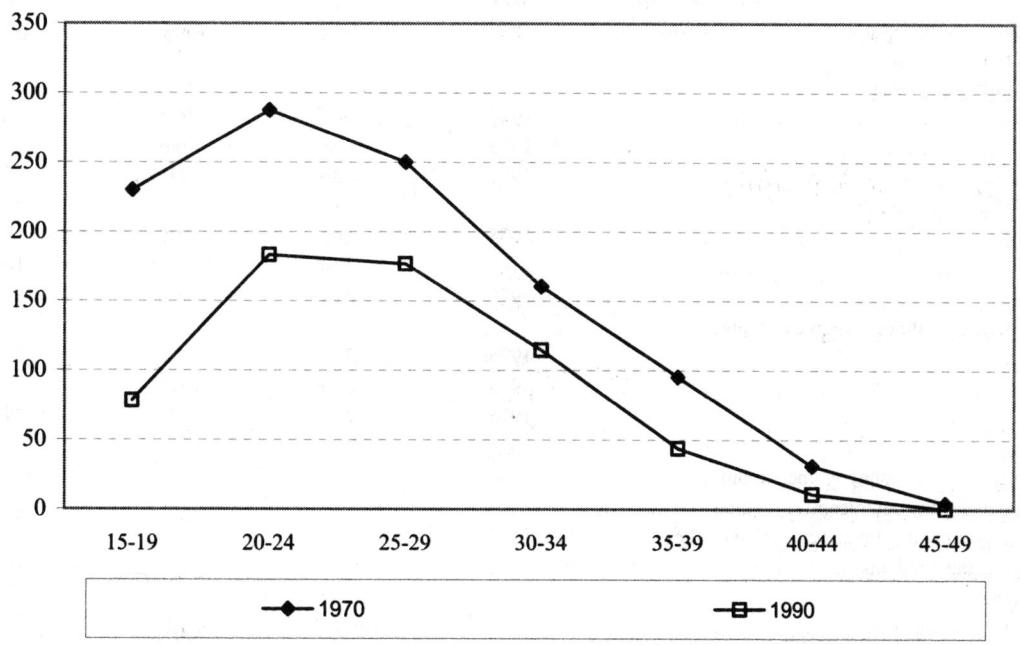

Indicator	Period					
	Earlier year			**Later year**		
	Year	Value		Year	Value	
Nuptiality						
Annual number of marriages (*thousands*) ....….........	1970	23.7		2000	13.9	
Annual number of divorces (*thousands*)	1970	2.9		2000	6.8	
	Year	Male	Female	Year	Male	Female
Total first marriage rate (per person)	..	..	..	1997	0.6	0.6
Total divorce rate (per person)	..	..	..	..	..	..
Mean age at first marriage (years) ....…...	..	..	..	1997	28.5	26.2
SMAM (years)	1975	25.4	22.5	1996	25.6	23.3
Percentage ever married by age group						
15-19	1975	1.9	12.4	1996	3.5	12.8
20-24	1975	27.0	51.1	1996	26.9	44.8
25-29	1975	62.1	75.8	1996	59.7	73.0
30-34	1975	77.4	84.9	1996	79.1	85.6
35-39	1975	81.3	88.0	1996	86.2	89.4
40-44	1975	83.7	89.2	1996	88.3	90.8
45-49	1975	85.1	89.3	1996	88.7	91.4
Fertility	Year	Value		Year	Value	
Annual number of births (*thousands*).............................	1970	54.9		2000	52.8	
Crude birth rate (per 1 000 population)	1970	19.5		2000	15.8	
Percentage of extra-marital births among all births	1970	21.1		1997	47.4	
Total fertility rate (births per woman)	1970	2.7		2000	2.2	
Age-specific fertility rate (per 1 000 women)						
15-19	1970	63		2000	65	
20-24	1970	148		2000	106	
25-29	1970	142		2000	107	
30-34	1970	105		2000	100	
35-39	1970	57		2000	48	
40-44	1970	24		2000	13	
45-49	1970	3		2000	1	
Mean age at childbearing (years)	1970	27.8		2000	27.5	
Mean age at first birth (years)	..	..		1996	23.8	
Children ever born per woman						
35-39	1975	2.5		1996	2.4	
40-44	1975	2.6		1996	2.6	
45-49	1975	2.6		1996	2.7	
Percentage of childless women						
35-39	1975	16.5		1996	11.8	
40-44	1975	15.8		1996	10.6	
45-49	1975	17.6		1996	11.1	
Percentage of women with parity three or higher						
35-39	1975	39.1		1996	38.4	
40-44	1975	39.6		1996	43.4	
45-49	1975	37.5		1996	44.7	
Family Planning						
Contraceptive prevalence among women in union						
Percentage using any contraceptive method	..	..		..	..	
Percentage using a modern contraceptive method	..	..		..	..	
Percentage using condoms ....…...	..	..		..	..	
Population policies						
Government's view on the level of fertility	1976	Too low		2001	Too low	
Government's policy regarding level of fertility	1976	Raise		2001	Raise	
Government's support for contraceptive methods	1976	No support		2001	Direct support	

Total fertility rates

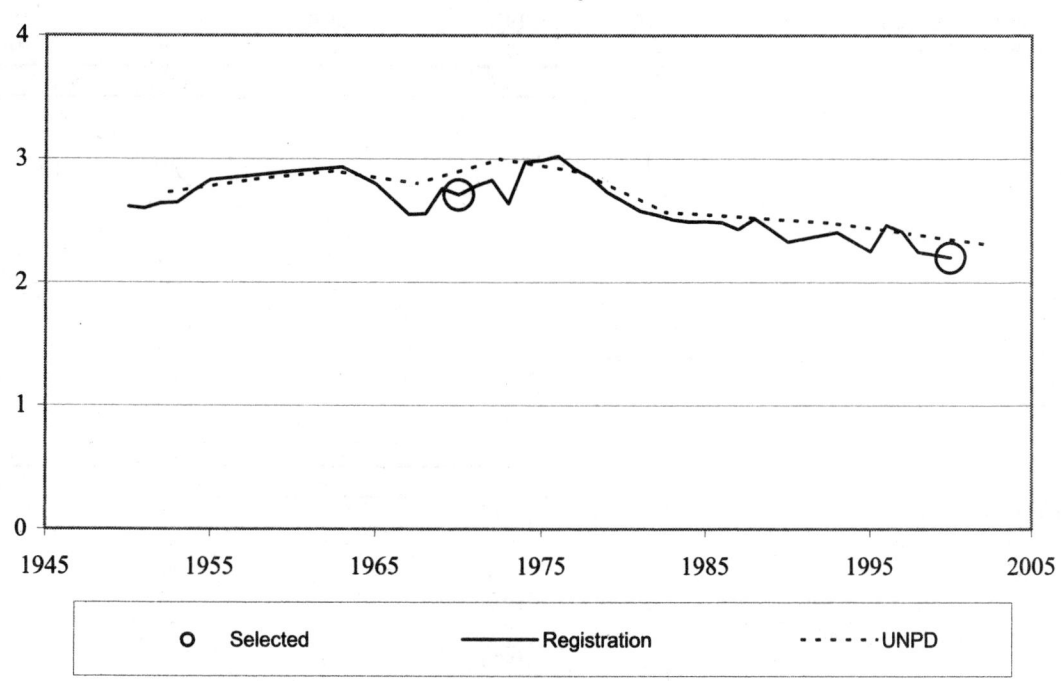

Age-specific fertility rates

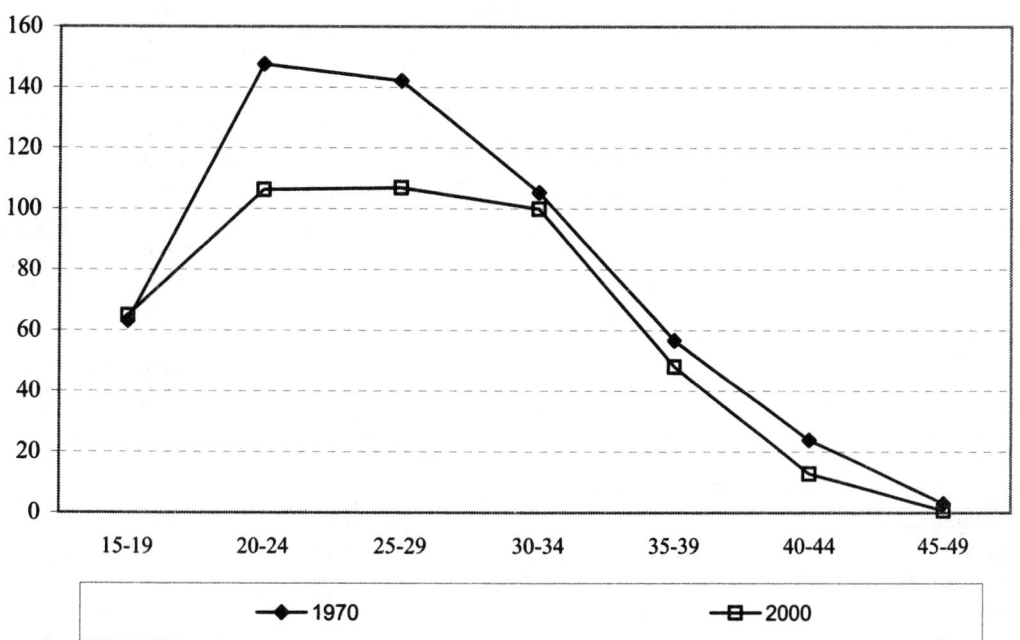

Uzbekistan

Indicator	Period					
	Earlier year			Later year		
	Year	Value		Year	Value	
Nuptiality						
Annual number of marriages (*thousands*)	1970	109.0		1997	181.1	
Annual number of divorces (*thousands*)	1970	13.0		2000	19.9	
	Year	Male	Female	Year	Male	Female
Total first marriage rate (per person)	..	..	..	1999	0.8	0.7
Total divorce rate (per person)	..	..	..	..	..	..
Mean age at first marriage (years)	..	..	..	1999	24.1	21.3
SMAM (years)	..	..	..	1996	..	20.6
Percentage ever married by age group						
15-19	..	..	..	1996	..	13.0
20-24	..	..	..	1996	..	77.2
25-29	..	..	..	1996	..	94.8
30-34	..	..	..	1996	..	98.1
35-39	..	..	..	1996	..	98.8
40-44	..	..	..	1996	..	99.6
45-49	..	..	..	1996	..	98.6
Fertility	Year	Value		Year	Value	
Annual number of births (*thousands*)	1970	401.6		2000	527.6	
Crude birth rate (per 1 000 population)	1970	33.6		2000	21.4	
Percentage of extra-marital births among all births	1980	4.0		1999	8.4	
Total fertility rate (births per woman)	1970	5.6		2000	2.6	
Age-specific fertility rate (per 1 000 women)						
15-19	1970	42		2000	21	
20-24	1970	261		2000	205	
25-29	1970	265		2000	161	
30-34	1970	246		2000	90	
35-39	1970	195		2000	31	
40-44	1970	92		2000	7	
45-49	1970	27		2000	1	
Mean age at childbearing (years)	1970	30.5		2000	26.8	
Mean age at first birth (years)	..	..		1999	23.4	
Children ever born per woman						
35-39	..	..		1996	4.1	
40-44	..	..		1996	4.5	
45-49	..	..		1996	4.7	
Percentage of childless women						
35-39	..	..		1996	2.3	
40-44	..	..		1996	1.9	
45-49	..	..		1996	2.8	
Percentage of women with parity three or higher						
35-39	..	..		1996	81.8	
40-44	..	..		1996	81.9	
45-49	..	..		1996	78.2	
Family Planning						
Contraceptive prevalence among women in union						
Percentage using any contraceptive method	..	..		2000	67.2	
Percentage using a modern contraceptive method	..	..		2000	62.5	
Percentage using condoms	..	..		2000	0.8	
Population policies						
Government's view on the level of fertility	..	--		2001	Satisfactory	
Government's policy regarding level of fertility	..	--		2001	Maintain	
Government's support for contraceptive methods	..	--		2001	Direct support	

Total fertility rates

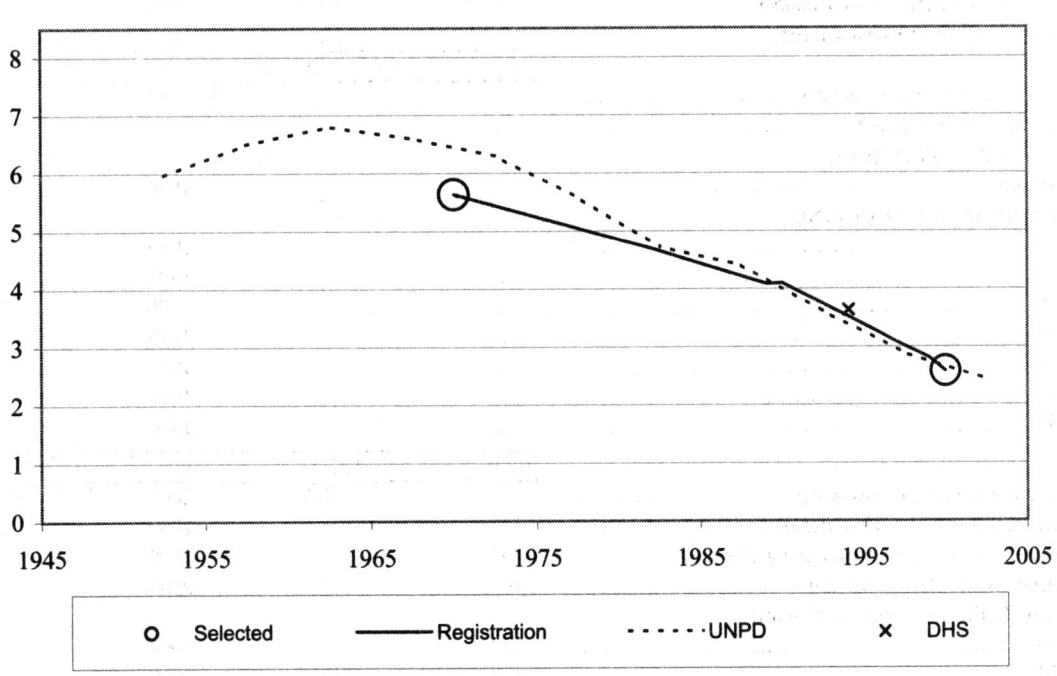

Age-specific fertility rates

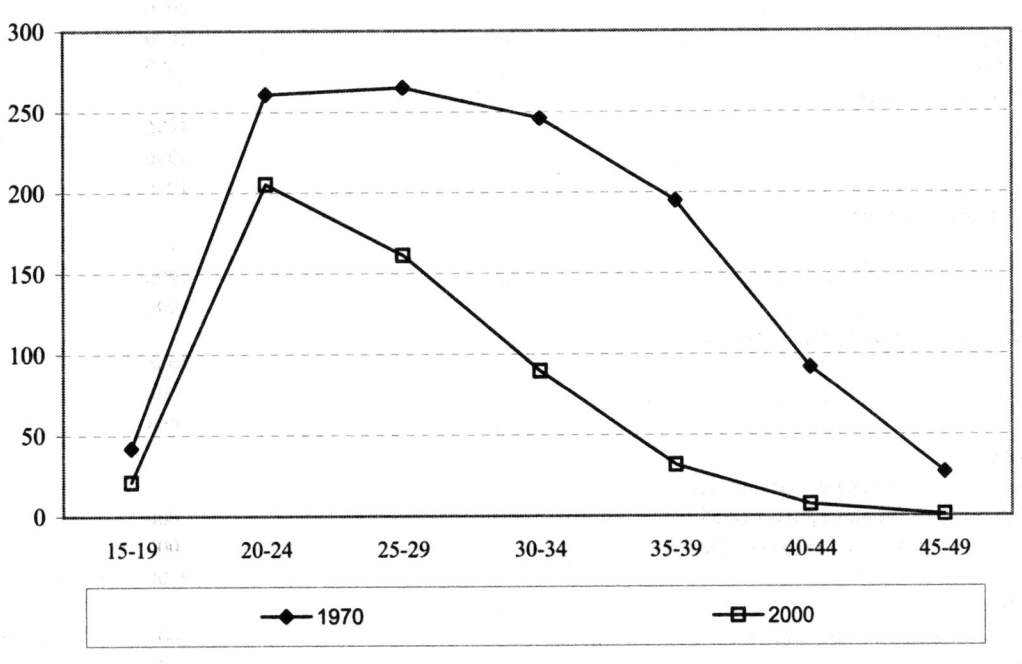

Indicator	Period					
	Earlier year			Later year		
	Year	Value		Year	Value	

Nuptiality

Indicator	Year	Value		Year	Value	
Annual number of marriages (*thousands*)	..	..		..	..	
Annual number of divorces (*thousands*)	..	..		..	..	

Indicator	Year	Male	Female	Year	Male	Female
Total first marriage rate (per person)	..	..	..	..	..	..
Total divorce rate (per person)	..	..	..	..	..	..
Mean age at first marriage (years)	..	..	..	..	..	..
SMAM (years)	1979	25.8	22.0	1989	25.3	22.6
Percentage ever married by age group						
15-19	1979	2.6	14.0	1989	2.4	11.9
20-24	1979	28.9	59.0	1989	29.1	56.9
25-29	1979	62.5	84.2	1989	69.2	82.6
30-34	1979	81.9	91.5	1989	87.0	92.8
35-39	1979	86.8	93.4	1989	92.8	95.0
40-44	1979	90.6	94.6	1989	93.6	96.3
45-49	1979	90.8	95.1	1989	94.4	97.0

Fertility

Indicator	Year	Value	Year	Value
Annual number of births (*thousands*)	..	..	..	..
Crude birth rate (per 1 000 population)	..	..	..	..
Percentage of extra-marital births among all births	..	..	..	..
Total fertility rate (births per woman)	1977	6.6	1989	4.9
Age-specific fertility rate (per 1 000 women)				
15-19	1976	91	1989	78
20-24	1976	294	1989	234
25-29	1976	327	1989	248
30-34	1976	265	1989	195
35-39	1976	179	1989	138
40-44	1976	110	1989	61
45-49	1976	45	1989	22
Mean age at childbearing (years)	1976	30.0	1989	29.3
Mean age at first birth (years)	..	..	..	..
Children ever born per woman				
35-39	1967	5.7	1989	4.5
40-44	1967	5.7	1989	5.2
45-49	1967	5.9	1989	..
Percentage of childless women				
35-39	1967	7.1	..	..
40-44	1967	8.9	..	..
45-49	1967	10.0	..	..
Percentage of women with parity three or higher				
35-39	1967	83.4	..	..
40-44	1967	79.8	..	..
45-49	1967	79.8	..	..

Family Planning

Indicator	Year	Value	Year	Value
Contraceptive prevalence among women in union				
Percentage using any contraceptive method	..	..	..	..
Percentage using a modern contraceptive method	..	..	..	..
Percentage using condoms	..	..	..	..

Population policies

Indicator	Year	Value	Year	Value
Government's view on the level of fertility	1976	..	2001	Satisfactory
Government's policy regarding level of fertility	1976	..	2001	No intervention
Government's support for contraceptive methods	1976	..	2001	Direct support

Total fertility rates

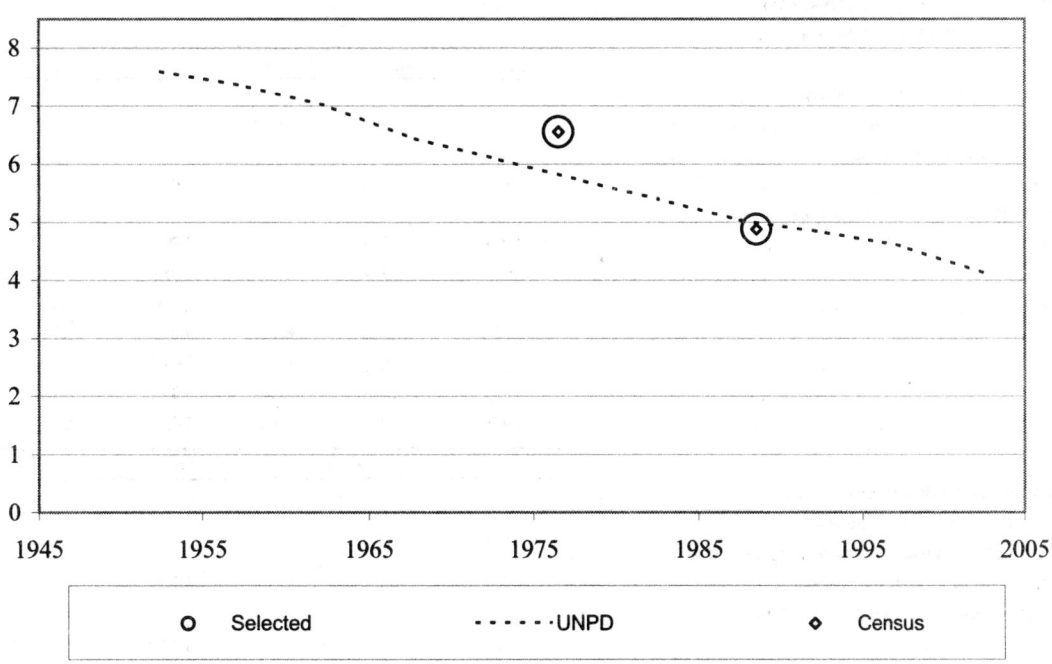

Age-specific fertility rates

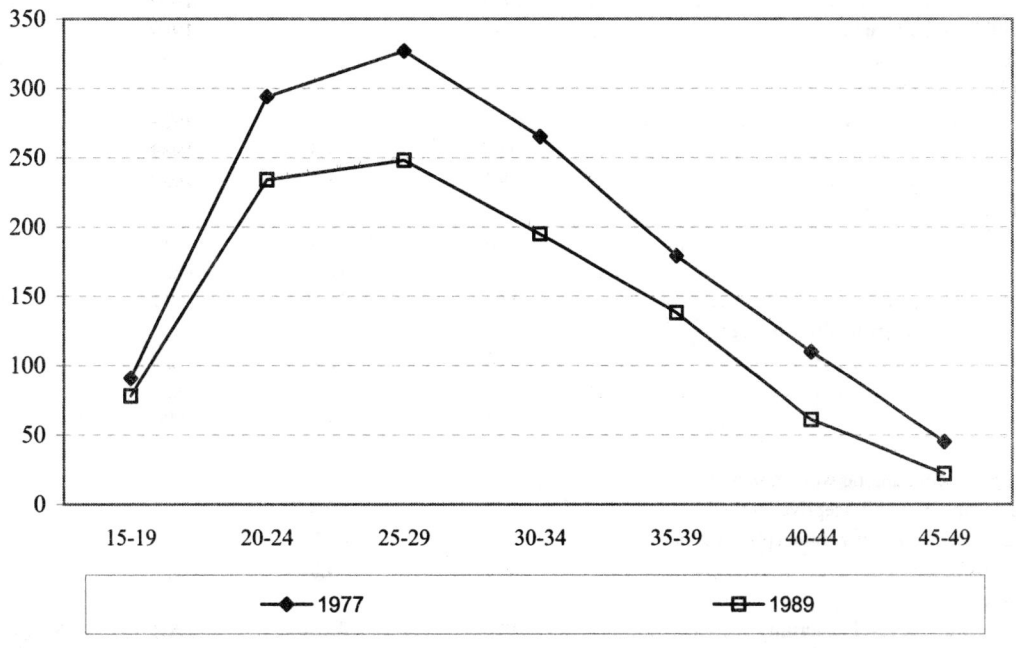

Venezuela

Indicator	Period					
	Earlier year			Later year		
	Year	Value		Year	Value	

Nuptiality

Indicator	Year	Value		Year	Value	
Annual number of marriages (*thousands*)	1970	60.1		2000	91.1	
Annual number of divorces (*thousands*)	1970	2.5		1989	21.9	

Indicator	Year	Male	Female	Year	Male	Female
Total first marriage rate (per person)	..	..	..	1990	0.6	0.6
Total divorce rate (per person)	1972	0.0	0.0	..	..	..
Mean age at first marriage (years)	..	..	..	1990	28.4	25.7
SMAM (years)	1971	25.6	20.1	1990	25.4	22.1
Percentage ever married by age group						
15-19	1971	2.6	16.1	1990	5.5	17.7
20-24	1971	25.0	49.3	1990	31.3	50.6
25-29	1971	58.3	71.9	1990	59.1	71.2
30-34	1971	75.2	80.3	1990	75.6	81.9
35-39	1971	81.1	82.2	1990	83.8	85.8
40-44	1971	83.7	80.9	1990	86.7	86.7
45-49	1971	84.7	79.0	1990	87.2	86.6

Fertility

Indicator	Year	Value	Year	Value
Annual number of births (*thousands*)	1970	392.6	2000	544.4
Crude birth rate (per 1 000 population)	1970	36.6	2000	22.5
Percentage of extra-marital births among all births	1970	38.8	..	..
Total fertility rate (births per woman)	1970	5.7	2000	2.7
Age-specific fertility rate (per 1 000 women)				
15-19	1970	114	2000	97
20-24	1970	281	2000	148
25-29	1970	288	2000	131
30-34	1970	210	2000	91
35-39	1970	167	2000	50
40-44	1970	61	2000	17
45-49	1970	14	2000	3
Mean age at childbearing (years)	1970	28.7	2000	26.7
Mean age at first birth (years)	1971	23.2	1998	23.6
Children ever born per woman				
35-39	1961	4.9	1990	3.4
40-44	1961	4.9	1990	4.0
45-49	1961	4.8	1990	4.6
Percentage of childless women				
35-39	1961	14.9	1990	7.7
40-44	1961	16.3	1990	6.7
45-49	1961	17.4	1990	6.4
Percentage of women with parity three or higher				
35-39	1961	68.3	1990	59.8
40-44	1961	66.3	1990	66.3
45-49	1961	64.4	1990	71.0

Family Planning

Indicator	Year	Value	Year	Value
Contraceptive prevalence among women in union				
Percentage using any contraceptive method	1977	49.3	..	..
Percentage using a modern contraceptive method	1977	37.7	..	..
Percentage using condoms	1977	4.8	..	..

Population policies

Indicator	Year	Value	Year	Value
Government's view on the level of fertility	1976	Satisfactory	2001	Satisfactory
Government's policy regarding level of fertility	1976	No intervention	2001	Lower
Government's support for contraceptive methods	1976	Direct support	2001	Direct support

Total fertility rates

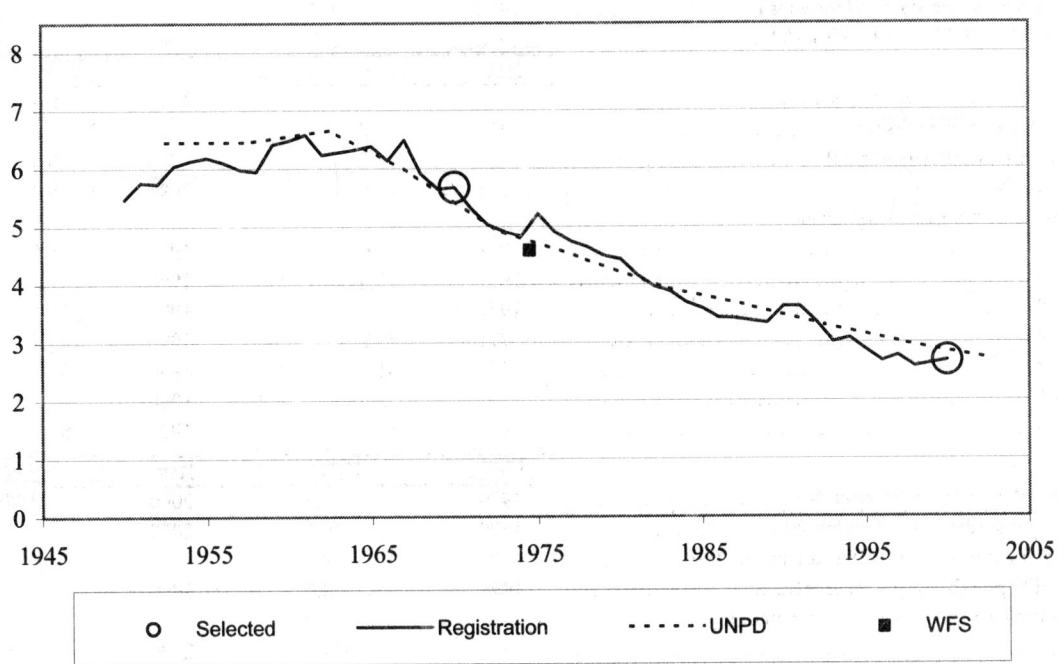

Age-specific fertility rates

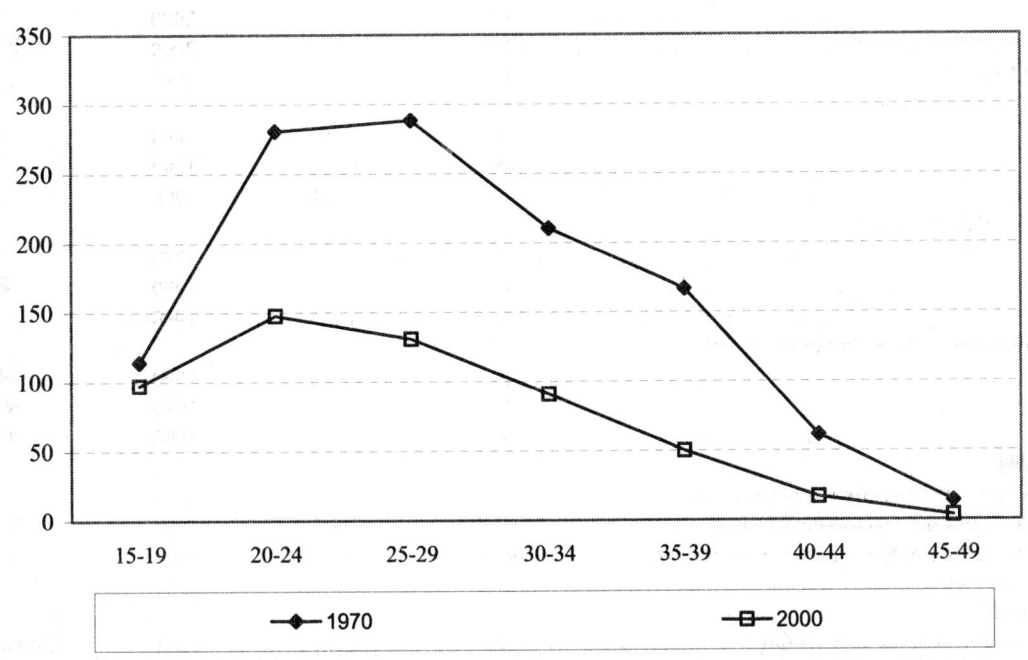

Indicator	Period					
	Earlier year			Later year		
	Year	Value		Year	Value	

Nuptiality

Indicator	Year	Value		Year	Value	
Annual number of marriages (*thousands*)	..	..		..	..	
Annual number of divorces (*thousands*)	..	..		..	..	

	Year	Male	Female	Year	Male	Female
Total first marriage rate (per person)	..	..	..	..	..	..
Total divorce rate (per person)	..	..	..	..	..	..
Mean age at first marriage (years)	..	..	..	..	..	..
SMAM (years)	..	..	..	1997	..	22.1
Percentage ever married by age group						
15-19	..	..	..	1997	..	7.7
20-24	..	..	..	1997	..	53.1
25-29	..	..	..	1997	..	78.9
30-34	..	..	..	1997	..	89.1
35-39	..	..	..	1997	..	91.3
40-44	..	..	..	1997	..	91.7
45-49	..	..	..	1997	..	90.1

Fertility

Indicator	Year	Value	Year	Value
Annual number of births (*thousands*)	..	..	1990	1 980.4
Crude birth rate (per 1 000 population)	..	..	1990	29.9
Percentage of extra-marital births among all births	..	..	..	..
Total fertility rate (births per woman)	1977	4.8	1994	2.7
Age-specific fertility rate (per 1 000 women)				
15-19	..	..	1994	39
20-24	..	..	1994	178
25-29	..	..	1994	148
30-34	..	..	1994	95
35-39	..	..	1994	52
40-44	..	..	1994	20
45-49	..	..	1994	4
Mean age at childbearing (years)	1977	27.7	1994	27.7
Mean age at first birth (years)	..	..	..	..
Children ever born per woman				
35-39	..	..	1999	2.8
40-44	..	..	1999	3.4
45-49	..	..	1999	..
Percentage of childless women				
35-39	..	..	1999	8.2
40-44	..	..	1999	7.5
45-49	..	..	1999	..
Percentage of women with parity three or higher				
35-39	..	..	1999	54.5
40-44	..	..	1999	66.9
45-49	..	..	1999	..

Family Planning

Indicator	Year	Value	Year	Value
Contraceptive prevalence among women in union				
Percentage using any contraceptive method	..	..	2000	74.2
Percentage using a modern contraceptive method	..	..	2000	55.7
Percentage using condoms	..	..	2000	6.1

Population policies

Indicator	Year	Value	Year	Value
Government's view on the level of fertility	1976	Too high	2001	Too high
Government's policy regarding level of fertility	1976	Lower	2001	Lower
Government's support for contraceptive methods	1976	Direct support	2001	Direct support

Total fertility rates

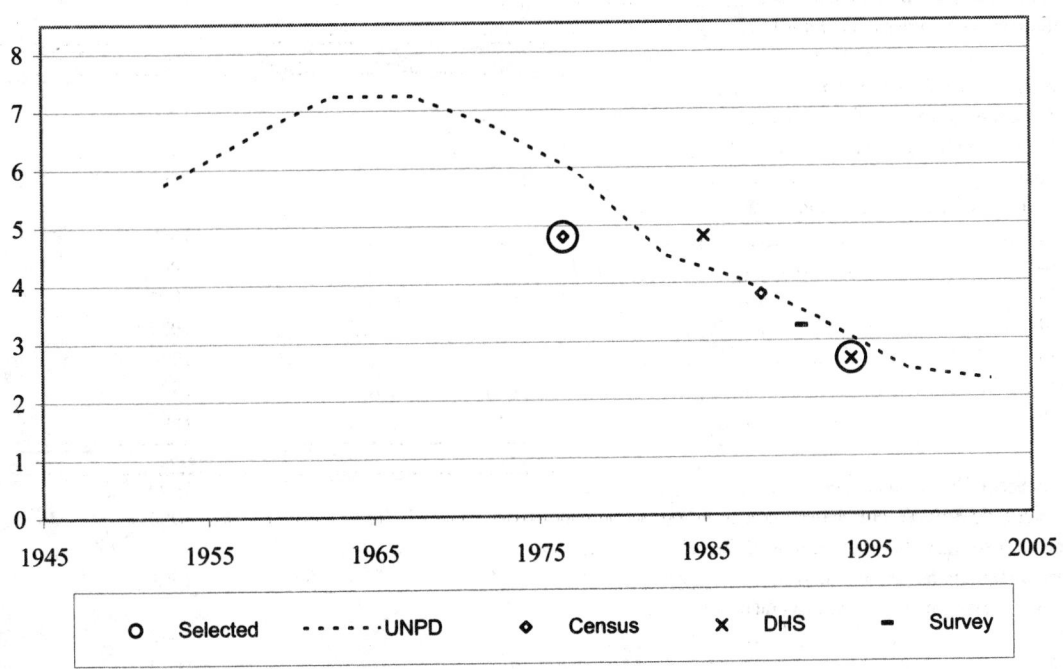

Age-specific fertility rates

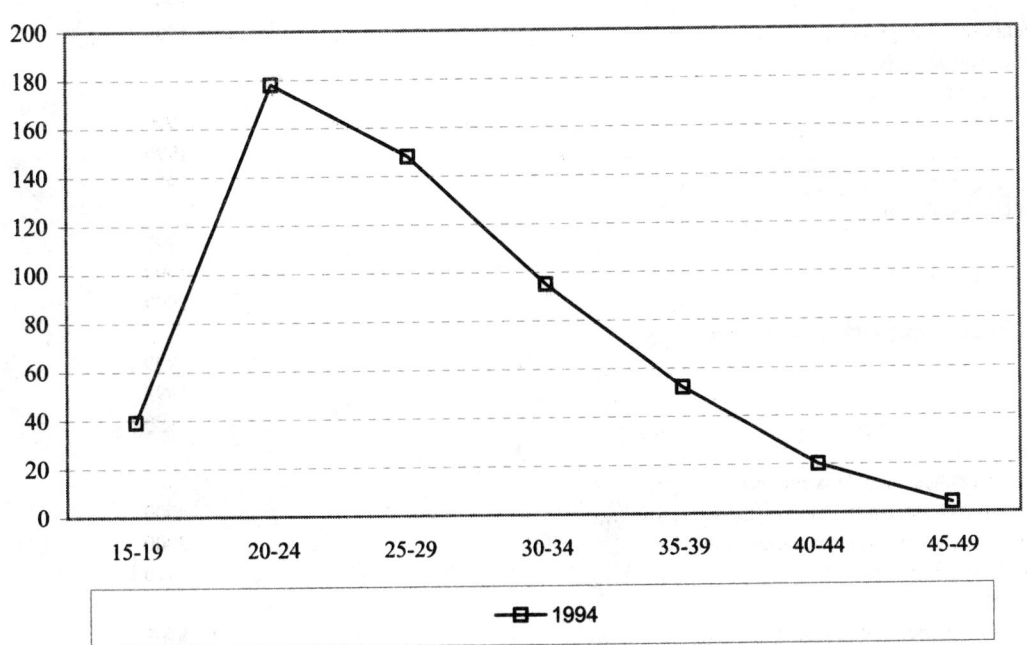

Indicator	Period					
	Earlier year			Later year		
	Year	Value		Year	Value	

Nuptiality

Indicator	Year	Value		Year	Value	
Annual number of marriages (*thousands*)	1970	0.5		..		..
Annual number of divorces (*thousands*)	1970	0.2		..		..

Indicator	Year	Male	Female	Year	Male	Female
Total first marriage rate (per person)	..	..	..	..	..	..
Total divorce rate (per person)	..	..	..	..	..	..
Mean age at first marriage (years)	..	..	..	..	..	..
SMAM (years)	1970	25.3	18.0	..	..	..
Percentage ever married by age group						
15-19	1970	1.3	60.6	..	..	..
20-24	1970	24.0	81.0	..	..	..
25-29	1970	72.4	87.1	..	..	..
30-34	1970	83.1	89.1	..	..	..
35-39	1970	87.4	93.7	..	..	..
40-44	1970	90.6	93.4	..	..	..
45-49	1970	90.6	93.1	..	..	..

Fertility

Indicator	Year	Value		Year	Value	
Annual number of births (*thousands*)	..	..		..	..	
Crude birth rate (per 1 000 population)	..	..		..	..	
Percentage of extra-marital births among all births	..	..		..	..	
Total fertility rate (births per woman)	..	..		..	..	
Age-specific fertility rate (per 1 000 women)						
15-19	..	..		..	..	
20-24	..	..		..	..	
25-29	..	..		..	..	
30-34	..	..		..	..	
35-39	..	..		..	..	
40-44	..	..		..	..	
45-49	..	..		..	..	
Mean age at childbearing (years)	..	..		..	..	
Mean age at first birth (years)	..	..		..	..	
Children ever born per woman						
35-39	..	..		..	..	
40-44	..	..		..	..	
45-49	..	..		..	..	
Percentage of childless women						
35-39	..	..		..	..	
40-44	..	..		..	..	
45-49	..	..		..	..	
Percentage of women with parity three or higher						
35-39	..	..		..	..	
40-44	..	..		..	..	
45-49	..	..		..	..	

Family Planning

Indicator	Year	Value		Year	Value	
Contraceptive prevalence among women in union						
Percentage using any contraceptive method	..	..		..	..	
Percentage using a modern contraceptive method	..	..		..	..	
Percentage using condoms	..	..		..	..	

Population policies

Indicator	Year	Value		Year	Value	
Government's view on the level of fertility	..	--		2001	--	
Government's policy regarding level of fertility	..	--		2001	--	
Government's support for contraceptive methods	..	--		2001	--	

Total fertility rates

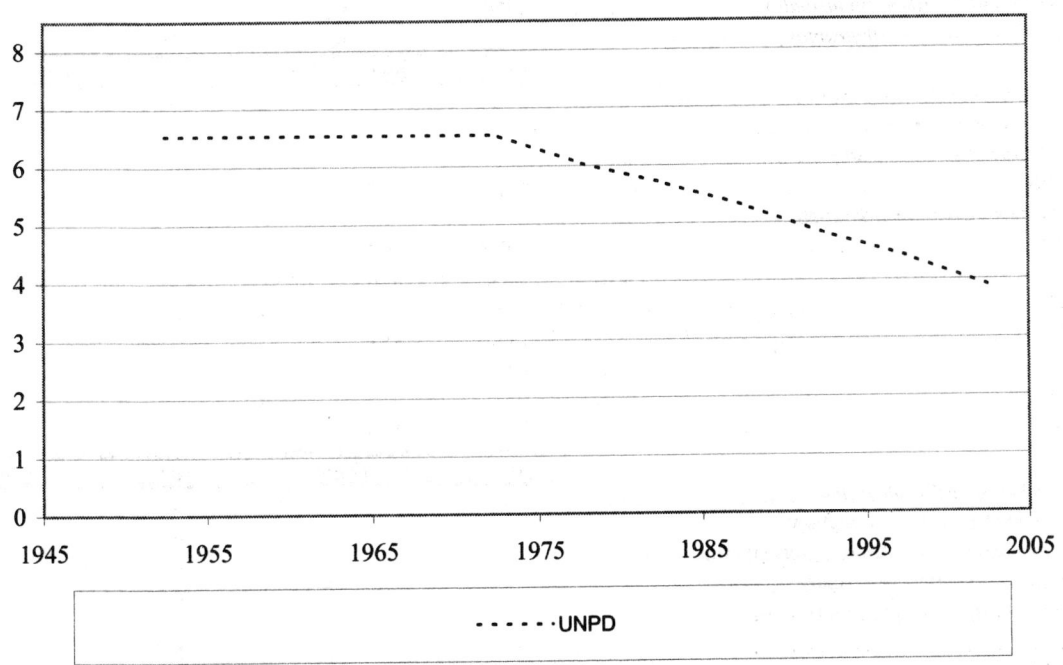

Indicator	Period			
	Earlier year		Later year	
	Year	Value	Year	Value
Nuptiality				
Annual number of marriages (*thousands*)	..	..	..	..
Annual number of divorces (*thousands*)	..	..	..	..

	Year	Male	Female	Year	Male	Female
Total first marriage rate (per person)	..	..	..	..	..	..
Total divorce rate (per person)	..	..	..	..	..	..
Mean age at first marriage (years)	..	..	..	..	..	..
SMAM (years)	..	..	..	1997	..	20.7
Percentage ever married by age group						
15-19	..	..	..	1997	..	26.9
20-24	..	..	..	1997	..	72.8
25-29	..	..	..	1997	..	90.5
30-34	..	..	..	1997	..	96.1
35-39	..	..	..	1997	..	97.9
40-44	..	..	..	1997	..	98.5
45-49	..	..	..	1997	..	99.2

	Year	Value	Year	Value
Fertility				
Annual number of births (*thousands*)............................	..	..	..	..
Crude birth rate (per 1 000 population)	..	..	..	..
Percentage of extra-marital births among all births	..	..	..	..
Total fertility rate (births per woman)	1977	8.5	1996	6.7
Age-specific fertility rate (per 1 000 women)				
15-19	1977	175	1996	110
20-24	1977	346	1996	286
25-29	1977	346	1996	304
30-34	1977	334	1996	267
35-39	1977	229	1996	200
40-44	1977	197	1996	115
45-49	1977	75	1996	62
Mean age at childbearing (years)	1977	30.4	1996	30.3
Mean age at first birth (years)[a]	..	..	1997	19.2
Children ever born per woman				
35-39	1979	6.0	1997	7.1
40-44	1979	6.4	1997	8.0
45-49	1979	7.2	1997	8.8
Percentage of childless women				
35-39	..	..	1997	4.3
40-44	..	..	1997	4.2
45-49	..	..	1997	2.3
Percentage of women with parity three or higher				
35-39	..	..	1997	91.1
40-44	..	..	1997	92.2
45-49	..	..	1997	95.9
Family Planning				
Contraceptive prevalence among women in union				
Percentage using any contraceptive method	1979	1.1	1997	20.8
Percentage using a modern contraceptive method	1979	1.1	1997	9.8
Percentage using condoms	1979	0.1	1997	0.3
Population policies				
Government's view on the level of fertility	1976	Satisfactory	2001	Too high
Government's policy regarding level of fertility	1976	No intervention	2001	Lower
Government's support for contraceptive methods	1976	Direct support	2001	Indirect support

[a]Median age at first birth among women aged 25-29 at the date of the survey

Total fertility rates

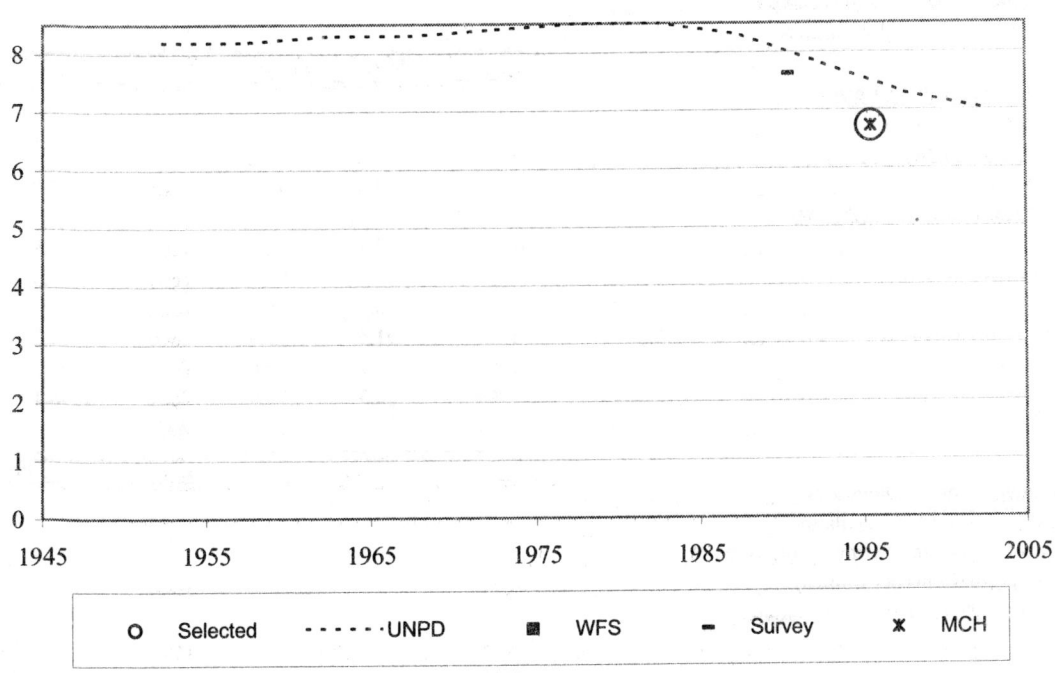

Age-specific fertility rates

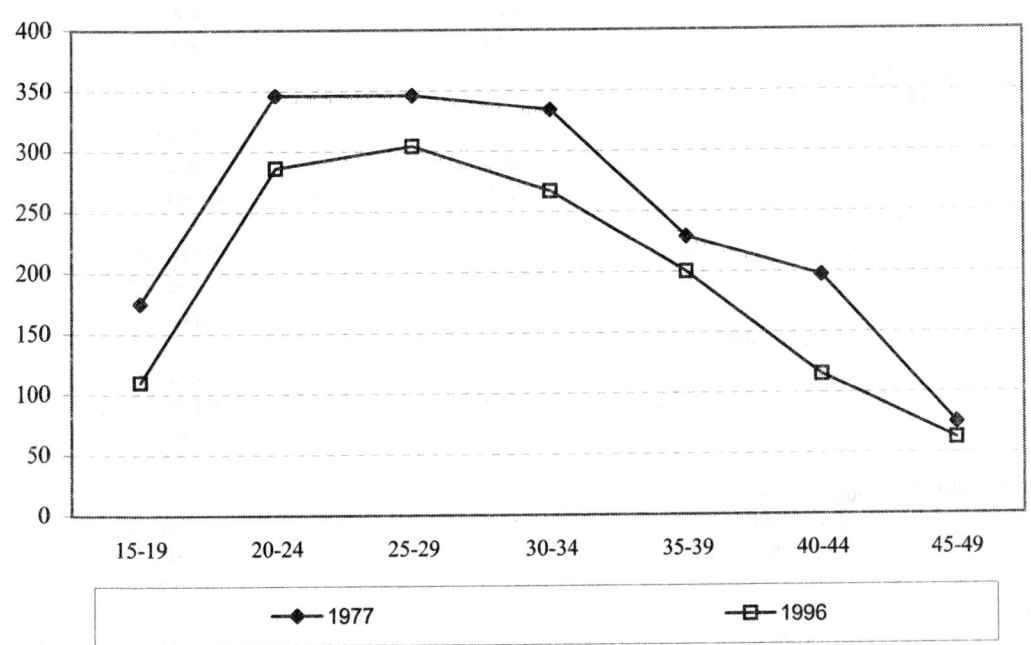

Indicator	Period					
	Earlier year			Later year		
	Year	Value		Year	Value	
Nuptiality						
Annual number of marriages (*thousands*)	..	..		..	..	
Annual number of divorces (*thousands*)	..	..		..	..	
	Year	Male	Female	Year	Male	Female
Total first marriage rate (per person)	..	..	..	..	..	..
Total divorce rate (per person)	..	..	..	..	..	..
Mean age at first marriage (years)	..	..	..	..	..	..
SMAM (years)	1969	24.5	18.2	2002	24.8	20.6
Percentage ever married by age group						
15-19	1969	2.7	41.3	2002	1.8	27.0
20-24	1969	36.2	90.4	2002	31.3	75.4
25-29	1969	78.2	96.2	2002	82.1	92.0
30-34	1969	91.4	97.8	2002	94.2	95.6
35-39	1969	94.7	98.0	2002	96.3	99.2
40-44	1969	96.3	98.0	2002	98.1	99.2
45-49	1969	97.0	97.8	2002	99.5	99.8
Fertility	Year	Value		Year	Value	
Annual number of births (*thousands*)	..	..		..	..	
Crude birth rate (per 1 000 population)	..	..		..	..	
Percentage of extra-marital births among all births	..	..		..	..	
Total fertility rate (births per woman)	1980	7.2		2000	5.9	
Age-specific fertility rate (per 1 000 women)						
15-19	1980	153		2000	161	
20-24	1980	318		2000	267	
25-29	1980	323		2000	247	
30-34	1980	289		2000	220	
35-39	1980	225		2000	168	
40-44	1980	115		2000	83	
45-49	1980	17		2000	28	
Mean age at childbearing (years)	1980	29.3		2000	28.9	
Mean age at first birth (years)[a]	..	..		2001-2002	19.0	
Children ever born per woman						
35-39	1969	6.7		2001-2002	5.7	
40-44	1969	6.8		2001-2002	6.9	
45-49	1969	6.7		2001-2002	7.4	
Percentage of childless women						
35-39	1969	2.5		2001-2002	2.5	
40-44	1969	2.9		2001-2002	1.7	
45-49	1969	4.1		2001-2002	1.8	
Percentage of women with parity three or higher						
35-39	1969	89.1		2001-2002	86.1	
40-44	1969	88.8		2001-2002	92.7	
45-49	1969	86.7		2001-2002	91.7	
Family Planning						
Contraceptive prevalence among women in union						
Percentage using any contraceptive method	..	..		2001-2002	34.2	
Percentage using a modern contraceptive method	..	..		2001-2002	22.6	
Percentage using condoms	..	..		2001-2002	..	
Population policies						
Government's view on the level of fertility	1976	Satisfactory		2001	Too high	
Government's policy regarding level of fertility	1976	No intervention		2001	Lower	
Government's support for contraceptive methods	1976	Direct support		2001	Direct support	

[a]Median age at first birth among women aged 25-29 at the date of the survey

Total fertility rates

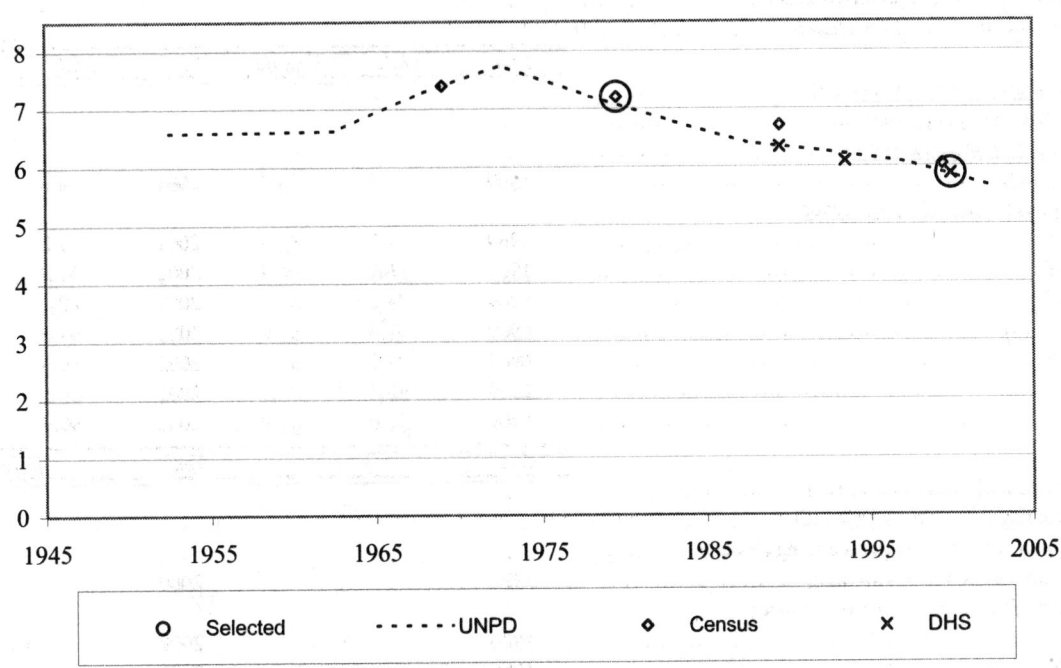

| Selected | UNPD | Census | DHS |

Age-specific fertility rates

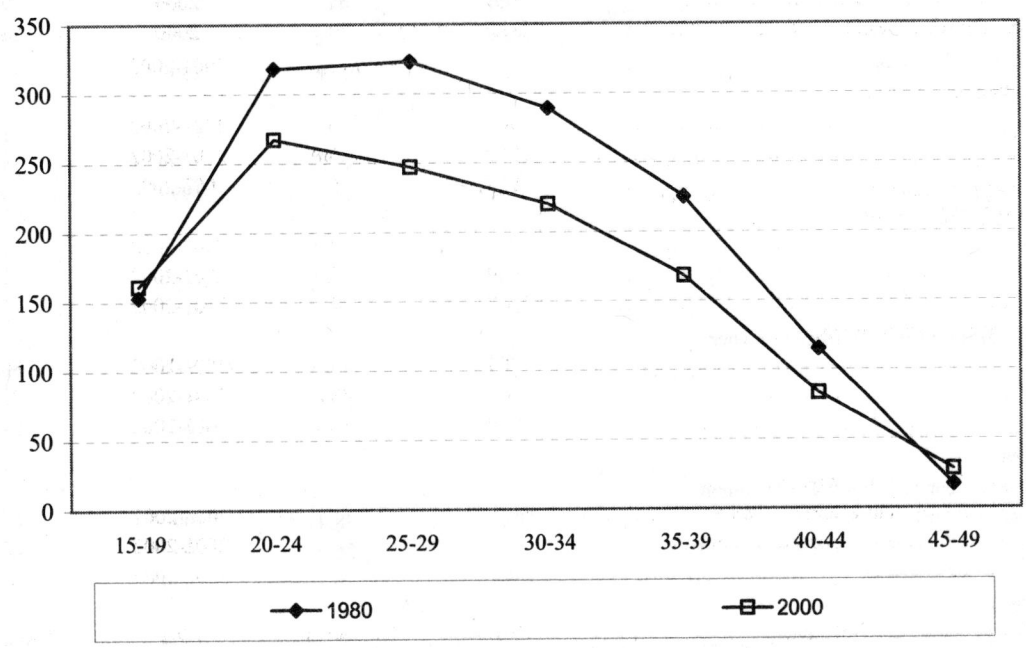

1980   2000

Indicator	Period					
	Earlier year			Later year		
	Year	Value		Year	Value	
Nuptiality						
Annual number of marriages (*thousands*)	..	..		..	..	
Annual number of divorces (*thousands*)	..	..		..	..	
	Year	Male	Female	Year	Male	Female
Total first marriage rate (per person)	..	..	..	..	..	..
Total divorce rate (per person)	..	..	..	..	..	..
Mean age at first marriage (years)	..	..	..	..	..	..
SMAM (years)	1982	25.2	20.3	1999	25.7	21.1
Percentage ever married by age group						
15-19	1982	2.0	26.1	1999	0.8	22.7
20-24	1982	29.9	76.5	1999	23.6	71.9
25-29	1982	72.6	90.7	1999	73.0	90.2
30-34	1982	88.1	94.5	1999	92.5	96.1
35-39	1982	92.5	96.4	1999	94.1	97.3
40-44	1982	94.6	97.0	1999	97.9	98.4
45-49	1982	95.3	97.2	1999	98.7	99.4
Fertility	Year	Value		Year	Value	
Annual number of births (*thousands*)...........................	..	..		..	..	
Crude birth rate (per 1 000 population)	..	..		..	..	
Percentage of extra-marital births among all births	..	..		..	..	
Total fertility rate (births per woman)	1969	6.7		1997	4.1	
Age-specific fertility rate (per 1 000 women)						
15-19	1969	79		1997	108	
20-24	1969	272		1997	201	
25-29	1969	304		1997	182	
30-34	1969	257		1997	145	
35-39	1969	218		1997	112	
40-44	1969	145		1997	49	
45-49	1969	73		1997	18	
Mean age at childbearing (years)	1969	31.2		1997	28.5	
Mean age at first birth (years)[a]	..	..		1999	20.3	
Children ever born per woman						
35-39	..	..		1999	4.5	
40-44	..	..		1999	5.5	
45-49	..	..		1999	6.3	
Percentage of childless women						
35-39	..	..		1999	3.7	
40-44	..	..		1999	2.7	
45-49	..	..		1999	1.9	
Percentage of women with parity three or higher						
35-39	..	..		1999	83.1	
40-44	..	..		1999	87.7	
45-49	..	..		1999	89.0	
Family Planning						
Contraceptive prevalence among women in union						
Percentage using any contraceptive method	1984	38.4		1999	53.5	
Percentage using a modern contraceptive method	1984	26.6		1999	50.4	
Percentage using condoms	1984	0.7		1999	1.8	
Population policies						
Government's view on the level of fertility	..	..		2001	Too high	
Government's policy regarding level of fertility	..	..		2001	Lower	
Government's support for contraceptive methods	..	..		2001	Direct support	

[a]Median age at first birth among women aged 25-29 at the date of the survey

Total fertility rates

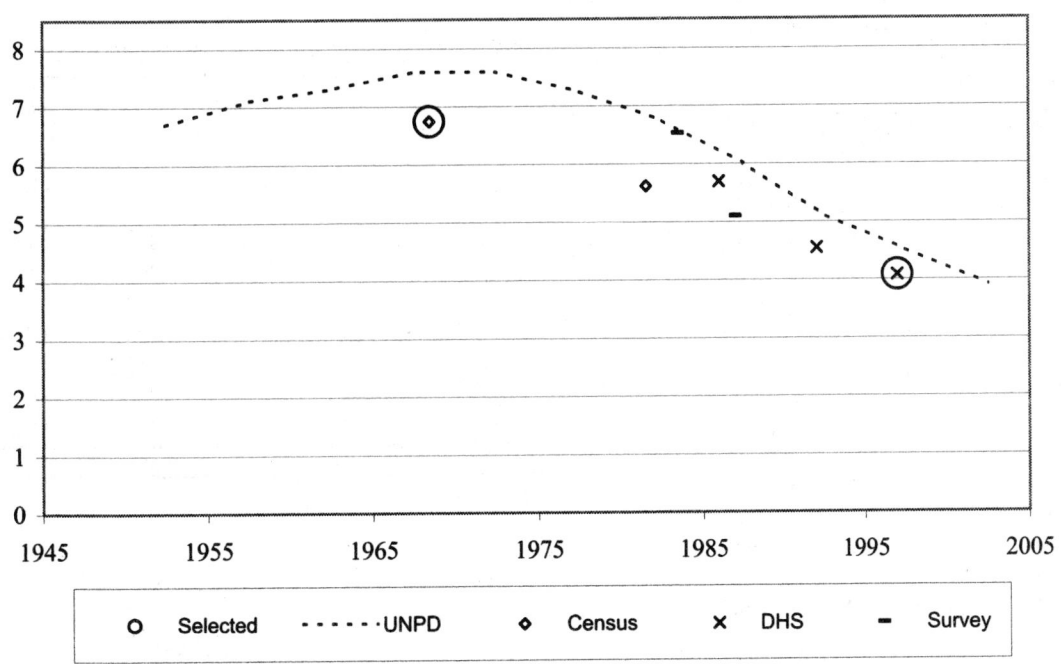

Age-specific fertility rates

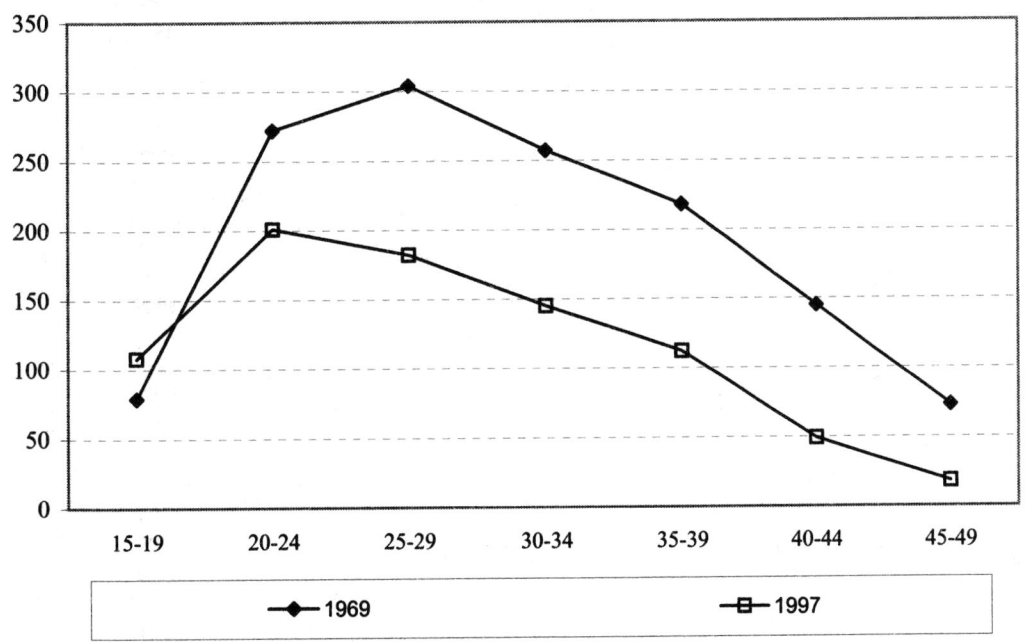

II. SELECTED INDICATORS

TABLE II.1. TOTAL FERTILITY RATE BY COUNTRY

Country	Year	Rate	Year	Rate
Africa				
Eastern Africa				
Burundi	1980	7.9	1985	7.0
Comoros	1980	7.1	1994	5.1
Djibouti	..	..	1991	6.0
Eritrea	..	..	2000	5.2
Ethiopia	1981	6.8	1998	5.9
Kenya	1969	7.6	1996	4.7
Madagascar	1975	6.4	1995	6.1
Malawi	1977	7.6	1998	6.4
Mauritius	1972	3.4	2000	2.0
Mozambique	1970	6.7	1995	5.6
Réunion	1970	4.4	1998	2.3
Rwanda	1970	7.7	1999	5.9
Somalia	1975	7.1	..	..
Uganda	1969	7.1	1999	7.0
United Republic of Tanzania	1971	7.1	1998	5.6
Zambia	1980	7.2	2000	5.9
Zimbabwe	1969	6.7	1997	4.1
Middle Africa				
Angola	..	..	..	..
Cameroon	1976	6.4	1996	5.2
Central African Republic	1975	5.8	1993	5.2
Chad	..	..	1995	6.6
Congo	1974	7.0	1984	5.9
Democratic Republic of the Congo	1971	6.3	1984	6.7
Equatorial Guinea	1983	5.5	..	..
Gabon	..	..	1998	4.3
Sao Tome and Principe	..	..	..	..
Northern Africa				
Algeria	1977	7.4	1996	3.1
Egypt	1970	5.4	1999	3.6
Libyan Arab Jamahiriya	1973	6.8	1993	4.1
Morocco	1977	5.9	1999	3.0
Sudan	1973	7.1	1992	4.6
Tunisia	1970	6.1	1999	2.1
Western Sahara	..	..	..	..
Southern Africa				
Botswana	1971	6.5	1986	5.0
Lesotho	1975	5.8	1991	4.8
Namibia	..	..	1990	5.2
South Africa	..	..	1996	2.9
Swaziland	1966	5.2	1986	5.0
Western Africa				
Benin	1980	7.1	1999	5.8
Burkina Faso	1985	7.2	1996	6.8
Cape Verde	1982	5.8	1996	4.2
Côte d'Ivoire	1978	7.4	1997	5.1
Gambia	1973	6.4	1988	5.9
Ghana	1968	7.1	1996	4.5
Guinea	1983	5.8	1997	5.8
Guinea-Bissau	..	..	..	..
Liberia	1984	6.6	..	..

TABLE II.1. *(continued)*

Country	Year	Rate	Year	Rate
Mali	1985	6.9	1994	7.0
Mauritania	1979	6.2	1999	4.7
Niger............	..	..	1997	7.5
Nigeria	1980	6.3	1997	5.1
Senegal	1976	7.2	1996	5.8
Sierra Leone	1973	6.5	1985	6.3
Togo	1970	6.6	1996	5.4
Asia				
Eastern Asia				
China	1970	5.7	2001	1.4
China, Hong Kong SAR	1970	3.3	2001	0.9
China, Macao SAR	1970	2.0	2000	0.9
Dem. People's Republic of Korea............	..	..	1993	2.2
Japan............	1970	2.1	2000	1.3
Mongolia	1973	7.5	2000	2.3
Republic of Korea	1970	4.3	2000	1.5
South-Central Asia				
Afghanistan	1973	8.2	..	..
Bangladesh	1973	6.1	1997	3.4
Bhutan	..	..	1993	5.6
India............	1981	4.9	1997	3.3
Iran (Islamic Republic of)............	1975	6.4	2000	2.2
Kazakhstan	1970	3.3	1997	2.1
Kyrgyzstan	1970	4.9	2000	2.4
Maldives............	..	..	1990	6.4
Nepal	1974	6.0	2000	4.3
Pakistan	1970	6.0	1999	4.8
Sri Lanka	1971	4.2	1996	2.3
Tajikistan	1970	5.9	1993	4.2
Turkmenistan............	1970	5.7	1998	3.0
Uzbekistan............	1970	5.6	2000	2.6
South-Eastern Asia				
Brunei Darussalam	1970	5.8	2000	2.4
Cambodia	1960	7.0	1996	5.2
Democratic Republic of Timor-Leste............	..	..	1993	4.7
Indonesia	1969	5.6	2003	2.6
Lao People's Democratic Republic............	..	..	1997	4.9
Malaysia............	1970	4.7	1998	3.1
Myanmar	1973	5.7	1994	2.9
Philippines............	1971	6.0	1996	3.8
Singapore............	1970	3.1	2000	1.7
Thailand............	1967	6.2	1995	2.0
Viet Nam	1977	4.8	1994	2.7
Western Asia				
Armenia	1970	3.2	1998	1.9
Azerbaijan	1970	4.6	2000	2.1
Bahrain	1971	6.7	1999	2.8
Cyprus	1970	2.7	2000	1.6
Georgia	1970	2.7	1998	1.7
Iraq	1974	7.1	1989	5.2
Israel	1970	3.9	2000	3.0
Jordan	1974	7.6	2001	3.7
Kuwait	1970	6.7	1994	4.3
Lebanon............	1970	4.6	1993	2.5

TABLE II.1. *(continued)*

Country	Year	Rate	Year	Rate
Occupied Palestinian Territory	1970	7.5	1997	6.1
Oman	..	..	1993	7.4
Qatar	..	..	1996	4.1
Saudi Arabia	..	..	1994	6.1
Syrian Arab Republic	1970	7.7	1991	4.7
Turkey	1970	5.7	2000	2.5
United Arab Emirates	..	..	1993	5.0
Yemen	1977	8.5	1996	6.7
Europe				
Eastern Europe				
Belarus	1970	2.3	2001	1.3
Bulgaria	1970	2.2	2001	1.2
Czech Republic	1970	1.9	2001	1.1
Hungary	1970	2.0	2001	1.3
Poland	1971	2.3	2001	1.3
Republic of Moldova	1969	2.6	2001	1.3
Romania	1970	2.9	2000	1.3
Russian Federation	1978	2.0	2001	1.3
Slovakia	1970	2.4	2001	1.2
Ukraine	1970	2.1	1998	1.2
Northern Europe				
Channel Islands	..	..	..	..
Denmark	1970	2.0	2001	1.7
Estonia	1970	2.2	2001	1.3
Finland	1970	1.8	2001	1.7
Iceland	1970	2.8	2000	2.1
Ireland	1970	3.9	2001	2.0
Latvia	1970	2.0	2001	1.2
Lithuania	1970	2.4	2001	1.3
Norway	1970	2.5	2001	1.8
Sweden	1970	1.9	2001	1.6
United Kingdom	1972	2.2	2000	1.6
Southern Europe				
Albania	1970	5.1	1999	2.1
Bosnia and Herzegovina	1970	2.7	1998	1.6
Croatia	1970	1.8	2001	1.4
Greece	1970	2.4	1999	1.3
Italy	1970	2.4	2000	1.2
Malta	1975	2.2	2001	1.5
Portugal	1970	3.0	2001	1.5
Serbia and Montenegro	1970	2.3	2000	1.7
Slovenia	1970	2.1	2001	1.2
Spain	1970	2.9	2000	1.2
TFYR Macedonia	1970	3.0	2000	1.9
Western Europe				
Austria	1970	2.3	2001	1.3
Belgium	1970	2.3	1995	1.5
France	1970	2.5	1999	1.8
Germany	1978	2.0	2000	1.4
Luxembourg	1970	2.0	2001	1.7
Netherlands	1970	2.6	2001	1.7
Switzerland	1970	2.1	2001	1.4

TABLE II.1. *(continued)*

Country	Year	Rate	Year	Rate
Latin America and the Caribbean				
Caribbean				
Bahamas	1970	3.5	1996	2.3
Barbados	1970	3.0	1988	1.6
Cuba	1970	3.7	2000	1.6
Dominican Republic	1973	5.7	1999	2.9
Guadeloupe	1970	4.6	1991	2.2
Haiti	1975	5.5	1998	4.7
Jamaica	1970	5.5	1996	2.9
Martinique	1970	4.4	1992	1.9
Netherlands Antilles	..	..	..	..
Puerto Rico	1970	3.2	2000	2.0
Saint Lucia	1975	5.5	2000	2.0
Saint Vincent and the Grenadines	..	..	..	..
Trinidad and Tobago	1971	3.6	1997	1.7
United States Virgin Islands	1970	5.3	1990	3.0
Central America				
Belize	1970	6.2	1998	3.2
Costa Rica	1970	4.9	1999	2.4
El Salvador	1971	6.0	1996	3.6
Guatemala	1972	6.3	1997	5.1
Honduras	1972	7.5	1994	5.0
Mexico	1974	6.2	1996	2.7
Nicaragua	1983	5.8	1999	3.3
Panama	1970	5.0	2000	2.7
South America				
Argentina	1970	3.2	2000	2.5
Bolivia	1974	6.5	1996	4.4
Brazil	1980	3.9	1994	2.6
Chile	1970	3.3	1999	2.1
Colombia	1974	4.7	1998	2.6
Ecuador	1977	5.3	1997	3.3
French Guiana	1973	3.9	1999	4.1
Guyana	1973	4.9	..	..
Paraguay	1977	5.0	1997	4.3
Peru	1975	5.5	1998	3.0
Suriname	1970	5.6	2000	2.7
Uruguay	1970	2.7	2000	2.2
Venezuela	1970	5.7	2000	2.7
Northern America				
Canada	1970	2.3	1997	1.6
United States of America	1970	2.5	2000	2.1
Oceania				
Australia/New Zealand				
Australia	1970	2.9	2000	1.7
New Zealand	1970	3.1	2000	2.0
Melanesia				
Fiji	1972	4.1	1986	3.4
New Caledonia	1970	5.3	1999	2.5
Papua New Guinea	1980	6.0	1994	4.8
Solomon Islands	1973	7.4	1985	6.1
Vanuatu	1977	6.6	1989	4.9

TABLE II.1. (*continued*)

Country	Year	Rate	Year	Rate
Micronesia				
Guam..	1970	4.8	1992	3.7
Micronesia Federated States of......................	..	..	..	..
Polynesia				
French Polynesia	1968	6.7	..	..
Samoa...	..	..	1991	4.9
Tonga..	..	..	..	..

TABLE II.2.   AGE-SPECIFIC FERTILITY RATES BY COUNTRY

Country	Year	15-19	20-24	25-29	30-34	35-39	40-44	45-49	Year	15-19	20-24	25-29	30-34	35-39	40-44	45-49
Africa																
Eastern Africa																
Burundi	1980	93	282	336	328	261	200	82	1985	52	271	324	292	238	131	82
Comoros	..	..	..	..	..	..	..	..	1994	66	196	237	246	164	78	29
Djibouti	..	..	..	..	..	..	..	..	1991	31	155	270	317	257	121	44
Eritrea	..	..	..	..	..	..	..	..	2000	85	199	214	213	183	102	51
Ethiopia	1981	115	273	299	264	225	125	65	1998	110	244	264	248	183	100	24
Kenya	1969	132	331	337	294	223	135	68	1996	111	246	222	185	107	54	16
Madagascar	1975	132	272	280	232	195	122	45	1995	173	278	264	216	166	93	26
Malawi	1977	165	341	334	304	241	119	16	1998	167	307	276	219	169	99	50
Mauritius	1972	50	189	191	130	88	32	3.8	2000	39	122	122	77	34	8	1
Mozambique	1970	133	294	271	235	196	140	71	1995	173	270	235	198	126	95	25
Réunion	1970	62	239	217	171	125	59	8	1998	36	108	131	101	58	19	1
Rwanda	..	..	..	..	..	..	..	..	1999	55	245	278	256	192	122	38
Somalia	..	..	..	..	..	..	..	..	..	..	..	..	..	..	..	..
Uganda	1969	198	341	322	253	189	87	35	1999	190	334	299	261	187	84	39
United Republic of Tanzania	1971	152	336	325	263	200	102	43	1998	137	271	233	210	148	89	32
Zambia	1980	153	318	323	289	225	115	17	2000	161	267	247	220	168	83	28
Zimbabwe	1969	79	272	304	257	218	145	73	1997	108	201	182	145	112	49	18
Middle Africa																
Angola	..	..	..	..	..	..	..	..	..	..	..	..	..	..	..	..
Cameroon	1976	187	295	277	220	155	106	41	1996	142	237	244	189	136	63	20
Central African Republic	1975	172	278	251	209	136	78	45	1993	157	234	232	196	123	61	27
Chad	..	..	..	..	..	..	..	..	1995	194	314	313	255	168	68	13
Congo	1974	156	305	305	255	203	122	52	1984	138	250	267	240	176	89	28
Democratic Republic of the Congo	..	..	..	..	..	..	..	..	..	..	..	..	..	..	..	..
Equatorial Guinea	..	..	..	..	..	..	..	..	..	..	..	..	..	..	..	..
Gabon	..	..	..	..	..	..	..	..	1998	144	193	178	176	101	48	11
Sao Tome and Principe	..	..	..	..	..	..	..	..	..	..	..	..	..	..	..	..
Northern Africa																
Algeria	1977	97	285	342	336	267	129	27	1996	19	109	150	154	125	58	13

TABLE II.2. *(continued)*

Country	Year	15-19	20-24	25-29	30-34	35-39	40-44	45-49	Year	15-19	20-24	25-29	30-34	35-39	40-44	45-49
Egypt	1970	22	157	288	257	213	96	45	1999	19	193	226	163	88	26	7
Libyan Arab Jamahiriya	1973	201	334	328	241	161	65	31	1993	7	74	181	229	193	109	24
Morocco	1977	93	265	296	222	178	98	29	1999	10	71	128	139	130	77	39
Sudan	1973	142	337	355	277	195	72	36	1992	51	169	214	212	161	66	37
Tunisia	1970	46	254	302	273	206	96	40	1999	8	67	123	121	73	23	3
Western Sahara	..	:	:	:	:	:	:	:	..	:	:	:	:	:	:	:
Southern Africa																
Botswana	1971	96	277	276	243	198	138	71	1986	125	212	202	191	148	83	38
Lesotho	1975	102	268	258	233	173	94	30	1991	54	186	214	212	149	100	38
Namibia	..	:	:	:	:	:	:	:	1990	101	197	236	197	171	99	38
South Africa	..	:	:	:	:	:	:	:	1996	78	136	138	108	72	30	10
Swaziland	..	:	:	:	:	:	:	:	1986	54	205	221	210	175	88	45
Western Africa																
Benin	1980	151	314	329	278	193	99	51	1999	108	255	267	243	165	87	31
Burkina Faso	1985	152	328	321	279	215	104	38	1996	144	305	293	264	214	112	28
Cape Verde	1982	77	225	279	261	200	88	23	1996	104	208	188	159	113	61	2
Côte d'Ivoire	1978	216	313	300	248	203	132	60	1997	126	210	234	195	148	78	33
Gambia	1973	200	300	290	210	160	70	40	1988	167	270	238	228	130	78	78
Ghana	1968	132	257	266	242	169	135	50	1996	90	192	206	183	143	79	16
Guinea	1983	161	267	269	211	149	72	39	1997	172	249	253	231	151	75	37
Guinea-Bissau	..	:	:	:	:	:	:	:	..	:	:	:	:	:	:	:
Liberia	1984	184	285	272	223	181	114	63	..	:	:	:	:	:	:	:
Mali	1985	201	291	288	260	193	112	40	1994	198	310	303	262	208	98	27
Mauritania	1979	155	264	290	242	168	86	44	1999	83	170	215	204	146	85	33
Niger	..	:	:	:	:	:	:	:	1997	216	322	319	293	206	96	42
Nigeria	1980	173	284	274	231	147	100	60	1997	111	220	239	226	138	71	24
Senegal	1976	188	304	331	270	197	106	36	1996	104	225	247	246	191	108	42
Sierra Leone	1973	212	296	280	210	169	81	54	1985	202	283	271	214	163	80	47
Togo	1970	122	292	288	245	194	117	71	1996	88.6	224	251	214	172	93	37

TABLE II.2. (continued)

Country	Year	15-19	20-24	25-29	30-34	35-39	40-44	45-49	Year	15-19	20-24	25-29	30-34	35-39	40-44	45-49
Asia																
Eastern Asia																
China	1970	39	278	308	252	179	83	10	2001	3	108	115	40	9	2	1
China, Hong Kong SAR	1970	18	135	230	159	86	30	5	2001	4	29	58	61	28	5	0
China, Macao SAR	1970	3	68	130	90	78	35	4	2000	5	26	64	56	26	5	0
Dem. People's Republic of Korea	..	..	..	..	..	..	..	..	1993	0	49	265	101	19	3	1
Japan	1970	5	97	209	86	20	3	0	2000	5	39	98	91	31	4	0
Mongolia	1973	83	202	364	368	300	137	44	2000	28	148	136	86	40	14	4
Republic of Korea	1970	13	174	298	207	111	43	8	2000	3	40	156	89	18	3	0
South-Central Asia																
Afghanistan	1973	168	359	355	307	235	137	81	..	..	..	..	..	..	..	..
Bangladesh	1973	219	304	260	214	142	64	12	1997	147	193	163	103	50	20	5
Bhutan	..	..	..	..	..	..	..	..	1993	120	267	242	195	174	95	24
India	1981	75	256	253	186	120	63	29	1997	54	226	188	109	55	26	8
Iran (Islamic Republic of)	1975	174	278	263	230	177	124	36	2000	35	110	131	90	48	16	4
Kazakhstan	1970	30	192	178	135	83	34	9	1997	44	166	115	63	29	6	0
Kyrgyzstan	1970	41	261	225	199	155	70	20	2000	35	165	135	88	46	14	3
Maldives	..	..	..	..	..	..	..	..	1990	106	286	303	270	199	96	23
Nepal	1974	131	283	287	236	159	79	27	2000	116	260	213	144	84	36	8
Pakistan	1970	58	223	261	252	200	124	85	1999	65	211	258	206	128	61	26
Sri Lanka	1971	40	184	232	199	131	40	6	1996	29	89	129	111	82	20	2
Tajikistan	1970	40	261	268	251	216	109	36	1993	54	272	225	160	94	36	7
Turkmenistan	1970	32	271	276	251	213	62	31	1998	29	192	204	113	50	12	1
Uzbekistan	1970	42	261	265	246	195	92	27	2000	21	205	161	90	31	7	1
South-Eastern Asia																
Brunei Darussalam	1970	78	323	302	233	153	57	23	2000	31	93	129	113	84	28	2
Cambodia	1960	102	306	323	295	233	118	25	1996	23	221	246	236	182	103	26
Democratic Republic of Timor-Leste	..	..	..	..	..	..	..	..	1993	49	213	243	212	153	51	16
Indonesia	1969	155	286	273	211	124	55	17	2003	51	131	143	99	66	19	4
Lao People's Democratic Republic	..	..	..	..	..	..	..	..	1997	102	228	224	172	127	70	53
Malaysia	1970	54	233	236	216	126	54	15	1998	15	115	204	168	96	33	4

TABLE II.2. (continued)

Country	Year	15-19	20-24	25-29	30-34	35-39	40-44	45-49	Year	15-19	20-24	25-29	30-34	35-39	40-44	45-49
Myanmar	..	..	..	..	..	..	..	..	1994	32	121	156	137	93	37	4
Philippines	1971	56	228	302	268	212	100	28	1996	50	177	210	161	106	43	8
Singapore	1970	26	140	210	139	75	27	5	2000	9	43	113	114	45	8	0
Thailand	1967	89	267	299	260	206	100	19	1995	70	119	108	66	26	6	0
Viet Nam	..	..	..	..	..	..	..	..	1994	39	178	148	95	52	20	4
Western Asia																
Armenia	1970	41	216	169	115	66	21	5	1998	57	169	97	39	15	2	0
Azerbaijan	1970	37	233	234	205	143	50	10	2000	44	151	133	58	19	9	..
Bahrain	1971	288	411	328	188	95	24	6	1999	14	113	157	136	100	40	9
Cyprus	1970	21	150	181	113	60	19	4	2000	9	70	120	83	30	7	0
Georgia	1970	36	190	155	94	47	12	2	1998	64	112	92	47	21	7	0
Iraq	..	..	..	..	..	..	..	..	1989	87	211	240	215	173	86	31
Israel	1970	50	210	232	177	90	21	3	2000	17	117	187	162	86	21	2
Jordan	1974	124	343	365	332	240	103	19	2001	28	150	202	184	122	43	5
Kuwait	1970	130	315	339	276	208	57	15	1994	30	183	237	201	141	61	16
Lebanon	1970	40	184	259	214	134	65	18	..	..	..	..	..	..	..	..
Occupied Palestinian Territory	1970	55	242	340	343	330	129	56	..	..	..	..	..	..	..	..
Oman	..	..	..	..	..	..	..	..	1993	100	293	340	315	231	120	79
Qatar	..	..	..	..	..	..	..	..	1996	28	154	221	208	136	48	17
Saudi Arabia	..	..	..	..	..	..	..	..	1994	61	224	287	264	195	119	70
Syrian Arab Republic	1970	83	357	389	335	236	123	12	1991	71	184	229	202	155	81	17
Turkey	1970	89	293	283	222	157	62	31	2000	56	165	145	82	36	12	1
United Arab Emirates	..	..	..	..	..	..	..	..	1993	44	188	257	222	164	92	41
Yemen	1977	175	346	346	334	229	197	75	1996	110	286	304	267	200	115	62
Europe																
Eastern Europe																
Belarus	1970	20	162	135	87	43	12	1	2001	27	104	73	37	12	2	0
Bulgaria	1970	72	188	111	46	15	3	0	2001	45	87	72	33	10	2	0
Czech Republic	1970	48	173	102	41	13	3	0	2001	11	60	91	47	15	3	0
Hungary	1970	53	159	109	51	19	4	0	2001	23	65	91	58	21	4	0
Poland	1971	30	171	129	72	36	11	1	2001	16	74	89	52	21	5	0
Republic of Moldova	1969	28	164	135	100	62	21	3	2001	35	98	67	36	12	3	0
Romania	1970	66	202	151	96	48	13	2	2000	39	90	78	37	14	3	0

TABLE II.2. *(continued)*

Country	Year	15-19	20-24	25-29	30-34	35-39	40-44	45-49	Year	15-19	20-24	25-29	30-34	35-39	40-44	45-49
Russian Federation........	1970	30	152	108	68	33	9	1	2001	28	95	72	39	13	2	0
Slovakia......................	1970	40	195	137	70	30	8	1	2001	21	73	84	43	15	3	0
Ukraine......................	1970	35	165	113	68	31	7	1	1998	41	101	58	26	9	2	0
Northern Europe																
Channel Islands........	:	:	:	:	:	:	:	:	:	:	:	:	:	:	:	:
Denmark....................	1970	32	129	139	67	25	5	0	2001	8	51	126	115	43	7	0
Estonia......................	1970	33	159	131	73	30	7	1	2001	24	81	83	53	22	4	0
Finland......................	1970	32	117	112	64	31	9	1	2001	11	60	114	103	48	10	0
Iceland......................	1970	74	166	142	101	57	20	4	2000	22	88	131	112	51	11	1
Ireland......................	1970	16	144	227	202	132	45	4	2001	19	50	92	140	79	14	1
Latvia........................	1970	28	147	119	70	32	8	1	2001	18	75	77	47	20	5	0
Lithuania..................	1970	24	159	143	88	48	15	1	2001	22	86	83	45	19	4	0
Norway......................	1970	46	166	149	88	41	11	1	2001	11	62	123	108	45	7	0
Sweden......................	1970	33	119	128	69	28	6	0	2001	7	47	104	103	44	8	0
United Kingdom........	1972	48	141	143	71	30	8	0	2000	29	69	95	88	40	8	0
Southern Europe																
Albania......................	1970	38	263	273	212	146	68	23	1999	16	122	158	89	30	6	1
Bosnia and Herzegovina...	1970	47	178	145	94	54	20	3	1998	26	113	91	51	24	6	1
Croatia......................	1970	48	136	98	54	23	6	1	2001	15	72	97	62	24	4	0
Greece........................	1970	38	143	152	94	42	9	1	1999	11	51	88	74	28	5	1
Italy...........................	1970	27	129	153	99	53	16	1	2000	7	33	76	84	40	8	0
Malta.........................	1975	17	119	150	91	42	14	0	2001	17	53	111	77	26	6	0
Portugal....................	1970	31	154	177	124	80	33	3	2001	20	55	92	83	35	6	0
Serbia and Montenegro...	1970	62	166	123	67	30	9	2	2000	25	105	109	62	25	5	0
Slovenia....................	1970	42	152	114	70	34	10	1	2001	6	51	98	63	20	3	0
Spain..........................	1970	14	123	199	133	77	27	3	2000	9	26	67	95	43	7	0
TFYR Macedonia	1970	43	198	185	103	49	16	3	2000	32	128	133	62	19	3	0
Western Europe																
Austria......................	1970	59	155	116	76	41	11	1	2001	14	61	91	66	25	5	0
Belgium......................	1970	32	150	144	77	36	10	1	1995	9	61	132	81	23	4	0
France........................	1970	37	167	150	88	41	11	1	1999	10	61	133	105	42	8	0

TABLE II.2. *(continued)*

Country	Year	15-19	20-24	25-29	30-34	35-39	40-44	45-49	Year	15-19	20-24	25-29	30-34	35-39	40-44	45-49
Germany	1971	49	136	111	68	33	8	1	2000	13	57	93	79	30	5	0
Luxembourg	1970	28	133	126	65	33	9	1	2001	12	60	110	102	41	7	0
Netherlands	1970	23	137	183	107	49	14	1	2001	8	41	108	129	50	7	0
Switzerland	1970	22	125	140	84	38	10	1	2001	6	43	93	95	39	6	0
Latin America And The Caribbean																
Caribbean																
Bahamas	1970	77	199	183	112	82	33	4	1996	62	114	115	96	55	13	4
Barbados	1970	94	164	156	102	60	25	4	1988	44	87	89	65	28	3	0
Cuba	1970	128	227	164	116	73	26	4	2000	51	97	89	55	22	4	0
Dominican Republic	1973	123	286	265	233	166	54	15	1999	60	150	157	108	57	26	29
Guadeloupe	1970	65	197	232	209	139	64	9	1991	34	98	136	100	53	14	1
Haiti	1975	57	204	266	226	178	116	54	1998	80	187	204	219	153	75	18
Jamaica	1970	167	302	268	190	127	47	8	1996	112	163	112	101	55	25	4
Martinique	1970	59	191	232	191	130	68	7	1992	28	89	114	93	50	12	1
Netherlands Antilles	..	..	..	..	..	..	..	..	..	..	..	..	..	..	..	..
Puerto Rico	1970	73	194	182	103	56	21	3	2000	74	128	110	65	27	6	0
Saint Lucia	1975	162	275	271	195	128	59	9	2000	57	100	94	86	50	18	1
Saint Vincent and the Grenadines	..	..	..	..	..	..	..	..	..	..	..	..	..	..	..	..
Trinidad and Tobago	1971	85	199	194	131	83	28	4	1997	43	97	88	70	35	9	1
United States Virgin Islands	1970	230	288	250	161	96	31	4	1990	78	183	177	115	44	11	1
Central America																
Belize	1970	142	309	302	239	173	75	9	1998	80	187	173	112	64	21	5
Costa Rica	1970	103	237	231	188	144	69	12	1999	84	131	122	84	46	14	1
El Salvador	1971	143	291	273	226	181	71	22	1996	116	211	167	118	68	29	8
Guatemala	1972	145	304	285	235	184	80	20	1997	123	277	229	191	136	61	3
Honduras	1972	171	317	339	307	221	127	18	1994	136	243	210	169	142	78	12
Mexico	1974	114	290	294	254	178	84	21	1996	75	146	144	102	56	19	3
Nicaragua	1983	182	275	264	208	150	62	17	1999	119	182	149	114	67	10	0
Panama	1970	134	280	246	174	115	40	8	2000	96	149	128	95	51	14	2
South America																
Argentina	1970	68	163	175	123	71	26	7	2000	66	117	127	106	60	18	2
Bolivia	..	..	..	..	..	..	..	..	1996	88	209	208	171	120	60	18

TABLE II.2. (*continued*)

Country	Year	15-19	20-24	25-29	30-34	35-39	40-44	45-49	Year	15-19	20-24	25-29	30-34	35-39	40-44	45-49
Brazil	1980	58	182	204	160	109	52	13	1994	88	153	126	81	45	16	3
Chile	1970	69	173	168	118	81	40	7	1999	65	100	106	84	49	13	1
Colombia	1974	101	230	221	172	130	62	23	1998	85	146	131	94	49	17	3
Ecuador	1977	103	240	261	203	163	81	17	1997	89	172	155	119	76	37	10
French Guiana	1973	101	263	177	120	80	34	6	1999	97	178	230	187	105	29	0
Guyana	1973	114	283	242	184	112	42	6	..	..	..	..	..	..	..	..
Paraguay	1977	86	221	239	207	150	74	16	1997	87	216	214	167	132	37	15
Peru	1975	86	232	266	237	169	91	28	1998	70	148	143	122	83	34	7
Suriname	..	..	..	..	..	..	..	..	2000	68	150	148	104	56	16	2
Uruguay	1970	63	148	142	105	57	24	3	2000	65	106	107	100	48	13	1
Venezuela	1970	114	281	288	210	167	61	14	2000	97	148	131	91	50	17	3
Northern America																
Canada	1970	42	138	143	79	38	11	1	1997	20	64	104	84	33	5	0
United States of America	1970	68	168	145	73	32	8	1	2000	49	112	121	94	40	8	0
Oceania																
Australia/New Zealand																
Australia	1970	51	172	190	102	45	12	1	2000	17	56	107	110	49	9	0
New Zealand	1970	62	209	200	100	45	12	1	2000	29	78	116	116	53	10	0
Melanesia																
Fiji	1972	58	248	215	162	90	43	10	1986	62	207	191	122	66	24	8
New Caledonia	1970	127	311	243	180	126	62	8	1999	14	113	156	127	70	22	1
Papua New Guinea	..	..	..	..	..	..	..	..	1994	77	229	234	189	122	82	35
Solomon Islands	1973	146	296	328	305	225	141	42	1985	101	280	295	252	177	84	25
Vanuatu	1976	91	294	327	265	179	110	45	1989	78	234	248	195	138	61	22
Micronesia																
Guam	1970	96	280	267	161	103	41	3	1992	110	217	201	124	61	17	1
Micronesia Federated States of	..	..	..	..	..	..	..	..	..	..	..	..	..	..	..	..
Polynesia																
French Polynesia	1968	109	379	353	249	156	79	11	..	..	..	..	..	..	..	..
Samoa	..	..	..	..	..	..	..	..	1991	26	165	251	221	182	103	39
Tonga	..	..	..	..	..	..	..	..	..	..	..	..	..	..	..	..

TABLE II.3. MEAN AGE AT CHILDBEARING BY COUNTRY

Country	Year	Age	Year	Age
Africa				
Eastern Africa				
Burundi	1980	31.6	1985	31.5
Comoros	..	..	1994	30.4
Djibouti	..	..	1991	32.3
Eritrea	..	..	2000	30.9
Ethiopia	1981	30.6	1998	29.8
Kenya	1969	30.2	1996	28.3
Madagascar	1975	30.0	1995	28.8
Malawi	1977	29.3	1998	29.1
Mauritius	1972	28.4	2000	27.2
Mozambique	1970	30.4	1995	28.5
Réunion	1970	29.0	1998	28.6
Rwanda	..	..	1999	30.9
Somalia	..	..	..	..
Uganda	1969	28.5	1999	28.7
United Republic of Tanzania	1971	29.3	1998	29.1
Zambia	1980	29.3	2000	28.9
Zimbabwe	1969	31.2	1997	28.5
Middle Africa				
Angola	..	..	..	..
Cameroon	1976	28.8	1996	28.5
Central African Republic	1975	28.7	1993	28.4
Chad	..	..	1995	28.0
Congo	1974	29.7	1984	29.4
Democratic Republic of the Congo	..	..	..	..
Equatorial Guinea	..	..	..	..
Gabon	..	..	1993	28.0
Sao Tome and Principe	..	..	..	..
Northern Africa				
Algeria	1977	30.5	1996	31.3
Egypt	1970	31.9	1999	29.0
Libyan Arab Jamahiriya	1973	28.0	1993	33.3
Morocco	1977	29.8	1999	33.3
Sudan	1973	28.9	1992	30.8
Tunisia	1970	30.7	1999	30.7
Western Sahara	..	..	..	..
Southern Africa				
Botswana	1971	30.8	1986	29.6
Lesotho	1975	29.7	1991	31.0
Namibia	..	..	1990	30.3
South Africa	..	..	1996	28.3
Swaziland	..	..	1986	31.0
Western Africa				
Benin	1980	29.4	1999	29.6
Burkina Faso	1986	29.4	1996	29.5

TABLE II. 3. *(continued)*

Country	Year	Age	Year	Age
Cape Verde	1979	30.8	1996	28.5
Côte d'Ivoire	1978	29.4	1992	29.4
Gambia	1973	28.3	1988	29.3
Ghana	1978	30.2	1996	29.7
Guinea	1983	28.8	1997	28.8
Guinea-Bissau	..	..	..	..
Liberia	1984	29.5	..	..
Mali	1985	29.1	1994	28.8
Mauritania	1979	29.3	1999	30.4
Niger	..	..	1997	28.9
Nigeria	1980	29.2	1997	29.3
Senegal	1976	29.1	1996	30.5
Sierra Leone	1973	28.6	1985	28.6
Togo	1970	30.3	1996	30.2
Asia				
Eastern Asia				
China	1970	29.9	2001	26.7
China, Hong Kong SAR	1970	29.5	2001	30.1
China, Macao SAR	1970	31.1	2000	29.8
Dem. People's Republic of Korea	..	..	1993	28.7
Japan	1970	27.8	2000	29.7
Mongolia	1973	31.5	2000	27.7
Republic of Korea	1970	29.8	2000	28.9
South-Central Asia				
Afghanistan	1973	30.0	..	..
Bangladesh	1973	27.5	1997	26.0
Bhutan	..	..	1993	29.4
India	1981	29.2	1997	27.5
Iran (Islamic Republic of)	1975	29.3	2000	28.3
Kazakhstan	1970	28.9	1997	26.1
Kyrgyzstan	1970	29.8	2000	27.5
Maldives	..	..	1990	29.6
Nepal	1974	29.0	2000	27.3
Pakistan	1970	31.8	1999	29.6
Sri Lanka	1971	29.5	1996	29.6
Tajikistan	1980	30.9	1993	28.1
Turkmenistan	1970	30.4	1998	27.5
Uzbekistan	1970	30.5	2000	26.8
South-Eastern Asia				
Brunei Darussalam	1970	28.9	2000	29.8
Cambodia	1960	30.0	1996	31.1
Democratic Republic of Timor-Leste	..	..	1993	29.8
Indonesia	1969	27.9	1996	28.1
Lao People's Democratic Republic	..	..	1997	29.6
Malaysia	1970	29.4	1998	30.1
Myanmar	..	..	1994	29.8
Philippines	1971	30.7	1996	29.2
Singapore	1970	29.1	2000	30.0

TABLE II.3. *(continued)*

Country	Year	Age	Year	Age
Thailand	1967	29.9	1995	26.0
Viet Nam	1977	27.7	1994	27.7
Western Asia				
Armenia	1970	27.8	2001	24.8
Azerbaijan	1970	29.6	2000	26.1
Bahrain	1971	25.6	1999	30.6
Cyprus	1970	28.6	2000	28.7
Georgia	1970	27.2	2000	25.6
Iraq	..	..	1989	30.2
Israel	1970	28.3	2000	29.6
Jordan	1974	29.5	2001	30.0
Kuwait	1970	28.8	1994	30.3
Lebanon	1970	30.2	..	..
Occupied Palestinian Territory	1970	31.7	..	..
Oman	..	..	1993	30.7
Qatar	..	..	1996	30.5
Saudi Arabia	..	..	1994	31.4
Syrian Arab Republic	1970	29.8	1991	30.1
Turkey	1970	29.1	2000	26.6
United Arab Emirates	..	..	1993	31.0
Yemen	1977	30.4	1996	30.3
Europe				
Eastern Europe				
Belarus	1970	27.7	2001	25.8
Bulgaria	1970	24.7	2001	25.1
Czech Republic	1970	25.0	2001	27.5
Hungary	1970	25.5	2001	27.6
Poland	1971	26.9	2001	27.6
Republic of Moldova	1969	28.2	2001	25.6
Romania	1970	26.7	2000	25.7
Russian Federation	1970	26.9	2001	25.9
Slovakia	1970	26.3	2001	26.8
Ukraine	1970	26.5	1998	24.7
Northern Europe				
Channel Islands	..	..	..	..
Denmark	1970	26.8	2001	29.7
Estonia	1970	26.7	2001	27.2
Finland	1970	27.1	2001	29.6
Iceland	1970	27.3	2000	28.9
Ireland	1970	30.4	2001	30.7
Latvia	1970	27.0	2001	27.4
Lithuania	1970	27.8	2001	26.8
Norway	1970	27.0	2001	29.4
Sweden	1970	27.0	2001	30.0
United Kingdom	1972	26.6	2000	28.5
Southern Europe				
Albania	1970	29.8	1999	29.8

TABLE II. 3. *(continued)*

Country	Year	Age	Year	Age
Bosnia and Herzegovina	1970	27.5	1998	26.7
Croatia	1970	26.0	2001	27.9
Greece	1970	27.4	1999	28.9
Italy	1970	28.3	2000	30.3
Malta	1975	28.2	2001	28.6
Portugal	1970	29.0	2001	28.8
Serbia and Montenegro	1970	26.1	2000	27.1
Slovenia	1970	26.7	2001	28.5
Spain	1970	29.5	2000	30.7
TFYR Macedonia	1970	27.3	2000	26.4
Western Europe				
Austria	1970	26.7	2001	28.4
Belgium	1970	27.1	1995	28.5
France	1970	27.2	1999	29.4
Germany	1971	26.6	2000	28.8
Luxembourg	1970	27.2	2001	29.3
Netherlands	1970	28.2	2001	30.3
Switzerland	1970	27.8	2001	30.0
Latin America And The Caribbean				
Caribbean				
Bahamas	1970	27.8	1996	27.8
Barbados	1970	27.2	1988	26.8
Cuba	1970	26.7	2000	26.1
Dominican Republic	1973	28.6	1999	28.7
Guadeloupe	1970	29.6	1991	28.5
Haiti	1975	31.3	1998	30.0
Jamaica	1970	27.4	1996	26.8
Martinique	1970	29.6	1992	28.6
Netherlands Antilles	..	..	..	..
Puerto Rico	1970	27.1	2000	25.8
Saint Lucia	1975	27.8	2000	27.9
Saint Vincent and the Grenadines	..	..	..	..
Trinidad and Tobago	1971	27.7	1997	27.3
United States Virgin Islands	1970	26.2	1990	26.7
Central America				
Belize	1970	28.5	1998	27.3
Costa Rica	1970	29.0	1999	26.7
El Salvador	1971	28.8	1996	27.0
Guatemala	1972	28.8	1997	28.2
Honduras	1972	29.3	1994	28.6
Mexico	1974	29.2	1996	27.4
Nicaragua	1983	27.1	1999	26.4
Panama	1970	27.5	2000	26.6
South America				
Argentina	1970	28.1	2000	27.9
Bolivia	..	..	1996	29.1
Brazil	1980	29.4	1994	26.5

TABLE II.3. *(continued)*

Country	Year	Age	Year	Age
Chile	1970	28.4	1999	27.4
Colombia	1974	29.0	1998	26.9
Ecuador	1977	29.3	1997	28.0
French Guiana	1973	27.1	1999	28.2
Guyana	1973	27.7	..	..
Paraguay	1977	29.5	1997	28.7
Peru	1975	30.0	1998	28.6
Suriname	..	..	2000	27.4
Uruguay	1970	27.8	2000	27.5
Venezuela	1970	28.7	2000	26.7
Northern America				
Canada	1970	27.1	1997	28.5
United States of America	1970	26.1	2000	27.4
Oceania				
Australia/New Zealand				
Australia	1970	27.1	2000	29.6
New Zealand	1970	26.7	2000	29.0
Melanesia				
Fiji	1972	28.4	1986	27.7
New Caledonia	1970	27.9	1999	29.5
Papua New Guinea	..	..	1994	29.8
Solomon Islands	1973	30.1	1985	29.5
Vanuatu	1976	30.0	1989	29.3
Micronesia				
Guam	1970	27.7	1992	26.6
Micronesia Federated States of	..	..	..	..
Polynesia				
French Polynesia	1968	28.4	..	..
Samoa	..	..	1991	31.7
Tonga	..	..	..	..

TABLE II.4. MEAN AGE AT FIRST BIRTH BY COUNTRY

Country	Year	Age	Year	Age	
Africa					
Eastern Africa					
Burundi	..	..	1997	20.9	a
Comoros	..	..	1996	22.4	a
Djibouti	..	..	..	..	
Eritrea	..	..	2002	20.6	a
Ethiopia	..	..	2000	20.1	a
Kenya	..	..	1998	19.6	a
Madagascar	..	..	1997	19.8	a
Malawi	..	..	2000	19.2	a
Mauritius	1967	22.5	1997	24.5	
Mozambique	..	..	1997	18.7	a
Réunion	1970	24.1	..	..	
Rwanda	..	..	2000	22.0	a
Somalia	..	..	..	..	
Uganda	..	..	2000-2001	18.9	a
United Republic of Tanzania	..	..	1999	19.5	a
Zambia	..	..	2001-2002	19.0	a
Zimbabwe	..	..	1999	20.3	a
Middle Africa					
Angola	..	..	..	..	
Cameroon	..	..	1998	20.3	a
Central African Republic	..	..	1994-1995	19.4	a
Chad	..	..	1996-1997	18.2	a
Congo	..	..	..	..	
Democratic Republic of the Congo	..	..	..	..	
Equatorial Guinea	..	..	..	..	
Gabon	..	..	2000	18.7	a
Sao Tome and Principe	..	..	..	..	
Northern Africa					
Algeria	..	..	1992	24.9	a
Egypt	1976	26.6	1995	27.1	
Libyan Arab Jamahiriya	..	..	..	..	
Morocco	..	..	1995	23.3	a
Sudan	..	..	1990	22.8	a
Tunisia	1970	23.7	1997	26.9	
Western Sahara	..	..	..	..	
Southern Africa					
Botswana	..	..	..	..	
Lesotho	..	..	..	..	
Namibia	..	..	1992	21.2	a
South Africa	..	..	1998	20.9	a
Swaziland	..	..	..	..	
Western Africa					
Benin	..	..	2001	20.2	a
Burkina Faso	..	..	1999	19.0	a

TABLE II.4. (continued)

Country	Year	Age	Year	Age	
Cape Verde	..	..	..	..	
Côte d'Ivoire	..	..	1998-1999	19.5	b
Gambia	..	..	..	..	
Ghana	..	..	1998	20.9	a
Guinea	..	..	1999	18.6	a
Guinea-Bissau	..	..	..	..	
Liberia	..	..	1986	19.0	a
Mali	..	..	2001	18.6	a
Mauritania	..	..	2000-2001	21.9	a
Niger	..	..	2001	19.6	a
Nigeria	..	..	1999	20.4	a
Senegal	..	..	1997	20.4	a
Sierra Leone	..	..	..	..	
Togo	..	..	1998	18.9	a
Asia					
Eastern Asia					
China	..	..	..	..	
China, Hong Kong SAR	1970	25.2	1998	28.3	
China, Macao SAR	1970	25.0	1998	28.3	
Dem. People's Republic of Korea	..	..	..	..	
Japan	1970	25.9	1998	27.9	
Mongolia	..	..	..	..	
Republic of Korea	1978	25.2	1998	27.1	
South-Central Asia					
Afghanistan	..	..	..	..	
Bangladesh	1975-1976	16.5	1999-2000	18.2	b
Bhutan	..	..	..	..	
India	..	..	1998-1999	19.5	a
Iran (Islamic Republic of)	..	..	..	..	
Kazakhstan	..	..	1998	23.5	
Kyrgyzstan	..	..	1998	23.3	
Maldives	..	..	1996	22.1	
Nepal	1976	19.8	2001	19.7	b
Pakistan	1975	19.9	1990-1991	22.0	b
Sri Lanka	1981	25.2	1995	26.2	
Tajikistan	..	..	..	..	
Turkmenistan	..	..	2000	23.3	a
Uzbekistan	..	..	1999	23.4	
South-Eastern Asia					
Brunei Darussalam	1978	23.5	1988	24.8	
Cambodia	..	..	2000	21.5	a
Democratic Republic of Timor-Leste	..	..	..	..	
Indonesia	1976	19.4	2003	20.2	b
Lao People's Democratic Republic	..	..	..	..	
Malaysia	1974	22.3	..	..	a
Myanmar	..	..	..	..	
Philippines	1978	23.3	1998	23.9	b
Singapore	1970	25.0	1998	28.1	

TABLE II.4 *(continued)*

Country	Year	Age	Year	Age
Thailand	1970	23.0	2001	24.3
Viet Nam	..	..	..	..
Western Asia				
Armenia	1985	22.5	2000	23.0
Azerbaijan	..	..	2001	24.7
Bahrain	..	..	1997	25.3
Cyprus	1975	24.0	2001	28.6
Georgia	..	..	2000	24.2
Iraq	..	..	..	..
Israel	1970	22.9	1997	21.7
Jordan	1976	19.8	1997	24.7 [b]
Kuwait	1970	22.4	1986	24.1
Lebanon	..	..	..	..
Occupied Palestinian Territory	..	..	..	..
Oman	..	..	..	..
Qatar	..	..	1997	24.9
Saudi Arabia	..	..	..	..
Syrian Arab Republic	..	..	..	..
Turkey	1970	20.1	1985	21.7
United Arab Emirates	..	..	..	..
Yemen	..	..	1997	19.2 [b]
Europe				
Eastern Europe				
Belarus	..	..	2001	23.4
Bulgaria	1970	22.1	2001	23.1
Czech Republic	1970	22.5	2001	25.3
Hungary	1970	22.8	2001	25.3
Poland	1970	22.8	2001	24.8
Republic of Moldova	..	..	2001	22.8
Romania	1970	22.6	2000	23.6
Russian Federation	1979	23.0	1998	23.1
Slovakia	1970	22.6	2001	24.3
Ukraine	..	..	..	..
Northern Europe				
Channel Islands	..	..	..	..
Denmark	1970	23.8	1995	27.4
Estonia	1970	24.1	2001	24.2
Finland	1970	24.4	2001	27.5
Iceland	1970	21.3	2000	25.5
Ireland	1975	25.5	2001	28.0
Latvia	1980	22.9	2001	24.6
Lithuania	1980	23.8	2001	24.1
Norway	1970	24.0	2001	27.0
Sweden	1970	25.9	2001	28.2
United Kingdom	..	..	2000	29.1 [a]

TABLE II.4. (continued)

Country	Year	Age	Year	Age	
Southern Europe					
Albania	1967	22.9	1989	24.7	
Bosnia and Herzegovina	1970	23.0	1990	23.6	
Croatia	1970	23.1	2000	25.5	
Greece	1970	25.0	1999	27.3	
Italy	1970	25.0	1995-1996	28.0	
Malta	..	..	..	..	
Portugal	1970	24.8	2001	26.7	
Serbia and Montenegro	1970	22.7	2000	25.0	
Slovenia	1970	23.7	2001	26.7	
Spain	1975	25.3	2000	29.1	
TFYR Macedonia	1975	22.1	1987	23.0	b
Western Europe					
Austria	1985	24.3	2001	23.0	
Belgium	1970	24.3	1990	26.4	c
France	1970	24.4	1999	28.7	c
Germany	1970	24.0	2000	28.2	c
Luxembourg	1970	24.4	2001	28.3	c
Netherlands	1970	24.8	2001	28.6	
Switzerland	1970	25.3	2001	28.8	c
Latin America And The Caribbean					
Caribbean					
Bahamas	1970	22.8	1996	23.5	
Barbados	..	..	..	..	
Cuba	1982	21.9	1996	23.1	
Dominican Republic	1975	19.8	1999	21.1	b
Guadeloupe	1967	25.1	..	..	
Haiti	..	..	2000	21.9	a
Jamaica	1975-1976	19.2	..	..	a
Martinique	1967	26.7	..	..	
Netherlands Antilles	..	..	..	..	
Puerto Rico	1972	22.7	1998	23.3	
Saint Lucia	1960	20.5	1998	23.1	
Saint Vincent and the Grenadines	1960	19.8	1997	22.1	
Trinidad and Tobago	1970	22.2	1997	23.8	
United States Virgin Islands	..	..	..	..	
Central America					
Belize	..	..	..	..	
Costa Rica	1973	22.5	1997	22.6	
El Salvador	1971	22.1	1998	23.0	
Guatemala	1970	22.0	1998-1999	22.7	b
Honduras	..	..	..	..	
Mexico	1972	24.4	1995	23.8	
Nicaragua	..	..	1997-1998	19.8	a
Panama	1970	21.7	1997	22.3	
South America					
Argentina	..	..	1987	23.7	

TABLE II.4 *(continued)*

Country	Year	Age	Year	Age	
Bolivia	..	..	1998	21.0	a
Brazil	..	..	1996	22.1	a
Chile	1970	24.1	1998	23.4	
Colombia	1976	21.3	2000	21.8	b
Ecuador	1970	22.7	1998	23.0	
French Guiana	1967	24.1	..	..	
Guyana	1977	20.4	..	..	a
Paraguay	..	..	1990	21.6	a
Peru	1977/78	23.0	2000	22.2	b
Suriname	..	..	1995	24.2	
Uruguay	..	..	1996	23.8	
Venezuela	1971	23.2	1998	23.6	
Northern America					
Canada	1970	23.7	1997	26.7	
United States of America	1969	22.5	1998	25.0	
Oceania					
Australia/New Zealand					
Australia	..	..	1996	27.7	
New Zealand	1970	24.0	1998	29.6	
Melanesia					
Fiji	1970	23.3	1987	22.3	
New Caledonia	1976	23.6	..	..	
Papua New Guinea	..	..	..	..	
Solomon Islands	..	..	..	..	
Vanuatu	..	..	..	..	
Micronesia					
Guam	..	..	..	..	
Micronesia Federated States of	..	..	..	..	
Polynesia					
French Polynesia	..	..	2000	24.2	
Samoa	1976	27.8	..	..	
Tonga	..	..	..	..	

[a] Median age at first birth among women aged 25-29 at the date of the survey

[a] Median age at first birth among women aged 25-29 at the date of the survey for both dates

[c] Mean age at first birth within current marriage

TABLE II.5. PERCENTAGE OF EXTRA-MARITAL BIRTHS AMONG ALL BIRTHS BY COUNTRY

Country	Year	Percentage	Year	Percentage
Africa				
Eastern Africa				
Burundi	..	..	..	..
Comoros	..	..	..	..
Djibouti	..	..	..	..
Eritrea	..	..	..	..
Ethiopia	..	..	..	..
Kenya	..	..	..	..
Madagascar	..	..	..	..
Malawi	..	..	..	..
Mauritius	1967	0	1997	18
Mozambique	..	..	..	..
Réunion	1970	24	1986	49
Rwanda	1978	5	..	..
Somalia	..	..	..	..
Uganda	..	..	..	..
United Republic of Tanzania	..	..	..	..
Zambia	..	..	..	..
Zimbabwe	..	..	..	..
Middle Africa				
Angola	..	..	..	..
Cameroon	..	..	..	..
Central African Republic	..	..	..	..
Chad	..	..	..	..
Congo	..	..	..	..
Democratic Republic of the Congo	..	..	..	..
Equatorial Guinea	..	..	..	..
Gabon	..	..	..	..
Sao Tome and Principe	1970	85	..	..
Northern Africa				
Algeria	1964	0	..	..
Egypt	1969	0	..	..
Libyan Arab Jamahiriya	..	..	..	..
Morocco	..	..	..	..
Sudan	..	..	..	..
Tunisia	1970	0	..	..
Western Sahara	..	..	..	..
Southern Africa				
Botswana	..	..	..	..
Lesotho	..	..	..	..
Namibia	..	..	..	..
South Africa	..	..	..	..
Swaziland	..	..	..	..
Western Africa				
Benin	..	..	..	..
Burkina Faso	..	..	..	..

TABLE II.5. *(continued)*

Country	Year	Percentage	Year	Percentage
Cape Verde..................................	1970	51	..	..
Côte d'Ivoire...............................	..	..	..	..
Gambia.......................................	..	..	..	..
Ghana...	..	..	..	..
Guinea	..	..	..	..
Guinea-Bissau	..	..	..	..
Liberia..	..	..	..	..
Mali..	..	..	..	..
Mauritania..................................	..	..	..	..
Niger	..	..	..	..
Nigeria..	..	..	..	..
Senegal	..	..	..	..
Sierra Leone	..	..	..	..
Togo	..	..	..	..
Asia				
Eastern Asia				
China	..	..	..	..
China, Hong Kong SAR........................	1970	0	1998	5
China, Macao SAR................................	1970	1	..	..
Dem. People's Republic of Korea............	..	..	..	..
Japan	1970	1	1998	1
Mongolia....................................	..	..	1989	19
Republic of Korea	..	..	..	..
South-Central Asia				
Afghanistan	..	..	..	..
Bangladesh	..	..	..	..
Bhutan	..	..	..	..
India	..	..	..	..
Iran (Islamic Republic of)	..	..	..	..
Kazakhstan.................................	1980	10	1998	22
Kyrgyzstan	1980	11	1998	27
Maldives.....................................	..	..	1996	1
Nepal..	..	..	..	..
Pakistan	..	..	..	..
Sri Lanka....................................	..	..	1996	1
Tajikistan....................................	1980	7	1994	9
Turkmenistan	1980	3	..	..
Uzbekistan..................................	1980	4	1999	8
South-Eastern Asia				
Brunei Darussalam.....................	..	..	1982	0
Cambodia	..	..	..	..
Democratic Republic of Timor-Leste......	..	..	..	..
Indonesia	..	..	..	..
Lao People's Democratic Republic..........	..	..	..	..
Malaysia.....................................	..	..	..	..
Myanmar	..	..	..	..
Philippines..................................	..	..	..	..
Singapore	..	..	..	..

TABLE II.5. *(continued)*

Country	Year	Percentage	Year	Percentage
Thailand	1970	6	2001	10
Viet Nam	..	..	..	..
Western Asia				
Armenia	1970	2	2001	15
Azerbaijan	1970	3	2001	7
Bahrain	..	..	..	..
Cyprus	1970	0	2000	2
Georgia	1975	0	2001	44
Iraq	..	..	..	..
Israel	1970	1	1996	3
Jordan	..	..	..	..
Kuwait	..	..	..	..
Lebanon	..	..	..	..
Occupied Palestinian Territory	..	..	..	..
Oman	..	..	..	..
Qatar	..	..	..	..
Saudi Arabia	..	..	..	..
Syrian Arab Republic	..	..	..	..
Turkey	1975	4	1990	5
United Arab Emirates	..	..	..	..
Yemen	..	..	..	..
Europe				
Eastern Europe				
Belarus	1970	7	2001	21
Bulgaria	1970	9	2001	42
Czech Republic	1970	5	2001	24
Hungary	1970	5	2001	30
Poland	1970	5	2001	13
Republic of Moldova	1980	7	1998	17
Romania	1970	4	2001	27
Russian Federation	1970	11	2001	29
Slovakia	1970	6	2001	20
Ukraine	1970	9	2001	18
Northern Europe				
Channel Islands	1964	11	1995	27
Denmark	1970	11	1997	45
Estonia	1970	14	2001	56
Finland	1970	6	2001	40
Iceland	1970	30	2000	65
Ireland	1970	3	2001	31
Latvia	1970	11	2001	42
Lithuania	1970	5	2001	25
Norway	1970	7	2001	50
Sweden	1970	18	2001	56
United Kingdom	1970	8	2001	40
Southern Europe				
Albania	..	..	..	..

TABLE II.5. *(continued)*

Country	Year	Percentage	Year	Percentage
Bosnia and Herzegovina	1970	5	1990	7
Croatia	1970	5	2001	9
Greece	1970	1	1999	4
Italy	1970	2	2000	10
Malta	1970	1	2001	13
Portugal	1970	7	2001	24
Serbia and Montenegro	1970	12	2000	20
Slovenia	1970	9	2001	39
Spain	1970	1	2000	18
TFYR Macedonia	..	..	..	..
Western Europe				
Austria	1970	13	2001	33
Belgium	1970	3	1995	17
France	1970	7	2000	43
Germany	1970	9	2000	23
Luxembourg	1970	4	1998	17
Netherlands	1970	2	2001	27
Switzerland	1970	4	2001	11
Latin America And The Caribbean				
Caribbean				
Bahamas	1970	29	1996	56
Barbados	1970	71	..	..
Cuba	..	..	..	..
Dominican Republic	1970	63	..	..
Guadeloupe	1970	43	1991	61
Haiti	..	..	..	..
Jamaica	1964	74	1989	86
Martinique	1970	51	1992	66
Netherlands Antilles	1970	31	1991	55
Puerto Rico	1970	19	1998	47
Saint Lucia	1971	72	1998	86
Saint Vincent and the Grenadines	..	..	..	..
Trinidad and Tobago	1970	41	..	..
United States Virgin Islands	1970	45	1990	63
Central America				
Belize	1970	44	1997	58
Costa Rica	1970	29	1997	48
El Salvador	1970	68	1998	73
Guatemala	1970	62	..	..
Honduras	..	..	..	..
Mexico	1970	27	1993	38
Nicaragua	..	..	..	..
Panama	1970	71	1997	80
South America				
Argentina	..	..	1998	53
Bolivia	..	..	..	..
Brazil	..	..	..	..

TABLE II.5. *(continued)*

Country	Year	Percentage	Year	Percentage
Chile...	1970	19	1998	46
Colombia...	..	..	..	..
Ecuador	1966	32	..	..
French Guiana.................................	1970	63	1986	75
Guyana	1970	37	..	..
Paraguay...	1970	43	..	..
Peru	1972	41	..	..
Suriname	1962	34	1997	66
Uruguay...	1970	21	1997	47
Venezuela..	1970	39	..	..
Northern America				
Canada..	1970	10	2000	38
United States of America	1970	11	1999	33
Oceania				
Australia/New Zealand				
Australia..	1970	8	1996	27
New Zealand	1970	13	1998	42
Melanesia				
Fiji...	1978	17	..	..
New Caledonia.................................	1982	46	1994	63
Papua New Guinea...........................	..	..	..	..
Solomon Islands...............................	..	..	..	..
Vanuatu...	..	..	..	..
Micronesia				
Guam...	1970	9	1992	41
Micronesia Federated States of	..	..	..	..
Polynesia				
French Polynesia..............................	1968	55	..	..
Samoa..	1975	59	..	..
Tonga	..	..	..	..

TABLE II.6. AVERAGE NUMBER OF CHILDREN EVER BORN BY AGE OF WOMEN AND COUNTRY

Country	Year	Age of women			Year	Age of women		
		35-39	40-44	45-49		35-39	40-44	45-49
Africa								
Eastern Africa								
Burundi...		..	..	..	1987	5.6	6.6	7.3
Comoros		..	..	..	1996	5.3	6.4	7.1
Djibouti...		..	..	..		..	..	..
Eritrea		..	..	..	2002	4.7	5.7	6.2
Ethiopia...		..	..	..	2000	5.7	6.7	7.2
Kenya..	1969	6.2	6.7	7.0	1998	5.3	6.4	6.9
Madagascar.......................................		..	..	..	1997	5.6	6.4	7.0
Malawi	1977	6.0	6.7	6.9	2000	5.6	6.6	7.0
Mauritius...		..	..	..	2000	2.3	2.6	3.0
Mozambique	1980	5.2	5.6	5.6	1997	5.0	5.7	5.9
Réunion...	1967	4.9	5.4	5.4		..	..	..
Rwanda	1978	6.2	7.1	7.3	2000	5.3	6.4	7.4
Somalia...		..	..	..		..	..	..
Uganda..		..	..	..	2000-2001	6.1	6.9	7.4
United Republic of Tanzania	1967	4.8	5.0	5.2	1999	5.0	6.4	7.0
Zambia..	1969	6.7	6.8	6.7	2001-2002	5.7	6.9	7.4
Zimbabwe		..	..	..	1999	4.5	5.5	6.3
Middle Africa								
Angola		..	..	..		..	..	..
Cameroon..	1978	4.9	5.2	5.2	1998	5.2	6.1	6.4
Central African Republic	1975	4.5	4.7	4.8	1994-1995	4.8	5.7	5.8
Chad..		..	..	..	1996-1997	6.3	6.7	6.9
Congo		..	..	..		..	..	..
Democratic Republic of the Congo...		..	..	..		..	..	..
Equatorial Guinea.............................		..	..	..		..	..	..
Gabon		..	..	..	2000	4.9	5.9	6.1
Sao Tome and Principe	1980	5.7	5.9	5.8	1991	5.3	5.9	6.2
Northern Africa								
Algeria		..	..	..	1992	5.4	6.8	7.6
Egypt...	1976 [a]	4.4	4.7	5.0	2000	4.2	4.9	5.4
Libyan Arab Jamahiriya....................	1973 [a]	7.0	7.5	7.7	1995	6.1	8.0	9.0
Morocco..	1979-1980	6.1	7.1	7.1	1995	3.9	5.5	6.8
Sudan	1978-1979	5.8	5.9	6.2	1990	6.0	7.0	7.5
Tunisia	1978	5.7	6.3	6.5		..	..	..
Western Sahara		..	..	..		..	..	..
Southern Africa								
Botswana	1971	5.1	5.6	5.6	1991	4.6	5.6	6.1
Lesotho	1977	4.6	5.0	5.2		..	..	..
Namibia...		..	..	..	1991	4.6	5.6	6.1
South Africa......................................		..	..	..	1998	3.2	3.5	4.0
Swaziland..		..	..	..	1997	4.7	5.5	6.0
Western Africa								
Benin...	1982	5.7	6.1	6.3	2001	5.6	6.4	7.2

TABLE II.6. *(continued)*

Country	Year	Age of women			Year	Age of women		
		35-39	*40-44*	*45-49*		*35-39*	*40-44*	*45-49*
Burkina Faso.................................	1985	4.8	4.8	4.8	1999	6.2	7.2	7.7
Cape Verde		..	..	..		..	..	..
Côte d'Ivoire	1980	5.9	6.7	6.9	1998-1999	5.4	6.3	6.6
Gambia	1973	5.4	5.4	5.5		..	..	..
Ghana...	1979-1980	5.4	6.1	6.7	1998	4.5	5.4	5.9
Guinea		..	..	..	1999	5.5	6.2	6.9
Guinea-Bissau...............................		..	..	..		..	..	..
Liberia..		..	..	..	1986	5.3	5.9	6.8
Mali	1984	5.5	5.8	5.9	2001	6.3	7.3	7.9
Mauritania.....................................	1981	5.7	5.9	5.9	2000-2001	5.1	5.6	6.2
Niger..		..	..	..	1998	6.9	7.4	7.6
Nigeria		..	..	..	1999	5.2	6.0	6.3
Senegal	1978	5.9	6.8	7.2	1997	5.8	6.7	7.6
Sierra Leone..................................		..	..	..		..	..	..
Togo...		..	..	..	1998	5.1	6.1	6.7
Asia								
Eastern Asia								
China...		..	..	..	1990	2.5	3.2	4.0
China, Hong Kong SAR	1971[a]	3.8	4.2	4.0		..	..	..
China, Macao SAR	1960[a]	3.4	2.9	2.4		..	..	..
Dem. People's Republic of Korea	1970	4.5	5.3	5.6		..	..	..
Japan...	1970[a]	2.0	2.3	2.7		..	..	..
Mongolia..		..	..	..		..	..	..
Republic of Korea..........................	1970[a]	4.5	5.3	5.6	1990	2.3	2.8	3.4
South-Central Asia								
Afghanistan....................................		..	..	..		..	..	..
Bangladesh.....................................	1975-1976	6.7	7.1	6.8	1999-2000	4.3	5.1	6.1
Bhutan..		..	..	..		..	..	..
India...	1981[a]	4.3	4.8	5.1	1998-1999	3.8	4.3	4.6
Iran (Islamic Republic of)..............		..	..	..	1986	5.6	6.4	6.8
Kazakhstan.....................................		..	..	..	1999	2.4	2.7	3.0
Kyrgyzstan		..	..	..	1997	3.7	4.3	4.9
Maldives	1977	6.4	6.4	6.3	2000	5.1	6.3	7.2
Nepal...	1976	5.1	5.5	5.8	2001	4.5	5.2	5.7
Pakistan..	1974-1975	5.9	6.9	6.8	1990-1991	5.5	6.3	6.4
Sri Lanka	1971[a]	4.7	5.5	5.5	1993	2.6	3.0	3.8
Tajikistan		..	..	..	1989	5.0	5.6	6.0
Turkmenistan		..	..	..	2000	3.6	4.7	5.1
Uzbekistan		..	..	..	1996	4.1	4.5	4.7
South-Eastern Asia								
Brunei Darussalam	1960	4.6	4.7	5.0		..	..	..
Cambodia		..	..	..	2000	4.4	5.2	5.6
Democratic Republic of Timor-Leste		..	..	..		..	..	..
Indonesia..	1971[a]	5.1	5.2	5.2	2003	3.0	3.8	4.3
Lao People's Democratic Republic ...		..	..	..		..	..	..

TABLE II.6. *(continued)*

Country	Year	Age of women			Year	Age of women		
		35-39	40-44	45-49		35-39	40-44	45-49
Malaysia	1970[a]	5.5	5.8	5.6		..	..	..
Myanmar	1983[a]	4.4	5.2	5.4		..	..	..
Philippines	1978	5.2	6.4	6.6	1998	3.8	4.2	4.7
Singapore	1980[a]	2.9	3.7	4.7	1990[a]	1.9	2.2	2.9
Thailand	1970[a]	5.3	6.1	6.4	2000	2.0	2.2	2.5
Viet Nam		..	..	..	1999	2.8	3.4	..
Western Asia								
Armenia		..	..	..	2000	2.5	2.6	2.7
Azerbaijan		..	..	..	2001	2.6	3.0	..
Bahrain	1971	6.1	6.1	6.0	1995	4.3	5.2	6.1
Cyprus	1973[a]	3.1	3.6	3.7	1992[a]	2.2	2.2	2.3
Georgia		..	..	..		..	..	..
Iraq		..	..	..	1987[a]	5.8	6.5	6.7
Israel	1961[a]	3.3	3.5	3.3		..	..	..
Jordan	1976	7.1	8.4	8.6	1997	5.0	6.5	7.2
Kuwait	1975[a]	5.2	5.7	5.8		..	..	..
Lebanon		..	..	..		..	..	..
Occupied Palestinian Territory		..	..	..	1997[a]	6.3	7.4	7.5
Oman		..	..	..	1995	7.9	8.6	8.6
Qatar		..	..	..	1998	4.6	5.6	6.6
Saudi Arabia		..	..	..	1996	6.8	7.7	8.2
Syrian Arab Republic	1970[a]	6.6	7.4	7.8		..	..	..
Turkey	1970[a]	4.8	5.2	5.1	1998	3.3	4.0	4.5
United Arab Emirates	1975[a]	4.7	4.6	4.6	1995[a]	6.6	7.6	7.9
Yemen	1979[a]	6.0	6.4	7.2	1997[a]	7.1	8.0	8.8
Europe								
Eastern Europe								
Belarus		..	..	..	1999	1.8	1.9	1.9
Bulgaria	1975[a]	2.0	2.0	2.0	1997-1998	1.6	1.7	..
Czech Republic		..	..	..	1991	2.0	2.0	2.0
Hungary	1970	1.9	2.0	2.1	1990	1.9	1.9	1.9
Poland	1970[a]	2.6	2.9	2.9	1991	2.1	2.2	2.3
Republic of Moldova		..	..	..	1989	2.2	2.2	2.4
Romania	1966	2.2	2.5	2.7	1992	2.1	2.3	2.3
Russian Federation		..	..	..	1994	1.8	1.9	1.8
Slovakia		..	..	..		..	..	..
Ukraine		..	..	..	1989	1.8	1.9	1.9
Northern Europe								
Channel Islands	1961[a]	1.9	1.9	2.0		..	..	..
Denmark		..	..	..		..	..	..
Estonia		..	..	..	1994	2.1	2.1	2.0

TABLE II.6. *(continued)*

Country	Year	Age of women 35-39	Age of women 40-44	Age of women 45-49	Year	Age of women 35-39	Age of women 40-44	Age of women 45-49
Finland		..	..	..	2000	1.8	1.9	1.9
Iceland		..	..	..		..	..	..
Ireland		..	..	..	2002	1.7	2.0	2.0
Latvia		..	..	..	1995	1.9	1.8	1.7
Lithuania		..	..	..	1994-1995	1.8	1.7	1.8
Norway	1960	2.2	2.4	2.3	1988-1989	1.8	2.1	2.2
Sweden		..	..	..	1992-1993	2.0	2.0	..
United Kingdom		..	..	..		..	..	..
Southern Europe								
Albania		..	..	..		..	..	..
Bosnia and Herzegovina		..	..	..		..	..	..
Croatia		..	..	..	1991	1.9	1.9	2.0
Greece		..	..	..		..	..	..
Italy		..	..	..	1995-1996	1.6	1.9	2.0
Malta		..	..	..		..	..	..
Portugal	1970	2.5	2.8	2.9	1991	1.9	2.1	2.3
Serbia and Montenegro		..	..	..		..	..	..
Slovenia		..	..	..	1994-1995	1.7	2.0	2.0
Spain		..	..	..	1994-1995	1.9	2.1	2.5
TFYR Macedonia	1970	5.3	6.1	6.4	2000	2.0	2.2	2.5
Western Europe								
Austria	1981	2.0	2.2	2.4	1995-1996	1.7	2.0	2.0
Belgium	1970	2.2	2.3	2.2	1992 [a]	1.8	..	..
France		..	..	..	1994	2.1	2.2	2.2
Germany		..	..	..		..	..	..
Luxembourg	1970 [a]	1.9	1.9	1.8	1991	1.5	1.7	1.8
Netherlands		..	..	..	1993	1.8	..	..
Switzerland		..	..	..	1994-1995	1.7	1.7	1.8
Latin America And The Caribbean								
Caribbean								
Bahamas	1980	4.1	4.8	5.2	1990	3.0	3.6	4.3
Barbados	1980	3.3	3.9	4.3		..	..	..
Cuba	1981	3.0	3.4	3.7		..	..	..
Dominican Republic	1970	5.6	5.8	6.0	1999	3.1	3.9	4.2
Guadeloupe	1967	5.1	6.0	5.7		..	..	..
Haiti	1977	4.5	5.6	5.9	2000	4.6	5.2	5.5
Jamaica	1975-1976	5.1	5.4	5.5	1991	3.4	4.1	4.6
Martinique	1967	5.3	5.8	5.5		..	..	..
Netherlands Antilles	1971	3.9	4.7	5.1	2001	2.0	2.2	2.3
Puerto Rico	1970	3.7	3.9	4.3	1990	2.4	2.7	3.1
Saint Lucia	1980	5.1	5.8	6.2	1992	3.3	3.9	4.3
Saint Vincent and the Grenadines	1980	5.4	6.4	6.4	1991	3.6	4.3	4.9
Trinidad and Tobago	1977	4.3	5.2	5.8	1990	3.0	3.5	4.1
United States Virgin Islands	1970 [a]	3.0	2.9	2.7		..	..	..

TABLE II.6. *(continued)*

Country	Year	Age of women 35-39	40-44	45-49	Year	Age of women 35-39	40-44	45-49
Central America								
Belize	1980	6.0	6.9	6.9	1991	5.0	5.7	6.3
Costa Rica	1973	5.5	6.4	6.7		..	..	..
El Salvador	1971	5.6	6.3	6.4	1998	3.7	4.2	4.9
Guatemala	1973	5.6	6.2	6.5	1998-1999	4.9	5.6	5.7
Honduras	1974	6.2	7.0	7.2		..	..	..
Mexico	1970	5.6	5.9	5.8	2000	3.2	3.8	4.4
Nicaragua	1971	6.2	6.7	6.8	2001	4.3	5.1	5.7
Panama	1975-1976	4.9	5.6	5.8	1990	3.6	4.2	4.8
South America								
Argentina	1970	2.7	2.9	2.9	1991	2.7	2.8	2.8
Bolivia	1976	5.1	5.7	5.9	1998	4.2	5.0	5.1
Brazil	1970	4.8	5.3	5.5	1996	3.0	3.5	3.9
Chile	1982	3.1	3.8	4.3	1992	2.5	2.9	3.2
Colombia	1973	5.4	6.1	6.4	2000	2.7	3.2	3.7
Ecuador	1974	5.6	6.4	6.7	2001	3.2	3.7	4.2
French Guiana	1967	3.7	3.7	3.4		..	..	..
Guyana	1970	5.9	6.0	5.7		..	..	..
Paraguay	1979	4.6	5.8	6.3	1992	4.3	4.9	5.4
Peru	1972	5.6	6.3	6.6	2000	3.5	4.2	4.7
Suriname	1964	4.9	5.1	5.0		..	..	..
Uruguay	1975	2.5	2.6	2.6	1996	2.4	2.6	2.7
Venezuela	1961	4.9	4.9	4.8	1990	3.4	4.0	4.6
Northern America								
Canada	1961 [a]	2.8	2.9	2.8	1991	1.8	2.0	2.2
United States of America	1980	2.4	2.9	3.1	2000	1.8	1.9	..
Oceania								
Australia/New Zealand								
Australia	1976 [a]	2.7	3.0	2.9	1986	2.2	2.5	2.7
New Zealand	1976 [a]	2.9	3.2	3.2		..	..	..
Melanesia								
Fiji	1966	5.8	6.3	6.4	1986	3.7	4.3	4.9
New Caledonia		..	..	..		..	..	..
Papua New Guinea	1980	4.3	4.6	4.6		..	..	..
Solomon Islands	1970	5.0	5.7	5.9		..	..	..
Vanuatu	1967	5.7	5.7	5.9	1989	4.5	5.2	..
Micronesia								
Guam	1960 [a]	3.9	4.1	..		..	..	..
Micronesia Federated States of		..	..	..	1994	4.7	5.7	..
Polynesia								
French Polynesia		..	..	..		..	..	..
Samoa	1971	6.2	6.7	6.8		..	..	..
Tonga	1966	5.3	6.5	6.7	1996	4.1	4.9	..

TABLE II.7. PERCENTAGE OF CHILDLESS WOMEN AMONG ALL WOMEN BY AGE OF WOMEN AND COUNTRY

Country	Year	Age of women			Year	Age of women		
		35-39	*40-44*	*45-49*		*35-39*	*40-44*	*45-49*
Africa								
Eastern Africa								
Burundi		..	..	..	1987	2.8	1.7	2.1
Comoros		..	..	..	1996	5.4	4.7	2.4
Djibouti		..	..	..		..	..	..
Eritrea		..	..	..	2002	5.3	3.1	3.4
Ethiopia		..	..	..	2000	3.5	1.8	2.4
Kenya	1969	4.1	3.9	4.2	1998	2.4	1.7	2.6
Madagascar		..	..	..	1997	4.5	6.0	5.4
Malawi	1977	3.5	3.7	3.8	2000	2.2	1.8	2.0
Mauritius		..	..	..	2000	5.0	4.6	4.6
Mozambique	1980	9.3	10.8	12.3	1997	7.1	7.7	8.4
Réunion	1967	16.8	18.5	20.6		..	..	..
Rwanda	1978	2.1	1.8	2.0	2000	2.4	1.3	1.5
Somalia		..	..	..		..	..	..
Uganda		..	..	..	2000-2001	3.6	4.7	3.7
United Republic of Tanzania	1967	10.7	11.8	11.3	1999	3.3	1.9	0.6
Zambia	1969	2.5	2.9	4.1	2001-2002	2.5	1.7	1.8
Zimbabwe		..	..	..	1999	3.7	2.7	1.9
Middle Africa								
Angola		..	..	..		..	..	..
Cameroon	1978	..	..	..	1998	5.7	4.4	8.0
Central African Republic	1975	15.2	17.0	17.0	1994-1995	7.5	7.9	8.4
Chad		..	..	..	1996-1997	2.7	4.0	4.3
Congo		..	..	..		..	..	..
Democratic Republic of the Congo		..	..	..		..	..	..
Equatorial Guinea		..	..	..		..	..	..
Gabon		..	..	..	2000	4.5	3.1	7.0
Sao Tome and Principe	1980	5.7	6.5	7.8	1991	2.9	3.3	3.5
Northern Africa								
Algeria		..	..	..	1992	9.7	6.4	3.9
Egypt	1976[a]	8.4	9.2	9.0	2000	6.3	5.2	4.8
Libyan Arab Jamahiriya	1973[a]	3.3	3.6	3.8	1995	13.5	5.7	4.3
Morocco	1979-1980	..	..	..	1995	16.9	9.3	3.7
Sudan	1978-1979	5.8	7.5	7.1	1990	8.0	7.0	4.4
Tunisia	1978	3.4	2.9	..		..	..	..
Western Sahara		..	..	..		..	..	..
Southern Africa								
Botswana	1971	6.1	6.2	6.5	1991	3.9	3.9	3.9
Lesotho	1977	..	..	..		..	..	..
Namibia		..	..	..	1991	5.4	4.7	4.7
South Africa		..	..	..	1998	4.9	4.7	5.2
Swaziland		..	..	..	1997	6.4	5.7	4.9
Western Africa								
Benin	1982	..	..	..	2001	1.3	1.0	2.5
Burkina Faso	1985	4.4	5.7	6.0	1999	1.6	1.2	1.1

TABLE II.7. *(continued)*

Country	Year	Age of women			Year	Age of women		
		35-39	40-44	45-49		35-39	40-44	45-49
Cape Verde		..	..	..		..	..	..
Côte d'Ivoire	1980	..	..	..	1998-1999	3.1	2.5	2.2
Gambia	1973	7.5	9.3	7.9		..	..	..
Ghana	1979-1980	..	..	..	1998	3.2	1.1	2.5
Guinea		..	..	..	1999	2.2	2.4	2.1
Guinea-Bissau		..	..	..		..	..	..
Liberia		..	..	..	1986	3.2	3.4	2.6
Mali	1984	3.6	3.7	3.7	2001	3.0	2.6	2.1
Mauritania	1981	..	..	..	2000-2001	8.3	6.9	7.0
Niger		..	..	..	1998	1.6	2.9	5.6
Nigeria		..	..	..	1999	3.5	4.2	3.0
Senegal	1978	..	..	..	1997	2.9	2.4	1.7
Sierra Leone		..	..	..		..	..	..
Togo		..	..	..	1998	2.7	1.6	2.1
Asia								
Eastern Asia								
China		..	..	..	1990	1.2	1.1	1.2
China, Hong Kong SAR	1971 [a]	3.8	3.9	5.0		..	..	..
China, Macao SAR	1960 [a]	..	..	..		..	..	..
Dem. People's Republic of Korea	1970	2.3	1.8	2.2		..	..	..
Japan	1970 [a]	5.9	6.8	7.4		..	..	..
Mongolia		..	..	..		..	..	..
Republic of Korea	1970 [a]	1.9	1.7	2.1	1990	2.1	1.5	1.3
South-Central Asia								
Afghanistan		..	..	..		..	..	..
Bangladesh	1975-1976	1.6	2.7	2.7	1999-2000	2.5	2.2	1.7
Bhutan		..	..	..		..	..	..
India	1981 [a]	4.3	4.6	4.5	1998-1999	4.5	3.8	3.8
Iran (Islamic Republic of)		..	..	..	1986	..	..	..
Kazakhstan		..	..	..	1999	7.7	5.8	5.1
Kyrgyzstan		..	..	..	1997	3.1	3.1	2.7
Maldives	1977	4.8	6.1	6.2	2000	4.7	4.1	3.2
Nepal	1976	3.1	4.4	4.5	2001	4.2	2.9	3.1
Pakistan	1974-1975	4.4	4.2	2.9	1990-1991	5.4	5.5	5.5
Sri Lanka	1971 [a]	6.3	4.0	2.7	1993	15.4	13.2	7.9
Tajikistan		..	..	..	1989	4.3	4.1	4.3
Turkmenistan		..	..	..	2000	5.1	2.6	1.4
Uzbekistan		..	..	..	1996	2.3	1.9	2.8
South-Eastern Asia								
Brunei Darussalam	1960	6.0	6.6	6.8		..	..	..
Cambodia		..	..	..	2000	8.1	7.6	8.2
Democratic Republic of Timor-Leste		..	..	..		..	..	..
Indonesia	1971 [a]	4.8	5.9	6.6	2003	6.6	5.5	4.9
Lao People's Democratic Republic		..	..	..		..	..	..

TABLE II.7. *(continued)*

Country	Year	Age of women 35-39	40-44	45-49	Year	Age of women 35-39	40-44	45-49
Malaysia	1970[a]	2.2	2.7	3.2		..	..	..
Myanmar	1983[a]	4.9	4.9	5.4		..	..	..
Philippines	1978	2.2	2.2	2.4	1998	9.4	9.7	8.7
Singapore	1980[a]	2.9	2.6	2.3	1990[a]	5.4	4.0	2.7
Thailand	1970[a]	1.3	1.4	1.6	2000[a]	7.6	6.9	6.7
Viet Nam		..	..	..	1999	8.2	7.5	..
Western Asia								
Armenia		..	..	..	2000	7.2	8.8	8.9
Azerbaijan		..	..	..	2001	12.4	11.8	..
Bahrain	1971	8.2	9.5	9.1	1995	12.3	9.6	8.9
Cyprus	1973[a]	3.0	3.4	4.4	1992[a]	3.4	3.5	4.2
Georgia		..	..	..		..	..	..
Iraq		..	..	..	1987[a]	5.2	5.4	5.9
Israel	1961[a]	4.2	6.2	7.1		..	..	..
Jordan	1976	2.4	2.3	2.3	1997	14.6	8.6	7.1
Kuwait	1975[a]	4.9	4.9	5.6		..	..	..
Lebanon		..	..	..		..	..	..
Occupied Palestinian Territory		..	..	..	1997[a]	4.7	4.6	5.2
Oman		..	..	..	1995	3.8	2.3	2.1
Qatar		..	..	..	1998	14.7	11.6	6.2
Saudi Arabia		..	..	..	1996	4.4	3.3	3.2
Syrian Arab Republic	1970[a]	3.3	3.6	3.6		..	..	..
Turkey	1970[a]	5.0	5.4	6.0	1998	6.0	3.8	3.7
United Arab Emirates	1975[a]	5.7	7.8	7.1	1995[a]	5.3	2.8	3.0
Yemen	1979[a]	..	..	..	1997	4.3	4.2	2.3
Europe								
Eastern Europe								
Belarus		..	..	..	1999	6.8	6.0	6.1
Bulgaria	1975	3.0	3.2	4.3	1997-1998	8.3	8.2	..
Czech Republic		..	..	..	1991	5.8	5.5	6.2
Hungary	1970	10.9	12.8	14.6	1990	8.9	8.5	8.8
Poland	1970	3.8	4.5	6.0	1991	9.5	6.1	7.2
Republic of Moldova		..	..	..	1989	8.4	9.2	10.5
Romania	1966	14.8	15.6	16.5	1992	10.6	9.7	10.6
Russian Federation		..	..	..	1994	7.5	7.0	7.7
Slovakia		..	..	..		..	..	..
Ukraine		..	..	..	1989	7.4	7.2	7.8
Northern Europe								
Channel Islands	1961	15.7	17.8	18.1		..	..	..
Denmark		..	..	..		..	..	..
Estonia		..	..	..	1994	7.8	6.6	10.8
Finland		..	..	..	2000	21.1	16.8	15.7
Iceland		..	..	..		..	..	..
Ireland		..	..	..	2002	13.9	7.6	9.0

TABLE II.7. *(continued)*

Country	Year	Age of women 35-39	Age of women 40-44	Age of women 45-49	Year	Age of women 35-39	Age of women 40-44	Age of women 45-49
Latvia		..	..	..	1995	5.3	6.9	8.3
Lithuania		..	..	..	1994-1995	9.4	12.2	8.9
Norway	..	..	..	..	1988-1989	15.8	9.4	6.6
Sweden		..	..	..	1992-1993	11.5	11.5	..
United Kingdom		..	..	..		..	..	..
Southern Europe								
Albania		..	..	..		..	..	..
Bosnia and Herzegovina		..	..	..		..	..	..
Croatia		..	..	..	1991	10.7	9.3	9.3
Greece		..	..	..		..	..	..
Italy		..	..	..	1995-1996	16.6	10.5	9.2
Malta		..	..	..		..	..	..
Portugal	1970	15.6	16.2	17.4	1991	10.6	10.0	10.8
Serbia and Montenegro		..	..	..		..	..	..
Slovenia		..	..	..	1994-1995	6.9	3.5	2.6
Spain		..	..	..	1994-1995	9.2	10.5	7.0
TFYR Macedonia	1970	1.3	1.4	1.6	2000	7.6	6.9	6.7
Western Europe								
Austria	1981	15.4	14.2	15.1	1995-1996	13.9	7.6	9.0
Belgium	1970	9.1	10.2	12.0	1992 [a]	12.4	..	..
France		..	..	..	1994 [a]	11.3	7.7	12.0
Germany		..	..	..		..	..	..
Luxembourg	1970	8.6	9.7	11.8	1991	22.9	18.8	17.9
Netherlands		..	..	..	1993	17.0	..	..
Switzerland		..	..	..	1994-1995	22.5	20.4	15.6
Caribbean								
Bahamas	1980	9.1	9.1	8.2	1990	10.9	8.3	8.2
Barbados	1980	11.5	10.7	11.6		..	..	..
Cuba	1981	7.3	7.6	9.1		..	..	..
Dominican Republic	1970	12.9	15.7	15.1	1999	7.9	2.5	4.5
Guadeloupe	1967	10.8	12.1	14.0		..	..	..
Haiti	1977	..	..	..	2000	8.9	9.9	8.8
Jamaica	1975-1976	4.7	6.2	8.2	1991	8.8	7.3	9.0
Martinique	1967	12.0	14.4	17.6		..	..	..
Netherlands Antilles	1971	15.7	15.3	15.8	2001	18.0	15.7	15.1
Puerto Rico	1970	4.3	5.4	6.4	1990	12.6	10.9	9.7
Saint Lucia	1980	7.5	8.3	9.9	1992	10.8	10.7	9.9
Saint Vincent and the Grenadines	1980	5.8	5.8	6.9	1991	8.6	6.4	7.7
Trinidad and Tobago	1977	..	..	..	1990	11.7	9.5	8.3
United States Virgin Islands	1970	6.9	8.2	10.1		..	..	..
Central America								
Belize	1980	5.5	4.4	6.4	1991	6.1	5.4	6.1
Costa Rica	1973	9.9	9.5	10.7		..	..	..
El Salvador	1971	5.4	5.9	6.0	1998	4.2	4.0	4.5
Guatemala	1973	5.2	5.0	5.0	1998-1999	4.1	5.5	3.6

TABLE II.7. *(continued)*

Country	Year	Age of women			Year	Age of women		
		35-39	*40-44*	*45-49*		*35-39*	*40-44*	*45-49*
Honduras	1974	5.2	5.1	5.1		..	..	..
Mexico	1970	12.3	12.4	12.9	2000	8.9	7.1	6.6
Nicaragua	1971	..	..	..	2001	4.1	2.8	4.0
Panama	1975-1976	1.5	2.5	4.1	1990	6.3	5.4	5.2
South America								
Argentina	1970	13.8	12.8	13.8	1991	..	..	..
Bolivia	1976	7.9	7.0	7.0	1998	5.4	3.9	4.2
Brazil	1970	13.7	13.4	13.5	1996	9.8	7.9	8.8
Chile	1982	9.9	9.3	10.1	1992	8.7	7.9	8.4
Colombia	1973	9.0	8.6	8.7	2000	7.9	7.8	8.1
Ecuador	1974	7.8	7.3	7.5	2001	9.0	7.8	7.5
French Guiana	1967	17.9	21.6	23.2		..	..	..
Guyana	1970	6.8	8.0	9.8		..	..	..
Paraguay	1979	..	..	..	1992	7.6	6.8	6.5
Peru	1972	6.8	6.9	7.4	2000	7.7	6.3	6.3
Suriname	1964	..	..	..		..	..	..
Uruguay	1975	16.5	15.8	17.6	1996	11.8	10.6	11.1
Venezuela	1961	14.9	16.3	17.4	1990	7.7	6.7	6.4
Northern America								
Canada	1961	8.3	9.4	11.9	1991	19.8	15.9	13.7
United States of America	1980	13.3	10.8	10.9	2000	20.1	19.0	..
Oceania								
Australia/New Zealand								
Australia	1976	3.8	3.7	4.8	1986	11.9	9.7	9.0
New Zealand	1976	5.2	5.2	6.2		..	..	..
Melanesia								
Fiji	1966	6.8	7.6	8.2	1986	7.3	5.7	5.8
New Caledonia		..	..	..		..	..	..
Papua New Guinea	1980	6.5	6.2	6.8		..	..	..
Solomon Islands	1970	10.4	10.5	10.4		..	..	..
Vanuatu	1967	7.1	8.9	10.0	1989	..	..	..
Micronesia								
Guam	1960	6.9	10.3	..		..	..	..
Micronesia Federated States of		..	..	..	1994	..	..	..
Polynesia								
French Polynesia		..	..	..		..	..	..
Samoa	1971	6.8	6.2	7.1		..	..	..
Tonga	1966	11.5	9.5	10.2	1996	14.2	9.8	..

Note [a] Percentage of childless women among ever married women

TABLE II.8. PERCENTAGE OF WOMEN WITH PARITY THREE OR HIGHER BY AGE OF WOMEN AND COUNTRY

Country	Year	Age of women			Year	Age of women		
		35-39	*40-44*	*45-49*		*35-39*	*40-44*	*45-49*
Africa								
Eastern Africa								
Burundi..............................		..	..	..	1987	91.4	90.6	93.6
Comoros		..	..	..	1996	81.3	82.6	87.6
Djibouti.............................		..	..	..		..	..	..
Eritrea...............................		..	..	..	2002	79.7	84.5	87.4
Ethiopia		..	..	..	2000	87.8	91.2	91.2
Kenya	1969	87.0	87.0	87.1	1998	87.7	92.7	91.1
Madagascar........................		..	..	..	1997	81.4	81.5	84.3
Malawi..............................	1977	87.0	87.5	87.5	2000	87.1	91.5	90.5
Mauritius		..	..	..	2000	36.5	48.1	57.4
Mozambique.......................	1980	77.2	76.7	75.1	1997	78.4	80.1	79.1
Réunion	1967	69.8	70.2	67.7		..	..	..
Rwanda.............................	1978	93.1	94.5	94.2	2000	90.1	91.6	96.1
Somalia.............................		..	..	..		..	..	..
Uganda..............................		..	..	..	2000-2001	86.4	86.5	91.2
United Republic of Tanzania	1967	72.3	71.7	71.8	1999	81.7	88.5	91.0
Zambia..............................	1969	89.1	88.8	86.7	2001-2002	86.1	92.7	91.7
Zimbabwe..........................		..	..	..	1999	83.1	87.7	89.0
Middle Africa								
Angola		..	..	..		..	..	..
Cameroon	1978	..	..	..	1998	80.9	83.6	81.8
Central African Republic...........	1975	64.9	63.7	63.5	1994-1995	74.8	78.7	75.9
Chad		..	..	..	1996-1997	90.8	89.0	88.6
Congo		..	..	..		..	..	..
Democratic Republic of the Congo		..	..	..		..	..	..
Equatorial Guinea.................		..	..	..		..	..	..
Gabon		..	..	..	2000	80.7	82.3	81.8
Sao Tome and Principe..............	1980	85.2	84.1	82.5	1991	83.2	83.2	82.7
Northern Africa								
Algeria..............................		..	..	..	1992	81.5	87.3	90.2
Egypt	1976[a]	74.8	74.9	76.4	2000	78.7	83.1	84.4
Libyan Arab Jamahiriya	1973[a]	91.3	90.9	90.9	1995	81.0	91.6	92.2
Morocco............................	1979-1980	..	..	..	1995	65.6	80.3	85.8
Sudan...............................	1978-1979	80.5	79.9	79.5	1990	84.9	87.1	90.7
Tunisia..............................	1978	84.1	88.2	..		..	..	..
Western Sahara....................		..	..	..		..	..	..
Southern Africa								
Botswana	1971	80.1	80.6	77.9	1991	80.5	83.9	84.3
Lesotho.............................	1977	..	..	..		..	..	..
Namibia		..	..	..	1991	76.7	81.6	82.8
South Africa.......................		..	..	..	1998	60.8	64.5	70.2
Swaziland		..	..	..	1997	75.6	79.3	82.3

TABLE II.8. *(continued)*

Country	Year	Age of women			Year	Age of women		
		35-39	*40-44*	*45-49*		*35-39*	*40-44*	*45-49*
Western Africa								
Benin	1982	..	..	..	2001	89.8	92.3	91.4
Burkina Faso	1985	86.7	85.3	85.3	1999	93.7	94.3	95.8
Cape Verde		..	..	..		..	..	..
Côte d'Ivoire	1980	..	..	..	1998-1999	83.4	86.3	86.5
Gambia	1973	78.2	75.4	76.9		..	..	..
Ghana	1979-1980	..	..	..	1998	80.5	86.9	90.2
Guinea		..	..	..	1999	88.8	90.3	91.6
Guinea-Bissau		..	..	..		..	..	..
Liberia		..	..	..	1986	82.0	80.0	84.6
Mali	1984	85.3	85.6	86.1	2001	89.0	90.6	93.5
Mauritania	1981	..	..	..	2000-2001	78.6	80.2	85.2
Niger		..	..	..	1998	93.1	93.1	87.7
Nigeria		..	..	..	1999	85.6	89.5	88.6
Senegal	1978	..	..	..	1997	86.1	90.1	92.0
Sierra Leone		..	..	..		..	..	..
Togo		..	..	..	1998	84.2	91.3	92.7
Asia								
Eastern Asia								
China		..	..	..	1990	42.9	68.1	84.0
China, Hong Kong SAR	1971 [a]	72.6	73.3	67.1		..	..	..
China, Macao SAR	1960 [a]	..	..	..		..	..	..
Dem. People's Republic of Korea	1970 [a]	87.0	87.8	87.6		..	..	..
Japan	1970 [a]	28.8	40.7	53.6		..	..	..
Mongolia		..	..	..		..	..	..
Republic of Korea	1970 [a]	87.0	87.7	87.6	1990	35.8	58.1	75.7
South-Central Asia								
Afghanistan		..	..	..		..	..	..
Bangladesh	1975-1976	93.5	91.1	89.5	1999-2000	80.1	86.2	92.4
Bhutan		..	..	..		..	..	..
India	1981 [a]	79.0	80.8	81.6	1998-1999	73.3	78.4	81.5
Iran (Islamic Republic of)		..	..	..	1986	..	..	..
Kazakhstan		..	..	..	1999	41.2	46.3	47.8
Kyrgyzstan		..	..	..	1997	74.1	73.8	77.3
Maldives	1977	87.4	86.1	85.5	2000	82.5	87.7	90.3
Nepal	1976	83.1	83.6	83.7	2001	86.4	88.0	89.9
Pakistan	1974-1975	84.9	89.4	88.5	1990-1991	86.9	90.0	88.4
Sri Lanka	1971 [a]	74.2	79.0	81.4	1993	52.3	61.5	70.4
Tajikistan		..	..	..	1989	72.6	71.3	72.0
Turkmenistan		..	..	..	2000	75.3	84.5	83.1
Uzbekistan		..	..	..	1996	81.8	81.9	78.2
South-Eastern Asia								
Brunei Darussalam	1960	78.1	76.8	76.1		..	..	..
Cambodia		..	..	..	2000	77.7	80.5	82.5

TABLE II.8. *(continued)*

Country	Year	Age of women			Year	Age of women		
		35-39	40-44	45-49		35-39	40-44	45-49
Democratic Republic of Timor-Leste		..	..	..		..	..	..
Indonesia	1971 [a]	77.8	75.6	73.5	2003	59.6	71.7	78.6
Lao People's Democratic Republic		..	..	..		..	..	..
Malaysia	1970 [a]	82.0	82.1	80.5		..	..	..
Myanmar	1983 [a]	73.5	77.4	77.4		..	..	..
Philippines	1978 [a]	80.0	85.4	85.0	1998	67.9	72.8	74.9
Singapore	1980 [a]	56.9	68.6	77.6	1990 [a]	29.5	40.5	59.3
Thailand	1970 [a]	81.9	84.4	84.1	2000 [a]	25.1	35.2	45.3
Viet Nam		..	..	..	1999	54.5	66.9	..
Western Asia								
Armenia		..	..	..	2000	48.9	53.6	55.3
Azerbaijan		..	..	..	2001	53.5	63.1	..
Bahrain	1971	81.4	79.2	79.0	1995	76.9	63.1	64.3
Cyprus	1973 [a]	61.1	68.5	67.5	1992 [a]	38.0	39.1	42.4
Georgia		..	..	..		..	..	..
Iraq		..	..	..	1987 [a]	81.7	83.8	83.5
Israel	1961 [a]	47.9	49.3	47.2		..	..	..
Jordan	1976	90.9	90.9	93.4	1997	78.1	87.5	88.1
Kuwait	1975 [a]	79.7	80.3	79.6		..	..	..
Lebanon		..	..	..		..	..	..
Occupied Palestinian Territory		..	..	..	1997 [a]	89.1	90.2	89.6
Oman		..	..	..	1995	93.6	93.3	93.4
Qatar		..	..	..	1998	76.6	82.0	88.0
Saudi Arabia		..	..	..	1996	90.8	92.3	92.2
Syrian Arab Republic	1970 [a]	88.0	88.7	89.7		..	..	..
Turkey	1970 [a]	80.6	80.6	78.6	1998	57.1	68.3	76.1
United Arab Emirates	1975 [a]	73.8	71.0	70.2	1995 [a]	92.3	91.7	92.0
Yemen	1979 [a]	..	..	..	1997 [a]	91.1	92.2	95.9
Europe								
Eastern Europe								
Belarus		..	..	..	1999	12.3	15.6	17.3
Bulgaria	1975 [a]	16.9	17.2	20.1	1997-1998	10.2	13.0	..
Czech Republic		..	..	..	1991	23.0	24.2	23.6
Hungary	1970	23.0	28.0	31.6	1990	18.2	19.0	18.6
Poland	1970 [a]	44.6	52.9	54.4	1991	26.6	33.1	35.3
Republic of Moldova		..	..	..	1989	31.8	31.9	37.2
Romania	1966	32.3	38.8	42.9	1992	29.2	33.5	36.3
Russian Federation		..	..	..	1994	17.4	17.4	15.3
Slovakia		..	..	..		..	..	..
Ukraine		..	..	..	1989	16.3	17.9	20.4

TABLE II.8. *(continued)*

Country	Year	Age of women			Year	Age of women		
		35-39	*40-44*	*45-49*		*35-39*	*40-44*	*45-49*
Northern Europe								
Channel Islands	1961[a]	26.5	27.1	28.9		..	..	..
Denmark		..	..	..		..	..	..
Estonia		..	..	..	1994	32.1	25.2	27.7
Finland		..	..	..	2000	26.4	29.4	26.2
Iceland		..	..	..		..	..	..
Ireland		..	..	..	2002	19.2	27.3	28.4
Latvia		..	..	..	1995	20.3	17.3	15.0
Lithuania		..	..	..	1994-1995	17.8	16.3	15.4
Norway	1960	..	..	..	1988-1989	21.2	28.8	35.8
Sweden		..	..	..	1992-1993	32.4	29.6	..
United Kingdom		..	..	..		..	..	..
Southern Europe								
Albania		..	..	..		..	..	..
Bosnia and Herzegovina		..	..	..		..	..	..
Croatia		..	..	..	1991	16.7	18.8	21.3
Greece		..	..	..		..	..	..
Italy		..	..	..	1995-1996	14.5	22.5	26.1
Malta		..	..	..		..	..	..
Portugal	1970	38.2	41.6	43.2	1991	22.0	26.9	32.8
Serbia and Montenegro		..	..	..		..	..	..
Slovenia		..	..	..	1994-1995	10.5	19.5	19.4
Spain		..	..	..	1994-1995	21.5	28.3	44.2
TFYR Macedonia	1970	81.9	84.4	84.1	2000	25.1	35.2	45.3
Western Europe								
Austria	1981	29.2	36.9	39.8	1995-1996	19.2	27.3	28.4
Belgium	1970	35.8	36.3	33.8	1992[a]	22.6	..	..
France		..	..	..	1994	31.9	36.7	30.2
Germany		..	..	..		..	..	..
Luxembourg	1970[a]	28.3	28.3	26.5	1991	17.5	20.6	23.0
Netherlands		..	..	..	1993	24.0	..	..
Switzerland		..	..	..	1994-1995	22.5	21.9	21.9
Latin America And The Caribbean								
Caribbean								
Bahamas	1980	67.6	73.7	73.8	1990	54.6	64.1	70.2
Barbados	1980	56.9	64.2	66.7		..	..	..
Cuba	1981	51.7	57.9	59.4		..	..	..
Dominican Republic	1970	74.8	71.4	71.8	1999	67.3	78.7	77.2
Guadeloupe	1967	69.7	69.6	64.8		..	..	..
Haiti	1977	..	..	..	2000	71.8	75.6	78.8
Jamaica	1975-1976	73.3	73.7	73.9	1991	60.3	69.2	72.7
Martinique	1967	68.1	67.0	60.4		..	..	..
Netherlands Antilles	1971	62.8	67.9	68.5	2001	29.4	35.3	38.5
Puerto Rico	1970	60.4	60.7	62.0	1990	47.5	54.2	59.3
Saint Lucia	1980	75.9	77.0	76.7	1992	61.8	68.3	73.6
Saint Vincent and the Grenadines	1980	80.6	84.6	81.5	1991	67.2	75.1	78.7

TABLE II.8. *(continued)*

Country	Year	Age of women 35-39	Age of women 40-44	Age of women 45-49	Year	Age of women 35-39	Age of women 40-44	Age of women 45-49
Trinidad and Tobago	1977	..	..	..	1990	55.2	63.5	70.3
United States Virgin Islands	1970 [a]	56.4	53.0	46.8		..	..	..
Central America								
Belize..	1980	83.2	85.9	82.4	1991	77.9	81.1	85.0
Costa Rica....................................	1973	76.2	78.0	76.9		..	..	..
El Salvador	1971	82.2	82.9	81.2	1998	68.1	75.1	78.7
Guatemala....................................	1973	82.6	83.6	83.7	1998-1999	78.5	82.6	87.4
Honduras	1974	85.3	86.4	86.2		..	..	..
Mexico...	1970	77.2	76.9	75.7	2000	61.1	68.9	73.7
Nicaragua.....................................	1971	..	..	..	2001	73.0	79.8	84.6
Panama	1975-1976	70.8	81.1	81.5	1990	64.4	71.4	76.3
South America								
Argentina.....................................	1970	41.1	42.8	41.7	1991	..	..	..
Bolivia...	1976	78.4	80.8	80.9	1998	74.3	77.6	77.9
Brazil...	1970	68.7	69.7	69.7	1996	53.8	62.8	67.5
Chile..	1982	57.6	65.2	67.4	1992	..	..	..
Colombia	1973	..	..	..	2000	50.0	57.6	66.6
Ecuador..	1974	80.3	82.0	81.8	2001	58.6	66.8	71.5
French Guiana	1967	58.4	55.4	50.2		..	..	..
Guyana...	1970	81.4	79.0	75.8		..	..	..
Paraguay	1979	..	..	..	1992	68.9	72.4	74.4
Peru..	1972	82.1	82.9	82.9	2000	61.8	70.7	74.7
Suriname.......................................	1964	..	..	..		..	..	..
Uruguay..	1975	39.1	39.6	37.5	1996	38.4	43.4	44.7
Venezuela.....................................	1961	68.3	66.3	64.4	1990	59.8	66.3	71.0
Northern America								
Canada	1961 [a]	49.7	49.0	44.6	1991	25.2	29.4	37.8
United States of America	1980	43.2	55.4	58.0	2000	27.8	29.6	..
Oceania								
Australia/New Zealand								
Australia	1976 [a]	54.2	58.8	56.0	1986	38.6	46.0	54.5
New Zealand.................................	1976 [a]	59.0	63.6	61.4		..	..	..
Melanesia								
Fiji	1966	80.3	80.1	78.9	1986	72.5	78.0	80.2
New Caledonia		..	..	..		..	..	..
Papua New Guinea	1980	76.1	77.7	77.4		..	..	..
Solomon Islands	1970	77.6	79.4	79.1		..	..	..
Vanuatu	1967	83.4	79.8	79.8	1989	..	..	..
Micronesia								
Guam..	1960 [a]	60.0	56.7	..		..	..	..
Micronesia Federated States of..		..	..	..	1994	..	..	..

TABLE II.8. *(continued)*

Country	Year	Age of women			Year	Age of women		
		35-39	40-44	45-49		35-39	40-44	45-49
Polynesia								
French Polynesia		..	..	..		..	..	..
Samoa	1971	84.2	84.9	83.2		..	..	..
Tonga	1966	76.0	79.2	78.2	1996	71.2	78.6	..

Note [a] Percentage of ever married women with parity three or higher

TABLE II.9. PERCENTAGE OF WOMEN WHO ARE EVER MARRIED BY AGE GROUP AND COUNTRY

Country	Year	15-19	20-24	25-29	30-34	35-39	40-44	45-49	Year	15-19	20-24	25-29	30-34	35-39	40-44	45-49
Africa																
Eastern Africa																
Burundi	1971	12.0	66.2	92.6	96.5	98.3	98.0	98.9	1990	7.0	60.2	86.5	94.4	96.5	97.4	98.0
Comoros	1980	31.0	77.8	94.5	98.4	99.1	99.0	99.2	1996	11.5	48.4	76.9	92.8	98.6	99.5	100.0
Djibouti	..	..	..	..	..	..	..	..	..	..	..	..	..	..	..	..
Eritrea	..	..	..	..	..	..	..	..	1995	37.7	78.1	92.1	95.7	98.2	97.3	98.1
Ethiopia	1984	60.9	94.4	98.6	99.0	99.2	99.3	99.2 [40-49]	2000	30.0	73.1	90.4	97.5	98.8	99.6	99.9
Kenya	1969	35.9	81.4	93.5	96.2	96.7	97.2	98.9	1998	16.7	65.1	87.3	93.9	97.2	97.2	98.3
Madagascar	1975	34.4	69.3	85.9	92.3	94.4	95.1	95.7	1997	33.7	74.3	87.6	93.9	94.4	97.6	98.7
Malawi	1977	51.0	92.6	97.8	98.7	99.0	99.0	99.1	2000	36.8	87.7	98.2	99.1	99.7	99.6	100.0
Mauritius	1972	13.2	53.9	82.7	92.1	95.0	95.6	96.3	1990	11.3	51.3	76.1	85.8	88.8	91.5	94.5
Mozambique	1970	30.8	78.9	89.5	93.4	94.9	95.7	96.0	1997	47.1	88.8	94.1	97.5	99.0	97.4	97.1
Réunion	1974	8.6	47.4	76.4	84.9	87.0	87.7	87.6	1990	2.1	19.4	44.7	63.3	74.5	80.8	84.1
Rwanda	1970	17.6	82.0	98.2	99.6	99.9	99.9	99.9	2000	7.2	58.5	86.7	95.2	97.8	98.1	98.9
Somalia	..	..	..	..	..	..	..	..	..	..	..	..	..	..	..	..
Uganda	1969	49.7	86.8	93.2	94.3	94.7	94.0	94.2	2001	32.3	84.7	93.8	97.4	97.8	99.4	99.5
United Republic of Tanzania	1978	37.6	83.9	94.6	97.1	98.1	98.4	98.6	1996	25.3	75.5	92.6	95.5	98.3	98.6	99.3
Zambia	1969	41.3	90.4	96.2	97.8	98.0	98.0	97.8	2002	27.0	75.4	92.0	95.6	99.2	99.2	99.8
Zimbabwe	1982	26.1	76.5	90.7	94.5	96.4	97.0	97.2	1999	22.7	71.9	90.2	96.1	97.3	98.4	99.4
Middle Africa																
Angola	1970	35.7	82.8	88.4	91.3	90.0	95.3	95.4	..	..	..	..	..	..	..	..
Cameroon	1976	45.6	80.2	90.8	93.9	94.9	95.4	95.7	1998	35.8	73.6	89.1	94.7	96.7	98.9	98.5
Central African Republic	1975	46.8	81.7	90.4	93.6	94.9	95.3	95.0	1995	42.3	81.2	90.8	94.2	95.3	98.3	98.1
Chad	1964	72.6	97.6	99.2	99.7	99.7	99.8	99.8	1996	48.6	92.2	98.4	99.6	99.7	100.0	99.9
Congo	1984	18.1	53.6	76.3	86.1	90.8	92.8	93.1	..	..	..	..	..	..	..	..
Democratic Republic of the Congo	1984	32.3	74.2	89.1	93.4	95.4	96.0	96.4	..	..	..	..	..	..	..	..
Equatorial Guinea	1983	26.3	62.8	79.3	86.3	90.7	93.5	93.4	..	..	..	..	..	..	..	..
Gabon	1961	62.7	87.0	95.1	96.5	98.2	98.4	98.4	2001	22.4	61.3	82.0	92.1	95.9	96.0	98.2
Sao Tome and Principe	1981	24.4	57.2	70.6	73.5	74.8	73.4	69.2	1991	19.9	61.7	74.8	78.5	78.4	78.8	75.4
Northern Africa																
Algeria	1977	23.6	69.0	89.1	96.4	98.2	98.7	99.0	1992	3.6	29.6	65.2	86.8	93.6	96.9	98.1
Egypt	1976	21.8	61.1	86.0	92.9	95.3	95.1	96.1	1996	14.5	56.1	87.1	94.9	97.4	98.1	98.6

TABLE II.9. (continued)

Country	Year	15-19	20-24	25-29	30-34	35-39	40-44	45-49	Year	15-19	20-24	25-29	30-34	35-39	40-44	45-49
Libyan Arab Jamahiriya	1973	39.6	88.0	97.4	98.9	99.4	99.4	99.5	1995	1.0	12.2	41.4	72.1	89.5	96.8	98.6
Morocco	1971	33.8	81.7	95.0	97.6	98.2	98.2	97.7	1994	12.8	44.1	64.9	81.7	90.8	95.1	97.9
Sudan	1973	43.1	85.0	95.4	97.3	98.2	98.2	98.3	1993	20.6	55.4	80.3	89.7	96.0	97.7	98.4
Tunisia	1975	10.5	54.5	85.5	95.2	97.6	98.4	98.5	1994	3.0	27.7	62.3	81.9	91.1	95.3	97.7
Western Sahara	1970	60.6	81.0	87.1	89.1	93.7	93.4	93.1	..	..	..	..	..	..	..	..
Southern Africa																
Botswana	1971	12.7	43.6	63.3	72.8	79.7	83.2	86.5	1991	5.4	27.2	48.0	61.6	68.9	74.7	77.5
Lesotho	1976	29.4	79.6	90.1	93.3	94.9	95.6	96.5	1986	18.1	70.4	88.2	92.8	94.5	95.5	96.8
Namibia	1960	11.2	53.5	79.6	87.5	89.5	89.9	88.6	1992	7.7	31.0	53.0	74.2	80.8	81.1	88.1
South Africa	1980	5.6	35.8	62.8	76.6	83.9	87.7	90.4	1996	3.4	22.3	47.5	64.1	73.1	78.9	82.8
Swaziland	..	..	..	..	..	..	..	..	1991	9.1	39.7	59.9	74.7	81.8	84.7	91.0
Western Africa																
Benin	1979	52.2	90.1	97.1	98.4	98.6	98.3	98.2	1996	29.1	79.5	94.3	98.4	99.4	99.8	99.7
Burkina Faso	1975	53.9	92.6	96.9	97.9	98.1	97.9	98.0	1999	34.8	90.3	97.9	99.4	99.6	99.8	99.8
Cape Verde	1980	4.6	31.7	59.3	72.5	79.2	80.6	80.0	1990	6.7	32.3	53.4	65.6	70.2	74.6	77.7
Côte d'Ivoire	1978	53.8	82.9	91.8	95.5	96.7	97.6	98.4	1999	25.4	64.2	82.7	92.3	95.1	98.8	99.3
Gambia	1983	55.2	85.1	94.9	97.6	98.3	[35-44]	98.7	1993	38.8	74.8	90.9	95.6	97.3	97.7	97.7
Ghana	1971	31.7	84.0	96.5	98.6	99.1	99.4	99.5	1998	16.4	71.0	88.8	97.7	99.1	99.8	98.6
Guinea	..	..	..	..	..	..	..	..	1999	46.1	84.6	96.8	98.6	99.7	99.8	100.0
Guinea-Bissau	..	..	..	..	..	..	..	..	..	..	..	..	..	..	..	..
Liberia	1970	50.5	84.5	92.8	95.2	96.6	97.2	98.3	1986	36.0	75.3	92.1	93.8	98.8	98.3	99.5
Mali	1976	51.1	88.0	95.9	97.5	98.0	98.1	98.3	1996	49.7	87.6	95.8	98.7	99.5	99.9	99.8
Mauritania	1977	43.0	75.6	90.2	93.8	96.2	96.2	96.6	2001	27.8	60.4	79.6	93.3	96.1	98.0	98.0
Niger	1959	86.3	98.7	99.5	99.8	100.0	99.8	99.9	1998	61.9	88.9	97.4	99.0	100.0	99.7	99.8
Nigeria	..	..	..	..	..	..	..	..	1999	27.5	63.5	87.0	94.9	98.1	98.7	98.9
Senegal	1970	43.3	85.4	97.6	99.2	99.5	99.4	99.7	1997	29.0	62.8	83.6	95.3	98.5	99.6	99.9
Sierra Leone	..	..	..	..	..	..	..	..	1992	47.4	73.1	88.7	92.9	97.2	96.7	98.3
Togo	1970	68.6	[15-24]	96.9	98.0	98.3	98.2	98.0	1998	19.9	63.4	92.3	97.6	98.9	99.5	99.7
Asia																
Eastern Asia																
China	1982	4.4	53.5	94.7	99.3	99.7	99.8	99.8	2000	1.2	42.5	91.3	98.7	99.5	99.7	99.8
China, Hong Kong SAR	1971	2.9	32.4	79.9	94.4	97.0	97.1	96.2	1996	1.7	14.7	48.0	73.5	85.4	91.0	94.1

TABLE II.9. (continued)

Country	Year	15-19	20-24	25-29	30-34	35-39	40-44	45-49	Year	15-19	20-24	25-29	30-34	35-39	40-44	45-49
China, Macao SAR	1970	2.0	28.5	59.6	88.5	93.6	95.2	95.6	1991	2.3	22.3	67.0	86.0	91.4	93.1	96.0
Dem. People's Republic of Korea	..	..	..	..	..	..	..	..	..	..	..	..	..	..	..	..
Japan	1970	2.1	28.3	81.9	92.8	94.2	94.7	96.0	2000	0.9	12.1	46.0	73.4	86.2	91.4	93.7
Mongolia	..	..	..	..	..	..	..	..	2000	5.6	48.3	79.1	90.0	93.5	95.1	96.0
Republic of Korea	1970	2.9	42.8	90.3	98.6	99.6	99.8	99.9	1995	0.8	16.7	70.4	93.3	96.7	98.1	99.0
South-Central Asia																
Afghanistan	1979	53.7	90.7	97.2	98.6	99.1	99.0	99.0	2000	48.1	81.5	95.8	99.9	99.8	100.0	100.0
Bangladesh	1974	75.5	96.8	99.1	99.4	99.6	99.5	99.7	1994	26.6	69.9	87.6	91.6	94.5	93.7	93.1
Bhutan	..	..	..	..	..	..	..	..	1999	30.0	78.0	94.3	97.9	98.7	98.9	99.2
India	1971	57.0	90.9	98.0	99.1	99.5	99.4	99.6	1996	17.9	60.5	85.2	93.6	96.7	98.1	98.7
Iran (Islamic Republic of)	1976	34.3	78.6	93.2	97.3	98.7	99.0	99.2	1999	12.9	48.2	73.3	85.6	92.3	95.3	96.7
Kazakhstan	1979	..	64.9	90.1	95.8	98.3	98.6	98.4	1999	11.5	65.9	88.4	94.8	96.6	97.5	98.0
Kyrgyzstan	1979	..	70.9	93.1	97.2	98.8	99.1	99.1	2000	12.0	64.1	91.6	96.2	98.4	98.7	99.2
Maldives	1977	56.2	93.3	98.6	99.3	99.6	99.3	99.4	2001	40.3	82.9	95.5	97.5	98.1	98.9	98.6
Nepal	1971	60.7	92.1	97.4	98.6	98.9	99.1	99.2	1998	20.6	61.4	93.9	92.8	95.6	96.3	97.5
Pakistan	1972	34.4	78.7	92.8	96.4	97.9	98.1	98.5	1993	7.1	38.8	66.3	82.3	88.9	90.8	94.8
Sri Lanka	1971	10.6	46.8	75.4	89.1	94.2	95.3	95.9	1989	11.6	76.9	94.0	97.5	98.3	98.7	98.9
Tajikistan	1979	..	79.6	95.6	98.1	99.0	99.2	99.3	2000	5.9	47.3	84.8	95.8	97.5	99.2	99.5
Turkmenistan	1979	..	68.3	94.5	98.0	99.0	99.2	99.2	1996	13.0	77.2	94.8	98.1	98.8	99.6	98.6
Uzbekistan	..	..	..	..	..	..	..	..	..	..	..	..	..	..	..	..
South-Eastern Asia																
Brunei Darussalam	1971	14.7	55.7	82.4	90.3	93.4	94.7	95.5	1991	8.0	38.2	67.5	80.5	85.4	88.4	91.3
Cambodia	1962	14.9	68.4	90.6	95.8	97.1	97.8	97.9	1998	12.4	60.6	83.2	90.0	93.2	94.6	95.8
Democratic Republic of Timor-Leste	..	..	..	..	..	..	..	..	..	..	..	..	..	..	..	..
Indonesia	1971	37.4	81.5	95.0	97.8	98.6	98.8	99.0	2000	13.3	56.9	83.3	93.1	96.5	97.6	98.0
Lao People's Democratic Republic	..	..	..	..	..	..	..	..	2000	26.8	73.0	90.8	95.4	96.6	97.6	98.2
Malaysia	1970	17.5	58.6	86.6	94.3	96.5	97.8	98.4	2000	4.9	31.5	70.2	87.3	92.2	93.9	95.0
Myanmar	1973	22.0	64.5	83.4	90.7	93.0	93.8	94.1	1991	10.7	44.0	67.6	80.4	86.2	89.6	90.9
Philippines	1970	10.9	49.8	78.5	88.4	92.0	92.7	93.3	1995	9.6	42.3	71.8	85.7	91.3	93.2	93.8
Singapore	1970	4.8	35.4	77.4	90.4	94.9	96.7	96.9	2001	1.0	16.2	59.8	80.5	84.9	86.4	87.5
Thailand	1970	18.9	62.0	84.4	91.9	94.7	96.1	97.0	1990	14.7	51.6	74.5	85.8	90.4	92.9	94.8
Viet Nam	..	..	..	..	..	..	..	..	1997	7.7	53.1	78.9	89.1	91.3	91.7	90.1

TABLE II.9. (continued)

Country	Year	15-19	20-24	25-29	30-34	35-39	40-44	45-49	Year	15-19	20-24	25-29	30-34	35-39	40-44	45-49
Western Asia																
Armenia	1979	..	57.1	82.4	91.6	95.5	96.1	96.4	2000	8.6	52.5	86.5	94.7	94.2	93.1	94.3
Azerbaijan	1979	..	48.8	82.4	92.8	96.6	97.6	97.9	1999	12.8	49.0	76.1	86.7	90.7	93.9	96.1
Bahrain	..	..	..	..	..	..	..	..	1991	6.7	40.9	68.8	80.9	88.3	92.3	96.2
Cyprus	1973	3.8	39.4	74.5	90.2	92.2	95.4	95.0	1992	7.5	50.8	81.1	89.7	92.1	93.0	94.0
Georgia	1979	..	57.3	79.4	87.9	92.2	93.5	94.1	1999	15.8	52.5	76.9	86.3	91.1	92.0	..
Iraq	1977	32.5	67.1	86.1	92.3	94.9	96.3	96.8	1987	20.7	56.5	80.3	90.0	94.6	95.5	96.0
Israel	1972	8.7	54.3	84.2	93.3	96.2	97.1	97.7	1999	4.2	34.2	70.2	86.2	91.0	93.2	94.1
Jordan	1979	20.5	64.4	86.7	93.7	96.2	97.4	97.6	1994	8.2	38.8	66.2	80.7	89.8	94.3	96.1
Kuwait	1970	37.7	79.0	90.9	95.1	96.7	96.5	96.8	1996	5.4	42.0	71.9	83.2	88.7	92.8	94.9
Lebanon	1970	13.2	49.1	74.9	85.8	89.9	92.4	93.1	..	..	..	..	..	..	..	..
Occupied Palestinian Territory	1967	17.2	60.7	86.2	92.0	95.4	96.6	97.0	1997	24.2	64.0	80.1	83.4	88.1	91.2	92.4
Oman	..	..	..	..	..	..	..	..	1995	15.5	61.3	90.3	97.5	99.3	99.2	99.5
Qatar	1982	15.8	64.3	91.3	95.4	95.9	97.0	98.1	1998	4.2	32.2	66.8	80.2	89.3	93.3	97.0
Saudi Arabia	..	..	..	..	..	..	..	..	1987	16.1	61.1	87.5	89.9	95.3	97.0	98.1
Syrian Arab Republic	1970	27.7	70.2	89.0	94.3	96.3	96.8	97.6	..	..	..	..	..	..	..	..
Turkey	1975	22.0	74.2	91.1	93.9	96.9	95.9	97.1	1998	15.5	60.7	87.1	93.5	97.6	98.2	98.3
United Arab Emirates	1975	56.5	87.8	94.6	97.4	98.4	98.4	98.6	1987	18.5	52.2	74.5	90.1	96.0	97.7	98.5
Yemen	..	..	..	..	..	..	..	..	1997	26.9	72.8	90.5	96.1	97.9	98.5	99.2
Europe																
Eastern Europe																
Belarus	1979	..	60.3	87.9	94.0	95.8	95.5	94.1	1999	6.3	54.9	84.4	92.5	95.0	96.0	96.3
Bulgaria	1975	17.8	72.0	91.8	96.1	97.6	98.0	97.8	1985	16.5	71.6	90.6	95.2	97.0	97.7	98.2
Czech Republic	..	..	..	..	..	..	..	..	2000	1.2	27.2	72.4	90.3	94.3	95.8	96.5
Hungary	1970	12.5	67.7	89.6	94.1	95.4	94.9	94.6	2000	1.9	24.7	62.3	83.5	91.4	94.4	95.3
Poland	1978	4.9	53.0	84.9	91.4	94.2	95.1	94.7	1999	1.8	31.4	70.3	85.6	90.7	93.1	93.9
Republic of Moldova	1979	..	66.9	89.7	94.0	95.3	95.8	95.9	1989	11.6	72.2	91.2	95.1	96.1	96.4	96.7
Romania	1977	15.9	66.4	90.1	95.3	96.5	96.8	96.5	2000	5.6	40.8	78.6	90.0	94.3	95.9	96.5
Russian Federation	1979	..	64.1	88.0	93.4	96.1	96.6	96.0	1989	10.9	66.3	87.9	93.0	94.7	95.5	96.5
Slovakia	..	..	..	..	..	..	..	..	2001	1.8	28.3	68.2	85.6	90.5	92.3	92.8
Ukraine	1979	..	67.4	90.1	94.7	96.2	95.9	94.8	1999	10.0	64.1	92.4	97.0	97.5	98.1	..
Northern Europe																
Channel Islands	..	..	..	..	..	..	..	..	..	..	..	..	..	..	..	..
Denmark	1970	4.1	55.3	86.2	92.6	93.7	93.4	93.1	2001	0.7	9.1	32.6	61.6	73.9	81.1	86.8

TABLE II.9. *(continued)*

Country	Year	15-19	20-24	25-29	30-34	35-39	40-44	45-49	Year	15-19	20-24	25-29	30-34	35-39	40-44	45-49
Estonia	1979	..	59.0	84.9	90.5	92.2	93.0	92.4	1989	9.4	59.4	83.7	89.9	92.6	93.3	93.2
Finland	1970	5.4	48.0	78.2	86.1	88.0	88.2	87.9	2000	0.5	10.5	37.8	60.3	72.7	80.4	85.9
Iceland	1974	3.8	49.9	82.9	90.3	91.1	90.7	89.5	2000	0.9	8.2	27.0	49.2	59.9	67.2	70.9
Ireland	1971	2.1	31.1	68.8	80.6	82.9	82.2	81.8	2002	0.4	3.0	25.0	61.1	80.6	85.9	89.7
Latvia	1979	..	57.8	85.2	91.7	93.8	94.3	93.6	2002	1.3	20.6	55.0	78.0	86.4	89.3	90.6
Lithuania	1979	..	52.9	84.8	91.6	93.5	93.5	92.6	2001	2.4	34.9	73.8	86.8	91.0	92.7	93.7
Norway	1970	4.9	52.4	84.0	92.1	93.5	93.1	91.7	2002	0.5	8.7	31.5	56.7	71.2	81.5	88.7
Sweden	1970	2.3	40.0	77.0	88.5	91.7	92.4	92.2	2001	0.4	6.7	23.6	47.7	61.4	71.9	79.3
United Kingdom	1971	8.6	59.7	86.1	92.2	92.8	92.3	91.7	1991	1.7	24.6	61.6	81.8	89.8	93.6	94.8
Southern Europe																
Albania	..	..	..	..	..	..	..	..	1989	8.3	52.2	85.9	94.0	96.8	98.2	98.6
Bosnia and Herzegovina	..	..	..	..	..	..	..	..	..	..	..	..	..	..	..	..
Croatia	..	..	..	..	..	..	..	..	2001	2.4	25.8	61.5	82.2	89.5	92.2	93.5
Greece	1981	13.8	52.9	79.3	89.0	92.3	93.0	93.7	1991	5.5	36.3	72.5	87.9	92.6	94.1	94.9
Italy	1971	6.4	43.5	76.8	85.5	87.2	87.0	86.2	1999	0.9	13.3	45.6	73.3	84.5	89.1	91.5
Malta	1967	2.7	32.8	66.6	73.6	76.0	77.1	79.1	1985	3.0	33.1	75.0	84.9	84.8	83.3	80.7
Portugal	1970	5.3	39.3	75.0	85.0	87.5	87.4	87.5	1991	5.7	38.6	74.8	88.3	92.1	92.9	93.1
Serbia and Montenegro	..	..	..	..	..	..	..	..	1991	11.3	50.8	78.8	90.6	94.0	95.4	96.1
Slovenia	..	..	..	..	..	..	..	..	2001	0.3	8.3	38.7	65.6	76.9	79.5	85.6
Spain	1970	3.1	31.7	73.3	86.3	88.4	88.0	87.9	1991	2.4	22.4	61.3	82.8	88.8	90.9	91.8
TFYR Macedonia	..	..	..	..	..	..	..	..	1994	9.1	51.3	84.5	93.9	96.0	96.6	97.2
Western Europe																
Austria	1971	7.0	55.0	81.4	87.7	89.4	89.6	88.4	1991	2.7	25.7	61.4	79.9	87.8	91.5	92.4
Belgium	1970	6.9	59.9	88.3	92.7	93.4	92.9	92.3	2000	1.1	16.5	53.7	76.2	85.3	90.3	93.2
France	1975	3.5	45.1	80.4	89.5	92.0	92.3	91.8	2000	0.3	8.8	38.8	62.0	74.6	83.6	88.6
Germany	..	..	..	..	..	..	..	..	..	..	..	..	..	..	..	..
Luxembourg	1970	6.1	55.9	85.4	91.1	91.9	91.4	89.6	1991	2.4	26.2	62.6	82.8	89.3	92.3	93.4
Netherlands	1971	5.2	54.8	86.0	92.0	92.7	92.5	91.9	2002	0.7	11.1	37.6	64.6	78.6	85.1	89.9
Switzerland	1970	3.7	45.2	78.1	87.0	88.7	88.6	87.8	2001	0.7	12.7	39.9	67.0	80.3	85.9	88.8
Latin America And The Caribbean																
Caribbean																
Bahamas	1970	10.1	52.0	74.0	81.6	83.5	83.5	85.6	1990	3.7	25.2	50.8	64.5	72.6	79.0	82.8
Barbados	1970	0.9	12.0	34.2	49.1	55.4	61.5	63.6	1990	0.6	6.7	21.4	35.7	47.3	53.3	59.8
Cuba	1970	29.6	70.4	86.0	89.9	90.7	90.5	89.9	..	..	..	..	..	..	..	..

TABLE II.9. *(continued)*

Country	Year	15-19	20-24	25-29	30-34	35-39	40-44	45-49	Year	15-19	20-24	25-29	30-34	35-39	40-44	45-49
Dominican Republic	1970	22.4	60.8	78.0	83.1	84.6	83.5	82.7	1996	28.9	66.1	86.1	94.6	95.5	97.3	98.9
Guadeloupe	1967	3.4	26.5	50.6	59.5	63.3	66.4	67.8	1990	1.1	11.7	33.0	48.4	58.1	65.9	69.8
Haiti	1971	5.5	38.2	67.2	78.5	82.3	81.7	80.3	2000	19.4	57.3	79.9	92.5	98.5	97.8	98.0
Jamaica	1970	16.5	51.5	69.9	77.5	80.8	79.8	78.9	1991	0.7	5.3	15.8	28.2	39.6	48.8	54.1
Martinique	1967	1.6	18.8	44.8	57.4	63.9	65.7	66.7	1990	0.5	6.7	24.3	41.9	54.9	62.8	67.2
Netherlands Antilles	1971	3.5	28.8	57.5	70.9	75.0	76.8	78.9	2001	0.8	12.3	32.8	46.3	53.7	59.0	66.4
Puerto Rico	1970	15.6	54.7	81.3	89.8	92.3	92.8	93.5	1996	19.5	55.0	83.9	89.5	92.4	94.4	96.9
Saint Lucia	1970	1.2	12.8	33.9	49.0	58.1	65.7	67.9	1991	0.7	4.8	15.9	29.8	42.6	51.6	58.8
Saint Vincent and the Grenadines	1970	2.3	14.4	27.6	37.5	44.7	47.3	49.4	1991	0.8	7.6	21.8	34.5	48.1	54.2	58.3
Trinidad and Tobago	1970	6.8	36.1	62.2	72.4	76.6	78.0	79.6	1990	9.0	27.5	49.6	63.1	70.2	74.9	79.3
United States Virgin Islands	1960	16.3	57.9	75.3	78.5	82.2	85.0	82.6	1995	3.2	15.5	41.4	58.0	73.7	77.3	88.5
Central America																
Belize	1970	11.4	41.1	59.8	63.8	66.6	67.0	67.9	1991	7.9	30.9	48.2	59.5	67.5	72.1	76.0
Costa Rica	1973	15.1	51.3	73.5	82.3	85.2	85.8	85.4	1986	20.0	59.0	83.0	91.0	92.0	93.0	91.0
El Salvador	1971	20.4	56.3	74.6	79.9	81.5	79.2	77.7	2000	15.9	49.9	71.9	81.3	85.2	85.9	86.3
Guatemala	1973	28.4	67.2	82.9	88.1	89.9	89.5	89.2	1999	26.0	69.5	89.2	92.7	96.4	94.6	95.4
Honduras	1974	29.2	72.0	88.5	93.3	95.0	95.0	95.1	1996	30.5	68.3	86.8	93.7	95.6	96.4	95.6
Mexico	1970	21.2	61.5	82.6	89.6	92.2	92.7	92.9	2000	17.1	52.3	75.1	85.6	89.7	91.4	92.2
Nicaragua	1971	22.1	62.0	80.8	86.2	88.0	87.3	87.3	1998	31.9	69.0	85.9	93.7	96.8	96.0	97.9
Panama	1970	26.6	66.5	84.9	91.2	93.2	93.4	93.1	2000	22.0	57.6	75.9	85.0	88.7	90.6	91.0
South America																
Argentina	1970	10.8	44.0	72.6	83.8	87.2	88.4	89.0	1991	12.4	45.2	73.8	85.2	89.5	90.8	91.3
Bolivia	1976	16.1	57.0	79.1	87.5	90.3	92.0	92.3	1998	12.2	53.4	80.5	90.7	94.3	96.1	96.3
Brazil	1970	12.6	49.2	75.2	85.2	89.2	90.3	91.2	1996	16.8	52.6	78.5	89.8	91.8	93.8	94.8
Chile	1970	9.2	43.9	70.3	80.2	85.4	86.6	87.0	1992	11.7	43.8	69.8	79.9	84.1	86.1	86.6
Colombia	1973	13.5	48.8	70.9	80.0	83.2	84.1	85.1	2000	17.6	50.1	74.1	83.7	90.0	89.9	92.4
Ecuador	1974	19.5	59.3	78.7	85.7	88.0	88.5	88.9	2001	22.0	57.0	75.5	83.6	86.4	87.1	87.9
French Guiana	1967	3.0	25.0	41.4	47.7	49.8	50.3	53.2	1999	0.8	6.5	21.3	31.6	41.2	45.4	51.4
Guyana	1970	14.6	53.3	75.2	81.1	83.4	83.6	83.9	1991	6.9	26.6	45.4	60.8	70.0	76.3	81.7
Paraguay	1972	11.7	45.1	68.8	78.9	81.4	81.3	80.1	1992	16.6	53.5	74.4	82.9	85.7	85.8	85.5
Peru	1972	17.0	55.5	77.7	86.0	88.9	89.4	89.8	1996	12.5	52.3	77.1	89.3	92.5	94.7	95.7
Suriname	1964	19.8	61.3	79.3	83.9	84.1	83.4	78.8	:	:	:	:	:	:	:	:
Uruguay	1975	12.4	51.1	75.8	84.9	88.0	89.2	89.3	1996	12.8	44.8	73.0	85.6	89.4	90.8	91.4
Venezuela	1971	16.1	49.3	71.9	80.3	82.2	80.9	79.0	1990	17.7	50.6	71.2	81.9	85.8	86.7	86.6

TABLE II.9. *(continued)*

Country	Year	15-19	20-24	25-29	30-34	35-39	40-44	45-49	Year	15-19	20-24	25-29	30-34	35-39	40-44	45-49
Northern America																
Canada	1971	7.5	56.5	84.6	90.9	92.7	93.1	93.0	2002	3.2	26.7	57.6	74.9	82.6	86.3	89.4
United States of America	1970	11.9	63.7	87.8	92.6	94.1	94.6	94.7	2000	4.1	27.2	61.1	78.1	85.7	88.2	90.0
Oceania																
Australia/New Zealand																
Australia	1971	8.8	64.3	88.4	93.5	95.0	95.2	95.1	2000	0.6	13.0	47.2	72.9	83.8	89.3	92.8
New Zealand	1976	10.3	62.5	88.2	93.8	95.3	95.6	95.3	1996	6.9	36.7	67.5	82.4	89.2	93.3	95.3
Melanesia																
Fiji	1976	14.0	63.4	86.9	94.1	95.8	96.7	96.9	1996	10.3	54.1	81.6	89.5	92.4	94.4	95.4
New Caledonia	1969	18.5	59.1	78.4	85.3	87.9	87.9	89.1	1996	1.2	13.1	35.7	53.7	65.9	74.9	81.1
Papua New Guinea	1980	17.6	73.4	93.4	97.0	98.0	98.1	98.6	1996	20.8	75.1	92.8	96.6	99.0	98.7	99.8
Solomon Islands	1970	15.6	58.7	82.1	90.2	93.4	95.0	95.9	..	..	..	..	..	..	..	..
Vanuatu	1979	14.0	59.0	84.2	91.5	93.4	94.6	95.1	1989	11.9	56.9	82.6	92.8	95.0	96.3	97.0
Micronesia																
Guam	1980	9.9	59.9	84.8	92.2	93.8	[35-44]	94.9	1990	5.8	45.3	72.3	84.5	90.8	93.1	94.8
Micronesia Federated States of	1980	20.1	60.8	81.7	88.6	93.8	[35-44]	95.6	1994	10.2	43.4	77.3	[25-34]	91.5	[35-44]	94.5
Polynesia																
French Polynesia	1977	3.7	28.1	55.7	71.1	75.4	76.9	80.4	1996	1.5	15.2	37.1	55.9	67.3	75.2	81.0
Samoa	1971	10.3	62.2	89.1	95.3	96.1	97.2	97.3	1999	8.3	50.8	77.4	87.4	91.5	93.9	96.6
Tonga	1976	4.9	41.0	73.7	86.3	92.1	93.0	93.6	1996	5.0	33.4	66.8	79.8	87.3	90.7	92.9

TABLE II.10. MEAN AGE OF WOMEN AT FIRST MARRIAGE AMONG WOMEN BY COUNTRY

Country	Year	Age	Year	Age
Africa				
Eastern Africa				
Burundi	..	..	..	..
Comoros	..	..	..	..
Djibouti	..	..	..	..
Eritrea	..	..	..	..
Ethiopia	..	..	..	..
Kenya	..	..	..	..
Madagascar	..	..	..	..
Malawi	..	..	..	..
Mauritius	..	..	1997	25.2
Mozambique	..	..	..	..
Réunion	..	..	..	..
Rwanda	..	..	..	..
Somalia	..	..	..	..
Uganda	..	..	..	..
United Republic of Tanzania	..	..	..	..
Zambia	..	..	..	..
Zimbabwe	..	..	..	..
Middle Africa				
Angola	..	..	..	..
Cameroon	..	..	..	..
Central African Republic	..	..	..	..
Chad	..	..	..	..
Congo	..	..	..	..
Democratic Republic of the Congo	..	..	..	..
Equatorial Guinea	..	..	..	..
Gabon	..	..	..	..
Sao Tome and Principe	..	..	..	..
Northern Africa				
Algeria	..	..	..	..
Egypt	1973	21.2	1996	23.6
Libyan Arab Jamahiriya	..	..	..	..
Morocco	..	..	..	..
Sudan	..	..	..	..
Tunisia	..	..	1997	26.1
Western Sahara	..	..	..	..
Southern Africa				
Botswana	..	..	..	..
Lesotho	..	..	..	..
Namibia	..	..	..	..
South Africa	..	..	1995	30.1
Swaziland	..	..	..	..
Western Africa				
Benin	..	..	..	..
Burkina Faso	..	..	..	..

TABLE II.10. *(continued)*

Country	Year	Age	Year	Age
Cape Verde	..	..	..	..
Côte d'Ivoire	..	..	..	..
Gambia	..	..	..	..
Ghana	..	..	..	..
Guinea	..	..	..	..
Guinea-Bissau	..	..	..	..
Liberia	..	..	..	..
Mali	..	..	..	..
Mauritania	..	..	..	..
Niger	..	..	..	..
Nigeria	..	..	..	..
Senegal	..	..	..	..
Sierra Leone	..	..	..	..
Togo	..	..	..	..

Asia
  Eastern Asia

Country	Year	Age	Year	Age
China	..	..	..	..
China, Hong Kong SAR	1975	24.8	1998	26.7
China, Macao SAR	..	..	1998	27.9
Dem. People's Republic of Korea	..	..	..	..
Japan	1975	24.5	1998	26.7
Mongolia	..	..	..	..
Republic of Korea	..	..	1998	26.2

  South-Central Asia

Country	Year	Age	Year	Age
Afghanistan	..	..	..	..
Bangladesh	..	..	..	..
Bhutan	..	..	..	..
India	..	..	..	..
Iran (Islamic Republic of)	..	..	..	..
Kazakhstan	..	..	1998	23.3
Kyrgyzstan	1982	22.5	1998	22.8
Maldives	..	..	..	..
Nepal	..	..	..	..
Pakistan	..	..	..	..
Sri Lanka	..	..	..	..
Tajikistan	..	..	1994	20.9
Turkmenistan	..	..	..	..
Uzbekistan	..	..	1999	21.3

  South-Eastern Asia

Country	Year	Age	Year	Age
Brunei Darussalam	1977	23.5	1986	26.5
Cambodia	..	..	..	..
Democratic Republic of Timor-Leste	..	..	..	..
Indonesia	..	..	..	..
Lao People's Democratic Republic	..	..	..	..
Malaysia	..	..	..	..
Myanmar	..	..	..	..
Philippines	1974	23.8	1986	24.6

TABLE II.10 *(continued)*

Country	Year	Age	Year	Age
Singapore..	1976	24.6	1998	26.0
Thailand...	..	..	..	..
Viet Nam..	..	..	..	..
Western Asia				
Armenia..	1982	22.8	1997	22.9
Azerbaijan	1982	23.5	1998	23.3
Bahrain...	..	..	1997	24.2
Cyprus...	1975	23.8	1997	26.0
Georgia...	1980	26.1	2000	24.6
Iraq	..	..	..	..
Israel...	1975	22.2	1996	23.9
Jordan	1975	20.7	1997	23.0
Kuwait	..	..	1989	22.2
Lebanon..	..	..	..	..
Occupied Palestinian Territory	..	..	..	..
Oman	..	..	..	..
Qatar...	..	..	..	..
Saudi Arabia.......................................	..	..	..	..
Syrian Arab Republic	..	..	..	..
Turkey	1970	19.9	1999	22.3
United Arab Emirates	..	..	..	..
Yemen	..	..	..	..
Europe				
Eastern Europe				
Belarus...	1978	22.2	1998	22.4
Bulgaria..	1970	21.4	1997	23.1
Czech Republic...................................	1970	21.6	2001	24.8
Hungary..	1975	21.1	1998	23.9
Poland...	1970	22.8	2001	24.1
Republic of Moldova...........................	1980	25.6	2001	21.9
Romania	1970	21.9	1998	23.1
Russian Federation	1970	23.2	1995	22.0
Slovakia..	1970	22.0	2001	24.2
Ukraine...	1976	21.8	1998	21.7
Northern Europe				
Channel Islands	..	..	..	..
Denmark..	1970	22.8	1997	29.3
Estonia..	1970	23.5	1997	24.1
Finland..	1973	23.6	1998	27.6
Iceland..	1975	23.2	2000	29.9
Ireland..	1974	25.0	1995	27.9
Latvia...	1975	23.3	1998	23.9
Lithuania...	1970	24.0	1998	22.9
Norway	1975	22.9	1998	28.3
Sweden	1975	24.9	1997	29.1
United Kingdom..................................	1970	22.4	1996	26.6

TABLE II.10. *(continued)*

Country	Year	Age	Year	Age
Southern Europe				
Albania	1970	21.6	1999	23.5
Bosnia and Herzegovina	1980	22.0	1991	22.4
Croatia	1970	21.4	1997	24.4
Greece	1975	23.7	1998	26.6
Italy	1974	23.8	1996	26.8
Malta	1975	24.3	1998	24.9
Portugal	1976	23.3	1997	25.0
Serbia and Montenegro	1970	22.0	1997	24.2
Slovenia	1970	23.1	1998	26.0
Spain	1974	24.1	1997	27.4
TFYR Macedonia	1970	22.1	1997	23.1
Western Europe				
Austria	1975	22.7	1998	26.7
Belgium	1975	22.1	1995	25.3
France	1974	22.6	1996	27.9
Germany	1970	22.5	1997	26.8
Luxembourg	1975	22.2	1996	26.5
Netherlands	1975	22.6	1998	27.6
Switzerland	1975	24.4	1996	27.3
Latin America And The Caribbean				
Caribbean				
Bahamas	..	..	..	..
Barbados	1978	28.0	1991	29.9
Cuba	1972	25.8	1996	27.1
Dominican Republic	1984	29.8	..	..
Guadeloupe	..	..	..	..
Haiti	..	..	..	..
Jamaica	..	..	..	..
Martinique	..	..	1992	29.9
Netherlands Antilles	1975	26.4	..	..
Puerto Rico	1975	23.3	1998	23.7
Saint Lucia	..	..	1998	31.7
Saint Vincent and the Grenadines	..	..	1998	32.5
Trinidad and Tobago	1985	25.9	..	..
United States Virgin Islands	..	..	1993	30.3
Central America				
Belize	..	..	..	..
Costa Rica	..	..	1991	27.2
El Salvador	1974	26.2	1997	28.3
Guatemala	..	..	1997	28.2
Honduras	..	..	..	..
Mexico	..	..	1997	24.4
Nicaragua	..	..	..	..
Panama	1975	24.6	..	..

TABLE II.10 *(continued)*

Country	Year	Age	Year	Age
South America				
Argentina	..	..	..	..
Bolivia	..	..	..	..
Brazil	1978	25.6	1995	24.6
Chile	1974	24.8	1998	25.5
Colombia	..	..	..	..
Ecuador	..	..	1989	24.7
French Guiana	1976	22.7	..	..
Guyana	..	..	..	..
Paraguay	..	..	..	..
Peru	..	..	..	..
Suriname	..	..	..	..
Uruguay	..	..	1997	26.2
Venezuela	..	..	1990	25.7
Northern America				
Canada	1975	22.8	1997	28.8
United States of America	1975	22.1	1990	24.5
Oceania				
Australia/New Zealand				
Australia	1976	22.5	1996	26.4
New Zealand	1975	22.4	1998	27.1
Melanesia				
Fiji	1975	23.5	1987	23.6
New Caledonia	1976	22.8	..	..
Papua New Guinea	..	..	..	..
Solomon Islands	..	..	..	..
Vanuatu	..	..	..	..
Micronesia				
Guam	1975	24.5	1992	25.2
Micronesia Federated States of	..	..	..	..
Polynesia				
French Polynesia	..	..	..	..
Samoa	1978	28.2	..	..
Tonga	..	..	..	..

TABLE II.11. SINGULATE MEAN AGE AT FIRST MARRIAGE FOR WOMEN BY COUNTRY

Country	Year	Age	Year	Age
Africa				
Eastern Africa				
Burundi	1971	21.7	1990	22.5
Comoros	1980	19.8	1996	23.6
Djibouti	..	..	..	..
Eritrea	..	..	1995	19.6
Ethiopia	1984	17.1	2000	20.5
Kenya	1969	19.2	1998	21.7
Madagascar	1975	20.3	1997	20.6
Malawi	1977	17.8	2000	18.9
Mauritius	1972	22.5	1990	23.8
Mozambique	1970	19.9	1997	18.0
Réunion	1974	22.5	1990	28.2
Rwanda	1970	20.1	2000	22.7
Somalia	..	..	..	..
Uganda	1969	17.7	2001	19.6
United Republic of Tanzania	1978	19.1	1996	20.5
Zambia	1969	18.2	2002	20.6
Zimbabwe	1982	20.3	1999	21.1
Middle Africa				
Angola	1970	19.4	..	..
Cameroon	1976	18.8	1998	20.2
Central African Republic	1975	18.4	1995	19.7
Chad	1964	16.5	1996	18.1
Congo	1984	22.6	..	..
Democratic Republic of the Congo	1984	20.0	..	..
Equatorial Guinea	1983	21.7	..	..
Gabon	1961	17.7	2001	22.1
Sao Tome and Principe	1981	15.6	1991	17.8
Northern Africa				
Algeria	1977	21.0	1992	25.9
Egypt	1976	21.4	1996	22.3
Libyan Arab Jamahiriya	1973	18.7	1995	29.2
Morocco	1971	19.1	1994	25.3
Sudan	1973	18.7	1993	22.7
Tunisia	1975	22.6	1994	26.6
Western Sahara	1970	18.0	..	..
Southern Africa				
Botswana	1971	24.9	1991	26.9
Lesotho	1976	20.1	1986	21.3
Namibia	1960	21.8	1992	26.4
South Africa	1980	25.7	1996	27.9
Swaziland	..	..	1991	26.0
Western Africa				
Benin	1979	17.7	1996	19.9
Burkina Faso	1975	17.4	1999	18.9

TABLE II.11. *(continued)*

Country	Year	Age	Year	Age
Cape Verde	1980	23.6	1990	25.7
Côte d'Ivoire	1978	18.7	1999	22.0
Gambia	1983	..	1993	19.6
Ghana	1971	19.4	1998	21.2
Guinea	..	..	1999	18.7
Guinea-Bissau	..	..	..	..
Liberia	1970	18.7	1986	20.2
Mali	1976	18.1	1996	18.4
Mauritania	1977	19.5	2001	22.1
Niger	1959	15.8	1998	17.6
Nigeria	..	..	1999	21.4
Senegal	1970	18.7	1997	21.5
Sierra Leone	..	..	1992	19.8
Togo	1970	..	1998	21.3

Asia
  Eastern Asia

Country	Year	Age	Year	Age
China	1982	22.4	2000	23.3
China, Hong Kong SAR	1971	23.8	1996	28.6
China, Macao SAR	1970	25.6	1991	27.1
Dem. People's Republic of Korea	..	..	..	..
Japan	1970	24.7	2000	28.6
Mongolia	..	..	2000	23.7
Republic of Korea	1970	23.3	1995	26.1

  South-Central Asia

Country	Year	Age	Year	Age
Afghanistan	1979	17.8	..	..
Bangladesh	1974	16.4	2000	18.7
Bhutan	..	..	1994	20.5
India	1971	17.7	1999	19.9
Iran (Islamic Republic of)	1976	19.7	1996	22.1
Kazakhstan	..	..	1999	23.4
Kyrgyzstan	..	..	1999	21.9
Maldives	1977	17.5	2000	21.8
Nepal	1971	17.5	2001	19.0
Pakistan	1972	19.7	1998	21.3
Sri Lanka	1971	23.5	1993	25.3
Tajikistan	..	..	1989	21.2
Turkmenistan	..	..	2000	23.4
Uzbekistan	..	..	1996	20.6

  South-Eastern Asia

Country	Year	Age	Year	Age
Brunei Darussalam	1971	22.4	1991	25.1
Cambodia	1962	21.3	1998	22.5
Democratic Republic of Timor-Leste	..	..	..	..
Indonesia	1971	19.3	2000	22.5
Lao People's Democratic Republic	..	..	2000	20.8
Malaysia	1970	22.1	2000	25.1
Myanmar	1973	21.3	1991	24.5
Philippines	1970	22.8	1995	24.1
Singapore	1970	24.2	2001	26.5

TABLE II.11. *(continued)*

Country	Year	Age	Year	Age
Thailand	1970	22.0	1990	23.5
Viet Nam	..	..	1997	22.1
Western Asia				
Armenia	1979	..	2000	23.0
Azerbaijan	..	..	1999	23.9
Bahrain	..	..	1991	25.6
Cyprus	1973	24.2	1992	23.1
Georgia	1979	23.2	1999	24.3
Iraq	1977	20.8	1987	22.3
Israel	1972	22.8	1999	25.0
Jordan	1979	21.5	1994	24.0
Kuwait	1970	19.6	1996	25.2
Lebanon	1970	23.2	..	..
Occupied Palestinian Territory	1967	21.9	1997	21.7
Oman	..	..	1995	21.7
Qatar	1982	21.4	1998	26.3
Saudi Arabia	..	..	1987	21.7
Syrian Arab Republic	1970	20.7	..	..
Turkey	1975	20.1	1998	22.0
United Arab Emirates	1975	18.0	1987	23.1
Yemen	..	..	1997	20.7
Europe				
Eastern Europe				
Belarus	..	..	1999	22.8
Bulgaria	1975	20.8	1985	21.1
Czech Republic	..	..	2000	25.3
Hungary	1970	20.9	2000	26.3
Poland	1978	22.5	1999	25.2
Republic of Moldova	..	..	1989	21.1
Romania	1977	21.1	2000	24.1
Russian Federation	..	..	1989	21.8
Slovakia	..	..	2001	25.4
Ukraine	1979	21.4	1999	21.7
Northern Europe				
Channel Islands	..	..	..	..
Denmark	1970	22.1	2001	30.7
Estonia	..	..	1989	22.1
Finland	1970	22.5	2000	30.2
Iceland	1974	21.9	2000	30.5
Ireland	1971	23.5	2002	30.9
Latvia	..	..	2002	26.9
Lithuania	..	..	2001	24.8
Norway	1970	21.9	2002	31.4
Sweden	1970	23.7	2001	32.3
United Kingdom	1971	21.3	1991	26.4
Southern Europe				
Albania	..	..	1989	22.9

TABLE II.11. *(continued)*

Country	Year	Age	Year	Age
Bosnia and Herzegovina	..	..	..	..
Croatia	..	..	2001	26.2
Greece	1981	22.5	1991	24.5
Italy	1971	22.6	1999	28.4
Malta	1967	24.0	1985	22.2
Portugal	1970	23.2	1991	23.9
Serbia and Montenegro	..	..	1991	23.1
Slovenia	..	..	2001	29.8
Spain	1970	23.7	1991	26.0
TFYR Macedonia	..	..	1994	22.9
Western Europe				
Austria	1971	21.9	1991	26.1
Belgium	1970	21.4	2000	27.9
France	1975	23.0	2000	30.2
Germany	..	..	..	..
Luxembourg	1970	21.4	1991	26.0
Netherlands	1971	21.9	2002	29.9
Switzerland	1970	22.6	2001	29.1
Latin America And The Caribbean				
Caribbean				
Bahamas	1970	22.4	1990	27.2
Barbados	1970	28.5	1990	31.8
Cuba	1970	19.5	..	..
Dominican Republic	1970	19.6	1996	21.3
Guadeloupe	1967	25.4	1990	29.5
Haiti	1971	22.4	2000	22.3
Jamaica	1970	21.1	1991	33.2
Martinique	1967	26.2	1990	31.0
Netherlands Antilles	1971	24.9	2001	30.2
Puerto Rico	1970	22.1	1996	22.6
Saint Lucia	1970	28.7	1991	33.7
Saint Vincent and the Grenadines	1970	28.4	1991	30.9
Trinidad and Tobago	1970	24.0	1990	26.8
United States Virgin Islands	1960	20.8	1995	29.9
Central America				
Belize	1970	22.6	1991	26.2
Costa Rica	1973	21.7	1986	20.9
El Salvador	1971	19.0	2000	22.3
Guatemala	1973	19.7	1999	20.5
Honduras	1974	20.0	1996	20.4
Mexico	1970	21.2	2000	22.7
Nicaragua	1971	20.2	1998	20.6
Panama	1970	20.4	2000	21.9
South America				
Argentina	1970	23.1	1991	23.3
Bolivia	1976	22.1	1998	22.8
Brazil	1970	23.0	1996	23.4

TABLE II.11. *(continued)*

Country	Year	Age	Year	Age
Chile..	1970	23.4	1992	23.4
Colombia......................................	1973	22.5	2000	23.1
Ecuador	1974	21.2	2001	21.5
French Guiana	1967	24.4	1999	31.7
Guyana	1970	21.5	1991	27.8
Paraguay.......................................	1972	21.7	1992	21.5
Peru	1972	21.8	1996	23.1
Suriname	1964	18.6	..	..
Uruguay..	1975	22.5	1996	23.3
Venezuela.....................................	1971	20.1	1990	22.1
Northern America				
Canada	1971	22.0	2002	26.8
United States of America	1970	21.5	2000	26.3
Oceania				
Australia/New Zealand				
Australia.......................................	1971	21.5	2000	28.7
New Zealand	1976	21.5	1996	25.4
Melanesia				
Fiji...	1976	21.7	1996	22.9
New Caledonia..............................	1969	21.6	1996	30.4
Papua New Guinea........................	1980	20.6	1996	20.8
Solomon Islands...........................	1970	22.3	..	..
Vanuatu..	1979	22.0	1989	22.6
Micronesia				
Guam..	1980	22.2	1990	24.4
Micronesia Federated States of	1980	..	1994	..
Polynesia				
French Polynesia..........................	1977	25.8	1996	29.9
Samoa...	1971	22.0	1999	23.9
Tonga	1976	24.3	1996	25.5

TABLE II.12. TOTAL FIRST MARRIAGE RATE AMONG WOMEN BY COUNTRY

Country	Year	Rate	Year	Rate
Africa				
Eastern Africa				
Burundi	..	..	..	..
Comoros	..	..	..	..
Djibouti	..	..	..	..
Eritrea	..	..	..	..
Ethiopia	..	..	..	..
Kenya	..	..	..	..
Madagascar	..	..	..	..
Malawi	..	..	..	..
Mauritius	..	..	1997	1.02
Mozambique	..	..	..	..
Réunion	..	..	..	..
Rwanda	..	..	..	..
Somalia	..	..	..	..
Uganda	..	..	..	..
United Republic of Tanzania	..	..	..	..
Zambia	..	..	..	..
Zimbabwe	..	..	..	..
Middle Africa				
Angola	..	..	..	..
Cameroon	..	..	..	..
Central African Republic	..	..	..	..
Chad	..	..	..	..
Congo	..	..	..	..
Democratic Republic of the Congo	..	..	..	..
Equatorial Guinea	..	..	..	..
Gabon	..	..	..	..
Sao Tome and Principe	..	..	..	..
Northern Africa				
Algeria	..	..	..	..
Egypt	..	..	..	..
Libyan Arab Jamahiriya	..	..	..	..
Morocco	..	..	..	..
Sudan	..	..	..	..
Tunisia	..	..	1997	0.66
Western Sahara	..	..	..	..
Southern Africa				
Botswana	..	..	..	..
Lesotho	..	..	..	..
Namibia	..	..	..	..
South Africa	..	..	..	..
Swaziland	..	..	..	..
Western Africa				
Benin	..	..	..	..
Burkina Faso	..	..	..	..

TABLE II.12. *(continued)*

Country	Year	Rate	Year	Rate
Cape Verde	..	..	..	..
Côte d'Ivoire	..	..	..	..
Gambia	..	..	..	..
Ghana	..	..	..	..
Guinea	..	..	..	..
Guinea-Bissau	..	..	..	..
Liberia	..	..	..	..
Mali	..	..	..	..
Mauritania	..	..	..	..
Niger	..	..	..	..
Nigeria	..	..	..	..
Senegal	..	..	..	..
Sierra Leone	..	..	..	..
Togo	..	..	..	..
Asia				
Eastern Asia				
China	..	..	..	..
China, Hong Kong SAR	1975	0.83	1998	0.50
China, Macao SAR	..	..	1998	0.75
Dem. People's Republic of Korea	..	..	..	..
Japan	1975	0.82	1998	0.70
Mongolia	..	..	..	..
Republic of Korea	..	..	1998	0.66
South-Central Asia				
Afghanistan	..	..	..	..
Bangladesh	..	..	..	..
Bhutan	..	..	..	..
India	..	..	..	..
Iran (Islamic Republic of)	..	..	..	..
Kazakhstan	..	..	1998	0.65
Kyrgyzstan	1982	0.98	1998	0.58
Maldives	..	..	..	..
Nepal	..	..	..	..
Pakistan	..	..	..	..
Sri Lanka	..	..	..	..
Tajikistan	..	..	1994	0.70
Turkmenistan	..	..	..	..
Uzbekistan	..	..	1999	0.73
South-Eastern Asia				
Brunei Darussalam	..	..	..	..
Cambodia	..	..	..	..
Democratic Republic of Timor-Leste	..	..	..	..
Indonesia	..	..	..	..
Lao People's Democratic Republic	..	..	..	..
Malaysia	..	..	..	..
Myanmar	..	..	..	..
Philippines	..	..	..	..

TABLE II.12. *(continued)*

Country	Year	Rate	Year	Rate
Singapore	1976	0.86	1998	0.82
Thailand	..	..	..	..
Viet Nam	..	..	..	..
Western Asia				
Armenia	1982	0.97	1997	0.39
Azerbaijan	1982	0.89	1998	0.60
Bahrain	..	..	1997	0.84
Cyprus	1975	1.14	1997	1.13
Georgia	1980	0.99	2000	0.41
Iraq	..	..	..	..
Israel	1975	0.97	1996	0.71
Jordan	1975	0.75	1997	0.76
Kuwait	..	..	1989	0.50
Lebanon	..	..	..	..
Occupied Palestinian Territory	..	..	..	..
Oman	..	..	..	..
Qatar	..	..	..	..
Saudi Arabia	..	..	..	..
Syrian Arab Republic	..	..	..	..
Turkey	..	..	1999	0.76
United Arab Emirates	..	..	..	..
Yemen	..	..	..	..
Europe				
Eastern Europe				
Belarus	1978	1.04	1998	0.74
Bulgaria	1975	1.00	1997	0.52
Czech Republic	1970	0.91	1997	0.52
Hungary	1975	1.04	1998	0.47
Poland	1975	0.93	1997	0.64
Republic of Moldova	1980	1.11	1998	0.61
Romania	1970	0.84	1998	0.68
Russian Federation	1970	1.06	1995	0.75
Slovakia	1970	0.86	2001	0.47
Ukraine	1976	0.92	1998	0.64
Northern Europe				
Channel Islands	..	..	..	..
Denmark	1974	0.66	1997	0.64
Estonia	1970	1.04	1997	0.36
Finland	1973	0.79	1998	0.57
Iceland	1975	0.80	1997	0.59
Ireland	1974	1.04	1995	0.59
Latvia	1975	1.01	1998	0.39
Lithuania	1970	1.14	1998	0.56
Norway	1975	0.80	1998	0.54
Sweden	1975	0.63	1997	0.42
United Kingdom	1970	1.04	1996	0.53

TABLE II.12. *(continued)*

Country	Year	Rate	Year	Rate
Southern Europe				
Albania..	1970	0.75	1990	0.99
Bosnia and Herzegovina.....................	1980	0.69	1991	0.67
Croatia..	1970	0.87	1997	0.67
Greece...	1975	1.15	1998	0.64
Italy	1974	1.00	1996	0.61
Malta	1975	0.98	1998	0.88
Portugal	1978	0.96	1997	0.77
Serbia and Montenegro.......................	1970	0.92	1997	0.63
Slovenia...	1970	0.96	1998	0.47
Spain...	1974	1.01	1997	0.59
TFYR Macedonia...............................	1970	0.91	1997	0.85
Western Europe				
Austria..	1975	0.76	1998	0.53
Belgium...	1975	0.89	1995	0.57
France...	1974	0.84	1996	0.54
Germany..	1970	0.98	1997	0.57
Luxembourg	1975	0.79	1996	0.58
Netherlands......................................	1970	1.06	1998	0.58
Switzerland......................................	1975	0.64	1996	0.65
Latin America And The Caribbean				
Caribbean				
Bahamas	..	..	..	..
Barbados..	1978	0.29	1991	0.73
Cuba	1972	1.08	1996	0.67
Dominican Republic...........................	1984	0.58	..	..
Guadeloupe......................................	..	..	..	..
Haiti..	..	..	..	..
Jamaica..	..	..	..	..
Martinique	..	..	1992	0.49
Netherlands Antilles	1975	0.94	..	..
Puerto Rico.......................................	1975	0.78	1998	0.52
Saint Lucia.......................................	..	..	1998	0.38
Saint Vincent and the Grenadines........	..	..	1998	0.56
Trinidad and Tobago	1985	0.67	1997	0.59
United States Virgin Islands	..	..	..	..
Central America				
Belize..	..	..	1997	0.81
Costa Rica	..	..	1991	0.53
El Salvador	1974	0.50	1997	0.43
Guatemala..	..	..	1997	0.61
Honduras..	..	..	..	..
Mexico..	..	..	1995	0.73
Nicaragua	..	..	..	..
Panama..	1975	0.34	..	..

TABLE II.12. *(continued)*

Country	Year	Rate	Year	Rate
South America				
Argentina	..	..	..	..
Bolivia	..	..	..	..
Brazil	..	..	..	..
Chile	1974	0.87	1998	0.58
Colombia	..	..	..	..
Ecuador	..	..	1989	0.67
French Guiana	..	..	..	..
Guyana	..	..	..	..
Paraguay	..	..	..	..
Peru	..	..	..	..
Suriname	..	..	..	..
Uruguay	..	..	1997	0.58
Venezuela	..	..	1990	0.62
Northern America				
Canada	1975	0.81	1997	0.66
United States of America	1975	0.62	1990	0.59
Oceania				
Australia/New Zealand				
Australia	1976	0.78	1996	0.60
New Zealand	1975	0.81	1998	0.52
Melanesia				
Fiji	1975	0.90	1987	0.83
New Caledonia	1976	0.59	..	..
Papua New Guinea	..	..	..	..
Solomon Islands	..	..	..	..
Vanuatu	..	..	..	..
Micronesia				
Guam	1975	..	1992	0.88
Micronesia Federated States of	..	..	..	..
Polynesia				
French Polynesia	..	..	..	..
Samoa	..	..	..	..
Tonga	..	..	..	..

TABLE II.13. TOTAL DIVORCE RATE AMONG WOMEN BY COUNTRY

Country	Year	Rate	Year	Rate
Africa				
Eastern Africa				
Burundi	..	..	..	..
Comoros	..	..	..	..
Djibouti	..	..	..	..
Eritrea	..	..	..	..
Ethiopia	..	..	..	..
Kenya	..	..	..	..
Madagascar	..	..	..	..
Malawi	..	..	..	..
Mauritius	..	..	..	..
Mozambique	..	..	..	..
Réunion	1970	0.04	..	..
Rwanda	..	..	..	..
Somalia	..	..	..	..
Uganda	..	..	..	..
United Republic of Tanzania	..	..	..	..
Zambia	..	..	..	..
Zimbabwe	..	..	..	..
Middle Africa				
Angola	..	..	..	..
Cameroon	..	..	..	..
Central African Republic	..	..	..	..
Chad	..	..	..	..
Congo	..	..	..	..
Democratic Republic of the Congo	..	..	..	..
Equatorial Guinea	..	..	..	..
Gabon	..	..	..	..
Sao Tome and Principe	..	..	..	..
Northern Africa				
Algeria	..	..	..	..
Egypt	1970	0.23	1996	0.14
Libyan Arab Jamahiriya	..	..	..	..
Morocco	..	..	..	..
Sudan	..	..	..	..
Tunisia	1971	0.13	..	..
Western Sahara	..	..	..	..
Southern Africa				
Botswana	..	..	..	..
Lesotho	..	..	..	..
Namibia	..	..	..	..
South Africa	..	..	..	..
Swaziland	..	..	..	..
Western Africa				
Benin	..	..	..	..
Burkina Faso	..	..	..	..

TABLE II.13. *(continued)*

Country	Year	Rate	Year	Rate
Cape Verde	..	..	..	..
Côte d'Ivoire	..	..	..	..
Gambia	..	..	..	..
Ghana	..	..	..	..
Guinea	..	..	..	..
Guinea-Bissau	..	..	..	..
Liberia	..	..	..	..
Mali	..	..	..	..
Mauritania	..	..	..	..
Niger	..	..	..	..
Nigeria	..	..	..	..
Senegal	..	..	..	..
Sierra Leone	..	..	..	..
Togo	..	..	..	..
Asia				
Eastern Asia				
China	..	..	..	..
China, Hong Kong SAR	..	..	..	..
China, Macao SAR	..	..	1997	0.13
Dem. People's Republic of Korea	..	..	..	..
Japan	1970	0.06	1997	0.16
Mongolia	..	..	..	..
Republic of Korea	1979	0.05	1997	0.18
South-Central Asia				
Afghanistan	..	..	..	..
Bangladesh	..	..	..	..
Bhutan	..	..	..	..
India	..	..	..	..
Iran (Islamic Republic of)	..	..	..	..
Kazakhstan	..	..	1997	0.28
Kyrgyzstan	..	..	1996	0.19
Maldives	..	..	..	..
Nepal	..	..	..	..
Pakistan	..	..	..	..
Sri Lanka	..	..	..	..
Tajikistan	..	..	1994	0.10
Turkmenistan	..	..	..	..
Uzbekistan	..	..	..	..
South-Eastern Asia				
Brunei Darussalam	..	..	..	..
Cambodia	..	..	..	..
Democratic Republic of Timor-Leste	..	..	..	..
Indonesia	..	..	..	..
Lao People's Democratic Republic	..	..	..	..
Malaysia	..	..	..	..
Myanmar	..	..	..	..
Philippines	..	..	..	..
Singapore	1980	0.07	1997	0.15

TABLE II.13. *(continued)*

Country	Year	Rate	Year	Rate
Thailand..	..	..	..	..
Viet Nam	..	..	..	..
Western Asia				
Armenia..	..	..	1996	0.08
Azerbaijan	..	..	1996	0.09
Bahrain	1976	0.17	1995	0.15
Cyprus	1980	0.04	2000	0.21
Georgia	..	..	1996	0.05
Iraq	..	..	..	..
Israel..	1971	0.11	1996	0.15
Jordan	1970	0.12	1997	0.17
Kuwait	1970	0.22	1992	0.22
Lebanon	..	..	..	..
Occupied Palestinian Territory	..	..	..	..
Oman	..	..	..	..
Qatar	..	..	1993	0.20
Saudi Arabia....................................	..	..	..	..
Syrian Arab Republic	..	..	..	..
Turkey	1970	0.04	1996	0.12
United Arab Emirates	..	..	..	..
Yemen	..	..	..	..
Europe				
Eastern Europe				
Belarus..	..	..	..	..
Bulgaria	1970	0.29	1997	0.15
Czech Republic.................................	..	..	1997	0.41
Hungary	1970	0.55	1997	0.33
Poland..	1970	0.13	1997	0.14
Republic of Moldova..........................	..	..	1991	0.39
Romania	1970	0.05	1997	0.19
Russian Federation	1970	0.34	1995	0.57
Slovakia...	..	..	1995	0.58
Ukraine..	1981	0.44	1995	0.48
Northern Europe				
Channel Islands	..	..	..	..
Denmark...	1970	0.51	1997	0.28
Estonia...	..	..	1996	0.50
Finland...	1970	0.33	1997	0.32
Iceland	1970	0.18	2000	0.40
Ireland..	..	..	..	..
Latvia...	..	..	1997	0.32
Lithuania..	..	..	1997	0.34
Norway	1970	0.13	1997	0.27
Sweden	1970	0.21	1996	0.29
United Kingdom................................	..	..	1996	0.33
Southern Europe				
Albania..	..	..	..	..

TABLE II.13. *(continued)*

Country	Year	Rate	Year	Rate
Bosnia and Herzegovina	..	..	1991	0.04
Croatia	..	..	1997	0.11
Greece	1970	0.01	1997	0.09
Italy	1978	0.03	1994	0.05
Malta	..	..	..	..
Portugal	1970	0.01	1997	0.17
Serbia and Montenegro	..	..	1995	0.10
Slovenia	..	..	1996	0.12
Spain	..	..	..	..
TFYR Macedonia	..	..	1997	0.07
Western Europe				
Austria	1970	0.20	1997	0.27
Belgium	1970	0.10	1995	0.42
France	1970	0.09	1993	0.24
Germany	..	..	1996	0.26
Luxembourg	1970	0.09	1996	0.22
Netherlands	1970	0.10	1996	0.25
Switzerland	1970	0.13	1996	0.26
Latin America And The Caribbean				
Caribbean				
Bahamas	1975	0.05	1996	0.17
Barbados	1970	0.06	1991	0.18
Cuba	1971	0.41	1996	0.39
Dominican Republic	1970	0.05	1984	0.06
Guadeloupe	..	..	..	..
Haiti	..	..	..	..
Jamaica	1970	0.05	1995	0.06
Martinique	1970	0.10	..	..
Netherlands Antilles	1970	0.25	..	..
Puerto Rico	..	..	..	..
Saint Lucia	..	..	..	..
Saint Vincent and the Grenadines	..	..	..	..
Trinidad and Tobago	1972	0.04	1995	0.10
United States Virgin Islands	1972	0.36	1993	0.53
Central America				
Belize	..	..	..	..
Costa Rica	1970	0.02	1981	0.12
El Salvador	1970	0.03	1997	0.06
Guatemala	1965	0.01	1993	0.02
Honduras	..	..	..	..
Mexico	1976	0.03	1997	0.05
Nicaragua	..	..	..	..
Panama	1970	0.11	1997	0.01
South America				
Argentina	..	..	..	..
Bolivia	..	..	..	..
Brazil	..	..	..	..

Population Division, DESA, United Nations

TABLE II.13. *(continued)*

Country	Year	Rate	Year	Rate
Chile	1984	0.04	1997	0.05
Colombia	..	..	..	..
Ecuador...	1970	0.03	1997	0.10
French Guiana	..	..	..	..
Guyana	..	..	..	..
Paraguay	..	..	..	..
Peru	..	..	..	..
Suriname..	..	..	1991	0.36
Uruguay...	..	..	..	..
Venezuela...	1972	0.04	..	..
Northern America				
Canada...	1973	0.21	1995	0.29
United States of America....................	1970	0.23	1990	0.25
Oceania				
Australia/New Zealand				
Australia	1970	0.13	1996	0.33
New Zealand......................................	1970	0.13	1997	0.30
Melanesia				
Fiji	..	..	..	..
New Caledonia	1976	0.09	1993	0.15
Papua New Guinea	..	..	..	..
Solomon Islands	..	..	..	..
Vanuatu	..	..	..	..
Micronesia				
Guam..	..	..	1992	0.71
Micronesia Federated States of............	..	..	..	..
Polynesia				
French Polynesia	..	..	..	..
Samoa...	..	..	..	..
Tonga..	..	..	..	..

TABLE II.14. ESTIMATES OF THE TOTAL FERTILITY RATE AS PRESENTED IN THE COUNTRY TABLES OF THIS REPORT AND AS ESTIMATED FROM THE 2002 REVISION OF WORLD POPULATION PROSPECTS

Country or area	Reference date	Total fertility rate				Reference date	Total fertility rate			
		From World Fertility Report 2003	Calculated from the 2002 Revision	Difference	Percentage difference		From World Fertility Report 2003	Calculated from the 2002 Revision	Difference	Percentage difference
Africa										
Eastern Africa										
Burundi	1980	7.91	6.80	-1.11	-16.31	1985	6.95	6.80	-0.15	-2.21
Comoros	1980	7.05	7.05	0.00	-0.04	1994	5.10	5.72	0.62	10.84
Djibouti	..	..	..	..	..	1991	5.97	6.31	0.34	5.39
Eritrea	..	..	..	..	..	2000	5.24	5.73	0.50	8.65
Ethiopia	1981	6.83	6.83	-0.01	-0.08	1998	5.87	6.50	0.64	9.77
Kenya	1969	7.60	8.12	0.52	6.40	1996	4.71	4.92	0.22	4.37
Madagascar	1975	6.39	6.56	0.17	2.59	1995	6.08	6.16	0.08	1.30
Malawi	1977	7.60	7.56	-0.04	-0.53	1998	6.44	6.46	0.03	0.39
Mauritius	1972	3.42	3.45	0.03	0.78	2000	2.02	2.01	-0.01	-0.45
Mozambique	1970	6.70	6.54	-0.16	-2.45	1995	5.61	6.08	0.47	7.73
Réunion	1970	4.40	4.46	0.06	1.34	1998	2.26	2.30	0.04	1.68
Rwanda	1970	7.70	8.24	0.54	6.51	1999	5.93	6.11	0.18	2.92
Somalia	1975	7.10	7.25	0.15	2.07	..	..	..	..	..
Uganda	1969	7.13	7.10	-0.03	-0.35	1999	6.97	7.10	0.13	1.83
United Republic of Tanzania	1971	7.11	6.77	-0.34	-5.01	1998	5.60	5.70	0.10	1.75
Zambia	1980	7.20	7.07	-0.13	-1.84	2000	5.90	5.89	-0.01	-0.25
Zimbabwe	1969	6.74	7.60	0.86	11.32	1997	4.08	4.62	0.55	11.80
Middle Africa										
Angola	..	..	..	..	..	..	..	..	..	..
Cameroon	1976	6.41	6.36	-0.04	-0.71	1996	5.16	5.34	0.19	3.46
Central African Republic	1975	5.85	5.79	-0.06	-1.00	1993	5.15	5.60	0.45	8.04
Chad	..	..	..	..	..	1995	6.63	6.65	0.03	0.38
Congo	1974	6.99	6.29	-0.70	-11.08	1984	5.90	6.29	0.39	6.20
Democratic Republic of the Congo	1971	6.30	6.39	0.09	1.41	1984	6.70	6.70	0.00	0.00
Equatorial Guinea	1983	5.50	5.79	0.29	5.01	..	..	..	..	..
Gabon	..	..	..	..	..	1998	4.26	4.50	0.25	5.44
Sao Tome and Principe	..	..	..	..	..	..	..	..	..	..
Northern Africa										
Algeria	1977	7.4	7.22	-0.20	-2.76	1996	3.1	3.54	0.40	11.25

Population Division, DESA, United Nations

TABLE II.14. (continued)

Country or area	Total fertility rate					Total fertility rate				
	Reference date	From World Fertility Report 2003	Calculated from the 2002 Revision	Difference	Percentage difference	Reference date	From World Fertility Report 2003	Calculated from the 2002 Revision	Difference	Percentage difference
Egypt	1970	5.4	6.22	0.82	13.23	1999	3.6	3.47	-0.14	-3.92
Libyan Arab Jamahiriya	1973	6.8	7.59	0.78	10.27	1993	4.1	4.10	0.02	0.49
Morocco	1977	5.9	6.10	0.19	3.16	1999	3.0	2.95	-0.02	-0.75
Sudan	1973	7.1	6.67	-0.40	-6.00	1992	4.6	5.36	0.81	15.11
Tunisia	1970	6.1	6.62	0.53	8.04	1999	2.1	2.26	0.17	7.58
Western Sahara	..	..	..	..	..	..	..	..	..	..
Southern Africa										
Botswana	1971	6.5	6.70	0.21	3.06	1986	5.0	5.48	0.48	8.77
Lesotho	1975	5.8	5.74	-0.05	-0.85	1991	4.8	4.91	0.11	2.28
Namibia	..	..	..	..	..	1990	5.2	5.84	0.65	11.04
South Africa	..	..	..	..	..	1996	2.9	3.10	0.24	7.74
Swaziland	1966	5.2	6.90	1.70	24.64	1986	5.0	6.42	1.43	22.27
Western Africa										
Benin	1980	7.1	7.09	0.01	0.20	1999	5.8	6.06	0.28	4.55
Burkina Faso	1985	7.2	7.68	0.50	6.45	1996	6.8	6.97	0.17	2.49
Cape Verde	1982	5.8	6.22	0.45	7.31	1996	4.2	4.16	-0.01	-0.36
Côte d'Ivoire	1978	7.4	7.41	0.05	0.67	1997	5.1	5.44	0.32	5.88
Gambia	1973	6.4	6.50	0.15	2.25	1988	5.9	6.20	0.26	4.11
Ghana	1968	7.1	6.90	-0.23	-3.41	1996	4.5	4.88	0.34	6.86
Guinea	1983	5.8	7.00	1.16	16.57	1997	5.8	6.30	0.46	7.27
Guinea-Bissau	..	..	..	..	..	..	..	..	..	..
Liberia	1984	6.6	6.90	0.29	4.20	..	..	..	..	..
Mali	1985	6.9	7.00	0.08	1.07	1994	7.0	7.00	-0.03	-0.43
Mauritania	1979	6.2	6.46	0.22	3.33	1999	4.7	5.96	1.28	21.45
Niger	..	..	..	..	..	1997	7.5	8.00	0.53	6.63
Nigeria	1980	6.3	6.90	0.56	8.17	1997	5.1	6.01	0.87	14.42
Senegal	1976	7.2	7.00	-0.16	-2.23	1996	5.8	5.66	-0.15	-2.67
Sierra Leone	1973	6.5	6.50	-0.01	-0.22	1985	6.3	6.50	0.20	3.08
Togo	1970	6.6	7.10	0.46	6.41	1996	5.4	5.96	0.56	9.43
Asia										
Eastern Asia										
China	1970	5.7	5.58	-0.17	-3.04	2001	1.4	1.82	0.43	23.55
China, Hong Kong SAR	1970	3.3	3.57	0.26	7.30	2001	0.9	1.04	0.11	10.96
China, Macao SAR	1970	2.0	3.08	1.04	33.70	2000	0.9	1.13	0.22	19.69

TABLE II.14. *(continued)*

Country or area	Total fertility rate					Total fertility rate				
	Reference date	From World Fertility Report 2003	Calculated from the 2002 Revision	Difference	Percentage difference	Reference date	From World Fertility Report 2003	Calculated from the 2002 Revision	Difference	Percentage difference
Dem. People's Republic of Korea..	..	..	..	..	..	1993	2.2	2.31	0.12	5.21
Japan	1970	2.1	2.03	-0.07	-3.28	2000	1.3	1.36	0.02	1.23
Mongolia	1973	7.5	7.33	-0.16	-2.14	2000	2.3	2.59	0.33	12.86
Republic of Korea	1970	4.3	4.54	0.24	5.23	2000	1.5	1.47	-0.07	-4.72
South-central Asia										
Afghanistan	1973	8.2	7.40	-0.81	-10.95	..	..	..	..	..
Bangladesh	1973	6.1	6.15	0.08	1.22	1997	3.4	4.04	0.64	15.72
Bhutan	..	..	..	..	..	1993	5.6	5.75	0.17	2.87
India	1981	4.9	4.62	-0.29	-6.38	1997	3.3	3.52	0.20	5.70
Iran (Islamic Republic of)	1975	6.4	6.44	0.03	0.47	2000	2.2	2.45	0.28	11.47
Kazakhstan	1970	3.3	3.59	0.28	7.84	1997	2.1	2.17	0.06	2.63
Kyrgyzstan	1970	4.9	4.90	0.04	0.86	2000	2.4	2.79	0.36	13.01
Maldives	..	..	..	..	..	1990	6.4	6.40	-0.02	-0.31
Nepal	1974	6.0	5.77	-0.24	-4.10	2000	4.3	4.50	0.19	4.24
Pakistan	1970	6.0	6.28	0.27	4.22	1999	4.8	5.40	0.63	11.57
Sri Lanka	1971	4.2	4.31	0.15	3.52	1996	2.3	2.22	-0.09	-4.09
Tajikistan	1970	5.9	6.77	0.86	12.71	1993	4.2	4.43	0.23	5.21
Turkmenistan	1970	5.7	6.28	0.60	9.60	1998	3.0	3.03	0.00	0.00
Uzbekistan	1970	5.6	6.48	0.84	12.96	2000	2.6	2.70	0.12	4.43
South-eastern Asia										
Brunei Darussalam	1970	5.8	5.73	-0.12	-2.04	2000	2.4	2.61	0.21	8.15
Cambodia	1960	7.0	6.30	-0.71	-11.33	1996	5.2	5.33	0.15	2.72
Democratic Republic of Timor-Leste	..	..	..	..	..	1993	4.7	4.75	0.07	1.37
Indonesia	1969	5.6	5.49	-0.11	-2.01	1996	2.8	2.76	-0.04	-1.29
Lao People's Democratic Republic	..	..	..	..	..	1997	4.9	5.40	0.52	9.63
Malaysia	1970	4.7	5.62	0.96	17.00	1998	3.1	3.26	0.14	4.18
Myanmar	1973	5.7	5.75	0.05	0.87	1994	2.9	3.70	0.80	21.62
Philippines	1971	6.0	6.20	0.23	3.71	1996	3.8	3.84	0.07	1.77
Singapore	1970	3.1	3.12	0.02	0.73	2000	1.7	1.48	-0.18	-12.24
Thailand	1967	6.2	6.08	-0.12	-1.97	1995	2.0	2.04	0.06	3.09
Viet Nam	1977	4.8	6.05	1.25	20.66	1994	2.7	3.14	0.46	14.65
Western Asia										
Armenia	1970	3.2	3.28	0.12	3.59	1998	1.9	1.42	-0.48	-33.45
Azerbaijan	1970	4.6	4.68	0.11	2.41	2000	2.1	2.22	0.15	6.76

TABLE II.14. (continued)

Country or area	Total fertility rate					Total fertility rate				
	Reference date	From World Fertility Report 2003	Calculated from the 2002 Revision	Difference	Percentage difference	Reference date	From World Fertility Report 2003	Calculated from the 2002 Revision	Difference	Percentage difference
Bahrain	1971	6.7	6.36	-0.35	-5.43	1999	2.8	2.91	0.07	2.29
Cyprus	1970	2.7	2.67	-0.07	-2.53	2000	1.6	1.94	0.34	17.58
Georgia	1970	2.7	2.61	-0.07	-2.67	1998	1.7	1.58	-0.14	-8.54
Iraq	1974	7.1	7.00	-0.12	-1.77	1989	5.2	6.06	0.85	13.94
Israel	1970	3.9	3.78	-0.13	-3.51	2000	3.0	2.85	-0.11	-3.83
Jordan	1974	7.6	7.71	0.08	1.01	2001	3.7	3.78	0.11	3.00
Kuwait	1970	6.7	7.21	0.50	6.98	1994	4.3	3.14	-1.21	-38.46
Lebanon	1970	4.6	5.60	1.03	18.35	1993	2.5	2.83	0.33	11.66
Occupied Palestinian Territory	1970	7.5	7.89	0.41	5.25	1997	6.1	6.08	-0.02	-0.26
Oman	:	:	:			1993	7.4	6.49	-0.90	-13.87
Qatar	:	:	:			1996	4.1	3.86	-0.20	-5.18
Saudi Arabia	:	:	:			1994	6.1	5.63	-0.47	-8.43
Syrian Arab Republic	1970	7.7	7.56	-0.12	-1.55	1991	4.7	5.23	0.53	10.16
Turkey	1970	5.7	5.48	-0.20	-3.63	2000	2.5	2.59	0.11	4.25
United Arab Emirates	:	:	:			1993	5.0	3.80	-1.24	-32.63
Yemen	1977	8.5	8.48	-0.03	-0.35	1996	6.7	7.50	0.78	10.40
Europe										
Eastern Europe										
Belarus	1970	2.3	2.33	0.03	1.20	2001	1.3	1.23	-0.05	-3.83
Bulgaria	1970	2.2	2.16	-0.01	-0.60	2001	1.2	1.12	-0.13	-11.38
Czech Republic	1970	1.9	2.05	0.15	7.18	2001	1.1	1.17	0.03	2.74
Hungary	1970	2.0	2.02	0.04	2.03	2001	1.3	1.27	-0.04	-3.22
Poland	1971	2.3	2.26	0.00	0.00	2001	1.3	1.35	0.06	4.45
Republic of Moldova	1969	2.6	2.64	0.08	2.84	2001	1.3	1.46	0.21	14.34
Romania	1970	2.9	2.82	-0.07	-2.41	2000	1.3	1.32	0.01	0.98
Russian Federation	1978	2.0	1.94	-0.06	-3.09	2001	1.3	1.18	-0.07	-5.66
Slovakia	1970	2.4	2.50	0.10	4.03	2001	1.2	1.33	0.13	9.49
Ukraine	1970	2.1	2.09	-0.01	-0.34	1998	1.2	1.25	0.06	5.12
Northern Europe										
Channel Islands	:					:				
Denmark	1970	2.0	2.14	0.15	6.92	2001	1.7	1.76	0.02	0.95
Estonia	1970	2.2	2.07	-0.09	-4.44	2001	1.3	1.24	-0.09	-7.56
Finland	1970	1.8	1.88	0.06	2.95	2001	1.7	1.74	0.01	0.55
Iceland	1970	2.8	3.03	0.22	7.18	2000	2.1	2.01	-0.07	-3.26
Ireland	1970	3.9	3.85	0.00	-0.03	2001	2.0	1.90	-0.08	-4.05

TABLE II.14. *(continued)*

Country or area	Reference date	Total fertility rate				Reference date	Total fertility rate			
		From World Fertility Report 2003	Calculated from the 2002 Revision	Difference	Percentage difference		From World Fertility Report 2003	Calculated from the 2002 Revision	Difference	Percentage difference
Latvia	1970	2.0	1.89	-0.13	-6.89	2001	1.2	1.13	-0.08	-7.45
Lithuania	1970	2.4	2.29	-0.10	-4.37	2001	1.3	1.30	0.01	0.54
Norway	1970	2.5	2.53	0.03	1.05	2001	1.8	1.82	0.04	1.94
Sweden	1970	1.9	2.05	0.13	6.50	2001	1.6	1.60	0.04	2.25
United Kingdom	1972	2.2	2.14	-0.06	-2.86	2000	1.6	1.66	0.01	0.72
Southern Europe										
Albania	1970	5.1	4.93	-0.19	-3.79	1999	2.1	2.40	0.30	12.31
Bosnia and Herzegovina	1970	2.7	2.95	0.25	8.36	1998	1.6	1.35	-0.21	-15.56
Croatia	1970	1.8	2.04	0.21	10.35	2001	1.4	1.63	0.26	15.83
Greece	1970	2.4	2.36	-0.04	-1.78	1999	1.3	1.29	0.01	0.93
Italy	1970	2.4	2.43	0.04	1.76	2000	1.2	1.22	-0.03	-2.20
Malta	1975	2.2	2.05	-0.12	-5.60	2001	1.5	1.81	0.35	19.57
Portugal	1970	3.0	2.81	-0.20	-7.06	2001	1.5	1.46	0.00	-0.26
Serbia and Montenegro	1970	2.3	2.40	0.10	4.20	2000	1.7	1.72	0.06	3.72
Slovenia	1970	2.1	2.27	0.15	6.70	2001	1.2	1.18	-0.03	-2.11
Spain	1970	2.9	2.90	0.02	0.66	2000	1.2	1.17	-0.06	-5.45
TFYR Macedonia	1970	3.0	3.24	0.25	7.82	2000	1.9	1.91	0.03	1.36
Western Europe										
Austria	1970	2.3	2.33	0.03	1.40	2001	1.3	1.31	0.00	0.02
Belgium	1970	2.3	2.17	-0.08	-3.53	1995	1.5	1.61	0.06	3.63
France	1970	2.5	2.49	0.02	0.65	1999	1.8	1.79	-0.01	-0.36
Germany	1970	2.0	2.05	0.02	1.12	2000	1.4	1.34	-0.04	-2.98
Luxembourg	1970	2.0	2.13	0.15	7.06	2001	1.7	1.73	0.07	4.05
Netherlands	1970	2.6	2.50	-0.07	-2.73	2001	1.7	1.67	-0.04	-2.30
Switzerland	1970	2.1	2.09	-0.02	-0.76	2001	1.4	1.44	0.02	1.67
Latin America and the Caribbean										
Caribbean										
Bahamas	1970	3.5	3.65	0.20	5.56	1996	2.3	2.48	0.18	7.33
Barbados	1970	3.0	3.17	0.14	4.45	1988	1.6	1.75	0.17	9.71
Cuba	1970	3.7	3.99	0.30	7.42	2000	1.6	1.55	-0.04	-2.66
Dominican Republic	1973	5.7	5.63	-0.08	-1.48	1999	2.9	2.85	-0.08	-2.90
Guadeloupe	1970	4.6	4.93	0.35	7.13	1991	2.2	2.24	0.06	2.72
Haiti	1975	5.5	5.84	0.34	5.75	1998	4.7	4.38	-0.30	-6.80
Jamaica	1970	5.5	5.47	-0.08	-1.41	1996	2.9	2.60	-0.26	-9.83

TABLE II.14. (continued)

Country or area	Reference date	Total fertility rate				Reference date	Total fertility rate			
		From World Fertility Report 2003	Calculated from the 2002 Revision	Difference	Percentage difference		From World Fertility Report 2003	Calculated from the 2002 Revision	Difference	Percentage difference
Martinique	1970	4.4	4.63	0.24	5.26	1992	1.9	1.98	0.04	2.27
Netherlands Antilles	..	..	..	..	..	..	..	..	..	..
Puerto Rico	1970	3.2	3.24	0.08	2.54	2000	2.0	1.95	-0.10	-5.05
Saint Lucia	1975	5.5	5.49	0.00	0.03	2000	2.0	2.35	0.31	13.37
Saint Vincent and the Grenadines	..	..	..	..	..	..	..	..	..	..
Trinidad and Tobago	1971	3.6	3.59	-0.04	-1.17	1997	1.7	1.74	0.02	1.27
United States Virgin Islands	1970	5.3	3.44	-1.86	-54.06	1990	3.0	2.31	-0.74	-31.89
Central America										
Belize	1970	6.2	6.31	0.06	0.99	1998	3.2	3.60	0.39	10.84
Costa Rica	1970	4.9	5.22	0.30	5.73	1999	2.4	2.52	0.11	4.43
El Salvador	1971	6.0	6.31	0.28	4.44	1996	3.6	3.31	-0.28	-8.31
Guatemala	1972	6.3	6.48	0.21	3.26	1997	5.1	5.02	-0.06	-1.28
Honduras	1972	7.5	7.12	-0.37	-5.21	1994	5.0	4.79	-0.16	-3.28
Mexico	1974	6.2	6.28	0.10	1.63	1996	2.7	2.90	0.17	5.93
Nicaragua	1983	5.8	6.20	0.41	6.61	1999	3.3	4.21	0.88	20.97
Panama	1970	5.0	5.35	0.36	6.78	2000	2.7	2.75	0.08	3.03
South America										
Argentina	1970	3.2	3.09	-0.08	-2.50	2000	2.5	2.55	0.07	2.75
Bolivia	1974	6.5	6.36	-0.14	-2.20	1996	4.4	4.51	0.14	3.20
Brazil	1980	3.9	4.08	0.19	4.59	1994	2.6	2.53	-0.03	-0.99
Chile	1970	3.3	4.12	0.84	20.32	1999	2.1	2.42	0.33	13.81
Colombia	1974	4.7	4.87	0.17	3.55	1998	2.6	2.80	0.18	6.32
Ecuador	1977	5.3	5.52	0.18	3.27	1997	3.3	3.18	-0.11	-3.36
French Guiana	1973	3.9	4.18	0.27	6.39	1999	4.1	3.73	-0.40	-10.76
Guyana	1973	4.9	4.90	-0.01	-0.31	..	..	..	..	..
Paraguay	1977	5.0	5.25	0.29	5.43	1997	4.3	4.24	-0.06	-1.35
Peru	1975	5.5	5.75	0.21	3.59	1998	3.0	3.20	0.17	5.16
Suriname	1970	5.6	5.68	0.08	1.45	2000	2.7	2.55	-0.17	-6.70
Uruguay	1970	2.7	2.88	0.17	5.91	2000	2.2	2.36	0.16	6.75
Venezuela	1970	5.7	5.52	-0.16	-2.88	2000	2.7	2.88	0.19	6.67
Canada	1970	2.3	2.29	0.04	1.53	1997	1.6	1.59	0.04	2.47
United States of America	1970	2.5	2.33	-0.14	-6.03	2000	2.1	2.08	-0.05	-2.37

TABLE II.14. *(continued)*

Country or area	Total fertility rate					Total fertility rate				
	Reference date	*From World Fertility Report 2003*	*Calculated from the 2002 Revision*	*Difference*	*Percentage difference*	*Reference date*	*From World Fertility Report 2003*	*Calculated from the 2002 Revision*	*Difference*	*Percentage difference*
Oceania										
Australia	1970	2.9	2.74	-0.12	-4.46	2000	1.7	1.74	-0.01	-0.35
New Zealand	1970	3.1	3.15	0.00	-0.08	2000	2.0	1.99	-0.02	-1.16
Melanesia										
Fiji	1972	4.1	4.36	0.23	5.28	1986	3.4	3.60	0.20	5.62
New Caledonia	1970	5.3	5.06	-0.23	-4.45	1999	2.5	2.57	0.05	2.12
Papua New Guinea	1980	6.0	5.69	-0.31	-5.52	1994	4.8	4.96	0.12	2.42
Solomon Islands	1973	7.4	7.23	-0.18	-2.54	1985	6.1	6.23	0.16	2.54
Vanuatu	1977	6.6	5.82	-0.73	-12.59	1989	4.9	5.00	0.12	2.36
Micronesia										
Guam	1970	4.8	4.48	-0.27	-6.05	1992	3.7	3.11	-0.55	-17.61
Micronesia (Federated States of)	..	..		..		..	..		..	
Polynesia										
French Polynesia	1968	6.7	6.20	-0.48	-7.78	1991	4.9	4.75	-0.19	-3.94
Samoa	..	..		..		..	..		..	
Tonga	..	..		..		..	..		..	

Population Division, DESA, United Nations

TABLE II.15. COMPARISON OF TOTAL FERTILITY ESTIMATES AS PRESENTED IN THE COUNTRY TABLES OF THIS REPORT AND AS ESTIMATED FROM THE 2002 REVISION OF *WORLD POPULATION PROSPECTS* FOR REFERENCE DATES WITHIN 1960-1985

Rank	Country or area	Reference date	Total fertility rate		Difference	Percentage difference
			From World Fertility Report 2003	*Calculated from the 2002 Revision*		
1	United States Virgin Islands	1970	5.30	3.44	-1.86	-54.06
2	Burundi..	1980	7.91	6.80	-1.11	-16.31
3	Afghanistan	1973	8.21	7.40	-0.81	-10.95
4	Vanuatu	1977	6.56	5.82	-0.73	-12.59
5	Cambodia.......................................	1960	7.01	6.30	-0.71	-11.33
6	Congo	1974	6.99	6.29	-0.70	-11.08
7	French Polynesia	1968	6.68	6.20	-0.48	-7.78
8	Sudan..	1973	7.07	6.67	-0.40	-6.00
9	Honduras	1972	7.50	7.12	-0.37	-5.21
10	Bahrain	1971	6.70	6.36	-0.35	-5.43
11	United Republic of Tanzania	1971	7.11	6.77	-0.34	-5.01
12	Papua New Guinea	1980	6.00	5.69	-0.31	-5.52
13	India...	1981	4.91	4.62	-0.29	-6.38
14	Guam	1970	4.75	4.48	-0.27	-6.05
15	Nepal	1974	6.01	5.77	-0.24	-4.10
16	Ghana	1968	7.14	6.90	-0.23	-3.41
17	New Caledonia	1970	5.29	5.06	-0.23	-4.45
18	Algeria	1977	7.42	7.22	-0.20	-2.76
19	Turkey	1970	5.68	5.48	-0.20	-3.63
20	Portugal	1970	3.01	2.81	-0.20	-7.06
21	Albania	1970	5.12	4.93	-0.19	-3.79
22	Solomon Islands	1973	7.42	7.23	-0.18	-2.54
23	China	1970	5.75	5.58	-0.17	-3.04
24	Mozambique...................................	1970	6.70	6.54	-0.16	-2.45
25	Venezuela......................................	1970	5.68	5.52	-0.16	-2.88
26	Mongolia	1973	7.49	7.33	-0.16	-2.14
27	Senegal	1976	7.16	7.00	-0.16	-2.23
28	United States of America..................	1970	2.47	2.33	-0.14	-6.03
29	Bolivia..	1974	6.50	6.36	-0.14	-2.20
30	Israel...	1970	3.91	3.78	-0.13	-3.51
31	Zambia..	1980	7.20	7.07	-0.13	-1.84
32	Latvia...	1970	2.02	1.89	-0.13	-6.89
33	Iraq	1974	7.13	7.00	-0.12	-1.77
34	Australia..	1970	2.86	2.74	-0.12	-4.46
35	Thailand..	1967	6.20	6.08	-0.12	-1.97
36	Syrian Arab Republic	1970	7.68	7.56	-0.12	-1.55
37	Brunei Darussalam	1970	5.84	5.73	-0.12	-2.04
38	Malta..	1975	2.17	2.05	-0.12	-5.60
39	Indonesia	1969	5.61	5.49	-0.11	-2.01
40	Lithuania.......................................	1970	2.39	2.29	-0.10	-4.37
41	Estonia..	1970	2.16	2.07	-0.09	-4.44
42	Dominican Republic	1973	5.71	5.63	-0.08	-1.48
43	Argentina.......................................	1970	3.16	3.09	-0.08	-2.50
44	Jamaica...	1970	5.55	5.47	-0.08	-1.41

TABLE II.15. *(continued)*

Rank	Country or area	Reference date	Total fertility rate		Difference	Percentage difference
			From World Fertility Report 2003	Calculated from the 2002 Revision		
45	Belgium	1970	2.25	2.17	-0.08	-3.53
46	Georgia	1970	2.68	2.61	-0.07	-2.67
47	Netherlands	1970	2.57	2.50	-0.07	-2.73
48	Romania	1970	2.89	2.82	-0.07	-2.41
49	Cyprus	1970	2.74	2.67	-0.07	-2.53
50	Japan	1970	2.10	2.03	-0.07	-3.28
51	United Kingdom	1972	2.20	2.14	-0.06	-2.86
52	Russian Federation	1978	2.00	1.94	-0.06	-3.09
53	Central African Republic	1975	5.85	5.79	-0.06	-1.00
54	Lesotho	1975	5.79	5.74	-0.05	-0.85
55	Cameroon	1976	6.41	6.36	-0.04	-0.71
56	Trinidad and Tobago	1971	3.63	3.59	-0.04	-1.17
57	Greece	1970	2.40	2.36	-0.04	-1.78
58	Malawi	1977	7.60	7.56	-0.04	-0.53
59	Yemen	1977	8.51	8.48	-0.03	-0.35
60	Uganda	1969	7.13	7.10	-0.03	-0.35
61	Switzerland	1970	2.10	2.09	-0.02	-0.76
62	Guyana	1973	4.92	4.90	-0.01	-0.31
63	Sierra Leone	1973	6.51	6.50	-0.01	-0.22
64	Bulgaria	1970	2.17	2.16	-0.01	-0.60
65	Ukraine	1970	2.10	2.09	-0.01	-0.34
66	Ethiopia	1981	6.83	6.83	-0.01	-0.08
67	Comoros	1980	7.05	7.05	0.00	-0.04
68	New Zealand	1970	3.15	3.15	0.00	-0.08
69	Ireland	1970	3.85	3.85	0.00	-0.03
70	Poland	1971	2.26	2.26	0.00	0.00
71	Saint Lucia	1975	5.49	5.49	0.00	0.03
72	Benin	1980	7.08	7.09	0.01	0.20
73	France	1970	2.47	2.49	0.02	0.65
74	Spain	1970	2.88	2.90	0.02	0.66
75	Singapore	1970	3.10	3.12	0.02	0.73
76	Germany	1970	2.03	2.05	0.02	1.12
77	Norway	1970	2.50	2.53	0.03	1.05
78	Mauritius	1972	3.42	3.45	0.03	0.78
79	Belarus	1970	2.30	2.33	0.03	1.20
80	Iran (Islamic Republic of)	1975	6.41	6.44	0.03	0.47
81	Austria	1970	2.29	2.33	0.03	1.40
82	Canada	1970	2.26	2.29	0.04	1.53
83	Hungary	1970	1.98	2.02	0.04	2.03
84	Kyrgyzstan	1970	4.86	4.90	0.04	0.86
85	Italy	1970	2.38	2.43	0.04	1.76
86	Côte d'Ivoire	1978	7.36	7.41	0.05	0.67
87	Myanmar	1973	5.70	5.75	0.05	0.87
88	Finland	1970	1.83	1.88	0.06	2.95
89	Réunion	1970	4.40	4.46	0.06	1.34
90	Belize	1970	6.25	6.31	0.06	0.99

TABLE II.15. *(continued)*

Rank	Country or area	Reference date	Total fertility rate		Difference	Percentage difference
			From World Fertility Report 2003	Calculated from the 2002 Revision		
91	Mali	1985	6.93	7.00	0.08	1.07
92	Bangladesh	1973	6.08	6.15	0.08	1.22
93	Republic of Moldova	1969	2.57	2.64	0.08	2.84
94	Jordan	1974	7.63	7.71	0.08	1.01
95	Puerto Rico	1970	3.16	3.24	0.08	2.54
96	Suriname	1970	5.60	5.68	0.08	1.45
97	Democratic Republic of the Congo	1971	6.30	6.39	0.09	1.41
98	Slovakia	1970	2.40	2.50	0.10	4.03
99	Serbia and Montenegro	1970	2.30	2.40	0.10	4.20
100	Mexico	1974	6.18	6.28	0.10	1.63
101	Azerbaijan	1970	4.56	4.68	0.11	2.41
102	Armenia	1970	3.17	3.28	0.12	3.59
103	Sweden	1970	1.92	2.05	0.13	6.50
104	Barbados	1970	3.03	3.17	0.14	4.45
105	Gambia	1973	6.35	6.50	0.15	2.25
106	Czech Republic	1970	1.90	2.05	0.15	7.18
107	Denmark	1970	1.99	2.14	0.15	6.92
108	Somalia	1975	7.10	7.25	0.15	2.07
109	Luxembourg	1970	1.98	2.13	0.15	7.06
110	Sri Lanka	1971	4.16	4.31	0.15	3.52
111	Slovenia	1970	2.12	2.27	0.15	6.70
112	Madagascar	1975	6.39	6.56	0.17	2.59
113	Uruguay	1970	2.71	2.88	0.17	5.91
114	Colombia	1974	4.70	4.87	0.17	3.55
115	Ecuador	1977	5.34	5.52	0.18	3.27
116	Brazil	1980	3.89	4.08	0.19	4.59
117	Morocco	1977	5.91	6.10	0.19	3.16
118	Bahamas	1970	3.45	3.65	0.20	5.56
119	Botswana	1971	6.50	6.70	0.21	3.06
120	Peru	1975	5.55	5.75	0.21	3.59
121	Croatia	1970	1.83	2.04	0.21	10.35
122	Guatemala	1972	6.27	6.48	0.21	3.26
123	Mauritania	1979	6.25	6.46	0.22	3.33
124	Iceland	1970	2.81	3.03	0.22	7.18
125	Philippines	1971	5.97	6.20	0.23	3.71
126	Fiji	1972	4.13	4.36	0.23	5.28
127	Republic of Korea	1970	4.30	4.54	0.24	5.23
128	Martinique	1970	4.39	4.63	0.24	5.26
129	Bosnia and Herzegovina	1970	2.71	2.95	0.25	8.36
130	TFYR Macedonia	1970	2.98	3.24	0.25	7.82
131	China, Hong Kong SAR	1970	3.31	3.57	0.26	7.30
132	Pakistan	1970	6.02	6.28	0.27	4.22
133	French Guiana	1973	3.91	4.18	0.27	6.39
134	El Salvador	1971	6.03	6.31	0.28	4.44
135	Kazakhstan	1970	3.31	3.59	0.28	7.84

TABLE II.15. *(continued)*

Rank	Country or area	Reference date	Total fertility rate		Difference	Percentage difference
			From World Fertility Report 2003	Calculated from the 2002 Revision		
136	Paraguay	1977	4.97	5.25	0.29	5.43
137	Equatorial Guinea	1983	5.50	5.79	0.29	5.01
138	Liberia	1984	6.61	6.90	0.29	4.20
139	Cuba	1970	3.70	3.99	0.30	7.42
140	Costa Rica	1970	4.92	5.22	0.30	5.73
141	Haiti	1975	5.51	5.84	0.34	5.75
142	Guadeloupe	1970	4.58	4.93	0.35	7.13
143	Panama	1970	4.98	5.35	0.36	6.78
144	Nicaragua	1983	5.79	6.20	0.41	6.61
145	Occupied Palestinian Territory	1970	7.47	7.89	0.41	5.25
146	Cape Verde	1982	5.77	6.22	0.45	7.31
147	Togo	1970	6.65	7.10	0.46	6.41
148	Burkina Faso	1985	7.19	7.68	0.50	6.45
149	Kuwait	1970	6.70	7.21	0.50	6.98
150	Kenya	1969	7.60	8.12	0.52	6.40
151	Tunisia	1970	6.09	6.62	0.53	8.04
152	Rwanda	1970	7.70	8.24	0.54	6.51
153	Nigeria	1980	6.34	6.90	0.56	8.17
154	Turkmenistan	1970	5.68	6.28	0.60	9.60
155	Libyan Arab Jamahiriya	1973	6.81	7.59	0.78	10.27
156	Egypt	1970	5.39	6.22	0.82	13.23
157	Chile	1970	3.28	4.12	0.84	20.32
158	Uzbekistan	1970	5.64	6.48	0.84	12.96
159	Zimbabwe	1969	6.74	7.60	0.86	11.32
160	Tajikistan	1970	5.91	6.77	0.86	12.71
161	Malaysia	1970	4.67	5.62	0.96	17.00
162	Lebanon	1970	4.57	5.60	1.03	18.35
163	China, Macao SAR	1970	2.04	3.08	1.04	33.70
164	Guinea	1983	5.84	7.00	1.16	16.57
165	Viet Nam	1977	4.80	6.05	1.25	20.66
166	Swaziland	1966	5.20	6.90	1.70	24.64

TABLE II.16. COMPARISON OF TOTAL FERTILITY ESTIMATES AS PRESENTED IN THE COUNTRY TABLES OF THIS REPORT AND AS ESTIMATED FROM THE 2002 REVISION OF WORLD POPULATION PROSPECTS FOR REFERENCE DATES WITHIN 1984-2001

Rank	Country or area	Reference date	Total fertility rate		Difference	Percentage difference
			From World Fertility Report 2003	Calculated from the 2002 Revision		
1	United Arab Emirates	1993	5.0	3.80	-1.24	-32.63
2	Kuwait	1994	4.3	3.14	-1.21	-38.46
3	Oman	1993	7.4	6.49	-0.90	-13.87
4	United States Virgin Islands	1990	3.0	2.31	-0.74	-31.89
5	Guam	1992	3.7	3.11	-0.55	-17.61
6	Armenia	1998	1.9	1.42	-0.48	-33.45
7	Saudi Arabia	1994	6.1	5.63	-0.47	-8.43
8	French Guiana	1999	4.1	3.73	-0.40	-10.76
9	Haiti	1998	4.7	4.38	-0.30	-6.80
10	El Salvador	1996	3.6	3.31	-0.28	-8.31
11	Jamaica	1996	2.9	2.60	-0.26	-9.83
12	Bosnia and Herzegovina	1998	1.6	1.35	-0.21	-15.56
13	Qatar	1996	4.1	3.86	-0.20	-5.18
14	Samoa	1991	4.9	4.75	-0.19	-3.94
15	Singapore	2000	1.7	1.48	-0.18	-12.24
16	Suriname	2000	2.7	2.55	-0.17	-6.70
17	Honduras	1994	5.0	4.79	-0.16	-3.28
18	Senegal	1996	5.8	5.66	-0.15	-2.67
19	Burundi	1985	7.0	6.80	-0.15	-2.21
20	Egypt	1999	3.6	3.47	-0.14	-3.92
21	Georgia	1998	1.7	1.58	-0.14	-8.54
22	Bulgaria	2001	1.2	1.12	-0.13	-11.38
23	Israel	2000	3.0	2.85	-0.11	-3.83
24	Ecuador	1997	3.3	3.18	-0.11	-3.36
25	Puerto Rico	2000	2.0	1.95	-0.10	-5.05
26	Estonia	2001	1.3	1.24	-0.09	-7.56
27	Sri Lanka	1996	2.3	2.22	-0.09	-4.09
28	Latvia	2001	1.2	1.13	-0.08	-7.45
29	Dominican Republic	1999	2.9	2.85	-0.08	-2.90
30	Ireland	2001	2.0	1.90	-0.08	-4.05
31	Republic of Korea	2000	1.5	1.47	-0.07	-4.72
32	Russian Federation	2001	1.3	1.18	-0.07	-5.66
33	Iceland	2000	2.1	2.01	-0.07	-3.26
34	Guatemala	1997	5.1	5.02	-0.06	-1.28
35	Spain	2000	1.2	1.17	-0.06	-5.45
36	Paraguay	1997	4.3	4.24	-0.06	-1.35
37	United States of America	2000	2.1	2.08	-0.05	-2.37
38	Belarus	2001	1.3	1.23	-0.05	-3.83
39	Cuba	2000	1.6	1.55	-0.04	-2.66
40	Hungary	2001	1.3	1.27	-0.04	-3.22
41	Germany	2000	1.4	1.34	-0.04	-2.98
42	Netherlands	2001	1.7	1.67	-0.04	-2.30
43	Indonesia	1996	2.8	2.76	-0.04	-1.29
44	Mali	1994	7.0	7.00	-0.03	-0.43
45	Italy	2000	1.2	1.22	-0.03	-2.20

TABLE II.16. *(continued)*

Rank	Country or area	Reference date	Total fertility rate		Difference	Percentage difference
			From World Fertility Report 2003	Calculated from the 2002 Revision		
46	Brazil	1994	2.6	2.53	-0.03	-0.99
47	Slovenia	2001	1.2	1.18	-0.03	-2.11
48	New Zealand	2000	2.0	1.99	-0.02	-1.16
49	Morocco	1999	3.0	2.95	-0.02	-0.75
50	Maldives	1990	6.4	6.40	-0.02	-0.31
51	Occupied Palestinian Territory	1997	6.1	6.08	-0.02	-0.26
52	Cape Verde	1996	4.2	4.16	-0.01	-0.36
53	Zambia	2000	5.9	5.89	-0.01	-0.25
54	Mauritius	2000	2.0	2.01	-0.01	-0.45
55	France	1999	1.8	1.79	-0.01	-0.36
56	Australia	2000	1.7	1.74	-0.01	-0.35
57	Portugal	2001	1.5	1.46	0.00	-0.26
58	Democratic Republic of the Congo	1984	6.7	6.70	0.00	0.00
59	Turkmenistan	1998	3.0	3.03	0.00	0.00
60	Austria	2001	1.3	1.31	0.00	0.02
61	Lithuania	2001	1.3	1.30	0.01	0.54
62	Finland	2001	1.7	1.74	0.01	0.55
63	United Kingdom	2000	1.6	1.66	0.01	0.72
64	Greece	1999	1.3	1.29	0.01	0.93
65	Romania	2000	1.3	1.32	0.01	0.98
66	Japan	2000	1.3	1.36	0.02	1.23
67	Denmark	2001	1.7	1.76	0.02	0.95
68	Libyan Arab Jamahiriya	1993	4.1	4.10	0.02	0.49
69	Trinidad and Tobago	1997	1.7	1.74	0.02	1.27
70	Switzerland	2001	1.4	1.44	0.02	1.67
71	Malawi	1998	6.4	6.46	0.03	0.39
72	Chad	1995	6.6	6.65	0.03	0.38
73	TFYR Macedonia	2000	1.9	1.91	0.03	1.36
74	Czech Republic	2001	1.1	1.17	0.03	2.74
75	Norway	2001	1.8	1.82	0.04	1.94
76	Sweden	2001	1.6	1.60	0.04	2.25
77	Réunion	1998	2.3	2.30	0.04	1.68
78	Canada	1997	1.6	1.59	0.04	2.47
79	Martinique	1992	1.9	1.98	0.04	2.27
80	New Caledonia	1999	2.5	2.57	0.05	2.12
81	Kazakhstan	1997	2.1	2.17	0.06	2.63
82	Belgium	1995	1.5	1.61	0.06	3.63
83	Poland	2001	1.3	1.35	0.06	4.45
84	Guadeloupe	1991	2.2	2.24	0.06	2.72
85	Thailand	1995	2.0	2.04	0.06	3.09
86	Ukraine	1998	1.2	1.25	0.06	5.12
87	Serbia and Montenegro	2000	1.7	1.72	0.06	3.72
88	Democratic Republic of Timor-Leste	1993	4.7	4.75	0.07	1.37
89	Bahrain	1999	2.8	2.91	0.07	2.29
90	Philippines	1996	3.8	3.84	0.07	1.77
91	Luxembourg	2001	1.7	1.73	0.07	4.05

TABLE II.16. *(continued)*

Rank	Country or area	Reference date	Total fertility rate		Difference	Percentage difference
			From World Fertility Report 2003	Calculated from the 2002 Revision		
92	Argentina	2000	2.5	2.55	0.07	2.75
93	Madagascar	1995	6.1	6.16	0.08	1.30
94	Panama	2000	2.7	2.75	0.08	3.03
95	United Republic of Tanzania	1998	5.6	5.70	0.10	1.75
96	Turkey	2000	2.5	2.59	0.11	4.25
97	Costa Rica	1999	2.4	2.52	0.11	4.43
98	Lesotho	1991	4.8	4.91	0.11	2.28
99	Jordan	2001	3.7	3.78	0.11	3.00
100	China, Hong Kong SAR	2001	0.9	1.04	0.11	10.96
101	Vanuatu	1989	4.9	5.00	0.12	2.36
102	Uzbekistan	2000	2.6	2.70	0.12	4.43
103	Papua New Guinea	1994	4.8	4.96	0.12	2.42
104	Dem. People's Republic of Korea	1993	2.2	2.31	0.12	5.21
105	Slovakia	2001	1.2	1.33	0.13	9.49
106	Uganda	1999	7.0	7.10	0.13	1.83
107	Malaysia	1998	3.1	3.26	0.14	4.18
108	Bolivia	1996	4.4	4.51	0.14	3.20
109	Cambodia	1996	5.2	5.33	0.15	2.72
110	Azerbaijan	2000	2.1	2.22	0.15	6.76
111	Solomon Islands	1985	6.1	6.23	0.16	2.54
112	Uruguay	2000	2.2	2.36	0.16	6.75
113	Bhutan	1993	5.6	5.75	0.17	2.87
114	Peru	1998	3.0	3.20	0.17	5.16
115	Barbados	1988	1.6	1.75	0.17	9.71
116	Tunisia	1999	2.1	2.26	0.17	7.58
117	Mexico	1996	2.7	2.90	0.17	5.93
118	Burkina Faso	1996	6.8	6.97	0.17	2.49
119	Colombia	1998	2.6	2.80	0.18	6.32
120	Rwanda	1999	5.9	6.11	0.18	2.92
121	Bahamas	1996	2.3	2.48	0.18	7.33
122	Cameroon	1996	5.2	5.34	0.19	3.46
123	Nepal	2000	4.3	4.50	0.19	4.24
124	Venezuela	2000	2.7	2.88	0.19	6.67
125	Sierra Leone	1985	6.3	6.50	0.20	3.08
126	India	1997	3.3	3.52	0.20	5.70
127	Fiji	1986	3.4	3.60	0.20	5.62
128	Republic of Moldova	2001	1.3	1.46	0.21	14.34
129	Brunei Darussalam	2000	2.4	2.61	0.21	8.15
130	Kenya	1996	4.7	4.92	0.22	4.37
131	China, Macao SAR	2000	0.9	1.13	0.22	19.69
132	Tajikistan	1993	4.2	4.43	0.23	5.21
133	South Africa	1996	2.9	3.10	0.24	7.74
134	Gabon	1998	4.3	4.50	0.25	5.44
135	Gambia	1988	5.9	6.20	0.26	4.11
136	Croatia	2001	1.4	1.63	0.26	15.83

TABLE II.16. *(continued)*

Rank	Country or area	Reference date	Total fertility rate		Difference	Percentage difference
			From World Fertility Report 2003	Calculated from the 2002 Revision		
137	Benin...............................	1999	5.8	6.06	0.28	4.55
138	Iran (Islamic Republic of)......................	2000	2.2	2.45	0.28	11.47
139	Albania............................	1999	2.1	2.40	0.30	12.31
140	Saint Lucia	2000	2.0	2.35	0.31	13.37
141	Côte d'Ivoire....................	1997	5.1	5.44	0.32	5.88
142	Lebanon	1993	2.5	2.83	0.33	11.66
143	Mongolia..........................	2000	2.3	2.59	0.33	12.86
144	Chile................................	1999	2.1	2.42	0.33	13.81
145	Ghana..............................	1996	4.5	4.88	0.34	6.86
146	Djibouti	1991	6.0	6.31	0.34	5.39
147	Cyprus.............................	2000	1.6	1.94	0.34	17.58
148	Malta	2001	1.5	1.81	0.35	19.57
149	Kyrgyzstan	2000	2.4	2.79	0.36	13.01
150	Congo..............................	1984	5.9	6.29	0.39	6.20
151	Belize..............................	1998	3.2	3.60	0.39	10.84
152	Algeria	1996	3.1	3.54	0.40	11.25
153	China...............................	2001	1.4	1.82	0.43	23.55
154	Central African Republic	1993	5.2	5.60	0.45	8.04
155	Guinea.............................	1997	5.8	6.30	0.46	7.27
156	Viet Nam..........................	1994	2.7	3.14	0.46	14.65
157	Mozambique	1995	5.6	6.08	0.47	7.73
158	Botswana	1986	5.0	5.48	0.48	8.77
159	Eritrea	2000	5.2	5.73	0.50	8.65
160	Lao People's Democratic Republic	1997	4.9	5.40	0.52	9.63
161	Niger	1997	7.5	8.00	0.53	6.63
162	Syrian Arab Republic............................	1991	4.7	5.23	0.53	10.16
163	Zimbabwe	1997	4.1	4.62	0.55	11.80
164	Togo................................	1996	5.4	5.96	0.56	9.43
165	Comoros...........................	1994	5.1	5.72	0.62	10.84
166	Pakistan...........................	1999	4.8	5.40	0.63	11.57
167	Ethiopia...........................	1998	5.9	6.50	0.64	9.77
168	Bangladesh.......................	1997	3.4	4.04	0.64	15.72
169	Namibia............................	1990	5.2	5.84	0.65	11.04
170	Yemen..............................	1996	6.7	7.50	0.78	10.40
171	Myanmar..........................	1994	2.9	3.70	0.80	21.62
172	Sudan	1992	4.6	5.36	0.81	15.11
173	Iraq.................................	1989	5.2	6.06	0.85	13.94
174	Nigeria	1997	5.1	6.01	0.87	14.42
175	Nicaragua.........................	1999	3.3	4.21	0.88	20.97
176	Mauritania........................	1999	4.7	5.96	1.28	21.45
177	Swaziland.........................	1986	5.0	6.42	1.43	22.27

PART THREE: DEFINITIONS AND SOURCES

I. DEFINITIONS

<u>Age-specific fertility rate</u> is the annual number of births to women in a particular age group per 1000 women in that age group. In all developed countries and in several developing countries, data on births by age of mother are obtained from civil registration covering 90 per cent or more of all live births. In developing countries lacking a civil registration system or where the coverage of that system is lower than 90 per cent of all live births, age-specific fertility rates are obtained from data gathered by surveys or censuses.

<u>Annual number of births</u> is the number of live births[1] registered over a calendar year by the civil registration system of a country. This report presents data on births only when national statistical offices estimate that their respective civil registration systems cover at least 90 per cent of all live births.

<u>Annual number of divorces</u> is the number of divorces granted (not the number of persons divorcing) during a calendar. The data are obtained from court records or from the civil registration system, following national practice. Divorce is the final legal dissolution of a marriage, that is, the separation of husband and wife which confers on the parties the right to remarry under civil, religious and/or other provisions, according to the laws of each country.[2]

<u>Annual number of marriages</u> is the number of all marriages over a calendar year, including both first marriages and remarriages after divorce, widowhood or annulment. The data are obtained from the civil registration system. Marriage is the act, ceremony or process by which the legal relationship of husband and wife is constituted. The legality of a union may be established by civil, religious, or other means as recognized by the laws of each country.[3]

<u>Children ever born by age of mother</u> is the average number of live births that women in a particular age group have ever had. It is derived from data gathered by censuses or surveys.

<u>Crude birth rate</u> is the annual number of live births per 1 000 population present at mid-year. It is usually derived from data on births from civil registration and data on population from a census.

<u>Government's policy regarding level of fertility</u> is the official response to the question "Does the Government wish to raise, lower or maintain the fertility level?" included in the Third (1976) or Eighth (2001) United Nations Inquiry among Governments on Population and Development.

<u>Government's support for contraceptive methods</u> is the official reply on that issue to the Third (1976) or Eighth (2001) United Nations Inquiry among Governments on Population and Development. "Direct support" means that the Government directly provides contraceptives through governmental agencies. "Indirect support" means that the Government indirectly supports provision of contraceptives by non-governmental sources.

---

[1] "Live birth is the complete expulsion or extraction from its mother of a product of conception, irrespective of the duration of pregnancy, which after such separation breathes or shows any other evidence of life such as beating of the heart, pulsation of the umbilical cord, or definitive movement of voluntary muscles, whether or not the umbilical cord has been cut or the placenta is attached; each product of such a birth is considered live-born regardless of gestational age" in *1999 Demographic Yearbook* (United Nations publication, Sales No. E/F.01.XIII.1), technical note 4.1.1.1.

[2] *1999 Demographic Yearbook* (United Nations publication, Sales No. E/F.01.XIII.1), technical note 4.1.1.5.

[3] *1999 Demographic Yearbook* (United Nations publication, Sales No. E/F.01.XIII.1), technical note 4.1.1.4.

Government's view on the level of fertility is the official reply to the question "What is the view of the Government concerning the present fertility level?" included in the Third (1976) or Eighth (2001) United Nations Inquiry among Governments on Population and Development.

Mean age at childbearing is the mean age of mothers at the birth of their children if women were subject throughout their lives to the age-specific fertility rates observed in a given year. It is computed as the sum of age-specific fertility rates weighted by the mid-point of each age group.

Mean age at first birth is the mean age of mothers at the birth of the first child. It is obtained from age-specific fertility rates derived from information on first births only. Data on first births by age of mother are normally obtained from a civil registration system. For developing countries lacking a reliable civil registration system, the median age at the birth of the first child for women aged 25-29 at the time of a survey has been used instead of the mean age at first birth. In this case, the indicator refers to a period located about ten years before the survey.

Mean age at first marriage is the average age at which men or women marry. It is derived from the distribution of first marriages by age group of husband or wife derived from civil registration data.

Percentage ever married by age group is the number of persons who are not single in a particular age group divided by all persons in that age group. These percentages are derived from census data on the population classified by current marital status, sex and age group. The ever married include those currently married, divorced or widowed.

Percentage of childless women by age group is the proportion of women in a particular age group who have never had a live birth. It is usually derived from census or survey data on women classified by the number of children ever born.

Percentage of extramarital births among all births is the number of live births whose parents, according to national law, were not married at the time of the birth,[4] divided by all live births and expressed in percentage terms.

Percentage of women with parity three or higher by age group is the number of women in a particular age group having had at least three live births over their lifetime divided by all women in that age group and expressed in percentage terms. This indicator is usually derived from data gathered by censuses or surveys.

Percentage using a modern contraceptive method is the percentage of women currently married or in union and aged 15-49 using a modern method of contraception. Modern contraceptive methods include sterilization (female or male), the pill, injectables, intra-uterine devices (IUDs), condoms, vaginal barrier methods and implants. Data on use of modern contraceptives are usually derived from surveys.

Percentage using any contraceptive method is the percentage of women currently married or in union and aged 15-49 using a modern or a traditional contraceptive method. Traditional contraceptive methods include rhythm (also called periodic abstinence or calendar method), withdrawal, breastfeeding, douching and various folk methods. Modern contraceptive methods include sterilization (female or male), the pill, injectables, intra-uterine devices (IUDs), condoms, vaginal barrier methods and implants.

Singulate mean age at marriage (SMAM) is the average length of single life in years among those who marry before age 50. This indicator is calculated from census data on the proportion of single men or women by age.

---

[4] *United Nations. Principles and Recommendations for a Vital Statistics System* (United Nations publication, Sales No. E.73.XVII.9), para. 136.

Total divorce rate is the number of divorces that men or women would have gone through by age 50 if the age-specific divorce rates observed in a given year applied throughout their life. This measure is expressed as number of divorces per person.

Total fertility rate is the average number of live births a woman would have by age 50 if she were subject, throughout her life, to the age-specific fertility rates observed in a given year. Its calculation assumes that there is no mortality. The total fertility rate is expressed as number of children per woman.

Total first marriage rate is the proportion of men or women who would have married at least once by age 50 if they had been subject throughout their lives to the age-specific first-marriages rates observed in a given year. It is expressed as the number of first marriages per person.[5]

The three cohort fertility indicators (children ever born by age of mother, percentage of childless women by age group and percentage of women by parity three or higher) are presented on ever married women (instead of all women) for the following countries/areas and years:

Australia (1976)
Belgium (1992)
Bulgaria (1975)
Canada (1961)
Channel Islands (1961)
China, Hong Kong SAR (1971)
China, Macao SAR (1960)
Cyprus (1973 and 1992)
Egypt (1976)
Guam (1960)
India (1981)
Indonesia (1971)
Iraq (1987)
Israel (1961)
Japan (1970)
Kuwait (1975)
Libyan Arab Jamahiriya (1973)
Luxembourg (1970)
Malaysia (1970)
Myanmar (1983)
New Zealand (1976)
Occupied Palestinian Territory (1997)
Poland (1970)
Republic of Korea (1970)
Singapore (1980 and 1990)
Sri Lanka (1971)
Syrian Arab Republic (1970)
Thailand (1970 and 2000)
Turkey (1970)
United Arab Emirates (1975 and 1995)
United States Virgin Islands (1970)
Yemen (1979 and 1997)

---

[5] Since the total first marriage rate is sensitive to changes in the timing of marriage, it may exceed 1.

II. Sources of Data

This volume presents only data that satisfy certain reliability criteria. Data on births, divorces and marriages derived from civil registration systems are retained only if the Statistics Division of the Department of Economic and Social Affairs of the United Nations Secretariat reports that they are "virtually complete", that is, they attain at least 90 per cent coverage of the relevant events. In a few cases, provisional figures or figures derived from sources of unknown or questionable reliability have been included provided they fall within a 10 per cent range of the estimates published in *World Population Prospects: The 2002 Revision*[6].

The indicators displayed in the country tables are normally derived from data from civil registration systems that satisfy the reliability criteria mentioned above or from censuses or nationally representative surveys. When several sources are available for the same period, the data presented are those judged to be the most reliable. In a few cases, indicators derived from survey data were considered to be better than those obtained from civil registration.

Tables III.1 to III.4 provide information on the sources of the data leading to the indicators presented in this report. In addition, data on the annual numbers of births, extra-marital births, marriages and divorces as well as on crude birth rates were obtained from demographic databases maintained by the Statistics Division, by the Council of Europe or by national statistical offices. Information on population policies was obtained from the Third (1976) and the Eighth (2001) United Nations Inquiries among Governments on Population and Development.

The availability of reliable data to calculate the different indicators varies widely. Tables III.5, III.6 and III.7 summarize such availability. They show that the availability of data has generally improved since the 1970s, particularly with respect to fertility indicators. Age-specific fertility data are available for at least one point in time within the period 1986-2000 for nearly 90 per cent of all countries. In order to provide some indication of fertility trends for as many countries as possible, the "recent" estimates for five countries in sub-Saharan Africa refer to 1984 or 1985 and therefore fall outside the period 1986-2000 to which the indicators of all other countries refer. Data on trends in total fertility are available for 83 per cent of all countries and those on trends of age-specific fertility are available for 78 per cent of all countries.

In spite of the large number of demographic surveys carried out during the 1990s, data on children ever born are not as widely available as those on total fertility, covering about 70 per cent of all countries in the period 1986-2000. Moreover, data on changes in children ever born are available for only 40 per cent of all countries. These data are more commonly available for developing countries than for developed countries because the censuses of the latter tend not to include questions on lifetime fertility.

Age-specific nuptiality data remain scarce in developing countries: total first marriage and divorce rates could be computed for less than one-quarter of all developing countries whereas they were available for all developed countries. There is better availability of data allowing the estimation of the singulate mean age at marriage (SMAM) and the percentages of ever-married persons by age group, especially for developing countries. In the 1970s, data on the percentage ever married and the SMAM were available for 80 per cent of all countries, in the 1990s the coverage had increased to 90 per cent.

Availability of data on contraceptive use in developing countries has shown the greatest improvement: data referring to the 1990s were available for nearly twice as many developing countries as those referring to the early 1970s. However, data on trends in contraceptive use are scarce and cover only about a third of all developing countries. Even for developed countries the coverage of available data on contraceptive use is far from ideal. Data on trends of contraceptive use are available for just about half of

---

[6] *World Population Prospects: The 2002 Revision*, volume I: Comprehensive Tables (United Nations publication, E.03.XIII.6).

all developed countries and although there has been an improvement in data availability between the early 1970s and the late 1990s, coverage is still far from complete in the 1990s.

In addition to the country profiles presented in tabular form this report includes, for each country, a plot of available estimates of total fertility that includes those presented in *World Population Prospects: The 2002 Revision*, a publication containing the official United Nations estimates and projections for all countries of the world. The total fertility estimates presented in the *2002 Revision* result from an assessment of available data on total fertility adjusted, as necessary, to be consistent with other relevant information. In contrast, the total fertility figures presented in this report have not been adjusted. Furthermore, whereas the estimates presented in the *2002 Revision* have been adjusted to refer to specific quinquennial periods, those in this report have different reference dates according to the sources from which they are derived. Hence, there is not a perfect comparability between the total fertility estimates in this report and the evaluated and adjusted figures presented in the *2002 Revision*. Nevertheless, the consistency between the two sets of information is high. Table II.14 in this report presents a comparison of the total fertility rates presented in the country profiles of this report and those estimated from the 2002 Revision figures so that their reference dates coincide with those presented in this report. Tables II.15 and II.16 present the same figure but ordered according to the size of the difference between the total fertility estimates derived from the *2002 Revision* and those presented in this report.

According to table II.15, for 61 of the 166 countries with data available for periods within 1960-1985, the absolute difference between the total fertility figures presented in this report and those derived from the *2002 Revision* is at most 0.1 of a child. Absolute differences of more than 0.4 children are found in 30 countries. If differences are gauged in percentage terms, only for 19 countries do they surpass 10 per cent. In general, the *2002 Revision* estimates tend to be higher than those obtained from national sources, especially in the case of countries with deficient data. However, in 7 countries, the *2002 Revision* estimates are markedly lower than the total fertility values obtained from national sources. These include countries such as Afghanistan, Burundi, Cambodia, the Congo and French Polynesia, where there is great paucity of data and the validation of existing estimates is difficult.

Regarding the estimates whose reference dates fall within the period 1985-2001, which are available for 177 countries, very close agreement between the total fertility rates presented in this volume and those derived from the *2002 Revision* occurs in 71 countries, where the difference between the two figures is at most 0.1 child per woman in absolute terms. Differences of more than 0.4 children in absolute terms occur in just 32 countries, in 25 of which the estimates of the *2002 Revision* are higher than those presented in this volume. Among the latter group, 15 countries are located in Africa and 9 in Asia and most of them are known to have deficient data. In the case of the 7 countries for which the *2002 Revision* estimates are markedly lower than national data, four are countries of the Gulf Cooperation Council whose data reflect the fertility of country nationals only, whereas the *2002 Revision* estimates represent the fertility of both nationals and foreigners, many of whom are childless women, thus being lower.

In sum, although agreement between the total fertility figures presented in this report and comparable figures derived from the *2002 Revision* is not perfect, the level of consistency of the two sets is very high. The data compiled for the preparation of this volume are already being used as basis for the preparation of the 2004 Revision of *World Population Prospects* so as to ensure that all relevant information is taken into account in revising the past estimates of fertility trends at the country level.

TABLE III.1. SOURCES OF DATA ON AGE-SPECIFIC FERTILITY RATES, TOTAL FERTILITY RATE AND MEAN AGE AT CHILDBEARING

Country name	Earlier period	Later period
Afghanistan	Survey 1973 [a]	...
Albania	Registration	Registration
Algeria	Registration	Registration
Angola	...	...
Argentina	Registration	Registration
Armenia	Registration	DHS 2000
Australia	Registration	Registration
Austria	Registration	Registration
Azerbaijan	Registration	RHS 2001
Bahamas	Registration	Registration
Bahrain	Census 1971	Registration
Bangladesh	WFS 1975	DHS 1999-2000
Barbados	Registration	Registration
Belarus	Registration	Registration
Belgium	Registration	Registration
Belize	Registration	Registration
Benin	WFS 1982	DHS 2001
Bhutan	...	Survey 1994 [t]
Bolivia	Census 1976	DHS 1998
Bosnia and Herzegovina	Registration	Registration
Botswana	Census 1971	FHS 1988
Brazil	Census 1980	DHS 1996
Brunei Darussalam	Registration	Registration
Bulgaria	Registration	Registration
Burkina Faso	Census 1985	DHS 1998-1999
Burundi	Census 1980	DHS 1987
Cambodia	Survey 1960 [b]	Survey 1996 [u]
Cameroon	WFS 1978	DHS 1998
Canada	Registration	Registration
Cape Verde	Registration	RHS 1998
Central African Republic	Census 1975	DHS 1994-1995
Chad	...	DHS 1996-1997
Channel Islands	...	...
Chile	Registration	Registration
China	Survey 1970 [c]	Survey 2001 [v]
China: Hong Kong SAR	Registration	Registration
China: Macao SAR	Registration	Registration
Colombia	WFS 1976	DHS 2000
Comoros	Census 1980	DHS 1996
Congo	Census 1974	...
Costa Rica	Registration	Registration

TABLE III.1. *(continued)*

Country name	Earlier period	Later period
Côte d'Ivoire	WFS 1980-1981	DHS 1998-1999
Croatia	Registration	Registration
Cuba	Registration	Registration
Cyprus	Registration	Registration
Czech Republic	Registration	Registration
Democratic People's Republic of Korea	...	Survey 1993 [w]
Democratic Republic of the Congo	Survey 1971 [d]	Census 1984
Democratic Republic of Timor-Leste	...	DHS 1994 (Indonesia)
Denmark	Registration	Registration
Djibouti	...	Survey 1991 [x]
Dominican Republic	WFS 1975	Registration
Ecuador	WFS 1979	MCH 1999
Egypt	Registration	Registration
El Salvador	Registration	Survey 1998 [y]
Equatorial Guinea	Census 1983	...
Eritrea	...	DHS 2002
Estonia	Registration	Registration
Ethiopia	Survey 1981 [e]	DHS 2000
Fiji	WFS 1974	Census 1986
Finland	Registration	Registration
France	Registration	Registration
French Guiana	Registration	Registration
French Polynesia	Registration	...
Gabon	...	DHS 2000
Gambia	Census 1973	CPS 1990
Georgia	Registration	RHS 1999-2000
Germany	Registration	Registration
Ghana	WFS 1979-80	DHS 1998
Greece	Registration	Registration
Guadeloupe	Registration	Registration
Guam	Registration	Registration
Guatemala	Registration	MCH 1998-1999
Guinea	Census 1983	DHS 1999
Guinea-Bissau	...	...
Guyana	WFS 1975	...
Haiti	WFS 1977	Survey 2000 [z]
Honduras	CPS 1972	Survey 1995 [aa]
Hungary	Registration	Registration
Iceland	Registration	Registration
India	Census 1981	DHS 1998-1999
Indonesia	Census 1970	DHS 2003
Iran (Islamic Republic of)	Survey 1976-1977 [f]	DHS 2000

TABLE III.1 *(continued)*

Country name	Earlier period	Later period
Iraq	Survey 1974 [g]	AHS 1989
Ireland	Registration	Registration
Israel	Registration	Registration
Italy	Registration	Registration
Jamaica	Census 1970	RHS 1997
Japan	Registration	Registration
Jordan	WFS 1976	DHS 2002
Kazakhstan	Registration	DHS 1999
Kenya	Census 1969	DHS 1998
Kuwait	Registration	AHS 1996
Kyrgyzstan	Registration	Registration
Lao People's Democratic Republic	...	RHS 2000
Latvia	Registration	Registration
Lebanon	Survey 1981 [h]	AHS 1996
Lesotho	WFS 1977	DHS 1991
Liberia	DHS 1986	...
Libyan Arab Jamahiriya	Registration	AHS 1995
Lithuania	Registration	Registration
Luxembourg	Registration	Registration
Madagascar	Survey 1975 [i]	DHS 1997
Malawi	Census 1977	DHS 2000
Malaysia	Registration	Registration
Maldives	...	Census 1990
Mali	DHS 1987	DHS 1995-1996
Malta	Registration	Registration
Martinique	Registration	Registration
Mauritania	WFS 1981	DHS 2000-2001
Mauritius	Registration	Registration
Mexico	WFS 1976	Survey 1997 [ab]
Micronesia Federated States of	Registration	...
Mongolia	Census 1973	Registration
Morocco	WFS 1979	Registration
Mozambique	Census 1970	DHS 1997
Myanmar	Census 1973	RHS 1997
Namibia	...	DHS 1992
Nepal	WFS 1976	DHS 2001
Netherlands	Registration	Registration
Netherlands Antilles	...	...
New Caledonia	Registration	Registration
New Zealand	Registration	Registration
Nicaragua	Survey 1985 [j]	DHS 2001
Niger	Registration	DHS 1998
Nigeria	WFS 1982	DHS 1999

TABLE III.1 *(continued)*

Country name	Earlier period	Later period
Norway	Registration	Registration
Occupied Palestinian Territory	Registration	Census 1997
Oman	...	AHS 1995
Pakistan	Survey 1970 [k]	RHS 2000-2001
Panama	Registration	Registration
Papua New Guinea	Survey 1980 [l]	DHS 1996
Paraguay	WFS 1979	MCH 1998
Peru	WFS 1976	DHS 2000
Philippines	Survey 1973 [m]	DHS 1998
Poland	Registration	Registration
Portugal	Registration	Registration
Puerto Rico	Registration	Registration
Qatar	...	AHS 1998
Republic of Korea	Census 1970	Registration
Republic of Moldova	Registration	Registration
Réunion	Registration	Registration
Romania	Registration	Registration
Russian Federation	Registration	Registration
Rwanda	Survey 1970 [n]	DHS 2000
Saint Lucia	Registration	Registration
Saint Vincent and the Grenadines	Registration	...
Samoa	Registration	Survey 1991 [ac]
Sao Tome and Principe	Registration	...
Saudi Arabia	Registration	AHS 1996
Senegal	WFS 1978	DHS 1997
Serbia and Montenegro	...	...
Sierra Leone	Survey 1973 [o]	Census 1985
Singapore	Registration	Registration
Slovakia	Registration	Registration
Slovenia	Registration	Registration
Solomon Islands	Census 1986	Census 1986
Somalia	Census 1975	...
South Africa	...	DHS 1997
Spain	Registration	Registration
Sri Lanka	Census 1971	...
Sudan	Census 1973	MCH 1992-1993
Suriname	Survey 1970 [p]	Registration
Swaziland	Census 1966	Survey 1988 [ad]
Sweden	Registration	Registration
Switzerland	Registration	Registration
Syrian Arab Republic	Survey 1970 [q]	MCH 1998
Tajikistan	Registration	Registration
TFYR of Macedonia	Registration	Registration

TABLE III.1 *(continued)*

Country name	Earlier period	Later period
Thailand	Census 1970	CPS 1996
Togo	Survey 1970 [r]	DHS 1998
Tonga	...	...
Trinidad and Tobago	Registration	Registration
Tunisia	Registration	Registration
Turkey	Registration	Registration
Turkmenistan	Registration	DHS 2000
Uganda	Census 1969	DHS 2000-2001
Ukraine	Registration	Registration
United Arab Emirates	Registration	AHS 1993
United Kingdom	Registration	Registration
United Republic of Tanzania	Survey 1973 [s]	RHS 1999
United States of America	Registration	Registration
United States Virgin Islands	Registration	Registration
Uruguay	Registration	Registration
Uzbekistan	Registration	Registration
Vanuatu	Census 1979	Census 1989
Venezuela	Registration	Registration
Viet Nam	Census 1979	DHS 1997
Western Sahara	Registration	...
Yemen	WFS 1979	MCH 1997
Zambia	Census 1980	DHS 2001-2002
Zimbabwe	Census 1969	DHS 1999

Notes

[a] James Trussell and Eleanor Brown, 1979. A close look at the demography of Afghanistan. Demography, vol. 16, table 4, p. 144

[b] G. S. Siampos. The population of Cambodia, 1945-80. *The Milbank Memorial Fund Quarterly*, vol. LXVII, no. 3, 1970.

[c] One-per-thousand sample survey

[d] Etude demographique de l'ouest du Zaire, 1975-76

[e] Demographic Survey 1981

[f] Fertility Survey 1976-1977

[g] UN ECWA(1980) The Population Situation in the ECWA Region. Iraq,T.5.4, p.5-10

[h] UN ECWA(1980) The Population Situation in the ECWA Region. Lebanon, T.8-2, p.8-8

[i] United Nations, Economic Commission for Africa, Second African Population Conference, Country Statement (Addis Ababa, 1984), table II, p. 214.

[j] ESDENIC 1985

[k] Fertility levels and trends as assessed from twenty World Fertility Surveys (United Nations 1983 publication, Series No. ST/ESA/SER.R/50) Table PK-3, p. 224.

[l] W. K. A. Agyei, *Fertility and Family Planning in the Third World: A Case Study of Papua New Guinea* (New York, Croom Helm, 1988), p.61, table 5.2.

[m] Demographic Survey 1973

[n] Enquête démographique 1970

[o] United Nations, Economic Commission for Africa, Second African Population Conference, Country Statements (Addis Ababa, 1984), p. 320.

TABLE III.1 *(continued)*

[p]   Survey or Estimate: National Report on Population and Development prepared for the International Conference Home Affairs of the Republic of Suriname, December 1993.

[q]   Omran, Abdel-Rahim, *Population in the Arab World: Problems and Prospects* (New York and London: United Nations Fund for Population Activities and Croom Helms Ltd., 1980), table 4.5, pp. 86-87.

[r]   World Population Trends, Population and Development Interrelations and Population Policies. 1993 Monitoring Report, vol. 1, Population Trends (United Nations publication, Sales No. E.84.XIII.10), table 12, p. 39.

[s]   Survey 1973

[t]   Health Survey 1994

[u]   Demografic Survey of Cambodia 1996

[v]   Sample Survey on Population Change 2001

[w]   *Population Today*, vol. 22, No. 11 (Nov. 1994).

[x]   1991 Demographic Survey

[y]   Family Health Survey 1998

[z]   Enquête mortalité, morbidité et utilisation des services 2000

[aa]   Encuesta Nacional de Salud Masculina 1995

[ab]   Encuesta de la Dinámica Demográfica 1997

[ac]   Personal communication from Andreas Demmke, South Pacific Commission (Noumea, New Caledonia), February 1997.

[ad]   Family Health Survey 1988

TABLE III.2. SOURCES OF DATA ON CHILDREN EVER BORN, PROPORTION OF CHILDLESS WOMEN AND PROPORTION OF WOMEN WITH PARITY THREE OR HIGHER

Country name	Earlier period	Later period
Afghanistan	..	..
Albania	..	..
Algeria	..	MCH 1992
Angola	..	..
Argentina	Census 1971	Census 1991
Armenia	..	DHS 2000
Australia	Census 1976	Census 1986
Austria	Census 1981	FFS 1995-1996
Azerbaijan	..	DHS 2001
Bahamas	Census 1980	Census 1980
Bahrain	Census 1971	AHS 1995
Bangladesh	WFS 1975-1976	DHS 1999-2000
Barbados	Census 1980	..
Belarus	..	Census 1991
Belgium	Census 1970	FFS 1992 [a]
Belize	Census 1980	Census 1991
Benin	WFS 1982	DHS 2001
Bhutan	..	..
Bolivia	Census 1976	DHS 1998
Bosnia and Herzegovina	..	..
Botswana	Census 1971	Census 1991
Brazil	Census 1970	DHS 1996
Brunei Darussalam	Census 1960	..
Bulgaria	Census 1975	FFS 1997-1998
Burkina Faso	Census 1985	DHS 1999
Burundi	..	DHS 1987
Cambodia	..	DHS 2000
Cameroon	WFS 1978	DHS 1998
Canada	Census 1961	Census 1991
Cape Verde	..	..
Central African Republic	Census 1975	DHS 1994-1995
Chad	..	DHS 1996-1997
Channel Islands	Census 1961	..
Chile	Census 1982	Census 1992
China	..	Census 1990
China: Hong Kong SAR	Census 1971	..
China: Macao SAR	Census 1960	..
Colombia	Census 1973	DHS 2000
Comoros	..	DHS 1996
Congo	..	..
Costa Rica	Census 1973	..
Côte d'Ivoire	WFS 1980	DHS 1998-1999
Croatia	..	Census 1991

TABLE III.2. *(continued)*

Country name	Earlier period	Later period
Cuba	Census 1981	..
Cyprus	Census 1973	Census 1992
Czech Republic	..	Census 1991
Democratic People's Republic of Korea	Census 1970	..
Democratic Republic of the Congo	..	..
Democratic Republic of Timor-Leste	..	..
Denmark	..	..
Djibouti	..	..
Dominican Republic	Census 1970	DHS 1999
Ecuador	Census 1974	Census 2001
Egypt	Census 1976	DHS 2000
El Salvador	Census 1971	FHS 1998
Equatorial Guinea	..	..
Eritrea	..	DHS 2002
Estonia	..	FFS 1994
Ethiopia	..	DHS 2000
Fiji	Census 1966	Census 1986
Finland	..	Census 2000
France	..	FFS 1994
French Guiana	Census 1967	..
French Polynesia	..	..
Gabon	..	DHS 2000
Gambia	Census 1973	..
Georgia	..	..
Germany	..	..
Ghana	WFS 1979-1980	DHS 1998
Greece	..	..
Guadeloupe	Census 1967	..
Guam	Census 1960	..
Guatemala	Census 1973	DHS 1998-99
Guinea	..	DHS 1999
Guinea-Bissau	..	..
Guyana	Census 1970	..
Haiti	WFS 1977	Survey 2000 [c]
Honduras	Census 1974	..
Hungary	Census 1970	Census 1990
Iceland	Census 1970	..
India	Census 1981	DHS 1998-1999
Indonesia	Census 1971	DHS 2003
Iran (Islamic Republic of)	Census 1976	Census 1986
Iraq	..	Census 1987
Ireland	..	Census 2002

TABLE III.2. *(continued)*

Country name	Earlier period	Later period
Israel	Census 1961	..
Italy	..	FFS 1995-1996
Jamaica	WWF 1975-1976	Census 1991
Japan	Census 1970	..
Jordan	WWS 1976	DHS 1997
Kazakhstan	..	Census 1999
Kenya	Census 1969	DHS 1998
Kuwait	Census 1975	..
Kyrgyzstan	..	DHS 1997
Lao People's Democratic Republic	..	..
Latvia	..	FFS 1995
Lebanon	..	..
Lesotho	WFS 1977	..
Liberia	..	DHS 1986
Libyan Arab Jamahiriya	Census 1973	AHS 1995
Lithuania	..	FFS 1994-1995
Luxembourg	Census 1970	Census 1991
Madagascar	..	DHS 1997
Malawi	Census 1977	DHS 2000
Malaysia	Census 1970	..
Maldives	Census 1977	Census 2000
Mali	Census 1984	DHS 2001
Malta	..	..
Martinique	Census 1967	..
Mauritania	WFS 1981	DHS 2000-2001
Mauritius	..	Census 2000
Mexico	Census 1970	Census 2000
Micronesia Federated States of	..	Census 1994
Mongolia	..	..
Morocco	WFS 1979-1980	DHS 1995
Mozambique	Census 1980	DHS 1997
Myanmar	Census 1983	..
Namibia	..	Census 1991
Nepal	WFS 1976	DHS 2001
Netherlands	..	FFS 1993
Netherlands Antilles	Census 1971	Census 2001
New Caledonia	..	..
New Zealand	Census 1976	..
Nicaragua	Census 1971	DHS 2001
Niger	..	DHS 1998
Nigeria	..	DHS 1999
Norway	Census 1960	FFS 1988-1989
Occupied Palestinian Territory	..	Census 1997

TABLE III.2. *(continued)*

Country name	Earlier period	Later period
Oman	..	AHS 1995
Pakistan	CPS 1974-1975	DHS 1990-1991
Panama	WFS 1975-76	Census 1990
Papua New Guinea	Census 1980	..
Paraguay	WFS 1979	Census 1992
Peru	Census 1972	DHS 2000
Philippines	WFS 1978	DHS 1998
Poland	Census 1970	FFS 1991
Portugal	Census 1970	Census 1991
Puerto Rico	Census 1970	Census 1990
Qatar	..	AHS 1998
Republic of Korea	Census 1970	Census 1990
Republic of Moldova	..	Census 1989
Réunion	Census 1967	..
Romania	Census 1966	Census 1992
Russian Federation	..	Survey 1994 [d]
Rwanda	Census 1978	DHS 2000
Saint Lucia	Census 1970	Census 1992
Saint Vincent and the Grenadines	Census 1980	Census 1991
Samoa	Census 1971	..
Sao Tome and Principe	Census 1980	Census 1991
Saudi Arabia	..	AHS 1996
Senegal	WFS 1978	DHS 1997
Serbia and Montenegro	..	..
Sierra Leone	..	..
Singapore	Census 1980	Census 1990
Slovakia	..	..
Slovenia	..	FFS 1994-1995
Solomon Islands	Census 1970	..
Somalia	..	..
South Africa	..	DHS 1998
Spain	..	FFS 1994-1995
Sri Lanka	Census 1971	DHS 1993
Sudan	WFS 1978-1979	DHS 1990
Suriname	Census 1964	..
Swaziland	..	Census 1997
Sweden	..	FFS 1992-1993
Switzerland	..	FFS 1994-1995
Syrian Arab Republic	Census 1970	..
Tajikistan	..	Census 1989
Thailand	Census 1970	Census 2000
The Former Yugoslav Rep. of Macedonia	Census 1970	Census 2000
Togo	..	DHS 1998

TABLE III.2. *(continued)*

Country name	Earlier period	Later period
Tonga	Census 1966	Census 1996
Trinidad and Tobago	WFS 1977	Census 1990
Tunisia	WFS 1978	..
Turkey	Census 1970	DHS 1998
Turkmenistan	..	DHS 2000
Uganda	..	DHS 2000-2001
Ukraine	..	Census 1989
United Arab Emirates	Census 1975	AHS 1995
United Kingdom	..	..
United Republic of Tanzania	Census 1967	RHS 1999
United States of America	Census 1980	Survey [e]
United States Virgin Islands	Census 1970	..
Uruguay	Census 1975	Census 1996
Uzbekistan	..	DHS 1996
Vanuatu	Census 1967	Census 1989
Venezuela	Census 1961	Census 1990
Viet Nam	..	Census 1999
Western Sahara	..	..
Yemen	Census 1979	MCH 1997
Zambia	Census 1969	DHS 2001-2002
Zimbabwe	..	DHS 1999

Notes

[a]   Dutch-speaking community of the Flemish Region only

[b]   Family Health Survey 1998

[c]   Enquête mortalité, morbidité et utilisation des services 2000

[d]   Microcensus 1994

[e]   Current Population Survey 2000

TABLE III.3. SOURCES OF DATA ON PROPORTION EVER-MARRIED AND SINGULATE MEAN AGE AT MARRIAGE

Country	Earlier period	Later period
Afghanistan	Census 1979	..
Albania	..	Census 1989
Algeria	Census 1977	Survey [b]
Angola	Census 1970	..
Argentina	Census 1970	Census 1991
Armenia	Census 1979	DHS 2000
Australia	Census 1971	Estimate 2000
Austria	Census 1971	Census 1991
Azerbaijan	Census 1979	Census 1999
Bahamas	Census 1970	Census 1990
Bahrain	..	Census 1991
Bangladesh	Census 1974	DHS 1999-2000
Barbados	Census 1970	Census 1990
Belarus	Census 1979	Census 1999
Belgium	Census 1970	Census 2000
Belize	Census 1970	Census 1991
Benin	Census 1979	DHS 1996
Bhutan	..	Survey 1994 [c]
Bolivia	Census 1976	DHS 1998
Bosnia and Herzegovina	..	..
Botswana	Census 1971	Census 1991
Brazil	Census 1970	DHS 1996
Brunei Darussalam	Census 1971	Census 1991
Bulgaria	Census 1975	Census 1985
Burkina Faso	Census 1975	DHS 1999
Burundi	Census 1970-1971	Census 1990
Cambodia	Census 1962	Census 1998
Cameroon	Census 1976	DHS 1998
Canada	Census 1971	Census 2000
Cape Verde	Census 1980	Census 1990
Central African Republic	Census 1975	DHS 1994-1995
Chad	Census 1964	DHS 1996-1997
Channel Islands	..	..
Chile	Census 1970	Census 1992
China	Census 1982	Census 2000
China: Hong Kong SAR	Census 1971	Census 1996
China: Macao SAR	Census 1970	Census 1991
Colombia	Census 1973	DHS 2000
Comoros	Census 1980	DHS 1996
Congo	Census 1984	..
Costa Rica	Census 1973	RHS 1986

TABLE III.3. *(continued)*

Country name	Earlier period	Later period
Côte d'Ivoire	Census 1978	DHS 1998-1999
Croatia	..	Census 2001
Cuba	Census 1970	..
Cyprus	Census 1973	Census 1992
Czech Republic	..	Eurostat estimate
Democratic Censusople's Republic of Korea	..	..
Democratic Republic of the Congo	Census 1984	..
Democratic Republic of Timor-Leste	..	..
Denmark	Census 1970	Estimate 2001
Djibouti	..	..
Dominican Republic	Census 1970	DHS 1996
Ecuador	Census 1974	Census 2001
Egypt	Census 1976	Census 1996
El Salvador	Census 1971	Census 2000
Equatorial Guinea	Census 1983	..
Eritrea	..	DHS 1995-1996
Estonia	Census 1979	Census 1989
Ethiopia	Census 1984	DHS 2000
Fiji	Census 1976	Census 1996
Finland	Census 1970	Census 2000
France	Census 1975	Census 2000
French Guiana	Census 1967	Census 1999
French Polynesia	Census 1977	Census 1996
Gabon	Census 1961	DHS 2000
Gambia	Census 1983	Census 1993
Georgia	Census 1979	Census 1999
Germany	..	..
Ghana	Survey[a]	DHS 1998
Greece	Census 1971	Census 1991
Guadeloupe	Census 1967	Census 1990
Guam	Census 1980	Census 1990
Guatemala	Census 1973	DHS 1998-1999
Guinea	..	DHS 1999
Guinea-Bissau	..	..
Guyana	Census 1970	Census 1991
Haiti	Census 1971	DHS 2000
Honduras	Census 1974	EHS1996
Hungary	Census 1970	Eurostat estimate
Iceland	Census 1974	Eurostat estimate
India	Census 1971	DHS 1998-1999

TABLE III.3. *(continued)*

Country name	Earlier period	Later period
Indonesia	Census 1971	Census 2000
Iran (Islamic Republic of)	Census 1976	Census 1996
Iraq	Census 1977	Census 1987
Ireland	Census 1971	Census 2002
Israel	Census 1972	Census 1999
Italy	Census 1971	Eurostat estimate
Jamaica	Census 1970	Census 1991
Japan	Census 1970	Census 2000
Jordan	Census 1979	DHS 1994
Kazakhstan	Census 1979	Census 1999
Kenya	Census 1969	DHS 1998
Kuwait	Census 1970	AHS 1996
Kyrgyzstan	Census 1979	Census 1999
Lao People's Democratic Republic	..	RHS 2000
Latvia	Census 1979	Estimate 2002
Lebanon	Census 1970	..
Lesotho	Census 1976	Census 1986
Liberia	Census 1970	DHS 1986
Libyan Arab Jamahiriya	Census 1973	MCH 1995
Lithuania	Census 1979	Census 2001
Luxembourg	Census 1970	Census 1991
Madagascar	Census 1975	DHS 1997
Malawi	Census 1977	DHS 2000
Malaysia	Census 1970	Census 2000
Maldives	Census 1977	Census 2000
Mali	Census 1976	DHS 1995-1996
Malta	Census 1967	Census 1985
Martinique	Census 1967	Census 1990
Mauritania	Census 1977	DHS 2000-2001
Mauritius	Census 1972	Census 1990
Mexico	Census 1970	Census 2000
Micronesia Federated States of	Census 1980	Census 1994
Mongolia	..	RHS 1998
Morocco	Census 1971	Census 1994
Mozambique	Census 1970	DHS 1997
Myanmar	Census 1973	Survey 1991 [d]
Namibia	Census 1960	DHS 1992
Nepal	Census 1971	DHS 2001
Netherlands	Census 1971	Census 2002
Netherlands Antilles	Census 1971	Census 2001
New Caledonia	Census 1969	Census 1996
New Zealand	Census 1976	Census 1996

TABLE III.3. *(continued)*

Country name	Earlier period	Later period
Nicaragua	Census 1971	Census 1998
Niger	Census 1959	DHS 1998
Nigeria	..	DHS 1999
Norway	Census 1970	Census 2002
Occupied Palestinian Territory	Census 1967	Census 1997
Oman	..	AHS 1995
Pakistan	Census 1972	Census 1998
Panama	Census 1970	Census 2000
Papua New Guinea	Census 1980	Survey 1996 [e]
Paraguay	Census 1972	Census 1992
Russian Federation	Census 1972	DHS 1996
Philippines	Census 1970	Census 1995
Poland	Census 1978	Census 1999
Portugal	Census 1970	Census 1991
Puerto Rico	Census 1970	RHS 1995-1996
Qatar	Survey 1982	AHS 1998
Republic of Korea	Census 1970	Census 1995
Republic of Moldova	Census 1979	Census 1989
Réunion	Census 1974	Census 1990
Romania	Census 1977	Census 2000
Russian Federation	Census 1979	Census 1989
Rwanda	Census 1970	DHS 2000
Saint Lucia	Census 1970	Census 1991
Saint Vincent and the Grenadines	Census 1970	Census 1991
Samoa	Census 1971	Census 1999
Sao Tome and Principe	Census 1981	Census 1991
Saudi Arabia	..	AHS 1996
Senegal	Census 1970	DHS 1997
Serbia and Montenegro	..	Census 1991
Sierra Leone	..	Survey 1992 [f]
Singapore	Census 1970	Census 2001
Slovakia	..	Census 2001
Slovenia	..	Census 2001
Solomon Islands	Census 1970	Census 1986
Somalia	..	..
South Africa	Census 1980	Census 1996
Spain	Census 1970	Census 1991
Sri Lanka	Census 1971	DHS 1993
Sudan	Census 1973	Census 1993
Suriname	Census 1964	..
Swaziland	..	Census 1991
Sweden	Census 1970	Census 2001
Switzerland	Census 1970	Census 2001
Syrian Arab Republic	Census 1970	..

TABLE III.3. *(continued)*

Country name	Earlier period	Later period
Tajikistan	Census 1979	Census 1989
Thailand	Census 1970	Census 1990
The Former Yugoslav Republic of Macedonia	..	Census 1994
Togo	Census 1970	DHS 1998
Tonga	Census 1976	Census 1996
Trinidad and Tobago	Census 1970	Census 1990
Tunisia	Census 1975	Census 1994
Turkey	Census 1975	DHS 1998
Turkmenistan	Census 1979	DHS 2001
Uganda	Census 1969	DHS 2000-2001
Ukraine	Census 1979	RHS 1999
United Arab Emirates	Census 1975	AHS 1995
United Kingdom	Census 1971	Census 1991
United Republic of Tanzania	Census 1978	DHS 1996
United States of America	Census 1970	Survey [g]
United States Virgin Islands	Census 1960	Survey [h]
Uruguay	Census 1975	Census 1996
Uzbekistan	..	DHS 1996
Vanuatu	Census 1979	Census 1989
Venezuela	Census 1971	Census 1990
Viet Nam	..	DHS 1997
Western Sahara	Census 1970	..
Yemen	..	MCH 1997
Zambia	Census 1969	DHS 2001-2002
Zimbabwe	Census 1982	DHS 1999

Notes

[a] Data from the United States Bureau of the Census (unspecified survey)

[b] Survey. Pan-Arab Project for Child Development, 1992

[c] Data from the United States Bureau of the Census (unspecified survey)

[d] Population Change and Fertility Survey 1991

[e] Data from the United States Bureau of the Census (unspecified survey)

[f] Demographic and Social Monitoring Survey 1992

[g] Current Population Survey

[h] Data from the United States Bureau of the Census (unspecified survey)

TABLE III.4. SOURCES OF DATA ON CONTRACEPTIVE USE

Country name	Earlier period	Later period
Afghanistan	Survey 1973 [a]	MICS 2000
Albania	..	MICS 2000
Algeria	..	MICS 2000
Angola	..	MICS 2001
Argentina	..	..
Armenia	..	DHS 2000
Australia	..	Australia Family Project 1986
Austria	Survey 1982 [b]	FFS 1996
Azerbaijan	..	RHS 2001
Bahamas	..	CPS 1988
Bahrain	..	AHS 1995
Bangladesh	WFS 1975-1976	DHS 1999-2000
Barbados	CPS 1981	CPS 1988
Belarus	..	Survey of married women 18-34, 1995
Belgium	Survey 1976 [c]	FFS 1992
Belize	..	FHS 1991
Benin	WFS 1982	DHS 2001
Bhutan	..	Health Survey 1994
Bolivia	CPS 1983	MICS 2000
Bosnia and Herzegovina	..	MICS 2000
Botswana	FHS 1984	MICS 2000
Brazil	..	DHS 1996
Brunei Darussalam	..	..
Bulgaria	WFS 1976	FFS 1997
Burkina Faso	..	DHS 1999
Burundi	..	MICS 2000
Cambodia	..	DHS 2000
Cameroon	WFS 1978	DHS 1998
Canada	National Fertility Survey 1984	FFS 1995
Cape Verde	..	RHS 1998
Central African Republic	..	MICS 2000
Chad	..	MICS 2000
Channel Islands	..	..
Chile	..	..
China	1982 National One-per-Thousand Population Sample Survey in Birth Rate	National Population and Reproductive Health Sample Survey 1997
China: Hong Kong SAR	KAP 1972	KAP 1992
China: Macao SAR	..	..
Colombia	WFS 1976	DHS 2000
Comoros	..	MICS 2000
Congo	..	..
Costa Rica	WFS 1976	Fertility and family formation Survey 1993
Côte d'Ivoire	WFS 1981	DHS 1998-1999

TABLE III.4. *(continued)*

Country name	Earlier period	Later period
Croatia	..	..
Cuba	National Fertility Survey 1987	MICS 2000
Cyprus	..	..
Czech Republic	WFS 1970	WFS 1977
Democratic People's Republic of Korea	..	Survey 1992 [d]
Democratic Republic of the Congo	..	MICS 2001
Democratic Republic of Timor-Leste	..	..
Denmark	National Survey 1970	CPS 1988
Djibouti	..	..
Dominican Republic	WFS 1975	MICS 2000
Ecuador	WFS 1979	Demographic and Maternal and Child Health Survey 1999
Egypt	WFS 1980	DHS 2000
El Salvador	CPS 1975	FHS 1998
Equatorial Guinea	..	..
Eritrea	..	DHS 2002
Estonia	..	FFS 1994
Ethiopia	..	DHS 2000
Fiji	WFS 1974	..
Finland	National Survey 1971	FFS 1989
France	National Survey 1972	FFS 1994
French Guiana	..	..
French Polynesia	..	..
Gabon	..	DHS 2000
Gambia	..	MICS 2000
Georgia	..	RHS 2000
Germany	KAP 1985	FFS 1992
Ghana	WFS 1979-1980	DHS 1999
Greece	..	..
Guadeloupe	Fertility and Contraceptive Use Survey 1976	..
Guam	..	..
Guatemala	CPS 1978	DHS 1998-1999
Guinea	..	DHS 1999
Guinea-Bissau	..	MICS 2000
Guyana	WFS 1975	MICS 2000
Haiti	WFS 1977	Enquête Mortalité, Morbidité et Utilisation des Services 2000
Honduras	CPS 1981	Epidemiologic and Family Health Survey 2001
Hungary	Fertility, Family Planning and Birth Control Study 1974	FFS 1993
Iceland	..	..
India	All India Survey 1970	FHS 1998-1999

TABLE III.4. *(continued)*

Country name	Earlier period	Later period
Indonesia	Fertility and Mortality Survey 1973	DHS 2003
Iran (Islamic Republic of)	Fertility Survey 1976-1977	Family Planning Survey 1997
Iraq	Survey 1974 [e]	AHS 1989
Ireland	..	..
Israel	..	1987-1988 Study of Fertility and Family Formation
Italy	WFS 1979	FFS 1996
Jamaica	WFS 1975-1976	RHS 1997
Japan	Family Planning and Public Opinion Survey 1971	FHS 2000
Jordan	FHS 1972	DHS 2002
Kazakhstan	..	DHS 1999
Kenya	WFS 1978	DHS 1998
Kuwait	..	AHS 1996
Kyrgyzstan	..	DHS 1997
Lao People's Democratic Republic	..	FHS 2000
Latvia	..	FFS 1995
Lebanon	National Fertility and Family Planning Survey 1971	AHS 1996
Lesotho	WFS 1977	MICS 2000
Liberia	..	DHS 1986
Libyan Arab Jamahiriya	..	AHS 1995
Lithuania	..	FFS 1995
Luxembourg	..	..
Madagascar	..	MICS 2000
Malawi	FHS 1984	DHS 2000
Malaysia	WFS 1974	Socio-economic Survey 1994
Maldives	..	..
Mali	..	DHS 2001
Malta	..	..
Martinique	FHS 1976	..
Mauritania	WFS 1981	DHS 2000-2001
Mauritius	National Survey of Family Planning 1975	CPS 1991
Mexico	WFS 1976	Encuesta de la Dinámica Demográfica 1997
Micronesia Federated States of	..	..
Mongolia	..	MICS 2000
Morocco	WFS 1979-1980	DHS 1995
Mozambique	..	DHS 1997
Myanmar	..	Fertility and Reproductive Health Survey 1997
Namibia	..	DHS 1992
Nepal	WFS 1976	DHS 2001
Netherlands	WFS 1975	FFS 1993
Netherlands Antilles	..	..

TABLE III.4. *(continued)*

Country name	Earlier period	Later period
New Caledonia	..	..
New Zealand	Survey 1976 [f]	New Zealand Women: Family, Employment and Education Survey 1995
Nicaragua	CPS 1981	DHS 2001
Niger	..	MICS 2000
Nigeria	WFS 1982	DHS 1990
Norway	WFS 1977	FFS 1989
Occupied Palestinian Territory	..	..
Oman	..	AHS 1995
Pakistan	WFS 1974-1975	Reproductive and Family Planning Survey 2001
Panama	WFS 1975-1976	..
Papua New Guinea	..	FHS 1996
Paraguay	CPS 1977	RHS 1998
Peru	CPS 1970	DHS 2000
Philippines	Demographic Survey 1973	DHS 1998
Poland	WFS 1972	FFS 1991
Portugal	WFS 1980	..
Puerto Rico	Family Planning Survey 1974-75	RHS 1996
Qatar	..	AHS 1998
Republic of Korea	FHS 1971	Fertility and Family Health Survey 1997
Republic of Moldova	..	MICS 2000
Réunion	..	General Fertility and Family Planning Survey 1990
Romania	WFS 1978	RHS 1999
Russian Federation	..	..
Rwanda	Enquête démographique 1970	DHS 2000
Saint Lucia	CPS 1981	CPS 1988
Saint Vincent and the Grenadines	CPS 1981	CPS 1988
Samoa	..	..
Sao Tome and Principe	..	MICS 2000
Saudi Arabia	..	AHS 1996
Senegal	WFS 1978	DHS 1997
Serbia and Montenegro	..	..
Sierra Leone	..	MICS 2000
Singapore	Survey on Family Planning 1973	Family Planning and Population Survey 1997
Slovakia	..	KAP 1991
Slovenia	..	FFS 1994
Solomon Islands	..	..
Somalia	..	..
South Africa	Survey 1976 [g]	DHS 1998
Spain	WFS 1977	FFS 1995

TABLE III.4. *(continued)*

Country name	Earlier period	Later period
Sri Lanka	WFS 1975	DHS 1993
Sudan	WFS 1978-1979	AHS 1993
Suriname	..	MICS 2000
Swaziland	..	MICS 2000
Sweden	FFS 1981	..
Switzerland	Survey 1980[h]	FFS 1994-1995
Syrian Arab Republic	WFS 1978	AHS 1993
Tajikistan	..	MICS 2000
Thailand	Longitudinal Study of Social, Economic and Demographic Change 1969/1970	CPS 1996-1997
The Former Yugoslav Republic of Macedonia	..	..
Togo	..	MICS 2000
Tonga	..	..
Trinidad and Tobago	CPS 1971	MICS 2000
Tunisia	WFS 1978	AHS 1994
Turkey	Fertility Survey 1978	DHS 1998
Turkmenistan	..	DHS 2000
Uganda	..	DHS 2000-2001
Ukraine	..	RHS 1999
United Arab Emirates	..	AHS 1995
United Kingdom	General Household Survey 1970	General Household Survey 1993
United Republic of Tanzania	..	DHS 1999
United States of America	National Survey of Family Growth 1973	National Survey of Family Growth 1995
United States Virgin Islands	..	..
Uruguay	..	..
Uzbekistan	..	MICS 2000
Vanuatu	..	..
Venezuela	WFS 1977	..
Viet Nam	..	MICS 2000
Western Sahara	..	..
Yemen	WFS 1979	DHS 1997
Zambia	..	DHS 2001-2002
Zimbabwe	FHS 1984	DHS 1999

Notes

[a] James Trussell and Eleanor Brown, 1979. A close look at the demography of Afghanistan. Demography, vol. 16, table 4, p. 144

[b] Rainer, Münz, Leben mit Kindern: Wunsch und Wirklichkeit (Vienna, Franz Deuticke, 1985) Annex Table 6.2

[c] R. Cliquet and E. Lodewijckx, "The contraceptive transition in Flanders", *European Journal of Population* (Amsterdam), vol.2, No. 1 (May 1986), Tables 1 and 2.

[d] *Population Today*, vol. 22, No. 11 (Nov. 1994).

[e] UN ECWA(1980) The Population Situation in the ECWA Region. Iraq, T.5.4, p.5-10.

Table III.4. *(continued)*

[f]   J. Kukwood and others (1976) "Contraceptive practice among New Zealand women", *New Zealand Medical Journal*, vol.90 (Welligton, 1979) pp. 108-111.

[g]   1975/76: National Research Council, Factors Affecting Contraceptive Use in Sub-saharan Africa , Table 2-4

[h]   1980: Franz Kuhne, Kontrazeption inder Schweiz, table 5

TABLE III.5. DISTRIBUTION OF INDICATORS BY NUMBER OF OBSERVATIONS: NUPTIALITY DATA

Indicator	Earlier year		Later year		Both years	
Developing countries						
Annual number of marriages (thousands)	72		75		65	
Annual number of divorces (thousands)	62		62		54	
	Male	*Female*	*Male*	*Female*	*Male*	*Female*
Total first marriage rate (per person)	20	21	34	37	16	17
Total divorce rate (per person)	31	34	28	30	21	24
Mean age at first marriage (years)	26	27	40	42	20	21
SMAM (years)	120	120	110	131	93	109
Percentage ever married by age group	128	129	112	132	102	118
Developed countries	*Earlier year*		*Later year*		*Both years*	
Annual number of marriages (thousands)	40		44		40	
Annual number of divorces (thousands)	39		43		39	
	Male	*Female*	*Male*	*Female*	*Male*	*Female*
Total first marriage rate (per person)	27	41	42	43	27	40
Total divorce rate (per person)	25	38	36	39	23	37
Mean age at first marriage (years)	27	42	41	42	26	39
SMAM (years)	28	28	40	41	26	27
Percentage ever married by age group	34	34	40	41	32	33

TABLE III.6. DISTRIBUTION OF INDICATORS BY NUMBER OF OBSERVATIONS: FERTILITY DATA

Indicator	Developing countries			Developed countries		
	Earlier year	*Later year*	*Both years*	*Earlier year*	*Later year*	*Both years*
Annual number of births (thousands)	77	82	69	44	44	44
Crude birth rate (per 1 000 population)	77	82	69	44	44	44
Percentage of extra-marital births among all births	53	38	33	42	42	42
Total fertility rate (births per woman)	123	134	117	43	43	43
Age-specific fertility rates (per 1 000 women)	111	131	105	43	43	43
Mean age at childbearing (years)	111	131	105	43	43	43
Mean age at first birth (years)	48	94	39	37	41	36
Children ever born per woman						
35-39	93	102	66	16	31	12
40-44	93	102	66	16	29	12
45-49	92	97	64	16	26	9
Percentage of childless women						
35-39	78	98	51	15	31	14
40-44	78	98	51	15	29	10
45-49	76	95	51	15	26	8
Percentage of women with parity three or higher						
35-39	77	97	50	15	31	14
40-44	77	97	50	15	29	10
45-49	75	94	49	15	26	8

TABLE III.7. DISTRIBUTION OF INDICATORS BY NUMBER OF OBSERVATIONS: CONTRACEPTIVE DATA AND POPULATION POLICY DATA

Indicator	Developing countries			Developed countries		
	Earlier year	*Later year*	*Both years*	*Earlier year*	*Later year*	*Both years*
Contraceptive prevalence among women in union						
Percentage using any contraceptive method	66	117	61	23	33	21
Percentage using a modern contraceptive method	65	117	60	23	32	20
Percentage using condoms	66	115	60	22	33	21
Population policy data	111	132	111	30	43	30

كيفية الحصول على منشورات الأمم المتحدة

يمكن الحصول على منشورات الأمم المتحدة من المكتبات ودور التوزيع في جميع أنحاء العالم . استعلم عنها من المكتبة
التي تتعامل معها أو اكتب إلى : الأمم المتحدة ، قسم البيع في نيويورك أو في جنيف .

如何购取联合国出版物

联合国出版物在全世界各地的书店和经售处均有发售。请向书店询问或写信到纽约或日内瓦的
联合国销售组。

HOW TO OBTAIN UNITED NATIONS PUBLICATIONS

United Nations publications may be obtained from bookstores and distributors throughout the
world. Consult your bookstore or write to: United Nations, Sales Section, New York or Geneva.

COMMENT SE PROCURER LES PUBLICATIONS DES NATIONS UNIES

Les publications des Nations Unies sont en vente dans les librairies et les agences dépositaires
du monde entier. Informez-vous auprès de votre libraire ou adressez-vous à : Nations Unies,
Section des ventes, New York ou Genève.

КАК ПОЛУЧИТЬ ИЗДАНИЯ ОРГАНИЗАЦИИ ОБЪЕДИНЕННЫХ НАЦИЙ

Издания Организации Объединенных Наций можно купить в книжных магазинах
и агентствах во всех районах мира. Наводите справки об изданиях в вашем книжном
магазине или пишите по адресу: Организация Объединенных Наций, Секция по
продаже изданий, Нью-Йорк или Женева.

COMO CONSEGUIR PUBLICACIONES DE LAS NACIONES UNIDAS

Las publicaciones de las Naciones Unidas están en venta en librerías y casas distribuidoras en
todas partes del mundo. Consulte a su librero o diríjase a: Naciones Unidas, Sección de Ventas,
Nueva York o Ginebra.

Litho in United Nations, New York
46373—October 2004—6,535
ISBN 92-1-151400-2

United Nations publication
Sales No. E.04.XIII.10
ST/ESA/SER.A/234